Randy J. Larsen
WASHINGTON UNIVERSITY IN ST. LOUIS

David M. Buss
UNIVERSITY OF TEXAS AT AUSTIN

Personality Psychology

Sixth Edition

DOMAINS

OF

KNOWLEDGE

ABOUT

HUMAN

NATURE

McGraw Hill Education

PERSONALITY PSYCHOLOGY: DOMAINS OF KNOWLEDGE ABOUT HUMAN NATURE,
SIXTH EDITION

ISBN: 978-1-260-08391-0
MHID: 1-260-08391-8

Dedication

To Tommy and Ana.

RL

To my father Arnold H. Buss.

DB

Brief Contents

Contents

Top Left: © moswyn/Getty Images RF; Top Right: © Svisio/Getty Images RF; Middle Left: © Science Photo Library RF/Getty Images RF; Middle Right: © Corbis/ SuperStock RF; Bottom Left: © Arthimedes/Shutterstock.com RF; Bottom Right: © Colin Anderson/Blend Images LLC RF

PART I

The Dispositional Domain

© moswyn/Getty Images RF

Chapter 3

Traits and Trait Taxonomies   56

Chapter 4

Theoretical and Measurement Issues in Trait Psychology   86

Chapter 5
Personality Dispositions over Time: Stability, Coherence, and Change   122

© Svisio/Getty Images RF

© *Science Photo Library RF/*
Getty Images RF

Chapter 10

Psychoanalytic Approaches: Contemporary Issues   296

Chapter 11

Motives and Personality   326

© Corbis/SuperStock RF

© Arthimedes/Shutterstock.
com RF

PART V
The Social and Cultural Domain

Chapter 15
Personality and Social Interaction   460

Chapter 16
Sex, Gender, and Personality   488

© Colin Anderson/Blend Images
LLC RF

CONCLUSION

Chapter 20

Summary and Future Directions   622

© Colin Anderson/Blend Images LLC RF

About the Authors

Randy J. Larsen received his PhD in Personality Psychology from the University of Illinois at Champaign-Urbana in 1984. In 1992, he was awarded the Distinguished Scientific Achievement Award for Early Career Contributions to Personality Psychology from the American Psychological Association, and in 1987 he received a Research Scientist Development Award from the National Institute of Mental Health. He has been an associate editor at the *Journal of Personality and Social* *Psychology* and the *Personality and Social Psychology Bulletin,* and has been on the editorial boards of the *Journal of Research in Personality, Review of General Psychology,* and the *Journal of Personality.* He has published over 100 scientific articles in personality psychology and is on the Institute of Scientific Information's list of the top 25 most cited scientists in his discipline. His books include The Science of Subjective Well-Being and Taking Sides in Personality Psychology. Randy Larsen has served on several Scientific Review Groups for the National Institute of Mental Health and the National Research Council. He is a Fellow in the Association for Psychological Science and the American Psychological Association. His research on personality has been supported by the National Institute of Mental Health, the National Science Foundation, the National Institute of Aging, the McDonnell Foundation for Cognitive Neuroscience, and the Solon Summerfield Foundation. In 2000 he was elected president of the Midwestern Psychological Association. He has served on the faculty at Purdue University and the University of Michigan. Currently Randy Larsen is the William R. Stuckenberg Professor of Human Values and Moral Development at Washington University in St. Louis, where he teaches Personality Psychology and other courses. He lives in St. Louis with his wife and two children.

David M. Buss received his PhD from the University of California at Berkeley. He served on the faculties of Harvard University and the University of Michigan before accepting a professorship at the University of Texas at Austin, where he currently teaches. Buss received the American Psychological Association (APA) Distinguished Scientific Award for Early Career Contribution to Personality Psychology, the APA G. Stanley Hall Award, and the APA Distinguished Scientist Lecturer Award. Books by David Buss include *The Evolution of Desire: Strategies of Human Mating* (Revised Edition) (Basic Books, 2016), which has been translated into 10 languages; *Evolutionary Psychology: The New Science of the Mind* (5th ed.) (Allyn & Bacon, 2015), which was presented with the Robert W. Hamilton Book Award; *The Dangerous Passion: Why Jealousy Is as Necessary as Love and Sex* (Free Press, 2000), which has been translated into 13 languages; and two editions of *The Handbook of Evolutionary Psychology* (Wiley, 2005, 2016). Buss has authored more than 300 scientific publications and has also written articles for *The New York Times* and the *Times Higher Education Supplement.* He appears in the ISI List of Most Highly Cited Psychologists Worldwide, has been cited as one of the most eminent psychologists of the modern era, and has been cited as one of the 30 most influential living psychologists. The American Psychological Society (APS) awarded David Buss the Mentor Award for Lifetime Achievement in 2017. He lectures widely throughout the United States and abroad and has extensive cross-cultural research collaborations. David Buss greatly enjoys teaching, and had the honor of winning the President's Teaching Excellence Award at the University of Texas.

Preface

We have devoted our lives to the study of personality and believe this field is one of the most exciting in all of psychology. Thus we were enormously gratified to see the volume of e-mails, letters, and comments from satisfied consumers of our first, second, third, and fourth editions. At the same time, preparing the sixth edition proved to be a humbling experience. The cascade of exciting publications in the field of personality is formidable, requiring not merely updating but also the addition of major sections of new material. Moreover, in important ways our first edition proved prescient.

Rather than organize our text around the traditional grand theories of personality, we devised a framework of six important domains of knowledge about personality functioning. These six domains are the *dispositional domain* (traits, trait taxonomies, and personality dispositions over time), the *biological domain* (physiology, genetics, evolution), the *intrapsychic domain* (psychodynamics, motives), the *cognitive-experiential domain* (cognition, emotion, and the self), the *social and cultural domain* (social interaction, gender, and culture), and the *adjustment domain* (stress, coping, health, and personality disorders). We believed these domains of knowledge represented the contemporary state of affairs in personality psychology, and progress in the field since publication of our first edition has continued to bear out that belief.

Our previous editions differed from other texts in the importance placed on *culture, gender,* and *biology,* and these areas of personality have shown substantial growth in recent years. But we have also been fascinated to witness the growth in *each* of the six major domains of personality that form the organizational core of the book.

We have always envisioned our text as a reflection of the field. Our desire has always been to capture the excitement of what the science of personality is all about. For the sixth edition, we did our best to remain true to that vision. We believe that the field of personality psychology is now entering a golden age of sorts, and we hope that the changes we've made to the fifth edition convey a discipline that is vibrant in a way it never has been before. After all, no other field is devoted to the study of all that it means to be human.

For this edition, each chapter has been streamlined through judicious trimming. This provided room for discussing new research conducted within the past three years and made the book a bit shorter and more economical. Significant additions to the sixth edition are described below.

Chapter 1: Introduction to Personality Psychology
- Minor editing, streamlining the writing a bit, and updating the language to reflect modern usage, such as referring to "gender" rather than "sex."

Chapter 2: Personality Assessment, Measurement, and Research Design
- New discussion of Experience Sampling methods in personality, including Facebook, Instagram, and Twitter postings, as well as Smartphone and Fitbit recordings. Discusses the strengths and limitations of these new forms of data sources.
- New discussion of Social Desirability response set; finding that highly religious people tend to exaggerate their level of Agreeableness, in part because they see this trait as highly socially desirable.

Chapter 3: Traits and Trait Taxonomies
- Expanded coverage of "the dark triad," a personality cluster marked by Psychopathy, Narcissism, and Machiavellianism.
- Expanded coverage of the correlates of major personality traits and combinations of personality traits. For example, Extraverts are less likely to save money for retirement; Introverts prefer the solitude of mountains to oceans in their leisure time. High Conscientious people are more likely to do volunteer work in retirement. Emotionally unstable people are more likely to "choke" under pressure. People high in Openness are more likely to be politically liberal. Academic dishonesty is predicted by low Conscientiousness and low Agreeableness.
- HEXACO model of personality added: Honesty-Humility (H), Emotionality (E), Extraversion (X), Agreeableness (A), Conscientiousness (C), and Openness to Experience (O). Cross-cultural work suggests that this model is more comprehensive than the Five Factor model. Fascinating correlates of the new factor, Honesty-Humility are discussed. It predicts: propensity to cooperative versus cheat in experimental games; sincere religious beliefs; offering of sincere apologies; the low end predicts tendencies to sabotage other people's work, criminal activities, and other exploitative actions.

Chapter 4: Theoretical and Measurement Issues in Trait Psychology
- New material on person-situation interaction and personality consistency.
- New material on personality traits as density distributions of specific behaviors over time.
- New material on integrity testing in the workplace, distinguishing between overt and covert measures of integrity.
- New Exercise on job analysis for personnel selection using personality.

Chapter 5: Personality Dispositions Over Time: Stability, Coherence, and Change
- A 21-year longitudinal study of activity level in boys and girls shows moderate stability over time.
- Another Finish study shows adult personality stability of the five factor model.
- Increase in emotional stability (decrease in Neuroticism) with increasing age found in Germany and Japan.
- Reciprocal or bi-directional links between Neuroticism and stressful life events; high Neuroticism predicts who will experience stressful life events, but reciprocally, those who experience a lot of stressful life events show an increase in Neuroticism with age.
- Women who choose not to have children show lower femininity scores than those who choose to have children.
- Large meta-analysis of the predictive power of Grit to forecast education success and achievement; shows that Grit heavily overlaps with Conscientiousness, but the perseverance component of Grit (but not the passion for goals component) does show some incremental predictive power.
- Several study show that moving into adult roles—getting into a serious romantic relationship, transitioning to parenthood, and investing a lot in work—cause an increase in the personality trait of Conscientiousness.

Chapter 6: Genetics and Personality
- Summaries of recent large-scale meta-analyses of the heritability of personality.
- New findings on the heritability of political attitudes (conservative to liberal) in five different countries.

- Expanding the section on the role of genetics in marriage outcomes , such as relationship satisfaction, to include the role of genetics in well-being and life satisfaction.
- Addition of studies of gene x environment interaction; for example, a study of the link between early puberty and depressive symptoms occurred only in higher socioeconomic groups, but not among lower socioeconomic groups. Also included an interesting study showing that personality is expressed differently in happy versus unhappy marriages.
- One meta-analysis found that children showing antisocial behavior, a moderately heritable trait, tend to elicit harsh discipline from parents who attempt to curb their behavior.
- Discussion of a promising method known as genome-wide association studies (GWAS), which can rapidly examine the entire genome for links with personality, may yield faster scientific advances.

Chapter 7: Physiological Approaches to Personality
- New material on imaging brain structure and brain connectivity in relation to personality, featuring a new Closer Look at the Human Connectome Project.
- New material on dopamine function and its connection to the trait of extraversion.
- New material on morningness–eveningness in relationships.
- Updated summary of frontal brain asymmetry research.

Chapter 8: Evolutionary Perspectives on Personality
- Additional discussion of the emotion of DISGUST, as part of the behavioral immune system; evidence is reviewed that supports the hypothesis that this emotion serves an important disease-avoidance function, such as avoiding contaminated food and even infected people. Added is a new "Closer Look" on the emotion of Disgust.
- Discussion of new studies showing the adaptations for "the need to belong" emerge quite early in life; discusses research on the effects of social ostracism on children's anxiety and attempts to imitate in order to be re-included in the in-group.
- Importances of kinship: study found that people are willing to endure more physical pain—maintaining a painfully awkward physical position for as long as possible—as a function of closeness of kinship or genetic relatedness.
- More on kinship: people write their wills to leave their cash and other assets to close genetic relatives more than to distant ones.
- Gender differences in jealousy: new research shows that the gender differences emerge robustly in cultures that are highly sexually egalitarian such as Sweden and Norway, as well is in traditional cultures such as the Himba of Namibia.
- Gender differences in mate preferences: these psychological gender differences are large, roughly the same magnitude as gender differences in height and upper body muscle strength. Biological sex (male or female) can be predicted with 92% accuracy solely from knowing a person's mate preferences.
- Consenting to sex with strangers: Importantly, the gender differences in consenting to sex with strangers have been robustly replicated in other countries, including France, Germany, and Denmark.
- Expanded review of research and theory on condition-dependent personality (reactive heritability) as a function of body strength and physical attractiveness.

Chapter 9: Psychoanalytic Approaches to Personality
- New material on unconscious decision-making and deliberation outside of awareness.
- Summary of new research on repressive coping style, including its benefits and underlying brain mechanisms.
- New research on ego depletion and its connection to Freud's idea of psychic energy.

Chapter 10: Psychoanalytic Approaches: Contemporary Issues
- New material on life stories and identity.
- New research on early attachment experiences and adult romantic functioning, plus recent extensions of attachment theory.
- New research establishing that attachment styles are best conceptualized and measured as dimensions rather than categories.

Chapter 11: Motives and Personality
- New research on validity of the TAT for assessing motives.
- Expanded definition of the need for power.
- New material on the role of hormones in human motivation.
- New discussion of recent declines in empathy, asking whether Internet use is creating an empathy deficit in young people whose primary mode of interaction is online.

Chapter 12: Cognitive Topics in Personality
- New material on field dependence/independence in relation to modern digital technology developments (e.g., digital mapping, virtual reality) and occupations that require perceptual focus in stimulating environments (e.g., air traffic controllers, bomb disposal technicians).
- New material on locus of control in situations where technology may control a portion of our lives, e.g., autonomous vehicles.
- New material on the application of explanatory style to groups (sports teams, business organizations).

Chapter 13: Emotion and Personality
- New discussion of income inequality in relation to studies of the influence of wealth on happiness.
- New research on pro-social spending and happiness.
- Expanded coverage of brain imaging studies of trait anxiety/neuroticism and trait anger.

Chapter 14: Approaches to the Self
- New material on problematic internet use and shyness/social anxiety, with a general discussion of online versus offline social interaction.
- Expanded coverage of research on implicit self-esteem.
- New research on self-esteem variability.

Chapter 15: Personality and Social Interaction
- Extraverts choose to spend more time in social situations, whereas highly conscientious people select more work-related activities—choices that continue from adolescence through young adulthood (Wrzus, 2016). Agreeable people choose to spend more time looking at photos and media depicting positive images; disagreeable people expose themselves to more negative photos and media images (Bresin & Robinson, 2014).

- The priority placed on personality traits such as Agreeableness, Conscientiousness, and Emotional Stability occur regardless of sexual orientation; they are as strong among non-heterosexual men and women as they are among heterosexual men and women (Valentova et al., 2016). Low scores on these personality traits tend to be relationship "dealbreakers" (Jonason et al., 2015).
- High neuroticism in one or both members of the couple leads to relationship dissatisfaction.
- A key predictor of marital satisfaction is mate value—whether one succeeds in selecting a mate whose personality embodies qualities most people want. Those mated with high mate-value individuals tend to be happier in their relationship than those mated with lower mate value individuals (Conroy-Beam et al., 2016).
- Those high on Neuroticism also create more conflict and disagreement and their emotional upset after a fight tends to last longer (Solomon & Jackson, 2014).
- Those high on sensation seeking gravitate toward risky gambling bets and risky sexual situations (Webster & Crysel, 2012).
- Expanded discussion of evocation: An example comes from the evocation of trust and cooperativeness by those high on Honesty-Humility (Thielmann & Hilbig, 2014). Perhaps because high scorers tend to trust others, they evoke trustworthy expectations in others. Another study found that low agreeable individuals, because of their anger, jealousy, and antisocial behavior, tend to evoke high levels of relationship conflict (Lemay & Dobush, 2014). Agreeable people tend to evoke trust and cooperation in laboratory-based economic games (Zhao & Smillie, 2015).
- Married couples with highly agreeable wives tend to have more frequent sex, perhaps because they are receptive to, evoke more, sexual overtures (Meltzer & McNulty, 2016).
- Expanded discussion of personality and tactics of manipulation. For example: parents sometimes try to manipulate the mate choices of their sons and daughters, and use tactics specific to that context such as "chaperoning"; for example, sticking around when offspring is with a potential mate (Apostalou, 2014). A study of how children manipulation their parents regarding their choice of a mate revealed that highly agreeable children used the reason tactic, and also convinced their parents to trust them (Apostalou et al., 2015).
- Expanded discussion of Narcissism: Narcissists post more "selfies," update their online profile photos more often, and spend more time on Instagram (Marshall et al., 2015; Moon et al., 2016; Sorokowski et al., 2015; Weiser, 2015). In the mating domain, they engage in manipulative game-playing and are more likely to use sexually coercive and aggressive tactics (Blinkhorn et al., 2015; Haslam & Montrose 2015).

Chapter 16: Sex, Gender, and Personality
- Major update on studies of gender differences in temperament; for example, robust effect of gender on impulsivity, with boys scoring much higher. Girls scoring higher on temperament of fearfulness, boys higher on anger.
- Major update on the facets of the five factor model of personality; specifically, discoveries of gender differences in facets of warmth and gregariousness (women higher than men), assertiveness and excitement seeking (men higher),
- Expanded discussion of gender differences in depression; although women ruminate more than men, this gender difference is small and cannot fully explain the gender difference in depression that emerges during adolescence.

- New discussion of the dimension of Empathizing—Systemizing. **Empathizing** refers to tuning in to other people's thoughts and feelings. **Systemizing** is the drive to comprehend how things work, how systems are built, and how inputs into systems produce outputs (Baron-Cohen, 2003). Women score higher on empathizing, men higher on systemizing, which may partially explain gender differences in occupational preferences—women more than men prefer the teaching and helping professions; men more than women gravitate toward construction and engineering.
- Added discussion of sexual harassment in the workplace, a violation more likely to be inflicted on women than on men.

Chapter 17: Culture and Personality
- New studies find that Chinese individuals are somewhat less self-enhancing than Americans.
- New section on the accuracy and inaccuracy of personality stereotypes. Stereotypes about gender differences and age differences in personality traits tend to be accurate; stereotypes about national character, in contrast, tend to be inaccurate.
- New work on social class differences; those from lower socioeconomic classes tend to be more charitable and give more, despite having less.
- Update on cultural change in using internet dating sites.
- Recent cross-cultural work has confirmed the universality of some basic forms of emotional expression. One study compared non-verbal emotional vocalizations (e.g., "yuck," "huh") of the "basic emotions" of anger, disgust, fear, joy, sadness, surprise) among Namibian and Western participants. These vocal expressions were bi-directionally recognized—Namibians correctly identified the emotion that corresponded with the nonverbal vocalizations uttered by Westerners and vice-versa. These findings lend further support to the notion that some emotions are universal across cultures.

Chapter 18: Stress, Coping, Adjustment, and Health
- Introduces the concepts of "moderation" and "mediation" in personality psychology, with special reference to how personality can influence health. Other general examples of moderation and mediation are given, to highlight the value of these concepts to understanding how personality works.
- Updated research on conscientiousness, longevity, and health behavior.

Chapter 19: Disorders of Personality
- New case presentation of the dependent personality disorder.
- Updated research on dimensional model of personality disorders as an alternative the current categorical model.
- Discussion of the controversial concept of the "successful" psychopath.
- New coverage of the Triarchic model of psychopathy, which includes the components of boldness, meanness, and lack of inhibition.
- New neuroscientific research on brain activity in specific regions that appear to underlie the distinct components of psychopathy.
- New information of female psychopaths.

Chapter 20: Summary and Future Directions
- Genetics of personality turning out to be more complex than initially envisioned.
- Progress in linking the six domains of human nature to each other via research collaborations.

Acknowledgments

We would like to thank our own mentors and colleagues who, over the years, generated in us a profound interest in psychology. These include Arnold Buss, Joe Horn, Devendra Singh, and Lee Willerman (*University of Texas*); Jack Block, Ken Craik, Harrison Gough, Jerry Mendelsohn, and Richard Lazarus (*University of California, Berkeley*); Roy Baumeister (*Florida State University–Tallahassee*); Brian Little, Harry Murray, and David McClelland (*Harvard University*); Sam Gosling, Bob Josephs, Jamie Pennebaker, and Bill Swann (now at *University of Texas*); Ed Diener (*University of Illinois*); Gerry Clore (*University of Virginia*); Chris Peterson (*University of Michigan*); Hans Eysenck and Ray Cattell (both deceased); Tom Oltmanns, Roddy Roediger, and Mike Strube (*Washington University*); Alice Eagly (*Northwestern University*); Janet Hyde (*University of Wisconsin*); Robert Plomin (*King's College London*), Lew Goldberg (*Oregon Research Institute*), and Jerry Wiggins (Formerly *University of British Columbia*) as mentors from afar. Special thanks go to Bill Graziano and Ken Thompson, LtCol, USMC (retired), for helpful comments on the text. We would also like to thank our team at McGraw-Hill, including Brand Manager Jamie Laferrera, Editorial Coordinator Jasmine Staton, Content Project Manager Christina Gimlin, and Development Editors Reshmi Rajeesh, Erin Guendelsberger, and the entire resource development team.

Finally, RL would like to acknowledge family members who supported him and tolerated his neglect while he concentrated on this book, including his wife, Zvjezdana, and his children, Tommy and Ana. DB would like to thank his ".50" genetic relatives: his parents Arnold and Edith Buss; his siblings Arnie and Laura Buss; and his children Ryan and Tara Buss.

A project of this scope and magnitude requires the efforts of many people. We are greatly indebted to our colleagues who reviewed this manuscript in its various stages. We sincerely appreciate the time and effort that the following instructors gave in this regard:

Michael Botwin
California State University, Fresno
Tammy Crow
Southeastern Oklahoma State University
Jennifer R. Daniels
Lyon College
Katherine Lau
SUNY Oneonta
Lynda Mae
Arizona State University
William Pavot
Southwest Minnesota State University

Justin W. Peer
University of Michigan–Dearborn
Lisa Rapalyea
University of California–Davis
Jonathan C. Smith
Roosevelt University
Lyra Stein
Rutgers University
Sarah Wood
University of Wisconsin–Stout

We also continue to be grateful to the reviewers of our previous editions for their valuable comments.

Michael Ashton
Brock University
Timothy Atchison
West Texas A&M University

Nicole E. Barenbaum
University of the South
Michael D. Botwin
California State University–Fresno

Fred B. Bryant
Loyola University Chicago
Joan Cannon
*University of Massachusetts
at Lowell*
Mark S. Chapell
Rowan University
Jeff Conte
San Diego State University
Eros DeSouza
Illinois State University
Scott J. Dickman
*University of Massachusetts at
Dartmouth*
Wayne A. Dixon
*Southwestern Oklahoma State
University*
Katherine Ellison
Montclair State University
Richard Ely
Boston University
Stephen G. Flanagan
University of North Carolina
Irene Frieze
University of Pittsburgh
Barry Fritz
Quinnipiac University
Lani Fujitsubo
Southern Oregon State College
Steven C. Funk
Northern Arizona University
Glenn Geher
*State University of New York–New
Paltz*
Susan B. Goldstein
University of Redlands
Jane E. Gordon
*The McGregor School of Antioch
College*
Marjorie Hanft-Martone
Eastern Illinois University
Evan Harrington
*John Jay College of Criminal
Justice*
Gail A. Hinesley
Chadron State College
Christopher Hopwood
Michigan State University
Alisha Janowsky
University of Central Florida

Marvin W. Kahn
University of Arizona
Jill C. Keogh
University of Missouri–Columbia
Carolin Keutzer
University of Oregon
Laura A. King
Southern Methodist University
John E. Kurtz
Villanova University
Alan J. Lambert
Washington University
Michael J. Lambert
Brigham Young University
Mark R. Leary
Wake Forest University
Len B. Lecci
*University of North Carolina at
Wilmington*
Christopher Leone
University of North Florida
Brian Little
Harvard University
Kenneth Locke
University of Idaho
Charles Mahone
Texas Tech University
Gerald Matthews
University of Cincinnati
Gerald A. Mendelsohn
University of California at Berkeley
Todd Nelson
*California State
University–Stanislaus*
Julie K. Norem
Wellesley College
Stephen J. Owens
Ohio University
William Pavot
Southwest State University
Bill E. Peterson
Smith College
David Pincus
Chapman University
Tracy Richards
Colorado State University
Alan Roberts
Indiana University
Mark E. Sibicky
Marietta College

Jeff Simpson
Texas A&M University
Stephanie Sogg
Massachusetts General Hospital;
Harvard Bipolar Research
Program
Robert M. Stelmack
University of Ottawa
Steven Kent Sutton
University of Miami
Kristy Thacker
University at Albany

Vetta L. Sanders Thompson
University of Missouri at St. Louis
Forrest B. Tyler
University of Maryland at College
Park
Jennifer Wartella
Virginia Commonwealth University
Barbara Woike
Barnard College
David Harold Zald
Vanderbilt University

Connect Logo

The 6th edition of *Personality Psychology* is now available online with Connect, McGraw-Hill Education's integrated assignment and assessment platform. Connect also offers SmartBook for the new edition, which is the first adaptive reading experience proven to improve grades and help students study more effectively. All of the title's website and ancillary content is also available through Connect, including:

- An Instructor's Manual for each chapter with chapter outlines, lecture topics and suggestions, ideas for classroom activities and demonstrations, questions for us in classroom discussions, ideas for student research papers, and lists of current research articles.
- A full Test Bank of multiple choice questions that test students on central concepts and ideas in each chapter.
- Lecture Slides for instructor use in class.

McGraw-Hill Connect®
Learn Without Limits

Connect is a teaching and learning platform that is proven to deliver better results for students and instructors.

Connect empowers students by continually adapting to deliver precisely what they need, when they need it, and how they need it, so your class time is more engaging and effective.

73% of instructors who use **Connect** require it; instructor satisfaction **increases** by 28% when **Connect** is required.

Connect's Impact on Retention Rates, Pass Rates, and Average Exam Scores

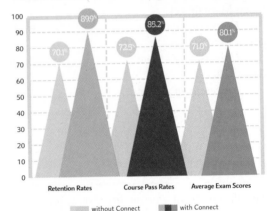

Using **Connect** improves retention rates by **19.8%**, passing rates by **12.7%**, and exam scores by **9.1%**.

Analytics —

Connect Insight®

Connect Insight is Connect's new one-of-a-kind visual analytics dashboard—now available for both instructors and students—that provides at-a-glance information regarding student performance, which is immediately actionable. By presenting assignment, assessment, and topical performance results together with a time metric that is easily visible for aggregate or individual results, Connect Insight gives the user the ability to take a just-in-time approach to teaching and learning, which was never before available. Connect Insight presents data that empowers students and helps instructors improve class performance in a way that is efficient and effective.

Impact on Final Course Grade Distribution

without Connect		with Connect
22.9%	A	31.0%
27.4%	B	34.3%
22.9%	C	18.7%
11.5%	D	6.1%
15.4%	F	9.9%

Students can view their results for any **Connect** course.

Mobile —

Connect's new, intuitive mobile interface gives students and instructors flexible and convenient, anytime–anywhere access to all components of the Connect platform.

Adaptive

THE **ADAPTIVE READING EXPERIENCE** DESIGNED TO TRANSFORM THE WAY STUDENTS READ

More students earn **A's** and **B's** when they use McGraw-Hill Education **Adaptive** products.

SmartBook®

Proven to help students improve grades and study more efficiently, SmartBook contains the same content within the print book, but actively tailors that content to the needs of the individual. SmartBook's adaptive technology provides precise, personalized instruction on what the student should do next, guiding the student to master and remember key concepts, targeting gaps in knowledge and offering customized feedback, and driving the student toward comprehension and retention of the subject matter. Available on tablets, SmartBook puts learning at the student's fingertips—anywhere, anytime.

Over **8 billion questions** have been answered, making McGraw-Hill Education products more intelligent, reliable, and precise.

www.mheducation.com

STUDENTS WANT

SMARTBOOK®

95% of students reported **SmartBook** to be a more effective way of reading material.

100% of students want to use the Practice Quiz feature available within **SmartBook** to help them study.

100% of students reported having reliable access to off-campus wifi.

90% of students say they would purchase **SmartBook** over print alone.

95% of students reported that **SmartBook** would impact their study skills in a positive way.

Mc Graw Hill Education

*Findings based on 2015 focus group results administered by McGraw-Hill Education

Personality Psychology

Top Left: © moswyn/Getty
Images RF; Top Right: © Svisio/
Getty Images RF; Middle Left:
© Science Photo Library RF/
Getty Images RF; Middle Right:
© Corbis/SuperStock RF;
Bottom Left: © Arthimedes/
Shutterstock.com RF; Bottom
Right: © Colin Anderson/Blend
Images LLC RF

1

Introduction to Personality Psychology

INTRODUCTION

Each person is, in certain respects, like all other persons, like some other persons, and like no other person.
© SuperStock/Ingram Publishing RF

Those who carry humor to excess are thought to be vulgar buffoons, striving after humor at all costs, not caring about pain to the object of their fun; . . . while those who can neither make a joke themselves nor put up with those who do are thought to be boorish and unpolished. But those who joke in a tasteful way are called ready-witted and tactful . . . and it is the mark of a tactful person to say and listen to such things as befit a good and well-bred person.

Aristotle, in *The Nicomachean Ethics,* expressed these wise observations on the subject of humor and the ways in which people do or do not express it. In this quote, we see Aristotle behaving much as a personality psychologist. Aristotle is analyzing the characteristics of persons who have an appropriate sense of humor and providing some details about what features are associated with a sense of humor. Aristotle adds to this description by comparing people who are extreme, having either too much or too little sense of humor. In his book on ethics, Aristotle analyzed many personality characteristics, including truthfulness, courage, intelligence, self-indulgence, anger proneness, and friendliness.

We might conclude that Aristotle was an amateur personality psychologist. But aren't we all amateur personality psychologists to some extent? Aren't we all curious about the characteristics people possess, including our own? Don't we all use personality characteristics in describing people? And haven't we all used personality terms to explain behavior, either our own or others'?

When we say that our friend goes to a lot of parties because she is outgoing, we are using personality to explain her behavior. When we refer to another friend as conscientious and reliable, we are describing features of his personality. When we characterize ourselves as thoughtful, intelligent, and ambitious, we are describing features of our personalities.

Features of personality make people different from one another, and these features usually take the form of adjectives, such as John is lazy, Mary is optimistic, and Fred is anxious. *Adjectives that can be used to describe characteristics of people are called* **trait-descriptive adjectives.** There are nearly 20,000 such trait-descriptive adjectives in the English language. This astonishing fact alone tells us that, in everyday life, there are compelling reasons for trying to understand and describe those we interact with, as well as ourselves.

Notice that the adjectives describing personality refer to several very different aspects of people. Words such as *thoughtful* refer to inner qualities of mind. Words such as *charming* and *humorous* refer to the effects a person has on other people. Words such as *domineering* are relational and signify a person's position, or stance, toward others. Words such as *ambitious* refer to the intensity of desire to reach our goals. Words such as *creative* refer both to a quality of mind and to the nature of the products we produce. Words such as *deceitful* refer to the strategies a person uses to attain his or her goals. All of these features describe aspects of personality.

Exercise

Think of someone you know well—say, a friend, family member, or roommate. Consider the many characteristics that make this person unique. List the five adjectives you think best capture this person's personality. For example, if you were to describe this person to someone, what five adjectives would you use? Now, ask your target person to list the five adjectives *he or she* thinks best describe himself or herself. Compare your lists.

Personality Defined

Establishing a definition for something as complex as human personality is difficult. The authors of the first textbooks on personality—Gordon Allport (1937) and Henry Murray (1938)—struggled with the definition. The problem is how to establish a definition that is sufficiently comprehensive to include all of the aspects mentioned earlier, including inner features, social effects, qualities of the mind, qualities of the body, relations to others, and inner goals. Because of these complexities, some textbooks on personality omit a formal definition entirely. Nonetheless, the following definition captures the essential elements of personality: **Personality** *is the set of psychological traits and mechanisms within the individual that are organized and relatively enduring and that influence his or her interactions with, and adaptations to, the intrapsychic, physical, and social environments.* Let's examine the elements of this definition more closely.

Personality Is the Set of Psychological Traits . . .

Psychological traits are characteristics that describe ways in which people are different from each other. Saying that someone is *shy* is to mention one way in which he or she differs from others who are more outgoing. Traits also define ways in which people are *similar* to some others. For example, people who are shy are similar to each other in that they are anxious in social situations, particularly when there is an audience focusing attention on them.

People are different from each other in many ways. The science of Personality Psychology provides an understanding of the psychological ways that people differ from one another.
© Rawpixel.com/Shutterstock.com RF

Consider another example—the trait of talkativeness. This characteristic can be meaningfully applied to people and describes a dimension of difference among them. Typically, a talkative person is that way from day to day, from week to week, and from year to year. Certainly, even the most talkative person can have quiet moments, quiet days, or even quiet weeks. Over time, however, those with the trait of talkativeness tend to emit verbal behavior with greater frequency than those who are low on talkativeness. In this sense, traits describe the **average tendencies** of a person. On average, a high-talkative person starts more conversations than a low-talkative person.

Research on personality traits asks four kinds of questions:

- How many traits are there?
- How are the traits organized?
- What are the origins of traits?
- What are the correlations and consequences of traits?

One primary question is *how many* fundamental traits there are. Are there dozens or hundreds of traits, or merely a few? The second research question pertains to the *organization,* or structure, of traits. For example, how is talkativeness related to other traits, such as impulsivity and extraversion? A third research question concerns the *origins* of traits—where they come from and how they develop. Does heredity influence talkativeness? What sorts of cultural and child-rearing practices affect the development of traits such as talkativeness? A fourth key question pertains to the *correlations and consequences* of traits in terms of experience, behavior, and life outcomes. Do talkative persons have many friends? Do they have a more extended social network to draw upon in times of trouble? Do they annoy people who are trying to study?

The four research questions constitute the core of the research program of many personality psychologists. Psychological traits are useful for at least three reasons. First, they help *describe* people and help understand the dimensions of difference among people. Second, traits are useful because they help *explain* behavior. The reasons people act may be partly a function of their personality traits. Third, traits are useful because

Figure 1.1

Psychological mechanisms have three essential ingredients. Our personalities contain many such mechanisms.

they can help *predict* future behavior—for example, the sorts of careers individuals will find satisfying, who will tolerate stress better, and who is likely to get along well with others. Thus, personality is useful in *describing, explaining,* and *predicting* differences among individuals. All good scientific theories enable researchers to describe, explain, and predict in their domains. Just as an economic theory might be useful in describing, explaining, and predicting fluctuations in the economy, personality traits describe, explain, and predict differences among persons.

And Mechanisms . . .

Psychological mechanisms are like traits, except that the term *mechanisms* refers more to the processes of personality. For example, most psychological mechanisms involve an information-processing activity. Someone who is extraverted, for example, may look for and notice opportunities to interact with other people. That is, an extraverted person is prepared to notice and act on certain kinds of social information.

Most psychological mechanisms have three essential ingredients: *inputs, decision rules,* and *outputs.* A psychological mechanism may make people more sensitive to certain kinds of information from the environment (input), may make them more likely to think about specific options (decision rules), and may guide their behavior toward certain categories of action (outputs). For example, an extraverted person may look for opportunities to be with other people, may consider in each situation the possibilities for human contact and interaction, and may encourage others to interact with him or her. Our personalities contain many psychological mechanisms of this sort—information-processing procedures that have the key elements of inputs, decision rules, and outputs (see Figure 1.1).

Courage is an example of a trait that is activated only under particular circumstances. For example, Hurlburt Field Medics Continue to Save Lives in Haiti—2010.

Source: U.S. Air Force photo by Tech. Sgt. James L. Harper Jr.

This does not mean that all of our traits and psychological mechanisms are activated at all times. In fact, at any point in time, only a few are activated. Consider the trait of courageousness. This trait is activated only under particular conditions, such as when people face serious dangers and threats to their lives. Some people are more courageous than others, but we will never know which people are courageous unless and until the right situation presents itself. Look around next time you are in class: Who do you think has the trait of courageousness? You won't know until you are in a situation that provides the potential for courageous behavior.

Within the Individual...

Within the individual means that personality is something a person carries with him- or herself over time and from one situation to the next. Typically, we feel that we are today the same people we were last week, last month, and last year. We also feel that we will continue to have these personalities into the coming months and years. And, although our personalities are certainly influenced by our environments, and especially by the significant others in our lives, we feel that we carry with us the same personalities from situation to situation in our lives. The definition of personality stresses that the important sources of personality reside within the individual and, hence, are at least somewhat stable over time and somewhat consistent over situations.

That Are Organized and Relatively Enduring...

Organized means that the psychological traits and mechanisms for a given person are not simply a random collection of elements. Rather, personality is organized because the mechanisms and traits are linked to one another in a coherent fashion. Imagine the simple case of two desires—a desire for food and a desire for intimacy. If you have not eaten for a while and are experiencing hunger pangs, then your desire for food might override your desire for intimacy. On the other hand, if you have already eaten, then your desire for food may temporarily subside, allowing you to pursue intimacy. Our personalities are organized in the sense that they contain decision rules that govern which needs or motives are activated, depending on the circumstances.

Psychological traits are also relatively **enduring** over time, particularly in adulthood, and are somewhat consistent over situations. To say that someone is angry at this moment is not saying anything about a trait. A person may be angry now, but not tomorrow or may be angry in one situation, but not in others. Anger is more of a *state* than a trait. To say that someone is anger prone or generally hot tempered, however, is to describe a psychological trait. Someone who is anger prone is *frequently* angry, relative to others, and shows this proneness time and time again in many different situations (e.g., the person is argumentative at work, is hostile and aggressive while playing team sports for recreation, and quarrels a lot with family members).

There may be some occasions when this generalization about the consistency of personality from situation to situation does not hold. Some situations may be overpowering and suppress the expression of psychological traits. Persons who are generally talkative, for example, may remain quiet during a lecture, at the movies, or in an elevator—although you undoubtedly have experienced someone who could not or would not keep quiet in any of these circumstances!

The debate about whether people are consistent across situations in their lives has a long history in personality psychology. Some psychologists have argued that the evidence for consistency is weak (Mischel, 1968). For example, honesty measured in one situation (say, cheating on a test) may not correlate with honesty measured in another situation (say, cheating on income taxes). We will explore this debate more fully later in the book. For now we will simply say that most personality psychologists maintain that although people are not perfectly consistent, there is enough consistency to warrant including this characteristic in a definition of personality.

The fact that personality includes relatively enduring psychological traits and mechanisms does not preclude change over time. Indeed, describing precisely the ways in which we change over time is one goal of personality psychologists.

And That Influence . . .

In the definition of personality, an emphasis on the **influential forces** of personality means that personality traits and mechanisms can have an effect on people's lives. Personality influences how we act, how we view ourselves, how we think about the world, how we interact with others, how we feel, how we select our environments (particularly our social environment), what goals and desires we pursue in life, and how we react to our circumstances. People are not passive beings merely responding to external forces. Rather, personality plays a key role in affecting how people shape their lives. It is in this sense that personality traits are forces that *influence* how we think, act, and feel.

His or Her Interactions with . . .

This feature of personality is perhaps the most difficult to describe, because the nature of **person–environment interaction** is complex. In Chapter 15, we examine interactionism in greater detail. For now, however, it is sufficient to note that interactions with situations include perceptions, selections, evocations, and manipulations. *Perceptions* refer to how we "see," or interpret, an environment. Two people may be exposed to the same objective event, yet what they pay attention to and how they interpret the event may be very different. And this difference is a function of their personalities. For example, two people can look at an inkblot, yet one person sees two cannibals cooking a human over a fire, whereas the other perceives a smiling clown waving hello. As another example, a stranger may smile at someone on the street; one person might perceive the smile as a smirk, whereas another person might perceive the smile as a friendly gesture. It is the same smile, just as it is the same inkblot, yet how people interpret these situations can be determined by their personalities.

Selection describes the manner in which we choose situations to enter—how we choose our friends, romantic partners, hobbies, college classes, and careers. How we go about making these selections is, at least in part, a reflection of our personalities. How we use our free time is especially a reflection of our traits. One person may take up the hobby of parachute jumping, whereas another may prefer to spend time quietly listening to a podcast alone. We select from what life offers us, and these choices are partly a function of personality.

Evocations are the reactions we produce in others, often quite unintentionally. To some extent, we create the social environment that we inhabit. A child with a high activity level, for example, may evoke in parents attempts to constrain the child, even though these attempts are not intended or desired by the child. A person who is physically large may evoke feelings of intimidation in others, even if intimidation is not the goal. Our evocative interactions are also essential features of our personalities.

Manipulations are the ways in which we intentionally attempt to influence others. Someone who is anxious or frightened easily may try to influence their group to avoid scary movies or risky activities. Someone who is highly conscientious may insist that everyone follow the rules. Or a husband who is very neat and orderly may insist that his wife pick up her things. The ways in which we attempt to manipulate the behavior, thoughts, and feelings of others are essential features of our personalities. All of these forms of interaction—perceptions, selections, evocations, and manipulations—are central to understanding the connections between the personalities of people and the environments they inhabit.

And Adaptations to . . .

An emphasis on **adaptation** conveys the notion that a central feature of personality concerns adaptive functioning—accomplishing goals, coping, adjusting, and dealing with the challenges and problems we face as we go through life. Few things are more obvious about human behavior than the fact that it is goal directed, functional, and purposeful. Even behavior that does not appear functional—such neurotic behavior as excessive worrying—may, in fact, be functional. For example, people who worry a lot often receive lots of support from others. Consequently, what appears on the surface to be maladaptive (worrying) may, in fact, have some rewarding characteristics for the person (eliciting social support). In addition, some aspects of personality processes represent deficits in normal adaptations, such as breakdowns in the ability to cope with stress, to regulate one's social behavior, or to manage one's emotions. Although psychologists' knowledge of the adaptive functions of personality traits and mechanisms is currently limited, it remains an indispensable key to understanding the nature of human personality.

The Environment

The physical **environment** often poses challenges for people. Some of these are direct threats to survival. For example, food shortages create the problem of securing adequate nutrients for survival. Extremes of temperature pose the problem of maintaining thermal homeostasis. Heights, snakes, spiders, and strangers can all pose threats to survival. Human beings, like other animals, have evolved solutions to these adaptive problems. Hunger pangs motivate us to seek food, and taste preferences guide our choices of which foods to consume. Shivering mechanisms help combat the cold, and sweat glands help fight the heat. At a psychological level, our fears of heights, snakes, spiders, and strangers—the most common human fears—help us avoid or safely interact with these environmental threats to our survival.

Our social environment also poses adaptive challenges. We may desire the prestige of a good job, but there are many other people competing for the same positions. We may desire interesting friends and mates, but there are many others competing for them. We may desire greater emotional closeness with others, but may not know how to achieve closeness. The ways in which we cope with our social environment—the challenges we encounter in our struggle for belongingness, love, and esteem—are central to an understanding of personality.

The particular aspect of the environment that is important at any moment in time is frequently determined by personality. A person who is talkative, for example, will notice more opportunities in the social environment to strike up conversations than will someone who is low on talkativeness. A person who is disagreeable will occupy a social environment where people frequently argue with him or her. A person for whom status is very important will pay attention to the relative hierarchical positions of others—who is up, who is down, who is ascending, who is sliding. In short, from among the potentially infinite dimensions of the environments we inhabit, our "effective environment" represents only the small subset of features that our psychological mechanisms direct us to attend and respond to.

In addition to our physical and social environments, we have an intrapsychic environment. *Intrapsychic* means "within the mind." We all have memories, dreams, desires, fantasies, and a collection of private experiences that we live with each day. This intrapsychic environment, although not as objectively verifiable as our social or physical environment, is nevertheless real to each of us and makes up an important part of our psychological reality. For example, our self-esteem—how good or bad we feel about ourselves at any given moment—may depend on our assessment of the degree to which we are succeeding in attaining our goals. Success at work and success at friendship may provide two different forms of success experience and, hence, form different intrapsychic memories. We are influenced by our memories of these experiences whenever we think about our own self-worth. Our intrapsychic environment, no less than our physical and social environments, provides a critical context for understanding human personality.

Exercise

Write a one-page essay about a good friend, someone you know well, in which you describe what is characteristic, enduring, and functional about that person. Include in this description those elements of the ways in which he or she interacts with, or adapts to, the physical, social, and intrapsychic environments.

Three Levels of Personality Analysis

Although the definition of personality used in this book is quite broad and encompassing, personality can be analyzed at three levels. These three levels are well summarized by Kluckhohn and Murray, in their 1948 book on culture and personality, in which they state that every human being is, in certain respects,

1. like all others (the human nature level);
2. like some others (the level of individual and group differences); and
3. like no others (the individual uniqueness level).

Another way to think of these distinctions is that the first level refers to "universals" (the ways in which we are all alike), the middle level refers to "particulars" (the ways in which we are like some people but unlike others), and the third level refers to "uniqueness" (the ways in which we are unlike any other person) (see Table 1.1).

Human Nature

The first level of personality analysis describes **human nature** in general—the traits and mechanisms of personality that are typical of our species and are possessed by everyone or nearly everyone. For example, nearly every human has language skills, which allow him or her to learn and use a language. All cultures on earth speak a

Table 1.1 Three Levels of Personality Analysis

Level of Analysis	Examples
Human Nature	Need to belong
	Capacity for love
Individual and Group Differences	Variation in need to belong (individual difference)
	Men more physically aggressive than women (group difference)
Individual Uniqueness	Letisha's unique way of expressing her love
	John's unique way of expressing aggression

language, so spoken language is part of the universal human nature. At a psychological level, all humans possess fundamental psychological mechanisms—for example, the desire to live with others and belong to social groups—and these mechanisms are part of general human nature. There are many ways in which each person is like most or all other people, and by understanding those ways we may achieve an understanding of the general principles of human nature.

Individual and Group Differences

The second level of personality analysis pertains to individual and group differences. Some people are gregarious and love parties; others prefer quiet evenings reading. Some people take great physical risks by jumping out of airplanes, riding motorcycles, and driving fast cars; others shun physical risks. Some people enjoy high self-esteem and live life relatively free from anxiety; others worry constantly and are plagued by self-doubt. These are dimensions of **individual differences**, ways in which each person is like *some* other people (e.g., extraverts, sensation seekers).

Personality can also be observed by studying **differences among groups**. That is, people in one group may have certain personality features in common, and these common features make that group of people different from other groups. Examples of groups studied by personality psychologists include different cultures, different age groups, different political parties, and groups from different socioeconomic backgrounds. Another important set of differences studied by personality psychologists concerns those between men and women. Although many traits and mechanisms of humans are common to both genders, a few are different for men and women. For example, there is accumulated evidence that, across cultures, men are typically more physically aggressive than women. Men are responsible for most of the violence the world over. One goal of personality psychology is to understand why certain aspects of personality differ among groups, such as understanding how and why women are different from men and why people from one culture differ from those from another culture.

Personality psychologists sometimes study group differences, such as differences between men and women.

© Eric Audras/Getty Images RF

Individual Uniqueness

No two individuals, not even identical twins raised by the same parents in the same home in the same culture, have exactly the same personalities. Every individual has personal qualities not shared by any other person in the world. One of the goals of personality psychology is to allow for individual uniqueness and to develop ways to capture the richness of unique individual lives.

One debate in the field concerns whether individuals should be studied *nomothetically*—that is, as individual instances of general characteristics that are distributed in the population, or should be studied *idiographically,* as single, unique cases. **Nomothetic** research typically involves statistical comparisons of individuals or groups, requiring samples of participants on which to conduct research. Nomothetic research is typically applied to identify universal human characteristics and dimensions of individual or group differences. **Idiographic** (translated literally as "the description of one") research typically focuses on a single person, trying to observe general principles that are manifest in a single life over time. Often, idiographic research results in case studies or the psychological biography of a single person (Runyon, 1983). Sigmund Freud, for example, wrote a psychobiography of Leonardo da Vinci (1916/1947). An example of another version of idiographic research is provided by Rosenzweig (1986, 1997), in which he proposes to analyze people in terms of the sequence of events in their lives, trying to understand critical life events within each persons' own history.

The important point is that personality psychologists have been concerned with all three levels of analysis: the universal level, the level of individual and group differences, and the level of individual uniqueness. Each contributes valuable knowledge to the total understanding of the nature of personality.

A Fissure in the Field

Different personality psychologists focus on different levels of analysis. And there is a gap within the field that has not yet been successfully bridged. It is the gap between the human nature level of analysis and the analysis of group and individual differences. Many psychologists have theorized about what human nature is like in general. However, when doing research, psychologists most often focus on individual and group differences in personality. As a consequence, there is a fissure between the grand theories of personality and contemporary research in personality.

Grand Theories of Personality

Most of the grand theories of personality address the human nature level of analysis. That is, these theories attempt to provide a universal account of the fundamental psychological processes and characteristics of our species. Sigmund Freud (1915/1957), for example, emphasized universal instincts of sex and aggression; a universal psychic structure of the id, ego, and superego; and universal stages of psychosexual development (oral, anal, phallic, latency, and genital). Statements about the universal core of human nature lie at the center of grand theories of personality.

Many of the textbooks used in teaching college courses in personality psychology are structured around grand theories. These books have been criticized, however, because many of those theories are primarily of historical interest. Only parts of them have stood the test of time and guide personality research today. Although the grand theories are an important part of the history of personality psychology, there is much interesting personality research going on today that is not directly relevant to the historical grand theories.

Contemporary Research in Personality

Most of the empirical research in contemporary personality addresses the ways in which individuals and groups differ. For example, the extensive research literature on extraversion and introversion, on anxiety and neuroticism, and on self-esteem all focuses on the ways in which people differ from one another. The extensive research on masculinity and femininity deals with the psychological ways in which men and women differ and the ways in which people acquire sex-typed social roles. Cultural research shows that one major dimension of difference concerns whether individuals endorse a collectivistic versus an individualistic attitude. Eastern cultures tend to be more collectivistic and Western cultures more individualistic (see Chapter 17).

One way to examine personality psychology would be to pick a dozen or so current research topics and explore what psychologists have learned about each. For example, a lot of research has been done on self-esteem—what it is, how it develops, how people maintain high self-esteem, and how it functions in relationships. There are many other interesting topics in contemporary personality psychology—shyness, aggression, trust, dominance, hypnotic susceptibility, depression, intelligence, attributional style, goal setting, anxiety, temperament, sex roles, self-monitoring, extraversion, sensation seeking, agreeableness, impulsivity, sociopathic tendencies, morality, locus of control, optimism, creativity, leadership, prejudice, and narcissism.

A course that just surveys current topics in personality research seems unsatisfactory. It would be like going to an auction and bidding on everything—soon you would be overwhelmed. Just picking topics to cover would not result in any sense of the connections among the aspects of personality. Indeed, the field of personality has been criticized for containing too many independent areas of investigation, with no sense of the whole person behind the separate topics of investigation. What holds personality together as a coherent field would be missing in such an approach.

You have probably heard the ancient legend of the three blind men who were presented with an elephant. They tried to figure out what the whole elephant was like. The first blind man approached cautiously; walking up to the elephant and putting his hands and then arms around the animal's leg, he proclaimed, "Why, the whole elephant is much like a tree, slender and tall." The second man grasped the trunk of the elephant and exclaimed, "No, the whole elephant is more like a large snake." The third blind man grasped the ear of the elephant and stated, "You are both wrong; the whole elephant more closely resembles a fan." The three blind men proceeded to argue with one another, each insisting that his opinion of the whole elephant was the correct one. In a sense, each blind man had a piece of the truth, yet each failed to recognize that his perceptions of the elephant captured only a narrow part of the truth. Each failed to grasp the whole elephant. Working together, however, the blind men could have assembled a reasonable understanding of the whole elephant.

The topic of personality is like the elephant, and personality psychologists are somewhat like the blind men, examining only one perspective at a time. For example, some psychologists study the biological aspects of personality. Others study ways that culture promotes personality differences among people and among groups. Still other psychologists study how various aspects of the mind interact and work together to produce personality. And others study relationships among people and believe that social interaction is where personality manifests its most important effects. Each of these perspectives on personality captures elements of truth, yet each alone is inadequate to describe the entire realm of human personality—the whole elephant, so to speak.

Six Domains of Knowledge About Human Nature

The various views of researchers in personality stem *not* from the fact that one perspective is right and the others wrong, but rather from the fact that they are studying different domains of knowledge. A **domain of knowledge** is a specialty area of science and scholarship in which psychologists have focused on learning about some specific and limited aspects of human nature. A domain of knowledge delineates the boundaries of researchers' knowledge, expertise, and interests.

This degree of specialization is reasonable. Indeed, specialization characterizes many scientific fields. The field of medicine, for example, has heart specialists and brain specialists, focusing in great detail on their own domains. It is likewise reasonable for the field of personality psychology to have intrapsychic specialists, trait origins specialists, cultural specialists, and personality and social interaction specialists. Each of these domains of personality has accumulated its own base of knowledge. Nonetheless, it is desirable to integrate these diverse domains to see how they all fit together.

The whole personality, like the whole elephant, is the sum of the various parts and the connections among them. For personality, each part is a domain of knowledge representing a collection of knowledge about certain aspects of personality. How are the domains of knowledge defined? For the most part, natural boundaries have developed in the field of personality psychology. That is, researchers have formed natural clusters of topics that fit together and are distinct from other clusters of knowledge. Within these identifiable domains, researchers have developed common *methods for asking questions;* have accumulated a foundation of *known facts;* and have developed *theoretical explanations* that account for what is known about personality from the perspective of each domain.

The field of personality can be cleaved into six distinct domains of knowledge about human nature: personality is influenced by traits the person is born with and how they develop over time (*dispositional domain*); by biological events (*biological domain*); by processes within the person's own mind (*intrapsychic domain*); by personal and private thoughts, feelings, desires, beliefs, and other subjective experiences (*cognitive-experiential domain*); by social, cultural, and gendered positions in the world (*social and cultural domain*); and by the adjustments that the person must make to the inevitable challenges of life (*adjustment domain*).

Personality psychologists working within each domain often use different theoretical perspectives and focus on different facts. As a consequence, psychologists from different domains can sometimes appear to contradict one another. The psychoanalytic perspective of Sigmund Freud, for example, views the personality as consisting of irrational sexual and aggressive instincts which motivate human activity. The cognitive perspective on personality, in contrast, views humans as rational "scientists," calmly trying to anticipate, predict, and control the events that occur in their worlds.

On the surface, these perspectives appear incompatible. How can humans be both irrational and rational? How can humans be driven by desire yet be cool and detached in their quest for accurate prediction? On deeper examination, the contradictions may be more apparent than real. It is entirely possible, for example, that humans have both powerful sexual and aggressive motivations and cognitive mechanisms designed to perceive and predict events with accuracy. It is entirely possible that sometimes basic emotions and motivations are activated and at other times the cool cognitive mechanisms are activated. And it is possible that the two sets of mechanisms sometimes become linked with one another, such as when the rational mechanisms are used in the service of fulfilling fundamental desires. In short, although each theoretical perspective may be focused on a critically important part of human psychological functioning, each perspective by itself does not capture the *whole* person.

This book is organized around the six domains of personality functioning— dispositional, biological, intrapsychic, cognitive-experiential, social and cultural, and adjustment. Within each of these domains of personality, we focus on two key elements: (1) the *theories* that have been proposed within each domain, including the basic assumptions about human nature, and (2) the *empirical research* that has been accumulating within each of these domains. In an attempt to bridge the gap between theory and research in personality, we focus primarily on the theories that have received the greatest research attention and the topics within each domain for which there is the greatest cumulative knowledge base.

Dispositional Domain

The **dispositional domain** deals centrally with the ways in which individuals differ from one another. As such, the dispositional domain cuts across all the other domains. The reason is that individuals can differ in their habitual emotions, their habitual concepts of self, their physiological propensities, and even their intrapsychic mechanisms. However, what distinguishes the dispositional domain is an interest in the number, nature, and consequences of fundamental dispositions. The central goal of personality psychologists working in the dispositional domain is to identify and measure the most important ways in which individuals differ from one another. They are also interested in the origins of the important individual differences and in how they develop and are maintained.

Biological Domain

The core assumption within the **biological domain** is that humans are, first and foremost, collections of biological systems, and these systems provide the building blocks for behavior, thought, and emotion. As personality psychologists use the term, *biological approaches* typically refers to three areas of research within this general domain: genetics, psychophysiology, and evolution.

The first area of research consists of the genetics of personality. Because of advances in behavioral genetic research, a fair amount is known about the genetics of personality. Some questions this research addresses include the following: Are identical twins more alike than fraternal twins in their personalities? What happens to identical twins when they are reared

Identical twins Alvin (left) and Calvin (right) Harrison, age 26, celebrate their first and second place finishes in the 400-meter race in Brisbane, Australia, August 8, 2000. Psychologists are studying twins to determine whether some aspects of personality are influenced by genetics.

© Greg Wood/AFP/Getty Images

apart versus when they are reared together? Can we identify the specific genes underlying traits using molecular genetic methods? Behavioral genetic research permits us to ask and provisionally answer these questions.

The second biological approach is best described as the psychophysiology of personality. Within this domain, researchers summarize what is known about the basis of personality in terms of nervous system functioning. Examples of such topics include cortical arousal and neurotransmitters, cardiac reactivity, strength of the nervous system, pain tolerance, circadian rhythms (whether you are a morning or night person), and the links between hormones, such as testosterone, and personality.

The third component of the biological approach concerns how evolution may have shaped human psychological functioning. This approach assumes that the psychological mechanisms that constitute human personality have evolved over thousands of years because they were effective in solving adaptive problems linked to survival and reproduction. An evolutionary perspective sheds light on the functional aspects of personality. We also highlight some fascinating research on personality in nonhuman animals (Gosling, 2001; Sih et al., 2015; Vazire & Gosling, 2003).

Intrapsychic Domain

The **intrapsychic domain** deals with mental mechanisms of personality, many of which operate outside of conscious awareness. The dominant theory in this domain is Freud's theory of psychoanalysis. This theory begins with fundamental assumptions about the instinctual system—the sexual and aggressive forces that are presumed to drive and energize much of human activity. Considerable research reveals that sexual and aggressive motives are indeed powerful, and their manifestations in actual behavior can be studied empirically. The intrapsychic domain also includes defense mechanisms, such as repression, denial, and projection—some of which have been examined in laboratory studies. Although the intrapsychic domain is most closely linked with the psychoanalytic theory of Sigmund Freud, there are modern versions as well. For example, much of the research on the power motives, achievement motives, and intimacy motives is based on a key intrapsychic assumption—that these forces often operate outside the realm of consciousness.

Cognitive-Experiential Domain

The **cognitive-experiential domain** focuses on thought processes and subjective experience, such as conscious ideas, feelings, beliefs, and desires about oneself and others. The psychological mechanisms involved in subjective experience differ, however, in form and content from one another. One important element of our experience entails the self and self-concept. Descriptive aspects of the self organize how we view ourselves: knowledge of ourselves, images of past selves, and images of possible future selves. Do we see ourselves as good or as evil? Are our past successes or past failures prominent in our self-views? Do we envision ourselves in the future as married with children or as successful in a career? How we evaluate ourselves—our self-esteem—is another facet of the cognitive-experiential domain.

A somewhat different aspect of this domain pertains to the goals we strive for. Some personality psychologists, for example, view human nature as inherently goal-directed, stressing the organizing influence of fundamental needs or strivings, such as the need for affiliation and the striving for status. Recent research within this tradition includes approaching personality through the personal projects, that is the tasks that individuals are trying to accomplish in their daily lives. These can range from the commonplace, such as getting a date for Saturday night, to the grandiose, such as changing social injustice in Western civilization.

Another important aspect of subjective experience entails our emotions. Are we happy or sad? What makes us angry or fearful? Do we keep our emotions bottled up inside, or do we express them at the drop of a hat? Joy, sadness, feelings of triumph, and feelings of despair all are essential elements in our subjective experience and are subsumed by the cognitive-experiential domain.

Social and Cultural Domain

One of the special features of this book is an emphasis on the **social and cultural domain** of personality. The assumption is that personality is not something that merely resides within the heads, nervous systems, and genes of individuals. Rather, personality affects, and is affected by, the social and cultural context.

At a cultural level, it is clear that groups differ tremendously from one another. Cultures such as the Yanomamö Indians of Venezuela are somewhat aggressive; indeed, a Yanomamö man does not achieve full status as a man until he has killed another man. In contrast, cultures such as the !Kung San of Botswana are relatively peaceful and agreeable. Overt displays of aggression are discouraged and bring social shame on the perpetrator. Personality differences among these groups are most likely due to cultural influences. In other words, different cultures may bring out different facets of our personalities in manifest behavior. Everyone may have the capacity to be peaceful as well as the capacity to be aggressive, as documented by the dramatic changes in violence and peacefulness over time (Pinker, 2012). Which one of these capacities we display may depend on what is acceptable in and encouraged by the culture.

By studying people in different cultures, psychologists are learning how society shapes personality by encouraging or discouraging specific behaviors. An indigenous man along the Amazon River, near Iquitos, Peru.
© *Dave Moyer RF*

At the level of individual differences within cultures, personality plays itself out in the social sphere. Whether we are dominant or submissive affects such diverse parts of our lives as the conflicts we get into with our partners and the tactics we use to manipulate others. Whether we tend to be anxious and depressed or buoyant and optimistic affects the likelihood of social outcomes, such as marital stability and divorce. Whether we are introverted or extraverted affects how many friends we will have and our popularity within the group. Many important individual differences are played out in the interpersonal sphere.

One important social sphere concerns relationships between men and women. At the level of differences between the genders, personality may operate differently for men than for women. Gender is often an essential part of our identities.

Adjustment Domain

The **adjustment domain** refers to the fact that personality plays a key role in how we cope, adapt, and adjust to the ebb and flow of events in our day-to-day lives. Evidence, for example, shows that personality is linked with important health outcomes, such as heart disease. Personality is also linked with health-related behaviors, such as smoking, drinking, and risk-taking. Some research has even demonstrated that personality is linked with how long we live.

Personality relates to health by influencing health-related behaviors, such as smoking.
© Martin Novak/Alamy Stock Photo RF

In addition to health, many important problems in coping and adjustment can be traced to personality. In this domain, certain personality features are related to poor adjustment and have been designated as personality disorders. Chapter 19 is devoted to the personality disorders, such as narcissistic personality disorder, antisocial personality disorder, and avoidant personality disorder. An understanding of "normal" personality functioning can be deepened by examining the disorders of personality, much as in the field of medicine, in which an understanding of normal physiological functioning is often illuminated by the study of disease.

Exercise

Think of a behavior pattern or characteristic that you find interesting in yourself or someone you know. Characteristics such as procrastination, narcissism, and perfectionism are good examples, but any personality characteristic that catches your interest is good. Then write six sentences about this characteristic, one to represent each of the six domains: dispositional, biological, intrapsychic, cognitive-experiential, social and cultural, and adjustment. Each sentence should make a statement or ask a question about the characteristic from the perspective of a particular domain.

The Role of Personality Theory

One of the central aims of this book is to highlight the interplay between personality theory and research. In each domain of knowledge, there are some prevailing theories, so we close this chapter with a discussion of theories. Theories are essential in all scientific endeavors, and they serve several useful purposes. A **good theory** is one that fulfills three purposes in science:

- provides a guide for researchers,
- organizes known findings, and
- makes predictions.

One of the most important purposes of theories is that they serve as a *guide for researchers,* directing them to important questions within an area of research.

A second useful function of theories is to *organize known findings.* In physics, for example, there is a bewildering array of events—apples fall from trees, planets exert attraction on each other, black holes suck down light. The theory of gravity neatly and powerfully accounts for all these observations. By accounting for known findings, theories bring both coherence and understanding to the known world. The same applies to personality theories. Theories are viewed as powerful if they succeed in accounting for known findings, in addition to guiding psychologists to important domains of inquiry.

A third purpose of theories is to *make predictions* about behavior and psychological phenomena that no one has yet documented or observed. Einstein's theory of relativity, for example, predicted that light will bend around large stars long before we had the technology to test this prediction. When researchers finally confirmed that light does, indeed, bend when going around stars such as our sun, that finding bore out the power of Einstein's theory.

Finally, we need to distinguish between scientific **theories** and **beliefs**. For example, astrology is a collection of beliefs about the relationship between personality and the position of the stars at birth. Some people hold that such relationships are true, even in the absence of supporting evidence. To date, psychologists have not found reliable factual support, using standard research methods and systematic observations, for the idea that the positions of the stars at a person's birth influence personality. As such, astrology remains a *belief,* not a scientific theory. Beliefs are often personally useful and crucially important to some people, but they are based on faith, not on reliable facts and systematic observations. Theories, on the other hand, are tested by systematic observations that can be repeated by others and that yield similar conclusions.

In sum, three key criteria of personality theories highlight the interplay of theory and research. They guide researchers to important domains of inquiry, account for known findings, and make predictions about new phenomena.

Standards for Evaluating Personality Theories

As we explore each of the six domains, it will be useful to bear in mind five **scientific standards for evaluating personality theories:**

- comprehensiveness
- heuristic value
- testability
- parsimony
- compatibility and integration across domains and levels

The first standard is **comprehensiveness**—does the theory do a good job of explaining all of the facts and observations within its domain? Theories that explain more empirical findings are generally superior to those that explain fewer findings.

A second evaluative standard is **heuristic value**—does the theory provide a guide to important new discoveries about personality that were not known before? Theories that steer scientists to making these discoveries are generally superior to theories that fail to provide this guidance. Plate tectonic theory in geology, for example, guided researchers to discover regions of volcanic activity that were unknown prior to the theory. Similarly, a good personality theory will guide personality researchers to make discoveries that were previously unknown.

A third important standard for evaluating theories is **testability**—does the theory provide precise predictions that can be tested empirically? Some theories—for example, certain aspects of Freud's theory of intrapsychic conflict—have been criticized on the grounds that they are difficult or impossible to test; other aspects of Freud's theory are testable (see Chapters 9 and 10). As a general rule, the testability of a theory rests with the precision of its predictions. Precise theoretical predictions aid progress in the science because they allow inadequate theories to be discarded (those whose predictions are falsified) and good theories to be retained (those whose predictions are empirically confirmed). If a theory does not lend itself to being tested empirically, it is generally judged to be a poor theory.

A fourth standard for evaluating personality theories is **parsimony**—does the theory contain few premises and assumptions (parsimony) or many premises and assumptions (lack of parsimony)? As a general rule, theories that require many premises and assumptions to explain a given set of findings are judged to be poorer than theories that can explain the same findings with fewer premises and assumptions. Although parsimony is important, bear in mind that this does not mean that simple theories are always better than complex theories. Indeed, simple theories often crash and burn because they fail to meet one or more of the other five standards described here; for example, they may fail to be comprehensive because they explain so little. It is our view that human personality is genuinely complex, and so a complex theory—one containing many premises—may ultimately be necessary.

A fifth standard is **compatibility and integration across domains and levels**. A theory of cosmology in astronomy that violated known laws of physics, for example, would be incompatible across levels and hence judged to be fundamentally flawed. A theory of biology that violated known principles of chemistry similarly would be judged to be fatally flawed. In the same way, a personality theory in one domain that violated well-established principles in another domain would be judged highly problematic. For example, a theory of the development of personality dispositions that was inconsistent with well-established knowledge in physiology and genetics would be judged to be problematic. Similarly, a theory of evolutionary influences on personality that contradicted what is known about cultural influences, or vice versa, would be problematic. Although the criterion of *compatibility and integration across domains and levels* is a well-established principle in most sciences (Buss, 2015; Tooby & Cosmides, 1992), it has rarely been used to evaluate the adequacy of personality theories. We believe that the "domains" approach taken in this book highlights the importance of the evaluative criterion of compatibility across levels of personality analysis.

In sum, as you progress through the six domains of personality functioning, keep in mind the five standards by which theories within each domain can be evaluated—comprehensiveness, heuristic value, testability, parsimony, and cross-domain compatibility (see Table 1.2).

Table 1.2 Five Standards for Evaluating Personality Theories

Standard	Definition
Comprehensiveness	Explains most or all known facts.
Heuristic value	Guides researchers to important new discoveries.
Testability	Makes precise predictions that can be empirically tested.
Parsimony	Contains few premises or assumptions.
Compatibility and integration	Consistent with what is known in other domains; can be coordinated with other branches of scientific knowledge.

Is There a Grand Ultimate and True Theory of Personality?

The field of biology contains a grand unifying theory—the theory of evolution by natural selection, originally proposed by Darwin (1859) and further refined in its neo-Darwinian form as inclusive fitness theory (Hamilton, 1964). This theory is comprehensive, guides biologists to new discoveries, has led to thousands of empirical tests, is highly parsimonious, and is compatible with known laws in adjacent scientific disciplines. Evolutionary theory provides the grand unifying framework within which most biologists conduct their work. Ideally, the field of personality psychology would also contain such a grand unifying theory. Alas, at the current time, it does not.

Perhaps Sigmund Freud, the inventor of psychoanalytic theory, provided the most ambitious attempt at a grand unifying theory of personality (see Chapter 9). And many grand theories have followed Freud's. But over the past several decades, most personality researchers have come to the realization that the field currently lacks a grand unifying theory. Instead, most have focused on more specific domains of functioning. It is precisely for this reason that our book is organized around the six domains—these represent the domains in which progress, scientific findings, and new discoveries are being made.

In our view, an ultimate grand theory of personality psychology will have to unify all six domains. It will have to explain personality characteristics and how they develop over time (dispositional domain). It will have to explain evolutionary, genetic, and physiological underpinnings of personality (biological domain). It will have to explain deeply rooted motives and dynamic intrapsychic processes (intrapsychic domain). It will have to explain how people experience the world and process information about it (cognitive-experiential domain). It will have to explain how personality affects, and is affected by, the social and cultural context in which people conduct their lives (social and cultural domains). And it will have to explain how people cope and function—as well as how adjustment fails—as they encounter the numerous adaptive problems they face over the sometimes bumpy course of their lives (the adjustment domain).

Although the field of personality psychology currently lacks a grand theory, we believe that work in these six domains will ultimately provide the foundations on which such a unified personality theory will be built. We are excited to report that there have been tremendous developments and discoveries in all six domains. We hope you share our excitement about discovering these domains of human personality.

KEY TERMS

trait-descriptive adjectives 4
personality 4
psychological traits 5
average tendencies 5
psychological mechanisms 6
within the individual 7
organized 7
enduring 7
influential forces 8
person–environment interaction 8
adaptation 9
environment 9

human nature 10
individual differences 11
differences among groups 11
nomothetic 12
idiographic 12
domain of knowledge 14
dispositional domain 15
biological domain 15
intrapsychic domain 16
cognitive-experiential domain 16
social and cultural domain 17
adjustment domain 17

good theory 18
theories 19
beliefs 19
scientific standards for evaluating
    personality theories 19
comprehensiveness 19
heuristic value 19
testability 19
parsimony 20
compatibility and integration across
    domains and levels 20

Personality Assessment, Measurement, and Research Design

INTRODUCTION

 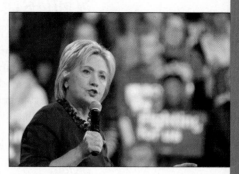

Much of the discussion surrounding political candidates involves their personalities.
Left © actionsports/123RF RF; Right © a katz/Shutterstock. com RF

I magine that a presidential election is looming. You are faced with a choice between two candidates. The personalities of the candidates may prove to be critical to your decision. How will they hold up under stress? What are their attitudes toward abortion or gun control? Will they stand tough in negotiating with leaders from other countries? This chapter is concerned with the means by which we gain information about other people's personalities—the sources from which we gather personality data and the research designs we use in the scientific study of personality.

When deliberating between the two presidential candidates, you might want to know what they say about their values and attitudes—through a *self-report*. You might want to know what others say about their strengths in dealing with foreign leaders—through an *observer report*. You also might want to place the candidates in a more controlled situation, such as a debate, and see how each performs—to acquire *test data* (T-data). Furthermore, you might want to know about certain events in their lives, such as whether they have ever used illegal drugs, been arrested, dodged the draft, been divorced, or have ever been caught in an embarrassing sexual scandal—*life history data*.

Each of these sources of data reveals something about the personalities of the presidential candidates, yet each alone is incomplete and may be biased. (For fascinating personality analyses of presidential candidates, see Immelman, 2002; O'Donnell & Rutherford, 2016; Post, 2003; and Renshon, 1998, 2005.) The candidate may self-report a grandiose record of successful business dealings, for example, but then the actual records show a history of bankruptcy filings and unpaid bills. Observers may report that the candidate is honest, yet they may be unaware of lies the candidate has told. A debate may show one candidate in a positive light, but perhaps the other candidate happened to have a cold that day. And the public record of serving in the military reserve may not reveal the family connections that enabled the candidate to avoid combat. Each source of data provides important information. But each source, by itself, is of limited value, an incomplete picture.

This chapter covers three topics related to personality assessment and research. The first concerns where we get our information—the sources of personality data and the actual measures that personality psychologists use. The second topic concerns how we evaluate the quality of those measures. The third topic pertains to how we use these measures in actual research designs to study personality.

Sources of Personality Data

Perhaps the most obvious source of information about a person is **self-report data** **(S-data)**—the information a person reveals. Clearly, individuals may not always provide accurate information about themselves for a variety of reasons, such as the desire to present themselves in a positive light. Nevertheless, the journals that publish the latest research in personality reveal that self-report is the most common method for measuring personality (Connelly & Ones, 2010).

S-Data

Self-report data can be obtained through a variety of means, including interviews that pose questions to a person, periodic reports by a person to record the events as they happen, and questionnaires. The questionnaire method, in which individuals respond to a series of items that request information about them, is by far the most commonly used self-report assessment procedure.

There are good reasons for using self-report. The most obvious reason is that individuals have access to a wealth of information about themselves that is inaccessible to anyone else, such as their habitual level of anxiety (e.g., Vazire, 2010). Individuals can report about their feelings, emotions, desires, beliefs, and private experiences. They can report about their self-esteem, as well as their perceptions of the esteem in which others hold them. They can report about their innermost fears and fantasies. And they can report about immediate and long-term goals. Because of this potential wealth of information, self-report is an indispensable source of personality data.

Self-report can take a variety of forms, ranging from open-ended "fill in the blanks" to forced-choice true-or-false questions. Sometimes these are referred to as **unstructured** (open-ended, such as "Tell me about the parties you like the most") and **structured** ("I like loud and crowded parties"—answer "true" or "false") personality tests. A prime example of the open-ended form of self-report is called the Twenty Statements Test (TST) (see A Closer Look on the next page for more information). In this test, a participant receives a sheet of paper that is essentially blank, except for the words "I am" repeated 20 times. There is a space after each of these partial statements, and participants are asked to complete them. For example, a person might say, in this order: *I am a woman; I am 19 years old; I am shy; I am intelligent; I am someone who likes quiet nights at home; I am introverted;* and so on. Personality instruments that use open-ended formats require coding schemes for classifying the responses they obtain. In other words, psychologists must devise a way to score or interpret the participant's open-ended responses. To get an idea of how outgoing the woman in our example is, the psychologist might count how many statements refer to social characteristics.

More common than open-ended questionnaires are structured personality questionnaires, in which the response options are provided. The simplest form of the structured self-report questionnaire involves a series of trait-descriptive adjectives, such as *active, ambitious, anxious, arrogant, artistic, generous, gregarious, greedy, good-natured, xenophobic,* and *zany.* Individuals indicate whether each adjective describes them. The simplest format for presenting these terms is a checklist, such as the Adjective Check List (ACL) (Gough, 1980). In completing the ACL, the individuals merely place a check beside adjectives that they feel accurately describe

A Closer Look   Who Am I?

The TST was published by a pair of sociologists. Manford Kuhn and Thomas McPartland were interested in attitudes people had toward themselves. In 1954, they published the "Who am I?" test. This test asked the participant to simply answer this question by completing the phrase "I am _____" 20 times. Kuhn and McPartland developed a way of scoring the test by analyzing the content of the person's responses. The order of each response was thought to be significant (e.g., something mentioned earlier might be more important to the self-definition than something mentioned later).

In early use by psychologists, the TST was applied mainly to clinical and personality research questions. For example, one study used the TST to see if the self-concepts of persons in "unadjusted" marriages differed from the self-concepts of persons in "well-adjusted" marriages (Buerkle, 1960). Results showed that people in adjusted marriages tended to mention their partner, their marriage, and their family more often in their self-definitions than those in unadjusted marriages. This finding implies that part of a successful marriage is incorporating the marriage role into one's definition of oneself.

In the 1970s, researchers turned a more critical eye on the TST. It is an open-ended questionnaire, so people with low verbal ability do not complete it as quickly or as thoroughly as persons with high verbal ability, leading the test scores to be biased by intelligence differences in participants (Nudelman, 1973). However, if people are given enough time to complete the 20 questions—at least 15 minutes—then it appears that the intelligence bias is eliminated. The TST survived and emerged as a measure that the field deemed useful for assessing how people defined themselves.

In the 1980s, the TST was used in the study of timely personality topics, such as the influence of gender and other social roles in people's self-definitions. For example, one study compared married and single women (Gigy, 1980). Married women tended to respond to the "Who am I?" question by mentioning relationships (*I am a mother, I am a wife*), acquired roles in family life (*I am the one who feeds the children*), and household activities (*I am the one who buys groceries*). Clearly, marriage can mean a large change in self-concept, and studies such as this one document the link between social roles and how individuals see themselves.

There has been a trend toward using culture and ethnicity in self-definitions (Bochner, 1994). One cross-cultural study using the TST compared people from Kenya with people from the United States. Several groups were compared on the percentage of responses that included references to social group categories (e.g., *I am a member of the local school board* or *I am a player on the local softball team*). U.S. college students mentioned social groups in their self-definitions 12 percent of the time. In Kenya, university students mentioned social groups 17 percent of the time. However, for traditional rural Kenyan citizens, results were quite different. Massai tribespersons in Kenya mentioned social groups 80 percent of the time in their responses, and Samburu tribespersons mentioned social groups 84 percent of the time in their TST responses (Ma & Schoeneman, 1997). Results such as these show how culture may influence how we view ourselves. The TST is a useful way to measure how people define themselves. The TST has proven especially effective at identifying the most important components of a person's identity—the ingredients that provide a person with a sense of self-esteem, meaning in life, and sense of belonging in the world of other people (Vignoles et al., 2006).

them and leave blank items that don't describe them. A more complex method involves requesting participants to indicate in numerical form the degree to which each trait term characterizes them, say on a 7-point rating scale of 1 (least characteristic) to 7 (most characteristic). This is called a **Likert rating scale** (after the person who invented it), and it is simply a way for someone to express with numbers the degree to which a particular trait describes him or her. A typical Likert rating scale looks like this:

ENERGETIC

1	2	3	4	5	6	7

Least characteristic   Most characteristic

Most commonly, a *personality scale* consists of summing the scores on a series of individual rating scales. A personality scale for activity level, for example, might consist of summing up scores from rating scales on *energetic, active,* and *vigorous.*

Exercise

DIRECTIONS: This list contains a series of adjectives. Please read them quickly and put an X in the box beside each one you consider to be self-descriptive. Try to be honest and accurate.

___	absent-minded	___	cheerful	___	dependent
___	active	___	civilized	___	despondent
___	adaptable	___	clear-thinking	___	determined
___	adventurous	___	clever	___	dignified
___	affected	___	coarse	___	discreet
___	affectionate	___	cold	___	disorderly
___	soft-hearted	___	touchy	___	zany

More common than adjective checklists, however, are self-report questionnaires in the form of statements. Examples of widely used self-report inventories are the NEO Personality Inventory (Costa & McCrae, 2005) and the California Psychological Inventory (CPI) (Gough, 1957/1987). Sample items from the CPI are: *I enjoy social gatherings just to be with people; I looked up to my father as an ideal man; A person needs to "show off" a little now and then; I have a very strong desire to be a success in the world; I am very slow in making up my mind.* Participants read each statement and then indicate on an answer sheet whether they agree with the statement and feel that it is true of them or disagree with the statement and feel that it is false about them. Sample items from the NEO Personality Inventory are: *I like most people I meet; I laugh easily; I often get disgusted with people I have to deal with.* Participants indicate the degree to which they agree the item describes them, using a 1 to 5 Likert scale, with 1 anchored with the phrase *strongly disagree* and 5 anchored with *strongly agree.*

Exercise

Pick a personality characteristic you would like to measure. Start by writing down a clear definition of that characteristic. For example, you might choose such characteristics as friendly, conscientious, anxious, or narcissistic. Then write a short questionnaire, about five items long, to measure this characteristic. Your items can be statements or adjectives, and they can be open-ended, true–false, or on a Likert response scale. Then give your questionnaire to other people. How easy was it to write items? Do you think your measure accurately assesses the trait?

Self-report measures, like all methods, have limitations and weaknesses. For the self-report method to be effective, respondents must be both willing and able to answer the questions put to them. Yet people are not always honest, especially when asked about unconventional experiences, such as unusual desires, unconventional sex practices, and undesirable traits. Some people may lack accurate self-knowledge. Because of these limitations, personality psychologists often use sources of data that do not rely on the honesty or insight of the participant. One of those sources is observers.

Application

Experience sampling—a wrinkle in self-report. One source of data in personality research is called **experience sampling** (e.g., Barrantes-Vidal & Kwapil, 2014; Hormuth, 1986; Larsen, 1989; Mehl & Pennebaker, 2003). In this method, people answer some questions, perhaps about their moods or physical symptoms, every day for several weeks or longer. People are usually contacted electronically (paged) one or more times a day at random intervals to complete the measures. In one study, 74 college students reported on their moods every day for 84 consecutive days (Larsen & Kasimatis, 1990). The investigators were interested in discovering the links between the day of the week and mood. They found a strong weekly cycle in the moods of the college students, with positive moods peaking on Friday and Saturday and negative moods peaking on Tuesday and Wednesday (Monday was not the worst day of the week). The introverts turned out to have a much more regular weekly mood cycle than extraverts. That is, the moods of the introverts were more predictable from this 7-day rhythm than the moods of the extraverts. This difference was probably due to the fact that extraverts are less likely to wait for the weekend to do things that put them in a good mood—partying, socializing, or going out for a special meal with friends. Extraverts typically avoid routine in their daily lives, and introverts typically lead more predictable lives.

Although experience sampling uses self-report as the data source, it differs from more traditional self-report methods in being able to detect patterns of behavior over time. Thus, experience sampling provides information not readily available using questionnaires taken at just one point in time. It's an excellent method, for example, for obtaining information about how a person's self-esteem may go up and down over time or how a person reacts to the stress of life day after day. Experience sampling is increasingly being used in personality research using technologies such as smartphones, Facebook, Twitter, and Instagram postings, and even Fitbit records. One study in Korea, for example, found that people high on narcissism posted more selfies and updated their profile pictures more often than those low on narcissism (e.g., Moon et al., 2016).

Observer-Report Data (O-Data)

In everyday life, we form impressions of others with whom we come into contact. For each individual, there are typically dozens of observers who form impressions. Our friends, families, teachers, and casual acquaintances are all potential sources of information about our personalities. **Observer-report data (O-data)** capitalizes on these sources for gathering information about a person's personality.

Observer reports offer both advantages and disadvantages as sources of personality data. One advantage is that observers may have access to information not attainable through other sources. For example, observers can report about the impressions people make on others, their social reputation, whether interactions with others are smooth or conflict-ridden and their status within the group hierarchy. Indeed, one study found that altruistic traits can be identified by observers with some accuracy by a mere 20-second exposure (Fetchenhauer et al., 2010). As noted by Santayana (1905/1980), "[The observer] sometimes reaches truths about people's character and destiny which they themselves are far from divining" (p. 154).

A second advantage of observer-reports is that multiple observers can be used to assess each individual, whereas in self-report only one person provides information (Connelly & Ones, 2010; Paunonen & O'Neill, 2010). The use of multiple observers allows investigators to evaluate the degree of agreement among observers—also known as **inter-rater reliability**. Furthermore, statistical procedures, such as averaging the assessments of multiple observers, have the advantage of reducing the idiosyncratic features and biases of single observers. Typically, a more valid and reliable assessment of personality can be achieved when multiple observers are used.

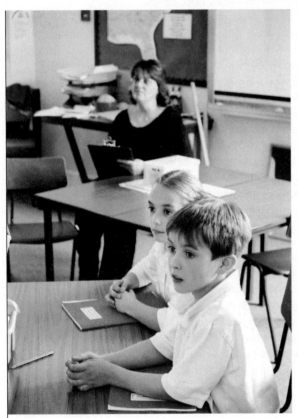

Observer reports can be used as one source of personality information.

© *Bananastock/age fotostock RF*

Selection of Observers

A key decision point that researchers face when using observers is how to select them. Personality researchers have developed two strategies. One strategy is to use professional personality assessors who do not know the participant in advance. The other strategy is to use individuals who actually know the target participants.

One setting in which professional observers are used is the Institute for Personality and Social Research (IPSR) at the University of California at Berkeley. Participants go to the institute for periods of time ranging from one to five days so that a wide variety of in-depth personality assessments can take place. One study contacted a set of architects who were judged by their peers to be highly creative, to determine the personality predictors of creativity. Another study looked at novelists judged to be creative. A third assessed graduate students in an MBA program to determine the personality predictors of success in business. During studies at the IPSR, trained personality assessors observe the participants in many contexts. Subsequently, each observer provides an independent personality description of the participants.

A second strategy for obtaining observational data is to use individuals who actually know the target participants. For example, close friends, spouses, mothers, and roommates have all been used to provide personality data on participants (e.g., Buss, 1984; Connelly & Ones, 2010; Vazire & Mehl, 2008). The use of observers who have existing relationships with the participant has advantages and disadvantages when compared with professional assessors. One advantage is that such observers are in a better position to observe the target's natural behavior. In the relatively public context of an IPSR assessment, in contrast, professional observers cannot witness the more private actions of a person and must settle for observing public actions. A spouse or close friend has access to privileged information often inaccessible through other sources.

A second advantage of using intimate observers is that **multiple social personalities** can be assessed (Craik, 1986, 2008). Each one of us displays different sides of ourselves to different people—we may be kind to our friends, ruthless to our enemies, loving toward a spouse, and conflicted toward our parents. Our manifest personalities, in other words, vary from one social setting to another, depending on the nature of relationships we have with other individuals (Lukaszewski & Roney, 2010). The use of multiple observers provides a method for assessing the many aspects of an individual's personality.

Although there are advantages in using intimate observers in personality assessment, there are also drawbacks (Vazire, 2010). Because intimate observers have relationships with the target person, they may be biased in certain ways. A participant's mother, for example, may overlook the negative and emphasize the positive features of her child.

Naturalistic Versus Artificial Observation

In addition to deciding the type of observers to use, personality researchers must determine whether the observation occurs in a natural or an artificial setting. In **naturalistic observation,** observers witness and record events that occur in the normal course of the lives of their participants. For example, a child might be followed throughout an entire day, or an observer may sit in a participant's home. In contrast, observation can take place in artificial settings, such as occur at the IPSR. Experimenters can instruct participants to perform a task, such as participation in a group discussion, and then observe how individuals behave in these constructed settings. For example, psychologists John Gottman and Robert Levenson have had married couples go to their laboratory and discuss a topic on which they disagree. The psychologists then observe the couple having a small argument. The way in which a couple conducts an argument can predict the likelihood that the couple will remain together or get divorced (Gottman, 1994). Even the facial expressions displayed during these laboratory conflicts predict subsequent marital outcomes (Coan & Gottman, 2007; Gottman, Levenson, & Woodin, 2001).

Naturalistic observation offers researchers the ability to secure information in the realistic context of a person's everyday life, but at the cost of not being able to control the events and behavioral samples witnessed. Observation in experimenter-generated situations has the advantage of controlling conditions and eliciting the relevant behavior. But this advantage comes at a cost—sacrificing the realism of everyday life.

In summary, there are many dimensions along which O-data, differ such as decisions about whether to use (1) professional assessors or intimate observers and (2) a naturalistic or an artificial setting. The strengths and weaknesses of the options must be evaluated with the goals of the investigation in mind. No single method is ideally suited for all assessment purposes.

Test Data (T-Data)

Beyond self-report and O-data, a third common source of personality-relevant information comes from standardized tests—**test data (T-data).** Participants are placed in a standardized testing situation. The idea is to see if different people react differently to an identical situation. The situation is designed to elicit behaviors that serve as indicators of personality variables (Block, 1977). An interesting example is the bridge-building test found in Henry Murray's (1948) classic book *The Assessment of Men.* In this test, the person being assessed is given two assistants and a collection of wood, rope, and tools, and he or she has the task of building a bridge over a small creek. The person being assessed cannot do the work alone, but must instruct the two assistants on how to build the bridge. Unbeknownst to the person being assessed, the two assistants are role-playing: one is acting dim-witted and has trouble understanding instructions; the other is a "know-it-all," who has his or her own ideas about how the bridge should be built and often contradicts the person being assessed. These two "helpers" actually are there to frustrate the person being assessed. Although the person being assessed thinks he or she is being observed on leadership skills, the person is actually being evaluated on tolerance of frustration and performance under adversity.

One fascinating example of the use of T-data is Edwin Megargee's (1969) study of manifestations of *dominance*. Megargee wanted to devise a laboratory test situation to examine the effect of dominance on leadership. He first administered the California Psychological Inventory Dominance scale to a large group of men and women. He then selected only men and women who scored either very high or very low on dominance. Megargee then took pairs of individuals into the laboratory, in each case pairing a high-dominant participant with a low-dominant participant. He created four conditions: (1) a high-dominant man with a low-dominant man; (2) a high-dominant woman with a low-dominant woman; (3) a high-dominant man with a low-dominant woman; and (4) a high-dominant woman with a low-dominant man.

Megargee then presented each pair with a large box containing many red, yellow, and green nuts, bolts, and levers. Participants were told that the purpose of the study was to explore the relationship between personality and leadership under stress. Each pair had to work as a team of troubleshooters to repair the box as fast as possible—by removing nuts and bolts with certain colors and replacing them with other colors. They were told that one person from the team had to be the *leader,* a position which entailed giving instructions. The second person was to be the *follower,* who had to go inside the box and carry out the menial tasks requested by the leader. The experimenter then told the participants that it was up to them to decide who would be the leader and who would be the follower.

Who takes the leadership role when people work together is often a function of personality.
© Sam Edwards/Getty Images RF

The key variable of interest for Megargee was who would become the leader and who would become the follower. He simply recorded the percentage of high-dominant participants within each condition who became leaders. He found that 75 percent of the high-dominant men and 70 percent of the high-dominant women took the leadership role in the same-sex pairs. When high-dominant men were paired with low-dominant women, however, 90 percent of the men became leaders. But the most startling result occurred when the woman was high in dominance and the man was low in dominance. In this condition, only 20 percent of the high-dominant women assumed the leadership role.

Megargee tape-record the conversations while they were deciding who would be the leader. When he analyzed these tapes, he made a startling finding: the high-dominant women were *appointing* their low-dominant partners to the leadership position. In fact, the high-dominant women actually made the final decision about the roles 91 percent of the time. This finding suggests that women were *expressing* their dominance in a different manner than the men in the mixed-sex condition.

Megargee's study highlights several key points about laboratory studies. First, it shows that it is possible to set up conditions to reveal key indicators of personality. Second, it suggests that laboratory experimenters should be sensitive to manifestations of personality that occur in incidental parts of the experiment, such as the discussions among the participants. And, third, there are often interesting links between S-data obtained through questionnaires and T-data obtained through controlled testing conditions. Such links help to establish the validity of both the questionnaire and the laboratory test of dominance.

Like all data sources, T-data have limitations. First, some participants might try to guess what trait is being measured and then alter their responses to create a specific impression of themselves. A second challenge is the difficulty in verifying that the research participants define the testing situation in the same way as the experimenter. An experiment designed to test for "obedience to authority" might be misinterpreted as a test for "intelligence," perhaps raising anxiety in ways that distort subsequent responses. Failure to confirm the correspondence between the conceptions of experimenters and those of participants may introduce error.

A third caution in the use of T-data is that these situations are inherently *interpersonal,* and a researcher may inadvertently influence how the participants behave. A researcher with an outgoing and friendly personality, for example, may elicit more cooperation from participants than a cold or aloof experimenter (see Kintz, Delprato, Mettee, Parsons, & Schappe, 1965). The choice of who runs the experiment, in short, including the personality and demeanor of the experimenter, may inadvertently introduce effects that alter the obtained results.

Despite these limitations, T-data remain a valuable and irreplaceable source of personality information. Procedures used to obtain T-data can be designed to *elicit behavior* difficult to observe in everyday life. They allow investigators to *control the context* and to eliminate extraneous sources of influence. And they enable experimenters to *test specific hypotheses* by exerting control over the variables that are predicted to have causal influence. For these reasons, T-data procedures remain an indispensable set of tools for the personality researcher (Elfenbein et al., 2008).

Mechanical Recording Devices

Personality psychologists have been enterprising in adapting technological innovations. An example is the use of the "actometer" to assess personality differences in activity or energy level. The actometer is essentially a modified self-winding watch, which can be strapped to the arms or legs of participants (typically, children). Movement activates the winding mechanism, registering the person's activity on the hands of the dial. Of course, day-to-day and even hour-to-hour fluctuations in mood, physiology, and setting limit the usefulness of any single sample of activity level. However, several samples can be recorded on different days to generate composite scores, reflecting, for each person, whether he or she is hyperactive, normally active, or sedentary (Buss, Block, & Block, 1980).

In one study, preschool children ages 3 and 4 wore actometers on the wrist of the nonfavored hand for approximately two hours (Buss et al., 1980). The dial of each actometer was covered with tape, so the children would not be distracted. Indeed, in pretesting, the children who could observe the dial became preoccupied with it—sitting in one spot, shaking the device back and forth—a practice that interfered with the usefulness of the measure. Several separate recording sessions were held, and the actometer readings were aggregated to obtain a more reliable index of each child's activity level.

The experimenters then sought answers to three questions: (1) Does activity level measured with the actometer yield the same results as activity level measured through observation? (2) To what extent is activity level stable over time? (3) Do activity level measurements using this mechanical recording device relate to observer-based judgments of personality functioning? To answer these questions, the children's teachers provided observer evaluations using the children's version of the California Q-Sort—an instrument designed to produce a wide-ranging description of children's personality characteristics (Block & Block, 1980). Examples of items on the Q-Sort are: *is a talkative individual; behaves in a giving way toward others; is basically submissive; is*

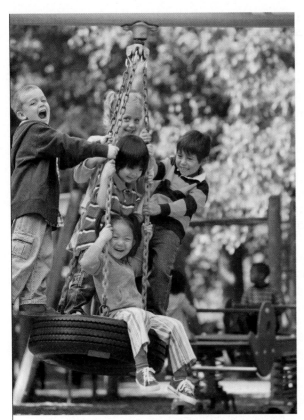

Activity level is stable over time and correlates with teacher ratings of vital, energetic, and active.

© *Ariel Skelley/Getty Images RF*

guileful and deceitful, manipulative, opportunistic; has a high energy level. These observations were made when the children were 3, 4, and 7 years old, whereas the actometer measures were recorded at ages 3 and 4.

It turns out that there was a strong correspondence between actometer measures of activity level and the observer-based measures. Activity level also turns out to be moderately stable over time. For example, actometer measures at age 3 showed a moderate correspondence with actometer measures at age 4. Is there any relationship between actometer measurements of activity level and observer-based judgments of personality? The highly active children, as assessed with the actometer, were judged by their teachers to be vital, energetic, and active. In addition, the highly active children were judged to be restless and fidgety. The active children were also seen by teachers as uninhibited, assertive, competitive, aggressive physically and verbally, attention-getting, and manipulative of others. Thus, actometer-based activity scores are linked to *other* personality characteristics, traits that have important consequences for social interaction.

In sum, some aspects of personality can be assessed through mechanical recording devices, such as the actometer (Wood et al., 2007). These forms of T-data have several advantages and disadvantages. They provide a mechanical means of assessing personality, unhampered by the biases that might be introduced when a human observer is involved. A second advantage is that they can be obtained in relatively naturalistic settings— such as a children's playground. Their primary disadvantage is that few personality dispositions lend themselves to being assessed by mechanical devices. There are no mechanical devices, for example, to directly measure introversion or conscientiousness.

Electronic and Internet Recording Devices

Electronic recording devices are increasingly being used in personality assessment. These include monitoring through Smart Phones, Instagram, Facebook, Twitter, and fitness devices such as Fitbit. One study using the Electronic Activated Recorder found that moral behavior, as indicated by showing sympathy and gratitude, was highly stable over time (Bollich et al., 2016). Another found that people high on narcissism updated their Instagram profile pictures with great regularity (Moon et al., 2016).

Electronic and internet recordings cut across the categories of T-data, S-data, and O-data. For example, experimenters can introduce an experimental manipulation (T-data), such as prompting participants to discuss a traumatic experience and compare that group with a control group simply asked to write about their day, and then compare the two groups on subsequent physical and psychological health (e.g., Pennebaker & Chung, 2011). Or researchers can ask participants to self-report what they are doing when prompted (S-data), or simply observe behavior such as number of selfies and correlate those with self-reported narcissism (O-data).

Electronic recording devices have the strong advantages in that they can assess naturally occurring behavior in ways not obtainable through laboratory or self-report methods. Nonetheless, because participants are aware that they are being monitored electronically, their behavior may still be sensitive to what they think experimenters want to see, and so act in ways they think are socially desirable.

Physiological Data

A critical source of personality data is physiological measurement. Physiological measures can provide information about a person's level of arousal, reactivity to various stimuli, and the speed at which he or she takes in new information—all potential indicators of personality. Sensors can be placed on different parts of a person's body, for example, to measure sympathetic nervous system activity, blood pressure, heart rate, and muscle contraction. Brain waves, such as reactivity to stimuli, also can be assessed. And even physiological changes associated with sexual arousal can be measured via instruments such as a penile strain gauge (Geer & Head, 1990) or a vaginal bloodflow meter (Hamilton, Rellini, & Meston, 2008).

In Chapter 7, we go into some detail on physiological measures. For our purposes here—examining alternative ways of measuring personality—we look at only one example of using physiological data as a source of personality information. Psychologist Christopher Patrick (1994, 2005) has been studying psychopaths, particularly men in prison who have committed serious crimes against other people. One theory about psychopaths is that they do not have the normal fear or anxiety response that most people have. Things that might make most people anxious may not make the psychopath anxious. To test this idea, Patrick used a technique called the "eyeblink startle reflex," which had previously been used in studies of fear.

When people are startled, as when a loud noise occurs, they show the startle reflex, which consists of blinking their eyes, lowering the chin toward the chest, and inhaling suddenly. If people are already anxious, they exhibit the startle reflex faster than when feeling normal. It makes adaptive sense that they will be prepared to have a faster defensive startle if they are already in a fearful or anxious state. You can demonstrate this by showing people pictures of frightening or unpleasant scenes, such as a snake, a vicious dog, or spiders, which most people find make them a little anxious. If they are startled while looking at these scenes, they will startle faster than when looking at nonfeared objects, such as a house, a tree, or a table. Interestingly, Patrick found that psychopaths who were in prison for violent crimes did not exhibit the faster eyeblink response while viewing the anxiety-producing photographs. Perhaps psychopaths commit their crimes because they don't have the normal level of anxiety or guilt that prevents most of us from doing anything wrong. This is a good example of how physiological measures can be used to examine and understand various personality characteristics.

A more recent physiological data source comes from **functional magnetic resonance imaging (fMRI)**, a technique used to identify the areas of the brain that "light up" when performing certain tasks such as verbal problems or spatial navigation problems. It works by gauging the amount of oxygen brought to particular places in the brain. When a certain part of the brain is highly activated, it draws large amounts of blood. The oxygen carried by the blood accumulates in that region of the brain. The fMRI is able to detect concentrations of iron carried by the oxygen contained in the red blood cells and thus determine the part of the brain that is used in performing certain tasks. The colorful images that emerge from fMRI brain scans are often quite dramatic.

In principle, fMRI provides a physiological data source that can be linked with personality dispositions, intelligence, or psychopathology. In practice, however, the method has limitations on what it reveals. Because fMRI must compare the "activated" state with a "resting" state, it becomes critical to know what the resting state really is. If men's resting state turns more to sports and women's resting state turns more to social

Measures of physiological responses, such as these fMRI brain scans, are a source of data in personality research. As the fMRI on monitor of NIH researcher.

interactions, for example, it is possible that a comparison of a task such as looking at faces to the resting state would suggest that men and women are performing the task differently, when in fact the difference is due entirely to a sex difference in the resting state (Kosslyn & Rosenberg, 2004).

One of the key benefits of physiological data is that it is difficult for participants to fake responses, particularly on measures of arousal or reflexive responses, such as the eyeblink startle reflex. Nonetheless, physiological recording procedures share most of the same limitations as other laboratory T-data. In particular, recording is typically constrained by a relatively artificial laboratory situation.

Projective Techniques

Another type of T-data is **projective techniques,** in which the person is given a standard stimulus and asked what he or she sees. The most famous projective technique for assessing personality is the set of inkblots developed by Hermann Rorschach. The hallmark of any projective technique is that the person is presented with an ambiguous stimulus, such as an inkblot, and then asked to impose structure on this stimulus by describing what he or she sees—for example, what is in the inkblot. The idea behind projective techniques is that what the person sees in the stimulus reveals something about his or her personality. Presumably, the person "projects" his or her concerns, conflicts, traits, and ways of seeing or dealing with the world onto the ambiguous stimulus.

A person interpreting an inkblot may project his or her personality into what is "seen" in the image.

Projective techniques are considered T-data, because all persons are presented with a standard testing situation, all are given the same instructions, and the test situation elicits behaviors that are thought to reveal personality.

To the psychologist interpreting a person's responses to the inkblots, the content of those responses is important. Someone with a "dependent personality," for example, might produce a high frequency of responses such as food, food providers, passively being fed, nurturers, oral activity, passivity, helplessness, and "baby talk" (Bornstein, 2005).

In sum, all projective measures present participants with ambiguous stimuli, asking them to provide structure by interpreting, drawing, or telling a story about the stimuli. Psychologists who advocate projective measures argue that they are useful for getting at wishes, desires, fantasies, and conflicts that the participants themselves may be unaware of and so could not report on a questionnaire. Others are critical of projectives, questioning their validity and reliability as accurate measures of personality (Wood, Nezworski, & Stejskal, 1996).

Life-Outcome Data (L-Data)

Life-outcome data (L-data) refers to information that can be gleaned from the events, activities, and outcomes in a person's life that are available to public scrutiny. For example, marriages and divorces are a matter of public record. Personality psychologists can sometimes secure information about the clubs a person joins, how many speeding tickets a person has received, and whether he or she owns a handgun. Whether a person gets arrested for a violent or white-collar crime is a matter of public record. Success at one's job, whether one is

The tendency to have frequent temper outbursts in childhood has been linked with negative adult outcomes, such as increased likelihood of divorce.
© Chris Knapton/Alamy Stock Photo RF

upwardly or downwardly mobile, and the creative products one produces, such as books published and music recorded, are often important outcomes in a person's life. These can all serve as important sources of information about personality.

Personality psychologists often use S-data and O-data to predict L-data. An example that illustrates how O-data can be used to predict important life events is provided by Avshalom Caspi and his colleagues (Caspi, Elder, & Bem, 1987). Based on clinical interviews with mothers of children ages 8, 9, and 10, researchers created two personality scales to measure ill-temperedness. One was based on the *severity* of temper tantrums; it noted physical behaviors such as biting, kicking, striking, and throwing things, and verbal expressions such as swearing, screaming, and shouting. The other scale assessed the *frequency* of these temper tantrums. Caspi and his colleagues summed these two scales to create a single measure of temper tantrums. This measure represents O-data because it is based on the mothers' actual observations. Then, in adulthood, when the participants were 30 to 40 years old, the researchers gathered information about life outcomes, such as education, work, marriage, and parenthood. They examined whether ill-temperedness, measured in childhood as O-data, predicted significant life outcomes two to three decades later, measured as L-data.

The results proved to be remarkable. For the men, early temper tantrums were linked with many negative outcomes in adult life. The men who had exhibited temper tantrums in childhood achieved significantly lower rank in their military service. They tended to have erratic work lives—changing jobs more frequently and experiencing more unemployment than those who had not been judged to be ill-tempered as children. Furthermore, such men were less likely than their even-tempered counterparts to have a satisfying marriage. Fully 46 percent of the ill-tempered men were divorced by age 40, whereas only 22 percent of the men in the low temper-tantrum category were divorced by the age of 40.

For the women, early temper tantrums did not have a bearing on their work lives, in contrast to the men. However, the women who had had temper tantrums as children tended to marry men who were significantly lower than themselves in occupational status; fully 40 percent of the women who had showed temper tantrums as children "married down," compared with only 24 percent of the women who had been even-tempered as children. As with the men, childhood temper tantrums were linked with frequency of divorce for the women. Roughly 26 percent of the women who had had childhood tantrums were divorced by age 40, whereas only 12 percent of the even-tempered women were divorced by that age.

In addition to empirical studies that predict marriage and divorce outcomes, life-outcome data are used in other ways that affect our everyday lives. Our driving records, including speeding tickets and traffic accidents, are used by insurance companies to determine how much we pay for car insurance. Our histories of credit card usage are sometimes tracked by businesses to determine our behavioral preferences, which influence the advertisements we get exposed to on social network sites such as Facebook. And more recently, advertisers sometimes track the Web sites we visit and use e-mail "spam" and pop-up advertisements based on our patterns of Internet surfing. Indeed, even a person's e-mail address can reveal personality. People who adopt e-mail addresses such as honey.bunny77@hotmail.com tend to be somewhat more extraverted than those who adopt blander e-mail addresses (Back, Schmukle, & Egloff, 2008). Thus, driving records, credit card usage, and patterns of Internet usage have become modern sources of L-data. Do you think we can predict these patterns of publicly traceable data from personality variables, such as impulsivity (more driving accidents), status striving (credit card purchase of prestige possessions), and sex drive (more frequent visiting of pornography Web sites)? Future studies of L-data will soon answer these questions.

In sum, L-data can serve as an important source of real-life information about personality. Personality characteristics measured early in life are often linked to important life outcomes several decades later. In this sense, life outcomes, such as work, marriage, and divorce, are, in part, manifestations of personality. Nonetheless, it must be recognized that life outcomes are caused by a variety of factors, including one's gender, culture, economic status, race, and ethnicity and the opportunities to which one happens to be exposed. Personality characteristics represent only one set of causes of these life outcomes.

Exercise

Think of a personality characteristic that you find interesting. For example, you might consider such characteristics as activity level, risk taking, temper, or cooperativeness. Using the four main data sources, think of ways that you might gather information on this characteristic. Give specific examples of how you could assess this characteristic using S-, O-, T-, and L-data as sources of information on people's level of this characteristic. Be specific in providing examples of how and what you might do to assess your chosen personality characteristic.

Issues in Personality Assessment

Now that we have outlined the basic data sources, it is useful to take a step back and consider two broader issues in personality assessment. The first issue involves using two or more data sources within a single personality study. What are the links among the various sources of personality data? The second issue involves the fallibility of personality measurement and how the use of multiple data sources can correct some of the problems associated with single data sources.

Links Among Various Data Sources

A key issue that personality psychologists must address is how closely the findings obtained from one data source correspond to findings from another data source. If, for example, a person rates herself as dominant, do observers, such as her friends and spouse, also view her as dominant? Do findings obtained from electronic recording devices, such as Facebook or Instagram, correspond to data obtained from observer reports or self-reports of narcissism?

Depending on the personality variable under consideration, agreement across data sources tends to range from low to moderate. Ozer and Buss (1991) examined the relationships between self-report and spouse report for eight dimensions of personality. They found that the degree of agreement varied depending on the particular trait and on the observability of the trait. Traits such as extraversion showed moderate agreement across data sources. The trait of "calculating," on the other hand, showed low self–spouse agreement. Traits that are easily observable (such as extraversion) show a higher degree of self–observer agreement than do traits (such as calculating) that are difficult to observe and require inferences about internal mental states (see Vazire, 2010).

One of the central advantages of using multiple measures is that each measure has unique idiosyncrasies that have nothing to do with the underlying construct of interest. By using multiple measures from various data sources, researchers are able to average out these idiosyncrasies and home in on the key variable under study.

A major issue in evaluating linkages among the sources of personality data is whether the sources are viewed as alternative measures of the same construct or as assessments of different phenomena. A person self-reporting about her relative dominance, for example, has access to a wealth of information—namely, her interactions with dozens of other people in her social environment. Any particular observer—a close friend, for example—has access to only a limited and selective sample of relevant behavior. Thus, if the friend rates a woman as highly dominant, whereas the woman rates herself as only moderately dominant, the disagreement may be due entirely to the different behavioral samples on which each person is basing the ratings. Thus, lack of agreement does not *necessarily* signify an error of measurement (although it certainly might).

In summary, the interpretation of links among the sources of personality data depends heavily on the research question being posed. Strong agreement between two sources of data leads researchers to be confident that their alternative measures are tapping into the same personality phenomenon, as proves true with extraversion and activity level. Lack of strong agreement, on the other hand, may mean that the different data sources are assessing different phenomena, or it may indicate that one or more data sources have problems—an issue to which we now turn.

The Fallibility of Personality Measurement

Each data source has problems and pitfalls that limit its utility. This is true of all methods in science. Even so-called objective scientific instruments, such as telescopes, are less than perfect because minor flaws, such as a slight warping in the lens, may introduce errors into the observations. The fallible nature of scientific measures is no less true in personality research.

One powerful strategy of personality assessment, therefore, is to examine results that transcend data sources—a procedure sometimes referred to as *triangulation*. If a particular effect is found—for example, the influence of dominance on the assumption of leadership—does the effect occur when dominance is measured with self-report as well as with observer reports? If extraverts are more easily bored than introverts, does this show up when boredom is assessed with physiological recording devices as well as via self-report? Throughout this book, we pay special attention to findings that transcend the limitations of single-data-source assessment.

Evaluation of Personality Measures

Once personality measures have been identified, the next task is to subject them to scientific scrutiny to determine how good the measures are. In general, three standards are used to evaluate personality measures: reliability, validity, and generalizability. Although these three standards are discussed here in the context of evaluating personality questionnaires, these standards are applicable to all measurement methods within personality research, not merely to those involving self-report personality questionnaires.

Reliability

Reliability can be defined as the degree to which an obtained measure represents the true level of the trait being measured. Assume for a moment that each person has some true amount of the trait you wish to measure and that you could know this true level. If your measure is reliable, then it will correlate with the true level. For example, if a person has a true IQ of 115, then a perfectly reliable measure of IQ will yield a score of 115 for that person. Moreover, a reliable measure of IQ will yield the same score of 115 each time it is administered to the person. A less reliable measure would yield a score, say, in a range of 112 to 118. An even less reliable measure would yield a score in an even broader range, between 100 (which is average) and 130 (which is borderline genius). Personality psychologists prefer reliable measures, so that the scores accurately reflect each person's true level of the personality characteristic.

There are several ways to estimate reliability. One is through **repeated measurement.** There are different forms of repeated measurement. A common procedure is to repeat a measurement over time—for example, at intervals of one month—for the same people. If the two tests are highly correlated, yielding similar scores for most people, the resulting measure is said to have high *test-retest reliability*.

A second way to gauge reliability is to examine the relationships among the items themselves at a single point in time. If the items within a test—viewed as a form of repeated measurement—all correlate well with each other, then the scale is said to have high *internal consistency reliability*. The reliability is internal because it is assessed within the test itself. The rationale for using internal consistency as an index of reliability is that psychologists constructing various measures assume that all items on a scale are measuring the same characteristic. If they are, then the items should be positively correlated with each other.

A third way to measure reliability—applicable only to the use of observer-based personality measures—is to obtain measurements from multiple observers. When different observers agree with each other, the measure is said to have high *inter-rater reliability*. When different raters fail to agree, the measure is said to have low inter-rater reliability.

It is important to demonstrate that a personality measure is reliable, whether through test-retest, internal consistency, or inter-rater reliability. One factor that can reduce measurement reliability, especially for self-report questionnaires, is response sets, to which we now turn.

Response Sets

When participants answer questions, psychologists typically assume that they are responding to the content of the questions. For example, when participants are confronted with the item "I have never felt like smashing things," psychologists assume that participants think of all the times when they were angry and then recall whether on those occasions they have ever felt like smashing something. Psychologists also assume that participants make a deliberate and conscious effort to consider the content of the question and then answer "True" or "False" to honestly reflect their behavior. This assumption may sometimes be incorrect.

The concept of **response sets** refers to the tendency of some people to respond to the questions on a basis that is unrelated to the question content. Sometimes this is also referred to as **noncontent responding**. One example is the response set of **acquiescence,** or yea saying. This is the tendency to simply agree with the questionnaire items, regardless of the content of those items. Psychologists counteract acquiescence by intentionally reverse-scoring some of the questionnaire items, such as an extraversion item that states, "I frequently prefer to be alone." **Extreme responding** is another response set, which refers to the tendency to give endpoint responses, such as "strongly agree" or "strongly disagree" and to avoid the middle part of response scales, such as "slightly agree" or "slightly disagree."

Personality psychologists worry about the effects of response sets on the reliability of measurement. Response sets may invalidate self-report measures of personality, so psychologists have looked for ways to detect and counteract their effects.

The response set known as **social desirability** has received the greatest amount of research and evaluation by personality psychologists. Socially desirable responding is the tendency to answer items in such a way as to come across as socially attractive or likable. People responding in this manner want to make a good impression, to appear to be well adjusted, to be good citizens. For example, imagine being asked to answer "True" or "False" to the statement "Most of the time I am happy." A person might actually be happy only 45 percent of the time yet answer "True" because this is the well-adjusted thing to say in our culture. People like happy people, so the socially desirable response is "Yes, I am happy most of the time." This is an example of responding not to the content of the item but to the kind of impression a "True" or "False" answer would create, and it represents a response set. An interesting new study found that highly religious individuals were more prone to exaggerate their level of Agreeableness, in part because they saw Agreeableness as a highly desirable trait (Ludeke & Carey, 2015).

There are two views regarding the interpretation of social desirability. One is that it represents distortion and should be eliminated or minimized. The other view is that social desirability is a valid part of other desirable personality traits, such as happiness, conscientiousness, or agreeableness.

Some rare individuals, like the late Mother Teresa of Calcutta, might score high on social desirability because they are in fact truly good, not because they want to create a good impression of themselves by lying on a personality questionnaire.

© David Bagnall/Alamy Stock Photo

Table 2.1 Crowne/Marlowe Scale for Measuring Social Desirability

Instructions: Listed below are a number of statements concerning personal attitudes and traits. Read each item and decide whether the statement is true or false as it pertains to you personally.

	True	False
1. I'm always willing to admit it when I make a mistake.	____	____
2. I always try to practice what I preach.	____	____
3. I never resent being asked to return a favor.	____	____
4. I have never been irked when people expressed ideas very different from my own.	____	____
5. I have never deliberately said something that hurt someone's feelings.	____	____
6. I like to gossip at times.	____	____

Source: Crowne & Marlowe, 1964.

Viewing social desirability as distortion does not assume that the person is consciously trying to create a positive impression. A social desirability response set may not actually be an outright effort to distort responses and, so, is different from faking or lying. Some people may simply have a distorted view of themselves or have a strong need to have others think well of them. For this reason, most psychologists have resisted calling this response set "lying" or "faking" (cf. Eysenck & Eysenck, 1972, for a different opinion). Nevertheless, many personality psychologists believe that socially desirable responding introduces inaccuracies into test scores and should be eliminated or controlled.

One approach to the problem of socially desirable responses is to assume that they are erroneous or deceptive, to measure this tendency, and to remove it statistically from the other questionnaire responses. There are several social desirability measures available. Items from a popular measure developed by Crowne and Marlowe (1964) are shown in Table 2.1. Crowne and Marlowe thought of social desirability as reflecting a need for approval, and they published the social desirability scale in their book *The Approval Motive.* Looking at the items on their scale, you can see that they typically refer to minor transgressions that most of us have committed or inadequacies that many of us suffer from. In addition, some items refer to almost saintlike behavior. To the extent that a person denies common faults and problems and endorses a lot of perfect and well-adjusted behaviors, he or she will get a high score on social desirability. A person's score on social desirability can be used to statistically adjust his or her scores on other questionnaires, thereby controlling for this response set.

A second way to deal with the problem of social desirability is by developing questionnaires that are less susceptible to this type of responding. For example, in choosing questions to put on a questionnaire, the researcher may select only the items that have been found *not* to correlate with social desirability.

A third approach to minimizing the effects of socially desirable responding is to use a **forced-choice questionnaire** format. In this format, test takers are confronted with pairs of statements and are asked to indicate which statement in each pair is more true of them. Each statement in the pair is selected to be similar to the other in social desirability, forcing participants to choose among statements that are equally socially desirable (or undesirable). The following items from the Vando Reducer Augmenter

Scale (Vando, 1974) illustrate the forced-choice format: Which would you most prefer (a or b)?

1. **a.** to read the book
   b. to see the movie
2. **a.** eat soft food
   b. eat crunchy food
3. **a.** continuous anesthesia
   b. continuous hallucinations
4. **a.** a job that requires concentration
   b. a job that requires travel

If one answers all *b*s, this scale measures the preference for arousing or strong stimulation. The two choices presented in each item are of approximately the same value in terms of social desirability. Consequently, participants must decide on an answer based on something other than social desirability. They should respond to the *content* of the item and hence provide accurate information about their personalities.

Although many psychologists view socially desirable responding as error to be avoided or eliminated, others see it as part of an important trait, one that is correlated with positive traits such as happiness, adjustment, and conscientiousness. These psychologists suggest that being mentally healthy may, in fact, entail possessing an overly positive view of oneself and one's abilities. In her book *Positive Illusions,* social psychologist Shelly Taylor (1989) summarizes much research suggesting that self-enhancing illusions about oneself, the world, and one's future can promote psychological adjustment and mental health. Indeed, research finds that unrealistic beliefs about the self (positive illusions) are related to better physical health, such as slower progression of disease in men infected with HIV. If psychologists were to measure such positive illusions in the form of social desirability and remove them from other personality measures, they might, in effect, be throwing the baby out with the bathwater. That is, social desirability may be part of being high on adjustment and positive mental health.

Work on social desirability has attempted to disentangle self-deceptive optimism from impression management. Psychologist Delroy Paulhus has developed a social desirability inventory called the Balanced Inventory of Desirable Responding, which contains two separate subscales (Paulhus, 1984, 1990). The Self-Deceptive Enhancement subscale was designed to tap self-deceptive overconfidence and contains items such as "My first impressions of other people are always right." The Impression Management subscale was designed to measure the tendency to present oneself favorably, as in the distortion interpretation of social desirability, and contains items such as "I don't gossip about other people's business." This subscale was intended to be sensitive to self-presentation motives, such as those that lead someone to want to create a good impression in others.

To the extent that response sets, such as social desirability, are considered error, they can reduce measurement reliability (Paulhus & Vazire, 2007). That is, a personality questionnaire that is influenced by response sets would not reflect the true level of the trait being measured. Personality psychologists worry about response sets for this reason, especially for self-report questionnaires. Indeed, new measures of personality are often designed in ways that minimize participants' efforts to fake or present themselves in a socially desirable light (e.g., McDaniel et al., 2009). Response sets also can influence a measure's validity, a topic to which we now turn.

Validity

Validity refers to the extent to which a test measures what it claims to measure (Cronbach & Meehl, 1955; Wiggins, 2003). Establishing whether a test actually measures what it is designed to measure is a complex and challenging task. There are five types of validity: face validity, predictive validity, convergent validity, discriminant validity, and construct validity. The simplest type of validity is **face validity**, which refers to whether the test, on the surface, appears to measure what it is supposed to measure. For example, a scale measuring manipulativeness might include the following face-valid items: *I made a friend just to obtain a favor; I tricked a friend into giving me personal information; I managed to get my way by appearing cooperative; I pretended that I was hurt to get someone to do me a favor.* Because most people agree that these acts are manipulative, the scale containing them is highly face valid.

A more important component of validity is **predictive validity**, which refers to whether the test predicts criteria external to the test (thus it is sometimes called **criterion validity**). A scale intended to measure sensation seeking, for example, should predict which individuals actually take risks to obtain thrills and excitement, such as parachute jumping or motorcycle riding. One study, for example, found that a measure of sensation seeking successfully predicted a variety of gambling behaviors, such as playing the lottery, betting on sporting events, playing video poker, and using slot machines—attesting to the predictive validity of the sensation-seeking measure (McDaniel & Zuckerman, 2003). A scale created to measure conscientiousness should predict which people actually show up on time for meetings and follow rules. Scales that successfully predict what they should predict have high predictive validity.

A third aspect of validity, called **convergent validity**, refers to whether a test correlates with other measures that it should correlate with. For example, if a self-report measure of tolerance corresponds well with peer judgments of tolerance, then the scale is said to have high convergent validity. Early in this chapter, we described a study of "activity level," in which mechanical recordings of activity level correlated highly with observer-based judgments of activity level—another example of convergent validity. Convergent validity is high to the degree that alternative measures of the same construct correlate or converge with the target measure.

A fourth kind of validity, called **discriminant validity**, is often evaluated simultaneously with convergent validity. Whereas *convergent validity* refers to what a measure *should* correlate with, *discriminant validity* refers to what a measure *should not* correlate with. For example, a psychologist might develop a measure of life satisfaction, the tendency to believe one's life is happy, worthwhile, and satisfying. However, there is another trait called social desirability, the tendency to say nice things about oneself; thus the psychologist might be concerned with the discriminant validity of his or her life-satisfaction measure and try to show that this measure is different from measures of social desirability. Part of knowing what a measure actually measures consists of knowing what it does not measure.

A final type of validity is **construct validity**, defined as a test that measures what it claims to measure, correlates with what it is supposed to correlate with, and does not correlate with what it is not supposed to correlate with. Thus, construct validity is the broadest type of validity, subsuming face, predictive, convergent, and discriminant validity. This form of validity is called construct validity because it is based on the notion that personality variables are **theoretical constructs**. If asked to "show your intelligence" or "show your extraversion," you would be hard-pressed to respond. That is because there is not any one thing you can produce and say, "This is my intelligence" or "This is my extraversion." Intelligence and extraversion, like almost all personality variables, are abstractions. Nevertheless, these theoretical constructs are useful to psychologists in describing and explaining differences among people. Determining whether actual measures can claim to be valid ways of assessing the constructs is the essence of construct validity.

How then do we know if a measure has construct validity? If a measure converges with other measures of the same construct, if it relates to other variables that a theory of the construct says it should, and if it does *not* relate to phenomena that the theory says it should not relate to, then we have the beginnings of construct validity. For example, say that a researcher has developed a questionnaire measure of creativity and is wondering about its construct validity. Do the questionnaire scores correlate with other measures of creativity gathered on the same sample, such as ratings of creativity provided by friends (convergent validity), or awards or grades obtained in fine arts classes (predictive validity)? Do the results correlate with behavioral tests in which participants are asked to name creative uses for common objects, such as a hammer and string?

Finally, if creativity is hypothesized to be different from intelligence, it will be important to prove that the measure of creativity does *not* correlate with measures of intelligence (discriminant validity). When a large number of known relations is built up around a measure, then we begin to believe that the measure is credible as a measure of a specific personality construct.

Generalizability

A third criterion for evaluating personality measures is **generalizability** (Cronbach & Gleser, 1965; Wiggins, 1973). Generalizability is the degree to which the measure retains its validity across various contexts. One context of interest might be different groups of *persons*. A personality psychologist, for example, might be interested in whether a questionnaire retains its predictive validity across age groups, genders, cultures, or ethnic groups. Is a particular scale equally valid when used on men versus women? Is a test equally valid for African Americans and European Americans? Is it equally valid among Japanese and Javanese? Does the scale measure the same trait or quality among college students as among middle-aged adults? If the scale is widely applicable across these person and cultural contexts, then the scale is said to have high generalizability across populations of people.

Another facet of generalizability refers to *different conditions*. Does a dominance scale, for example, predict who becomes the leader in business settings as well as in informal, after-work settings? Does a scale designed to measure conscientiousness predict who will show up for class on time, as well as who will keep their bedrooms tidy? Scales have high generalizability to the degree that they apply widely over different persons, situations, cultures, and times.

Research Designs in Personality

In this chapter, we have examined the *types of personality measures* and the *means for evaluating the quality* of those measures. The next step in personality research is to use these measures in actual *research designs*. Although the variations are nearly infinite, there are three basic research designs in the field of personality psychology: experimental, correlational, and case study. Each has strengths and weaknesses. Each provides information that complements the information provided by the others.

Experimental Methods

Experimental methods are typically used to determine causality—that is, to find out whether one variable *influences* another variable. A *variable* is simply a quality that differs, or can take different values, for different people. Height, for example, is a variable because individuals differ in height. Aggressiveness is a variable because individuals differ in their levels of aggressiveness. Personality characteristics, such as extraversion and agreeableness, are other examples of variables. In order to establish the influence of one variable on another, two key requirements of good experimental design must be met: (1) **manipulation** of one or more variables and (2) ensuring that participants in each experimental condition *are equivalent to each other at the beginning of the study.*

In the first requirement, manipulation, the variable thought to be the influence is manipulated as part of the experiment. For example, if a drug is hypothesized to influence memory, then some participants get the drug and other participants get pills containing no active substances; then all participants have their memories tested. The second requirement, equivalence, is accomplished in one of two ways. If the experiment has manipulation among groups, then the **random assignment** of participants to experimental groups is a procedure that helps ensure that all groups are the same at the beginning of the study. However, in some experiments, manipulation is within each single group. For example, in the memory experiment, participants might get the drug and have their memories tested, then later take the blank pills and have their memories tested again. In this case, each participant is in both conditions. In this kind of experiment (called a within-participant design), equivalence is obtained by **counterbalancing** the order of the conditions, with half of the participants getting the drug first and blank pill second, and the other half getting the blank pill first and the drug second.

The meaning of each of these features will become clear through an example of a personality experiment. Perhaps you are curious about why some people like to study with music or a TV on, whereas others need total silence for studying. A personality theory predicts that extraverts prefer lots of stimulation and introverts prefer very little. Imagine being interested in testing the hypothesis that extraverts function best under conditions of high external stimulation, whereas introverts function best under conditions of low stimulation. To test this hypothesis, you could first give a group of participants a self-report questionnaire that measures extraversion–introversion. Then you could select only those individuals who score at either extreme—as very introverted or very extraverted—to participate in your experiment. Next you would take these participants into the laboratory and have them work on math and sentence comprehension problems under two different conditions—in one condition, a radio would be blaring in the background, and in the other there would be total silence. Half of each group (that is, half of the extraverts and half of the introverts) should be randomly placed in the noisy condition first and the quiet condition second. The other half should be placed in the quiet condition first and the noisy condition second. Then, you would measure the number of errors each group makes under each of the two conditions. If the personality theory you are testing is correct, you should get a pattern of results like that in Figure 2.1. The hypothetical results in Figure 2.1 show that the extraverts made few errors in the noisy condition and more errors when it was quiet. The introverts showed the opposite pattern—noise hampered their performance, whereas they functioned best under conditions of silence.

This study, although hypothetical, highlights the key features of good experimental design. The first is manipulation. In this case, the external condition (the *independent variable*) was manipulated—whether there was a lot of or a little ambient noise in the laboratory. The second feature is counterbalancing—half of the participants received the noisy condition first, and the other half received the quiet condition first. Counterbalancing is critical because there might be *order effects* as a consequence of being exposed to one condition first. Counterbalancing allows the experimenter to rule out order effects as an explanation for the results. The third feature is random assignment. Through random assignment, all persons have an equal chance of being selected for a given condition. Randomization can occur by flipping a coin or, more commonly, by the use of a table of random numbers. Randomization ensures that there are no predetermined patterns linked with condition assignment that could account for the final results.

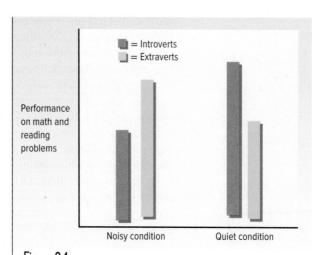

Figure 2.1

Performance on math and reading problems.

In experimental designs, it is desirable to establish whether the groups in the different conditions are *significantly* different. In the introversion–extraversion example, we want to know if the performance of introverts and extraverts in the noisy condition is significantly different. Is the performance of the introverts significantly different from that of the extraverts in the quiet condition? To answer these questions, we need to know five things: sample size, the mean, the standard deviation, the *t*-test, and the *p*-value (significance of the differences among the conditions).

The *mean* refers to the average—in this case, the average number of errors within each condition. The *standard deviation* is a measure of variability within each condition. Because not all participants make the same average number of errors, we need a way to estimate how much participants within each condition vary; this estimate is the standard deviation. Using these numbers, we can use a statistical formula—called the *t-test*—to calculate the difference between two means.

The next step is to see whether the difference is large enough to be called significantly different (the *p*-value). Although "large enough" is a somewhat arbitrary concept, psychologists have adopted the following convention: if the difference between the means would be likely to occur *by chance alone* (i.e., due to random fluctuations in the data) only 1 time out of 20 or less, then the difference is **statistically significant** at

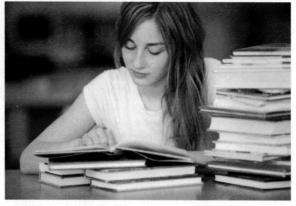

People who study alone in a library are likely to be introverted, whereas those who do their studying in groups tend to be extraverted.
Left © Stockbroker/Purestock/SuperStock RF; Right © Leah Warkentin/Design Pics RF

the $p < .05$ level (the .05 refers to 5 percent chance level, or 1 time in 20). A difference between means that is significant at the .05 level implies that the finding would be likely to occur by chance alone only 5 times out of 100. Another way to think about this is to imagine that, if the experiment were repeated 100 times, we would expect to find these results by chance alone only 5 times.

In sum, the experimental method is effective at demonstrating *relationships among variables*. Experiments similar to the one described, for example, have established a link between extraversion–introversion and performance under conditions of high versus low noise. The procedures of manipulating the conditions, counterbalancing the order in which the conditions occur, and randomly assigning participants to conditions help to ensure that extraneous factors are canceled out. Then, after calculating means and standard deviations, *t*-tests and *p*-values are used to determine whether the differences between the groups in the two conditions are statistically significant. These procedures determine whether personality influences how people perform.

Correlational Studies

A second major type of research design in personality is the correlational study. In the **correlational method** a statistical procedure is used for determining whether there is a relationship between two variables. For example, do people with a high need for achievement in college go on to earn higher salaries in adulthood than people lower on need for achievement? Correlational research designs attempt to identify the relationships between two or more variables, without imposing the sorts of manipulations seen in experimental designs. Correlational designs typically try to determine what goes with what in nature. We might be interested, for example, in the relationship between self-esteem, as assessed through S-data, and the esteem in which a person is held by others, as assessed through O-data. Or we might be interested in how achievement motivation relates to grade point average. A major advantage of correlational studies is that they allow us to identify relationships among variables as they occur naturally. To continue the example of extraversion–introversion and performance under noise conditions, we might measure people's preferences for studying with or without music in real life, then see if there is a correlation with their scores on a measure of introversion–extraversion.

The most common statistical procedure for gauging relationships between variables is the **correlation coefficient.** Consider the relationship between height and weight. We can take a sample of 100 college students and measure their height and weight. If we chart the results on a scatterplot, we see that people who are tall also tend to be relatively heavy and that people who are short tend to be less heavy. But there are exceptions, as you can see in Figure 2.2.

Correlation coefficients can range from +1.00 through 0.00 to −1.00. That is, the variables of interest can be positively related to each other (+.01 to +1.00), unrelated to each other (0.00), or negatively related to each other (−.01 to −1.00). Height and weight happen to be strongly positively correlated with each other—with a calculated correlation coefficient of +.60, for the data shown in Figure 2.2.

Consider a more psychological example. Suppose we are interested in the relationship between people's self-esteem and the amount of time they are unhappy. We might see a scatterplot as depicted in Figure 2.3. This scatterplot was obtained from a sample of college students using a standard questionnaire measure of self-esteem. As the second variable, a measure of unhappiness, the participants were asked to keep a diary for two months, noting for each day whether that day was generally good (felt happy) or generally bad (felt unhappy). Then the percentage of days for each participant

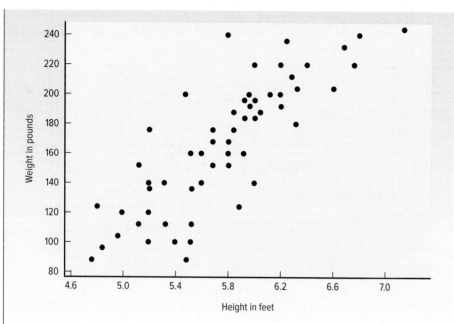

Figure 2.2

Fifty-five cases plotted, showing a strong positive correlation between height and weight. Each symbol (•) represents one person who was measured on both height and weight. Heavier persons tend to be taller; lighter persons tend to be shorter.

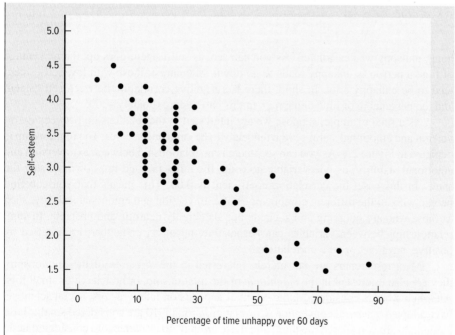

Figure 2.3

Fifty-eight cases plotted to illustrate the negative correlation between self-esteem and the percentage of time reported as being unhappy over two months. The correlation is −.60, indicating that people with higher self-esteem tend to be less unhappy than people with low self-esteem.

48

IntroductionIntroduction

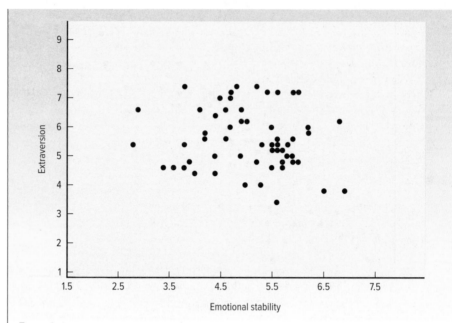

Figure 2.4

Fifty-seven cases plotted to show the relationship between emotional stability and extraversion. The correlation between these two variables is essentially 0.00, meaning that there is no relationship. Consequently, in the scatterplot, we see that people fall fairly equally in all sections of the plot, with no clear pattern.

being unhappy was calculated. As you can see, as self-esteem goes up, the percentage of time a person is unhappy tends to go down. In contrast, those with low self-esteem tend to be unhappy a lot. In short, there is a negative correlation between self-esteem and the percentage of time unhappy—in this case, approximately −.60.

As a final example, suppose we are interested in the relationship between extraversion and emotional stability (the tendency to be calm and secure). The relationship is depicted in Figure 2.4. As you can see, there is no relationship between extraversion and emotional stability; as one variable goes up, the other may go up, down, or stay the same. In this case, the correlation coefficient is 0.00. This means that you can find people with all the different combinations of extraversion and emotional stability, such as those who are outgoing and sociable but also highly neurotic and unstable. In sum, relationships between variables can be positive, negative, or neither, as signified by positive, negative, or zero correlations.

Most researchers are not merely interested in the *direction* of the relationship; they are also interested in the *magnitude* of the relationship, or how large or small it is. Although what is considered large or small depends on many factors, social scientists have adopted a general convention. Correlations around .10 are considered small; those around .30 are considered medium; and those around .50 or greater are considered large (Cohen & Cohen, 1975). Using the examples in Figures 2.2 and 2.3, the +.60 correlation between height and weight is considered large, as is the −.60 correlation between self-esteem and percentage of time unhappy. These correlations have the same magnitude but are different in sign.

The concept of statistical significance can also be applied to correlation values. This is basically part of the statistical calculation, and it results in a numerical statement about how likely you are to find a correlation this size by chance, given the variables measured and the size of the sample. Here psychologists also require a probability of .05 or less before referring to a correlation as significant.

It is important to keep in mind that one cannot infer causation from correlations. There are at least two reasons correlations can never prove causality. One is called the **directionality problem.** If *A* and *B* are correlated, we do not know if *A* is the cause of *B* or if *B* is the cause of *A*. For example, we know there is a correlation between extraversion and happiness. From this fact alone, we do not know if being extraverted causes people to be happy or if being happy causes people to be extraverted.

The second reason that correlations can never prove causality is the **third variable problem.** Two variables might be correlated because a third, unknown variable is causing both. For example, the amount of ice cream sold on any given day may be correlated with the number of people who drown on that particular day. Does this mean eating ice cream causes drowning? Not necessarily, because there is most likely a third variable at work: hot weather. On very hot days, many people eat ice cream. Also, on very hot days many people go swimming who otherwise don't swim very much, so more are likely to drown. Drowning has nothing to do with eating ice cream; rather, these two variables are likely to be caused by a third variable: hot weather.

Case Studies

Sometimes a personality researcher is interested in examining the life of one person in-depth as a case study. There are advantages to the **case study method.** Researchers can find out about personality in great detail, which rarely can be achieved if the study includes large samples. Case studies can give researchers insights into personality that can then be used to formulate a more general theory to be tested on a larger population. They can provide in-depth knowledge of particularly outstanding individuals, such as Mahatma Gandhi or Martin Luther King. Case studies also can be useful in studying rare phenomena, such as a person with a photographic memory or a person with multiple personalities.

One case study occupied an entire issue of the *Journal of Personality* (Nasby & Read, 1997), the case of Dodge Morgan, who, at the age of 54, completed a nonstop solo circumnavigation of the earth by small boat. The case study is a highly readable account of this interesting man undertaking an almost impossible task. The focus is on how Mr. Morgan's early life experiences formed a particular adult personality, which led him to undertake the extreme act of going around the world alone in a small boat. The psychologists used Morgan's voyage log book, autobiographical material, interviews, and even standard personality questionnaires in conducting their case study. The report is noteworthy in that the psychologists also discussed the strengths and weaknesses of the case study method for advancing the science of personality psychology. The authors concluded that personality theories provide a language for discussing individual lives; analysis of individual lives, in turn, provides a means for evaluating personality theories on how they help us understand specific individuals.

Case study design can use a wide array of tools. One can develop coding systems to be applied to written texts, such as personal letters and

Dodge Morgan was 54 when he completed a nonstop, solo circumnavigation of the earth in his boat **American Promise.** *An extensive case study of this fascinating man was conducted by psychologists William Nasby and Nancy Read and reported in their paper "The Voyage and the Voyager" published in the Journal of Personality, 1997, volume 65, pages 823–852.*

Courtesy of Dodge Morgan

correspondence. One can interview dozens of people who know the individual. One can interview the participant for hours and at great depth. One can follow the person around with a video camera and record, with sound and image, the actions in his or her everyday life.

Case Study: An Attention-Seeking Boy

One of the strongest advocates of the case study method was Gordon Allport, one of the founders of the field of modern personality psychology. Allport firmly believed that important hypotheses about personality could come from examining single individuals in great depth. He also believed that one could test hypotheses about the underlying personality characteristics of a single individual using case study methods. The following example illustrates this sort of hypothesis formation and testing:

> *A certain boy at school showed exemplary conduct; he was orderly, industrious, and attentive. But at home he was noisy, unruly, and a bully toward the younger children . . . .*
>
> *Now the psychologist might make the hypothesis: This boy's central disposition is a craving for attention. He finds that he gains his end best at school by conforming to the rules; at home, by disobeying them.*
>
> *Having made this hypothesis, the psychologist could then actually count the boy's acts during the day (being checked by some independent observer) to see how many of them were "functionally equivalent," i.e., manifested a clear bid for attention. If the proportion is high, we can regard the hypothesis as confirmed, and the p.d. [personality disposition] as established. (Allport, 1961, p. 368)*

Case Study: The Serial Killer Ted Bundy

Although Ted Bundy was convicted of killing three women, he was suspected of raping and killing as many as 36 women during his half-decade murder spree in the states of Oregon, Washington, Colorado, and Florida in the 1970s (Rule, 2000). Case studies have been devoted to explaining what drove Bundy to rape and kill. Some traced it back to the fact that he was adopted and felt a burning shame over the fact that he never knew his biological parents. Some tied it to his failed aspirations as a lawyer—where a status-striving motive was frustrated. Some traced it to the fact that he developed a deep-seated hostility toward women after being rejected by his fiancée—a woman who was considerably higher than he in socioeconomic status and who he felt was impossible to replace. All case studies of Bundy revealed, however, that he shared many traits with other serial killers. He had a "classic" sociopathic personality—characterized by grandiosity, extreme sense of entitlement, preoccupation with unrealistic fantasies of success and power, lack of empathy for other people, a long history of deceitfulness, repeated failures to meet normally expected obligations of school and work, and high levels of interpersonal exploitativeness. Furthermore, Ted Bundy showed early behavior and personality dispositions that are known to be associated with serial killers, the so-called serial killer triad: (1) torturing animals while young, (2) starting destructive fires, and (3) bedwetting. Case studies such as those of Ted Bundy can reveal unique aspects of his

Ted Bundy, a convicted serial killer, showed the personality characteristics of a classic sociopath.
© Bill Frakes/The LIFE Images Collection/Getty Images

life (e.g., being rejected by a higher status fiancée, failure to achieve status as an attorney), as well as the common personality dispositions that are often linked with serial killers (e.g., torturing animals, bedwetting; see also the case of Keith Hunter Jesperson, who confessed to raping and killing eight women, in Olson, 2002).

Despite the strengths of the in-depth case study method, it has some critical limitations. The most important one is that findings based on one individual cannot be generalized to other people. A case study is to the other research designs what a study of the planet Mars is to the study of planetary systems. We may find out a great deal about Mars (or a particular person), but what we find out may not be applicable to other planets (or other people). For this reason, case studies are most often used as a *source of hypotheses* and as a *means to illustrate* a principle by bringing it to life.

When to Use Experimental, Correlational, and Case Study Designs

Each of the three major types of research designs has strengths and weaknesses or, more precisely, questions that each is good at answering and questions that each is poor at answering. The experimental method is ideally suited for establishing causal relationships among variables. For example, it can be used to determine whether noisy conditions hamper the performance of introverts, but not of extraverts. On the other hand, the experimental method is poor at identifying the relationships among variables as they occur naturally in everyday life. Moreover, it may be impractical or unethical to use the experimental method for some questions. For example, if a researcher is interested in the role of nutrition in the development of intelligence, it is unethical to conduct an experiment in which half of the participants are put on a starvation diet for several years as children to see if it affects their IQs as adults.

Exercise

Think of a question about one aspect of personality. Most questions take the form of "Is variable *A* related to or caused by variable *B*?" For example, are extraverted persons better than introverts at coping with stress? Are people with high self-esteem more likely to be successful than people with low self-esteem? Do narcissistic persons have problems getting along with others? Write down your question about personality. Now think about how you might approach your question using an experiment, using the correlational method, and doing a case study. Briefly describe how you would use each of these three research designs to try to answer your question.

However, there are people who, for whatever unfortunate circumstances, have had several years of very poor nutrition. Thus a correlational study could be done on whether level of nutrition is related to the development of intelligence. The weakness of the experimental research design is precisely the strength of the correlational design. Correlational designs are ideally suited for establishing the relationships between two or more variables that occur in everyday life, such as between height and dominance, conscientiousness and grade point average, or anxiety and frequency of illness. But correlational designs are poor at establishing causality.

Case studies are ideally suited for generating hypotheses that can be tested subsequently using correlational or experimental methods. Case studies can be used to identify patterns in individual psychological functioning that might be missed by the more rigorous but artificial experimental approach and the limited correlational designs. Furthermore, case studies are wonderful in depicting the richness and complexity of human experience. Despite these strengths, case studies cannot establish causality, as can experimental methods, nor can they identify patterns of covariation across individuals as they occur in nature. Case studies also cannot be generalized to anyone beyond the single individual being studied. Together, all three designs provide complementary methods for exploring human personality.

SUMMARY AND EVALUATION

Personality assessment and measurement start with identifying the sources of personality data—the places from which we obtain information about personality. The four major sources of personality data are self-report (S-data), observer report (O-data), laboratory tests (T-data), and life history outcomes (L-data). Each of these data sources has strengths and weaknesses. In self-report, for example, participants might fake or lie. Observers in the O-data mode may lack access to the relevant information. Laboratory tests may be inadequate for identifying patterns that occur naturally in everyday life. Each source of personality data is extremely valuable, however, and each provides information not attainable through the other sources. Furthermore, new measurement techniques continue to be invented and explored; recent examples include assessments through electronic and internet technologies such as Smart Phones, Instagram, and Facebook.

Once sources of data have been selected for measuring personality, the researcher then evaluates their quality. Personality measures, ideally, should be reliable in the sense of attaining the same scores through repeated measurement. They should be valid, measuring what they are supposed to measure. And researchers should establish how generalizable their measures are—determining the people, settings, and cultures to which the measure is most applicable. Scales applicable only to college students in the United States, for example, are less generalizable than scales applicable to people of differing ages, economic brackets, ethnic groups, and cultures.

The next step in personality research involves selecting a particular research design within which to use the measures. There are three basic types of research designs. The first, the experimental research design, which involves controlling or manipulating the variables of interest, is best suited to determining causality between two variables. The second, correlational research design, is best for identifying relationships between naturally occurring variables but is poorly suited to determining causality. The third is the case study method, which is well suited to generating new hypotheses about personality and to understanding single individuals.

Perhaps the most important principle of personality assessment and measurement is that the decisions about data source and research design depend heavily on the purpose of the investigation. There are no perfect methods; there are no perfect designs. But there are data sources and methods that are better suited for some purposes than for others.

KEY TERMS

self-report data (S-data) 24
structured 24
unstructured 24
Likert rating scale 25
experience sampling 27
observer-report data (O-data) 27
inter-rater reliability 28
multiple social personalities 28
naturalistic observation 29
test data (T-data) 29
functional magnetic resonance
    imaging (fMRI) 33
projective techniques 34
life-outcome data (L-data) 35

reliability 38
repeated measurement 38
response sets 39
noncontent responding 39
acquiescence 39
extreme responding 39
social desirability 39
forced-choice questionnaire 40
validity 42
face validity 42
predictive validity 42
criterion validity 42
convergent validity 42
discriminant validity 42

construct validity 42
theoretical constructs 42
generalizability 43
experimental methods 44
manipulation 44
random assignment 44
counterbalancing 44
statistically significant 45
correlational method 46
correlation coefficient 46
directionality problem 49
third variable problem 49
case study method 49

PART ONE

The Dispositional Domain

© *moswyn/Getty Images RF*

The dispositional domain concerns those aspects of personality that are stable over time, are relatively consistent over situations, and make people different from each other. For example, some people are outgoing and talkative; others are introverted and shy. The introverted and shy person tends to be that way most of the time (is stable over time) and tends to be introverted and shy at work, at play, and at school (is consistent over situations).

The study of traits makes up the dispositional domain. The term *disposition* is used because it refers to an inherent tendency to behave in a specific way. The term *trait* is used interchangeably with the term *disposition*. The major questions for

I

psychologists working in the dispositional domain are these: How many personality traits exist? What is the best taxonomy, or classification system, for traits? How can we best discover and measure these traits? How do personality traits develop? How do traits interact with situations to produce behaviors?

In this domain, traits are seen as the building blocks of personality. A person's personality is viewed as being built out of a set of common traits. Psychologists have been concerned with identifying the most important traits, the ones out of which all differences among people can be formed.

The next step is to develop taxonomies, or classification systems. Taxonomies are very useful in all areas of science. Currently, the most popular taxonomy of personality has five fundamental traits: extraversion, neuroticism, agreeableness, conscientiousness, and openness to experience.

In the dispositional domain there is a unique conception of how people change yet remain stable at the same time. We will discuss how the traits that underlie behavior can remain stable, yet how the traits expressed in behavior can change over a person's life span. Consider the trait of dominance. Suppose that a girl who is dominant at age 8 grows into a young woman who is dominant at age 20. As an 8-year-old this person might display her high level of dominance by showing a readiness for rough-and-tumble play, referring to her less dominant peers as sissies and insisting on monopolizing whatever interesting toys are available. By age 20, however, she manifests her dominance in quite different behaviors, perhaps by persuading others to accept her views in political discussions, boldly asking others out on dates, and deciding on the restaurants they will go to on these dates. Consequently, trait levels can stay the same over long time periods, yet the behaviors expressing those traits change as the person ages.

We will discuss the ways in which personality psychologists have studied the development of dispositions as well as studies of how dispositions can change across the life span.

Traits and Trait Taxonomies

3

THE DISPOSITIONAL DOMAIN

People readily form impressions of others that can be described using a few traits of personality, such as whether the person is friendly, generous, and poised. Portrait of large group of students cheering at college sporting event.
© Hero Images/Hero Images/ Corbis RF

Suppose that you walk into a party with a friend, who introduces you to the host, an acquaintance of hers. The three of you chat for 10 minutes, and then you mingle with the other guests. Later, as you leave the party with your friend, she asks what you thought of the host. As you mull over the 10-minute interaction, what springs to mind? Perhaps you describe the host as *friendly* (she smiled a lot), *generous* (she told you to help yourself to the bountiful spread of food), and *poised* (she was able to juggle the many demands of her guests as they came and went). These words are all examples of *trait-descriptive adjectives*—words that describe *traits, attributes* of a person that are reasonably *characteristic* of the person and perhaps *enduring* over time. Just as you might describe a glass as *brittle* or a car as *reliable* (enduring characteristics of the glass and the car), trait-descriptive adjectives imply consistent and stable characteristics. For much of the past century, psychologists have focused on identifying the basic traits that make up personality and identifying the nature and origins of those traits.

Most personality psychologists hypothesize that traits (also called *dispositions*) are reasonably stable over time and at least somewhat consistent over situations. The host of the party just described, for example, might be friendly, generous, and poised at other parties later on—illustrating stability over time. And she might also show these traits in other situations—perhaps showing friendliness by smiling at people on elevators, generosity by giving homeless people money, and poised by maintaining her composure when called on in class. However, the actual degree to which traits show stability over time and consistency across situations has been the subject of considerable debate and empirical research.

Three fundamental questions guide those who study personality traits: The first question is "How should we *conceptualize* traits?" Every field needs to define its key terms explicitly. In biology, for example, *species* is a key concept, so the concept of species is defined explicitly (i.e., a group of organisms capable of reproducing with each other). In physics, the basic concepts of mass, weight, force, and gravity are defined explicitly. Because traits are central concepts in personality psychology, they, too, must be precisely formulated.

The second question is "How can we identify which traits are the *most important* traits from among the thousands of ways in which individuals differ?" Individuals differ in many ways that are both characteristic and enduring. Some individuals are extremely extraverted, enjoying loud and crowded parties; others are introverted, preferring quiet evenings spent reading. Some like rock music, whereas others like rap music. A crucial goal of personality psychology is to identify the most important ways in which individuals differ.

The third question is "How can we formulate a *comprehensive taxonomy* of traits—a system that includes within it *all* of the major traits of personality?" Once the important traits have been identified, the next step is to formulate an organized scheme—a *taxonomy*—within which to assemble the individual traits. The periodic table of elements, for example, is not merely a random list of all the physical elements that have been discovered. Rather, it is a taxonomy that organizes the elements using a coherent principle—the elements are arranged according to their atomic numbers (which refer to the number of protons in the nucleus of a given atom). Within biology, to use another example, the field would be hopelessly lost if biologists were to merely list all of the thousands of species that exist, without relying on an underlying organizational framework. Thus, the individual species are organized into a taxonomy—all the species of plants, animals, and microbial species are linked systematically through a single tree of descent. Likewise, a central goal of personality psychology is to formulate a comprehensive taxonomy of all important traits. This chapter describes how personality psychologists have addressed these three fundamental questions of trait psychology.

What Is a Trait? Two Basic Formulations

When you describe someone as *impulsive, unreliable,* and *lazy,* what specifically are you referring to? Personality psychologists differ in their formulations of what these traits mean. Some personality psychologists view these traits as *internal* (or hidden) *properties* of persons that *cause* their behavior. Other personality psychologists make no assumptions about causality and simply use these trait terms to *describe* the enduring aspects of a person's behavior.

Traits as Internal Causal Properties

When we say that Dierdre has a *desire* for material things, that Dan has a *need* for stimulation, or that Dominick *wants* power over others, we are referring to something inside of each that causes him or her to act in particular ways. These traits are presumed to be *internal* in the sense that individuals carry their desires, needs, and wants from one situation to the next (e.g., Alston, 1975). Furthermore, these desires and needs are presumed to be *causal* in the sense that they explain the behavior of the individuals who possess them. Dierdre's desire for material things, for example, might cause her to spend a lot of time at the shopping mall, work extra hard to earn more money, and acquire many household possessions. Her internal desire *influences* her external behavior, presumably causing her to act in certain ways.

Psychologists who view traits as internal dispositions do not equate traits with the external behavior in question. This distinction is most easily explained using a food example. Harry may have a strong desire for a large hamburger and french fries. However, because he is trying to lose weight, he refrains from expressing his desire in behavioral terms—he looks at the food hungrily but resists the temptation to eat it. Similarly, Dominick may have a desire to take charge in most social situations, even if he does not always express this desire. For example, some situations may have an already identified leader, such as in a class discussion with his psychology professor. Note that this formulation assumes that we can measure Dominick's need for power independently of measuring Dominick's actual behavioral expressions.

These examples are analogous to that of a glass, which has the trait of being brittle. Even if a particular glass never shatters (i.e., expresses its brittleness), it still possesses the trait of being brittle. In sum, psychologists who view traits as internal dispositions believe that traits can lie dormant in the sense that the *capacities* remain present even when particular behaviors are not actually expressed. Traits—in the sense of internal needs, drives, desires, and so on—are presumed to exist, even in the absence of observable behavioral expressions.

The scientific usefulness of viewing traits as causes of behavior lies in ruling out other causes. When we say that Joan goes to lots of parties *because* she is extraverted, we are implicitly ruling out other potential reasons for her behavior (e.g., that she might be going to a lot of parties simply because her boyfriend drags her to them, rather than because she herself is extraverted). The formulation of traits as internal causal properties differs radically from an alternative formulation that considers traits as merely descriptive summaries of actual behavior.

Traits as Purely Descriptive Summaries

Proponents of this alternative formulation define traits simply as *descriptive summaries* of attributes of persons; they make no assumptions about internality or causality (Hampshire, 1953; Saucier & Goldberg, 2001). Consider an example in which we ascribe the trait of *jealousy* to a young man named George. According to the descriptive summary viewpoint, this trait merely describes George's *expressed behavior*. For example, George might glare at other men who talk to his girlfriend insist that she wear his ring, and require her to spend all of her free time with him. The trait of jealousy, in this case, accurately *summarizes* the general trend in George's expressed behavior, yet no assumptions are made about what causes George's behavior.

Although it is possible that George's jealousy stems from an internal cause, perhaps deeply rooted feelings of insecurity, his jealousy might instead be due to *social situations*. George's expressions of jealousy might be caused by the fact that other men are flirting with his girlfriend and she is responding to them (a situational cause), rather than because George is intrinsically a jealous person. The important point is that those who view traits as descriptive summaries do not prejudge the cause of someone's behavior. They merely use traits to describe, in summary fashion, the trend in a person's behavior. Personality psychologists of this persuasion (e.g., Saucier & Goldberg, 1998; Wiggins, 1979) argue that we must first identify and describe the important individual differences among people, then subsequently develop causal theories to explain them.

The Act Frequency Formulation of Traits—An Illustration of the Descriptive Summary Formulation

A number of psychologists who endorse the descriptive summary formulation of traits have explored the implications of this formulation in a program of research called the "act frequency approach" (Amelang, Herboth, & Oefner, 1991; Angleiter, Buss, & Demtroder, 1990; Buss & Craik, 1983; Church et al., 2007; Jackson et al., 2010; Romero et al., 1994).

The act frequency approach starts with the notion that *traits are categories of acts*. Just as the category "birds" has specific birds as members of the category (e.g., robins, sparrows), trait categories such as "dominance" or "impulsivity" have specific acts as members. The category of dominance, for example, might include specific acts such as the following:

He issued orders that got the group organized.
She managed to control the outcome of the meeting without the others being
    aware of it.
He assigned roles and got the game going.
She decided which programs they would watch on TV.

Dominance is a trait category with these and hundreds of acts as members. A dominant person, according to the act frequency approach, is someone who performs a large number of dominant acts relative to others. For example, if we videotaped Mary and a dozen of her friends over a period of three months and then counted up how many times each person performed dominant acts, Mary would be considered dominant if she performed more dominant acts than her friends. Thus, in the act frequency formulation, a trait such as dominance is a descriptive summary of the general trend in a person's behavior—a trend that consists of performing a large number of acts within a category relative to other persons.

Act Frequency Research Program

The act frequency approach to traits involves three key elements: act nomination, prototypicality judgment, and the recording of act performance.

Act Nomination

Act nomination is a procedure designed to identify which acts belong in which trait categories. Consider the category of "impulsive." Now think of someone you know who is impulsive. Then list the specific acts or behaviors this person has performed that exemplify his or her impulsivity. You might say, "He decided to go out with friends on the spur of the moment, even though he had to study," "He immediately accepted the dare to do something dangerous, without thinking about the consequences," or "He blurted out his anger before he had time to reflect on the situation." Through act nomination procedures such as this one, researchers can identify hundreds of acts belonging to various trait categories.

Prototypicality Judgment

The second step involves identifying which acts are most central to, or *prototypical* of, each trait category. Consider the category of "bird." When you think of this category, which birds come to your mind first? Most people think of birds such as *robins* and *sparrows*. They do not think of *turkeys* and *penguins*. Even though penguins and turkeys are members of the category bird, robins and sparrows are considered to be more

Table 3.1 Self-Report of Creative Acts

Instructions. Following is a list of acts. Read each act and circle the response that most accurately indicates how often you typically perform each act. Circle "0" if you never perform the act; circle "1" if you occasionally perform the act; circle "2" if you perform the act with moderate frequency; and circle "3" if you perform the act very frequently.

Circle	Acts	
0 1 2 3	1.	I came up with a funny nickname for someone.
0 1 2 3	2.	I sat down and drew or painted from my imagination.
0 1 2 3	3.	I took photos just for fun.
0 1 2 3	4.	I carried a sketchpad all day long.
0 1 2 3	5.	I listened to a great variety of musical styles.
0 1 2 3	6.	I wrote a song.
0 1 2 3	7.	I made a card for someone.
0 1 2 3	8.	I kept a journal of thoughts and turned them into poems.
0 1 2 3	9.	I told a joke that made people laugh.
0 1 2 3	10.	I gave self-made drawings as presents for people's birthdays.

Source: Adapted from Ivcevic, 2007. From among the most prototypical everyday and artistic creative acts. Items 1, 3, 5, 7, and 9 are prototypical everyday creative acts. Items 2, 4, 6, 8, and 10 are artistic creative acts. According to the act frequency approach, you would be judged to be "creative" if you performed a high overall frequency of these creative acts, relative to your peer group.

prototypical of the category—they are better examples, more central to what most people mean by "bird" (Rosch, 1975).

In a similar way, acts within trait categories differ in their prototypicality of the trait. Panels of raters judge how prototypical each act is as an example of a particular concept. For example, raters find the acts *She controlled the outcome of the meeting without the others being aware of it* and *She took charge after the accident* to be more prototypically dominant than the act *She deliberately arrived late for the meeting.*

Recording Act Performance

The third and final step in the research program consists of securing information on the actual performance of individuals in their daily lives. As you might imagine, obtaining information about a person's daily conduct is difficult. Most researchers have used self-reports of act performance or reports from close friends or spouses. As shown in Table 3.1, you can provide your own responses to this measure of everyday and artistic creative acts. Similar measures have been developed for conscientious acts (Jackson et al., 2010) and extraverted acts (Rauthmann & Denissen, 2011). In the same way, observational measures of dominant acts have been developed in the context of face-to-face groups (Anderson & Kilduff, 2009). Interestingly, traditional trait measures do a moderately good job of predicting manifest behavior in everyday life (Fleeson & Gallagher, 2009).

Evaluation of the Act Frequency Formulation

The formulation of traits as purely descriptive summaries, as in the act frequency approach, has been criticized on several grounds (see Angleitner & Demtroder, 1988; Block, 1989). Most of the criticisms have been aimed at the technical implementation of the approach. For example, the act frequency approach does not specify how much context should be included in the description of a trait-relevant act. Consider the following dominant act: *He insisted that the others go to his favorite restaurant.* To understand this act as a dominant act, we might need to know (1) the relationships among the people involved, (2) the occasion for going out to eat, (3) the history of restaurant going for these people, and (4) who is paying for the dinner. How much context is needed to identify the act as a dominant act?

Another criticism of the approach is that it seems applicable to overt actions, but what about *failures* to act and covert acts that are not directly observable? For example, a person may be very courageous, but we will never know this under ordinary life circumstances in which people have no need to display courageousness.

Despite these limitations, the act frequency approach has produced some noteworthy accomplishments. It has been especially helpful in making explicit the *behavioral phenomena* to which most trait terms refer—after all, the primary way that we know about traits is through their expressions in actual behavior. As noted by several prominent personality researchers, "Behavioral acts constitute the building blocks of interpersonal perception and the basis for inferences about personality traits" (Gosling et al., 1998). Thus the study of behavioral manifestations of personality remains an essential and indispensable part of the agenda for the field, despite the difficulties entailed by their study (Furr, 2009). The act frequency approach is also helpful in identifying behavioral regularities—phenomena that must be explained by any comprehensive personality theory (Furr, 2009). And it has been helpful in exploring the *meaning* of some traits that have proven difficult to study, such as impulsivity (Romero et al., 1994), conscientiousness (Jackson et al., 2010), and creativity (Amelang et al., 1991). It has also proven useful in identifying cultural similarities and differences in the behavioral manifestation of traits (Church et al., 2007). Initiating a conversation with a shy person, for example, is a greater reflection of extraversion in the Philippines than in the United States, whereas smiling at a stranger is a greater reflection of extraversion in the United States than in the Philippines.

Explorations of the act frequency approach have helped to identify the domains in which it provides insight into personality. One study, for example, examined the relationship between self-reported act performance and observer codings of the individual's actual behavior (Gosling et al., 1998). Some acts showed high levels of self–observer agreement, such as "Told a joke to lighten a tense moment," "Made a humorous remark," "Took charge of things at the meeting." Acts that reflect the traits of extraversion and conscientiousness tend to show high levels of self–observer agreement. Acts that reflect the trait of agreeableness, on the other hand, tend to show lower levels of self–observer agreement. The more observable the actions, the higher the agreement between self-report and observer codings.

Other research has demonstrated that the act frequency approach can be used to predict important outcomes in everyday life such as job success, salary, and how rapidly individuals are promoted within business organizations (Kyl-Heku & Buss, 1996; Lund et al., 2006). Others have used the act frequency approach to explore topics such as *acts of deception* in social interaction (Tooke & Camire, 1991) and acts of *"mate guarding"* that predict violence in dating and marital relationships (Shackelford et al., 2005).

In sum, there are two major formulations of traits. The first considers traits to be internal causal properties of persons that affect overt behavior. The second considers traits to be descriptive summaries of overt behavior, with the causes of those trends in conduct to be determined subsequently. However traits are formulated, all personality psychologists must confront the next vexing challenge—identifying the most important traits.

Identification of the Most Important Traits

Three fundamental approaches have been used to identify important traits. The first is the **lexical approach**. According to this approach, all traits listed and defined in the dictionary form the basis of describing differences among people (Allport & Odbert, 1936). Thus the logical starting point for the lexical strategy is the natural language. The second method of identifying important traits is the **statistical approach**. This approach uses factor analysis, or similar statistical procedures, to identify major personality traits. The third method is the **theoretical approach** in which researchers rely on theories to identify important traits.

Lexical Approach

The lexical approach to identifying important personality traits starts with the **lexical hypothesis**: *all important individual differences have become encoded within the natural language*. Over time, differences among people that are important are noticed, and words are invented to talk about those differences. People invent words such as *dominant, creative, reliable, cooperative, hot-tempered,* or *self-centered* to describe these differences. People find these trait terms helpful in describing people and for communicating information about them. And so, usage of these trait terms spreads and becomes common within the group. The trait terms that are not useful to people in describing and communicating with others fail to become encoded within the natural language.

If we consider the English language, we find an abundance of trait terms codified as adjectives, such as *manipulative, arrogant, slothful,* and *warm.* A perusal of the dictionary yields about 18,000 trait-descriptive adjectives (Norman, 1967). The key implication of this finding, according to the lexical approach, is clear: trait terms are extraordinarily important for people in communicating with others.

The lexical approach yields two criteria for identifying important traits—**synonym frequency** and **cross-cultural universality**. The criterion of synonym frequency means that if an attribute has not merely one or two trait adjectives to describe it but rather many words, then it is a more important dimension of individual difference. "The more important is such an attribute, the more synonyms and subtly distinctive facets of the attribute will be found within any one language" (Saucier & Goldberg, 1996, p. 24). Consider individual differences in "dominance." There are many terms to describe it: *dominant, bossy, assertive, powerful, pushy, forceful, leaderlike, domineering, influential, ascendant, authoritative,* and *arrogant.* The prevalence of many synonyms, each term conveying a subtle difference in dominance, suggests that dominance is an important trait and that different shades of dominance are important in social communication. Thus, synonym frequency provides one criterion of importance (see Wood, 2015, for a contrary position).

Cross-cultural universality is the second key criterion of importance within the lexical approach: "The more important is an individual difference in human transactions, the more languages will have a term for it" (Goldberg, 1981, p. 142). The logic is that if a trait is sufficiently important in all cultures that its members have codified terms to describe the trait, then the trait must be universally important in human affairs. In contrast, if a trait term exists in only one or a few languages, then it may be of only local relevance. Such a term is unlikely to be a candidate for a universal taxonomy of personality traits (McCrae & Costa, 1997).

The Yanomamö Indians of Venezuela, for example, have the words *unokai* and *"non-unokai,"* which mean, roughly, "a man who has achieved manhood by the killing of another man" (*unokai*) and "a man who has not achieved manhood status by the killing of another man" (*non-unokai*) (Chagnon, 1983). In Yanomamö culture, this individual difference is of critical importance, for the unokai have elevated status, are widely feared, have more wives, and are looked to for leadership. In mainstream American culture, by contrast, there is the generic *killer,* but there is no single word that has the specific connotations of *unokai.* Thus, although this individual difference is of critical importance to the Yanomamö, it is unlikely to be a candidate for a universal taxonomy of personality traits.

One problem with the lexical strategy concerns the fact that personality is conveyed through different parts of speech, including adjectives, nouns, and adverbs. For example, there are dozens of noun terms encoded within the English language to describe someone who is not too smart: *birdbrain, blockhead, bonehead, chucklehead, cretin, deadhead, dimwit, dolt, dope, dullard, dumbbell, dummy, dunce, jughead, lunkhead, moron, peabrain, pinhead, softhead, thickhead,* and *woodenhead.* Although they have not been explored much, personality nouns remain a viable source of potential information about important dimensions of individual differences.

The lexical strategy has proven to be a remarkably generative starting point for identifying important individual differences (Ashton & Lee, 2005). To discard this information "would require us needlessly to separate ourselves from the vast sources of knowledge gained in the course of human history" (Kelley, 1992, p. 22). The lexical approach represents a good starting point for identifying important individual differences but should not be used exclusively. Two other commonly used approaches are the statistical and theoretical strategies.

Statistical Approach

The statistical approach to identifying important traits starts with a pool of personality items. These can be trait words or questions about behavior, experience, or emotion. Most researchers using the lexical approach turn to the statistical approach to distill self-ratings of trait adjectives into basic categories of personality traits. However, the starting point can also be self-ratings on a large collection of personality-relevant sentences (e.g., *I find that I am easily able to persuade people to my point of view*). Once a large and diverse pool of items has been assembled, the statistical approach is applied. It consists of having people rate themselves (or others) on the items, then using a statistical procedure to identify groups or clusters of items. The goal of the statistical approach is to identify the major dimensions, or "coordinates," of the personality map, much the way latitude and longitude provide the coordinates of the map of Earth.

The most commonly used statistical procedure is **factor analysis**. Although the complex mathematical procedures underlying factor analysis are beyond the scope of this text, the essential logic is simple. Factor analysis essentially identifies groups of items that *covary* (i.e., go together) but tend not to covary with other groups of items. Consider, as a spatial metaphor, the office locations of physicists, psychologists, and sociologists on your campus. Although these may be spread out, in general the offices of the psychologists tend to be closer to one another than they are to the offices of the physicists or sociologists. And the physicists are closer to one another than they are to the sociologists or psychologists. Thus, a factor analysis might reveal three clusters of professors.

Similarly, a major advantage of identifying clusters of personality items that covary is that it provides a means for determining which personality variables have some common property. Factor analysis can also be useful in reducing the large array of diverse personality traits into a smaller and more useful set of underlying factors. It provides a means for organizing the thousands of personality traits.

Table 3.2 A Sample Factor Analysis of Personality Adjective Ratings

Adjective Rating	Factor 1 (Extraversion)	Factor 2 (Ambition)	Factor 3 (Creativity)
Humorous	**.66**	.06	.19
Amusing	**.65**	.23	.02
Popular	**.57**	.13	.22
Hard-working	.05	**.63**	.01
Productive	.04	**.52**	.19
Determined	.23	**.52**	.08
Imaginative	.01	.09	**.62**
Original	.13	.05	**.53**
Inventive	.06	.26	**.47**

Note: The numbers refer to factor loadings, which indicate the degree to which an item correlates with the underlying factor (see text).
Source: Adapted from Matthews & Oddy, 1993.

Let's examine how factor analysis works in an example shown in Table 3.2. This table summarizes the data obtained from a sample of 1,210 subjects who rated themselves on a series of trait-descriptive adjectives. Among the adjectives rated were *humorous, amusing, popular, hard-working, productive, determined, imaginative, original,* and *inventive*.

The numbers in Table 3.2 are called **factor loadings**, indexes of how much of the variation in an item is "explained" by the factor. Factor loadings indicate the degree to which the item correlates with, or "loads on," the underlying factor. In this example, three clear factors emerge. The first is an "extraversion" factor, with high loadings on *humorous, amusing,* and *popular*. The second is an "ambition" factor: *hard-working, productive,* and *determined*. The third is a "creativity" factor, with high loadings on *imaginative, inventive,* and *original*. Factor analysis is quite useful in identifying three distinct groups of trait terms that covary with each other but are relatively independent of (tend not to covary with) other groups. Without this statistical procedure, a researcher might be forced to consider the nine traits as all separate from each other. Factor analysis tells us that *hard-working, productive,* and *determined* all covary sufficiently that they can be considered a single trait, rather than three separate traits.

A cautionary note should be made about using the statistical approach for identifying important traits: you get out of it only what you put into it. If an important personality trait happens to be left out of a factor analysis, it will not show up in the subsequent results. Thus, it is critical that researchers pay close attention to their initial selection of items.

Factor analysis and similar statistical procedures have been extremely valuable to personality researchers. Perhaps their most important contribution has been the ability to reduce a large, cumbersome array of diverse personality items into a smaller, more meaningful set of broad, basic factors.

Theoretical Approach

The theoretical approach to identifying important dimensions of individual differences starts with a theory that determines which variables are important. In contrast to the statistical strategy, which can be described as atheoretical in the sense that there is no prejudgment about which variables are important, the theoretical strategy dictates which variables are important to measure.

To a Freudian, for example, it is critical to measure "the oral personality" and "the anal personality" because these represent important, theory-driven constructs. Or, to a self-actualization theorist such as Maslow (1968), it is critical to measure individual differences in the degree to which people are motivated to self-actualize (see Williams & Page, 1989, for one such measure). The theory, in short, strictly determines which variables are important.

As an example of the theoretical strategy, consider the theory of **sociosexual orientation** (Simpson & Gangestad, 1991; Penke & Asendorph, 2008a). According to the theory, men and women will pursue one of two alternative sexual relationship strategies. The first entails seeking a single committed relationship characterized by monogamy and tremendous investment in children. The second sexual strategy is characterized by a greater degree of promiscuity, more partner switching, and less investment in children. (When applied to men, one easy way to remember these two strategies is to label them as "dads" and "cads.") Because the theory of sociosexual orientation dictates that the mating strategy one pursues is a critical individual difference, Gangestad and Simpson have developed a measure of sociosexual orientation (see the Exercise following).

Exercise

INSTRUCTIONS: Please answer all of the following questions honestly. For the questions dealing with behavior, *write* your answers in the blank spaces provided. For the questions dealing with thoughts and attitudes, *circle* the appropriate number on the scales provided.

1. With how many different partners have you had sex (sexual intercourse) within the past year? _____

2. How many different partners do you foresee yourself having sex with during the next five years? (Please give a *specific, realistic* estimate.)

   _____

3. With how many different partners have you had sex on *one and only one* occasion? _____

4. How often do you fantasize about having sex with someone other than your current partner? (circle one).
   1. never
   2. once every two or three months
   3. once a month
   4. once every two weeks
   5. once a week
   6. a few times a week
   7. nearly every day
   8. at least once a day

5. Sex without love is okay.

        1   2   3   4   5   6   7   8   9

   I strongly disagree   I strongly agree

6. I can imagine myself being comfortable and enjoying "casual" sex with different partners.

  1   2   3   4   5   6   7   8   9
  I strongly disagree   I strongly agree

7. I would have to be closely attached to someone (both emotionally and psychologically) before I could feel comfortable and fully enjoy having sex with him or her.

  1   2   3   4   5   6   7   8   9
  I strongly disagree   I strongly agree

Source: From Simpson & Gangestad (1991). Copyright © 1991 by the American Psychological Association. Reproduced with permission. No further reproduction or distribution is permitted without written permission from the American Psychological Association.

Evaluating the Approaches for Identifying Important Traits

In sum, the theoretical approach lets the theory determine which dimensions of individual differences are important. Like all approaches, the theoretical approach has strengths and limitations. Its strengths coincide with the strengths of the theory. If we have a powerful theory that tells us which variables are important, then it saves us from wandering aimlessly like a sailor without a map or compass. A theory charts the course to take. At the same time, its weaknesses coincide with the weaknesses of the theory. To the extent that the theory contains gaps or biases, the subsequent identification of important individual differences will reflect omissions and distortions.

The current state of the field of personality trait psychology is best characterized as "letting a thousand flowers bloom." Some researchers start with a theory and let their measurement of individual differences follow from that theory. Others believe that factor analysis is the only sensible way to identify important individual differences. Still other researchers believe that the lexical strategy, by capitalizing on the collective wisdom of people over the ages, is the best method of ensuring that important individual differences are captured.

In practice, many personality researchers use a combination of the three strategies. Norman (1963), Goldberg (1990), and Saucier (2009), for example, started with the lexical strategy to identify their first set of variables for inclusion. They then applied factor analysis to this initial selection of traits to reduce the set to a smaller, more manageable number (five or six). This solved two problems that are central to the science of personality (Saucier & Goldberg, 1996): the problem of identifying the domains of individual differences and the problem of figuring out a method for describing structure that exists among the individual differences identified. The lexical strategy can be used to sample trait terms, and then factor analysis supplies a powerful statistical approach to providing structure and order to those trait terms.

Taxonomies of Personality

Over the past century, dozens of taxonomies of personality traits have been proposed. Many have been merely lists of traits, often based on the intuitions of personality psychologists. As personality psychologist Robert Hogan observed, "The history of personality theory consists of people who assert that their private demons are public afflictions" (Hogan, 1983). Indeed, two editors of a book on personality traits (London & Exner, 1978) expressed despair at the lack of agreement about a taxonomy of traits, so they

Hans Eysenck at his London office.

Courtesy of Randy J. Larsen

simply listed the traits alphabetically. Clearly, we can develop a firmer basis for organizing personality traits. The taxonomies of traits presented in the rest of this chapter are not random samplings from the dozens available. Rather, they represent taxonomies that have solid empirical and theoretical justification.

Eysenck's Hierarchical Model of Personality

Of all the taxonomies of personality, the model of Hans Eysenck, born in 1916, is most strongly rooted in biology. Eysenck was raised in Germany at the time when Hitler was rising to power. Eysenck showed an intense dislike for the Nazi regime, so at age 18 he migrated to England. Although intending to study physics, Eysenck lacked the needed prerequisites, so almost by chance he began to study psychology at the University of London. He received his PhD in 1940 and after World War II became director of the psychology department at the Maudsley Hospital's new Institute of Psychiatry in London. Eysenck's subsequent productivity was enormous, with more than 40 books and 700 articles. Eysenck was the most cited living psychologist until he died in 1998.

Eysenck developed a model of personality based on traits that he believed were highly heritable (see Chapter 6) and had a likely psychophysiological foundation. The three main traits that met these criteria, according to Eysenck, were *extraversion–introversion* (E), *neuroticism–emotional stability* (N), and *psychoticism* (P). Together, they can be easily remembered by the acronym PEN.

Description

Let us begin by describing these three broad traits. Eysenck conceptualizes each of them as sitting at the top of its own hierarchy, as shown in Figure 3.1. *Extraversion,* for example, subsumes a large number of narrow traits—sociable, active, lively, venturesome,

"You should get out more."

Introverts prefer to spend more time alone than extraverts.

Source: Richard Jolley/www.CartoonStock.com

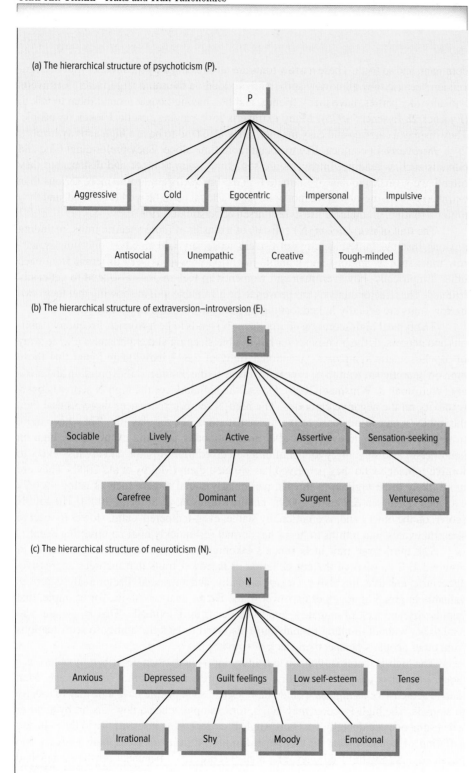

(a) The hierarchical structure of psychoticism (P).

(b) The hierarchical structure of extraversion–introversion (E).

(c) The hierarchical structure of neuroticism (N).

Figure 3.1

Eysenck's hierarchical structure of major personality traits. Each "super-trait" (P, E, and N) occupies the highest level in the hierarchy, representing broad personality traits. Each of these broad traits subsumes more narrower traits in the hierarchy. (a) The hierarchical structure of psychoticism (P); (b) the hierarchical structure of extraversion–introversion (E); (c) the hierarchical structure of neuroticism–emotional stability (N).

dominant, and so forth. These narrow traits are all subsumed by the broader trait of extra-version because they all covary sufficiently to load on the same large factor. Extraverts typically like parties, have many friends, and like having people around them to talk to (Eysenck & Eysenck, 1975). Many extraverts love playing practical jokes on people. They display a carefree and easy manner. They also tend to have a high activity level.

Introverts, in contrast, like to spend more time alone. They prefer quiet time and pursuits such as reading. Introverts are sometimes seen as aloof and distant, but they often have a small number of intimate friends. Introverts tend to be more serious than extraverts and to prefer a more moderate pace. They tend to be well organized, and they prefer a routine, predictable lifestyle (Larsen & Kasimatis, 1990).

The trait of *neuroticism* (N) consists of a cluster of more specific traits, including anxious, irritable, guilty, lacking self-esteem, tense, shy, and moody. Conceptually, nar-row traits such as anxious and irritable might be viewed as very different from each other. Empirically, however, men and women who feel anxious also tend to get easily irritated. Thus, factor analysis has proven to be a valuable tool in showing that these two narrow traits are actually linked together, tending to co-occur in people.

The typical high scorer on neuroticism (N) tends to be a worrier. Frequently anxi-ous and depressed, the high-N scorer has trouble sleeping and experiences a wide array of psychosomatic symptoms. A national study of 5,847 individuals found that those high on neuroticism tend to be especially prone to the disorders of depression and anxi-ety (Weinstock & Whisman, 2006). One of the hallmarks of the high-N scorer is over-reactivity on the negative emotions. The high-N scorer experiences more arousal than the low-N scorer in response to the normal stresses of everyday life. They have more trouble returning to an even keel after an emotionally arousing event. Those high on neuroticism also stay angry longer after a perceived transgression and are less likely to forgive someone who they perceived has violated them (Maltby et al., 2008). They are more likely to be vigilant to threats, particularly social threats such as being socially excluded (Denissen & Penke, 2008b; Tamir, Robinson, & Solberg, 2006). The low-N scorer, on the other hand, is emotionally stable, even-tempered, calm, slower to react to stressful events, and returns to his or her normal self quickly after an upsetting event.

The third large trait in Eysenck's taxonomy is *psychoticism* (P). As shown in Figure 3.1, P consists of the constellation of narrower traits that includes aggressive, egocentric, creative, impulsive, lacking empathy, and antisocial. Factor analysis proves valuable in grouping together narrower traits. Factor analyses show, for example, that impulsivity and lack of empathy tend to co-occur in individuals. That is, people who tend to act without thinking (impulsivity) also tend to lack the ability to see situations from other people's perspectives (lack of empathy).

The high-P scorer is typically a solitary individual, often described by others as a "loner." Because they lack empathy, high-P scorers may be cruel or inhumane. Men tend to score twice as high as women on P. Often, such people have a history of cruelty to animals. The high-P scorer may laugh, for example, when a dog gets hit by a car or when someone accidentally gets hurt. High-P scorers show insensitivity to the pain and suffering of others, including their own kin. They are aggressive, both verbally and physically, even with loved ones. The high-P scorer has a penchant for the strange and unusual and may disregard danger in pursuit of novelty. They like to make fools of other people and are often described as having antisocial tendencies.

Empirically, the P-scale predicts a number of fascinating criteria. Those who score high on P tend to show a strong preference for violent films and rate violent scenes from films more enjoyable than those who score low on P (Bruggemann & Barry, 2002). High-P individuals prefer unpleasant paintings and photographs more than do low-P individuals (Rawling, 2003). Men, but not women, who score high on Machiavellianism (which is highly correlated with P) endorse promiscuous and hostile sexual attitudes—they divulge sexual secrets to third parties, pretend to be in love when they are not, ply potential sex partners with alcoholic drinks, and even report trying to force others into sex acts (McHoskey, 2001). Indeed, those high in P tend are more likely to become sexual predators (O-Connell & Marcus, 2016). Those who are low in P tend to be more deeply religious, whereas high-P scorers tend to be somewhat cynical about religion (Saroglou, 2002). Finally, high-P scorers are disposed to getting into dangerous activities, such as violence, theft, and vandalism (Carrasco et al., 2006; Pickering et al., 2003).

The labels Eysenck has given to these super-traits, especially P, have generated controversy. Indeed, some suggest that more accurate and appropriate labels for psychoticism might be "antisocial personality" or "psychopathic personality." Regardless of the label, P has emerged as an important trait in normal-range personality research. In modern personality research, P has made a resurgence in the form of "the dark triad," which consists of psychopathy, narcissism, and Machiavellianism (Furnham et al., 2013). Dark Triad traits have been linked to bad bosses and toxic leadership in the workplace; cheating in the classroom; deception and coercion in the mating domain; and a host of other forms of antisocial behaviors, including white-collar crime.

Let's look more closely now at two aspects of Eysenck's system that warrant further comment—its hierarchical nature and its biological underpinnings.

Hierarchical Structure of Eysenck's System

Figure 3.1 shows the levels in Eysenck's hierarchical model, with each super-trait at the top and narrower traits at the second level. Subsumed by each narrow trait, however, is a third level—that of *habitual acts*. For example, one habitual act subsumed by sociable might be talking on the phone; another might be taking frequent breaks to socialize with other students. Narrow traits subsume a variety of habitual acts.

At the very lowest level in the hierarchy are *specific acts* (e.g., *I talked with my friend during class* and *I took a coffee break to chat at 10:30 a.m.*). If enough specific acts are repeated frequently, they become habitual acts at the third level. Clusters of habitual acts become narrow traits. And clusters of narrow traits become super-traits at the tops of the hierarchy. This hierarchy has the advantage of locating each specific personality-relevant act within a precise nested system. Thus, the fourth-level act *I danced wildly at the party* can be described as extraverted at the highest level, sociable at the second level, and part of a regular habit of party-going behavior at the third level.

Biological Underpinnings

There are two aspects of the biological underpinnings of Eysenck's personality system: *heritability* and *identifiable physiological substrate*. For Eysenck a key criterion for a "basic" dimension of personality is that it has reasonably high heritability. The behavioral genetic evidence confirms that all three super-traits in Eysenck's taxonomy—P, E, and N—do have moderate heritabilities, although this is also true of many personality traits (see Chapter 6).

The second biological criterion is that basic personality traits should have an identifiable physiological substrate—that is, that one can identify properties in the brain and central nervous system that are presumed to be part of the causal chain that produces personality traits. In Eysenck's formulation, extraversion is supposed to be linked with central nervous system arousal or reactivity. Eysenck predicted that introverts would be more easily aroused (and more autonomically reactive) than extraverts (see Chapter 7). In contrast, he proposed that neuroticism was linked with the degree of *lability* (changeability) of the autonomic nervous system. Finally, high-P scorers were predicted to be high in testosterone levels and low in levels of MAO, a neurotransmitter inhibitor.

In sum, Eysenck's personality taxonomy has many distinct features. It is hierarchical, starting with broad traits, which subsume narrower traits, which in turn subsume specific actions. The broad traits within the system have been shown to be moderately heritable. And Eysenck has attempted to link these traits with physiological functioning—adding an important level of analysis not included in most personality taxonomies.

Despite these admirable qualities, Eysenck's personality taxonomy has several limitations. One is that many other personality traits also show moderate heritability, not just extraversion, neuroticism, and psychoticism. A second limitation is that Eysenck may have missed some important traits in his taxonomy—a point argued by other personality psychologists, such as Raymond B. Cattell, and more recently by authors such as Lewis Goldberg, Paul Costa, and Robert McCrae.

Circumplex Taxonomies of Personality

People have been fascinated with circles for centuries. They have no beginning and no end, and they symbolize wholeness and unity. Circles have also fascinated personality psychologists as representations of the personality sphere.

In the twentieth century, the two most prominent advocates of circular representations of personality were Timothy Leary (also known for his LSD experiments at Harvard) and Jerry Wiggins, who formalized the circular model with modern statistical techniques. (Circumplex is simply a fancy name for circle.)

Wiggins (1979) started with the lexical assumption—the idea that all important individual differences are encoded within the natural language. But he went further in his efforts at taxonomy by arguing that trait terms specify different *kinds* of ways in which individuals differ. One kind of individual difference pertains to what people do to and with each other—**interpersonal traits**.

Other kinds of individual differences are specified by the following types of traits: *temperament* traits, such as nervous, gloomy, sluggish, and excitable; *character* traits, such as moral, principled, and dishonest; *material* traits, such as miserly and stingy; *attitude* traits, such as pious and spiritual; *mental* traits, such as clever, logical, and perceptive; and *physical* traits, such as healthy and tough.

Because Wiggins was concerned primarily with *interpersonal* traits, he carefully separated these from the other categories of traits. Then, based on the earlier theorizing of Foa and Foa (1974), he defined *interpersonal* as interactions among people involving exchanges. The two resources that define social exchange are *love* and *status:* "interpersonal events may be defined as *dyadic interactions that have relatively clear-cut social (status) and emotional (love) consequences for both participants*" (Wiggins, 1979, p. 398, italics original). Hence, the dimensions of status and love define the two major axes of the Wiggins circumplex, as shown in Figure 3.2.

There are three clear advantages to the Wiggins circumplex. The first is that it provides an *explicit definition* of interpersonal behavior. Thus it should be possible to locate any transaction in which the resources of status or love are exchanged within a specific area of the circumplex pie. These include not just giving love (e.g., giving a friend a hug) or granting status (e.g., showing respect or honor to a parent). They also include denying love (e.g., yelling at a boyfriend) and

Jerry Wiggins developed measurement scales to assess the traits in the circumplex model.
Courtesy of Krista Trobst

Figure 3.2

The circumplex model of personality.

Source: Adapted from "Circular Reasoning About Interpersonal Behavior," by J. S. Wiggins, N. Phillips, and P. Trapnell, 1989, *Journal of Personality & Social Psychology,* 56, p. 297. Copyright 1989 by the American Psychological Association. Reprinted with permission.

denying status (e.g., dismissing someone as too inconsequential to talk to). Thus the Wiggins circumplex model has the advantage of providing an explicit and precise definition of interpersonal transactions.

The second advantage of Wiggins's model is that the circumplex *specifies the relationships between each trait and every other trait within the model.* There are basically three types of relationships specified by the model. The first is **adjacency**, or how close the traits are to each other in the circumplex. The variables that are adjacent, or next, to each other within the model are positively correlated. Thus gregarious-extraverted is correlated with warm-agreeable. Arrogant-calculating is correlated with hostile-quarrelsome.

The second type of relationship is **bipolarity**. Traits that are bipolar are located at opposite sides of the circle and are negatively correlated with each other. Dominant is the opposite of submissive, so the two are negatively correlated. Cold is the opposite of warm, so they are negatively correlated. Specifying this bipolarity is useful because nearly every interpersonal trait has another trait that is its opposite.

The third type of relationship is **orthogonality**, which specifies that traits that are perpendicular to each other on the model (at 90° of separation, or at right angles to each other) are entirely unrelated to each other. In other words, there is a zero correlation between such traits. Dominance, for example, is orthogonal to agreeableness, so the two are uncorrelated. This means that dominance can be expressed in a quarrelsome manner (e.g., *I yelled in order to get my way*) or in an agreeable manner (e.g., *I organized the group in order to get help for my friend*). Similarly, aggression (quarrelsome) can be expressed in an active/dominant manner (e.g., *I used my position of authority to punish* *my enemies*) or in an unassured/submissive way (e.g., *I gave him the silent treatment when I was upset*). Orthogonality allows one to specify with greater precision the different ways in which traits are expressed in actual behavior.

The third key advantage of the circumplex model is that it *alerts investigators to gaps* in investigations of interpersonal behavior. For example, whereas there have been many studies of dominance and aggression, personality psychologists have paid little attention to traits such as unassuming and calculating. The circumplex model, by providing a map of the interpersonal terrain, directs researchers to these neglected areas of psychological functioning.

In sum, the Wiggins circumplex model provides an elegant map of major individual differences in the social domain. The circumplex structure of interpersonal traits has been discovered in children as well as adults (Di Blas, 2007). It has been used to discover interpersonal sensitivities (Hopwood et al., 2011). For example, people tend to find others unpleasant who have personalities that are the polar opposite of their own. And it has been used to identify some maladaptive aspects of interpersonal functioning: Those who are submissive and agreeable, for example, may be overly accommodating (e.g., allowing themselves to be shortchanged at the store without saying anything) or passively aggressive (e.g., giving others the "silent treatment") (Hennig & Walker, 2008). Despite these positive qualities, the circumplex also has some limitations. The most important limitation is that the interpersonal map is limited to two dimensions. Other traits, not captured by these two dimensions, also have important interpersonal consequences. The trait of conscientiousness, for example, is interpersonal in that persons high on this trait are very dependable in their social obligations to friends, mates, and children. Even a trait such as neuroticism or emotional stability may show up most strongly in interpersonal transactions with others (e.g., *He overreacted to a subtle interpersonal slight when the host took too long to acknowledge his presence,* and *He insisted that he and his partner leave the party*). A more comprehensive taxonomy of personality that includes these dimensions is known as the five-factor model.

Five-Factor Model

In the past few decades, the taxonomy of personality traits that has received the most attention and support from personality researchers has been the **five-factor model**—variously labeled the five-factor model, the Big Five, and even in a humorous vein The High Five (Costa & McCrae, 1995; Goldberg, 1981; McCrae & John, 1992; Saucier & Goldberg, 1996). The broad traits composing the Big Five have been provisionally named (I) *surgency* or *extraversion,* (II) *agreeableness,* (III) *conscientiousness,* (IV) *emotional stability,* and (V) *openness-intellect.* This five-dimensional taxonomy of personality traits has accrued some persuasive advocates (e.g., John, 1990; McCrae & John, 1992; Rammstetd, Goldberg, & Borg, 2010; Saucier & Goldberg, 1998; Wiggins, 1996), as well as some strong critics (e.g., Block, 1995; McAdams, 1992).

The five-factor model was originally based on a combination of the lexical approach and statistical approaches. The lexical approach started in the 1930s, with the pioneering work of Allport and Odbert (1936), who laboriously went through the English dictionary and identified 17,953 trait terms. Allport and Odbert then divided the trait terms into four lists: (1) *stable traits* (e.g., secure, intelligent), (2) *temporary states, moods, and activities* (e.g., agitated, excited), (3) *social evaluations* (e.g., charming, irritating), and (4) *metaphorical, physical, and doubtful terms* (e.g., prolific, lean).

The terms from the first category, 4,500 presumably stable traits, were subsequently used by Cattell (1943) as a starting point for his lexical analysis of personality traits. Because of the limited power of computers at the time, however, Cattell could not subject this list to a factor analysis. Instead, he reduced the list to a smaller set of

Table 3.3 Norman's Markers for the Big Five

I. Extraversion or Surgency
Talkative–silent
Sociable–reclusive
Adventurous–cautious
Open–secretive

II. Agreeableness
Good-natured–irritable
Cooperative–negativistic
Mild/gentle–headstrong
Not jealous–jealous

III. Conscientiousness
Responsible–undependable
Scrupulous–unscrupulous
Persevering–quitting
Fussy/tidy–careless

IV. Emotional stability
Calm–anxious
Composed–excitable
Not hypochondriacal–hypochondriacal
Poised–nervous/tense

V. Culture—Intellect, Openness
Intellectual–unreflective/narrow
Artistic–nonartistic
Imaginative–simple/direct
Polished/refined–crude/boorish

Source: Norman, 1963.

171 clusters (groups of traits) by eliminating some and lumping together others. He ended up with a smaller set of 35 clusters of personality traits.

Fiske (1949) then took a subset of 22 of Cattell's 35 clusters and discovered, through factor analysis, a five-factor solution. However, this single study of relatively small sample size was hardly a robust foundation for a comprehensive taxonomy of personality traits. In historical treatments of the five-factor model, therefore, Fiske is noted as the first person to discover a version of the five-factor model, but he is not credited with having identified its precise structure.

Tupes and Christal (1961) made the next major contribution to the five-factor taxonomy. They examined the factor structure of the 22 simplified descriptions in eight samples and emerged with the five-factor model: *surgency, agreeableness, conscientiousness, emotional stability,* and *culture*. This factor structure was subsequently replicated by Norman (1963), then by a host of other researchers (e.g., Botwin & Buss, 1989; Digman & Inouye, 1986; Goldberg, 1981; McCrae & Costa, 1985; Rammstetd et al., 2010). The key markers that define the Big Five, as determined by Norman (1963), are shown in Table 3.3.

The past 30 years have witnessed an explosion of research on the Big Five. Indeed, the Big Five taxonomy has achieved a greater degree of consensus than any other trait taxonomy in the history of personality trait psychology. But it has also generated some controversy. We consider three key issues: (1) What is the empirical evidence for the five-factor taxonomy of personality? (2) What is the identity of the fifth factor? (3) Is the Big Five taxonomy really comprehensive, or are there major trait dimensions that lie beyond the Big Five?

What Is the Empirical Evidence for the Five-Factor Model?

The five-factor model has proven to be astonishingly replicable in studies using English-language trait words as items (Goldberg, 1981, 1990; John et al., 2008; McCrae & Costa, 2008). The five factors have been found by dozens of researchers using different samples. This model has been replicated in every decade for the past half-century. It has been replicated in different languages and in different item formats (Rammstetd et al., 2010).

In its modern form, the Big Five taxonomy has been measured in two major ways. One way is based on self-ratings of single-word trait adjectives, such as *talkative, warm, organized, moody*, and *imaginative* (Goldberg, 1990), and one way is based on self-ratings of sentence items, such as "*My life is fast-paced*" (McCrae & Costa, 1999). We will discuss these in turn.

Lewis R. Goldberg has done the most systematic research on the Big Five using single-word trait adjectives. According to Goldberg (1990), key adjective markers of the Big Five are as follows:

1. Surgency or extraversion: *talkative, extraverted, assertive, forward, outspoken* versus *shy, quiet, introverted, bashful, inhibited.*
2. Agreeableness: *sympathetic, kind, warm, understanding, sincere* versus *unsympathetic, unkind, harsh, cruel.*
3. Conscientiousness: *organized, neat, orderly, practical, prompt, meticulous* versus *disorganized, disorderly, careless, sloppy, impractical.*
4. Emotional stability: *calm, relaxed, stable* versus *moody, anxious, insecure.*
5. Intellect or imagination: *creative, imaginative, intellectual* versus *uncreative, unimaginative, unintellectual.*

In addition to measures of the Big Five that use single trait words as items, the most widely used measure using a sentence-length item format has been developed by Paul T. Costa and Robert R. McCrae. It's called the NEO-PI-3: the neuroticism-extraversion-openness (NEO) Personality Inventory (PI) Revised (R) (McCrae, Costa, & Martin, 2005). Sample items from the NEO-PI-3 are neuroticism (N): *I have frequent mood swings;* extraversion (E): *I don't find it easy to take charge of a situation* (reverse scored); openness (O): *I enjoy trying new and foreign foods;* agreeableness (A): *Most people I know like me;* and conscientiousness (C): *I keep my belongings neat and clean.*

Exercise?

Your job is to develop a way to measure the Big Five traits in someone you know, such as a friend, a roommate, or a family member. Read the adjectives in Table 3.3 carefully until you

	Very low	Somewhat low	Average	Somewhat high	Very high
Extraversion					
Agreeableness					
Conscientiousness					
Emotional stability					
Openness–intellect					

have an understanding of each of the Big Five traits. Then, consider the different sources of personality data described in Chapter 2:

1. Self-report—typically, asking questions on a questionnaire.
2. Observer-report—typically, asking someone who knows the subject to report what the subject is like.
3. Test data—typically, objective tasks, situations, or physiological recordings that get at manifestations of the trait in question.
4. Life-outcome data—aspects of the person's life that may reveal a trait, such as introverted people selecting careers in which there is little contact with others.

Your job is to assess your target person on each of the Big Five traits, using a combination of data sources. You should first list, for each of the five traits, the way you measured that trait, such as the items on your questionnaire or interview or the life-outcome data. Then, in the second part of your report, indicate how high or low you think your examinee is on each of the five traits.

You might be thinking at this point that five factors may be too few to capture all of the fascinating complexity of personality. And you may be right. But consider this. Each of the five global personality factors has a host of specific "facets," which provide a lot of subtlety and nuance. The global trait of conscientiousness, for example, includes these six facets: competence, order, dutifulness, achievement striving, self-discipline, and deliberation. The global trait of neuroticism has these six facets: anxiety, angry hostility, depression, self-consciousness, impulsivity, and vulnerability. These facets of each global factor go a long way toward adding richness, complexity, and nuance to personality description.

Although the NEO-PI-3 traits are presented in a different order (N, E, O, A, and C) than the Goldberg order, and in a few cases the traits are given different names, the underlying personality traits being measured are nearly identical to those found by Goldberg. This convergence between the factor structures of single-trait item formats and sentence-length item formats provides support for the robustness and replicability of the five-factor model (Rammstetd et al., 2010).

What Is the Identity of the Fifth Factor?

Although the five-factor model has achieved impressive replicability across samples, investigators, and item formats, there is still some disagreement about the content and replicability of the fifth factor. Different researchers have variously labeled this fifth factor as *culture, intellect, intellectance, imagination, openness, openness to experience,* and even *fluid intelligence* and *tender-mindedness* (see Brand & Egan, 1989; De Raad, 1998). A major cause of these differences is that different researchers start with different item pools to factor analyze. Those who start with the lexical strategy and use adjectives as items typically endorse *intellect* as the meaning and label of the fifth factor (Saucier & Goldberg, 1996). In contrast, those who use questionnaire items tend to prefer *openness* or *openness to experience* because this label better reflects the content of those items (McCrae & Costa, 1997, 1999, 2008).

One way to resolve these differences is to go back to the lexical rationale to begin with and to look *across cultures* and *across languages*. According to the lexical approach, traits that emerge universally in different languages and cultures are more important than those that lack cross-cultural universality. What do the cross-cultural data show? In a study conducted in Turkey, a clear fifth factor emerged that is best described as *openness* (Somer & Goldberg, 1999). A different Dutch study found a fifth factor marked by *progressive* at one end and *conservative* at the other (DeRaad et al., 1998). In German, the fifth factor represents *intelligence, talents,* and *abilities* (Ostendorf, 1990). In Italian, the fifth factor is *conventionality,* marked by the items *rebellious* and *critical* (Caprara & Perugini, 1994). Looking across all these studies, the fifth factor has proven difficult to pin down, although *openness* and *intellect* best describe the most common content (John, Naumann, & Soto, 2008).

In summary, although the first four factors are highly replicable across cultures and languages, there is uncertainty about the content, naming, and replicability of the fifth factor (De Raad et al., 2010). Perhaps some individual differences are more relevant to some cultures than to others—intellect in some cultures, conventionality in other cultures, and openness in yet other cultures. Clearly, more extensive cross-cultural work is needed, particularly in African cultures and in more traditional cultures that are minimally influenced by Western culture.

What Are the Empirical Correlates of the Five Factors?

Over the past 20 years, a tremendous volume of research has been conducted on the empirical correlates of each of the five factors. This section summarizes some of the most recent interesting findings.

Extraversion. Extraverts love to party—they engage in frequent social interaction, take the lead in livening up dull gatherings, and enjoy talking a lot. Indeed, evidence suggests that **social attention** is the cardinal feature of extraversion (Ashton, Lee, & Paunonen, 2002). From the perspective of the extravert, "the more the merrier." Extraverts have a greater impact on their social environment, often assuming leadership positions, whereas introverts tend to be more like wallflowers (Jensen-Campbell & Graziano, 2001). Extraverted men are more likely to be bold with women they don't know, whereas introverted men tend to be shy with women (Berry & Miller, 2001). Extraverts tend to be happier, and this positive affect is experienced most intensely when a person acts in an extraverted manner with other people (Fleeson, Malanos, & Achille, 2002; Oelermns & Bakker, 2014). Extraversion also has an impact in the workplace. Extraverts tend to be more involved and enjoy their work (Burke, Mattheiesen, & Pallesen, 2006) and show more commitment to their work organization (Erdheim, Wang, & Zickar, 2006). Experiments also show that extraverts are more cooperative than introverts (Hirsh & Peterson, 2009), which might contribute to their positive work experiences. Extraverts tend to be physically stronger than introverts, in part because they engage in more vigorous and frequent physical activity (Fink et al., 2016; Tolea et al., 2012). But there are also downsides—extraverts like to drive fast and listen to music while driving, and as a consequence, tend to get into more car accidents, and even road fatalities, than their more introverted peers (Lajunen, 2001). They are less likely than introverts to save money for retirement (Hirsh, 2015). When given a choice, extraverts prefer to spend leisure time on beaches and near oceans, whereas introverts enjoy the solitude of mountains (Oishi et al., 2015).

Agreeableness. Whereas the motto of the extravert might be "let's liven things up," the motto of the highly agreeable person might be "let's all get along." Those who score high on agreeableness favor using negotiation to resolve conflicts; low-agreeable persons try to assert their power to resolve social conflicts (Graziano & Tobin, 2002; Jensen-Campbell & Graziano, 2001). The agreeable person is also more likely to withdraw from social conflict. Agreeable individuals like harmonious social interaction and cooperative family life. They are also highly prosocial and empathic, and enjoy helping others in need (Caprara et al., 2010). They value prosocial behaviors in others, but at the same time tend to judge harshly those who commit antisocial acts (Kammrath & Scholer, 2011). Agreeable children tend to be less often victimized by bullies during early adolescence (Jensen-Campbell et al., 2002). As you might suspect, politicians, at least in Italy, tend to score high on scales of agreeableness (Caprara et al., 2003). Those high on agreeableness seem to be good at reading other people's minds (Nettle & Liddle, 2008), an empathic ability that leads to more forgiveness of the transgressions of other people (Strelan, 2007).

At the other end of the scale of agreeableness lies aggressiveness. Wu and Clark (2003) found that aggressiveness was strongly linked to many everyday behaviors. Examples include hitting someone else in anger, blowing up when things don't work properly, slamming doors, yelling, getting into arguments, clenching fists, raising voices, being intentionally rude, damaging someone's property, pushing and hitting others, and slamming down the phone. So the next time you think about getting into an argument with someone, you might want to find out where they are on the agreeable–aggressiveness disposition.

Agreeable individuals, in short, get along well with others, are well liked, avoid conflict, strive for harmonious family lives, and may selectively prefer professions in which their likeability is an asset. Disagreeable individuals are aggressive and seem to get themselves into a lot of social conflict.

Conscientiousness. If extraverts party up and agreeable people get along, then conscientious individuals are industrious and get ahead. The hard work, punctuality, and reliable behavior exhibited by conscientious individuals result in a host of life outcomes such as a higher grade point average (Conrad, 2006; Noftle & Robins, 2007; Poropat, 2009), greater job satisfaction, greater job security, and more positive and committed social relationships (Langford, 2003). Those who score low on conscientiousness, in contrast, are likely to perform more poorly at school and at work. The fact that highly conscientious individuals succeed in the work domain is likely due to three key correlates. They do not procrastinate, in contrast to their low-conscious peers whose motto might be "never put off until tomorrow what you can put off until the day after tomorrow" (Lee, Kelly, & Edwards, 2006). Second, they tend to be perfectionists, setting high standards for themselves (Cruce et al., 2012; Stoeber, Otto, & Dalbert, 2009) and score high on achievement motivation (Richardson & Abraham, 2009). And those high in conscientiousness are exceptionally industrious, putting in the long hours of diligent hard work needed to get ahead (Lund et al., 2006). Those high on conscientiousness are more likely to stick with good plans for physical exercise (Bogg, 2008) and consequently are less likely to gain weight when they reach middle age (Brummett et al., 2006). High scorers on conscientiousness also display more passion and perseverance for long-term goals (Duckworth et al., 2007). And they are more likely to do volunteer work when they retire from their jobs (Mike et al., 2014).

Low C is linked with risky sexual behaviors, such as failing to use condoms (Trobst et al., 2002) and being more responsive to other potential partners while already in an existing romantic relationship (Schmitt & Buss, 2001). Among a sample of prisoners, low-C scorers tend to have frequent arrests (Clower & Bothwell, 2001). The high-C individual, in sum, tends to perform well in school and work, avoids breaking the rules, and has a more stable and secure romantic relationship. But there does appear to be at least one downside to being highly conscientious—high scorers, compared to low scorers, experience a more substantial drop in psychological well-being when they are unemployed for extended periods of time (Boyce et al., 2010).

Emotional stability. Life poses stresses and hurdles that everyone must confront. The dimension of emotional stability taps into the way people cope with these stresses. Emotionally stable individuals are like boats that remain on course through choppy waters. Emotionally unstable people get buffeted about by the waves and are more likely to get knocked off course. The hallmark of emotional instability, or neuroticism, is variability of moods over time—such people swing up and down more than emotionally stable individuals (Murray, Allen, & Trinder, 2002).

Emotionally unstable individuals experience more fatigue over the course of the day (De Vries & Van Heck, 2002) and experience more grief and depression after the death of a loved one (Winjgaards-de Meij et al., 2007). Psychologically, emotionally unstable individuals are more likely to have dissociate experiences such as an inability to recall important life events, feeling disconnected from life and other people, and feeling like they've woken up in a strange or unfamiliar place (Kwapil, Wrobel, & Pope, 2002). Those high on neuroticism also tend to have more frequent suicidal ideation (Chioqueta & Stiles, 2005; Stewart et al., 2008). Those high on neuroticism report poorer physical health, more physical symptoms, and fewer attempts to engage in health-promoting behaviors (Williams, O'Brien, & Colder, 2004). They also engage in health-impairing behaviors, such as drinking alcohol as a means of coping with their problems (Theakston et al., 2004).

Interpersonally, those high on emotional instability have more ups and downs in their social relationships. In the sexual domain, for example, emotionally unstable individuals experience more sexual anxiety (e.g., worried about performance) as well as a greater fear of engaging in sex (Heaven et al., 2003; Shafer, 2001). And with highly stressful events, such as an unwanted loss of a pregnancy, emotionally unstable individuals are more likely to develop "posttraumatic stress disorder," in which the psychological trauma of the loss is experienced profoundly and for a long time (Englelhard, van den Hout, & Kindt, 2003).

Emotional instability augers poorly for professional success. This may be partly due to the fact that emotionally unstable people are thrown off track by the everyday stresses and strains that we all go through. It may be partly due to their experience of greater fatigue. But it may also be attributable to the fact that they engage in a lot of "self-handicapping" (Ross, Canada, & Rausch, 2002). Self-handicapping is defined as a tendency to "create obstacles to successful achievement in performance or competitive

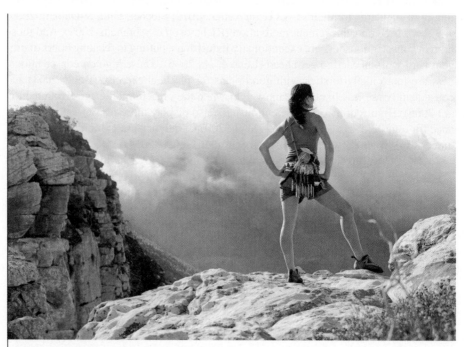

Personality characteristics predict who will climb mountains, literally and metaphorically.
© *OJO/Getty Images RF*

situations in order to protect one's self-esteem" (Ross et al., 2002, p. 2). Emotionally unstable individuals are also more likely to choke under pressure, such as a time deadline to complete a task (Byrne et al., 2015). Nonetheless, those high on neuroticism actually outperform their more emotionally stable counterparts in an office setting when changes in the work needs create an unusually busy work environment (Smillie et al., 2006). In sum, the affective volatility that comes with being low on emotional stability affects many spheres of life, from sexuality to achievement.

Intellect-Openness. Would you agree or disagree with the following statements? "Upon awakening during the night, I am unsure whether I actually experienced something or only dreamed about it," "I am aware that I am dreaming, even as I dream," "I am able to control or direct the content of my dreams," "A dream helped me to solve a current problem or concern" (Watson, 2003). If you tend to agree with these statements, you probably score high on openness. Those who are high on openness tend to remember their dreams more, have more waking dreams, have more vivid dreams, have more prophetic dreams (dreaming about something that later happens), and have more problem-solving dreams (Watson, 2003).

Openness has been linked to experimentation with new foods, a liking for novel experiences, and even "openness" to having extramarital affairs (Buss, 1993). One possible cause of openness may lie in individual differences in the processing of information. Those high in openness have more difficulty ignoring previously experienced stimuli (Peterson, Smith, & Carson, 2002). It's as though the perceptual and information processing "gates" of highly open people are literally more "open" to receiving information coming at them from a variety of sources. Perhaps that is why high openness is linked with measures of creativity (Nusbaum & Silva, 2010). Less-open people have more tunnel vision and find it easier to ignore competing stimuli. Those high in openness exhibit less prejudice against minority groups and are less likely to hold negative racial stereotypes (Flynn, 2005). They also are more likely to get tattoos and body piercings (Nathanson, Paulhus, & Williams, 2006; Tate & Shelton, 2008). High open people tend to be more politically liberal, especially when there is an external threat such as terrorism (Sibley et al., 2012). They also excel in achievement in the arts (Kaufman et al., 2016), and show higher levels of musical sophistication (Greenberg et al., 2015). Openness also predictions more cross-sex friendships on social networks such as Facebook (Lonnqvist et al., 2014). In sum, openness has been correlated with a host of other fascinating variables from intrusive stimuli to possible alternative sex partners.

Combinations of Big Five variables. Many life outcomes, of course, are better predicted by combinations of personality dispositions than by single personality dispositions. Here are a few examples.

- *Good grades* are best predicted by Conscientiousness (high) and Emotional Stability (high) (Chamorro-Premuzic & Furnham, 2003a, 2003b). One reason might be that emotionally stable and conscientious people are less likely to procrastinate (Watson, 2001).
- *Academic dishonesty* is more likely among those low in Conscientiousness and low in Agreeableness (Giluk et al., 2015).
- *What makes a good computer wiz?* High Conscientiousness, high Openness, and Introversion.
- Obedience to authority in a Milgram-like experiment is more likely among people high in Conscientiousness and high in Agreeableness (Begue et al., 2014).
- *Educational attainment and earnings* are predicted by high Emotional Stability, Openness, and Conscientiousness (O'Connell & Sheikh, 2011).

- *Risky sexual behaviors,* such has having many sex partners and not using condoms, are best predicted by high Extraversion, high Neuroticism, low Conscientiousness, and low Agreeableness (Miller et al., 2004; Trobst et al., 2002).
- *Alcohol consumption* is best predicted by high Extraversion and low Conscientiousness (Paunonen, 2003; Hong & Paunonen, 2009). A study of more than 5,000 workers in Finland found that low Conscientiousness also predicts *increases* in alcohol consumption over time, that is, who ends up becoming a heavy drinker (Grano et al., 2004).
- *Substance abuse disorders,* such as illegal drug abuse, are linked to high neuroticism and low conscientiousness (Kotov et al., 2010).
- *Pathological gambling* is best predicted by a combination of high Neuroticism and low Conscientiousness (Bagby et al., 2007; Myrseth et al., 2009; MacLaren et al., 2011).
- *Aggression* against other people when angry is well predicted by Neuroticism, but being high on Agreeableness appears to cool the tempers that these emotionally unstable people sometimes experience (Ode, Robinson, & Wilkowski, 2008).
- *Mount Everest mountain climbers* tend to be extraverted, emotionally stable, and high on Psychoticism (Egan & Stelmack, 2003).
- *Happiness* and experiencing positive affect in everyday life are best predicted by high Extraversion and low Neuroticism (Cheng & Furnham, 2003; Steel & Ones, 2002; Stewart, Ebmeier, & Deary, 2005; Yik & Russell, 2001).
- *Proclivity to engage in volunteer work,* such as campus or community services, is best predicted by a combination of high Agreeableness and high Extraversion (Carlo et al., 2005).
- *Forgiveness,* the proclivity to forgive those who have committed some wrong, characterizes individuals who are high on Agreeableness and high on Emotional Stability (Brose et al., 2005; Steiner et al., 2012).
- *Leadership effectiveness* in business settings is best predicted by high Extraversion, high Agreeableness, high Conscientiousness, and high Emotional Stability (Silverthorne, 2001).
- *Propensity to migrate* within and among states within the USA is predicted by high Openness and low Agreeableness (Jokela, 2009), although some studies show that high Openness combined with high Extraversion predicts intentions to emigrate to a new country (Canache et al., 2013).
- *Propensity to have children* is predicted by high Extraversion (sociability) and high Emotional Stability (Jokela et al., 2009).
- *Favorable attitudes toward being touched by an intimate partner* are most strongly felt by those high in Agreeableness and high in Openness to experience (Dorros, Hanzel, & Segrin, 2008).

We should not be surprised that combinations of personality variables often do better than single variables in predicting important life outcomes, and we can expect future research to focus increasingly on these combinations.

Is the Five-Factor Model Comprehensive?
Critics of the five-factor model argue that it leaves out important aspects of personality. Almagor, Tellegen, and Waller (1995), for example, present evidence for seven factors. Their results suggest the addition of two factors: *positive evaluation* (e.g., *outstanding* versus *ordinary*) and *negative evaluation* (e.g., *awful* versus *decent*). Goldberg, one of the

proponents of the five-factor model, has discovered that factors such as *religiosity* and *spirituality* sometimes emerge as separate factors, although these are clearly smaller in size (accounting for less variance) than those of the Big Five (Goldberg & Saucier, 1995).

Lanning (1994), using items from the California Adult Q-Sort, has found a replicable sixth factor, which he labels *attractiveness,* including the items *physically attractive, sees self as attractive,* and *charming.* In a related vein, Schmitt and Buss (2000) have found reliable individual differences in the sexual sphere, such as *sexiness* (e.g., sexy, stunning, attractive, alluring, arousing, sensual, and seductive) and *faithfulness* (e.g., faithful, monogamous, devoted, and not adulterous). These individual difference dimensions are correlated with the five factors: *sexiness* is positively correlated with *Extraversion,* and *faithfulness* is positively correlated with both *Agreeableness* and *Conscientiousness.* But these correlations leave much of the individual variation unaccounted for, suggesting that these individual differences in sexuality are not completely subsumed by the five-factor model.

Paunonen and colleagues have identified 10 personality traits that appear to fall outside of the five-factor model: Conventionality, Seductiveness, Manipulativeness, Thriftiness, Humorousness, Integrity, Femininity, Religiosity, Risk Taking, and Egotism (Paunonen, 2002; Paunonen et al., 2003). Other researchers have confirmed that these traits are not highly correlated with the Big Five and that they highlight many interesting facets of personality at a more specific level than the "global" factors represented by the five-factor model (Lee, Ogunfowora, & Ashton, 2005).

Proponents of the five-factor model are typically open-minded about the potential inclusion of factors beyond the five factors, if and when the empirical evidence warrants it (Costa & McCrae, 1995; Goldberg & Saucier, 1995). Nonetheless, these researchers have not found the evidence for additional factors beyond the Big Five to be compelling. *Positive* and *negative evaluation,* some have argued, are not really separate factors but, rather, false factors that emerge simply because raters tend to evaluate all things as either good or bad (McCrae & John, 1992). With respect to the *attractiveness* factor found by Lanning (1994), Costa and McCrae (1995) argue that *attractiveness* is not ordinarily considered to be a personality trait, although the *charming* item that loads on this factor surely would be considered part of personality.

One approach to personality factors beyond the Big Five has been to explore **personality-descriptive nouns** rather than adjectives. Saucier (2003) has discovered eight fascinating factors within the domain of personality nouns such as: *Dumbbell* (e.g., dummy, moron, twit), *Babe/Cutie* (e.g., beauty, darling, doll), *Philosopher* (e.g., genius, artist, individualist), *Lawbreaker* (e.g., pothead, drunk, rebel), *Joker* (e.g., clown, goof, comedian), and *Jock* (e.g., sportsman, tough, machine). A study of personality nouns in the Italian language revealed a somewhat different organization than that of the Big Five, discovering factors such as Honesty, Humility, and Cleverness (Di Blas, 2005). As Saucier concludes, "Personality taxonomies based on adjectives are unlikely to be comprehensive, because type-nouns have different content emphases" (Saucier, 2003, p. 695).

The HEXACO Model

Another approach to personality factors beyond the Big Five has been to go back to the lexical approach, focusing on large pools of trait adjectives in different languages (De Raad & Barelds, 2008). In an exciting development, several studies have converged on six rather than five factors. One study of seven languages (Dutch, French, German, Hungarian, Italian, Korean, and Polish) found variants of the Big Five, plus a sixth factor, Honesty–Humility (Ashton et al., 2004). At one end of the Honesty–Humility factor lie trait adjectives such as honest, sincere, trustworthy, and unselfish; the other end is anchored by adjectives such as arrogant, conceited, greedy, pompous, self-important, and egotistical. Independent investigators have also found versions of this sixth factor in Greece (Saucier et al., 2005) and Italy (Di Blas, 2005).

So much evidence has accumulated that some argue that the most comprehensive cross-language taxonomy of personality is best captured by **the HEXACO model**: Humility-Honesty (H), Emotionality (E), Extraversion (X), Agreeableness (A), Conscientiousness (C), and Openness to Experience (O) (Ashton et al., 2014). In this model, five of the six factors are very close to those of the Big Five, although there are subtle differences. The largest difference, of course, is the addition of the **Honesty–Humility** factor. This six-factor taxonomy has emerged in lexical-based studies of the major world languages, the most recent emerging from Poland (Gorbaniuk et al., 2013). The Honesty–Humility factor has also accrued strong construct validity. High scorers are more likely to offer sincere and humble apologies (Dunlop et al., 2015), even though they are less likely to violate social rules. It predicts cooperation in experimental games (Ashton et al., 2014). Those high on Honesty–Humility are also more likely to be sincerely religious (Silvia et al., 2014) and more easily show sexual and moral disgust (Tybur et al., 2013).

Those low on Honesty–Humility tend to be interpersonally exploitative, are more likely to sabotage others in their work environment, and are even more likely to engage in criminal activity (Johnson et al., 2011; Zettler & Hilbig, 2010). They are more likely to violate social contracts and cheat in games (Fiddick et al., 2016). They are more boastful (Hilbig et al., 2014). Moreover, be wary of romantically rejecting someone low on Honesty–Humility; such people are more likely to seek revenge against their former romantic partner (Sheppard & Boon, 2012).

The low end of Honesty–Humility captures several unpleasant interpersonal traits, including egotism, narcissism, and an exploitative interpersonal style. This cluster, sometimes called "the dark triad" (narcissism, Machiavellianism, and psychopathy), increasingly appears to be an important dispositional domain beyond that captured by the five-factor model (Paulhus & Williams, 2002; Veselka, Schermer, & Vernon, 2012). These findings point to an expansion of the basic factors of personality within the dispositional domain (Ashton & Lee, 2008, 2010; Lee & Ashton, 2008).

The expansion of the five-factor model to the six-factor HEXACO model is an exciting new development in personality psychology, and illustrates important progress in this vibrant science.

SUMMARY AND EVALUATION

This chapter focused on three fundamental issues for a personality psychology based on traits: how to conceptualize traits, how to identify the most important traits, and how to formulate a comprehensive taxonomy of traits.

There are two basic conceptualizations of traits. The first views traits as the internal properties of persons that cause behavior. In this conception, traits cause the outward behavioral manifestations. The second conceptualization views traits as descriptive summaries of overt behavior. The summary view does not assume that traits cause behavior; rather, it treats the issue of cause separately, to be examined after the behavioral summaries are identified.

There have been three major approaches to identifying the most important traits. The first is the lexical approach, which views all the important traits as captured by the natural language. The lexical approach uses synonym frequency and cross-cultural universality as the criteria for identifying important traits. The second approach, the statistical approach, adopts statistical procedures, such as factor analysis, and attempts to identify clusters of traits that covary. The third approach, the theoretical approach, uses an existing theory of personality to determine which traits are important. In practice, personality psychologists sometimes use blends of these three approaches—for example, by starting with the lexical approach to identify the universe of traits and then applying statistical procedures to identify groups of traits that covary and form larger factors.

The third fundamental issue—formulating an overarching taxonomy of personality traits—has yielded several solutions. Eysenck developed a hierarchical model in which the broad traits *extraversion, neuroticism,* and *psychoticism* subsume more narrow traits, such as activity level, moodiness, and egocentricity. Eysenck's taxonomy is based on a factor analysis but is also explicitly anchored in biological underpinnings, including a heritable basis for the traits and the identification of the underlying physiological basis for the traits.

Circumplex taxonomies of personality have been more narrowly targeted toward the domain of interpersonal traits as opposed to the entire personality sphere. Circumplex models are circular arrangements of traits organized around two key dimensions—status (dominance) and love (agreeableness).

The five-factor model of personality is a taxonomy that subsumes the circumplex in that the first two traits in the model—*extraversion* and *agreeableness*—are roughly the same as the circumplex dimensions of *dominance* and *agreeableness*. In addition, however, the five-factor model includes *conscientiousness, emotional stability,* and *openness–intellect.* The five-factor model has been criticized for not being comprehensive and for being inadequate for understanding underlying psychological processes. Recent evidence points to the exciting discovery of a sixth factor—*Honesty–Humility*—that necessitates an expansion of the Big Five. Some now argue for the cross-cultural robustness of a six-factor personality structure, the HEXACO Model: Honesty–Humility (H), Emotionality (E), Extraversion (X), Agreeableness (A), Conscientiousness (C), and Openness to Experience (O). This development is likely the most important advance in personality taxonomy in the past 20 years.

KEY TERMS

Theoretical and Measurement Issues in Trait Psychology

4

Theoretical Issues

Meaningful Differences Among Individuals
Stability over Time
Consistency Across Situations
Person–Situation Interaction
Aggregation

Measurement Issues

Carelessness
Faking on Questionnaires
Beware of Barnum Statements in Personality Test Interpretations

Personality and Prediction

Applications of Personality Testing in the Workplace
Legal Issues in Personality Testing in Employment Settings
Personnel Selection—Choosing the Right Person for the Job
Selection in Business Settings—The Myers-Briggs Type Indicator
Selection in Business Settings—The Hogan Personality Inventory

SUMMARY AND EVALUATION
KEY TERMS

THE DISPOSITIONAL DOMAIN

4

Signing up for an Internet dating service often involves answering a personality trait questionnaire.
© Wavebreak Media Ltd /123RF RF

Sarah was a junior in college with a double major in math and computer science. She was a bit shy, especially with men her own age. Although she wanted to date more, she was very particular about the characteristics she looked for in a man. She decided that a Web-based dating service might be an efficient way to find someone to date. She signed up with an Internet dating service and discovered that the first step was to complete an extensive personality inventory. She answered a lot of questions about her likes and dislikes, her habits, traits, and what others thought of her. She even answered questions about the kind of car she owned and her driving style. After this, the site returned the personality profiles of a few men who, the site claimed, would be good matches for her. One looked particularly interesting to her, so she spent a couple of hours with him online. Sarah decided to call him a couple of times on the phone. They had a lot in common, and Sarah found it easy to talk to him. She enjoyed the conversations, as did he, so they decided to take the next step and meet in person for a dinner date. When they made arrangements to meet, she was surprised to learn that they lived in the same apartment complex and that they had probably already seen one another, perhaps had even spoken to one another. But it took an Internet dating service, using a program that matches people according to personality, for them to actually find each other.

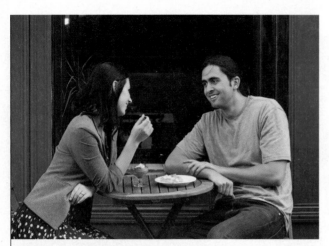

A key task for a first date is determining what you have in common with the other person—that is, how similar your personalities are.

© Alan Bailey/Getty Images RF

There are many Internet-based dating services, and many of these use personality psychologists to help them do a better job of matching people. For example, the Web site eHarmony.com uses a 480-item personality questionnaire. This dating service uses a combined matching system that relies on selecting matches on major personality traits. Other Internet dating services, such as Chemistry.com, PerfectMatch.com, or okcupid.com, also gather extensive personality data and engage in sophisticated matching routines. Personality psychologists have been accumulating evidence over the past half-century that personality similarity is a significant predictor of whether people will be attracted to each other (see Chapter 15) and whether they will be satisfied with their relationship once it is established (Decuyper, De Bolle, & De Fruyt, 2012).

Matching on personality traits sounds like a great idea, but it works only to the extent that the measures of personality are valid. People can represent themselves falsely in terms of physical characteristics (e.g., say they are petite when they are not, say they have thick, wavy hair when they are in fact bald), and they may represent themselves falsely in terms of their personality. They may, for example, try to cover up an aggressive, abusive personality. Consequently, some of these dating services are very concerned about safety and are using techniques from personality assessment to detect potential problem clients. For example, some sites ask about minor misbehaviors, such as "I never resent being asked to return a favor" or "I have, on occasion, told a white lie." People who deny a lot of these common faults raise a red flag because they are probably misrepresenting themselves on all the questionnaires. In fact, eHarmony.com claims that 16 percent of its clients are asked to leave the site based on their answers to such questionnaires (reported in *U.S. News & World Report,* September 29, 2003).

This use of personality testing brings into focus several questions about measurement of traits. Do traits represent consistent behavior patterns, such that we could make accurate predictions about a person's future behavior based on her or his trait standings? How do personality traits interact with situations, particularly social situations? Are there ways to detect that someone is not telling the truth on a personality questionnaire? Are some people motivated to fake good or to fake bad on questionnaires?

Personality measures are also used in other selection situations, such as for jobs or for prison parole or for placement within an organization. What are some of the legal issues in using personality measures to make such decisions? Are there some common problems with selection procedures? Can an employer use a measure of "integrity" to screen out potentially dishonest employees? What about selecting people for admission into college, law school, or medical school on the basis of aptitude tests or other so-called intelligence tests?

Although many of these questions seem abstract, they are important for how we think about personality traits. They are important for understanding controversial issues, such as the use of personality measures in business, industry, and education for the selection, training, and promotion of candidates.

Theoretical Issues

Trait theories of personality offer a collection of viewpoints about the fundamental building blocks of human nature. As we saw in Chapter 3, there are differences among the various theories concerning what constitutes a trait, how many traits exist, and what are the best methods for discovering basic traits. Despite their differences, trait theories share three important assumptions about personality traits. These assumptions go beyond any one theory or taxonomy of personality traits and, so, form the basic foundation for trait psychology. These three important assumptions are

- meaningful individual differences,
- stability over time, and
- consistency across situations.

Meaningful Differences Among Individuals

Trait psychologists are primarily interested in determining the ways in which people are *different from each other*. Any meaningful way in which people differ from each other may potentially be identified as a personality trait. Some people like to talk a lot; others don't. Some people are active; others are couch potatoes. Some people enjoy working on difficult puzzles; others avoid mental challenges. Because of its emphasis on the study of differences among people, trait psychology has sometimes been called **differential psychology** in the interest of distinguishing this field from other branches of personality psychology (Anastasi, 1976). Differential psychology includes the study of other forms of individual differences in addition to personality traits, such as abilities, aptitudes, and intelligence. In this chapter, however, we focus mainly on personality traits.

The trait perspective historically has been concerned with accurate measurement. It takes a quantitative approach, which emphasizes how much a given individual differs from average. Of all the perspectives and strategies for studying personality, the trait approach is the most mathematically and statistically oriented due to its emphasis on amount (Paunonen & Hong, 2015).

You might be wondering how the vast differences among people could be captured and represented by a few key personality traits. How is it that the uniqueness of every individual can be portrayed by just a few traits? Trait psychologists are somewhat like chemists. They argue that by combining a few primary traits in various amounts, they can recreate the unique qualities of every individual. This process is analogous to that of combining the three primary colors. Every visible color in the spectrum, from dusty mauve to burnt umber, is created through various combinations of the three primary colors: red, green, and blue. According to trait psychologists, every personality, no matter how complex or unusual, is the product of a particular combination of a few basic and primary traits.

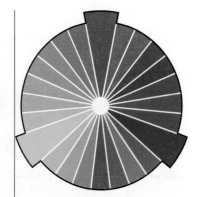

The Color Wheel. The infinite hues of color are created from a combination of three primary colors. Similarly, trait psychologists hold that the infinite variety of personalities are created from a combination of a few primary traits.

Stability over Time

The second assumption made by all trait theories is that there is a degree of stability in personality over time. If someone is highly extraverted during one period of observation, trait psychologists tend to assume that he or she will be extraverted tomorrow, next week, a year from now, or even decades from now. The view that many broad-based personality traits show considerable stability over time has been supported by a large number of research studies, which we review in Chapter 5. Traits such as intelligence, emotional reactivity, impulsiveness, shyness, and aggression show high test-retest correlations, even with years or decades between measurement occasions. Personality traits that are thought to have a biological basis, such as extraversion, sensation seeking, activity level, and shyness, also show remarkable consistency over time. Attitudes, however, are much less stable over time, as are interests and opinions (Conley, 1984a, 1984b). Of course, people do change in important behavioral ways throughout adulthood, especially after encountering some important life "turning point," such as serving in the military. For example, Jackson and colleagues (2012) showed that people lower in agreeableness and openness in high school were more likely to enter the military upon graduation. After training, the military recruits were even lower on agreeableness, and this low agreeableness persisted at least five years after training, when most of the recruits were no longer in the military and had either started college or entered the labor force. However, in the absence of major life "turning points," when it comes to broad personality traits, stability over time is more often the rule than the exception (Allemand, Gomez, & Jackson, 2010).

Although a trait might be stable over time, the way in which it manifests itself in actual behavior might change substantially. Consider the trait of disagreeableness. As a child, a highly disagreeable person might be prone to temper tantrums and fits of breath holding, fist pounding, and undirected rage. As an adult, a disagreeable person might be difficult to get along with and hence might have trouble sustaining personal relationships and holding down a job. Researchers have found, for example, a correlation of −.45 between throwing temper tantrums in childhood and being able to hold a job as an adult 20 years later (Caspi, Elder, & Bem, 1987). This finding is evidence of stability in the underlying trait (disagreeableness), even though the *manifestation* of that trait changes over time.

What about traits that decrease in intensity with age, such as activity level, impulsiveness, or sociopathy? How can there be stability in a trait if it is known to change with age? For example, criminal tendencies usually decrease with age, so a 20-year-old sociopath becomes much less dangerous to society as he or she ages. The

The Hartshorne and May study examined cross-situational consistency in academic and play situations in children. While they found little evidence for consistency in such traits as honesty, the study has been criticized for measuring behavior on one occasion in each situation. Studies that aggregate measurements over several occasions in each situation find much higher levels of cross-situational consistency.

Left © Image Source/Alamy Stock Photo RF; Right © McGraw-Hill Education

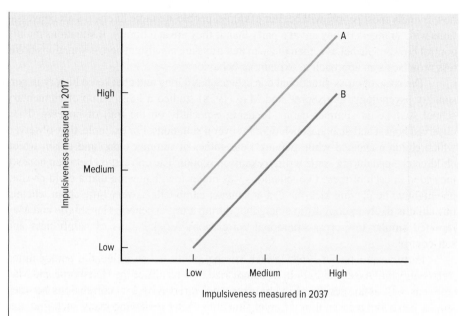

Figure 4.1

Hypothetical regression lines between impulsiveness measured 20 years apart. Line A represents an age change in impulsiveness, with all persons scoring as less impulsive in later life. Line B represents no change in impulsiveness over 20 years. Both lines represent rank order stability, however, and thus high test-retest correlations.

answer to this question lies in the concept of **rank order stability.** If all people show a decrease in a particular trait at the same rate over time, they might still maintain the same rank order relative to each other. Accounting for general change with age can be compared to subtracting or adding a constant to each participant's score on the trait measure. Figure 4.1 illustrates how a general decrease in impulsiveness with age might have no real effect on the correlation between measures obtained 20 years apart. People in general can show a decrease in impulsiveness as they get older, yet those individuals who were the most impulsive at an earlier age are still the ones who are most impulsive at a later age. We revisit the idea of rank order stability, as well as the whole notion of stability and change, in Chapter 5.

Consistency Across Situations

The third assumption made by trait psychologists is that traits will exhibit some **consistency** across situations. Although the evidence for stability in traits *over time* is substantial, the question of consistency in traits *from situation to situation* has been more hotly debated (for a recent review, see Leikas, Lonnqvist, & Verkasalo, 2012). Trait psychologists have traditionally believed that people's personalities show consistency from situation to situation. For example, if a young man is "really friendly," he is expected to be friendly at work, friendly at school, and friendly during recreation activities. This person might be friendly toward strangers, people of different ages, and authority figures.

Even though someone is "really friendly," there are, of course, situations in which the individual will not act friendly. Perhaps a particular situation exerts an influence on how friendly most people will be. For example, people are more likely to start conversations with strangers if they are at a party than if they are at a library. If situations mainly control how people behave, then the idea that traits are consistent across situations holds less promise as an approach to explaining behavior.

The issue of cross-situational consistency has a long and checkered history in personality psychology. Hartshorne and May (1928) studied a large group of elementary school students at summer camp, focusing especially on the trait of honesty. They observed honest and dishonest behavior in several situations. For example, they observed which children cheated while playing field games at summer camp and again, which children cheated during some written exams in school. The correlation between honesty measured in each of these two situations was rather low. Knowing that a child cheated one night while playing kick-the-can at summer camp tells us very little about whether this child is likely to copy from a neighbor during a test at school. Hartshorne and May reported similar low cross-situational correlations for the traits of helpfulness and self-control.

Forty years later, in 1968, Walter Mischel published an influential book entitled *Personality and Assessment.* In it, he summarized the results of the Hartshorne and May study, as well as the results of many other studies reporting low correlations between similar behaviors measured in different situations. After reviewing many such findings, Mischel concluded that "behavioral consistencies have not been demonstrated, and the concept of personality traits as broad predispositions is thus untenable" (p. 140).

Mischel's 1968 book questioned the very foundation of personality traits—the notion that people are consistent from situation to situation. He suggested that personality psychologists should abandon their efforts to explain behavior in terms of personality traits and recommended that they shift their focus to situations. If behavior differs from situation to situation, then it must be situational differences, rather than underlying personality traits, that determine behavior. This position, called **situationism,** can be illustrated with the following examples. A young woman may be friendly at school with people she knows but reserved with strangers. Or a young man may want to achieve good grades at school but may not care whether he excels in sports.

Mischel's challenge to the trait approach preoccupied the field of trait psychology for the 20 years following publication of his 1968 book. Many researchers responded to Mischel's situationist approach by formulating new theoretical perspectives and gathering new data designed to rescue the idea of traits (e.g., A. H. Buss, 1989; Endler & Magnusson, 1976). Mischel, in turn, countered with new ideas and new data of his own, intended to reinforce his position that the trait concept was limited in its usefulness (e.g., Mischel, 1984, 1990; Mischel & Peake, 1982).

Although the dust is still settling from this long-running debate (for a summary of the current situation, see Benet-Martinez et al., 2015), it is safe to say that both trait psychologists *and* Mischel have modified their views as a result. Mischel has tempered his position that situations are always the strongest determinants of behavior. However, he still maintains that trait psychologists have been guilty of overstating the importance of broad traits (Mischel & Shoda, 2010). Prior to Mischel's critique, it was common for trait psychologists to make statements about the predictability of people's behavior from their scores on personality tests. Mischel points out that psychologists simply are not very good at predicting how *an individual* will behave *in particular situations.* Trait psychologists, too, have modified their views. Two of the most lasting changes that trait psychologists have embraced have been the notion of **person–situation interaction** and the practice of **aggregation,** or averaging, as a tool for assessing personality traits.

A Closer Look

Situationism Today

The popular science writer Malcolm Gladwell (author of *The Tipping Point* and *Blink*) came out with a new book in 2008, titled *Outliers*. (The term *outlier* comes from statistics and refers to an individual in a sample who is markedly different from all others in that sample.) In this book Gladwell tackles the issue of being exceptional: why some people are exceedingly successful in some area of life, such as sports, science, or business, whereas most others are only mediocre. This question embodies the very concept of individual differences and lies at the heart of personality psychology. It also is a useful example to illustrate the extreme situational perspective.

Gladwell takes the position that most exceptional people get that way because of special opportunities or life situations that give them some advantage. His view is that the successful among us were presented with a beneficial life situation and ran with it. For example, the founders of many major computer companies (e.g., Microsoft, Apple, Sun Microsystems) were all born between 1953 and 1956 and therefore were exposed to early prototype computers when they were geeky teenage boys with lots of time on their hands. They all spent countless hours with these early prototypes and grew up to be exceptionally successful in the computing industry.

Gladwell presents case after case like this, arguing that exposure to critical life situations, at the right time, is what matters most in understanding why some people are so successful. This is an entirely situational explanation, in that the cause of the success lies not in the person but in the situations to which she or he was exposed. In Gladwell's view, success is all about opportunity, timing, luck, and hard work. It has nothing to do with traits within the person, such as aptitude, intelligence, interest, motivation, or personality. Gladwell is a modern situationist, presenting a one-sided perspective on understanding exceptional success.

The authors of the book you are presently reading were also both born between 1953 and 1956, just like Bill Gates, Steve Jobs, and Bill Joy. We also were exposed to primitive computers when we were geeky teenagers with lots of discretionary time on our hands. However, neither of us grew up to be corporate giants in the computing industry, even though we were exposed to the same kinds of life situations Gladwell argues were responsible for the exceptional success of these computing magnates. What explains this discrepancy? Well, we are both extremely interested in people, and we both were motivated to learn as much as we could about human nature when we were growing up. We must have had some innate ability in this field because we both went on to earn PhDs in psychology and to conduct award-winning research in the field of personality. Clearly, our interests, motivations, abilities, and personalities are very different from those of Bill Gates and Steve Jobs, even though we experienced many similar life situations. We might argue that it is precisely these personal characteristics that determined why we became personality psychologists and why Jobs and Gates became computing tycoons. This would be a strictly personality position, arguing that personal characteristics—ability, intelligence, interest, personality—entirely determine outcomes. Books presenting this perspective, which are as one-sided as Gladwell's, have also been written by nonscientists (e.g., *The Personality Code*, by Travis Bradberry, Putnam Press, 2007).

The real answer to understanding most life outcomes can be found in the interaction between personal characteristics and life situations: exceptional things happen when chance situations meet the prepared person. If someone had all the personal characteristics of Bill Gates or Steve Jobs, yet was from a poor, inner-city school that did not get those early prototype computers, he or she would most likely not go into this career. However, if someone had the exact same life experiences as Jobs and Gates, yet differed from them in basic interests, aptitudes, and personality (like us), then it is also likely that he or she would not go into computing as a career. It takes the right situations happening to people with the right personal characteristics to produce the exceptional outcome. Gladwell's book tells only half of the story, the situational half. The whole story is more complicated—and more interesting—than he portrays. For an integrated perspective on person–situation interaction, see Funder (2006).

Person–Situation Interaction

We first looked at the topic of person–situation interaction in Chapter 1. In this section, we examine this topic in a bit more detail, focusing on interactionism as a response to Mischel's challenge to trait consistency. As Mischel's debate with trait psychologists made clear, there are two possible explanations for behavior, or why people do what they do in any given situation:

1. Behavior is a function of personality traits, $B = f(P)$.
2. Behavior is a function of situational forces, $B = f(S)$.

Clearly, there is some truth in both of these statements. For example, people behave differently at funerals than they do at sporting events, illustrating that situational forces direct behavior in certain ways, as Mischel emphasized. Some people, however, are consistently quiet, even at sporting events, whereas other people are talkative and sociable, even at funerals. These examples lend support to the traditional trait position, which stresses that personality determines why people do what they do.

The obvious way to integrate these two points of view is to declare that both personality and situations interact to produce behavior, or

$$B = f(P \times S)$$

This formula suggests that behavior is a function of the *interaction* between personality traits and situational forces. Consider, for example, the trait of having a hot temper, a tendency to respond aggressively to minor frustrations. Acquaintances of a person high on this trait might be unaware of her short temper as long as they did not encounter her having to deal with a frustrating situation. The trait of having a short temper might be expressed only under the right situational conditions, such as in frustrating situations. If a person is frustrated by a situation (e.g., a vending machine takes the person's money but does not give him or her the product) *and* the person happens to have a quick temper (personality forces), then he or she will become upset and perhaps strike out at the source of the frustration (e.g., kick the vending machine repeatedly while cursing loudly). Any explanation of why such people get so upset would have to take into account both particular situations (e.g., frustration) and personality traits (e.g., hot temper). This point of view is called person–situation interaction, and it has become a fairly standard view in modern trait theory. Another way to view this is in the form of "If . . . , if . . . , then . . . ." statements (Shoda, Mischel, & Wright, 1994). For example, "**If** the situation is frustrating, and **if** the person has a hot temper, **then** aggression will be the result."

In the interactional view, differences among people are understood to make a difference only under the right circumstances. Some traits are specific to certain situations. Consider the trait of test anxiety. A young man might be generally easygoing and confident. However, under a set of *very specific* situational conditions, such as when he has to take an important exam, he becomes very anxious. In these particular circumstances, someone who is otherwise easygoing might become distressed, anxious, and quite upset. This example illustrates how certain very specific situations can provoke behavior that is otherwise out of character for the individual. This is referred to as **situational specificity,** in which a person acts in a specific way under particular circumstances implying that his or her behavior is caused by the situation.

Some trait–situation interactions are rare because the kinds of situations that elicit behavior related to those traits are themselves rare. For example, you would find it difficult to identify which of your classmates were high in courageousness. It would take a certain kind of *situation,* such as a hostage situation at your school, for you to find out just who is courageous and who is not.

The point is that personality traits interact with situational forces to produce behavior. Personality psychologists have given up the hope of predicting "all of the people all of the time" and have settled on the idea that they can predict "some of the people some of the time." For example, given the trait of anxiety, we might be able to predict who is likely to be anxious in some situations (e.g., evaluation situations, such as tests) but not anxious in other situations (e.g., when relaxed at home with family).

An interesting example of person X situation interaction is provided in a study by Debbie Moskowitz (1993). It has long been thought that the personality traits of dominance (the disposition to try to influence others) and friendliness (the degree to which a person is cordial and congenial) show large gender differences, with men being more dominant than women, and women being more friendly than men (Eagly, 1987). However, the study by Moskowitz showed that these traits interact with situation variables. Specifically, a person's level of dominance or friendliness may depend on who he or she is interacting with at the time, for example, whether the individual is interacting with a same-sex or opposite-sex person, and whether that person is someone known or a stranger. Moskowitz's (1993) study showed that women are more friendly than men, but only when they are interacting with other women; when interacting with opposite-sex strangers, women were not more friendly than men. As for dominance, the men were more dominant than women, but only when interacting with a same-sex friend; when interacting with strangers, the men were not more dominant than women. This study shows that who a person is interacting with will influence the expression of the personality traits of dominance and friendliness, and that this expression may or may not differ for men and women, depending on the social setting. A recent summary of her research on person–situation interaction, along with additional examples, can be found in Moskowitz and Fournier, 2015.

Some situations are so strong, however, that nearly everyone reacts in the same way. For example, in a study of emotional reactions to life events, Larsen, Diener, and Emmons (1986) were interested in finding out who tended to overreact emotionally to everyday events. Participants in this study kept a daily diary of life events for two months. They also rated their emotions each day. Based on a trait measure of emotional reactivity, these researchers were able to predict who would overreact to a minor or moderately stressful event, such as getting a flat tire, being stood up for a date, or having an outdoor event get rained out. When *really* bad things happened, such as the death of a pet, virtually everyone reacted with strong emotion. Researchers have coined the term **strong situation** to refer to situations in which nearly all people react in similar ways.

Certain strong situations, such as funerals, religious services, and crowded elevators, seem to pull for uniformity of behavior. By contrast, when situations are weak or ambiguous, personality has its strongest influence on behavior. The Rorschach inkblot cards are a classic example of a weak or ambiguous situation. A person being asked to interpret these inkblots is, in effect, being asked to provide structure by describing what he or she sees in the inkblot. Many situations in real life are also somewhat ambiguous. When a stranger smiles at you, is it a friendly smile or is there a bit of a sneer in the smile? When a stranger looks you right in the eye and holds the stare for a bit too long, what does it mean? Many social situations, like these two, require us to interpret the actions, motives, and intentions of others. As with interpretations of inkblots, how we interpret social situations may reveal our personalities. For example, people with a Machiavellian character (e.g., the tendency to use others, to be manipulative and

Personality plays a role in determining which situations a person chooses to enter. For example, whether one chooses team activities for recreation, such as soccer, or individual activities, such as long-distance running, is a function of one's level of extraversion. Studies show that extraverts prefer team activities and introverts prefer solitary activities for recreation.

© Corbis/Glow Images RF

calculating) often think others are out to get them (Golding, 1978). Especially in ambiguous social interactions, Machiavellian persons are likely to see others as threatening. This is a rather straightforward version of P × S interaction; not all people react the same to a given situation. Kihlstrom (2013) called this the static version of interaction, where personality traits and situational characteristics are thought as separate influences that, when acting together, explain more than either one considered one at a time.

Situational Selection

There are, however, more dynamic forms of P × S interaction, where the situation is not really separate from personality (Kihlstrom, 2013). In these dynamic versions, personality plays a role in constructing the situations that people find themselves in. We call this "dynamic" because the causal effects between personality and situations runs in both directions. That is, situations are, in part, a function of personality just as much as personality is, in part, a function of situations.

There are at least three distinct kinds of dynamic P × S interactions, and they each refer to different ways that personality affects situations. These concepts come up in later chapters, so we'll spend some time on them now. The first form of dynamic interactionism is **situational selection,** the tendency to choose the situations in which one finds oneself (Ickes, Snyder, & Garcia, 1997; Snyder & Gangestad, 1982). In other words, people typically do not find themselves in random situations. Instead, they select the situations in which they will spend their time. Snyder (1983) states this idea concisely: "Quite possibly, one's choice of the settings in which to live one's life may reflect features of one's personality; an individual may choose to live his or her life in serious, reserved, and intellectual situations precisely because he or she is a serious, reserved, and thoughtful individual" (p. 510).

Researchers have examined whether specific personality traits predict how often people enter into specific situations (Diener, Larsen, & Emmons, 1984). These researchers had participants wear pagers so that the participants could be signaled electronically throughout the day for six weeks. They were paged twice each day, resulting in a sample of 84 occasions for each participant. Each time the pager went off, the participants had to complete a brief questionnaire. One question inquired about the kind of situation each participant was in when the pager went off. Over the 84 times when the participants were "caught," the researchers predicted that certain personality traits would predict how many times they were caught in certain situations. For example, the researchers found that the trait of need for achievement correlated with spending more time in work situations, the need for order with spending time in more familiar situations, and extraversion with choosing social forms of recreation (e.g., team sports, such as baseball or volleyball, rather than solitary sports, such as long-distance running or swimming).

The idea that personality influences the kinds of situations in which people spend their time suggests that we can investigate personality by studying the choices people make in life. When given a choice, people typically choose situations that fit their personalities (Snyder & Gangestad, 1982). The personality effect does not have to be large to result in substantial life-outcome differences. For example, choosing to enter into work situations just 10 percent more of the time (e.g., studying 10 percent longer, or working 10 percent more hours) may result in very large differences in real-life outcomes, such as achieving a degree or a higher salary. Think, for example, about how you choose to spend your free time and about whether your choices reflect your own personality, to a degree.

The relationship between persons and situations goes in both directions. So far, we have been emphasizing how personality affects situational selection. However, once in the situation, that situation can affect the person's personality. A study by psychologist Will Fleeson and colleagues (Fleeson, Malanos, & Achille, 2002) illustrates how situations can influence personality. It has long been known that the trait of extraversion is related to positive emotions. We discuss this more in Chapter 13, but for now it is important simply to know that a strong correlation exists between extraversion and frequently feeling high levels of positive emotions. In their study, Fleeson and colleagues had subjects come to the lab in groups of three to participate in a group discussion. They were randomly assigned to an "introverted" or an "extraverted" condition. Instructions for the extraverted condition emphasized that they should behave in a talkative, bold, and energetic manner for the group discussion. Instructions for the introverted condition emphasized that they should behave in a reserved, compliant, and unadventurous manner for the group discussion. They were then asked to have a discussion of either the 10 most important items needed after an airplane crash or to come up with 10 possible solutions to the parking problem on their campus.

During the discussion, observers rated how positive each participant appeared. Also, following the discussion, each participant self-reported how positive he or she felt during the discussion. For both of these variables—observed positivity and self-reported positive feelings—the participants in the extraverted condition were substantially higher than those in the introverted condition. Moreover, this effect did not depend on the person's actual levels of trait extraversion. This study shows that being in an extraverted situation (being with a group of energetic, talkative people) can raise a person's level of positive affect. The study clearly illustrates that, when it comes to person × situation interactions, situations can influence persons just as much as persons can influence situations.

Evocation

The second form of dynamic person–situation interaction is **evocation,** the idea that certain personality traits may evoke specific responses from the environment. For example, people who are disagreeable and manipulative may evoke certain reactions in others, such as hostility and avoidance. In other words, people may create their own environments by eliciting certain responses from others. Consider the case of a male patient who had trouble sustaining relationships with women, such that he was divorced three times (Wachtel, 1973). He complained to his therapist that every woman with whom he became involved turned out to be bad-tempered, vicious, and spiteful. He complained that his relationships started out satisfying but always ended with the women becoming angry and leaving him. Wachtel (1973) speculated that the *man* must have been doing something to *evoke* this response from the women in his life.

The idea of evocation is similar to the idea of transference, discussed in Chapter 9 on psychoanalysis. Transference occurs when a patient in psychoanalysis re-creates, with the analyst, the interpersonal problems he or she is having with significant others. In doing so, the patient may evoke in the therapist the reactions and feelings that he or she typically evokes in other persons. Malcolm (1981) reported on a male psychoanalyst who found one female patient to be particularly boring. The analyst could hardly stay awake during the therapy sessions because the patient and her problems seemed so dull and trivial to him. After experiencing this reaction for a few weeks, however, the analyst realized that the patient was making him feel bored, just as she made other men in her life feel bored. She made herself dull, he concluded, to avoid the attentions of men and drive them away. However, she was in therapy, in part, because she complained of being lonely. This case illustrates how people can evoke reactions in others—creating and re-creating certain kinds of social situations in their everyday lives.

Manipulation

A third form of dynamic person–situation interaction is **manipulation,** which can be defined as the various means by which people influence the behavior of others. Manipulation is the intentional use of certain tactics to coerce, influence, or change others. Manipulation changes the social situation. Manipulation differs from selection in that selection involves choosing existing environments, whereas manipulation entails altering those environments already inhabited. Individuals differ in the tactics of manipulation they use. Researchers have found, for example, that some individuals use a charm tactic—complimenting others, acting warm and caring, and doing favors for others in order to influence them. Other people use a manipulation tactic sometimes referred to as the silent treatment, ignoring or failing to respond to the other person. A third tactic is coercion, which consists of making demands, yelling, criticizing, cursing, and threatening the other to get what one wants (Buss et al., 1987).

Aggregation

We've seen how their debate with Mischel led trait psychologists to appreciate that behavior is an outcome of the interaction between personality traits and situations. Another important lesson learned by trait psychologists is the value of aggregation when it comes to measuring personality traits. Aggregation is the process of adding up, or averaging, several single observations, resulting in a better (i.e., more reliable) measure of a personality trait than a single observation of behavior. This approach usually provides psychologists with a better measure of a personality trait than does using a single observation. Consider the concept of batting average, which is seen as a measure of a baseball player's batting ability (a trait). It turns out that batting average is not a very good predictor of whether or not a player will get a hit during any *single* time at bat. In fact, psychologist Abelson (1985) analyzed single batting occasions over the whole season. He found that batting average accounted for only .3 percent of the variance in getting a hit. This is a remarkably poor relationship, so why do people pay such close attention to batting average, and why do players with a good batting average earn so much more money? Because what matters is how a player performs *over the long run,* over an entire season. This is the principle of aggregation in action.

To draw an analogy between batting average and personality, let's say you decide to marry someone, in part, because of that person's cheerful disposition. Clearly, there will be days when your spouse is not going to be cheerful. However, what matters to you is your spouse's behavior over the long term (i.e., how cheerful your spouse will be in general) and not his or her mood on any given day or occasion.

Imagine taking an intelligence test that has only one item. Do you think this one-item test would be a good measure of your overall intelligence? You would be right if you concluded that a single question was probably not a very accurate or fair measure of overall intelligence. A related example might be if the instructor in your personality course were to decide that your entire grade for a course would be determined by asking you only one question on the final exam. Surely one question could not possibly measure your knowledge of the course material. Single questions or single observations are rarely good measures of anything.

Recall the Hartshorne and May (1928) study in which the researchers measured honesty by assessing whether or not a child cheated during a game on one occasion during summer camp. Do you think this one-item measure of honesty was an accurate reflection of the participants' true levels of honesty? It probably was not. This is likely the main reason why Hartshorne and May found such small correlations among their various measures of honesty (that is, because they were all single-item measures).

Personality psychologist Seymour Epstein published several papers (1979, 1980, 1983) showing that aggregating several questions or observations results in better trait measures. Longer tests are more reliable than shorter ones (reliability was introduced in Chapter 2) and hence are better measures of traits. If we want to know how conscientious a person is, we should observe many conscientious-related behaviors (e.g., how neat he or she is or how punctual) on many occasions and aggregate, or average, the responses. Any single behavior on any single occasion may be influenced by all sorts of extenuating circumstances unrelated to personality. But the average, or trend, of the person's behavior may be the best indicator of his or her personality.

Imagine that a trait psychologist is developing a questionnaire to measure how helpful, caring, and conscientious respondents are. She includes the following item on the questionnaire: "How often in the past few years have you stopped to help a person whose car was stuck in the snow?" Imagine further that you live in a place where it rarely snows. You answer "never," even though you are generally a helpful person. Now imagine being asked a whole set of questions, such as how often you donate money to charity, participate in blood donation programs, and do volunteer work in your community. Your answers to that whole series of questions provides a better indicator of your true level of helpfulness than does your answer to any single question.

Psychologists "rediscovered" aggregation in the 1980s. Charles Spearman published a paper back in 1910, explaining that tests with more items are generally more reliable than tests with fewer items. Spearman provided a formula—now called the Spearman-Brown prophesy formula—for determining precisely how much a test's reliability will increase as it is made longer. Although this formula appeared in all the major textbooks on measurement and statistics, personality psychologists seemed to have forgotten about the principle of aggregation until Epstein (1980, 1983) published his reminders in the early 1980s. Since then, other researchers have provided ample demonstrations of how the principle of aggregation works to increase the strength of correlations between measures of personality and measures of behavior. For example, according to a study by Diener and Larsen (1984), measures of activity level on one day correlated with activity level on another day at a correlation of only .08. However, when activity level was averaged over a three-week period and then correlated with activity level averaged over another three-week period, that correlation went up to .66. Clearly, aggregation provides a more stable and reliable measure of a person's average standing on a trait than any single observation can.

Besides being an important measurement principle, the notion of aggregation has profound implications for how we conceptualize personality traits and their effects in our daily lives. The biggest implication is that traits are really about averages, not about what a person does at any given point in time. In other words, traits are best at predicting trends or averages, and will never be good at predicting single behaviors on single occasions. If we say a person is punctual, for example, in means they are usually on time when they have an appointment. However, from time to time they might show up late (for example, if they got a flat tire on the way to the appointment). We will never know ahead of time if they will be on time for the appointment tomorrow (on one occasion), but our best guess, knowing they are a punctual person, would be to predict that they will be on time. We would be wrong on those occasions when something happens to disrupt their schedule.

Nevertheless, what matters most is a person's average tendency. When we are writing a letter of recommendation, for example, we might say that this person is highly reliable and punctual, ignoring the few occasions they showed up late through no fault of their own. Traits are about average tendencies, not about what happens on any given occasion.

The notion of traits as **density distributions of states** was developed by psychologist Will Fleeson (e.g., 2001, 2004) to understand the implications of aggregation for how we think about personality traits. Take the trait of extraversion, for example, which is associated with frequently engaging in specific behaviors like talking a lot, acting vigorously, being enthusiastic, etc. Focus on one of those behaviors, say talking, and imagine measuring that by outfitting 100 people with a micro-recorder that assesses how much they talked during each waking hour for a month straight. For each person you could count how many words they spoke each hour, and plot a frequency distribution of their talking behavior. Figure 4.2 illustrates two hypothetical density distributions of talking behavior from such a study. Person A's distribution in this figure has a lower mean level of talking behavior than Person B's, so we say that Person B is likely higher on the trait of extraversion (they talk more, and more frequently). However, Person A has some hours during this period when they actually talked quite a bit, even more than Person B's mean level. In other words, viewing each persons' talking behavior as a distribution illustrates that people vary quite a bit over time; sometimes a person is talkative, sometimes they are not. What matters is their mean level, how much they talk on average. Implicit in this is the acknowledgement that a person will sometimes behave below, and sometimes above, their own mean level on any given trait. Situations likely explain much of this within-person variability, whereas personality traits likely explain

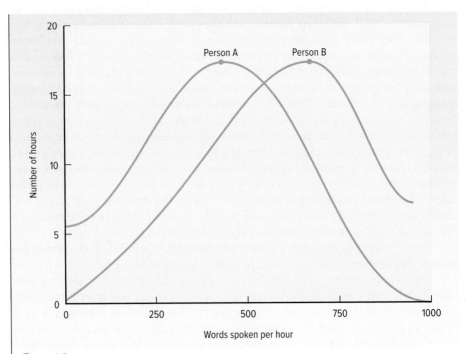

Figure 4.2

Two hypothetical density distributions of talking behavior showing differences in mean level. Note, however, a great deal of overlap, with the more talkative person (B) sometimes talking less than the less talkative person's (A) mean level, and vice versa.

the person's mean level (Fleeson & Law, 2015). Viewing traits as density distributions of states in a person's daily life acknowledges that in real life people are variable, their behavior varies from moment to moment, hour to hour, day to day. Nevertheless, within this variability is the person's true mean, their average, and the trait conception is really about average levels. This is similar to the set-point concept in body weight; a person's weight fluctuates day to day, but it fluctuates around their set-point, or average level, to which he or she returns.

Measurement Issues

More than any other approach to personality, the trait approach relies on self-report questionnaires to measure personality. Although trait psychologists can use other measurement methods (e.g., projective techniques, behavioral observation), questionnaires are the most frequently used method for measuring traits (Craik, 1986). Personality psychologists assume that people differ from each other in the *amounts* of various traits they possess, so the key measurement issue is determining *how much* of a particular trait a person possesses.

Traits are represented as dimensions along which people differ from each other. One of the most efficient ways to assess people's standing on any personality trait dimension is simply to ask them about their characteristics. If the right questions are asked, as the trait view holds, an accurate assessment of a person's standing on the trait dimension will be obtained.

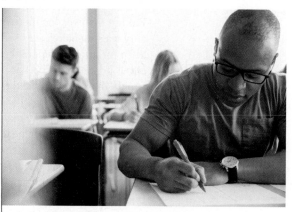

As compelling as this view of trait assessment is, it assumes that people generally are willing and able to report accurately on their behavior. However, some people may be unwilling to disclose information about themselves or may be motivated for some reason to distort or otherwise falsify their self-reports, such as during an employment interview or a parole hearing. Trait psychologists have long concerned themselves with the circumstances that affect the accuracy, reliability, validity, and utility of trait measures. We will now consider some important measurement issues in trait research.

Personality tests are frequently administered in large group settings. In such settings, some people may be careless or even fake their responses. Psychologists have developed ways of detecting faking and carelessness in the answers from individual test takers.
© Hero Images/Getty Images RF

Carelessness

Some participants filling out a trait questionnaire might not be motivated to answer carefully or truthfully. For example, some colleges and universities require introductory psychology students to participate in psychology experiments, many of which involve personality questionnaires. These volunteer participants may not be motivated to complete the questionnaires carefully; they may rush through the questionnaire, answering randomly. Other participants may be motivated to answer correctly but might accidentally invalidate their answer sheets. For example, when participants are asked to put their answers on optical scanning sheets by filling in circles with a number 2 lead pencil, it is not uncommon for participants to inadvertently neglect to fill in a circle or two, which means that all subsequent answers are then out of order. Another problem arises when, for some reason, the participant is not reading the questions carefully but is nevertheless providing answers. Perhaps the participant has difficulty reading, is tired, or even is hallucinating.

A common method for detecting these problems is to embed an **infrequency scale** within the set of questionnaire items. An infrequency scale contains items that all or almost all people will answer in a particular way. Using such items, if a person endorses more than one or two of these items in the "wrong" direction, then his or her test is flagged as suspicious. For example, on the Personality Research Form (Jackson & Messick, 1967), the infrequency scale contains items such as the following: "I do not believe that wood really burns," "I make all my own clothes and shoes," and "Whenever I walk up stairs, I always do so on my hands." These questions are answered "False" by over 95 percent of the people in samples from the United States and Canada. If a participant answers more than one or two of these as "True," we may begin to suspect that his or her answers do not represent valid information.

Another technique used to detect carelessness is to include duplicate questions spaced far apart in the questionnaire. The psychologist can then determine the number of times the participant answered identical questions with different responses. If this happens often, the psychologist might suspect carelessness or another problem that invalidates the person's answers.

Faking on Questionnaires

Faking involves the motivated distortion of answers on a questionnaire. When personality questionnaires are used to make important decisions about people's lives (e.g., hire them for a job, promote them, decide that they are not guilty by reason of insanity, or allow prisoners to be paroled), then there is always the possibility of faking. Some people may be motivated to "fake good" in order to appear to be better off or better adjusted than they really are. Others may be motivated to "fake bad" in order to appear to be worse off or more maladjusted than they really are. For example, a worker suing a company for mental anguish caused by a poor working condition might be motivated to appear very distressed to the court-appointed psychologist.

Questionnaire developers have attempted to devise ways to detect faking good and faking bad. In constructing the 16 Personality Factor questionnaire, for example, Cattell, Eber, and Tatsouoka (1970) had groups of participants complete the questionnaire under specific instructions. One group of participants was instructed to fake good, to appear to be

	The person being tested really is being . . .	
	Honest	Dishonest
The psychologist concludes he or she is . . . Honest	Correct	False positive "incorrect"
Dishonest	False negative "incorrect"	Correct

Two ways to make a mistake when deciding whether a person was faking his or her responses to a personality questionnaire.

as well adjusted as possible. Another group of participants was instructed to fake bad, to try to appear as maladjusted as possible. The data for these two groups were then used to generate a "faking good profile" and a "faking bad profile." The data from real participants can then be compared with those in these two faking profiles, and the psychologist can calculate just how much a person's responses fit the profile of the groups asked to fake their answers. This approach offers psychologists an imperfect but nevertheless reasonable method for determining the likelihood that a person is faking his or her responses to the questionnaire.

A recent study of military cadets applying for pilot training clearly illustrates that, when an important outcome is based on personality scores, people are motivated to "fake good" while answering the questions (Galic, Jerneic, & Kovacic, 2012). These researchers showed in three samples of military cadets applying to pilot school that the applicant's scores were more similar to scores obtained by persons who were asked to fake the most desirable person's responses. They warn that whenever important decisions are based on responses to questionnaires, care must be taken to account for desirable responding, or "faking good," on the part of the test takers.

There are two ways for psychologists to make a mistake when seeking to distinguish between genuine and faked responses. They may conclude that a truthful person was faking and reject that person's data (called a **false negative**). Or they may decide that a person who was faking was actually telling the truth (called a **false positive**). Psychologists do not know for certain how well their faking scales perform when it comes to minimizing the percentages of false positives and false negatives. Because of this problem of undetected faking, many psychologists are suspicious of self-report questionnaire measures of personality.

Beware of Barnum Statements in Personality Test Interpretations

"We have something for everyone."

—P. T. Barnum

Barnum statements are generalities—statements that could apply to anyone—though they often appear to the readers of astrology advice columns to apply specifically to them. Astrology predictions are very popular in newspapers and magazines. For example: "You sometimes have doubts about whether you have done the right thing" or "You have a need for others to like or admire you" or "Although you are able to deal with confrontation in a pinch, you typically like to avoid it if you can." These are Barnum statements. People read such statements and think, "Yes, that's me all right," when in fact such statements could apply to anyone.

Personality test interpreters also sometimes offer interpretations that consist of Barnum statements. To illustrate this, one of the authors of this textbook completed an online version of the Meyers-Briggs Type Indicator, a very popular personality test. He then submitted his answers to three different online interpretation services to get feedback about his personality. Reading the results of the first interpretation, he felt it had it right: "You advance toward good and retreat from evil; you hate to miss out on what is going on around you; you always try to tell the truth to those around you; you strive to be authentic and genuine, and you communicate well with others." The second interpretation also sounded accurate: "You want to be liked and admired by others; you are interested in new ideas; you have a great deal of charm, and others genuinely like you; at times your attention span can be short; you dislike bureaucracy." The third interpretation, too, seemed to apply: "You are fun to be around; while you can be intellectual, serious, and all business, you are also capable of flipping the switch and becoming childlike, interested in fun; you enjoy learning new things and have good self-discipline."

A Closer Look   Lying, Lie Detection, and Integrity Testing

Throughout history, employers have been concerned about employee theft. Such thefts could be avoided or at least minimized if there were a way to tell whether a person was generally honest or dishonest before hiring him or her. Over two centuries ago, the Chinese developed a test to determine whether a person was lying. The test consisted of asking the suspect a question, waiting for the answer, and then placing rice powder in the suspect's mouth. If the suspect could not swallow the rice powder, it was viewed as a sure sign that he or she was lying. This may sound like superstition, but if you think of the dry mouth that usually accompanies nervousness, then there might be some face validity to this early lie detection technique.

The modern lie detector, a polygraph, is a mechanical device that relies on psychophysiological measures, such as heart rate, respiration, and skin conductance (see Chapter 7). The use of physiological measures for lie detection started early in the 1900s in the United States. The idea behind this approach is that physiological measures may be useful in detecting the nervous arousal (e.g., guilt feelings) that often accompanies lying. The origin of the modern lie detection machine is shrouded in mystery. Some attribute it to a police officer from Berkeley, California, named Larson, who constructed the prototype of the multichanneled polygraph between 1917 and 1921 and also published a manual on how to use the machine. Others trace the idea of using psychophysiological recordings—in particular, systolic blood pressure—to measure deception in laboratory and legal settings to William Moulton Marston, who worked on this problem while he was a graduate student at Harvard University from 1915 to 1921. The lie detector gained widespread attention in the 1930s when it was introduced in the trial of Bruno

Hauptman, who was accused of murdering the Lindbergh baby. Businesses began using the polygraph widely in the 1970s.

The polygraph was originally designed to detect guilt reactions that arise from denying specific criminal acts. However, many employers began to use polygraph and other so-called lie detector tests to screen potential employees for general *honesty*. That is, the original purpose was to assess a state (guilt), whereas the polygraph was often pressed into usage to assess a trait (honesty). At any rate, participants were connected to these devices and asked various incriminating questions, such as whether they had ever taken anything that did not belong to them. If they showed any signs of nervousness or arousal (e.g., increased heart rate or shallower breathing), they might not have been hired. Employers also routinely used lie detector tests to question employees who were already on the job. Fast-food chains were among the largest users of polygraph tests in employment settings during this era (1970 to 1988). Managers hired polygraphers to connect employees to these devices, then ask questions such as whether they had taken any hamburgers or money in the past few months. If the polygraphs indicated any signs of nervousness, the employee might have been fired.

Polygraph exams were widely used in employment screening until they were banned by Congress in 1988 from use in private-sector employment settings. The government, however, still uses polygraphs in employment screening as well as periodic honesty verification of persons in sensitive positions. In fact, the U.S. government runs several training institutes that certify persons to administer standard polygraph exams.
© RIA Novosti/TopFoto/The Image Works

Through the 1970s and 1980s, more than 3 million polygraph tests were administered each year in the United States alone (Murphy, 1995). If you went into a large class of college students in the 1980s and asked if anyone had ever taken a polygraph exam, it was common to see at least a couple of hands go up for every hundred or so persons. Most said that they took the polygraph test as part of an employment screening procedure, often when applying for jobs in fast-food outlets.

A scientific evaluation of the polygraph as a lie detector was undertaken in 1983 by the U.S. federal government's Office of Technology Assessment. Its report concluded that there was no such device as a lie detector. Technically, this is true, as the polygraph detects physiological arousal, and sometimes lying is not accompanied by physiological arousal. In addition, sometimes physiological arousal is not accompanied by lying. The government evaluators also concluded that none of the methods used for lie detection were foolproof and that there were several effective ways to beat the device. Moreover, the polygraph's use in employment settings to screen for honesty may have resulted more in employment discrimination than in honesty detection.

In 1988, the U.S. Congress banned the use of the polygraph for most employment purposes in the private sector. Interestingly, the government still uses polygraphs for employee selection in several government service branches, such as the Secret Service, the CIA, the FBI, the DEA, Customs, and even the Postal Service. The government also maintains several polygraph schools, where people go to be trained in the use of the polygraph. In the private sector, however, the use of the polygraph in employment settings is highly restricted at this time.

This leaves the private sector employer with no mechanical means for detecting whether potential employees are honest. However, since the ban on polygraphs, many publishing companies have developed and promoted questionnaire measures to use in place of the polygraph (DeAngelis, 1991). These questionnaires, called **integrity tests,** are designed to assess whether a person is generally honest or dishonest. Many of these tests are considered to be reasonably reliable and valid and so may be legally used for employment screening (DeAngelis, 1991). Integrity tests measure attitudes related to one or more of the following psychological constructs: tolerating others who steal, beliefs that many others engage in theft, rationalizations that theft may be acceptable, interthief loyalty, antisocial beliefs and behaviors, and admission to stealing in the past.

One review of integrity questionnaires (Ones & Viswesvaran, 1998) concluded that the measures are reliable (have test-retest correlations in the range of 0.85) and valid (integrity test scores predict the following theft criteria: (a) supervisors' ratings of employees' dishonesty, (b) applicants who are likely to get caught stealing once hired, (c) applicants who have a criminal history, and (d) applicants who are likely to admit theft in an anonymous testing situation). In one study, a group of convenience stores started using an integrity test to select employees and experienced a 50 percent reduction in inventory shrinkage due to theft over an 18-month period. A more recent review (Berry, Sackett, & Wiemann, 2007) concludes that integrity tests are improving in terms of validity and resistance to faking and coaching, that they do not show adverse impact on protected groups (see following), and that they continue to be legal for use in employment settings. Moreover, new testing formats are being developed, such as using items that assess ethical decision making to various scenarios or that look at how people justify the decisions that they make. Integrity testing is a very active area of applied personality psychology, where the principles of personality psychology are used to improve the workplace and worker productivity.

These interpretations all sounded personally relevant. The only problem was that the answers to the questionnaire were filled in at random. That is, the author of this book did not read the questions, but merely clicked "true" or "false" randomly. How then did these test interpretations seem to apply so personally and directly? Read the interpretations again and you will see that they are Barnum statements. They could apply to just about anyone.

This example is not meant to suggest that the MBTI is not a good test. Rather, it is the personality feedback or test interpretations that can sometimes not be accurate. Recall that these interpretations were obtained from free online services. So this example could also be an illustration of the advice "you get what you pay for." Most reliable test interpretation services charge a fee for this service.

Reliable test interpretation services typically make statements that are quantitative or that provide information about a person's standing on a trait relative to others. So, for example, an interpretation might state: "Your scores on extraversion put you in the highest or most extraverted 10% of the population." Or the statement might refer to research results, such as: "Persons with extraversion scores such as yours were found to be extremely satisfied in careers that involved frequent social contact, such as salespersons, teachers, or public relations work." Also, reliable test interpretation services typically include checks for careless responding, as discussed earlier in this chapter. They typically provide an assessment of how suspicious one should be regarding the validity of the person's responses. None of the free test interpretation services used in this example provided such checks, and so none of them detected that the responses were random.

So far we have discussed some of the theoretical and measurement issues in trait psychology. Trait psychologists do not only concern themselves with these somewhat esoteric and academic issues. Trait psychology also has some real-world applications. We turn now to a consideration of the practical uses to which personality trait measures have been put.

Personality and Prediction

Personality measures have a long history of use in industry and government. They are used in the federal and state prison systems to make decisions about inmates. They are also widely used in industry to match people with particular jobs, to help screen people for employment, and to select people for promotion. An employer may feel that emotional stability is a requirement for a specific job (e.g., firefighter) or that the personality trait of honesty is especially important (e.g., for a clerk in a jewelry store or for a driver for a money delivery truck). Other jobs may require strong organizational or social skills or the ability to work in a distracting environment. Whether someone does well in employment settings may be determined, in part, by whether the individual's personality traits mesh with the job requirements. In short, personality traits may predict who is likely to do well in a particular job, so it makes some sense to try to select people for employment based on measures of these traits.

Applications of Personality Testing in the Workplace

In an increasingly competitive business environment, many employers resort to employment testing to improve their workforce. The majority of the Fortune 100 companies use some form of employment selection that includes psychological testing. A survey by the American Management Association revealed that 44 percent of its responding members used testing to screen or select employees. Although cognitive ability testing (e.g., comprehension, reading speed) is the most commonly used form of psychological testing in the workplace, personality tests are being used more and more frequently.

The personality tests used in the workplace are mostly self-report measures of specific traits or dispositions. A very large number of personality measures are available. Some personality measures characterize people within the normal range of personality functioning; others focus on the identification of psychopathology or abnormal levels of functioning. Many personality tests, such as the Minnesota Multiphasic Personality Inventory (MMPI) or the California Personality Inventory (CPI), assess a large number of personality characteristics; others measure single traits in which the employer is specifically interested.

Employers use different types of personality tests for different purposes. They use personality assessment in the workplace for three main reasons: personnel selection, integrity testing, and concerns over negligent hiring.

Personnel Selection
Employers sometimes use personality tests to select people especially suitable for a specific job. For example, an insurance company might use a measure of extraversion–introversion to select applicants high on extraversion for a sales job so that their characteristics match successful incumbents in their sales department. Alternatively, the employer may want to use personality assessments to deselect, or screen out, people with specific traits. For example, a police department might use the MMPI or a similar test to screen out applicants who have high levels of mental instability or psychopathology. A number of personality tests and applications can aid employers in **personnel selection.**

Integrity Testing

Personality tests that assess honesty or integrity are probably the most widely used form of personality assessment in the business world. They are commonly used in the retail and financial services industries in selecting people for low-paying entry level jobs where the employee handles money or merchandise in an unsupervised setting. Integrity tests are designed to predict a tendency toward theft or other forms of counterproductive behaviors in work settings, such as absenteeism (see the Closer Look box on "Lying, Lie Detection, and Integrity Testing").

The annual economic losses to American business from employee theft are estimated at between $15 billion and $25 billion per year. Moreover, a substantial proportion of annual business failures have been blamed on employee theft. Because of this, many employers are interested in any technique that could detect those employees most likely to commit theft on the job. There are two kinds of integrity measures—**overt and covert integrity tests.** Both are based on self-report. Overt measures ask about past counterproductive workplace behaviors, such as theft and absenteeism, as well as general criminal history, delinquency, or school disciplinary problems. They also ask about attitudes towards theft and punishment, whether they had ever thought about stealing from an employer, and a general self-assessment of their honesty. Overt measures, on the other hand, do not directly ask about counterproductive behaviors per se, but rather assess aspects of personality that are correlated with counterproductive work behaviors. Of the Big Five traits, conscientiousness has the strongest correlations (negatively) with workplace problems (Berry et al., 2007), and so covert measures include many conscientiousness items. They also typically include items reflecting the traits of dependability, sociability, agreeableness, and (negatively weighted) hostility toward authority, thrill seeking, and social insensitivity (Sackett et al., 1989). In a cross-cultural study of workplace integrity in 27 countries, researchers found that countries with the highest country-level corruption levels (corruption in government and corporations) had workers with the lowest levels of workplace integrity (Fine, 2010).

Concerns over Negligent Hiring

A third reason some employers use personality testing arises from the fact that should an employee assault a customer or another coworker on the job, the employer may be held accountable in a court case. In such a case, the employer could be charged with **negligent hiring,** that is, hiring someone who is unstable or prone to violence. With cases of negligent hiring now being tried in the courts of most states, employers are defending themselves against a growing number of suits seeking compensation for crimes committed by their employees. In such cases, the employer is charged with negligently hiring an applicant with traits that posed a threat of injury to others. Such cases hinge on whether the employer should have discovered those traits ahead of time, before hiring such a person into a position where he or she posed a threat to others. Personality testing may provide evidence that the employer did in fact try to reasonably investigate an applicant's fitness for the workplace, and thus lessen their negligence.

Legal Issues in Personality Testing in Employment Settings

Legal issues surrounding the use of personality and other tests in employment settings can be traced to the Civil Rights Act of 1964, which barred racial discrimination in public places, including theaters, restaurants, hotels, and polling places. **Title VII of the Civil Rights Act of 1964** also required employers to provide equal employment opportunities to all persons. The first test of the Civil Rights Act in employment law occurred

A Closer Look   The Female Underprediction Effect

A selection situation almost all of you are familiar with is selection into college on the basis of entrance exam scores, typically the SAT or ACT exams. These exams are known to predict performance in college, and colleges and universities find them useful when selecting students from the pool of applicants for admission.

College entrance exams typically predict grade point average (GPA) in college in the range of .30 to .50 correlations between SAT scores and GPA (College Board Online, 2009). In a recent analysis of students at Washington University in St. Louis, for example, one of the authors found that SAT scores correlated .33 with first-semester GPA among freshmen. Hence we conclude that SAT scores have a degree of predictive validity when it comes to forecasting grades in college.

However, the prediction of college GPA from SAT scores works a bit differently for women than for men. It turns out that SAT scores underpredict GPA for women relative to men. That is, women tend to do better in college than one might predict from their SAT scores. This has been known for over 30 years and has come to be called the **female underprediction effect** (Hyde & Kling, 2001).

What does the female underprediction effect mean for women? One thing it means is that, as a group, women tend to do better than men in terms of overall college grades. Psychologists have proposed several explanations for this finding. For example, women may simply be better students than men, getting more out of their education. Or it might be that women score higher on conscientiousness than men, giving them a collection of traits that contribute to success in college, such as being punctual, well-organized, and hard-working.

The female underprediction effect also has another implication for women. If universities use a strict cutoff SAT score for admission, and apply this equally to both men and women, then some women will be rejected from admission who otherwise would have performed better than some men who were admitted. Because women as a group tend to perform better than men, and because their SAT scores under-predict their performance in college, women just below the cutoff SAT score might actually do better than some of the men at or above the cutoff score. This has led some researchers to conclude that the SAT is biased against women as a selection tool for colleges and universities (Hyde & Kling, 2001).

You might think that one way to correct for gender bias in SAT scores would be to use different cutoff scores for men and women. However, using different cutoff scores for different groups is illegal. Consequently, most universities and colleges make up for gender bias in SAT scores by incorporating other information and creating an admissions index, which takes into account many pieces of information about each applicant, including high school grades (where women as a group do better than men). Thus admission decisions are not based solely on SAT scores. Admissions decisions at most colleges and universities are based on an integration of many pieces of information about the applicant and use a composite index designed to balance bias in any single measure.

in the case of *Griggs v. Duke Power.* Prior to 1964 the Duke Power Company had used clearly discriminatory practices in hiring and work assignment, including barring Blacks from certain jobs. After passage of the Civil Rights Act, Duke Power instituted various requirements for such jobs, including passing certain aptitude tests. The effect was to perpetuate discrimination. In 1971 the Supreme Court ruled that the seemingly neutral testing practices used by Duke Power were unacceptable because they operated to maintain discrimination. Moreover, the court ruled that any selection procedure could not produce disparate impact for a group protected by the act (e.g., racial groups, women). This Supreme Court decision put the burden of proof on the employer to demonstrate that selection procedures were not discriminatory and did not produce disparate impact on specific groups.

The next major event in employee selection occurred in 1978 when the Department of Labor released the **Uniform Guidelines on Employee Selection Procedures.** These guidelines were widely adopted and are still in use today by the Department of Justice. The purpose of the guidelines is to provide a set of principles for employee selection that meet the requirements of all federal laws, especially those that prohibit discrimination on the basis of race, color, religion, sex, or national origin. They provide details on the proper use of personality tests and other selection procedures in employment settings. The guidelines define discrimination and adverse impact, describe how to evaluate and document the validity evidence for tests, and instruct employers on what records to keep.

Another important legal case in employment law is that of ***Ward's Cove Packing Co. v. Atonio.*** Ward's Cove Packing Co. was a salmon cannery operating in Alaska. Cannery jobs were filled predominantly by non-Whites. Noncannery jobs were filled predominantly with White workers. Virtually all of the noncannery jobs paid more than cannery positions. In 1974 the non-White cannery workers started legal action against the company, alleging that a variety of the company's hiring and promotion practices—for example, nepotism, a rehire preference, a lack of objective hiring criteria, separate hiring channels—were responsible for the racial stratification of the workforce. The claim was advanced under the disparate impact portion of Title VII of the Civil Rights Act. In 1989 the Supreme Court decided that employees filing discrimination lawsuits must expose specific hiring practices that led to disparities in the workplace. However, the Court also decided that even if the employees can prove discrimination, the hiring practices may still be considered legal if they serve "legitimate employment goals of the employer."

The *Ward's Cove* case watered down the effects of the *Griggs* decision and allowed companies a loophole to continue with discriminatory employment practices as long as they could prove such practices served the needs of the company. For example, if a test excluded most Black applicants, yet the company could prove that the test was job relevant, then the company could continue using this test. This case prompted Congress to pass the Civil Rights Act of 1991, which contained several important modifications to Title VII of the original act. The 1991 act expanded protected groups to include those based on race, color, religion, sex, or national origin. The new act also prohibited use of different cutoff scores based on race in employment tests (see the A Closer Look box titled "The Female Underprediction Effect"). Most important, however, the new act shifted the burden of proof onto the employer by requiring that it must prove a close connection between disparate impact and the ability to actually perform the job in question.

Another important case, one with clear personality connections, was the case of ***Price Waterhouse v. Hopkins,*** also decided in 1989 by the Supreme Court. Ann Hopkins was a senior manager at an accounting firm, who was being considered for promotion to partnership in the firm. Following its usual promotion practice, the firm asked each existing partner to evaluate Ms. Hopkins. Many of the evaluations came in as negative, criticizing her interpersonal skills and accusing her of being abrasive and too masculine for a woman (they felt she needed to wear more makeup, to walk and talk more femininely, etc.). She sued the company, charging that they had discriminated against her on the basis of sex, on the theory that her evaluations had been based on sexual stereotyping. The case eventually rose to the Supreme Court. Price Waterhouse acknowledged discrimination but maintained that sexual stereotypes were just one factor and argued that there were other reasons to deny partnership to Hopkins. They argued that even without any sex discrimination, Hopkins still would have been passed over.

The other legal issue, the one that won the case for Hopkins, was that she had been passed over for partner because of gender stereotyping within the company. In essence, she argued, the voting partners compared her to a cultural stereotype of how a woman is supposed to behave in the workplace, and they decided that Hopkins did not fit that image. The American Psychological Association joined the case and provided expert evidence that such stereotypes do exist and that women who deviate from the cultural expectations are often penalized for violating these standards. The Supreme Court accepted the argument that gender stereotyping does exist and that it can create a bias against women in the workplace that is not permissible. By court order Ann Hopkins was made a full partner in her accounting firm. She went on to describe her long court case, both from a legal and personal perspective, in a book titled *So Ordered: Making Partner the Hard Way* by Ann Branigar Hopkins (Amherst: University of Massachusetts Press, 1996).

Disparate Impact

To prove a case of **disparate impact,** a plaintiff must show that an employment practice disadvantages people from a protected group. The Supreme Court has not defined the size of the disparity necessary to prove disparate impact. Most courts define disparity as a difference that is sufficiently large that it is unlikely to have occurred by chance. Tests of statistical significance are generally used to establish this. Some courts, however, have preferred the 80 percent rule contained in the Uniform Guidelines on Employee Selection Procedures. Under this rule, adverse impact is established if the selection rate for any race, sex, or ethnic group is less than four-fifths (or 80 percent) of the rate for the group with the highest selection rate.

Once the court accepts that adverse impact has occurred, the burden shifts to the employer to prove that the selection practice is job-related and consistent with business necessity. The Uniform Guidelines suggests three methods by which an employer can show job-relatedness: content validity, criterion validity, and construct validity. Content validity is used when the test closely approximates the job, as in a typing exam for a typist position. This form of validation is not generally applicable to personality testing because such tests measure general traits not specific abilities. Criterion validity compares performance on the test with performance on critical or important job behaviors. It is the preferred method of validation under the Uniform Guidelines but is not always technically feasible. Construct validity establishes relationships between aspects of satisfactory job performance and a specific trait, then measures of that trait are used for selection. For example, the job of customer service representative may require a specific interpersonal style to function effectively. This form of validation is the most appropriate for personality testing because it focuses on the link between a particular trait and different aspects of job performance. If a test is job-related and satisfies the validity requirements of the Uniform Guidelines, then, in most cases the disparate impact claim is dropped by the court.

There have been relatively few disparate impact cases involving personality tests because such tests generally do not disadvantage any protected group. Integrity tests may have the best record of any selection technique in demonstrating freedom from adverse impact. Moreover, integrity test publishers typically have extensive statistical evidence demonstrating the validity of integrity tests in predicting theft and job-relevant counterproductive behavior, which would satisfy the employer's burden. Similar data supporting the job relevance for other personality tests also exist. In some cases, however, an employer may need to perform its own validity studies.

Race or Gender Norming

The Civil Rights Act of 1991 forbids employers from using different norms or cutoff scores for different groups of people. For example, it would be illegal for a company to set a higher threshold for women than men on their selection test. A few personality test publishers, including versions of the Myers-Briggs Type Indicator (MBTI), recommend different scoring practices based on **race or gender norming.** This practice is clearly illegal, and employers should avoid tests of this sort in favor of personality tests with standard norms applied equally to all applicants.

Americans with Disabilities Act (ADA)

The **Americans with Disabilities Act** states that an employer cannot conduct a medical examination, or even make inquiries as to whether an applicant has a disability, during the selection process. Moreover, even if a disability is obvious, the employer cannot ask about the nature or severity of that disability. Consequently, employers should be careful when they administer psychological testing to job applicants to make sure that the testing is not a medical examination. Psychological testing can be considered a medical examination if it provides evidence that would lead to a diagnosis or the identification of mental disorder or impairment.

Consider the following example: A psychological test (like the MMPI) is constructed to diagnose mental illnesses, but a particular employer says she does not use the test to disclose mental illness. Instead, the employer says she uses the test to disclose preferences and habits of job applicants. However, the test also is interpreted by a psychologist working for the company. In addition, the test is routinely used in clinical settings to provide evidence that would lead to a diagnosis of a mental disorder or impairment (for example, whether a person has paranoid tendencies or is depressed). Under these conditions, this test might be considered a medical examination and may violate the ADA laws.

The use of clinically oriented personality measures designed primarily to diagnose psychopathology, such as the MMPI, would probably violate the ADA's prohibition on medical examinations. Consequently, employers should avoid the MMPI and similar measures for selection purposes. Tests of normal-range personality functioning, and measures of integrity, have never been considered equivalent to a medical examination.

Right to Privacy

Perhaps the largest issue of legal concern for employers using personality testing is privacy. The **right to privacy** in employment settings grows out of the broader concept of the right to privacy. Cases that charge an invasion-of-privacy claim against an employer can be based on the federal constitution, state constitutions and statutes, and common law.

In the case of *McKenna v. Fargo,* a federal district court in New Jersey upheld the right of a city fire department to use personality testing to select applicants for the position of firefighter. The case was based on an invasion-of-privacy claim. The court determined that although the test did infringe on the applicant's right to privacy, the city's interest in screening out applicants who would be unstable under the pressures of the job was sufficient to justify the intrusion. The *McKenna* ruling establishes that personality test questions that inquire about an applicant's sexual, religious, or political attitudes may intrude on an applicant's right to privacy. However, the ruling also recognizes that a government can justify this intrusion if it has a compelling need, such as the need for firefighters who can protect the safety of the public.

In another case, a California Court of Appeals found that certain items on a personality test administered to security guard applicants violated the state constitutional right to privacy. In *Saroka v. Dayton Hudson,* the plaintiff had applied for a security guard position with the Target Stores chain and was required to complete both the MMPI and the California Psychological Inventory (CPI). The two tests are widely used

Exercise

Think of a job or career where personality might play a role in how well a person does in that job, or how satisfied they would be in that career. It can be any job or career—investment banking, programming, car salesperson—just pick one for this exercise. Now, think about the requirements for doing well in this career or job and make a list of two or three key requirements. This step is called **job analysis**, and in it you try to identify the key requirements associated with a particular job. For example, social skills might be a key part of being a car sales person. Now take each of the key requirements and see if you can identify a personality or ability trait that might contribute to that job requirement. For an example, look over the material on selecting police officers in the section on "Personnel Selection." If you can link the key requirements identified in your job analysis with specific personality traits, then there is a good chance the personality measures would be useful in selecting employees for that job. This exercise is one of the real-world applications that personality psychologists working in industry do all the time.

to assess personality traits and adjustment, and they contain items asking about very personal topics such as religion, sexual behavior, and political beliefs. The plaintiff argued that the questions required him to reveal very private thoughts and highly personal behaviors and were not job related. The court agreed. Target tried to mount a defense by arguing that they had a compelling business interest in the outcome of the selection process. The court acknowledged that Target had an interest in employing emotionally stable persons as store security officers. However, the court ruled that Target did not show how questions about an applicant's religious beliefs or sexual orientation would have any bearing on his or her emotional stability. Because Target Stores could not provide evidence on the construct or criterion validity of the specific items in question, they lost the case.

Personnel Selection—Choosing the Right Person for the Job

The job of a police officer can illustrate the importance of selecting the right person for the job. Recent high-profile shootings of unarmed suspects by police, such as in Ferguson, MO in 2014, as well as numerous such events highlight the importance of selecting the right persons for this occupation (or equally important, screening the wrong ones out). Personality tests are frequently used to screen out the wrong individuals from the pool of applicants for police officers. One of the most frequently given tests is the revised Minnesota Multiphasic Personality Inventory (MMPI II), which was designed to detect various mental illnesses. The MMPI II has 550 items, and its primary use is to identify persons with significant psychological problems. Individuals with elevated scores indicating mental or emotional difficulties can be screened out of the pool of potential officers (Barrick & Mount, 1991).

Little was known about which personality traits contribute to the successful performance of the job of police officers until Hargrave and Hiatt (1989) examined the California Personality Inventory (CPI) in relation to police officer performance. In their study, they found that 13 percent of the cadets in training were found to be "unsuitable" by their instructors. Moreover, these unsuitable cadets differed from the "suitable" group on 9 scales of the CPI, including the conformity and social presence scales. In another sample of 45 officers on the job who were having serious problems, Hargrave and Hiatt (1989) found that the CPI also discriminated this group from other police officers who were not having problems. These findings provided evidence that the CPI is useful in the selection of police officers, and it, as well as other personality questionnaires, are being used for this purpose (e.g., Black, 2000; Coutts, 1990; Grant & Grant, 1996; Lowry, 1997; Mufson & Mufson, 1998).

The 16 Personality Factor (16 PF) questionnaire, described in Chapter 3, is also being used in vocational advising and selection. The 16 PF profile that best matches police officers is one that emphasizes boldness and self-confidence, qualities that facilitate one's abilities to direct or control others and to achieve goals (Krug, 1981). A heightened need for adventure and a strong need to influence others are linked with the enjoyment of careers that provide challenge and opportunities to take charge. The police officer personality profile is low on the need for support from others, which suggests a very self-assured personality. All of these personality characteristics appear to combine into a "masculine" profile. Nevertheless, the profile that matches the police prototype occurs equally often among "normal" men and women in U.S. samples (Krug, 1981). Psychologically, men and women appear about equally equipped with the personality traits that most match the police officer prototype.

The personality profile that characterizes police officers emphasizes boldness and self-confidence (qualities that facilitate the direction or control of others), a heightened need for adventure, and a low need for support from others (suggestive of self-assurance). The personality traits associated with being a good police officer are distributed equally among men and women (Krug, 1981).
© *Getty Images RF*

Selection in Business Settings—The Myers-Briggs Type Indicator

Businesses confront critical decisions on which success or failure hinge. Different jobs pose different demands, and it's likely that personality plays a critical role in determining success in different positions. By far the most widely used personality assessment device in business settings is the **Myers-Briggs Type Indicator (MBTI)** (Myers et al., 1998). The test was developed by a mother-daughter team, Katherine Briggs and Isabel Myers, anchored in Jungian concepts (see Chapter 10). The test provides information about personality by testing for eight fundamental preferences. A sample item: "Do you usually value sentiment more than logic, or value logic more than sentiment?" This type of item is an example of a "forced-choice" format, in which individuals must respond in one way or another, even if they feel that their preferences might be somewhere in the middle. The eight fundamental preferences are shown in Table 4.1.

These eight fundamental preferences reduce to four scores—you are either extraverted OR introverted; sensing OR intuitive; thinking OR feeling; judging OR perceiving. These four scores are then combined to yield *types*. Indeed, each person is placed into one of the 16 types yielded by their four scores. For example, you could be an *ESTP* type: Extraverted, Sensing, Thinking, and Perceiving. This type, according to the MBTI authors, has a distinctive leadership style in business settings. She likes to take charge when a crisis occurs; she's good at persuading others to adopt her point of view; she is

Table 4.1   Eight Fundamental Preferences Measured by the Myers-Briggs Type Indicator

Extraversion
Draws energy from the outside; involved with people; likes action and activity

Introversion
Draws energy from internal world of thoughts and ideas

Sensing
Prefers taking in information through all five senses; attends to what actually exists

Intuition
Prefers information derived from a "sixth sense"; notices what's possible rather than what is

Thinking
Prefers logic, organization, and clean objective structure

Feeling
Prefers a person- and value-oriented way of processing information

Judging
Prefers living a well-ordered and controlled life

Perceiving
Prefers to live spontaneously, with room for flexible spur-of-the-moment activities

Sources: Myers et al. (1998); Hirsh & Kummerow (1990).

assertive and leads the group to the most direct route to the goal; and she wants to see immediate results.

Contrast this with another type, an *INFJ:* Introverted, Intuitive, Feeling, and Judging. This type, according to the authors of the instrument, has a fundamentally different leadership style. Rather than take charge and assert, INFJs are more likely to develop a *vision* for the organization; get others to cooperate rather than demand cooperation; work to inspire others rather than command others; and work solidly and with integrity and consistency to achieve business goals. One can readily imagine that different types of business leaders would be better in different organizational settings. In a time of crisis, for example, an ESTP might be better at organizing others to deal with immediate threats. On a plateau in business, an INFJ might be better at pausing to reflect on a long-term vision for the organization.

It is estimated that over 3 million people a year take the MBTI (Gardner & Martinko, 1996). Although it was developed for applications in education, counseling, career guidance, and workplace team-building, it is also widely used in personnel selection settings (Pittenger, 2005). Its wide use most likely comes from its intuitive appeal; people can readily understand the relevance of the personality traits supposedly measured by this test.

There are, however, several problems with the MBTI. The first problem is that the theory on which it is based—Jung's theory of **psychological types**—is not widely endorsed by academic or research-oriented psychologists. For one thing, people don't come in "types," such as extraverted types and introverted types. Instead, most personality traits are normally distributed. Figure 4.3 illustrates the difference between data that would support a type model of introversion–extraversion (called a bimodal distribution) and the real data on introversion–extraversion, which is normally distributed according to a bell-shaped curve. Very few characteristics of persons follow a typological or bimodal distribution. Biological sex is one characteristic that does conform to a bimodal distribution; there are many female-type people, as well as many male-type people, and very few people in between. The distribution of extraversion–introversion is not like this at all; it has only one peak, right in the middle, suggesting that the majority of people are neither purely

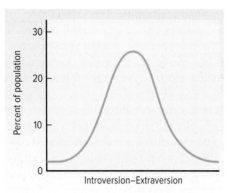

A. Hypothetical data on the trait of introversion–extraversion if it followed a truly typelike distribution in the population. There would be a large number of introverts, a large number of extraverts, and few people in between.

B. Typical data on the trait of introversion–extraversion, which follows a bell curve or normal distribution in the population. There are a large number of people in between the relatively rare extreme introverts and extreme extraverts.

Figure 4.3

Examples illustrating what the trait of introversion–extraversion would look like in terms of distributions in the population if it followed a type model (Panel A) or a normal distribution model (Panel B). Real data support the normal distribution model, not the type model.

introverted nor purely extraverted, but are somewhere in between. Virtually all personality traits follow this normal distribution, so the concept of personality "types" is simply not justified.

One consequence of forcing a typology onto a trait that is normally distributed concerns the importance of cutoff scores for classifying people into one category or the other (e.g., as introverted or extraverted). Most users of the MBTI use the median score (the score at which 50 percent fall above and 50 percent fall below) from some standardization sample as the cutoff. The problem lies in the fact that a large percentage of people in any sample will be clustered right around the median score. If that median score moves a point or two in either direction, because of differences in sample characteristics used to determine the cutoff score, a very large number of people will be reclassified into their opposite category. In fact, a person with an introversion–extraversion score of 20 might be classified as an introvert in one sample (if it had a median of 21) and classified as an extravert in another sample (if it had a median of 19). So, the same individual score (a 20) will be interpreted very differently depending on the median used to perform the cutoff for classification. Despite this problem with cutoff scores and typologies, the majority of users of the MBTI continue to follow the scoring system that classifies persons into letter category groups, a practice that has been soundly criticized in the professional consulting literature (e.g., Pittenger, 2005).

Another related consequence of using a typology scheme for scoring the MBTI is that the scores will be unreliable. Reliability is often estimated by testing a group of people twice, separated by a period of time. With the MBTI, because cutoff scores are used to categorize people into groups, and because many people are very close to the cutoff scores, slight changes in people's raw scores on retesting can result in a large percentage being reclassified into different personality types. Indeed, a study of the test-retest reliability of the MBTI (McCarley & Clarskadon, 1983) showed that, across a five-week test-retest interval, 50 percent of the participants received a different classification on one or more of the type categories. These results are not surprising, and this is one reason most scientific personality psychologists do not recommend using typological scoring systems for any personality measure.

Another problem with typological scoring systems is that it assumes large between-category differences, and no within-category differences, among people. For example, all extraverted types are assumed to be alike, and introverted types are assumed to be very different from extraverted types. This, however, is not necessarily the case. Imagine two people who score as extraverted types, yet one of these is just one point above the median and the other is 31 points above the median. These two extraverted types are likely to be very different from each other (they differ by 30 points on the scale yet are given the same type category). Now imagine an introverted type who scored one point below the median, and an extraverted type who scored one point above the median. This introvert and this extravert are likely to be indistinguishable from each other (they differ by only 2 points on the scale yet are given different type categories). This is another reason psychologists who know about measurement issues avoid using type scoring systems for any personality test.

Dozens of validity studies of the MBTI have been published, mostly relating type categories to occupational preferences. These studies have been criticized, however, because most fail to report statistical details necessary to determine whether the differences are significant. For example, Gardner and Martinko (1996) review 13 studies that examined the distribution of MBTI types in managerial professions. All of these studies reported the frequencies of types in different categories, yet none reported scale score means that would have allowed strong statistical tests of mean personality differences among the different managerial categories. Moreover, other reviewers (e.g., Hunsley, Lee, & Wood, 2003) point out that no adequate tests have been done on the predictive validity of the MBTI (e.g., that the MBTI can predict *future* career choices or job satisfaction). Also, virtually no studies have been done examining the incremental validity of the MBTI (e.g., whether the MBTI can add meaningfully to the prediction of career choice or job satisfaction above and beyond that obtained with more traditional personality measures).

Every few years psychologists take a fresh look at the evidence for the MBTI and summarize what they find. In 1991, Bjork and Druckman reviewed the evidence and concluded: "At this time, there is not sufficient, well-designed research to justify the use of the MBTI in career counseling programs" (p. 99). A few years later, Boyle (1995) also reviewed the literature and found no strong scientific evidence supporting the utility of the MBTI. In 2003, Hunsley, Lee, and Wood reviewed the latest evidence and summarized their findings: "One can only conclude that the MBTI is insufficient as a contemporary measure of personality" (pp. 63–64). And in an even more recent review paper, Pittenger (2005) evaluated all of the scientific literature on the MBTI and concluded: "Using the MBTI to select employees, to assign employees to work groups or assignments, or for other forms of employment evaluation are [sic]not justified for the simple reason that there are no available data to recommend such decisions" (p. 219).

Given the highly negative reviews on the scientific merit of the MBTI, why does it continue to be a hugely popular tool in consulting and career counseling? There are probably several reasons. First, the popularity of the MBTI may reflect the success of the publisher's marketing campaign. In addition, the test comes with rather simple scoring and interpretation instructions, making it usable and understandable by people without advanced training in personality psychology. Moreover, the interpretations the test offers are readily translated into seemingly sensible predictions about work and interpersonal relations. Like the popularity of horoscopes, people like hearing about themselves and their futures, even if little or no scientific evidence exists for those descriptions and predictions.

Is there any legitimate use for the MBTI? Although it should definitely not be used as the single piece of evidence on which to base employment selections or career decisions, it may have a role in such areas as team-building, career exploration, or relationship counseling. The test can get people thinking about differences among people. People with vastly different personalities see the world differently, and if the test fosters an appreciation for this diversity, then it may be useful. The test might also be useful if it gets people thinking about the relationship between personality and behavior. If we understand that how we act toward others, and they toward us, is influenced in part by our personalities, then this increases our ability to understand and relate well to others. For example, if teachers take the MBTI as part of a "teacher development workshop," they may think about their own teaching style or may gain an awareness that not all pupils are alike in how they relate to teachers. The test may even act as a catalyst for group exercises or team building that foster esprit de corps among group members. For example, at a "corporate retreat" a group of managers may take the test and then explore ways that they can work better as a team given the differences in their personalities. So the test may indeed have some utility for getting people to think about personality, even though the test does not appear adequate as an instrument for selection.

Selection in Business Settings—The Hogan Personality Inventory

Because of the problems noted earlier, the Myers-Briggs Type Indicator test should probably not be used to select employees. Which tests are good alternatives? There are literally thousands of published personality tests (Spies & Plake, 2005) and hundreds of companies that use personality tests to help other companies select employees. We have chosen one of these companies and one of their personality tests to describe here, mainly because the procedures they use are based on a solid scientific foundation. The company is called Hogan Assessment Systems, and its main personality test is called the Hogan Personality Inventory.

The founder of this assessment company, Robert Hogan, was a professor of psychology at the University of Tulsa for many years. He had been teaching and doing research in personality psychology through the 1970s and 1980s, even becoming the head editor of the most prestigious scientific journal in personality psychology, the *Journal of Personality and Social Psychology*. During this time, Hogan's own research concerned efforts to identify aspects of personality important in contemporary business settings. He started with the Big Five model of personality but focused on how these traits might work in the business world. He developed a theory about the social aspects of personality that are important to business and concluded that the dominant themes in social life are the motive to get along with others and the motive to get ahead of others.

In most business settings, people work in groups, and every group has a status hierarchy. Hogan's theory states that, within such groups, people want three things: (1) acceptance, including respect and approval; (2) status and the control of resources; and (3) predictability (Hogan, 2005). Some of Hogan's research showed that business problems often occur when a manager violates one or more of these motives within a work group, for example, by treating staff with disrespect, by micromanaging in a way that takes away the staff's sense of control, or by not communicating or providing feedback, thereby making the workplace unpredictable.

Hogan developed a questionnaire measure of personality, called the **Hogan Personality Inventory (HPI)**, that measures aspects of the Big Five traits that are relevant to the above three motives important to business. For the details on why and how this inventory was developed, see Hogan and Hogan (2002). The traits this inventory measures are described in Table 4.2. Hogan and his wife, Joyce Hogan, also a research psychologist, started using this inventory in research on the effectiveness of people working in a variety of businesses. They began to look at how specific job requirements fit with specific combinations of these personality traits. Soon they were doing validity studies, exploring how the personality test predicted how well people fit into specific business cultures. They also conducted outcome studies, to see how well the personality inventory predicted occupational performance in a wide variety of jobs. Across a large number of studies, the test achieved high levels of reliability and acceptable levels of validity for predicting a number of important occupational outcomes, including organizational fit and performance. Joyce Hogan and J. Holland (2003) provide a meta-analysis of 28 validity studies on the Hogan Personality Inventory, the results of which strongly support the validity of the personality scales for predicting several important job-relevant criteria.

In 1987, Robert and Joyce Hogan started their own company, Hogan Assessment Systems, to consult with businesses that wanted to use personality measures to select employees. Soon afterward, Robert Hogan left his position at the University of Tulsa to devote his full effort toward helping companies successfully use personality measures in business applications. The Hogans continue to use a scientific approach to improve and validate the use of their personality inventory in the business community. For a

Table 4.2 The Hogan Personality Inventory (HPI) Contains Seven Primary Scales and Six Occupational Scales

Primary Scales	Occupational Scales
Adjustment—self-confidence, self-esteem, and composure under pressure. The opposite of neuroticism.	*Service Orientation*—being attentive, pleasant, and courteous to customers.
Ambition—initiative, competitiveness, and the desire for leadership roles.	*Stress Tolerance*—being able to handle stress, remaining even-tempered and calm under fire.
Sociability—extraversion, gregariousness, and a need for social interaction.	*Reliability*—honesty, integrity, and positive organizational citizenship.
Interpersonal Sensitivity—warmth, charm, and the ability to maintain good relationships.	*Clerical Potential*—following directions, attending to detail, and communicating clearly.
Prudence—self-discipline, responsibility, and conscientiousness.	*Sales Potential*—energy, social skills, and the ability to solve customers' problems.
Inquisitiveness—imagination, curiosity, vision, and creative potential.	*Managerial Potential*—leadership ability, planning, and decision-making skills.
Learning Approach—enjoying learning, staying current on business and technical matters.	

recent review of predicting career success from personality, with an interesting discussion of how some traits predict getting a job whereas other traits predict keeping a job, see Hogan and Chamorro-Premuzic (2015).

Why is the Hogan Personality Inventory (HPI) a better choice than the MBTI when it comes to employee selection? First, the HPI is based on the Big Five model, which has been modified specifically for applications to the workplace. The construction and development of the HPI followed standard statistical procedures, resulting in an inventory with a high level of measurement reliability (test-retest correlations range from .74 to .86). To date, there have been more than 400 validity studies of the HPI. These studies have examined the ability of the test to predict a wide variety of important business results in a large number of job categories, such as employee turnover, absenteeism, improved sales performance, customer service, employee satisfaction, customer satisfaction, and overall business performance. The test has been able to predict occupational success in a wide variety of job categories. Personality profiles on the HPI are available for over 200 different work categories that span the range of jobs in the U.S. economy. The company maintains a database from over a million people who have taken the HPI.

The HPI itself consists of true–false items and takes about 20 minutes to administer. None of the items are invasive or intrusive, and none of the scales show adverse impact on the basis of gender or race or ethnicity. The test is also available in a number of foreign languages. Hogan Assessment Systems maintains a research archive and record-keeping practice that scrupulously follows the procedures outlined by the Uniform Guidelines on Employee Selection Procedures discussed earlier. If a company using the HPI is sued by a job applicant, Hogan Assessment Systems will provide reports and records on test development and validity necessary to defend the case. The selection procedures and validation research on the HPI have never been successfully challenged in court. The test authors are members of the American Psychological Association and the Society of Industrial/Organizational Psychology, both of which mandate professional levels of ethical, legal, and scientific standards with regard to assessment practices.

Because of all these positive qualities, including the research base and demonstrated effectiveness of the test, use of the HPI in business and industry has grown tremendously in the last 20 years. Hogan Assessment Systems has consulted with 60 percent of the Fortune 100 companies and has provided assessment services to more than a thousand other customers around the world. Currently, in any given month, between 300 and 500 companies utilize their services to select or develop employees.

While Hogan Assessment Systems provides other services, such as employee development, we will describe one case example of the use of the HPI in employee selection applications. A leading financial services company approached Hogan Assessment Systems to develop a preemployment assessment procedure to select financial consultants. The job requirements were analyzed and compared to known validity research on performance in related jobs, and a personality selection profile was determined. After new people were hired and on the job for a few years, the company evaluated the effectiveness of the selection procedure by comparing the performance of financial consultants hired before and after the selection procedure went into effect. They found that those financial consultants hired on the basis of their personality profiles earned 20 percent more in commissions annually, conducted 32 percent more volume in dollar terms annually, and made 42 percent more trades annually. Obviously, selecting those applicants with the "right stuff" was beneficial to this company. Other business examples of the use of the HPI in selecting employees can be found at www.hoganassessments.com.

It is clear that personality factors can play an important role in predicting who does well in specific employment settings. When it comes to using personality tests to select employees for specific positions, one should realize that not all personality tests do the job equally well. Clearly those assessment systems with a strong scientific base, grounded in an accepted theory of personality, with acceptable reliability and strong evidence of validity relative to the needs of the company will have the best potential for helping business users achieve positive results.

SUMMARY AND EVALUATION

This chapter described some important issues and concepts that the various trait theories have in common. The hallmark of the trait perspective is an emphasis on differences among people. Trait psychology focuses on the study of differences, the classification of differences, and the analysis of the consequences of differences among people. Trait psychology assumes that people will be relatively consistent over time in their behavior because of the various traits they possess. Trait psychologists also assume a degree of cross-situational consistency for traits. Psychologists assume that people will be *more or less* consistent in their behavior, depending on the particular trait being studied and the situations in which it is observed. Nevertheless, some situations are very strong in terms of their influence on behavior. Some situations are so strong that they overpower the influence of personality traits. One important lesson is that traits are more likely to influence a person's behavior when situations are weak and ambiguous and don't push for conformity from all people.

Most trait psychologists agree that personality trait scores refer primarily to average tendencies in behavior. A score on a trait measure refers to how a person is likely to behave, on average, over a number of occasions and situations. Trait psychologists are better at predicting average tendencies in behavior than specific acts on specific occasions. For example, from a person's high score on a measure of trait hostility, a personality psychologist could not predict whether this person is likely to get into a fight tomorrow. However, the psychologist could confidently predict that such a person is more likely to be in more fights in the next few years than a person with a lower score on hostility. Traits represent average tendencies in behavior.

Trait psychologists are also interested in the accuracy of measurement. More than any other personality perspective, trait psychology has occupied itself with efforts to improve the measurement of traits, particularly through self-report questionnaire measures. Psychologists who devise questionnaires work hard at making them less susceptible to lying, faking, and careless responding.

A particularly important measurement issue is social desirability, or the tendency to exaggerate the positivity of one's personality. Currently, trait psychologists hold that one motive for socially desirable responding is the test taker's desire to convey a certain impression (usually positive). This behavior is sometimes referred to as impression management. Many psychologists worry about social desirability as a response set, thinking that it lowers the validity of the trait measure. However, another view on social desirability is that socially desirable responding is a valid response by some people who simply view themselves as better or more desirable than most, or who actually have deceived themselves into thinking they are better off psychologically than they probably are. As is typical, trait psychologists have devised measures to identify and distinguish between these two types of socially desirable responding.

Finally, their interest in measurement and prediction has led trait psychologists to apply these skills to the selection and screening of job applicants and other situations in which personality might make a difference. There are legal issues employers must keep in mind when using trait measures as a basis for making important hiring or promotion decisions. For example, tests must not discriminate unfairly against protected groups, such as women and certain minorities. In addition, the tests must be shown to be related to important real-life variables, such as job performance. We considered a number of important legal cases in employment law that are relevant to personality testing. We also considered two specific instruments that are popular in employment selection settings. One instrument, the Myers-Briggs Type Indicator, is widely used but also widely criticized in the scientific literature for its low levels of measurement reliability and unproven validity. The other instrument, the Hogan Personality Inventory, can be considered a "best practice" case when it comes to the use of personality in employee selection.

KEY TERMS

differential psychology 89
consistency 91
rank order stability 91
situationism 92
person–situation interaction 92
aggregation 92
situational specificity 94
strong situation 95
situational selection 96
evocation 97
manipulation 98
density distributions of states 100
infrequency scale 102
faking 102

false negative 103
false positive 103
Barnum statements 103
integrity tests 105
overt and covert integrity
    measures 107
personnel selection 106
negligent hiring 107
female underprediction effect 108
Title VII of the Civil Rights Act of
    1964 107
Griggs v. Duke Power 108
Uniform Guidelines on Employee
    Selection Procedures 108

Ward's Cove Packing Co. v. Atonio 109
Price Waterhouse v. Hopkins 109
disparate impact 110
race or gender norming 111
Americans with Disabilities Act
    (ADA) 111
right to privacy 111
job analysis 112
Myers-Briggs Type Indicator
    (MBTI) 113
psychological types 114
Hogan Personality Inventory
    (HPI) 118

Personality Dispositions over Time: Stability, Coherence, and Change

© moswyn/Getty Images RF

5

THE DISPOSITIONAL DOMAIN

Even though people change and develop as they age, each person still has a sense of self as the same person from year to year. As we see in this chapter on development, when it comes to personality, some things change and some things stay the same.
© Andrea Laurita/Getty Images RF

Think back to your days in middle school. Can you remember what you were like then? Try to recall what you were most interested in, how you spent your time, what things were most important to you. If you are like most people, you probably feel that, in many ways, you are a different person now than you were in middle school. Your interests have probably changed somewhat. Different things may be important to you. Your attitudes about school, family, and relationships have probably all changed at least a bit. Perhaps now you are more mature and have a more experienced view of the world.

As you think about what you were like then and what you are like now, you probably also feel that there is a core of "you" that is essentially the same over the years. If you are like most people, you have a sense of an enduring part of you, a feeling that you are "really" the same person now as then. Certain inner qualities seem the same over these several years.

In this chapter, we explore the psychological continuities and changes over time, which define the topic of personality development. When it comes to personality, "Some things change; some things stay the same." In this chapter, we discuss how psychologists think about personality development, with a primary focus on personality traits or dispositions.

Conceptual Issues: Personality Development, Stability, Coherence, and Change

This section defines personality development, examines the major ways of thinking about personality stability over time, and explores what it means to say that personality has changed. The study of personality development has attracted a lot of research attention, with two entire scientific journals devoting special issues to the topic, one in the *Journal of Personality* (Graziano, 2003), and one in the *European Journal of Personality* (Denissen, 2014; Specht et al., 2014).

What Is Personality Development?

Personality development can be defined as the continuities, consistencies, and stabilities in people over time *and* the ways in which people change over time. Each of these two facets— stability and change—requires definitions and qualifications. There are many forms of personality stability and, correspondingly, many forms of personality change. The three most important forms of stability are rank order stability, mean level stability, and personality coherence. We discuss each of these in turn. Then we examine personality change.

Rank Order Stability

Rank order stability is the maintenance of individual position within a group. Between ages 14 and 20, most people become taller, but the rank order of heights tends to remain fairly stable because this form of development affects all people pretty much the same, adding a few inches to everyone. The tall people at 14 fall generally toward the tall end of the distribution at age 20. The same can apply to personality traits. If people tend to maintain

Exercise

To illustrate the phrase "Some things change; some things stay the same," consider the period just before high school (your middle school years) and compare that with the period just after high school—typically, your college years. Identify three characteristics that have changed noticeably during that period. These characteristics might be your interests, your attitudes, your values, and what you like to do with your time. Then list three characteristics about you that have not changed. Again, these characteristics could reflect certain traits of your personality, your interests, your values, or even your attitudes about various topics. Write them down in the following format:

	What I was like in middle school:	What I was like after high school:
Characteristics that have changed	1. _____	1. _____
	2. _____	2. _____
	3. _____	3. _____
Characteristics that have not changed	1. _____	
	2. _____	
	3. _____	

their positions on dominance or extraversion relative to the others over time, then there is high rank order stability to those personality characteristics. Conversely, if people fail to maintain their rank order—if the submissive people rise up and put down the dominants, for example—then the group is displaying rank order instability, or rank order change.

Mean Level Stability

Another kind of personality stability is constancy of level, or **mean level stability.** Consider political orientation. If the average level of liberalism or conservatism in a group remains the same over time, the group exhibits high mean level stability. If the average degree of political orientation changes—for example, if people tend to get increasingly conservative as they get older—then that population is displaying **mean level change.**

Personality Coherence

A more complex form of personality development involves changes in the *manifestations* of a trait. Consider the trait of dominance. Suppose that the people who are dominant at age 8 are the same people who are dominant at age 20. The 8-year-old boys, however, manifest their dominance by showing toughness in rough-and-tumble play, calling their rivals "sissies," and insisting on monopolizing the computer games. At the age of 20, they manifest their dominance by persuading others to accept their views in political discussions, boldly asking someone out on a date, and insisting on the restaurant at which the group will eat.

This form of personality development—maintaining rank order in relation to other individuals but changing the manifestations of the trait—is called **personality coherence.** Notice that this form of personality coherence does not require that the precise behavioral manifestations of a trait remain the same. Indeed, the manifestations may be so different that there is literally no overlap between age 8 and age 20. The act

The manifestation of disagreeableness may differ across the life span, ranging from temper tantrums in infancy to being argumentative and having a short temper in adulthood. Even though the behaviors are different at the different ages, they nevertheless express the same underlying trait. This kind of consistency is called personality coherence.

Left © Kristy-Anne Glubish/Design Pics RF; Right © Chris Ryan/age fotostock RF

A Closer Look

A Case of Personal Stability

Mohandas Karamchand Gandhi was born in 1869 into a family of modest means in India. His mother was devoutly religious, and she impressed young Mohandas with her beliefs and practices. The Gandhi family not only practiced traditional Hinduism but also practiced Buddhist chants, read from the Koran, and even sang traditional Christian hymns. Mohandas developed a personal philosophy of life that led him to renounce all personal desires and to devote himself to the service of his fellow human beings.

After studying law in England, and practicing for a few years in South Africa, Gandhi returned to India. At that time, India was under British rule, and most Indians resented the oppression of their colonial rulers. Gandhi devoted himself to the ideal of Indian self-rule and to freedom from British oppression. When the British decided to fingerprint all Indians, for example, Gandhi came up with an idea he called passive resistance—he encouraged all Indians to simply refuse to go in for fingerprinting. During the period of 1919–1922, Gandhi led widespread but nonviolent strikes and boycotts throughout India. He coordinated campaigns of peaceful noncooperation with anything British—he urged Indians not to send their children to the British-run schools, not to participate in the courts, even not to adopt the English language. In their frustration, British soldiers sometimes attacked crowds of boycotting or striking Indians, and many Indians were killed. The people of India loved Gandhi. They followed him in droves, recording everything he did and said. He became a living legend, and the people referred to him as Maha Atma, or the Great Soul. We know him today as Mahatma Gandhi.

In 1930, Gandhi led the Indian people in nonviolent defiance of the British law forbidding Indian people from making their own salt. He started out with a few of his followers on a march to the coast of India, intending to make salt from seawater. By the time Gandhi had reached the sea, several thousand people had joined him in this act of civil disobedience. By this time, the British had jailed more than 60,000 Indians for disobedience to British law. The jails of India were bursting with native people put there by foreign rulers for breaking foreign laws. The British rulers were finally coming to some sense of embarrassment and shame for this situation. In the eyes of the world, this frail man Gandhi and his nonviolent followers were shaking the foundation of the British Empire in India.

Gandhi was not an official of the Indian government. Nevertheless, the British began negotiations with him to free India from British rule. During negotiations, the British played tough and put Gandhi in jail. The Indian people demonstrated and nearly a thousand of them were killed by the British, bringing shame on the colonial rulers in the eyes of the world. Gandhi was finally freed and a few years later, in 1947, Britain handed India its independence.

Gandhi negotiated a mostly peaceful transition from British rule to self-rule for the people of India. In his lifetime, he was one of the most influential leaders in the world. His ideas have influenced the struggles of many oppressed groups since.

In 1948, an assassin fired three bullets into Gandhi at point-blank range. The assassin was a Hindu fanatic who believed that Gandhi should have used his position to preach hatred of the Muslims of India. Gandhi instead preached tolerance and trust, urging Muslims and Hindus to participate together in the new nation of India. This most nonviolent and tolerant man became a victim of violence.

Mahatma Gandhi lived in a tumultuous period and led one of the largest social revolutions in human history. Despite the changing conditions of his life, his personality remained remarkably stable. For example, he practiced self-denial and self-sufficiency throughout his adult life, preferring a simple loincloth and shawl to the suit and tie worn by most leaders of the world's great nations.
© Dinodia Photos/Hulton Archive/Getty Images

Even though Gandhi became the "Father of India," he remained essentially the same person throughout his adult life. Each day of his life, he washed himself in ashes instead of expensive soap, and he shaved with an old, dull straight razor rather than with more expensive blades. He cleaned his own house and swept his yard almost every day. Each afternoon he spun thread on a hand-wheel for an hour or two. The thread was then made into cloth for his own clothes and for the clothes of his followers. He practiced the self-denial and self-sufficiency he learned early in his life. In most ways, his personality was remarkably stable over his life, even though he was at the center of one of the most tumultuous social revolutions in history.

manifestations have all changed, but something critical has remained the same—the overall level of dominant acts. Thus, personality coherence includes both elements of continuity and elements of change—continuity in the underlying trait but change in the outward manifestation of that trait.

Personality Change

The notion of personality development in the sense of change over time also requires elaboration. To start with, not all change qualifies as development. For instance, if you walk from one classroom to another, your relationship to your surroundings has changed. But we do not speak of your "development" in this case because the change is external to you and not enduring.

And not all internal changes can properly be considered development. When you get sick, for example, your body undergoes important changes: your temperature may rise, your nose may run, and your head may ache. But these changes do not constitute development because the changes do not last—you soon get healthy, your nose stops running, and you spring back into action. In the same way, temporary changes in personality—due to taking alcohol or drugs, for example—do not constitute personality development unless they produce more enduring changes in personality.

If you were to become consistently more conscientious or responsible as you aged, however, this would be a form of personality development. If you were to become gradually less energetic as you aged, this also would be a form of personality development.

In sum, personality change has two defining qualities. First, the changes are typically *internal* to the person, not merely changes in the external surroundings, such as walking into another room. Second, the changes are relatively *enduring* over time, rather than being merely temporary.

Three Levels of Analysis

We can examine personality over time at three levels of analysis: the population as a whole, group differences within the population, and individual differences within groups. As we examine the empirical research on personality development, it is useful to keep these three levels in mind.

Population Level

Several personality psychologists have theorized about the changes that we all go through in navigating from infancy to adulthood. Freud's theory of psychosexual development, for example, contained a conception of personality development that was presumed to apply to *everyone* on the planet. All people, according to Freud, go through an invariant stage sequence, starting with the oral stage and ending with the mature genital stage of psychosexual development (see Chapter 9).

This level of personality development deals with the changes and constancies that apply more or less to everyone. For example, almost everyone in the population tends to increase in sexual motivation at puberty. Similarly, there is a general decrease in impulsive and risk-taking behaviors as people get older. This is why auto insurance rates go down as people age, because a typical 30-year-old is much less likely than a typical 16-year-old to drive in a risky manner. This change in impulsivity is part of the population level of personality change, describing a general trend that might be part of what it means to be human and go through life.

Group Differences Level

Some changes over time affect different groups of people differently. Sex differences are one type of group differences. In the realm of physical development, for example, females go through puberty, on average, two years earlier than males. At the other end of life, men in the United States tend to die seven years earlier than women. These are sex differences in development.

Analogous sex differences can occur in the realm of personality development. As a group, men and women suddenly develop differently from one another during adolescence in their average levels of risk taking (men become more risk taking). Men and women also develop differently in the degree to which they show empathy toward others (women develop a stronger awareness and understanding of others' feelings). These forms of personality development are properly located at the group differences level of personality analysis.

Other group differences include cultural or ethnic group differences. For example, in the United States, there is a large difference in body image satisfaction between European American women and African American women. European American women tend to be, as a group, much less satisfied with their bodies than are African American women with theirs. Consequently, European American women are much more at risk for developing eating disturbances, such as anorexia or bulimia, compared with women in other groups. This group difference emerges primarily around puberty, when more European American women develop feelings of dissatisfaction with their physical appearance, compared with African American women.

Individual Differences Level

Personality psychologists also focus on individual differences in personality development. For example, can we predict, based on their personalities, which individuals will go through a midlife crisis? Can we predict who will be at risk for a psychological disturbance later in life based on earlier measures of personality? Can we predict which individuals will change over time and which ones will remain the same? These issues are located at the individual differences level of personality analysis.

Some changes affect different groups of people differently. For example, European American women tend to be, as a group, much less satisfied with their bodies than are African American women with theirs. Consequently, European American women have a higher risk for developing eating disorders, such as anorexia or bulimia, compared with women in other groups.
Left © wavebreakmedia/ Shutterstock.com RF; Right © Sam Edwards/Glow Images RF

Personality Stability over Time

This section examines the research on the stability of personality over the lifetime. We first examine stability in infancy, then explore stability during childhood, and finally look at stability during the decades of adulthood.

Stability of Temperament During Infancy

Many parents of two or more children will tell you that their children had distinctly different personalities the day they were born. For example, Albert Einstein, the Nobel Prize–winning father of modern physics, had two sons with his first wife. These two boys were quite different from each other. The older boy, Hans, was fascinated with puzzles as a child and had a gift for mathematics. He went on to become a distinguished professor of hydraulics. The younger son, Eduard, enjoyed music and literature as a child. As a young adult, however, he ended up in a Swiss psychiatric hospital, where he died. Although this is an extreme example, many parents notice differences among their children, even as infants. Do the intuitions of parents square with the scientific evidence?

By far the most commonly studied personality characteristics in infancy and childhood fall under the category of temperament. Although there is some disagreement about what the term means, most researchers define **temperament** as the individual differences that emerge very early in life, are likely to have a heritable basis (see Chapter 6), and are often involved with emotionality or arousability.

Mary Rothbart (1981, 1986; Rothbart & Hwang, 2005) studied infants at different ages, starting at 3 months of age. She examined six factors of temperament, using ratings completed by the caregivers:

1. *Activity level:* the infant's overall motor activity, including arm and leg movements.
2. *Smiling and laughter:* How much does the infant smile or laugh?
3. *Fear:* the infant's distress and reluctance to approach novel stimuli.
4. *Distress to limitations:* the child's distress at being refused food, being dressed, being confined, or being prevented access to a desired object.
5. *Soothability:* the degree to which the child reduces stress, or calms down, as a result of being soothed.
6. *Duration of orienting:* the degree to which the child sustains attention to objects in the absence of sudden changes.

The caregivers, mostly mothers, completed observer-based scales designed to measure these six aspects of temperament. Table 5.1 shows the cross-time correlations over different time intervals. If you scan the correlations in the table, you will notice first that they are all positive. This means that infants who tend to score high at one time period on activity level, smiling and laughter, and the other personality traits, also tend to score high on these traits at later time periods.

Next, notice that the correlations in the top two rows of Table 5.1 tend to be higher than those in the bottom four rows. This means that activity level and smiling and laughter tend to show higher levels of stability over time than the other personality traits.

Now notice that the correlations in the right-most two columns are generally higher than those in the left-most columns. This suggests that personality traits tend to become more stable toward the end of infancy (from 9 to 12 months), compared with the earlier stages of infancy (from 3 to 6 months).

Table 5.1 Stability Correlations for Temperament Scales

	MONTHS					
Scale	3–6	3–9	3–12	6–9	6–12	9–12
AL—activity level	0.58	0.48	0.48	0.56	0.60	0.68
SL—smiling and laughter	0.55	0.55	0.57	0.67	0.72	0.72
FR—fear	0.27	0.15	0.06	0.43	0.37	0.61
DL—distress to limitations	0.23	0.18	0.25	0.57	0.61	0.65
SO—soothability	0.30*	0.37*	0.41	0.50	0.39	0.29
DO—duration of orienting	0.36*	0.35*	0.11	0.62	0.34	0.64

Source: Adapted from Rothbart, 1981.

*Correlations based on only one cohort.

Like all studies, this one has limitations. Perhaps most important, the infants' caregivers may have developed certain conceptions of their infants, and it may be their conceptions rather than the infants' behaviors that show stability over time. Nonetheless, these findings reveal four important points. First, stable individual differences appear to emerge very early in life, when they can be assessed by observers. Second, for most temperament variables, there are moderate levels of stability over time during the first year of life. Third, the stability of temperament tends to be higher over short intervals of time than over long intervals of time—a finding that occurs in adulthood as well. And, fourth, the level of stability of temperament tends to increase as infants mature (Goldsmith & Rothbart, 1991; Rothbart & Hwang, 2005).

Stability During Childhood

Longitudinal studies, which examine the same groups of individuals over time, are costly and difficult to conduct. As a result, there are few studies to draw on. A major exception is the Block and Block Longitudinal Study, which initiated the testing of a sample of more than 100 children from the Berkeley-Oakland area of California when the children were 3 years old (see, e.g., Block & Robbins, 1993). Since that time, the sample has been followed and repeatedly tested at ages 4, 5, 7, 11, and into adulthood.

One of the first publications from this project focused on individual differences in activity level (Buss, Block, & Block, 1980). When the children were 3 years old, and then again at 4, their activity levels were assessed in two ways. The first was through the use of an **actometer,** a recording device attached to the wrists of the children during several play periods. Motoric movement activated the recording device—essentially a self-winding wristwatch. Independently, the children's teachers completed ratings of their behavior and personalities. The behavioral measure of activity level contained three items that were directly relevant: "is physically active," "is vital, energetic, active," and "has a rapid personal tempo." These items were summed to form a total measure of teacher-observed activity level. This observer-based measure was obtained when the children were 3 and 4 and then again when they reached age 7.

Table 5.2 shows the correlations among the activity level measures, both at the same ages and across time to assess the stability of activity level during childhood. The

Table 5.2 Intercorrelations Among Activity Measures

	ACTOMETER		JUDGE-BASED		
	Age 3	Age 4	Age 3	Age 4	Age 7
Actometer:					
Age 3	. . .	.44*	.61***	.56***	.19
Age 4	.43**	. . .	.66***	.53***	.38**
Judge-based:					
Age 3	.50***	.36**	. . .	.75***	.48***
Age 4	.34*	.48***	.51***	. . .	.38**
Age 7	.35*	.28*	.33*	.50***	. . .

Source: Buss, Block, & Block, 1980.

*p < .05. **p < .01. ***p < .001 (two-tailed). Correlations above the ellipses (. . .) are based on boys' data, those below the ellipses (. . .) are based on girls' data.

correlations between the same measures obtained at two different points in time are called **stability coefficients** (these are also sometimes called test-retest reliability coefficients). The correlations between different measures of the same trait obtained at the same time are called **validity coefficients.**

Several key conclusions about validity and stability can be drawn from these findings. First, the actometer-based measurements of activity level have significant positive validity coefficients with the judge-based measurements of activity level. Activity level in childhood can be validly assessed through both observational judgments and activity recordings from the actometers. The two measures are moderately correlated at each age, providing cross-validation of each type of measure.

Second, notice that the correlations of the activity level measurements are all positively correlated with measurements of activity level taken at later ages. We can conclude that activity level shows moderate stability during childhood. Children who are highly active at age 3 are also likely to be active at ages 4 and 7. Their less active peers at age 3 are likely to remain less active at ages 4 and 7. A 21-year-study tracking physical activity of Finish boys and girls found that this level of moderate stability carries throughout childhood and into adulthood (Telama et al., 2005).

Finally, the size of the correlations tends to decrease as the time interval between the different testings increases. As a general rule, the longer the time between testings, the lower the stability coefficients. In other words, measures taken early in life can predict personality later in life, but the predictability decreases over time.

These general conclusions apply to other personality characteristics as well. Aggression and violence have long been a key concern of our society from school shootings to suicide bombers. What causes some children to act so aggressively?

As it turns out, numerous studies of childhood aggression have been conducted by personality psychologists. Dan Olweus (1979) reviewed 16 longitudinal studies of aggression during childhood. The studies varied widely on many aspects, such as age at which the children were first tested (2–18), length interval between first testing and final testing (half a year to 18 years), and the specific measures of aggression used (e.g., teacher ratings, direct observation, and peer ratings).

Figure 5.1 shows a summary graph of the results of all these studies. The graph depicts the stability coefficients for aggression as a function of the interval between

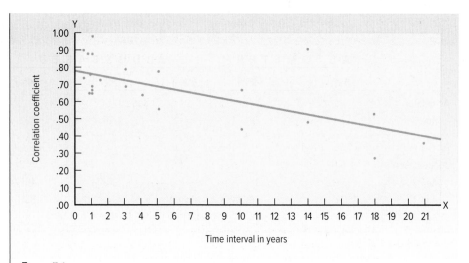

Figure 5.1

The figure shows the stability of aggression in males over different time intervals. Aggression shows the highest levels of stability over short time intervals such as from one year to the next. As the time interval between testings increases, however, the correlation coefficients decline, suggesting that aggressiveness changes more over long time intervals than over short time intervals.

Source: Olweus, 1979.

first and final testing. Marked individual differences in aggression emerge very early in life, certainly by the age of 3 (Olweus, 1979). Individuals retain their rank order stability on aggression to a substantial degree over the years. Moderate levels of rank order stability have also been documented for major personality traits from early childhood to adolescence (Hampson et al., 2007), from middle childhood to adolescence (Tackett et al., 2008), and from adolescence to early adulthood (Blonigen et al., 2008). Longitudinal studies of aggression continue to support the conclusion of moderate levels of stability (Piquero et al., 2012). And, as we have seen with infant temperament and childhood activity level, the stability coefficients tend to decline as the interval between the two times of measurement increases.

In sum, we can conclude that individual differences in personality emerge very early in life—most likely in infancy for some traits and by early childhood for other traits, such as aggression. These individual differences tend to be moderately stable over time, so that people who are high on a particular trait tend to remain high. Indeed, childhood personality at age 3 turns out to be a good predictor of adult personality at age 26 (Caspi, Harrington, et al., 2003). Finally, the stability coefficients gradually decline over time as the distance between testings increases.

Rank Order Stability in Adulthood

Many studies have been conducted on the stability of adult personality. Longitudinal studies span as many as four decades of life. Furthermore, many age brackets have been examined, from age 18 through older cohorts ranging up to age 84.

A summary of these data is shown in Table 5.4, assembled by Costa and McCrae (1994; see also McCrae & Costa, 2008). This table categorizes the measures of personality into the five-factor model of traits, described in Chapter 3. The time intervals between the first and last personality assessments for each sample range

A Closer Look   Bullies and Whipping Boys from Childhood to Adulthood

The individual differences that emerge early in life sometimes have profound consequences, both for the life outcomes of individuals and for the impact on the social world. Norwegian psychologist Dan Olweus has conducted longitudinal studies of "bullies" and "whipping boys" (Olweus, 1978, 1979, 2001). The meanings of these terms are precisely what they sound like. Bullies pick on and victimize other children. They trip victims in the hallway, push them into lockers, elbow them in the stomach, demand their lunch money, and call them names.

Although the victims, or "whipping boys," do not have any external characteristics that appear to set them apart, they do have certain psychological characteristics. Most commonly, victims tend to be anxious, fearful, insecure, and lacking in social skills. They are emotionally vulnerable and may be physically weak as well, making them easy targets who don't fight back. The victims suffer from low self-esteem, lose interest in school, and often show difficulties establishing or maintaining friendships. They seem to lack social support that might buffer them against bullies. It has been estimated that 10 percent of all schoolchildren are afraid of bullies during the school day, and most

children have been victimized by bullies at least once (Brody, 1996).

In one longitudinal study, bullies and victims were identified through teacher nominations in Grade 6. A year later, the children attended different schools in different settings, having made the transition from elementary school to junior high school. At this different setting during Grade 7, a different set of teachers categorized the boys on whether they were bullies, victims, or neither. The results are shown in Table 5.3. As you can see from looking at the circled numbers in the diagonal in Table 5.3, the vast majority of the boys received similar classifications a year later, despite the different school, different setting, and different teachers doing the categorizing.

The bullying, however, does not appear to stop in childhood. When Olweus followed thousands of boys from grade school to adulthood, he found marked continuities. The bullies in childhood were more likely to become juvenile delinquents in adolescence and criminals in adulthood. An astonishing 65 percent of the boys who were classified by their Grade 6 teachers as bullies ended up having felony convictions by the time they were 24 years old (Brody, 1996). Many of the bullies apparently

remained bullies throughout their lives. Unfortunately, we don't know the fate of the victims, other than that they tended not to get involved in criminal activities.

A study of 228 children, ranging in age from 6 to 16, found several fascinating personality and family relationship correlates of bullying (Connolly & O'Moore, 2003). A total of 115 children were classified as "bullies" based on both their own self-ratings and on the basis of at least two of their classmates categorizing them as bullies. These were then compared with 113 control children, who both did not nominate themselves as bullies and were not categorized as bullies by any of their classmates. The bullies scored higher on the Eysenck scales of Extraversion, Neuroticism, and Psychoticism (see Chapter 3). Bullies, in short, tended to be more outgoing and gregarious (extraversion); emotionally volatile and anxious (neuroticism); and impulsive and lacking in empathy (psychoticism). In addition, the bullies, relative to the controls, expressed more ambivalence and conflict with their family members, including their brothers, sisters, and parents. Conflicts in the home, in short, appear to be linked to conflicts these children get into during school, pointing to a degree of consistency across situations.

Table 5.3   Longitudinal Classification of Boys in Aggressive Behaviors

Grade 6	GRADE 7		
	Bully	Neither	Victim
Bully	(24)	9	2
Neither	9	(200)	15
Victim	1	10	(16)

from a low of 3 years to a high of 30 years. The results yield a strong general conclusion: across self-report measures of personality, conducted by different investigators and over differing time intervals of adulthood, the traits of Neuroticism, Extraversion, Openness, Agreeableness, and Conscientiousness all show moderate to high levels of stability. The average correlation across these traits, scales, and time intervals is roughly +.65.

These studies all rely on self-report. What are the stability coefficients when other data sources are used? In one six-year longitudinal study of adults using spouse ratings,

Table 5.4 Stability Coefficients for Selected Personality Scales in Adult Samples

Factor/Scale	Interval	r
Neuroticism		
NEO-PI N	6	.83
16PF Q4: Tense	10	.67
ACL Adapted Child	16	.66
Neuroticism	18	.46
GZTS Emotional Stability (low)	24	.62
MMPI Factor	30	.56
	Median:	.64
Extraversion		
NEO-PI E	6	.82
16PF H: Adventurous	10	.74
ACL Self-Confidence	16	.60
Social Extraversion	18	.57
GZTS Sociability	24	.68
MMPI Factor	30	.56
	Median:	.64
Openness		
NEO-PI O	6	.83
16PF I: Tender-Minded	10	.54
GZTS Thoughtfulness	24	.66
MMPI Intellectual Interests	30	.62
	Median:	.64
Agreeableness		
NEO-PI A	3	.63
Agreeableness	18	.46
GZTS Friendliness	24	.65
MMPI Cynicism (low)	30	.65
	Median:	.64
Conscientiousness		
NEO-PI C	3	.79
16PF G: Conscientious	10	.48
ACL Endurance	16	.67
Impulse Control	18	.46
GZTS Restraint	24	.64
	Median:	.67

Note: Interval is given in years; all retest correlations are significant at $p < .01$. NEO-PI = NEO Personality Inventory, ACL = Adjective Check List, GZTS = Guilford Zimmerman Temperament Survey, MMPI = Minnesota Multiphasic Personality Inventory.

Source: Costa & McCrae, 1994. These stability coefficients are similar to those of all subsequent studies. A longitudinal study in Finland, for example, found that the five factors showed adult rank order stability ranging from .65 to .97 (Rantanen et al., 2007).

stability coefficients were +.83 for Neuroticism, +.77 for Extraversion, and +.80 for Openness (Costa & McCrae, 1988). Another study used peer ratings of personality to study stability over a seven-year interval. Stability coefficients ranged from +.63 to +.81 for the five-factor taxonomy of personality (Costa & McCrae, 1992). In sum, moderate to high levels of personality stability, in the individual differences sense, are found whether the data source is self-report, spouse-report, or peer-report.

Studies continue to confirm the rank order stability of personality during the adult years. In one study, Richard Robins and his colleagues (Robins et al., 2001) examined 275 college students during their freshman year, and then again in their senior year. Across the four years of college, the rank order stability obtained was .63 for Extraversion, .60 for Agreeableness, .59 for Conscientiousness, .53 for Neuroticism, and .70 for Openness. A study of 2,141 German students tested over a two-year period from college to employment found stabilities of .70 for Extraversion, .65 for Agreeableness, .69 for Conscientiousness, .65 for Neuroticism, and .75 for Openness (Ludtke, Trautwein, & Husemann, 2009). In sum, the moderate levels of rank order stability of the Big Five are highly replicable across different populations and investigators.

Similar findings emerge for personality dispositions that are not strictly subsumed by the Big Five. In a massive meta-analytic study of the stability of self-esteem—how good people feel about themselves—Trzesniewski, Donnellan, and Robins (2003) found high levels of continuity over time. Summarizing 50 published studies involving 29,839 individuals and four large national studies involving 74,381 individuals, they found stability correlations ranging from the .50s to the .70s. How people feel about themselves—their level of self-confidence—appears very consistent over time. Similar findings have been obtained with measures of prosocial orientation and interpersonal empathy (Eisenberg et al., 2002). In sum, personality dispositions, whether the standard Big Five or other dispositions, show moderate to considerable rank order stability over time in adulthood.

Researchers have posed an intriguing question about rank order personality stability in the individual differences sense: When does personality consistency peak? That is, is there a point in life when people's personality traits become so firm that they don't change much relative to those of other people? To address this question, Roberts and DelVecchio (2000) conducted a meta-analysis of 152 longitudinal studies of personality. The key variable Roberts and DelVecchio (2000) examined was "personality consistency," which was defined as the correlation between Time 1 and Time 2 measures of personality (e.g., the correlation between a personality trait at age 15 and the same trait at age 18).

Roberts and DelVecchio (2000) found two key results. First, personality consistency tends to increase with increasing age. For example, the average personality consistency during the teenage years was +.47. This jumped to +.57 during the decade of the twenties and +.62 during the thirties (see Vaidya et al., 2008, for similar results). Personality consistency peaked during the decade of the fifties at +.75. As the authors conclude, "trait consistency increases in a linear fashion from infancy to middle age where it then reaches its peak after age 50" (p. 3). As people age, personality appears to become more and more "set."

Mean Level Stability and Change in Adulthood

The five-factor model of personality also shows fairly consistent mean level stability over time, as shown in Figure 5.2. Especially after age 50, there is little change in the average level of stability in Openness, Extraversion, Neuroticism, Conscientiousness, and Agreeableness.

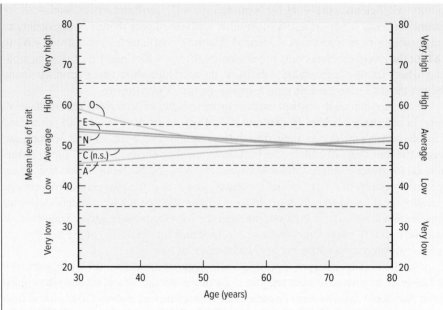

N = Neuroticism, E = Extraversion, O = Openness, A = Agreeableness, C = Conscientiousness

Figure 5.2

The figure shows the mean level of five traits over the life span. Although the average scores on each trait are quite stable over time, Openness, Extraversion, and Neuroticism show a gradual decline from age 30 to 50. In contrast, Agreeableness shows a gradual increase over these ages.

Source: Costa & McCrae, 1994.

Little change, however, does not mean no change. In fact, there are small but consistent changes in these personality traits, especially during the decade of the twenties. As you can see in Figure 5.2, there is a tendency for Openness, Extraversion, and Neuroticism to gradually decline with increasing age until around age 50. At the same time, Conscientiousness and Agreeableness show a gradual increase over time—effects found in Switzerland, Germany, as well as in the United States (Anusic, Lucas, & Donnellan, 2012; Specht, Egloff, & Schmukle, 2011). The magnitude of these age effects is not large.

Studies confirm that mean level personality traits change in slight, but nonetheless important, ways during adulthood. By far the most consistent change is a good one—people score lower on Neuroticism or Negative Affect as they grow older. From freshman to senior years in college, for example, students show a decrease in Neuroticism corresponding to roughly half a standard deviation (d = −.49) (Robins et al., 2001). Students reported experiencing less negative affect and more positive affect over time (Vaidya et al., 2002). A study from adolescence to midlife also found a decrease in the experience of Negative Affect—individuals feel less anxious, less distressed, and less irritable as they move into midlife (McCrae et al., 2002). Emotional stability even increases from middle adulthood (ages 42–46) to older age (ages 60–64) (Alleman, Zimprich, & Hertzog, 2007). Similar findings were obtained in a longitudinal study of 2,804 individuals over a 23-year time span—Negative Affect decreased consistently as the participants got older (Charles, Reynolds, & Gatz, 2001).

A massive meta-analysis of 92 different samples found that both women and men gradually become more emotionally stable as they grow older, with the largest changes occurring between the ages of 22 and 40 (Roberts, Walton, & Viechtbauer, 2006). These increases in emotional stability (or decreases in Neuroticism) with age also have been found in Germany (Lehmann et al., 2013) and Japan (Kawamoto, 2016). A study of 1,600 men found that those who got married showed above-average increases in emotional stability compared to their bachelor peers (Mroczek & Spiro, 2003). In sum, most people become less emotionally volatile, less anxious, and generally less neurotic as they mature—a nice thing to look forward to for people whose current lives contain a lot of emotional turmoil.

Some people, however, change more than others (Johnson et al., 2007; Neyer, 2006; Vaidya et al., 2008). People who experience very few stressful life events show the largest decreases in Neuroticism over time (Jeronimus et al., 2014). In contrast, those who experience a lot of stressful life events tend to increase in Neuroticism over time. At the same time, being high on Neuroticism seems to cause people to get themselves into stressful life events. So the link between Neuroticism and stress seems to be bidirectional. Entering into a stable romantic relationship, transitioning to becoming a parent, and investing heavily in work all seem to have the effect of increasing levels of Conscientiousness compared to those who do not enter into these adult roles (Bleidorn, 2012; Hudson & Roberts, 2016; van Scheppingen et al., 2016; Wagner et al., 2015).

While Neuroticism and Negative Affect decline with age, people score higher on Agreeableness and Conscientiousness as they grow older. One study found an increase in Agreeableness of nearly half a standard deviation (d = +.44), and Conscientiousness increased roughly one-quarter of a standard deviation (d = +.27) (Robins et al., 2001). The facets of Conscientiousness that increase most with age are industriousness (working hard), impulse control, and reliability (Jackson et al., 2009). Similar findings have been discovered by other researchers: College students become more agreeable, extraverted, and conscientious from freshman year to two and a half years later (Vaidya et al., 2002); Agreeableness and Conscientiousness increase throughout early and middle adulthood (Srivastava et al., 2003); Positive Affect increases from the late teen years through the early fifties (Charles et al., 2001). Increases in Agreeableness over the course of adulthood have been found in Germany and Japan (Lehmann et al., 2013; Kawamoto, 2016). Some studies find increases in the trait of Openness with age, although these are less robust than changes in traits such as emotional stability. One study found an increase in Openness from adolescence to young adulthood (Pullman, Raudsepp, & Allik, 2006), whereas another study found this Openness increase in a similar age group only for women (Branje, van Lieshout, & Geris, 2006). Perhaps a good summary of the mean level personality changes comes directly from the longitudinal researchers: "The personality changes that did take place from adolescence to adulthood reflected growth in the direction of greater maturity; many adolescents became more controlled and socially more confident and less angry and alienated" (Roberts, Caspi, & Moffitt, 2001, p. 670). Indeed, these personality changes have been dubbed the *maturity principle* (Caspi, Roberts, & Shiner, 2005).

Finally, the Big Five personality dispositions may be changeable through therapy. Ralph Piedmont (2001) evaluated the effects of an outpatient drug rehabilitation program on personality dispositions, as indexed by the Big Five. The therapy, administered to 82 men and 50 women over a six-week period, revealed fascinating findings. Those who went through the program showed a decrease in Neuroticism, and increases in Agreeableness and Conscientiousness (d = .38). These personality changes were largely maintained in a follow-up assessment 15 months later, although not quite as dramatically (d = 28). Programs to help people change their personality traits when they want change, notably to become lower on Neuroticism, have met with some success (Hudson & Fraley, 2015).

In sum, although personality dispositions generally show high levels of mean stability over time, predictable changes occur with age and perhaps also with therapy—lower Neuroticism and Negative Affect, higher Agreeableness, higher Conscientiousness.

Exercise?

Each person's personality is, in some ways, stable over time; however, in other ways, it changes over time. In this exercise, you can evaluate yourself in terms of what describes you now and how you think you will be in the future (Markus & Nurius, 1986). Following is a list of items. For each one, simply rate it on a 1 to 7 scale, with 1 meaning "does not describe me at all" to 7 meaning "is a highly accurate description of me." Give a rating for each of two questions: (1) Does this describe me now? and (2) Will this describe me in the future?

Items	Describes Me Now	Will Describe Me in the Future
Happy		
Confident		
Depressed		
Lazy		
Travels widely		
Has lots of friends		
Destitute (poor)		
Sexy		
In good shape		
Speaks well in public		
Makes own decisions		
Manipulates people		
Powerful		
Unimportant		

Compare your answers to the two questions. Items you gave the same answers to indicate that you believe this attribute will remain stable over time. The items that change, however, may reflect the ways in which your personality will change over time.

You can view your possible self in a number of ways, but two are especially important. The first pertains to the *desired self*—the person you wish to become. Some people wish to become happier, more powerful, or in better physical shape. The second pertains to your *feared self*—the sort of person you do not wish to become, such as poor or rigid. Which aspects of your possible self do you desire? Which aspects do you fear?

Personality Change

Global measures of personality traits, such as those captured by the five-factor model, give us hints that personality can change over time. But it is also true that researchers who have focused most heavily on personality stability have generally not explicitly designed studies and measures to assess personality change. It is important to remember that knowledge about personality change is sparse.

One reason for the relative lack of knowledge about change is that there might be a bias among researchers against even looking for personality change (Helson & Stewart, 1994). As Block (1971) notes, even the terms used to describe stability and change are laden with evaluative meaning. Terms that refer to absence of change tend to be positive: *consistency, stability, continuity,* and *constancy* all seem like good things to have. On the other hand, *inconsistency, instability, discontinuity,* and *inconstancy* all seem undesirable or unpredictable.

Changes in Self-Esteem from Adolescence to Adulthood

In a unique longitudinal study, Block and Robbins (1993) examined self-esteem and the personality characteristics associated with those whose self-esteem had changed over time. **Self-esteem** was defined as "the extent to which one perceives oneself as relatively close to being the person one wants to be and/or as relatively distant from being the kind of person one does not want to be, with respect to person-qualities one positively and negatively values" (Block & Robbins, 1993, p. 911). Self-esteem was measured by use of an overall difference between a *current* self-description and an *ideal* self-description: the researchers hypothesized that the smaller the discrepancy, the higher the self-esteem. Conversely, the larger the discrepancy between current and ideal selves, the lower the self-esteem.

The participants were first assessed on this measure of self-esteem at age 14, roughly the first year of high school. Then they were assessed again at age 23, roughly five years after high school.

For the sample as a whole, there was no change in self-esteem with increasing age. However, when males and females were examined separately, a startling trend emerged. Over time, the genders departed from each other, with men's self-esteem tending to increase and women's self-esteem tending to decrease. The males tended, on average, to increase in self-esteem by roughly a fifth of a standard deviation, whereas the females tended, on average, to decrease in self-esteem by roughly a standard deviation. This is an example of personality change at the group level—the two subgroups (women and men) changed in different directions over time.

In sum, the transition from early adolescence to early adulthood appears to be harder on women than on men, at least in terms of self-esteem. As a whole, females tend to decrease in self-esteem, showing an increasing gap between their current self-conceptions and their ideal selves. As a whole, males tend to show a smaller discrepancy between their real and ideal selves over the same time period.

Autonomy, Dominance, Leadership, and Ambition

Another longitudinal study examined 266 male managerial candidates at the business AT&T (Howard & Bray, 1988). The researchers first tested these men when they were in their twenties (in the late 1950s) and then followed them up periodically over a 20-year time span when they were in their forties (in the late 1970s).

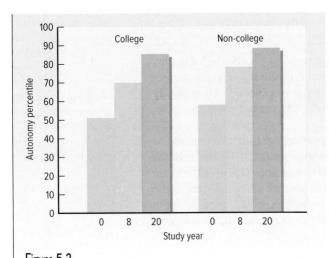

Figure 5.3

The figure shows change with age in autonomy scores of men in the AT&T study. Both college-educated and non-college-educated men tend to become more autonomous or independent as they grow older.

Several dramatic personality changes were observed for the sample as a whole. The most startling change was a steep drop in the *ambition* score. This drop was steepest during the first 8 years but continued to drop over the next 12 years. The drop was steepest for the college men, less so for the non-college men, although it should be noted that the college men started out higher on ambition than did the non-college men. Supplementary interview data suggested that the men had become more realistic about their limited possibilities for promotion in the company. It is not that these men lost interest in their jobs or became less effective. Indeed, their scores on *autonomy, leadership motivation, achievement,* and *dominance* all increased over time (see Figure 5.3).

Sensation Seeking

Conventional wisdom has it that people become more cautious and conservative with age. Studies of sensation seeking confirm this view. The Sensation-Seeking Scale (SSS) contains four subscales, each containing items and phrases as a forced-choice between two distinct options. First is *thrill and adventure seeking,* with items such as "I would like to try parachute jumping" versus "I would never want to try jumping out of a plane, with or without a parachute." The other scales are *experience seeking* (e.g., "I am not interested in experience for its own sake" versus "I like to have new and exciting experiences and sensations even if they are a little frightening, unconventional, or illegal"); *disinhibition* (e.g., "I like wild, uninhibited parties" versus "I prefer quiet parties with good conversation"); and *boredom susceptibility* (e.g., "I get bored seeing the same old faces" versus "I like the comfortable familiarity of everyday friends").

Sensation seeking increases with age from childhood to adolescence and peaks in late adolescence around ages 18–20; then it falls more or less continuously as people get older (Zuckerman, 1974). This age trend of sensation seeking has been replicated within the United States and across many cultures (Chan et al., 2012; Steinberg et al., 2008). Parachute jumping and wild, uninhibited parties seem to be less appealing to older folks.

Femininity

In a longitudinal study of women from Mills College in the San Francisco bay area, Helson and Wink (1992) examined changes in personality between the early forties and early fifties. They used the California Psychological Inventory at both time periods. The most dramatic change occurred on the *femininity* scale (now called the femininity/masculinity scale). High scorers on femininity tend to be described by observers as dependent, emotional, feminine, gentle, high-strung, mild, nervous, sensitive, sentimental, submissive, sympathetic, and worrying (Gough, 1996). Low scorers (i.e., those who score in the masculine direction), in contrast, tend to be described as aggressive, assertive, boastful, confident, determined, forceful, independent, masculine, self-confident, strong, and

A Closer Look

Day-to-Day Changes in Self-Esteem

Most personality psychologists who study self-esteem focus on a person's average level, whether the person is generally high, low, or average in terms of his or her self-esteem. A few studies have been done on changes in self-esteem over long time spans in people's lives—for example, in the years from adolescence to adulthood. However, with some reflection, most of us would realize that we often change from day to day in how we feel about ourselves. Some days are better than other days when it comes to self-esteem. Some days we feel incompetent, that things are out of our control, and that we even feel a little worthless. Other days we feel satisfied with ourselves, that we are particularly strong or competent, and that we are satisfied with who we are and what we can become. In other words, it seems that feelings of self-esteem can change, not just from year to year but also from day to day.

Psychologist Michael Kernis has become interested in how changeable or variable people are in their self-esteem in terms of day-to-day fluctuations. *Self-esteem variability* is the magnitude of short-term changes in ongoing self-esteem (Kernis, Grannemann, & Mathis, 1991). Self-esteem variability is measured by having people keep records of how they feel about themselves for several consecutive days, sometimes for weeks or months. From these daily records, the researchers can determine just how much each person fluctuates, as well as his or her average level of self-esteem.

Researchers make a distinction between level and variability of self-esteem. These two aspects of self-esteem turn out to be unrelated to each other and are hypothesized to interact in predicting important life outcomes, such as depression (Kernis, Grannemann, & Barclay, 1992). For example, variability in self-esteem is an indicator that the person's self-esteem, even if high, is fragile, and the person is vulnerable to stress. Consequently, we can think of level and variability as defining two qualities of self-esteem as in the figure below.

Kernis et al. (1991, 1992) have suggested that self-esteem variability is related to the extent to which one's self-view can be influenced by events, particularly social events. Some people's self-esteem is pushed and pulled by the happenings of life more than is other people's self-esteem. For example, for some people, self-esteem might soar with a compliment and plummet with a social slight, whereas others, who can better roll with the punches of life, might be more stable in their self-esteem, weathering both the slights as well as the uplifts of life without much change in their self-view. This stability versus changeability of self-esteem is the psychological disposition referred to as self-esteem variability.

Several studies have been conducted to examine whether self-esteem variability predicts life outcomes, such as depressive reactions to stress, differently than does self-esteem level. In one study

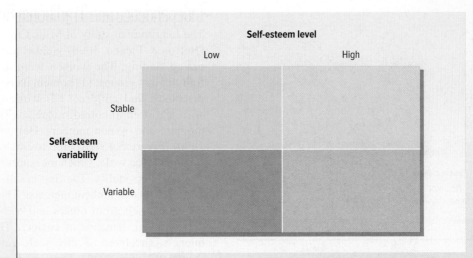

Level of self-esteem (whether one is high or low) and variability in self-esteem (whether one is stable or variable from day to day) are unrelated to each other. This makes it possible to find people with different combinations, such as a person who has a high level of self-esteem but is also variable.

(Continued)

A Closer Look (*Continued*)

(Kernis et al., 1991), self-esteem level was related to depression, but this relation was much stronger for those higher in self-esteem variability than for those lower in self-esteem variability. In other words, at all levels of self-esteem, the participants who were low in variability showed less of a relation between self-esteem and depression than did the participants who were high in variability. Similar results were obtained by Butler, Hokanson, and Flynn (1994), who showed that self-esteem variability is a good predictor of who

would become depressed six months later, especially when there was life stress in the intervening months. These authors also concluded that variability indicates that the person may have a fragile sense of self-value and that, with stress, he or she may become more chronically depressed than someone whose self-esteem is more stable.

Based on findings from studies like these, researchers have come to view self-esteem variability as a vulnerability to stressful life events (Roberts & Monroe, 1992). That is, variability is thought to result

from a particular sensitivity in one's sense of self-worth. Psychologists Ryan and Deci (2000) have suggested that variable persons are dependent for their self-worth on the approval of others. Variable persons are very sensitive to social feedback, and they judge themselves primarily through the eyes of others. High-variability persons show (1) an enhanced sensitivity to evaluative events, (2) an increased concern about their self-concept, (3) an overreliance on social sources for self-evaluation, and (4) reactions of anger and hostility when things don't go their way.

tough. In terms of acts performed (recall the act frequency approach from Chapter 3), as reported by the spouses of these women, high scorers on the femininity scale tend to do such things as send cards to friends on holidays and remember an acquaintance's birthday, even though no one else did. Low scorers, in contrast, tend to take charge of committee meetings and take the initiative in sexual encounters (Gough, 1996).

A fascinating change occurred in this sample of educated women—they showed a consistent drop in femininity as they moved from their early forties to their early fifties—a group level change in this personality variable. Women who choose not to have children also score lower in femininity than women who do have children, although this may not reflect change so much as choices made based on this preexisting personality dimension (Newton & Stewart, 2013).

Independence and Traditional Roles

The longitudinal study of Mills College women (Helson & Picano, 1990) yielded another fascinating finding. The women were divided into four distinct groups: (1) homemakers with intact marriages and children, (2) working mothers with children (neotraditionals), (3) divorced mothers, and (4) non-mothers (Helson & Picano, 1990). Figure 5.4 shows the results for the CPI Independence scale, which measures two related facets of personality. The first is self-assurance, resourcefulness, and competence. The second is distancing self from others and not bowing to conventional demands of society. The act frequency correlates of this scale reflect these themes (Gough, 1996). Those high on the Independence scale tend to set goals for groups they are in, talk to many people at parties, and take charge of the group when the situation calls for it. High scorers also tend to interrupt

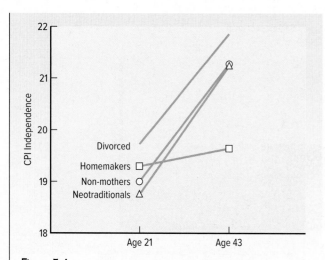

Figure 5.4

Means on the CPI Independence scale at ages 21 and 43 for homemakers (*n* = 17) and three groups of women with less traditional role paths: neotraditional, *n* = 35; divorced, *n* = 26; and non-mothers, *n* = 26.

conversations and do not always follow instructions from those who are in a position to lead (hence, distancing themselves from others in these ways).

For the divorced mothers, non-mothers, and working mothers, independence scores increased significantly over time. Only the traditional homemakers showed no increase in independence over time. These data, of course, are correlational, so we cannot infer causation. It is possible that something about the roles affected the degree to which the women became more independent. It is also possible that the women who were less likely to increase in independence were more content to remain in the traditional homemaking role. Regardless of the interpretation, this study illustrates the utility of examining subgroups within the population.

In sum, although the evidence is sparse, there are enough empirical clues to suggest that personality traits show some predictable changes with age. First, impulsivity and sensation seeking show predictable declines with age. Second, men tend to become somewhat less ambitious with age. There are indications that both men and women become somewhat more competent and independent with increasing age. Finally, there are hints that changes in independence are linked with the role and lifestyle adopted, with traditional homemaking women increasing less on independence than women who get divorced or lead less traditional work lives.

Personality Changes Across Cohorts: Assertiveness and Narcissism

One of the interesting issues in exploring personality change over time is determining whether the changes observed are due to true personal change that all people undergo as they age, as can be determined by longitudinal studies of the sort just presented, or, conversely, changes in the **cohort effects**— the social times in which they lived. Jean Twenge (2000, 2001a, 2001b) has been at the forefront in exploring personality change that is likely to be caused by cohort effects. She argues that American society has changed dramatically over the past seven decades. One of the most dramatic changes centers on women's status and roles. During the depression era of the 1930s, for example, women were expected to be self-sufficient, but during the 1950s and 1960s, women assumed a more domestic role. Then from 1968 through 1993, women surged into the workforce and American society increasingly adopted norms of sexual equality. For example, from 1950 to 1993, the number of women obtaining bachelor's degrees doubled roughly from 25 to 50 percent. And the number of women obtaining PhDs, medical degrees, and law degrees all more than tripled. Have these dramatic societal changes impacted women's personality?

Twenge (2001a) discovered that women's trait scores on *assertiveness* rose and fell dramatically, depending on the cohort in which the woman was raised. Women's assertiveness scores generally rose half a standard deviation from 1931 to 1945; fell by roughly that amount from 1951 to 1967; and then rose again from 1968 to 1993. On measures such as the California Psychological Inventory scale of Dominance, for example, women increased +.31 of a standard deviation from

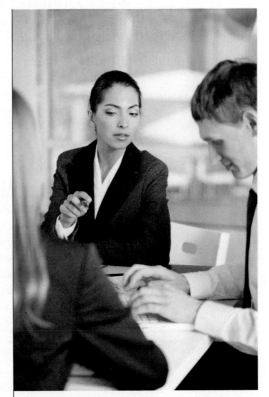

Women's assertiveness scores rose from 1968 to 1993, pointing to a cohort effect.

© Image Source/Getty Images RF

1968 to 1993. Men, in contrast, did not show significant cohort differences in their levels of assertiveness or dominance. Twenge (2001a) concludes that "social change truly becomes internalized with the individual . . . girls absorb the cultural messages they received from the world around them, and their personalities are molded by these messages" (p. 142).

Older people sometimes complain that the younger generation is too self-centered ("The kids these days!"). Is there any truth to these laments? Twenge and her colleagues (2008) explored this issue by analyzing the personality syndrome labeled *narcissism*—those who tend to be self-centered, exhibitionistic, self-aggrandizing, interpersonally exploitative, grandiose, lacking empathy, and having an undue sense of entitlement (Buss & Chiodo, 1991). Twenge and colleagues (2008) found that scores on narcissism increased by about a third of standard deviation between 1982 and 2006. Based on a study of 30,073 individuals, critics of this analysis concluded that the evidence for major cohort changes in narcissism is actually weak (ranging from +.02 to +.04) and that there is little evidence for "an emerging epidemic of narcissism" (Donnallan, Trzesniewski, & Robins, 2009). Although the debate about narcissism continues, cautious readers may wish to wait for further evidence before concluding that today's youth are truly more self-centered than their elders.

Personality Coherence over Time: Prediction of Socially Relevant Outcomes

The final form of personality development we will examine is called personality coherence, defined as predictable changes in the *manifestations* or *outcomes* of personality factors over time, even if the underlying characteristics remain stable. In particular, we focus on the consequences of personality for socially relevant outcomes, such as marital stability and divorce; alcoholism, drug use, and emotional disturbance; and job outcomes later in life.

Marital Stability, Marital Satisfaction, and Divorce

In a longitudinal study of unprecedented length, Kelly and Conley (1987) studied a sample of 300 couples from their engagements in the 1930s all the way through their status later in life in the 1980s. At the final testing, the median age of the subjects was 68 years. Within the entire sample of 300 couples, 22 couples broke their engagements and did not get married. Of the 278 couples who did get married, 50 ended up getting divorced sometime between 1935 and 1980.

During the first testing session in the 1930s, acquaintances provided ratings of each participant's personality on a wide variety of dimensions. Three aspects of personality proved to be strong predictors of marital dissatisfaction and divorce—the neuroticism of the husband, the lack of impulse control of the husband, and the neuroticism of the wife. High levels of neuroticism proved to be the strongest predictors. Neuroticism was linked with marital dissatisfaction of both the men and the women in the 1930s, again in 1955, and yet again in 1980.

Furthermore, the neuroticism of both the husband and the wife, as well as the lack of impulse control of the husband, were strong predictors of divorce. These three

Psychologists have identified personality variables that predict whether a marriage will turn out to be happy and satisfying or whether it will end in divorce. Although personality is not destiny, it does relate to important life outcomes, such as marital unhappiness and divorce.
Left © Ariel Skelley/Blend Images LLC RF; Right © Ingram Publishing RF

dimensions of personality accounted for more than half of the predictable variance in whether the couples split up. The couples who had a stable and satisfying marriage had neuroticism scores roughly half a standard deviation lower than the couples who subsequently got divorced.

The reasons for divorce themselves appear to be linked to the personality characteristics measured earlier in life. The husbands with low impulse control when first assessed, for example, tended later in life to have extramarital affairs—breaches of the marital vows that loomed large among the major reasons cited for the divorce. The men with higher impulse control appear to have been able to refrain from having sexual flings, which are so detrimental to marriages (Buss, 2003).

These results, spanning a 45-year period consisting of most of the adult lives of the participants, point to an important conclusion about personality coherence. Personality may not be destiny, but it leads to some predictable life outcomes, such as infidelity, marital unhappiness, and divorce.

Interestingly, neuroticism also plays a role in another important life outcome—resilience after losing a spouse. A fascinating longitudinal study showed that one of the best predictors of coping well with the death of a spouse was the personality disposition of emotional stability (Bonanno et al., 2002). A total of 205 individuals were assessed several years prior to the death of their spouse and again 18 months after their spouse's demise. Those high on emotional stability grieved less, showed less depression, and displayed the quickest psychological recovery. Individuals low on emotional stability (high on neuroticism) were still psychologically anguished a year and a half later. Personality, in short, affects many aspects of romantic life: who is likely to get involved in a successful romantic relationship (Shiner, Masten, & Tellegen, 2002); which marriages remain stable and highly satisfying (Kelly & Conley, 1987); which people are more likely to get divorced (Kelly & Conley, 1987); and how people cope following the loss of a spouse (Bonanno et al., 2002).

Alcoholism, Drug Use, and Emotional Disturbance

Personality also predicts the later development of alcoholism and emotional disturbance (Conley & Angelides, 1984). Of the 233 men in one longitudinal study, 40 were judged to develop a serious emotional problem or alcoholism. These 40 men had earlier been rated by their acquaintances as high on neuroticism. Specifically, they had neuroticism scores roughly three-fourths of a standard deviation higher than men who did not develop alcoholism or a serious emotional disturbance.

Furthermore, early personality characteristics were useful in distinguishing between the men who had become alcoholic and those who had developed an emotional disturbance. Impulse control was the key factor. The alcoholic men had impulse control scores a full standard deviation lower than those who had an emotional disturbance. Other studies also find that those high on Sensation Seeking and Impulsivity, and low on traits such as Agreeableness and Conscientiousness, tend to use and abuse alcohol more than their peers (Cooper et al., 2003; Hampson et al., 2001; Markey, Markey, & Tinsley, 2003; Ruchkin et al., 2002). Low levels of Agreeableness and Conscientiousness are also linked to substance abuse (prescription and illegal drugs) in mid-life (Turiano et al., 2012). In sum, neuroticism and impulsivity early in life are coherently linked with socially relevant outcomes later in life.

Religiousness and Spirituality

Another important life outcome pertains to spirituality—the degree to which individuals embrace religion or seek to lead a spiritual life. Personality traits in adolescence predict these outcomes in late adulthood. Adolescents who scored high on conscientiousness and agreeableness were more likely to score high on religiousness later in life (Wink et al., 2007). Openness to experience, in contrast, was the only personality trait in adolescence that predicted spirituality seeking in late life. Personality in youth, in short, appears to influence spirituality and religiousness later in life, regardless of the early socialization practices to which people are exposed.

Education, Academic Achievement, and Dropping Out

Impulsivity also plays a key role in education and academic achievement. Kipnis (1971) had a group of individuals self-report on their levels of impulsivity. He also obtained their SAT scores, which are widely regarded as measures of academic achievement and potential. Among those with low SAT scores, there was no link between impulsivity and subsequent grade point average. Among those with high SAT scores, however, the impulsive individuals had consistently lower GPAs than did their less impulsive peers. Furthermore, the impulsive individuals were more likely to flunk out of college than were those who were less impulsive. Another researcher found a similar link, showing a correlation of −.47 between peer ratings of impulsivity before entry into college and GPA subsequently (Smith, 1967). Impulsivity (or lack of self-control) continues to affect performance in the workplace. One longitudinal study looked at personality dispositions at age 18 and work-related outcomes at age 26 (Roberts, Caspi, & Moffitt, 2003). They found that those who were high on self-control at age 18 had higher occupational attainment, greater involvement with their work, and more financial security at age 26. Conversely, the impulsive 18-year-olds were less likely to progress in their work, showed less psychological involvement, and experienced lower financial security.

The personality trait of Conscientiousness turns out to be the single best predictor of successful achievement in school and work. High Conscientiousness at age 3 predicts successful academic performance nine years later (Abe, 2005). Observer-based assessment of children's conscientiousness at ages 4 to 6 predicts school grades nine years later (Asendorpf & Van Aken, 2003). Conscientiousness of children assessed between the ages of 8 and 12 predicts academic attainment two decades later (Shiner, Masten, & Roberts, 2003). Although other personality traits also predict successful academic performance, such as Emotional Stability (Chamorro-Premuzic & Furnham, 2003a, 2003b), and Agreeableness and Openness (Hair & Graziano, 2003), Conscientiousness is the most powerful longitudinal predictor of success in school and work. The predictive power of Conscientiousness on educational outcomes has been replicated in other countries such as Luxembourg (Spengler et al., 2013).

A relatively new much-hyped personality trait purported to predict education and achievement is *Grit*—defined by both perseverance and passion toward long-term goals (Duckworth et al., 2007). A massive meta-analysis of the Grit literature shows that it is highly correlated with Conscientiousness (Crede et al., 2016). Even after controlling for Conscientiousness, however, the perseverance facet of Grit does predict academic success, although the passion for long-term goals does not. Persistence seems to pay off more than pure passion when it comes to achievement.

Interestingly, work experiences also have an effect on personality change (Roberts et al., 2001). Those who attain high occupational status at age 26 have become happier, more self-confident, less anxious, and less self-defeating since they were 18 years old. Those who attain high work satisfaction also become less anxious and less prone to stress in their transition from adolescence to young adulthood.

Finally, what about people who attain financial success in the workplace? These individuals not only become less alienated and better able to handle stress, but they also increase their levels of social closeness—they like people more, turn to others for comfort, and like being around people. In sum, just as personality at age 18 predicts work outcomes at age 26 (e.g., self-control predicts income), work outcomes predict personality change over time. We see again that impulsivity is a critical personality factor that is linked in meaningful ways with later life outcomes.

Health and Longevity

How long people live and how healthy or sickly they become during their years of life are exceptionally important developmental outcomes. It may come as a surprise that your personality actually predicts how long you are likely to live. The most important traits conducive to living a long life are *high conscientiousness, positive emotionality (extraversion), low levels of hostility,* and *low levels of neuroticism* (Danner, Snowdon, & Friesen, 2001; Friedman et al., 1995; Miller et al., 1996; Mroczek et al., 2009). There are several paths through which these personality traits affect longevity (Ozer & Benet-Martinez, 2006). First, conscientious individuals engage in more health-promoting practices, such as maintaining a good diet and getting regular exercise; they also avoid unhealthy practices such as smoking and becoming a "couch potato." Conscientious children in elementary school, for example, end up smoking less and drinking less alcohol when they are adults fully 40 years later (Hampson et al., 2006). Conscientiousness at age 17 also predicts refraining from engaging in legal (nicotine, alcohol) and illegal drug use three years later (Elkins et al., 2006). Those low on Conscientiousness in adolescence are more likely to get addicted in young adulthood to drugs of all sorts. Moreover, conscientious individuals are more likely to follow doctors' orders and adhere to the treatment plans they recommend. Being low on Conscientiousness (being impulsive, or low on self-control) during the preschool years predicts high levels of risk-taking during adolescence (Honomichl & Donnellan, 2012). Being impulsive (undercontrolled) in childhood predicts an increased likelihood of high blood pressure and stroke 40 years

A Closer Look   Adult Outcomes of Children with Temper Tantrums

In a longitudinal study spanning 40 years, Caspi et al. (1987) explored the implications of childhood personality for adult occupational status and job outcomes. He identified a group of explosive, undercontrolled children, using interviews with their mothers as the data source. When the children were 8, 9, and 11, their mothers rated the frequency and severity of their temper tantrums. Severe tantrums were defined as behaviors involving biting, kicking, striking, throwing things, screaming, and shouting. From the sample, 38 percent of the boys and 29 percent of the girls were classified as having frequent and uncontrolled temper tantrums.

These children were followed throughout life, and the adult manifestations of childhood personality for men were especially striking. The men who as children had frequent and severe temper tantrums achieved lower levels of education in adulthood. The occupational status of their first job was also consistently lower than that of their calmer peers. The explosive children who had come from middle-class backgrounds tended to be downwardly mobile, and by midlife their occupational attainment was indistinguishable from that of their working-class counterparts. Furthermore, they tended to change jobs frequently, showed an erratic work pattern with more frequent breaks from employment, and averaged a higher number of months being unemployed.

Because 70 percent of the men in the sample served in the military, their military records could also be examined. The men who as children had been classified as having explosive temper tantrums attained a significantly lower military rank than their peers. Finally, nearly half (46 percent) of these men were divorced by the age of 40, compared with only 22 percent of the men without a childhood history of temper tantrums. In sum, early childhood personality shows coherent links with important adult social outcomes, such as job attainment, frequency of job switching, unemployment, military attainment, and divorce.

It is easy to imagine why explosive, undercontolled individuals tend to achieve less and get divorced more. Life consists of many frustrations, and people deal with their frustrations in different ways. Explosive undercontrollers are probably more likely to blow up and yell at the boss, for example, or to quit their jobs during an impulsive moment. Similarly, explosive undercontrollers are probably more likely to vent their frustrations on their spouses or perhaps even to impulsively have an extramarital affair. All of these events are likely to lead to lower levels of job attainment and higher levels of divorce.

later (Chapman & Goldberg, 2011). And being impulsive also predicts unhealthy weight gain and weight fluctuations in later adulthood (Sutin et al., 2011).

Second, extraverts are more likely to have lots of friends, leading to a good social support network—factors linked with positive health outcomes. And third, low levels of hostility, a component of neuroticism, put less stress on the heart and cardiovascular system—a topic explored in greater detail in Chapter 18. High levels of neuroticism are also linked with poor health behaviors, such as smoking, although neuroticism predicts mortality even after statistically controlling for smoking (Mroczek et al., 2009). It also aids intelligence. High childhood intelligence predicts lower morality risk over 40 years (Wrulich et al., 2015). In sum, the personality traits of conscientiousness, positive emotionality (extraversion), and low hostility predict both positive health outcomes and longevity.

Predicting Personality Change

Can we predict who is likely to change in personality and who is likely to remain the same? In a fascinating longitudinal study, Caspi and Herbener (1990) studied middle-aged couples over an 11-year period. The couples were tested twice, once in 1970 and again in 1981. All the subjects had been born in either 1920–21 or 1928–29 and were part of a larger longitudinal project.

The question that intrigued Caspi and Herbener was this: Is the choice of a marriage partner a cause of personality stability or change? Specifically, if you marry someone who is similar to you, do you tend to remain more stable over time than if you marry someone who is different from you? They reasoned that similarity between spouses would support personality stability, because the couple would tend to reinforce one another on their attitudes, seek similar external sources of stimulation, and perhaps even participate together in the same social networks. Marrying someone who is unlike oneself, in contrast, may offer attitudinal clashes, exposure to social and environmental events that one might not otherwise seek alone, and generally create an environment uncomfortable to maintaining the status quo.

Using personality measures obtained on both husbands and wives, Caspi and Herbener divided the couples into three groups: those who were highly similar in personality, those who were moderately similar in personality, and those who were low in similarity. Then they examined the degree to which the individuals showed stability in personality over the 11-year period of midlife in which they were tested. The results are shown in Figure 5.5.

As you can see in Figure 5.5, the people married to spouses who were highly similar to themselves showed the most personality stability. Those married to spouses least similar to themselves showed the most personality change. The moderate group fell in between. This study is important in pointing to a potential source of personality stability and change—the selection of spouses. It will be interesting to see whether future research can document other sources of personality stability and change—perhaps by examining the selection of similar or dissimilar friends, or by selecting college or work environments that show a good "fit" with one's personality traits upon entry into these environments (Roberts & Robins, 2004).

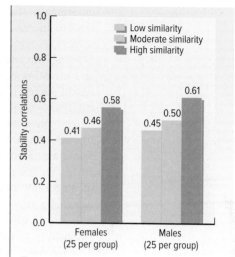

Figure 5.5

The figure shows the stability of personality over time as a function of the similarity (low, medium, or high) of the person to his or her spouse. Men and women who are married to someone similar to themselves in personality show the highest levels of personality stability over time.

Source: Caspi & Herbener, 1990.

SUMMARY AND EVALUATION

Personality development includes both the continuities and changes over time. There are three forms of personality stability: (1) rank order stability is the maintenance of one's relative position within a group over time; (2) mean level stability is the maintenance of the average level of a trait or characteristic over time; and (3) personality coherence is predictable changes in the manifestations of a trait. We can examine personality development at three levels of personality analysis: the population level, the group differences level, and the individual differences level.

There is strong evidence for personality rank order stability over time. Temperaments such as activity level and fearfulness show moderate to high levels of stability during infancy. Activity level and aggression show moderate to high levels of stability during childhood. Bullies in childhood tend to become juvenile delinquents in adolescence and criminals in adulthood. Personality traits, such as those captured by the five-factor model, show moderate to high levels of stability during adulthood. As a general rule, the stability coefficients decrease as the length of time between the two periods of testing increases.

Personality also changes in predictable ways over time. With respect to the Big Five, Neuroticism generally decreases over time; people become a bit more emotionally stable as they age. Furthermore, Agreeableness and Conscientiousness tend to increase over time. All these changes suggest increased maturity, as the sometimes tumultuous times of adolescence settle out into the maturity of adulthood. Moving into adult roles such as a serious romantic relationship, becoming a parent, and investing heavily in work appears to increase people's level of Conscientiousness. From early adolescence to early adulthood, men's self-esteem tends to increase, whereas women's self-esteem tends to decrease. In adulthood, there is some evidence from a study of creative architects that flexibility and impulsivity decline with increasing age. Sensation seeking also declines predictably with age. And in women, femininity tends to decrease over time, notably from the early forties to the early fifties. On the other hand, several studies suggest that the personality characteristics of autonomy, independence, and competence tend to increase as people get older, especially among women.

In addition to personality change due to age, there is also evidence that mean personality levels can be affected by the social cohort in which one grows up. Jean Twenge has documented several such effects, most notably on women's levels of assertiveness or dominance. Women's assertiveness levels were high following the 1930s, in which women had to be extremely independent; they fell during the 1950s and 1960s, when women were largely homemakers and fewer became professionals. From 1967 to 1993, however, women's levels of assertiveness increased, corresponding to changes in their social roles and increasing participation in professional occupations.

Personality also shows evidence of coherence over time. Early measures of personality can be used to predict socially relevant outcomes later in life. High levels of neuroticism in both sexes and impulsivity in men, for example, predict marital dissatisfaction and divorce. Neuroticism early in adulthood is also a good predictor of later alcoholism and the development of emotional problems. Impulsivity plays a key role in the development of alcoholism and the failure to achieve one's academic potential. Highly impulsive individuals tend to get poorer grades and drop out of school more than their less impulsive peers. Children with explosive temper tantrums tend to manifest their personalities as adults through downward occupational mobility, more frequent job switching, lower attainment of rank in the military, and higher frequencies of divorce. People who are impulsive at age 18 tend to do more poorly in the workplace—they attain less occupational success and less financial security. Work experiences, in turn, appear to affect personality change. Those who attain occupational success tend to become happier, more self-confident, and less anxious over time.

Although little is known about what factors maintain these forms of personality stability and coherence over time, one possibility pertains to our choices of marriage partners. There is evidence that we tend to choose those who are similar to us in personality, and the more similar our partners, the more stable our personality traits remain over time.

How can we best reconcile the findings of considerable personality stability over time with evidence of important changes? First, longitudinal studies have shown conclusively that personality traits, such as those subsumed by the Big Five, show substantial rank order stability over time. These personality traits also show evidence of coherence over time. Bullies in middle school, for example, tend to become criminals in adulthood. Those with self-control and conscientiousness in adolescence tend to perform well academically and well in the workplace later in life. In the context of these broad brushstrokes of stability, it is also clear that people show mean level changes with age—as a group people become less neurotic, less anxious, less impulsive, lower in sensation seeking, more agreeable, and more conscientious. Some changes are more pronounced in women—they become less feminine and more competent and autonomous over time. And some personality change affects only some individuals, such as those who succeed in the workplace. In short, although personality dispositions tend to be stable over time, they are not "set in plaster" in the sense that some change occurs in some individuals some of the time.

KEY TERMS

personality development 124

rank order stability 124

mean level stability 125

mean level change 125

personality coherence 125

temperament 129

longitudinal studies 130

actometer 130

stability coefficients 131

validity coefficients 131

self-esteem 139

cohort effects 143

The Biological Domain

© Svisio/Getty Images RF

The biological domain refers to those physical elements and biological systems within our bodies that influence or are influenced by our behaviors, thoughts, and feelings. For example, one type of physical element within our bodies that may influence our personalities is our genes. Our genetic makeup determines whether our hair is curly or straight, whether our eyes are blue or brown, and whether we have large, heavy bones or a slight build. Our genetic makeup influences how active we are, whether we are hot-tempered and disagreeable, and whether we like to be with others or prefer solitude. Understanding whether and how genetics contribute to personality falls squarely within the biological domain.

Another area in which biology and personality intersect is in the physiological systems, such as the brain, where subtle differences among people might contribute to personality differences. For example, some people might have more activity in the right half than in the left half of their brains. Empirically, we know that this imbalance of activation is linked with a tendency to experience distress and other negative emotions more strongly. Here, physical differences among people are associated with differences in emotional style. Because these differences represent enduring and stable ways that people differ from one another, these physiological features represent aspects of personality (see Chapter 7).

The literature in personality psychology contains many examples of physiological measures that are considered to be correlates of personality. The finding that shy children show elevated heart rates when in the presence of strangers, compared to nonshy children, is one example (Kagan & Snidman, 1991). Would eliminating the heart rate reactivity make the shy child less shy? Probably not. This is because the physiological response is a *correlate* of the traits in question,

rather than an underlying substrate that *produces* or *contributes* to the personality trait.

This is not to say that studying physiological correlates of personality is a worthless endeavor. On the contrary, physiological measures often reveal important *consequences* of personality. For example, the high cardiovascular reactivity of Type A persons may have serious consequences for developing heart disease. For this reason identifying physiological measures that are correlates of personality is also a scientifically useful and important task.

On the other hand, there are several modern theories of personality in which underlying physiology plays a more central role in *generating* or forming the substrate of specific personality differences. In Chapter 7, we consider several of these theories in detail. Each shares the notion that specific personality traits are based on underlying physiological differences. Each theory also assumes that if the underlying physiological substrate is altered, the behavior pattern associated with the trait will be altered as well.

The third biological approach we cover is based on Charles

Darwin's theory of evolution. Adaptations that helped members of the species to survive and reproduce were passed on as evolved characteristics. For example, primates who could walk upright could colonize open fields, and their hands were freed for using tools. Evidence for the evolution of such physical characteristics is solid.

Psychologists are now considering evidence for the evolution of psychological characteristics. They are taking the principles of evolution, such as natural selection, and applying them to an analysis of psychological traits. For example, natural selection may have operated on our ancestors to select for group cooperation; those early humans who were able to cooperate and work in groups were more likely to survive and reproduce, and those who preferred not to cooperate were less likely to become an ancestor. Consequently, the desire to be part of a cooperative group may be an evolved psychological characteristic that is present in today's population of humans. Evolutionary perspectives on personality are discussed in Chapter 8.

© Svisio/Getty Images RF

Genetics and Personality

6

THE BIOLOGICAL DOMAIN

A record of the past is written in the genetic blueprint.
© Lonely/Shutterstock.com RF

The Jim twins are identical twins separated at birth and raised in different adoptive families. They met for the first time when they were 39 years old, having been apart for their entire lives. One of the twins, Jim Springer, made the first phone call on February 9, 1979, after learning that he had a twin brother, Jim Lewis, who was living in the Midwest. They had an instant connection; three weeks after the phone call, Jim became the best man at his brother's wedding.

When they first met, the Jim twins displayed an astonishing set of similarities. Both weighed 180 pounds. Both were 6 feet tall. They had each been married twice, and in each case their first wives were named Linda and their second wives named Betty. Each had a son named James. Their jobs were also similar—each worked part-time as a sheriff. Both smoked Salem cigarettes and drank Miller Lite beer. Both suffered from the same kind of headache syndrome, and both had a habit of biting their fingernails. Both left love notes for their wives scattered around the house. And both had remarkably similar personality scores on standardized tests (Segal, 1999).

The Jim twins were not identical in all ways, of course. One was a better writer, the other a better speaker. They wore their hair differently; one combed his hair down over his forehead, and the other combed his hair back. But overall, the similarities were striking, especially since they had grown up from infancy in entirely different families. This is a single twin pair, and of course no conclusions can be drawn from one case. But the case of the Jim twins raises the intriguing question "What is the role of genetics in influencing personality?"

The Human Genome

Genome refers to the complete set of genes an organism possesses. The human genome contains between 20,000 and 25,000 genes. All these genes are located on 23 pairs of chromosomes. Each person inherits one set of each pair of chromosomes from the mother and one set from the father. One way to think about the human genome is to consider it to be a book containing 23 chapters, with each chapter being a chromosome pair. Each one of the chapters contains several thousand genes. And each gene consists of long sequences of DNA molecules. One astonishing fact is that the nucleus of each cell within the body contains two complete sets of the human genome, one from the mother and one from the father. The only exceptions are red blood cells, which do not contain any genes, and female egg cells and male sperm cells, each of which contains only one copy of the human genome. Because the body contains roughly 100 trillion cells (a million times a million), each of which is smaller than the head of a pin, each of us has roughly 100 trillion copies of our genome within our bodies.

The Human Genome Project is a multibillion-dollar research endeavor dedicated to sequencing the entire human genome—that is, to identifying the particular sequence of DNA molecules in the human species. On June 26, 2000, scientists made headlines by announcing that they had completed the first draft of the complete human genome. Identifying the sequence of DNA molecules does not mean identifying all the functions of these DNA molecules. Scientists now have the "book" of life, but they must still figure out what role the genes play in the body, mind, and behavior.

Some findings appear to be turning standard assumptions about the human genome on its head. Two findings are especially noteworthy. First, although the number of genes humans possess is similar to the number of genes estimated for mice and worms, the *manner* in which human genes get decoded into proteins turns out to be far more variable than in other species. These alternative forms of decoding create a tremendous variety of proteins—many more than seen in mice or worms—and may account for the complex differences we observe between rodents and humans (Plomin, 2002). Second, these protein-coding genes, making up roughly 2 percent of the human genome, are only part of the story. Many parts of the other 98 percent of the DNA in the human chromosomes used to be chalked up as **"genetic junk"** because scientists believed that these parts were functionless residues that served no purposes. Genetic researchers are discovering that this "junk DNA" is not junk at all. Rather, parts of these chunks of DNA have an impact on humans, potentially affecting everything from a person's physical size to personality (Gibbs, 2003; Plomin, 2002). These hidden layers of complexity in the human genome—given names such as "pseudogenes" and "riboswitches"—mean that we have a long way to go before understanding the complex and mysterious links between genes and human behavior.

Most of the genes within the human genome are the same for each individual on the planet. That is why all normally developing humans have many of the same characteristics: 2 eyes, 2 legs, 32 teeth, 10 fingers, a heart, a liver, 2 lungs, and so on. A small number of these genes, however, are different for different individuals. Thus, although all humans have two eyes, some people have blue eyes, some have brown eyes, and a few even have violet eyes. Some of the genes that differ from individual to individual influence physical characteristics, such as eye color, height, and bone width. Some genes that differ across individuals influence the behavioral characteristics that define human personality.

Controversy About Genes and Personality

Perhaps no other area of personality psychology has been fraught with as much controversy as the study of behavioral genetics. Researchers in this field attempt to determine the degree to which individual differences in personality are caused by genetic and environmental differences. Scientific reports on behavioral genetic studies often make headlines and cover stories. On January 2, 1996, for example, *The New York Times* caused a stir with reports of a scientific breakthrough: "Variant Gene Is Connected to a Love of the Search for New Thrills." It reported the discovery of a specific gene for novelty seeking—the tendency to be extraverted, impulsive, extravagant, quick-tempered, excitable, and exploratory. A November 5, 2012, news article proclaimed that "Being Perfectionist Lies in Your Genes" (http://www.newstrackindia .com/newsdetails/2012/11/05/161-Being-perfectionist-lies-in-your-genes.html). Some popular media sources are proposing "designer babies," where parents select from a genetic checklist the characteristics they would like in their children. These ideas are controversial because they suggest that genetic differences among individuals, rather than differences in parental socialization or personal experience, are responsible for shaping the core features of human personality.

Part of the reason for the controversy is ideological. Many people worry that findings from behavioral genetics will be used (or misused) to support particular political agendas. If individual differences in thrill seeking, for example, are caused by specific genes, then does this mean that we should not hold juvenile delinquents responsible for stealing cars for joy rides? If scientists trace a behavior pattern or personality trait to a genetic component, some people worry that such findings might lead to pessimism about the possibilities for change.

Another part of the controversy concerns the idea of eugenics. **Eugenics** is the notion that we can design the future of the human species by fostering the reproduction of persons with certain traits and by discouraging the reproduction of persons without those traits. Many people are concerned that findings from genetic studies might be used to support programs intended to prevent some individuals from reproducing or, even worse, to bolster the cause of those who would advocate that some people be eliminated in order to create a "master race."

However, modern psychologists who study the genetics of personality are typically extremely careful in their attempts to educate others about the use and potential misuse of their findings (Plomin et al., 2013). Knowledge is better than ignorance, they argue. If people believe that hyperactivity, for example, is caused by parenting behaviors when in fact hyperactivity turns out to be primarily influenced by genes, then attempts to influence hyperactive behavior by altering parental practices could cause frustration and resentment on the part of the parents. Furthermore, psychologists maintain that genetic findings need not lead to the evil consequences that some worry about. Finding that a personality characteristic has a genetic component, for example, does not mean that the environment is powerless to modify that characteristic. Let's now turn to the field of genetics and personality to discover what lies beneath the swirling controversy.

Goals of Behavioral Genetics

To understand the primary goals of the field of behavioral genetics, let's look at a concrete example—individual differences in height. Some individuals are tall, such as basketball player LeBron James (6 feet, 8 inches). Other individuals are short, such as actor Danny DeVito (around 5 feet). Geneticists focus on the key question, "What causes some individuals to be tall and others to be short?"

In principle, there can be a variety of causes of individual height differences. Differences in diet while growing up, for example, can cause differences in height among people. Genetic differences can also account for some of the differences in height. One of the central goals of genetic research is to determine the percentage of an individual difference that can be attributed to genetic differences and the percentage due to environmental differences.

In the case of height, both environmental and genetic factors are important. Clearly, children tend to resemble their parents in height—generally, tall parents have taller than average children and short parents have shorter than average children. And genetic research has confirmed that roughly 90 percent of the individual differences in height are indeed due to genetic differences. The environment, which contributes 10 percent to individual differences in height, is far from trivial. In the United States, average adult height has increased in the entire population by roughly 2 inches over the past century, most likely due to increases in the nutritional value of the food eaten by U.S. citizens. This example brings home an important lesson: even though some observed differences among people can be due to genetic differences, this does not mean that the environment plays no role in modifying the trait.

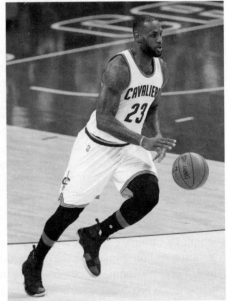

In determining height, genetics accounts for 90 percent of the variation, and environmental factors, such as diet, account for 10 percent of the variation. The actor Danny DeVito is nearly 2 feet shorter than basketball player LeBron James.

Left © Helga Esteb/Shuttertstock.com RF; Right © Jason Miller/Getty Images Sport/Getty Images

Exercise

Can you think of some human characteristics that you consider to be mostly under genetic influence? Consider, for example, individual differences in eye color. Can you think of other characteristics that are not very much influenced by genetic factors? Consider, for example, individual differences in eating with forks versus eating with chopsticks. How might you go about proving that some individual differences are, or are not, influenced by genetic differences?

The methods used by behavioral geneticists examined in this chapter can be applied to any individual difference variable. They can be used to identify the causes of differences in height and weight, differences in intelligence, differences in personality traits, and even differences in attitudes, such as liberalism or conservatism.

Behavioral geneticists typically are not content simply with figuring out the **percentage of variance** due to genetic and environmental causes. *Percentage of variance* refers to the fact that individuals vary, or are different from each other, and this variability can be partitioned into percentages that are due to different causes. Behavioral geneticists also are interested in determining the ways in which genes and the environment interact and correlate with each other. And they are interested in figuring out precisely where in the environment the effects are taking place—in parental socialization practices, for example; in the teachers to whom children are exposed; or even in peer influences (Harris, 2007). We turn to these more complex issues toward the end of this chapter. First, we must examine the fundamentals of behavioral genetics: What is heritability, and what methods do geneticists use to get their answers?

What Is Heritability?

Heritability is a statistic that refers to the proportion of observed variance in a *group* of individuals that can be accounted for by genetic variance (Plomin et al., 2001). It describes the degree to which genetic differences among individuals cause differences in an observed property, such as height, extraversion, or sensation seeking. Heritability may be one of the most frequently misunderstood concepts in psychology. If precisely defined, however, it provides useful information in identifying the genetic and environmental determinants of personality.

Heritability has a formal definition: *the proportion of phenotypic variance that is attributable to genotypic variance.* **Phenotypic variance** refers to observed individual differences, such as in height, weight, or personality. **Genotypic variance** refers to individual differences in the total collection of genes possessed by each person. Thus a heritability of .50 means that 50 percent of the observed phenotypic variation is attributable to genotypic variation. A heritability of .20 means that only 20 percent of the phenotypic variation is attributable to genotypic variation. In these examples, the environmental component is simply the proportion of phenotypic variance that is *not* attributable to genetic variance. Thus, a heritability of .50

means that the environmental component is .50. A heritability of .20 means that the environmental component is .80. These examples illustrate the simplest cases and assume that there is no correlation or interaction between genetic and environmental factors.

The environmental contribution is defined in a similar way. Thus, the percentage of observed variance in a *group* of individuals that can be attributed to environmental (nongenetic) differences is called **environmentality.** Generally speaking, the larger the heritability, the smaller the environmentality and vice versa.

Exercise

Discuss the meaning of the following statement: "All normally developing humans have language, but some people speak Chinese, others French, and others English." To what degree is variability in the language spoken due to variability in genes or variability in the environment in which one is raised?

Misconceptions About Heritability

One common misconception about heritability is that it can be applied to a single individual. It can't. It is meaningful to say that individual differences in height are 90 percent heritable, but it makes absolutely no sense to say, "Meredith's height is 90 percent heritable." You cannot say, for example, that the first 63 inches of her height are due to genes and the other 7 inches are due to the environment. For an individual, genes and environment are inextricably intertwined. Both play a role in determining height, and they cannot be separated. Thus, heritability refers only to differences in a sample or population, not to an individual.

Another common misconception about heritability is that it is constant. In fact, it is nothing of the sort. Heritability is a statistic that applies only to a population at one point in time and in a particular array of environments. If the environments change, then heritability can change. For example, in principle, heritability can be high in one population (e.g., among Swedes) but low in another (e.g., among Nigerians). And heritability can be low at one time and high at another time. Heritability always depends on both the range of genetic differences in the population and on the range of environmental differences in that population. To draw on a concept from Chapter 2, heritability does not always generalize across persons and places.

A final common misconception is that heritability is an absolutely precise statistic (Plomin et al., 2001). Nothing could be further from the truth. Error or unreliability of measurement, for example, can distort heritability statistics. And because heritability statistics are typically computed using correlations, which themselves fluctuate from sample to sample, further imprecision creeps in. In sum, heritability is best regarded merely as an *estimate* of the percentage of phenotypic differences due to genetic differences. It is not precise. It does not refer to an individual. And it is not eternally fixed (see Johnson et al., 2011, for a more detailed treatment of what heritability means and its limits).

Nature–Nurture Debate Clarified

Clarifying the meaning of the term *heritability*—what it is and what it is not—allows us to think more clearly about the **nature-nurture debate**—the arguments about whether genes or environments are more important determinants of personality. The clarification comes from clearly distinguishing between two levels of analysis: the level of the individual and the level of a population of individuals.

At the level of an individual, there is no nature-nurture debate. Every individual contains a unique constellation of genes. And those genes require environments during one's life to produce a recognizable individual. At this moment, each person reading these pages is the product of an inseparable intertwining of genes and environment. It makes no sense to ask "Which is more important, genes or environment, in accounting for Sally?" At the individual level of analysis, there is simply no issue to debate. As an analogy, consider baking a cake. Each particular cake consists of flour, sugar, eggs, and water. It makes no sense to ask whether the finished cake is "caused" more by the flour or more by the eggs. Both are necessary ingredients, inextricably combined and inseparable in the finished cake. Genes and environment for one individual are like flour and eggs for one cake—both ingredients are necessary, but we cannot logically disentangle them to see which is more important.

At the level of the population, however, we can disentangle the influence of genes and environments. This is the level of analysis at which behavioral geneticists operate. It makes perfectly good sense to ask, "Which is more important in accounting for individual differences in trait *X*—genetic differences or environmental differences?" At the population level, we can partition the differences into these two sources: differences in genes and differences in environments. And for a particular population at a given point in time, we can make sensible statements about which is more important *in accounting for the differences*. Consider the cake example. If you have 100 cakes, it makes sense to ask whether the differences among the cakes in, say, sweetness are caused more by differences in the amount of flour used or by differences in the amount of sugar used.

Now consider physical differences among people. Individual differences in height, for example, show a heritability of roughly .90. Individual differences in weight show a heritability of roughly .50. And individual differences in mate preferences—the qualities we desire in a marriage partner—show very low heritabilities of roughly .10 (Waller, 1994). Thus, it is meaningful to say that genetic differences are more important than environmental differences for height. Genetic and environmental factors are roughly equal when it comes to weight. And environmental differences are overwhelmingly important for mate preferences.

The next time you get into a debate with someone about the nature-nurture issue, be sure to ask, "Are you asking the question at the level of the individual or at the level of individual differences within a population?" Only when the level of analysis is specified can the answers make any sense.

Behavioral Genetic Methods

Behavioral geneticists have developed an array of methods for teasing apart the contributions of genes and environments as causes of individual differences. Selective breeding with animals is one method. Family studies provide a second method. A third, and perhaps the most well-known, method is that of twin studies. Adoption studies provide a fourth behavioral genetic method. We briefly discuss the logic of each of these methods, exploring where heritability estimates come from.

Selective Breeding—Studies of Humans' Best Friend

Artificial selection—as occurs when dogs are bred for certain qualities—can take place only if the desired characteristics are under the influence of heredity. **Selective breeding** occurs by identifying the dogs that possess the desired characteristic and having them mate only with other dogs that also possess the characteristic. Dog breeders have been successful precisely because many of the qualities they wish specific dog breeds to have are moderately to highly heritable.

Some of these heritable qualities are physical traits, characteristics that we actually see, such as size, ear length, wrinkled skin, and coat of hair. Other characteristics we might try to breed for are more behavioral and can be considered personality traits (Gosling, Kwan, & John, 2003). Some dogs, such as pit bulls, are, on average, more aggressive than most other dogs. Other breeds, such as the Labrador, are, on average, very sociable and agreeable. And others, such as the Chesapeake Bay retriever, have a strong desire to please their owners by retrieving objects. All of these behavioral traits—aggressiveness, agreeableness, and the desire to please—are characteristics that have been established in these animals through selective breeding.

If the heritability for these personality traits in dog breeds is literally zero, then attempts to breed dogs selectively for such traits will be doomed to fail. On the other hand, if the heritability of these personality traits is high (e.g., >80 percent), then selective breeding will be highly successful and will occur rapidly. The fact that selective breeding has been so successful with dogs tells us that heredity must be a factor in the personality traits, such as aggressiveness, agreeableness, and desire to please, that were successfully selected. For obvious ethical reasons, we cannot do selective breeding experiments on people. Fortunately, however, there are other methods of behavioral genetics that can be used to study humans.

The Labrador retriever and the Chesapeake Bay retriever have been selectively bred for certain characteristics. Both have webbed feet, for example, which makes them strong swimmers and excellent water retrievers. They have also been selectively bred for certain "personality" characteristics. The Labrador was bred to be sociable and friendly, whereas the Chesapeake Bay dog was bred to be loyal to only one owner and suspicious of strangers. Consequently, the Chesapeake Bay retriever makes a good watch dog in addition to its skills as a sporting dog. The Labrador, however, is the most popular family dog in America, most likely due to the unrestrained friendliness and cheerful disposition of this breed.

Left © Comstock Images/Alamy Stock Photo RF; Right Courtesy of Randy J. Larsen

Family Studies

Family studies correlate the degree of genetic relatedness among family members with the degree of personality similarity. They capitalize on the fact that there are known degrees of genetic relatedness among family members. Parents are usually not related to each other genetically. However, each parent shares 50 percent of his or her genes with each of the children. Similarly, siblings share 50 percent of their genes, on average. Grandparents and grandchildren share 25 percent of their genes, as do uncles and aunts with their nieces and nephews. First cousins share only 12.5 percent of their genes.

If a personality characteristic is highly heritable, then family members with greater genetic relatedness should be more similar to each other than are family members with less genetic relatedness. If a personality characteristic is not at all heritable, then even family members who are closely related genetically, such as parents and children, should not be any more similar to each other than are family members who are less genetically related to each other.

Family members who share the same genes also typically share the same environment. Two members of a family might be similar to each other not because a given personality characteristic is heritable, but rather because of a shared environment. For example, certain brothers and sisters may be similar on shyness not because of shared genes, but because of shared parents. For this reason, results from family studies alone can never be viewed as definitive. A more compelling behavioral genetic method is that of twin studies.

The family study method assumes that for traits with a large genetic component, the degree of similarity among relatives on that trait will be in proportion to the amount of genetic relatedness or degree of kinship, among them.
© John Lund/Tiffany Schoepp/Blend Images LLC RF

Twin Studies

Twin studies estimate heritability by gauging whether identical twins, who share 100 percent of their genes, are more similar to each other than are fraternal twins, who share only 50 percent of their genes. Twin studies, and especially studies of twins reared apart, have received tremendous media attention. The Jim twins, described at the beginning of this chapter, are identical twins given up for adoption at birth. Because they were adopted into different families, they were unaware that they had a twin. When they met for the first time, to everyone's astonishment these men shared many behavioral habits—having the same favorite TV shows, using the same brand of toothpaste, owning a Jack Russell terrier dog, and so on. They also shared many personality traits, such as being highly conscientious and emotionally stable, as measured by valid personality scales. Is this coincidence? Perhaps, but these coincidences seemed to happen with unusual regularity in the course of studying twins (Segal, 1999).

Twin studies take advantage of a fascinating quirk of nature. Nearly all individuals come from a single fertilized egg, and humans—as contrasted with some other mammals, such as mice—typically give birth to a single child at a time. Occasionally, however, twins are born, occurring only once in 83 births (Plomin et al., 2013). Twins come in two distinct types: identical and fraternal.

Twins come in two varieties: monozygotic and dizygotic. Can you identify which of these two pairs of twins is more likely to be monozygotic? Which pair is definitely dizygotic? What is the clue that helps you answer these questions?

Left © by golf9c9333/Getty Images RF; Right © Digital Vision/Getty Images RF

Identical twins, technically called **monozygotic (MZ) twins**, come from a single fertilized egg (or zygote—hence, *monozygotic*), which divides into two at some point during gestation. No one knows why fertilized eggs occasionally divide. They just do. Identical twins are remarkable in that they are genetically identical, like clones, coming from the same single source. They share literally 100 percent of their genes.

The other type of twin is not genetically identical to the co-twin; instead, such twins share only 50 percent of their genes. They are called fraternal twins, or **dizygotic (DZ) twins,** because they come from two eggs that were separately fertilized (*di* means "two," so *dizygotic* means "coming from two fertilized eggs"). Fraternal twins can be same sex or opposite sex. In contrast, identical twins are always the same sex because they are genetically identical. Dizygotic twins are no more alike than regular siblings in terms of genetic relatedness. They just happen to share the same womb at the same time and have the same birthday; otherwise, they are no more similar than are ordinary brothers and sisters. Of all the twins born, two-thirds are fraternal, or dizygotic, and one-third are identical, or monozygotic.

The twin method capitalizes on the fact that some twins are genetically identical, sharing 100 percent of their genes, whereas other twins share only 50 percent of their genes. If fraternal twins are just as similar to each other as identical twins are, in terms of a particular personality characteristic, then we can infer that the characteristic under consideration is not heritable: the greater genetic similarity of identical twins, in this case, is not causing them to be more similar in personality. Conversely, if identical twins are substantially *more similar* to each other than are fraternal twins on a given characteristic, then this provides evidence that is compatible with a heritability interpretation. In fact, studies have shown that identical twins are more similar than fraternal twins in dominance, height, and the ridge count on their fingertips (Plomin et al., 2008), suggesting that heritability plays a causal role in influencing these individual differences. For dominance, identical twins are correlated +.57, whereas fraternal twins are correlated only +.12 (Loehlin & Nichols, 1976). For height, identical twins are correlated +.93, whereas fraternal twins are correlated only +.48 (Mittler, 1971).

There are several formulas for calculating heritability from twin data, each with its own problems and limitations. One simple method, however, is to double the difference between the MZ correlation and DZ correlation:

$$\text{heritability}^2 = 2(r_{mz} - r_{dz})$$

In this formula, r_{mz} refers to the correlation coefficient computed between pairs of monozygotic twins, and r_{dz} refers to the correlation between the dizygotic twins. Plugging in the correlations for height, for example, leads to the following heritability estimate: heritability of height $= 2(.93 - .48) = .90$. Thus, according to this formula, height is 90 percent heritable and 10 percent environmental (as the total has to add up to 100 percent). The basic logic of this method can be applied to any characteristic: personality traits, attitudes, religious beliefs, sexual orientation, drug use habits, and so on.

We must note an important assumption of the twin method. This assumption is known as the **equal environments assumption**. The twin method assumes that the environments experienced by identical twins are no more similar to each other than are the environments experienced by fraternal twins. If they are more similar, then the greater similarity of the identical twins could be due to the fact that they experience more similar environments rather than the fact that they have more genes in common. If identical twins are treated by their parents as more similar than fraternal twins are treated by their parents—for example, if the parents of identical twins dress them in more similar clothing than do the parents of fraternal twins—then the greater similarity of the identical twins might be due to more similar treatment.

Behavioral geneticists have been worried about the validity of the equal environments assumption and so have designed studies to test it. One approach is to examine twins who have been misdiagnosed as identical or fraternal (Scarr, 1968; Scarr & Carter-Saltzman, 1979). That is, some twins who were believed to be identical by their parents were really just fraternal. And some twins whose parents believed them to be fraternal turned out to be identical. These mistakes in labeling allowed the researchers to examine whether fraternal twins who were *believed* to be identical were in fact more similar to each other than accurately labeled fraternal twins. Similarly, it allowed the researchers to examine whether the identical twins, believed to be fraternal, were in fact less similar to each other than identical twins correctly labeled as identical. The findings on a variety of cognitive and personality tests supported the validity of the equal environments assumption. The parents' beliefs and labeling of the twins did not affect their actual similarity on the personality and cognitive measures. This means that, however twins are labeled, the environments experienced by identical twins do not seem to be functionally more similar to each other than the environments experienced by fraternal twins.

Additional studies over the years have continued to support the equal environments assumption (e.g., Loehlin & Nichols, 1976; Lytton, Martin, & Eaves, 1977). Although it is true that identical twins do tend to dress more alike than fraternal twins, spend more time together, and have more friends in common, there is no evidence that these environmental similarities cause them to be any more similar in their personalities than they are to begin with (Plomin et al., 2008).

Adoption Studies

Adoption studies is one of the most powerful behavioral genetic methods available. In an adoption study, one can examine the correlations between adopted children and their adoptive parents, with whom they share no genes. If one finds a positive correlation between adopted children and their adoptive parents, then this provides strong evidence for environmental influences on the personality trait in question.

Similarly, we can examine the correlations between adopted children and their genetic parents, who had no influence on the children's environments. If we find a zero correlation between adopted children and their genetic parents, again this is strong evidence for a lack of heritable influence on the personality trait in question. Conversely, if we find a positive correlation between parents and their adopted-away children, with whom they have had no contact, then this provides evidence for heritability.

Adoption studies are especially powerful because they allow us to get around the equal environments assumption, which must be made in twin studies. In twin studies, because parents provide both genes and environments to their children, and may provide more similar environments for identical than for fraternal twins, there is a potential compromise of the equal environments assumption. In adoption studies, however, genetic parents provide none of the environmental influences on their children, thus unconfounding genetic and environmental causes.

Adoption studies, however, have potential problems of their own. The most important potential problem is the assumption of representativeness. Adoption studies assume that adopted children, their birth parents, and their adoptive parents are representative of the general population. For example, these studies assume that couples who adopt children are not any different from couples who do not adopt children. Fortunately, the assumption of representativeness can be tested directly. Several studies have confirmed that the assumption of representativeness holds for cognitive abilities, personality, education level, and even socioeconomic status (Plomin & DeFries, 1985; Plomin, DeFries, & Fulker, 1988).

Another potential problem with adoption studies is **selective placement**. If adopted children are placed with adoptive parents who are similar to their birth parents, then this may inflate the correlations between the adopted children and their adoptive parents. Fortunately, there does not seem to be selective placement, so this potential problem is not a problem in actual studies (Plomin et al., 2008).

One of the most powerful behavioral genetic designs is one that combines the strengths of twin and adoption studies at the same time, by studying twins reared apart. In fact, the correlation between identical twins reared apart can be interpreted directly as an index of heritability. If identical twins reared apart show a correlation of +.65 for a particular personality characteristic, then that means that 65 percent of the individual differences are heritable. Unfortunately, identical twins reared apart are exceedingly rare. Painstaking efforts have been undertaken to find such twins and study them (Segal, 1999). The effort has been well worth it, as such studies have yielded a bounty of fascinating results, to which we now turn. A summary of the traditional behavioral genetic methods, along with their advantages and limitations, is shown in Table 6.1.

Table 6.1 Summary of Traditional Behavioral Genetic Methods

Method	Advantages	Limitations
Selective breeding studies	Can infer heritability if selective breeding works	Are unethical to conduct on humans
Family studies	Provide heritability estimates	Violate equal environments assumption
Twin studies	Provide both heritability and environmentality estimates	Sometimes violate equal environments assumption
Adoption studies	Provide both heritability and environmentality estimates; get around the problem of equal environments assumption	Adopted kids might not be representative of population; problem of selective placement

Major Findings from Behavioral Genetic Research

This section summarizes what is known about the heritability of personality. The results may surprise you.

Personality Traits

The most commonly studied personality traits in behavioral genetic designs are Extraversion and Neuroticism. Recall that Extraversion is a dimension containing people who are outgoing and talkative at one end and people who are quiet and withdrawn at the other (introverted) end. Neuroticism is a dimension with one end characterized by people who are anxious, nervous, and emotionally volatile and at the other end calm and emotionally stable. Henderson (1982) reviewed the literature on more than 25,000 pairs of twins. He found substantial heritability for both traits. In one study involving 4,987 twin pairs in Sweden, for example, the correlations for Extraversion were +.51 for identical twins and +.21 for fraternal twins (Floderus-Myrhed, Pedersen, & Rasmuson, 1980). Using the simple formula of doubling the difference between the two correlations yields a heritability of .60.

The findings for Neuroticism is similar (Floderus-Myrhed et al., 1980). The identical twin correlation for Neuroticism is +.50, whereas the fraternal twin correlation is only +.23. This suggests a heritability of .54. Twin studies have yielded very similar results, suggesting that Extraversion and Neuroticism are traits that are approximately half due to genetics. A large-scale twin study, conducted in Australia, found a heritability for Neuroticism of 47 percent (Birley et al., 2006). Similar moderate heritabilities continue to be found for Neuroticism and Extraversion in more recent samples using diverse measurement methods (Loehlin, 2012; Moore et al., 2010).

The findings for Extraversion and Neuroticism from adoption studies suggest somewhat lower heritabilities. Pedersen (1993), for example, found heritability estimates based on comparisons of adoptees and their biological parents of about 40 percent for Extraversion and about 30 percent for Neuroticism. Correlations between adoptive parents and their adopted children tend to be around zero, suggesting little *direct* environmental influence on these traits.

Individual differences in *activity level* have also been subjected to behavioral genetic analysis. You may recall from Chapter 5 that individual differences in activity level, measured with a mechanical recording device called an actometer, emerge early in life and show stability in children over time. Activity level was assessed in an adult sample of 300 monozygotic and dizygotic twin pairs residing in Germany (Spinath et al., 2002). The researchers measured the physical energy each individual expended through body movements, recorded mechanically with motion recorders analogous to self-winding wristwatches. Movement of a person's limbs activates the device, which records the frequency and intensity of body activity. Activity level showed a heritability of .40, suggesting that a moderate proportion of the individual differences in motor energy are due to genetic differences.

The trait of activity level—how vigorous and energetic a person is—shows a moderate degree of heritability

© Maskot/Alamy Stock Photo RF

Activity level is one among several temperaments that show moderate heritability. A study of 1,555 twins in Poland found 50 percent heritability, on average, for all temperaments, including activity, emotionality, sociability, persistence, fear, and distractibility (Oniszczenko et al., 2003). A study of Dutch twins, at ages 3, 7, and 10, found even higher heritabilities for aggressiveness, ranging from 51 to 72 percent (Hudziak et al., 2003).

Behavioral genetic studies also have examined other personality dispositions. Using 353 male twins from the Minnesota Twin Registry, researchers explored the heritability of psychopathic personality traits (Blonigen et al., 2003). These include traits such as Machiavellianism (e.g., enjoys manipulating other people), Coldheartedness (e.g., has a callous emotional style), Impulsive Nonconformity (e.g., indifferent to social conventions), Fearlessness (e.g., a risk taker; lacks anticipatory anxiety concerning harm), Blame Externalization (e.g., blames others for one's problems), and Stress Immunity (e.g., lacks anxiety when faced with stressful life events). All of these "psychopathic" personality traits showed moderate to high heritability. For example, for Coldheartedness, the r_{mz} was +.34, whereas the r_{dz} was −.16; for Fearlessness, the r_{mz} was +.54, whereas the r_{dz} was only .03. Using the method of doubling the difference between the MZ and DZ correlations suggests *substantial* heritability to all of these psychopathic-related personality dispositions (Vernon et al., 2008; Niv et al., 2012). The heritability of psychopathic personality traits, which predispose individuals to criminal activity, may be the key reason that a massive study from Sweden of more than a million individuals showed the heritability of violent crime to be roughly 50% (Frisell et al., 2012).

Interestingly, heritability of personality might not be limited to our own species. In a study of chimpanzees, Weiss, King, and Enns (2002) explored the heritability of dominance (high extraversion, low neuroticism) and well-being (e.g., seems happy and contented), as indexed by trained observer judgments. Individual differences in chimpanzee well-being showed a moderate heritability of .40, whereas dominance showed an even stronger heritability of .66. These findings suggest that the importance of genes in influencing personality may not be restricted to humans but instead may extend to other primates.

Behavioral genetic studies using more comprehensive personality inventories have been carried out in many different countries as personality research expands to include more and more cross-cultural work. A study of 296 twin pairs in Japan revealed moderate heritability for Cloninger's Seven-Factor model of temperament and character, which includes dispositions such as novelty seeking, harm avoidance, reward dependence, and persistence (Ando et al., 2002). A study of twins in Germany, using observational methodology, revealed a 40 percent heritability to markers of the Big Five (Borkenau et al., 2001). Similar findings for the Big Five personality traits have been documented in Canada and Germany using self-report measures (Jang et al., 2002; Moore et al., 2010).

One of the most fascinating studies to examine personality traits is the Minnesota Twin Study (Bouchard & McGue, 1990; Tellegen et al., 1988). This study examined 45 sets of identical twins reared apart and 26 sets of fraternal twins reared apart. The researchers found the correlations shown in Table 6.2 between identical twins reared apart. These findings startled many people. How could traditionalism, for example, which reflects an attitude or a preference for the established ways of doing things, show such strong heritability? Traits that we intuitively think of as environmentally determined, such as self-esteem, have moderate heritabilities (Kamakura, Ando, & Ono, 2007). Even character traits that we sometimes think of as instilled by parents and teachers—compassion, integrity, courage, and tolerance—turn out to be strongly linked

Table 6.2 Correlations Between Identical Twins Reared Apart

Personality Trait	Twin Correlation
Sense of well-being	.49
Social potency	.57
Achievement orientation	.38
Social closeness	.15
Neuroticism	.70
Sense of alienation	.59
Aggression	.67
Inhibited control	.56
Low risk taking	.45
Traditionalism	.59
Absorption or imagination	.74
Average twin correlation	**.54**

Sources: Bouchard & McGue, 1990; Tellegen et al., 1988.

to traditional personality traits and show moderate heritabilities (Steger et al., 2007). And how could neuroticism have such a high heritability, given the traditional view that it is parents who make their children neurotic by their inconsistency of reinforcement and improper attachment? These behavioral genetic findings caused some researchers to question long-held assumptions about the origins of individual differences, a topic we consider later in this chapter under the heading "Shared Versus Nonshared Environmental Influences: A Riddle."

Summaries of the behavioral genetic data for many of the major personality traits—Extraversion, Agreeableness, Conscientiousness, Neuroticism, Openness to experience—yield heritability estimates of approximately 50 percent (Bouchard & Loehlin, 2001; Caspi, Roberts, & Shiner, 2005). A recent meta-analysis of personality traits in more than 100,000 participants revealed a slightly lower heritability of 40 percent (Vukasovic & Bratko, 2015). A different meta-analysis, however, showed heritabilities of 48 percent for Neuroticism and 49 percent for Extraversion (van den Berg et al., 2014). Furthermore, it is clear that the heritability of personality is heavily responsible for the fact that personality traits remain fairly stable over time (Blonigen et al., 2006; Briley & Tucker-Drob, 2014; Caspi et al., 2005; Johnson et al., 2005; Kamakura et al., 2007; Kandler et al., 2010; van Beijsterveldt et al., 2003). Overall, major personality traits show a modest degree of heritability. The same studies, however, also suggest that a substantial portion of the variance in personality traits is environmental in origin.

Attitudes and Preferences

Stable attitudes are generally regarded to be part of personality: they show wide individual differences; they tend to be stable over time; and at least sometimes they are linked with actual behavior. Behavioral geneticists have examined the heritability of attitudes.

The Minnesota Twin Study showed that traditionalism—as evidenced by attitudes favoring conservative values over modern values—showed a heritability of .59.

A longitudinal study of 654 adopted and nonadopted children from the Colorado Adoption Project revealed significant genetic influence on conservative attitudes (Abrahamson, Baker, & Caspi, 2002). Markers of conservative attitudes included whether participants agreed or disagreed with specific words or phrases such as "death penalty," "gay rights," "censorship," and "Republicans." Significant genetic influence emerged as early as 12 years of age in this study. Other studies confirm the moderate heritability of values (Renner et al., 2012). For example, twin studies of 19 measures of political ideologies from five different countries revealed heritabilities ranging between 30 and 60 percent (Hatemi, 2014).

Genes also appear to influence occupational preferences. Occupational preferences are not mere whims, but can have important effects on a person's life work, wealth, and eventual social status. In a study of 435 adopted and 10,880 genetic offspring residing in Canada and the United States, Ellis and Bonin (2003) had participants respond to 14 different aspects of prospective jobs, using a scale ranging from 1 (not at all appealing) to 100 (extremely appealing). The 14 job aspects were high income, competition, prestige, envied by others, taking risks, element of danger, controlling others, feared by others, little supervision, independence, job security, part of a team, clear responsibilities, and help others. These occupational preferences were then correlated with seven measures of parental social status, including mother's and father's education level, occupational status, and income. A full 71 percent of the correlations were statistically significant for the genetic children, whereas only 3 percent were significant for the adopted children (suggesting that rearing environment does not create the effect). The authors conclude that "this study not only suggests that the genes influence various preferences related to occupations, but that these preferences have an effect on the social status attainment" (p. 929). In short, occupational preferences such as desire for competition and wealth can lead to choosing occupations in which more status and income are actually achieved. The jobs in which we spend a large portion of our lives and the prestige and income that comes from those jobs are at least partly influenced by the genes we inherit from our parents.

Not all attitudes and beliefs show these levels of moderate heritability, however. One study of 400 twin pairs yielded heritabilities of essentially zero for beliefs in God, involvement in religious affairs, and attitudes toward racial integration (Loehlin & Nichols, 1976). A study of adopted and nonadopted children confirmed that there is no evidence of a heritable influence on *religious* attitudes (Abrahamson et al., 2002). Another study also found extremely low heritability (12 percent) for religiousness, as measured by items such as "frequency of attending religious services," during adolescence (Koenig et al., 2005). In adulthood (average age of 33), however, the heritability of religiousness had increased to 44 percent. These and other findings suggest that genes have an increasingly important role in religiousness as people move from adolescence into adulthood (Button et al., 2011).

No one knows why some attitudes appear to be partly heritable. Are there specific genes that predispose people to be more conservative? Or are these heritabilities merely incidental byproducts of genes for other qualities? Future research in behavioral genetics will be able to address these questions and provide an answer to the mystery of why some attitudes appear to be partly heritable.

Drinking and Smoking

Drinking and smoking are often regarded as behavioral manifestations of personality dispositions, such as sensation seeking (Zuckerman & Kuhlman, 2000), extraversion

A Closer Look

Sexual Orientation

Sexual orientation refers to the object of a person's sexual desires, whether the person is sexually attracted to those of the same sex or the opposite sex. These differences tend to be relatively stable over time. Moreover, these differences are associated with important life outcomes, such as the social groups with which one affiliates, the leisure activities one pursues, and the lifestyle one adopts. By the definition of personality provided in Chapter 1, sexual orientation clearly falls well within the scope of personality.

Is homosexuality inherited? Psychologist Michael Bailey has conducted the most extensive studies of this issue. Bailey and his colleagues examined the twin brothers of a sample of homosexuals, as well as the adoptive brothers of another sample of homosexuals. Heritability estimates from all studies ranged from 30 percent to a strikingly high 70 percent. Similar heritabilities were found in a sample of lesbians and their adoptive sisters (Bailey et al., 1993).

These heritability findings come on the heels of another startling discovery, which was published in *Science* magazine (LeVay, 1991). Brain researcher Simon LeVay discovered that homosexual and heterosexual men differ in a specific area of the brain known as the hypothalamus. One area of the hypothalamus, the medial preoptic region, appears to be partially responsible for regulating male-typical sexual behavior (LeVay, 1993, 1996). LeVay obtained the brains of gay men who had died of AIDS and compared them with the brains of heterosexual men who had died of AIDS or other causes. He found that the size of the medial preoptic region of the hypothalamus—the region believed to regulate male-typical sexual behavior— was two to three times *smaller* in the gay

men, compared with that of the heterosexual men. Unfortunately, given the extremely expensive nature of brain research, the samples in this study were quite small. Moreover, no one has yet replicated these findings.

Behavioral geneticist Dean Hamer has published some evidence that male sexual orientation is influenced by a gene on the X chromosome (Hamer & Copeland, 1994). However, this finding also needs to be replicated, and several researchers have debated its validity (e.g., see Bailey, Dunne, & Martin, 2000).

Obviously, this research area is controversial, and the findings are hotly debated. Moreover, the genetic studies of homosexuality have attracted their share of critics. The studies have been challenged on the grounds that the samples, which were secured from advertisements in lesbian and gay publications, were unrepresentative (Baron, 1993).

Another weakness in past studies was a neglect of the correlates of sexual orientation. For example, childhood gender nonconformity is strongly related to adult sexual orientation. Gay men as adults recall having been feminine boys, and lesbian women as adults recall being masculine girls. This association is strong and has been established with many sources of data (e.g., using peer reports of childhood gender non-conformity).

Results of recent, well-controlled studies find concordance rates for homosexual orientation to be about 20 percent, much lower than previously thought.
© Jakob Helbig/Getty Images RF

Regarding the importance of gender nonconformity in childhood, a leading researcher has remarked that "it is difficult to think of other individual differences that so reliably and so strongly predict socially significant outcomes across the life span, and for both sexes, too" (Bem, 1996, p. 323).

Bailey and his colleagues set out to clear up these weaknesses— unrepresentative samples and lack of accounting for childhood gender nonconformity—by conducting one of the largest twin studies of adult sexual orientation to date (Bailey, Dunne, et al., 2000). The

(Continued)

A Closer Look (*Continued*)

participants were from a sample of almost 25,000 twin pairs in Australia, out of which approximately 1,000 MZ and 1,000 DZ twins participated. Their average age at time of participation was 29 years. The participants completed a questionnaire about childhood (before age 12) participation in a variety of sex-stereotyped activities and games. They also completed a detailed questionnaire on adult sexual orientation and activity, such as "when you have sexual daydreams, how often is your sexual partner male? how often female?"

The women were more likely than the men to have slight homosexual feelings without being exclusively homosexual, whereas the men tended to be either exclusively heterosexual or exclusively homosexual. Just over 3 percent of the men, but

only 1 percent of the women, were predominantly or exclusively homosexual in sexual attraction and sexual fantasy.

Regarding whether homosexual orientation runs in families, this study found lower rates than previous studies, at 20 percent concordance for the identical twin men and 24 percent concordance for the identical twin women. Concordance is the probability that one twin is gay if the other is also gay. Previous studies typically found concordance rates ranging between 40 and 50 percent. Bailey argues that previous studies overestimate genetic contributions due to selecting participants by advertising in gay and lesbian magazines.

In the Bailey, Dunne, et al. (2000) study, participants were randomly selected from a large pool of twins, so there was no

selection bias. It seems likely that the real rate of genetic contribution to sexual orientation is lower than previously thought. Childhood gender non-conformity did, however, show significant heritability for both men (50 percent heritability) and women (37 percent heritability). This finding provides some support for Bem's (1996) theory that childhood gender non-conformity may be the inherited component of adult sexual orientation.

In summary, the findings from behavioral genetics and brain research point to the fascinating possibility that sexual orientation—an individual difference that is linked with the social groups one associates with, the leisure activities one pursues, and the lifestyle one adopts—may be partly heritable.

(Eysenck, 1981), and neuroticism (Eysenck, 1981). Individuals differ widely in their smoking and drinking habits, and although consumers sometimes quit for good and abstainers sometimes start, these differences tend to be stable over time. Individual differences in drinking and smoking habits also show evidence of heritability. In one study of Australian twins, an MZ twin who smoked was roughly 16 times more likely than an MZ twin who did not smoke to have a twin who smoked (Hooper et al., 1992). The comparable figures for DZ twins were only a sevenfold increase, suggesting evidence of heritability. Similar findings were obtained in a sample of 1,300 Dutch families of adolescent Dutch twins (Boomsma et al., 1994). These studies also point simultaneously to the importance of environmental factors—a point taken up in the following section.

Heritability studies of alcohol drinking are more mixed. Some studies find heritability for boys, but not for girls (Hooper et al., 1992). Other studies find heritability for girls, but not for boys (Koopmans & Boomsma, 1993). Most studies, however, show moderate heritability for both sexes, ranging from .36 to .56 (Rose, 1995).

Heritability studies of alcoholism, as opposed to everyday drinking habits, show even stronger heritabilities. Indeed, nearly all show heritabilities of .50 or greater (Kendler et al., 1992). In one study, the heritabilities of alcoholism were 67 percent in women and 71 percent in men (Heath et al., 1994). Interestingly, the same study found a genetic linkage between alcoholism and "conduct disorder" (antisocial behavior), suggesting that the genes for both tend to occur in the same individuals.

Marriage and Satisfaction with Life

A fascinating study revealed that genes can even influence the propensity to marry or stay single (Johnson et al., 2004). The heritability estimate for propensity to marry turned out to be an astonishing 68 percent! One causal path is through personality characteristics. Men who got married, compared to their single peers, scored higher on social potency and achievement—traits linked with upward mobility, success in careers, and financial success. These traits are also highly valued by women in selecting marriage partners (Buss, 2016). Thus, a genetic proclivity to marry occurs, at least in part, through heritable personality traits that are desired by potential marriage partners.

Genes also play an interesting role in marital satisfaction. First, individual differences in women's marital satisfaction are roughly 50 percent heritable (Spotts et al., 2004) (this study could not evaluate the heritability of a husband's marital satisfaction). Second, the personality characteristics of wives, notably dispositional optimism, warmth, and low aggressiveness, accounted for both their own marital satisfaction and their husband's marital satisfaction (Spotts et al., 2005). Thus, the marital satisfaction of both women and men seems partly to depend on the moderately heritable personality dispositions of the wives. Interestingly, husbands' personality did not explain as much of their own or their wives' marital satisfaction. Taken together, these results suggest that genes play a role in the quality of marriages, and even who gets divorced versus staying married (Jerskey et al., 2010), in part through heritable personality characteristics.

If heritable personality contributes to marital satisfaction, what about overall satisfaction with life overall? Heritable personality characteristics play a key role here too (Bartels, 2015). Four moderately heritable personality factors—having a sense of purpose, an orientation toward personal growth, feeling your life is under your own control, and having positive social relationships—predict psychological well-being and overall satisfaction with life (Archontaki et al., 2012). Nonetheless, the same studies show that environmental influences also play a key role in life satisfaction (Hahn et al., 2013), a topic to which we now turn.

Shared Versus Nonshared Environmental Influences: A Riddle

With all of the findings on the moderate heritability of so many personality characteristics, it is important not to lose sight of one important fact: the same studies that suggest moderate heritability also provide the best evidence for the importance of environmental influences. If many personality characteristics show heritabilities in the range of 30 to 50 percent, this means that the same characteristics show a substantial degree of environmentality—as much as 50 to 70 percent. This conclusion must be tempered, however, by the fact that all measures contain errors of measurement; some of the differences in personality might be attributable to *neither* environmental nor genetic differences, but rather to errors of measurement.

One critical distinction behavioral geneticists make is between **shared** and **nonshared environmental influences.** Consider siblings—brothers and sisters in the same family. Some features of their environment are shared: the number of books in the home; the presence or absence of a TV, DVD player, or computer; the quality and quantity of food in the home; the parents' values and attitudes; and the schools, church, synagogue, or mosque the parents send the children to. All of these are features of the shared environment. On the other hand, the same brothers and sisters do not share *all* features of their environment. Some children might get special treatment from their parents. They might have different groups of friends. They might occupy different rooms in the house. One might go to summer camp, whereas the others stay home each summer. All of these features are called nonshared because they are *experienced differently* by different siblings.

Exercise

Make a list of five shared environmental influences you have in common with your siblings (or, if you are an only child, what things might be shared environmental influences if you had siblings). Then list five nonshared environmental influences. Which had the strongest influence on your personality, attitudes, or behavior?

We know that the environment exerts a major influence on personality. But *which* environment matters most—the shared or the nonshared environment? Some behavioral genetic designs allow us to figure out whether the environmental effects come more from shared or from nonshared sources. The details of how this is done are too technical to examine in this book, but, if you are interested, you can check out Plomin and colleagues (2013) for more details.

The bottom line is this: for most personality variables, the shared environment has either little or no impact. Adoption studies show that the average correlation for personality variables between adopted siblings who share much of their environment, but who share no genes, is only .05. This suggests that even though these siblings grow up together—with the same parents, same schools, same religious training, and so on—whatever is happening in their shared environment (e.g., parenting, rearing practices, values education) is not causing them to be similar in personality.

Instead, most environmental causes appear to stem from the aspects of the environment that siblings experience differently. Thus, it's not the number of books in the home. It's not parental values or parental attitudes toward child rearing. In fact, it's not what most psychologists have long believed it is. Rather, the critical environmental influences on personality appear to lie in the unique experiences of individual children.

Which unique experiences are important? Well, here we run into a brick wall. Most theories of socialization over the decades have focused exclusively on the shared environment, such as poverty and parental attitudes toward child rearing. It is only recently that psychologists have begun to study nonshared environments.

There are two possibilities of what they will find. One possibility is a major breakthrough—a discovery of a critically important environmental variable that has been overlooked by psychologists who for years focused only on the shared environment. Different peer influences may be one good candidate (Harris, 2007). The other possibility is less satisfying. It is conceivable that there are so many environmental variables that exert an impact on personality that each one alone might account only for a tiny fraction of the variance (Willerman, 1979). If this is the case, then we are stuck with the discovery of many small effects.

Does this mean that the shared environment accounts for nothing? Have psychologists been entirely misguided in their thinking by their focus on shared effects? The answer is no. In some areas, behavioral genetic studies have revealed tremendously important shared environmental influences: attitudes, religious beliefs, political orientations, health behaviors, and to some degree verbal intelligence (Segal, 1999). As an example, adoptive siblings reared together but genetically unrelated are correlated .41 (girls) and .46 (boys) in their patterns of smoking and drinking (Willerman, 1979).

Thus, although smoking and drinking have a substantial genetic component, there is also a large shared environmental component.

Another study found that shared environments accounted for several personality clusters in the "adjustment" domain (Loehlin, Neiderhiser, & Reiss, 2003). These include antisocial behavior (e.g., showing behavior problems and breaking rules), depressive symptoms (e.g., moody, withdrawn), and autonomous functioning (e.g., being able to care for self in basic needs and recreational activities). And a study of adult twins using observational measurement—trait ratings of videotaped behaviors—suggests that shared environment might be more important in explaining Big Five personality traits than is typically revealed by studies using self-report (Borkenau et al., 2001). If this study is replicated by future research, it may have the far-reaching consequence of challenging the now conventional wisdom that shared environments have little effect on personality traits.

Exercise

Discuss what you think might represent shared environmental influences that contribute to the tendency to smoke. That is, what in the environment might have influenced most people who smoke to start and maintain their smoking habit?

In summary, environments shared by siblings are important in some domains. But, for many personality traits, such as extraversion and neuroticism, shared environments do not seem to matter. Instead, it is the unique environment experienced by each sibling that carries the causal weight.

Genes and the Environment

As important as it is to identify sources of environmental and genetic influence on personality, the next step requires an understanding of how genetic and environmental factors interact. More complex forms of behavioral genetic analysis involve the concepts of *genotype–environment interaction* and *genotype–environment correlation.*

Genotype–Environment Interaction

Genotype–environment interaction refers to the differential response of individuals with different genotypes to the same environments. Consider introverts and extraverts, who have somewhat different genotypes. Introverts tend to perform well on cognitive tasks when there is little stimulation in the room, but they do poorly when there are distractions, such as music blaring or people walking around. In contrast, extraverts do just fine with the music blasting, the phone ringing, and people walking in and out. But the same extraverts make a lot of errors in these cognitive tasks when there is little stimulation—when the task they are working on is boring or monotonous.

Extraversion–introversion is a perfect example of genotype–environment interaction, whereby individuals with different genotypes (introverts and extraverts) respond differently to the same environment (e.g., noise in the room). Individual differences *interact* with the environment to affect performance. You may want to take this into consideration when you arrange your studying environment. Before turning on the music, first determine whether you lie on the introverted or extraverted end of the continuum. If you are an introvert, you would likely do better studying in a quiet environment with few interruptions.

Studies have begun to identify other genotype–environment interactions. One examined the effects of abusive parenting on whether children developed antisocial personalities (Caspi, Sugden, et al., 2003). Abused children who had a genotype that produced low levels of the brain neurotransmitter monoamine oxidase A (MAOA) frequently developed conduct disorders, antisocial personalities, and violent dispositions. In contrast, maltreated children who had high levels of MAOA were far less likely to develop aggressive antisocial personalities. This study and replications of it (Kim-Cohen et al., 2006) provide excellent examples of genotype–environment interaction—exposure to the same environment (abusive parenting) produces different effects on personality, depending on the differences in genotype. Interestingly, this suggests that violent parents may create violent children *only* if the children have a genotype marked by low levels of MAOA. Similar G x E interactions have been discovered between the 5-HTT gene and childhood maltreatment in predicting persistent depression later in life. Only individuals with two short 5-HTT forms of the gene who had experienced maltreatment as children developed persistent depression (Uher et al., 2011). The empirical study of genotype–environment interactions represents one of the most exciting developments in the behavior genetics of personality (Jang et al., 2005; Moffitt, 2005), psychological disorders (McGue, 2010), health depression linked with early puberty in girls depending on socioeconomic status (Mendle et al., 2015; Johnson, 2007), and the ways in which personality is expressed in satisfied versus dissatisfied romantic relationships (South et al., 2016).

Genotype–Environment Correlation

Just as interesting is the concept of **genotype–environment correlation,** the differential exposure of individuals with different genotypes to different environments. Consider, for example, a child who has a genotype for high verbal ability. Her parents may notice this and provide her with lots of books to read, engage in intellectual discussions with her, and give her word games and crossword puzzles. Parents of children with less verbal skill, who presumably have different genotypes than those with high verbal abilities, may be less inclined to provide this stimulation. This is an example of genotype–environment correlation; individuals with different genotypes (e.g., those with high versus low verbal abilities) are exposed to different environments (e.g., high versus low stimulation). In another example, parents might promote sports activities for athletically inclined children more than for less athletically inclined children.

Plomin, DeFries, and Loehlin (1977) describe three very different kinds of genotype–environment correlation: passive, reactive, and active. **Passive genotype–environment correlation** occurs when parents provide both genes and the environment to children, yet the children do nothing to obtain that environment. Suppose, for example, that parents who are verbally inclined pass on genes to their children that make them verbally inclined. However, because the parents are highly verbal, they buy a lot of books. Thus, there is a correlation between the children's verbal ability and the number of books in their home, but it is passive in the sense that the child has done nothing to cause the books to be there.

In sharp contrast, the **reactive genotype–environment correlation** occurs when parents (or others) respond to children differently, depending on the child's genotypes. A good example is cuddlers versus non-cuddlers. Some babies love to be touched—they giggle, smile, laugh, and show great pleasure when they are handled. Other babies are more aloof and simply do not like to be touched very much. Imagine that a mother starts out touching and hugging each of her two children a lot. One child loves it; the other hates it. Over the course of several months, the mother reacts by continuing to hug the cuddler but cuts down on hugging the noncuddler. This example illustrates the reactive genotype–environment correlation, which is achieved because people react to children differently, based in part on the children's heritable dispositions.

Active genotype–environment correlation occurs when a person with a particular genotype creates or seeks out a particular environment. High sensation seekers, for example, expose themselves to risky environments: skydiving, motorcycle jumping, and drug taking. Highly intellectual individuals are likely to attend lectures, read books, and engage others in verbal discussions. This active creation and selection of environments has also been called "niche picking" (Scarr & McCartney, 1983). Active genotype–

Modern views on the nature-nurture debate suggest more complex answers to the question of the origins of personality. One view is that genes and environments interact in determining personality.
© Ingram Publishing RF

environment correlation highlights the fact that we are not passive recipients of our environments; we mold, create, and select the environments we subsequently inhabit, and some of these actions are correlated with our genotypes.

These genotype–environment correlations can be positive or negative. That is, the environment can encourage the expression of the disposition, or it can discourage its expression. Adolescents who have personalities marked by positive emotionality (e.g., an upbeat, optimistic stance) tend to evoke high levels of helpful and affirmative regard from their parents, so that genotypes for positive emotionality are positively correlated with environments of high parental regard (Krueger et al., 2008). The positive link between personality and parenting, in short, is genetically mediated (South et al., 2008). Conversely, parents of highly active children may try to get them to sit still and calm down, and parents of less active children may try to get them to perk up and be more lively, in which case there is a negative genotype–environment correlation because the parents' behavior opposes the children's traits (Buss, 1981). One meta-analysis found that children showing antisocial behavior, a moderately heritable trait, tend to elicit harsh discipline from parents who attempt to curb their behavior (Avinun & Knafo, 2014). Another example of negative genotype–environment correlation occurs when people who are too arrogant or dominant elicit negative reactions from others, who try to "cut them down" (Cattell, 1973). The key point is that environments can go against a person's genotype, resulting in a negative genotype–environment correlation, or they can facilitate the person's genotype, creating a positive genotype–environment correlation.

A study of 180 twins reared apart points to an intriguing potential example of genotype–environment correlation (Krueger, Markon, & Bouchard, 2003). The study assessed personality traits through the Multidimensional Personality Questionnaire (MPQ), which identifies three major factors of personality: Positive Emotionality (happy, content), Negative Emotionality (anxious, tense), and Constraint (controlled, conscientious). The researchers evaluated each individual's *perceptions* of the family environments in which they were raised, which yielded two main factors: Family Cohesion (e.g., parental warmth, absence of family conflict) and Family Status (e.g., parents provided intellectual and cultural stimulation, active recreational activities, and financial resources). The intriguing results were that the correlations between personality and perceptions of family environment were genetically mediated. In other words, the perceived environment in which the individuals were raised was largely due to heritable personality traits. Specifically, experiencing a cohesive family upbringing was explained by genetic influence on the two personality traits of Constraint and lack of Negative Emotionality. In contrast, recalling a family environment high in cultural and intellectual activity was explained by the heritable personality trait of Positive Emotionality.

These results may be subject to several interpretations. One interpretation is that personality affects the subjective manner in which people remember their early environments. Perhaps calm, controlled individuals are more likely to forget about real family conflict that was present during their childhood, and so may simply recall greater family cohesion than actually existed. An alternative interpretation is in terms of genotype–environment correlation: Individuals with calm, controlled personalities (high Constraint, low Negative Emotionality) may actually *promote* cohesion among family members—in essence, creating a family environment that further fosters their calm, controlled personality. Future studies of personality, parenting, and perceived family environments offer the promise of unraveling the complex ways in which genes interact and correlate with environments (Spinath & O'Connor, 2003).

Another promising avenue for exploring genotype–environment correlations is through peers (Burt, 2009; Loehlin, 2010). One study found a GE correlation for adolescent alcohol consumption based on the differential selection of peers, especially for females (Loehlin, 2010). Another found evidence for GE correlation between impulsivity, which leads to mild forms of rule breaking (e.g., drinking, smoking, vandalism), and popularity during adolescence (Burt, 2009). Thus, genes predispose some individuals to break rules, which in turn leads to greater popularity during adolescence—an example of reactive gene–environment correlation. Genes for impulsivity, in short, are correlated with a social environment of being popular—a correlation established, in part, through acts of rule breaking.

Molecular Genetics

The most recent development in the science of behavioral genetics has been the exploration of **molecular genetics.** The methods of molecular genetics are designed to identify the specific genes associated with personality traits. The details are quite technical, but the most common method, called the association method, is to identify whether individuals with a particular gene (or allele) have higher or lower scores on a particular trait than individuals without the gene (Benjamin et al., 1996; Ebstein et al., 1996).

The most frequently examined gene is called **DRD4,** which is located on the short arm of chromosome 11. This gene codes for a protein called a dopamine receptor. The function of this dopamine receptor, as you might guess, is to respond to the presence of dopamine, which is a neurotransmitter. When the dopamine receptor encounters dopamine from other neurons in the brain, it discharges an electrical signal, activating other neurons.

The most frequently examined association between the DRD4 gene and a personality trait has involved novelty seeking, the tendency to seek out new experiences, especially those considered risky, such as drug experiences, risky sexual experiences, gambling, and high-speed driving (Zuckerman & Kuhlman, 2000). Individuals with so-called long repeat versions of the DRD4 gene were found to be higher on novelty seeking than individuals with so-called short repeat versions of this gene (Benjamin et al.,

1996). The researchers hypothesized that the reason for this association is that people with long DRD4 genes tend to be relatively unre-
sponsive to dopamine. This causes them to seek out novel experiences
that give them a "dopamine buzz." In contrast, those with the short
DRD4 genes tend to be highly responsive to whatever dopamine is
already present in their brains, so they tend not to seek out novel
experiences, which might boost their dopamine to uncomfortable
levels.

Although the association between DRD4 and novelty seeking
has been replicated several times, there have also been several failures
to replicate (Plomin & Crabbe, 2000). One study, for example, found
that the DRD4 was *not* at all associated with measures of novelty
seeking (Burt et al., 2002). A second study of preschool children
found that DRD4 *was* significantly linked with mothers' reports of
their children's problems with aggression (a possible precursor to
novelty seeking) but was *not* significantly linked with observed
behavioral measures of aggression (Schmidt et al., 2002). And a third
study found that high novelty seeking was linked with a different allele of a *different*
gene—the A1 allele of the D2 dopamine receptor gene (DRD2) (Berman et al., 2002).

Part of the problem is that the size of the association is small. The original
researchers (Benjamin et al., 1996) estimate that the DRD4 gene explains only 4 percent
of the variation in novelty seeking. It has also been speculated that there may be 10 other
genes that are equally important in novelty seeking, none of which has yet been explored.
And perhaps there are 500 genes that vary with other aspects of human personality
(Ridley, 1999). It seems unlikely, therefore, that any single gene will ever be found to
explain more than a small percentage of variation in personality. One meta-analysis of
the dopamine D4 receptor (DRD4) gene has found reliable links with novelty seeking
and impulsivity (Munafo et al., 2008). As an illustration, one experiment found that men
with the 7-repeat (7R) allele of the DRD4 gene were more likely to engage in financial
risk taking than men lacking the 7R allele (Dreber et al., 2009), as shown in Figure 6.1.

Interestingly, the 7R allele of the DRD4 gene occurs at dramatically different
rates in different geographical regions. It occurs at higher rates in America than in Asia,
and has been hypothesized to be favored by evolutionary selection (see Chapter 7) when
people migrate to new environments or inhabit resource-rich environments (Chen et al.,
1999; Penke, Denissen, & Miller, 2007). Empirical evidence for this hypothesis comes
from a study of the migration patterns of 2,320 individuals from 39 groups (Chen et al.,
1999). Migratory populations showed a far higher proportion of the 7R allele of the
DRD4 gene than did sedentary populations, which could be caused by selective migration of individuals carrying those genes, selective favoring of those genes in the new
environments, or both. Evidence on sedentary and nomadic populations favors the
hypothesis that the 7R allele of the DRD4 gene is more advantageous among nomadic
than settled populations (Eisenberg et al., 2008). Men with the 7R allele may also have
an advantage in highly competitive societies in resource competition and in direct competition for access to mates (Harpending & Cochran, 2002).

As exciting as the results are from these molecular genetic methods, it is important to exercise caution when interpreting them. In several cases, researchers have found
an association between a particular gene and personality-related traits, such as anxiety
and attention deficit disorder, but subsequent researchers have failed to replicate these
associations (Plomin & Crabbe, 2000; McCue, 2010; Turkheimer et al., 2014). Furthermore, some gene-personality links are found for one gender, but not for the other. For

Figure 6.1

Men with DRD4 7R+ invest more money in a
financial risk game.

Source: Dreber et al. (2009).

example, one study found that women with one copy of the A allele at OXTR rs2254298 experienced greater attachment anxiety than did women with two copies of the G allele (Chen & Johnson, 2012). Nonetheless, this gene-personality link was not found among men. Research over the next decade or two, however, should reveal the degree to which specific genes for specific personality traits can be found. A promising method known as genome-wide association studies (GWAS), which can rapidly examine the entire genome for links with personality, may yield faster scientific advances (Turkheimer et al., 2014). A GWAS study of Extraversion produced one promising candidate (van den Berg et al., 2016). But it appears possible that personality traits may be linked to such a large number of genes, each accounting for only tiny effects, that understanding the molecular genetics of personality may be many years in the future.

Finally, rather than looking for direct links between single genes and personality or behavior, modern research in this area is beginning to explore gene-environment interactions using molecular genetic techniques (e.g., Caspi et al., 2003; South & Krueger, 2008). As noted above, stressful life events cause depressive symptoms, but *only* in people who carry the short version of the serotonin transporter (5-HTT) gene (Uher et al., 2011). For those carrying other variants of this gene, stressful life events did *not* produce depressive symptoms. This provides an illustration of the power of combining molecular genetic techniques with the important concept of gene–environment interaction.

Behavioral Genetics, Science, Politics, and Values

The history of behavioral genetic research has taken some fascinating twists and turns, which are worth noting (see Plomin et al., 2013, for an excellent summary of this history). During the past century in the United States, behavioral genetic research received what can be phrased as a "frosty reception." Findings that some personality traits were moderately heritable seemed to violate the dominant paradigm, which was environmentalism (and, especially, behaviorism). The prevailing **environmentalist view** was that personality was determined by socialization practices, such as parenting style. Furthermore, people worried about the potential misuse of findings emerging from behavioral genetics. Images of Nazi Germany sprang to mind, with the evil notions of a master race.

A large part of the controversy over genetic research on personality has centered around studies of intelligence, which has often been considered to be a personality variable. Many people have worried that findings from these studies will be misused to label some people intrinsically superior or inferior to others (e.g., see Herrnstein & Murray, 1994). Others worry that findings will be misused to give some people preferential treatment in education or job placement. Still others are concerned that standard tests of intelligence fail to capture many of the multiple facets of intelligence, such as social intelligence, emotional intelligence, and creativity. All of these are legitimate concerns, and they suggest that the findings from the field of behavioral genetics must be viewed with caution and interpreted responsibly, in terms of the larger picture of human nature and society.

In the past decade, attitudes have shifted, and the field of psychology now considers the findings from behavioral genetics as fairly mainstream. Behavioral genetic studies tend not to generate the intense controversy that they did in prior decades. Indeed, findings from sophisticated behavioral genetic research on personality are now seen as critical in combating important individual and social problems, such as the effects of stressful life events on depression.

The links between science and politics, between knowledge and values, are complex, but they need to be confronted. Because scientific research can be misused for political goals, scientists bear a major responsibility for presenting findings carefully and accurately. Science can be separated from values. Science is a set of methods for discovering what exists. Values are notions of what people *want* to exist—to be desired or sought after. Although scientists clearly can be biased by their values, the virtue of the scientific method is that it is self-correcting. The methods are public, so other scientists can check the findings, discover errors in procedure, and hence over time correct any biases that creep in. This does not imply, of course, that scientists are unbiased. Indeed, the history of science is filled with cases in which values influenced the nature of the questions posed and the acceptance or rejection of particular findings or theories. Nonetheless, the scientific method provides a system for correcting such biases in the long run.

SUMMARY AND EVALUATION

The behavioral genetic study of personality has a fascinating history. Early on, when behavioral genetic methods were being developed, the field of psychology was dominated by the behaviorist paradigm. In this context, findings from behavioral genetic research were not warmly received. Social scientists worried that findings from behavioral genetic research might be misused for ideological purposes.

Over the past two decades, the empirical evidence on heritability has become stronger and stronger, in part because of the convergence of evidence across behavioral genetic methods. There are four traditional behavioral genetic methods: selective breeding studies, family studies, twin studies, and adoption studies. Selective breeding studies cannot be ethically conducted on humans. Family studies are problematic because the genetic and environmental factors are often confounded. Twin studies have potential problems, such as violations of the equal environments assumption (the assumption that identical twins are not treated any more alike than fraternal twins) and the assumption of representativeness (the notion that twins are just like non-twins). Adoption studies also have potential problems, such as the non-random placement of adopted-away children in particular families. Empirical tests of these assumptions suggest that they are not violated much or are violated in ways that do not seem to make much difference. However, the most compelling evidence on the heritability of personality comes from looking across methods that do not share methodological problems. Thus, if the findings from twin studies *and* adoption studies converge on the same result, then we can have more confidence in the results than we can when only a single method is used.

The study of large samples of twins reared together, the study of smaller samples of identical twins reared apart, and sound adoption studies have added greatly to the credibility of behavioral genetic research. The empirical findings clearly show that personality variables, such as extraversion and neuroticism, as well as the other dimensions of the Big Five, have moderate heritability. Perhaps even more striking are the findings that drinking, smoking, attitudes, occupational preferences, and even sexual orientation appear to be moderately heritable. Equally important, however, is the finding that the same studies provide the best evidence for the importance of environmental influences. Overall, personality characteristics are 30 to 50 percent heritable and 50 to 70 percent environmental.

The environmental causes appear to be mostly of the nonshared variety—that is, the different experiences that siblings have even though they are in the same family. This finding is startling because nearly all theories of environmental influence—such as those that posit the importance of parental values and child-rearing styles—have been of the shared variety. Thus, behavioral genetic research may have provided one of the most important insights into the nature of nurture—the location of the most important environmental influences on personality. The next decade of personality research should witness progress in identifying the precise locations of these nonshared environmental influences. Separating perceived environments from objective environments will be an important part of this research program.

In interpreting the research findings, it is important to keep in mind the meaning of heritability and the meaning of environmentality. Heritability is the proportion of observed individual differences that are caused by genetic differences in a particular population or sample. It does not pertain to an individual; genetic and environmental influences are inextricably interwoven at the individual level and cannot be separated. Heritability does not mean that the environment is powerless to alter the individual differences. And heritability is not a fixed statistic—it can be low in one group and high in another, low at one time and high at another. Environmentality is the proportion of observed individual differences that is caused by environmental differences. Like heritability, environmentality is not a fixed statistic. It, too, can change over time and across situations. The discovery of a powerful environmental intervention, for example, could, in principle, dramatically increase environmentality while lowering heritability. The key point is that neither heritability nor environmentality is fixed in space and time.

In addition to providing estimates of heritability and environmentality, some behavioral genetic research examines the interactions and correlations among genetic and environmental variables. There are three major types of genotype–environment correlations: passive, reactive, and active. *Passive* genotype–environment correlation occurs when parents provide both genes and environment to their children in ways that just happen to be correlated—for example, parents who pass on genes for verbal ability and stock their houses with a lot of books. Books and verbal ability become correlated, but in a passive way because the children did not have to do anything for the correlation to occur. *Reactive* genotype–environment correlation occurs when parents, teachers, and others respond differently to some children than to others. Parents generally tickle and coo at smiley babies more than at nonsmiley babies, creating a correlation between genotypes for smiling and a cuddly social environment. The correlation occurs because parents react to babies differently. *Active* genotype–environment correlation occurs when individuals with certain genotypes seek out environments nonrandomly. Extraverted individuals, for example, might throw a lot of parties, thus surrounding themselves with a different social environment than that of the more reclusive introverts. The correlation occurs because individuals actively create it.

The more complex and interesting behavioral genetic concepts such as genotype–environment correlation have received relatively little research attention. One possible exception is the fascinating finding that individuals low on Negative Emotionality and high on Constraint recall their early family environment as being extremely cohesive. One interpretation is in terms of genotype–environment correlation: Calm, nonneurotic individuals may actually promote calmness and cohesion in their family environment, thus creating an upbringing that further fosters their calm, controlled personality.

Molecular genetics represents the most recent development in the realm of personality psychology. The research techniques attempt to establish an association between specific genes and scores on personality traits. The DRD4 gene, for example, is linked with novelty seeking. One of the most promising new developments is combining molecular genetics with the search for *gene-environment interactions*—the ways in which people with different genes react differently to the same environment. Stressful environments, for example, appear to produce depressive symptoms, but primarily in people with the short version of the serotonin transporter (5-HTT) gene.

KEY TERMS

genome 156
genetic junk 156
eugenics 157
percentage of variance 159
heritability 159
phenotypic variance 159
genotypic variance 159
environmentality 160
nature-nurture debate 161
selective breeding 162
family studies 163

twin studies 163
monozygotic (MZ) twins 164
dizygotic (DZ) twins 164
equal environments assumption 165
adoption studies 165
selective placement 166
shared environmental influences 173
nonshared environmental
  influences 173
genotype–environment
  interaction 175

genotype–environment
  correlation 176
passive genotype–environment
  correlation 176
reactive genotype–environment
  correlation 176
active genotype–environment
  correlation 177
molecular genetics 178
DRD4 gene 178
environmentalist view 180

© Svisio/Getty Images RF

Physiological Approaches to Personality

THE BIOLOGICAL DOMAIN

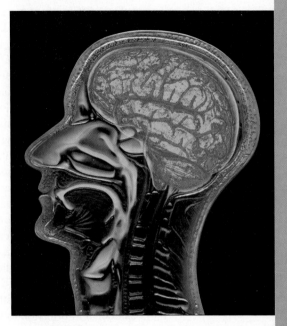

Brain imaging techniques have enabled researchers to learn more about the brain's role in behavior and personality than previously thought possible.
© Don Farrall/Getty Images RF

Elliot was a successful businessman, a proud father, and a good husband. At his firm, he was a role model for his younger colleagues. Personally, he was charming and pleasant. His social skills were such that he often was called on to settle disputes at work. Elliot was respected by others. His position in the community, his satisfying personal life, and his prosperity and professional status were all enviable.

One day Elliot began to have severe headaches. After a few days, he went to his doctor, who suspected a brain tumor. This suspicion was confirmed when a small tumor was found growing not on his brain, but on the lining of tissue that covers the brain. The location was just above his eyes, behind his forehead. The tumor was, however, pushing against his brain and had damaged a small portion of the front of his brain, part of the prefrontal cortex, which had to be removed with the tumor.

The operation went smoothly and Elliot recovered quickly, with no apparent lasting damage, at least none that could be found with ordinary tests. Elliot's IQ was tested after the operation and was found to be superior, as it was before his operation. His memory was tested and was found to be excellent. His ability to use and understand language was also unaffected by the operation. His ability to do arithmetic, to memorize lists of words, to visualize objects, to make judgments, and to read a map all remained unaffected by the operation. All his cognitive functions remained normal or above normal, completely unaffected by the removal of a small portion of his prefrontal cortex.

Elliot's family, however, reported that his personality had changed. He began to behave differently at work as well. He could not seem to manage his time properly. He needed lots of prompting from his wife to get going in the morning. Once at work, he had problems finishing tasks. If he was interrupted in a task, he had difficulty starting back up where he had left off. Often he would get captivated by one part of a task and get sidetracked for hours. For example, in refiling some books, which should have taken 15 minutes, he stopped to read one of the books and returned to his desk hours later. He knew his job but just had trouble putting all the actions together in the right order.

Soon Elliot lost his job. He tried various business schemes on his own and finally took his life savings and started an investment management business. He teamed up with a disreputable character, against the advice of many of his friends and family members. This business went bankrupt, and he lost all his savings. To his wife and children Elliot appeared to be behaving impulsively, and they had trouble coping with the difficulties he was getting into. A divorce followed. Elliot quickly remarried, but to a woman whom none of his friends or family approved of. This marriage ended quickly in another divorce. Without a source of income, and without a family to support him, Elliot became a drifter.

Elliot came to the attention of Dr. Antonio Damasio, a neurologist at the University of Iowa, who later wrote a book about Elliot's condition (Damasio, 1994). It seems that the small bit of brain matter destroyed by Elliot's tumor was essential in transmitting emotional information to the higher reasoning centers of the brain. Elliot reported that the only change in himself that he noticed was that, after his operation, he did not feel any strong emotion, or much of any emotion for that matter.

The case of Elliot shows us that the body and the mind are intimately connected. Indeed, after Elliot's operation, the biggest change in him was in his personality, not in his memory, his reasoning, or his knowledge.

Studies have shown that traumatic brain injury can lead to large changes in personality (Edmundson et al., 2015). One of the most common changes in personality following brain injury is a diminished ability to inhibit or control one's impulses. This has been found in children who experienced brain trauma (Gerring & Vasa, 2016), in adults with traumatic brain injuries (Kim, 2002), and in elderly persons whose brains have been injured by stroke (Freshwater & Golden, 2002). This increased impulsivity and lack of self-control is most likely due to disruptions between the frontal lobes, which serve as the executive control center of the brain, and other parts of the brain. As a result, persons with extensive brain injury can retain most of their cognitive abilities, yet lose some degree of self-control (Lowenstein, 2002). Persons with personality changes following traumatic brain injuries often have spontaneous outbursts, sudden changes in mood, and episodes of aggression and can become quite disruptive to their families (Beer & Lombardo, 2007). Indeed, this is the personality profile of one of the most famous brain injury patients, Phineas Gage, who was injured by an iron rod that was blasted through his brain while he was working as a railway builder in the mid-1800s (see A Closer Look).

An advantage of the physiological approach is that physiological characteristics can be measured mechanically and reliably. The term *physiological characteristics* refers to the functioning of organ systems within the body. Examples of **physiological systems** are the nervous system (including the brain and nerves), the cardiac system (including the heart, arteries, and veins), and the musculoskeletal system (including the muscles and bones, which make all movements and behaviors possible). To get an idea

A Closer Look   The Brain Injury of Phineas Gage

Phineas Gage was a nineteenth-century rail worker, serving as foreman on a construction gang preparing the way for the Rutland and Burlington Railroad in Vermont. His work involved blasting large rocks with dynamite, and one day he was injured in a serious accident. Prior to his accident, Phineas was an industrious worker, highly agreeable and conscientious, and seen by his employers as one of their most capable and efficient foremen. On September 13, 1848, he was tamping dynamite into a hole in a rock using an iron rod. The dynamite accidentally ignited and the explosion shot the iron rod out of the hole like a bullet. Phineas was bending over the work area. The iron rod he was working with was 1¼ inches in diameter, 3-feet, 7-inches long, and weighed almost 14 pounds. It was tapered at one end almost to a point. The heavy iron rod came out of the tamping hole point first. It shot up through Gage's left cheek, just below the cheek bone, passed behind his left eye and exited the top of his skull, landing approximately 75 feet away. Gage was knocked off his feet but did not lose consciousness. The iron rod destroyed a large portion of the front part of his brain. Remarkably, Gage survived this accident. He spent 10 weeks under a doctor's care,

then returned to his home in New Hampshire. Even more remarkably, most of his intellectual functions remained intact. However, his personality changed dramatically. His doctor, John Harlow, described the new Phineas Gage as "obstinate, capricious, and vacillating, devising many plans of future operations which are no sooner arranged than they are abandoned, a child, yet with the passions of a strong man" (cited in Carter, 1999). He lacked the ability to direct himself nor could he devise plans to achieve goals. He was impulsive and aggressive. He started using profane language and disregarded social conventions, behaving impolitely toward those around him. Women were advised to avoid him. He never worked as a foreman again. Instead, he had various farm jobs, mostly caring for horses and cleaning stables. He died on May 21, 1860, almost 12 years after his devastating accident. His skull and the iron rod are

Photo of Phineas Gage holding the iron rod that inflicted the serious head injury described in this Closer Look.
© Science Source

on display at Harvard's Countway Library of Medicine. See Macmillan (2000) for a modern perspective on this famous case.

---

of the importance of these physiological systems, imagine the result of removing any one of them. Without a brain, a person could not think or respond to the environment; without the musculoskeletal system, a person could not move or act on the environment; and without a cardiac system, the result is obvious. All of the physiological systems are important to the maintenance of life, and their study has resulted in the fields of medicine, anatomy, and physiology.

From the perspective of personality psychology, physiology is important to the extent that differences in physiology create, contribute to, or indicate differences in psychological functioning. For example, people differ from one another in how sensitive their nervous systems are to stimulation. Given exposure to loud noise, for example, some people find it quite irritating, whereas other people are not bothered at all.

A person who is particularly sensitive might frequent quiet environments (e.g., the library), avoid crowds (e.g., not go to loud parties), and limit the amount of stimulation in their environments (e.g., never play loud rock-and-roll music). The physiologically oriented personality psychologist would say that this person is introverted (a psychological characteristic) because he or she has an overly sensitive nervous system (a physiological characteristic). Thus, this approach assumes that differences in physiological characteristics are related to differences in important personality characteristics and behavior patterns.

Application

Individual Differences in Digit Ratio. Scholars have speculated on connections between bodily shapes and personality traits for centuries. Most simple theories have been discredited (Stelmack & Stalkas, 1991), such as the system of phrenology that related bumps on the head to aspects of personality. However, one bodily difference that is receiving attention these days is the ratio of the index finger to the ring finger, commonly called the "digit ratio" index. This ratio is easy to calculate by measuring the index and ring fingers (see graphic), and there has been a wide variety of research on the correlates of digit ratio.

One common and reliable finding is that women have a higher digit ratio than men. Women tend to have index fingers that are longer than their ring fingers, resulting in a digit ratio greater than 1.0, whereas men tend to have index fingers that are shorter than their ring fingers, resulting in a digit ratio less than 1.0. Why might this be so? Research with humans and animals (those with measurable digits, such as mice and monkeys) has confirmed that digit ratio is determined prior to birth through exposure of the fetus to testosterone in utero. Testosterone in utero also influences the development of the gonads and sexual development of the fetus. Consequently, the digit ratio after birth is thought to be a lifelong indicator of the amount of prenatal testosterone that the fetus was exposed to. The more testosterone exposure, the smaller the index finger relative to the ring finger (i.e., the smaller the digit ratio).

Prenatal testosterone exposure is greater for male fetuses than female fetuses, and hence there is a lifelong difference between the sexes in digit ratio. However, even within a single gender, the differences in digit ratio appears related to the kinds of personality traits hypothesized to be related to testosterone. These traits are described by Wilson and Daly (1985) as the "young male syndrome" and include risk taking, a tendency toward violence, and competitiveness. Using terms more connected with personality psychology, some of which are discussed in this chapter, the relevant personality traits would have to do with impulsive sensation seeking, extraversion/assertiveness/social dominance, and aggression. Although males do score higher on all three of these traits than women, research linking digit ratio to these traits is mixed.

A recent study by Wacker, Mueller, and Stemmler (2012) hypothesized that perhaps more specific traits related to aspects of the "young male" syndrome might correlate with digit ratio. Moreover, they thought this relationship might be stronger in males than females. In a study of over 200 young adult males, they administered a large number of personality scales related to the "young male" syndrome and used factor analysis to distill relatively pure and specific measures of these traits. They found a strong relationship between digit ratio and impulsive sensation seeking (men with longer ring fingers relative to their index fingers (lower digit ratio) scored higher in impulsive sensation seeking). This finding is consistent with a number of other studies that found lower digit ratio was associated with risk taking, such as participating in riskier lotteries (Garbarino, Slonim, & Sydnor, 2011), receiving more traffic violations (Schwerdtfeger, Heims, & Heer, 2010), and choosing riskier careers in finance (Sapienza, Singales, & Maestripieri, 2009). Results with women tend to be less clear, though some studies have reported that, in females, a lower digit ratio (similar to the male digit ratio) is associated with higher levels of risk taking (Honekopp, 2011). One study of female rhesus macaques monkeys found that females with lower digit ratios achieved a higher dominance status in their group (Nelson et al., 2010).

There is a vast amount of information on digit ratio on the Internet. Just enter this term in an Internet search and you will find many reports and articles. However, the research should be viewed skeptically, with an eye toward evaluating the quality of the studies reported. Looking at the best studies, we conclude that this bodily difference is very likely a lifelong signature of testosterone exposure prenatally and that it does correlate modestly with risk taking and sensation seeking as well as forms of social dominance in adulthood. There is a large gender difference in digit ratio, and within genders the correlates tend to be similar, though somewhat weaker for women. We return to a discussion of testosterone in Chapter 16 when we cover sex and gender in personality psychology.

HOW TO MEASURE YOUR FINGER

☐ With your palm up and fingers straight, measure the base of your index finger to its tip.

☐ Do the same with your ring finger.

To calculate digit ratio, divide index finger length by ring finger length.

Source: Adapted from Michael Hanlon, "What the Length of Your Index Finger Says about You," *Daily Mail.* December 3, 2010.

Another characteristic of the physiological approach to personality is simplicity or parsimony. Physiological theories often propose to explain a good deal of behavior with a few constructs. Often the theories state that a physiological difference results in a given personality difference or a difference in an important behavior pattern. Why, for example, do some people take up skydiving, race car driving, and other high-risk behaviors? One theory states that they do so because they have a deficiency of a certain chemical in their nervous systems. Despite the obvious simplicity of theories such as these, human nature is actually more complicated. For example, two people could be equally high on sensation seeking, yet one of them has satisfied this need in a socially approved manner (for instance, by becoming an emergency room doctor), whereas the other satisfies it in a socially unacceptable manner (for example, through various exciting but illegal behaviors, such as illegal gambling or drug use). Most physiologically oriented psychologists would *not* argue that "physiology is destiny." Most would agree that physiology is only one cause among many for explaining behavior.

190

As you know from Chapter 1, Gordon Allport wrote one of the first textbooks on personality (1937), and in it he argued that "[t]he organization (of personality) entails the operation of both body and mind, inextricably fused into a personal unity" (p. 48). Because personality consists of both bodily and mental aspects, its study can be approached from either direction. In this chapter, we focus on an approach to personality that focuses on underlying physiological systems.

A Physiological Approach to Personality

Most physiological personality psychologists today focus on measures of distinct physiological systems, such as heart rate or brain waves. The typical research question posed by contemporary psychologists concerns whether some people will exhibit more or less of a specific physiological response than others under certain conditions. For example, people who are introverted may avoid loud parties because they easily become overwhelmed by the social and physical stimulation at such parties. Notice that this statement specifies which particular environmental conditions (i.e., loud parties) affect which particular personality trait (i.e., introversion) to produce a particular physiological response (i.e., overwhelmed, indicated by increased heart rate), which then promotes a specific behavioral response (i.e., avoidance). These connections are depicted in Figure 7.1.

Specific statements—about which traits are connected to which psychological reactions under which conditions or in response to which stimuli—are now the

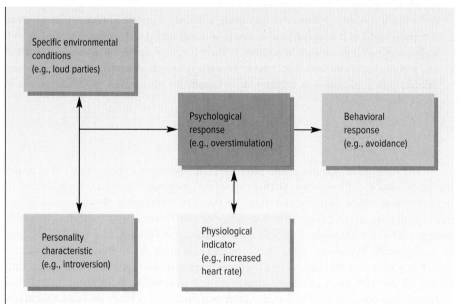

Figure 7.1

Theoretical bridge between personality and physiology: Connections among environmental conditions, personality traits, and responses build a theoretical bridge that links personality to specific situations in terms of evoking a certain psychological response, which can be identified and measured using specific physiological measures. A theory specifies which conditions or stimuli will interact with which personality traits to produce specific responses, which can be observed physiologically.

way personality psychologists talk about physiology. Researchers must be able to build such a **theoretical bridge** between the personality dimension of interest and physiological variables in order to use physiological concepts to help explain personality (Levenson, 1983; Yarkoni, 2015). Let's turn now to a brief review of physiological variables, with an emphasis on how they are measured in personality research.

Physiological Measures Commonly Used in Personality Research

Most of the common physiological measures in personality research are obtained from **electrodes,** or sensors placed on the surface of a participant's skin. They are noninvasive in that they do not penetrate the skin, and these electrodes cause practically no discomfort. One drawback to such measures is that the participant is literally wired to the physiological recording machine (often called a polygraph), so movement is constrained. A new generation of electrodes will, however, overcome this limitation through the use of **telemetry,** a process by which electrical signals are sent from the participant to the polygraph through Bluetooth, WiFi, or other radio waves instead of by wires. This is already being used with astronauts whose physiological systems are monitored constantly on Earth. Three physiological measures of particular interest to personality psychologists are electrodermal activity (skin conductance of electricity), cardiovascular measures, and activity in the brain. Other biological measures, such as the amounts of hormones in the blood are also of interest. We will discuss each of these in turn.

Electrodermal Activity (Skin Conductance)

The skin on the palms of the hands (and the soles of the feet) contains a high concentration of sweat glands. These sweat glands are directly influenced by the **sympathetic nervous system**, the branch of the **autonomic nervous system** that prepares the body for action—that is, the fight-or-flight mechanism. When the sympathetic nervous system is activated (such as during episodes of anxiety, startle, or anger), the sweat glands begin to fill with salty water. If the activation is sufficiently strong or prolonged, the sweat may actually spill out onto the palms of the hands, causing the person to develop sweaty palms. Interestingly, all mammals have a similarly high concentration of sweat glands on the friction surfaces of their hands/paws.

Even before the sweat is visible, however, it can be detected by the clever application of a small amount of electricity because water (i.e., sweat) conducts electricity. The more water present in the skin, the more easily the skin carries, or conducts, electricity. This bioelectric process, known as **electrodermal activity** (*dermal* means "of the skin"), or **skin conductance,** makes it possible for researchers to directly measure sympathetic nervous system activity.

In this technique, two electrodes are placed on the palm of one hand. A very low voltage of electricity is then put through one electrode into the skin, and the researcher measures how much electricity is present at the other electrode. The difference in the amount of electricity that is passed into the skin at one electrode and the amount detected at the other electrode tells researchers how well the skin is conducting electricity. The more sympathetic nervous system activity there is, the more water is produced by the sweat glands in the skin, and the better the skin conducts the electricity. The levels of electricity involved are so small that the participant does not feel anything.

Electrodermal responses can be elicited by all sorts of stimuli, including sudden noises, emotional images, conditioned stimuli, mental effort, pain, and emotional reactions such as anxiety, fear, and guilt (as in the so-called lie detector test, which uses skin conductance). One phenomenon of interest to personality psychologists is the observation that some people show skin conductance responses in the *absence* of any external stimuli. Imagine a participant sitting quietly in a dimly lit room who is instructed to just relax. Most people in this situation exhibit very little in the way of autonomic nervous system activity. However, some participants in this situation exhibit spontaneous electrodermal responses, even though there is nothing objectively causing these responses. Not surprisingly, the personality traits most consistently associated with nonspecific electrodermal responding are anxiety and neuroticism (Cruz & Larsen, 1995). A person who is high in anxiety and neuroticism appears to have a sympathetic nervous system that is in a state of chronic activation. This is just one example of how electrodermal measures have been used by personality psychologists to ascertain differences in personality among people.

Cardiovascular Activity

The cardiovascular system involves the heart and associated blood vessels, and examples of measures of cardiovascular activity include blood pressure and heart rate. Blood pressure is the pressure exerted by the blood on the inside of the artery walls, and it is typically expressed with two numbers: diastolic and systolic pressure. The systolic pressure is the larger number, and it refers to the maximum pressure within the cardiovascular system produced when the heart muscle contracts. The diastolic pressure is the smaller number, and it refers to the resting pressure inside the system between heart contractions. Blood pressure can increase in a number of ways—for example, the heart may pump with larger strokes generating more volume or through a narrowing of the artery walls. Both of these actions occur through activation of the sympathetic nervous system in the fight-or-flight response. Blood pressure is responsive to a number of conditions, and personality researchers have been especially interested in blood pressure response to stress.

Another easily obtained cardiovascular measure is heart rate, often expressed in beats-per-minute (BPM). Heart rate can change beat by beat, so a technique with a degree of sophistication is needed to ensure accurate measurement. One approach is to measure the time interval between successive beats. If that interval is exactly one second, then the heart rate is 60 BPM. As the time interval between beats becomes shorter, the heart is beating faster, and vice versa. By measuring the intervals between successive heartbeats, the psychologist can get a readout of heart rate on a beat-by-beat basis. Heart rate is important because as it increases, it indicates that the person's body is preparing for action—to flee or to fight, for example. It tells us that the person is distressed, anxious, fearful, or otherwise more aroused than normal. Heart rate also increases with cognitive effort, as when people try to solve a difficult math problem. People differ from each other in heart rate responses, with some showing large increases and others only minor increases in response to the same stimuli or task.

Researchers have been interested in what happens to a person's cardiovascular system when he or she is challenged by having to perform a stressful task in front of an audience. One technique used to induce temporary stress is to have participants perform backwards serial subtraction (e.g., "take the number 784 and subtract 7, take the result and subtract 7, and keep doing so until you are told to stop"). Having to carry out a serial subtraction task is stressful, especially if the experimenter is standing there, writing down the answers and telling the participant to "work faster; come on, I know you can try harder." Not surprisingly, everyone's blood pressure and heart rate goes up during this task, but some people show much larger increases than others. This phenomenon has been called **cardiac reactivity** and has been associated with the **Type A personality**—a behavior pattern characterized by impatience, competitiveness, and hostility. Evidence suggests that chronic cardiac reactivity contributes to coronary artery disease, which may be why the Type A personality trait, especially the hostility part of being Type A, is associated with a higher likelihood of heart disease and heart attacks (see Chapter 18). The relation between cardiovascular reactivity and Type A is one example of how physiological measures have been used in the study of personality.

Brain Activity

The brain spontaneously produces small amounts of electricity, which can be measured by electrodes placed on the scalp. This measure is called the electroencephalogram (EEG), and EEG recordings can be obtained for various regions of the brain while the participant is asleep, is relaxed but awake, or is doing a task. Such measures of regional brain activity can provide useful information about patterns of activation in various parts of the brain, which may be associated with different types of cognitive tasks (e.g., processing verbal versus spatial information, as in receiving directions from someone verbally or being shown a map of where to go). Personality psychologists have been especially interested in whether different regions of the brain show different activity for different people (e.g., introverts versus extraverts).

Another technique in measuring brain activity is called the evoked potential technique, in which the brain EEG is measured but the participant is given a stimulus, such as a tone or a flash of light, and the researcher assesses the participant's brain responsiveness to that stimulus. Several examples of how measurement of brain activity has contributed to our understanding of personality differences are presented in the section on brain asymmetry later in this chapter.

The powerful brain imaging techniques currently being used are another class of physiological measures that are particularly useful in personality research. For example, positron emission tomography (PET) and functional magnetic resonance imaging (fMRI) are noninvasive imaging techniques used for mapping the structure and function of the brain. In fact, the 2003 Nobel Prize for medicine was awarded to two researchers—Paul C. Lauterbur and Sir Peter Mansfield—for their discoveries leading to the development of fast functional magnetic resonance imaging (fMRI). This powerful imaging tool, which was

fMRI imagery tracks brain activity by monitoring glucose metabolism in the brain. When an area of the brain is used, it consumes energy in the form of glucose (Beer & Lombardo, 2007).
© Miguel Medina/AFP/Getty Images

developed primarily for medical diagnosis, allows physicians and psychologists to look inside the working brains of their patients and subjects. This tool can show exactly which portions of the brain are active while the person is performing a particular task. For example, if we wanted to know what part of the brain is involved in memory, we would have a sample of people perform a memory task (such as remember a phone number for five minutes) while their brains were scanned by fMRI. Traditional fMRI measures the activity level in areas of the brain in terms of glucose consumption; more glucose consumption in a region indicates that the neurons there are more active. It provides very fine spatial resolution and is able to pinpoint specific areas of activation that are associated with specific cognitive or emotional tasks.

Powerful brain imaging techniques are now being applied to the study of personality (Herrington et al., 2006), creating a new subfield called personality neuroscience (DeYoung & Gray, 2009). An important study was published by Canli and colleagues (2001), in which they used fMRI to scan the brains of people as they looked at 20 negative pictures (e.g., spiders, people crying) and 20 positive pictures (a happy couple, cute puppies). They found specific brain changes associated with viewing the different emotion-inducing photographs. More important, however, they found that personality correlated with the degree of brain activation in response to the positive and negative images. Specifically, neuroticism correlated with increased frontal brain activation to the negative images, and extraversion correlated with increased frontal brain activation to the positive images. Correlations between personality and other brain structures were also found, and the pattern of findings is consistent with the notion that personality is associated with brain reactivity to emotional stimuli. Brain imaging tools are very likely to revolutionize what we know about the brain and personality over the next few years, making this a particularly exciting area of research (Beer & Lombardo, 2007; Canli & Amin, 2002).

A relatively new use of imaging techniques is to assess brain structure instead of function, to see whether personality correlates with the size of various areas of the brain. So, instead of measuring how active a region is, fMRI can be used instead to measure the volume of various brain areas. In a recent study, DeYoung and colleagues (2012) used the Big Five model of personality to generate predictions about which areas of the brain would be responsible for generating the behaviors or responses relevant to each trait. They then assessed brain structure in a large (for neuroscience studies; $N = 116$ subjects) sample of healthy young adults. They found support for many of their predictions about the volume of certain brain regions being associated with specific personality traits. For example, extraversion correlated with the volume of medial orbitofrontal cortex, a brain region involved in processing reward information. Neuroticism correlated with the volume of brain regions that have been associated with threat and punishment. Overall, they argue that their findings support a biologically based explanatory model of the Big Five personality traits. The article has, however, been widely criticized on several points. For example, the size of a brain region is not necessarily correlated with increased functioning of that region. The authors implicitly assumed that structure and function are related, whereas there is no evidence of this fact. Even the popular press criticized the article as a modern incarnation of phrenology, a discredited discipline that held that the size of various bumps on the head could be used to infer a person's personality. Although skepticism is healthy in science, at the very least we can say that this recent paper demonstrates a new approach in the neuroscience of personality. Pioneering papers are often criticized, but over the long term their potential to guide the field is realized.

An even newer brain imaging technique is to focus, not on brain regions *per se*, but on the connections between specific regions. For example, there is a brain region associated with emotion, and another region associated with decision-making. Researchers are now able to image the circuitry that connects these two regions and measure the size of the connectivity between these regions. The size of the connectivity relates to the amount of communication or interaction between these two regions. Personality correlates may be found in the strength of connections between brain areas. For example, some people may have more of a connection between reason and emotion, whereas for others emotion and reason are less connected (i.e., emotions figure very little if at all in their decision-making). This new approach, focusing on the functional connectivity between brain regions, is an important development in neuroscience, and is just now being extended into personality psychology, where the emphasis will be on individual differences in the strength of connections between brain regions.

As an example of one interesting finding emerging from this brain connectivity approach, variation in the default brain network—the background total spontaneous communication between the brain's many regions—has been related to the personality trait of openness to experience (Beaty et al., 2016). This finding suggests that the brains of people high on openness (who tend to be imaginative, creative, and enjoy abstract reasoning) show more total connectivity between all their brain regions than persons low on openness. This new area of research holds much promise for understanding the biological foundation of personality traits (see the Closer Look on the Human Connectome Project).

A Closer Look

The Human Connectome Project

Mapping the human brain is one of the greatest scientific challenges of this century. Much work has already been done identifying key areas of the brain associated with various functions, such as memory, perception, and emotion. However, mapping the neural pathways that connect these various regions is just getting started. As an analogy, think about the electrical system of a house, where you know about the various electrical devices (e.g., lights, TV, computer, refrigerator, etc.) and the wiring diagram of the house, which tells you how they are all connected to the electrical grid, remains a mystery to you. Decoding the complex wiring diagram that is the human brain is an amazingly challenging task, like

determining the wiring diagram for a whole city. The Human Connectome Project is an effort to decode the wiring diagram of the human brain, and is formed from a consortium of three universities working together (Washington University, University of Minnesota, and Oxford University). Their goal is to comprehensively map the human brain circuitry of 1,200 healthy adults and to develop improved imaging tools along the way. Their official web site is (**http://humanconnectome. org**).

The Human Connectome Project started in 2010 and is making all of its data publically available. It also makes available the software for extracting information from the brain scan data.

The project has built an open-source web-accessible neuroinformatics platform to allow others to access and work with the vast amount of data the project is generating. The goal is not just to have a wiring diagram for the human brain (the structure of circuitry), but to also know the functions of the connections identified.

A large part of the project is directed at understanding individual differences. That is, not everyone's brain is wired the same. There is variation from person to person in brain circuitry, and this variation may relate to personality differences, or to various medical conditions. Some of the initial publications coming out of this project focus on such individual

(Continued)

A Closer Look (*Continued*)

differences. One important paper (Smith et al., 2015) assesses the link between positive life outcomes and patterns of brain connectivity in 460 participants between the ages of 22 and 35. The researchers defined positive life outcomes by grouping measures of positive characteristics like vocabulary, intelligence, education, life satisfaction, financial income, and subtracting negative characteristics like smoking, trait anger, and self-reports of delinquency or rule breaking. Each subject receives a ranking on this single positive-negative life outcome dimension, with higher rank indicating more positive outcomes in the person's life. They then correlated the strength of connections between various brain regions to this overall positive life outcome. They found that the connectivity strength of over thirty brain circuits correlated with higher rank on the positive life outcome dimension. In general, those persons with stronger brain connectivity had more positive characteristics, such as larger vocabulary, better memory, higher life satisfaction, larger income, and better education. Conversely, those with weaker network connections in their brains had more of the negative characteristics, such as anger, rule breaking, and substance use.

While this initial result sounds promising, we need to remind ourselves that correlation does not establish causation, and it does not prove that the stronger brain connections "cause" the person to be more intelligent, have a better vocabulary, etc. It could well be that developing a larger vocabulary causes the brain connections to develop. So there is a lot left to be learned about the development of both brain connectivity and the development of positive characteristics, and how the two are linked together. This kind of work however, illustrates the promise of a physiological approach to personality, with the possibility in the future of using brain scans to predict the kinds of skills, abilities, and personalities we might expect from a particular individual. If the nature of causal influences of biology and environment are understood well enough, it may lead to the design of better schools or other interventions to help people change their behavior (and their brains) toward the more positive end of the life outcome dimension.

3D probabilistic trajectories of white matter fibers arising from a seed in the left frontal cortex, superimposed on the right cortical graymatter surface for reference. The orientation vectors are color-coded (red: Left-right, green: anterior posterior, blue: inferior-superior) and have opacity representative of the underlying number of streamlines that took the particular fiber orientation brain scan.

Source: S. Sotiropoulos and T. E. J. Behrens for the WU-Minn HCP consortium - http://humanconnectome.org

A map of the average "functional connectivity" in the human cerebral cortex collected on healthy subjects while "at rest" in the MRI scanner. Regions in yellow/red are functionally connected to the "seed" location in the right frontal cortex (black circle, arrow), whereas regions in green and blue are weakly connected or not connected at all.

Source: M. F. Glasser and S. M. Smith for the WU-Minn HCP consortium - http://humanconnectome.org

Other Measures

Although skin conductance, heart rate, and brain activity are the most commonly used measures in physiological studies of personality, other biological measures have also proven useful (see Table 7.1). One important class of measures includes biochemical analyses of blood and saliva. For example, from saliva samples, biochemists can extract indicators of how competently a person's immune system is functioning (Miller & Cohen, 2001). The quality of immune system functioning may go up and down with stress or emotions and thereby may relate to personality. Hormones, such as testosterone, that play a role in important behaviors can also be extracted from saliva samples. Testosterone has been linked to uninhibited, aggressive, and risk-taking behavior patterns (Dabbs & Dabbs, 2000). Cortisol, a byproduct of the hormone noradrenaline, can be readily assessed from saliva samples. Researchers have found, for example, that shy children have high levels of cortisol in their systems (Kagan & Snidman, 1991), suggesting that they experience more stress than less shy children. Monoamine oxidase (MAO) is an enzyme found in the blood that is known to regulate neurotransmitters, the chemicals that carry messages between nerve cells. MAO may be a causal factor in the personality trait of sensation seeking. Other theories of personality are based directly on different amounts of neurotransmitters in the nervous system. One particular

Table 7.1 Common Physiological Measures Used in Personality Research

Physiological Measure	Physiological System	Psychological Response System	Examples of Stimuli Used in Research
Electrodermal activity	Sweat gland activity controlled by sympathetic nervous system	Anxiety, startle, guilt, effort, pain	Noise, mental effort, emotional stimuli, painful stimuli
Cardiovascular activity	Blood pressure and heart rate controlled by autonomic nervous system	Flight-or-fight response, mental effort, stress	Stress, social anxiety, effort, high cognitive load
Electroencephalogram (EEG)	Brain's spontaneous electrical activity	Brain activation, alertness	Resting with eyes closed, reading
Evoked EEG	Brain's electrical activity in response to specific stimuli	Attention, recognition, cognitive processing	Brief sensory stimuli, emotional stimuli
Neuroimaging (e.g., fMRI, PET)	Brain's energy metabolism	Specific brain areas responsible for cognitive control, emotion, memory, pain, decision making, sensory processing	Wide variety of tasks that activate these psychological response systems
Antibodies	Immune system	Immune response to infection, stress	Virus, bacteria, stress
Testosterone	Hormone system (steroid)	Aggression, competitiveness, psychological drive and libido, muscle bulk	Tasks involving competition, aggression, attraction
Cortisol	Hormone system (adrenal)	Stress response	Life events, stress, anxiety stimuli
Serotonin, dopamine, MAO, etc.	Neurotransmitters	Transmission of specific nerve signals	Rewarding stimuli, emotions

neurotransmitter—dopamine—plays a role in several neurological functions, one of which is responding to rewarding or pleasurable stimuli and is associated with such psychological states as "liking," "wanting," and "enjoyment" (Smillie & Wacker, 2014). Evidence is accumulating that the personality trait of extraversion is related to increased dopamine function, with extraversion scores significantly predicting how people respond to drugs that manipulate dopamine levels (Wacker & Smillie, 2015). Researchers have known for some time that extraverts tend to have more positive emotions and are happier than introverts (see Chapter 13 on Emotions and Personality), and this may be due in part to dopamine function in extraverts being different from introverts. A recent special issue of the journal *Frontiers in Human Neurocience* (2014, vol 8) published 16 papers on individual differences in the dopamine system, primarily in reference to the personality trait of extraversion. There are, however, several other physiological theories of extraversion, to which we now turn.

Physiologically Based Theories of Personality

Now that we have covered the basic physiological measures used in personality research, we turn to some of the theories that have generated interest and attention among personality psychologists. We begin with what is perhaps the most widely studied physiological theory of personality—the theory that proposes a biological explanation for why some people are introverted and others extraverted.

Extraversion–Introversion

Among the people you know, someone probably fits the following description: is talkative and outgoing, likes meeting new people and going new places, is active, is sometimes impulsive and venturesome, gets bored easily, and hates routine and monotony. Such a person would score as an extravert on an extraversion–introversion questionnaire. See Table 7.2 for items from a popular extraversion–introversion questionnaire—the Eysenck Personality Inventory.

You probably also know someone who is just the opposite, someone who is quiet and withdrawn, who prefers being alone or with a few friends to being in large crowds, who prefers routines and schedules, and who prefers the familiar to the unexpected. Such a person would score in the introverted direction on an extraversion–introversion questionnaire. If you are wondering *why* introverts and extraverts are so different from each other, physiologically minded personality psychologists have an intriguing explanation: Eysenck's theory.

An early example of a physiologically based theory of personality was put forward by H. J. Eysenck (1967) in his book *The Biological Basis of Personality*. Eysenck proposed that introverts are characterized by higher levels of activity in the brain's **ascending reticular activating system (ARAS)** than are extraverts. The ARAS is a structure in the brain stem thought to control overall cortical arousal. In the 1960s, the ARAS was thought of as a gateway through which nervous stimulation entered the cortex. If the gate were somewhat closed, then the resting **arousal level** of the cortex would be lower, and if the gate were more open, then the resting arousal level would be higher. Introverts, according to this theory, have higher resting levels of cortical arousal because their ARAS lets in too much stimulation. Introverts engage in introverted behaviors (are quiet and seek low-stimulation settings, such as libraries) because they need to keep their already heightened level of arousal in check. Conversely, extraverts engage in extraverted behaviors because they need to increase their level of arousal (Claridge, Donald, & Birchall, 1981).

Are you a talkative person? Do you like mixing with people? Do you like plenty of bustle and excitement around you? Answering no to such questions suggests an introverted personality.

© Kennan Harvey/Getty Images RF

Do you like telling jokes and funny stories to your friends? Do you like mixing with people? Can you get a party going? Answering yes to such questions suggests an extraverted personality. Interestingly, Eysenck's extraversion–introversion theory is based not on a need to be with people, but rather on a need for arousal and stimulation.

© Blend Images/Getty Images RF

Eysenck also incorporated Hebb's (1955) notion of "optimal level of arousal" into his theory. By optimal level of arousal, Hebb meant a level that is just right for any given task. For example, imagine going into a final exam in an underaroused state (e.g., sleepy, tired). Being sleepy and underaroused would be just as bad for your performance as going into the exam in an overaroused state (e.g., extremely anxious and agitated). There is an optimal level of arousal for taking an exam, one in which you are focused, alert, and attentive, but not aroused to the point of anxiety.

Table 7.2   Items from the Eysenck Personality Questionnaire Extraversion Scale

Extraversion Items

For every question, circle just one response.

YES	NO	Are you a talkative person?
YES	NO	Are you rather lively?
YES	NO	Can you usually let yourself go and enjoy yourself at a lively party?
YES	NO	Do you enjoy meeting new people?
YES	NO	Do you tend to keep in the background on social occasions? (reversed)
YES	NO	Do you like going out a lot?
YES	NO	Do you prefer reading to meeting people? (reversed)
YES	NO	Do you have many friends?
YES	NO	Would you call yourself happy-go-lucky?

Scoring directions: Reverse your answers to the items marked "reversed"; then count how many questions you endorsed with a "yes." The average college student scores about 6 on this questionnaire.

Source: Eysenck, Eysenck, & Barrett, 1985.

If introverts have a higher baseline level of arousal than extraverts (i.e., level of arousal while at rest), then introverts are above their optimal level of arousal more often than extraverts. According to the theory, the generally overaroused condition of introverts leads them to be more restrained and inhibited. They avoid active social interactions that might aggravate their already overstimulated condition. Extraverts, on the other hand, need to get their arousal level higher and so seek out stimulating activities and engage in more unrestrained behaviors. The qualities that typically characterize introverts (e.g., quiet, withdrawn) and extraverts (e.g., outgoing, engaging) are understood to be attempts to regulate arousal downward (in the case of introverts) or upward (in the case of extraverts) to maintain an optimal level of arousal.

In the decades following publication of Eysenck's theory, many studies were conducted to test it (see reviews by Eysenck, 1991; Matthews & Gilliland, 1999; Stelmack, 1990). If it is true that introverts are more cortically aroused than extraverts, then introverts should display enhanced responsiveness on measures of cortical activity, such as the electroencephalogram (EEG), as well as on measures of autonomic nervous system activity, such as electrodermal response. Studies designed to test this hypothesis typically have taken the form of comparing introverts with extraverts on physiological measures gathered under conditions of various degrees of stimulation (Gale, 1986). In conditions where participants were presented with either no stimulation or very mild stimulation, differences between introverts and extraverts turned out to be small or nonexistent. However, in studies that looked at nervous system responsiveness to moderate levels of stimulation, introverts showed larger or faster responses than extraverts, as predicted by Eysenck's theory (Bullock & Gilliland, 1993; Gale, 1983).

The fact that introverts and extraverts are not different at resting levels, but *are* different under moderate levels of stimulation, led Eysenck to revise his arousal theory (Eysenck & Eysenck, 1985). When he first stated his theory in 1967, Eysenck did not distinguish between resting, or *baseline,* levels of arousal and arousal *responses* to stimulation. A good deal of evidence now suggests that the real difference between introverts and extraverts lies in their **arousability**, or arousal response, not in their baseline

Exercise

The Lemon Juice Demonstration: This demonstration is designed to illustrate that introverts are more reactive to stimulation than extraverts. Although some teachers have tried this in the classroom, it can be a bit messy and so might best be done as a thought experiment to illustrate the point of individual differences in reactivity. Here is how it would go: Take a double-tipped cotton swab and tie a thread exactly in its center so that it hangs perfectly in balance (i.e., is horizontal). Swallow three times and put one end on your tongue for exactly 20 seconds. After removing the swab, place 4 drops of lemon juice under your tongue. Place the other end of the cotton swab on your tongue for 20 seconds. Remove the swab and let it hang by the thread. If you are an extravert it is likely that the swab will remain horizontal, indicating that you did not react strongly to the lemon juice by producing more saliva. If you are an introvert, it is likely that the swab will no longer balance horizontally and will instead be heavier on the end placed on the tongue following the lemon juice. This would indicate that you produced more saliva in response to the lemon juice. Eysenck conducted a similar experiment (Eysenck & Eysenck, 1967) as did Corcoran (1964).

arousal level. Extraverts and introverts do not differ in their level of brain activity while sleeping, for example, or while lying quietly in a darkened room with their eyes shut (Stelmack, 1990). However, when presented with moderate levels of stimulation, introverts show enhanced physiological reactivity compared with extraverts (Gale, 1987).

An important corollary of the theory is that, when given a choice, extraverts should prefer higher levels of stimulation than do introverts. Indirect evidence supports this prediction. For example, laboratory studies have shown that extraverts will press a button at a higher rate than introverts when the button pressing produces changes in the visual environment (such as change the channel on a TV, change the slide on a projector) (e.g., Brebner & Cooper, 1978). In a more naturalistic study, done in a university library, persons studying in a noisy reading room scored as more extraverted than did students studying in the quieter rooms (Campbell & Hawley, 1982). Findings such as these suggest that, when given a choice, extraverts tend to seek greater levels of stimulation than introverts.

A clever study designed by psychologist Russell Geen (1984) tested the hypothesis that, when allowed to control the noise level during a learning task, extraverts would choose a louder level than introverts. In this experiment, participants were told they would engage in a learning task in a noisy environment (like studying with the TV on). However, they were allowed to control the volume of the noise (though they could not turn it completely off). Extraverts did choose a louder noise level than introverts. In their preferred noise levels (the levels chosen), the performance of extraverts and introverts did not differ. However, in another condition, the introverts were given the noise level chosen by the extraverts, and in this condition their performance declined. Similarly, when the extraverts were given the noise level chosen by the introverts, their performance also declined. This study shows not only that extraverts prefer more intense stimulation than introverts, but that stimulation outside of their preferred level (higher for introverts, lower for extraverts) resulted in performance declines, supporting the notion of an optimal level of stimulation, which differs for extraverts (where optimal is more intense) and introverts (where optimal is less intense).

Sensitivity to Reward and Punishment

Jeffrey Gray has proposed an influential alternative biological theory of personality (Gray, 1972, 1990), called **reinforcement sensitivity theory**. Based on brain function research with animals, Gray has constructed a model of human personality based on two hypothesized biological systems in the brain. The first is the **behavioral activation system (BAS),** which is responsive to incentives, such as cues for reward, and regulates approach behavior, most likely through the dopamine system, as noted above. When the BAS recognizes a stimulus as potentially rewarding, it triggers approach behavior. For example, as a child, you might have learned about an ice cream truck that made deliveries to your neighborhood while playing music. When you heard that music (cues of reward), your BAS created the urge to run out into the street to find the ice cream truck (approach motivation). The other system in the brain postulated by Gray (1975) is the **behavioral inhibition system (BIS)**, which is responsive to cues for punishment, frustration, and uncertainty. The effect of BIS activation is to cease or inhibit behavior or to bring about avoidance behavior. You may have been scolded or punished by your mother for running into the street. The street becomes a punishment cue to the BIS, which causes you to inhibit your behavior. A rough analogy is that the BAS is like an accelerator that motivates approach behavior, whereas the BIS is like brakes that inhibit behavior or help a person stop what he or she is doing.

According to Gray, people differ from each other in the relative sensitivity of their BIS or BAS system. A person with a reactive BIS is especially sensitive to cues of punishment, frustration, or novelty. He or she is vulnerable to unpleasant emotions, including anxiety, fear, and sadness. According to Gray, the BIS is responsible for the personality dimension of **anxiety**. A person with a reactive BAS, on the other hand, is especially sensitive to reward. Such a person is vulnerable to positive emotions and tends to approach stimuli. The ability of an individual with a reactive BAS to inhibit behavior decreases as he or she approaches a goal. According to Gray, the BAS is responsible for the personality dimension of **impulsivity**, the inability to inhibit responses.

Some debate has focused on exactly where to locate BAS (impulsivity) and BIS (anxiety) in the conceptual space defined by Eysenck's dimensions of extraversion and introversion (see Figure 7.2). In fact, one of the authors of this book has had a series of exchanges with Gray and his colleagues about this issue (Pickering, Corr, & Gray, 1999; Rusting & Larsen, 1997, 1999). It appears that the relation between Gray's constructs and Eysenck's constructs is direct, with BAS being equivalent to extraversion and BIS being equivalent to neuroticism. In fact, the Canli and colleagues (2001) study cited earlier showed that the brains of extraverts (compared to introverts) were more reactive to pleasant, rewarding images, and the brains of persons high on neuroticism were more reactive (than those low on neuroticism) to images associated with negative emotions. Many researchers view the BIS and BAS constructs as similar to neuroticism and extraversion in that both refer to dispositional tendencies to withdraw from punishment or to approach reward, respectively (e.g., Davidson, 2003; Kosslyn et al., 2002; Knutson & Bhanji, 2006; Sutton, 2002). Gray has revised his model and now locates

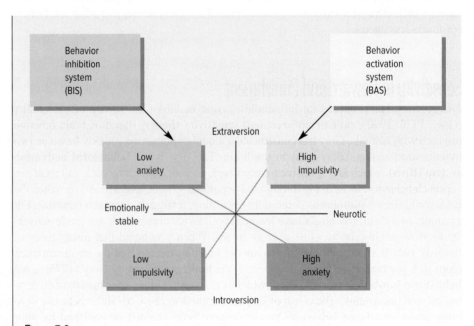

Figure 7.2

Relation between Eysenck's dimensions of extraversion and neuroticism and Gray's dimensions of impulsivity and anxiety.

BIS much closer to neuroticism and locates BAS much closer to extraversion (Pickering et al., 1999).

Gray believes that differences among people in sensitivity to reward and punishment are responsible for generating the varieties of behavior associated with being anxious/neurotic and with being impulsive/extraverted. If we ask why some people are more susceptible than others to anxiety attacks, fears, worry, depressions, phobias, obsessions, or compulsions, Gray would argue that their susceptibility is due to an overly sensitive behavioral inhibition system. Such people tend to notice and are sensitive to punishment and other frustrations. Moreover, they are distressed by uncertainty and novelty. Then, if we ask why some people are more susceptible than others to positive emotions, to approach behaviors, to seeking out and interacting with others, Gray would argue that this is due to an overly sensitive behavioral activation system.

One team of researchers, stimulated by Gray's theory, constructed a questionnaire to measure BIS sensitivity—a tendency toward anxiety and fearfulness and the avoidance of uncertainty and risk (MacAndrew & Steele, 1991). The researchers identified a high and a low fearful group and determined which questions discriminated between the groups. Some examples of questions on this questionnaire are "I have been quite independent and free from family rule," "I am entirely self-confident," and "I do not blame a person for taking advantage of someone who lays himself open to it." For the high BIS group, the researchers selected a group of female psychiatric patients who had a history of anxiety and panic attacks. The low BIS group called for a sample of persons who had little regard for their own safety, who took risks and disregarded danger. To represent this group, the researchers used a sample of convicted prostitutes—persons who regularly engaged in illegal, high-risk sexual and drug-taking behavior. The prostitutes and anxiety patients were found to be significantly different in their responses to the questionnaire. The prostitutes scored lower than the anxiety patients on this measure. Such a finding indicates that the questionnaire has some validity as a measure of tolerance for risky situations, danger, and fearlessness.

A second research group making use of Gray's theory consists of psychologist Charles Carver and his colleagues (Carver, Sutton, & Scheier, 1999; Carver & White, 1994). Carver and White developed and validated a scale to measure individual differences in the strength of the BIS and BAS. Other researchers are adding to the validity evidence behind this scale. For example, Zelenski and Larsen (1999) found this scale to be one of the best measures of BIS and BAS. Carver et al. (1999) reviewed Gray's theory, emphasizing individual differences in approach or incentive motivation (extraversion or impulsivity) and individual differences in withdrawal or aversive motivation (neuroticism or anxiety). They showed how several programs of research can be integrated into the theme that humans appear to possess separate systems for responding to incentives and threats. For example, these systems show reliable individual differences, they relate to major affective dispositions, they may be lateralized in our cerebral architecture, and they may relate differently to learning by punishment and learning by reward. Carver and his colleagues consider these the "Big Two" personality dimensions. This review paper shows the remarkable integrating power of Gray's theory of personality.

Gray has primarily conducted research with animals. With animals, you can use drugs or surgery to eliminate certain areas of the brain, then test whether this affects the animal's ability to learn through punishment or reward. Gray's theory relates anxiety and impulsivity to the two principles of learning: reinforcement (both positive and negative) and punishment (and the loss of reinforcement). There is some evidence that these two forms of learning are under separate neural control. It appears likely that different brain mechanisms may be involved when a person or an animal learns through reinforcement or through punishment (Gray, 1991). Thus, there should be people with varying degrees of sensitivity (high, medium, or low) to punishment and to reward.

In a study of reward and punishment, participants were required to complete hundreds of trials of a difficult reaction time task (Larsen, Chen, & Zelenski, 2003). They had to name the colors of words that popped up on a computer screen, as quickly and accurately as possible. It is a difficult task, and people can get only about half the trials correct given that they have to respond in less than one second on each trial. One group was rewarded for each correct and fast response, and they earned $5 during the course of a 20-minute experiment. Another group was punished after incorrect or slow responses, and although they started the experiment with $10, proceeded to lose $5. As such, everyone finished the experiment with $5, but one group was rewarded on a trial-by-trial basis, whereas the other group was punished on a trial-by-trial basis. It turned out that BAS scores predicted better performance in the reward condition, with high BAS persons working faster and becoming more accurate when they were working for reward. BIS scores, on the other hand, predicted performance in the punishment condition, with high-BIS persons responding with better performance when they were being punished, compared to low BIS participants.

Much of the work carried out to test Gray's theory has focused on impulsivity (the inability to inhibit responses). Our jails are full of people who are deficient in the ability to control their behavior, especially behavior that may be immediately rewarding. For example, a 17-year-old male sees an expensive sports car parked on the street. As he looks at the car and thinks about how much fun it would be to drive, he notices that the keys are in the ignition. The owner appears nowhere in sight and the street is fairly deserted. He starts to reach for the door handle. The ability to stop this approach behavior, even though it is immediately rewarding, separates the average person from the impulsive person.

Impulsive individuals can be characterized as having stronger approach than avoidance tendencies and are less able to inhibit approach behavior, especially in the presence of desirable goals or rewards. You probably know people who often say things that get them into trouble or who hurt other people's feelings without even thinking. Even though they know they might hurt someone's feelings and feel bad themselves (i.e., are "punished" by feelings of remorse), why can't they control what they do and say?

According to Gray's theory, impulsive people do not learn well from punishment because they have a weak behavioral inhibition system. If this is true, then researchers should be able to demonstrate that in a task that involves learning from punishment, impulsive persons do less well than nonimpulsive persons. Studies have been conducted on impulsive college students, juvenile delinquents, psychopaths, and criminals in jail (Newman, 1987; Newman, Widom, & Nathan, 1985). The typical finding is that such persons are, in fact, deficient in learning through punishment. Impulsive persons, it seems, do not learn as well from punishment as from reward.

Let's say you have a roommate and would like to teach her to clean her part of the apartment. You could try rewarding with candy and praise every time she picked

Exercise

Think of a situation in which you are trying to teach someone something new. For example, perhaps you want to teach your roommate to keep her or his part of the room neat and tidy. Discuss an example of how you might use reward to teach that behavior. Then discuss how you might use mild punishment to teach the same behavior. Which do you think would work better? Could the effectiveness of the reward or the punishment depend on the personality of your roommate?

something up. Or you could try punishing by yelling and scolding every time she left something out of place. If your roommate is an impulsive person, chances are that you would do better using the reward strategy than the punishment strategy. On the other hand, if your roommate is an anxious person, it might be more effective to use punishment than reward.

Sensation Seeking

Sensation seeking is another dimension of personality postulated to have a physiological basis. Sensation seeking is the tendency to seek out thrilling and exciting activities, take risks, and avoid boredom. Research on the need for sensory input grew out of studies on **sensory deprivation.** Let's begin, then, with a description of sensory deprivation research.

Imagine volunteering for a study in which you are put into a small chamber where there is no light, no sound, and only minimal tactile sensations. Imagine further that you agree to do this for 12 hours straight. What would this experience be like? Research suggests that at first you would feel relaxed, then bored, then anxious as you started to hallucinate and have delusions. Early research by Hebb (1955) showed that

in such a situation, college students chose to listen over and over to a taped lecture intended to convince 6-year-olds about the dangers of alcohol. Other participants in these early sensory deprivation experiments who were offered a recording of an old stock market report opted to listen to it over and over again, apparently to avoid the unpleasant consequences of sensory deprivation. Persons in sensory deprived environments appear motivated to acquire *any* sensory input, even if ordinarily such input would be perceived as boring.

Hebb's Theory of Optimal Level of Arousal

Hebb developed the theory of **optimal level of arousal,** which was used by Eysenck in his theory of extraversion. Hebb's theory states that people are motivated to reach an optimal level of arousal. If they are underaroused, relative to this level, an

The theory of sensation seeking was proposed to explain why some people routinely seek out thrilling experiences, even though such experiences may come with certain risks.

© Purestock/ SuperStock RF

increase in arousal is rewarding; conversely, if they are overaroused, a decrease in arousal is rewarding. For its time, Hebb's theory was controversial because most researchers thought that tension *reduction* was the goal of all motives, yet Hebb was saying that we are motivated to *seek out* tension and stimulation. How else can we explain the fact that people *like* to work on puzzles, enjoy mild frustration, and occasionally take risks or do something to arouse mild fears, such as going on a roller coaster ride. Hebb's belief that people need stimulation and sensory input is consistent with the results of sensory deprivation research. The nervous system appears to need at least some sensory input.

Zuckerman's Research

Early on in sensory deprivation research, Zuckerman and Haber (1965) noted that some people were not as distressed as others by the sensory deprivation experience. In these early experiments, some people found sensory deprivation extremely unpleasant. These participants requested lots of sensory material (tapes, reading material) during the experiment and quit the experiment relatively early. Zuckerman believed that such persons had a particularly *high need for sensation* because they were the least tolerant of deprivation. He called them sensation seekers because they appeared to seek out stimulation, not just in the sensory deprivation experiment but in their everyday lives as well.

Zuckerman developed a questionnaire designed to measure the extent to which a person needs novel or exciting experiences and enjoys the thrills and excitement associated with them. He called the questionnaire the Sensation-Seeking Scale, and items from it appear in Table 7.3 (Zuckerman & Aluja, 2015).

As it turned out, Zuckerman's questionnaire about preferences for stimulation in everyday life predicted how well people tolerated the sensory deprivation sessions. High sensation seekers found sensory deprivation to be particularly unpleasant, whereas low sensation seekers were able to tolerate it for longer periods of time. In the early 1960s, Zuckerman left the sensory deprivation laboratory and began to study the other

Table 7.3 Items from the Sensation-Seeking Scale

There are several aspects of sensation seeking that are reflected in the items on this scale.

Thrill and adventure seeking—reflected in items that ask about desire for outdoor sports or activities involving elements of risk, such as flying, scuba diving, parachute jumping, motorcycle riding, and mountain climbing—for example, "I sometimes like to do things that are a little frightening" (high) versus "A sensible person avoids activities that are dangerous" (low).

Experience seeking—reflected in items that refer to the seeking of new sensory or mental experiences through unconventional or nonconforming lifestyle choices—for example, "I like to have new and exciting experiences and sensations even if they are frightening, unconventional, or illegal" (high) versus "I am not interested in experience for its own sake" (low).

Disinhibition—reflected in items indicating a preference for getting "out of control" or an interest in wild parties, gambling, and sexual variety—for example, "Almost everything enjoyable is illegal or immoral" (high) versus "The most enjoyable things are perfectly legal and moral" (low).

Boredom susceptibility—reflected in items that refer to a dislike for repetition, routine work, monotony, predictable and dull people, and a restlessness when things become unchanging—for example, "I get bored seeing the same old faces" (high) versus "I like the comfortable familiarity of everyday friends" (low).

All of the items on the Sensation-Seeking Scale, as well as scoring instructions, can be found in Zuckerman (1978).

A Closer Look   Personality and Problem Behaviors: Gambling

Greg Hogan, age 19, was president of his sophomore class at Lehigh University in Pennsylvania and the son of a Baptist pastor. He played cello in the Lehigh orchestra, was a member of Sigma Phi Epsilon fraternity, and acted as an assistant to the university chaplain. On December 9, 2005, Hogan walked into the Wachovia Bank in Allentown, Pennsylvania, and passed a note to the teller, saying he was armed and wanted money. He walked out with $2,871. He then went to a movie, *The Chronicles of Narnia,* with two friends. Later that day, while preparing to go to rehearsal with his university orchestra, seven police cars surrounded his fraternity house. Greg Hogan never made it to rehearsal that evening. Instead, he was arrested and charged with bank robbery. At his trial he plead guilty and was sentenced to 10 years in prison. He was released on probation on June 16, 2008, after serving 22 months. As part of his probation, Hogan is not allowed to enter a casino or place a gambling bet until his probation ends in 2016.

Greg Hogan had run up over $5,000 in gambling debt, mostly at Internet gambling sites. Due to his gambling compulsion, he was in a desperate, but not unique, situation. A study done by PokerPlus.com estimates that more than 1.8 million people play online poker each month, wagering an average total of $200 million a day. Considering all forms of card gambling, more than 3 million students a week engage in gambling for money, according to the National Council on Problem Gambling estimates. This study also estimates that, out of every 10 college students who play poker regularly, 2 will develop an addiction. Of these gambling addicts, about 80 percent will commit a crime to fund their gambling debt. A common view is that problematic gambling is an expression of an addictive personality.

Is there any evidence for an "addictive personality"? Are certain people more prone than others to get hooked on gambling? Before answering this question, we briefly review the scope of the gambling problem in the United States. Pathological gambling disorder (PGD) is characterized by gambling behavior that is persistent over time and that causes significant problems in the person's life, such as with family members, or at school or work. The diagnosis of PGD is made when at least 5 out of 10 criteria are present (American Psychiatric Association, 1994). These criteria include a preoccupation with or inability to control or stop gambling, the need to gamble more often or to make larger bets to obtain a level of excitement, continuing to gamble despite problems, lying to conceal gambling involvement, committing illegal acts to obtain gambling money, "withdrawal" symptoms of restlessness and irritability when unable to gamble, and gambling to escape negative moods. These criteria look very similar to criteria for drug and alcohol addictions. Other gambling-specific criteria include "chasing losses" (i.e., continuing to bet in an attempt to recover losses) and relying on others for financial help following gambling losses.

Pathological gambling behavior often co-occurs with other addictions, including nicotine dependence, cannabis use, drug addiction, and alcohol dependence

For some people, playing cards is a form of recreation. For others, however, it can result in compulsive gambling.
© *JGI/Jamie Grill/Blend Images LLC RF*

(Slutske, Caspi, et al., 2005). In fact, persons with pathological or problem gambling are two to four times more likely to develop alcohol dependence than nongamblers. This is an example of **comorbidity**, where two or more disorders simultaneously occur within the same individual.

We return now to the question of whether any specific personality traits are associated with problem gambling. Several correlational studies have found that measures of impulsiveness and sensation seeking correlate with problem gambling (McDaniel & Zuckerman, 2003; Vitaro, Arsenault, & Tremblay, 1997). From correlational data, we don't really know if the personality traits are causing the gambling or if gambling is causing people to become more impulsive and sensation seeking. In a longitudinal study, however, the psychologist Wendy Slutske, Eisen, and colleagues (2005) found that problem gambling at age 21 was associated with the personality traits of risk taking and impulsivity at age 18. This study strengthens the conclusion that the personality traits of high impulsivity and risk taking (or sensation seeking)

(Continued)

A Closer Look (*Continued*)

put a person at risk for developing problem gambling.

Genetic studies suggest that the risk for developing problem gambling and the risk for developing other addictions (e.g., alcohol) may be explained by largely overlapping genetic risk factors. These genetic factors may give rise to the specific personality traits related to low behavioral control (impulsivity and risk taking), and these traits may in turn be responsible for the comorbidity of pathological gambling and other addictive disorders.

The Iowa Gambling Task is a laboratory procedure developed to study impulsivity and insensitivity to consequences. In this task, the subject is confronted with various decks of cards, from which they can choose. Some of the decks have very high initial rewards but also high punishments, such that over time the person drawing from these decks would lose money. Other decks have lower initial rewards, but also lower and less frequent punishments, such that if choices were made from these decks, the person would ultimately win money. Most people pick up on the pattern and learn to avoid the risky decks and select from the safer decks (less rewarding but also fewer losses). People with high levels of impulsive sensation seeking (Crone, Vendel, & van der Molen, 2003), as well as people with alcohol and drug addictions (Bechara et al., 2001), often stay with the riskier decks and end up losing money. Interestingly, people with specific damage to their brains (in the region of the prefrontal cortex) also will stick with the riskier decks and not learn to avoid the frequent losses that come with the infrequent gains (Bechara, Tranel, & Damasio, 2005). Studies of age changes in the Iowa Gambling Task show that performance continues to improve through adolescence, consistent with findings that the prefrontal cortex continues to develop through adolescence. By implication, adolescence is not a time one should be experimenting with gambling because the brain centers that help one appreciate consequences are still developing.

In summary, even casual or recreational gambling can reach problem proportions for certain individuals. The personality traits of impulsivity and sensation seeking appear to put people at risk for developing gambling problems and other addictions (Zuckerman, 2012). Moreover, these traits also put people at risk for developing other addictions, such as alcohol, nicotine, and drug dependence. It may be that both the personality traits and addictive behaviors are expressions of a common genetic pathway. Moreover, this pathway may also be expressed in a specific brain area—the prefrontal cortex—that has been associated with the ability to anticipate consequences and to engage in self-regulation.

unique characteristics associated with the personality dimension of sensation seeking. Notice that this theoretical explanation of sensation seeking is very similar to that Eysenck offered for extraversion. In fact, there is a moderately strong positive correlation between extraversion and sensation seeking.

In the 40-plus years that Zuckerman and his colleagues and others have been doing research on sensation seeking, many interesting findings have emerged. Police officers who volunteer for riot duty have higher sensation-seeking scores on Zuckerman's scale than officers who do not volunteer for riot duty. Skydivers score higher on sensation-seeking measures than non-skydivers. Among college students who volunteered to be in psychology experiments, the students with high sensation-seeking scores volunteered to participate in the more unusual studies (studies on ESP, hypnosis, or drugs) than in the typical studies (on learning, sleep, or social interaction). In studies of gambling behavior, the participants with high sensation-seeking scores tended to make riskier bets. High sensation seekers also report having a larger number of sex partners, engaging in a wider variety of sex acts, and beginning to have sex at an earlier age than low sensation seekers. The list of correlates of sensation seeking is quite long, and you may consult various reviews to learn more about this personality trait (e.g., Zuckerman, 1978, 1984, 1991b).

According to Zuckerman, there is a physiological basis for sensation-seeking behavior. Zuckerman's more recent work (1991b, 2005, 2006) focuses primarily on the role played by neurotransmitters in bringing about differences in sensation seeking. **Neurotransmitters** are chemicals in the nerve cells that are responsible for the transmission of a nerve impulse from one cell to another. As you may recall from your introductory psychology class, nerve cells are separated from one another by a slight gap, called a synapse. A nerve impulse must jump across this gap if it is to continue toward its destination. Neurotransmitters are the chemicals released by the nerves that allow nerve impulses to jump across the synapse and continue on their way.

The neurotransmitter must be broken down after the impulse has passed, or too many nerve transmissions would occur. As an analogy, think of the turnstyle at a movie theater or subway, which lets in one person at a time. If it were left open, many people could run through, allowing too many people in. If it were stuck closed, however, no one could get through. The neurotransmitter system is similar in that the chemical balance in the synapse has to be just right in order for the correct amount of nervous transmission to get through and continue on.

Certain enzymes, particularly **monoamine oxidase (MAO),** are responsible for maintaining the proper levels of neurotransmitters. MAO works by breaking down the

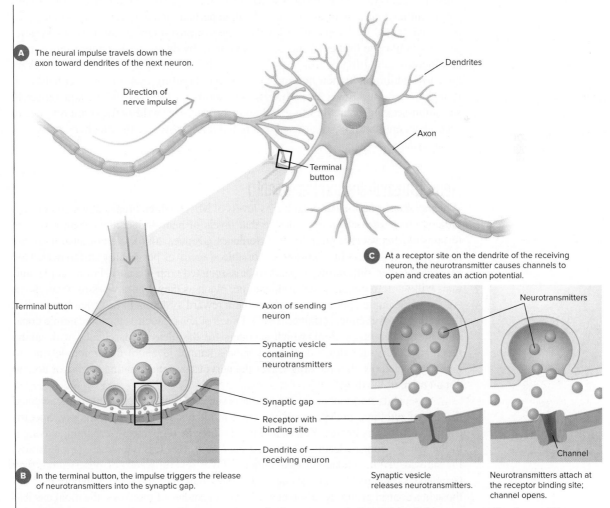

A · The neural impulse travels down the axon toward dendrites of the next neuron.

Direction of nerve impulse

Dendrites

Axon

Terminal button

C · At a receptor site on the dendrite of the receiving neuron, the neurotransmitter causes channels to open and creates an action potential.

Neurotransmitters

Terminal button

Axon of sending neuron

Synaptic vesicle containing neurotransmitters

Synaptic gap

Receptor with binding site

Dendrite of receiving neuron

Channel

B · In the terminal button, the impulse triggers the release of neurotransmitters into the synaptic gap.

Synaptic vesicle releases neurotransmitters.

Neurotransmitters attach at the receptor binding site; channel opens.

Illustration of a synapse, the junction between two nerve cells. Synapses transmit electrical signals from one nerve cell to the next. When an electrical signal reaches a synapse, it triggers the release of chemicals called neurotransmitters (pink) from vesicles (purple). The vesicles burst through the membrane, and neurotransmitters cross a microscopic gap called the synaptic gap and bind to the receptor nerve cell, causing it to propagate an electrical impulse.

neurotransmitter after it has allowed a nerve impulse to pass. If an excessive amount of MAO were present, it would break down too much of the neurotransmitter, and nerve transmission would be diminished. If there were too little MAO present, an excessive amount of the neurotransmitter would be left in the synapse, allowing for too much nervous transmission to take place. Suppose that you had to do a fine movement with your fingers, such as pick up a dime off a flat surface. With too little MAO in your system, your fingers might be shaking and your movements jerky (too much nervous transmission). With too much MAO, however, your fingers might be clumsy because of dulled sensation and lethargic movement control. When MAO levels are just right, neurotransmitter levels are regulated appropriately, and the nervous system works properly to control the muscles, thoughts, and emotions.

High sensation seekers tend to have low levels of MAO in their bloodstream, compared with low sensation seekers. Across studies, the correlation tends to be small to moderate but is consistently negative (Zuckerman, 1991b, 2005). If high sensation seekers tend to have low MAO levels, and low MAO means more neurotransmitter available in the nerve cells, then perhaps sensation seeking is caused by or is maintained by having high levels of neurotransmitters in the nervous system. MAO acts like the brakes of the nervous system, by decomposing neurotransmitters and thereby inhibiting neurotransmission. With low MAO levels, sensation seekers have less inhibition in their nervous systems and therefore less control over behavior, thoughts, and emotions. According to Zuckerman's (1991a) theory and research, sensation-seeking behaviors (e.g., illicit sex, drug use, wild parties) are due not to seeking an optimal level of arousal, but to having too little of the biochemical brakes in the synapse.

Neurotransmitters and Personality

Whereas Zuckerman's theory concerns levels of MAO, which breaks down neurotransmitters, other researchers hypothesize that levels of neurotransmitters themselves are responsible for specific individual differences (Depue, 2006). Neurotransmitters are receiving a great deal of attention as possible sources of personality differences. One neurotransmitter, **dopamine,** appears to be associated with pleasure. For example, animals will work to obtain doses of dopamine, much as they would work to obtain food. As such, dopamine appears to function like a reward system and has even been called the feeling good chemical (Hamer, 1997). Drugs of abuse, such as cocaine, mimic dopamine in the nervous system, which accounts for the pleasure associated with taking them. However, such drugs deplete a person's natural levels of dopamine, leading to unpleasant feelings after the drug leaves the nervous system, creating a drive or urge to obtain more of the drug.

A second important neurotransmitter is **serotonin.** Researchers have documented the role of serotonin in depression and other mood disorders, such as anxiety. Specifically, drugs such as Prozac, Zoloft, and Paxil block the reuptake of serotonin, leaving it in the synapse longer, leading depressed persons to feel less depressed. In one study, Prozac was given to nondepressed subjects. Over several weeks of observation, they reported less negative affect and engaged in more outgoing and social behavior than did those in a control group (Knutson et al., 1998). In studies of monkeys, the monkeys that were higher in dominance and that engaged in more grooming had higher levels of serotonin. The monkeys low in serotonin were frequently fearful and aggressive (Rogness & McClure, 1996). In summarizing animal studies, Depue (1996) notes that low serotonin is associated with irritable behavior.

A third important neurotransmitter, **norepinephrine**, is involved in activating the sympathetic nervous system for fight-or-flight. Not surprisingly, personality theories have been proposed based on the neurotransmitters dopamine, serotonin, and norepinephrine. Probably the most comprehensive is Cloninger's **tridimensional personality model** (Cloninger, 1986, 1987; Cloninger, Svrakic, & Przybeck, 1993), in which three personality traits are tied to levels of the three neurotransmitters. The first trait, **novelty seeking**, is based on low levels of dopamine. Recall that low levels of dopamine create a drive state to obtain substances or experiences that increase dopamine. Novelty, thrills, and excitement can make up for low levels of dopamine, so novelty-seeking behavior is thought to result from low levels of this neurotransmitter.

The second personality trait identified in Cloninger's model is **harm avoidance**, which he associates with abnormalities in serotonin metabolism. Although various descriptions of the theory indicate increased or decreased serotonin levels are associated with increased harm avoidance, Cloninger himself (personal communication, October 2003) states that it is unwise to suggest a simple linear correlation between harm avoidance and absolute levels of serotonin. Very low levels of the principal serotonin metabolite 5-HIAA in cerebrospinal fluid are associated with risk of severe depression, but serotonin levels can also be elevated in states of anxiety or stress. The selective serotonin uptake inhibitors (like the antidepressants Prozac, Zoloft, or Paxil) result in increased levels of serotonin at synapses, which may increase anxiety initially but then lead to decreased vulnerability to overreact to stress, probably by down-regulating sensitivity to serotonin when it is released in response to stress. So we have to distinguish the acute role of serotonin, which is increased in states of acute stress, and the role of serotonin down-regulation over the life span, which is associated with lower levels of harm avoidance. People low in harm avoidance are described as energetic, outgoing, and optimistic, whereas people high in harm avoidance are described as cautious, inhibited, shy, and apprehensive. They seem to expect that harmful and unpleasant events will happen to them, so they are constantly on the lookout for signs of such threatening events.

The third trait in Cloninger's model is **reward dependence**, which Cloninger sees as related to low levels of norepinephrine. People high on this trait are persistent; they continue to act in ways that produce reward. They work long hours, put a lot of effort into their work, and often continue striving after others have given up.

Genes Work Through Neurotransmitter Systems to Influence Personality

Although we discussed behavior genetics in more detail in Chapter 6, it is worth mentioning here that many researchers interested in personality and genetics are focusing on the genes involved in regulating our neurotransmitter systems. For example, if low levels of dopamine are related to novelty seeking, then perhaps the genes involved in dopamine transmission would be a good place to start in the search for the genetic basis of this personality trait. Keltikangas-Järvinen and her colleagues (2003) in Finland have found that the type 4 dopamine receptor gene (DRD4) is associated with heightened levels of novelty seeking. An early meta-analysis of genetic studies of novelty seeking has suggested that very specific types of repeated genetic codes on the DRD4 gene (Schinka, Letsch, & Crawford, 2002) are reliably associated with novelty seeking. A later meta-analysis (Munafo, Yalcin, Willis-Owen, & Flint, 2008) concluded that specific variants of DRD4 are reliably associated with novelty seeking and impulsivity, implying that genetic variations of DRD4 are involved in this personality trait. These findings imply that many genes are involved in the creation of any single personality trait. So, although looking for one gene as the basis of a personality trait is like looking for the proverbial needle in the haystack, now the researchers are looking for many different needles in the same big haystack. That is, they are looking for multiple genes that interact in complex ways to influence neurotransmitter systems. A prominent researcher in this area, Dean Hamer, once commented, "After 10 years, it is quite clear to me that at least for most traits there are a very large number of genes involved" (quoted in Azar, 2002). As new technology for analyzing gene sequences is developed, the search will likely become more tractable. Nevertheless, any answers that are found in the future are likely to reveal complicated and multiple interacting genetic contributions, possibly requiring environmental triggers, for the expression of any biologically based personality trait.

It is probably clear that Cloninger's model has much in common with Gray's, Eysenck's, and Zuckerman's. For example, novelty seeking seems a lot like the reward sensitivity associated with the BAS of Gray's theory. All of these theories have different explanatory bases for the traits (Depue & Collins, 1999). For example, Gray suggests that brain systems involved in learning through reward and punishment are important in determining these traits. Eysenck also implicates the brain and nervous system. Zuckerman focuses on the synapse and the neurochemicals found there. And Cloninger specifies particular neurotransmitters. All are perhaps describing the same behavioral traits but focusing on different levels of explanation within the body, ranging from the synapse to the brain that influence reactivity to various kinds of stimuli.

Let's turn now to a consideration of two other personality dimensions that appear to have a biological base that is not related to physiological reactivity—morningness–eveningness and brain asymmetry.

Morningness–Eveningness

Perhaps you are the kind of person who likes to sleep late and stay up late, saving your important schoolwork for late afternoon or evening, when you are feeling at your peak. Or perhaps you are more of a morning person, regularly getting up early without the aid of an alarm clock. Moreover, perhaps you tend to do all your important work early in the day, when you are feeling at your best, and get to sleep fairly early in the evening. Being a morning type or an evening type of person appears to be a stable characteristic. Personality psychologists have become interested in such stable differences among persons in preferences for different times of the day and have coined the term **morningness–eveningness** to refer to this dimension (Horne & Ostberg, 1976).

Differences between morning and evening types of persons, sometimes called "larks" and "owls," appear to be due to differences in underlying biological rhythms. Many biological processes have been found to fluctuate around an approximate 24- to 25-hour cycle. These have been called **circadian rhythms** (*circa* means "around," *dia* means "day," or "24 hours"). Of particular interest have been circadian rhythms in body temperature and endocrine secretion rates. For example, on average, body temperature shows a peak around mid-evening (between 8 and 9 p.m.) and a trough in the early morning (around 6 a.m.). Figure 7.3 presents a graph of body temperature by time of day.

Researchers use a temporal-isolation design to study such circadian rhythms. In this design, participants volunteer to live in an environment totally controlled by the experimenter with respect to time cues. There are no windows, so the participants do not know if it is day or night. There are no regularly scheduled meals, so the participants do not know if it is breakfast-, lunch-, or suppertime. Participants are given food whenever they ask for it. There is no access to live television or radio. Instead, the participants

Figure 7.3

Circadian rhythm in body temperature.

have a large collection of videotapes and audiotapes for entertainment. Volunteers live in this environment for several weeks or longer. Often, the participants are students who want to use the time in isolation as an opportunity to study for an important exam or who need to write a PhD thesis.

Imagine being a participant in such a study. You would go to sleep whenever you wanted, sleep as long as you wanted, eat whenever you felt like it, work or watch movies as the inclination struck, and so on. This is called **free running** in time, in which there are no time cues to influence your behavior or biology. If you were in such a situation and your temperature were taken every hour, and if you were like the average person, you would find that your temperature followed an approximate 24- to 25-hour cycle, starting to rise before waking up and falling before going to sleep (Aschoff, 1965; Finger, 1982; Wever, 1979).

Note that 24- to 25-hour rhythms are the average; there are wide differences among persons in the actual length of their biological rhythms (Kerkhof, 1985). Circadian rhythms in temporal-isolation studies have been found to be as short as 16 hours in one person and as long as 50 hours in another person (Wehr & Goodwin, 1981). While free running in a temporal-isolation experiment, the first person would complete a sleep-wake cycle every 16 hours, whereas the second person's sleep-wake cycle would last 50 hours.

Such wide differences among persons are evident only in a temporal isolation situation. In real life, there are time cues all around us that fluctuate in a 24-hour rhythm—most notably, the light-dark cycle. These cues entrain us and make us fit into the 24-hour day. Even though people with short and long biological cycles entrain quite well to the 24-hour cycle, there nevertheless are differences between those people in terms of the timing of peaks and valleys in their biological rhythms. Imagine someone with a slightly long circadian rhythm (such as 26 hours) and someone with a slightly short rhythm (such as 22 hours). They both may entrain to the same 24-hour day, but the peak in body temperature might occur relatively late for the first person (perhaps at 10 p.m.), whereas the peak would occur relatively early for the second person (perhaps around 6 p.m.).

Individuals with short biological rhythms hit their peak body temperature and alertness levels earlier in the day and thus begin to get sleepy earlier than do persons with longer circadian rhythms (Bailey & Heitkemper, 1991). A person with a 26-hour rhythm would have a harder time getting up at 6 in the morning, because his or her 26-hour biological rhythm still has 2 hours to go, even though the 24-hour clock is telling him or her to start a new day. A person with a 22-hour rhythm would have an easier time getting up early because he or she has completed a biological "day" in 22 hours and is ready to start another day even *before* the 24-hour clock is up.

Do you know someone who you think is a morning type of person? What specific evidence makes you come to this conclusion? Do you think people with a morning type of rhythm are different in other ways from evening-type people? For example, are there other personality characteristics associated with being a morning type? Benjamin Franklin is quoted as saying that "early to bed, early to rise, makes a man healthy, wealthy, and wise." Do you think it is possible that morning types are actually wiser or that they have better outcomes in life? How would you design a study to answer this question?

Research on individual differences in circadian rhythms provides the ground-work for understanding why some people are morning types and others are evening types. As you know, those with *shorter* biological rhythms tend to be morning persons, and those with *longer* biological rhythms tend to be evening persons. Horne and Ostberg (1976, 1977) developed a 19-item questionnaire to measure morningness–eveningness (see Table 7.4). The items ask about preferences for activities earlier or later in the day. In a sample of 48 participants, who took their body temperature every hour for several days, the researchers found that the scores on this questionnaire correlated –.51 with time of day that peak body temperature was reached. While the original study was done in Sweden, the negative correlation between self-reported preferences for activities in the morning and timing of peak body temperature has been replicated in the United States (Monk et al., 1983), Italy (Mecacci, Scaglione, & Vitrano, 1991), Spain (Adan, 1991, 1992), Croatia (Vidacek et al., 1988), and Japan (Ishihara, Saitoh, & Miyata, 1983).

These cross-cultural replications are consistent with the idea that preferences for morning or evening activities, and the time of day people are at their best, is a stable disposition with a biological basis. Scores on the Horne and Ostberg measure of morningness–eveningness are stable over time. Croatian researchers tested 90 college students on this measure and then tested them again seven years later, when they had finished college (Sverko & Fabulic, 1985). They found a significant positive correlation, suggesting that the morningness–eveningness characteristic is fairly stable over time. There was, however, a general shift in the whole sample toward morningness, which might be expected in a group that moves from being college students to persons having jobs.

Many studies have been done on the validity of the morningness–eveningness construct. In one study (Larsen, 1985), college students completed a report every day for 84 consecutive days, stating what time they felt at their best each day and what time they got up and went to bed each day. The Horne and Ostberg questionnaire correlated strongly with average rise and retire times, as well as with the time of day the participants reported feeling at their best. The morning persons got up earlier, went to bed earlier, and reportedly felt at their best earlier, on average, than the evening persons.

What would happen if people who had to live together, such as college roommates, were mismatched on morningness–eveningness? One person likes to stay up late and sleep late, whereas the other likes to get up early, even on weekends, as well as go to bed early. How happy do you think these people would be with their rooming situation? This was the topic of a study by Watts (1982), who selected first-year college students living on the campus of Michigan State University. The participants had to

Table 7.4 Items from the Morningness–Eveningness Questionnaire

Instructions

Please read each question carefully before answering. Each question should be answered independently of others. Do *not* go back and change or check your answers.

All questions have a selection of answers. For each question, circle the number in front of only one answer. Please answer each question as honestly as possible.

1. Considering only your "feeling best" rhythm, at what time would you get up if you were entirely free to plan your day?
   1. between 11:00 a.m. and noon
   2. between 9:30 a.m. and 11 a.m.
   3. between 7:30 a.m. and 9:30 a.m.
   4. between 6:00 a.m. and 7:30 a.m.
   5. before 6:00 a.m.

2. Considering only your "feeling best" rhythm, at what time would you go to bed if you were entirely free to plan your evening?
   1. after at least 1:30 in the morning
   2. between midnight and 1:30 a.m.
   3. between 10:30 p.m. and midnight
   4. between 9:00 p.m. and 10:30 p.m.
   5. before 9:00 p.m.

3. On the average, how easy do you find getting up in the morning?
   1. not at all easy
   2. not very easy
   3. fairly easy
   4. very easy

4. How alert do you feel during the first half-hour after having awakened in the morning?
   1. not at all alert
   2. not very alert
   3. fairly alert
   4. very alert

5. How is your appetite during the first half-hour after having awakened in the morning?
   1. very poor
   2. fairly poor
   3. fairly good
   4. very good

Source: Adapted from Horne & Ostberg, 1976.

have only one roommate. The roommate pairs completed the Morningness–Eveningness Questionnaire (MEQ), and they rated various aspects of their roommate relationship. Watts found that, the greater the difference between the roommates' MEQ scores, the lower ratings they gave to the quality of their relationship. Roommates who were very different on morningness–eveningness said that they did not get along very well with each other, that they did not enjoy their relationship and were not good friends, and that they were unlikely to continue living together. It appears that differences in morningness–eveningness, or chronotype incompatibility, create stress for people having to live together.

It is not surprising that chronotype compatibility is also found in intimate relationships. Randler and Kretz (2011) studied 84 couples and found a correlation between the couples' scores on a M–E questionnaire, implying that couples pair up on chronotype. This correlation did not change as a function of length of the relationship, implying that assertive mating on M–E occurs at the start of the relationship. The authors speculate that, because morning-types and evening-types inhabit different temporal environments, they are likely to meet and mate with others who have similar time-of-day preferences. For example, morning types have been found to start social contact earlier in the day than evening types (Randler & Jankowski, 2014). Who are they likely to come in contact with at that early time of day? Other morning-types, most likely.

Being a morning type or evening type refers to preferences for time of day that may have a biological basis; however, sometimes situations occur that go against such preferences. Imagine a college student who is definitely an evening type, yet a class he or she needs to take is offered only at 8 a.m., or a morning type of person who takes a job in a factory and is assigned to the late shift (4 p.m. to midnight). Going against one's natural circadian preferences is difficult, but not impossible. People do adjust to shift work and changes in sleep-wake schedule, and there is some evidence that evening types adjust to disruptions in sleep-wake cycles better than morning types (Ishihara et al., 1992). Such disruptions as transmeridian airline flights (which create jet lag) or working all night without sleeping (i.e., pulling an all-nighter) may be better tolerated by an evening type than a morning type of person.

In summary, the preference for being active and doing important or demanding work earlier or later in the day may be rooted in the length of a person's inherent biological circadian temperature rhythm. This is a good example of a physiological approach to personality because it highlights the notion of a behavior pattern (i.e., preference for different times of the day) being based on an underlying physiological mechanism (i.e., circadian rhythms).

Brain Asymmetry and Affective Style

As you are probably aware, the left and right sides of the brain are specialized, with asymmetry in the control of various psychological functions. One type of asymmetry that is receiving research attention is the relative amount of activity in the front part of the left and right brain hemispheres. The brain constantly produces small amounts of electrical activity, which can be measured on the scalp with sensitive electrical recording equipment. A recording of such electrical activity is called an **electroencephalograph,** or **EEG.** Moreover, such electrical activity is rhythmic and exhibits waves that are fast or slow, depending on neurological activation in the brain. One particular type of brain wave, called an **alpha wave,** oscillates at 8 to 12 times a second. The amount of alpha wave present in a given time period is an inverse indicator of brain activity during that time period. The alpha wave is given off when a person is calm and is relaxed and is feeling a bit sleepy and not attentive to the environment. In a given time period of brain wave recording, the *less* alpha wave activity present, the *more* we can assume that part of the brain was active.

EEG waves can be measured over any region or part of the brain. In emotion research, particular attention has been directed toward the frontal part of the brain, comparing the amount of activation in the right and left hemispheres. Study results suggest that the left hemisphere is relatively more active than the right when a person is experiencing pleasant emotions and vice versa, that the right frontal hemisphere is more active than the left when the person is experiencing unpleasant emotions. For example, in a study by Davidson and colleagues (1990), they showed film clips to the participants in an attempt to amuse some of the participants and disgust the others. The participants were also videotaped while they watched the funny or disgusting films. EEGs were taken while the participants looked at the films. When the participants were smiling at the amusing films, they had relatively more activation in their left than right frontal hemispheres. Similarly, when the participants were exhibiting a facial expression of disgust (lower lip pulled down, tongue protruding, nose wrinkled), their brains were more active in the right than left hemispheres.

Similar results have also been obtained in very young children. Instead of using films, Fox and Davidson (1986) used sweet and bitter solutions placed in the mouths of 10-month-old infants to produce pleasant and unpleasant affective reactions. The infants showed relatively more left- than right-brain activation to the sweet solution and more right- than left-brain activation to the bitter solution. In another study of 10-month-old infants, the infants' mothers left them alone in the testing room, whereupon a stranger entered the room (Fox & Davidson, 1987). In this standard anxiety-producing procedure, some infants become distressed but some do not; some infants cry and fuss but others do not. The researchers divided their sample of infants into those who cried during separation from their mothers and those who did not cry. They found that the criers exhibited more right-brain activation, relative with the left, compared with the noncriers. These results suggest that this tendency to become distressed or not (and the associated brain EEG asymmetry) is a stable characteristic of infants. Fox and colleagues (Fox, Bell, & Jones, 1992) studied a group of infants at age 7 months and again at age 12 months and found that the EEG measures of hemisphere asymmetry taken at those two time periods were highly correlated, suggesting stability over time in frontal brain asymmetry. Similar results have been found with adults, showing that measures of EEG asymmetry show test-retest correlations in the range of .66 to .73 across studies (Davidson, 1993, 2003). These findings suggest that individual differences in **frontal brain asymmetry** exhibit enough stability and consistency to be considered as indicative of an underlying biological disposition or trait.

Other studies suggest that EEG asymmetry indicates a vulnerability to pleasant or unpleasant affective states. Tomarken and colleagues (Tomarken, Davidson, & Henriques, 1990) and Wheeler and colleagues (Wheeler, Davidson, & Tomarken, 1993) examined the relation between individual differences in frontal asymmetry and reactions to affective film clips in normal participants. In these studies, EEG asymmetry was measured while the participants were resting. Then the participants were shown either happy and amusing films or disgusting and fearful films. For the dependent variable, the participants were asked to rate how the films made them feel. The hypothesis was that the participants with greater right-side activation at rest (measured before watching the films) would report more intense *negative* affective reactions to the fear and disgust films, compared with the participants with relatively more left-side activation. The opposite prediction was made for the participants with greater left-side activation—they should report stronger *positive* emotions in response to the happy and amusing films. The predictions were essentially supported, with frontal asymmetry measures taken *before* the films were seen predicting the participants' *subsequent* self-reported affective reactions to the films, with the right-side-dominant participants reporting more distress to the unpleasant films and the left-side-dominant participants reporting more pleasant reactions to the films.

Similar results have also been found with monkeys. Because monkeys cannot tell you how positive or negative they are feeling, researchers have used measures of **cortisol** to assess emotional reactivity. Cortisol is a stress hormone that prepares the

Application

Assessing brain asymmetry without an EEG. An EEG is not the only way to obtain an index of asymmetry in brain activation. Research suggests that a person's characteristic level of left- or right-sided activation may be indicated by the direction in which their eyes drift as they concentrate on answering difficult questions. When answering a difficult question (e.g., "Make up a sentence using the words *rhapsody* and *pleasure*"), people's eyes drift one way or the other as they reflect on their answer (Davidson, 1991). Among right-handed persons, eyes drifting to the right signify left-sided activation, and eyes drifting to the left signify right-sided activation. If you ask a person several difficult questions (e.g., "How many turns do you make from your house or apartment to the nearest store?") and note which way his or her eyes usually drift, you may get an indication of whether he or she tends to be right- or left-sided asymmetric. Of course, this quick measure is not as reliable as an EEG. It nevertheless may be a rough gauge of whether a person is left- or right-side asymmetric.

Perhaps you could make some observations of a few friends or acquaintances, asking them several difficult questions and observing which way they move their eyes as they think through their answers. Most people will not show completely consistent patterns of going one way or the other. That is why it is important to ask several questions and see which way they *usually* move their eyes. You will also need to decide whether they are more vulnerable to positive or negative emotions (see Figure 7.4). Persons who glance frequently to the right are more likely to be left-hemisphere dominant and should be more vulnerable to the pleasant emotions (e.g., happiness, joy, enthusiasm). Persons who frequently glance to the left while engaging in reflective thought are more likely to be right-hemisphere dominant and, by implication, should be more vulnerable to the negative emotions (e.g., distress, anxiety, sadness).

Certainly, many factors influence how people feel and which emotions they experience. The findings reviewed here suggest that the characteristic pattern of brain activation is one factor that may influence our affective lives by contributing to the likelihood that we will experience certain emotions.

Figure 7.4

These gaze patterns illustrate left and right gaze direction, associated with opposite brain hemisphere activation, for use in completing the exercise in the text.

© *McGraw-Hill Education. Mark Dierker, photographer*

body to fight or flee, and increases in cortisol mean that the animal has recently experienced stress. Davidson and his colleagues (reviewed in Kosslyn et al., 2002) have found that monkeys with greater right-sided activation had higher levels of cortisol. Identical results have been found with 6-month-old children. These researchers induced fear in the infants by having a male stranger enter the room, slowly approach the infant, and stare at the infant for two minutes. Those infants who had greater right-sided activation at baseline showed increased cortisol responses to the stranger. Also, those infants who showed the most right-sided activation during the stranger approach phase also displayed more crying and facial expressions of fear, and tried to escape more, compared to infants with less right-sided activation (Buss et al., 2003).

Over 100 studies of frontal EEG asymmetry have been published to date, most of them treating asymmetry as an individual difference variable related to differences in emotional responding to positive or negative situations or stimuli. One useful way to think about frontal asymmetry is as a moderator of the relation between an emotional stimulus and emotional response (Coan & Allen, 2004). A positive stimulus should produce a positive emotional response, but this effect will be especially strong (i.e., produce a higher correlation) for people with a left frontal asymmetry. For example, Wheeler et al. (1993) showed that the correlation between watching happy and amusing video and self-reported positive emotions was much stronger among people with left frontal asymmetry (compared to right frontal asymmetry). Similarly, a negative stimulus should produce a negative emotional response, but this effect will be especially strong for persons with right frontal asymmetry. An example of this is that going away to college for the first time often causes the negative emotion of homesickness, and homesickness has been found to be stronger in college freshmen who have more right (compared to left) frontal asymmetry (Steiner & Coan, 2011). The point of this information is that frontal asymmetry, a measure of underlying brain physiology, acts much like a traditional personality when it comes to explaining differences in how people respond emotionally to pleasant and unpleasant events in their lives.

The importance of brain asymmetry research is that different portions of the brain may respond with pleasant or unpleasant emotions, given the appropriate affective stimulus. Fox and Calkins (1993) discuss this notion in terms of thresholds for responding. The concept of thresholds implies that persons with a left- or right-sided pattern require less of the affective stimulus to evoke the corresponding emotion. The person who displays a right-frontal-activation pattern may have a lower threshold for responding with negative emotions when an unpleasant event happens. It may take less of a negative affective event to evoke unpleasant feelings for right-dominant persons. For an individual who displays a left-frontal-activation pattern, the threshold for experiencing pleasant emotions in response to positive events is lowered. A person's affective lifestyle may have its origins in, or at least may be predicted by, his or her pattern of asymmetry in frontal brain activation.

SUMMARY AND EVALUATION

The study of personality can be approached biologically. Theorizing about the biological influences on personality has a long history, and there are two ways to think about how physiological variables can be useful in personality theory and research. One way to view physiological measures is as variables that may be correlated with personality traits. For example, in a sample of college students, there may be a negative correlation between resting heart rate and scores on a neuroticism questionnaire (perhaps due to the heightened level of chronic anxiety associated with neuroticism). Here a physiological variable is seen as a correlate of a personality dimension, as something that is associated with being neurotic. Does an elevated heart rate cause a person to become neurotic? Probably not. Instead, a pounding heart goes along with, or is a correlate of, being neurotic.

A second way to think about physiological approaches to personality is to view physiological events as contributing to or providing the physiological substrate for the personality characteristic. This chapter covered six such examples of theories about the biological underpinnings of specific personality dimensions: extraversion (and neuronal excitability or arousability), sensitivity to cues of reward and punishment (based on brain circuits of the BIS and BAS systems), sensation seeking (and level of MAO and hormones in the bloodstream), tridimensional personality theory (based on neurotransmitters), morningness–eveningness (and circadian rhythms in body temperature), and affective style (and hemispheric asymmetry in the frontal cortex of the brain). In these theories, the physiological variables are assumed to be more than just correlates of the personality traits; they are assumed to be substrates of the biological underpinnings for the behavior pattern that defines the personality trait (see Table 7.5).

Table 7.5 Biological Theories of Specific Personality Traits

RELATED TO PHYSIOLOGICAL REACTIVITY

Personality Trait	Biological Underpinnings
Extraversion–Introversion	Arousal level of brain (early theory) Arousability of nervous system
Sensitivity to reward and punishment	Behavioral activation system (BAS) responds to incentives and reward Behavioral inhibition system (BIS) responds to threat and punishment
Sensation seeking	Optimal arousal level (early theory) Monoamine oxidase (MAO) levels
Tridimensional personality model	
Novelty seeking	Dopamine
Harm avoidance	Serotonin
Reward dependence	Norepinephrine

NOT RELATED TO PHYSIOLOGICAL REACTIVITY

Personality Trait	Biological Underpinnings
1. Morningness–eveningness	Length of circadian rhythm shorter = morning type longer = evening type
2. Affective style	Asymmetry in frontal brain activation Left = tendency toward positive Right = tendency toward negative

KEY TERMS

physiological systems 186
theoretical bridge 191
electrodes 191
telemetry 191
sympathetic nervous system 191
autonomic nervous system 191
electrodermal activity
    (skin conductance) 191
cardiac reactivity 193
type A personality 193
ascending reticular activating system
    (ARAS) 198
arousal level 198
arousability 200

reinforcement sensitivity theory 201
behavioral activation system
    (BAS) 201
behavioral inhibition system
    (BIS) 201
anxiety 202
impulsivity 202
sensation seeking 205
sensory deprivation 205
optimal level of arousal 205
comorbidity 207
neurotransmitters 208
monoamine oxidase (MAO) 209
dopamine 210

serotonin 210
norepinephrine 211
tridimensional personality model 211
novelty seeking 211
harm avoidance 211
reward dependence 211
morningness–eveningness 212
circadian rhythms 212
free running 213
electroencephalograph (EEG) 216
alpha wave 216
frontal brain asymmetry 217
cortisol 217

© Svisio/Getty Images RF

Evolutionary Perspectives on Personality

8

How much of human nature today is the result of behavior patterns that evolved as our ancestors solved the problems of surviving and reproducing?
© P. Rotger/Iberfoto/The Image Works

Imagine living as our ancestors did a million years ago. You awaken at dawn and shrug off the coldness of night. A few warm embers glow in the fire, so you stoke it with kindling. The others in your group gather around the fire as the sun breaks the horizon. Stomachs start growling. Your thoughts turn to food. Small groups set off in search of berries, nuts, and small game animals.

After a long day of hunting and gathering, the members converge back at their temporary home site. As night begins to fall, the group gathers around the fire. The day's foraging has been successful and the mood is warm and animated. Tales of the hunt are reenacted, the bounty of gathered goods admired. With bellies full, discussion turns to whether the group should move the next day or stay a bit longer. A successful hunter makes eye contact with his young lover, but she shyly looks away. Others notice this flirtation. Mating universally draws interest. As people grow sleepy and children are put to sleep, the young lovers quietly slip away from the group to be alone. Their warm embrace echoes millions of past events as people partake of life's cycle.

Evolutionary psychology is a new and rapidly growing scientific perspective, and it offers important insights into human personality. In this chapter, we look at some of these insights in three areas: human nature, sex differences, and individual differences. We will see how theories of evolutionary psychology fit with the discoveries of personality psychologists and generate new lines of research. We begin by reviewing some basic information about the theory of evolution.

Evolution and Natural Selection

All of us come from a long and unbroken line of ancestors who accomplished two critical tasks: they survived to reproductive age, and they reproduced. If any one of your ancestors had failed at reproduction, you would not be here today to contemplate their existence. In this sense, every living human is an evolutionary success story. As descendants of successful ancestors, we carry with us the genes for the adaptations that led to their success. From this perspective, our human nature—the collection of adaptations that defines us as human—is the product of the evolutionary process.

Long before Charles Darwin it was known that change takes place over time in organic structures. The fossil record showed the bones of long extinct dinosaurs, suggesting that not all species in the past are with us today. The paleontological record showed changes in animals' body forms, suggesting that nothing remains static. Moreover, the structures of species seemed extraordinarily well adapted to their environments. The long necks of giraffes enabled them to eat leaves from tall trees. The turtle's shell seemed designed for protection. The beaks of birds seemed suited for cracking nuts to get at their nutritious meat. What could account for change over time and apparent adaptation to environmental conditions?

Natural Selection

Darwin's contribution was not in observing change over time, nor in noticing the adaptive design of mechanisms. Rather, Darwin proposed a theory of the *process* by which adaptations are created and change takes place over time. He called it the theory of **natural selection**.

Darwin noticed that species seemed to produce many more offspring than could possibly survive and reproduce. He reasoned that changes, or *variants,* that better enabled an organism to survive and reproduce would lead to more descendants. The descendants would inherit the variants that led to their ancestors' survival and reproduction. Through this process, the successful variants were selected and unsuccessful variants weeded out. Natural selection, therefore, results in gradual changes in a species over time, as successful variants increase in frequency and eventually spread throughout the gene pool, replacing the less successful variants. Over time, these successful variants come to characterize the entire species; unsuccessful variants decrease in frequency and vanish from the species.

This process of natural selection, sometimes called *survival selection,* led Darwin to focus on the events that impede survival, which he called the **hostile forces of nature**. These hostile forces included food shortages, diseases, parasites, predators, and extremes of weather. Variants that helped organisms survive these hostile forces of nature led to an increased likelihood of successful reproduction. Food preferences for substances rich in fat, sugar, and protein, for example, helped organisms survive food shortages. An immune system teeming with antibodies helped organisms survive diseases and parasites. The behavioral immune system, including the emotion of disgust, helped to avoid contact with disease-carrying organisms, including other humans (Schaller, 2016). Fear of snakes and spiders helped them survive poisonous bites. These mechanisms, resulting from a long and repeated process of natural selection, are called adaptations, inherited solutions to the survival and reproductive problems posed by the hostile forces of nature.

Even after Darwin came up with his theory of natural selection, there remained many mysteries that puzzled him. He noticed that many mechanisms seemed contrary to survival. The elaborate plumage, large antlers, and other conspicuous features displayed by the males of many species seemed costly in terms of survival. He wondered how the brilliant plumage of peacocks could evolve, and become common, when it posed such an obvious threat to survival, acting as a neon advertisement to predators. In response to puzzles of this sort, Darwin proposed a second evolutionary theory—the theory of sexual selection.

Sexual Selection

Darwin's answer to the mysteries of the peacock's tail and the stag's antlers was that they evolved because they contributed to an individual's mating success, providing an advantage in the competition for desirable mates. The evolution of characteristics because of their mating benefits, rather than because of their survival benefits, is known as **sexual selection**.

Sexual selection, according to Darwin, takes two forms. In one form, members of the same sex compete with each other, and the outcome of their contest gives the winner greater sexual access to members of the opposite sex. Two stags locking horns in combat is the prototypical image of this **intrasexual competition**. The characteristics that lead to success in contests of this kind, such as greater strength, intelligence, or attractiveness to allies, evolve because the victors are able to mate more often and, hence, pass on their genes.

In the other type of sexual selection—**intersexual selection**—members of one sex choose a mate based on their preferences for particular qualities. These characteristics evolve because those that possess them are chosen more often as mates, and their genes thrive. Animals that lack the desired characteristics are excluded from mating, and their genes perish.

Success at same-sex competition leads to success at mating; traits that help to win these battles are passed on in greater numbers and hence evolve in the population.

Source: NPS photo by Jeff Foot.

Genes and Inclusive Fitness

Genes are packets of DNA that are inherited by children from their parents in distinct chunks. Genes are the smallest discrete units that are inherited by offspring intact, without being broken up. According to modern evolutionary biologists, evolution operates by the process of **differential gene reproduction**, defined by reproductive success relative to others. The genes of organisms that reproduce more than others get passed down to future generations at a greater frequency than do the genes of those that reproduce less. Survival is usually critical for reproductive success, so characteristics that lead to greater survival get passed along. Success in mating is also critical for reproductive success, and the qualities that lead to success in same-sex competition or to success at being chosen as a mate get passed along. Successful survival and successful mate competition, therefore, are both paths to differential gene reproduction. The characteristics that lead to the greater reproduction of genes that code for them are selected and, hence, evolve over time.

The modern evolutionary theory based on differential gene reproduction is called **inclusive fitness theory** (Hamilton, 1964). The "inclusive" part refers to the fact that the characteristics that facilitate reproduction need not affect the personal production of offspring. They can affect the survival and reproduction of genetic relatives as well. For example, if you take a personal risk to defend or protect your sister or another close relative, then this might enable her to better survive and reproduce. Because you share genes with your sister—50 percent on average in the case of siblings—then helping her survive and reproduce will also lead to successful gene reproduction.

A critical condition for such helping to evolve is that the cost to your reproduction as a result of the helping must be less than the benefits to the reproduction of your genes that reside in your relative. If helping your sister survive—for example, by jumping into rushing rapids to save her from drowning—puts your own life at risk, the odds of saving her must exceed twice the odds of your dying in order for evolution to select for mechanisms underlying this helping behavior. Thus, inclusive fitness can be defined as one's personal reproductive success (roughly, the number of children you produce) *plus* the effects you have on the reproduction of your genetic relatives, weighted by the degree of genetic relatedness. Inclusive fitness can lead to adaptations that incline you to take some risk for the welfare of your genetic relatives, but not too great a risk. Inclusive fitness theory, as an expansion and elaboration of Darwin's theory, represented a major advance in understanding human traits, such as some forms of altruism.

Traits for helping can evolve through inclusive fitness.
© UpperCut Images/Getty Images RF

Products of the Evolutionary Process

All living humans are products of the evolutionary process, the descendants of a long line of ancestors who succeeded in surviving, reproducing, and helping their genetic relatives. The evolutionary process acts as a series of filters. In each generation, only a small subset of genes passes through the filter. The recurrent filtering process lets only three things pass through: adaptations; byproducts of adaptations; and noise, or random variations.

Adaptations

Adaptations are the primary product of the selective process. An adaptation can be defined as a "reliably developing structure in the organism, which, because it meshes with the recurrent structure of the world, causes the solution to an adaptive problem" (Tooby & Cosmides, 1992, p. 104). Known human adaptations include a taste for sweet and fatty foods, the drive to defend close relatives, and preferences for specific mates, such as those that are healthy.

Let's examine the components of the definition of adaptation. The focus on reliably developing structure means that an adaptation tends to emerge with regularity during the course of a person's life. The mechanisms that allow humans to see, for example, develop reliably. But this does not mean that vision develops invariantly. The development of the eye can be perturbed by genetic anomalies or by environmental trauma. The emphasis on reliable development suggests that evolutionary approaches are *not* forms of "genetic determinism." Environments are always needed for the development of an adaptation, and environmental events can always interfere with or enhance such development.

The emphasis on meshing with recurrent structures of the world means that adaptations emerge from, and are structured by, the selective environment. Features of the environment must be recurrent over time for an adaptation to evolve. The venomous snakes must be recurrently dangerous, ripe fruit must be recurrently nutritious, and enclosed caves must be recurrently protective before adaptations to them can emerge.

Finally, an adaptation must facilitate the solution to an adaptive problem. An **adaptive problem** is anything that impedes survival or reproduction, or anything whose solution increases the odds of survival or reproduction. Stated more precisely, all adaptations must contribute to fitness during the period of time in which they evolve, by helping an organism survive, reproduce, or facilitate the reproductive success of genetic relatives.

The hallmark of adaptation is *special design*. That is, the features of an adaptation are recognized as components of specialized problem-solving machinery. Factors such as *efficiency* in solving a specific adaptive problem, *precision* in solving the adaptive problem, and *reliability* in solving the adaptive problem are key criteria in recognizing the special design of an adaptation. Adaptations are like keys that fit only specific locks. The tines of the key (adaptation) show special design features, which mesh with the specific mirror-image elements within the lock (adaptive problem).

For most of our evolutionary past, humans lived in small, close-knit groups, usually of less than 150 people. This form of group living is relatively rare today.
© ranplett/Getty Images RF

All adaptations are products of a history of selection. In this sense, we live with an ancient brain in a modern world, which is in some ways different from the world in which we evolved. For example, ancestral humans evolved in relatively small groups of 50 to 150, using both hunting and gathering as methods of acquiring food (Dunbar, 1993). In the modern world, by contrast, many people live in large cities surrounded by thousands or millions of people. Characteristics that were probably adaptive in ancestral environments—such as **xenophobia**, or fear of strangers—are not necessarily adaptive in modern environments. Some of the personality traits that make up human nature may be vestigial adaptations to an ancestral environment that no longer exists.

Byproducts of Adaptations

The evolutionary process also produces things that are not adaptations—such as **byproducts of adaptations**. Consider the design of a lightbulb. A lightbulb is designed to produce light—that is its function. But it also may produce heat, not because it is designed to produce heat, but rather because heat is an incidental byproduct, which occurs as a consequence of design for light. In the same way, human adaptations can also have **evolutionary byproducts**, or incidental effects that are not properly considered to be adaptations. The human nose, for example, is clearly an adaptation designed for smelling. But the fact that we use our noses to hold up our eyeglasses is an incidental byproduct. The nose was designed for smelling odors, not for holding up glasses. Notice that the hypothesis that something is a byproduct (e.g., by holding up eyeglasses) requires specifying the adaptation (e.g., the nose) of which it is a byproduct. Thus, both sorts of evolutionary hypotheses—adaptation and byproduct hypotheses—require a description of the nature of the adaptation.

Noise, or Random Variations

The third product of the evolutionary process is **evolutionary noise**, or random variations that are neutral with respect to selection. In the design of a lightbulb, for example, there are minor variations in the surface texture of the bulb that do not affect the functioning of the design elements. Neutral variations introduced into the gene pool through mutation, for example, are perpetuated over generations if they do not hinder the functioning of adaptations.

In sum, there are three products of the evolutionary process: adaptations, byproducts, and noise. Adaptations are the primary product of the selective process, so evolutionary psychology is primarily focused on identifying and describing human psychological adaptations. The hypothesis that something is a byproduct requires specifying the adaptation of which it is a byproduct. The analysis of byproducts, therefore, leads us back to the need to describe adaptations. And noise is the residue of nonfunctional variation that is selectively neutral.

Evolutionary Psychology

The basic elements of the evolutionary perspective apply to all forms of life on Earth, from slime molds to people. We will turn now to the application of this perspective to human psychology. This branch of psychology is referred to as evolutionary psychology.

Premises of Evolutionary Psychology

Evolutionary psychology involves three key premises: domain specificity, numerousness, and functionality.

Domain Specificity

Adaptations are hypothesized to be **domain specific** because they are designed by the evolutionary process to solve a particular adaptive problem. Consider the problem of food selection—choosing the right foods to eat from among a large array of possible objects in the world. A general decision rule, such as "eat the first thing you encounter," would be highly maladaptive because it would fail to guide you to choose the small subset of objects that are edible and nutritious. Such a general rule would result in the consumption of poisonous plants, twigs, dirt, or feces, which would interfere with successful survival. The mechanisms favored by the evolutionary process are more specialized. In the area of food selection, domain specificity is seen in our preferences for calorically rich fat and in our evolved sweet tooth, which leads us to objects rich in sugar, such as ripe fruit and berries. General mechanisms cannot guide us to the small islands of successful adaptive solutions that are surrounded by oceans of maladaptive solutions.

Another reason for domain specificity is that different adaptive problems require different sorts of solutions. Our taste preferences, which guide us to successful food choices, do not help us solve the adaptive problem of choosing successful mates. If we were to use our food preferences as a general guide to the choice of mates, we would select strange mates indeed. Successful mate choices require different mechanisms. Domain specificity implies that selection tends to fashion at least somewhat specialized mechanisms for each adaptive problem.

Numerousness

Our ancestors faced many sorts of adaptive problems in the course of human evolution, so we have numerous adaptive mechanisms. If you look at a textbook on the body, for example, you will discover a large number of physiological and anatomical mechanisms. We have a heart to pump our blood, a liver to detoxify poisons, a larynx to prevent us from choking, and sweat glands to keep the body thermally regulated.

Evolutionary psychologists suggest that the human mind, our evolved psychology, also contains a large number of mechanisms—psychological adaptations. Consider the most common fears and phobias. We tend to be scared of snakes, heights, darkness, spiders, cliff edges, and strangers. Just in the domain of fears, we have a large number of psychological mechanisms because the number of hazardous hostile forces of nature has been so large. We also have psychological mechanisms for the selection of mates, the detection of cheaters in social exchanges, the favoring of habitats, the rearing of children, and the formation of strategic alliances. Evolutionary psychologists expect there to be a large number of domain-specific psychological adaptations to correspond to the large number of distinct adaptive problems humans have recurrently confronted.

Functionality

The third key premise of evolutionary psychology is **functionality**, the notion that our psychological mechanisms are designed to accomplish particular adaptive tasks. If you were a medical researcher studying the liver, you could not get very far in your understanding unless you understood the functions of the liver (e.g., filtering out toxins). Evolutionary psychologists suggest that understanding adaptive function is also critical to insight into our evolved *psychological* mechanisms. We can't understand our preferences for certain mates, for example, without inquiring about the function of such preferences (e.g., to select a healthy or fertile mate). The search for function involves identifying the specific adaptive problem for which the mechanism is an evolved solution.

Empirical Testing of Evolutionary Hypotheses

To understand how evolutionary psychologists test hypotheses, it is necessary to consider the hierarchy of levels of evolutionary analysis depicted in Figure 8.1. At the top of the hierarchy is evolution by selection. The theory has been tested directly in many cases. New species can be formed in the laboratory by its application, and dogs can be selectively bred using its principles. Because there has never been a single case in which the general theory has been proved to be incorrect, most scientists take the general theory for granted and proceed with a more specific form of hypothesis testing.

At the next level down are middle-level evolutionary theories, such as the theory of parental investment and sexual selection. According to this theory, the sex (male or female) that invests more in offspring is predicted to be more discriminating or "choosy" about its mating partners. And the sex that invests less in offspring is predicted to be more competitive with members of its own sex for sexual access to the high-investing sex. From these hypotheses, specific predictions can be derived and tested empirically. In the human case, women bear the heavy parental investment

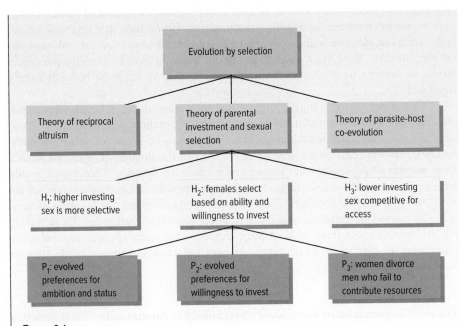

Figure 8.1

The evolutionary analysis hierarchy depicts the conceptual levels of evolutionary analysis. At the top of the hierarchy is natural selection theory. At the next level down are middle-level evolutionary theories from which specific hypotheses and predictions can be derived. Each level of the hierarchy is evaluated by the cumulative weight of the empirical evidence from tests of the predictions derived from it.

Source: Adapted from Buss, 1995a.

burdens of internal fertilization and nine-month pregnancy. Women are the high-investing sex; thus, according to the theory, they should exert more selectivity in their choice of mates than should men, who require only the contribution of sperm in order to reproduce. Two specific predictions can be derived from this hypothesis: (1) women will choose as mates men who are willing to invest resources in them and their children, and (2) women will divorce men who fail to continue providing resources to them and their children.

Using this method of deriving specific testable predictions, researchers can carry out the normal scientific business of empirical research. If the data fail to support the predictions and hypotheses, then the middle-level theory from which they were derived is called into question. If the findings support the predictions and hypotheses, then the middle-level theory from which they were derived increases in credibility.

The **deductive reasoning approach**, or the "top down," theory-driven method of empirical research is one approach to scientific investigation. Another method, which is equally valid, is called the **inductive reasoning approach**, or the "bottom-up," data-driven method of empirical research. In the inductive reasoning approach, a phenomenon is first observed, and then the researchers develop a theory to fit the observations. Just as astronomers observed the galaxies in the universe expanding before they had a theory to explain why, psychologists notice and empirically document a number of phenomena before they have theories to explain them. In the domain of personality, for example, we might notice that men tend to be more physically aggressive than women. Although nothing in the theory of evolution by selection would have predicted this sex difference in advance, it is fair game for subsequent theorizing. The dual inductive and deductive approaches, of course, can apply to all theories in personality psychology, not just evolutionary theories.

Once a theory is proposed to explain the sex difference in aggression, however, we can ask, "If the theory is true, then what *further* predictions follow from it that we have not already observed?" It is in these further deduced predictions that the value and tenability of the theory rest. If the theory generates a wealth of new predictions, which are then confirmed empirically, we know that we are on the right explanatory track. If the theory fails to generate further testable predictions, or if its predictions fail to be confirmed empirically, then the theory is called into question. For example, one theory of sexual aggression against women has proposed that men who have experienced deprivation of sexual access to women are more likely to use aggressive tactics. This has been called the *mate deprivation hypothesis* (Lalumiere et al., 1996). The evidence so far, however, has failed to support this hypothesis—men who have difficulty attracting women are no more likely to use sexual aggression than are men who are highly successful at attracting women. The mate deprivation hypothesis, in short, appears to be false.

Evolutionary hypotheses have sometimes been criticized as being vague, speculative "just-so stories," implying that they are like fairy tales that have little scientific value. Most evolutionary hypotheses have been framed in a precise and testable manner, so this criticism is not valid (Buss, 2005a; Confer et al., 2010; Kenrick & Luce, 2004). Individual scientists bear a responsibility to formulate evolutionary (and nonevolutionary) hypotheses in as precise and testable manner as possible.

With this theoretical background in mind, let's now turn to the implications of an evolutionary perspective for the three key levels of personality analysis: human nature, sex differences, and individual differences.

Human Nature

In the history of psychology, "grand" theories of personality were proposed about the universal contents of human nature. Sigmund Freud's theory of psychoanalysis, for example, proposed that humans had the core motives of sex and aggression. Alfred Adler proposed that humans had the striving for superiority as a core motive. Robert Hogan suggests that humans are driven by the desire for status and acceptance by the group—getting ahead and getting along. Even the most radical behaviorist, B. F. Skinner, had a theory of human nature, consisting of a few domain-general learning mechanisms. Thus, all personality theories attempt to answer the question: If humans have a nature that is different from the nature of gorillas, dogs, or rats, what are its contents and how can we discover them?

The perspective of evolutionary psychology offers a set of tools for discovering the human nature component of personality. From this perspective, human nature is the primary product of the evolutionary process. Psychological mechanisms that are successful in helping humans survive and reproduce tend to out-replicate those that are less successful. Over evolutionary time, these successful mechanisms spread throughout the population and come to characterize a species. Let's examine a few evolutionary hypotheses about the contents of human nature.

Need to Belong

Hogan (1983) argues that the most basic human motivators are status and acceptance by the group. According to Hogan, the most important social problems early humans had to solve in order to survive and reproduce involved establishing cooperative relations with other members of the group and negotiating hierarchies. Achieving status and popularity likely conferred a host of reproductively relevant resources on an individual, including better protection, more food, and more desirable mates.

According to Hogan's theory, being ostracized from a group would have been extremely damaging. Therefore, it can be predicted that humans have evolved psychological mechanisms to prevent being excluded. Baumeister and Tice (1990) propose that this is the origin and function of **social anxiety**, defined as distress or worry about being negatively evaluated in social situations. They propose that social anxiety is a species-typical adaptation that prevents social exclusion. People who were indifferent to being excluded by others may have suffered in the currency of survival by lacking the protection of the group. They may also have suffered by failing to find mates. These individuals may have experienced lower reproductive success than those whose psychological mechanisms caused them to maintain inclusion in the group by avoiding doing things that elicit criticism.

If this hypothesis is correct, what testable predictions might follow from it? One set of testable predictions pertains to the *events* that elicit social anxiety (Buss, 1990). Groups can be expected to shun those who inflict costs on others within the group. Showing cowardice in the face of danger, displaying aggression toward in-group members, trying to lure away the mates of in-group members, and stealing from in-group members would all have inflicted costs on particular members of the group.

Baumeister and Leary (1995) present empirical evidence that the need to belong is a central motive of human nature. They argue that the group serves several key adaptive functions for individuals. First, groups can share food, information, and other resources. Second, groups can offer protection from external threat, or defense against

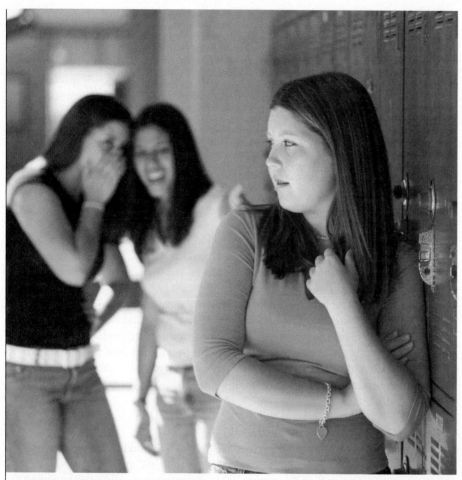

Humans evolved to live in groups. Consequently, an individual who is shunned by a group will feel anxious.
© *SW Productions/Getty Images RF*

rival groups. Third, groups contain concentrations of mates, which are needed for reproduction. And, fourth, groups usually contain kin, which provide opportunities to receive altruism and to invest in genetic relatives.

Several lines of empirical research support Baumeister and Leary's theory about the need to belong. First, external threats have been shown repeatedly to increase group cohesion (Stein, 1976). In one study, World War II veterans were examined for enduring social ties (Elder & Clipp, 1988). Remarkably, their strongest social ties 40 years after the war were with comrades who had experienced combat together. This effect was intensified among the units in which some comrades had died, suggesting that the more intense the external threat, the greater the social bonding.

The opportunity to acquire resources also seems to be a powerful context for triggering group cohesion. In one study, participants were randomly assigned to two groups (Rabbie & Horwitz, 1969). The assignment to groups alone produced no increase in group cohesion. When one group was given a prize—a transistor radio—based on the flip of a coin, however, both the rewarded group and the deprived group showed an increase in in-group preference. When resources are linked with group membership, people become increasingly bonded with their groups.

Further support for the importance of the need to belong as a fundamental human motive comes from a cross-cultural study on the effects of social interactions on self-esteem (Denissen et al., 2008). Those who spend a lot of time with others enjoy higher self-esteem. Day-to-day fluctuations in self-esteem are linked with quality and quantity of social interactions. And even at the level of nations, countries whose inhabitants frequently interact with friends and relatives enjoy higher self-esteem than countries with less frequent social interactions. These findings point to the notion that self-esteem functions, at least in part, as an internal tracking device that monitors social inclusion (Denissen et al., 2008).

Adaptations for the need to belong appear to emerge quite early in life. In a clever laboratory study of children 5 to 6 years old, some were ostracized from a video game which others were apparently playing; another group was socially included in the game (Watson-Jones et al., 2016). Subsequently, the ostracized children showed more anxiety, conformity, and imitation. These reactions, the authors argue, function to motivate in-group inclusion after being shunned.

Researchers have begun to make progress in identifying the underlying brain circuitry for the pain caused by social exclusion (MacDonald & Leary, 2005; Panksepp, 2005). Social rejection or exclusion has often been described as literally painful. Brain research suggests that social exclusion is mediated by components of the physical pain system, such as the anterior cingulate cortex. The fact that people use words like *hurt, wounded,* and *damaged* when they are socially excluded may reflect the shared brain circuitry through which physically induced pain and socially induced pain are mediated.

Humans have always been intensely group living, and lack of a group almost surely would have meant death in ancestral environments, so it is not surprising that we have a strong need to belong—a part of our human nature.

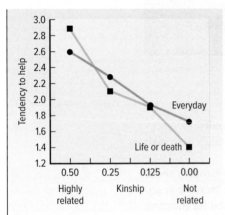

Figure 8.2

Tendency to help kin under life-or-death versus everyday conditions. Genetic overlap predicts the tendency to help, especially under life-or-death conditions.

Source: Adapted from "Some Neo-Darwinian Decision Rules for Altruism: Weighing Cures for Inclusive Fitness as a Function of the Biological Importance of the Decision," by E. Burnstein, C. Crandall, and S. Kitayama, 1994, *Journal of Personality & Social Psychology, 67,* pp. 773–789, Figure 2, p. 778. Copyright © 1994 by the American Psychological Association. Reprinted with permission.

Helping and Altruism

An evolutionary perspective provides a straightforward set of predictions about the human nature of helping and altruism (Burnstein, Crandall, & Kitayama, 1994). Burnstein and colleagues hypothesized that helping others is a direct function of the recipients' ability to enhance the inclusive fitness of the helpers. Helping should decrease, according to this hypothesis, as the degree of genetic relatedness decreases between the helper and the recipient. Thus, you should be more likely to help your sibling, who shares 50 percent of your genes, on average, than your nieces and nephews, who share only 25 percent of your genes, on average. Helping is expected to be lower still between individuals who share only 12.5 percent of their genes, such as first cousins. No other theory in psychology generates this precise helping gradient as a function of genetic relatedness or specifies kinship as one underlying principle for altruism.

Studies in the United States and Japan support these predictions. In one study, participants were asked to imagine different individuals asleep in different rooms of a rapidly burning building. The participants imagined that they had time to rescue only one of them. They circled the target they were most likely to help. As shown in Figure 8.2, the tendency to help is a direct function of the degree of genetic relatedness. This is especially true in a life-or-death context, as confirmed by independent researchers (Fitzgerald & Colarelli, 2009).

Genetic relatedness represents just the start of an evolutionary analysis of the altruistic component of human nature. Burnstein et al.,

(1994) predicted that people should help younger relatives more than older relatives because helping older kin would have less impact, on average, on their reproductive success than would helping a younger person. Furthermore, individuals of higher reproductive value (ability to produce children) should be helped more than individuals of lower reproductive value.

In one study, 1-year-olds were helped more than 10-year-olds, who in turn were helped more than 45-year-olds (Burnstein et al., 1994). Least helped were 75-year-old individuals. These findings, replicated across both Japanese and American samples, provide further support for the hypothesis that life-or-death helping decreases as the kin member gets older. Interestingly, these results were strongest in the life-or-death situation, but showed a reversal in a trivial helping condition. For everyday helping, such as running a small errand for someone, the 75-year-olds were helped more than the 45-year-olds (see Figure 8.3).

The tendency to help younger people depended on a critical survival context—famine conditions (Burnstein et al., 1994). When the participants imagined themselves living in a sub-Saharan African country that suffered widespread famine and disease, they reported a curvilinear relationship between age and helping. Infants in this condition were helped *less* than 10-year-olds, who were helped the most. But then helping began to drop, with the least helped being the 75-year-olds. Another study found that people are willing to endure more physical pain—maintaining a painfully awkward physical position for as long as possible—as a function of closeness of kinship (Madsen et al., 2007). Moreover, studies confirm that in real-life situations in which life is in danger, having kin in close proximity literally increases the odds of surviving compared to people in the same situation who lack kin in close proximity (Grayson, 1993; Sear & Mace, 2008). Moreover, people write their wills to leave their cash and other assets to close genetic relatives more than to distant ones (Judge & Hrdy, 1992).

These studies suggest that a central component of human nature is helping other people, but in highly domain-specific ways. The ways in which humans help others—the distribution of helping acts across individuals—is highly predictable from an evolutionary perspective. The importance of genetic relatedness on helping others has even been documented for patterns of grandparental investment (Laham, Gonsalkorale, & von Hippel, 2005).

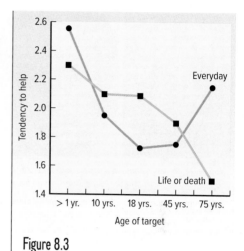

Figure 8.3

Tendency to help as a function of the recipient's age under life-or-death versus everyday conditions. When helping is relatively trivial, people tend to help those most in need, such as the young and the elderly. Under costly forms of help, however, the young are helped more than the old.

Source: Adapted from "Some Neo-Darwinian Decision Rules for Altruism: Weighing Cures for Inclusive Fitness as a Function of the Biological Importance of the Decision," by E. Burnstein, C. Crandall, and S. Kitayama, 1994, *Journal of Personality & Social Psychology, 67,* pp. 773–789, Figure 3, p. 779. Copyright © 1994 by the American Psychological Association. Reprinted with permission.

Universal Emotions

Evolutionary psychologists have taken three distinct perspectives on the study of emotions, such as fear, rage, and jealousy. One view is to examine whether facial expressions of emotion are interpreted in the same ways across cultures, on the assumption that universality is one criterion for adaptation (Ekman, 1973, 1992a, 1992b). If all humans share an adaptation, such as smiling to express happiness, that adaptation is likely to be a core part of human nature. A second evolutionary view is that emotions are adaptive psychological mechanisms that signal various "fitness affordances" in the social environment (Ketelaar, 1995). According to this perspective, emotions guide the person toward goals that would have conferred fitness in ancestral environments (e.g., the pleasure one feels having one's status rise within a group) or to avoid conditions that would have interfered with fitness (e.g., getting beaten up or abused or ostracized). A third evolutionary

Photos of the seven emotional expressions that are correctly identified by people from many diverse cultures. Can you identify which photo is associated with the following emotions: happiness, disgust, anger, fear, surprise, sadness, and contempt?

© *Paul Ekman Group LLC*

perspective on social emotions is the "manipulation hypothesis," which suggests that emotions are designed to exploit the psychological mechanisms of other people. For example, expressions of rage might be designed to make a verbal threat more credible than the same threat made without displaying rage (Sell et al., 2009).

All these evolutionary perspectives on emotions hinge on the proposition that they are universal and universally recognized in the same way. Ekman (1973, 1992a, 1992b) pioneered the cross-cultural study of emotions. He assembled pictures of several different faces, each of which showed one of seven emotions: happiness, disgust, anger, fear, surprise, sadness, and contempt. When these pictures were shown to subjects in Japan, Chile, Argentina, Brazil, and the United States, all showed tremendous agreement on which emotions corresponded to which face. Subsequent research has confirmed the universal recognition of these emotional expressions in Italy, Scotland, Estonia, Greece, Germany, Hong Kong, Sumatra, and Turkey (Ekman et al., 1987).

Especially impressive is the study of the Fore of New Guinea—a cultural group with practically no contact with outsiders. They spoke no English, had seen no TV or movies, and had never lived with Caucasians. Nonetheless, the Fore also showed the universal pairing of emotions and faces. Subsequent research has also shown the universality of the facial expression of contempt (Ekman et al., 1987). Ekman's work suggests that emotions, as central components of personality, are universally expressed and recognized, thus fulfilling an important criterion for adaptation. They are good candidates for evolved components of human nature.

We have reviewed only a few hypotheses about the components of human nature from an evolutionary perspective: the need to belong, social anxiety about ostracism, the urge to help, and the universality of emotions. An evolutionary perspective may shed light on many other possible components of human nature, such as childhood fears of loud noises, darkness, spiders, and strangers; emotions such as anger, envy, passion, and love; the universality of play among children; retaliation and revenge for perceived personal violations; status striving as a fundamental motive; psychological pain on the loss of status and reputation; and perhaps many more. Human nature, however, represents only one level of personality analysis. We now turn to the second level—sex differences.

A Closer Look

The Emotion of Disgust: The Disease-Avoidance Hypothesis

The emotion of disgust is a hypothesized adaptation that serves as a defense against microbial attacks, protecting people from the risk of disease (Curtis et al., 2004; Oaten, Stevenson, & Case, 2009). Disgust is an emotion that involves feelings of revulsion and sometimes nausea. It motivates strong withdrawal from the disgust-producing stimulus. If the emotion of disgust is an evolved defense against disease, several predictions follow. One is that disgust should be evoked most strongly by disease-carrying substances. The second is that these disgust elicitors should be universal across cultures. Empirical research supports both predictions (Curtis & Biran, 2001). People from cultures ranging from the Netherlands to West Africa find foods potentially contaminated by parasites or unhygienic preparation to be exceptionally disgusting. Examples are rotting flesh, dirty food, bad-smelling food, food leftovers, moldy food, dead insects in food, and witnessing food preparation by someone with dirty hands. Foods that have had contact with worms, cockroaches, or feces evoke especially strong disgust reactions. A third prediction is that disgust should activate the immune system. One study found that showing people images of contaminated food actually elevated their body temperature—one of the key features of immune response to disease (Stevenson et al., 2012).

A cross-cultural study asked Americans and Japanese to list the things they found most disgusting. Feces and other body wastes were the most frequently mentioned items, at 25 percent of the written responses (Rozin, 1996). Feces in particular are known to harbor harmful elements, including parasites and toxins, and are particularly dangerous to humans. Another study found that students refuse to drink from a glass that has been thoroughly cleaned and sterilized when told that it once held dog feces (Rozin & Nemeroff, 1990). Other evidence of the universality of disgust comes from studies that find that the facial expression of disgust is universally recognized; it is expressed by people who are blind from birth; and it is interpreted correctly by people who are born deaf (Oaten et al., 2009).

Another prediction from the disease-avoidance hypothesis of disgust is a gender difference: Since women typically care for their infants and children, they need to protect them from disease, as well as themselves. And indeed, women find images depicting disease-carrying objects to be more disgusting than men do, and also perceive that the risk of disease is greater from those objects than men do (Curtis et al., 2004). Individuals differ in disgust sensitivity—a prime candidate for an important personality variable. Individuals who have especially heightened sensitivity to contamination and who were most easily disgusted have significantly fewer infections—a finding that provides evidence for the protective function of disgust (Stevenson et al., 2009). Interestingly, individuals who score high on a measure of pathogen disgust find relatively unattractive faces to be especially unattractive compared with people low on pathogen disgust (Park et al., 2012).

Potential contact with people who have poor hygiene, who appear diseased, or have body boundary violations such as gaping wounds, and who engage in practices such as anal sex—all of which are possible conduits for disease transmission—often evokes disgust (Tyber et al., 2009). Indeed, sexual contact is an important source of disease transmission (Tyber et al., 2013). The mouth, the skin, the anus, and the genitals are all key entry and exit points for microorganisms to move from host to host. Kissing, touching, oral–genital contact, genital–genital contact, and other sexual behaviors put individuals at risk of contracting diseases. Recent empirical studies suggest that sexual disgust may be a specialized adaptation to avoid potentially infected sex partners, above and beyond the disgust adaptation designed to avoid contaminated food and infectious animals and insects (Tyber et al., 2013). Much empirical evidence, in short, supports the disease-avoidance hypothesis of disgust. It is an emotion that evolved to avoid predictable classes of disease conduits that jeopardized survival.

Sex Differences

Evolutionary psychology predicts that males and females will be *the same* or *similar* in domains in which the sexes have faced the same or similar adaptive problems. Both sexes have sweat glands because both sexes have faced the adaptive problem of thermal regulation. Both sexes have similar taste preferences for fat, sugar, and salt, because both sexes have faced similar food consumption problems.

In other domains, men and women have faced substantially different adaptive problems over human evolutionary history. Women have faced the problem of childbirth; men have not. Women, therefore, have evolved particular adaptations that are lacking in men, such as mechanisms for producing labor contractions through the release of oxytocin into the bloodstream.

Men and women have also faced different information-processing *problems* in some adaptive domains. Because fertilization occurs internally within the woman, for example, men have faced the adaptive problem of uncertainty of paternity in their offspring. Men who failed to solve this problem risked investing resources in children who were not their own. We are all descendants of a long line of ancestral men whose characteristics led them to behave in ways that increased their likelihood of paternity and decreased the odds of investing in children who were presumed to be theirs but whose genetic fathers were other men.

This does not imply that men were or are consciously aware of the adaptive problem of compromised paternity. A man does not think, "Oh, if my wife has sex with someone else, then my certainty that I'm the genetic father will be jeopardized, and this will endanger the replication of my genes; I'm really mad." Or if a man's wife is taking birth-control pills, he does not think, "Well, because Joan is taking the pill, it doesn't really matter whether she has sex with other men; after all, my certainty in paternity is secure." Instead, jealousy is a blind passion, just as our hunger for sweets, disgust at contaminated food, and craving for companionship are blind passions. The "wisdom" of jealousy is passed down to us over millions of years by our successful forebears (Buss, 2000a).

Women faced the problem of securing a reliable or replenishable supply of resources to carry them through pregnancy and lactation, especially when food resources were scarce, such as during droughts and harsh winters. We are all descendants of a long and unbroken line of women who successfully solved this adaptive challenge—for example, by preferring mates who showed the ability to accrue resources and the willingness to channel them toward particular women (Buss, 2003). The women who failed to solve this problem failed to survive, imperiled the survival chances of their children, and hence failed to become our ancestors.

Evolutionary-predicted sex differences hypothesis holds that the sexes will differ in precisely those domains where women and men have faced different sorts of adaptive problems (Buss, 2009a, 2009b). To an evolutionary psychologist, the likelihood that the sexes are psychologically identical in domains in which they have recurrently confronted different adaptive problems over the long expanse of human evolutionary history is essentially zero (Symons, 1992). The key question therefore is not "Are men and women different psychologically?" Rather, the key questions about sex differences, from an evolutionary psychological perspective, are the following:

1. In what *domains* have women and men faced different adaptive problems?
2. What are the *sex-differentiated psychological mechanisms* of women and men that have evolved in response to these sex-differentiated adaptive problems?
3. Which social, cultural, and contextual inputs affect the magnitude of expressed sex differences?

This section reviews some of the key domains in which the sexes have been predicted to differ: aggression, jealousy, desire for sexual variety, and mate preferences.

Sex Differences in Aggression

The earliest known homicide victim was a Neanderthal man who died 50,000 years ago (Trinkaus & Zimmerman, 1982). He was stabbed in the left front of his chest, indicating a right-handed attacker. As paleontological detective work has become increasingly sophisticated, evidence of prehistoric violence among our forebears has mushroomed (Buss, 2005b). Ancient skeletal remains contain cranial and rib fractures that appear inexplicable except by the force of clubs and weapons that stab. Weapon fragments are occasionally found lodged in skeletal rib cages. Humans apparently have a long evolutionary history of violence.

Men tend to engage in riskier tactics of competition, such as aggression and violence.
© *Ollyy/Shutterstock.com RF*

In a sample of homicides committed in Chicago from 1965 through 1980, 86 percent were committed by men (Daly & Wilson, 1988). Of these, 80 percent of the victims were also men. Although the exact percentages vary from culture to culture, cross-cultural homicide statistics reveal strikingly similar findings. In all cultures studied to date, men are overwhelmingly more often the killers, and most of their victims are other men. Any reasonably complete theory of aggression must provide an explanation for both facts—why men engage in violent forms of aggression so much more often than women do and why men comprise the majority of their victims.

An evolutionary model of intrasexual competition provides the foundation for such an explanation. It starts with the theory of parental investment and sexual selection (Archer, 2009; Trivers, 1972). In species in which females invest more heavily in offspring than males do, females become the valuable limiting resource on reproduction for males. Males become constrained in their reproduction not so much by their own ability to survive but rather by their ability to gain sexual access to the high-investing females. In other words, in a species in which females can bear only a small number of offspring, such as the human species, females will express great care in their choice of mates, and males will be forced to compete for access.

Because female mammals bear the physical burden of gestation and lactation, there is a considerable sex difference in minimum obligatory parental investment. Therefore, males can have many more offspring than females can. Stated differently, the ceiling on reproduction is much higher for males than for females. This difference leads to differences in the *variances* in reproduction between the sexes. The differences between the haves and have-nots therefore become greater for males than for females. Among males, a few males will sire multiple offspring, whereas some will have none at all. This is known as **effective polygyny**.

As a general rule, the greater the variance in reproduction, the more ferocious the competition within the sex that shows higher variance. In an extreme case such as the elephant seals off the coast of northern California, 5 percent of the males sire 85 percent of all offspring produced in a given breeding season (Le Boeuf & Reiter, 1988). Species that show high variance in reproduction within one sex tend to be highly **sexually dimorphic**, highly different in size and structure. The more intense the effective polygyny, the more dimorphic the sexes are in size and form (Plavcan, 2012; Trivers, 1985). Elephant seals are highly size dimorphic: males are four times larger than females (Le Boeuf & Reiter, 1988). Chimpanzees are less sexually dimorphic: males are roughly twice as large as females. Humans are mildly dimorphic, with males roughly 12 percent larger than females, although some specific body components, such as upper body strength, show much larger sexual dimorphism (Lassek & Gaulin, 2009). Within primate species, the greater the effective polygyny, the more the sexual dimorphism and the greater the reproductive variance between the sexes (Alexander et al., 1979; Plavcan, 2012).

Effective polygyny means that some males gain more than their fair share of copulations, whereas other males are shut out entirely, banished from contributing to the ancestry of future generations. Such a system leads to ferocious competition within the high-variance sex. In essence, polygyny selects for risky strategies, including those that lead to violent combat with rivals and those that lead to increased risk taking to acquire the resources needed to attract members of the high-investing sex.

Indeed, greater body size and strength in males is also likely due to a long history of females who select as mates males with these qualities (Buss, 2012; Plavcan, 2012). One study found that women who fear crime are especially likely to prefer long-term mates who are aggressive and physically formidable (Snyder et al., 2011). Another study found that men with more muscle mass had a larger number of sex partners and an earlier age of first sexual intercourse (Lassek & Gaulin, 2009). And a third study found that men who experienced aggressive victimization in adolescence at the hands of other males have fewer sex partner (Gallup et al., 2009).

This evolutionary account provides an explanation for facts revealed in the cross-cultural homicide record. Males are more often the perpetrators of violence because they are the products of a long history of effective polygyny. Throughout human evolution, male strategies have been characterized by risky intrasexual competition for females or for the social status and resources that attract females. The fact that men die, on average, five to seven years earlier than women is one of the many markers of this aggressive and risk-taking intrasexual strategy (Promislow, 2003).

Men are the victims of aggression far more than women because men are in competition primarily with other men. It is other men who block any given man's access to women. With increased aggression comes a greater likelihood of injury and early death. The patterns of aggression, in summary, are well predicted by the evolutionary theory of intrasexual competition (Buss & Duntley, 2006; Griskevicius et al., 2009). Even psychologists who argue that most psychological and behavioral sex differences are due to social roles concede that sex differences in aggression are most likely caused by a long evolutionary history in which women and men have confronted different adaptive problems in the context of mating and mate competition (Archer, 2009).

Sex Differences in Jealousy

Another difference between the sexes in the nature of the adaptive problems they have faced stems from the fact that fertilization occurs internally (and unseen) within women. This means that, over human evolutionary history, men have risked investing in children who were not their own. Few women, however, have ever been uncertain about which children were their own. From this perspective, a reproductively damaging act, from an ancestral man's point of view, would have been if his mate had had a pregnancy through sexual intercourse with another man. That is the act that would have jeopardized his certainty of passing on his genes.

From an ancestral woman's point of view, however, the fact that her mate was having sex with another woman, by itself, would not jeopardize her certainty in that she is the mother of her own children. Such an infidelity, however, could be extremely risky to the woman's reproductive success: she could risk losing her mate's resources, time, commitment, and investment, all of which could be diverted to another woman.

For these reasons, evolutionary psychologists have predicted that men and women should differ in the weighting they give to cues that trigger jealousy.

Specifically, men have been predicted to become more jealous than women in response to cues to a sexual infidelity. Women have been predicted to become more jealous than men in response to cues to the long-term diversion of a mate's commitment, such as emotional involvement with someone else. To test these predictions, participants were put in an agonizing dilemma, which you can participate in as well. Take a look at the Exercise that follows.

Exercise?

Think of a serious, committed romantic relationship that you had in the past, that you currently have, or that you would like to have. Imagine that you discover that the person with whom you've been seriously involved has become interested in someone else. Of the following, what would distress or upset you more?

1. Imagining your partner forming a deep emotional attachment to that person.
2. Imagining your partner enjoying passionate sexual intercourse with that other person.

As shown in Figure 8.4, men are far more distressed than women when imagining their partners having sexual intercourse with someone else (Buss et al., 1992). The overwhelming majority of women, in contrast, are more distressed when imagining their partners becoming emotionally involved with someone else. This does not mean that women are indifferent to their partners' sexual infidelities or that men are indifferent to their partners' emotional infidelities—far from it. Both events upset both sexes. However, when forced to choose which one is more upsetting, a large sex difference emerges, precisely as predicted by the evolutionary hypothesis of sex differences in the nature of the adaptive problems. These results also show up in measures of physiological distress (Buss et al., 1992; Pietrzak et al., 2002). When imagining partners having sex with someone else, men's heart rate goes up five beats per minute, which is like drinking three cups of coffee at one time. Their skin conductance increases, and their frown response is visible. Women, in contrast, show greater physiological distress at imagining their partners becoming emotionally involved with someone else.

Are these sex differences found across cultures? Thus far, researchers have replicated these sex differences in Germany, the Netherlands, and Korea (Buunk et al., 1996), as shown in Figure 8.5. Other researchers have replicated these sex differences in Korea and Japan (Buss et al., 1999). The sex differences in jealousy appear to be robust across a range of cultures.

Not every psychologist agrees with the evolutionary explanation. DeSteno and Salovey (1996) have proposed that men and women

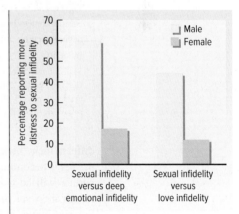

Figure 8.4

Percentage reporting more distress to sexual infidelity than to emotional or love infidelity. A large sex difference is found, with far more men than women reporting more distress to sexual infidelity, and the overwhelming majority of women reporting more distress to emotional or love infidelity.

Source: From "Sex Differences in Jealousy: Evolution, Physiology, and Psychology," by D. M. Buss, R. Larsen, J. Semmelroth, and D. Weston, 1992, *Psychological Science, 3*, pp. 251–255, Figure 1, top panel, p. 252. Copyright © 1992 Association for Psychological Science. Reprinted by permission of SAGE Publications, Inc.

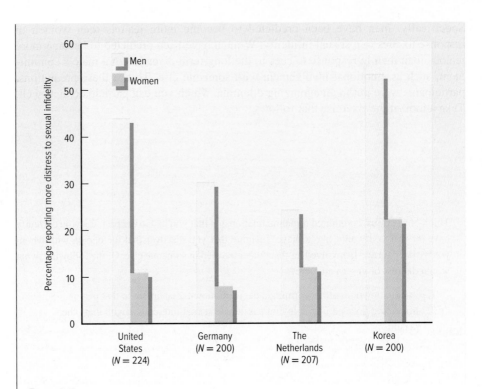

Figure 8.5

Sex differences in jealousy across four cultures. In all four cultures, more men than women are distressed about imagining a partner's sexual infidelity; most women are more distressed by a partner's emotional infidelity.

Source: From "Sex Differences in Jealousy in Evolutionary and Cultural Perspective: Tests from the Netherlands, Germany, and the United States," by A. P. Buunk, A. Angleitner, V. Oubaid, and D. M. Buss, 1996, *Psychological Science, 7,* pp. 359–363, Figure 1, p. 361. Copyright © 1996 Association for Psychological Science. Reprinted by permission of SAGE Publications, Inc.

differ in their "beliefs" about sexual and emotional involvement. When a man thinks that his partner is becoming sexually involved with a rival, for example, he might also think that his partner will be getting emotionally involved—a so-called double shot of infidelity. The reason men get more upset about sexual rather than emotional infidelity, DeSteno and Salovey argue, is not because men are really more jealous about sexual infidelity—it's because men "believe" that a sexual infidelity will result in the double shot of infidelity, which includes emotional infidelity.

Women, DeSteno and Salovey argue, have different beliefs, although they fail to explain why. Women believe in a reverse double-shot, that if their partners become emotionally involved with a rival, they will also become sexually involved. It's women's beliefs about this double shot of infidelity that upset them, DeSteno and Salovey argue, and not that women really are more upset about an emotional betrayal.

The evolutionary explanation opposes the double-shot explanation. Given the large sex differences stemming from fundamental differences in reproductive biology, according to evolutionary psychologists, it would be unlikely for selection to have failed to produce psychological sex differences about the two forms of infidelity. The hard hand of data, however, usually settles scientific disagreements. Buss and his colleagues (1999) conducted four empirical studies in three different cultures to pit the predictions of evolutionary theory against the predictions of the double-shot hypothesis. One of the studies involved 1,122 participants from a liberal arts college in the southeastern United States. The researchers asked them to imagine their partners becoming interested in someone else and asked: What would upset or distress you more: (a) imagining your partner forming a deep emotional *(but not sexual)* relationship with that person? or (b) imagining your partner enjoying a sexual *(but not emotional)* relationship with that person? The men and women differed by roughly 35 percent in their responses, as predicted by the evolutionary model. The women continued to express greater upset about a partner's emotional infidelity, even if it did not involve sex. The men continued to show more upset than the women about a partner's sexual infidelity, even if it did not involve emotional involvement. If the double-shot hypothesis were the correct explanation for the initial sex differences that were found, then the sex difference should have disappeared when the sexual and emotional components of infidelity were isolated. It did not.

In a second study of 234 women and men (Buss et al., 1999), the researchers used a different strategy for pitting the competing hypotheses against each other. They asked participants to imagine that their worst nightmare had occurred—that their partners had become both sexually *and* emotionally involved with someone else. They then asked the participants to state *which aspect* they found more upsetting. The results were conclusive. The researchers found large sex differences, precisely as predicted by the evolutionary explanation—63 percent of the men but only 13 percent of the women found the sexual aspect of the infidelity to be more upsetting. In contrast, 87 percent of the women, but only 37 percent of the men, found the emotional aspect of the infidelity to be more upsetting. No matter how the questions were worded, no matter which method was used, the same sex difference emerged in every test. Several other scientists have now confirmed these results using somewhat different methods and different cultures, such as Sweden (e.g., Wiederman & Kendall, 1999). Wiederman and Kendall concluded that, "contrary to the double-shot explanation, choice of scenario was unrelated to attitudes regarding whether the other gender was capable of satisfying sexual relations outside of a love relationship" (p. 121).

These and similar sex differences have now been replicated in China, Germany, the Netherlands, Korea, Japan, England, and Romania (Brase, Caprar, & Voracek, 2004). The gender differences emerge robustly in cultures that are highly sexually egalitarian such as Sweden and Norway (e.g., Bendixen, 2015), as well is in traditional cultures such as the Himba of Namibia (Scelza, 2014). The cross-cultural findings support the theory that these are universal sex differences. The double-shot theory cannot explain why these sex differences are universal. Based on the available evidence, the double-shot theory has failed to be supported both from the cross-cultural findings and from the studies that test its predictions in direct competition with those from the evolutionary theory.

In an ingenious study, Schutzwohl and Koch (2004) used an entirely new method that has never been used in jealousy research. They had participants listen to a story about their own romantic relationship in which an infidelity was said to have occurred. Embedded within the story were five cues that had been previously determined to be cues highly diagnostic of *sexual infidelity* (e.g., He suddenly has difficulty becoming sexually aroused when you and he want to have sex) and five cues highly diagnostic of *emotional infidelity* (e.g., He doesn't respond any more when you tell him that you love him). In a surprise recall test a week later, men spontaneously remembered more cues to sexual than to emotional infidelity (42 percent vs. 29 percent), whereas women remembered more cues to emotional than to sexual infidelity (40 percent vs. 24 percent). These findings support the hypothesis that sex differences in jealousy are quite real and cannot be dismissed as an "experimental artifact" (Schutzwohl & Koch, 2004).

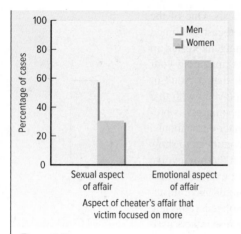

Figure 8.6

Men and women differ in which aspects of their
partner's infidelity they focus on more.

Source: Kuhle, 2011.

Other studies have discovered other design features of sex differences in the psychology of jealousy. One found that women experienced more *psychological relief* when they discovered that their
partner was not emotionally unfaithful, whereas men experienced
greater relief upon the disconfirmation of a partner's sexual infidelity
(Schutzwohl, 2008). Women more than men inquire about the emotional nature of a partner's extra-pair relationship, whereas men more
than women inquire about the sexual nature of a partner's extra-pair
relationship (Kuhle, Smedley, & Schmitt, 2009). And those who are
dispositionally or chronically more jealous tend to show even larger
sex differences in jealous responses to sexual versus emotional infidelity (Miller & Maner, 2009). This latter finding highlights the
importance of integrating stable individual differences with evolutionary theories of sex differences in personality (Miller & Maner,
2009).

The gold standard in science is independent replication, and by
this criterion the evolutionary explanation has fared well. After each
challenge, additional research by independent scientists has continued to find support for the existence of sex differences in jealousy
and the evolutionary explanations for them (e.g., Brase et al., 2004;
Buss & Haselton, 2005; Cann, Mangum, & Wells, 2001; Dijkstra & Buunk, 2001; Fenigstein & Pelz, 2002; Geary et al., 2001; Maner & Shackelford, 2008; Murphy et al., 2006;
Pietrzak et al., 2002; Sagarin, 2005; Sagarin et al., 2003, 2009; Schutzwohl & Koch,
2004; Shackelford, Buss, & Bennett, 2002; Shackelford et al., 2004; Strout et al., 2005).
Indeed, a meta-analysis of 47 independent samples provided strong support for the evolutionarily predicted sex differences across methods, including studies that evaluated
reactions to actual infidelities (Sagarin et al., 2012; Zengel, Edlund, & Sagarin, 2013).

Finally, in using a novel method of content coding jealous interogations of romantic partners, Kuhle (2011) discovered that men tended to interrogate partners more
about the sexual aspects ("Did you have sex with him?"), whereas women interrogated
partners about the emotional aspects ("Do you love her?") (see Figure 8.6).

Sex Differences in Desire for Sexual Variety

Another sex difference predicted by evolutionary psychological theories is a difference
in the desire for sexual variety (Figure 8.7). This prediction stems from parental investment and sexual selection theory. The members of the sex that invests less in offspring,
according to this theory, are predicted to be less discriminating in their selection of
mates and more inclined to seek multiple mates. In ancestral times, men could increase
their reproductive success by gaining sexual access to a variety of women.

If you were given your ideal wish, how many sex partners would you like to have in
the next month? How about the next year? How about over your entire lifetime? When
unmarried college students were asked these questions, the women indicated that they
wanted about 1 in the next month and 4 or 5 in their entire lifetimes (Buss & Schmitt,
1993). The men, in contrast, thought that 2 would be about right in the next month, 8 over
the next couple of years, and 18 in their lifetimes. In terms of expressed desires, men and
women differ in the ways predicted by the evolutionary account.

The sex differences in number of partners desired has now been replicated in
a massive cross-cultural study. David Schmitt and his colleagues (2003) studied
16,288 individuals from 10 world regions, representing 52 different nations from

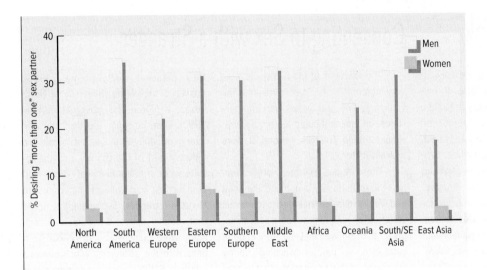

Figure 8.7

"Ideally, how many different sexual partners would you like to have in the next month?"

Total sample size 16, 288.

Source: Data from International Sexuality Description Project, courtesy of David P. Schmitt.

Argentina to Slovakia to Zimbabwe. They used instruments identical to those used for Figure 8.7, translated into the appropriate language for each culture. For the time interval of the next 30 years, men worldwide expressed a desire for roughly 13 sex partners, whereas women expressed a desire for roughly 2.5 partners (see Figure 8.7 for illustrative findings). The sex difference in the desire for sexual variety, in short, appears to be large and universal. The sex difference extends to how often men and women think about sex. One study found that women, on average, think about sex 9 times per week; men, on average, think about sex 37 times per week (Regan & Atkins, 2006).

Sex Differences in Mate Preferences

Evolutionary psychologists have also predicted that men and women differ in the qualities they desire in a long-term mate. Because women bear the burdens of the heavy obligatory parental investment, they are predicted to place more value on a potential mate's financial resources and the qualities that lead to such resources. Men, in contrast, are predicted to place greater value on a woman's physical appearance, which provides a wealth of observable cues to her fertility. In a sample of college students, the men ranked physical attractiveness an average of 4.04, whereas the women ranked it lower, giving it 6.26 (the highest possible rank would be a "1," whereas the lowest possible rank would be "13"). On the dimension of good earning capacity, the women ranked it 8.04, whereas the men ranked it 9.92 (Buss & Barnes, 1986). Thus, it is clear that women and men both place many qualities above looks and resources. In particular, "kind and understanding" (rank: 2.20) and having an "exciting personality" (rank: 3.50) are more valued by both sexes. Interestingly, people prefer the trait of "kindness" in mates when the kindness is directed toward them, but not necessarily when it is directed toward others (Lukaszewski & Roney, 2010). Personality, in short, plays a key role in what people want in a marriage partner.

Nonetheless, in the study, the men and women differed in their rankings of looks and resources in the predicted direction. These sex differences have been found across

A Closer Look

Consenting to Sex with a Stranger

The sex difference in desire for sexual variety shows up in behavioral data. In one study conducted at a university in Florida, experimental confederates approached people of the opposite sex (Clark & Hatfield, 1989). After introducing themselves, they said, "Hi, I've been noticing you around campus lately, and I find you very attractive. Would you go out on a date with me tonight?" A different group was asked, "Would you go back to my apartment with me tonight?" And a third group was asked, "Would you have sex with me tonight?"

Experimenters simply recorded the percentage of people approached who agreed to the request. Of the women who were approached by the male confederate, 55 percent agreed to the date, 6 percent agreed to go back to the man's apartment, and 0 percent agreed to have sex with him. Of the men approached by the female confederate, 50 percent agreed to go out on the date, 69 percent agreed to go back to her apartment, and 75 percent agreed to have sex with her.

The reactions of the two sexes were very different in the sex condition. The women approached for sex were often insulted, and many thought the request was simply strange. The men, in contrast, were typically flattered.

These studies and many others support the evolutionary hypothesis that men and women differ in their desire for sexual variety. Men tend to have more sexual fantasies than do women, and they engage more often in "partner switching" during the course of those fantasies—that is, they fantasize about two or more sex partners during the course of a single fantasy episode (Buss, 2003). In fact, one meta-analysis found that attitudes toward casual sex was one of the two largest sex differences in the sexual domain, with men typically much more positive than women about casual sex (Oliver & Hyde, 1993).

Journalist Natalie Angier questions these results, arguing that women would hop into bed as easily as men in these situations but are deterred by a concern for

their personal safety (Angier, 1999). Russell Clark, of the University of North Texas, explored this possibility (Clark, 1990). First, he replicated the "sex with strangers" study on a different sample in a different part of the country, and the results were virtually identical—more men than women were willing to have sex with a virtual stranger. Second, Clark noted that roughly half of the women in each study were quite willing to go out on a date with the strangers, which seemed puzzling if they were concerned about their safety. Third, when Clark's experimenters asked the participants to describe the reason for their refusal (if they refused), women's and men's answers were nearly identical—both mentioned that they had a boyfriend or girlfriend or that they did not know the person well enough.

Importantly, the gender differences in consenting to sex with strangers have been robustly replicated in other countries, including France, Germany, and Denmark (e.g., Hald et al., 2010; Guéguen, 2011).

37 cultures (Buss, 1989; Kamble et al., 2014; Souza et al., 2016). Zambian, Chinese, Indonesian, Brazilian, Indian, and Norwegian men rank physical attractiveness as more important than do their female counterparts, just like the American samples. Similarly, worldwide, women rank a potential partner's good financial prospects to be more important than do their male counterparts. Taken together, these psychological gender differences are large, roughly the same magnitude as gender differences in height and upper body muscle strength (Conroy-Beam & Buss, 2015; see Figure 8.8). Importantly, these gender differences have remained robust throughout all cultures studied over the past decade, including Brazil, China, India, and Iran. Perhaps even more important, the personality characteristics that contribute to financial success—ambition, industriousness, and dependability—are also highly valued by women worldwide. Whereas men prioritize physical attractiveness, women prioritize social status as a "necessity" in selecting long-term mates (Li et al., 2011).

In summary, personality plays a key role in mate preferences across the globe, and on a few dimensions there are universal gender differences in what people want in a marriage partner. Although the evolutionary hypotheses for these sex differences have so far received support in cross-cultural research, competing hypotheses have been proposed to explain them, and these are currently being tested.

Perhaps a date seems safer than sex, and women really do want sex with strangers, if only they could be assured of their safety. To explore this possibility, Clark (1990) conducted yet another experiment. Men and women participants were contacted by close personal friends who testified about the integrity and character of the stranger. The participants were assured by their friends that the stranger was warm, sincere, trustworthy, and attractive. The participants were then asked one of two questions: "Would you be willing to go on a date?" or "Would you be willing to go to bed?" After being debriefed, the participants were asked for their reasons for their decisions.

The overwhelming majority of both sexes agreed to the date—91 percent of the women and 96 percent of the men. In the sex condition, however, a large sex difference emerged—50 percent of the men but only 5 percent of the women agreed. Not a single woman indicated a concern for safety. Clearly, making conditions safer for women increases the odds that they will consent to sex with a stranger—from 0 to 5 percent—so safety concerns are not irrelevant, but the sex

difference remains large. Most women agree to date strangers when a close friend vouches for the man's warmth and integrity, but 95 percent still refuse to consent to sex.

It's not that women lack interest in sex. The evidence is compelling, however, that most women are careful about whom they choose to sleep with and for the most part avoid jumping into bed with total strangers. Men are more willing. Most men responded to the sexual request by saying, "What time?" or "Why not?" and then asking for the requester's telephone number and directions to her house.

These findings have now been replicated in a study involving three countries—Italy, Germany, and the United States (Schutzwohl et al., 2009). The new twist in this study involved varying the attractiveness of the requestor, which increased acceptance rates for both sexes. For the "exceptionally attractive" requestor, 83 percent of the men agreed to sex, whereas 24 percent of the women agreed to sex. So although there are indeed circumstances in which some women consent to sex with strangers, men are still much more likely to do so.

These differences hold with equal force in lust for affairs. In one study by Ralph Johnson (1970) of Sacramento State College, 48 percent of American men, but only 5 percent of American women, expressed a desire to engage in extramarital sex. In a classic older study by Lewis Terman (1938) of 769 American men and 770 American women, 72 percent of the men, but only 27 percent of the women, admitted that they sometimes desired sex with someone outside of their marriage. Germans revealed similar tendencies—46 percent of married men but only 6 percent of married women admit that they would take advantage of a casual sexual opportunity with someone else if the chance arose (Sigusch & Schmidt, 1971).

Women, of course, may be more reluctant to confide their sexual desires to a surveyor, so the figures are likely to underestimate women's sexual impulses. Nonetheless, the sex difference proves so robust across studies and methods of inquiry that there is no reason to doubt that men and women differ in desire for a variety of sex partners.

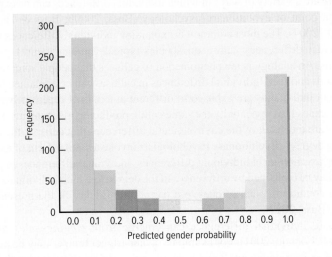

Figure 8.8

We can predict biological sex, whether one is male or female, with 92.4% accuracy solely from knowing a person's expressed preferences for good financial prospects, good looks, chastity, ambition, and age in a potential mate.

Source: Findings and graph courtesy of Daniel Conroy-Beam; for more information, see Conroy-Beam, Buss, Pham, & Shackelford, 2015

Exercise

Following is a list of characteristics that might be present in a potential mate or marriage partner. Rank them on their desirability in someone you might marry. Give a 1 to the most desirable characteristic in a potential mate, a 2 to the second most desirable characteristic in a potential mate, a 3 to the third most desirable characteristic, and so on down to 13 for the 13th most desirable characteristic in a potential mate.

___ kind and understanding   ___ good housekeeper   ___ college graduate

___ religious   ___ intelligent   ___ physically attractive

___ exciting personality   ___ good earning capacity   ___ healthy

___ creative and artistic   ___ wants children

___ easygoing   ___ good heredity

Individual Differences

The study of individual differences, which is central to personality psychology, has been the most challenging level of analysis for evolutionary psychologists. Unlike sex differences, for which scientists have accumulated a large empirical foundation, there is less of a foundation for adaptive individual differences. Thus, this section must necessarily be more speculative than previous sections.

There are a variety of ways in which individual differences can be explained from the vantage point of evolutionary psychology (Buss, 2009b; Buss & Hawley, 2011; Penke et al., 2007). The most common is explaining individual differences as a result of environmental differences acting on species-typical (human nature) psychological mechanisms. An analogy is the phenomenon of calluses that people sometimes develop on their hands and feet. Individual differences in calluses can be explained by proposing that different individuals are exposed to different amounts of repeated friction to their skin. All humans have essentially the same callus-producing mechanisms, so individual differences are the result of the environmental differences that activate the mechanisms to differing degrees. Evolutionary psychologists invoke a similar form of explanation to account for psychological individual differences. Individual differences in jealousy, for example, may be explained by differences in the degree to which individuals are exposed to evoking conditions, such as cues to a partner's infidelity or the presence of "mate poachers" (Buss, 2012).

Second, individual differences can emerge from *contingencies among traits* (Bouchard & Loehlin, 2001). For example, "a hair-trigger temper may be advantageous if one is big and strong but not if one is small and weak" (p. 250). Rather than the trait's expression being contingent on the environment, however, its expression is contingent on other traits the person has—in this case, the size and strength of one's body.

A third source of individual difference stems from *frequency–dependent selection:* the process whereby the reproductive success (fitness) of a trait depends on its frequency relative to other traits in the population. For example, in a large population of people with a cooperative disposition, selection may favor those with a cheating disposition as long as they are not too common. As the frequency of cheaters gets more common, cooperators evolve defenses to punish cheaters, and so the success of cheating goes down. Thus, heritable individual differences can be created through frequency–dependent selection.

A fourth source of individual differences comes from the fact that *the optimum level of a personality trait can vary over time and space.* Consider as an example differences over evolutionary time (or space) in the abundance of food, perhaps due to droughts or ice ages. In times of food scarcity, selection favors a risk-taking personality trait—one that prompts a person to risk encountering predators in order to venture widely to get food and prevent starvation. In times of food abundance, selection favors a more cautious personality disposition to reduce the risk of venturing widely in the environment. Variations over time and space in the optimum level of a trait can create heritable individual differences in personality that are maintained in the population.

In sum, the evolutionary framework identifies several sources of individual differences: (1) those that arise from individuals possessing universal adaptations whose expression is contingent on the environment; (2) those that arise from contingencies with other traits; (3) those due to variation over time and space in the optimum value of a trait; and (4) those due to frequency–dependent selection. Next we explore some examples of these individual differences.

Environmental Triggers of Individual Differences

According to one theory, the critical event of early father presence versus father absence triggers specific sexual strategies in individuals (Belsky, Steinberg, & Draper, 1991). Children who grow up in father-absent homes during the first five years of life, according to this theory, develop expectations that parental resources will not be reliably or predictably provided. Furthermore, these children come to expect that adult pair bonds will not be enduring. Such individuals cultivate a sexual strategy marked by early sexual maturation, early sexual initiation, and frequent partner switching—a strategy designed to produce a larger number of offspring. Extraverted and impulsive personality traits may accompany and facilitate this sexual strategy. Other people are perceived as untrustworthy and relationships as transitory. Resources sought from brief sexual encounters are opportunistically attained and immediately extracted.

In contrast, individuals who experience a reliable, investing father during the first five years of life, according to the theory, develop a different set of expectations about the nature and trustworthiness of others. People are seen as reliable and trustworthy, and relationships are expected to be enduring. These early environmental experiences predispose individuals toward a long-term mating strategy, marked by delayed sexual maturation; a later onset of sexual activity; a search for long-term, securely attached adult relationships; and heavy investment in a small number of children.

There is some empirical support for this theory. Children from divorced homes, for example, are more sexually promiscuous than children from intact homes (Belsky et al., 1991). Furthermore, girls from father-absent homes reach menarche (age of first menstruation) earlier than girls from father-present homes (Kim, Smith, & Palermiti, 1997). Nonetheless, these findings are correlational, so causation cannot be inferred. Men or women who are genetically predisposed to pursue a short-term mating strategy may be more likely to get divorced and more likely to pass on to their children genes for that strategy (Bailey, Kirk, et al., 2000). However, despite the current lack of conclusive data (Del Giudice & Belsky, 2011), this theory and modest provisional support for it nicely illustrates an evolutionary approach to the emergence of consistent individual differences—in this case, the effects of different environments on species-typical mechanisms.

Heritable Individual Differences Contingent on Other Traits

Another type of evolutionary analysis of personality involves evaluating one's personal strengths and weaknesses. Suppose, for example, that men could pursue two different strategies in social interaction—an aggressive strategy marked by the use of physical force and a nonaggressive strategy marked by cooperativeness. The success of these strategies, however, hinges on an individual's size, strength, and fighting ability. Those who happen to be muscular in body build can more successfully carry out an aggressive strategy than those who are skinny or chubby. If humans have evolved ways to evaluate themselves on their physical formidability, they can determine which social strategy is the more successful to pursue—an aggressive strategy or a cooperative strategy. Adaptive self-assessments, therefore, can produce stable individual differences in aggression or cooperativeness. In this example, the tendency toward aggression is not directly heritable. Rather, it is **reactively heritable**: it is a secondary consequence of heritable body build (Tooby &

Cosmides, 1990). There is some evidence to support this idea that body build enters into a man's decision of whether to pursue an aggressive strategy (Ishikawa et al., 2001). Body weight, which is highly correlated with strength, predicts aggression both among pro hockey players and among young men more generally (Archer & Thanzami, 2009; Deaner et al., 2012). Physically stronger males are also quicker to anger and are more likely to believe in the utility of warfare (Sell et al., 2012). Even more interesting when it comes to personality, the combination of physical strength and physical attractiveness predicted the traits of extraversion, leadership orientation, and amount of bargaining power in social interactions—a prime example of how a personality trait can be contingent on other traits (Lukaszewski, 2013; Lukaszewski & Roney, 2011; von Rueden et al., 2015). These traits, in turn, predict men's (but not women's) proclivity to be oriented toward a short-term mating strategy (Lukaszewski et al., 2014). The notion of self-assessment of heritable qualities remains a fascinating avenue for understanding the adaptive patterning of individual differences, and is now being extended beyond traits like aggressiveness and extraversion to a wider array of condition-dependent models of personality (Lewis, 2015).

According to reactive heritability, a man with a slim, wiry build is less likely than a stocky man to engage in aggressive behavior.
© Radius Images/Alamy Stock Photo RF

Frequency-Dependent Strategic Individual Differences

The process of evolution by selection tends to use up heritable variation. In other words, heritable variants that are more successful tend to replace those that are less successful, resulting in species-typical adaptations that show little or no heritable variation. The universal human design is to have two eyes, for example.

In some contexts, two or more heritable variants can evolve within a population. The most obvious example is biological sex itself. Within sexually reproducing species, the two sexes exist in roughly equal numbers because of **frequency–dependent selection**. If one sex becomes rare relative to the other, evolution will produce an increase in the numbers of the rarer sex. Frequency–dependent selection causes the frequency of men and women to remain roughly equal.

Some propose that human individual differences in women's mating strategies have been caused by frequency–dependent selection (Gangestad & Simpson, 1990; Gangestad & Thornhill, 2008). They start with the observation that competition tends to be most intense among individuals who are pursuing the same mating strategy (Maynard Smith, 1982). This lays the groundwork for the evolution of alternative strategies.

According to Gangestad and colleagues, women's mating strategies should center on two key qualities of potential mates: the parental investment a man could provide and the quality of his genes. A man who is able and willing to invest in a woman and her children can be an extraordinarily valuable reproductive asset. Similarly, independent of a man's ability to invest, women could benefit by selecting men who have high-quality genes, which can be passed down to her children. Men may carry genes for good health, physical attractiveness, or sexiness, which are then passed on to the woman's sons or daughters.

There may be a trade-off, however, between selecting a man for his parenting abilities and selecting a man for his genes. Men who are highly attractive to many women, for example, may be reluctant to commit to any one woman. Thus, a woman who is seeking a man for his genes may have to settle for a short-term sexual relationship without parental investment.

These various selection forces, according to theorists, gave rise to two alternative female mating strategies. A woman seeking a high-investing mate would adopt a **restricted sexual strategy** marked by delayed intercourse and prolonged courtship. This would enable her to assess the man's level of commitment, detect the existence of prior commitments to other women or children, and simultaneously signal to the man her sexual fidelity and hence assure him of his paternity of future offspring.

A woman seeking a man for the quality of his genes, on the other hand, has less reason to delay sexual intercourse. A man's level of commitment to her is irrelevant, so prolonged assessment of his prior commitments is not necessary. This is referred to as an **unrestricted mating strategy**.

According to this theory, the two mating strategies of women—restricted and unrestricted—evolved and are maintained by frequency–dependent selection. As the number of unrestricted females in the population increases, the number of "sexy sons" in the next generation also increases. As the number of sexy sons increases, however, the competition among them also increases. Then, because there are so many sexy sons competing for a limited pool of women, their average success declines.

Now consider what happens when the number of restricted females seeking investing men increases in the population. Because there are now so many women seeking investment, they end up competing with each other for men willing to invest. Therefore, as the number of women seeking investment increases, the average success of their strategy declines. In short, the key idea behind frequency–dependent selection is that the success of each of the two strategies depends on how common each strategy is in the population. As a given strategy becomes more common, it becomes less successful; when it becomes less common, it becomes more successful.

There is some evidence for this theory (Thornhill & Gangestad, 2008). Individual differences in female mating strategy (restricted vs. unrestricted) have been shown to be heritable. Women who pursue an unrestricted sexual strategy have been shown to place more value on qualities of men linked with good genes, such as physical attractiveness and good health (Greiling & Buss, 2000; Thornhill & Gangestad, 2008). There is also evidence that sexual strategy is somewhat flexible and responsive to aspects of the social situation. Thus, people shift in the *restricted* direction of sociosexual desire when they enter a new relationship and become more *unrestricted* again when they break up with an existing romantic partner (Penke & Asendorpf, 2008a). Nonetheless, the dispositional components of sociosexual desire are reflected in the findings that unrestricted individuals tend to dissolve romantic relationships more quickly, become sexually involved with new partners more readily, and are more likely to be sexually unfaithful within existing mateships (Penke & Asendorpf, 2008a).

Another hypothesized example of personality differences originating from frequency–dependent selection centers on **psychopathy**—a cluster of personality traits marked by irresponsible and unreliable behavior, egocentrism, impulsivity, an inability to form lasting relationships, superficial social charm, and a deficit in social emotions such as love, shame, guilt, and empathy (Cleckley, 1988; Lalumiere, Harris, & Rice, 2001). Psychopaths pursue a deceptive "cheating" strategy in their social interactions. Psychopathy is more common among men than women, but occurs in both sexes (Mealey, 1995). Psychopaths pursue a strategy of exploiting the cooperative proclivities of other people. After feigning cooperation, psychopaths typically defect, cheat, or violate the presumed relationship. This cheating strategy might be pursued by those who are unlikely to out-compete others in more mainstream or traditional social hierarchies (Mealey, 1995).

According to one evolutionary theory of this individual difference, a psychopathic strategy can be maintained by frequency–dependent selection. As the number of cheaters increases, and hence the average cost to the cooperative hosts increases, adaptations will evolve in cooperators to detect and punish cheating, thus lowering its overall effectiveness (Price, Cosmides, & Tooby, 2002). As psychopaths get detected and punished, the average success of the strategy declines. As long as the frequency of psychopaths is not too large, however, it can be maintained in a population composed primarily of cooperators.

There is some empirical evidence consistent with this theory of the evolution of this individual difference cluster. First, behavioral genetic studies suggest that psychopathy is moderately heritable (Willerman, Loehlin, & Horn, 1992). Second, psychopaths often pursue an exploitative sexual strategy, which could be the primary route by which genes for psychopathy increase or are maintained (Rowe, 2001). Psychopathic men, for example, tend to be more sexually precocious, have sex with higher numbers of women, have more illegitimate children, and are more likely to get divorced if they marry than nonpsychopathic men (Rowe, 2001). This short-term exploitative sexual strategy would increase in populations marked by high geographic mobility, in which the costs to reputation associated with this strategy are muted (Buss, 2012). This leads to the alarming idea that we may be witnessing an increase in psychopaths in modern times, as society becomes increasingly geographically mobile. Evidence supports the frequency–dependent theory of this individual difference cluster—that it is part of normal personality variation and is not due to "pathology" (Lalumiere et al., 2001). In sum, individual differences in this cluster of personality traits—unreliability, egocentrism, impulsivity, superficial social charm, and a deficit in empathy and other social emotions—may originate evolutionarily from frequency–dependent selection (see also Millon, 1990, 1999, for additional explorations of personality from an evolutionary perspective).

The most recent effort to explore individual differences from the perspective of frequency–dependent selection focuses on *life history strategy* (Figueredo et al., 2005a, 2005b, 2012; Gladden, Figueredo, & Jacobs, 2009; Rushton, 1985; Rushton, Cons, & Hur, 2008). According to this approach, individuals have evolved differences in the effort they allocate to reproductively relevant problems, such as survival, mating, and parenting. The core idea is that there are trade-offs among these problems. Effort allocated to mating, for example, is effort taken away from parenting. On one end of the continuum, individuals favor what is called a *K-strategy*—greater effort is allocated to survival and heavy parenting over effort allocated to obtaining many mates (van der Linden, 2012). These high-K individuals are hypothesized to have formed strong attachments to their biological parents, avoid risk taking that would imperil survival, pursue long-term mating rather than short-term mating, and invest heavily in children. Low-K individuals, at the other end, are hypothesized to have formed weaker attachments to their biological parents, have a risk-taking personality, pursue short-term mating, and invest little in their children. Some empirical research supports the hypothesis that these variables do indeed covary or cluster together (Figueredo et al., 2005b; Gladden et al., 2009; Rushton et al., 2008; Templor, 2008). Others have criticized this theory on conceptual grounds (e.g., Penke et al., 2007).

In sum, we have examined several ways in which evolutionary psychologists study individual differences that might be adaptively patterned. First, different environments can direct individuals into different strategies, as in the case of father absence directing individuals toward a short-term sexual strategy. Second, there can be adaptive self-assessment of heritable traits, as is the case when individuals who are muscular in body build pursue a more aggressive strategy than those who are skinny. Third, two heritable strategies can be supported by frequency–dependent selection.

Fourth, the forces of selection can be different in different places, for example, or different times. This can result in evolved individual differences that are due to different evolutionary selection pressures in different local ecologies. We know, for example, that individual differences in the presence or absence of "sickle cells" in the blood, an adaptation to protect against mosquito-borne malaria, have been caused by different selection pressures in different local ecologies. Although no individual differences in personality have yet been empirically traced to this particular evolutionary source, it remains a viable theoretical possibility in the evolutionary arsenal of explanatory options.

The Big Five, Motivation, and Evolutionarily Relevant Adaptive Problems

Evolutionary psychologists have attempted to understand the importance of the Big Five personality dispositions within an evolutionary framework (Buss, 1991b, 1996; Buss & Greiling, 1999; Denissen & Penke, 2008a; Ellis, Simpson, & Campbell, 2002; Nettle, 2006). One approach views stable individual differences on the five-factor model as individual differences in "motivational reactions," or solutions, to particular classes of adaptive problems (Buss, 2009a; Denissen & Penke, 2008a, 2008b; Ellis et al., 2002; Nettle, 2006). Thus, Agreeableness reflects differences in the proclivity to cooperate versus to act selfishly in conflicts over resources. Emotional Stability reflects differences in sensitivity to the adaptive problem of social exclusion; high neuroticism, for example, can be beneficial in causing increased vigilance to social danger but at a cost of increased stress and depression (Nettle, 2006; Tamir et al., 2006). Extraversion reflects pursuit of a risk-taking social strategy marked by success in short-term mating versus adopting a more stable family life marked by long-term mating (Nettle, 2006). Conscientiousness reflects a long-term strategy of delayed gratification and tenacity of goal pursuit versus a more impulsive solution that involves grabbing immediate adaptive benefits.

Heritable individual differences on these dimensions can be maintained in the population because different levels are adaptive under different conditions; the optimum level varies over time and space. In technical terms, these personality differences are maintained by **balancing selection** (Penke et al., 2007), which occurs when genetic variation is maintained by selection because different levels on a trait dimension are adaptive in different environments.

A complementary evolutionary approach is to conceptualize major factors of personality as clusters of the most important features of the "adaptive landscape" of other people (Buss, 1991b, 2011). Humans, according to this perspective, have evolved "difference-detecting mechanisms" designed to notice and remember individual differences that have the most relevance for solving social adaptive problems. Specifically, the five factors may provide important answers to questions such as these:

- Who is likely to rise in the social hierarchy and hence gain access to status and position in the social hierarchy? *(Dominance, Extraversion)*
- Who is likely to be a good cooperator and reciprocator, and who will be a loyal friend or romantic partner? *(Agreeableness)*
- Who will be reliable and dependable in times of need and work industriously to provide resources? *(Conscientiousness)*
- Who will drain my resources, encumber me with their problems, monopolize my time, and fail to cope well with adversity? *(Emotional Stability)*
- Who can I go to for sage advice? *(Openness, Intellect)*

In one study, Ellis and his colleagues (Ellis et al., 2002) developed a theoretical synthesis of the Big Five and evolutionary psychology, and conducted studies to see whether positioning on the five factors was correlated with these adaptively relevant individual differences. They included two additional individual differences that are relevant to romantic relationships: physical attractiveness (a sign of health and fertility) and physical prowess (a sign of the ability to protect a friend or romantic partner from danger). Using factor analysis, they discovered that the Big Five were indeed closely linked with solutions to these critical adaptive problems. In romantic relationships, those who were high on Agreeableness, for example, were also judged to be highly cooperative, devoted to their partners, and in love with their partners. Those who were high on Extraversion were also judged to be socially ascendant, taking leadership roles in the group and showing proclivities to elevate themselves in social hierarchies. People highly responsible and efficient (signs of Conscientiousness) were dependable in times of need, were well organized, and showed good potential for future earning.

This study is just the start of exploring the five-factor model within an evolutionary framework. But it does highlight the important point that individual differences of people who inhabit one's social environment are adaptively consequential. It's reasonable to hypothesize that humans have evolved psychological sensitivities to noticing, detecting, naming, and remembering precisely those individual differences that are most relevant to solving critical social adaptive problems—problems ultimately linked to survival and reproduction.

Limitations of Evolutionary Psychology

Like all approaches to personality, the evolutionary perspective carries a number of important limitations. First, adaptations are forged over the long expanse of thousands or millions of generations, and we cannot go back in time and determine with absolute certainty what the precise selective forces on humans have been. Scientists make inferences about past environments and past selection pressures. Nonetheless, our current mechanisms provide windows for viewing the past. Our fear of snakes and heights, for example, suggests that these were hazards in our evolutionary past. Humans seem to come into the world prepared to learn some things quite easily (e.g., fear of snakes, spiders, and strangers) (Seligman & Hager, 1972). Intense male sexual jealousy suggests that uncertain paternity was an adaptive problem in our evolutionary past. The intense pain we feel on being ostracized from a group suggests that group membership was critical to survival and reproduction in our evolutionary past. Learning more and more about our evolved mechanisms is thus a major tool for overcoming the limitation of sparse knowledge of the environments of our ancestors.

A second limitation is that evolutionary scientists have just scratched the surface of understanding the nature, details, and design features of evolved psychological adaptations. In the case of jealousy, for example, there is a lack of knowledge about the range of cues that trigger it, the precise nature of the thoughts and emotions that are activated when a person is jealous, and the range of behaviors, such as vigilance and violence, that are manifest outcomes. As more research is conducted, this limitation can be expected to be circumvented.

A third limitation is that modern conditions differ from ancestral conditions in many respects, so that what was adaptive in the past might not be adaptive in the present. Ancestral humans lived in small groups of perhaps 50 to 150 in the context of close extended kin (Dunbar, 1993). Today we live in large cities in the context of thousands of strangers. Thus, it's important to keep in mind that selection pressures have changed. In this sense, humans can be said to live in the modern world with an ancient brain.

A fourth limitation is that it is sometimes easy to come up with different and competing evolutionary hypotheses for the same phenomena. To a large extent, this is true of all of science, including personality theories that do not invoke evolutionary explanations. The existence of competing theories is not an embarrassment but rather is an essential element of science. The critical obligation of scientists is to render their hypotheses in a sufficiently precise manner so that specific empirical predictions can be derived from them. In this way, the competing theories can be pitted against each other, and the hard hand of empirical evidence can be used to evaluate the competing theories.

Finally, evolutionary hypotheses have sometimes been accused of being untestable and hence unfalsifiable. The specific evolutionary hypotheses on aggression, jealousy, and so on presented in this chapter illustrate that this accusation is certainly false for some of them (see Buss, 2009a and 2012, for a list of others). Nonetheless, there is no doubt that some evolutionary hypotheses (like some standard "social" hypotheses) have indeed been framed in ways that are too vague to be of much scientific value. The solution to this problem is to hold the same high scientific standards for all competing theories. To be scientifically useful, theories and hypotheses should be framed as precisely as possible, along with attendant predictions, so that empirical studies can be conducted to test their merits.

SUMMARY AND EVALUATION

Selection is the primary key to evolution, or change in life forms over time. Variants that lead to greater survival, reproduction, or the reproductive success of genetic relatives tend to be preserved and spread through the population.

Evolutionary psychology starts with three fundamental premises. First, adaptations are presumed to be domain specific; they are designed to solve specific adaptive problems. Adaptations good for one adaptive problem, such as food selection, offer little help in solving other adaptive problems, such as mate selection. Second, adaptations are numerous, corresponding to the many adaptive problems humans have faced over evolutionary history. Third, adaptations are functional. We cannot understand them unless we figure out what they were designed to do—the adaptive problems they were designed to solve.

The empirical science of testing evolutionary hypotheses proceeds in two ways. First, middle-level evolutionary theories, such as the theory of parental investment and sexual selection, can be used to derive specific predictions in a top-down method of investigation. Second, we can observe a phenomenon and then develop a theory about its function in a process known as bottom-up investigation. Using this method, specific predictions are then derived based on the theory about phenomena that have not yet been observed.

Evolutionary psychological analysis can be applied to all three levels of personality analysis: human nature, sex differences, and individual differences. At the level of human nature, there is good evidence that people have evolved the need to belong to groups; to help specific others, such as genetic relatives; and to possess basic emotions, such as happiness, disgust, anger, fear, surprise, sadness, and contempt. There is good evidence that disgust, for example, is a universal human emotion that functions to avoid disease vectors, including contaminated food and disease-infected people. At the level of sex differences, men and women diverge only in domains in which they have faced recurrently different adaptive problems over evolutionary history. Examples include proclivities toward violence and aggression, desire for sexual variety, events that trigger jealousy, and specific mate preferences for qualities such as physical appearance and resources.

Individual differences can be understood from an evolutionary perspective using several approaches. First, individual differences can result from different environmental inputs into species-typical mechanisms. Second, individual differences can be contingent on other traits, such as when being large and strong inclines one to an aggressive disposition, whereas being small and weak inclines one to be less aggressive. Third, individual differences can result from frequency–dependent selection. Fourth, individual differences can be caused by variations over time or space in the optimum value for a trait.

The Big Five personality dispositions have begun to be examined through the lens of evolutionary psychology. One approach is to view individual differences as variations in strategic solutions to adaptive problems. Agreeableness, for example, reflects individual differences in adopting a strategy of cooperation versus acting selfishly when there are conflicts over resources. Emotional Instability reflects high levels of vigilance to social threats, which can be adaptive under some circumstances but carries a cost of high levels of stress and fatigue. These adaptive individual differences can be maintained by *balancing selection,* which occurs when genetic variation is maintained by selection because different levels on a trait dimension are adaptive in different environments.

A second approach proposes that evaluating other people on the five factors provides adaptively relevant information to solving key problems of social living: Whom can I trust for cooperation, devotion, and reciprocation (those high on Agreeableness)? Who is likely to ascend social hierarchies (those high on Extraversion)?

Who will be likely to work hard, be dependable, and accrue resources over time (those high on Conscientiousness)? Future evolutionary research will undoubtedly explore individual differences in the important social adaptive problems humans face in the context of group living.

Evolutionary psychology has several critical limitations at this stage of scientific development. The first is the lack of precise knowledge about the environments in which humans evolved and the selection pressures our ancestors faced. We are also limited in our knowledge about the nature, details, and workings of evolved mechanisms, including the features that trigger their activation and the manifest behavior that they produce as output. Nonetheless, the evolutionary perspective adds a useful set of theoretical tools to the analysis of personality at the levels of human nature, sex differences, and individual differences.

KEY TERMS

natural selection 224
hostile forces of nature 224
sexual selection 225
intrasexual competition 225
intersexual selection 225
genes 226
differential gene reproduction 226
inclusive fitness theory 226
adaptive problem 227
xenophobia 228

byproducts of adaptations 228
evolutionary byproducts 228
evolutionary noise 228
domain specific 229
functionality 229
deductive reasoning approach 231
inductive reasoning approach 231
social anxiety 232
evolutionary-predicted sex
   differences 238

effective polygyny 239
sexually dimorphic 239
reactively heritable 250
frequency–dependent
   selection 251
restricted sexual strategy 251
unrestricted mating strategy 251
psychopathy 252
balancing selection 254

PART THREE

The Intrapsychic Domain

© Science Photo Library RF/Getty Images RF

We now turn to the intrapsychic domain. This domain concerns the factors within the mind that influence behavior, thoughts, and feelings. The pioneer of this domain was Sigmund Freud. Freud was a medical doctor and neurologist and was highly influenced by biology. He often applied biological metaphors to the mind—for example, proposing that the mind had separate "organ systems," which operated independently from each other yet that influenced each other. His goal was to analyze the elements within the mind and describe how the elements worked together. He named this enterprise psychoanalysis, which refers both to his intrapsychic theory of personality and his method of helping people change.

In this domain, we devote two chapters to psychoanalysis. In Chapter 9, we cover the foundations of classical psychoanalysis, primarily in terms of Freud's original ideas and formulations. We will present Freud's most influential ideas, including the notion that the human mind is divided into two parts, the conscious part and the unconscious part. Moreover, Freud proposed three forces in the human mind—the id, the ego, and the superego—and these forces were constantly interacting over taming the twin motives of sex and aggression, or the life and death instincts. We also present Freud's ideas on personality development and how he stressed the importance of childhood events in determining the adult personality.

Some of Freud's ideas, such as repression, unconscious processing, and recalled memories, have stood the test of time and are active research topics in personality today. However, many students of Freud have modified some of his ideas, so we devote Chapter 10 to a discussion of contemporary topics in psychoanalytic theory. These include the idea of personality development as continuing through adulthood rather than stopping in childhood as Freud originally proposed. Another key development in contemporary psychoanalysis concerns the importance of a child's attachments to caregivers in influencing his or her subsequent relationships.

The intrapsychic domain differs from all the other domains in that it is concerned with the forces within the mind that work together and interact with each other and the environment. To some extent, this domain is similar to the biological domain in that the biological domain also emphasizes forces within the person. However, in the intrapsychic domain, the concern is with aspects of *psychic* functioning. In the biological domain, we are concerned

with aspects of *physical* functioning, such as the brain, genes, and the chemicals in the bloodstream.

One fundamental assumption of psychologists working in the intrapsychic domain is that there are areas of the mind that are outside awareness. Within each person, there is a part of him- or herself that even he or she does not know about. This is called the unconscious mind. Moreover, according to classical psychoanalysis, the unconscious mind is thought to have a life of its own, with its own motivation, its own will, and its own energy.

Another assumption within the intrapsychic domain is that most things do not happen by chance. That is, every behavior, every thought, and every experience means something or reveals something about the person's personality. A slip of the tongue, for example, occurs not by accident, but because of an intrapsychic conflict. A person forgets someone's name not by accident, but because of something about the person whose name cannot be remembered. Or a person dreams of flying, not because dreams are random, but because of an unconscious wish or desire being expressed in the dream. Everything a person does, says, or feels has meaning and can be analyzed in terms of intrapsychic elements and forces.

We will also examine the life and ideas of one of Freud's more famous female students, Karen Horney. Freud's ideas have been criticized for neglecting women, and Horney was among the first to take women's issues seriously from a psychoanalytic perspective. She developed a feminist interpretation of Freud's ideas.

In Chapter 11, we examine work on motivational aspects of personality. Here psychologists emphasize the common motives that most people have to varying degrees.

Individual differences in motives help psychologists answer the question "Why do people want what they want?" The three most common motives studied in this domain are the desire to achieve, the need to have close relationships with other people, and the desire to have power and influence over others. We present some of the basic findings on each of these three motives, as well as describe a projective technique that has been developed for assessing these needs. We also describe a contemporary notion that suggests that motives can be conscious or unconscious and that unconscious motives affect different kinds of behavior than conscious motives.

Most of the research on motives emphasizes deficit motives—that is, motives that arise because something is lacking. There is, however, the notion that one particular motive is not based on a deficit, but rather is based on growth and change. This motive refers to the more abstract need to become who we are, to actualize our potential as the persons we were meant to be. The need to self-actualize can also operate outside awareness, and we may engage in certain behaviors, not because we have thought everything through, but because it just feels like the right thing to be doing at the moment.

In Part 3 of this book, we explore some of the major ideas and findings from the intrapsychic domain of personality. As you read, it is important to keep in mind that the intrapsychic domain, as well as all the other domains, refers to just one set of factors that influence personality. Personality is determined by many factors; like a jigsaw puzzle, it is made up of many parts. Let's now consider the part that dwells in the deeper reaches of the human mind.

© *Science Photo Library RF/*
Getty Images RF

9

Psychoanalytic Approaches to Personality

THE INTRAPSYCHIC DOMAIN

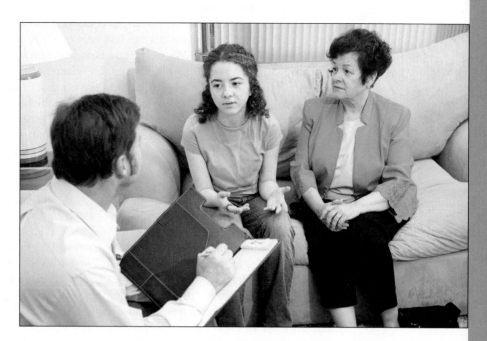

Events from childhood often form the topics for discussion during therapy sessions.
© Lisa F. Young/Alamy Stock Photo RF

Dr. Ross Cheit is a professor of political science and international and public affairs at Brown University. In 1992, he received a phone call from his sister, saying that his nephew had joined a boys' choir, just as Professor Cheit had done when he was a boy. Instead of being happy at the news that his nephew was following in his footsteps, Professor Cheit was strangely unhappy. Over the next few weeks, Professor Cheit became increasingly depressed and irritable and began to have marital difficulties. He did not connect any of his troubles to the phone call from his sister.

Shortly thereafter, Professor Cheit recalled a memory of a man he had not seen or thought about for 25 years. The man he remembered was William Farmer. Mr. Farmer had been the administrator of the San Francisco Boys Chorus summer camp, which Professor Cheit had attended between the ages of 10 and 13. Professor Cheit was now 38, and for the first time in 25 years he was recalling how Mr. Farmer would come into his cabin at night, sit on his bed, and begin stroking his chest and then his stomach, and then reach into his pajamas.

Intent on gathering objective information about his abuse, Professor Cheit hired a private investigator. The director of the boys' chorus at the time Professor Cheit was there, Madi Bacon, now 87 years old, was located in Berkeley. When Professor Cheit first talked to her and mentioned Farmer's name, she spontaneously remarked how she had almost had to fire Farmer for "hobnobbing" with the boys. For the first time, Professor Cheit felt that his memory of being molested was authentic. Moreover, after talking with Madi Bacon, he realized that he might not have been the only young boy abused by Farmer.

Using chorus records, Professor Cheit located dozens of the 118 boys who had been at camp with him 25 years earlier. In contacting them, he soon found that others had been molested by Mr. Farmer but had kept quiet. A professor at a university in Michigan, a librarian in the Midwest, and a homeless man living in San Francisco—all had allegedly been abused by Mr. Farmer. The camp nurse at the time recalled catching Mr. Farmer in bed with a sick child in the camp infirmary. The nurse claims to have reported the incident to the camp director, Madi Bacon, who took no action. Professor Cheit obtained documentation that, on at least four occasions, the camp director was informed of molestation of the boys by staff members but took no steps to address the problem.

Now more sure than ever that his memory of abuse was authentic, Professor Cheit wanted to talk directly with Mr. Farmer, who was finally located in the tiny town of Scio, Oregon. Professor Cheit phoned him. Mr. Farmer had no trouble remembering Professor Cheit as one of the boys in summer camp 25 years earlier. "What can I do for you?" Farmer inquired. "You can tell me whether you have any remorse for what you did to me and the other boys at summer camp," replied Professor Cheit. With a tape recorder running, Professor Cheit kept Mr. Farmer on the phone for nearly an hour. Mr. Farmer admitted molesting Professor Cheit in his cabin at night, and he acknowledged that the camp director had known of the abuse but had allowed him to stay on at the camp. He also admitted that he had since lost other jobs for molesting children and conceded that he knew the acts he had committed with children were criminal.

On August 19, 1993, Professor Cheit and his parents filed a lawsuit against the San Francisco Boys Chorus, charging that the chorus had "negligently or intentionally" allowed staff members to molest children in its care. Lawyers for the chorus at first denied the charges. Professor Cheit's lawsuit asked the boys chorus to meet three conditions: to apologize, thereby admitting guilt; to institute protective measures for current campers; and to pay $450,000 to Professor Cheit as financial compensation. During the litigation, Professor Cheit produced five corroborating witnesses and the tape-recorded admission from Mr. Farmer himself. Just over a year later, the lawsuit was settled. The boys chorus agreed to apologize to Professor Cheit, to put safeguards in place to protect present chorus members from possible molestation, and to pay Professor Cheit $35,000. Professor Cheit is currently on the faculty at Brown University, is the chair of the Rhode Island Ethics Commission, and is affiliated with the Taubman Center for Public Policy and American Institutions at Brown University. He has authored several important papers and book chapters about childhood sexual abuse (e.g., Cheit, Shavit, & Reiss-Davis, 2010) and motivated forgetting (e.g., DePrince et al., 2012).

Professor Cheit was fortunate in that the state of California had just changed its statute of limitations laws, allowing for criminal charges of child abuse to be filed anytime within three years of the time that the alleged victim *remembered* the abuse, with independent corroboration. On July 12, 1994, Mr. Farmer was arrested at his home, then in Texas, and extradited to Plumas County, California, the site of the boys chorus camp. According to the county district attorney, Mr. Farmer was charged with six counts of child molestation involving three boys, including Professor Cheit, in 1967 and 1968. Mr. Farmer was charged with committing crimes over a quarter of a century earlier. He pleaded not guilty. The details of this fascinating case are discussed in several books, including Chu (1998) and Schachter (1997).

Is it possible that a person can forget something as traumatic as sexual abuse? Can a forgotten memory lie dormant for years, only to be aroused later by an event, such as a chance phone call? Once aroused, can such a memory cause a person to start having symptoms, such as feelings of depression and irritability, without his or her knowing the cause of those difficulties? Some psychologists believe that people sometimes are unaware of the reasons for their own problematic behaviors. When treating a person for a psychological problem, some therapists believe that the cause of the problem resides in the person's unconscious, the part of the mind outside the person's immediate awareness. They contend that a memory of a past traumatic event can be completely forgotten yet nevertheless cause a psychological problem years later (Bass & Davis, 1988). This reasoning has led many states, such as California, to place the statute of limitations on child abuse at three years from when the abuse is *remembered* by the person. Furthermore, such therapists believe that if they can help make this unconscious memory conscious— that is, if they can help the patient recall a forgotten traumatic memory—they can put the patient on the road to recovery (Baker, 1992).

This perspective on the causes and cures of psychological problems has its origin in a theory of personality developed by Sigmund Freud (1856–1939), commonly called psychoanalysis. In this chapter, we examine the basic elements of classical psychoanalytic theory and explore some of the empirical studies conducted to test certain aspects of the theory. We consider the scientific evidence for the repression of childhood memories, for the concept of unconscious motivation, and for other aspects of psychoanalytic theory. Whereas many of Freud's ideas have not stood the test of time, other ideas are still with us and are topics of contemporary research. Because this theory is so much the result of one person's thinking, let's first look at a brief biographical sketch of Freud.

Sigmund Freud: A Brief Biography

Although Freud was born in 1856 in Freiberg, Moravia (now part of the Czech Republic), his family moved to Vienna when he was 4 years old, and he spent virtually the remainder of his life there. Freud excelled in school and obtained his medical degree from the University of Vienna. Although he started out as a researcher in neurology, he realized that he could make more money to support his wife and growing family if he entered into private medical practice. After studying hypnosis with Jean-Martin Charcot in Paris, Freud returned to Vienna and started a private practice, treating patients with "nervous disorders." During that time, Freud began developing the idea that portions of the human mind were outside conscious awareness. The unconscious is the part of the mind about which the conscious mind has no awareness. Freud sought to study empirically the implications of the unconscious for understanding people's lives and their problems with living. From his early contact with patients, Freud began to surmise that the unconscious mind operated under its own power, subject to its own motivations and according to its own logic. Freud devoted the rest of his career to exploring the nature and logic of the unconscious mind.

Sigmund Freud at age 82. He most likely insisted this photo be taken from the side in order not to show the ravages of his jaw and throat cancer, and the many operations he underwent in an unsuccessful attempt to cure that disease. He died in 1939, less than a year after this photo was taken.

© Keystone/Archive Photos/Getty Images

Freud's first solo-authored book, *The Interpretation of Dreams,* was published in 1900. In it, he described how the unconscious mind was expressed in dreams and how dreams contained clues to our innermost secrets, desires, and motives. The analysis of dreams became a cornerstone of his treatment. This book sold poorly at first but nevertheless attracted the attention of other medical doctors seeking to understand psychological problems. By 1902, there was a small group of followers (e.g., Alfred Adler) who met with Freud every Wednesday evening. At these meetings, Freud talked about his theory, shared insights, and discussed patients' progress, all the while smoking one of the 20 or so cigars he smoked each day. During this period, Freud was systematically building his theory and testing its acceptance by knowledgeable peers. By 1908, the membership of the Wednesday Psychological Circle had grown significantly, prompting Freud to form the Vienna Psychoanalytic Society (Grosskurth, 1991).

In 1909, Freud made his only visit to the United States, to present a series of lectures on psychoanalysis at the invitation of psychologist G. Stanley Hall, who was then president of Clark University. Rosenzweig (1994) describes Freud's trip to the United States in fascinating detail. In 1910, the International Psychoanalytic Association was formed. Freud's theories were gaining recognition around the world.

Freud and his work drew both praise and criticism. Whereas some accepted his ideas as brilliant insights into the workings of human nature, others opposed his views on various scientific and ideological grounds. To some, his treatment approach (the so-called talking cure) was absurd. Freud's theory that the adult personality was a result of how the person as a child coped with his or her sexual and aggressive urges was considered politically incorrect by the standards of Victorian morality. Even some of the founding members of his Vienna Psychoanalytic Society grew to disagree with developments in his theory. Nevertheless, Freud continued to refine and apply his theory, writing 20 books and numerous papers during his career.

Germany invaded Austria in 1938, and the Nazis began their persecution of the Jews there. Freud, who was Jewish, had reasons to fear the Nazis. The Nazi party burned his books and the books of other modern intellectuals. With the assistance of wealthy patrons, Freud, his wife, and their six children fled to London. Freud died the following year after a long, painful, and disfiguring battle with cancer of the jaw and throat.

Freud's London house continued to be occupied by his daughter, Anna Freud, herself a prominent psychoanalyst, until her death in 1982. The house is now part of the Freud Museum in London. Visitors can walk through Freud's library and study, which remain largely as he left them when he died. The study, which is where Freud treated his patients, still contains his celebrated couch, covered with an Oriental rug. It also contains the many ancient artifacts and small statues and icons that seemed to fascinate him and reveal his secret passion for archeology. Freud has been referred to as the original archeologist of the human mind.

Fundamental Assumptions of Psychoanalytic Theory

Freud's model of human nature relied on the notion of **psychic energy** to motivate all human activity. What were the forces that motivated people to do one thing and not another or that motivated people to do anything at all? Freud proposed a source of energy that is within each person and used the term *psychic energy* to refer to this wellspring of motivation. Freud believed that psychic energy operated according to the law of conservation of energy: The amount of psychic energy an individual possessed remained constant throughout his or her lifetime. Personality change was viewed as a redirection of a person's psychic energy.

Basic Instincts: Sex and Aggression

What was the basic source of psychic energy? Freud believed that there were strong innate forces that provided *all* the energy in the psychic system. He called these forces **instincts**. Freud's original theory of instincts was profoundly influenced by Darwin's theory of evolution. Darwin had published his book on evolution just a few years after Freud was born. In Freud's initial formulation, there were two fundamental categories of instincts: self-preservation instincts and sexual instincts. Curiously, these corresponded exactly to two major components of Darwin's theory of natural selection: selection by survival and selection by reproduction. Thus Freud's initial classification of instincts could have been borrowed from Darwin's two forms of evolution by selection (Ritvo, 1990).

In his later formulations, however, Freud collapsed the self-preservation and sexual instincts into one, which he called the life instinct. And due in part to his witnessing the horrors of World War I, he developed the idea of a death instinct. Freud postulated that humans had a fundamental instinct toward destruction and that this instinct was often manifest in aggression toward others. The two instincts were usually referred to as **libido** for the life instinct and **thanatos** for the death instinct. Although the libido was generally considered sexual, Freud also used this term to refer to any need-satisfying, life-sustaining, or pleasure-oriented urge. Similarly, thanatos was considered to be the death instinct, but Freud used this term in a broad sense to refer to any urge to destroy, harm, or aggress against others or oneself. Freud wrote more about the libido early in his career, when this issue was perhaps relevant to his own life. Later in his career, Freud wrote more about thanatos, when he faced his own impending death.

Although Freud initially believed that the life and death instincts worked to oppose one another, he later argued that they could combine in various ways. Consider the act of eating. Eating obviously serves the life instinct, entailing the consumption of nutrients necessary for survival. At the same time, eating also involves acts of tearing, biting, and chewing, which Freud thought could be seen as aggressive manifestations of thanatos. As another example, Freud viewed rape as an expression of extreme death instinct, directed toward another person in a manner that is fused with sexual energy. The combination of erotic and aggressive instincts into a single motive is a particularly volatile mixture.

Because each person possesses a fixed amount of psychic energy, according to Freud, the energy used to direct one type of behavior is not available to drive other types of behaviors. The person who directs his or her death instinct into a socially acceptable channel, such as competitive sports, has less energy to expend toward more destructive manifestations of this instinct. Because psychic energy exists in a fixed and limited amount within each person, it can be directed and redirected in various ways.

Unconscious Motivation: Sometimes We Don't Know Why We Do What We Do

According to Freud, the human mind consists of three parts. The **conscious** mind is the part that contains all the thoughts, feelings, and perceptions that you are presently aware of. Whatever you are currently perceiving or thinking about is in your conscious mind. These thoughts represent only a small fraction of the information available to you.

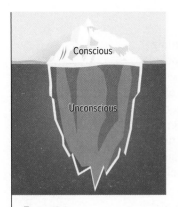

Figure 9.1

The iceberg metaphor of the human mind; the conscious part is what is above the waterline, the preconscious is what is below water but still visible from above, and the unconscious, the largest part, is that part hidden well below the surface.

You also have a vast number of memories, dreams, and thoughts that you could easily bring to mind if you so desired. What were you wearing yesterday? What was the name of your best friend in seventh grade? What is the earliest memory you have of your mother? This information is stored in the **preconscious** mind. Any piece of information that you are not presently thinking about, but that could easily be retrieved and made conscious, is found in the preconscious mind.

The **unconscious** is the third and, according to Freud, largest part of the human mind. The metaphor of an iceberg is often used to describe the topography of the mind. The part of the iceberg above the water represents the conscious mind. The part that you can see just below the water surface is the preconscious mind. And the part of the iceberg totally hidden from view (the vast majority of it) represents the unconscious mind. In Figure 9.1, we reproduce a drawing made by Freud in 1932, in which he graphically presented the three levels of consciousness. The top level is perception and consciousness, which he abbreviated "pcpt-cs." The middle level is the preconscious, and the lower level is the unconscious. Residing in the unconscious mind is unacceptable information, hidden from conscious view so well that it cannot even be considered preconscious. Those memories, feelings, thoughts, or urges are so troubling or even distasteful that being aware of them would make the person anxious. Many of the cases reported in the psychoanalytic literature involve distressing unconscious themes—such as incest; hatred toward siblings, parents, or spouses; and memories of childhood traumas.

Society does not allow people to express freely all of their sexual and aggressive instincts. Individuals must learn to control their urges. One way to control these urges, according to Freud, is to keep them from entering conscious awareness in the first place. Consider a child who has gotten extremely angry with a parent. This child might have a fleeting wish that the parents die. Such thoughts would be very distressing to a child—so distressing that they might be held back from conscious awareness and banished instead to the unconscious—the part of the mind holding thoughts and memories about which the person is unaware. All kinds of unacceptable sexual and aggressive urges, thoughts, and feelings might accumulate in the unconscious during the course of a typical childhood.

Exercise

Think back to the first house or apartment you lived in as a child. If you are like most people, you can probably remember as far back as your fourth or fifth year of age. Try to recall the structure of the house or apartment, the location of the rooms relative to each other. Draw a floor plan, starting with the basement if there was one, then the first floor, then the upstairs rooms (if the house had a second floor). On your floor plan, label each room. Now think about each room, letting the memories of events that happened in each of them come back to you. It is likely that you will recall some people and events that you have not thought about for a decade or more. You also might notice that many of your memories have an emotional quality; some memories are pleasant, whereas others are unpleasant. The memories that you can bring to conscious awareness are in your preconscious. You may have memories of events that occurred that do not come back to you during this exercise because they are in your unconscious.

Psychic Determinism: Nothing Happens by Chance

Freud maintained that nothing happens by chance or by accident. There is a reason behind every act, thought, and feeling. Everything we do, think, say, and feel is an expression of the mind—the conscious, preconscious, or unconscious mind. In his book *The Psychopathology of Everyday Life,* Freud introduced the idea that the little "accidents" of daily life are often expressions of the **motivated unconscious**, such as calling someone by the wrong name, missing an appointment, and breaking something that belongs to another. Texas Republican Dick Armey once referred to the openly homosexual congressman from Massachusetts, Barney Frank, as "Barney Fag." Once, a psychology professor referred to Sigmund Freud as "Sigmund Fraud." Such mix-ups can often be embarrassing, but, according to Freud, they represent the motivated activity of the unconscious. There is a reason for every slip of the tongue, for being late, for forgetting a person's name, and for breaking something that belongs to another. The reasons can be discovered if the contents of the unconscious can be examined.

Freud taught that most symptoms of mental illnesses are caused by unconscious motivations. Freud provided detailed case histories of 12 patients, as well as dozens of shorter discussions of specific patients. In these case studies, he found support for his theory that psychological problems were caused by unconscious memories or desires. For example, Freud wrote about the case of Anna O. Although Freud did not directly treat or even meet Anna O., her physician, Joseph Breuer, consulted with Freud.

At the time, Anna O. was a 21-year-old woman who had fallen ill while taking care of her sick father who eventually died of tuberculosis. Anna's illness began with a severe cough, and later included the loss of movement in her right side, disturbances of vision, hearing, and the inability to drink liquids. Dr. Breuer diagnosed Anna O's illness as hysteria and developed a form of therapy that appeared effective in relieving her symptoms. This form of therapy consisted of Breuer talking with Anna O. about her symptoms, and in particular about her memories of events that happened before the onset of the symptoms. For example, in talking about her severe cough, they talked about her memories of caring for her father, and the severe cough he had from his tuberculosis. As she explored these memories, and especially her feelings toward her father and about his death, her own cough lessened and disappeared. Similarly, when talking about her inability to drink liquids (she had been quenching her thirst with fruit and melons), she suddenly recalled the memory of seeing a dog drink from a woman's glass, an incident that completely disgusted her at the time but about which she had forgotten. Soon after describing this memory, she asked for a drink of water and immediately regained her ability to drink liquids.

To Breuer, and to Freud, hysterical symptoms did not occur by chance. Rather, they were physical expressions of repressed traumatic experiences. From the experience treating Anna O., Breuer concluded that the way to cure hysterical symptoms was to help the person recall the memory of the incident that had originally led to the symptoms. By the patient's recalling the traumatic incident (e.g., her father's death), an emotional catharsis or release can be achieved by having her or him express any feelings associated with that memory. This then removes the cause of the symptom and hence the symptom disappears.

Freud adopted and refined the technique developed by Breuer for effecting the "talking cure." Freud believed that for a psychological symptom to be cured, the unconscious cause of the symptom must first be discovered. Often the process involves discovering a hidden memory of an unsettling, disagreeable, or even repulsive experience

A Closer Look

Examples of the Unconscious: Blindsight and Deliberation-Without-Awareness

Following an injury or stroke that damages the primary vision center in the brain, people will lose some or all of their ability to see. In this kind of blindness the eyes still work to bring information into the brain; it is just that the brain center responsible for object recognition fails. People who suffer this kind of "cortical" blindness often display an interesting capacity to make judgments about objects that they truly cannot see. This phenomenon is termed **blindsight,** and it has fascinated psychologists since it was first documented in the 1960s (Leopold, 2012).

Imagine having a person with cortical blindness as a subject. You could hold a red ball in front of her open eyes and ask if she can see it. She would reply no, which is consistent with the fact that she is blind. Now you ask her to point to the red ball (which she has just denied seeing). What happens? She points directly to the red ball even though she does not have the ability to see it!

Blindsight is taken as evidence of the unconscious. Here one part of the mind knows about something that another part of the mind does not know about. There are many demonstrations of people with blindsight. For example, when an object is placed in front of a person with blindsight—that is, a person who does not know for sure whether it is there or not—that person can guess the color of that object at levels much better than merely by chance. In other words, such a condition illustrates that information that is

unconscious (whether an object is or is not in front of the person) is actually being processed somewhere in the mind (because the person knows the color of objects that are presented).

An explanation for such "unconscious" perception has been offered in terms of nerve pathways from the eyes into the brain. The optic nerve carries information from the eye into the brain, and the majority of this information is transferred to the primary visual center in the striate cortex. However, pathways split off of the optic nerve before getting to the visual center and carry some of this visual information to other parts of the brain. These other centers may be involved in movement recognition or color recognition or even emotional evaluation. If the vision center were completely destroyed, the person would not recognize *what* the object was, but the person might know if it was moving or how he or she felt about it.

One of the most interesting and robust examples of blindsight concerns the perception of the emotional significance of something that one does not see. In one study, a person with blindsight underwent a conditioning procedure where a visual cue that the person could not see (a picture of a circle) was accompanied by an unpleasant shock, whereas other visual cues (pictures of squares, rectangles, etc.) were not paired with shock. Following a period of conditioning, the stimuli shapes were later

"shown" to the blind subject, and the subject exhibited a fear response to the circle but not the squares or rectangles (Hamm et al., 2003). These researchers argue that emotional conditioning does not require a conscious representation in the mind of the subject. Other studies of people with cortical blindness demonstrate that, when "shown" pictures of facial expressions, they can "guess" the emotions expressed in the faces even when they cannot see the faces being presented. Obviously, a lot of emotional processing occurs at some level in the brain that does not involve the primary visual center. People could have feelings about (i.e., like or dislike) something that they are not even aware of.

Another example of the unconscious at work concerns the phenomenon of **deliberation-without-awareness,** or the "let me sleep on it" effect. The notion here is, if a person confronted with a difficult decision can put it out of his or her conscious mind for a period of time, then the unconscious mind will continue to deliberate on it outside of the person's awareness, helping him or her to arrive at a "sudden" and often correct decision sometime later. This is sometimes called "unconscious decision making."

The phenomenon of unconscious decision making was the topic of several clever studies published in the prestigious journal *Science* by a team of Dutch researchers (Dijksterhuis et al., 2006). These researchers

that has been repressed or pushed into the unconscious (Masson, 1984). Freud always acknowledged the importance of the case of Anna O. on his thinking, and gave credit to the careful observations of Dr. Breuer:

> *If it is a merit to have brought psychoanalysis into being, that merit is not mine. I had no share in its earliest beginnings. I was a student and working for my final examinations at the time when another Viennese physician, Dr. Josef Breuer, first made use of this procedure on a girl who was suffering from*

hypothesized that, for simple decisions, conscious deliberation would work best, but when decisions were complex, involving many factors, then unconscious deliberation would work best. They presented subjects with the task of deciding on the best car out of four different cars. Subjects in the simple condition considered 4 attributes of the cars, whereas subjects in the complex condition considered 12 attributes of the cars. In all cases, one car was characterized by 75 percent positive attributes (i.e., the best car), two by 50 percent positive attributes, and one by 25 percent positive attributes. After reading all the information about the cars, half of the subjects were assigned to the conscious deliberation condition and the other half were assigned to the unconscious deliberation condition. In the conscious deliberation condition, subjects were asked to think about the information for four minutes before deciding on the best car. In the unconscious deliberation condition, subjects were distracted for four minutes by being asked to solve anagram puzzles, then immediately asked to decide on the best car.

As shown in Figure 9.2, in the simple decision condition, with only 4 attributes to consider on each car, subjects who consciously deliberated made the best decisions. However, when the decision was complex, involving 12 different attributes of the cars, subjects in the "unconscious" deliberation condition made the best decisions. The authors demonstrate similar effects in three additional studies. Even though the studies concern consumer items (e.g., cars), there is reason to believe that the unconscious deliberation effect might apply to any type of decision (e.g., what career path to

pursue, who to vote for, whom to marry, etc.). The authors (Dijksterhuis et al., 2006) argue that, with any decision, it would "benefit the individual to think consciously about simple matters and to delegate thinking about more complex matters to the unconscious" (p. 1007).

A recent review of the unconscious decision-making literature urges caution in interpreting results, and shows how alternative explanations (other than that the unconscious is an intelligent decision-maker) can account for some findings (Newell, 2014). However, this review leaves out several recent studies that have employed functional brain imaging to investigate unconscious decision-making (Brooks & Stein, 2014). For example, one study (Creswell, Bursley, & Satpute, 2013) used brain imaging while half the subjects were consciously deliberating on a decision, and the other half were doing a distractor task and supposedly unconsciously deliberating (since they knew they would have to make a decision when finished with the distractor task). A third group just did the distractor task. When the researchers subtracted out the brain activation pattern identified in the distractor task group, from the distractor task/unconscious deliberation group, they found residual brain activation that matched

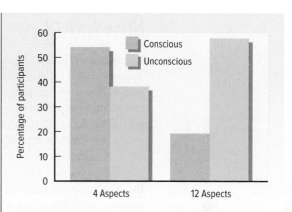

Figure 9.2

Percentage of participants who chose the most desirable car as a function of complexity of decision and mode of thought.

Source: Dijksterhuis, A., Bos, M. W., Nordgren, L. F., and van Baaren, R. B. (2006). On making the right choice: The deliberation without-attention effect. *Science, 311,* 1005–1007.

the deliberation group. In other words, the group that was being distracted so they could not deliberate, nevertheless showed brain activation patterns consistent with the notion that they were in fact deliberating in one part of their brains, while other parts of their brains were occupied with the distractor task.

Research on deliberation without awareness is not without its critics. Some have argued that the results do not prove that the subjects' "unconscious" actively arrives at the correct decision (Aczel et al., 2011). Others have argued that decisions are memory based, and thus offer an explanation for the findings that do not rely on anything like an "unconscious" (Lassiter et al., 2009). As you will see throughout this chapter, much that is connected with psychoanalysis is contentious and a matter of debate. Nevertheless, psychoanalytic ideas are stimulating research into novel and interesting phenomena.

hysteria. (From Freud's lectures presented at Clark University in Massachusetts, 1909.)

Freud is uncharacteristically modest in the preceding quote. He adapted the notions of symptom formation and the talking cure from Breuer, and combined these with other ideas about the unconscious, about repression, about stages of development and many other notions, and, from these, he formulated a grand theory of personality that has yet to be rivaled by a single unitary theory of personality.

Structure of Personality

Psychoanalytic personality theory describes how people cope with their sexual and aggressive instincts within the constraints of a civilized society. Sexual and aggressive instincts often lead to drives and urges that conflict with society and with reality. One part of the mind creates these urges; another part has a sense of what civilized society expects; and another part tries to satisfy the urges within the bounds of reality and society. How is it that the mind can have so many parts, and how do these parts work together to form personality?

A metaphor may be helpful in answering this question. Think of the mind as a plumbing system, which contains water under pressure. The pressure is the metaphor for the psychic energy from the sexual and aggressive instincts, which builds up and demands release. According to Freud's theory, when it comes to this internal pressure, there are three schools of plumbing: one plumber suggests that we open all the valves at the slightest pressure, another offers ways to redirect the pressure so that the strain is relieved without making much of a mess, and the third plumber wants to keep all the valves closed. Let's discuss each of these "psychic plumbers" in some detail, using Freud's terminology.

Id: Reservoir of Psychic Energy

Freud taught in the beginning there was id, the most primitive part of the human mind. Freud saw the **id** (German for "it") as something we are born with and as the source of all drives and urges. Using the plumbing metaphor, the id is the plumber who wants to let off all pressure at the slightest hint of strain or tension. The id is like a spoiled child—selfish, impulsive, and pleasure-loving. According to Freud, the id operates according to the **pleasure principle**, which is the desire for immediate gratification. The id cannot tolerate any delays in satisfying its urges. During infancy, the id dominates. When an infant sees an attractive toy, it will reach for the toy and will cry and fuss if it cannot get it. Infants can sometimes appear unreasonable in their demands. Because the id operates according to the pleasure principle, it does not listen to reason, does not follow logic, has no values or morals (other than immediate gratification), and has very little patience.

The id also operates with **primary process thinking**, which is thinking without logical rules of conscious thought or an anchor in reality. Dreams and fantasies are examples of primary process thinking. Although primary process thought does not follow the normal rules of reality (e.g., in dreams, people fly and walk through walls), Freud believed that there were principles at work in primary process thought and that these principles could be discovered. If an urge from the id requires an external object or person, and that object or person is not available, the id may create a mental image or fantasy of that object or person to satisfy its needs. Mental energy is invested in that fantasy, and the urge is temporarily satisfied. This process is called **wish fulfillment**, whereby something unavailable is conjured up and the image of it is temporarily satisfying. Someone might be very angry, for example, but the target of the anger is too powerful to attack. In this case, engaging in wish fulfillment might produce an imagined fantasy of revenge for past wrongs. This strategy of wish fulfillment works only temporarily to gratify the id because the need is not satisfied in reality. A person must find other ways to gratify id urges or hold them in check.

Ego: Executive of Personality

The ego is the plumber who works to redirect the pressure produced by the id instincts into acceptable or at least less problematic outlets. The **ego** is the part of the mind that constrains the id to reality. According to Freud, it develops within the first two or three years

In the psychoanalytic theory of personality, conflicts between children and parents are normal, necessary, and an important part of personality development.
© georgerudy/123RF RF

of life (after the "terrible 2s"). The ego operates according to the **reality principle**. Perhaps you have heard the phrase "reality check" which comes from the notion that the ego, while trying to satisfy the id, has to take the reality of the person's situation into account, it cannot just focus on the childlike urges of the id. The ego understands that the urges of the id are often in conflict with social and physical reality. A child cannot just grab a candy bar off the shelf at the grocery store or hit his sister whenever she makes him angry. Although such acts might reduce immediate tension in the child, they conflict with society's and parents' rules about stealing and beating up little sisters. The ego understands that such actions can lead to problems and that *direct* expression of id impulses must therefore be avoided, redirected, or postponed, depending on the situation.

The ego works to postpone the discharge of id urges until an appropriate situation arises. The ego engages in **secondary process thinking**, which is the development of strategies for solving problems and obtaining satisfaction. Often this process involves taking into account the constraints of physical reality about when and how to express a desire or an urge. For example, teasing one's sister is more acceptable than hitting her, and this can perhaps satisfy the id's aggressive urge almost as well. There may be some urges, however, that simply remain unacceptable according to social reality or conventional morality, *regardless* of the situation. The third part of the mind, the superego, is responsible for upholding social values and ideals.

Superego: Upholder of Societal Values and Ideals

Around the age of 5, a child begins to develop the third part of the mind, which Freud called the superego. The **superego** is the part of the mind that internalizes the values, morals, and ideals of society. Usually, these are instilled into the child by society's various socializing agents, such as parents, schools, and organized religions. Freud emphasized the role of parents in particular in children's development of self-control and

A Closer Look

Ego Depletion: Is Self-Control a Limited Resource?

In Freud's structure of the mind, the ego is that part that must deal with reality by resolving conflicts between inner and outer pressures. For example, a man walking through a "red-light" district in a city might feel the urge of his id to walk over to a prostitute, and he might simultaneously feel the urge from his superego to find a church. It is up to his ego, however, to start him moving in one direction or the other. Freud also taught that the mind is a closed energy system; the more energy used by one self-control activity, the less energy is available for other self-control activities. This implies that the psychic energy used to resolve a conflict among reality, the id, and the superego would leave less psychic energy available for resolving other conflicts.

Psychologist Roy Baumeister and his colleagues have subjected this basic notion—that psychic energy can be depleted by efforts toward self-control, leaving less energy available for subsequent self-control situations—to a series of experimental tests. In general, the findings are supportive of Freud's basic notion about the ego and psychic energy. Let's take a closer look at some of these studies.

In one study, participants signed up for a study on taste perception and were asked to skip a meal just prior to their session (to ensure that they would be hungry). Arriving at the laboratory, participants were left alone in a room; on the table was a bowl of radishes and a stack of freshly baked chocolate chip cookies (Baumeister, Bratslavsky, et al., 1998). One group of participants was instructed to "eat two or three radishes and avoid eating the cookies while waiting for the experiment to start." Another group was instructed to "eat two or three cookies and avoid eating the radishes." And a third group, the control group, was not exposed to any food while waiting. Following this waiting period, where presumably the "radish eating" group would have had to exercise self-control over the

immediate gratification of eating some cookies, the participants then attempted to solve a geometrical puzzle that was, unbeknown to them, impossible to solve. Participants were told that they could quit working on the puzzle at any time. Results showed that participants in the radish condition gave up on the puzzle sooner than participants in either the cookie condition or the noneating control condition. Importantly, participants in the cookie condition did not differ from those in the no-food control condition in their persistence on the puzzle. Participants in the radish condition also reported being more tired after the puzzle task than those in the cookie or noneating conditions. These findings are consistent with the theory of **ego depletion**. In the radish condition, the participants' exertion of self-control in the face of temptation to eat cookies resulted in a decrease of psychic energy available to work on the difficult puzzle, leading them to give up sooner and report being more tired after the experiment.

To date, hundreds of studies have been published on ego depletion (Baumeister, 2014). Most take the form of breaking research participants into two groups: one group performs a self-control task, and the second group performs a similar task that does not require self-control. Next, all participants go on to perform a second, unrelated self-control task. If self-control depletes a limited psychic resource, then performing the first self-control task should deplete this groups' resource, leaving less available for the second self-control task and causing poorer performance on that task for this group compared to the group that did not perform the first self-control task (Baumeister, Vohs, & Tice, 2007). Many studies have looked at depletion effects on the self-control of cognitive effort; others have looked at the effects of ego depletion on more id-like self-control tasks,

such as self-control of sexual impulses (Gailliot & Baumeister, 2007) and the self-control of aggressive and violent responding (DeWall et al., 2007; Stucke & Baumeister, 2006). For example, in one experiment on aggression the ego depletion group had to resist the urge to eat tempting food, whereas the control group could eat as much as they wanted. Later, in a second task, the ego depletion group reacted more aggressively to an insult than did the control group (Stucke & Baumeister, 2006). In studies of sexual restraint, ego-depleted subjects were found to be less likely than a group that did not undergo ego depletion to stifle inappropriate sexual thoughts, and were more likely to consider engaging in sexual activity with someone other than their primary relationship partner (Gailliot & Baumeister, 2007).

All of us have to resist unacceptable impulses all the time: resist falling asleep in a boring class, eating forbidden foods, playing when we should be working, resting when we should be exercising, saying something that might hurt a relationship partner, engaging in inappropriate aggressive or sexual activities, or any one of a long list of problematic behaviors (such a list, based on studying people in their everyday lives resisting everyday temptations, can be found in Hoffman, Baumeister, et al., 2012, and in Hoffman, Vohs, & Baumeister, 2012). To resist these behaviors we call upon our powers of self-control, which Freud taught was the main function of the ego. Freud also taught that the psyche is a closed energy system, such that the energy used to cope with a specific conflict would not be available to cope with another conflict that presented itself very close in time to the first.

Results from a large number of ego depletion experiments show that exercising self-control in one situation often lessens the amount of self-control that can be exerted in a subsequent situation. Studies range from research on athletes engaging in second efforts following an initial attempt (Englert & Bertrams, 2014) to business leaders' ethical behaviors on one day, being followed by more abusive behavior on the subsequent day. Most produce evidence that ego depletion is a state of reduced willpower that is brought about by a prior exertion of self-control. It can make people less inhibited but also produce sub-optimal performance, all by way of diminishing self-control. Freud, who felt that psychic energy existed in a fixed amount in a closed system, and could therefore be depleted, would have predicted such findings. Interesting lines of recent research include studies on factors that protect against depletion (such as the trait of optimism; In Den Bosch-Meevissen, Peters, & Alberts, 2014) or that help people recover faster from ego depletion (such as being in nature; Chow & Lau, 2015).

Are we doomed to go through life with a chronically exhausted ego due to the serial temptations we encounter? Baumeister is optimistic about our self-control ability and has introduced a muscle metaphor of ego depletion (e.g., Baumeister et al., 2007). In this metaphor, self-control is like a muscle. If it is overused, it can become temporarily weak and unable to respond adequately to self-control challenges. However, even mildly tired athletes can summon strength for major exertion at decisive moments in a competition. Recent evidence is coming in that people can, with some effort or external motivation (e.g., cash incentives), increase their intentions to exert self-control and overcome multiple temptations. Moreover, like training a muscle, Baumeister believes that self-control can be trained through practice. People who practice mild but regular self-control in one area of life (e.g., dieting) exhibit better self-control in other areas of their lives (e.g., regular exercise). Moreover, Baumeister has identified conditions that can counteract the effects of ego depletion, including states of positive emotion and humor, forming plans for how to behave in tempting situations prior to entering them, and being guided by a strong set of social values. In Table 9.1 we list several of the key variables identified in the research on ego depletion.

Table 9.1 Key Variables Identified in Research on Ego Depletion

Responses That Require Self-Control

- Controlling thoughts
- Managing emotions
- Overcoming unwanted impulses
- Controlling attention
- Guiding behavior
- Making many choices

Behaviors That Are Sensitive to Ego Depletion

- Eating among dieters
- Overspending
- Aggression after being provoked
- Sexual impulses
- Logical and intelligent decision making

Social Behaviors That Demand Self-Control

- Self-presentation for impression management
- Kindness in response to bad behavior
- Dealing with demanding or difficult people
- Interracial interactions

Ways to Counteract the Harmful Effects of Ego Depletion

- Humor and laughter
- Other positive emotions
- Cash incentives
- Implementing intentions to cope with temptations with a specific plan
- Pursuing social values (e.g., wanting to help people, wanting to be a good relationship partner)

conscience, suggesting that the development of the superego was closely linked to a child's identification with his or her parents.

To return to the plumbing metaphor, the superego is the plumber who wants to keep the valves closed all the time and even wants to add more valves to keep the pressure under control. The superego is the part of personality that makes us feel guilty, ashamed, or embarrassed when we do something "wrong" and makes us feel pride when we do something "right." The superego determines what is right and what is wrong: it sets moral goals and ideals of perfection and so is the source of our judgments that some things are good and some are bad. It is what some people refer to as conscience. The main tool of the superego in enforcing right and wrong is the emotion of guilt.

Like the id, the superego is not bound by reality. It is free to set standards for virtue and for self-worth, even if those standards are perfectionistic, unrealistic, and harsh. Some children develop low moral standards and consequently do not feel guilty when they hurt others. Other children develop very powerful internal standards, due to a superego that demands perfection. The superego burdens them with almost impossibly high moral standards. Such persons might suffer from a chronic level of shame because of their continual failures to meet their unrealistic standards.

Interaction of the Id, Ego, and Superego

The three parts of the mind—id, ego, and superego—are in constant interaction. They have different goals, provoking internal conflicts within an individual. Consequently, one part of a person can want one thing, whereas another part wants something else. For example, imagine that a young woman is last in line at a fast-food counter. The man in front of her unknowingly drops a $20 bill from his wallet and does not notice. The woman sees the money on the floor in front of her. The situation sets off a conflict among the three parts of her personality. The id says, "Take it and run! Just grab it; push the person out of the way if you have to." The superego says, "Thou shalt not steal." And the ego is confronted with the reality of the situation as well as the demands from the id and the superego, saying "Did the clerk see the $20 fall? Do any of the other customers see the $20 on the floor? Could I put my foot over it without being noticed? Maybe I should just pick it up and return it to the person; perhaps he will even give me a reward." The young woman in this situation is bound to experience some anxiety. Anxiety is an unpleasant state, which acts as a signal that things are not right and something must be done. It is a signal that the control of the ego is being threatened by reality, by impulses from the id, or by harsh controls exerted by the superego. Such anxiety might be expressed as physical symptoms, such as a rapid heart rate, sweaty palms, and irregular breathing. A person in this state might also feel herself on the verge of panic. Regardless of the symptoms displayed, a person whose desires are in conflict with reality or with internalized morals will appear more anxious in such a situation.

A well-balanced mind, one that is free from anxiety, is achieved by having a strong ego. It is the ego that balances the competing forces of the id, on the one hand, and the super-ego on the other. If either of these two competing forces overwhelms the ego, then anxiety is the result.

Dynamics of Personality

Because it is unpleasant, people try to resolve the conditions that give rise to anxiety. These efforts to defend oneself from anxiety are called **defense mechanisms**, and they are used to defend against all forms of anxiety.

Types of Anxiety

Freud identified three types of anxiety: objective, neurotic, and moral anxiety.

Objective anxiety is fear. Such anxiety occurs in response to a real, external threat to the person. For example, being confronted by a large, aggressive-looking man with a knife while taking a shortcut through an alley would elicit objective anxiety (fear) in most people. In this case, the control of the ego is being threatened by an external factor rather than by an internal conflict. In the other two types of anxiety, the threat comes from within.

The second type of anxiety, **neurotic anxiety**, occurs when there is a direct conflict between the id and the ego. The danger is that the ego may lose control over an unacceptable desire of the id. For example, a woman who becomes anxious whenever she feels sexually attracted to someone, who panics at even the thought of sexual arousal, is experiencing neurotic anxiety. As another example, a man who worries excessively that he might blurt out an unacceptable thought or desire in public is also beset by neurotic anxiety.

The third type of anxiety, **moral anxiety**, is caused by a conflict between the ego and the superego. For example, a person who suffers from chronic shame or feelings of guilt over not living up to "proper" standards, even though such standards might not be attainable, is experiencing moral anxiety. A young woman with bulimia, an eating disorder, might run 3 miles and do 100 sit-ups in order to make up for having eaten a "forbidden" food. People who punish themselves, who have low self-esteem, or who feel worthless and ashamed most of the time are most likely suffering from moral anxiety, from an overly powerful superego, which constantly challenges the person to live up to higher and higher expectations.

The ego faces a difficult task in attempting to balance the impulses of the id, the demands of the superego, and the realities of the external world. It is as if the id is saying, "I want it now!" The superego is saying, "You will never have it!" And the poor ego is caught in the middle, saying, "Maybe, if I can just work things out." Most of the time, this conversation is going on outside a person's awareness. Sometimes the conflicts among the id, ego, and superego are expressed in a disguised way in various thoughts, feelings, and behaviors. In most cases, such conflicts are accompanied by anxiety, and so we turn now to a discussion of various mechanisms that people use to defend themselves against anxiety.

Defense Mechanisms

In all three types of anxiety, the function of the ego is to cope with threats and to defend against the dangers they pose in order to reduce anxiety. The ego accomplishes this task through the use of various defense mechanisms, which enable the ego to control anxiety, even objective anxiety. Although intrapsychic conflicts frequently evoke anxiety, people can successfully defend themselves from conflict and never consciously feel the anxiety. For example, in conversion reaction, where a conflict is converted to a symptom, the conflict is expressed in the form of physical symptoms, an illness or weakness in a part of the body. Curiously, such people may be indifferent to the symptom, not anxious about losing feeling in a leg or having a headache that will not go away. The symptoms help them avoid the anxiety, and even the symptoms do not make them anxious. Defense mechanisms serve two functions: (1) to protect the ego and (2) to minimize anxiety and distress. Let's turn now to a discussion of one of the defense mechanisms that Freud wrote about extensively and that has received a good deal of attention from researchers in personality psychology.

Repression

Early in his theorizing, Freud used the term **repression** to refer to the process of pre-venting unacceptable thoughts, feelings, or urges from reaching conscious awareness. Repression was the forerunner of all other forms of defense mechanisms. Repression is defensive in the sense that, through it, a person avoids the anxiety that would arise if the unacceptable material were made conscious. From his clinical practice, Freud learned that people often tended to remember the pleasant circumstances surrounding an event more easily than the unpleasant ones. He concluded that unpleasant memories were often repressed.

Freud first developed the concept of repression as a global strategy that the ego uses to maintain forbidden impulses in the unconscious. The term is still used today to refer to "forgotten" wishes, urges, or events—recall the account of "repressed" trau-matic memories with which the chapter opened. Later, Freud articulated several more specific kinds of defense mechanisms. All of these specific forms involved a degree of repression in that some aspect of reality is denied or distorted in the service of reducing anxiety and protecting the control of the ego over the psychic system.

Other Defense Mechanisms

Freud's daughter Anna Freud (1895–1982), herself an accomplished psychoanalyst, played a large role in identifying and describing other mechanisms of defense (A. Freud, 1936/1992). She believed that the ego could muster some very creative and effective mechanisms to protect against blows to self-esteem and threats to psychic existence. A few of these defense mechanisms will be described in detail in this section.

A student of Freud's named Fenichel (1945) revised the idea of defense to focus more on how these mechanisms function to protect self-esteem. That is, people have a preferred view of themselves, and they will defend against any unflattering changes or blows to that self-view. Obviously, realizing that one has unacceptable sexual or aggres-sive wishes might be a blow to one's self-view, especially for persons in the Victorian era. However, in today's society there may be other events that threaten self-esteem, such as failure, embarrassment, or being "unfriended" on Facebook. Most modern psy-chologists believe that people defend themselves against these threats to their self-esteem (Baumeister & Vohs, 2004). Much of the contemporary research on self-esteem maintenance can thus be thought of as having roots in the psychoanalytic concept of defense mechanisms (Baumeister, Dale, & Sommer, 1998). There is a questionnaire measure of defense mechanisms (Cramer, 1991) and empirical research is accumulating on their use. For example, in adolescence identification is a common defense mecha-nism (identification is covered in the next section, as it is the resolution of the phallic stage of psychosexual development), whereas later in life denial, covered next, becomes the most common defense mechanism (Cramer, 2012).

Denial   When the reality of a situation is extremely anxiety provoking, a person may resort to the defense mechanism of **denial**. In contrast to repression, which involves keeping an *experience* out of memory, a person in denial insists that things are not the way they seem. Denial involves refusing to see the facts. A man whose wife has left him might still set a place at the dinner table for her and insist that she is supposed to come home at any time. Playing out this scenario night after night might be more acceptable than acknowledging that she is, in reality, gone. Denial can also be less extreme, as when someone reappraises an anxiety-provoking situation so that it seems less daunt-ing. For example, a man might convince himself that his wife *had* to leave him for some reason, that it really was *not* her fault, and that she *would* return if only she could. In this case, he is denying that his wife freely chose to leave him.

A common form of denial is to dismiss unflattering feedback as wrong or irrelevant. When people are given a poor evaluation, say by a supervisor, some will reject the evaluation rather than change their view of themselves. They might blame their difficulties on bad luck or problems with the situation, anything but accepting personal responsibility and having to alter their view of themselves. Indeed, the tendency to blame events outside one's control for failure but to accept responsibility for success is so common that psychologists refer to this as the **fundamental attribution error**. It may be interpreted, however, as a specific form of denial.

Health psychologists are also interested in denial. How can a person smoke two packs of cigarettes a day and not worry about his or her health? One answer would be to deny one's personal vulnerability, or to deny the evidence linking smoking to illness, or to deny that one wants to live a long and healthy life. Baumeister and colleagues (1998) review evidence that people often minimize the risks they see in the various unhealthy behaviors that they engage in.

Denial often shows up in daydreams and fantasies. Daydreams are frequently about how things might have been. To some extent, daydreams deny the present situation by focusing on how things could have been otherwise. In doing so, they may lessen or defend against the potentially anxiety-provoking circumstances of one's present situation. For example, a person who has done something embarrassing might daydream about how things might have gone had he or she not done that stupid, embarrassing thing.

Displacement In **displacement**, a threatening or an unacceptable impulse is channeled or redirected from its original source to a nonthreatening target. Consider, for example, a woman who has an argument with her supervisor at work. She is really angry with the supervisor, but her ego keeps her in check because, after all, the supervisor is the boss and can make her work life difficult, so she goes home and displaces her anger onto her husband, perhaps yelling and nagging at him or belittling him. Although this approach may contribute to marital problems, it will most likely avoid the difficulties associated with losing one's temper at one's boss. Sometimes displacement has a domino effect, whereby one spouse berates another, who in turn yells at the children, who then abuse the family dog. Moreover, although displacement is often thought of as a defense mechanism involving the redirection of aggressive instincts, it can also involve sexual urges that are redirected from a less acceptable to a more acceptable target. For example, a man may have a strong sexual attraction toward a woman who is subordinate to him at work, but this woman has no interest in him. Rather than harass the woman, he may redirect this sexual energy toward his wife and rediscover that he is still attracted to her. Freud also noted that sometimes even fears are redirected through displacement and cited as an example the case of a boy who feared his father but who redirected that fear toward horses.

Although these examples seem to involve conscious awareness and a calculating choice of how to express the unacceptable emotion, the process of displacement takes place outside of awareness. *Deliberately* redirecting one's anger, for example, is not displacement, even though someone might do this to manage a situation. Real displacement is an unconscious means of avoiding the recognition that one has certain inappropriate or unacceptable feelings (e.g., anger or sexual attraction) toward a specific other person or a specific object. Those feelings then are displaced onto another person or object that is more appropriate or acceptable.

A Closer Look   Empirical Studies of Repression

Although psychoanalysts have been interested in repression since Freud introduced the concept, empirical research on this topic has been relatively sparse until the 1990s. Perhaps this has been due to the difficulty of defining repression in such a way that it may actually be measured for research purposes. Researchers have developed questionnaires to identify individuals who typically use repression as a mechanism for coping with threatening, stressful, or anxiety-producing situations.

Freud held that the essential aspect of repression was the motivated unavailability of unpleasant, painful, or disturbing emotions (Bonanno, 1990). He wrote that repression was a process whereby unpleasant emotions are turned away and kept "at a distance from the conscious" (Freud, 1915/1957, p. 147). Almost 65 years later, Weinberger, Schwartz, and Davidson (1979) were the first to propose that repression, as a style of coping with unpleasant emotions, can be measured by examining various combinations of scores on questionnaires of anxiety and defensiveness. These researchers administered a questionnaire measure of anxiety and a questionnaire measure of defensiveness to a group of subjects. The anxiety questionnaire contained items that inquired about whether one has strong symptoms of anxiety (e.g., heart pounding) when engaging in various behaviors, such as public speaking. The defensiveness questionnaire contained items inquiring about common faults, such as whether respondents had ever gossiped, had ever become so angry that they wanted to break something, or had ever resented someone's asking them for a favor. Clearly, almost everyone is guilty of these minor offenses at one time or another. Therefore, subjects who consistently deny engaging in these somewhat undesirable behaviors score high on defensiveness. The researchers combined the subjects' anxiety and defensiveness

scores, which resulted in the fourfold typology portrayed in Figure 9.3. Most of the subsequent research on repression involved comparing the repressor group to the other three groups on a dependent measure.

In the initial study, after subjects had completed the questionnaires, Weinberger and colleagues (1979) had the subjects engage in a phrase association task in which they match phrases in one list with phrases in another list that have similar meaning; several phrases contained angry and sexual overtones. As the subjects attempted to match the phrases, the researchers measured their physiological reactions. The researchers also measured the subjects' self-reported levels of distress immediately after their performance. They found that the repressors reported the lowest levels of subjective distress yet were found to exhibit the highest levels of physiological arousal (heart rate, skin conductance). In short, repressors *verbally* say they are not distressed yet *physiologically* appear to be very distressed. Other researchers have obtained similar findings (e.g., Asendorpf & Scherer, 1983; Davis & Schwartz, 1987). These experimental results are consistent with Freud's view that repression keeps unpleasant experiences out of conscious awareness. Moreover, the results are consistent with Freud's ideas that such repressed unpleasant experiences still affect the individual, in spite of being outside of awareness (in this case, the repressed experiences affect the person's level of physiological arousal, even though the person is not consciously aware of being anxious).

Another way to examine repression is to ask subjects to recall childhood experiences associated with pleasant and unpleasant

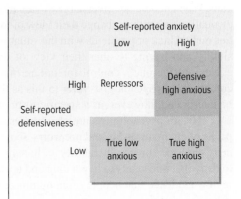

Figure 9.3
Finding repressors by measuring anxiety and defensiveness. The subjects who deny being anxious, but who are high on defensiveness, are most likely repressors.

emotions. This is exactly what psychologists Penelope Davis and Gary Schwartz did in 1987. They asked their subjects to recall and describe childhood experiences that they associated with happiness, sadness, anger, fear, and wonder. The researchers' findings showed that the repressors, defined as high defensive–low anxious persons, did recall fewer negative emotional experiences than the other subjects and that the repressors were substantially older at the time of their earliest negative emotional memories. Somewhat surprisingly, the repressors also had limited access to positive memories. This finding illustrates what may be one of the costs of repression—pleasant as well as unpleasant emotional memories may be diminished or lost to conscious recall.

Penelope Davis (1987) expanded on the general idea that repressors have limited access to emotional memories. First, she found that the effect is strongest for memories about the *self*. The repressors in her study had no trouble remembering bad things that had happened to *other* people (e.g., siblings), but they did have limited recollection about unpleasant events that they themselves had experienced. Second, the effects of repression appeared to be strongest for the memories associated with feelings of fear and self-consciousness. Although Freud (1915/1957) wrote "the motive and purpose of repression was nothing else than the avoidance of unpleasure" (p. 153), according to Davis, the motive to repress is particularly strong for experiences associated with fear and self-consciousness. Why might this be the case? These emotions are often evoked in situations where the focus of attention is on the self in an evaluative or threatening way. In fear, for example, there is a threat to the very existence of the self. In self-consciousness, the threat of being negatively evaluated by others looms large, leading a person to feel exposed and vulnerable.

Hansen and Hansen (1988) found that repressors' memories are relatively less elaborate when it comes to emotion than are those of nonrepressors. That is, repressors have memories for emotional events that are less developed, less refined, and less rich than those of nonrepressors. These authors raise the intriguing question of what might account for this impoverished emotional memory on the part of repressors. It could come about in one of two ways. First, repressors may have limited *recall* of their emotional experiences. That is, repressors may have actually *had* varied emotional experiences and those experiences may actually be *in* their memories, but they just have trouble retrieving or recalling them. Alternatively, repressors could actually have blocked certain emotional experiences from entering into their memories in the first place. The effect of repression could have occurred at the *encoding* rather than the recall stage.

Although most studies of repression have examined memory for past events, a few studies (e.g., Hansen, Hansen, & Shantz, 1992) suggest that the effect of repression may occur not only as diminished *memory* for negative events but also in the person's actual reaction to negative events when they occur. This is what Freud would have predicted, that repressors actually do not experience negative emotions as strongly as nonrepressors do. We can ask whether repressors simply have poor memories for bad events or whether, when bad events happen, they actually experience less negative emotion than nonrepressors do, or both.

In a study by Cutler, Larsen, and Bunce (1996), repressors and nonrepressors kept daily diaries of 40 different emotions for 28 consecutive days. After reporting on their emotions every day for a month, the subjects were then asked to think back over the month and to rate how much of each emotion they recalled experiencing, on average, during the course of that month. The researchers thus had a measure of actual day-to-day emotion, recorded close to the time when the subjects experienced the emotions, as well as a measure of recalled emotion. This approach allowed the researchers to test whether the repressors reported less negative emotion, recalled less negative emotion, or both. The results showed that the repressors, compared with the nonrepressors, actually reported *experiencing* fewer and less intense unpleasant emotions on a day-to-day basis. The repressors' memories for unpleasant emotions, however, were only slightly less accurate than the memories of the nonrepressors. The effect of

repression seems to occur during the *experience* of unpleasant events, whereby repressors somehow dampen their emotional reactions to bad events.

Almost 40 years since Weinberg et al. (1979) proposed measuring repression as a combination of high defensiveness and low anxiety, a good amount of empirical research has been done (Myers, 2010). Much of it has focused on the negative consequences of this way of coping. More recent research, however, has focused on the potential benefits of repression. For example, a study of rescue workers in Israel, who work often involves handling human remains after terrorist attacks, found that those workers with a repressive coping style displayed more resilience, and fewer stress symptoms, than workers without a repressive style (Solomon & Ginzburg, 2007). Other work has confirmed that the effects of repression occur more at encoding experiences than at memory recall (Derakshan, Eysenck, & Myers, 2007; Myers, 2015), suggesting that repression is not so much about a failure of memory as it is about an inhibited experience of negative emotions in the first place. And finally, researchers are beginning to uncover the brain circuits associated with the trait of repressive coping style (Klucken, Kruse, Schweckendiek, & Stark, 2015).

Freud said that the function of repression was to keep unpleasant experiences out of conscious awareness. We now know more specifically that the blunting effect of repression occurs primarily during the reaction to bad events. Repressors do not have bad memories; rather, somehow they keep unpleasant events from entering into their memories in the first place.

Researchers have tried to study the displacement of aggressive impulses. In one study, student participants were frustrated (or not, if they were in the control group) by the experimenter. Later they had the opportunity to act aggressively toward the experimenter, the experimenter's assistant, or another participant. The frustrated participants were more aggressive, but they were equally aggressive toward the experimenter, the assistant, or the other student (Hokanson, Burgess, & Cohen, 1963).

The target did not matter. Other studies have replicated this finding. In one study subjects were angered, not by the experimenter, but by another participant, then given an opportunity to act aggressively toward that subject or toward a friend of that participant. Again, angered participants were more aggressive in general, but it did not seem to matter who the target was.

Are these results evidence for displacement? Baumeister and colleagues (1998) conclude they are not. Angered people act aggressively, they argue, and there is no evidence that it is defensive. They argue that, although displacement is an interesting dynamic concept, there is little empirical support for the idea that urges are like hydraulic fluid in a closed system being shunted this way or that depending on displacement.

Rationalization   Another common defense mechanism, especially among educated persons, such as college students, is **rationalization**. It involves generating acceptable reasons for outcomes that might otherwise appear socially unacceptable. In rationalization, the goal is to reduce anxiety by coming up with an explanation for an event that is easier to accept than the real reason. For example, a student who receives a failing grade on a term paper might explain it away by insisting that the teacher did not give clear directions for how to write the paper. Or perhaps a woman whose boyfriend has broken up with her explains to her friends that she never really liked him that much to begin with. These reasons are a lot more emotionally acceptable than the alternatives that one is not as smart or as desirable as one thinks.

Reaction Formation   In an attempt to stifle the expression of an unacceptable urge, a person may continually display a flurry of behavior that indicates the opposite impulse. Such a tactic is known as **reaction formation**. For example, imagine the woman who is angry with her supervisor, described in the discussion of displacement. If, instead of displacing her anger, her ego unconsciously resorts to reaction formation, then she might go out of her way to be overly kind to her boss, to show the boss special courtesy and consideration.

An interesting example of reaction formation is provided by Cooper (1998), who discusses the concept of "killing someone with kindness." Consider a man who is angry with his girlfriend, but the anger is not conscious; he is not aware of how angry he really is. It is raining outside so he offers her his umbrella. She refuses to take it, but he insists. She keeps refusing, and he keeps insisting that she take it. Here he is replacing his hostility with apparent kindness. However, his aggression is coming out in his persistent insistence and his ignoring her wishes not to take the umbrella. According to psychoanalysis, this dynamic can often be found when defenses are being used; people may try to cover up their wishes and intention and yet unwittingly express them.

The mechanism of reaction formation makes it possible for psychoanalysts to predict that sometimes people will do exactly the opposite of what you might otherwise think they would do. It also alerts us to be sensitive to instances when a person is doing something in excess, such as when someone is being overly nice to us for no apparent reason. Perhaps in such cases the person really means the opposite of what he or she is doing.

Projection   Another type of defense mechanism, **projection**, is based on the notion that sometimes we see in others the traits and desires we find most upsetting in ourselves. We literally "project" (i.e., attribute) our own unacceptable qualities onto others. We can then hate them, instead of hating ourselves, for having those unacceptable qualities or desires. At the same time, we can disparage the tendencies or characteristics in question without admitting that we possess them. Other people become the target by virtue of their having qualities that we intensely dislike in ourselves. For instance, a thief is often worried about the prospect of others stealing from him and claims that others are not to be trusted. Or a woman denies having any interest in sexuality yet insists that all the men she knows "have nothing but sex on their minds." Married men who have affairs are more suspicious than other husbands that their wives are unfaithful. What a person intensely dislikes in or gets upset about with others is often revealing of his or her innermost insecurities and conflicts. A person who always insults others by calling them "stupid" may, in fact, harbor some insecurity about his or her own intelligence.

In projection, we see in others those traits or desires we find most upsetting in ourselves. We can then disparage them for having the undesirable characteristic, without admitting that we have that very characteristic.
© Westend61 GmbH/Alamy Stock Photo RF

As another example, consider people who become involved in anti-homosexuality campaigns. Some people publicly express moral outrage or even propose violence against persons with this sexual orientation. Trent Lott was Senate Majority Leader in June 1998 when he stated on television that homosexuals had an illness similar to alcoholism or kleptomania. At the same time, Christian fundamentalists were airing TV advertisements stating that homosexuality was a disease and that gay persons should be cured. Pat Robertson, a fundamentalist preacher on the Christian Broadcasting Network, said that a hurricane might strike Orlando, Florida, because of a recent gathering of homosexual persons there. Could it be that homophobic persons are engaging projection as a defense mechanism against their own questionable sexual orientation?

In modern psychological research there is an effect, similar to projection, called the **false consensus effect**. This was first described by Ross, Greene, and House in 1977. It refers to the tendency many people have to assume that others are similar to them. That is, extraverts think many other people are extraverted, and conscientious persons think many other people are conscientious. To think that many other people share your own preferences, motivations, or traits is to display the false consensus effect.

Baumeister and colleagues (1998) argue that having a false consensus about one's unflattering traits could be ego defensive. For example, to be the only person whose credit card is over the limit would imply that one is unique in this moral deficiency. But if one believes that many people are over their credit limits, or close to it, then this false consensus belief might be protective of one's self-concept. The adolescent who explains some misbehavior with the phrase, "Gee, everyone else was doing it," is perhaps engaging in defensive false consensus, essentially saying, "I'm not so bad because everyone is bad too."

Sublimation   According to Freud, **sublimation** is the most adaptive defense mechanism. Sublimation is the channeling of unacceptable sexual or aggressive instincts into socially desired activities. A common example is going out to chop wood when you are angry rather than acting on that anger or even engaging in other less adaptive defense mechanisms, such as displacement. Watching football or boxing is more desirable than beating someone up. Mountain climbing or volunteering for combat duty in the army might be forms of sublimating a death wish. Freud, during his only visit to the US, reportedly remarked about all the sublimated sexual energy that must have gone into building the skyscrapers of New York City. One's choice of occupation (e.g., athlete, mortician, or emergency room nurse) might be interpreted as the sublimation of certain unacceptable urges. The positive feature of sublimation is that it allows for some limited expression of id tendencies, so the ego does not have to invest energy in holding the id in check. Freud maintained that the greatest achievements of civilization were due to the effective sublimation of sexual and aggressive urges.

Defense Mechanisms in Everyday Life

Life provides each of us with plenty of psychological bumps and bruises. We don't get a job we badly wanted; an acquaintance says something hurtful; we realize something about ourselves that is not flattering. In short, we must face unexpected or disappointing events all the time. Defense mechanisms may be useful in coping with these occurrences and the emotions they generate (Larsen, 2000a, 2000b; Larsen & Prizmic, 2004). We all have to deal with stress, and to the extent that defense mechanisms help, so much the better (see Valliant, 1994, for a discussion and categorization of defense mechanisms).

It is not too difficult, however, to imagine circumstances that are made worse by the use of defense mechanisms (Cramer, 2000, 2002). Others may avoid a person who projects a lot. A person who displaces frequently may have few friends. Moreover, the use of defense mechanisms takes psychic energy that is therefore not available for other pursuits. How do you know when the use of defense mechanisms is becoming a problem? The answer is twofold: you know a behavior is becoming a problem if it begins inhibiting the ability to be *productive* or if it begins limiting the ability to *maintain relationships*. If either one of these areas in life is negatively affected—work or relationships—then you might wonder about a psychological problem. Moreover, there is much to be said in favor of directly confronting difficult issues and taking action directed at solving problems. Nevertheless, sometimes problems simply cannot be solved or a person does not have the energy or resources to directly confront a problem. Under these temporary circumstances, defense mechanisms may be very useful. When used occasionally, defense mechanisms most likely will not interfere with work or social life. According to Freud, the hallmark of mature adulthood is the ability to work productively and to develop and maintain satisfying relationships. Reaching mature adulthood, however, involves passing through several stages of personality development.

Psychosexual Stages of Personality Development

Freud believed that all persons passed through a set series of stages in personality development. Each of these stages involves a conflict, and how the person resolves this conflict gives rise to various aspects of his or her personality. So in psychoanalytic theory, the source of individual differences lies in how the child comes to resolve conflicts in each of the stages of development. The end result, after going through all the stages, is a fully formed personality. Because all of this happens in childhood, the famous phrase "The child is father to the man" captures a key Freudian idea.

At each of the first three stages, young children must face and resolve specific conflicts. The conflicts revolve around ways of obtaining a type of sexual gratification. For this reason, Freud's theory of development is called the **psychosexual stage theory**. According to the theory, children seek sexual gratification at each stage by investing libidinal energy in a specific body part. Each stage in the developmental process is named after the body part in which sexual energy is invested.

If a child fails to fully resolve a conflict at a particular stage of development, he or she may get stuck in that stage, a phenomenon known as **fixation**. Each successive stage represents a more mature mode of obtaining sexual gratification. If a child is fixated at a particular stage, he or she exhibits a less mature approach to obtaining sexual gratification. In the final stage of development, mature adults obtain pleasure from healthy intimate relationships and from work. The road to this final stage, however, is fraught with developmental conflicts and the potential for fixation. Let's examine these stages and discuss the conflicts that arise, as well as the consequences of fixation at each stage.

The first stage, which Freud called the **oral stage**, occurs during the initial 18 months after birth. During this time, the main sources of pleasure and tension reduction are the mouth, lips, and tongue. You don't have to be around many babies to realize how busy they are with their mouths (e.g., whenever they come across something new, such as a rattle or toy, they usually put it into their mouths first). The main conflict during this stage is weaning, withdrawing from the breast or bottle. This conflict has both a biological and a psychological component. From a biological standpoint, the id wants the immediate gratification associated with taking in nourishment and obtaining pleasure through the mouth. From a psychological perspective, the conflict is one of excessive pleasure versus dependency, with the fear of being left to fend for oneself. Sometimes a child has a painful or traumatic experience during the weaning process, resulting in a degree of fixation at the oral stage. Adults who still obtain pleasure from "taking in," especially through the mouth, might be fixated at this stage (e.g., people who overeat or smoke). Problems with nail biting, thumb sucking, or pencil chewing might also occur. At a psychological level, people who are fixated at the oral stage may be overly dependent: they may want to be babied, to be nurtured and taken care of, and thus to have others make decisions for them. Some psychoanalysts also believe that drug addiction (because it involves pleasure from "taking in") is a sign of oral fixation.

There is another possible conflict of the oral stage that is associated with biting. This conflict can occur after the child grows teeth and finds that he or she can obtain pleasure from biting and chewing. Parents typically discourage a child from biting, particularly if the child bites other children or adults. Thus, the child has the conflict between the urge to bite and parental restrictions. People who fixate during this stage might develop adult personalities that are hostile, quarrelsome, or mocking. They continue to draw gratification from being psychologically "biting" and verbally attacking.

The second stage of development is the **anal stage**, which typically occurs between the ages of 18 months and 3 years of age. At this stage, the anal sphincter is the source of sexual pleasure. During this time, the child obtains pleasure from first expelling feces and then, during toilet training, from retaining feces. At first, the id desires immediate tension reduction whenever there is any pressure in the rectum. This is achieved by defecating whenever and wherever the urge arises. Parents, however, work to instill in the child a degree of self-control through the process of toilet training. Many conflicts arise around this issue of the child's ability to achieve some self-control. Some children achieve too little control and grow up to be sloppy and dirty. Other children have the opposite problem: they develop too much self-control and begin to take pleasure in little acts of self-control. Adults who are compulsive, overly neat, rigid, and never messy are, according to psychoanalysts, likely to be fixated at the anal stage. After all, toilet training usually presents a child with the first opportunity to exercise choice and willpower. When a parent puts the child on the potty seat and says, "Now, do your business," the child has the opportunity to say, "No!" and to withhold. This might signal the beginnings of being stingy, holding back, not giving others what they want, and being overly willful and stubborn.

The third stage, which occurs between 3 and 5 years of age, is called the **phallic stage**, because the child discovers that he has (or she discovers that she does not have) a penis. In fact, the major event during this stage is children's discovery of their own genitals and the realization that some pleasure can be derived from touching them. This is also the awakening of sexual desire directed outward, and according to Freud, it is first directed toward the parent of the opposite sex. Little boys fall in love with their mothers, and little girls fall in love with their fathers. But children feel more than just parental love, according to Freud's theory. A little boy lusts for his mother and wants to have sex with her. His father is seen as the competitor, as the one who is preventing the little boy from possessing his mother and receiving *all* of her attention. For the boy, the main conflict, which Freud called the **Oedipal conflict**, is the unconscious wish to have his mother all to himself by eliminating the father. (Oedipus is a character in Greek mythology who unknowingly kills his father and marries his mother.) Daddy is the competitor for Mommy's attention, and he should be beaten and driven from the home or killed. But killing or beating Daddy is wrong.

Part of the Oedipal conflict, then, is that the child loves, yet is competing with, the parent of the same sex. Moreover, the little boy grows to fear his father because surely this big and powerful person could prevent this all from happening. In fact, Freud argued that little boys come to believe that their fathers might make a preemptive strike by taking away the thing that is at the root of the conflict: the boy's penis. This fear of losing his penis, called **castration anxiety**, drives the little boy into giving up his sexual desire for Mommy. The boy decides that the best he can do is to become like the guy who has Mommy—in other words, like his father. This process of wanting to become like Daddy, called **identification**, marks the beginning of the resolution of the Oedipal conflict and the successful resolution of the phallic stage of psychosexual development for boys. Freud believed that the resolution of the Oedipal conflict was the beginning of both the superego and morality, as well as the male gender role.

For little girls, the situation is at once similar and different. One similarity is that the conflict centers on the penis, or actually the lack thereof, on the part of the little girl. According to Freud, a little girl blames her mother for the fact that she lacks a penis. She desires her father yet at the same time envies him for his penis. This is called **penis envy**, and it is the counterpart of castration anxiety. Penis envy is different in that the little girl does not necessarily fear the mother, as the boy fears the father. Thus, for girls, there is no strong motivation to give up her desire for her father.

Freud's student Carl Jung termed this stage the **Electra complex**, for girls. Electra was also a character in a Greek myth. Electra convinced her brother to kill their mother after the mother had murdered the father. Freud actually rejected the idea of the Electra complex, and he was vague about how the phallic stage is resolved for girls. He wrote that it drags on later in life for girls and may never fully be resolved. Because successful resolution results in the development of the superego, Freud believed that women must therefore be morally inferior to men. This aspect of Freud's developmental theory is not widely accepted today, and Freud has been strongly criticized for his beliefs about sex differences (e.g., Helson & Picano, 1990).

The next stage of psychosexual development is called the **latency stage**. This stage occurs from around the age of 6 until puberty. Little psychological development is presumed to occur during this time. It is mainly a period when the child is going to school and learning the skills and abilities necessary to take on the role of an adult.

Because of the lack of specific sexual conflicts during this time, Freud believed that it was a period of psychological rest, or latency. Subsequent psychoanalysts have argued instead that much development occurs during this time, such as learning to make decisions for oneself, learning to interact and make friends with others, developing an identity, and learning the meaning of work. Because this is a more contemporary modification of Freud's theory, we examine it in Chapter 10.

The latency period ends with the sexual awakening brought about by puberty. If the Oedipus or Electra complex has been resolved, the person goes on to the next and final stage of psychosexual development, the **genital stage**. This stage begins around puberty and lasts through one's adult life. Here the libido is focused on the genitals, but not in the manner of self-manipulation associated with the phallic stage. This differs from the earlier stages in that it is not accompanied by a specific conflict. People reach the genital stage only if they have resolved the conflicts at the prior stages. It is in this sense that personality development, according to Freud, is largely complete at around the age of 5 or 6: the adult personality is dependent on how the conflicts that arise during infancy and early childhood are resolved.

Freud's psychosexual stage theory is a theory about personality development, both normal and abnormal. In a nutshell, the theory states that we are all born with a drive for sexual pleasure (the id) but that the constraints of civilized society limit the ways we can satisfy that drive. We all go through a series of predictable clashes or conflicts between our desire for pleasure and the demands placed on us by our parents and by society in general. The nature of the conflicts and the stages we go through are universal, but the specific instances and outcomes are each unique. Parts of our personalities are shaped at each stage by the particular ways we resolve the conflict. If, for example, at the oral stage, a person did not receive enough gratification (was weaned early) or received too much gratification (was weaned too late), then he or she might continue to have inappropriate demands for oral gratification throughout the rest of his or her life (perhaps in the form of being a dependent personality or developing an eating disorder or developing an alcohol or drug problem).

Freud developed the metaphor of an army whose troops are called into battle during each stage of psychosexual development. If the resolution of a stage is incomplete, then some soldiers must be left behind to monitor that particular conflict. It is as if some psychic energy must stand guard, lest the psychosexual conflict break out again. The poorer the resolution at a particular stage, the more psychic soldiers have to be left behind. One consequence of this is that less psychic energy is available for the subsequent tasks of maturity. The more soldiers brought forward to the genital stage, the more psychic energy that can be invested in mature intimate and productive relationships and the better the adult personality adjustment. It is interesting to note that neither happiness nor life satisfaction was directly a part of Freud's conception of successful personality development. Successful personality development instead was defined by the ability to be productive and to maintain mature adult sexual relationships.

Personality and Psychoanalysis

Psychoanalysis, besides being a theory of personality, is also a method of psychotherapy, a technique for helping individuals who are experiencing a mental disorder or even relatively minor problems with living. Psychoanalysis can be thought of as a method for deliberately restructuring the personality. The connection between the psychoanalytic theory of personality and psychoanalytic therapy is very strong. Principles of psychoanalytic therapy are based directly on the psychoanalytic theory about the structure and functioning of personality. Freud developed his theory of personality while treating patients in therapy. Similarly, many modern psychoanalysts, even those in academic settings, maintain a practice of seeing patients. Most psychoanalysts have themselves undergone psychoanalytic psychotherapy, which Freud held to be a requirement for becoming a psychoanalyst.

Techniques for Revealing the Unconscious

The goal of psychoanalysis is to make the unconscious conscious. Mental illness, problems with living, and unexplained physical symptoms can all be viewed as the result of unconscious conflicts. Thoughts, feelings, urges, or memories have been forced into the unconscious because of their disturbing or threatening nature. Due to the dynamic nature of the human mind, and the motivated unconscious, these conflicts or restrained urges may slip out of the unconscious in ways that cause trouble. They often obtain expression as psychological or physical symptoms.

The first aim of psychoanalysis is to identify these unconscious thoughts and feelings. Once the patient can be made aware of this material, the second aim is to enable the person to deal with the unconscious urges, memories, or thoughts realistically and maturely. The major challenge facing the psychoanalyst is determining how to penetrate the unconscious mind of the patient. By its very definition, the unconscious mind is the part of which the person has no awareness. How can one person (the therapist) come to know something about another person (the patient) which that other person does not know? Freud and other psychoanalysts have developed a set of standard techniques that can be used to dredge up material from the unconscious minds of patients.

Free Association

If you were to relax, to sit back in a comfortable chair, to let your mind wander, and then to say whatever came into your mind, you would be engaging in **free association**. Chances are, you would say some things that would even surprise you, and you might be embarrassed by what comes out. If you were able to resist the urge to censor your thoughts before speaking, then you would have an idea of how a patient spends much of his or her time in psychoanalysis. The typical psychoanalytic session lasts 50 minutes and may be repeated several times a week; the sessions may continue for years. The goals of the sessions are to enable patients to identify unconscious material that might be causing unwanted symptoms and to help them cope with that material in an adult fashion.

By relaxing the censor that screens our everyday thoughts, the technique of free association allows potentially important material into conscious awareness. This takes some practice. Patients are encouraged to say whatever comes to mind, no matter how absurd, trifling, or obscene. The technique is a bit like looking for a needle in a haystack in that the psychoanalyst is likely to be subjected to a barrage of trivial material before stumbling on an important clue to an unconscious conflict.

In free association, the psychoanalyst must be able to recognize the subtle signs that something important has just been mentioned—a slight quiver in the way a word is pronounced, a halting sentence, the patient's immediate discounting of what he or she has just said, a false start, a nervous laugh, or a long pause. An effective psychoanalyst

The Process of Psychoanalysis

With the help of free association, dream analysis, and projective techniques, the psychoanalyst gradually comes to understand the unconscious source of the patient's problems. The patient must also come to understand the unconscious dynamics of his or her situation. Toward this end, the psychoanalyst offers the patient **interpretations** of the psychodynamic causes of the problems. The patient is led to view problematic thoughts, dreams, behaviors, symptoms, or feelings as all having unconscious roots and as expressions of unconscious conflicts or repressed urges. The psychoanalyst might say, "Could it be that the reason you feel so sleepy when you go out with your boyfriend is that you are afraid of being sexually attractive to him?" The patient is confronted with an explanation of something she has been keeping from herself. Through many interpretations, the patient is gradually led to an understanding of the unconscious source of her problems. This is the beginning of **insight**. Insight, in psychoanalysis, is more than a simple cognitive understanding of the intrapsychic basis of one's troubles, though this certainly is a part of insight. Insight refers to an intense emotional experience that accompanies the release of repressed material. When this material is reintegrated into conscious awareness, and the person experiences the emotions associated with that previously repressed material, then we say that some degree of insight has been achieved.

Projective techniques, such as the inkblots developed by the Swiss psychiatrist Hermann Rorschach, are popular methods for assessing unconscious aspects of personality, such as repressed desires, wishes, or conflicts.
© Science & Society Picture Library/SSPL/Getty Images

As you might imagine, none of this is easy. The patient, or at least the patient's ego, has expended much energy to repress the root of the problem in order to keep anxiety at bay. As the therapist pokes at the unconscious material through free association and dream analysis, and begins to offer interpretations, the patient typically feels threatened. The forces that have worked to repress the disturbing impulse or trauma now work to resist the psychoanalytic process, in a stage of psychoanalysis called **resistance**. As the patient's defenses are threatened by the probing psychoanalyst, the patient may unconsciously set up obstacles to progress. The patient may come up with all sorts of clever ways to misdirect or derail the psychoanalyst. The patient may forget appointments, not pay the analyst's bill, or go very late to a session. Sometimes during a session, a patient in resistance might spend a great deal of time on trivial matters, thereby avoiding important issues. A patient might waste lots of time recalling the names of and other details about every classmate he or she knew in grade school, a process that could take weeks of session time. Or a patient who is being pressed by the analyst and confronted with interpretations might become angry and insult the analyst.

When an analyst detects a patient's resistance, it is usually a welcome sign that progress is being made. Resistance signifies that important unconscious material is coming to the fore. The resistance itself then becomes an integral part of the interpretations the analyst offers to the patient. For example, the analyst might say, "Perhaps you are insulting me because you want to avoid discussing the various ways in which you have been trying to make yourself sexually unattractive to men. Let's talk some more about what you are trying to avoid by starting an argument with me."

Another important step in most analyses is called **transference**. In this stage, the patient begins reacting to the analyst as if he or she were an important figure from the patient's own life. The patient displaces past or present feelings toward someone from his or her own life onto the analyst. For example, a patient might feel and act toward his analyst the way he felt or acted toward his father. The feelings that the patient transfers onto the analyst can be either positive or negative. For example, a patient may express her admiration for the analyst's powerful intellect and keen mind and offer the sort of adoration that a child is likely to have toward a parent. Old conflicts and old reactions then are played out during the therapy sessions.

The idea behind transference is that the interpersonal problems between a patient and the important people in his or her life will be reenacted in the therapy session with the analyst. Freud called this the "**repetition compulsion**," whereby the person reenacts his or her interpersonal problems with new people, including the psychoanalyst. Transference may be one source of clues about the person's unconscious conflicts, and it provides the analyst with opportunities for offering interpretations about the patient's behavior.

Exercise?

Transference can occur in everyday life as well as in psychoanalysis. The nature of our everyday interactions with others can be influenced by past relationship patterns. For example, a student might work hard on a paper to please a favorite professor. Earning less than a perfect grade on that paper—say, a B+—might cause distress, a tearful scene with the professor, or a temper tantrum. The surprised professor might wonder what this person is really reacting to, since a B+ is actually a pretty good grade. Perhaps the student is replaying a childhood pattern of reacting immaturely whenever he or she disappoints a person from whom he or she desperately seeks approval, such as a demanding parent.

Think of a time when you or someone you know overreacted to an event. Once you have identified such a situation, can you think of any similarities it has to past situations, particularly from childhood? Are there any reasons to suppose that you or someone you know who is overreacting is repeating a conflict from the past?

Movies and other modern media often portray psychoanalysis as resulting in a flash of insight, in which the patient is suddenly and forever cured. Real life is not so simple. A thorough psychoanalysis can take years, sometimes a decade or longer. The analyst provides interpretation after interpretation, illustrating to the patient the unconscious source of his or her problems. Along the way, the patient may exhibit resistance. Transference also typically becomes an issue for interpretation. Through long and laborious work by both patient and analyst, the patient gradually gains insight. The successfully analyzed patient then has available the psychic energy that his or her ego has formerly been expending in repressing conflicts. This energy may be directed into those twin pursuits Freud said were the hallmarks of adult personality development—to love and to work.

Why Is Psychoanalysis Important?

Throughout much of the twentieth century, Freud's ideas had a profound influence on how the mind was understood to operate. His continuing influence can be seen in several areas. First, psychoanalytic ideas influence the practice of psychotherapy even today. The second largest division of the American Psychological Association is the Division of Psychoanalysis. The basic idea of the "talking cure" can be traced back to Freud. Even if a psychotherapist does not engage in classic psychoanalysis, many rely on a few psychoanalytic ideas, such as free association (saying whatever comes to mind as a part of therapy) or transference (that the patient will re-create interpersonal problems with the therapist) in their practice of therapy.

Another area of influence concerns the resurgence of interest in some Freudian ideas on the part of research psychologists. Research psychologists are showing a revival of interest in such topics as the unconscious (e.g., Bornstein, 1999), psychic energy (Baumeister et al., 2007), and defense mechanisms (Cramer & Davidson, 1998). Although they may not endorse the whole of Freudian theory, such researchers are nevertheless finding empirical support for several of his ideas, either in their original form or as they have been modified by others.

A third area of influence can be found in our popular culture, where many of Freud's ideas have been incorporated into everyday language and the logic of understanding our own and others' behavior. For example, if someone says, "He cannot get along with his teacher because he has a conflict with authority," this comment draws on Freudian ideas. Or if someone explains a person's current problems as being the result of poor parenting, this is a Freudian interpretation. Or if you think a person is avoiding dating and putting all her time into needlepoint work because she is conflicted over sexuality, then you are following a Freudian theme. Many of Freud's ideas have made it into everyday explanations of behavior and everyday forms of speech, such that you probably know more about Freud's theory than you actually realize.

A final reason Freud's ideas are important is that he laid the foundation for many of the topics and questions that psychologists are still addressing. He proposed a developmental sequence in the growth of personality. He devised a method to resolve internal conflicts. He proposed a structure of the basic elements of personality and described what he thought were the main dynamic relationships among these elements. He noted that the mind has regions about which it does not itself have awareness. All these ideas have continued to be areas of inquiry among contemporary psychologists.

Freud started one of the more interesting, influential, and even controversial approaches to understanding human nature. Consequently, no student of personality should skip over this theory, even if the theory does not play a large role in contemporary studies of personality. Pieces of it have survived and inform various parts of current personality research and theory, so it is worth taking a good look at Freud's classic theory as well as the contemporary modifications of it.

Evaluation of Freud's Contributions

Among contemporary personality psychologists, Freud's theory of personality remains controversial. Some personality psychologists (e.g., Eysenck, 1985; Kihlstrom, 2003b) suggest that psychoanalysis be abandoned. Others contend that psychoanalysis is alive and well (Westen, 1992, 1998; Weinberger, 2003). Opinions among personality psychologists differ dramatically on the accuracy, worth, and importance of psychoanalytic theory, and discussions about the merits of psycho-analysis often provoke passionate debate among those on both sides of the issue (Barron, Eagle, & Wolitsky, 1992).

The controversy surrounding psychoanalysis is covered in *Taking Sides: Clashing Views in Personality Psychology,* by Newman and Larsen (2011). Indeed, that book, or at least Chapter 11 in that book, would make excellent supplementary reading to the current chapter. At one extreme are the critics who hold that psychoanalysis is a stupendous con job by Freud and is totally and completely without merit. At the other extreme are the proponents who argue that it is the most complete theory of human nature to have arisen in recent centuries. Of course, like most controversies, the truth is probably somewhere between the extreme positions.

Proponents of psychoanalysis point to the major impact that Freud's theory has had on Western thought. Many psychoanalytic terms—id, ego, superego, Oedipal conflict, penis envy, anal character, etc.—have entered our everyday language. In addition to their influence in psychology, Freud's writings have played a significant role in sociology, literature, fine arts, history, anthropology, and medicine, to name only a few disciplines. Within psychology, Freud's works are among the most frequently cited sources in the literature. Many subsequent developments in the discipline of psychology have borrowed or built on the foundation laid by Freud. Freud shaped modern personality psychology and set the course of advancement for perhaps half a century, and Freud's ideas on psychosexual development played a significant role in initiating the field of developmental psychology. His views on anxiety, defense, and the unconscious show up in modified forms across many areas of modern clinical psychology. The psycho-therapy techniques he pioneered are frequently practiced, even if sometimes in modified form. Although many modern therapists have done away with the couch, they still inquire about their patients' dreams, ask their patients to free associate, identify and interpret forms of resistance, and work through transference. Moreover, if we think Freud overemphasized sex and aggression, we need merely to look at the popular movies, violent video games, and the proliferation of Internet pornography.

Critics of psychoanalysis also have strong arguments (e.g., Kihlstrom, 2003b). They maintain that Freud's theory is primarily of historical value, that it does not inform much of the contemporary research in personality psychology. If you were to look in the pages of mainstream personality journals that publish research, you would find very little that had direct relevance to classical psychoanalysis. Critics insist that without holding psychoanalysis up to scrutiny from outsiders, its merits cannot be fairly evaluated on scientific grounds. Freud himself did not believe in the value of experimentation or hypothesis testing in establishing the validity of psychoanalysis (Rosenzweig, 1994). The scientific method is self-correcting in that experiments are conducted to try to disprove theories. If psychoanalysis is not examined scientifically, is not subjected to tests of disproof, then it is simply not supported by scientific fact. Consequently, in the view of some psychologists, psychoanalysis is more a matter of belief than scientific fact.

Another criticism of psychoanalysis pertains to the nature of the evidence on which it was built. Freud relied primarily on the case study method, and the cases he studied were his patients. Who were his patients? They were primarily wealthy, highly educated, and highly verbal women who had lots of free time to spend in frequent sessions with Freud and lots of disposable income to pay his bills. His observations were made during the therapy sessions only. These are limited observations, obtained on a narrow segment of humanity. However, from these observations, Freud constructed a universal theory of human nature. In his writings, he provided as evidence not original observations, but his *interpretations* of those observations. Unlike scientists, who make their raw data available so that the results of their experiments can be checked and verified by others, Freud wrote about his interpretations of the patients' behavior rather than reporting or describing their behavior per se. If the actual raw observations were made available, it would be interesting to see if readers would come to the same conclusions that Freud did. Psychoanalysts today could record therapy sessions for use as evidence. This is rarely done, however, as analysts argue that patients who know they are being recorded do not respond naturally.

According to classic Freudian theory, human nature is powered by the twin motives of sex and aggression. These two motives are woven throughout much of contemporary literature, movies, video games, and Internet content.
© David McNew/Getty Images News/Getty Images

There are other specific disagreements with Freudian theory. For example, many believe that Freud's emphasis on sexual drives in his theory of childhood development is inappropriate and perhaps reflects more of a preoccupation of Freud, and the times in which he lived, than an actual topic of childhood development. Others disagree with the notion that personality development pretty much ends at around the age of 5, as Freud held. Those psychologists point to the sometimes profound changes in personality that can occur in adolescence and even throughout adulthood. In Chapter 10, we take up alternative conceptions of personality development that build on, but significantly extend, Freud's ideas. We examine other issues in contemporary psychoanalytic thought as well, including a modern view of the unconscious and the importance of relationships in determining personality development (Kihlstrom, Barnhardt, & Tataryn, 1992).

Some personality psychologists take issue with Freud's generally negative view of human nature. At heart, Freud's theory suggests that human nature is violent, sexual, self-centered, and impulsive. Freud suggested, in effect, that without the inhibiting influence of society, mediated by the superego, humans would self-destruct. Other personality psychologists suggest a more neutral or even positive core to human nature, which we cover in Chapter 11. Finally, Freud's view of women, when he wrote about them at all, implied that they were inferior to men (Kofman, 1985). He suggested that women developed weaker superegos than men (making them more primitive, with weaker moral character), that women's problems were more difficult to cure than men's, and even that women universally had an unconscious wish to become like men (the penis envy component of the Electra complex). Feminist writers have criticized Freud for confusing women's true capacities and potential with the role they were assigned in an oppressive, male-dominated society, an idea we discuss further in Chapter 10. For a strong feminist critique of Freud, see *Feminism and Psychoanalytic Theory* (Chodorow, 1989).

SUMMARY AND EVALUATION

Freud proposed a theory of human nature that has become highly influential. The theory is unique in its emphasis on how the psyche is compartmentalized into conscious and unconscious portions. Freud's theory holds that there are three main forces in the psyche—the id, ego, and superego—which constantly interact in taming the two motives of sex and aggression. These motives may generate urges, thoughts, and memories that arouse so much anxiety that they are banished to the unconscious. Keeping these unacceptable thoughts, desires, and memories out of conscious awareness requires defense mechanisms, such as repression. Several of these defense mechanisms are topics of contemporary research by academic personality psychologists. Freud also theorized about a series of developmental stages that all persons went through, with each stage involving a conflict over expressions of sexuality. How the person resolves these conflicts and learns to satisfy his or her desires within the constraints of a civilized society is the development of personality. That is, adults are different from each other because as children they learned different strategies for dealing with specific kinds of conflicts.

Freud also developed a theory and technique of psychotherapy, also called psychoanalysis. The goals of this form of therapy are to make the patient's unconscious conscious and to help the patient understand the traumatic basis of his or her problems. There has been a lively debate in the field about the value of psychoanalysis. However, as psychoanalytic ideas undergo more scientific examination, and as researchers undertake tests on psychoanalytic hypotheses using controlled laboratory experiments, they will undoubtedly learn more about the value and validity of Freud's theory.

The theory of personality proposed by Freud is one of the most comprehensive views on the working of human nature ever proposed; however, most modern personality psychologists do not totally and uncritically accept the entire theory as it was proposed, word for word, by Freud. Instead, most psychologists accept portions of the theory or agree with modifications to Freud's theory. For example, many psychologists agree that there is an unconscious mind that exists outside awareness, yet many disagree that it is motivated in the way Freud proposed. In Chapter 10, we discuss how this influences the debate over repressed memories.

KEY TERMS

psychic energy 264
instincts 265
libido 265
thanatos 265
conscious 265
preconscious 266
unconscious 266
motivated unconscious 267
blindsight 268
deliberation-without-awareness 268
id 270
pleasure principle 270
primary process thinking 270
wish fulfillment 270
ego 270
reality principle 271
secondary process thinking 271
superego 271
ego depletion 272

defense mechanisms 274
objective anxiety 275
neurotic anxiety 275
moral anxiety 275
repression 276
denial 276
fundamental attribution error 277
displacement 277
rationalization 280
reaction formation 280
projection 280
false consensus effect 281
sublimation 281
psychosexual stage theory 282
fixation 282
oral stage 283
anal stage 283
phallic stage 284
Oedipal conflict 284

castration anxiety 284
identification 284
penis envy 284
Electra complex 284
latency stage 284
genital stage 285
psychoanalysis 285
free association 286
dream analysis 287
manifest content 287
latent content 287
symbols 287
projective hypothesis 288
interpretations 289
insight 289
resistance 289
transference 290
repetition compulsion 290

© Science Photo Library RF/
Getty Images RF

Psychoanalytic Approaches: Contemporary Issues

The Neo-Analytic Movement

Ego Psychology

Object Relations Theory

SUMMARY AND EVALUATION
KEY TERMS

10

Gary Ramona, left, and his attorney walk to Napa County Superior Court on March 24, 1994, for the start of a trial accusing his daughter's therapist of implanting molestation memories using improper suggestion and drugs. © Al Francis/AP Images

T he following information is drawn from a case decided in a California court in 1994 (*Ramona v. Isabella,* California Superior Court, Napa, C61898). The case is described in detail in Johnston, 1999.

Holly Ramona was a 23-year-old woman being treated through counseling for bulimia. One of her counselors, Marche Isabella, acknowledges telling Holly Ramona that an overwhelming majority of women with bulimia were sexually abused during childhood. During the course of therapy, which included sessions during which a hypnotic drug (sodium amytal) was administered, Holly Ramona began recalling incidents of sexual abuse that had occurred during her childhood. More specifically, in response to leading questions from her therapists, Holly began "recovering" memories of her father repeatedly raping her between the ages of 5 and 8. The therapist admitted telling Holly that, because sodium amytal is a "truth serum," if she recalled sexual abuse while under its influence, it *must* have really taken place.

Holly's father, Gary Ramona, was severely affected by his daughter's accusations. When Holly went public with the allegations of incest, his wife divorced him, the rest of his family left him, he lost his well-paying job as an executive at a large winery, and his reputation in the community was ruined. Mr. Ramona claimed he was innocent and accused his daughter's therapists of implanting false memories of incest in her mind.

In an unprecedented legal case, Gary Ramona decided to sue the therapists for the damage they had caused him and his family. He charged that his daughter's recovered memories of being raped by him were, in fact, created by the therapists through repeated suggestions that this was the cause of her bulimia and that she wouldn't get better until she actually remembered having been abused. Mr. Ramona held that implanting these false memories was a form of negligence on the part of the therapists, so he filed a malpractice suit against them.

The therapists claimed that Gary Ramona had no legal grounds on which to sue for malpractice because he was not their patient. In an important landmark decision, however, the trial judge held that, as a family member of the patient, and especially as one who had been substantially affected by the therapists' alleged malpractice, Mr. Ramona *did* have the right to file a malpractice suit against the defendants.

During the trial, which lasted seven weeks, Mr. Ramona denied abusing his daughter, whereas Holly repeated her allegations that he had raped her many times during her childhood. It appeared to be a classic case of one person's word against another's. As often happens in such cases, expert witnesses were called in to try to clarify the issues. Psychologist Elizabeth Loftus, a prominent memory researcher, testified during the trial that "there is no support for the idea that you can be raped . . . over a period of years and totally forget about it." A psychiatrist specializing in legal issues, Park Dietz, testified that although Holly Ramona recalled being abused, she could not at first recall who the abuser was. It was only after the sodium amytal session, during which the therapists suggested to Holly that the abuser was her father, that she "remembered" it was her father. Martin Orne, a psychiatrist, psychologist, and authority on hypnosis, also testified that sodium amytal interviews are "inherently untrustworthy and unreliable" and that "Holly Ramona's memory is so distorted that she no longer knows what the truth is." Finally, Harvard psychiatry professor Harrison Pope offered his opinion that Holly Ramona had been "grossly and negligently treated, with catastrophic results."

The jury decided that the therapists were guilty of malpractice and awarded Mr. Ramona $475,000 in damages. The jury foreman was quoted in media sources as having said that the verdict was intended to "send a message about false child abuse memories." Mr. Ramona's attorney saw the verdict as a warning to other therapists, especially to those who believe that adult psychological problems are the result of repressed childhood traumas. One defendant, therapist Marche Isabella, described the verdict as a blow to the mental health profession, adhering to the position that "repressed memories are a reality."

Why did this case turn out so differently from the case of Professor Cheit, described at the start of Chapter 9? The major difference between the two cases is that Ross Cheit provided substantial corroborating evidence in support of his recovered memory. Unlike Holly Ramona, Ross Cheit's memory fragment was corroborated by many other persons and even by a tape-recorded confession from the abuser himself.

But what do these cases tell us about the psychoanalytic idea of the motivated unconscious, the idea that the mind can bury memories of horrifying events and then, decades later, accurately retrieve those memories? By themselves, single cases do not prove anything for or against unconsciously motivated repression. People forget all sorts of things. Can you remember what you ate for dinner last Tuesday? With the right cues, however, could you be led to remember accurately? With other cues, could you be led to inaccurately remember what you had for dinner last Tuesday?

What is the difference between ordinary forgetting and motivated repression? Is there good scientific evidence for motivated repression? Could people be motivated to "remember" events that did not actually happen, as apparently was the case with Holly Ramona? To answer these questions we examine contemporary revisions to classical psychoanalysis, collectively known as the neo-analytic movement.

The Neo-Analytic Movement

As proposed by Freud, classical psychoanalysis is a detailed and comprehensive theory, developed in the early 1900s, of the totality of human nature. Many of Freud's ideas are out of date; however, contemporary psychoanalyst Drew Westen (1998) argues that they *should* be out of date; after all, Freud died in 1939 and "he has been slow to undertake further revisions" (p. 333) of his theory. Westen goes on humorously to note that "Freud, like Elvis, has been dead for a number of years but continues to be cited with some regularity" (p. 333). Whereas many of Freud's ideas have not stood the test of time, others have and have been incorporated into a contemporary version of psychoanalysis. Today, psychoanalysis is probably best thought of as a theory containing ideas variously inspired by Sigmund Freud but modified and advanced by others.

Westen (e.g., 1990, 1998) is one of the most active proponents of contemporary psychoanalysis. Writing on the scientific legacy of Freud, Westen notes that contemporary psychoanalysts no longer write much about ids, superegos, and repressed sexuality; nor do they liken treatment to an archeological expedition in search of forgotten memories. Instead, most contemporary psychoanalysts focus their attention on childhood relationships and adult conflicts with others, such as difficulties becoming intimate or readily becoming intimate with the wrong kinds of persons (Greenberg & Mitchell, 1983). Westen (1998) defines contemporary psychoanalysis as being based on the following five postulates:

1. The unconscious still plays a large role in life, although it may not be the ubiquitous influence that Freud held it was.
2. Behavior often reflects compromises in conflicts among mental processes, such as emotions, motivations, and thoughts (Westen & Gabbard, 2002a).
3. Childhood plays an important part in personality development, particularly in terms of shaping adult relationship styles.
4. Mental representations of the self and relationships guide our interactions with others (Westen & Gabbard, 2002b).
5. Personality development involves not just regulating sexual and aggressive feelings but also moving from an immature, socially dependent way of relating to others to a mature, independent relationship style.

This neo-analytic viewpoint has wider currency and better empirical support, in some cases, than Freud's original ideas. To start our coverage of contemporary issues in psychoanalysis, we begin with a discussion of repression and memory.

Repression and Contemporary Research on Memory

It is easy to find conflicting opinions among respected psychologists on the issue of motivated repression. One review of the clinical literature on motivated repression concluded "the evidence for repression is overwhelming and obvious" (Erdelyi & Goldberg, 1979, p. 384). Another review of the same literature concluded "the concept of repression has not been validated with experimental research" (Holmes, 1990, p. 97).

Elizabeth Loftus, a professor of psychology and world-renowned memory researcher, has perhaps conducted the most research on the authenticity of recovered memories. Loftus has been the one psychologist most connected to the repressed memory debate, and summarizes scientific status of the concepts of "repressed" and

Professor Elizabeth Loftus testified in the Ramona trial and has contributed a good deal of scientific information to the debate over repressed memories.

© *Don Shrubshell, Pool/AP Images*

"recovered" memories of sexual abuse (Loftus, 2009). In her article titled "The Reality of Repressed Memories" (Loftus, 1993), she discusses many cases of individuals who suddenly recover memories of important events: some of these turn out to be true memories, whereas others are false or inaccurate accounts, which are later recanted. However, she argues that we should not conclude that *all* recovered memories are **false memories,** just because some, such as Holly Ramona's, have turned out apparently to be false. Similarly, we should not assume that *all* recovered memories are true, just because some, such as Ross Cheit's that we explored in Chapter 9, have turned out to be true. Loftus believes that what is important is being aware of the processes that may contribute to the possible creation of inaccurate or false memories. Loftus (1992, 1993, 2011) suggests that many variables contribute to the construction of false memories.

One factor that might influence people to have false memories is the popular press. Many books purport to be guides for survivors of abuse; these are undoubtedly of some comfort to people who have been living with painful memories of abuse. For those who have no such memories, these books often provide strong suggestions that abuse could have happened, even if there is no memory of the abuse. For example, one book in this category is *The Courage to Heal* (Bass & Davis, 1988), which states:

> *You may think you don't have memories. . . . To say, "I was abused," you don't need the kind of recall that would stand up in a court of law. Often the knowledge that you were abused starts with a tiny feeling, an intuition. . . . Assume your feelings are valid. . . . If you think you were abused and your life shows the symptoms, then you were. (p. 22)*

What are some of the symptoms *The Courage to Heal* suggests indicate a person is likely to have been abused? The book lists, among other things, low self-esteem, self-destructive thoughts, depression, and sexual dysfunction. This book, and others like it, provides a strong message that even in the absence of a specific memory, many people should conclude that they have been abused. However, there are many causes of low self-esteem, depression, and sexual dysfunction. In addition, these symptoms are associated with many other psychological disorders, such as phobias and anxieties, and these disorders certainly can occur without a history of abuse.

This quote is a powerful suggestion that may lead some persons to conclude falsely that they must have been abused. A person who starts with this idea may embellish this suggestion by filling in details to make a convincing or consistent story of abuse. If he or she is led further along these lines by a questioning therapist, his or her false memories may become more and more convincing. Loftus (1993) has demonstrated in the lab that subjects questioned in a leading manner after watching a video of a car accident can be led to conclude that one car ran a stop sign, even though there was no stop sign in the video. And with more leading questioning, subjects increase their confidence that one car is to blame because it ran the stop sign (Bernstein & Loftus, 2009).

Another factor that may contribute to false memories is the behavior of some therapists. Loftus tells of a woman who wrote to her after the woman's therapist had concluded that her depression was caused by childhood sexual abuse. The patient stated that her therapist was certain of that diagnosis, even though the patient had no memory of the abuse. The patient further stated that she could not understand how something so terrible could have happened without her being able to remember the event. Loftus tells of another case of a man who went to a therapist because he was distraught over his father's suicide. The patient talked about painful events in his life, but the therapist kept suggesting that there must be something else. Not knowing what this "something else" was, the patient became even more depressed. Then, during a therapy session, the therapist stated that "you display the same kinds of characteristics as some of my patients who are victims of . . . ritualistic abuse" (cited in Loftus, 1993, p. 528).

A variety of techniques are used in therapy that encourages patients to reflect on their childhoods. Hypnosis is one technique used to get patients to recall freely childhood experiences within the protection of a relaxed, suggestion-induced, trancelike state. An extensive scientific literature, however, shows that hypnosis does not improve memory (Nash, 1987, 1988). This explains why hypnotizing witnesses is not allowed in courts of law; hypnotized witnesses do not recall facts with any greater accuracy than nonhypnotized witnesses (Kihlstrom, 2003c; Wagstaff, Vella, & Perfect, 1992). In fact, hypnosis may be associated with increased distortions in memory (Spanos & McLean, 1986). In one case, a highly suggestible man was led under hypnosis to develop "memories" for crimes that had not even been committed (Ofshe, 1992). Under hypnosis, people are often more imaginative, more spontaneous, and more emotional and often report unusual bodily sensations (Nash, 2001). After being taken back to childhood through hypnosis, people have been known to recall being abducted by alien creatures with fantastic spaceships (Loftus, 1993).

Loftus and colleagues have pointed to specific techniques in psychotherapy that can contribute to the creation of false memories (Loftus, 2000; Lynn et al., 2003). These include the use of hypnosis, suggestive interviewing, the interpretation of symptoms as signs of past trauma, pressure from an authority figure to recall trauma, and dream interpretation. Such practices can be used to foster the recollection of events that did not actually happen (Tsai, Loftus, & Polage, 2000). In laboratory studies, Loftus and colleagues have shown that having persons imagine various events can lead them to later rate those events as more familiar, leading subjects to have a more elaborate memory representation, which in turn leads them to rate those imagined events as likely to have happened (Thomas, Bulevich, & Loftus, 2003). This effect is called the **imagination inflation effect**, and it occurs when a memory is elaborated upon through imagination, leading the person to confuse the imagined event with events that actually happened. For example, by showing people an advertisement suggesting that they shook hands with Mickey Mouse as a child, those people later had higher confidence that they had personally shaken hands with Mickey as a child. Another study had persons imagining shaking hands with Bugs Bunny and produced a similar effect (Braun, Ellis, & Loftus, 2002). Having persons imagine something, even something as unusual as shaking hands with Bugs Bunny, can lead them to have a false confidence that it actually may have happened. Loftus and others have pointed out the implications of this research for the admissibility of allegedly repressed memories in courts (Hyman & Loftus, 2002; Loftus, 2003). Loftus has also developed a misinformation paradigm whereby false memories can be instilled in laboratory settings by exposing subjects to misinformation when questioning them about some event. She has shown that this technique can alter memory for even very personally stressful events (Morgan et al., 2012), and that such false memories were found to persist over a one and a half years later when subjects were followed up (Zhu et al., 2012).

Why would some therapists suggest false memories to their patients? Many therapists believe that effective treatment must result in a patient's overcoming repressed memories and reclaiming a traumatic past. Therapists, like many other people, can also suffer from a **confirmatory bias**—the tendency to look only for evidence

A Closer Look

So, You Want to Have a False Memory

Imagine you are a subject in a psychology experiment in which you are assigned to listen carefully to a list of 15 words, knowing that you will later be tested on these words. The words are *bed, rest, awake, tired, dream, wake, snooze, blanket, doze, slumber, snore, nap, peace, yawn,* and *drowsy.* Now cover the list of words and indicate whether or not each of the following words was on the list:

	On the List?	
	Yes	No
snooze	——	——
mother	——	——
bed	——	——
television	——	——
sleep	——	——
chair	——	——

If you are like most people, you checked yes following the word *sleep.* Indeed, many people are so certain that *sleep* was on the first list that they argue with the experimenter when they are told that, in fact, it was not. Thus, if you checked yes, indicating that sleep was on the list during the recall phase of the task, and you really remember seeing the word *sleep,* then you just had a false memory. Approximately 80 percent of normal subjects are induced to have this false memory—that is, they believe that *sleep* was on the original list (Roediger, Balota, & Watson, 2001; Roediger, McDermott, & Robinson, 1998).

The procedure you just completed was developed by psychologists Henry Roediger and Kathleen McDermott (1995). They devised the technique based on the **spreading activation** model of memory. This model of memory holds that mental elements (such as words or images) are stored in memory along with associations

to other elements in memory. For example, *doctor* is associated with *nurse* in most people's memories, because of the close connection or similarity between these concepts. The mental association between these two concepts can be demonstrated easily; the speed of deciding that a letter string *(doctor)* is a word or not is faster if it is preceded by an associated concept *(nurse)* relative to an unrelated word *(table).* The explanation is that the activation of *nurse* in your memory spreads through an association network and activates other related concepts, such as *doctor,* allowing them to be recognized faster.

How does this explain the false memory for *sleep* in the exercise? Like any concept, *sleep* is stored in your memory in a network of associations to other words, such as *bed, rest, awake, tired, dream, wake, snooze, blanket,* and *doze.* This network of associations is depicted in Figure 10.1.

Activation from the multiple words on the first list spreads or primes the critical concept on the recall list *(sleep)* in the memory network of the person studying the list. The activation from all the words related to *sleep* (e.g., *bed, rest,* and *tired)* sums up and makes the concept of *sleep* more likely to be recalled or recognized later, even though the actual word *sleep* was not on the original list.

Researchers have also shown that the probability of a false memory in this task is a function of the number of words on the first list that are associated with the critical word (e.g., *sleep).* That is, the sum of the association strength from the list items to the critical item determines false recall of the critical item. Association strength is determined by how frequently the critical word (e.g., *sleep)* is named when people are asked for the

first word that comes to mind from some other word (e.g., *bed).* In fact, psychologists have determined lists of common associates to a whole variety of words, and the sum of association strength of the listed items to the critical item is what determines the probability of false recall (Roediger et al., 2001).

How is this material related to the psychoanalytic idea of false memories? First, this material highlights how most cognitive psychologists, even those with strong scientific values, believe that false memories can occur. It is accepted as fact that humans have a **constructive memory**; that is, memory contributes to or influences in various ways (adds to, subtracts from, and so on) what is recalled. Rather than referring to pristine and objective retrieval of facts from the past, human memory is fallible and open to error and corruption. Moreover, the corruption is most likely to occur when elements with strong associations to each other converge repeatedly in experience. In this condition, the person is likely to recognize or recall something associated to those elements, even if that new element never occurred. For example, during interrogation, imagine that a person is repeatedly asked about an event in many different leading ways. After some time, the person is asked something that is new but related to the first information. The person may then be more likely to recall this new event as happening, not because it did happen, but because it is associated with the previously presented information. This is how innocent mistakes of recognition on word lists might help us understand the larger and more dramatic false memories that have been documented in certain legal cases, such as that of Holly Ramona.

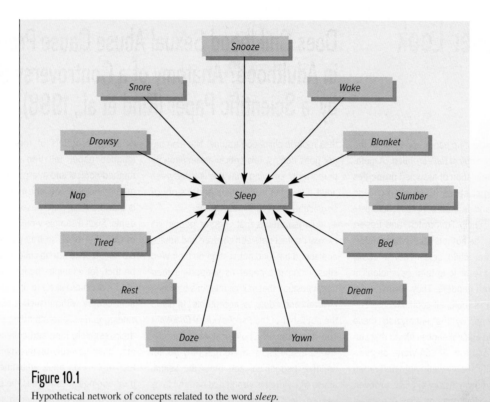

Figure 10.1

Hypothetical network of concepts related to the word *sleep*.

Source: Adapted from Roediger, Balota, & Watson, 2001.

that confirms their previous hunch and to not look for evidence that might disconfirm their belief. If a therapist believes that childhood trauma is the cause of most adult problems, he or she will most likely probe for memories of childhood trauma. Compliant and suggestible patients are then often induced to spend long periods of time trying to imagine what events must have happened in their childhoods to produce their current difficulties. Meanwhile, the therapist relates stories of other patients with similar problems who were helped by recalling and coping with memories of childhood abuse. The therapist, as an "authority" on how to get better, stands ready to authenticate any possible memory of trauma that the patient might produce. These are the ideal conditions for constructing a shared reality that, even though both parties are confident of its authenticity, is not true.

However, this position must be balanced with some known facts about the rates of various forms of child abuse. Surveys suggest that a remarkable amount of trauma is inflicted on children. For example, in 2006 there were approximately 905,000 child victims of maltreatment in the United States. Of these, 64 percent were for neglect, 16 percent involved physical abuse, 9 percent were sexual abuse cases, and approximately 9 percent each involved psychological abuse and medical neglect. In this reporting year, an estimated 1,530 children died of abuse and neglect. Of these fatalities, 78 percent were under the age of 4 years! (All statistics are from U.S. Department of Health and Human Services, 2008.)

A Closer Look

Does Childhood Sexual Abuse Cause Problems in Adulthood? Anatomy of a Controversy Started by a Scientific Paper (Rind et al., 1998)

In 1998, a scientific paper appeared in the journal *Psychological Bulletin* titled "A meta-analytic examination of assumed properties of child sexual abuse (CSA) using college samples," and authored by psychologists Bruce Rind, Philip Tromovitch, and Robert Bauserman. The authors' goal was to determine whether child sexual abuse (CSA) causes intense or long-term psychological harm for both genders. They reviewed 59 studies on this topic, all conducted on college students. By meta-analyzing these studies, Rind and colleagues found that students with a history of CSA were, on average, slightly less well adjusted than students without a history of CSA. However, poor family environment also correlated with a history of CSA, making it impossible to argue that CSA in itself causes adjustment problems (independent from poor family environment). In general, the authors concluded that CSA does not appear to cause as much intense or long-lasting psychological harm as might be assumed.

This paper ignited a firestorm of controversy that took several years to play out. Most people assume that the sexual abuse of children is bad because of the long-term harm such abuse holds for children. Yet here was a study saying that it was difficult to document any substantial harm over the long run for childhood sexual abuse. Consequently, many people entered the debate because they were simply outraged over the conclusions that childhood sexual abuse was not so bad.

Other groups were outraged by the Rind and colleagues paper for other reasons. Psychologists with a psychoanalytic bent start with the critical assumption that psychological problems in adulthood often have

their roots in childhood trauma. The Rind paper goes against this critical assumption by purportedly showing that the link between adult adjustment difficulties and history of sexual abuse in childhood is weak.

Organizations that endorse pedophilia (sexual contact between children and adults) applauded the Rind publication on their Web sites, citing this paper as supporting their moral position that sexual relations between children and adults is acceptable. In 1999 the publisher of the *Psychological Bulletin*—The American Psychological Association—issued a statement saying that they do not endorse pedophilia, and that "the sexual abuse of children is wrong and harmful to its victims." In 1999 the U.S. House of Representatives passed a resolution condemning the Rind and colleagues (1998) study, declaring that child–adult sex was inherently "abusive and destructive" and the resolution was passed unanimously in the Senate.

What can we say about the Rind and colleagues study in light of this controversy? The authors attacked a common assumption that CSA causes harm and leads to long-term problems. Most cultures around the world consider it wrong for adults to have sexual contact with children. However, Rind and colleagues argued that the "wrongfulness" of CSA may be in question because its "harmfulness" is in dispute. In other words, because the act may not produce harmful *consequences,* we might question whether CSA is actually *wrong.* Moreover, the authors were quite provocative in interpreting their results, for example, arguing that discussions of CSA should not include such terms as *victim* or *perpetrator* or even *abuse* because these are moral, not scientific, terms.

The rebuttals of the Rind and colleagues paper fall into two categories: methodological and interpretational. On the methodological side, one important concern is that the data were based on college students. Such a sample would exclude victims of CSA that were so traumatized that they did not go on to attend college. Also, it could be that, for example, people with a history of CSA are more likely to drop out of college than people without such a history. By excluding non-college-attending persons from their research, Rind and colleagues (1998) may have severely underestimated the effect of CSA on adult adjustment. Another methodological concern is the broad definition they used of CSA, which included acts ranging from forced sexual intercourse to being verbally propositioned. By including such "mild" abuses as being verbally propositioned (without sexual contact) in their definition of CSA, it could be that Rind and colleagues diluted the effects of real CSA on adjustment.

A final methodological concern involves the fact that most of the studies analyzed by Rind and colleagues relied completely on retrospective self-report of college students as the only source of data. A much better (though also much more difficult) approach would be a prospective design, where children identified as having been recently abused would be followed over the years until they are adults and then adjustment is assessed and compared with a control group that was not abused.

One can also disagree with how Rind and colleagues interpret their findings. For example, they argue that because poor family environment correlates with CSA, one cannot know that it is CSA that is causing the poorer adjustment outcomes. It could be that people from poor family backgrounds (those that have other forms of abuse or neglect, high levels of conflict, mental illness, etc.) are at risk of poor adjustment outcomes regardless of whether CSA occurs. However, Rind and colleagues never seriously consider whether poor family background is caused by, or is a consequence of, the child sexual abuse. Because most of the studies are based on retrospective self-report, we cannot know which of these possibilities is the correct interpretation for the relationship between poor family background and CSA (Lilienfeld, 2002).

Another interpretation issue concerns the meaning of "small" when the authors describe the relation between CSA and such adjustment outcomes as anxiety, depression, suicide, divorce, or paranoia. It is true that the effect sizes conform to the statistical definition of small (e.g., effect sizes less than .30). However, even small effects can reflect very important consequences for people and impact large percentages of persons. Moreover, individuals may exhibit elevated levels of one type of symptom, but the symptoms may differ from person to person, such that any one symptom may not be very elevated in the CSA population as a whole, even though individuals themselves suffer

greatly. In certain ways, statistical effect sizes do not convey clinical significance and in this regard can be misleading.

A final interpretation issue concerns the fact that, because their data suggest that CSA is not intensely harmful, Rind and colleagues (1998) go on to allude that CSA is morally benign. However, this is a slippery slope. Such a position holds that in order for something to be wrong, it must be shown to be harmful. It replaces a moral standard with a scientific standard, and science can only document relations, not decide on what is right or wrong. Ultimately, the question boils down to how do we decide if something is wrong? Legally, the definition of most wrongs is given by society's norms, by what most people feel is wrong or inappropriate. Ultimately we need to rely on the wisdom of societal beliefs to help us determine what is wrong. When it comes to children, society generally believes that they are incapable of making rational and informed life decisions. For example, in U.S. society, children are not allowed to enter into financial contracts, to decide whether they want to attend school, to consent to medical procedures, to participate in research, or to consume tobacco or alcohol. In addition, add to this list the sociological belief that children cannot

consent to sexual relations. The real moral basis for deeming sexual acts with children inappropriate is based on the social belief that children cannot give consent to sex because they have little knowledge about what is being consented to, and when it is an adult forcing the issue, they may not have the absolute freedom to accept or decline. This position is well summarized in a 1999 public letter written by the then American Psychological Association CEO Raymond Fowler to Congressman Delay, holding "that children cannot consent to sexual activity with adults" and that such activity "should never be considered or labeled as harmless or acceptable" (American Psychological Association, 1999). Because society believes that children lack the maturity to make important life decisions, they need to be protected from those who would exploit their immaturity. In this sense, the data from the Rind and colleagues article are irrelevant to whether CSA is wrong. The huge controversy surrounding the article was not so much an attempt to censure unpopular results, though there were methodological problems with the study. Much of the controversy can be traced to the authors' use of science to replace morality, their confusing "harmfulness" with "wrongness."

Contemporary Views on the Unconscious

The idea of a motivated unconscious is at the core of classical psychoanalytic theory. Most contemporary psychologists also believe in the unconscious, although it is a different version of the unconscious than that found in classical psychoanalytic theory. Consider the views of psychologist John Bargh (2005), a social psychologist whose research on unconscious processes has had a large impact on psychology: "People are often unaware of the reasons and causes of their own behavior. In fact, recent experimental evidence points to a deep and fundamental dissociation between conscious awareness and the mental processes responsible for one's behavior" (p. 38). This can be illustrated with one of Bargh's own experiments in which college student subjects took part in what they thought was an experiment on language, where they were presented with many different words. Half of the participants were presented with words synonymous with rudeness; the other half were presented with words synonymous with politeness. After finishing the language experiment, they went to another experiment in another room and encountered a staged situation where it was possible to act in either a rude or polite way. Although the participants showed no awareness of the possible influence of the language experiment, they nevertheless behaved in the staged situation in a manner that was consistent with the kinds of words they were exposed to in the "previous" experiment (Bargh, 2005). Most psychologists believe that the unconscious can influence our behavior, but not all agree with Freud that the unconscious can have its own autonomous motivation (Bargh, 2006, 2008).

We can term these two differing views on the unconscious the **cognitive unconscious** view and the **motivated unconscious** view. Those with the cognitive unconscious view readily acknowledge that information can get into our memories without our ever being aware of the information (Kihlstrom, 1999). For example, in the phenomenon of **subliminal perception**, some information—such as the phrase "Buy a Coke"—is flashed on a screen so quickly that you don't recognize the actual words. That is, you would say that you had seen a flash but were not able to distinguish what was written. Indeed, you could not even guess that the word *Coke* was presented better than chance compared to guessing that some other nonpresented word, say *House,* was presented. However, if you were asked to judge whether a string of letters is a word or not a word, and the dependent variable were reaction time (how quickly you can make this judgment), then you would judge *Coke* as a word faster than words unrelated to Coke or soft drinks in general. Thus, subliminal information primes associated material in memory. **Priming** makes that associated material more accessible to conscious awareness than is material that is not primed. Results such as these using subliminal primes clearly demonstrate that information can get into the mind and have some influence, without going through conscious experience. (A demonstration of subliminal priming can be found at www.millisecond.com/products/demos/subliminal/subliminal.web.)

If someone were given the subliminal message "Buy a Coke," would they be more likely to spontaneously go out and do so? After all, this is consistent with the psychoanalytic idea of the motivated unconscious—that something in the unconscious can motivate behavior. Can advertisers use subliminal messages to unconsciously motivate consumers? Similar questions arise concerning the influence of subliminal rock music messages that supposedly advocate suicide or violence. The vast majority of research on subliminal perception, however, suggests that unconscious information does not influence people's motivations. That is, the average teen exposed to subliminal messages of violence in a song is unlikely to go out and commit a violent act. Similarly, the average person subliminally exposed to the phrase "Buy a Coke" is unlikely to do so.

In the cognitive view of the unconscious, the content of the unconscious mind is assumed to operate just like thoughts in consciousness. Thoughts are unconscious because they are not in conscious awareness, not because they have been repressed or because they represent unacceptable urges or wishes. For example, we might say that buttoning a shirt is unconscious because we can do it without focusing any conscious attention on the act. Typing can also be unconscious for the person who is good at it. Other kinds of mental content, such as beliefs and values, might also be unconscious. Such elements are not in our unconscious because they are threatening; nor are they there to exert influence on our behavior. And although unconscious material can influence subsequent thoughts or behavior, as in the priming examples, these influences are not consistent with the motivated unconscious of classical psychoanalytic theory (Kihlstrom, 2003b; Nash, 1999). As such, the cognitive unconscious as viewed by contemporary psychologists is quite different from that put forward by Freud a hundred years ago. According to Freud, the unconscious was a torrid and fuming cauldron of

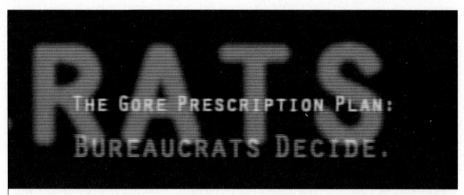

In the 2000 U.S. presidential election campaign, a Republican team released a commercial describing some of the questionable fund-raising efforts of Al Gore, the Democratic opponent. During the commercial, the word RATS was subliminally presented, along with information about Gore. When the Gore campaign team discovered this, they responded with outrage and a public denouncement of this subliminal attempt to influence voter opinion on the part of the Bush campaign. The Bush campaign quickly pulled the commercial, with Bush himself denying he had had any role in ordering subliminal propaganda. The fact that both campaign teams believed that such subliminal messages would have a wide impact on voter motivation shows that many people believe in unconscious motivation. Researchers are debating the power of subliminal political advertisements to influence public opinion (Weinberger & Westen, 2007).
© Reuters/Newscom.

anger and eroticism. It operated according to its own primitive and irrational rules, and it had broad, sweeping influence over our conscious behavior, thoughts, and feelings. In contemporary psychology, the unconscious is peaceful, gentle, and much more rational than Freud's version. Moreover, although the unconscious is still viewed as having an influence on behavior, thoughts, and feelings, that influence is seen as more bounded, rule governed, and specific, as in unconscious priming, than was taught by Freud (Bargh & Morsella, 2008, 2010).

Ego Psychology

Another major modification to psychoanalysis concerns a shift in focus from id to ego. Freud's version of psychoanalysis focused on the id, especially the twin instincts of sex and aggression, and how the ego and superego respond to the demands of the id. We might characterize Freudian psychoanalysis as **id psychology**. Later psychoanalysts felt that the ego deserved more attention, that it performed many constructive functions. One prominent student of Freud—Erik Erikson—emphasized the ego as a powerful, independent part of personality. Moreover, Erikson noted that the ego was involved in mastering the environment, achieving one's goals, and hence establishing one's identity. It is no wonder, then, that the approach to psychoanalysis started by Erikson is called **ego psychology**.

Establishing a secure identity is seen as the primary function of the ego. Identity can be thought of as an inner sense of who we are, of what makes us unique, and a sense of continuity over time and a feeling of wholeness. You have probably heard the term **identity crisis**. This term comes from Erikson's work, and it refers to the desperation and confusion a person feels when he or she has not developed a strong sense of identity. Maybe you have even felt such feelings when you were uncertain about yourself, uncertain about who you were or how you wanted others to view you, what you valued and wanted out of life, and where you were going in terms of the direction of your life. A period of identity crisis is a common experience during adolescence, but for some people it occurs later in life or lasts for a longer period. The so-called midlife crisis, discussed more in Chapter 11, often begins with an identity crisis (Sheldon & Kasser, 2001).

One of Erikson's lasting contributions was developing the notion of identity as an important developmental achievement in everyone's personality. Identity has been thought of as a story that a person develops about himself or herself (McAdams, 1999, 2008, 2010, 2011). The story answers the following questions: Who am I? What is my place in the adult world? What are the unifying themes of my life? What is the purpose of my existence? McAdams (e.g., 2016, McAdams & Manczak, 2015) sees identity as a narrative story that a person constructs. Although a person may rearrange and reconstruct the plot of his or her life story, it nevertheless takes on importance as the person's unique story. According to McAdams, once the story has evolved to have coherent themes, the person may make very few changes to his or her story. However, certain events can cause large changes to identity and are incorporated into the narrative, such as graduation, marriage, birth of a child, turning 40, or retirement. Unexpected events can become a part of the story too, such as the death of a marriage partner, loss of a job, or unexpected wealth. A study by Cox and McAdams (2012) showed that even volunteering over spring break to work with people living in poverty can transform the narrative identity that college students write about themselves. McAdams (2008) describes how all of us construct a life story, and that part of becoming an adult is taking ownership of this story:

> People begin to construct narrative identities in adolescence and young adulthood and continue to work on these stories across the adult life course. . . . The stories we construct to make sense of our lives are fundamentally about our struggle to reconcile who we imagine we were, are, and might be in our heads and bodies with who we were, are, and might be in the social contexts of family, community, the workplace, ethnicity, religion, gender, social class, and culture writ large. The self comes to terms with society through narrative identity. (pp. 242–243)

Erikson's Eight Stages of Development

Whereas Freud taught that our personalities were formed by around the age of 5 years, Erikson disagreed and felt that important periods of development occurred throughout the life span. For example, Freud called the period from age 6 to puberty the latency period because he believed not much psychologically was going on. However, this is a period when children are starting to go to school; they are learning to work and to gain satisfaction from success and from accomplishments; they are learning to be sociable, to share, and to cooperate with peers; and they are learning about social structures, such as the fact that teachers are in charge and represent authorities. Erikson (1963, 1968) argued that much development occurred during the years that Freud thought were quiet. Indeed, Erikson believed that the development of personality lasted well into adulthood and even old age (Erikson, 1975). He outlined **eight stages of development** through which we all pass (Figure 10.2).

Not only did Erikson disagree with Freud about the time span of development, but he also disagreed with Freud about the conflict, or crisis, that occurs at each stage. Whereas Freud felt that the crises were inherently sexual, Erikson believed that the crises were of a social nature. After all, he argued, the persons with whom we have our

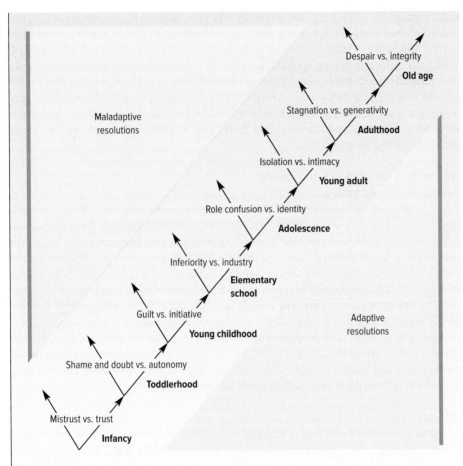

Figure 10.2
Erikson's eight stages of development.

first social relationships are our parents. Thus, there could be crises of learning to trust our parents, learning to be autonomous from them, learning from them how to act as an adult. He called these **psychosocial conflicts** rather than the psychosexual conflicts that formed Freud's developmental stages.

Although Erikson disagreed with Freud on these two issues of development, he did agree with Freud on several other points. First, like Freud, Erikson kept a **stage model of development**, implying that people go through the stages in a certain order and that there is a specific issue that characterizes each stage. Second, Erikson believed that each stage represented a conflict, a **developmental crisis**, that needed to be resolved. Third, Erikson maintained the notion of fixation, meaning that if the crisis was not successfully and adaptively resolved, then personality development could become arrested and the person would continue to be preoccupied by that crisis in development. Let's now briefly consider each of the eight stages.

Trust Versus Mistrust
When children are born, they are completely dependent on those around them. Their first questions would most likely be "Who's going to take care of me, and will they do a good job? Can I trust that they will feed me when I am hungry, clothe me when I am

cold, comfort me when I cry, and generally take care of me?" If children are well taken care of, if their basic needs are met, then they will develop a sense of trust in their care-givers. This sense of trust, according to Erikson, forms the basis of future relationships, with such children growing up believing that other people are approachable, trustable, and generally good and loving. However, some infants are not well taken care of, for various reasons, and they never receive the love and care they need. Such infants may develop a sense that others are not to be trusted and may develop a lifelong pattern of mistrust in others, suspiciousness, and feelings of estrangement, isolation, or social discomfort when around others.

Autonomy Versus Shame and Doubt

Around the second year, most children are on their feet and on the go. This is the stage many parents call the "terrible twos." Children begin experimenting with their new abili-ties, including running when the parents tell them to walk, screaming when the parents tell them to be quiet, and generally just testing their powers. They are trying to answer the question "How much of the world do I control?" A good outcome is when a child feels a sense of control and mastery over things and develops self-confidence and a sense of autonomy that lets the child explore and learn. If parents inhibit such autonomy, per-haps by being strict, restrictive, or punishing when the child is independent, then the child may feel shame and doubt over the goals he or she is contemplating. Overly protec-tive parents can also cause problems, in that they can hinder the child's natural urge to explore and to encounter a wide variety of life events and experiences. For example, parents who prevent their child from rough-and-tumble play with other children may cause their child to grow up doubting his or her ability to get along with others.

Initiative Versus Guilt

Children at this stage—around 3 years of age—often imitate adults, dressing in adult clothes, playing adults, and acting as adults. Children at this stage receive their first practice in adult tasks during play. As adults, we must learn how to work together, to follow leaders, and to resolve disputes. When children play, they practice these skills by organizing games, choosing leaders, and forming goals. Then, during school activities they also take the initiative to accomplish goals and to work with a distinct purpose in mind. If all goes well, children at this stage develop a sense of initiative, which trans-lates into ambition and goal seeking. If things do not go well, children may become resigned to failure or to not even take the initiative to pursue goals.

Industry Versus Inferiority

It is good to have experiences of success, but we all have limits, and there is a lot of competition. Starting around age 4, children begin comparing themselves to each other, especially those their own age, and many (although not all) develop a sense of compe-tence and achievement. If people have enough success experiences, then they believe in their strength and abilities and assume that if they just work hard enough, they can do most things they desire to do. This sense of industry—feeling as if they can work to achieve what they want—sets children on their way to being productive members of society. However, with enough failure experiences, children might develop a sense of inferiority, feeling that they don't have the talent or ability to get ahead in life.

Identity Versus Role Confusion

During adolescence, people go through a whole series of drastic physical changes. This can be an especially difficult time of life, in which people emerge from childhood into adulthood, whether they are ready or not. Erikson gave this period special attention in his work, referring to identity achievement as one of the most important goals of development.

At this stage, adolescents begin to ask themselves the questions "Who am I?" and "Do others recognize me for who I think I am?" Many people do a lot of experimentation at this stage, trying on many different identities. One semester, a high school student might try on the role of athlete; the next semester, the role of punk rocker; the next semester, born-again Christian; and the next semester, Goth. Experimenting with identities is common at this time of life, with teenagers searching for identity in all sorts of ways and places. One student said he was going to Hawaii to "find himself." In actuality, no matter where you go, there you are, so the search for identity really has no special place. But many people at this stage join groups, drift around the country, commit themselves to various causes or ideals, or experiment with drugs, politics, or religion, all in an effort to find the true "me." Eventually, most people make some decisions about what is important and what they value and want out of life, and they acquire a sense of "who they are," achieving some degree of consistent self-understanding. People who fail in this stage develop role confusion and enter adulthood without a solid sense of who they are or what they think is the meaning of their lives. Such people bounce around among all sorts of roles and are generally unstable in their relationships, in their jobs, and in their goals and values.

People differ from one another in the extent to which they commit themselves to their values, careers, relationships, and ideologies (Marcia, 2002). Most people will pass through a period of **identity confusion**, which refers to not having a strong sense of who one really is. Some cultures institute a **rite of passage** ritual, usually around adolescence, which typically is a ceremony that initiates a child into adulthood. For example, some southwestern American Indians send adolescent males to be alone in the wilderness, fasting, until they have a vision. After such ceremonies, the adolescent is sometimes given a new name, bestowing a new adult identity. Secular American culture does not provide common rite of passage rituals, though certain religions do, such as the Confirmation ritual in Roman Catholicism or Bar/Bat Mitzvah in Judaism.

In resolving the identity crisis, some persons develop a **negative identity**, an identity founded on undesirable social roles, such as street gang member. Unfortunately, modern culture provides many undesirable role models. Because this is a time of life when youngsters are looking for models, most are very impressionable. This is one reason most states keep their juvenile court system separate from the adult court system, so that young persons do not come into contact with adult criminals.

Identity is something that must be achieved. If a person commits to an identity they did not work for or that was handed to them, then that identity is likely to be shallow or changeable (Marcia, 1966). Indeed, Marcia (2002) holds that mature identity development involves going through a crisis and emerging with a firm sense of commitment to one's values, relationships, or career. If a person does not have a crisis, or if he or she forms an identity without exploring alternatives, such as accepting the values of parents, then this is called **identity foreclosure**. People in identity foreclosure are often moralistic and conventional, but when asked to back up their positions, they often cannot provide a good rationale for their beliefs and opinions.

A final concept relevant to identity development, especially to college students, concerns the notion of a **moratorium**. This refers basically to taking time to explore options before making a commitment to an identity. In some ways, college can be thought of as a socially approved period in which a young person is able to explore a variety of roles and responsibilities before taking any one set on "for real." One can

Lee Malvo (Left) and John Muhammad were arrested for the sniper murders of several people in the Washington, D.C., area in 2002. Lee Malvo, who was 17 years old at the time of the crimes, pled that he was so much under the influence of the older man, John Muhammad, that he, Lee Malvo, should not be held responsible for any of the shootings. Malvo was most likely in a period of identity confusion.
Left © Davis Turner-Pool/Getty Images News/Getty Images; Right © Jahi Chikwendiu-Pool/ Getty Images News/Getty Images

change majors, change social groups, explore different relationships, meet people from diverse backgrounds, spend a semester studying abroad, and learn about a variety of fields of study before committing to any ideals and values. Erikson himself emphasized exploring alternatives before making a commitment to a particular identity (1968). He held that only after considering alternatives and spending time "shopping around" was a person ready to make commitments and to spend the rest of his or her life honoring those commitments. This is what it means to say that the development of an identity takes work (Newman & Newman, 1988).

Intimacy Versus Isolation

Connecting with others, both in terms of friendships and intimate relationships, becomes a prime concern toward the latter half of the teenage years. People at this stage appear to have a need to develop relationships that are mutually satisfying and intimate. In such relationships, people grow emotionally and develop into caring, nurturing, and providing adults. For many people, this takes the form of making a commitment to one person through marriage. But many others find intimacy without the social contract of marriage. And of course, marriage is no guarantee of intimacy, as it is certainly possible to have a marriage that is devoid of intimate feelings.

Isolation is the result of a failure to find or maintain intimacy. In the United States, the percentage of married people has dropped, from 72 percent in 1970 to 59 percent in 2000. The total number of divorced persons in the United States was 4.3 million in 1970, but that number had risen to 20 million by 2000. In 2006, the number of never-married persons aged 18 and over reached 55 million. Certainly, being single has its benefits (DePaulo, 2006); however, most people report that a satisfying intimate relationship is something they desire. Failing to achieve this level of relationship is often a serious impairment to one's happiness and life satisfaction (Diener & Biswas-Diener, 2008).

Generativity Versus Stagnation

At this stage, occupying most of the adult years, the main question concerns whether or not the person has generated something that he or she really cares about in life. Often this takes the form of a career that one cares about. Other times, it is a family that has generated children that the parent cares about. Sometimes caring is achieved in a hobby or a volunteer activity that is particularly generative and that gives the person something to care about. The crisis at this stage is that when people step back and look at their adult years, they might get the feeling they are just spinning their wheels, stagnating. In other words, without anything to really care about, people may feel that their lives really don't matter, that they are just "going along to get along," and that they really don't care how it all works out. The people who don't really care about what they are doing, who are just going through the motions, are easily seen as phonies. For example, maybe you've had a teacher who really didn't care about the course material, who just came in, lectured blandly, and left. You have probably also had teachers who cared deeply about their topic, whose lectures were enlivened by their interest and enthusiasm, and who obviously drew satisfaction and meaning from their role as teacher or professor (see Professor Randy Pausch's "Last Lecture" on YouTube). This is the difference between generativity and stagnation.

Integrity Versus Despair

This is the last stage of development, occurring toward the end of life, and even this stage contains a crisis, an issue to face. This occurs when we let go of the generative role; maybe we retire from the jobs we loved, maybe the children we loved and raised leave home and start their own lives, or maybe the hobbies or volunteer activities we found so meaningful are no longer possible for us. We start the process of withdrawing from life, pulling back from our adult roles, and preparing to face death. At this stage, we look back on our lives and pass judgment—"Was it all worth doing?" "Did I accomplish most of what I wanted to do in life?" If we can take some satisfaction in our lives, then we can face the inevitability of our passing with a measure of integrity (again, see Professor Randy Pausch's "Last Lecture" on YouTube for an example of integrity at the end of life). However, if we are dissatisfied with our lives, if we wish we had more time to make changes, to repair relationships, and to right wrongs, then we experience despair. People who have a lot of regrets at the end of their lives become bitter old people who have a lot of contempt and irritation. On the other hand, if people feel that their one go-around was acceptable, that they pretty much did it all up right and have no regrets, then they face their end with integrity.

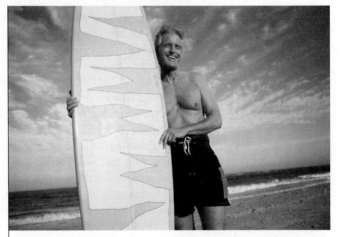

Late in life there is still one more developmental stage, one more set of questions to be faced: "Was it all worthwhile? Did I accomplish most of what I wanted out of life?" How one answers these questions determines whether the remaining time is filled with bitterness and despair or satisfaction and integrity.

© Purestock/SuperStock RF

Fredrick Nietzsche, a German philosopher, wrote a story in his book *Thus Spoke Zarathustra* (1891/1969) about a person walking on a mountain trail. Along the trail, a troll suddenly jumps out and kills the person. The person, however, is immediately reborn to the same parents, is given the same name, and lives the same life as before. Then one day, again the person is walking on a mountain trail and a troll suddenly jumps out and slays the person, who is reborn to the same parents, is given the same name as before, and lives the same life. The point, Nietzsche says, concerns what a person would think about this eternal return of our lives. If you would not want to live your life over and over again, then perhaps you should make some changes in it now, as you are living it. The person who says, "Yes, I wouldn't mind another go-around of my life, even if it were all the same," is someone who would go through Erikson's last stage and achieve integrity.

Karen Horney and a Feminist Interpretation of Psychoanalysis

Karen Horney (pronounced Horn-eye) was another early proponent of ego psychology. She was a medical doctor and a psychoanalyst at a time when most doctors and practically all psychoanalysts were men, practicing from the 1930s up to about 1950. She questioned some of the more paternalistic notions of Freudian psychoanalysis and reformulated some of the ideas to generate a more feminist perspective on personality development. For example, she reacted against Freud's notion of penis envy. Recall that Freud interpreted the phallic stage for women as a sexual conflict, starting when a little girl realizes she does not have a penis. Horney taught that the penis was a symbol of **social power** rather than an organ women actually desired. Horney wrote that girls realize, at an early age, that they are being denied social power because of their gender. She argued that girls did not really have a secret desire to become boys. Rather, she taught, girls desired the social power and preferences given to boys in the culture at that time. **Culture** is a set of shared standards for many behaviors. For example, whether a person should feel ashamed about promiscuous sexual behavior is determined by a cultural norm. Moreover, culture might contain different standards for males and females, such that girls should be ashamed if they engage in promiscuous sex, whereas boys should be proud of such behavior, with it being culturally acceptable for them even to brag about such behavior.

Horney was among the first psychoanalysts to stress the cultural and historical determinants of personality, which we explore in more detail in Chapters 16 and 17. Horney noted that many gender roles were defined by culture. For example, she coined the phrase **fear of success** to highlight a gender difference in response to competition and achievement situations. Many women, she argued, felt that if they were to succeed they would lose their friends. Consequently many women, she thought, harbored an unconscious fear of success. She held that men, on the other hand, believed they would actually gain friends by being successful and hence were not at all afraid to strive and pursue achievement. This points to an important cultural influence on behavior.

Horney stressed the point that, although biology determines sex, cultural norms are used to determine what is acceptable for a typical male and female in that culture. Partly because of Horney, today we use the terms **masculine** and **feminine** to refer to traits or roles typically associated with being male or female in a particular culture, and we refer to differences in such culturally ascribed roles and traits as **gender differences**, not *sex differences*. This distinction, so important to modern feminism, can be traced back to Karen Horney. It is unfortunate that Horney died in 1952 and did not see the progress made by the women's movement, of which she can truly be counted as an early leader.

Horney had very personal knowledge of the social and cultural forces that oppressed women in her era. Colleagues in the male-dominated profession of psychoanalysis were disapproving of her skeptical attitudes toward classical Freudian ideas. In 1941, the members of the New York Psychoanalytic Institute voted to remove Horney from her position as instructor there. Horney left immediately and went on to establish her own American Institute for Psychoanalysis, which was very successful. Indeed, she went on to develop a major reconceptualization of psychoanalysis, which stressed social influences over biology and gave special attention to interpersonal processes in the creation and maintenance of mental disorders and other problems with living. Her intriguing theories were laid out in a series of highly readable books (Horney, 1937, 1939, 1945, 1950).

Karen Horney was the first psychoanalyst to recognize that cultural forces, not biology, restrict the social roles that women may fill. Today these cultural forces are sometimes called "glass ceilings" and are increasingly being recognized as artificial barriers, relics of past cultural practices. Quite recently, one of these glass ceilings was broken when Hillary Clinton became the first woman to become the presidential nominee of a major political party in the United States.
© 승일 류/123RF RF

Emphasis on Self and the Notion of Narcissism

Ego psychology generally emphasizes the role of identity, which is experienced by the person as a sense of self. Contemporary psychoanalysts Otto Kernberg (1975) and Heinz Kohut (1977) are important contributors to the psychoanalytic conception of the role of the self in normal personality functioning and in disorders. In normal personality functioning, most people develop a stable and relatively high level of self-esteem, they have some pride in what they have so far accomplished, they have realistic ambitions for the future, and they feel that they are getting the attention and affection from others that they deserve. Most of us have a healthy level of self-esteem; we consider ourselves worthwhile, we like ourselves, and we believe that others like us as well. And most of us engage in **self-serving biases**, which refers to the common tendency for people to take credit for successes yet to deny responsibility for failure.

Some take self-esteem too far, however, trying to increase their self-worth in various problematic ways. For example, they may constantly try to appear more powerful than others, more independent, or more liked by others. This style of inflated self-admiration and constant attempts to draw attention to the self and to keep others focused on oneself is called **narcissism**. Sometimes narcissism is carried to extremes and becomes narcissistic personality disorder (see Chapter 19). However, narcissistic tendencies can be found in normal range levels, characterized as an extreme self-focus, a sense of being special, feelings of entitlement (that one deserves admiration and attention without earning it), and a constant search for others who will serve as one's private fan club.

There is a paradox, however, commonly called the **narcissistic paradox**: although a narcissist appears high in self-esteem, he or she actually has doubts about his or her worth as a person. Although the narcissist appears confident and sure of him- or herself, the person needs constant praise, reassurance, and attention from others. Although the narcissist appears to have a grandiose sense of self-importance, he or she is nevertheless very vulnerable to blows to his or her self-esteem and cannot handle criticism very well. In contemporary psychoanalysis, narcissism is seen as disturbance in the sense of self that has many implications for creating problems with living and relating to others.

An example of one problem associated with narcissism is that when narcissists are criticized or challenged, they may behave aggressively, trying to achieve some respect by attacking or belittling their critics. The *Diagnostic and Statistical Manual IV* (APA, 1994) suggests that persons with narcissistic personality disorder can become at risk for violence following blows to their self-esteem, such as getting reprimanded at work or having been left by a spouse. This tendency toward violence in response to criticism was illustrated in a laboratory study conducted by psychologists Brad Bushman and Roy Baumeister (1998). The subjects came to the laboratory and wrote a short essay on a topic given to them. Another person then commented on the essays they had just written, providing strong criticism of the subjects' opinions. Later in the experiment, the subjects were given the opportunity to play a computer game with their critic and were allowed to "blast" their opponent with loud bursts of noise during the game; that is, subjects could distract their opponents with irritating blasts of noise during the competition. The narcissistic subjects who had been insulted blasted the critic much more aggressively than did either the non-narcissistic persons or the narcissistic persons who had not received criticism. This finding suggests that narcissism can lead to aggression when the narcissist is provoked or criticized. People with secure and normally healthy levels of self-esteem, however, do not become distressed and aggressive when insulted (Rhodenwalt & Morf, 1998).

Exercise

A questionnaire measure of narcissism. The following items are from the Narcissistic Personality Inventory (NPI) (Raskin & Hall, 1979).

1. I think I am a special person.   True   or   False
2. I expect a great deal from other people.   True   or   False
3. I am envious of other people's good fortune.   True   or   False
4. I will never be satisfied until I get all that I deserve.   True   or   False
5. I really like to be the center of attention.   True   or   False

In one interesting study of narcissism, it was found that the number of first-person pronouns a person used in an essay *(I, mine, me)* was correlated positively with narcissism scores (Emmons, 1987). In another study it was found that when given the opportunity to watch themselves on videotape or to watch a tape of someone else, the narcissists spent more time watching the tape of themselves (Robins & John, 1997). This study also showed that narcissists rate their performance on the videotape much more positively than it is rated by others, implying an inflated sense of their own abilities.

In sum, narcissism is not the same as having high self-esteem (Brown & Ziegler-Hill, 2004). Studies have confirmed the theoretical notions that narcissists are preoccupied with self, are vulnerable to criticism and blows to their self-worth, and respond to such challenges with anger and aggression. Although narcissists appear to have high self-esteem, their internal or private self representations are fragile and vulnerable. Clearly, an important notion from contemporary psychoanalytic thought is that one's internal representation of self plays an important role in how one interacts with and reacts to the social environment. In the next section, you see how contemporary psychoanalysis also focuses on the internal representation of other persons and how this influences social interactions.

Object Relations Theory

Other changes to Freud's original ideas have been so sweeping that one new approach drops the term "analytic" altogether: object relations theory. Recall that Freud emphasized sexuality in the development of personality. He viewed the adult personality as the result of how people accommodate the inevitable conflicts between their desires for sexual pleasure from various body parts and the constraints of parents, social institutions, and civilized society. Freud's emphasis on sexuality has been completely rethought by recent generations of psychoanalysts. This new movement—**object relations theory**—emphasizes social relationships and their origins in childhood.

Consider the Oedipal phase of development. Freud stressed the sexual attraction for the parent of the opposite sex, and the accompanying fear, rage, anger, and jealousy toward the parent of the same sex. Psychoanalysts after Freud looked at the same childhood situation and saw, instead, the importance of forming social relationships to the developing personality. Later analysts emphasized not sexuality but, instead, the development of meaningful social relationships as the task that occurs at this stage of development. After all, the first persons with whom we have a meaningful relationship are our parents.

Although object relations theory has several versions, which differ from each other in emphasis, all the versions have at their core a set of basic assumptions. One assumption is that the internal wishes, desires, and urges of the child are not as important as his or her developing relationships with significant external others, particularly parents. A second assumption is that the others, particularly the mother, become **internalized** by the child in the form of mental objects. The child creates an unconscious mental representation of the mother. The child, thus, has an unconscious "mother" within, to whom he or she can relate. This allows the child to have a relationship with this internalized object, even in the absence of the real mother—hence the term *object relations* theory.

The relationship object the child internalizes is based on his or her developing relationship with the mother. If things are going well between the mother and the infant, the infant internalizes a caring, nurturant, trustworthy mother object. This image then forms the fundamentals for how children come to view others with whom they develop subsequent relationships. If the child internalizes a mother object who is not trustworthy, perhaps because the real mother has left the child alone too often or has not fed the child regularly, then the child might have difficulty learning to trust other people later in life. Children who are traumatically separated from their parents during childhood—who experience an attachment disruption—often become adults with distinct personality problems (Malone, Westen, & Levendosky, 2011). The first social attachments that the infant develops form the templates for all meaningful relationships in the future. This is consistent with the classic psychoanalytic idea that the "child is father to the man," in the sense that what develops in childhood determines the outcomes in adulthood. However, in the neo-analytic case, it is early childhood experience with caregivers, especially attachment to the primary caregiver, that determines adult personality.

Early Childhood Attachment

Work on early childhood attachment has drawn on a couple of lines of research in developmental psychology. The first line of research was the work by Harry Harlow and others on infant monkeys. Harlow's well-known experiments involved taking infant monkeys away from their real mothers and raising them with models of mother monkeys made of wire or

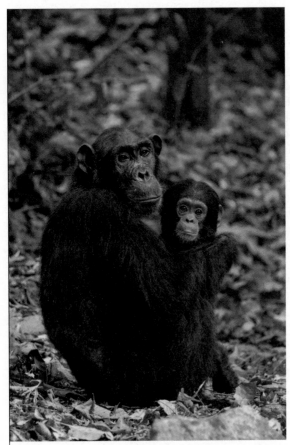

The strong bond between infant and primary caregiver, called attachment, is important in the development of all primates, including humans.

© *IMPALASTOCK/iStockphoto/Getty Images RF*

cloth. These fake mothers did not provide the grooming, cuddling, holding, or social contact of the real mothers. The infant monkeys raised with the fake mothers developed problems in adolescence and adulthood, growing into adults that were socially insecure, that were generally anxious, and that did not develop normal sexual relations as adults (Harlow, 1958; Harlow & Suomi, 1971; Harlow & Zimmerman, 1959). Moreover, the infant monkeys preferred their real mothers to the fake mothers, and they preferred the cloth mother to the wire mother when given the choice. Harlow concluded that **attachment** between infant and primary caregiver required physical contact with a warm and responsive mother and that it is vitally important to the psychological development of the infant.

Attachment to the mother or caregiver during the first six months of life appears to be crucial to all primates, including humans. Attachment in the human infant begins when he or she develops a preference for people over objects. For example, the child prefers to look at a human face rather than at a toy. Then the preference begins to narrow to familiar persons, so that the child prefers to see people he or she has seen before, compared with strangers. And finally the preference narrows even further, so that the child prefers the mother or primary caregiver over anyone else.

The ways in which young children develop attachments to their parents and caregivers was the primary topic of research for British psychologist John Bowlby (1969a, 1969b, 1980, 1988). Bowlby focused on the attachment relationship with the mother and how that relationship meets the needs of the infant for protection, nurturance, and support. Bowlby studied what happens when this attachment relationship is temporarily broken, as when the mother has to leave the infant alone for a short time. He noticed that some infants seem to trust that the mother will return and provide uninterrupted care—these infants are happy when the mother returns. Other infants, in contrast, react negatively to separation and become agitated and distressed when the mother leaves. They can be calmed only by the return of the mother. Bowlby said these infants experience **separation anxiety**. Bowlby also observed a third type of infants, who seem to become depressed when their mothers leave. Even when the mother returns, these infants seem to remain detached from, or angry at, their mothers.

Psychologist Mary Ainsworth and her colleagues developed a 20-minute procedure for studying separation anxiety—a procedure used for identifying differences among children in how they react to separation from their mothers. This is called the **strange situation procedure**. In this procedure, a mother and her baby enter the laboratory room, which is like a comfortable living room. The mother sits down, and the child is free to explore the toys and other things in the room. After a few minutes, a stranger, an unfamiliar but friendly adult, enters the room. The mother then gets up and leaves the baby alone with this unfamiliar adult. After a few minutes, the mother returns to the room and the stranger leaves. The mother is alone with the baby for several more minutes. All the while, the infant is being videotaped, so that his or her reactions can later be analyzed.

Across many studies, Ainsworth and her colleagues (e.g., Ainsworth, 1979; Ainsworth, Bell, & Stayton, 1972) found essentially the same three patterns of behavior noted by Bowlby. One group of infants, called **securely attached,** stoically endured the separation and went about exploring the room, waiting patiently or even approaching the stranger and sometimes wanting to be held by the stranger. When the mothers returned, these infants were glad to see them, typically interacted with them for a while, then went back to exploring the new environment. They seemed confident the mothers would return, hence the term *secure*. This group of infants was the largest of the three (66 percent fell into this group).

The second group, called the **avoidantly attached** group, consisted of infants who avoided the mothers when they returned. The infants in this group typically seemed unfazed when the mothers left and typically did not give them much attention when they returned, as if aloof from their mothers. Approximately 20 percent of the babies fell into this category.

Ainsworth called the third category of infant response to separation the **ambivalently attached** group. The infants in this group were very anxious about the mothers' leaving. Many started crying and protesting vigorously before the mothers even got out of the room. When the mothers were gone, these infants were difficult to calm. On the mothers' return, however, the infants behaved ambivalently. Their behavior showed both anger and a desire to be close to the mothers; they approached their mothers but then resisted by squirming and fighting against being held.

Mothers of babies in these three groups appear to behave differently. According to subsequent research, reviewed by Ainsworth and Bowlby (1991), mothers of securely attached infants provide more affection and stimulation to their babies, and are generally more responsive, than mothers of infants in the other groups. These studies have provided clear evidence that a caregiver's responsiveness to infants leads to a more harmonious relationship later in life between the child and parents. For example, in one study, responsiveness to infant crying in the early months of life was associated with less (not more) crying at 1 year of age. Although this finding was greeted with disbelief at first, especially by learning theorists, it eventually influenced recommendations for parenting practices (Bretherton & Main, 2000).

Mothers of babies from both the ambivalent and the avoidant groups tend to be less attentive to their children, less responsive to their needs. Such mothers appear to be less in tune or less engaged with their babies. Some children react to these less responsive mothers by becoming angry themselves (the ambivalent infants) or by trying to become emotionally detached (the avoidant infants). Fraley, Roisman, and Haltigan (2013) showed that maternal insensitivity assessed when the child was 3 years old was related to lower social competence and academic skills when the child was 15 years old. Although there may be alternative explanations for these findings, they are nevertheless consistent with the notion that the lack of maternal responsiveness can have negative childhood outcomes.

These early experiences and reactions of the infant to the parents, particularly the mother, become what Bowlby called **working models** for later adult relationships. These working models are internalized in the form of unconscious expectations about relationships. If children experience that they are not wanted, or that their mothers cannot be trusted to take care of them, then they may internalize the expectation that probably no one else wants them either. On the other hand, if children's needs are met, and they are confident that their parents really love them, then they will expect that others will find them lovable as well (Bowlby, 1988). These expectations about relationships, which are developed in our first contacts with our caregivers, are thought to become part of our unconscious and thereby exert a powerful influence on our adult relationships.

We might think that the "strange situation" paradigm is useful only for thinking about how children cope with the temporary separation from their caregivers. However, some researchers are studying an adult analogue of this paradigm, where married couples are temporarily separated by life circumstances (Cafferty et al., 1994). These researchers conducted a longitudinal study on members of the National Guard and other military reserve units who were separated from their spouses and deployed overseas during Operation Desert Storm. They found that attachment styles predicted individual differences in emotional reactions to the separation (securely attached persons were not as distressed) and to postreunion marital adjustments (ambivalently attached persons had the most difficulty). When adult marital relationships are temporarily disrupted, it may be that the persons in those relationships will react and adjust in ways that resemble how they coped with their earliest separations, both of which may be influenced by the style of attachment they developed early in life with their primary caregiver.

Adult Relationships

Research on attachment has tested object relations ideas by examining whether the attachment style developed in childhood is related to later adult relationship styles. In 2010, an entire issue of the *Journal of Social and Personal Relationships* was dedicated to research on how childhood attachment styles are related to adolescent and adult relationships (Shaver, 2012). In a study that started this line of research, psychologists Cindy Hazan and Philip Shaver (1987) showed that there are patterns of adult relationships that look similar to the secure, avoidant, and ambivalent childhood attachment patterns. In the adult **secure relationship style**, the person has few problems developing satisfying friendships and relationships. Secure people trust others and develop bonds with them. The adult **avoidant relationship style** is characterized by difficulty in learning to trust others. Avoidant adults remain suspicious of the motives of others, and they are afraid of making commitments. They are afraid of depending on others because they anticipate being disappointed, being abandoned, or being separated. Finally, the adult **ambivalent relationship style** is characterized by vulnerability and uncertainty about relationships. Ambivalent adults become overly dependent and demanding on their partners and friends. They display high levels of neediness in their relationships. They are high maintenance, in the sense that they need constant reassurance and attention.

Psychologist Philip Shaver and his colleagues have shown that there is a positive correlation between the parent–infant attachment style and the later relationship style developed in adulthood. In one study, for example, adults with an avoidant relationship style more frequently reported that their parents had unhappy marriages compared to adults with a secure relationship style (Brennan & Shaver, 1993). The adults with a secure relationship style, on the other hand, tended to report coming from a trusting and supportive family, with parents who were happily married. Those with an avoidant relationship style tended to report that their family members were aloof and distant, and that they did not feel very much warmth or trust either from or toward their parents.

You may recall from Chapter 4, we said that personality dimensions rarely were types; that people do not come in categories, but are best represented by scores along a dimension, usually a normal-curve shaped dimension. Yet in the attachment style area, there are three categories that people are put into: secure, avoidant, ambivalent. Are attachment styles really categories or types? Recent research shows how attachment style can be better represented by underlying dimensions, for example, degrees of security, degrees of avoidance, degrees of ambivalence (Fraley, Hudson, Heffernan, & Segal, 2015). Indeed, a measure based on dimensions of attachment styles was a better fit to real data than a

Exercise ?

Determining which adult attachment style a person has can be accomplished by having them report which style is most like them. Consider the following statements, and choose which is most descriptive of you:

1. I am typically comfortable with others and find it easy to become close friends with people. I can easily come to rely on others and enjoy it when they rely on me. I don't worry about being left out or abandoned and find it easy to let others get close to me.

2. I am sometimes tense when I get too close to others. I don't like to trust other people too much, plus I don't like it when people have to depend on me for something. It makes me anxious when people get close or want me to make an emotional commitment to them. People often want me to be more personal and intimate than I feel like being.

3. In relationships, I often worry that the other person does not really want to stay with me or that he or she doesn't really love me. I often wish that my friends would share more and be more of a confidante than they seem willing to be. Maybe I scare people away with my readiness to become close and make them the center of my world.

The first description is associated with a secure relationship style, the second with an avoidant relationship style, and the third with an ambivalent relationship style. It is possible that you have different styles with different people, or that none of these descriptions applies perfectly to your relationships.

measure based on categorical distinctions. This new approach to thinking about and measuring attachment styles as dimensions will likely have a large impact on how research is done, and on how psychologists think about and measure attachment style.

A dominant theme of attachment theory is that a person's romantic attachments in adulthood will be a reflection of his or her attachment patterns in the past, especially with their earliest relationships (for a recent review, see Fraley & Roisman, 2015). Representations of the earliest relationships can serve as prototypes for later relationships, with the early experiences retaining their influential role in attachment behaviors throughout the life span. The psychologist Chris Fraley has published meta-analyses of studies examining the long-term influence of attachment styles (Fraley, 2002a, 2002b). After reviewing a great deal of research, and evaluating different models of change and stability, Fraley concludes that the data are consistent with a moderate degree of stability in attachment security from infancy to adulthood. His best estimate of the correlation between early attachment security and attachment security at any later point in time is approximately .39, which can be described as significantly larger than zero, but moderate in magnitude. In a study that followed people for a year and assessed adult attachment style, peoples' attachment style was found to be fairly stable over that time period, about as stable as each of the Big Five personality traits (Fraley et al., 2012). Fraley has published an online quiz that people can take to assess the similarity among their attachment styles with different people in their lives (see www.yourpersonality.net/relstructures/).

Adult relationship styles may be most important for understanding romantic relationships. What do people look for in a romantic relationship? What do people expect from their romantic partners? How do people cope with abandonment by and separation

Object relations theorists believe that the characteristics and quality of adult relationships are determined, in part, by relationships experienced in early childhood.

Left © Purestock/SuperStock RF; right © Alexander Benz/Purestock/SuperStock RF

from their romantic partners either real or imagined? Research suggests that individuals with different attachment styles will answer these questions very differently from each other (e.g., Hazan & Shaver, 1987). Those with an avoidant attachment style tend to shun romance, believing that real love is rare and never lasts. They fear intimacy and rarely develop deep emotional commitments. They tend not to be very supportive of their partners, at least not emotionally.

Adults with an ambivalent attachment style tend to have frequent, but short-lived, romantic relationships. They fall in and out of love easily but rarely say that they are happy with their relationships. They develop a sort of desperation in their adult relationships and show fear of losing their partners. Their focus is often on keeping the other happy, and so they are quick to compromise, to change themselves for the sake of avoiding conflict with the other. As you might guess, ambivalent adults report that being separated from their partners is very stressful.

Adults with a secure attachment style can be separated from their partners without stress, just as secure attachment children can remain calm when their mothers leave the room. Secure adults are generally more warm and supportive in their romantic relationships, and their partners report more satisfaction with the relationship than do the partners of avoidant or ambivalent adults (Hazan & Shaver, 1994). Secure adults are also more likely to give emotional support to their partners when it is needed. Secure adults seek support when they need it more than do ambivalent or avoidant adults. In general, secure adults do a good job of navigating through the treacherous waters of adult romantic relationships. A study by Fraley and colleagues (Holland, Fraley, & Roisman, 2012) showed that the effects of attachment style on romantic relationships are more observable after the relationship has been developing for awhile, with stronger effects observed one year into the relationship than at the very start of the relationship. It takes awhile to really get to know someone.

An interesting study by psychologist Jeff Simpson illustrates the working of attachment styles in adult relationships (Simpson et al., 2002). In this study heterosexual dating couples served as subjects. The couple was told that the male would undergo a stressful and unpleasant experience as part of the experiment. They were separated and the male was taken to a room where an experimenter recorded his pulse while saying the following:

> In the next few minutes you are going to be exposed to a situation and set of experimental procedures that arouse considerable anxiety and distress in most people. Due to the nature of these procedures, I cannot tell you any more at this moment. Of course, I'll answer any questions or concerns you have after the experiment is over. (p. 603)

The purpose of this statement was to make the male subject anxious. Moreover, he was taken to a darkened, windowless room that contained some polygraphs. The experimenter remarked that the equipment was "not quite ready yet" and that the subject would have to wait a few minutes before the "stress phase" could start. Meanwhile, the female was told that her partner was going to be involved in a "stress and performance session" that would start in 5 or 10 minutes. The couple was brought together to wait, and during this time they were unobtrusively videotaped for 5 minutes. After 5 minutes the experimenter entered the room and told the subjects the experiment was over, explained the purpose of the experiment, and told the subjects that they could erase the videotape if they so desired (none did).

The experimenters coded the videotape for a number of behaviors. Mostly they were interested in the degree to which the women offered support to their partners, and the degree to which the men asked for support from their partners. Prior to the start of the experiment, the experimenters used an interview method to assess childhood recollections of experiences with parents and other attachment figures. From these interviews the experimenters rated the degree to which each subject was avoidantly or securely attached to his or her primary caregivers in early childhood.

Results showed that women who had avoidant attachment experiences with their parents were significantly less likely to offer support and encouragement to their male partners, even if the male asked for that. The securely attached women did provide support if the partner asked for it, but provided less if he did not ask for it. This is a contingent pattern of support, what some researchers consider ideal in relationships (George & Solomon, 1996). Regarding help seeking from the men, none of the attachment style variables predicted this behavior in this study. However, this was not a very intense or long-lasting stressor. Studies of real, intense, and chronic stress (persons under missile attacks, persons undergoing combat training) have found that attachment styles do relate to help seeking (Mikulincer, Florian, & Weller, 1993; Mikulincer & Florian, 1995). Specifically, secure men and women seek support from others when distressed, whereas avoidantly attached persons try to distance themselves from others, want to spend time alone when under stress, and distract themselves from the stressors. When stress is severe or chronic, it appears that a person's attachment style might relate to her or his pattern of support seeking.

Individual differences in attachment style may have implications beyond those for romantic relationships. Any area of life that involves closeness, getting along with others, confiding in others, and exploring relationships might be negotiated differently by persons with different attachment styles (Elliot & Reis, 2003). Attachment theory has been applied to understanding relationships between twins (Fraley & Tancredy, 2012), relationships with pets (Zilcha-Mano, Mikulincer, & Shaver, 2012), and even one's relationship with one's God (Granqvist et al., 2012). Of particular interest, how one was parented as a child may influence how one, later in life, parents one's own children. Szepsenwol et al. (2015) showed that this effect was strongest for men with men who developed an insecure attachment style when they were children going on to develop more negative and unsupportive parenting style when they became parents. Karantzas and Simpson (2015) extend the implications of attachment style theory to the situation where adult children become caregivers to their own aging parents, a situation that has been likened to role reversal; the children becoming parents to the parents. Any life situation that involves close, caring relationships may be impacted by how it went with the very first relationship that was experienced in life.

We want to close this chapter on a hopeful note with the answer to the following question: If a person develops a particular childhood attachment style, is he or she destined to live out the adult version of that style? This important question has been the topic of much theoretical debate and empirical research (Cassidy & Shaver, 1999; Simpson & Rholes, 1998). Attachment theorists believe that even the poorest childhood experiences with relationships can be overcome. Ainsworth and Bowlby (1991) argued that children were not necessarily damaged forever because of unfortunate parenting experiences in infancy. They felt that subsequent positive experiences could compensate for earlier negative relationships. Despite a bad start in life, a person exposed to a loving, nurturant relationship as an adult can revise his or her working model of object relations. If the relationship is positive and supportive enough, the person could internalize a new mental version of relationships, one that was more secure and trusting, with positive expectations about how people would relate to the person (Fraley, 2007).

SUMMARY AND EVALUATION

In this chapter, we explored alternative versions of some of Freud's original ideas. We began with an evaluation of repressed memories, examining a case in which the recalled memory turned out not to be true, at least as determined in a court of law. This case should not put doubt on the possibility of real cases of abuse and trauma causing memories to be forgotten or repressed. Indeed, such cases do exist and conform to the notion that traumatic experiences can be pushed out of consciousness. However, the material in this chapter is meant to lead you to a more balanced approach to the topic of repressed memories. Although repressed memories can occur, not all cases are truly of forgotten memories. Some memories can be implanted by well-meaning therapists and others interrogating a subject about an event. We also discussed how to discriminate real from false memories. The crucial element is corroboration, finding someone who can support the subject's version of the remembered event.

The view of repressed memories also highlights a more contemporary version of the unconscious. Although most modern cognitive psychologists believe in the unconscious, they do not believe in the motivated version of the unconscious proposed by Freud. Certainly, material can get into the mind without conscious experience, as through subliminal perception, but that material does not have the kind of sweeping motivational effects suggested by Freud.

Another reconstruction of Freud's theory concerns the emphasis on the role of the ego relative to the id. This is in stark contrast to Freud's emphasis on aggressive and sexual id urges as the twin engines powering psychic life. We discussed two proponents of ego psychology. The first, Erik Erikson, was well known for his alternative theory of personality development, which differed from Freud's in several important ways, including an emphasis on social tasks and an extension of development through the entire life span. A second important figure in ego psychology was Karen Horney, who was among the first psychoanalysts to consider the role of culture and social roles as central features in personality development. Horney also started a feminist reinterpretation of Freud's theories, which continues to this day. Ego psychology also generated an interest in the development of sense of self and the protection of self through various strategies.

Object relations theory is another major new development in this area, having been called the most important theoretical development in psychoanalysis since Freud's death. The term *object relations* is used to refer to enduring patterns of behavior in relationships with intimate others, as well as to the emotional, cognitive, and motivational processes that generate those patterns of behavior. The theory is about how relationship behaviors are determined by mental representations laid down in childhood through experiences with caregivers. This theory began with studies of attachment between children and primary caregivers—typically, mothers. This bond may set a pattern that continues into adulthood. Also important are the experiences the growing child has with the relationship he or she observes between the parents. This is also internalized in the form of a mental representation for how people get along and what is appropriate behavior in a relationship.

Parts and versions of Freud's psychoanalytic theory are alive and well today. However, instead of focusing on unconscious conflicts over id urges, contemporary psychoanalysts are more likely to focus on interpersonal patterns of behavior and the emotions and motives that accompany those. Instead of seeing personality as the result of a sequence of sexual conflicts with the parents, contemporary psychoanalysts are more likely to see personality as the result of solving a series of social crises and the ensuing movement toward increasingly more mature forms of relating to others. And, finally, unlike much of classical psychoanalytic theory, which was based on one man's views, much of contemporary psychoanalytic theory is connected to empirical studies and corroborated observations of many persons working to improve and expand on some of Freud's lasting contributions.

KEY TERMS

false memories 300
imagination inflation effect 301
confirmatory bias 301
constructive memory 302
spreading activation 302
cognitive unconscious 306
motivated unconscious 306
subliminal perception 306
priming 306
id psychology 307
ego psychology 307
identity crisis 307
Erikson's eight stages of development 308
psychosocial conflicts 309

stage model of development 309
developmental crisis 309
identity confusion 311
rite of passage 311
negative identity 311
identity foreclosure 311
moratorium 311
social power 314
culture 314
fear of success 314
masculine 314
feminine 314
gender differences 314
self-serving bias 315
narcissism 315

narcissistic paradox 315
object relations theory 317
internalized 317
attachment 318
separation anxiety 318
strange situation procedure 318
securely attached 319
avoidantly attached 319
ambivalently attached 319
working models 319
secure relationship style 320
avoidant relationship style 320
ambivalent relationship style 320

Motives and Personality

11

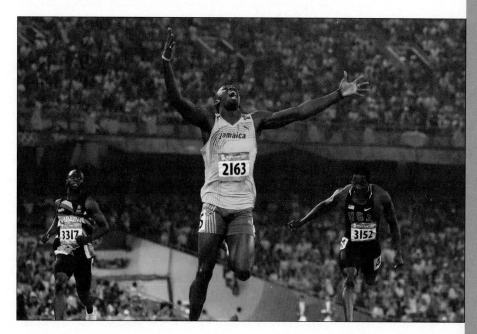

Olympic Gold-medalist Michael Johnson (on the right in above photo), who uses different strategies to motivate himself before a 200-meter race and a 400-meter race.
© Mark Dadswell/Getty Images Sport/Getty Images

One hot August night in 1996, a gun went off in Atlanta. It started the final of the 200-meter Olympic race. Michael Johnson, who had won a gold medal in the 400-meter race just a few days earlier, exploded from the starting blocks. Would he become the first man in history to win both the 400- and 200-meter races at the Olympics? Michael stumbled slightly at the start of the race but soon assumed the upright style that had come to characterize his running technique. As he went around the turn, his trademark golden shoes flashing, it became obvious to the crowd that he was running for more than just the gold medal. As Michael widened his lead over his opponents, people knew they were witnessing something special. Michael finished a full 5 meters ahead of his nearest competitor, and as he crossed the finish line, the timer read 19.32 seconds. People who knew the significance of that time, including Michael himself, gasped in disbelief. He had beaten the previous world record, which he had set earlier, by almost three-tenths of a second, a remarkable gap in short-distance running.

How did Michael motivate himself to set a world record in the 200-meter race and win a gold medal in the 400-meter race? The 400- and 200-meter races are very different, according to runners. In the 400-meter race, the runners can be strategic and take some time to plan a tactic. The 200, on the other hand, demands that the runners run flat-out and aggressively.

Before the 400-meter race, Michael reportedly listens to jazz on his headset; before the 200, he listens to gangsta rap. He tries to make himself feel aggressive before the 200-meter race. He tries to get into what he calls the "danger zone."

In warming up for the 200-meter race at Atlanta, Michael pulled on a T-shirt that read DANGER ZONE. "Now I have to think about the 200," he said. "I've got to get into the danger zone. I've got to get more aggressive." He approached the 200-meter race with a fighting instinct, taking the offense by running not just to beat his competitors but to beat them badly. As Michael approached the finish line in the 200-meter race, the aggression could be seen in his face, an expression that looked as if he could assault his opponents. The only thing he assaulted, however, was the world record. He had just motivated himself to run faster than any other living person.[1]

We saw in Chapter 1 that personality psychologists ask, "Why do people do what they do?" Motivational psychologists phrase the question a bit differently—"What do they want?" All personality psychologists seek to explain behavior. Personality psychologists interested in motivation, however, look specifically for a desire or motive that propels people to do the things they do (Cantor, 1990).

In this chapter, we cover some of the major theories on human motivation, and we examine some research findings on these theories. Some theories that we will look at are quite different from each other, such as the theories of Henry Murray and Abraham Maslow. In fact, most texts in personality cover these two theories in different chapters. However, all the theories we examine have two features in common. First, all view personality as consisting of a few general motives, which all people have to various degrees. Second, these motives operate mainly through mental processes, either inside or outside of awareness, generating an intrapsychic influence on a person's behavior (King, 1995).

Basic Concepts

Motives are internal states that arouse and direct behavior toward specific objects or goals. A motive is often caused by a deficit, a lack of something; for example, if a person has not eaten for many hours, he or she is motivated by hunger. Motives differ from each other in both type and amount. Hunger differs from thirst, for example, and both of these differ from the motive to achieve and excel. Motives differ in intensity, depending on the person and his or her circumstances. For example, the strength of the hunger motive varies considerably, depending on whether a person has merely skipped a meal or has not eaten for several days. Also, motives are often based on **needs**, states of tension within a person. As a need is satisfied, the state of tension is reduced. The need to eat creates the motive of hunger. The motive of hunger in turn causes the person to seek out food, to think about food constantly, and perhaps even to see food in objects not normally thought of as food. For example, a hungry person gazing at the sky might exclaim, "Wow, that cloud looks just like a hamburger!" Motives propel people to perceive, think, and act in specific ways that satisfy the need. Figure 11.1 illustrates the relation between needs and motives. As you will see in the section on self-actualization later in this chapter, some motives are not based on deficit needs, but rather are based on growth needs.

---

[1]In the 2000 Olympics at Sydney, Michael Johnson again won the gold medal in the 400-meter race but had to drop out of competition in the 200-meter race. Johnson subsequently retired from competition. However, he remains the only male athlete in history to have won both the 200- and 400-meter events at the same Olympics.

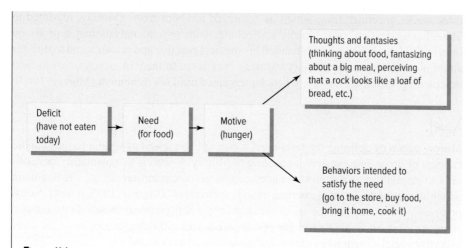

Figure 11.1

Deficits lead to a need, which leads to a motive to satisfy that need, either in reality, by fostering specific actions, or in fantasy, by creating thoughts that are satisfying.

Motives belong in the intrapsychic domain for several reasons. First, researchers who study motives have stressed the importance of *internal* psychological needs and urges that propel people to think, perceive, and act in certain predictable ways. Motives can be unconscious, in the sense that the person does not know explicitly what he or she wants. Just as people may not be fully aware of why they engage in particular fantasies, they may not be consciously aware of what compels them to act in certain ways. This similarity leads to another feature shared by psychologists interested in motives and other intrapsychic constructs—the reliance on projective techniques. Motive psychologists, like psychoanalysts, believe that fantasies, free associations, and responses to projective techniques reveal the unconscious motivation behind many thoughts, feelings, and behaviors (Barenbaum & Winter, 2003).

Motive psychologists also share some core ideas with dispositional psychologists, whose work we covered in Part 1 of this book. Like dispositional psychologists, motive psychologists stress that (1) people differ from one another in the type and strength of their motives; (2) these differences are measurable; (3) these differences cause or are associated with important life outcomes, such as business success or marital satisfaction; (4) differences among people in the relative amounts of various motives are stable over time; and (5) motives may provide one answer to the question "Why do people do what they do?" The motive approach can be thought of as a halfway point between the intrapsychic domain and the dispositional domain (Winter et al., 1998). We will discuss motives as we examine the intrapsychic domain because of the view that motives exist within the psyche and can operate outside of conscious awareness to affect everyday behaviors, thoughts, and feelings.

One of the first researchers to develop a modern theory of motivation was Henry Murray, a psychologist active in research from the 1930s through the 1960s. The path that ultimately led Murray to a career in psychology was decidedly untraditional. He went to medical school, became a physician, and interned in surgery. Murray then pursued research in embryology, followed by a PhD in biochemistry from Cambridge University. While studying in England, Murray went to Zurich during spring break in 1925, to visit the famous psychoanalyst Carl Jung. He met with Jung every day for three weeks, meetings from which he "emerged a reborn man" (Murray, reprinted in Shneidman, 1981, p. 54). Murray's encounter with psychoanalysis had a profound impact on him, leading him to abandon his medical practice and research and to turn his attention entirely to psychology. Murray was then trained in psychoanalysis and accepted a position at Harvard, where he remained until his retirement (Murray, 1967).

Need

Murray began by defining the term *need,* a concept he viewed as similar to the analytic concept of drive. In a nutshell, according to Murray, a need is a "potentiality or readiness to respond in a certain way under certain given circumstances. . . . It is a noun which stands for the fact that a certain trend is apt to recur" (Murray, 1938, p. 124). Needs organize perception, guiding us to see what we want (or need) to see. For example, someone who has a high need for power, a need to influence others, may see even everyday social situations as opportunities to boss others around.

A need also organizes action by compelling a person to do what is necessary to fulfill the need. A person who has a need to achieve, for example, often makes sacrifices and works hard at the task in which he or she wants to excel. Murray believed that needs referred to states of tension and that satisfying the need reduces the tension. According to Murray, however, it was the *process* of reducing tension that the person found satisfying, not the tensionless state per se. Murray believed that people might actually seek to increase tension (e.g., by going on a roller-coaster ride or viewing a horror movie) in order to experience the pleasure of reducing that tension (i.e., to end the roller-coaster ride or the horror movie).

Based on his research with the Office for Strategic Services (a forerunner of the Central Intelligence Agency), Murray proposed a list of fundamental human needs, some of which are described in Table 11.1. Each need is associated with (1) a specific desire or intention, (2) a particular set of emotions, and (3) specific action tendencies, and each need can be described with trait names. Consider the need for affiliation, which is the desire to win and maintain associations with people. The primary set of emotions associated with this need are interpersonal warmth, cheerfulness, and cooperativeness, and the associated action tendencies are accepting people, spending time with others, and making efforts to maintain contact with others. The associated traits that characterize people with a strong need for affiliation are attributes such as agreeableness, friendliness, loyalty, and goodwill.

Murray believed that each person had a unique **hierarchy of needs**. An individual's various needs can be thought of as existing at different levels of strength—for instance, a person might have a high need for dominance, an average need for affiliation, and a low need for achievement. Each need interacts with the various other needs within each person. This interaction is what makes the concept of motive **dynamic**. The term *dynamic* is used to refer to the mutual influence of forces within a person—in this case, the interaction of various motives within a person. To return to our person with a high need for dominance, it would make a big difference in her overall behavior if her need for dominance were accompanied with a high or low need for affiliation. If her high need for dominance were coupled with a high need for affiliation (e.g., a strong desire to develop and maintain relationships), then she would most likely develop the social and leadership skills to make others comfortable with her dominance. If her high need for dominance were combined with a weak need for affiliation, in contrast, then she might simply exercise power over others without regard to their feelings. She might impress others as argumentative, quarrelsome, and just plain disagreeable and bossy.

Table 11.1 A Brief Description of Several of Murray's Needs, Organized into Five Higher-Level Categories

Ambition Needs

- **Achievement:** To master, manipulate, or organize others, objects, or ideas. To accomplish difficult tasks, and to do this as rapidly and independently as possible. To overcome obstacles and excel. To surpass rivals by exercising talent.

- **Exhibition:** To be seen and heard, to be the center of attention. To make an impression on others. To excite, fascinate, entertain, intrigue, amuse, entice, or amaze others.

- **Order:** To put things in orderly arrangement, to desire cleanliness, organization, balance, neatness, and precision.

Needs to Defend Status

- **Dominance:** To seek to influence or direct the behavior of others by persuasion, command, suggestion, or seduction. To control one's environment, particularly the social environment. To restrain or prohibit others.

Needs Related to Social Power

- **Abasement:** To accept injury, criticism, and blame. To submit passively to external force, to resign oneself to fate. To admit inferiority, error, or wrongdoing. To confess and atone and seek pain and misfortune.

- **Aggression:** To overcome opposition forcefully. To avenge an injury. To attack, injure, or kill another. To forcefully punish or oppose another.

- **Autonomy:** To shake off restraint, break out of confines. To get free, to resist coercion and restriction. To avoid being domineered. To be free to act according to one's wishes and to remain unattached.

- **Blame-avoidance:** To avoid humiliation at all costs. To avoid situations that may lead to embarrassment or belittlement. To refrain from action because of fear of failure or worry over the scorn, derision, or indifference from others.

Social Affection Needs

- **Affiliation:** To enjoy cooperation or reciprocal interaction with similar others. To draw near to others. To please and win affection of those you like. To remain loyal to friends.

- **Nurturance:** To take care of others in need, to give sympathy and gratify the needs of helpless others, such as a child, or someone who is weak, disabled, inexperienced, infirm, humiliated, lonely, dejected, or confused. To assist persons in danger. To help, support, console, protect, comfort, nurse, feed, and heal others.

- **Succor:** To receive aid from others. To have one's needs gratified by another, to be nursed, supported, protected, advised, indulged, loved, and consoled. To always have a supporter or a devoted protector.

Source: Adapted from *Explorations in personality,* by J. H. Murray, New York, Oxford University Press.

Press

Another important contribution of Murray to personality psychology was a specific way of thinking about the environment. According to Murray, elements in the environment affected a person's needs. For example, a person with a high need for affiliation might be sensitive to the social aspects of his or her environment, such as how many people are present, whether they are interacting, and whether they look approachable and outgoing. Murray used the term **press** to refer to need-relevant aspects of the environment. A person's need for affiliation, for example, won't affect that person's behavior without an appropriate environmental press (such as the presence of friendly people). People with a high need for affiliation would be more likely to notice other people, and to see more opportunities for interaction with others, than someone with a low need for affiliation.

Murray also introduced the notion that there is a so-called real environment (which he called **alpha press**, or objective reality) and a perceived environment (called **beta press**, or reality as it is perceived). In any given situation, what one person sees may be different from what other people see. Consider what might happen if two people are walking down the street and a third person approaches and smiles at each of them. One person who is high on the need for affiliation might see the smile as a sign of friendliness and a nonverbal invitation to start a conversation. The other person who is low on the need for affiliation might see the same smile as a smirk and consequently become suspicious that the stranger is laughing at them. Objectively (alpha press), it was the same smile. Subjectively (beta press), it was a very different event for these two persons, due to their differences in the need for affiliation.

Apperception and the TAT

Murray held that a person's needs influenced how he or she perceived the environment, especially when the environment is ambiguous (as when a stranger smiles at the person). The act of interpreting the environment and perceiving the meaning of what is going on in a situation is termed **apperception** (Murray, 1933).

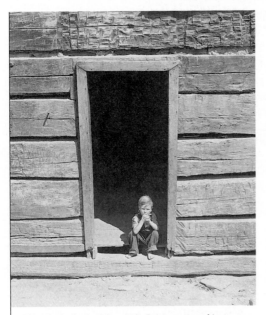

This photo, obtained from U.S. Government archives, was used by Morgan and Murray as one of the TAT pictures. Can you make up a story about the child in this photo? What do you believe he is thinking about? What happens next?
Source: Farm Security Administration - Office of War Information Photograph Collection, Library of Congress, LC-USF34-055829-D.

Because our needs and motives influence apperception, if we want to know about a person's primary motives, we might ask that individual to interpret what is going on in a variety of situations, especially ambiguous situations.

The simple insight that needs and motives influence how we perceive the world led Murray and his research associate Christiana Morgan to develop a formal technique for assessing these two constructs (Morgan & Murray, 1935). They called this the **Thematic Apperception Test** (or TAT, for short). The TAT consists of a set of black-and-white images that are ambiguous. The person is then asked to make up a story about what is happening in the picture. For example, in the drawing of a person on a windowsill, the person may be going in (to rob the house?) or going out (jumping to commit suicide?). Some pictures contain no people at all, such as a picture of a rowboat on the shore of a small creek. Such pictures are perhaps the most ambiguous: Who put the rowboat there? Are they coming or going? Why are they not in the picture right now? It is easy to make up a story because the picture is so ambiguous with respect to what is happening.

In administering the TAT, a person is shown each picture and told to be creative and make up a short story, interpreting what is happening in each picture. He or she is encouraged to tell a story that has a beginning, a middle, and an end. The psychologist then codes the stories for the presence of various types of imagery associated with particular motives. For example, a subject might write the following about the TAT card of the boat on the shore: "The boat in the picture is being used by a young boy to take produce to market. The boy has stopped to gather some wild berries to take to the market to sell along with his farm produce. This boy works very hard and eventually grows up, puts himself through college, and becomes a famous scientist, specializing in the study of plants, primarily agricultural crops." This story has a lot of achievement imagery, so the subject who wrote it would be seen to have a high need for achievement.

Morgan and Murray published the TAT in 1935. Since then, many researchers have modified its administration (e.g., using fewer cards, selecting other drawings, and using a data projector or computers to display the images to many people at once. Because the pictures in the original TAT are dated (e.g., clothing and hair are styles from the 1930s), newer versions of TAT-type pictures have been developed and found to function similarly to the original set in terms of soliciting need-relevant themes (Schultheiss & Brunstein, 2001). The essential features of the TAT and similar projective techniques are that (1) the subject is given an *ambiguous* stimulus, usually a picture, and (2) he or she is asked to describe and *interpret* what is going on.

Take the need for achievement motive, which can be scored by counting up the number of references in the person's story to wanting to do things better, anticipating success, feeling positive about succeeding, and overcoming obstacles (Schultheiss & Brunstein, 2001; Schultheiss & Pang, 2007). Studies of the TAT suggest that people do respond differentially to the themes of the picture, with, for example, high need for achievement people responding to the achievement pictures differently than low need for achievement people (Kwon, Campbell, & Williams, 2001; Tuerlinckz, De Boeck, & Lens, 2002).

Some personality researchers argue that projective tests in general, and the TAT in particular, are less reliable as measures of personality than other methods, such as questionnaires and informant report. Some even argue that the term *test* should not be used to refer to projective methods (McGrath & Carroll, 2012). Nevertheless, the TAT continues to be used particularly to assess psychoanalytic constructs, such as defense mechanisms (Hibbard et al., 2010), attachment styles (Berant, 2009), and psychosexual stages (Huprich, 2008), as well as for needs and motives. Research shows that, as measures of individual differences in motivation, the TAT (McAdams et al., 1996) and other picture story completion exercises (Schultheiss & Schultheiss, 2014) can be both reliable and valid when scored using specific criteria to identify themes of achievement, power, and intimacy.

We can make a distinction between using the TAT to assess state levels of needs and trait levels of needs. **State levels** of a need refer to a person's momentary amount of a specific need, which can fluctuate with specific circumstances. For example, a person who is failing at a task (e.g., a player on a baseball team that is down 5 to 4 in the ninth inning) might experience a sharp increase in the state of achievement motivation. The TAT has been shown to be sensitive to changes in state levels of various motives, particularly the needs for achievement, power, and intimacy (Moretti & Rossini, 2004). The assessment of **trait levels** of a need refers to measuring a person's average tendency, or their set point, on the specific trait. The idea is that people differ from each other in their typical or average amount of specific needs. Assessing trait levels of needs is the most frequent goal of personality psychologists who use such measures (Schultheiss, Liening, & Schad, 2008).

A newer form of assessing motives is the **Multi-Motive Grid**, which combines features of the TAT with features of self-report questionnaires (Schmalt, 1999). In this

A Closer Look

TAT and Questionnaire Measures of Motives: Do They Measure Different Aspects of Motives?

Psychologist David McClelland and his colleagues focused primarily on the TAT. Critics have argued that the TAT demonstrates poor test-retest reliability and that responses to one picture may not correlate with responses to other pictures—that is, the TAT has poor internal reliability (Entwisle, 1972). Moreover, when the TAT is used to predict actual motive-related behaviors (such as when TAT need for achievement scores are used to predict overall college grade point averages or performance on an achievement test), the correlations are frequently low and inconsistent (Fineman, 1977). Smith and Atkinson (1992) have reviewed the major criticisms of the TAT, as well as responses from its proponents.

These undesirable properties of the TAT have led some researchers to develop questionnaire measures of motives (Jackson, 1967). These questionnaires simply ask people directly about their motives and desires and about whether they engage in the kinds of behaviors that indicate high levels of the motives. These questionnaires turn out to have desirable measurement properties, such as adequate test-retest reliability and

predictive validity (Scott & Johnson, 1972). A troubling finding, however, is that TAT measures of motives and questionnaire measures of the same motives are often uncorrelated (Fineman, 1977; for an exception see Thrash & Elliot, 2002). Many researchers therefore suggest that the TAT measure and other projective measures should be abandoned.

McClelland and his colleagues did not silently accept these criticisms (McClelland, 1985; Weinberger & McClelland, 1990; Winter, 1999). In response, McClelland argued that, when the TAT is properly administered and scored, the motive scores *do* show acceptable test-retest reliability. In addition, he asserted that the TAT predicts long-term real-life outcomes, such as business success, better than questionnaire measures do. He argued that the questionnaire measures are better at predicting short-term behaviors, such as how competitive a person will behave while playing a game in a psychology laboratory. McClelland argued that the TAT measure and the questionnaire measures are uncorrelated because they measure *two different types of motivation*. Let's discuss each in turn.

One type of motive is called **implicit motivation**. These motives are based on needs, such as the need for achievement (nAch), the need for power (nPow), and the need for intimacy (nInt), as they are measured in fantasy-based (i.e., TAT) measures. When the TAT is used to measure these motives, they are called implicit, because the persons writing the stories are not explicitly telling the psychologist about themselves. Instead, they are telling stories about other people. The stories are thought to reflect the *implied* motives of the persons writing the stories—their unconscious desires and aspirations, their unspoken needs and desires (Schüler, Sheldon, & Fröhlich, 2010). What people write in response to the TAT pictures is presumed to reflect their real, although unconscious, motivations (Hofer, Bond, & Li, 2010).

The other type of motivation is called explicit, or **self-attributed motivation**, which McClelland argued reflects primarily a person's self-awareness of his or her own conscious motives or "normative beliefs about desirable goals and modes of conduct" (McClelland,

test, 14 pictures are selected to arouse one of the big three motives (achievement, power, or intimacy). The pictures are presented along with questions about important motivational states, and the person then answers those questions. The idea is that the photo will arouse the motive, which then will influence how the person will answer the questions. Although this technique is relatively new, initial results show promising levels of reliability (Langens & Schmalt, 2008; Sokolowski et al., 2000). Initial validity data are also promising, for example, showing that motive grid assessment of need for achievement predicted persistence and performance in laboratory tasks (Schmalt, 1999).

The TAT remains a popular personality assessment technique today, even though some researchers argue that it has low test-retest reliability (see, however, Smith & Atkinson, 1992). In addition, several researchers have reported extremely low correlations between TAT measures of certain needs and questionnaire measures of the same needs, leading them to question whether the TAT is a valid measure. This is the topic of our A Closer Look discussion above.

Koestner, & Weinberger, 1989, p. 690). These self-attributed motivations reflect a person's conscious *awareness* about what is important to him or her. As such, they represent part of the individual's conscious self-understanding.

McClelland argued that implicit and self-attributed motives represent fundamentally different aspects of motivation and that they should predict different life outcomes. Implicit motives predict long-term, spontaneous behavioral trends over time. For example, compared with questionnaire measures, TAT-assessed need for achievement is the better predictor of long-term entrepreneurial success, and TAT-assessed need for power is the better predictor of long-term success as a business manager (Chen, Su, & Wu, 2012; McAdams, 1990). Self-attributed motives, on the other hand, are better predictors of responses to immediate and specific situations and to choice behaviors and attitudes (because they measure the person's conscious desires and wants). For example, questionnaire-assessed need for achievement is the better predictor of how hard a person will work to obtain a reward in a psychology experiment, and questionnaire-assessed need for power is the better predictor of a person's self-reported attitudes about social inequality (Koestner & McClelland, 1990; Woike, 1995).

The research literature supports a distinction between implicit and explicit motives, at least for achievement motivation (Spangler, 1992; Thrash & Elliot, 2002). Spangler examined more than 100 studies of need for achievement and performed a meta-analysis of these studies. Half the studies meta-analyzed by Spangler used TAT measures (implicit motives), and the other half used questionnaire measures (self-attributed motives) of the achievement motive. Spangler then looked carefully at the variables being predicted by achievement. He sorted the studies into those that looked at short-term responses to specific tasks (e.g., grades in college courses, performance on ability tests, and performance in laboratory achievement tests) and those that looked at long-term achievements (e.g., lifetime income, job level attained in an organization, number of publications achieved, and participation in community organizations). Spangler found that the TAT-based measure was a better predictor of the long-term outcomes than was the questionnaire measure, whereas the questionnaire was a better predictor of the short-term responses. Understanding the congruence of implicit and explicit measures of motives is receiving a good deal of attention from personality psychologists (e.g., Thrash, Elliot, & Schultheiss, 2007).

A promising line of research is looking at specific hormones in relation to specific implicit motives (reviewed in Schultheiss, 2014). Several studies have found that gonadal steroid hormones are related to need for power, specifically testosterone in men, and estradiol in women. The need for intimacy has been related to release of the hormone progesterone. And there is some limited evidence that need for achievement may be related to vasopressin. These newer findings suggest that individual differences in hypothalamus functioning may produce, or at least may be related to, variability in the strength of implicit motives. Moreover, there are also hormones that are released when a person is under stress (particularly cortisol) and these have also been implicated in implicit motives. For example high need for power individuals, who find challenges to their dominance to be especially stressful, and who do not tolerate social defeat very well, release more cortisol under such conditions than persons low on need for power (Schultheiss, 2014). People high on implicit need for achievement are not as stressed (exhibit less cortisol release) during one-on-one competition as people low on need for achievement (Schultheiss, Wiemers, & Wolf, 2014). All in all, hormones are powerful biological regulators of behavior, and are proving to be linked in meaningful ways to individual differences in implicit motives.

Spangler's meta-analysis suggests that both the TAT and questionnaire measures may play important roles in helping psychologists understand the short- and long-term effects of motives. If you want to know how someone will react to achievement demands today or tomorrow, you might be best advised to use a questionnaire or to just ask the person about his or her achievement needs. However, if you want to make a prediction about who in a group of people will earn the largest lifetime income or climb the highest in an organizational setting, you might be better off using the TAT measure of need for achievement.

The Big Three Motives: Achievement, Power, and Intimacy

Although Murray proposed several dozen motives, researchers have focused most of their attention on a relatively small set. These motives are based on the needs for achievement, power, and intimacy. Let's review what we know about each of these fundamental human motives.

Need for Achievement

Behavior that is motivated by the need for achievement has long interested psychologists. Because it has received the most research attention, we begin with this motive.

Doing Things Better

Following Murray at Harvard, psychologist David McClelland carried on the tradition of motive research. McClelland was best known for his research on the **need for achievement**, defined as the desire to do better, to be successful, and to feel competent. Like all motives, we assume that the need for achievement will energize behavior in certain (achievement-related) situations. It is energized by the incentives of challenge and variety; it is accompanied by feelings of interest and surprise; and it is associated with the subjective state of being curious and exploratory (McClelland, 1985). People motivated by a high need for achievement obtain satisfaction from accomplishing a task or from the anticipation of accomplishing a task. They cherish the process of being engaged in challenging activities.

As the leader of two successful companies, Apple Computer and Pixar Animation, the late Steve Jobs was constantly striving to do things better. He is a good example of someone high in achievement motivation.

© Justin Sullivan/Getty Images New/Getty Images

In terms of trait levels, high nAch individuals prefer moderate levels of challenge, neither too high nor too low. This preference makes sense given that the high nAch person is motivated to do better than others. A task that is almost impossible to accomplish will not be attractive because it will not provide the opportunity to do better if everyone does poorly. A task that is too easy will be easy for everyone; the high nAch person will not do better if everyone is successful. Theoretically, we expect high nAch persons to have a preference for *moderately* challenging tasks. Dozens of studies have found support for this idea. One study examined children's preference for challenge in a variety of games (e.g., the ring-toss game, in which children attempt to toss rings around sticks that are placed at varying distances). Children high in nAch preferred a moderate challenge (e.g., tossed

Exercise?

Have a look at the TAT picture presented earlier, on page 332. Write a short story about what is happening in this picture. However, instead of writing off the top of your head, try to write a story that would score high on the need for achievement. What themes would you put in such a story? What actions and outcomes might be interpreted as indicating high nAch? What you consciously try to put into such a story are the themes and acts that psychologists look for in the stories of people writing naturally. Some put plenty of such themes and acts into their stories quite naturally and so seem to see achievement-related behaviors all around. Others reveal that their stories and the characters therein act in very nonstriving, nonachieving ways. And this comes perfectly naturally to them when they make up a story about an ambiguous situation.

their rings at the sticks in the middle), whereas children low in nAch tried either the very easy levels of the games (closer sticks) or the levels at which success was almost impossible (McClelland, 1958). This relationship has also been demonstrated outside the laboratory. Young adults high in nAch have been found to choose college majors that are of intermediate difficulty and to pursue careers that are of moderate difficulty (reviewed in Koestner & McClelland, 1990).

To summarize the characteristics of persons high in nAch, (1) they prefer activities that provide some, but not too much, challenge; (2) they enjoy tasks in which they are personally responsible for the outcome; and (3) they prefer tasks for which feedback on their performance is available.

Increasing the Need for Achievement

Research on the achievement motive typically takes the form of correlating TAT need for achievement (nAch) scores with other measures thought to be related to achievement. Demonstrating the relationship between nAch and success in entrepreneurial activities is one example of this type of research. Starting and managing a small business appears to offer a high degree of satisfaction for the person with a strong need to achieve. It provides an opportunity to engage in a challenging pursuit, assume responsibility for making decisions and taking action, and obtain swift and objective feedback about the success of one's performance. Studies in several countries have found that men with a high nAch are more attracted to business occupations than are their peers who have a low nAch (McClelland, 1965). A study of farmers (who are, in effect, small business operators) showed those with a high need to achieve were more likely than low nAch farmers to adopt innovative farming practices and to show improved rates of production over time (Singh, 1978). A study comparing self-employed entrepreneurs to workers for large corporations found that the self-employed were significantly higher on need for achievement (Lee-Ross, 2015).

Research on entrepreneurial talent has not been limited to business activities. Some studies have examined the work habits of college students. Students with high nAch appear to be more deliberate in their pursuit of good grades: they are more likely to investigate course requirements before enrolling in a class, speak with a professor prior to exams, and contact the professor about the exam after it was given to obtain feedback about their performance (Andrews, 1967). In a very different subject sample, blue-collar workers with high nAch engaged in more problem-solving activities after being laid off than did unemployed workers lower in nAch: they started looking for a new job sooner and used a greater number of job-seeking strategies (Koestner & McClelland, 1990).

More recent studies on entrepreneurial orientation examined achievement motives in a group of students of small business (a major considered to have high entrepreneurial potential) and compared them to a group of students of economics (considered to have much less entrepreneurial potential). Results showed that small business students were significantly higher on achievement motivation than the economics students (Sagie & Elizur, 1999). A study by Langens (2001) also supports the notion that training for high need for achievement can promote success in business. It seems that persons with high achievement motives are drawn to careers that have more potential risk and uncertainty, where success is a matter of personal responsibility and where emergency problem solving is routine.

There are also cultural differences in how the need for achievement is expressed. In the United States, most high-achieving high school students strive for good grades for themselves. Many students, and their parents, go to great lengths to achieve. Cheating can be common, and some students do not view cheating as wrong. The psychologist Demerath (2001) even reports that some parents of high-achieving students sought to have them classified as special-education students, which would entitle them to extra time on standardized tests. When he went to Papua New Guinea, Demerath found a very different norm among students. There, school is seen as a noncompetitive place where it is important for all to do well. Doing well as an individual, especially if it is at the expense of others, is frowned upon. In fact, New Guineans call this "acting extra" and view it as a form of vanity. Given the cultural differences between New Guinea and the United States, such differences in how the need for achievement is expressed make sense. People in Papua, New Guinea, make their living at farming and fishing, and they need to know that if they get sick or something happens and they cannot work their fields or nets, others will pitch in and help. In collectivist cultures, individual achievement is less valued than the person who helps his or her group achieve.

Determining Sex Differences

Much of the research on nAch, particularly that done in the 1950s and 1960s, was conducted on males only. Perhaps this was due to the fact that Harvard (where both Murray and McClelland did much of their research) was primarily a male institution at that time. Or it might have been due to the biased belief of that period that achievement was important only in the lives of men. Whatever the reason, little was known about achievement strivings in women until the 1970s and 1980s. Since then, some similarities and some differences have been found between men and women. Men and women high in nAch are similar in their preference for moderate challenge, personal responsibility for the outcome, and tasks with feedback. The major differences between such men and women occur in two areas: the life outcomes predicted by nAch and childhood experiences. Let's consider each of these in turn.

Research on men has focused primarily on achievement in business as a typical life outcome predicted by nAch. Research on women, however, has identified different "achievement trajectories," depending on whether the women value having a family or value having both family and work goals. Among women who value both work and family, nAch is related more to achieving better grades and to completing college, marrying, and starting a family later than it is among women low in nAch with career and family interests. Among women who are more exclusively focused on family, nAch is seen in the women's investment in activities related to dating and courtship, such as placing greater emphasis on physical appearance and talking with friends about their boyfriends more frequently (Koestner & McClelland, 1990). Such findings underscore researchers' need to know the subjects' goals before they can make predictions about success in particular areas.

The second major difference between men and women has been in the childhood experiences associated with nAch. Among women, nAch is associated with a stressful or difficult early family life. The mothers of girls high in nAch were found to be critical of their daughters and to be aggressive and competitive toward them (Kagan & Moss, 1962). The mothers of high-achieving schoolgirls were also less nurturant and affectionate toward their daughters than the mothers of less academically successful girls (Crandall et al., 1964). In contrast, the early lives of males high in nAch are characterized by parental support and care.

Condoleezza Rice was a straight-A student in grade school, began studying classical piano at age 10, and was a competitive ice skater, rising at 4:30 to practice for two hours before school each day. At age 38 she became provost at Stanford University, then became a National Security Advisor, and then Secretary of State from 2005 to 2009.

© Mark Wilson/Getty Images News/Getty Images

An interesting related finding concerns the levels of nAch in children who come from families in which the parents have divorced or separated. A nationally representative study found that women whose parents had divorced or separated when they were children had higher nAch scores than women whose parents had stayed together. The opposite outcome was found for men (Veroff et al., 1960). Living with a single mom may provide an achieving role model for young girls, whereas for boys it may demonstrate that men are unnecessary to family life and perhaps even to be resented.

Several recent studies have examined gender differences in competitive achievement settings. In one study the researchers had 40 men and 40 women solve simple addition problems as quickly as they could, paying them 50 cents for each correct answer (Niederle & Vesterlund, 2005). In one condition the participants simply played against the clock, trying to solve as many problems as they could. In another condition the game was changed to a tournament, where subjects were divided into teams of two women or two men each, and they played against each other. The winning team received $2.00 for each problem they solved and the losing team received nothing. The researchers found that men and women performed equally well in both conditions: the tournament setting and the individual setting. The experimenters then had a third round, where each person could choose whether he or she wanted to play individually or in a tournament setting. Interestingly, only 35 percent of the women chose the tournament setting, whereas 75 percent of the men chose the tournament setting. The authors concluded that even in settings where women perform just as well as men, they are less likely to want to engage in direct competition with others. Women may be more selective in how they express their achievement strivings, especially when winning for oneself means that others lose.

Promoting Achievement Motivation in Children

Despite the sex differences in childhood antecedents of achievement, McClelland believed that certain parental behaviors could promote high achievement motivation in children. One of these parenting practices is placing an emphasis on **independence training.** Parents can behave in ways that promote autonomy and independence in their children. For example, a young child who is taught to feed him- or herself becomes independent of the parents during feeding time; a child who is toilet trained early no longer relies on his or her parents for assistance with this task. One longitudinal study found that strict toilet training in early childhood is associated with high need for achievement 26 years later (McClelland & Pilon, 1983). Training a child to be independent in various tasks of life promotes a sense of mastery and confidence in the child. This may be one way that parents can promote a need for achievement in their children.

A second parental practice associated with need for achievement is setting challenging *standards* for the child (Heckhausen, 1982). Parents need to let the child know what is expected of him or her. These expectations should not exceed the child's abilities, however, or else the child may give up. The idea is for parents to provide goals that challenge the child, support the child in working toward these goals, and reward the child when the goal is attained (see Table 11.2). Positive and frequent success experiences appear to be part of the prescription for developing a heightened need for achievement. For example, learning the ABCs is a challenging task for a 4-year-old; parents might encourage a young child to undertake this task, enthusiastically sing the ABC song with the child, and reward the child with praise and hugs when he or she recites the alphabet independently for the first time.

Table 11.2 Raising High Need for Achievement Children

- Set tough but realistic standards.
- Applaud successes and celebrate accomplishments.
- Acknowledge but don't dwell on failures; stress that failures are part of learning.
- Avoid instilling a fear of failure, and instead emphasize the motive to succeed.
- Stress effort over ability: instead of saying "You can do it because you are smart" say "You can do it if you really try."

A developmental theory of achievement motivation has been proposed by the psychologist Carol Dweck (2002). This theory emphasizes the beliefs that people develop about their abilities and competencies. Briefly, the theory holds that the most adaptive belief system is that abilities are not fixed, but that they are malleable and can be developed through effort. Dweck (2002) argues that sometimes even "smart" people succumb to the belief that their abilities are fixed or given or genetically determined, that their current performance reflects their long-term potential, and that truly gifted persons do not need effort to achieve. She argues that this set of beliefs is "dumb" in the sense that people who hold such beliefs will consequently have a low need for achievement. It is more adaptive, Dweck holds, to believe that abilities are changeable, that one's performance is a temporary indicator of where one is, not where one will ultimately be, and that one's true potential will be realized only through sustained effort. This new theory is having an impact on schools and other educational settings (Elliot & Dweck, 2005). Dweck (2006) has also written a popular book on how this new theory relates to achievement in sports, business, and relationships.

In a recent large scale study, Dweck and her colleagues (Paunesku et al., 2015) showed that training students to view intelligence as a malleable and changeable quality, rather than viewing it as fixed or hereditary, lead to measureable increases in grades. We'll have more to say about Dweck's theory in the next chapter, when we discuss cognition and personality, but for now we'll simply say that believing one can become smarter with effort appears to be a prerequisite for actually becoming smarter (or at least achieving better grades).

Need for Power

Another motive of interest to psychologists is based on the need for power—the desire to have an impact on others.

Impact on Others

Although McClelland was known primarily for his studies of the achievement motive, both he and several of his students went on to study other motives. One of his students, David Winter, focused a good deal of his research on the **need for power** (nPow). Winter (1973) defines the need for power as a readiness or preference for having an impact on other people. A more detailed definition is provided by Fodor (2009); persons high on need for power have a need to impress, influence, or control other people, and to be recognized by others for their power-oriented actions. They achieve impact on others through various means, but most notably through forceful actions towards or against others, strong efforts to control others, or ostentatious displays of valued personal possessions. They want others to react to them, either with admiration, astonishment, or fear. One study investigated the hypothesis that high nPOW individuals would be faster at recognizing facial expressions of emotions in others (Donhauser, Rosch, & Schultheiss, 2015). Because of their desire to impact others, and because this impact often is registered in the faces of those around them, the high need for power person gauges the strength of their dominance by reading the emotions displayed by others. The researchers showed that need for power did correlate with faster recognition of facial expressions of emotions in others. This is most likely how high need for power people monitor whether they are being successful in having an impact, by reading the emotions displayed by those around them. As with the need to achieve, the need for power is assumed to energize and direct behavior when the person is in opportune situations for exerting power. The TAT has likewise been the predominant assessment tool for research on nPow. The subjects' stories are scored for the presence of images related to themes of power. These include descriptions of strong or vigorous actions, behaviors that bring about strong reactions in others, and statements that emphasize the importance of a character's status or reputation.

Research Findings
Many studies have examined the correlates of individual differences in nPow (e.g., Kuhl & Kazén, 2008). The need for power correlates positively with having arguments with others, being elected to student office in college, taking larger risks in gambling situations, behaving assertively and actively in a small-group setting, and acquiring more of what Winter calls "prestige possessions," such as sports cars, credit cards, and nameplates for dormitory doors (Winter, 1973).

It appears that an individual high in nPow is interested in control—control of situations and other people (Assor, 1989). Men high in nPow rate their "ideal wives" as those who are under the men's control and dependent on them, perhaps because such relationships offer them a sense of superiority (Winter, 1973). Men high in nPow are also more likely to abuse their spouses (Mason & Blankenship, 1987). A person with a high need for power prefers as friends people who are not well known or popular, perhaps because such people do not pose a threat to the person's prestige or status (Winter, 1973).

Sex Differences
Research on the power motive has found no sex differences in average levels of nPow or in the kinds of situations that arouse the power motive. Men and women also do not differ in the life outcomes that are associated with nPow, such as having formal social power (e.g., holding office), having power-related careers (e.g., being a manager), or gathering prestige possessions (e.g., sports cars).

The largest and most consistent sex difference is that high nPow men, but not women, perform a wide variety of impulsive and aggressive behaviors. Men high in nPow are more likely than men low in nPow to have dissatisfying dating relationships, arguments with others, and higher divorce rates. Men high in nPow are also more likely to engage in the sexual exploitation of women, have more frequent sex partners, and engage in sex at an earlier age than do their counterparts who are lower in nPow. Men with a strong need for power also abuse alcohol more than those with a low need for power (feelings of power often increase under the influence of alcohol). None of these correlates have been found for women.

"Profligate impulsive" behaviors (drinking, aggression, and sexual exploitation) are less likely to occur if an individual has had **responsibility training** (Winter & Barenbaum, 1985). Taking care of younger siblings is an example of responsibility training. Having one's own children provides another opportunity to learn to behave responsibly. Among people who have had such responsibility training, nPow is not related to profligate impulsive behavior (Winter, 1988). These findings have led Winter and others (e.g., Jenkins, 1994) to assert that socialization experiences, not biological sex per se, determine whether nPow will be expressed in these maladaptive behaviors.

Health Status and the Need for Power

As you might imagine, people high in nPow do not deal well with frustration and conflict. When high nPow people do not get their way or when their power is challenged or blocked, they are likely to show strong stress responses. McClelland (1982) called such obstacles **power stress** and hypothesized that people high in nPow were vulnerable to various ailments and diseases because of the stresses associated with inhibited power. In a study of college students, when power motives were inhibited or stressed, the subjects' immune function became less efficient and they reported more frequent illnesses, such as colds and the flu (see McClelland & Jemmott, 1980). A later study of male prisoners found similar results, with prisoners high in nPow showing the highest levels of illness and the lowest levels of immune antibodies (McClelland, Alexander, & Marks, 1982). Other studies have demonstrated that inhibiting the power motive among people high in nPow is linked with high blood pressure. This relationship was also found in a longitudinal study, which revealed that the inhibited power motive measured in men in their early thirties significantly predicted elevated blood pressure and signs of hypertension 20 years later (McClelland, 1979).

An interesting laboratory study induced power stress by having people lead a group discussion without knowing that the group's members were coached ahead of time to disagree with the leader and to display a lot of conflict (Fodor, 1985). The group leader was assessed for muscle tension. Consistent with McClelland's theory, the greatest tension responses were found for those leaders in the group conflict condition who were high in nPow.

War and Peace and Power

In a fascinating line of research, psychologist David Winter (1993, 2002) investigated nPow on a national level and related it to the broad areas of war and peace. Traditionally, nPow is measured by evaluating stories written in response to TAT pictures. However, nPow (as well as any motive) can be determined by assessing just about any written document, ranging from children's fairy tales to presidential speeches. Winter analyzed the content of 300 years of State of the Parliament speeches given by the prime ministers of England. Each of the speeches was rated for the presence of power images. He then used these image scores to predict warfare activity in these three centuries of British history. Winter found that wars were started when power imagery in the parliamentary speeches was high. Once under way, wars ended only after the levels of power imagery in the speeches ended. Similar analyses were done on the British–German communications during World War I, as well as on U.S.–Soviet communications during the Cuban missile crisis of the 1960s (Winter, 1993).

Speeches delivered by national leaders, including candidates for the presidency, can be analyzed for themes of power. Winter (2002) showed that words are often followed by actions, with the presence of high power imagery in national speeches often being followed by the onset of wars. The words politicians use can indicate their motives, which in turn can forecast their future actions.

© actionsports/123RF RF

In these cases, increases in power images preceded military actions, whereas decreases in power imagery preceded decreases in military threat.

In an extension of this research, Winter and his students examined how power images in communications may lead to escalation in conflict (Peterson, Winter, & Doty, 1994). Subjects were asked to write replies to letters taken from real conflict situations. The letters the subjects were responding to were altered to create two versions: one with high power imagery and the other with low power imagery. Otherwise, the content of the letters remained the same. The subjects' responses were then analyzed for themes of power. Subjects responded to power imagery with power images of their own. Assuming that the other side would similarly respond with more power images, it is easy to see how conflicts might escalate to violence.

More recent studies of communications among governments involved in crises have revealed similar motive patterns (Langner & Winter, 2001). Analyzing official documents during four international crises, Langner and Winter found that making concessions was associated with affiliative motives expressed in the communications, whereas power images were associated with making fewer concessions. In a laboratory study, they found that power or affiliative motives could be primed by having the subjects read different communications from their negotiation partner and that these primed motives predicted the likelihood that they would make a concession during the negotiation. Such personality research may have wide implications for understanding how governments could respond to each other to avoid crises.

To summarize, the need for power is the desire to have an impact on others. It can be measured from the TAT and from other verbal documents, such as speeches and other forms of communication, by looking for evidence of themes related to status seeking, concerns about reputation, or attempts to make others do what one wants. For example, Winter (1988) provides an interesting analysis of Richard Nixon's speeches in terms of the needs for achievement, power, and intimacy. Winter (1998) applies a similar analysis to the speeches of former president Bill Clinton, linking Clinton's motives to some of his problems as well as to his popularity. Krasno (2015) also analyzed the motives of president Bill Clinton, and found him to be particularly high on both the need for achievement as well as the need for intimacy.

Need for Intimacy

The last of the "Big Three" motives is based on the desire for warm and fulfilling relationships with others.

Intimacy

The third motive receiving a good deal of research attention is the need for intimacy (nInt). The researcher most closely associated with this motive is Dan McAdams, another McClelland student. McAdams defines the **need for intimacy** as the "recurrent preference or readiness for warm, close, and communicative interaction with others" (McAdams, 1990, p. 198). People high in nInt want more intimacy and meaningful human contact in their day-to-day lives than do those who are low in nInt.

Research Findings

McAdams and others have conducted a number of studies of nInt over the years in an effort to determine how people high and low in nInt differ from each other. As with the other motives, the TAT is often used to measure the strength of the intimacy motive. People high in nInt (compared to those who are low) have been found to (1) spend more time during the day thinking about relationships; (2) report more pleasant emotions when they are around other people; (3) smile, laugh, and make more eye contact; and (4) start up conversations more frequently and write more letters. We might think that the people high in nInt are simply extraverts, but the findings do not support this interpretation. Rather than being the loud, outgoing, life-of-the-party extravert, the person high in nInt is more likely to be someone with a few very good friends, who prefers sincere and meaningful conversations over wild parties. When asked to describe a typical time with a friend, people high in nInt tend to report one-on-one interactions instead of group interactions. When they get together with friends, people high in nInt are likely to listen to their friends and to discuss intimate or personal topics with them, such as their feelings, hopes, beliefs, and desires. Perhaps this is why people who are high in nInt are rated by their peers as especially "sincere," "loving," "not dominant," and "not self-centered" (McAdams, 1990).

A few studies have examined the relationship between nInt and well-being. In a longitudinal study, nInt measured at age 30 in a sample of male Harvard graduates was significantly related to overall adjustment (e.g., having a satisfying job and family life, coping well with life's stress, being free from alcohol problems) 17 years later (McAdams & Vaillant, 1982). Other studies have shown that nInt is associated with certain benefits and positive life outcomes for both men and women. Among women, nInt is associated with happiness and satisfaction with life. Among men, nInt is associated with less strain in life. Unlike the motives for power and achievement, for which no sex differences have been found as far as level of need is concerned, there does exist a consistent sex difference in need for intimacy—women have, on average, a higher need than men (McAdams, 1990; McAdams & Bryant, 1987).

To summarize, the need for intimacy is the desire for warm and intimate relationships with others. Individuals with a strong nInt enjoy the company of others and are more expressive and communicative toward others compared with people low in nInt. The intimacy motive is distinguished from extraversion in that persons high in nInt prefer having a few close friends to being a member of a rowdy group. In contrast to the need for achievement and power, for which men and women show comparable levels, women's need for intimacy tends to be higher than men's.

The motives we have covered so far—the needs for power, intimacy, and achievement—all fall within the tradition of academic personality psychology. There is, however, another motivational tradition, one that is rooted more in clinical psychology than in academic personality research. This tradition has come to inform the field of personality psychology, and concepts from this tradition are present or implied in several areas of contemporary research. We turn now to the humanistic tradition within personality psychology.

Humanistic Tradition: The Motive to Self-Actualize

In 1995, an American legend passed away—Jerry Garcia, lead guitarist of the Grateful Dead—reportedly of heart failure, at the age of 53. In the many newspaper stories recounting his life and times, reporters often suggested that Garcia lived longer than he should have, given his lifestyle. His band was constantly on the road for three decades, and Garcia was known to have abused a multitude of drugs, including cocaine, heroin, and alcohol, on a regular basis.

Other entertainers from the past have also abused drugs and alcohol—and died as a result—at much younger ages than Garcia, such as John Belushi (died at 33), Kurt Cobain (died at 27), Jimi Hendrix (died at 27), Janis Joplin (died at 27), Jim Morrison (died at 27),

Keith Moon (died at 31), and Elvis Presley (died at 42). With each such death, the public engages briefly in an age-old debate about personal responsibility and the self-destructiveness often seen in artists. Some people argue that such artists are victims of their times or their culture. Garcia, for example, was thought to carry the burden of representing the best (and worst) of the 1960s counterculture; he and his band were often viewed as a time capsule from that era.

Jerry Garcia of the Grateful Dead, who died in a drug rehabilitation center in 1995. Some argue he was a victim of his times and his mission to maintain a vision of the 1960s counterculture. Others argue that Garcia was a musical genius who also chose a very destructive lifestyle. The issue of personal responsibility is important in the humanistic approach to motivation.
© Bob Minkin/ZUMA Press/Newscom

Another view of the same situation is that Garcia did kill himself, that he slowly but willfully self-destructed. This view implies that Garcia was responsible for his own demise. In an MTV interview the week of Garcia's death, then-President Bill Clinton represented this view: "While he had great talent, he also had a terrible problem [heroin addiction]. . . . You don't have to have a destructive lifestyle to be a genius." The implication is that Garcia's genius and his self-destructive tendencies were two separate parts of his personality and that one did not necessarily produce the other. Garcia killed himself by his own free will, in President Clinton's perspective, and he was responsible for his own death due to the lifestyle choices he had made over the years.

Was Garcia a victim of his culture, or was he responsible for his own self-destruction? The answer depends on how one views free will in relation to motivation. Earlier, in our A Closer Look section we discussed unconscious (implicit) motives. These are motives that a person is largely unaware of yet guide his or her behavior, life choices, and responses to projective tests such as the TAT. Choices based on unconscious motives are, in most respects, made without free will. The Garcia question really becomes whether or not he was aware of his motives, whether he knew what he was doing when he made his many self-destructive life choices.

An emphasis on conscious awareness of needs, choice, and personal responsibility is one of the characteristics of the **humanistic tradition** approach to motivation. Humanistic psychologists emphasize the role of *choice* in human life, as well as the influence of *responsibility* on creating a meaningful and satisfying life. The meaning of any person's life, according to the humanistic approach, is found in the choices that person makes and the responsibility he or she takes for those choices. In midlife, for example, some people conclude that they are not exercising much choice in their daily lives, that they have fallen into a rut in their careers, their personal relationships, or both. For example, the 2000 Oscar-winning movie *American Beauty* portrays the desperation of a man who has realized he is living a life he has not chosen and his extreme attempts to reclaim and take responsibility for his life. Some people respond to such a realization with drastic efforts to resume responsibility for creating their own lives. Career changes, divorce, moves across the country, and other drastic choices are often symptoms of, and sometimes solutions to, the midlife crisis of responsibility for one's life.

A second major characteristic of the humanistic tradition is an emphasis on the human need for growth and the realization of one's full potential. Human nature, according to this view, is positive and life-affirming. This view stands in marked contrast to psychoanalysis, which takes a rather pessimistic view of human nature, one that views humans as seething cauldrons of primitive and destructive instincts. The humanistic tradition provides an optimistic counterpoint, one that stresses the process of positive growth toward a desired or even an idealized human potential. That human potential is summed up in the concept of the self-actualization motive.

We will define self-actualization shortly. First, we must note a third characteristic of the humanistic tradition that distinguishes it from other motivational approaches. The humanistic tradition views much of motivation as being based in a need to *grow,* to become who one is meant to be. The other traditions, including those of Freud, Murray, and McClelland, view motivation as coming from a specific *deficit,* or lack. This is a subtle but important distinction, and it represents a historical break in motivation theory and research. All the motives we have discussed—achievement, power, and intimacy— are deficiency motives. In the humanistic tradition, the most human of all motivations— the motive to self-actualize—is seen as *not* based on a deficiency. Rather, it is a growth-based motive, a motive to develop, to flourish, and to become more and more what one is destined to become. In the words of Abraham Maslow (1970), who coined the term in the 1960s, self-actualization is the process of becoming "more and more what one idiosyncratically is, to become everything that one is capable of becoming" (p. 46).

Maslow's Contributions

Any discussion of the motive to self-actualize has to begin with Maslow's contributions (see Maslow & Hoffman, 1996). Several of his ideas form the foundation for theory and research in this area.

Hierarchy of Needs

Maslow (1908–1970) began with the concept of need but defined needs primarily by their goals. Maslow believed that needs were hierarchically organized, with more basic needs found toward the bottom of the hierarchy and the self-actualization need at the top (see Figure 11.2). He divided the hierarchy of needs into five levels.

Figure 11.2

Maslow's hierarchy of needs in his theory of motivation. The needs are organized hierarchically into levels. Lower-level needs are more pressing (indicated by larger, bolder fonts) than are higher-level needs.

At the base of the need hierarchy are the **physiological needs**. These include needs that are of prime importance to the immediate survival of the individual (the need for food, water, air, and sleep), as well as to the long-term survival of the species (e.g., the need for sex). At the next highest level are the **safety needs**. These have to do with shelter and security, such as having a place to live and being free from the threat of danger. Maslow believed that building a life that was orderly, structured, and predictable also fell under safety needs. Having your automobile inspected prior to a long trip might be seen as an expression of your safety needs.

With only two levels mentioned so far, we can make a few important observations. One is that we typically must satisfy the lower needs before we proceed to satisfy the higher needs. One of Maslow's enduring contributions is that he assembled the needs in a specific order, providing an understanding of how they relate to one another. Obviously, we have to have enough food and water before we will worry about earning esteem and respect from our peers. It is possible, of course, to find examples of people who do not follow the hierarchy (e.g., starving artists, who frequently go without adequate food to continue expressing themselves in their art). Maslow's theory, like most personality theories, is meant to apply to the average person or to describe human nature in general. Although there are always exceptions to the rule, people appear, on average, to work their way up Maslow's hierarchy from the lowest to the highest level. Maslow also taught that the need hierarchy emerges during the course of human development, with the lower-level needs emerging earlier in life than the higher-level needs.

A second observation is that needs lower in the hierarchy are more powerful or more pressing when not satisfied than the needs toward the top of the hierarchy. The higher-level needs are less relevant to survival, so they are less urgent when not satisfied than the lower needs. Another way to put this is that when people are working on satisfying their higher needs, their motivation is weak and easily disrupted. Maslow (1968) stated that "this inner tendency [toward self-actualization] is not strong and overpowering and unmistakable like the instincts of animals. It is weak and delicate and subtle and easily overcome by habit, cultural pressures, and wrong attitudes toward it" (p. 191).

People typically work at satisfying multiple needs at the same time. It is easy to find examples of people engaging in a variety of tasks that represent different needs in a given period of time (e.g., eating, installing a new lock on the front door, going to a family reunion, and studying for an exam to earn a better grade). At any given time, however, we can determine the level at which a person is investing *most* of his or her energy. The point is that, even if we are working primarily on self-actualization needs, we need to do certain things (e.g., buy groceries) to make sure the lower needs continue to be satisfied.

The plots of many movies, particularly adventure movies, involve people who find themselves in situations that force them to take a step downward on the hierarchy of needs—circumstances that require a sudden shift in focus to safety or even physiological needs. The series of *Alien* and *Die Hard* movies are examples of films that illustrate this phenomenon. In the film *The Edge,* actors Anthony Hopkins and Alec Baldwin take a few steps down the hierarchy of needs when their

In the movie The Edge, *the plot involves two high-esteem men who are suddenly knocked several steps down on Maslow's hierarchy of needs by a large and persistent grizzly bear.*
© *Moviestore collection Ltd/Alamy Stock Photo*

plane crashes in the wilderness and they are pursued by a large, hungry, and very persistent grizzly bear.

The third level in Maslow's hierarchy consists of **belongingness needs**. Humans are a very social species, and most people possess a strong need to belong to groups (families, sororities/fraternities, churches, clubs, teams, etc.) (Baumeister & Leary, 1995). Being accepted by others and welcomed into a group represents a somewhat more psychological need than the physiological needs or the need for safety. Some observers have argued that modern society provides fewer opportunities for satisfying our need to belong than it did in the past, when ready-made groups existed and people were automatic members (e.g., multigenerational extended families and small towns in which virtually everyone felt like a member of the community). Loneliness is a sign that these needs are not being satisfied; alienation from one's social group is another. The popularity of so-called street gangs is a testament to the strength of belongingness needs. Gangs provide group membership to people who might otherwise feel alienated or excluded from groups available to members of the dominant culture.

One reason the need to belong is so basic comes from the theory of evolution. In our evolutionary past, belonging to a large social group was essential to survival. People hunted in groups, lived in groups, and moved around in groups. Belonging to a group allowed the individual members to share the workload and to protect each other, raise each others' young, and share important resources. Belonging to a group had survival value. Not only was each individual ensuring his or her own survival by living in a group, but all members of the group were invested in each other's survival because each member played an important role in the group. Today it is not necessarily the case that group living fosters survival; nevertheless, modern humans still have a strong desire to belong to specific groups, such as church groups, work groups, clubs, fraternities and sororities, and various interest groups.

The fourth level of need in Maslow's hierarchy contains **esteem needs**. There are really two types of esteem—esteem from others and self-esteem, the latter often depending on the former. We want to be seen by others as competent, strong, and able to achieve. We want to be respected by others for our achievements and our abilities. We also want this respect to translate into self-esteem; we want to feel good about ourselves, to feel that we are worthwhile, valuable, and competent. Much of the activity of adult daily life is geared toward achieving recognition and esteem from others and bolstering self-confidence.

The pinnacle of Maslow's need hierarchy is the **self-actualization need**, the need to develop one's potential, to become the person one was meant to be. You might think this is difficult, as it assumes that one must first figure out who one was meant to be. However, self-actualizers seem to just know who they are and have few doubts about the direction their lives should take. They tend to score higher on measures of general well-being (Bauer, Schwab, & McAdams, 2011).

Research Findings

Maslow developed his theory based on his ideas and thoughts about motivation, not on empirical research. He never, for example, developed a measure of self-actualization, though others did (Flett, Blankstein, & Hewitt, 1991; Jones & Crandall, 1986). How has his theory fared in the hands of researchers? Although not all the studies support Maslow's theory (e.g., Wahba & Bridwell, 1973), some studies support its main tenets (e.g., Hagerty, 1999). One group of researchers tested the idea that lower-level needs in the hierarchy are stronger than the higher-level needs when deprived (Wicker et al., 1993). These researchers presented subjects with a variety of goals that mapped onto

A Closer Look

A Re-Interpretation of Maslow's Hierarchy of Needs: An Evolution-Based Model

Psychologist Doug Kenrick and colleagues (Kenrick et al., 2010) proposed a reinterpretation of Maslow's hierarchical model of fundamental human needs. Because this is the first major overhaul of Maslow's key contribution, we chose it for a closer look. Although this reformulation merges Maslow's ideas with basic concepts from evolutionary psychology (covered in Chapter 8), only time will tell whether it provides a more useful framework for studying human needs and motives.

Maslow published his hierarchy of needs in 1943, and it had a large impact on many subfields of psychology, including personality and developmental psychology. However, today many see it as a

quaint bit of armchair theorizing that, although interesting, is largely disconnected from any contemporary theory. Kenrick and colleagues suggest that it can take on new significance if the hierarchy can be renovated by incorporating theoretical and empirical developments from evolutionary psychology. They propose a new model that retains several of Maslow's key ideas (i.e., it remains a hierarchical model; several original needs are retained; and it presumes a developmental order to the needs). However, what is added is a theoretical explanation for the model that is based on the evolutionary function of each particular need. This model is presented in the accompanying Figure 11.3.

A novel and enduring part of Maslow's model of needs is the idea of a hierarchy, the notion that certain motives take precedence over others. Hence the needs are arranged in a specific order. Also, the needs lower in the pyramid are, when unsatisfied, are stronger and more persistent than needs higher in the pyramid, presumably because they are more important for survival. Additionally, the needs are also related to development, such that as a person matures, he or she shifts from needs lower to higher in the hierarchy.

All of these elements are retained by Kenrick et al.'s 2010 reinterpretation. The basic needs related to physiological, safety or self-protection, affiliation, and esteem

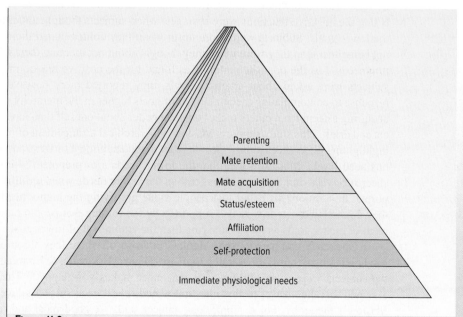

Figure 11.3

An updated hierarchy of fundamental human motives.

Source: "Renovating the Pyramid of Needs: Contemporary Extensions Built Upon Ancient Foundations," by D. T. Kenrick et al., *Perspectives on Psychological Science, 5,* 292–314.

motives are also retained because they are important to survival, a major evolutionary goal. But, as we learned in Chapter 8, survival is only part of the evolutionary process. More important is reproduction, since survival without reproduction is an evolutionary dead end. So Kenrick et al. add the important needs to find and retain a mate, and to succeed at parenting by raising one's children so that they may, in turn, reproduce, ensuring one's genes into future generations.

Kenrick et al. use functional explanations for each need in the hierarchy, with each need fulfilling a particular function with regard to evolution. Maslow's ultimate need—the need to self-actualize—has no apparent function with respect to surviving

and reproducing, and so Kenrick et al. leave that need off of their model.

The journal that published Kenrick et al.'s revised model of needs also published four articles critical of this new model. One criticism (Kesebir Graham, & Oishi, 2010) argued that a theory of human needs should be human-centered, and not animal-centered. After all, the Kenrick et al. model applies to rats and lizards as much as it applies to humans, ignoring what might be distinctively human about human nature. Others argued that self-actualization can be viewed as evolutionarily important, and should not be dropped off of the list of fundamental human needs (Peterson & Park, 2010). Others argued that the purpose of life, other than ensuring one's

genes into future generations, is missing from the Kenrick et al. model (Ackerman & Bargh, 2010). Kenrick and colleagues provide a thoughtful reply to these criticisms (Schaller, Neuberg, Griskevicius, & Kenrick, 2013), illustrating why and how evolution can be relevant to our understanding of uniquely human needs and motives.

The Kenrick et al. model of human needs does have a unifying theory it is built upon, something that was lacking in Maslow's version. Also, the theory on which the Kenrick model is based has a great deal of empirical support and is almost universally accepted among scientists. Whether it is the last word, or even whether or how it moves the field of personality needs and motives forward, remains to be seen.

Maslow's theory: having enough to eat and drink, feeling safe and unafraid, being part of a special group, being recognized by others as an outstanding student, and being mentally healthy and making full use of one's capabilities. They then asked subjects several questions about each goal, including "How good would you feel if you attained it?" and "How bad would you feel if you did not attain it?" What the researchers found is that the negative reactions were strongest when subjects thought about not attaining the lower goals. Subjects were more upset when they contemplated their safety needs not being met than they were when they thought about not meeting their self-actualization needs. Just the opposite pattern was found for the positive reaction ratings. When subjects were asked about attaining goals, they reported more positive emotions in response to contemplating the attainment of goals higher in the hierarchy. For example, acquiring esteem from others makes one feel better about oneself than having enough to eat and drink. This study supports Maslow's hierarchical arrangement of motives, while highlighting differences in how people react to the attainment or frustration in the various need levels. Maslow's idea that the lower needs are "prepotent"—imperative for sheer survival—and therefore stronger than the higher needs when unfulfilled was supported. In addition, his belief that people value gratifying the higher needs more than they do the lower needs was also supported by the finding that people rated the attainment of higher goals as more satisfying than the attainment of lower goals.

One study compared groups defined in terms of where they stood on Maslow's need hierarchy in terms of overall happiness (Diener, Horowitz, & Emmons, 1985). All the subjects were asked, "What is it that most makes you happy?" The researchers assumed that the answer to this question would reveal each subject's level of need in Maslow's hierarchy. For example, one subject said, "A good meal and the ability to digest it," which was scored as being at the physiological level. The results showed no relationship between level of need and overall happiness (which was gauged in this study by a questionnaire measure). For happiness, it does not appear to matter what level of need a person is working on. People working on self-actualization needs are not any more likely to be happier than people working on other needs. Maslow also notes in his book that happiness does not necessarily come with working on the self-actualizing need.

Given these findings, we might ask, "What *are* the characteristics that distinguish self-actualized persons from others?" Let's turn to a discussion of Maslow's research on the particular traits that best describe self-actualizing persons.

Characteristics of Self-Actualizing Persons

To learn more about self-actualization, Maslow conducted case studies of a number of people who he thought were self-actualizers. Maslow estimated about 1 percent of the population are growth motivated and are working on becoming all that they can become. Maslow's list of self-actualizing people whom he investigated included several living persons whom he kept anonymous. He also studied several historical figures through their writings and other biographical information, including Albert Einstein, Eleanor Roosevelt, and Thomas Jefferson. Maslow then looked for common characteristics that could be identified in this group. From this study, he produced a list of 15 characteristics that he suggested are commonly found among self-actualizers (see Table 11.3). Most of the people Maslow studied were famous, and many had made great contributions to science, politics, or the humanities. When reading over the list of characteristics in Table 11.3, bear in mind that the theory does not say "you must make great contributions" to become self-actualized. Students of personality often make this misinterpretation because of the special nature of the people studied by Maslow. It is possible for ordinary as well as extraordinary people to achieve self-actualization.

A notion related to self-actualization is the concept of flow, proposed by psychologist Mihaly Csikszentmihalyi (e.g., Csikszentmihalyi, Abuhamdeh, & Nakamura, 2005). **Flow** is defined as a subjective state that people report when they are completely involved in something to the point of forgetting time, fatigue, and everything else but the activity itself. In states of flow, a person is functioning at his or her fullest capacity.

Exercise ?

Think of a person you know or have met who impresses you. Try to identify someone who you think might be a self-actualizer. Review Maslow's list of the 15 characteristics he associated with self-actualized individuals (Table 11.3), and identify the characteristics that the person you've chosen appears to possess. Try to provide concrete examples from the person's life to illustrate the 15 characteristics.

Although flow experiences are somewhat rare, they occur under specific conditions; there is a balance between the person's skills and the challenges of the situation, there is a clear goal, and there is immediate feedback on how one is doing. The experience of flow itself can be a powerful motivating force and can be an indication that, at least for the moment, one is experiencing self-actualization.

Rogers's Contributions

Maslow focused on the characteristics of self-actualizing individuals, but psychologist Carl Rogers (1902–1987) focused on the ways to foster and attain self-actualization. During the four decades of his productive career, Rogers developed a theory of personality and a method of psychotherapy (client-centered therapy). Like Maslow, Rogers

Table 11.3 Characteristics of Self-Actualizers from Maslow's Case Studies

1. *Efficient perception of reality.* They do not let their own wishes and desires color their perceptions. Consequently, they are able to detect the deceitful and the fake.

2. *Acceptance of themselves, others, and nature or fate.* They realize that people, including themselves, make mistakes and have frailties, and they accept this fact. They accept natural events, even disasters, as part of life.

3. *Spontaneity.* Their behavior is marked by simplicity and honest naturalness. They do not put on airs or strain to create an effect. They trust their impulses.

4. *Problem focus.* They have an interest in the larger philosophical and ethical problems of their times. Petty issues hold little interest for them.

5. *Affinity for solitude.* They are comfortable with being alone.

6. *Independence from culture and environment.* They do not go in for fads. They prefer to follow their self-determined interests.

7. *Continued freshness of appreciation.* They have a "beginner's mind," for which every event, no matter how common, is experienced as if for the first time. They appreciate the ordinary and find pleasure and awe in the mundane.

8. *More frequent peak experiences.* A peak experience is a momentary feeling of extreme wonder, awe, and vision, sometimes called the "oceanic feeling." These are special experiences that appear to be very meaningful to the person who has one.

9. *Genuine desire to help the human race.* All self-actualizers tend to have a deep and sincere caring for their fellow humans.

10. *Deep ties with relatively few people.* Although they care deeply about others, they have relatively few very good friends. They tend to prefer privacy and allow only a few people to really know them.

11. *Democratic values.* They respect and value all people and are not prejudiced in terms of holding stereotypes about people based on superficial characteristics, such as race, religion, sex, and age. They treat others as individuals, not as members of groups.

12. *Ability to discriminate between means and ends.* They enjoy doing something for its own sake rather than simply doing something for the goals the activity can fulfill.

13. *Philosophical sense of humor.* Most humor is an attempt to make fun of a perceived inferiority of a person or group of people. Self-actualizers do not think such jokes are funny. Instead, what they find funny are examples of human foolishness in general.

14. *Creativity.* Creativity can be thought of as the ability to see connections among things—connections that no one has seen before. They are more likely to be creative because of their fresh perception of even ordinary things.

15. *Resistance to enculturation.* Cultures tell us how to behave, how to dress, and even how to interact with each other. Self-actualizers remain detached from culture-bound rules. They often appear different from and act differently from the crowd.

Source: Adapted from Maslow, 1954/1987.

believed that people were basically good and that human nature was fundamentally benevolent and positive. He felt that the natural human state was to be fully functioning, but under certain conditions people become stalled in their movement toward self-actualization. His theory explains how people lose their direction. Moreover, he proposed techniques for helping people get back on track toward achieving their potential. His general approach to self-actualization—the person-centered approach—has been expanded and applied to groups, to education, to corporate organizations, and even to government (see Rogers, 2002, for his posthumously published autobiography).

At the core of Rogers's approach is the concept of the **fully functioning person**, the person who is on his or her way toward self-actualization. The fully functioning person may not actually *be* self-actualized yet, but he or she is not blocked or side-tracked in moving toward this goal. Several characteristics describe the fully function-ing person. Such persons are open to new experiences, and they enjoy diversity and novelty in their daily lives. Fully functioning individuals are also centered in the pres-ent. They do not dwell on the past or their regrets. Neither do they live in the future. Fully functioning individuals also trust themselves, their feelings, and their own judg-ments. When faced with a decision, they don't automatically look around to others for guidance (e.g., "What would make my parents happy?"). Instead, they trust themselves to do the right thing. Fully functioning individuals are often unconventional, setting their own obligations and accounting to themselves.

How does someone become fully functioning? This is where Rogers's theory of the development of the self comes into play. An entire chapter of this book is devoted to an exploration of the self, and much of the work covered in Chapter 14 can be traced back to Carl Rogers, who strongly believed that there was one primary motive in life— the motive to self-actualize, to develop the self that was meant to be.

Journey into Selfhood: Positive Regard and Conditions of Worth

According to Rogers, all children are born wanting to be loved and accepted by their parents and others. He called this inborn need the desire for **positive regard**. Parents frequently make their positive regard contingent on conditions, such as the conditions expressed in the statements "Show me you are a good child and earn all As on your report card" and "I will really like it if you earn the star role in your school play." In another example, parents push children into sports, and the children might stay in the sports, not because they like sports, but to earn the love and positive regard of their parents. Of course, it is good for parents to have expectations for their children, but not to make their love contingent on the child's meeting those expectations.

The requirements set forth by parents or significant others for earning their posi-tive regard are called **conditions of worth**. Children may become preoccupied with living up to these conditions of worth rather than discovering what makes them happy. They behave in specific ways to earn the love, respect, and positive regard of parents and other significant people in their lives. Positive regard, when it must be earned by meeting certain conditions, is called **conditional positive regard**.

Children who experience many conditions of worth may lose touch with their own desires and wants. They begin living their lives in an effort to please others. They become what others want them to become, and their self-understanding contains only qualities that others condone. They are moving away from the ideals of a fully functioning person. What matters most is pleasing others. "What will *they* think?"—not "What do I really want in this situation?"—is a question such people ask themselves repeatedly.

As they reach adulthood, they remain preoccupied with what others think of them. They work primarily for approval from others, not out of their own sense of self-direction. They are dependent on others for positive regard and are constantly looking for the conditions of worth, which must be satisfied. They hide their weaknesses, distort their shortcomings, and perhaps even deny their faults. They act in ways that make everybody, except themselves, happy. They have been working to please others for so long that they have forgotten what they want out of life. They have lost self-direction and are no longer moving toward self-actualization.

How can one avoid this outcome? Rogers believed that positive regard from parents and significant others should have no strings attached. It should be given freely and liberally without conditions or contingencies. Rogers called this **unconditional positive regard**—when the parents and significant others accept the child without conditions, communicating that they love and value the child because the child just is. Parents need to show unconditional acceptance of the child, even when providing discipline or guidance. For example, if a child has done something wrong, the parent can still provide correction in combination with unconditional positive regard: "You have done something bad. *You* are not bad, and I still *love* you; it's just that the thing you have done is bad, and I don't want you to do that anymore."

With enough unconditional positive regard, children learn to accept experiences rather than deny them. They don't have to engage in efforts to distort themselves for others or alter their behaviors or experiences to fit a mold or model of what others want. Such persons are free to accept themselves, even their own weaknesses and shortcomings, because they have experienced unconditional **positive self-regard**. They are able to give themselves unconditional positive regard and accept themselves for who they are. They trust themselves, follow their own interests, and rely on their feelings to guide them to do the right thing. In short, they begin to take on the characteristics of a fully functioning person and begin to actualize the selves that they were meant to be.

Promotion of Self-Actualization in Self and Others

People who are not moving forward in terms of self-actualization experience frequent episodes of anxiety. **Anxiety**, according to Rogers, is the result of having an experience that does not fit with one's self-conception. Imagine a young woman who worked hard all through grade school and high school to earn good grades in an effort to make her parents happy. Part of her self-concept is that she "is smart and gets good grades." Then she enters college and obtains some less than perfect grades in some of her courses. This experience is alien; it does not fit with her self-concept as a person who is smart and gets good grades, so it makes her anxious. "What will *they* think," she says to herself, referring to her parents, "when they find out about these grades?" This new experience is a threat to her self-image, and that self-image is vitally important to her because in the past it brought her the positive regard of her parents. Rogers believed that people needed to defend themselves against anxiety, to reduce the discrepancy between their self-concept and their experiences. A fully functioning person could change his or her self-concept to incorporate the experience (e.g., "Perhaps I'm not so smart after all, or perhaps I don't always need to get perfect grades").

A less functional response to anxiety is to alter the experience by using a defense mechanism. Rogers emphasized the defense mechanism of **distortion**. Persons who engage in distortion modify their experience rather than their self-image to reduce the threat. For example, a person might say, "The professors in these classes are unfair," or "The grades really don't reflect how well I did," or in another way distort the experience. Or perhaps the person decides to take only "easy" classes, in which she is likely to earn high grades. Her decisions about which classes to take are based not on her own interests and desires (as would be the case for a self-actualizing reason) but on which classes are more likely to result in better grades to make her parents happy (a condition-of-worth reason). Taking classes merely to obtain easy grades is at odds with her self-concept of someone who is smart, and she may become anxious over the fact that so many of her experiences do not fit exactly with the way she would like to see herself.

A study found a relationship between the self-actualizing tendency and emotional intelligence (Bar-On, 2001). **Emotional intelligence** is a relatively new construct that has five components: the ability to know one's own emotions, the ability to regulate those emotions, the ability to motivate oneself, the ability to know how others are feeling, and the ability to influence how others are feeling. This may be an especially adaptive form of intelligence, which we describe in more detail in Chapter 12 on cognitive approaches. In the Bar-On (2001) study, the self-actualizing tendency was defined as working on actualizing one's talents and skills, and it was found that emotional intelligence correlated with this tendency. The author argues that emotional intelligence may be more important for self-actualizing than IQ, or cognitive intelligence. People may get off the path toward self-actualization, not because they lack IQ or education but because they have gotten out of touch with their emotions.

Application

Paul Gauguin is most famous for his paintings of South Pacific islanders using lush color, the denial of perspective, and the use of flat, two-dimensional forms. His powerfully expressive yet stylistically simple paintings helped form the basis of modern art. Gauguin was not always an artist, however. In 1872, Gauguin started a very successful career as a stockbroker in Paris. His marriage to his Danish wife Mette produced five children, and they led a content, upper-middle-class life in Paris. Gauguin always wanted to paint, however. He felt he could be a great painter, but his job as a stockbroker consumed all of his time (Hollmann, 2001).

In 1874, Gauguin attended the first Impressionist painting exhibition in Paris. He was entranced with this style of painting. He had a strong desire to become a painter, but instead he put all of his energy into his stockbroker's job and used the proceeds to purchase some paintings by Monet, Pissarro, and Renoir. This was the closest he could come, he felt, to realizing his potential as an artist.

Fortunately or unfortunately, the bank that employed Gauguin began having difficulties in 1884. Gauguin began to take time away from work and started painting. His income went down, and he had to move his family from expensive Paris to the town of Rouen, where the cost of living was lower. As Gauguin devoted more time to painting and less time to stockbrokering, his income went even lower and his marriage started to suffer. Neither Paul nor his wife were happy with their current situation, but for different reasons; Paul wanted more of the new life of painting he was discovering, and his wife wanted more of the old life and for him to return to the Paris life of stockbrokers, banks, and the upper middle class.

After a period of some marital discord, Paul Gauguin left his wife and five children and, with absolute sincerity and clarity of purpose, began to realize his potential as an artist. He fell in with the likes of van Gogh, Degas, and Pissarro, who mentored him in impressionism. In 1891, he decided to flee civilization in search of a new way of life, one that more matched his painting style: primitive, bold, and sincere. He sailed to Tahiti and the islands of the South Pacific, where, except for a brief visit back to France, he remained until his death in 1903 (Gauguin, 1985). In Tahiti, his paintings of indigenous people grew

Application (*Continued*)

more powerful and distinctive, and on a large scale he achieved his potential as one of the modern world's greatest artists.

   The ethical questions in Gauguin's life concern the competing responsibilities that are so evident; he had one life as a responsible banker and stockbroker, complete with a loving wife and five dependent children. On the other hand, Gauguin felt (correctly) that he had the potential to become a truly outstanding artist. Should he have been true to this inner calling, or should he have been true to his responsibilities as husband, father, and provider for his family? How should we judge his decision to abandon his family to pursue his self-actualization? What role does his success as an artist have in our judgment? What if, for example, he had abandoned his family then failed miserably as an artist? What should get priority in life when there is a conflict between one's immediate responsibilities and one's inner calling to become someone else? These are the difficult ethical questions of choice and responsibility that sometimes come to people on their way toward self-actualization.

A painting by Paul Gauguin titled "Self-Portrait with Yellow Christ" (1890), from a private collection. The life of Paul Gauguin raises several complicated questions about responsibility, choice, and self-actualization.
Source: National Gallery of Art, Washington

Rogers's approach to therapy is designed to get a person back on the path toward self-actualization. Rogers's therapy, sometimes called **client-centered therapy**, is very different from Freudian psychoanalysis. In client-centered therapy, the client (a term Rogers preferred over *patient*) is never given an interpretation of his or her problem. Nor is a client given any direction about what course of action to take to solve the problem. The therapist makes no attempts to change the client directly. Instead, the therapist tries to create the right conditions in which the client can change him- or herself.

There are three **core conditions** for client-centered therapy (Rogers, 1957). These conditions must be present in the therapy context in order for progress to occur. A film of Carl Rogers conducting a therapy session with "Gloria" is widely available and is sometimes used in training therapists. In this film, Rogers expertly sets up these three conditions in his conversation with Gloria (see the analysis of this film by Wickman & Campbell, 2003). The first core condition is an atmosphere of *genuine acceptance* on the part of the therapist. The therapist must be genuinely able to accept the client. Second, the therapist must express *unconditional* positive regard for the client. This means that the therapist accepts everything the client says without passing judgment on the client. Clients trust that the therapist will not reject them if they say the "wrong" thing, or if something unflattering comes out in the course of therapy. The atmosphere is safe for clients to begin exploring their concerns.

The third condition for therapeutic progress is *empathic understanding*. The client must feel that the therapist understands him or her. A client-centered therapist attempts to know the client's thoughts and feelings as if they were his or her own. **Empathy** is understanding the other person from his or her point of view (Rogers, 1975). The therapist conveys empathic understanding by restating the content and feelings of what the client has said. Instead of interpreting the meaning behind what the client says (e.g., "You have a harsh superego, which is punishing you for the actions of your id"), the client-centered therapist simply listens to what the client says and reflects it back. It is analogous to looking in a mirror; a good Rogerian therapist reflects back the person's feelings and thoughts, so that the person can examine them in full and undistorted detail. The client comes to understand him- or herself better by making the therapist understand.

Exercise

Empathic listening is a technique of conversation that can be rather easily developed. You might practice with a friend. Find someone to role-play with you, and ask the person to start by describing a small problem from his or her life. Your job is to role-play a client-centered approach to the conversation. That is, you will try to do the two activities involved in reflecting back: first, try to just restate the content of what your friend says. That is, repeat what the person has said, exactly as you understand it (e.g., "What I hear you saying is . . ."). The second reflecting-back action is to restate your friend's feelings. That is, take any feelings the friend mentions and state them back to him or her exactly as you understand those feelings (e.g., "It seems you are feeling . . . about this situation"). The friend will correct you or elaborate on the situation or feelings. After a few minutes, switch the roles and have your friend be the empathic listener while you describe a small problem. If done correctly, you should feel that your friend is really understanding you and that you are encouraged to explore your problem situation and your feelings about that situation.

The therapist expresses this understanding by restating the content ("What I heard you say is . . .") and by reflecting back the person's feelings ("It sounds as if you are feeling . . ."). This may sound simple, but it is a very effective approach to helping people understand themselves and helping them change how they think about themselves.

Ever since Rogers published his classic article describing empathy as one of the necessary conditions for therapeutic change (Rogers, 1957), many psychologists have

Application

The metaphor of a mirror is a useful one that can help us appreciate how the client-centered techniques work. Imagine that you want to adjust your outward appearance, so you look in a mirror to examine your appearance and see how the adjustment looks. Similarly, if you want to change your inner self, you can use the positive atmosphere and empathic understanding of a client-centered therapist to examine yourself and to contemplate changes. The following example demonstrates the technique of reflecting back:

Client: I just don't know which classes to take next year. I wish someone could make those decisions for me.

Therapist: You are looking for someone to tell you what to do.

Client: Yes, but I know that's impossible [sigh]. Nobody can decide what's right for me if even I don't have a clue.

Therapist: You find it exasperating that you are having so much trouble deciding on a class schedule.

Client: Well, none of my friends have this much trouble making decisions.

Therapist: You feel that your situation is not normal; it's not like the experience of your friends.

Client: Yeah, and it makes me mad. I should just be able to pick four or five courses and stick with my decision, but I can't seem to. I know it's silly.

Therapist: You think it is a trivial thing, yet it makes you angry that you cannot seem to make the decision.

Client: Well, you know, it really is trivial, isn't it? I know I can always change classes if they don't work out. I guess I just need to try them out.

Therapist: You see some options, that you can get out of a class if it isn't right for you.

The therapist never directs the client or offers an interpretation of the problem. This is why Rogerian therapy is sometimes called nondirective therapy—the focus is on the client's understanding of the situation, not the therapist's interpretation. The client works to clarify the therapist's understanding and, in so doing, increases his or her self-understanding. The client may come to accept that he or she has been denying or distorting experiences, such as taking classes for grades rather than for their own intrinsic interest. In helping the therapist understand why she is having so much trouble deciding on a class schedule, the person in the example may come to the realization that she has been taking classes primarily to make her parents happy. In an accepting atmosphere, she may come to this unflattering realization, and she might go on to explore how she can change her self-concept to accept this new understanding.

attempted to understand the nature of empathy. Are some people natural-born empathizers, or is empathy a skill that can be acquired and improved with training? A study of 839 twin pairs suggests that the ability to take the perspective of another person is not significantly heritable (Davis, Luce, & Kraus, 1994). This finding implies that people are not necessarily born with a predisposition to be good at the empathic understanding of others' points of view. Other studies have demonstrated that empathy can be taught effectively. For example, in one study the researchers measured empathic ability both before and after training in peer counseling (Hacher et al., 1994). They found that the training program, which emphasized listening skills (such as those in the previous Exercise and Application), produced significant increases in overall empathy scores. The training especially helped college and high school students improve their abilities to take the perspectives of other people and understand the others' concerns. Interestingly, these researchers found that, although college women initially had higher starting levels of empathic ability, men and women were equally teachable.

In another study, empathic ability increased with practice (Marangoni et al., 1995). College students watched videotapes of three individuals undergoing an interview about a personal problem (e.g., a recent divorce or the difficulties of being both a wife and a career woman). The researchers' hypothesis was supported; the subjects with more empathy were more accurate in their hunches about what the videotaped person was thinking and feeling, compared with the subjects who had less empathic ability. Moreover, the more practice the subjects had, the better they became at discerning what the videotaped individual was thinking and feeling. Finally, some subjects were simply better than others at empathic understanding. Even though everyone's performance could improve with practice, some subjects were consistently better than others. Trying to understand the characteristics that make someone particularly adept at empathic understanding is an important topic for future research.

Rogers's theory is important to personality psychology for a number of reasons (Bohart, 2013). His theory concerns the development of the self over the life span and includes specific processes that can interrupt or facilitate that development. He offers a new perspective on the importance of early experiences, similar to secure attachment, but which he calls unconditional positive regard. As in psychoanalysis, he assigns an important role to anxiety as a signal that things are not going well with the psychological system. Also as in classical psychoanalysis, he offers a system of psychotherapy for helping persons overcome personal setbacks on the road toward actualizing their full potential. His work has had a large impact on the practice of psychotherapy over the last half century (see Patterson, 2000).

SUMMARY AND EVALUATION

Motives can be used to explain why people do what they do. Motive explanations are unique in that they imply a goal that pulls people to think, act, and feel in certain ways. Many motives grow out of deficits. For example, someone motivated to achieve must feel that he or she has not yet achieved enough in life. The three motives discussed in detail—achievement, power, and intimacy—are all deficit motives. The fourth major motive—the motive to self-actualize—is not a deficit motive, but rather a growth motive because it refers to the desire to become more and more what one is destined to become.

Henry Murray was among the first to catalog the variety of human needs. He assumed that individuals differed in the strength of these needs and that the intensity of the needs also fluctuated over time and in different situations. Murray's emphasis was on how individuals differ from each other in terms of the basic needs, such as how some people have a more intense and lasting need for achievement than do other people.

Individual differences in the need for achievement have received a good deal of systematic attention from researchers. The need for achievement is the need to do things better and to overcome obstacles in the quest to attain one's goals. Those with high levels of the need for achievement differ from those low in this need in many important ways, such as the preference for moderate levels of challenge, the tendency to do well in situations where they have control and responsibility, and the interest in receiving feedback on their performance.

The need for power, another deficit motive, has also received research attention. This motive is the desire to have an impact on other people, to make other people respond, and to dominate others. Individuals who have a high need for power seek out positions in which they can influence others and acquire possessions that have all the markings of power, such as sports cars and expensive stereo equipment. They prefer friends who are not particularly powerful or popular. Men with a high need for power may sometimes engage in social influence tactics that are irresponsible or unethical.

The need for intimacy is the motive to acquire warm and communicative relationships. People high in this need tend to think about, and spend more time with, other people. Communication and self-disclosure characterize their interactions, and they prefer one-to-one interactions to large group activities.

The TAT is a projective technique for assessing levels of motivation in people. The technique is based on the idea that what people see is influenced by their needs. For example, a lonely person might see all situations as opportunities to be with people. The TAT was validated by showing that arousing a need in a person influences the person to write TAT stories consistent with that aroused need. Recent reviews of the literature suggest that the TAT assesses implicit motives, and it might be best suited for predicting long-term consequences of motives rather than short-term behaviors. Newer measures of motives, including the Multi-Motive Grid, are being developed.

The need to self-actualize represents a distinct tradition in the psychology of motivation, fundamentally different from the tradition that emphasizes deficit motivation. This humanistic approach emphasizes taking responsibility for decisions and making efforts to move and grow in a positive direction. The humanistic tradition assumes that human nature is positive and life-affirming and that most people would become fully functioning human beings if left to their own devices.

Abraham Maslow developed a hierarchical theory of motivation, the pinnacle of which is self-actualization, ranging from lower-level needs (physiological needs and safety needs) to higher-level needs (need for esteem and self-actualization). Maslow also studied the characteristics of self-actualizing persons and developed a list of the traits and behavior patterns that are common among the small percentage of the population working on becoming more of who they were meant to be.

Psychologist Carl Rogers theorized about obstacles to self-actualization and the therapeutic techniques that help people overcome those obstacles. Client-centered therapy is designed to help people regain their potential for growth and positive change. The therapist creates an atmosphere of unconditional positive regard and communicates empathic understanding to the client in order to enhance therapeutic effectiveness. It is clear from research that empathy is a skill that can be learned, supporting Rogers's theory.

KEY TERMS

The Cognitive/Experiential Domain

© Corbis/SuperStock RF

Part Four covers the cognitive/experiential domain, which emphasizes an understanding of people's perceptions, thoughts, feelings, desires, and other conscious experiences. The focus here is on understanding experience, especially from the person's point of view. However, distinctions can be made in terms of the kinds of experiences that people have.

One kind of experience that people have concerns cognitive experiences; what they perceive and pay attention to, how they interpret the events in their lives, and their goals and strategies and plans for getting what they want in the future.

People differ from each other when it comes to cognitively interpreting or making sense out of life events. We introduce a theory based on the idea that people construct

their experiences by applying personal constructs to their sensations. A related theory concerns how people decide on the causes of life events. Often people interpret events by making attributions of responsibility for those events. That is, "Why did this happen?" and "Whose fault is this?" Personality psychologists have extensively studied how people make attributions of responsibility, and how there may be stable individual differences in the tendency to blame oneself for bad events.

Cognitive experiences can also be studied in terms of the plans and goals that people formulate for themselves and for the strategies they develop for reaching their goals. People anticipate different futures and strive for different goals. Understanding people's goals and how their goals are expressions of personality as well as social standards also forms a part of the cognitive/experiential domain of knowledge about human nature.

A topic related to cognitive experience, and included in this part of the book, is intelligence. Currently there are several controversies about the concept of intelligence. For example, what is the best definition of intelligence—the accumulation of what a person has learned or the ability to learn new information? Is intelligence one quality, or are there several different kinds of intelligence?

A second broad but important category of experience, one that is associated with, but distinct from, cognition, is emotion. Psychology has seen a sharp rise in research on emotion in the past few decades. We can ask a straightforward question about emotional lifestyle: Is a person generally happy or generally sad? What makes a person anxious or fearful? Why is it that some people become enthusiastic so easily? What makes people angry, and why can some people control their anger, whereas others cannot?

Emotional experiences are often thought of as states that come and go; now you are anxious, now you are not, or now you are angry, now you are not. However, emotions can also be thought of as traits, as the frequent experiences of specific states. For example, a person may become anxious frequently or have a lower threshold for experiencing anxiety. And so we might talk of anxiety proneness as a personality trait—the tendency to easily and frequently become anxious.

When it comes to emotions as traits, we can divide the main topics into variables that refer to the content and variables that refer to the style of emotional life. When it comes to content, we are referring to the kinds of emotions a person is likely to experience. The content of emotional life can be divided into pleasant and unpleasant emotions. In terms of pleasant emotions, the typical personality-relevant trait is happiness. Psychologists have recently become very interested in happiness.

When it comes to unpleasant emotion traits, the research can be divided into three different dispositional emotions: anger, anxiety, and depression. Depression is a syndrome that is experienced by a large portion of the population, and it is of great importance in terms of public mental health implications. Trait anxiety has many different names in the personality literature, including neuroticism, negative affectivity, and emotional instability. Anger proneness is also a traitlike tendency, but this one refers to the tendency to easily or frequently become angry, a characteristic personality psychologists are keenly interested in.

People also differ from each other in the style of their emotional lives. Emotional style refers to how their emotions are typically experienced. Some people, for example, tend to experience their emotions at a higher intensity than other persons. For such high affect-intensity persons, a positive event makes them very, very happy, and a negative event makes them very, very unhappy. Consequently such people experience wider emotional swings from day to day or even within a day.

A third major category of experience is distinct from cognition and emotion yet is very important to the average person. This category of experience refers to experiences of the self. These experiences are unique in that individuals can focus on themselves as an object, pay attention to themselves, come to know themselves. The experience of self is unlike all of our other experiences, because in the experience of the self the knower and the known are one and the same. Psychologists have paid a great deal of attention to this unique object of our experience, self-knowing, and research and theorizing on the self has a long and rich tradition in personality psychology.

There are some useful distinctions among types of self-experiences. First there are descriptive aspects of the self: who are we, what are the important images we have of our past self, and what are the images of possible future selves? A second main component of the experience of self is evaluative: Do we like or dislike who we are? This is called self-esteem, and it is a central organizing force in much of what we do. And a third component of our self experience concerns the social roles we inhabit, the social selves we show to others, which we call identity. For example, many college students show one identity to their parents and another identity to their companions at school. And people sometimes go through identity crises, especially during transitions in life, such as starting college, getting married, or starting a new job.

© Corbis/SuperStock RF

Cognitive Topics in Personality

12

THE COGNITIVE/EXPERIENTIAL DOMAIN

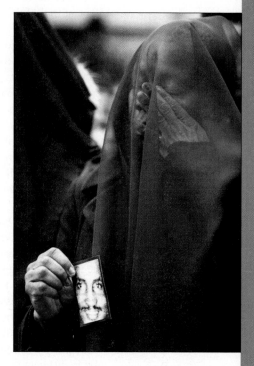

Mourners in New York City after the shooting of Amadou Diallo. Protests erupted over the killing of an unarmed African male by the police. The court ruled that what occurred the night Mr. Diallo was shot was a series of terrible accidents, errors in perception and cognition on the part of the police officers.
© Doug Kanter/AFP/Getty Images

O n February 4, 1999, just past midnight, Amadou Diallo, a 22-year-old immigrant from West Africa, was standing on the front stoop of his Bronx home after putting in a full day at work. An unmarked car carrying four plainclothes officers from the NYPD Street Crime Unit cruised by. The police officers were investigating crimes that had plagued that particular area, including a series of gunpoint rapes. This South Bronx neighborhood was one of the most dangerous in New York City. As they passed Mr. Diallo, he backed into a dark doorway. On noticing this, the officer driving put the car into reverse and backed up to a point directly in front of Mr. Diallo.

As Mr. Diallo stood in the doorway, the plainclothes officers exited their vehicle, and two approached Mr. Diallo saying, "Police Department. We'd like to have a word with you." At this point, Mr. Diallo started to back into the vestibule and the two officers then added the commands "Stay where you are," and "Keep your hands where we can see them."

Mr. Diallo reached his right hand into his front pocket. He turned toward the officers while pulling a black object out of his pocket and going into a crouching stance, bringing his hands toward each other. One officer yelled, "Gun!" Two officers fired. The closest officer, trying to back away from Mr. Diallo, fell backward down the steps. The other officers thought he had been shot.

In the next four seconds, the police officers fired a total of 41 bullets, 19 of which struck Mr. Diallo, killing him almost instantly. When the officers approached Mr. Diallo's body, they found him holding not a gun, but his wallet.

The details of this tragic and controversial case were made public during the subsequent trial of the police officers. Key documents from this trial, as well as news articles on which the above description is based, can be found at http://criminaldefense.homestead.com/Diallo.html. The jury concluded that what occurred that night was a series of terrible accidents, errors in perception and cognition that had catastrophic results. The officers "saw" a gun, they "thought" one of their own had been shot, and they "thought" Mr. Diallo was returning gunfire, when in fact it was their own ricocheting bullets. Their behavior then followed these cognitive errors. Many police academies now analyze the Diallo case during the training of new officers to understand what factors contributed to such misunderstandings and to avoid similar misperceptions in the future. The final chapter in this case closed in January 2004 when the City of New York settled a civil rights lawsuit by paying Mr. Diallo's family $3 million and offering an apology for the tragic misunderstanding.

The case of Mr. Diallo illustrates the connection between cognitive factors and behavior. People perceive and think and then act. Sometimes this all happens very quickly; sometimes we take our time thinking things through. We are processing information all the time and using this information to guide our actions. Most of the time, our information processing is fairly accurate, resulting in appropriate actions. Sometimes errors of information processing occur, and mistakes are made. Psychologists are very interested in understanding how humans process information. Personality psychologists take this interest a step further; they are interested in how people differ from each other in processing information. They are interested in different styles of perceiving and thinking and in different strategies people use to solve problems.

The following case illustrates individual differences in perception. It is not as dramatic as the Diallo case, but it nevertheless illustrates how two people can look at the same object and see two very different things.

There were several women from the same sorority in one class. The professor had heard that the sorority had adopted a dog. Curious, he asked one sorority member what kind of dog it was. She said, "He is big and friendly and loves to go for walks and likes to jump up and lick my face. I just love him." The next day, he had an opportunity to ask a different sorority member the same question. She responded, "Our new dog is a 3-year-old male golden retriever. He weighs about 90 pounds, is tall for the breed, and is rusty-red colored." It is interesting that the same question elicited such different information from these two people. The first student offered no information about the breed of dog; instead, she told how she *felt* about the dog. The second student gave details about the dog but said nothing about what she thought of the dog. These two women obviously processed quite different information when asked about the new dog. And it is also quite likely that they think very differently from each other about many things in life. Such differences in how people think are the focus of **cognitive approaches** to personality.

Many years ago, a study was done on what people think about when they are exposed to emotion-provoking stimuli (Larsen, Diener, & Cropanzano, 1987). The researchers showed people slides of emotion-provoking scenes, then asked the participants what they thought about when they looked at each slide (a technique called thought sampling). For example, one picture was of a mother holding a child who was bleeding from a severe head wound. In this study, the researchers were interested not in what the participants felt but in what they thought about—in the information that went through their minds—when exposed to such emotional scenes. One participant said, "My brother once had a bad gash on his head just like that, and I remember all the blood, and how upset my mother became, and my brother screaming and my mother trying to stop the bleeding, and me feeling helpless and confused." The next participant looked at the same picture and said, "Head wounds bleed quite a bit because, in the head, there is a high concentration of blood vessels close to the surface of the skin. I was thinking about the major artery groups in the head when I looked at that photo." The first person who looked at the picture engaged in what is called **personalizing cognition**. That is, the scene prompted him to recall a similar event from his own life. The second subject looked at the same picture and engaged in what is called **objectifying cognition**. That is, the scene prompted her to recall objective facts about the distribution of blood vessels in the human head. The difference between these two persons is a difference in cognition.

Cognition is a general term referring to awareness and thinking, as well as to specific mental acts such as perceiving, attending to, interpreting, remembering, believing, judging, deciding, and anticipating. All these mental behaviors add up to what is called **information processing**, or the transformation of sensory input into mental representations and the manipulation of such representations. If you have ever wondered whether other people think about things the same way you do, then you are a budding cognitive personality psychologist. Perhaps you have wondered if other people see colors the same as you do. Is the perception of green, for example, the same for everyone?

In this chapter, we cover three levels of cognition that are of interest to personality psychologists. The first level is **perception**, or the process of imposing order on the information our sense organs take in. You might think that there are few, if any, differences in how people perceive the world because our sensory and perceptual systems are all the same and what we perceive is an accurate representation of what is out there. But this is not true; two people can look at the same situation and actually see very different things.

Consider Figure 12.1. If you look at this illustration, you can see it in three dimensions. That is, instead of being a two-dimensional, flat drawing, you perceive it as having depth, as coming out of the page. This is because your perceptual system interprets cues of depth as representing a three-dimensional object. Another aspect of this figure—known as the Necker Cube—is that you may perceive the cube as extending out and upward to the right of the base, whereas others perceive the cube as extending outward and downward toward the left. Thus, not everyone sees the same object, even though the drawing is objectively the same. An especially interesting feature of the Necker Cube is that most people can actually see the cube reverse directions. If you stare at the cube long enough, you will see the two different three-dimensional cubes, and you should be able to see the two cubes flip back and forth, from up and rightward to down and leftward.

Figure 12.1

The Necker Cube.

Imagine how people might differ in what they see when they look at the much more complicated social world. Even at the level of perception, what we see in the world can be quite different from person to person. Moreover, these differences in what people see may be related to their personalities. It is this reasoning that underlies the rationale for such projective assessment techniques as the Rorschach inkblots. As we discussed in Chapters 2 and 9, what people see in the inkblots can be a function of their personalities. When looking at the same inkblot, one person might see a family of butterflies landing on a garden of flowers, and another person, looking at the same inkblot, might see a dog that has been hit by a car, with blood splattered all over the street. Do you think these two people might have dramatically different personalities?

The second level of cognition of interest to personality psychologists is **interpretation**, or the making sense of, or explaining, various events in the world. Interpretation concerns giving meaning to events. When you are confronted with an event and you are asked, "What does this mean?" or "How did this happen and how will it turn out?" you are likely to engage in the act of interpretation. For example, suppose you have a small mishap while driving your car, driving up a curb and scratching your fender. Someone might ask you, "Why did this happen?" You quickly and automatically make an interpretation and offer it to your inquisitor as a fact: "The street there is poorly laid out. It's too narrow and the curve is too sharp, and lots of people jump the curb there. It's the fault of the road department." However, maybe you offer a different interpretation, equally certain that it represents a fact: "I'm really a clumsy driver; I just can't handle the car. Maybe I should quit driving."

These are two of many possible interpretations, and which ones people offer may reveal aspects of their personalities. This notion of differences in interpretation underlies the rationale for such projective techniques as the Thematic Apperception Test (TAT), discussed in Chapter 11.

The third level of cognition that is of interest to personality psychologists is people's **conscious goals,** the standards that people develop for evaluating themselves and others. People develop specific beliefs about what is important in life and which tasks are appropriate to pursue. These tasks may be age specific and culture specific, such as, in Western cultures, establishing independence from one's family in early adulthood. A final topic in cognitive approaches is intelligence. Because this is a large and controversial topic in psychology, the student of personality should have some grasp of the basic issues and concepts in this area.

Personality Revealed Through Perception

Most people assume there is reality out there and that the representation we have of it in our minds is a precise duplicate, a flawless perception of the facts. This is simply not true; the perceiver contributes to the mental representations such that, even in perception, there are differences among people in what they see when they look at a scene. In this chapter, we expand on this notion and cover two topics that explore individual differences in perception. These topics show how perceptual differences can be stable, consistent, and meaningfully related to other areas of life.

Field Dependence

Have you ever heard the phrase that someone "can't see the forest for the trees"? This usually refers to the fact that someone cannot look beyond the details to get the big picture about a situation, that he or she cannot disengage his or her perception from the particular details to get a grasp of the general gist of the situation. Psychologist Herman Witkin studied such differences in perceptual style for almost 30 years. He came to call this topic *field dependence versus field independence.* Witkin's first book was titled *Personality Through Perception* (Witkin et al., 1954), and this title captures the idea that personality can be revealed through differences in how people perceive their environment.

Witkin was first interested in the cues that people use in judging orientation in space. If you see an object that is tilted, how do you know it is the object, and not your body, that is tilted? To make such judgments, some people rely on cues from the environment surrounding the object (are other things tilted as well?), whereas other people rely more on bodily cues that tell them that *they* are upright and therefore it must be the object that is tilted. To investigate this individual difference, Witkin devised an apparatus called the **Rod and Frame Test (RFT)**. Using this apparatus, the participant sits in a darkened room and is instructed to watch a glowing rod surrounded by a square frame, which is also glowing. The experimenter can adjust the tilt of the rod, the frame, and the participant's chair. The participant's task is to adjust the rod by turning a dial, so that the rod is perfectly upright. To do this accurately, the participant has to ignore cues in the visual field in which the rod appears (i.e., the square frame surrounding the rod, which the experimenter tilts). If the participant adjusts the rod so that it is leaning in the direction of the tilted frame, then that person is said to be dependent on the visual field, or **field dependent**. Other people disregard the external cues and, instead, use information from their bodies in adjusting the rod to upright. Such participants are said to be independent of the field, or **field independent**; they appear to rely on their own sensations, not the perception of the field, to make the judgment.

The Rod and Frame Test is a difficult and time-consuming way to measure field dependence/independence, so Witkin sought new ways to measure this perceptual difference (Witkin et al., 1962). One clever way of measuring field dependence/independence is to create a complex figure that contains many simple figures or shapes. You may have seen children's puzzles that consist of a large drawing with several smaller, hidden figures within it. The goal of such puzzles is to find as many of the hidden figures within the larger drawing as possible. An example of a hidden figures test is given in Figure 12.2. Witkin devised a similar test, called the Embedded Figures Test (EFT), which can be used to measure field dependence without relying on the cumbersome Rod and Frame Test. Some people, when given the EFT, have trouble locating the simple figures embedded within the more complex surrounding figure, apparently being bound up in the "forest" and unable to see the "trees." These people are said to be field dependent. Other people quickly spot many or all of the embedded figures and, so, are able to see objects independently from the background. Such people are said to be field independent. Performance on the EFT correlates strongly with performance on the RFT (Witkin, 1973).

Field Dependence/Independence and Life Choices

Are differences in perception related to other differences in personality functioning? Just before his death in 1979, Witkin wrote several papers summarizing his research in two broad domains in which field dependence/independence appears to have consequences: education and interpersonal relations. In one large study, 1,548 students were followed from their entry into college until several years after graduation. Choice of major in college was found to be related to field independence/dependence: the field-independent students tended to favor the natural sciences, math, and engineering, whereas the more field-dependent students tended to favor the social sciences and education (Witkin, 1977; Witkin et al., 1977).

Figure 12.2

An Embedded Figures Test, in which the objective is to find as many of the smaller figures hidden in the larger figure as possible.

A second major area of research reviewed by Witkin and Goodenough (1977) concerns the interpersonal correlates of field independence/dependence. Field-dependent people, as might be predicted, tend to rely on social information and frequently ask other people for their opinions. They are attentive to social cues and, in general, are oriented toward other people. They show a strong interest in others, prefer to be physically close to other people, gravitate to social situations, and get along well with others. Field-independent people, on the other hand, function with more autonomy and display a more impersonal or detached orientation toward others. They are not very interested in others' opinions, keep their distance from others, and show a preference for nonsocial situations.

Current Research on Field Dependence/Independence

After Witkin's death, little research was done on field independence/dependence for about a decade. However, starting in the 1990s, new research began to appear in the literature (Messick, 1994). One new area of research concerns how people react to situations that are rich in sensory stimulation and whether field-independent people can focus on a task and screen out distracting information from the field. For example, one study of 100 police officers examined their ability to disregard noise and distractions in simulated, though naturalistic, shooting situations. Similarities can be drawn between this study and the Diallo case presented at the beginning of this chapter. That night in the Bronx, the officers were trying to focus on Mr. Diallo. However, the light was dim, other people were around, the four officers needed to be aware of each other and aware of the commands being given, and so on. In short, they were in a stimulus-rich environment. Field-independent persons are predicted to be better at ignoring distracting information and focusing on the important details of the event. The researchers conducting the study of 100 police officers in simulated high-stimulation settings (Vrij, van der Steen, & Koppelaar, 1995) made exactly this prediction—that the more field-independent officers would perform better by noticing details more accurately, would be less distracted by the noise and activity, and would be more accurate in deciding when to shoot. Results showed that the field-independent officers performed better on the shooting task under these high-stimulation conditions and were able to give a better description of the witnessed event, compared with the field-dependent officers. Presumably, the field-independent officers could better focus on the target without being distracted by the noise and activity going on in the field around them. In another study, when presented with complex photographs of people, field-independent persons were better at noticing and decoding the facial expressions in the photographs, compared with field-dependent persons (Bastone & Wood, 1997).

Another area of high stimulation is in hypermedia- and multimedia-based computer instruction, such as educational materials on the World Wide Web, which come with sound and streaming video. Field dependence is related to different preferences for web-based instruction (Clewley, Chen, & Liu, 2011). This form of instruction involves the presentation of information in multiple media formats (text on a computer screen, graphics, video, sound) while students navigate through this maze of sensory information at their own pace.

In a study of eighth-graders, the researchers found that the field-independent students learned more effectively than the field-dependent subjects in a hypermedia-based instructional environment. Presumably, the field-independent students more easily found the thread that ran through the various media presentations of information. The experimenters concluded that field-independent students are able to get the

Studies have shown that individuals serving in bomb disposal units score higher in field independence than other terrorist response units. The ability to stay focused in a distracting environment would be an asset to a bomb disposal technician.

© deepspace/Shutterstock.com RF

points embedded within the various sources of media faster and are able to switch between educational media or sensory fields faster, compared with field-dependent students (Weller et al., 1995). Many studies of this perceptual style suggest that it leads to different styles of learning—for example, field-independent persons are good at selective attention in stimulus-rich environments (at processing specific information while blocking out what is not important), whereas field-dependent persons tend to process information in chunks and are good at seeing connections among categories of information (Nicolaou & Xistouri, 2011; Oughton & Reed, 1999; Richardson & Turner, 2000).

Some interesting research has also been done on the relation between field dependence and the ability to "read" or decode emotional facial expressions. On the one hand, because field-dependent people tend to be more socially oriented, we might think they should do especially well in reading emotional expressions. On the other hand, if we think of facial expressions as complex arrays of information, then maybe the field-independent persons would be better at analyzing and interpreting such patterns. In a study on this topic, psychologists Linda Bastone and Heather Wood (1997) had subjects indicate the emotion expressed in 72 different faces. However, to make the task difficult, some emotion displays showed only the eyes, and some showed only the mouth. The field-independent subjects were significantly better at interpreting facial expressions than the field-dependent subjects, but only when the tasks were difficult. This finding reinforces the notion that field-independent persons are good at tasks that require finding and interpreting patterns and making generalizations.

Another area that requires skill at seeing patterns, organizing information, and making generalizations is learning a second language. Psychologists interested in second language acquisition have examined the role of personality, and several studies have identified field-independent persons as making better progress than field-dependent persons when learning a second language. One study looked at American college students learning.

Is it better to be field independent or field dependent? Like most personality dimensions, there are pros and cons associated with both tendencies (and remember, we are describing points along a continuum, not two categories of people). Field-independent people are skillful at analyzing complex situations and extracting information from the clutter of background distractions. Field-independent people also tend to be more creative (Miller, 2007). However, they are somewhat low on social skills and prefer to keep their distance from others. Field-dependent people, on the other hand, have strong social skills, gravitate toward others, and are more attentive to the social context than are field-independent persons (Tamir & Nadler, 2007). It appears that each of these

Virtual reality can provide a stimulus rich environment for applications in education, science and elsewhere. It may be the field independent people are more able to function effectively in stimulus rich virtual realities.

© Rommel Canlas/123RF RF

contrasting perceptual styles is adaptive in particular situations, making it impossible to state which orientation is more valuable (Collins, 1994; Mathes et al., 2011).

Pain Tolerance and Sensation Reducing/Augmenting

The way in which people perceive their surroundings and navigate through information—whether they tend to focus on the whole or tend to notice the particulars—is a perceptual style. What about other individual differences in perception? One commonly noticed difference among people is in **pain tolerance**, in which people undergo the same physical stimulus (e.g., having to get an injection from the doctor) but react quite differently from each other in terms of the pain they report experiencing. This difference among people in their pain tolerance attracted the interest of psychologist Aneseth Petrie, whose book *Individuality in Pain and Suffering* describes her research on and theory of individual differences in tolerance for sensory stimulation (Petrie, 1967).

Petrie's Research
Petrie studied people in hospitals undergoing painful operations, as well as normal subjects in whom she induced pain—through applying heat or by piling weights on the middle joint of her subjects' fingers. In these studies, she was able to quantify how well each

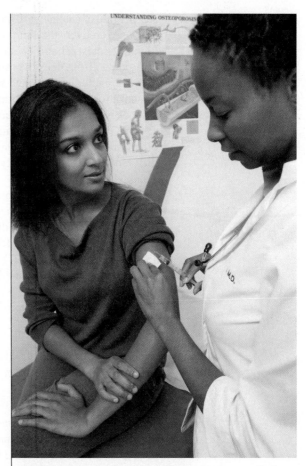

Understanding individual differences pain tolerance to medical procedures is what led psychologist Aneseth Petrie to develop her theory of sensory reducing-augmenting.
© moodboard/Getty Images RF

subject could tolerate pain. She developed a theory that people with low pain tolerance had a nervous system that amplified, or augmented, the subjective impact of sensory cues. In contrast, people who could tolerate pain well were thought to have a nervous system that dampened, or reduced, the effects of sensory stimulation. For these reasons, her theory came to be called the **reducer/augmenter theory**. This term refers to the dimension along which people differ in their reaction to sensory stimulation; some appear to reduce sensory stimulation, whereas some appear to augment stimulation.

Petrie believed that individual differences in pain tolerance originated in the nervous system. A few studies have examined nervous system reactivity directly in relation to augmenting/reducing. For example, researchers reported that reducers show relatively small brain responses to flashes of lights (Spilker & Callaway, 1969) as well as smaller brain responses to bursts of noise (Schwerdtfeger & Baltissen, 1999) in comparison with augmenters. In this last study, conducted in Germany, reducers also reported that the noise was less loud, compared with augmenters, though the noise was, in fact, identical for all the participants.

The brain evoked response increases with increasing stimulus intensity, but the rate of change differs for different individuals, with augmenters showing a steeper rate of change with increasing stimulus intensity (Schwerdtfeger & Baltissen, 2002). Moreover, the brain evoked potential augmenting/reducing measure shows high test-retest reliability, similar to other personality traits (Beauducel et al., 2000). Individual differences in brain augmenting/reducing have also been studied in other animals, including cats and rats (Siegel, 1997). In fact, rats that have been bred to be sensation seeking or sensation avoiding have been shown to display brain evoked responses that indicate reducing and augmenting, respectively (Siegel & Driscoll, 1996). Given that this individual difference in sensory reactivity can be observed in other mammals, it is not surprising that studies also show that this individual differences arises in infancy in humans (Evans, Nelson, & Porter, 2012; Fox & Polak, 2004).

Reducers should be motivated to seek strong stimulation to compensate for their lower sensory reactivity, related to optimal level of arousal, discussed in Chapter 6. Supporting this prediction, reducers have been found to drink more coffee, smoke more, and have a lower threshold for boredom, compared with augmenters (Clapper, 1990, 1992; Larsen & Zarate, 1991). Reducers also have been found to more frequently consume psychoactive drugs and listen to music at a louder level compared to augmenters (Schwerdtfeger, 2007).

Exercise

Researchers have developed questionnaire measures to assess people's standing on the reducing/augmenting dimension. One example is the questionnaire developed by Vando (1974) and modified by Clapper (1992), called the Revised Reducer Augmenter Scale (RRAS). This measure is based on the notion that if reducers dampen down stimulation, then they have a relatively high need for stimulation, compared with augmenters. Items on Clapper's RRAS questionnaire present test takers with a choice between a relatively stimulating and a nonstimulating experience. The test taker indicates his or her preference for either the stimulating or the nonstimulating experience. Subjects who prefer many of the stimulating choices are assumed to be reducers. Examples of these items follow. For each pair of activities or events, circle a number that best indicates your preference:

Hard-rock music	1	2	3	4	5	6	Soft pop music
Action movies	1	2	3	4	5	6	Comedy movies
Contact sports	1	2	3	4	5	6	Noncontact sports
A drum solo	1	2	3	4	5	6	A flute solo
Too much exercise	1	2	3	4	5	6	Too little exercise

Many researchers see a strong similarity between the augmenting/reducing construct and other personality constructs related to individual differences in how people respond to stimulation, such as those covered in Chapter 6 (e.g., sensation seeking), as well as Eysenck's theory of extraversion, covered in Chapters 3 and 6. For our purposes here, the reducer/augmenter research illustrates how personality psychologists have studied individual differences in perception, the most basic form of cognition. Let's turn now to a consideration of how people differ from one another in a higher level of cognition—interpretation.

Personality Revealed Through Interpretation

Trial lawyers are familiar with the fact that two or more people can witness the same event yet offer differing interpretations of that event. Trials often hinge on having the jury arrive at a particular interpretation of the facts, such as whether the suspect *intended* to harm someone, whether the suspect had *planned* the crime ahead of time, or whether the suspect is capable of *appreciating the consequences* of his or her behavior at the time of the criminal act. Many defense lawyers do not dispute that their clients committed their acts, but rather argue that the clients did not possess the required intention to be found guilty of a crime. For example, the Menendez brothers confessed to killing their parents with a shotgun. Their lawyers argued that the brothers acted in self-defense and therefore were not guilty of murder, which legally requires intent. The jury interpreted the facts to suggest that the brothers did not intend to murder their parents but did, in fact, act in self-defense.

Everyday life may not be as dramatic as the cases that make their way to courtrooms. Nevertheless, we often find ourselves interpreting everyday events: Why did I get a poor grade on my test? Can I really do anything to lose weight? Whose fault is it that I can't seem to get along with my girlfriend/boyfriend? Such interpretations often concern responsibility or blame—such as whose fault it is when someone gets a poor grade. Other times, such interpretations inquire about expectations for the future—such as if someone can lose weight. Both of these kinds of interpretations—about responsibility and about expectations for the future—have been studied by personality psychologists. However, before covering these topics, let's examine the theory that started the cognitive revolution in personality psychology: the work of George Kelly.

Kelly's Personal Construct Theory

Psychologist George Kelly (1905–1967), who spent most of his career at Ohio State University, played an important role in starting the cognitive tradition within personality psychology. Although a clinical psychologist, Kelly believed that all people are motivated to understand their circumstances and to be able to predict what will happen to them in the near future. He viewed psychoanalysis as effective because it provided people with a system for explaining psychological problems (e.g., "You are depressed because you have a hostile and sadistic superego, probably as the result of an improper anal stage resolution."). Kelly believed that the content of explanations was not as important as the fact that people believed them and could use them to understand their circumstances. Kelly felt that a primary motivation for all people was to find meaning in their life circumstances, and to use this meaning to predict their own future, to anticipate what is likely to happen next (Fransella & Neimeyer, 2003).

Kelly's view of human nature was that of humans as scientists. He felt that, just like scientists, people in general engage in efforts to understand, predict, and control the events in their lives. When people do not know why some event happened (e.g., "Why did my girlfriend break up with me?"), they experience greater distress than if they had an explanation. Thus, people seek explanations for the events in their lives just the way scientists seek explanations for phenomena in the laboratory.

Scientists employ **constructs** to interpret observations. A construct does not exist in itself; it is a word that summarizes a set of observations and conveys the meaning of those observations. Gravity, for example, is a scientific construct. We cannot show you gravity, but we can demonstrate the effects of gravity by observing other things, such as an apple falling from a tree. There are lots of constructs that could be applied to people: smart, outgoing, arrogant, shy, deviant. Like scientists interpreting the physical world, we use constructs all the time to give meaning to, or to interpret, the social world.

The constructs a person routinely uses to interpret and predict events are called, in Kelly's theory, **personal constructs**. Kelly's idea was that people have a few key constructs that they habitually apply in interpreting their world, particularly the social world. No two people have the same personal construct system, and so have their own unique interpretation of the world. For Kelly, personality consisted in differences in the way people construe the world, particularly the social world. These differences were the result of differences in the personal constructs that people habitually employed. What do you tend to notice when you meet a person for the first time? For you, it might be important how athletic versus nonathletic a person is, and this plays a large role in how you first construe the person. Another person, however, might apply the construct of intelligent versus nonintelligent to the same target person. As a result, that person will have a different construal of the target person than you have because you are each viewing the target person through the unique "lens" of your preferred construct systems (Hua & Epley, 2012).

For Kelly all constructs are bipolar. That is, they consist of some characteristic understood against its opposite, or what the person takes to be its opposite. So, a few typical constructs might be smart–not smart, cooperative–uncooperative, tall–short, and boring–interesting. People develop characteristic sets of constructs that they frequently use in interpreting the world. A person might apply smart–not smart to most people they meet and use this construct to parse their social world into groups. Moreover, they then behave differently toward people in the smart category compared to the not-so-smart category. However, it is the person's own construal that puts the acquaintances into those categories to begin with. Personal constructs are used to create the social groupings.

In many ways, Kelly was ahead of his times. He was postmodern before post-modernism became popular. **Postmodernism** is an intellectual position grounded in the notion that reality is constructed, that every person and certainly every culture has a version of reality that is unique, and that no single version of reality is any more privileged than another (Gergen, 1992). Kelly's emphasis on how personal constructs serve to create each person's psychological reality puts him in the postmodern camp (Raskin, 2001).

Kelly presented a highly complex but systematic theory of personality and personal constructs, which the interested student can pursue in Kelly's own work (e.g., 1955) or in summaries of his work (e.g., Fransella, 2003). We present some of the basic ideas here. His most basic idea was the *fundamental postulate,* which refers to the statement that "a person's processes are psychologically channelized by the ways in which he anticipates events" (Kelly, 1955, p. 46). To this fundamental postulate, Kelly added a number of corollaries. For example, if two people have similar construct systems, they would be psychologically similar (the commonality corollary). Some couples might be quite different in many ways, but if their personal construct systems are similar, then they are likely to get along quite well because they interpret the world similarly.

Like many personality theorists, Kelly also devoted a special place in his theory to the concept of anxiety. For Kelly, anxiety was the result of not being able to understand and predict life events. In his terms, anxiety is the result of our personal constructs failing to make sense of our circumstances. People are anxious when they don't understand what is happening to them and when they feel that events are unpredictable, outside of their control. How do constructs fail? Sometimes they are too rigid and impermeable to new experiences. Something comes along that they just cannot understand. Imagine a woman who, after raising the children and shipping them off to college, decides she wants to work. Her husband, whose conception of a good marriage is one in which "the wife does not have to work," cannot understand this experience. His construct of good versus bad marriage cannot make sense out of his wife's newfound desire for employment. Another way that constructs fail is if they are too permeable, if the person applies them too liberally. If a person categorizes everyone she encounters as either smart or not smart, and once categorized refuses to change her mind about them, even in the face of contradictory information, then her construct is too rigidly applied. A person knows that her construct system is in trouble when she starts having experiences that she cannot understand ("I just can't understand why you are leaving") or cannot anticipate ("That caught me by surprise.").

Kelly's ideas about how people construct their experiences based on construct systems that they "carry" through life was part of a cognitive revolution within personality psychology. Several self-report methods exist for the assessment of a person's personal construct system (e.g., Caputi, 2012; Hardison & Neimeyer, 2012). Another example of this cognitive emphasis can be seen in a development in learning theory, which occurred about the same time that Kelly was formulating his theory. We turn now to this other important development in the cognitive approach to personality.

Locus of Control

Locus of control is a concept that describes a person's perception of responsibility for the events in his or her life. More specifically, *locus of control* refers to whether people tend to locate that responsibility internally, within themselves, or externally, in fate, luck, or chance. For example, when you see a person who gets good grades, do you think it is because she is just plain lucky or because of her personal efforts? When you see someone in poor health, do you think it is because of fate, or is it because he does not take care of himself? Your answers to such questions may reveal your standing on the personality dimension of locus of control—the tendency to believe that events are or are not under one's personal control and responsibility.

Locus of control research started in the mid-1950s, when psychologist Julian Rotter was developing his social learning theory. Rotter was working within traditional learning theory, which emphasizes that people learn because of reinforcement. Rotter expanded these notions to suggest that learning also depended on the degree to which the person *expected* reinforcement—that obtaining a reward was under their control. Some people expect that certain behaviors will result in obtaining a reinforcer. In other words, they believe that they are in control of the outcomes of life. Other people fail to see the link between their behavior and reinforcement. This is Rotter's "expectancy model" of learning behavior. Interestingly, the expectation part involves characteristics that the individual brings to each situation. That is, *the expectancy of reinforcement* refers to characteristics that distinguish specific individuals. For example, suppose a person expects that acting in an assertive and demanding manner will get her what she wants. She wants a raise at work, so she expects that if she is assertive and demanding toward her boss, she will get her raise. Another person may have the opposite expectation, that acting in such a manner will be counterproductive, so he believes that being assertive will not produce the desired raise. These two individuals have different expectations for the outcome associated with the same assertive behavior pattern. She thinks she can do something to obtain a raise; he thinks he must just wait for the boss to make the decision. Differences in the subsequent behavior of these two people—for example, she is demanding and he is submissive at work—may be due to differences in their expectations of whether a certain behavior (assertiveness) will bring reinforcement (the desired raise).

Rotter published a questionnaire measure of internal versus external locus of control in 1966. Some items from that questionnaire are presented in Table 12.1.

Rotter emphasized that a person's expectations for reinforcement held across a variety of situations, what he called **generalized expectancies** (Rotter, 1971, 1990). When people encounter a new situation, they base their expectancies about what will happen on their generalized expectancies about whether they have the ability to influence events. For example, if a young man generally believes that he can do little to influence events, then in a new situation, such as entering college, he would have a generalized expectancy that things are outside of his control. He may, for example, assume that his grades will be due to luck or chance or fate, not to anything that he can actually control.

Table 12.1 Sample Items from the Locus of Control Scale

Yes	No	
_____	_____	1. Do you believe that most problems will solve themselves if you just don't fool with them?
_____	_____	2. Do you believe that you can stop yourself from catching a cold?
_____	_____	3. Are some people just born lucky?
_____	_____	4. Most of the time do you feel that getting good grades means a great deal to you?
_____	_____	5. Are you often blamed for things that just aren't your fault?
_____	_____	6. Do you believe that if somebody studies hard enough he or she can pass any subject?
_____	_____	7. Do you feel that most of the time it doesn't pay to try hard because things never turn out right anyway?
_____	_____	8. Do you feel that if things start out well in the morning, it's going to be a good day no matter what you do?
_____	_____	9. Do you feel that most of the time parents listen to what their children have to say?
_____	_____	10. Do you believe that wishing can make good things happen?

Source: Adapted from Rotter, 1982.

Such a generalized expectancy that events are outside of one's control is called an **external locus of control**. An **internal locus of control**, on the other hand, is the generalized expectancy that reinforcing events are under one's control and that one is responsible for the major outcomes in life. People high on internal locus of control believe that outcomes depend mainly on their own personal efforts, whereas people who have a more external locus of control believe that outcomes largely depend on forces outside of their personal control. Although problems can arise when a person with an internal locus of control confronts circumstances that truly are outside of one's control (Heidemeier & Göritz, 2013), an internal locus of control is, in general, conducive to well-being.

Internal locus of control has been found to be predictive of a variety of real-world outcomes. For example, people who displayed an internal locus of control at age 10 were found to have a reduced risk of obesity at age 30 compared to people with an external locus of control (Gale, Batty, & Deary, 2008). In another study of college students, those with an internal locus of control completed their degrees in a more timely manner than students with an external locus of control (Hall, Smith, & Chia, 2008). Another interesting study showed that adults with a more internal locus of control had higher credit ratings than those with a more external locus of control (Perry, 2008). In many ways, internal locus of control is associated with a tendency toward being more in charge of one's life, ranging from better control over one's weight to better control over one's spending habits and hence credit rating.

In an interesting case study, a 29-year-old man who sailed around the world solo in 260 days (Kjaergaard, Leone, & Venables, 2015) was found, as you might have guessed, to have a very internal score on a locus of control measure, quite literally the captain of his fate. Another activity where people's control over outcomes is sometimes

Exercise

Can you think of situations in which having an internal locus of control is a disadvantage? Under what circumstances would a person with an internal orientation experience relatively more stress than someone with an external orientation? What characteristics or situations would match the expectations of the person with an external locus of control? When might it be healthy to have an external locus of control?

Some situations are truly beyond our control and cannot be influenced by us, no matter what we do. For example, a loved one may be dying from an incurable disease. This is not anyone's fault, and there is nothing anyone can do to prevent the outcome. However, even in such situations some people, particularly close relatives, can feel that they are somehow to blame. In such situations, an internal locus of control might be a handicap to personal coping with the outcome.

Another example is the "survivor syndrome" often reported by persons who have lived through a tragedy in which many others were severely injured or killed, such as in a terrorist bombing or a mass shooting. Often, survivors report feeling that "if only" they had done something differently, they could have helped others make it to safety. They often report some feelings of personal responsibility for the outcome, even though the event was horrifically outside of their control.

at risk is stage acting, and a study of professional actors found that those with a more external locus of control suffered more from stage fright than actors with a more internal locus of control (Goodman, 2014).

When it comes to locus of control, the general finding is that an internal perspective is the more adaptive one, to see oneself as being in control of one's fate. However, what about situations that require giving up control? For example, the willingness to use autonomous cars requires that a person give up control of the driving to a machine, to turn over one's fate to a computer. Some people may be reluctant to try an autonomous car. A recent study showed that persons with an internal locus of control were more unwilling to try autonomous vehicles than persons with an external locus of control (Choi & Ji, 2015). Like with other personality traits, we can never say that one extreme of the dimension is entirely good or entirely bad; one can always find strengths and weakness associated with either high or low levels of any particular trait. As computers and machines do more and more for us, it may be adaptive to relinquish control for some aspects of our lives, and people with a more external locus of control may be more willing or more able to do so.

Learned Helplessness

We now turn to another individual difference in how people interpret the world—**learned helplessness**. Research on this topic also had its start in learning theory, similar to Rotter's start. Work on learned helplessness began when psychologists were studying avoidance learning in dogs and subjected the dogs to foot shocks from which the dogs could not escape. During the first few shocks, the dogs would pull at their harnesses, jump and twist, and try to escape. Eventually, however, they seemed to accept the shocks and did not try to escape anymore. The dogs, apparently knowing that they could not escape, would passively accept the shocks.

The dogs were then put into a different cage, a cage where they *could* escape the foot shocks by simply jumping over a small barrier into a different part of the cage. However, the dogs that had received inescapable shocks earlier did not even try to escape in this new situation. It was as if they had learned that their situation was hopeless, and they gave up seeking to avoid their painful circumstance. Other dogs that had not been shocked earlier quickly learned to avoid the shocks by jumping over the barrier. The researchers were surprised that the learned helplessness dogs did not even try to escape, and so they turned off the shock after one minute.

Next, the researchers tried lifting the dogs over the barrier to the safe part of the cage. After being shown how to reach safety, the dogs quickly learned to jump over and avoid the shocks. However, without such coaching, the learned helplessness dogs simply accepted their painful fates without attempting to remove themselves from the unpleasant situation.

Numerous studies document the learned helplessness phenomenon with humans (Seligman, 1992, 1994). Using unpleasant noise rather than shock, researchers set up the following learned helplessness situation. Participants are told that they will be given problems to solve and that they can avoid or turn off the blasts of unpleasant noise by solving the problems (for example, by pressing buttons in a correct order) (Garber & Seligman, 1980; Hiroto & Seligman, 1975). Some participants (the learned helplessness subjects) are given problems without solutions. Consequently, for these participants, the unpleasant blasts of noise are inescapable—nothing they can do will control the irritating and aversive blasts of noise. But do these participants generalize their helplessness to new situations?

Participants are then taken to a new situation and given a new set of problems to solve. This time there is no unpleasant noise. The researchers tell the participants that they are simply interested in how the participants will work on these new problems. Participants who were exposed to the learned helplessness condition in the earlier trials usually perform much worse on the subsequent problems. It is as if they are saying, "What's the use in trying to solve these problems? They are too difficult." Such participants appear to generalize their experiences of helplessness from one problem-solving situation to another.

In real life, learned helplessness can result whenever people are stuck in an unpleasant situation that is apparently outside of their control. For example, imagine a woman who tries everything she knows to get her husband to stop abusing her. She tries being nice to him, and it works for a while, but soon he is abusive again. She threatens to leave, and this works for a while, but he starts abusing her again. No matter what she does, nothing seems to solve the problem. A woman in such circumstances may develop learned helplessness. She may give up even trying to solve the problem: "What's the use," she may say, "nothing I do seems to help, so maybe I just have to take it."

However, people in learned helplessness don't have to "take it." They need an outside perspective, like coaching the learned helpless dogs to jump over the barrier to escape. They need someone who can see the situation objectively and who can recommend strategies for solving the problem. Whenever a problem situation looks as if it has no solution or is inescapable, that is the time to ask others for help, to seek an outside opinion (Seligman & Csikszentmihalyi, 2000).

The original model of learned helplessness began with experiments on dogs and was generalized to humans through experimental studies. Humans are more complex than dogs, at least when it comes to thinking about the events in their lives, analyzing situations, and forming new expectancies for behavior. What factors determine whether feelings of helplessness in one situation will spill over to other situations? Under what circumstances do people become motivated to take control of their lives? What factors influence people to decide that they do or do not have the ability to take control of a situation? In seeking answers to these questions, psychologists began to study what was going on in the minds of people who underwent learned helplessness conditioning (Peterson, Maier, & Seligman, 1993). Current research is examining the neurobiology of learned helplessness in humans (Hammack, Cooper, & Lezak, 2012) and animals (Bredemann, 2012).

Personality Revealed Through Goals

So far in this chapter, we have considered aspects of personality related to how a person perceives and interprets the world. We turn now to a third aspect of cognition, a person's goals and how these are related to personality. Such goals may range from minor ones, such as buying groceries for the week, to the more lofty, such as reducing world hunger. The focus in this approach is on intention, on *what persons want to happen*, on what they want to achieve in their lives. People differ in their goals, and these differences are part of and reveal their personalities.

Different psychologists have offered different terms, such as personal strivings (Emmons, 1989), current concerns (Klinger, 1977a, 1977b), personal projects (Little, 1999) and life tasks (Cantor, 1990). All of these constructs emphasize what people believe is worth pursuing in life, as well as the kinds of goal-directed behaviors they enact to achieve these desires. Other personality theories in this section emphasize self-guides, or the standards that people strive to meet (Higgins, 1996), their understanding of their own abilities and motivations (Dweck, Chiu, & Hong, 1995), or internal abilities related to goals, including people's expectations, beliefs, plans, and strategies (Mischel, 2004).

A Closer Look

Reformulated Learned Helplessness: Explanatory Style

The reformulation of learned helplessness theory focuses on the cognitions, or thoughts, a person has that may lead to feelings of helplessness. More specifically, the focus is on the *explanations* that people give for events in their lives, particularly the *unpleasant events* (Peterson et al., 1993). Imagine that you had submitted a paper in your class and that you received a surprisingly low grade on that paper. A common question you might ask yourself is "What *caused* the low grade on my paper?" Your explanation for the cause of the low grade might reveal something about your explanatory style. When things go wrong, who or what typically gets the blame? Psychologists prefer the term **causal attribution** to refer to a person's explanation of the cause of an event. To what cause would you attribute your paper's low grade? Was it because you happened to be in a rush and submitted a quickly written paper? Was it because you are simply a poor writer? Was it because the professor who graded it was unduly harsh in her grading? Or was it because your dog ate your original paper, so you quickly wrote another, which was not nearly as good as the one your dog ate? All of these explanations are causal attributions for the event.

Psychologists use the term **explanatory style** to refer to tendencies some people have to frequently use certain explanations for the causes of events. Explanations for the causes of events can be broken down along three broad dimensions. First, explanations for events can be either *internal* or *external*. The poor paper grade could be due to something pertaining to *you* (internal, such as your lack of skill) or something pertaining to the *environment* (external, such as the professor's being unduly harsh). Some people blame

themselves for all sorts of events and are constantly apologizing for events that are outside their control. The more internal your explanation, the more likely you are to blame yourself for unpleasant events, even those events over which you have little or no control.

A second dimension concerns whether the cause of the event is *stable* or *unstable*. For example, if you were temporarily set back by your dog eating the original version of your paper, then that would be an unstable cause (assuming your dog does not eat all of your papers). However, an explanation that concerns your lack of writing skill is a more or less *permanent*, or stable, characteristic. When bad events happen, some people tend to think that the causes of such situations are permanent, that the causes are stable and long-lasting.

The third important dimension of causes of events concerns whether the cause is *global* or *specific*. A specific cause is one that affects only the particular situation (e.g., writing papers), whereas a global cause affects many situations in life (all areas involving intellectual skills). For example, you might have explained the cause of your poor paper grade like this: "I am just unable to write; I can hardly put a noun and a verb together to form a sentence." This is a global explanation and might imply that you would be expected to do poorly in whatever task required writing.

Whenever someone offers an explanation for an event, that explanation can be analyzed in terms of the three dimensions: internal–external, stable–unstable, and global–specific. Most people use different combinations of explanations—sometimes blaming themselves, sometimes blaming external causes, sometimes blaming specific causes, and so forth. However, some

people develop a consistent explanatory style. For example, suppose someone consistently blames herself whenever *anything* goes wrong. After arriving at her destination on a plane that was late, the woman apologizes to her friend who picked her up at the airport, saying, "I'm sorry I'm late," when, in fact, *she* was not at all responsible for being late. She might say to her friend instead, "I'm sorry that *the plane I was on was late* and that you had to be inconvenienced. Next time I'll use a different airline." This might be a more appropriate external explanation for the real cause of being late.

The explanatory style that most puts a person at risk for feelings of helplessness and poor adjustment is one that emphasizes internal, stable, and global causes for bad events. This has been called the **pessimistic explanatory style**. This style is in contrast to the **optimistic explanatory style**, which emphasizes external, temporary, and specific causes of events. For example, one scenario on the Attributional Style Questionnaire (Peterson, 1991) asks you to imagine being on a date that goes badly, in which both you and your date have a lousy time. You are then asked why this might happen to you. If your explanation involves an external attribution to an unstable and highly specific cause (e.g., "I happened to choose a movie that neither one of us liked, then we went to a restaurant where the service was poor, and afterward my car got stuck in the mud."), then you are scored as more optimistic than someone who offers an internal, stable, and global interpretation (e.g., "I just have trouble relating to people, I cannot keep a conversation going, and I am completely shy when it comes to the opposite sex.") (see Figure 12.3).

	Internal/external	Stable/unstable	Global/specific
Optimistic style	External: "My girlfriend broke up with me because her parents forced her."	Unstable: "My girlfriend broke up with me because she needs all her time right now to devote to the charity drive, which only lasts one month."	Specific: "My girlfriend broke up with me because she found out I dated Julie last weekend."
Pessimistic style	Internal: "My girlfriend broke up with me because I'm from a low-class family, I'm not going to college, and I have very little ambition in life."	Stable: "My girlfriend broke up with me because I'm shorter than her, and she wants someone who is taller."	Global: "My girlfriend broke up with me because I'm an inconsiderate, two-timing, unfaithful jerk who couldn't keep a relationship going if his life depended on it."

Figure 12.3

The three dimensions underlying explanatory style, with their pessimistic and optimistic versions.

Is explanatory style a stable characteristic? One study examined explanatory style over the life span (Burns & Seligman, 1989). A group of participants, whose average age was 72 years, completed a questionnaire on explanatory style and provided diaries or letters written in their youth, an average of 52 years earlier. The diaries and letters were content analyzed for explanatory style. The correlation between these two measures of explanatory style for negative life events that were generated five decades apart, was .54, indicating a significant amount of stability in explanatory style.

Because an optimistic explanatory style correlates with beneficial effects in many areas of life, including earning better grades in college (Maleva et al., 2014), programs have been developed to train people to have a more optimistic explanatory style. For example, one program for college students (Gerson & Fernandez, 2013) is a three-session program that teaches students to adopt an optimistic explanatory style, and has been shown to increase student reports of optimism, resilience, and thriving in college. The majority of research on explanatory style focuses on how people adapt to traumatic events, with the general finding that an optimistic style is associated with better response. For example, researchers examined survivors of the 2004 tsunami that devastated two-thirds of the coast of Sri Lanka (Levy, Slade, & Ranasinghe, 2009), and found that a pessimistic explanatory style was associated with more symptoms of post-traumatic stress disorder.

An interesting extension of the concept of explanatory style is to extend it from individuals to groups. For example, recent studies have examined the explanatory style of sports teams (Carron, Shapcott, & Martin, 2014) and the explanatory style of business organizations (Smith, Caputi, & Crittenden, 2013). Results generally mirror those found with individuals, that team optimism was associated with better outcomes (higher percentage of winning, business success).

In Chapter 13, we discuss the role of explanatory style in depression, and in Chapter 18 we return to the topic of explanatory style, again in some detail, with reference to health.

Personal Projects Analysis

A **personal project** is a set of relevant actions intended to achieve a goal that a person has selected. Psychologist Brian Little (e.g., Little, 2007, 2011) believes that personal projects make natural units for understanding the workings of personality because they reflect how people face up to the serious business of navigating through daily life. Most people, if asked, are able to make a list of the important projects that they work on in their daily lives, such goals as to lose weight, do homework, make new friends, start and maintain an exercise program, send away for graduate school applications, develop a better relationship with God, or find some principles to live by. People typically have many goals that come and go in their day-to-day lives—one project is more important today, and a different one is important tomorrow—as well as other projects that are more ongoing.

Little developed the Personal Projects Analysis method for assessing personal projects. Participants first generate a list of their personal projects, as many or as few as they deem relevant. Most participants list an average of 15 personal projects that are currently important in their daily lives. Next, participants rate each project on several scales, such as how important the project is to them, how difficult it is, how much they enjoy working on it, how much progress they have made on it, and the negative and positive impacts it has had in their lives (Little & Gee, 2007).

Personal Projects Analysis has a number of interesting implications for understanding personality. Researchers have investigated the relation between the Big Five personality traits (discussed in Chapter 3) and aspects of personal projects. Little (1999) reports several interesting relationships. For example, people who score high on the trait of neuroticism are also likely to rate their personal projects as stressful, difficult, likely to end in failure, and outside of their control. Such people are also likely to state that they have made little progress toward achieving their goals. Apparently, part and parcel of being high on the neuroticism dimension is experiencing difficulty and dissatisfaction in accomplishing one's personal projects (Little, Lecci, & Watkinson, 1992).

Researchers have also been interested in which specific aspects of personal projects are most closely related to overall reports of life satisfaction and happiness. Little (1999, 2007) summarizes research suggesting that overall happiness is most related to feeling in control of one's personal projects, feeling unstressed about those projects, and being optimistic that projects will end successfully. These aspects of personal projects have also been found to predict well-being in an elderly sample (Lawton et al., 2002). These aspects of Personal Project Analysis (low stress, high control, high optimism) do indeed predict overall levels of happiness and life satisfaction (Palys & Little, 1983). Such findings have led Little to conclude that "bringing our personal projects to successful completion . . . seems to be a pivotal factor in whether we thrive emotionally or lead lives of . . . quiet desperation" (Little, 1999, p. 25). Recent work on personal projects is presented in an edited volume by Little, Salmela-Aro, and Phillips (2007).

Cognitive Social Learning Theory

A number of modern personality theories have expanded on the notion that personality is expressed in goals and in how people think about themselves relative to their goals. Collectively these theories form what has been called the **cognitive social learning approach** to personality, an approach that emphasizes the cognitive and social processes whereby people learn to value and strive for certain goals over others.

Albert Bandura and the Notion of Self-Efficacy   Albert Bandura was trained in classical behavioral psychology, popular in the 1940s, which viewed humans, and all organisms, as passive responders to the external environment, completely determined by external reinforcements. Bandura helped change this view by emphasizing the active nature of human behavior. He argued that people have intentions and forethought; they are reflective and can anticipate future events; they monitor their behavior and evaluate their own progress; plus they learn by observing others. Because he expanded on classical learning theory by adding cognitive and social variables, the movement he helped start is called cognitive social learning theory. Bandura referred to these distinctly human cognitive and social activities under the rubric of the self-system. The self-system exists for the self-regulation of behavior in the pursuit of goals (Bandura, 1997).

In Bandura's theory, one of the most important concepts is that of **self-efficacy**, which refers to the belief that one can execute a specific course of action to achieve a goal. For example, a child learning to bat a baseball may believe she can hit most balls pitched to her. We would say she has high self-efficacy beliefs for batting. A child who doubts his hitting ability, on the other hand, has low self-efficacy beliefs in this area. As it turns out, high self-efficacy beliefs often lead to effort and persistence on tasks, and to setting higher goals, compared to people with low self-efficacy beliefs (Bandura, 1989). As another example, college students who have higher self-efficacy beliefs about their studies are more persistent in their academic work and perform better in their classes than students with lower self-efficacy (Multon, Brown, & Lent, 1991).

Self-efficacy and performance mutually influence one another. Self-efficacy leads to better performance; then better performance leads to further increases in self-efficacy. As such, high self-efficacy is most important when starting out on some particular task. If the task is complex, it can be broken down into parts or subgoals, which can be accomplished. Accomplishing each subgoal along the way can increase overall self-efficacy. Self-efficacy can also be influenced by **modeling**, by seeing others engage in the performance with positive results.

Carol Dweck and the Theory of Mastery Orientation   We introduced the work of psychologist Carol Dweck in Chapter 11. Her early research focused on helpless and mastery-oriented behaviors in schoolchildren (Deiner & Dweck, 1978, 1980). She noted that some students persist in the face of failure, whereas others quit as soon as they encounter difficulties or their first failure. She started investigating the cognitive beliefs, particularly beliefs about ability, that lie behind these behavior patterns. For example, she discovered that students' implicit beliefs about the nature of intelligence had a significant impact on the way they approach challenging intellectual tasks: Students who view their intelligence as an unchangeable and fixed internal characteristic (what Dweck calls an "entity theory" of intelligence) tend to shy away from academic challenges, whereas students who believe that their intelligence can be increased through effort and persistence (what Dweck calls an "incremental theory" of intelligence) seek them out (Dweck, 1999a, 2002; Dweck, Chiu, & Hong, 1995).

It may sound like such a small thing, simply believing that intelligence is a fixed trait that cannot change, yet this belief is associated with putting less effort into school, with giving up earlier on academic challenges, and with lower academic success. Dweck's research illustrates the power of this belief in many studies of school children and college students (see review in Dweck, 2009, 2012). Having the opposite mindset—that intelligence is malleable and is something that can be changed with effort—is associated with better academic motivation and higher grades (Romero, Master, Pauneku, Dweck, & Gross, 2014). Moreover, Dweck and colleagues have designed and

Research by Carol Dweck clearly shows that praising a child for her effort is more effective than praising her for her intelligence. See text for the explanation of this.

© Andy Dean Photography/Shutterstock.com RF

tested several school-based interventions to change student's beliefs about their own intelligence, with students who have been trained to view intelligence as malleable subsequently putting more effort into academic performance and doing better in terms of grades (reviewed in Rattan, Savani, & Dweck, 2015).

Dweck's theory also has implications for how the praise of teachers and parents may unwittingly lead children to accept an entity view of intelligence. Praising a child for his or her intelligence may reinforce the notion that success and failure depend on something beyond the child's control. Comments such as "I'm so happy you got an A+ on your biology test, Mary! You are such a smart girl!" are interpreted by the child as "If good grades means that I'm intelligent, then poor grades must mean I am dumb." Or when trying to comfort a student, a teacher might say, "It's okay—not everyone can be good at math." This can reinforce an entity theory of math ability in the child, leading her to have lower motivation and lower expectations for her own math performance (Rattan, Good, & Dweck, 2012). When children with an entity view of intelligence do perform well, they have high self-esteem, but self-esteem diminishes as soon as they hit academic challenges that make them falter. Children who are admired for their effort are much more likely to view intelligence as changeable, and their self-esteem remains stable regardless of how hard they have to work to succeed. According to Dweck, it is much better to praise children for their effort ("Congratulations, your effort really paid off!") than for their ability ("Congratulations, you are really smart!"). Children who are praised for their effort learn to associate success with effort, not ability, and therefore become more confident that they can meet challenges through effort and hard work (Gunderson et al., 2013). Children with a view of intelligence and ability as changeable are more likely to work through frustrations and setbacks and reach their full academic potential (Dweck, 1999a, 2002).

E. Tory Higgins and the Theory of Regulatory Focus   Psychologist E. Tory Higgins has also developed a motivational theory concerning goals, called regulatory focus theory (Higgins, 2012). His theory adds the notion that people regulate their goal-directed behaviors in two distinct ways that serve two different needs. One focus of regulation is called **promotion focus,** in which the person is concerned with advancement, growth, and accomplishments. Behaviors with a promotion focus are characterized by eagerness, approach, and "going for the gold." The other focus of regulation is called **prevention focus**, in which the person is concerned with protection, safety, and the prevention of negative outcomes and failures. Behaviors with a prevention focus are characterized by vigilance, caution, and attempts to prevent negative outcomes.

When examined from a trait perspective, promotion focus correlates with such traits as extraversion and behavioral activation (which we discussed in Chapter 7). Prevention focus correlates with such traits as neuroticism and harm avoidance and (negatively) with impulsivity (Grant & Higgins, 2003). However, the concepts of prevention and promotion focus are more concerned with motivation and goal behaviors than the standard personality traits with which they correlate.

Walter Mischel and the Cognitive-Affective Personality System (CAPS)   As discussed in Chapter 4, psychologist Walter Mischel had a huge impact on personality psychology when he wrote a book in 1968, titled *Personality and Assessment,* that was highly critical of the evidence for personality traits. Recall that he argued that people's behavior was more strongly influenced by the situations they were in than by the personality traits they brought to those situations. In more recent years, Mischel and his former student—Youchi Shoda—have proposed a theory that personality variables (though not necessarily traits) do have an influence on behavior, mainly by interacting with and modifying the psychological meaning of situations.

In Michel and Shoda's cognitive-affective personality system (CAPS), they reconceptualize personality not as a collection of traits, but as an organization of cognitive and affective activities that influence how people respond to certain kinds of situations (Mischel, 2000, 2004; Shoda et al., 2013, 2015; Smith & Shoda, 2009). The emphasis is more on personality processes than on static traits. These cognitive and affective processes consist of such mental activities as construals (how one views a situation), goals, expectations, beliefs, and feelings as well as self-regulatory standards, abilities, plans, and strategies. According to this theory, each individual is characterized by a relatively stable network of such mental activities. Individuals acquire their specific set of these mental abilities through their learning history, their particular culture and subculture, their genetic endowment, and their biological history.

The CAPS theory argues that people differ from each other in the distinct organization of their cognitive and affective processes. As people move through the different situations in their lives, different cognitive and affective processes will be activated and mediate the impact of specific situations. For example, if a situation engenders frustration (e.g., being blocked from a goal), and the person has a specific cognitive-affective system (e.g., high expectations for success, the belief that aggression is permissible to obtain what you want), then he or she may respond with hostility. So, it is not the case that aggressive people would be aggressive in all situations (the trait view) but that aggressive people are sensitive to certain kinds of situations (e.g., frustration), and only then will they behave aggressively.

Mischel and Shoda present a contextualized view of personality as expressed in **"if . . . then . . ."** propositions: If situation A, then the person does X; but if situation B, then the person does Y. Personality leaves its signature, Mischel argues, in terms of the specific situational ingredients that prompt behavior from the person. To illustrate his approach, Mischel (2004) presents data gathered at a summer camp for delinquent children. All of the children had impulse control problems and had been aggressive in the past. The children were observed over many days and in many different situations in the summer camp. The researchers were interested in verbal aggression. They broke down the situations into five categories: when the child was "teased by a peer," "warned by an adult," "punished by an adult," "praised by an adult," and "approached by a peer." The children showed distinct profiles of verbal aggression across these different situations. For example, some children were aggressive only after being warned by an adult. Other children were aggressive only when approached by a peer. Mischel points out that verbal aggression was not consistent across all five situations and that specific "if . . . then . . ." profiles could be discerned for each child. These profiles were consistent, however, in the sense that kids who were aggressive when warned by an adult behaved that way repeatedly (Mischel, Shoda, & Mendoza-Denton, 2002).

The CAPS theory offers an important new way to think about personality, a way that emphasizes cognitive and affective processes that influence a person's behaviors relative to specific situational characteristics in terms of "if. . ., then . . ." propositions (for another example, see Smith et al., 2009). We present this theory in the chapter on cognitive approaches because it emphasizes the internal processes that people engage in to regulate their behavior. It is interesting that Mischel still argues that situations exert the most control over people's behavior but now believes that it is the psychological situation—that is, the meaning of the situation from the individual's perspective—that organizes behavior (Mischel, 2004, 2010).

Intelligence

No discussion of individual differences in cognition and information processing would be complete without at least some mention of intelligence. Intelligence has been defined in many ways, and there may be many different kinds of intelligence. One definition of intelligence is associated with educational attainment, how much knowledge a person has acquired relative to others in his or her age cohort. This is an **achievement view of intelligence**. Other definitions view intelligence less as the product of education and more as an ability to become educated, as the ability or aptitude to learn. This is the **aptitude view of intelligence**. Traditional measures of intelligence—so-called IQ tests—often have been used and interpreted as aptitude measures. For much of the past century, IQ tests were used to predict school performance and to select persons for educational opportunities. They are still used in this fashion today. For example, one study on college undergraduates found that general intelligence predicted 16 percent of the variability in grades, which translates into a correlation of about .40 between IQ and grades. Interestingly, need for achievement, which we discussed in Chapter 11, accounted for 11 percent of the variability in grades, beyond the variability accounted for by IQ (Lounsbury et al., 2003).

Early in the study of intelligence, most psychologists thought of this characteristic in traitlike terms, as a property of the individual. And individuals were thought to differ from each other in amount, in how much intelligence they possessed. Moreover, intelligence was thought of as a single broad factor—often called *g* for **general intelligence**. As tests were developed, however, researchers began to identify separate abilities—such as verbal ability, memory ability, perceptual ability, and arithmetic ability. The Scholastic Aptitude Test, or SAT, is one example that most college students are familiar with because they have taken this test. The SAT gives two scores—a verbal score and a mathematical score—and is an example of two differentiated kinds of intelligence. As the name implies, many believe the SAT is an aptitude measure, that it measures the ability to learn and acquire new information. However, the SAT contains questions that only persons already with an education can answer and, so, is really, some argue, an achievement test. Nevertheless, the SAT predicts college grade point average, which is useful in selecting persons who are likely to do well in higher education settings.

Other intelligence tests yield even more than two scores. For example, the Wechsler Intelligence Scale for Children—Revised (revised in 1991, originally published by Wechsler, 1949) yields 11 subtest scores, 6 of which require or depend on verbal ability and 5 of which are nonverbal, such as finding missing elements in a picture and assembling a puzzle. Also, the test yields 2 broad scores to represent verbal and performance intelligence. Psychologists use the multiple scores to evaluate a person's strengths and weaknesses, as well as to understand how the individual uniquely approaches and solves problems.

A widely accepted definition of intelligence, proposed by Gardner (1983), is that it is the application of cognitive skill and knowledge to solve problems, learn, and achieve goals that are valued by the individual and the culture. With intelligence defined this broadly, it is obvious that there are many kinds of intelligence, perhaps several more beyond the traditional verbal, mathematical, and performance distinctions. Howard Gardner has proposed a theory of **multiple intelligences**, which includes seven forms, such as interpersonal intelligence (social skills, ability to communicate, and get along with others) and intrapersonal intelligence (insight into oneself, one's emotions, and one's motives). Gardner also includes kinesthetic intelligence—describing the abilities of athletes, dancers, and acrobats—and musical intelligence (Gardner, 1999). Other experts are adding to the growing list of forms of intelligence, such as the concept of emotional intelligence, proposed by psychologists Peter Salovey and Jack Mayer (1990) and popularized by journalist Dan Goleman (1995). The concept of emotional intelligence is receiving a great deal of attention from researchers (see Zeidner et al., 2003, for a review).

Exercise

The concept of emotional intelligence has been proposed to explain why some people with a lot of academic intelligence do not appear to have a lot of practical intelligence, people skills, or what might be called street smarts. Goleman (1995), in his highly readable book *Emotional Intelligence,* presents many cases of people who have high levels of traditional intelligence yet fail in various areas of their lives, such as in relationships. Goleman also reviews the psychological literature and comes to the conclusion that traditional measures of intelligence, although predicting school performance fairly well, actually do a rather poor job of predicting later life outcomes, such as occupational attainment, salary, professional status, and quality of marriage (e.g., Vaillant, 1977). *Emotional intelligence,* Goleman argues, is more strongly predictive of these life outcomes.

Emotional intelligence is proposed as a set of five specific abilities:

- Awareness of one's own feelings and bodily signals and an ability to identify one's own emotions and to make distinctions (such as realizing the fear that lies behind anger)
- Ability to manage and regulate emotions, especially negative emotions, and to manage stress
- Control of one's impulses—directing one's attention and effort, delaying gratification, and staying on task toward goals
- Ability to decode the social and emotional cues of others, to listen, and to take the perspective of others (empathy)
- Leadership, the ability to influence and guide others without their becoming angry or resentful, the ability to elicit cooperation, and skill in negotiation and conflict resolution

It is easy to see how these skills and abilities relate to positive life outcomes and how they are so different from traditional concepts of intelligence, such as scholastic achievement and scholastic ability. Can you think of someone you know who is very high on scholastic ability yet deficient in one or more of the aspects of emotional intelligence? Such a person might be successful in school yet have problems in other areas of life, such as making friends or becoming independent from his or her family. Alternatively, can you think of someone you know who is high on emotional intelligence yet low on scholastic ability?

Gardner's concept of multiple intelligences is controversial. Some intelligence researchers feel that these separate abilities are correlated enough with each other (implying that they tend to co-occur in the same persons) to justify thinking of intelligence as *g,* a general factor (e.g., Herrnstein & Murray, 1994; Petrill, 2002; Rammsayer & Brandler, 2002). Other experts acknowledge a few broad distinctions, such as the verbal and mathematical intelligences that are so much a part of school systems in the United States. Other experts, including many educators, are examining the implications of the multiple intelligences notion. Some universities are considering using "noncognitive" measures of personality characteristics, like persistence, initiative, and conscientiousness, in addition to the traditional SAT scores, to inform admissions decisions (Hoover, 2013). Some schools are making curriculum changes designed to develop and strengthen various forms of intelligence in their students. For example, some schools are teaching units in emotional intelligence. Other schools offer classes for those high on nonverbal intelligence. Other schools are fostering character education, which can be thought of as a form of civic intelligence. These modern educational efforts are the direct outcomes of research being conducted by personality psychologists exploring the basic nature of intelligence.

We cannot leave the concept of intelligence without looking at the **cultural context of intelligence**. What is defined as "intelligent behavior" will obviously differ across cultures. For example, among the people who live on the islands of Micronesia, the ability to navigate the ocean and other maritime skills are considered superior forms of intelligence. Among Eskimos who hunt along the shores in their kayaks, the ability to develop a cognitive map of the complex shoreline in Alaska is a valued ability. Many psychologists define culture, in part, as the shared notions about what counts as efficient problem solving (Wertsch & Kanner, 1992). These skills then become part of the way successful people think in that culture. Western cultures, for example, emphasize verbal skills, both written and oral, as well as the mathematical and spatial skills necessary in a technologically advanced culture. Other cultures, however, might guide their members to develop different problem-solving skills, such as developing a sense of direction or a knowledge of animal behavior.

Because of these considerations, we should always view intelligence as comprised of the skills valued in a particular culture. However, Western culture—along with its economic, social, and political systems—is proliferating into countries around the world. Will the world become a monoculture? If so, will there become one form of intelligence, which is universally valued? Or will cultures maintain separate identities and define differences in what counts as intelligent behavior? For example, currently most people in Europe speak more than one language, and many speak three or more because of the problem-solving advantage a multilingual person has in Europe. Many Europeans consider Americans to be linguistically challenged or, less charitably, verbally unintelligent because most Americans know only one language.

Interestingly, average IQ scores have risen steadily the past several decades, at the rate of approximately 1 IQ point every 4 or 5 years within populations (Flynn, 2007, 2012). This rise in population IQ scores is known as the *Flynn effect,* named after the person who first documented this observation (Flynn, 1984). Various explanations have been put forward for rising population IQ scores, such as better nutrition around the world. Flynn's (2007, 2012) own explanation focuses on access to, and improvements in, quality of education over those decades. However, despite steady increases in average IQ over the last half of the twentieth century, psychologists have observed a decline in population IQ scores over the last decade, starting around 1998, in specific countries (Teasdale & Owen, 2008) as well as worldwide (Lynn & Harvey, 2008), a phenomenon called the *reverse Flynn effect.*

This decline in population IQ worries intelligence researchers because the average IQ in a country is correlated with many indicators of national well-being, including gross domestic product (the wealth of the nation, Gelade, 2008; Hunt & Wittmann,

2008), educational attainment, and technological advancements (Rindermann, 2008). Lower population IQ has also been associated with the prevalence of juvenile delinquency, adult crime, single parenthood, and poverty (Gordon, 1997). Each decline of one IQ point is associated with a reduction of income of about $425 per year (Zagorsky, 2007). Lynn and Harvey (2008) attribute this decline in national IQ scores around the world to increasing fertility rates, generalizing from the often-replicated observation that IQ and fertility are negatively correlated (i.e., people with lower IQ scores tend to produce more offspring than people with higher IQ scores) (Shatz, 2008; Vining, 1982).

A new variable in intelligence research is called **inspection time**, which refers to the time it takes a person to make a simple discrimination between two displayed objects. For example, two lines appear on a computer screen and the subject's task is to say which one is longer. The time it takes the subject to inspect the two lines, measured in milliseconds (thousandths of a second), before making the discrimination is the measure of inspection time. This variable is highly related to standard measures of general intelligence (Osmon & Jackson, 2002). Inspection time correlates with other measures of perceptual speed and reaction time to make decisions (Jensen, 2011), and these mental speed abilities contribute to higher IQ scores (Johnson & Deary, 2011). Inspection Time is also a sensitive leading indicator of the cognitive decline that occurs with old age for some people (Gregory, Nettelbeck, Howard, & Wilson, 2008). Another similar measure is the ability to discriminate auditory intervals that differ only in the range of a few milliseconds, which also is related to general intelligence (Rammsayer & Brandler, 2002). A recent review of 172 studies of the relationship between IQ and speed of information processing (Sheppard & Vernon, 2008) concluded that measures of intelligence are correlated with mental speed, with smarter people being generally faster on a wide variety of mental tasks. Findings such as these suggest that brain mechanisms specifically involved in information processing are more efficient in persons scoring high on intelligence measures.

There are many debates about intelligence that are beyond the scope of an introductory personality text. If you are interested, you can go to advanced sources, such as the journal *Intelligence,* or to books, such as Neisser's (1998) or Herrnstein and Murray's controversial *The Bell Curve* (1994) and the direct responses to the controversy created by *The Bell Curve*—such as Fraser (1995), Jacoby and Glauberman (1995), and Lynn (2008). Other alternatives to the Herrnstein and Murray position include works by Sternberg (1985), Gardner (1983), and Simonton (1991). You should know that there are several current debates about intelligence, including whether it can be measured accurately, whether measures of intelligence are biased to favor persons from the dominant majority group in the culture, the extent to which intelligence is heritable and the implications of heritability, whether different racial groups differ with respect to intelligence, and whether race differences should be interpreted as social class differences. These issues are politicized and have many implications for social and government policy, and so are generating much heated debate. Personality psychologists are playing an important role by doing the research necessary to provide a scientific approach to these issues.

SUMMARY AND EVALUATION

Cognitive topics in personality psychology are a broad class of subject matter. People differ from each other in many ways, in how they think as well as in how they perceive, interpret, remember, want, and anticipate the events in their lives. In this chapter, we organized the coverage into four broad categories: perception, interpretation, goals, and intelligence.

We began by examining some ways in which personality is related to perceptual differences among people. Field independence/dependence concerns the ability to see the trees despite the forest. This individual difference in perceptual style has to do with the ability to focus on the details despite the clutter of background information. This style of perceiving may have important implications for learning styles and career choices.

The second perceptual difference we discussed was sensory reducing/augmenting. This dimension originally referred to the tendency to reduce or augment painful stimuli and was first related to individual differences in pain tolerance. It is now more generally used to refer to individual differences in sensitivity to sensory stimulation, with some individuals (augmenters) being more sensitive than others (reducers). This individual difference may have important implications for the development of problem behaviors associated with seeking stimulation, such as smoking or other forms of drug abuse.

Another aspect of cognition is how people interpret events in their lives. This approach to personality has its roots in the work of George Kelly. His personal construct theory emphasizes how people construct their experiences by using their constructs to make sense out of the world. Another general difference among people is in locus of control, the tendency to interpret events either as under one's control or as not under one's control. Many researchers now apply the locus of control concept in particular life domains, such as health locus of control or relationship locus of control.

Learned helplessness is the feeling engendered when a person experiences an inescapable aversive situation. The feeling of helplessness may also generalize to new situations so that the person continues to act helplessly and fails to seek solutions to his or her problems. The theory of learned helplessness was reformulated to incorporate how people think about events in their lives, particularly unpleasant events. Psychologists have focused on specific dimensions of people's explanations, such as whether the cause is internal or external to the person, whether it is stable or unstable, and whether it is global or specific. A pessimistic explanatory style is internal, stable, and global.

Personality can also be revealed by how people select projects and tasks to pursue in life. If you know what a person really wants out of life, then you probably know that person fairly well. Our goals define us, and the strategies with which we pursue those desires illustrate the active aspects of personality in our daily lives.

Cognitive social learning theory was introduced and several specific examples of this approach were described. All of the example theories incorporate the concept of goals and related cognitive activities, such as expectancies, strategies, and beliefs about one's abilities. These theories are important new additions to the psychology of personality because they emphasize how the psychological situation is a function of characteristics of the person (e.g., their self-efficacy beliefs).

Intelligence was also discussed in this chapter, along with different views on intelligence (as academic achievement versus an aptitude for learning). We reviewed the historical development of intelligence as starting with the view of this as a single and general trait up to today's trend toward a multiple intelligences view. We also noted that culture influences which skills and achievements contribute toward intelligence and presented some results on a biological interpretation of intelligence. In addition, we briefly reviewed some of the controversies that are being debated in the area of intelligence.

KEY TERMS

cognitive approaches 366
personalizing cognition 367
objectifying cognition 367
cognition 367
information processing 367
perception 367
interpretation 368
conscious goals 368
rod and frame test (RFT) 369
field dependent 369
field independent 369
pain tolerance 373
reducer/augmenter theory 373

constructs 376
personal constructs 376
postmodernism 376
locus of control 377
generalized expectancies 378
external locus of control 379
internal locus of control 379
learned helplessness 380
causal attribution 382
explanatory style 382
pessimistic explanatory style 382
optimistic explanatory style 382
personal project 383

cognitive social learning approach 384
self-efficacy 385
modeling 385
promotion focus 386
prevention focus 386
"if . . . then . . ." propositions 387
achievement view of intelligence 388
aptitude view of intelligence 388
general intelligence 388
multiple intelligences 388
cultural context of intelligence 390
inspection time 391

© Corbis/SuperStock RF

13

THE COGNITIVE/EXPERIENTIAL DOMAIN

The emotion of fear is characterized by a distinct facial expression. Fear also has a distinctly unpleasant subjective feeling. There are also the associated changes in physiology, such as heart rate increases and increases in blood flow to the large muscles of the legs and arms. These changes prepare the frightened person for the intense action tendency associated with fear, for example, to flee or to fight.
© moodboard/Getty Images RF

Imagine you are traveling to visit a friend in a city to which you've never been before. You've taken a train to this city and are walking to your friend's apartment from the station. The train was late, so it is dark as you begin to make your way in the unfamiliar neighborhood. Your directions seem a little vague, and after 20 minutes of walking you are beginning to think they are incorrect. It is late and there are not many people on the street. You are certain that the directions are incorrect. You decide to take a shortcut through an alley and head back to the train station. The alley is dark, but short, and it will get you back to the train station faster, so you start down the alley. You are alert, a bit on edge, as you are really out of your element. You look over your shoulder and notice that someone has followed you down the alley. Your heart is pounding. You turn and look ahead, and you see that someone has entered the alley in front of you as well. You suddenly feel trapped and you freeze. You are in a real predicament, as your way is blocked in both directions. Your breathing is rapid and you feel confused and light-headed. Your mind is racing, but you are not sure what to do as the two people are closing in on you from both directions. Your palms are sweating and you feel the tension in your neck and throat, as if you might scream any second. The two people are getting closer and closer to you. You feel nervousness in your stomach as you look first in front, then behind. You want to run but cannot decide which way to go. You are paralyzed with fear; you stand there, trembling, not knowing whether you can run away or whether you will have to fight for your life. Suddenly, one of the persons calls out your name.

You realize it is your friend, who has come with his roommate to look for you between the train station and the apartment. You breathe a sigh of relief, and quickly your state of fear subsides, your body calms, your mind clears, and you greet your friend with an enthusiastic, "Am I glad to see you!"

In this example, you experienced the emotion of fear. You also experienced the emotion of relief, and perhaps even elation, at being rescued by your friend. **Emotions** can be defined by their three components. First, emotions have distinct subjective feelings, or affects, associated with them. Second, emotions are accompanied by bodily changes, mostly in the nervous system, and these produce associated changes in breathing, heart rate, muscle tension, blood chemistry, and facial and bodily expressions. And third, emotions are accompanied by distinct **action tendencies,** or increases in the probabilities of certain behaviors. With the emotional feeling of fear, there are subjective feelings of anxiety, confusion, and panic. There are also associated changes in bodily function, such as heart rate increases, decreased blood flow to the digestive system (making for stomach queasiness), and increased blood flow to the large muscles of the legs and arms. These changes prepare you for the intense activity sometimes associated with fear. The activity, or action tendency, associated with fear is to flee or to fight.

Why are personality psychologists interested in emotions? People differ from each other in their emotional reactions, even to the same events, so emotions are useful in distinguishing among persons. For example, imagine losing your wallet, which contains a large sum of money, your credit card, and all your identification, including your driver's license. What emotions do you think you would feel—anger, embarrassment, hopelessness, frustration, panic, fear, shame, guilt? Different people would have different emotional reactions to this life event, and understanding how and why people differ in their emotional reactions is part of understanding personality.

Other theories of emotion emphasize the functions that emotions play, such as generating short-term adaptive actions that help us survive. For example, the emotion of disgust has the adaptive value of prompting us to quickly spit out something that is not good for us. Interestingly, the expression of disgust, even when the feeling is evoked by a thought or something that is only psychologically distasteful, is to wrinkle the nose, open the mouth, and protrude one's tongue as if spitting something out.

In his 1872 book *The Expression of the Emotions in Man and Animals,* Charles Darwin proposed a **functional analysis** of emotions and emotional expressions. His analysis focuses on the "why" of emotions and expressions, in particular in terms of whether they increase the fitness of individuals (see Chapter 8 of this textbook). In his book he describes his observations of animals, his own children, and other people, linking particular expressions with specific emotions. He recognized that evolution by natural selection applied not only to anatomic structures but also to the "mind," including the emotions and their expressions. How do emotions increase evolutionary fitness? Darwin concluded that emotional expressions rapidly communicate information from one animal to another about what is likely to happen. The dog baring its teeth and bristling the hair on its back is communicating to others that he is likely to attack. If others recognize this communication, they may choose to back away, thereby avoiding the attack. Many modern emotion theorists accept this functional emphasis, but most personality psychologists approach emotion with an interest in how people differ from each other in terms of emotions.

Issues in Emotion Research

Several major issues divide the field of emotion research (Davidson, Scherer, & Goldsmith, 2003). Psychologists typically hold an opinion on each of these issues. We consider two of these issues, beginning with the distinction between emotional states and emotional traits.

Emotional States Versus Emotional Traits

We typically think of emotions as states that come and go (similar to motives, as we saw in Chapter 11). A person gets angry, then gets over it. A person becomes sad, then snaps out of it. **Emotional states** are *transitory*. Moreover, emotional states depend more on the situation a person is in than on the specific person. A man is angry *because* he was unfairly treated. A woman is sad *because* her bicycle was stolen. Most people would be angry or sad in these situations. Emotions as states are transitory; they have a specific cause, and that cause typically originates outside of the person (something happens in the environment).

We can also think of emotions as dispositions, or traits. For example, we often characterize people by stating what emotions they *frequently* experience or express: "Mary is cheerful and enthusiastic," or "John is frequently angry and often loses his temper." Here we are using emotions to describe dispositions, characteristic emotional traits. Emotional traits are consistencies in a person's emotional life. Traits, as you'll recall from Chapter 3, are patterns in a person's behavior or experience that are at least somewhat consistent from situation to situation and that are at least somewhat stable over time. Thus, an **emotional trait** is a pattern of emotional reactions that a person consistently experiences across a variety of life situations.

Categorical Versus Dimensional Approach to Emotion

Emotion researchers can be divided into two camps based on their answers to the following question: What is the best way to think about emotions? Some suggest emotions are best thought of as a small number of primary and distinct emotions (anger, joy, anxiety, sadness). Others suggest that emotions are best thought of as broad dimensions of experience (e.g., a dimension ranging from pleasant to unpleasant). Those who think that primary emotions are the key are said to take the **categorical approach**. Hundreds of terms describe different categories of emotions. Averill (1975), for example, compiled a list of 550 terms that describe different feeling states. This is similar to the situation with basic trait terms, in which psychologists started with thousands of trait adjectives and searched for the fundamental factors that underlie those many variations, concluding that there are probably about five primary personality traits that underlie the huge list of trait adjectives.

Emotion researchers who take the categorical approach have tried to reduce the complexity of emotions by searching for the primary emotions that underlie the great variety of emotional terms (Levenson, 2003). They have not reached the kind of consensus that is found in the personality trait domain, however. The lack of consensus found in this area of psychology results from different criteria that researchers use for defining an emotion as primary. Ekman (1992a), for example, requires that a primary emotion have a distinct facial expression that is recognized across cultures. The experience of

Happiness can be thought of as a state or as a trait. People high in trait happiness experience frequent happiness states, or have a lower threshold for becoming happy. Moreover, happiness is recognized around the world through the expression of smiling. People from all cultures smile when they are happy.
© Ollyy/Shutterstock.com RF

sadness is accompanied by frowning and knitting the brow. This facial expression is universally recognized as depicting the emotion of sadness. Similarly, clenching and baring the teeth is associated with anger and is universally recognized as anger. In fact, people who are blind from birth frown when sad, clench and bare their teeth when angry, and smile when they are happy. Because persons blind from birth have never seen the facial expressions of sadness, anger, or joy, it is not likely that they learned these expressions. Rather, it seems likely that the expressions are part of human nature. Based on these criteria of distinct and universal facial expressions, Ekman's list of primary emotions contains disgust, sadness, joy, surprise, anger, and fear.

Other researchers hold different criteria for counting emotions as primary. For example, Izard (1977) suggests that the primary emotions are distinguished by their unique motivational properties. That is, emotions are understood to guide behaviors by motivating a person to take specific adaptive actions. Fear is included as a primary emotion on Izard's list because it motivates a person to avoid danger and seek safety. Interest is similarly a fundamental emotion because it motivates a person to learn and acquire new skills. Izard's criteria result in a list of 10 primary emotions. In Table 13.1, various lists of primary emotions are based on various criteria.

Another approach to understanding the complexity of emotion has been based on empirical research rather than on theoretical criteria. In the **dimensional approach**, researchers gather data by having subjects rate themselves on a wide variety of emotions, then apply statistical techniques (usually factor analysis) to identify the basic dimensions underlying the ratings.

There is remarkable consensus among researchers on the basic dimensions that underlie self-ratings of affect (Judge & Larsen, 2001; Larsen & Diener, 1992; Watson, 2000). Most of the studies suggest that people categorize emotions using just two primary dimensions: how pleasant or unpleasant the emotion is and how high or low on arousal the emotion is. When these two dimensions are arrayed as axes in a two-dimensional coordinate system, the adjectives that describe emotions fall in a circle around the two dimensions, as shown in Figure 13.1.

This model of emotion suggests that every feeling state can be described as a combination of pleasantness/unpleasantness and arousal. For example, a person can feel unpleasant feelings in a very high-arousal way (nervous, anxious, terrified) or in a very low-arousal

Table 13.1 A Selection of Theorists Who Provide Lists of Primary Emotions

Theorists	Basic Emotions	Criteria
Ekman, Friesen, & Ellsworth, 1972	Anger, disgust, fear, joy, sadness, surprise	Universal facial expression
Frijda, 1986	Desire, happiness, interest, surprise, wonder, sorrow	Motivation to take specific actions
Gray, 1982	Rage, terror, anxiety, joy	Brain circuits
Izard, 1977	Anger, contempt, disgust, distress, fear, guilt, interest, joy, shame, surprise	Motivation to take specific actions
James, 1884	Fear, grief, love, rage	Bodily involvement
Mower, 1960	Pain, pleasure	Unlearned emotional states
Oatley & Johnson-Laird, 1987	Anger, disgust, anxiety, happiness, sadness	Little cognitive involvement
Plutchik, 1980	Anger, acceptance, joy, anticipation, fear, disgust, sadness, surprise	Evolved biological processes
Tomkins, 2008	Anger, interest, contempt, disgust, fear, joy, shame, surprise	Density of neural firing

Source: Adapted from Ortony & Turner, 1990.

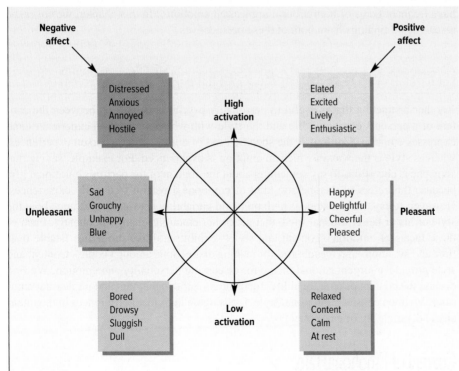

Figure 13.1

The dimensional approach to emotion, showing two primary dimensions: high to low activation and pleasantness to unpleasantness with emotions falling in a circular array. This is sometimes called the Circumplex model of emotion.

way (bored, fatigued, tired). Similarly, a person can feel pleasant feelings in a high-arousal way (excited, enthusiastic, elated) or in a low-arousal way (calm, relaxed). Thus the two dimensions of pleasantness and arousal are seen as fundamental dimensions of emotion.

The dimensional view of emotion is based on research studies in which subjects rate their emotional experiences. Emotions that occur together, which are experienced as similar to each other, are understood as defining a common dimension. For example, the emotions of distress, anxiety, annoyance, and hostility are very similar in terms of experience and thus seem to anchor one end of a dimension of high arousal negative affect. The dimensional approach to emotion refers more to how people *experience* their emotions than to how they *think* about their emotions. In contrast, the categorical approach relies more on conceptual distinctions between emotions. The dimensional approach, on the other hand, suggests that what we experience are various degrees of pleasantness and arousal and that every emotion we are capable of experiencing can be described as a combination of pleasantness and arousal (Larsen & Fredrickson, 1999; Larsen & Prizmic, 2006).

Some researchers prefer the categorical perspective, finding it useful to think about emotions as distinct categories rather than dimensions. For example, the emotions of anger and anxiety, although similar in terms of being high-arousal negative emotions, are nevertheless associated with different facial expressions, feelings, and action tendencies. Personality psychologists with a categorical perspective would be interested in how people differ from each other with respect to primary emotions, such as anger and anxiety. There are also personality psychologists who prefer to think about how people differ with respect to the primary dimensions of emotion. For example, who are the people who have a good deal of pleasantness in their lives? Who are the people who have frequent bouts of high-arousal unpleasant emotions? In this chapter, we cover the research and findings from both of these perspectives.

Content Versus Style of Emotional Life

Another distinction that is useful to personality psychologists is that between the content of a person's emotional life and the style with which that person experiences and expresses emotion. **Content** is the specific kind of emotion that a person experiences, whereas **style** is the way in which an emotion is experienced. For example, saying that someone is cheerful is to say something about the content of the person's emotional life, because this refers to the specific kind of emotions a person frequently experiences. However, to say that someone is high on mood variability is to say something about the style of his or her emotional life—that his or her emotions change frequently. Each of these facets of emotion—content and style—exhibits traitlike properties (stable over time and situations and meaningful for making distinctions among people). Content and style provide an organizational theme for discussing personality and emotion. We first discuss the content of emotional life, focusing on various pleasant and unpleasant emotions. We then consider emotional style, focusing on individual differences in the intensity and variability of emotional life.

Content of Emotional Life

Content of emotional life means the typical emotions a person is likely to experience over time. For example, someone characterized as an angry or hot-tempered person should have an emotional life that contains a good deal of anger, irritability, and hostility. Someone whose emotional life contains a lot of pleasant emotions we might characterize as happy, cheerful, and enthusiastic. Thus the notion of content leads us to consider the *kinds* of emotions that people are likely to experience over time and across situations in their lives. We begin with a discussion of the pleasant emotional dispositions.

Pleasant Emotions

In lists of primary emotions, happiness or joy are typically the only pleasant emotions mentioned (though some theorists include interest as a pleasant emotion). In trait approaches to emotion, the major pleasant disposition is happiness and the associated feelings of being satisfied with one's life. We begin with these concepts.

Definitions of Happiness and Life Satisfaction   Over 2,000 years ago, Greek philosopher Aristotle wrote that happiness was the supreme good and that the goal of life was to attain happiness. Moreover, he taught that happiness was attained by living a virtuous life and being a good person. Some modern researchers similarly emphasize eudaimonia, the creation of a life of meaning and purpose, as the route to happiness (e.g., King & Hicks, 2012). Other scholars and philosophers have offered other theories on the sources of human happiness. For example, unlike Aristotle, eighteenth-century French philosopher Jean-Jacques Rousseau speculated that the road to happiness lies in the satisfaction of one's desires and the hedonistic pursuit of pleasure. In the late nineteenth century, the founder of psychology in America, William James, taught that happiness was the ratio of one's accomplishments to one's aspirations. One could achieve happiness, James thought, in one of two ways: by accomplishing more in life or by lowering one's aspirations.

William James defined happiness as having a high ratio of one's accomplishments compared to one's aspirations.
© SPL/Science Source

Although philosophers and psychologists have speculated about the roots of happiness for centuries, the scientific study of happiness is relatively recent (see Eid & Larsen, 2008, for a review). Psychologists began the serious study of happiness (also called subjective well-being) in the mid-1970s. Since then, scientific research on the topic has grown by leaps and bounds. In recent years, hundreds of scientific articles on happiness have been published annually in the psychological literature (Diener & Seligman, 2002). Indeed, a new journal started in the year 2000, titled *Journal of Happiness Research,* publishes six volumes a year dedicated to the science of happiness. Another journal, the *Journal of Positive Psychology,* also publishes many scientific studies on happiness.

One way to define **happiness** is to examine how researchers measure it. Several questionnaire measures are widely used in surveys and other research. Because happiness is a subjective quality—it depends on an individual's own judgment of his or her life—researchers *have* to rely on questionnaires. Some of these questionnaires focus on judgments about one's life, such as "How satisfied are you with your life as a whole these days?" Other questionnaires focus on emotion, particularly on the balance between pleasant and unpleasant emotions in a person's life. An example of this type of questioning was proposed by Fordyce (1978), in which the subject is asked the following questions:

What percent of the time are you happy?   _____
What percent of the time are you neutral?   _____
What percent of the time are you unhappy?   _____
Make sure your percents add up to 100.

Among college students, data indicate that the average person reports being happy about 65 percent of the time, neutral 15 percent, and unhappy 20 percent (Larsen &

Diener, 1985). The percent happy scale is one of the better measures of happiness in terms of construct validity (see Chapter 2). For example, it predicts a wide range of other happiness-related aspects of a person's personality, such as day-to-day moods and peer reports of overall happiness (Larsen, Diener, & Lucas, 2002).

Researchers conceive of happiness as having two complementary components. One is more cognitive and consists of judgments that one's life has purpose and meaning and has been called the life-satisfaction component. The other component is affective and consists of the ratio of a person's positive emotions to his or her negative emotions averaged over time. This has been called the hedonic component and really refers to the balance of positive to negative emotions in a person's life over time. The two components—life satisfaction and hedonic balance—tend to be highly correlated. Although we can think of cases where a person could be high on one and low on the other (e.g., a starving artist who feels her life has a great deal of purpose and meaning, yet is suffering greatly day to day to produce her art), the fact is that most people who have a life of meaning and purpose also have more positive than negative emotions in their life. Consequently, most psychologists refer to the general construct of happiness to talk about this characteristic.

Can it be that happy people are just deluding themselves, that most people are really miserable and happy people just don't know it or are denying it? It would be easy to lie on a questionnaire and to portray oneself as being happy and satisfied. This is the idea of social desirability, as discussed in Chapter 4. It turns out that measures of happiness *do* correlate with social desirability scores. In other words, people who score high on social desirability also score high on self-reported happiness scales. Moreover, social desirability measures also correlate with non-self-report happiness scores, such as peer reports of happiness. This finding suggests that having a positive view of oneself is part of being a happy person. Said differently, part of being happy is to have **positive illusions** about the self, an inflated view of one's own characteristics as a good, able, and desirable person, as this characteristic appears to be part of emotional well-being (Taylor, 1989; Taylor et al., 2000).

Despite the correlation of self-report measures of happiness with social desirability, other findings suggest that these happiness measures are valid (Diener, Oishi, & Lucas, 2003). These findings concern the positive correlations found between self-report and non-self-report measures of happiness. People who report that they are happy tend to have friends and family members who agree (Sandvik, Diener, & Seidlitz, 1993). In addition, studies of the daily diaries of happy people find that they report many more pleasant experiences than do unhappy people (Larsen & Diener, 1985). When different clinical psychologists interview a sample of people, the psychologists tend to agree strongly about which are happy and satisfied and which are not (Diener, 2000). And, in an interesting experiment, Seidlitz and Diener (1993) gave the participants five minutes to recall as many happy events in their lives as possible and then gave them five minutes to recall as many unhappy events in their lives as possible. They found that the happy people recalled more pleasant events, and fewer unpleasant events, than did the unhappy people.

Questionnaire measures of happiness and well-being also predict other aspects of people's lives that we would expect to relate to happiness (Diener, Lucas, & Larsen, 2003). For example, compared with unhappy people, happy people are less abusive and hostile, are less self-focused, and report fewer instances of disease. They also are more helpful and cooperative, have more social skills, are more creative and energetic, are more forgiving, and are more trusting (Myers, 1993, 2000; Myers & Diener, 1995; Veenhoven, 1988). In summary, self-reports of happiness appear to be valid and trustworthy (Larsen & Prizmic, 2006). After all, who but the persons themselves are the best judge of their subjective well-being? See Table 13.2 for a sample "life satisfaction" questionnaire.

Table 13.2 Satisfaction with Life Scale

Below are five statements with which you may agree or disagree. Using the scale below, indicate your agreement with each item by placing the appropriate number on the line preceding that item. Please be open and honest in your responses.

Strong Disagreement 1	Moderate Disagreement 2	Slight Disagreement 3	Slight Agreement 4	Moderate Agreement 5	Strong Agreement 6

1. _____ In most ways my life is close to my ideal.

2. _____ If I could live my life over, I would change almost nothing.

3. _____ I am satisfied with my life.

4. _____ So far I have gotten the important things I want in life.

5. _____ The conditions of my life are excellent.

Source: Diener et al., 1985.

What Good Is Happiness?   It has long been known that happiness correlates with many positive outcomes in life, such as marriage, longevity, self-esteem, and satisfaction with one's job (Diener et al., 1999). These correlations between desirable outcomes in life and happiness are often interpreted to mean that success in some area of life (e.g., a good marriage) will make a person happy. As another example, the small correlation between personal wealth and happiness is often interpreted as meaning that having money can make one (slightly more) happy. The majority of researchers in this area have gone on the assumption that successful outcomes foster happiness and that the causal direction goes from being successful leading to increased happiness.

However, a group of researchers (Lyubomirsky, King, & Diener, 2005) questioned this assumption about the causal direction going from success to happiness. They suggested that there may be areas of life where the causality goes in the opposite direction, from happiness to success. For example, it could be that being happy leads one to get married, or to have a better marriage, instead of having a good marriage leading one to become happy.

In an extremely large meta-analysis of the happiness and well-being literature, Lyubomirsky and colleagues (2005) reviewed many studies that might be used to disentangle the causal direction between happiness and several different outcomes. Two kinds of studies are most useful in assessing causal direction. One type of study is longitudinal, in which people are measured on at least two occasions separated in time. If happiness precedes success in life, then we have some evidence that the causal direction might go from happiness to the outcome. A second type of study is experimental, in which happiness is manipulated (people are put in a good mood) for half the sample (the other half is the control group), and some outcome is measured. If the outcome is higher in the group undergoing the happiness induction than in the control group, then we have some evidence that the causal direction might go from happiness to the outcome.

Lyubomirsky and colleagues (2005) found that longitudinal studies provided evidence that happiness leads to, or at least comes before, positive outcomes in many areas of life, including fulfilling and productive work, satisfying relationships, and superior mental and physical health and longevity. Experimental studies also provide evidence that happiness can lead to several positive outcomes, including being more helpful and altruistic, wanting to be with others, increases in self-esteem and liking of others, a better

Does having a good marriage cause a person to be happy? Or does being happy cause one to have a good marriage?

© Antonio Guillem/Shutterstock.com RF

functioning immune system, more effective conflict resolution skills, and more creative or more original thinking.

Although happiness has been shown to lead to many positive outcomes in life, the situation with some outcomes might be more complex and involve **reciprocal causality,** which refers to the idea that causality can flow in both directions. For example, we know that happy people are more likely to help others who are in need. Also, from the experimental literature, we know that helping someone in need can lead to increases in happiness. This kind of reciprocal causality may apply to many areas of life, including having a satisfying marriage or intimate relationship, having a fulfilling job, or having high self-esteem.

What Is Known About Happy People   In an early article titled "Who Is Happy?" psychologists David Myers and Ed Diener (1995) reviewed what is known about happy people. For example, are women happier than men, or are men the happier gender? In the United States, women are diagnosed with depression twice as often as men. This might suggest that men are happier than women. However, men are at least twice as likely as women to become alcoholics. The use of alcohol may be one way men medicate themselves for depression, so the real rate of depression may be more similar for men and women. Researchers need to examine actual studies of happiness to address the gender difference question. Fortunately, an excellent and thorough review of the studies on gender and happiness has already been done. Haring, Stock, and Okun (1984) analyzed 146 studies on global well-being and found that gender accounted for less than 1 percent of the variation in people's happiness. This finding of practically no difference between men and women appears across cultures and countries as well. Michalos (1991) obtained data on 18,032 university students from 39 countries. He found that roughly equal proportions of men and women rated themselves as being satisfied with their lives. Diener (2000) also reports gender equality in overall happiness.

Is happiness more likely among young, middle-aged, or older people? We often think that certain age periods are more stressful than others, such as the midlife crisis or the stress of adolescence. This might lead us to believe that certain times of life are happier than others. Inglehart (1990) addressed this question in a study of 169,776 people from 16 nations. It was found that the circumstances that make people happy change with age. For example, financial security and health are important for happiness later in life, whereas, for younger adults, success at school or work and satisfying intimate relationships are important for happiness. However, in looking at overall levels of happiness, Inglehart concluded that there was no evidence to suggest that any one time of life was happier than any other.

Is ethnicity related to happiness? Are some ethnic groups happier than others? Many surveys have included questions about ethnic identity, so a wealth of data exists on this question. Summarizing many such studies, Myers and Diener (1995) conclude that ethnic group membership is unrelated to subjective well-being. For example, African Americans report roughly the same amount of happiness as European Americans and in fact have slightly lower levels of depression (Diener et al., 1993). Crocker and Major (1989) suggest that people from disadvantaged social groups maintain their happiness by valuing the activities they are good at, by comparing themselves with members of their own group, and by blaming their problems on events that are outside of their control.

What about national differences in well-being? Are people from certain nations happier than people from other nations? The answer here seems to be yes. An impressive study by Diener, Diener, and Diener (1995) examined well-being scores obtained using probability surveys in 55 nations. The nations sampled in this study represented 75 percent of the earth's population. The results are portrayed in Table 13.3, where the nations are rank-ordered on the well-being measure. Looking at the rankings, what do you think might account for the differences among the countries that were high and low on well-being?

The researchers were able to assemble a broad array of other environmental, social, and economic information on each of these countries, and they tested whether any of these variables correlated with average national happiness. At the national level, the poorer countries appeared to possess less happiness and life satisfaction than the countries that were wealthier. The nations also differed in the rights they provided their citizens. The researchers found that the countries that provided few civil and political rights tended to have lower well-being than did the countries where civil rights and individual freedoms were well protected by laws. Other national variables, such as population density and cultural homogeneity, showed only minor correlations with well-being. Diener and colleagues (1995) concluded that differences in the economic development of nations may be the primary source of differences in the subjective well-being of societies. Researchers who have conducted similar but smaller-scale national surveys have offered similar findings (Easterlin, 1974; Veenhoven, 1991a, 1991b).

Such findings might lead us to think that money or income makes people happy. People often think that if they had a bit more money or if they had a few more material goods, they would be happier. Some believe that if they win the lottery they will be happy for the rest of their lives. Researchers have found that there is no simple answer to the question about whether money makes people happy (Diener & Biswas-Diener, 2002, 2008).

Research on the objective circumstances of a person's life—age, sex, ethnicity, income, and so on—shows that these matter very little to overall happiness, yet we

Table 13.3 Country Scores of Average Subjective Well-Being

Country	Subjective Well-Being	Country	Subjective Well-Being
Iceland	1.11	Bangladesh	−.29
Sweden	1.03	France	−.38
Australia	1.02	Spain	−.41
Denmark	1.00	Portugal	−.41
Canada	.97	Italy	−.44
Switzerland	.94	Hungary	−.48
U.S.A.	.91	Puerto Rico	−.51
Colombia	.82	Thailand	−.62
Luxembourg	.82	South Africa	−.63
New Zealand	.82	Jordan	−.77
N. Ireland	.78	Egypt	−.78
Norway	.77	Yugoslavia	−.81
Finland	.74	Japan	−.86
Britain	.69	Greece	−.89
Netherlands	.68	Poland	−.90
Ireland	.57	Kenya	−.92
Brazil	.57	Turkey	−1.02
Tanzania	.51	India	−1.13
Belgium	.51	S. Korea	−1.15
Singapore	.43	Nigeria	−1.31
Bahrain	.36	Panama	−1.31
W. Germany	.18	E. Germany	−1.52
Austria	.15	U.S.S.R.	−1.70
Chile	.13	China	−1.92
Philippines	.10	Cameroon	−2.04
Malaysia	.08	Dominican Republic	−3.92
Cuba	.00		
Israel	−.18	Average	0.00
Mexico	−.28	Standard deviation	1.00

Source: Diener, Diener, & Diener, 1995.

know that people differ from each other and that, even through life's struggles and disappointments, some people are consistently happier than others. Costa, McCrae, and Zonderman (1987) found, in a study of 5,000 adults, that the people who were happy in 1973 were also happy 10 years later, in spite of undergoing many changes in life. What else might explain why some people are consistently happier than others?

Personality and Well-Being   In 1980, psychologists Paul Costa and Robert McCrae concluded that demographic variables, such as gender, age, ethnicity, and income, accounted for only about 10 to 15 percent of the variation in happiness, an estimate confirmed by others (Lyubomirski, 2007; Myers & Diener, 1995). This leaves a lot of the variance in subjective well-being unaccounted for. Costa and McCrae (1980) proposed that personality might have something to do with disposing certain people to be happy and so looked into that research. The few studies existing at that time suggested that happy people were outgoing and sociable (Smith, 1979), emotionally stable, and low on neuroticism (Wessman & Ricks, 1966).

Exercise

Recall and describe in writing a recent time when you purchased something for someone else. After writing a brief description of this, think of a time when you spent an equivalent amount of money on something for yourself. Now consider which of these two events produced the higher level of happiness in you? If you are like the participants in research reported in *Science* by Dunn, Aknin, and Norton (2008), you will find that spending one's money on other people has a larger effect on happiness than spending money on oneself. Why do you think this might be so? The effect is so reliable that these authors even found that participants randomly assigned to spend money on others experienced greater happiness than participants randomly assigned to spend money on themselves.

Costa and McCrae used such information to theorize that there may be two personality traits that influence happiness: extraversion and neuroticism. Moreover, Costa and McCrae made specific predictions about exactly how extraversion and neuroticism influenced happiness. Their idea was both simple and elegant. They began with the notion that happiness was the presence of relatively high levels of positive affect, and relatively low levels of negative affect, in a person's life over time. Extraversion, they held, influenced a person's positive emotions, whereas neuroticism determined a person's negative emotions.

Costa and McCrae (1980; McCrae & Costa, 1991) found that their model was supported by further research. Extraversion and neuroticism predicted the amounts of positive and negative emotions in people's lives and hence correlated with subjective well-being. In fact, extraversion and neuroticism accounted for up to three times as much of the variation in happiness among people compared with *all* of the common demographic variables (e.g., age, income, gender, education, ethnicity, religion) put together. It appears that having the right combination of personality traits (high extraversion and low neuroticism) may contribute much more to happiness than gender, ethnicity, age, and all the other demographic characteristics. Their model of well-being is portrayed in Figure 13.3.

Since Costa and McCrae's original study in 1980, more than a dozen studies have replicated the finding that extraversion and neuroticism are strong personality correlates of well-being (summarized in Rusting & Larsen, 1998b). All of these studies have been correlational, however, usually taking the form of administering personality and well-being questionnaires, then examining the correlations (Lucas & Dyrenforth, 2008).

Correlational studies cannot determine whether there is a direct causal connection between personality and well-being, or whether personality leads one to live a certain lifestyle and that lifestyle in turn makes one happy. For example, being neurotic may lead one to be a worrier and complainer. Other people dislike being around someone who worries a lot and is always complaining, so people may avoid the person who is high on neuroticism. Consequently, that person may be lonely and unhappy; however, that unhappiness may be due to the fact that the person drives people away by complaining all the time. The person's neuroticism leads him or her to create certain life situations, such as making others uncomfortable, and these situations in turn make the person unhappy (Hotard et al., 1989).

We can contrast this with a different view of the causal relation between personality and well-being, in which personality is viewed as directly causing people to react to the same situations with different amounts of positive or negative emotions, hence directly influencing their well-being. A neurotic person may respond with more negative emotion, even to the identical situation, compared to a person low in neuroticism.

A Closer Look   Does Money Make People Happy?

Pop singer Madonna, also known as "the Material Girl," has sung the praises of materialism. Americans are often thought of as materialistic. In fact, in surveys, the goal of being very well off financially is often rated as the top goal in life by first-year college students, surpassing other goals, such as being helpful to others, realizing potential as a person, and raising a family (Myers, 2000). This attitude is summarized by a bumper sticker seen on an expensive car towing a large boat, which read, "When the game is over, the person with the most toys wins." Does having more make one a winner? Does money lead to happiness?

Looked at in terms of national data, the answer seems to be that wealthier countries do indeed have higher average levels of life satisfaction than poorer countries. Myers and Diener (1995) report that the correlation between a nation's well-being score and its gross national product (adjusted for population size) is +.67. However, national wealth is confounded with many other variables that influence well-being, such as health care services, civil rights, women's rights, care for the elderly, and education. This is a classic example of how potential third variables might explain why two variables are related (see discussion of this problem in Chapter 2). For example, wealthier countries may have higher well-being *because* they also provide better health care for their citizens.

To counteract this research problem, we must look at the relationship between income and happiness within specific countries. Diener and Diener (1995) report that, in very poor countries, such as Bangladesh and India, financial status is a moderately good predictor of well-being. However, once people can afford life's basic necessities, it appears that increasing one's financial status matters very little to one's well-being. In countries that have a higher

standard of living, where most people have their basic needs met (such as in Europe or the United States), income "has a surprisingly weak (virtually negligible) effect on happiness" (Inglehart, 1990, p. 242).

What if we were to look within a country and examine changes in affluence over time, within a single economy, to see if people become happier as the country becomes more affluent? The United States, for example, has undergone huge increases in national wealth, income, and affluence over the past half-century. For example, from 1957 to the late 1990s, the average person's after-tax income (in constant 1995 dollars) more than doubled, going from $8,000 to $20,000 annually. Are Americans happier today than they were in 1957? Myers (2000) reports that Americans are *not* any happier today. This is illustrated by Figure 13.2, which shows that the percentage of Americans who describe themselves as very happy has stayed fairly constant over the decades, fluctuating right around 30 percent. This constant rate of personal happiness stands in contrast to the corresponding steep increase in national wealth experienced during those decades.

Of course, the national wealth portrayed in Figure 13.2 is not evenly distributed in the U.S. population. The United States has one of the highest wealth inequality rates in the world, an issue brought to light in the 2016 presidential race by candidate Bernie Sanders. Psychologists Oishi and Kesebir (2016) argue that the reason wealth and happiness are not correlated over time in the U.S. data is due to the unequal distribution of national wealth. They speculate that, if economic growth were more evenly shared in the population, with everyone benefiting from economic growth, perhaps the national level of happiness would increase with

increasing wealth. This remains to be seen, however, and the data at present show little effect of increasing wealth on national happiness.

This finding of a lack of relation between income and happiness contradicts the views of many politicians, economists, and policymakers. Moreover, it seems to run counter to common sense, as well as data on poverty and poor life outcomes. For example, people in the lowest levels of the economy have the highest rates of depression (McLoyd, 1998). Economic hardship takes a toll on people, increasing stress and conflict in people's lives (Kushlev, Dunn, & Lucas, 2015). Poverty is associated with elevations in a variety of negative life outcomes, ranging from infant mortality to increased violent crimes, such as homicide (Belle et al., 2000). How can poverty be associated with such unfortunate circumstances, yet income not be related to happiness? The answer, in part, lies in the notion of a threshold of income, below which a person is very unlikely to be happy, at least in the United States (Csikszentmihalyi, 2000). Once a person is above this threshold, however, the notion that having more money would make one happier does not seem to hold (Diener & Biswas-Diener, 2002).

Myers and Diener (1995) make the analogy between wealth and health: the absence of either health or wealth can bring misery, but their presence is no guarantee that happiness will follow. An interesting experiment to test this assertion for wealth would be to take a sample of people and randomly assign them to two groups. In Group 1, you give each member $1 million. In Group 2, you give each member $1. Then you see whether, six months later, the people in Group 1 (the new millionaires) are happier than the people in Group 2. Of course, this experiment would be impossible to

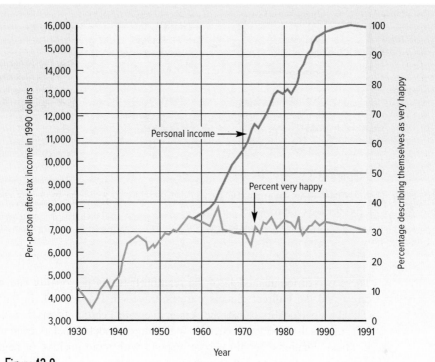

Figure 13.2

Has the large growth in average income been accompanied by an increase in average happiness within the United States? Keep in mind that the income data is averaged, and we know that there is great income inequality in the US population.

Source: Adapted from "The Funds, Friends, and Faith of Happy People," by D. G. Myers, 2000, *American Psychologist,* 55, pp. 56–67, Figure 5. Copyright © 2000 by the American Psychological Association. Reprinted with permission.

conduct, right? Wrong. With the advent of state lotteries in the United States, many people become millionaires overnight. Brickman, Coates, and Janoff-Bulman (1978) conducted a study of lottery winners, comparing their happiness levels with those of people from similar backgrounds who had not won large amounts of money. Within six months of winning, the newly rich lottery winners were found to be no more happy than the subjects in the control group. Apparently, winning the lottery is not as good as it sounds, at least not in terms of making a person permanently happy. External life circumstances have a surprisingly small effect on happiness and subjective well-being (Lucas, 2007).

What can we conclude about money and happiness? Probably the most

reasonable conclusion is that below a very low income level, a person is very unlikely to be happy. Being able to meet the basic needs of life (e.g., the needs on Maslow's hierarchy that are discussed in Chapter 8, including food, shelter, and security) appears crucial. However, once those needs are met, research suggests that there is little to the notion that further wealth will bring increased happiness. Support for this idea is provided in a study by Diener, Ng, Harter, and Arora (2010) that is based on a huge sample that is representative of almost everyone on planet Earth. Diener and colleagues (1995), for example, found that the correlation between personal income and happiness is +.12 in the United States. In a German sample that correlation was found to be .20 (Lucas & Schimmack, 2009). Fischer (2008) reports a correlation of .19

between median hourly wage and happiness in U.S. data between 1972 and 2004. Although these correlations are not negative, they are hardly large enough to think that having a huge income, in itself, will make you happy. What wealthy people choose to do with their money may have more to do with their potential happiness than does the mere fact of having a lot of money. For example, Dunn, Aknin, and Norton (2008) have shown that spending money on others can have a larger positive impact on happiness than spending the same amount on oneself. Across three separate studies, using data from 136 countries, Aknin et al. (2013) showed that using ones money to help others (called prosocial spending) may be a universally rewarding experience that contributes to the buyer's personal happiness.

410 PART FOUR The Cognitive/Experiential Domain

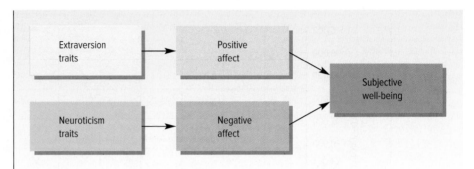

Figure 13.3

The influence of extraversion and neuroticism on subjective well-being by making a person susceptible to positive and negative affect.

Source: Adapted from Costa and McCrae, 1980.

These two different models of the relation between personality and well-being—the direct and the indirect models—are portrayed in Figure 13.4. In the indirect model (Panel b), personality causes the person to create a certain lifestyle, and the lifestyle, in turn, causes the emotional reaction. In the direct model (Panel a), even when exposed to identical situations, certain people respond with more positive or negative emotions, depending on their level of extraversion and neuroticism.

Larsen and his colleagues (e.g., Larsen, 2000a; Larsen & Ketelaar, 1989, 1991; Rusting & Larsen, 1998b; Zelenski & Larsen, 1999) have conducted several studies of whether the personality traits of extraversion and neuroticism have a direct effect on emotional responding. In these studies, the participants underwent a **mood induction** in the laboratory. In one study, the subjects listened to guided images of very pleasant scenes (a walk on the beach) or very unpleasant scenes (having a friend dying of an incurable disease). In other studies, the participants' emotions were manipulated by having them look at pleasant or unpleasant images. Prior to the laboratory session, their personality scores on extraversion and neuroticism were obtained by questionnaire, and mood was measured before and after the mood induction. The researchers were then able to determine if extraversion and neuroticism scores predicted responses to the laboratory mood inductions. Across several studies, the best predictor of responsiveness to the positive mood induction was the personality variable of extraversion. The best predictor of responses to the negative mood induction was neuroticism. It seems that it is easy to put an extravert into a good mood, and easy to put a high-neuroticism person into a bad mood. Moreover, these laboratory studies suggest that personality acts like an amplifier of life events, with extraverts showing amplified positive emotions to good events and high-neuroticism subjects showing amplified emotions to bad events. These findings are important because they suggest that personality has a direct effect on emotions and that, even under controlled circumstances, people respond differently to the emotional events in their lives, depending on their personalities.

The finding that extraverts get more positive emotional "bang" out of the emotion-inducing "buck" (or event) has been replicated in several other psychological laboratories (e.g., Gomez, Cooper, & Gomez, 2000; Gross et al., 1998). Some researchers, however, have failed to find the effect of extraversion on positive affective reactivity. For example, Lucas and Baird (2004) used clips of stand-up comedy to induce positive emotions and did not find that extraversion scores predicted a larger positive response (at least not in

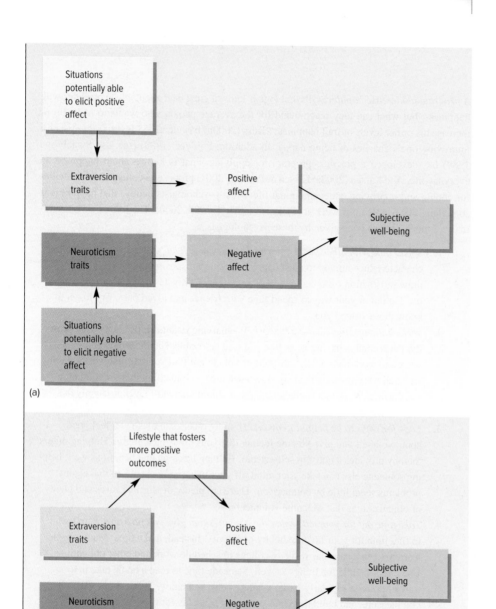

Figure 13.4

Two models of the relationship between personality variables and subjective well-being. Panel a: Model showing a direct effect of personality on emotional life, where life events are amplified by the personality traits, resulting in stronger positive or negative emotions for high extraversion or neuroticism subjects, respectively. Panel b: Model of the indirect relation between personality and emotional life. Here personality causes one to develop a lifestyle, and that lifestyle in turn fosters positive or negative affect for the high extraversion or neuroticism persons, respectively.

Application

A program to increase happiness. Psychologists know a great deal about what correlates with happiness, but what can they recommend for the average person who wants to maintain or increase his or her levels of trait happiness? Buss (2000b) has identified several strategies for improving one's chances of being happy. In addition, Fordyce (1988) (see also Swanbrow, 1989) has developed a practical program for applying what is known about happiness in everyday life. And Larsen (2000a; Larsen & Prizmic, 2004) proposes a collection of strategies for coping and improving one's emotional life. Most psychologists believe that happiness is something that people must work at (Csikszentmihalyi, 1999, 2000). The following is a summary of much of the advice given by these psychologists:

1. *Spend time with other people, particularly friends, family, and loved ones.* The one characteristic common to most happy people is a disposition to be sociable, to draw satisfaction from being with other people. Cultivate an interest in other people. Go out of your way to spend time with friends and loved ones. Try to get to know those around you.

2. *Seek challenge and meaning in work.* If satisfying relationships are the first priority, the second is having work that you find enjoyable. Happy people enjoy their work and work hard at what they do. If you do not find your current work (or college major) rewarding, then consider switching to something that you find more worthwhile. Work that is challenging, but within your skill level, is usually the most satisfying.

3. *Look for ways to be helpful to others.* Helping others can make you feel good about yourself and give you the feeling that your life is meaningful. Helping others thereby provides a boost in self-esteem. Helping has a second benefit as well; helping someone else can take your mind off your own problems or can make your problems seem little by comparison. There are plenty of worthy causes and plenty of organizations that welcome volunteers.

4. *Take time out for yourself; enjoy the activities that give you pleasure.* Don't wait to find time for your favorite hobby or activity. Instead, make time. Many people learn to keep a calendar while in college to schedule work and other obligations. Use it to schedule fun things as well. Set aside time to read a book, take in a movie, exercise regularly, or do whatever else you enjoy. Think about what gives you pleasure, and build time into your busy schedule for those activities.

5. *Stay in shape.* Exercise is positively associated with emotional well-being. Exercise need not be intense or all that frequent to provide the emotional benefit. Playing on team sports, dancing, biking, swimming, gardening, or even walking, if done at a brisk pace, is about all it takes. It doesn't seem to matter what the activity is, as long as you move around enough to keep in shape.

6. *Have a plan, but be open to new experiences.* Having an organized life allows a person to accomplish much. However, sometimes the most fun moments in life are unplanned. Be open to trying different things or having different experiences—try going somewhere you have never been, try doing a routine activity a little differently, or try doing something on the spur of the moment. Be flexible, rather than rigid, and try to avoid getting stuck in any ruts.

7. *Be optimistic.* Put on a smiling face, whistle a happy tune, look for the silver lining in every cloud. Sure, it sounds too good to be true, but acting happy and trying to

look on the bright side of things can go a long way toward making you feel happy. Try to avoid negative thinking. Don't make pessimistic statements, even to yourself. Convince yourself that the cup *really is* half full.

8. *Don't let things get blown out of proportion.* Sometimes when something bad happens, it seems like the end of the world. Happy people have the ability to step back and see things in perspective. Happy people think about their options and about the other things in their lives that *are* going well. They think about what they can do to work on their problems or what to avoid in the future. But they *don't* think it is the end of the world. Often asking yourself "What's the worst that can come of this?" will help put things in perspective.

Just wishing for happiness is not likely to make it so. Psychologists agree that people have to work at being happy; they have to work at overcoming the unpleasant events of life, the losses and failures that happen to everyone. The strategies in the previous list can be thought of as a personal program for working on happiness.

two out of four studies, whereas the fourth study did find the extraversion effect). Recently, Smillie and colleagues (2012) argued that the positive affect induction must involve a rewarding stimuli, such as winning a lottery or finding some money. Smillie and colleagues (2012) went on to demonstrate that, across five experiments, extraverts are more reactive to rewards (money) or situations involving desired outcomes (success feedback) or appetitive stimuli (delicious food). Having subjects do something that is merely pleasant, such as imagine they are relaxing at the beach or watch a "feel-good" movie clip, although enjoyable, does not involve rewards or appetitive stimuli and hence does not produce the larger positive emotional response in extraverts compared to introverts.

Unpleasant Emotions

Unlike pleasant emotion, the unpleasant emotions come in several distinct varieties. We discuss three important unpleasant emotions that are viewed by psychologists as having dispositional characteristics: anxiety, depression, and anger.

Trait Anxiety and Neuroticism   Recall that people who exhibit the trait of neuroticism are vulnerable to negative emotions. **Neuroticism** is one of the Big Five dimensions of personality, and it is present, in some form, in every major trait theory of personality.

Different researchers have used different terms for neuroticism, such as emotional instability, anxiety-proneness, and negative affectivity (Watson & Clark, 1984). Adjectives useful for describing persons high on the trait of neuroticism include moody, touchy, irritable, anxious, unstable, pessimistic, and complaining. Hans Eysenck (1967, 1990; Eysenck & Eysenck, 1985) suggested that individuals high on the neuroticism dimension tend to overreact to unpleasant events, such as frustrations or problems, and that they take longer to return to a normal state after being upset. They are easily irritated, worry about many things, and seem to be constantly complaining. You may have heard

People high on the personality trait of neuroticism tend to worry frequently. They may worry about their health, their social interactions, their work, their future, or just about anything. Worrying and complaining takes up a great proportion of their time.

© Blend Images/Dream Pictures/Getty Images RF

the phrase "She is not happy unless she has something to worry about." Well, it is unlikely that worrying actually makes a person happy. But the fact that some people worry almost all the time might suggest that worrying fulfills a need for them. Some people worry about their health ("Is this nagging cough really a sign that I have lung cancer? Could this headache really be a brain tumor?"). Others worry about their social interactions, ruminating after every conversation. And still others worry about their work.

In addition to worry and anxiety, the person high on the neuroticism dimension frequently experiences episodes of irritation. An interesting way to illustrate this is to ask people to list all the things that have irritated them in the past week. Perhaps seeing someone spit in public is irritating to many people. Or seeing someone with a pierced nose and eyebrows might be mentioned as irritating. Or seeing a couple kissing in public might be mentioned. If people were to write down all the things that irritated them, you would find that people high on neuroticism would have much longer lists than people low on neuroticism.

Eysenck's biological theory   As briefly discussed in Chapter 3, Eysenck (1967, 1990) argues that neuroticism has a biological basis. In his theory of personality, neuroticism is due primarily to a tendency of the **limbic system** in the brain to become easily activated. The limbic system is the part of the brain responsible for emotion and the fight-or-flight reaction. If someone has a limbic system that is easily activated, then that person probably has frequent episodes of emotion, particularly emotions associated with flight (such as anxiety, fear, and worry) and with fight (such as anger, irritation, and annoyance). High-neuroticism persons are anxious, irritated, and easily upset, so the theory goes, because their limbic systems are more easily aroused to produce such emotions.

Because the limbic system is located deep within the brain, its activity is not easily measured by EEG electrodes, which are placed on the surface of the scalp. Newer brain imaging technologies, such as MRI or PET, are allowing personality researchers to test this theory directly (DeYoung, 2010). Nevertheless, Eysenck (1990) has made several logical arguments in favor of a biological basis for neuroticism. First, many studies have shown a remarkable level of stability in neuroticism. For example, Conley (1984a, 1984b, 1985) found that neuroticism showed a high test-retest correlation after a period of 45 years. Although this does not prove a biological basis for neuroticism, stability is nevertheless consistent with a biological explanation. A second argument is that neuroticism is a major dimension of personality that is found in many different kinds of data sets (e.g., self-report, peer report) in many different cultures and environments by many different investigators. Again, although this ubiquity does not prove a biological basis, the fact that neuroticism is so widely found across cultures and data sources is consistent with a biological explanation. And a third argument in favor of a biological explanation is that many genetic studies find that neuroticism shows one of the higher heritability values. Trait negative affect shows relatively high levels of heritability, whereas trait positive affect shows a significant shared environment component (Goldsmith, Aksan, & Essex, 2001). A predisposition to be neurotic appears to be somewhat inherited. Most behavior geneticists believe that what is heritable in the heritability of emotion traits is individual differences in neurotransmitter function, such as in dopamine transport or serotonin reuptake (Canli, 2008).

Other biologically based research on emotion traits examines which areas of the brain are active when processing emotion information, such as looking at sad pictures or thinking about something that makes one anxious or angry (Sutton, 2002). Most of the studies reveal that emotion is associated with an increased activation of the anterior cingulate cortex (Bush, Luu, & Posner, 2000; Whalen, Bush, & McNally, 1998).

The **anterior cingulate** is the portion of the brain located deep inside toward the center of the brain, and it most likely evolved early in the evolution of the nervous system. DeYoung and colleagues (2010) measured the volume of brain tissue in different regions of the brain. Neuroticism was correlated with the volume of brain regions associated with the evaluation of threat and punishment and the production of negative emotions. Other studies of neuroticism and brain structure find it associated with larger (Kapogiannis et al., 2013) and thicker (Wright et al., 2006) prefrontal cortex regions, areas that are involved in the regulation of negative emotions and impulses. A meta-analysis of brain imaging studies and neuroticism (Servaas et al., 2013) concluded that neuroticism is associated with differences in brain activation during fear learning, anticipation of aversive events (e.g., shocks), and during the processing of unpleasant information (e.g., images).

Other researchers have focused on the biological basis of the self-regulation of negative emotions. For example, Levesque, Fanny, and Joanette (2003) had subjects watch a sad film. Half of them were told to do whatever they could to stop or prevent the sad feelings and to not show any emotional reactions during the film. Subjects who were successful at this exhibited increased activity in the right ventral medial **prefrontal cortex**, part of the so-called executive control center of the brain. Other studies also have identified this area as highly active in the control of emotion (Beauregard, Levesque, & Bourgouin, 2001). When specifically told to try to dampen their emotional responses to unpleasant images, the amount of activity in the prefrontal area correlated positively with neuroticism. This suggests that the high neuroticism persons were putting in extra effort to regulate their negative emotions (Harenski, Kim, & Hamann, 2009). Schuyler et al. (2014) looked at recovery time in amygdala activation following exposure to unpleasant images. Subjects higher in neuroticism showed slower amygdala recovery, implying that, at least at the level of amygdala activity, negative emotions last longer for high neuroticism individuals.

Cognitive theories   Another way to look at neuroticism is as a cognitive phenomenon. Some personality psychologists have argued that the cause of neuroticism lies not so much in the biology of the limbic brain but in the psychology of the person's overall cognitive system. These theorists have argued that neuroticism is caused by certain styles of information processing (such as attending, thinking, and remembering). Lishman (1972), for example, found that high-N (neuroticism) subjects were more likely to recall unpleasant information than were low-N subjects. There was no relation between neuroticism and the recall of pleasant information. After studying lists of pleasant and unpleasant words, high-N subjects also recalled the unpleasant words *faster* than the pleasant words. Martin, Ward, and Clark (1983) had subjects study information about themselves and about others. When asked to recall that information, the high-N subjects recalled more negative information about themselves but did not recall more negative information about others. There appear to be very specific information-processing characteristics associated with neuroticism: it appears to relate to the preferential processing of negative (but not positive) information about the self (but not about others). Martin and colleagues (1983) state that "high-N scorers recall more self-negative words than low-N scorers because memory traces for self-negative words are stronger in the high-N scorers" (p. 500).

As a related explanation for the relation between neuroticism and selective memory for unpleasant information, researchers use a version of the spreading activation concept, which was discussed in Chapter 10. Recall that this notion suggests that material is stored in memory by being linked with other, similar pieces of material. Many psychologists hold that emotional experiences are also stored in memory. Moreover, some individuals—those high in neuroticism—have richer networks of association surrounding memories of negative emotion. Consequently, for them, unpleasant material is more accessible, leading them to have higher rates of recall for unpleasant information.

One type of unpleasant information in memory concerns memory for illnesses, injuries, and physical symptoms. If high-N subjects have a richer network of associations surrounding unpleasant information in memories, then they are also likely to recall more instances of illness and bodily complaints. Try asking a high-N person the following question: "So, what's your health been like the past few months?" Be prepared for a long answer, with a litany of complaints and many details about specific symptoms. Study after study has established a link between neuroticism and self-reported health complaints. For example, Smith and colleagues (1989) asked subjects to recall whether they had experienced each of 90 symptoms within the past three weeks. Neuroticism correlated with the self-reported frequencies of symptoms, usually in the range of $r = .4$ to .5. This means that roughly 15 to 25 percent of the variation in health symptoms could be attributed to the personality variable of neuroticism.

Larsen (1992) examined the sources of bias in neurotics' reports of physical illnesses. He asked participants to report every day on whether they experienced any physical symptoms, such as a runny nose, cough, sore throat, backache, stomachache, sore muscles, headache, loss of appetite, and so on. The participants made daily reports for two months, providing the researcher with a day-by-day running report of physical symptoms. After the daily report phase was complete, Larsen then asked the participants to recall, as accurately as they could, how many times they reported each symptom during the two months of daily reporting. This unusual research design allowed the researcher to calculate the subjects' "true" total number of symptoms, as reported on a daily basis, as well as their remembered number of symptoms. It turned out that both of these scores were related to neuroticism. That is, the high-N participants reported more daily symptoms, *and* they recalled more symptoms, than did the stable low-N subjects. Moreover, even when controlling for the number of day-to-day symptoms reported, neuroticism was *still* related to elevated levels of recalled symptoms.

High-neuroticism persons recall and report more symptoms, but are they more likely than stable low-N individuals to actually *have* more physical illnesses? This is a tricky question to address, as even medical doctors rely on a person's self-reports of symptoms to establish the presence of physical disease. The answer is to look at objective indicators of illness and disease and to see if those are related to neuroticism. Major disease categories, such as coronary disease, cancer, or premature death, appear to have little, if any, relation to neuroticism (Watson & Pennebaker, 1989). Costa and McCrae (1985) reviewed this literature and concluded that "neuroticism influences perceptions of health, but not health itself" (p. 24). Similar conclusions were reached by Holroyd and Coyne (1987), who wrote that neuroticism reflects "a biased style of perceiving physiological experiences" (p. 372).

Research on the immune system, however, is showing that neuroticism does appear to be related to diminished immune function during stress (Herbert & Cohen, 1993). In a fascinating study by Marsland and colleagues (2001), subjects underwent vaccination for hepatitis B, and their antibody response to the injection was measured (this is a measure of how well the immune system responds to antigens in a vaccine). It was found that the subjects low in neuroticism mounted and maintained the strongest immune response to the vaccine. This finding suggests that persons high in neuroticism may, in fact, be more susceptible to immune-mediated diseases.

The immune system plays a role in many diseases, suggesting that neuroticism may affect health through compromising the body's ability to fight off foreign cells.

In a study of neuroticism and lung cancer, Augustine and colleagues (2008) found that age of onset of lung cancer was negatively related to neuroticism. This finding held even after statistically controlling for the age of subjects when they started smoking and the number of cigarettes smoked per day prior to contracting lung cancer. Smoking history and amount smoked were strongly related to earlier onset of lung cancer, but neuroticism was an additional and independent risk factor for earlier onset of this disease. Examining differences between persons one standard deviation above and below the mean on neuroticism showed that the high-N subjects contracted lung cancer an average of 4.33 years earlier than the low-N subjects. The authors speculate that neuroticism is related to the speed of cancer progression due to its impact on the immune system. The chronic stress associated with neuroticism can lead to depletion of the immune system (Irwin, 2002), which in turn can make a person less able to fight off the progression of cancer.

Psychologists have proposed a theory that high-neuroticism subjects pay more attention to threats and unpleasant information in their environment (e.g., Dalgleish, 1995; Matthews, 2000; Matthews, Derryberry, & Siegle, 2000). High-N subjects are thought to have a stronger behavioral inhibition system, compared to low-N persons, making them particularly vulnerable to cues of punishment and frustration and prompting them to be vigilant for signs of threat. These researchers argue that high-N subjects are on the lookout for threatening information in their environment, constantly scanning for anything that might be menacing, unsafe, or negative.

Researchers have incorporated a version of the Stroop effect into investigations of attentional bias and neuroticism. The Stroop effect (Stroop, 1935) describes the increased time it takes to name the color in which a word is written when that word names a different color, relative to when it is a matching color word or a patch of color. For example, if the word *blue* is written in red ink, then it takes longer to name the color of the ink (red) than it would take if the word *red* were written in red ink. Researchers agree that the relevant dimension (color of ink) and the irrelevant dimension (name of the word) produce a conflict within the attentional system. If a person's attentional system can efficiently suppress the irrelevant dimension (the word), then he or she should be faster in naming the color than someone who cannot suppress the word information.

The Stroop task has been modified to study individual differences in attention to emotion words. In the so-called emotion Stroop task, the content of the words is typically anxiety- or threat-related, such as *fear, disease, cancer, death, failure, grief,* or *pathetic* (Larsen, Mercer, & Balota, 2006). The words are written in colored ink, and the subject is asked to name the color of the ink and ignore the content of the words. Emotional interference is assumed when the time it takes to name the colors of the threat words is longer than the time it takes to name the colors of neutral words (Algom, Chajut, & Lev, 2004). Applied to neuroticism, the idea is that high-N persons have an attentional bias such that certain stimuli (the threat words) are more salient, or attention-grabbing. The threat words should be more difficult for them to ignore when naming the color. Therefore, neuroticism should correlate with response time to name the colors when the words refer to threat (e.g., *disease, failure*).

A thorough review of this literature was published by Williams, Mathews, and MacLeod (1996). These researchers reviewed more than 50 experiments that used a version of the emotion Stroop task. Many of the studies show that high-N groups (or participants with anxiety disorder) are often slower to name colors of anxiety- and threat-related words, compared with the color naming of control, nonemotion words. The explanation given for this effect is that the emotion words capture the attention of the high-N participants, but not of the low-N participants.

In summary, neuroticism is a trait that relates to a variety of negative emotions, including anxiety, fear, worry, annoyance, irritation, and distress. Persons high in neuroticism are unstable in their moods, are easily upset, and take longer to recover after being upset. There are both biological and cognitive theories about the causes of negative emotions in neuroticism, and each has some supportive evidence in the scientific literature. One particularly well-known finding concerns the tendency of persons high in neuroticism to complain of health problems. In addition, high-N persons are thought to be on the lookout for threatening information; they pay more attention to negative cues and events in life, however minor, compared with more emotionally stable persons.

Depression and Melancholia   **Depression** is another traitlike dimension. In this chapter, we cover only a small part of what is known about depression. There is a huge body of literature on the topic of depression, as is befitting a psychological disorder that is estimated to strike 20 percent of the people in the United States at some time in their lives (American Psychiatric Association, 1994). There are entire books on depression, graduate courses devoted to this topic, and clinicians who specialize primarily in the treatment of depression. There are thought to be many varieties of depression (e.g., Rusting & Larsen, 1998a), and researchers are attempting to categorize the kinds of depression and are looking for ways to help people who suffer from the debilitating effects of depression. See Table 13.4 for a list of symptoms that define depression.

Diathesis-stress model   One way to view depression is through a **diathesis-stress model**. This model suggests that there is a preexisting vulnerability, or diathesis, that is present among people who later become depressed. In addition to this vulnerability, a stressful life event must occur in order to trigger the depression, such as the loss of a loved one, a career failure, or another major negative life event. Neither element alone—the diathesis or the stress—is sufficient to trigger depression. Rather, they must occur together—something bad or stressful must happen to a person who has a vulnerability to depression.

Beck's cognitive theory   Many researchers have emphasized certain cognitive styles as one type of preexisting condition that makes people vulnerable to depression (Larsen & Cowan, 1988). One of these researchers is Aaron Beck (1976), who has written extensively on his cognitive theory of depression. He suggests that the vulnerability lies in a particular **cognitive schema**, or way of looking at the world. A schema is a way of processing incoming information, a way of organizing and interpreting the events of

Table 13.4 Signs of Depression

The signs of depression include having five or more of the following symptoms during the same two-week period:

- Depressed mood most of the day, nearly every day
- Diminished interest or pleasure in most activities
- Change in weight: significant weight loss when not dieting or a weight gain
- Change in sleep pattern: insomnia or sleeping much more than usual
- Change in movements: restlessness and agitation or feeling slowed down
- Fatigue or loss of energy nearly every day
- Feelings of worthlessness or guilt nearly every day
- Diminished ability to concentrate or make decisions nearly every day
- Recurrent thoughts of death or suicide

Source: Adapted from American Psychiatric Association, 2013.

daily life. The cognitive schema involved in depression, according to Beck, distorts the incoming information in a negative way, a way that makes the person depressed.

According to Beck, three important areas of life are most influenced by the depressive cognitive schema. This **cognitive triad** includes information about the self, the world, and the future. Information about these important aspects of life is distorted in specific ways by the depressive cognitive schema. For example, after doing poorly on a practice exam, a depressive person might say to himself, "I am a total failure." This is an example of the *overgeneralizing* distortion applied to the self. Overgeneralizing is taking one instance and generalizing to many or all other instances. The lay term for this is "blowing things out of proportion." The person might have failed at one exam, but that does not mean he is a total failure. The same overgeneralizing style can be applied to the world ("If anything can go wrong, it will.") and the future ("Why bother trying, when everything I do is doomed to fail?"). In Beck's (1976) theory, there are many other cognitive distortions, such as making *arbitrary inferences* (jumping to a negative conclusion, even when the evidence does not support it), *personalizing* (assuming that everything is your fault), and *catastrophizing* (thinking that the worst will always happen). These cognitive elements are portrayed in Figure 13.5.

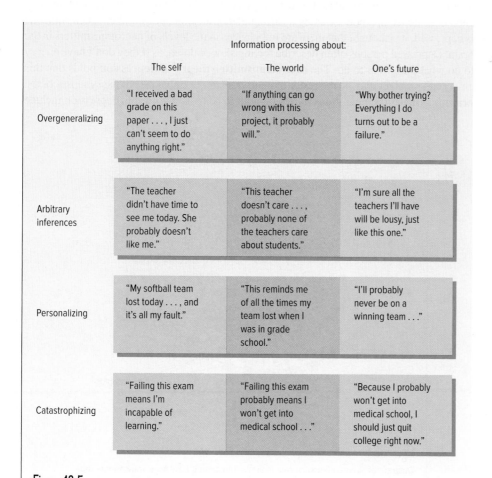

Information processing about:

	The self	The world	One's future
Overgeneralizing	"I received a bad grade on this paper . . . , I just can't seem to do anything right."	"If anything can go wrong with this project, it probably will."	"Why bother trying? Everything I do turns out to be a failure."
Arbitrary inferences	"The teacher didn't have time to see me today. She probably doesn't like me."	"This teacher doesn't care . . . , probably none of the teachers care about students."	"I'm sure all the teachers I'll have will be lousy, just like this one."
Personalizing	"My softball team lost today . . . , and it's all my fault."	"This reminds me of all the times my team lost when I was in grade school."	"I'll probably never be on a winning team . . ."
Catastrophizing	"Failing this exam means I'm incapable of learning."	"Failing this exam probably means I won't get into medical school . . ."	"Because I probably won't get into medical school, I should just quit college right now."

Figure 13.5

Beck's cognitive model of depression, showing how distortions are applied to processing information about the self, the world, and one's future. These cognitive distortions promote depression.

According to Beck's influential theory (1976), depression is the result of applying these cognitive distortions to the information from daily life. These distortions are applied quickly and outside of immediate awareness, resulting in a stream of automatic negative thoughts, which deeply affect how the person feels and acts ("I'm no good. The world is against me. My future is bleak."). The person who thinks he is a total failure will often act like a total failure and may even give up trying to do better, creating a **self-fulfilling prophecy**. Moreover, depressive feelings lead to more distortions, which in turn lead to more bad feelings, and so on, in a self-perpetuating cycle. Beck devised a form of therapy for changing people's cognitive distortions. In a nutshell, this involves challenging the person's distortions, such as by asking, "Does it really mean that you are a *total failure* because you flunked just this one exam?"

Biology of Depression   Nerve cells in the brain communicate with each other by way of chemical messengers called neurotransmitters (Chapter 6). These neurotransmitters are broken down and delivered from one neuron across a gap—called the synapse—to another neuron (Figure 13.6). The first neuron is called the presynaptic neuron, and the second neuron is called the postsynaptic neuron. If the neurotransmitter reaches the postsynaptic neuron in sufficient strength, the nerve signal continues on its way toward completing the action for which it is intended, for instance, changing the channel on the remote, reading another sentence in a book, casting a flirting glance at someone you like. When someone is depressed, it is thought that there are imbalances in the levels of neurotransmitters in the brain. Depressed persons often describe feeling slowed down, as if they don't have energy to do what they want to do. The **neurotransmitter theory of depression** holds that this emotional problem may be the result of neurotransmitter imbalance at the synapses of the nervous system. The neurotransmitters thought to be most involved in depression include

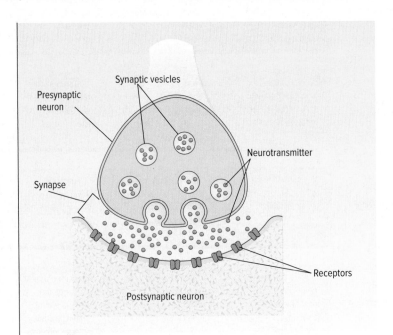

Figure 13.6

Diagram of synapse between two neurons, illustrating how neurotransmitters must be released, cross the synapse, and bond with the receptors on the postsynaptic neuron in order for a nerve impulse to pass on its way to completion.

norepinephrine (also called noradrenaline), serotonin, and, to a lesser degree, dopamine. Many of the drugs used to treat depression target exactly these neurotransmitters. For example, Prozac, Zoloft, and Paxil inhibit the reuptake of serotonin in the synapse, resulting in increased levels of this neurotransmitter in the nervous system. The medication Tofranil works to maintain a better balance between levels of both serotonin and norepinephrine. Not all persons with depression are successfully treated with these kinds of medications, suggesting that there may be varieties of depression, some more biologically based, others more reactive to stress or cognitively based.

Recent studies suggest that exercise might be usefully applied to the treatment of depression, at least for some persons (Dubbert, 2002). In his 1996 annual report, Surgeon General of the United States David Satcher documented the benefits of exercise for health promotion and disease prevention—including depression prevention. The use of exercise in counseling people with depression is described by Dixon, Mauzey, and Hall (2003).

Anger Proneness and Potential for Hostility   Another important negative emotion is anger and feelings of hostility. Psychologists have long been interested in what makes people hostile and aggressive. Social psychologists, for example, have examined conditions under which the average person will become aggressive (Baron, 1977). One finding is that most people are willing to strike out against someone who has treated them unfairly. Here the emphasis is on how certain situations, such as being treated unfairly, are likely to evoke aggression in *most* people. Personality psychologists agree that some circumstances tend to make most people angry, but their interest is more in terms of individual differences in anger proneness. They begin with the position that some people are characteristically more hostile than others in response to the same kinds of situations, such as frustration. **Hostility** is defined as a tendency to respond to everyday frustrations with anger and aggression, become irritable easily, feel frequent resentment, and act in a rude, critical, antagonistic, and uncooperative manner in everyday interactions (Dembrowski & Costa, 1987).

The scientific objectives, from the personality psychologist's perspective, are (1) to understand how hostile people became that way, what keeps them that way, and in what other ways they differ from nonhostile people and (2) to examine the consequences of hostility in terms of important life outcomes.

One consequence of hostility is its relation to coronary heart disease. We cover this topic in more detail in Chapter 18 on Type A behavior and health. It turns out that chronic hostility is the component of the Type A behavior pattern that most contributes to heart disease. Hostility as a personality trait can be measured with questionnaires that ask about the frequency and duration of anger episodes, whether anger is triggered by minor events (e.g., having to wait in line), or how easily one is bothered or irritated in everyday life (Siegel, 1986). For most people, even those high on the hostility dimension, the trait produces mostly feelings and urges that are uncomfortable and that create a negativistic and brooding outlook. For some these urges spill over into acts of aggression.

Anger is an emotion that causes some people to lose control. Most of the violent inmates in our prisons have trouble with the self-regulation of this potent emotion. Researchers have long speculated that there may be biological differences, particularly in brain function, between violent and nonviolent persons. The psychologist Adrian Raine has spent many years examining some of the most violent and aggressive members of our society (e.g., Raine, 2002; Brennan & Raine, 1997). He has focused on the brain structures associated with individual differences in violence and aggression, and has started a field called "neurocriminology" (Glenn & Raine, 2014). In one study of especially

Would a person with a long history of extreme violence be able to change completely into a gentle, loving father and pillar of his community?

© Twin Design/Shutterstock.com RF

violent murderers, Raine, Meloy, and Bihrle (1998) found that these persons showed decreased activity in the prefrontal areas of their brains, those areas mentioned earlier that are associated with normal emotional regulation. Psychologist Jonathan Pincus has also specialized in the study of violent criminals. In a review of his work, Pincus (2001) presents information on the lives of numerous serial killers, and in virtually all cases these murderers suffered from some damage to their brains, either through violence, accidental injuries, or excessive drug or alcohol abuse. In addition, practically all of these murderers came from severely abusive families. Pincus presents data that the presence of brain damage in violent criminals is most often in the prefrontal areas. Again, these are the areas involved in self-control (Densen et al., 2009). Interestingly, this is the area that was severely damaged in the case of Phineas Gage, discussed in Chapter 6.

In large studies not every violent or sadistic person is found to have brain abnormalities. However, the rates of brain abnormalities are much higher in violent persons than in those persons without a history of violence. For example, in a study of 62 criminals in Japan the researchers divided the inmates into those convicted of murder and those convicted of nonviolent offenses. Brain abnormalities were much more frequent among the murderers than among the nonviolent offenders (Sakuta & Fukushima, 1998). In a study done in Austria, a group of high-violence offenders were compared to a group of low-violence offenders. In the high-violence group, 66 percent were found to have brain abnormalities, whereas in the low-violence group only 17 percent were found to have the same brain abnormalities (Aigner et al., 2000). In a study of sexual offenders, criminals were divided into those who physically harmed their victims (e.g., committed murder or sadistically violent acts) and those who did not physically harm their victims (e.g., exposed themselves). In the group of violent sex offenders, 41 percent were found to have brain abnormalities, a rate significantly higher than in the nonviolent sex offenders (Langevin et al., 1988). In a particularly strong longitudinal study, a group of 110 hyperactive and 76 normal boys had their brain activity assessed when they were between 6 and 12 years of age. They were followed up between the ages of 14 and 20 years, with special attention to arrest records. Those adolescent boys with a history of delinquency turned out to have had unusual brain patterns in childhood compared to those adolescents without subsequent delinquency (Satterfield & Schell, 1984).

More recent studies (e.g., Hawes et al., 2016) document the trajectory of having poor anger management in childhood leading to higher rates of violence and aggression in adulthood. Such findings highlight the importance of developing anger control strategies which, for most people, naturally develop in childhood. Could it be that the brain abnormalities often seen in violent adults involve those brain regions that are responsible for self-control and the management of emotions, especially anger?

The kind of brain damage most often observed in hostile aggressive persons involves areas in the frontal lobe and, to a lesser extent, the temporal lobe. These areas are important in regulating impulses, particularly aggressive impulses, and fear conditioning. The damage may be developmentally caused or caused by injury. For example, sniffing glue or inhaling butane gas, which can induce intoxication similar to alcohol, can cause the kind of brain damage that has been related to antisocial behavior (Jung,

Lee, & Cho, 2004). Another example is a case report where a man developed a cyst in his brain. Prior to this development he was not a violent person. However, after the cyst grew, and presumably caused damage to his brain, he strangled his wife to death after she scratched his face (Paradis et al., 1994). A similar case is reported in Glenn and Raine (2014), along with actual brain scans, of a 40-year-old man who, with no prior history, suddenly became sexually aggressive and was arrested. He was found to have a large tumor in his prefrontal cortex and, when it was removed, his behavior returned to normal, with none of the sexual inappropriateness that got him into trouble with the police. The kind of brain abnormalities found in violent and aggressive persons appears to involve decrements in the person's ability to inhibit or control aggressive impulses.

Style of Emotional Life

So far in this chapter, we have discussed people's emotional lives in terms of emotional content, or the various characteristic emotions that define how one person is different from others. We examined four emotion traits: happiness, anxiety, depression, and anger. Now we turn to a discussion of emotional style. As a quick distinction, we might say that content is the *what* of a person's emotional life, whereas style is the *how* of that emotional life.

Affect Intensity as an Emotional Style

When we think about how emotions are experienced, probably the major stylistic distinction is one of intensity. You know from experience with your own emotional reactions that emotions can vary greatly in terms of magnitude. Emotions can be weak and mild, or strong and almost uncontrollable. To characterize a person's emotional style, we must inquire about the typical intensity of his or her emotional experiences. For emotional intensity to be useful to personality theory, we must establish that it describes a stable characteristic useful for making distinctions among persons.

Affect intensity can be defined by a description of persons who are either high or low on this dimension. Larsen (2009) describes *high affect intensity* individuals as people who typically experience their emotions strongly and are emotionally reactive and variable. High affect intensity subjects typically go way up when they are feeling up and go way down when they are feeling down. They also alternate between these extremes more frequently and rapidly than do low affect intensity individuals. Low affect intensity individuals, on the other hand, typically experience their emotions only mildly and with only gradual fluctuations and minor reactions. Such persons are stable and calm and usually do not suffer the troughs of negative emotions. But they also tend not to experience the peaks of enthusiasm, joy, and other strong positive emotions.

Note that these descriptions of high and low affect intensity persons make use of the qualifying terms *typically* and *usually*. This is because certain life events can make even the lowest affect intensity person experience relatively strong emotions. For example, being accepted into one's first choice of schools can cause elation in almost anyone. Similarly, the death of a loved pet can cause strong sadness in almost everyone. However, because such events are fairly rare, we want to know what people are usually or typically like: how they characteristically react to the normal sorts of everyday emotion-provoking events.

Figure 13.7 presents daily mood data for two subjects from a study by Larsen and Diener (1985). These subjects kept daily records of their moods for 84 consecutive days. Note that Subject A's emotions were fairly stable and did not depart too far from her baseline level of mood over the entire three-month reporting period. Actually, she

(a)

(b)

Figure 13.7

Data from individual subjects who kept a mood diary every day for three consecutive months. (a) Data
from subject A. (b) Data from Subject B, who has much more intense moods and larger day-to-day mood
swings than Subject A.

Source: Adapted from Larsen, 1991.

had a bad week at the beginning of the semester, which is denoted by the several low points at the left side of the graph. Otherwise, things were pretty stable for this subject.

Subject B, on the other hand, exhibited extreme changes in mood over time. This subject was hardly ever near his baseline level of mood. Instead, Subject B appears to have experienced both strong positive and strong negative affect frequently and to alternate between these extremes frequently and rapidly. In other words, this high affect intensity person exhibited a good deal of variability in his daily moods, fluctuating back and forth between positive and negative affect from day to day. Interestingly, Subject B was in the student hospital three times that semester, once for an infection and twice for feeling run down.

Assessment of Affect Intensity and Mood Variability

In early studies of affect intensity (e.g., Diener, Larsen, et al., 1985), this characteristic of emotional life was assessed using a daily experiential sampling method. That is, data were gathered much like that presented in Figure 13.7, panels a and b. Researchers would then compute a total score for each subject to represent how intense or variable that person was over the time period.

This longitudinal method of measuring affect intensity is straightforward and face valid, and it represents the construct of affect intensity quite well. However, it takes several weeks or longer of daily mood reporting to generate a reliable composite affect intensity score for each individual. Consequently, a questionnaire measure of affect intensity has been developed that allows a relatively quick assessment of a person's emotional style in terms of intensity. Table 13.5 lists 20 items from this questionnaire, called the Affect Intensity Measure (AIM) (Larsen & Diener, 1987).

An important aspect of the affect intensity trait is that we cannot really say whether it is bad or good to be low or high on this trait. Both positive and negative consequences are related to scoring either high or low. High-scoring persons, for example, get a lot of zest out of life, enjoying peaks of enthusiasm, joy, and positive emotional involvement. On the other hand, when things are not going well, high-scoring persons are prone to strong negative emotional reactions, such as sadness, guilt, and anxiety. In addition, because high-scoring persons have frequent experiences of extreme emotions (both positive and negative), they tend to suffer the physical consequences of this emotional involvement. Emotions activate the sympathetic nervous system, making the person aroused. Even strong *positive* emotions activate the sympathetic nervous system and produce wear and tear on the nervous system. High-scoring persons tend to exhibit physical symptoms that result from their chronic emotional lifestyles, such as muscle tension, stomachaches, headaches, and fatigue. An interesting finding is that, even though they report more of these physical symptoms, high-scoring persons are not particularly unhappy or upset by them (Larsen, Billings, & Cutler, 1996). Interviews with high-scoring persons usually show that they have no desire to change their level of emotional intensity. They seem to prefer the emotional involvement, the ups and downs, and the physiological arousal that accompanies their highly emotional lifestyle (Larsen & Diener, 1987).

Low affect intensity individuals, on the other hand, are stable and do not typically get upset very easily. Even when negative events happen, they maintain an even emotional state and avoid the troughs of negative affect. The price such people pay for this emotional stability, however, is that they fail to experience their positive emotions very strongly. They lack the peaks of zest, enthusiasm, emotional engagement, and joy that energize the lives of high affect intensity individuals. Low affect intensity individuals, however, do not pay the price of the physical and psychosomatic symptoms that go along with the high affect intensity personality.

Table 13.5　AIM Questionnaire

INSTRUCTIONS: The following statements refer to emotional reactions to typical life events. Please indicate how *you* react to these events by placing a number from the following scale in the blank space preceding each item. Please base your answers on how *you* react, *not* on how you think others react or how you think a person should react.

Never	Almost Never	Occasionally	Usually	Almost Always	Always
1	2	3	4	5	6

1. _____ When I accomplish something difficult, I feel delighted or elated.

2. _____ When I feel happy, it is a strong type of exuberance.

3. _____ I enjoy being with other people very much.

4. _____ I feel pretty bad when I tell a lie.

5. _____ When I solve a small personal problem, I feel euphoric.

6. _____ My emotions tend to be more intense than those of most people.

7. _____ My happy moods are so strong that I feel as if I were in heaven.

8. _____ I get overly enthusiastic.

9. _____ If I complete a task I thought was impossible, I am ecstatic.

10. _____ My heart races at the anticipation of an exciting event.

11. _____ Sad movies deeply touch me.

12. _____ When I'm happy, it's a feeling of being untroubled and content, rather than being zestful and aroused.

13. _____ When I talk in front of a group for the first time, my voice gets shaky and my heart races.

14. _____ When something good happens, I'm usually much more jubilant than others.

15. _____ My friends might say I'm emotional.

16. _____ The memories I like the most are of those times when I felt content and peaceful, rather than zestful and enthusiastic.

17. _____ The sight of someone who is hurt badly affects me strongly.

18. _____ When I'm feeling well, it's easy for me to go from being in a good mood to being really joyful.

19. _____ "Calm and cool" could easily describe me.

20. _____ When I'm happy, I feel as if I'm bursting with joy.

Research Findings on Affect Intensity

In a daily study of mood, Larsen, Diener, and Emmons (1986) had subjects record the events in their daily lives. Sixty-two subjects recorded the best and the worst events of the day for 56 consecutive days, resulting in almost 6,000 event descriptions. The subjects also rated these events each day in terms of how subjectively good or bad the events were for them. The same event descriptions were rated later by a team of raters for how objectively good or bad they would be for the average college student. Results showed that the subjects high on the affect intensity dimension rated their life events as significantly *more severe* than did the low affect intensity subjects. That is, events that were rated as only "moderately good" by the objective raters (such as receiving a compliment from a professor) were rated as "very good" by the high affect intensity subjects. Similarly, events that were rated as only "moderately bad" by the objective raters (such as losing a favorite pen) tended to be rated as "very bad" by the high affect intensity subjects. Thus, the high affect intensity subjects tended to evaluate the events in their lives—both good and bad events—as having significantly more emotional impact than did the low affect intensity subjects. High affect intensity individuals are thus more emotionally reactive to the emotion-provoking events in their lives, both the good and the bad events.

An aspect of these findings worth emphasizing is that high affect intensity individuals are more reactive to *both* positive and negative events in their lives. In other words, high affect intensity individuals should exhibit more **mood variability**, or more frequent fluctuations in their emotional lives over time. Larsen (1987) found that individuals high on the affect intensity dimension do, in fact, exhibit more frequent changes in their moods and that these changes tend to be larger in magnitude than are the mood changes of low affect intensity individuals.

The concept of affect intensity, containing as it does the notion of mood variability, is a general and broad characteristic of emotional life. Affect intensity has been found to relate to a variety of standard personality variables. For example, Larsen and Diener (1987) reported that affect intensity relates to the personality dimensions of high activity level, sociability, and arousability. High affect intensity individuals tend to have a vigorous and energetic lifestyle, tend to be outgoing and enjoy being with others, and tend to seek out stimulating and arousing things to do in their daily lives. During an interview, a high affect intensity subject reported that, to her, the worst thing in life was to be bored. She reported that she often did things to liven up her life, such as playing practical jokes on her roommates. Although such activities sometimes got her into trouble, she felt that it was worth it to obtain the stimulation. Another high affect intensity subject described himself as an "intensity junkie," hooked on the need for an emotionally stimulating lifestyle. A recent review of what is known about individual differences in affect intensity can be found in Larsen (2009).

Interaction of Content and Style in Emotional Life

People differ from each other in terms of the relative amounts of positive and negative emotional *content* in their lives over time, as well as in terms of the *stylistic* intensity of their emotional experiences. In trying to understand emotional life as an aspect of personality, it appears that the hedonic balance—the degree of pleasantness in a person's life over time—represents the content of emotional life. For example, Larsen (2000b) reported that the average college student had a positive hedonic balance on 7 out of 10 days. That is, out of every 10 days, 7 of them contained predominantly positive emotions, and 3 of them contained a predominance of negative emotions. However, there were wide individual differences, so that some people had as few as 20 percent positive days, whereas others had as many as 95 percent positive days. This hedonic balance between positive and negative affect, between the good and bad days in a person's life over time, best represents the content of emotional life (Zelenski & Larsen, 2000).

Affect intensity represents the style of emotional life and refers to the magnitude of a person's typical emotional reactions. Together, these two characteristics—content and style—provide a good deal of descriptive and explanatory power. An interesting aspect of these two dimensions is that hedonic balance and affect intensity are unrelated to each other (Larsen & Diener, 1985). This means that there are people who have frequent positive affect of low intensity and others who have frequent positive affect of high intensity. Similarly, there are people who have frequent negative affect of low intensity and others

Figure 13.8

Quality of emotional life as a function of content (hedonic balance) and style (affect intensity).

who have frequent negative affect of high intensity. In other words, hedonic balance interacts with affect intensity to produce specific types of emotional lives that may characterize different personalities. The effects of this interaction of hedonic balance and affect intensity in creating emotional life are illustrated in Figure 13.8.

In Figure 13.8, you can see that individuals high and low on the affect intensity dimension typically experience the content of their emotional lives in very different ways. A person low in affect intensity has an emotional life that is characterized by its enduringness, evenness, and lack of fluctuation. If such a person also happens to be a happy person (more positive than negative emotional content in life), then he or she experiences this happiness as a tranquil sort of enduring contentment. If he or she happens to be an unhappy person (less positive than negative emotional content in life), then his or her emotional life consists of a chronic and somewhat annoying or irritating level of negative affect over time. On the other hand, a person high on the affect intensity dimension has an emotional life characterized by abruptness, changeableness, and volatility. If this kind of person also happens to be a happy person, then he or she experiences this happiness as enlivened and animated spikes of enthusiasm and exhilaration. If this high affect intensity person is, instead, an unhappy person, then he or she experiences troughs of a variety of negative emotions, such as anxiety, guilt, depression, and loneliness.

SUMMARY AND EVALUATION

Emotions can be thought of either as states or as traits, and both of these are patterns of experience, physiological changes, and changes in behavior, or action tendencies. Emotional states are short-lived and are typically caused by an event in the environment. As traits, however, emotions are consistent and stable patterns of experience in a person's life, where these patterns are due mostly to the person's personality. In this chapter, we looked at emotions as traits. For example, people differ from each other in how often they are angry, happy, or depressed. Such differences can be useful in describing aspects of personality.

Emotional content is the types of emotional experiences that a person is likely to have. If we know, for example, the typical content of a person's emotional life, then we know the kinds of emotions he or she is likely to experience over time.

Emotional content can be broadly divided into the pleasant and the unpleasant emotions. In the pleasant emotion category are happiness and the associated judgment of life satisfaction. On most people's lists of primary emotions, there is only one major pleasant emotion, whereas there are many varieties of unpleasant emotions. From a trait perspective, under pleasant emotions we discussed dispositional happiness. Some people are happier than others, and psychologists are developing theories and gathering data to understand why people differ on happiness and how people might increase their level of trait happiness.

Under the content approach to dispositional unpleasant emotions, we discussed three dispositions: anxiety, depression, and anger. Trait anxiety has many names in the personality literature, including neuroticism and negative affectivity. This trait emotion appears to have distinct cognitive components and is related to ongoing health, especially self-reported health. Depression is also defined as a syndrome of associated experiences and behaviors, and we examined several cognitive theories of depression. Anger proneness and hostility were also discussed as a trait affect, and we examined the health and well-being implications of this disposition. Anxiety, depression, and anger are currently topics of intense interest for neuroscientists, and data are accumulating on the brain centers involved in the experience, as well as the regulation, of each of these emotions.

Emotional style is the typical way in which a person experiences emotions. We focused on the stylistic component of affect intensity, or the typical magnitude with which people experience emotions. Persons who score high on the affect intensity dimension have larger emotional reactions to the events in their lives, are reactive to both pleasant and unpleasant events, and are more variable in their day-to-day moods. Content and style interact within persons to produce distinct varieties of emotional lives.

KEY TERMS

emotions 396
action tendencies 396
functional analysis 396
emotional states 397
emotional traits 397
categorical approach 397
dimensional approach 398
content 400
style 400

happiness 401
positive illusions 402
reciprocal causality 404
mood induction 410
neuroticism 413
limbic system 414
anterior cingulate 415
prefrontal cortex 415
depression 418

diathesis-stress model 418
cognitive schema 418
cognitive triad 419
self-fulfilling prophecy 420
neurotransmitter theory of
   depression 420
hostility 421
affect intensity 423
mood variability 427

© Corbis/SuperStock RF

Approaches to the Self

14

THE COGNITIVE/EXPERIENTIAL DOMAIN

There are many aspects to the self: the way we see and define our selves, or our self-concept; the evaluation we make of that self-concept, which is called self-esteem; and our social identities, which are the outward reflections we show other people.
© B2M Productions/Getty Images RF

"**K**now thyself!" was the advice given by the Greek Oracle at Delphi. Do you know yourself? Who are you? How would you answer this question? Would you define yourself first as a student, as a son or daughter, or as someone's spouse or boy- or girlfriend? Or would you define yourself by listing your various characteristics: "I am smart, optimistic, and confident"? Or would you instead give a physical description: "I am a male, 6 feet 6 inches tall, about 200 pounds, with red hair and a ruddy complexion"? No matter how you respond to this question, your answer is an important part of your **self-concept**, your understanding of yourself. Moreover, some people are satisfied with who they are, whereas others are dissatisfied with their self-concept. How you feel about who you are is your self-esteem. On top of this, you have a **social identity** as you present yourself to others. Sometimes social identity does not match our self-concept, and the selves we present to others are not the selves we know ourselves to be, leading some of us to feel false or phony in our relationships.

In this chapter, we explore how psychologists have approached the notion of the self. We do this by considering the three main components of the self: self-concept, self-esteem, and social identity.

Why might we want to learn about the self? To most people, their sense of self is their anchor, their starting point for interpreting everything around them. For example, when you look at a group photo on a friend's Facebook page, whom in the group do you look at first? If you are like most people, you will say that you look at yourself first. And when looking at the photo of yourself, you immediately engage in an evaluation. You might think the picture is not a good representation, that it does not show you in the best light. Maybe you think that you have a nicer smile than that and that you are, in fact, a happier person than this picture portrays. Or you might think that you have put on a few pounds lately, that you are heavier than your friends in the photo. Maybe you dislike the fact that you have gotten heavier, and a small blow to your self-esteem occurs when you look at the photo. Or maybe you wonder how certain other people would view this photo of you. Would your parents like to see you this way? For example, would they approve of the self you portray in this group photo of yourself with your college friends?

Our sense of self is changing all the time. In infancy, we first distinguished ourselves from the world around us and began the lifelong process of constructing, evaluating, and presenting to others our sense of who we are. During this process, we constantly undergo challenges and changes to our self-concept. For example, in high school, a young man might try out for the basketball team and do poorly. His sense of himself as an athlete is challenged by this experience of failure. He will have to search for other ways of defining himself. Maybe he will dye his hair purple and start wearing a trench coat to school, beginning to define himself in terms of an alternative teen lifestyle. High school and college are years in which many people struggle with defining their self-concept, and it is a time when people are especially sensitive to events that challenge their sense of self.

Once people have a fairly stable sense of themselves, they begin to use that to evaluate events and objects in the world. For example, when something happens to a person, such as a young woman's breakup with a boyfriend, she evaluates that event from the perspective of her self-concept and whether the event is good or bad for who she thinks she is. If having this boyfriend was an important part of her self-concept ("I'm nothing without him.") (Aron et al., 2004), then she evaluates the breakup as devastating. On the other hand, if the young woman has a sense of herself that is rooted in other areas of her life (e.g., academics, friendships, sports) that are mostly independent of her relationship with the young man, then the breakup is less devastating.

Our sense of who we are leads us to evaluate events in the world in certain ways. Only events that are important to our sense of self will have any strong impact either way, as very good or very bad. For example, if doing well in school is not part of your self-concept (maybe you are in college for other reasons), then doing poorly on an academic assignment will not affect you much. You can quickly learn what is important to a person's self-concept by observing what evokes emotions in them. Who we are, our self-concept, determines how we respond to and evaluate the events in the world.

People do not always like or value what they see when they turn inward and assess their self-concept. That liking or value is self-esteem. For example, two people may both tend to save money rather than spend it, to not leave tips at restaurants, and to always buy the cheapest things. One of these persons views herself as frugal and conservative, and she evaluates these to be positive characteristics. She has positive self-esteem, at least as far as these attributes go. The second person may see himself as stingy, ungenerous, and without compassion. He views these characteristics as negative. Consequently, he has low self-esteem, at least as far as these attributes go. Both have the same self-concept, of being thrifty and hoarding their money, but differ in how they evaluate those characteristics and hence in their self-esteem.

Finally, social identity is the self that is shown to other people. This is the relatively enduring part of ourselves that we use to create an impression, to let other people know who we are and what can be expected from us. For instance, your driver's license, which is often used for social identification purposes, contains information about your social identity: your family name, your first name, your gender and racial identity, your date of birth, your address, your physical description, such as height, weight, and eye color. These characteristics differentiate you from other people and form some of the more visible and socially available aspects of your identity. Other, less available aspects of your social identity include how you like to be perceived by others and the impression that you want others to have of your personality. Maybe you are the kind of person who wants to be taken seriously, so it is important to you to have a very businesslike social identity. Maybe you are the kind of person who wants to be liked by most people, so you strive to have a social identity as a friendly and agreeable person.

The three components of the self—self-concept, self-esteem, and social identity—are all vitally important in our day-to-day lives. Personality psychologists have studied these aspects of the self and have generated a good deal of knowledge about them. We begin this chapter with a focus on the descriptive component of the self—the self-concept.

Descriptive Component of the Self: Self-Concept

Knowledge of the self does not happen all at once. It develops over years, starting in infancy, accelerating in adolescence, and reaching completion in old age. The self-concept is the basis for self-understanding, and it forms the answer to the question "Who am I?"

Development of the Self-Concept

The first glimmer of a self-concept occurs in infancy, when the child learns that some things are always there (e.g., its body) and some things are there only sometimes (e.g., the mother's breast). The child makes a distinction between its own body and everything else: it discovers that boundaries exist between what is "me" and what is "not me." Gradually, the infant comes to realize that it is distinct from the rest of the world. This distinction forms the rudimentary sense of self, awareness of one's body.

Have you ever seen a dog bark at its own reflection in a mirror? The dog barks because it does not recognize that the image is a reflection of itself. Dogs soon get bored with mirrors and ignore their reflections. Humans and some primates do recognize that the mirror is a self-reflection. Psychologists have devised a clever technique for studying whether a monkey or a human recognizes its own reflection. They place a small mark on the face that cannot be seen without a mirror. Then, when faced with the mirror, they look to see if the monkey or child uses the reflection to touch the mark on its own face. Chimpanzees and orangutans do exhibit self-recognition with mirrors and will find the mark after about two to three days with the mirror (Gallup, 1977a). Studies of lower primates, such as the macaque, do not find that they exhibit self-recognition with mirrors, even after 2,400 hours of exposure to the mirror (Gallup, 1977b). Animals that have passed the mirror test of self-recognition include all of the great apes (bonobos, chimpanzees, gorillas, orangutans, and humans), elephants, bottlenose dolphins, orcas, and one species of magpie (Prior, Schwarz, & Güntürkün, 2008).

In normal children, self-recognition with mirrors occurs on average at age 18 months (Lewis & Ramsay, 2004). There is, however, some variability in age of onset

Self-recognition in the mirror test is a criterion for determining whether a species has self-awareness.
© *Life on white/Alamy Stock Photo RF*

of self-recognition, with 15 months being the earliest documented case, and age 24 months being the point at which all or almost all children demonstrate self-recognition. Interestingly, pretend play appears to require self-recognition (Lewis & Ramsay, 2004). A child pretending to feed a doll imaginary food or a child drinking an imaginary liquid from a cup must know that what he or she is doing is not real. Pretending behavior requires that the child distinguish "this is what I pretend to be doing" from "this is what I actually am doing." In a study of children aged 15 to 21 months, only those children who exhibited self-recognition to a mirror were capable of pretend play (Lewis & Ramsay, 2004). Moreover, children do not begin using personal pronouns (I, me, mine) until they gain self-recognition abilities in the mirror test. Self-recognition is therefore an important cognitive developmental achievement that allows the child to go on to more complex manifestations of self-awareness, such as engaging in pretend play and representing the self in language with personal pronouns.

Although very young children are fascinated with their reflections, it takes a while for a child to be able to recognize photographs of him- or herself in a group. A child needs to be about 2 years old before he or she can pick his or her picture out of a crowd (Baumeister, 1991). Around this time, the second year of life, children begin to grasp the idea that other people have expectations for them. For example, this is about the time when children can follow rules set up by parents. Children learn that some behaviors are good and other behaviors are bad, and they evaluate their own behavior against these standards. They will smile when they do something good and frown when something bad occurs. They clearly are developing a sense of themselves relative to standards. This is the beginning of self-esteem.

Among the first aspects of the self that people learn to identify and associate with themselves are sex and age. This typically occurs between 2 and 3 years of age, when a child begins to call himself a boy or herself a girl and to refer to other children as boys or girls. A rudimentary knowledge of age also develops, with a child often learning to hold up the number of fingers that designate age. Children at this age also expand their self-concept to include reference to a family. "I'm Sarah's brother," a child might say, implying that part of his self-concept includes being in the same family as Sarah.

From age 3 to about 12, children's self-concepts are based mainly on developing talents and skills. The child thinks of him- or herself as someone who can do this or cannot do that, such as recite the alphabet, tie his own shoes, read, walk to school by herself, tell time, or write in cursive handwriting. At this age, the self-concept is defined mainly in terms of sex, age, family of origin, and what the child believes he or she can or cannot do.

Starting with the school years, ages 5 or 6 onward, children increasingly begin to compare their skills and abilities with those of others. They are now either better than or worse than other children. This is the beginning of **social comparison**, which most people engage in to varying degrees for the rest of their lives (Baumeister, 1997). Social comparison is the evaluation of oneself or one's performance in terms of a comparison with a reference group. "Am I faster, smarter, more popular, more attractive, and so on than my friends?" is the question that children repeatedly ask themselves during this period of development.

Also during this time, children learn that they can lie and keep secrets. This is based on the realization that there is a hidden side to the self, a side that includes private attributes, such as thoughts, feelings, and desires. The realization that "Mommy doesn't know everything about me" is a big step. The development of an inner, **private self-concept** is a major but often difficult development in the growth of the self-concept. It may start out with children developing an imaginary friend, someone only they can see or hear. This imaginary friend may actually be the children's first attempt to communicate to their parents that they know there is a secret part, an inner part, to their understanding of the self. Later, children develop the full realization that only they have access to their own thoughts, feelings, and desires and that no one else can know this part of themselves unless they choose to tell others. This is a big step in developing self-concept.

As children grow from childhood to adolescence, their self-concept changes from one based on such concrete characteristics as physical appearance and possessions to one that is based on more abstract psychological terms. We illustrate this below with examples drawn from Montemayor and Eisen (1977). The statements are from children of different ages all answering the question "Who am I?"

The following is from a 9-year-old boy in the fourth grade. Notice how concrete his description is and that he uses mostly tangible concepts such as age, sex, name, address, and other aspects of his physical self:

> *My name is Bruce. I have brown eyes and brown hair. And I have brown eyebrows. I am nine years old. I LOVE sports. I have seven people in my family. I have great eyesight and I have lots of friends. I will be 10 in September. I live at 1923 Pinecrest. I am a boy. I have an uncle that is almost 7 feet tall. My school is Pinecrest and my teacher is Mrs V. I play Hockey.*

The next statement is from a girl aged 11½ in the sixth grade. Notice that she frequently refers to her likes, and also emphasizes more abstract personality and social characteristics:

> *My name is Alice. I am a human being. I am a girl. I am a truthful person. I am not pretty. I do so-so in my studies. I am a very good cellist and a very good pianist. I am a little bit tall for my age. I like several boys and girls. I am old-fashioned. I play tennis and am a very good swimmer. I try to be helpful. I am always ready to be friends with anybody. Mostly I am good, but I lose my temper. I am not well-liked by some girls. I don't know if I'm liked by boys or not.*

The final example is from a 17-year-old girl in the twelfth grade. Notice how she emphasizes interpersonal characteristics, her typical mood states, and several ideological and belief references in her self-description:

> *I am a human being. I am a girl. I am an individual. I don't know who I am. I am a Pisces. I am a moody person. I am an indecisive person. I am an ambitious person. I am a very curious person. I am not an individual. I am a loner. I am an American (God help me). I am a Democrat. I am a liberal person. I am a radical. I am a conservative. I am a pseudoliberal. I am an atheist. I am not a classifiable person (i.e., I don't want to be classified).*

In the development of the self, children learn to compare themselves to others. "I'm faster than you" is a phrase commonly heard whenever a group of young children gather. This is the beginning of social comparison, whereby people define and evaluate themselves in comparison to others.

© Sergey Novikov/Shutterstock.com RF

A final unfolding of the self-concept, during the teen years, involves **perspective taking**: the ability to take the perspectives of others, or to see oneself as others do, to step outside of oneself and imagine how one appears to other people. This is why many teenagers go through a period of extreme self-consciousness during this time, focusing much of their energy on how they appear to others. You might vividly recall this period of your life, the strong emotions involved in episodes of **objective self-awareness**, of seeing yourself as an object of others' attention. Remember going to gym class in your funny gym uniform, or that first trip to the beach in your new swimsuit? Often, objective self-awareness is experienced as shyness, and for some people this is a chronic problem.

Because shyness is such a common problem, especially during the adolescent years, we added a "Closer Look" on this topic. We will mention here that, because shy people are anxious about interacting with others, they often avoid opportunities to socialize. One way to avoid face-to-face interaction is to socialize on-line, where the interaction is more controllable, proceeds more slowly, and provides limited information exchange (e.g., no non-verbal information, etc.). Also, when with others, one way to avoid having to interact with them is to take out your cell phone and give the device all your attention. Researchers have found that young adults with social anxiety (shyness) are more likely to use the Internet excessively (Weinstein et al., 2015). In fact, Internet use can reach problematic proportions for shy individuals, such that they can appear "addicted" to their smart phones (Bian & Leung, 2015); that is, become preoccupied and have trouble controlling the use of their phone, experience productivity loss, feel anxiety or "lost" without their phone, etc. Other studies of young adults focused on excessive use of Facebook (to the point of interfering with school work) and found that social anxiety was correlated with problematic Facebook usage (Lee-Won, Herzog, & Park, 2015). Other researchers have examined excessive online gaming, and again found that persons high in social anxiety spent more hours gaming per week than persons without social anxiety (Lee & Leeson, 2015). Several recent studies show that the strongest personality predictor of problematic Internet use is shyness or social anxiety (e.g., Carli & Durkee, 2016; Huan et al., 2014). While there are certainly socially beneficial ways to use the Internet (for communication, to stay in touch, to gather information), we all have had the experience of being socially ignored by someone preoccupied with their smart phones. Shy persons are at risk for developing these preoccupations, presumably because it gives them a means to avoid face-to-face socializing, the very behavior they should work on increasing.

In summary, the self-concept is a distinct knowledge structure made up of many different elements and stored in our memories much as we might store a cognitive map of our hometown. Part of developing a sense of self lies in being able to see yourself through the eyes of others and, while this perspective can be a valuable skill to have, it can sometimes make a person feel uncomfortable and produce shyness.

A Closer Look

Shyness: When Objective Self-Awareness Becomes Chronic

Garrison Keillor, the popular host of the *Prairie Home Companion* radio show, suffers from acute shyness and has openly discussed this in articles and in interviews. He says that when shy persons have to be in an interaction, they just want to become invisible. They dislike conversation because they lack social confidence, are made terribly anxious by the interaction, and are not good at promoting themselves. Because of these feelings, the shy person withdraws from social interaction.

Many accomplished people are shy, including singers Barbra Streisand and Bob Dylan, and writer J. D. Salinger (Stocker, 1997). What shy persons have in common is that they desire friendships and social interactions but are held back by their insecurities and fears. Consequently, they avoid the spotlight, avoid face-to-face interaction, and ruminate excessively after conversations, worrying about whether they said the right things, made a good impression, or sounded stupid. The inner experience of a shy person in an interaction is quite different from that of someone else in the same interaction who is not shy.

Shy people are not necessarily introverts (Cheek, 1989). Introverts prefer to be alone; they enjoy the peace and quiet of solitude. Shy people, on the other hand, want to have contact with others, to be socially involved, and to have friends and be part of the group. But shy persons' self-doubt and self-consciousness prompts them to pass up opportunities to socialize (Henderson & Zimbardo, 2001a, 2001b; see www.shyness.com). They handicap themselves; by not entering groups, not speaking to unfamiliar people, not approaching others, they deny themselves the opportunities to learn and practice the very social skills they need to overcome their shyness (see Table 14.1).

Psychologist Jerome Kagan has been studying shyness for decades (Kagan, 1981, 1994, 1999). In his studies of infants, he found that about 20 percent of 4-month-old babies exhibit signs of shyness—they flail their arms and legs and cry when presented with an unfamiliar object or person. Following up these infants for several years, Kagan found that most of them exhibited signs of shyness as young children. For example, in play situations they often did not move very far from their parents, and some even clung to their parents, not leaving their sides at all when there were unfamiliar children around. Following them a few more years, Kagan found that roughly half of the shy children were transformed and were no longer shy in later childhood. In looking at parenting practices, Kagan found that the parents of these formerly shy children had encouraged their children to socialize. That is, they often had pushed their children to join groups and to talk to other children, and they had given their children lots of praise for socializing. Often this had been "tough love," in that the parents had had to push the reluctant and complaining children to play with peers. However, a few years later, the result was children who were much less shy. The parents of the children who remained shy often had given in to the children's reluctance to join groups. That is, when the children complained or resisted joining a group, the parents often had given in, not pushing the children anyway. As a result, such children apparently never learned that they could overcome their self-doubt and lack of social confidence (Kagan, 1999). Other research has shown that parents who are too controlling and protective toward their children often have children who are shy and anxious (Wood et al., 2003).

Psychologists studying shyness sometimes prefer the term social anxiety, which is defined as discomfort related to social interactions, or even to the anticipation of social interactions (Chavira, Stein, & Malcarne, 2002). Adults with social anxiety report that they are nervous or that they feel awkward when talking to others, especially people with whom they are unfamiliar (Cheek & Buss, 1981). Socially anxious persons appear to be overly concerned about what others will think. After a conversation, they often conclude that they said something wrong, sounded foolish, or looked stupid (Ritts & Patterson, 1996). Sometimes the social anxiety is so strong that it shows in various outward signs, such as a trembling voice or jittery movements. Other people interacting with a socially anxious person often interpret their behavior as unfriendliness, rather than as shyness (Cheek & Buss, 1981). Sometimes shy persons are so overcome with anxiety that it hinders their ability to carry on a conversation. They may spend time staring at their shoes, rather than talking, because they cannot think of a thing to say. Pauses in a conversation can be very discomforting to shy persons.

In an interesting study, researchers asked participants to work on a unique task, one that could not be completed without having to ask another person for

(Continued)

A Closer Look (*Continued*)

help (DePaulo et al., 1989). The researchers deliberately created this task so they could investigate whether shy persons would reach out to others when they really needed to. They found that the socially anxious participants were reluctant to ask for help from another person, presumably because the shy person is anxious that the other may rebuff a request for help.

Shy people also tend to interpret social interactions negatively; they are more likely to interpret a comment as a criticism than as a helpful suggestion. For example, DePaulo et al. (1987) had students work in groups, then write reports on each other's performance. They were then individually interviewed about what they thought the others had said about them. It turns out that the shy participants thought that the others liked them less and that the others thought they were less competent. It seems that shy people are not only reluctant to enter into social interaction but also expect that others will dislike them. These expectations may lead them to avoid interactions or cut conversations short, losing the very opportunities they need to overcome their shyness.

What makes shy people so socially anxious? Kagan believes that some of it is due to genetics. After all, it shows up in some infants very early in life. However, some of this social anxiety must also be learned. What most researchers believe is that shy persons have learned to put too much stock in other people's judgments of them. This is called evaluation apprehension, the idea that shy persons are apprehensive about being evaluated by others. For example, shy persons believe that a person with whom they are talking will think they are dull, silly, or childish. They fear that others will evaluate them negatively. As a consequence, just the thought of going out on stage or leading a group meeting fills them with

dread. And so they avoid such situations. When forced into interaction, they try to limit it or cut it short. They avoid eye contact, which indicates to others that they prefer to end the conversation. When forced into conversation, they try to keep it impersonal and nonthreatening. They do a lot of agreeing, nodding their heads, without getting too involved in the conversation. They try not to give too much in the way of opinions or personal information, which can be evaluated by others. In sum, researchers believe that at the root of shyness is a fear of being evaluated negatively by others (Leary & Kowalski, 1995), which translates into a lack of confidence in social interactions and feeling that they lack the social skills necessary to navigate social situations (Cheek & Melchior, 1990).

Recent surveys estimate that 7–13 percent of persons in Western countries will experience social phobia, or extreme shyness, during their lifetime (Furmark, 2002). This suggests that shyness is not uncommon in the general population. Schmidt and Fox (2002) provide a review of the developmental course of shyness, as well as the varieties of shyness. For example, some shy persons are high in sociability and are distinguished by being especially anxious and fearful. Another type is shy persons who are low in sociability, who simply avoid others because of their excessive self-consciousness (Cheek & Krasnoperova, 1999). Empirically, however, it is difficult to distinguish owing to the overlap in the characteristics. Self-reports of shyness do correlate strongly with peer reports of shyness, suggesting that this characteristic can be well measured with questionnaires (Zarevski et al., 2002).

Psychologists studying the brain have suggested that shy persons have a more reactive **amygdala**, which is a section of the limbic or emotional system of the brain that is most responsible for fear.

A study by Kagan and colleagues followed up a group of adults who, at age 2 years, had been assessed for shyness. They found that the adults who were shy as children showed a greater fMRI response within the amygdala to novel versus familiar faces, compared to the nonshy adults (Schwartz et al., 2003). In another interesting study, researchers assessed cortisol (the stress hormone described in Chapter 6) on the first and fifth days of school among 35 first-graders (Bruce, Davis, & Gunnar, 2002). They found that most children showed an elevated cortisol response on the first day of school. However, the shy children showed an elevated and extended cortisol response even on the fifth day of school.

Whatever its causes, shyness can have problematic social implications for the shy person. Several studies have examined how shy persons use the Internet to avoid face-to-face social interaction (e.g., Caplan, 2002). One study found that shy persons were more likely to use the Internet for recreation rather than interact with others in face-to-face recreational settings (Scealy, Phillips, & Stevenson, 2002).

Stocker (1997) reviewed much of what is known about helping shy persons overcome their difficulties. She offers seven concrete steps a shy person can take:

1. *Show up.* Shy persons want to avoid the situations that make them anxious. However, if you really want to overcome shyness, you've got to enter those uncomfortable situations: go to a party or strike up a conversation with a stranger. Often, shy persons overestimate how uncomfortable they will feel; however, once they engage in an interaction, they find that it is not as bad as they had expected.

2. *Give yourself credit.* Stop being your own worst critic. In scorning

Table 14.1 Example Items from the Henderson/Zimbardo Shyness Questionnaire

INSTRUCTIONS: Rate each item using a number from the following scale to indicate how characteristic that statement is of you.

Not at all characteristic 1	Somewhat characteristic 2	Often characteristic 3	Very characteristic 4	Extremely characteristic 5

1. I am afraid of looking foolish in social situations.

2. I often feel insecure in social situations.

3. Other people appear to have more fun in social situations than I do.

4. If someone rejects me I assume that I have done something wrong.

5. It is hard for me to approach people who are having a conversation.

6. I feel lonely a good deal of the time.

7. I tend to be more critical of other people than I appear to be.

8. It is hard for me to say "no" to unreasonable requests.

9. I do more than my share on projects because I can't say no.

10. I find it easy to ask for what I want from other people.

or deriding their own social performance after the fact, shy persons are often very hard on themselves. If they make one little social faux pas, they often blow that misstep out of proportion, ignoring the fact that 99 percent of the interaction went well.

3. *Take baby steps.* It is useful to take big goals and break them into smaller steps. Instead of wanting to "become an engaging conversationalist," maybe try to set some smaller goals, such as going to a meeting of a group you've been wanting to join. The first time, you don't have to talk; just go and listen. The second time, maybe your goal will be to talk, not during the meeting but maybe to someone after the meeting is over. At the third meeting, try to ask a question during the actual meeting by speaking up. The point is to set small goals and experience some small successes along the way.

4. *Give unto others.* Shy people, because they are nervous, are focused on themselves during conversations. Shift your attention to others; look at them when they talk, listen carefully to what they say, try to find something interesting and connect to that, ask questions, and give a compliment or a word of support. Paying attention outwardly toward other people will also get your attention off yourself and your own nervousness.

5. *Exude warmth.* The nervousness that shy people feel is often interpreted by others as unfriendliness or tension. Try to create a more positive nonverbal impression by smiling, making eye contact, and staying relaxed.

6. *Anticipate failure.* Overcoming shyness is a learning process. It will take practice, and small failures are inevitable. If you say something wrong in a conversation, chalk it up to the learning process and get on with more practice.

7. *Join the crowd.* Nobody is perfect all the time. There are lots of people who are not perfect conversationalists. Also, you might think that making small talk is a big deal. However, when you really listen to other people's small talk, you'll realize that it really is just that—small talk, nothing more.

One way some people avoid social interaction is by directing all their attention to their smartphone. Studies show that shyness is often associated with smartphone "addiction."

© pathdoc/Shutterstock.com RF

Self-Schemata: Possible Selves, Ought Selves, and Undesired Selves

So far, we have considered some of the main steps in the development of a self-concept. Once formed, the self-concept provides a person with a sense of continuity and a framework for understanding the past and present and for guiding future behavior.

The self-concept is a network of information in memory, which organizes and provides coherence to the ways in which we experience the self (Markus, 1983). The self-concept also guides how each person processes information about him- or herself (Markus & Nurius, 1986). For example, people more easily process information that is consistent with their self-concepts; if you see yourself as highly masculine, then you will quickly agree with statements such as the following: "I am assertive" and "I am strong."

The term **self-schema** (*schema* is singular; *schemata* is plural) refers to the specific knowledge structure, or cognitive representation, of the self-concept. For example, a person might have a schema about what it means to be masculine, and this schema might include such attributes as assertiveness, strength, and independence. As such, self-schemata are cognitive structures that are built on past experiences and that guide the processing of information about the self, particularly in social interaction.

Self-schemata usually refer to past and current aspects of the self. However, there are also schemata for future selves, which people are able to imagine. The term **possible selves** describes the many ideas people have about who they might become, who they hope to become, or who they fear they will become (Markus & Nurius, 1987). People often have specific desires, anxieties, fantasies, fears, hopes, and expectations about their own future selves (Oyserman, Destin, & Novin, 2015). Although possible selves are not based on actual past experiences, they nevertheless are part of the overall self-concept. That is, possible selves are some of the building blocks of the general self-concept. For example, are you the kind of person who could envision yourself becoming a scientist—that is, is this a possible self for you? Buday, Stake, and Petersen (2012) showed that possessing such a possible self as a scientist in high school predicted whether the participants were actually in a science career 10 years later. Other researchers have shown that future career selves in college predicted proactive career behaviors (e.g., visiting the job center on campus, signing up early for career fairs, and so forth (Strauss, Griffin, & Parker, 2012). One's future work self can be a strong motivating force for engaging in behaviors that prepare one for specific careers. Even older persons who are retired can have possible selves, such as future images of themselves as healthier, slimmer, etc. (Bolkan Hooker, & Coehlo, 2015).

Because they play a role in defining the self-concept, possible selves may influence a person's behavior in certain ways. For example, a high school student may have no idea what it would be like to be an astronaut. Nevertheless, because this is one of her possible selves, she has many thoughts and feelings about this image of herself as astronaut. Information about astronauts, the space agency, aviation science, and so forth has personal significance for her, and she seeks it out every chance she gets. Thus, this possible self will influence her here and now in terms of her current decisions (e.g., to take an extra math course). Possible selves are like bridges between our present and our future; they are our working models of ourselves in the future (Oyserman & Markus, 1990). Such a working model might lead to problem behaviors, however, as when the possible self is a poor role model. In studying a group of juvenile delinquents, Oyserman and Saltz (1993) found that a high proportion had a possible self of *criminal,* and relatively few had such conventional possible selves as *having a job* or *getting along well in school.* A study of 8th graders found that those who could imagine themselves as problem drinkers (i.e., had a "problem drinker" possible self) were more likely, as 9th graders, to have experienced problematic alcohol use (Lee et al., 2015).

Possible selves allow us to stay on schedule, to work toward self-improvement. Behaviors that stem from possible selves (desired or undesired) can activate a host of intense feelings and emotions. For example, to a person who does not have a possible self with coronary artery disease, missing a few days of an exercise program will not be as distressing as it is to a person who has such a possible self.

Psychologist Tory Higgins (1987, 1997, 1999) has elaborated on the possible selves notion by distinguishing the **ideal self**, which is what persons themselves want to be, from the **ought self**, which is persons' understanding of what others want them to be. The ought self is built on what people take as their responsibilities and commitments to others—what they ought to do. It is related to Carl Rogers' notion of conditions of worth, which we covered in Chapter 11. The ideal self is built on one's own desires and goals—what one wants to become. Higgins refers to the ought and the ideal selves as **self-guides**, standards that one uses to organize information and motivate appropriate behavior. The self-guides get their motivating properties from emotions. Higgins argues that these two types of possible selves are at the root of different emotions. If one's real self does not fit one's ideal self, then one will feel sad, despondent, and disappointed. If, on the other hand, one's real self does not fit one's ought self, then one will feel guilty, distressed, and anxious.

To summarize, self-schemata are cognitive knowledge structures about the self-concept, and they consist of past, present, and future aspects of the self. The self-concept is the sum of people's self-schemata, what they know and believe about themselves. An important part of the self-concept concerns possible selves, which can be ideals that people desire or undesired selves that people strive to avoid. Who have I been, what am I like now, and what do I want to be like in the future—the answers to these questions define the self-concept.

Evaluative Component of the Self: Self-Esteem

The first glimmer of self-esteem occurs when children identify standards or expectations for behavior and live up to them. For example, parents have expectations for toilet training. When children finally master these expectations, it is a source of pride and self-esteem, at least until larger challenges are encountered. In later childhood, the next shift in the source of self-esteem occurs when children begin to engage in social comparison; children compare themselves to others, and if they are doing better than others, then they feel good about themselves. And later, people develop a set of internal standards, part of what they hold to be important to their self-concept. Behavior or experiences inconsistent with these internal standards can lead to decreases in self-esteem. In all cases, self-esteem results from an evaluation of oneself.

Evaluation of Oneself

Self-esteem is a general evaluation of self-concept along a good–bad or like–dislike dimension: Do you generally like yourself and feel you are a worthwhile, good person? Do you feel that others respect you? Do you feel you are basically a decent, fair person?

Do you take pride and satisfaction in what you have done, in who you are, and in who you would like to become? Self-esteem is the sum of your positive and negative reactions to all the aspects of your self-concept.

Most of us have a mixed reaction to ourselves; we have to take the bad with the good, and we acknowledge that we have both strengths and weaknesses. How we feel about ourselves can change from day to day and even from hour to hour. When we do something that is not consistent with our self-concept, such as hurt someone's feelings, then we may experience a dip in self-esteem. Such fluctuations, however, occur around our average level of self-esteem. Most personality psychologists are interested in self-esteem in terms of our average level of self-esteem, our characteristic standing on the self-esteem dimension. Average levels of self-esteem fluctuate across the lifespan in predictable ways. The average low point in self-esteem usually occurs in adolescence, followed by a gradual rise through midlife for most people (Donnellan et al., 2012; Wagner et al., 2013). Increases in self-esteem over time tend to accompany other positive life events, such as the development of intimate relationships and career success (Wagner et al., 2013).

Personality researchers have begun to acknowledge that people can evaluate themselves positively or negatively in different areas of their lives. For example, you may feel pretty good about your intellectual abilities, but perhaps you are shy with members of the opposite sex. Consequently, you may have high academic self-esteem but lower self-esteem when it comes to dating or feeling attractive to others. Global self-esteem may be a composite of several individual areas of self-evaluation. Each of these subareas can be assessed separately, and researchers can examine self-esteem about various areas of life. For example, there is a scale for measuring three aspects of self-esteem: performance self-esteem, appearance self-esteem, and social self-esteem (Heatherton & Polivy, 1991).

Although there are distinct areas of life in which people can feel more or less confident of themselves—such as friendships, academics, and appearance—self-esteem measures of these content areas are moderately correlated. This means that people who tend to have high self-esteem in one area also tend to have high self-esteem in the other areas. Sometimes researchers find it useful to examine specific areas of self-esteem, such as appearance self-esteem in persons at risk for eating disorders. However, the majority of researchers find it useful to think of self-esteem as the person's global or average evaluation of their whole self-concept. Table 14.2 shows a global self-esteem questionnaire that is widely used by researchers in this area. This measure assesses a person's overall self-esteem, and by reading and answering the items for yourself you will get an idea of what self-esteem means in terms of the measures used to assess this construct. High scores on self-esteem are obtained by answering items 1–4 as "True" and items 5–7 as "False."

Table 14.2 Items in a Global Self-Esteem Questionnaire

1.	True	False	I feel good about myself.
2.	True	False	I feel I am a person of worth, the equal of other people.
3.	True	False	I am able to do things as well as most other people.
4.	True	False	On the whole, I am satisfied with myself.
5.	True	False	I certainly feel useless at times.
6.	True	False	At times I think I am no good at all.
7.	True	False	I feel I do not have much to be proud of.

Source: Adapted from Marsh, 1996.

A Closer Look

"But How Do You Really Feel?" Measuring Implicit Self-Esteem

Recall the A Closer Look from Chapter 11 on implicit motivation and research that compares peoples' explicit and implicit levels on particular motives. Implicit motivation was used to refer to the person's unconscious desires and aspirations, their unspoken needs and wants. Researchers measured this with the TAT and then compared their level of implicit motivation to their explicit level of that same motivation, with particular attention to subjects who were discrepant (i.e., reported high levels of some motive, yet on the TAT showed low levels of that motive). A similar situation has arisen in the literature on self-esteem, with researchers developing an implicit measure of self-esteem to get at a person's unconscious view of their self-worth and to contrast this to the explicit level he or she reports on a questionnaire measure of self-esteem.

Greenwald and Farnham developed an implicit measure of self-esteem in the year 2000. It consists of a task done on the computer and does not rely on self-reports of how positively people see themselves. Instead, the task, called the Self-Esteem Implicit Association Test (SE-IAT), measures how quickly and consistently people associate positive words to themselves compared to how quickly and consistently they associate negative words to themselves. The task is described in detail in Greenwald and Farnham (2000).

Before actually undertaking the task, the participant is asked to generate 18 "me-type" items and 18 "not-me-type" items. Me-type items are things such as first and last name, phone number, birth month, birth year, and the zip code in which one lives. Not-me-type items are things like a state where one does not live, a street name that one does not live on, and so forth. The researcher also has two lists of words; one list contains positive words (e.g., smart, nice, joy, lucky, etc.) and the other list contains unpleasant words (e.g., stupid, despised, filth, poison, etc.).

When the task begins, the researcher presents pairs of words on the computer screen, with each pair containing either a me-type item or a not-me-type item paired with either a positive or a negative word. The participant is instructed to categorize each pair, as quickly as he or she can, according to some rule, such as "If a me item is paired with a positive word, press the left key, and if a not-me item is paired with a positive word, press the right key." Participants are presented with many pairs of words and categorize each pair as quickly as they can according to the rule. The time it takes them to perform the categorization is measured by the computer in milliseconds.

An implicit self-esteem score is calculated by taking the average time it takes to categorize me-pleasant word pairs and subtracting the average time it takes to categorize me-unpleasant word pairs. A person with a small number is someone who is fast at categorizing me with pleasant words and relatively slow at categorizing me with unpleasant words, and we say that he or she has high implicit self-esteem. Such persons easily associate positive attributes to themselves. We say the measure is "implicit" because it does not rely on some conscious understanding or some spoken verbalization of how positively they see themselves. Rather, it relies on the strength of associations they have in their cognitive system between positive concepts and their self-concept, relative to the strength of associations they have between negative concepts and their self-concept.

Researchers have compared implicit to explicit measures of self-esteem. Explicit measures are questionnaires, such as that presented in Table 14.2, where the person self-reports how good they feel about themselves. Because the method of measuring implicit self-esteem was developed in 2000, a good deal of research has accumulated on people with discrepant levels.

One particularly interesting line of research examines individuals who have high explicit self-esteem (they say they feel pretty good about themselves) yet have a low level of implicit self-esteem (they more quickly associate negative than positive words to themselves). This discrepancy in how one "really" feels about him- or herself is correlated with narcissism (Jordan et al., 2003). That is, on the outside, narcissists appear to have high self-esteem, but on the inside they are insecure about their self-esteem. Other researchers have replicated this finding of a discrepancy between outward and inward self-esteem, and have shown that people who exhibit an abundance of explicit self-esteem but a dearth of implicit self-esteem have a kind of fragile self-concept and are overly sensitivity to the opinions of others and other threats to their self-esteem (Gregg & Sedikides, 2012).

Other studies have examined discrepancies where explicit self-esteem is low (the person says they don't feel very good about themselves) yet implicit levels remain high (unconsciously they remain positive). This kind of discrepancy is associated with emotional problems, such as depression and feeling worthless (Leeuwis et al., 2015). These authors also found that being victimized by a bully can bring about declines in explicit self-esteem yet leave implicit levels intact. Another study found that psychotherapy (25 sessions of either cognitive therapy or psychoanalysis) elevated both implicit and explicit self-esteem (Ritrer et al., 2013).

As research accumulates on implicit and explicit self-esteem, and the discrepancies between the two, we will gain a better understanding of the dynamics of inner and outer manifestations of how people feel about themselves. Starting with a measure of some new concept, and then proceeding to ask questions about that new concept, is exactly how science progresses in personality psychology.

Research on Self-Esteem

Much of the research on self-esteem concerns how people respond to evaluation. Being evaluated is a very common occurrence, especially during the school years. Homework is evaluated, tests are given, and children receive regular reports on their performance. Even outside school, a lot of play in childhood also involves evaluation, such as occurs with competitive games. In adulthood, the games change but the evaluation continues. At most jobs, there is usually some form of evaluation done on a regular basis, and the workers receive feedback on their performance at least in the form of the size of the raise they get that year. There is also competition and evaluation in many other areas of adult life, such as finances, marriage, and children, where people often compare how they are doing with their neighbors. Because self-esteem is linked to evaluation, much of the research on this topic concerns how people react to criticism and negative feedback.

Reactions to Criticism and Failure Feedback

Many laboratory studies have been conducted on how people high and low on self-esteem react to failure and criticism. In general, participants are taken into the laboratory and instructed to complete an important task. For example, they may be given an intelligence test and told that norms are being developed and that they should try to do the very best they can. Usually this gets the participants very involved and motivates them to want to perform well. The researcher then scores the test when the subjects are finished, and the researcher is critical of the participants' performance, saying that they did very poorly. The research question is "How are high and low self-esteem persons affected by this criticism and personal failure?" The research has looked mainly at how failure feedback affects subsequent performance on similar tasks, and whether failure affects high and low self-esteem persons differently (Brown & Dutton, 1995; Stake, Huff, & Zand, 1995). The findings suggest that, following failure, low self-esteem persons are more likely to perform poorly and to give up earlier on subsequent tasks. For high self-esteem persons, on the other hand, failure feedback seems to spur them into action on subsequent tasks, and they are less likely to give up and more likely to work just as hard on the second task as they did on the first (Brown & Dutton, 1995).

Why is it that failure seems to incapacitate low self-esteem persons but seems to encourage high self-esteem persons into renewed effort? Researchers think that people readily accept feedback that is consistent with their self-concept, so for low self-esteem persons, failure feedback on the first task is consistent with their self-concept, and it confirms their views that they are the kind of people who fail more than succeed. And so, when confronted with the second task, low self-esteem persons, who have just had their negative self-view confirmed with failing on the first task, believe they will also fail on the second task, and so do not try so hard or just give up. For high self-esteem persons, however, failure is not consistent with their existing self-concept, so they are more likely *not* to accept this feedback. Also, it is likely that they will discount the feedback, perhaps thinking that failure on the first task must have been an accident or a mistake. Consequently, they are motivated to try just as hard the second time, and to not give up, because they do not see their self-concept as the kind of people who fail. Psychologist Roy Baumeister and his colleagues (e.g., Baumeister, Tice, & Hutton, 1989) argue that high self-esteem persons are concerned with projecting a successful, prosperous, and thriving self-image. Low self-esteem persons, on the other hand, are most concerned with avoiding failure. It is a difference of emphasis: high self-esteem persons fear not succeeding; low self-esteem persons fear failure.

Self-Esteem and Coping with Negative Events

Other research on high self-esteem persons has examined the strategies these people use to get through life. Unpleasant events happen to everyone. High self-esteem persons appear to maintain their positive evaluation through the ups and downs of everyday life. Have high self-esteem persons somehow figured out how to cope more effectively with these challenges of life? How do high self-esteem persons overcome the disappointments, shortcomings, losses, and failures that are a normal part of being human?

One strategy identified by Brown and Smart (1991) is that, following failure in one area of life, the high self-esteem person often will focus on other areas of life in which things are going well. Larsen (2000a; Larsen & Prizmic, 2004) identifies this strategy as one of the most effective but least used strategies for overcoming feelings of failure. For example, imagine you are a research psychologist and you are evaluated in this job by the number of research articles you publish each year. Imagine then that one of your articles is rejected by a publisher. This represents a small failure in your life. If you were a low self-esteem person, this failure would have a large effect, confirming your view that you are generally a failure in most things that you do, that this is just one more instance of how you are unworthy and inadequate. On the other hand, if you were a high self-esteem person, you would likely remind yourself that you are still a good teacher, a good faculty member at your university, and a good spouse and a good parent to your children; that you still play a good game of squash; and that your dog still loves you. Larsen and Prizmic (2004) have suggested that in order to cope with such failures, people should make a list of all the things in their lives that are going well and that they keep this list on their phones. Then, if a failure occurs in one area of life—for instance, at work—they can pull up this list and review it, just as a high self-esteem person might do naturally. This can help people cope with the inevitable bumps, bruises, and failures of everyday life.

This idea of compartmentalizing the self is consistent with the research on **self-complexity** started by psychologist Patricia Linville (1987). She holds the view that we have many roles and many aspects to our self-concept. However, for some of us, our self-concept is rather simple, being made up of just a few large categories, such as when a man says, "I am nothing without her," meaning that his whole self-concept is wrapped up in this one relationship. Other people may have a more complex, or differentiated, self-concept. Such a person would say he or she has many parts to his or her self-concept: relationships, family, work, hobbies, friends, sports, and so forth. For people with high self-complexity, a failure in any one aspect of the self (such as a relationship that breaks apart) is buffered because there are many other aspects of the self that are unaffected by that event. However, if a person is low in self-complexity, the same event might be seen as devastating because the person defines him- or herself mainly in terms of this one aspect. The relationship between having a complex self-concept and fairing better in the face of negative life events has been replicated by many researchers (e.g., Martins & Calheiros, 2012; McConnell et al., 2009). Some researchers have proposed programs for expanding the self-concept with the goal of improving a person's functioning in the face to threats to self-esteem, such as failures or losses (Walton, Paunesku, & Dweck, 2012). The old phrase "Don't put all your eggs into one basket" seems to apply to the self-concept as well. A meta-analysis and review of the self-complexity research (Rafaeli-Mor & Steinberg, 2002) concluded that under conditions of objective and identifiable stress, higher self-complexity is weakly but significantly associated with superior well-being. This suggests that other factors, in addition to self-complexity, influence how people react to stress and negative life events.

Protecting Versus Enhancing the Self

Imagine you are a graduating college senior; you have majored in computer science and have a lot of expertise in Web-based programming. You are being recruited by a

A Closer Look

The Six Myths of Self-Esteem

Most people naturally try to enhance and protect their self-esteem, believing that it is important to psychological health. In America in the past decade there has been a growing national concern with developing self-esteem, believing it is related to all manner of good things in life. For example, the State of California set up a task force on self-esteem, which ultimately produced a report titled "The Social Importance of Self-Esteem." In it the task force argued that "many if not most of the major problems plaguing society have roots in the low self-esteem of many of the people who make up society." As a result, self-esteem courses found their way into the grade schools and high schools around the country, fostering a "feel-good" version of self-esteem (e.g., feel good about yourself).

The Association of Psychological Science set up a task force charged with reviewing the scientific literature on self-esteem, particularly with respect to objective behaviors and outcomes. The report was published in 2003 (Baumeister et al., 2003). We have taken this report and distilled the findings into a series of myths about self-esteem that are not supported by scientific research.

Myth One: High self-esteem is correlated with all manner of positive characteristics, such as being physically attractive, smart, kind, generous, etc. It is true that, for example, when both self-esteem and physical attractiveness are assessed using self-report (e.g., rate how attractive you are, rate your self-esteem), then strong correlations are typically found. However, when objective measures of attractiveness are used, such as having raters rate photographs of people in terms of attractiveness, then the correlation between

self-reported self-esteem and other-rated physical attractiveness drops to zero. Those with high self-esteem may be gorgeous in their own eyes, but they are not necessarily gorgeous in the eyes of others. These kinds of findings are also obtained with a variety of other positive characteristics. For example, high self-esteem people may rate themselves as smart or high in kindness or generosity as well, yet others do not necessarily see them as being this way. In a sense, persons high in self-esteem may have an inflated or unrealistic view of their positive characteristics, a view that is not necessarily supported by those who know the person well.

Myth Two: High self-esteem promotes success in school. The issue here is really one of causality and causal direction; does self-esteem cause people to achieve success or does achieving success lead to self-esteem? Many of the educational movements imply that if only we could raise children's self-esteem then we would help them on their way to achieving success in life. Consequently teachers are sometimes taught to praise students all the time, even if they are not successful. However, there is very little empirical science to support the idea that self-esteem leads to academic success. For example, Baumeister and colleagues (2003) review a study which tested more than 23,000 high school students, first in the 10th grade, then again in the 12th grade. They found that self-esteem in the 10th grade only weakly predicted academic achievement in the 12th grade. Academic achievement in the 10th grade correlated higher with self-esteem in the 12th grade. Thus these results suggest that success causes increases in self-esteem, not the other way around. Many studies show

similar results, and none of them indicate that improving self-esteem offers students much benefit. In fact, some studies show that artificially boosting self-esteem (through unconditional praise, for example) may actually lower subsequent performance (Baumeister et al., 2003).

Myth Three: High self-esteem promotes success on the job. The same basic issues about causality apply here; does self-esteem promote success on the job, or vice versa? When people rate their own job performance, there is often a modest correlation with self-esteem, but when job performance is assessed objectively (e.g., supervisor ratings), the correlations drop to close to zero.

Myth Four: High self-esteem makes a person likable. Again, if we use self-reports of popularity (e.g., How much do other people like you?), then these self-ratings of likability do correlate with self-esteem (i.e., high self-esteem persons regard themselves as being popular and believe they have many friends). However, these self-perceptions do not reflect reality. Baumeister and colleagues (2003) report on a study of high-school students who were asked to nominate their most-liked peers. The person in the class receiving the most votes was ranked as most popular, the person with the second most votes was ranked as second most popular, and so on. When self-esteem scores were correlated with the objective peer-ranking of popularity, that correlation was approximately zero. Similar findings have been found with college students. In another study reported by Baumeister and colleagues (2003), college students self-reported their own interpersonal skills in several domains (e.g., initiating relationships, self-disclosure, being assertive when necessary, providing emotional support to their friends, and managing interpersonal conflict). The researchers also had the subject's roommates report what the subject was like on each of the above interpersonal skill domains. Although the subject's self-esteem scores correlated with all of the self-reported interpersonal skill domains, the correlations between self-esteem and the roommates' ratings were essentially zero for four out of five of the interpersonal skills. The only interpersonal skill area that the roommates noticed that was associated with self-esteem was the subject's ability to initiate new social contacts and friendships. This does seem to be the one area in which the confidence associated with self-esteem really matters. People who think that they are desirable and attractive should be good at striking up conversations with strangers. Persons with low self-esteem may shy away from trying to make new friends, perhaps fearing rejection. In most other areas of interpersonal skills, however, self-esteem is not associated with having an advantage over other people.

Myth Five: Low self-esteem puts a person at risk for drug and alcohol abuse and premature sexual activity. The scientific studies reviewed by Baumeister and colleagues (2003) do not support the idea that low self-esteem predisposes young people to more or earlier sexual activity. If anything, persons with high self-esteem are less inhibited, more willing to disregard risks, and more prone to engage in sex. There is, however, evidence that unpleasant sexual experiences and unwanted pregnancies appear to lower self-esteem. As for alcohol and illicit drugs, preventing these behaviors has been a major rationale for those calling for programs to promote self-esteem. The data, however, do not

conclusively show that low self-esteem causes, or even correlates with, the abuse of illicit drugs or alcohol. For example, in a longitudinal study, no correlation was found between self-esteem at age 13 and drinking or drug abuse at age 15. A few other studies have found small correlations between low self-esteem and drinking, but other studies have found the opposite. All in all, the results are not conclusive to make any statements about self-esteem protecting people from the dangers of drug and alcohol use or risky sexual behavior.

Myth Six: Only low self-esteem people are aggressive. For decades many psychologists thought that low self-esteem was an important factor underlying aggressive behavior. Under their tough exteriors, aggressive people were thought to suffer from insecurities and self-doubt. However, recent research has shown that aggressive persons often have quite favorable views of themselves. In fact, extremely high self-esteem can blend into narcissism, which has been associated with bouts of anger and aggression when the narcissist does not get his or her way. If self-esteem is threatened or disputed by someone or some event, especially among high self-esteem persons, then they may react with hostility or violence. People with a highly inflated view of their own superiority, those with narcissistic tendencies, may be the most prone to violent reactions. After a challenge to self-esteem (e.g., getting beaten at a game), people might protect their self-concept by directing their anger outward, attacking the victor. Baumeister and colleagues (2003) review the literature on bullying and conclude that bullies are often very self-confident and less socially anxious than average. The general pattern in these studies and those on adults is that even high self-esteem, especially when it blends into narcissism, can be associated with interpersonal aggression. In several

empirical studies, Baumeister, Bushman and colleagues have demonstrated that, when their self-esteem is threatened, persons who are narcissistic are more likely to retaliate or aggress against the source of the threat (e.g., Baumeister, Bushman, & Campbell, 2000; Bushman & Baumeister, 1998). In a study of men in prison, Bushman and Baumeister (2002) found that those prisoners who had a history of violent offenses were significantly higher on narcissism than those prisoners with no history of violence. All of these findings run counter to the notion that low self-esteem causes aggression and instead point to the counterintuitive notion that threatened egotism is a likely cause of aggression and violence.

After crushing these myths about self-esteem, we can ask the question: So, what good is self-esteem? As described elsewhere in this chapter, self-esteem improves persistence in the face of failure. Persons high in self-esteem perform better in groups than those with low self-esteem. Also, having a poor self-image is a risk factor for developing certain eating disorders, especially bulimia. Low self-esteem is also related to depression, with evidence suggesting that low self-esteem can lead to depression rather than the other way around (Sowislo & Orth, 2013). High self-esteem also is related to social confidence and taking the initiative in making new friends. It is most likely the case that successes in academics, in the interpersonal domain or in one's career, lead to both happiness and self-esteem. Consequently, efforts to artificially boost children's self-esteem (through unconditional praise, for example) might fail. Rather, we should encourage and praise children when they put effort into learning or achieving the skills necessary to succeed in the various areas of life.

hot Internet start-up company for a job managing its information technology department. You know there is a lot of potential for you in this company. In fact, it could make you a millionaire within a few years if the company were to go public. However, you also know that it will be a lot of hard work. You will have to put in lots of hours and dedicate yourself almost entirely to the company for several years. You know you will also need to have some luck to get the right team together, to have some successes on your first few projects. It is a high-stakes but also a high-risk position. You know you have a lot of skill in this area, but you also know it is quite possible for you to fail miserably. What would you do? Would you take this job?

Some people may decline this opportunity to try for a big success because they are motivated to protect their self-concept. That is, they are concerned with *not failing,* and, in situations in which failure is a good possibility, they prefer not to take the risk. In other words, for some people, not failing is much more important than succeeding wildly. It turns out that people low in self-esteem are like this, in that they are motivated to protect their self-concept by avoiding failure much more than they are motivated to enhance it with success (Tice, 1991, 1993).

Research support for this notion has been found in several studies. For example, in one study (Taylor et al., 2000) the participants took an intelligence test and then were given their scores, plus the scores of the other participants. The participants were led to believe they had done much better (false success feedback) or much worse (false failure feedback) than the others. They then had the opportunity to receive more feedback on how they compared with the others, feedback that was likely to be in the same direction as their test scores. The low self-esteem participants asked for more feedback only when they knew it would be good news, when they were sure that they already were doing above average. When they thought they were below average, the low self-esteem persons did not want any more feedback. This is consistent with the idea that low self-esteem persons are motivated to protect their self-concept; they wanted more feedback only if they were certain it would be positive. The high self-esteem persons, on the other hand, did not avoid more feedback after learning they were below average.

Low self-esteem persons sometimes put a lot of energy into evading any new negative information about themselves. One strategy is to simply expect to fail; then, when it happens, it is not anything new. **Defensive pessimism** is a strategy in which a person facing a challenge, such as an upcoming test, expects to do poorly. Defensive pessimists are motivated by their fear of failure, but they take this gloomy outlook because the impact of failure can be lessened if it is expected in advance. For example, a little boy who strikes out at bat is not so upset with himself if he expects to strike out in the first place. Psychologist Julie Norem, who has done most of the research on defensive pessimism, sees a positive side to this characteristic: defensive pessimists use their worry and pessimism in a constructive way, to motivate themselves to work on the thing they are pessimistic about. She gives the example of a man who must give a public speech (Norem, 1995). Even though he has done a lot of public speaking, and all his speeches have gone well, he nevertheless is anxious and convinces himself that this time he is surely going to make a fool of himself. Thus, he decides to work extra hard on this speech; he rehearses and rehearses, prepares and prepares. When it comes time to give the speech, he does great, as usual. By reflecting on the worst outcome, defensive pessimists work through ways to keep that worst case from happening. The downside to defensive pessimism is that the negativity of defensive pessimists annoys others (Norem, 1998, 2001).

Sometimes people go to great lengths to set up their failure. This is called self-handicapping (e.g., Tice & Baumeister, 1990). **Self-handicapping** is a process in which a person deliberately does the things that increase the probability that he or she will fail (Tice & Bratslavsky, 2000). For example, a young woman may have a pessimistic attitude toward her upcoming exam, so she uses this as an excuse for not studying. However, not studying for the exam provides a handicap, an excuse to fail. By not studying, she increases the chances that she will fail, but it also gives her an excuse for that failure. When she fails, she can then say that she was simply unprepared, not that she is unintelligent or lacks the ability to do well in her classes. For low self-esteem persons, failing is bad, but failing without an excuse is worse.

Self-Esteem Variability

Most of the research on self-esteem concerns the average level, or what people's evaluations of themselves are like on average. But we also know from Chapter 5 that people fluctuate on their self-esteem from day to day and even from hour to hour. **Self-esteem variability** is an individual difference characteristic; it is the magnitude of short-term fluctuations in ongoing self-esteem (Kernis, Grannemann, & Mathis, 1991). In this section, we stress two main points. First, researchers make a distinction between level and variability of self-esteem. These two aspects of self-esteem are unrelated to each other. Moreover, level and variability in self-esteem are hypothesized to be based on different psychological mechanisms and are often found to interact in predicting important life outcomes (Kernis, Grannemann, & Barclay, 1992).

A second point is that self-esteem variability is related to the extent to which one's self-evaluation is changeable. That is, some people's self-esteem is pushed and pulled by the events of life much more than other people's self-esteem. Studies have shown that people whose self-esteem hinges on the feedback they receive from others show higher levels of self-esteem variability (Leitner et al., 2014). Trying to make other people happy, as Carl Rogers said (see Chapter 11), can interfere with ones self-development. Psychologist Michael Kernis, who has written extensively about this characteristic, believes that self-esteem variability is high in some people because they

- have an enhanced sensitivity to social evaluation events.
- have an increased concern about their self-view.
- overrely on social sources of evaluation.
- react to evaluation with anger and hostility.

Several studies have been conducted to examine whether self-esteem variability moderates the relation between self-esteem level and other variables, such as depression (Gable & Nezlak, 1998). In one study (Kernis et al., 1991), self-esteem level was related to depression, but this relation was much stronger for persons higher in self-esteem variability. Based on such findings, researchers have come to view variability as a susceptibility to depression (Roberts & Monroe, 1992). Women tend to have higher self-esteem variability than men, and they have higher rates of depression than men (Wagner, Ludtke, & Trautwein, 2015), a finding discussed in Chapter 13.

Other studies are exploring the health correlates of chronic self-esteem variability, and typically finding that this characteristic is associated with various health risk factors (Ross et al., 2013). All in all, variability in self-esteem is turning out to be as consequential as level of self-esteem.

Social Component of the Self: Social Identity

Social identity is the self that is shown to other people. This is the part of ourselves that we use to create an impression, to let other people know who we are and what they can expect from us. Social identity is different from self-concept because identity contains elements that are socially observable, publicly available outward expressions of the self. Gender and ethnicity are aspects of social identity. This may or may not figure into a person's self-concept, but gender and ethnicity are parts of one's social self, one's identity that is available to others.

Identity has an element of continuity because many of its aspects, such as gender and ethnicity, are constant. People are recognized as being the same from day to day, week to week, and year to year. If you were asked for your "identification," you might produce a passport or a driver's license. These documents contain socially available facts about you, such as your height, weight, age, and eye color. They also contain your family name and your address. All of these pieces of information are aspects of your identity, and they provide others with a brief sketch of who you are.

The Nature of Identity

Identity has two important features: continuity and contrast. **Continuity** means that people can count on you to be the same person tomorrow as you are today. Obviously, people change in various ways, but many important aspects of social identity remain relatively stable, such as gender, surname (though some women elect to change this when they marry), language, ethnicity, and socioeconomic status.

Other aspects of identity can change but do so gradually, lending some sense of continuity (e.g., education, occupation, and marital status). Other aspects of identity refer to behavior patterns that are public, such as being an athlete, a delinquent, or a "party animal," which also contribute to a sense of continuity (Baumeister & Muraven, 1996).

Contrast means that your social identity differentiates you from other people. An identity is what makes you unique in the eyes of others. The combination of characteristics that make up your identity differentiates you from everyone else. For example, there may be other students who speak the way you do and work where you do, but you are the only one who likes a particular type of music and has your ethnic background and eye color. Some characteristics are more important to social identity for some people than others. We now turn to how people develop identity by selecting what they choose to emphasize about themselves in their social identities.

Identity Development

Although anything that provides a sense of sameness can potentially become part of identity, people have some latitude to choose what they want to be known for (or not known for). For example, a student may try out for the swimming team, thereby choosing the identity of an athlete. Another might break a lot of rules, thereby choosing the identity of a delinquent. One person might choose to "come out," making their gay sexual orientation a part of their public social identity, whereas another gay person might choose to "stay in the closet" and not have their sexual orientation part of their public identity. People also differ from each other in the strength of their identities. Some people feel a strong sense of reputation, whereas others feel adrift in their social relations, not knowing who they are expected to be. In fact, most people go through a period, usually in high school or college, in which they experiment with various identities. For many people, this is an uncomfortable time. They may feel socially insecure or sensitive while developing their social identity.

As mentioned in Chapter 10, the term *identity* was popularized in the 1960s by the psychoanalyst Erik Erikson (1968). He believed that identity resulted from efforts to separate oneself from one's parents, to stop relying on one's parents to make decisions about what values to hold and what goals to pursue in life. Erikson believed that achieving an identity took effort and work and that there was always a risk that an identity achieved could come undone, resulting in what he called role confusion. People need to continually work on achieving and maintaining their identity, Erikson taught.

Identity can be achieved in several ways, according to Erikson (1968). Many people struggle with identities, particularly during late adolescence and early adulthood. Experimenting with various identities can be compared to trying on different hats to see which one fits. In trying on identities, a young man in college might one semester be an athlete and the next semester join the debate and chess clubs; the following semester, he gets a tattoo, has some body parts pierced, and starts hanging with a crowd of similarly pierced and tattooed persons. People actively struggle to find a social identity that fits, one they are comfortable with. Usually, after a period of experimentation, most people settle into a comfortable social identity and attain some stability.

Application

The true story of the return of Martin Guerre is so interesting that several film depictions have been made. In the real story, which took place in the late middle ages in France, a peasant, Martin Guerre, leaves his wife to fight in the "Hundred Years War." His wife waits patiently for him, but after nine years without word, she presumes that Martin is dead. Believing herself a widow, she is astonished when Martin returns suddenly after being away so long. Although the neighbors have a big homecoming celebration for Martin, several are suspicious that the man is an impostor, that he is not really Martin, but someone who knew Martin well enough to steal his identity. To the lonely wife, however, he looks like her Martin, sounds like her Martin, and has a working knowledge of the intimate details of their prior relationship. In addition, the man in her house now is nicer, gentler, more loving, and more attentive than the man who went to war almost a decade earlier. And so she very much wants this man to be her Martin.

Telltale signs of a forged identity emerge bit by bit and unravel the clever facade around Martin's social self. The neighbors get the local magistrate involved. His wife tries to defend Martin as her husband, and even if he is not, she wants him to stay anyway. Nevertheless, the case is made that he is an impostor, that this Martin is not really Martin Guerre. The impostor is believed to have forced the real Martin to reveal details of his self-concept and social identity and then to have used this knowledge to create a social identity so similar to Martin's that he fooled even Martin's wife into believing he was truly her returning husband. The magistrate, convinced that this is not the "real" Martin, charges the impostor with adultery, a crime punishable by death. Martin's wife is not similarly charged because she believed this was her husband.

The 1993 French film based on this story, *The Return of Martin Guerre*, starring Gerard Depardieu, won three French Academy Awards. It is a stunningly filmed study in the portrayal of the self and social identity. In it, we see the small details that go into making a social identity. It shows how people form expectations for social behavior from others based on identity and how small violations of those expectations can create doubts and suspicions.

The French movie **The Return of Martin Guerre,** *starring Gerard Depardieu, portrays a true story from medieval times about the theft of social identity. The scene here shows the "new" Martin, who has just returned from a nine-year absence, embracing the "old" Martin's wife. The film won three French Academy Awards.*

© Jacky Coolen/Gamma-Rapho via Getty Images

For other people, the route to identity is not through experimentation. Instead, some people attain an identity by accepting and adopting a ready-made social role. Typically, such people adopt an identity that is practiced and provided by their parents or significant others. For example, they may take over the family business, buy a house in their hometown, and join the same church or synagogue as their parents. Such people appear stable and mature in their identities and have mature values, plans, and objectives even when they are teenagers. Another identity adoption example is arranged marriages, in which the parents decide whom their children will marry and the children accept this decision willingly, a practice still common in India today.

These kinds of instant identity adoptions can be risky, however, as they may be achieved with a certain amount of rigidity, making the person closed to new ideas or lifestyles. Such people may be inflexible and stubborn in their social roles, especially when they are under stress. Nevertheless, for many people, this route to identity is an acceptable and reasonable alternative, one that provides an identity for life.

Identity Crises

A person's identity is challenged from time to time. The answer to the question "Who do others think I am?" can change. For example, when a woman gets divorced, her social identity changes from "I am married" to "I am divorced and newly single." Or a man gives up a career as a business executive to pursue a vocation in small-scale farming, so his identity changes from "I am an executive" to "I am a farmer." Other challenges to identity would be events that change one's reputation, change one's family life, or change one's economic status.

Erikson (1968) coined the phrase identity crisis, meaning the feelings of anxiety that accompany efforts to define or redefine one's own individuality and social reputation. For most people, the process of going through an identity crisis is an important and memorable phase of life. Sometimes it happens early, in adolescence; sometimes it happens later, in midlife. And some people have identity crises multiple times in their lives. Psychologist Roy Baumeister suggests that there are two distinct types of identity crises: identity deficit and identity conflict (Baumeister, 1986, 1997).

Identity Deficit

An **identity deficit** arises when a person has not formed an adequate identity and thus has trouble making major decisions: Should I go to college or not? If I go to college, what major should I choose? Should I join the military service? Should I get married? A person without a secure, established identity would have trouble making such major decisions because he or she has no inner foundation. When facing a tough decision, many people turn inward to find the answer. In doing so, many people arrive at a course of action right away, because they know their own values and preferences very well; they know what "a person like me" would do in such situations. When people who have an identity deficit turn inward, however, they find little in the way of a foundation on which to base such life choices.

Identity deficits often occur when a person discards old values or goals. For example, college students often reject old opinions in favor of new ideas and new values to which they are exposed in college. In fact, some college courses are designed to encourage students to doubt or challenge their previous assumptions about themselves or the world. A popular bumper sticker, often seen on college campuses, is "Question Authority." But rejecting old beliefs and assumptions creates a void or an identity deficit, which is accompanied by feelings of emptiness and uncertainty. Such feelings prompt people to search for new beliefs, for new values and goals. People who are trying to fill this identity deficit may try on new belief systems, explore new relationships, and investigate new ideas and values. They may be alternately depressed and confused at one point in time and then euphoric about the possibilities in their lives.

People in identity deficit are particularly vulnerable to the propaganda of various groups. They are often very curious about other belief systems, so they are vulnerable to influence from other people. Because of their feelings of emptiness and their search for new values and ideas, they tend to be very persuadable during this period. As Baumeister (1997) points out, recruiters for cults are often especially successful at enlisting persons who are undergoing identity deficit crises.

Identity Conflict

An **identity conflict** involves an incompatibility between two or more aspects of identity. This kind of crisis often occurs when a person is forced to make an important and difficult life decision. For example, a person who immigrates to the United States may have an identity conflict between wanting to assimilate into the majority culture and wanting to maintain his or her ethnic identity. A similar identity conflict arises in working persons who also want to have a family. A person with a strong commitment to building a family might experience an identity conflict if he or she were offered a promotion at work that involved longer hours or frequent out-of-town travel. Whenever two or more aspects of identity clash (such as being both a high-power career woman and dedicated mother of multiple children), there is a potential for an identity conflict crisis.

Identity conflicts are "approach–approach" conflicts, in that the person wants to reach two mutually contradictory goals. Although these conflicts involve wanting two desirable identities, not much pleasure is experienced during identity conflicts. Identity conflicts usually involve intense feelings of guilt or remorse over perceived unfaithfulness to an important aspect of the person's identity. People in an identity conflict may feel as if they are letting themselves and others down.

Overcoming an identity conflict is often a difficult and painful process. One course of action is to put aside a part of one's identity, to abandon a formerly important aspect of the self. Some people are able to strike a balance in their lives. For example, a college professor may accept a lighter teaching load to have more time with his children; a business executive may telecommute to her job two days a week in order to spend more time with her children. Some people partition their lives in ways that prevent such conflicts from arising. For example, some people keep their work lives and their private lives entirely separate.

Resolution of Identity Crises

Identity crises—both deficits and conflicts—commonly occur during adolescence, though not all adolescents experience identity crises. Those who do find that resolution involves two steps (Baumeister, 1997). First, they decide which values are most important to them. Second, they transform these abstract values into desires and actual behaviors. For example, a person might arrive at the conclusion that what is really important is to have a family. The second step is to translate this value into actions, such as finding the right spouse, someone who also wants a family; working hard to maintain this relationship; preparing a career with which to support a family; and so forth. As the person begins working toward these goals, he or she assumes a secure identity and is unlikely to experience an identity crisis, at least during this early phase of life.

Application

The movie character Lester, played by Kevin Spacey in the Oscar-winning film *American Beauty,* undergoes an acute midlife identity crisis. In fact, the movie is about the havoc Lester wreaks on his family, neighbors, and coworkers during his identity crisis. Lester goes from being a complacent husband, a neglecting but "good-enough" father, and a submissive worker to someone who wants things his own way at home and at work. One day, Lester decides that he does not like what he has become and decides to make drastic changes in his life. During his transformation, Lester ruins his marriage, drives his daughter to contemplate running away, loses his job, experiments with drugs, pushes an unstable neighbor over the brink, and contributes to the delinquency of two minor children. Clearly, Lester's attempts to redefine himself are adolescent and dysfunctional throughout most of the movie. However, toward the end, Lester appears to be starting on the right track; he has finally found some integrity and is heading in a positive direction. It is the scene in which Lester decides not to have sex with his daughter's teenage girlfriend that he acknowledges that his new identity will at least be that of a mature adult.

In the Oscar-winning movie **American Beauty**, *actor Kevin Spacey plays Lester, a man undergoing a severe midlife identity crisis. In his effort to transform his social identity, Lester changes the way he interacts with his wife, his boss, his child, and even his neighbors. Although he makes some rash decisions along the way, toward the end of the movie we get a sense that Lester is finally forming a positive new identity.*

© AF archive/Alamy Stock Photo

A second phase of life in which identity crises commonly occur is during middle age. For some people, this is a period in which they experience dissatisfaction with their existing identities, perhaps at work or in a marriage. Whatever the reason, people undergoing a midlife identity crisis begin to feel that things are not working out as they wished. They may feel that their lives are inauthentic. People in the midlife identity crisis begin to doubt that they made the right choices early in life, and they reconsider those commitments: "If only I had done . . ." is a frequent complaint. It is a period of regret over time spent pursuing goals that turned out to be unsatisfying or impossible. Many people in this predicament decide to abandon their goals and experience an identity deficit because they give up the principles that have guided their lives so far.

People who undergo midlife crises often act as adolescents again. That is, an identity crisis often looks the same, whether it occurs at adolescence or at midlife: the person experiments with alternative lifestyles, forms new relationships and abandons old ones, and gives up previous ambitions and responsibilities. In midlife crises, people often change their careers, change their spouses, change their religions, change where they live, or do various combinations of these. Sometimes they simply change their priorities—for example, a woman might keep her job and her spouse but decide to spend more time with her spouse and less time working. A midlife identity crisis can be just as much of an emotional roller-coaster ride as an adolescent identity crisis.

To summarize, a social identity consists of the social or public aspects of yourself, the impression that you typically create in others. Many of your more visible characteristics—such as gender, ethnicity, and occupation—contribute to your identity. Other characteristics, including those that make up reputation, also go into the formation of identity. Your identity is what gives you and others a sense of continuity, of being the same person tomorrow as today. It also makes you unique in the eyes of others.

SUMMARY AND EVALUATION

This chapter presented an outline of what personality psychologists know about the self. This knowledge is neatly divided into three broad areas: self-concept, self-esteem, and social identity. These aspects of the self are important to understanding personality. The notion of a self makes sense in terms of our everyday lives and our experience. We frequently use terms such as *selfish, self-worship, selfless, self-conscious,* and *self-esteem* in everyday life. In the evolution of language, we developed a rich vocabulary for talking about the self. This reflects people's general preoccupation with themselves. Another reason psychologists are interested in the self is that it plays an important role in organizing a person's experiences of the world. What a person deems important, for example, are the things that are relevant to his or her self-concept. Moreover, people behave differently when they are self-involved than when they are not, so the concept of the self is important for understanding how people construe their world, their experiences, and their actions. The self is a major organizing force within the person.

Self-concept is a person's self-understanding—his or her own story. The self-concept has its start in infancy, when the child first makes a distinction between its body and everything else. This glimmer of self-concept goes on to develop, through repeated experiences of self-awareness, into a collection of characteristics that the child uses for self-definition, such as gender, age, and membership in a particular family. Children acquire skills and talents and start comparing themselves with others and refining their self-concept. They also develop a sense of privacy and a sense of their ability to keep secrets, so they begin to develop a private self-concept, things they know about themselves that no one else knows. Cognitive schemata then develop around aspects of the self; these knowledge structures are collections of characteristics associated with the self-concept. People also develop views of themselves in the future, their possible selves, which include both desirable (ideal self) and undesirable features. All in all, the self-concept is the person's answer to the questions "Who have I been, what am I like now, and who do I want to be in the future?"

Self-esteem is the evaluation a person makes of his or her self-concept along a good–bad dimension. People differ from each other in terms of whether they see themselves as worthwhile, valuable, and good. Research on self-esteem has emphasized how people respond to failure, and findings suggest that high self-esteem persons persevere in the face of failure, whereas low self-esteem persons often give up following failure. High self-esteem people seem particularly good at deflecting the bumps and bruises of everyday life. One strategy they seem particularly adept in using is, when something bad happens in one area of their lives, to remind themselves that other areas in their lives are going well. This puts negative events in perspective and helps them cope. Extremely high self-esteem, associated with narcissistic tendencies, can sometimes result in aggressive responses to threats to that self-esteem. Researchers have shown that narcissistic persons often retaliate following negative feedback. Another clinical problem associated with self-esteem is extreme shyness. Shyness does have some biological correlates, but it is also associated with an over-controlling parenting style. Shyness can often be changed through treatment efforts. Another area of research shows that high self-esteem people are often concerned with enhancing their self-concept, whereas low self-esteem persons are often concerned with protecting what they have from insult. Finally, in terms of self-esteem variability, variable persons seem especially sensitive to evaluative life events, such as social slights and public failures.

The final aspect of the self discussed in this chapter was social identity, as a person's outward manifestation or the impression he or she gives others. Identity develops over time through relations with others. For many people, the development of an identity follows a period of experimentation, but for others it happens more easily by adopting ready-made social roles. There are periods in life when some people undergo identity crises and have to redefine their social identities. Developing an identity is a lifelong task, as identity changes with the changing social roles that come with age.

Erikson coined the term *identity crisis* to refer to the anxiety that comes with having to redefine one's social reputation. There are two kinds of crises: identity deficit, not forming an adequate identity; and identity conflict, in which two or more aspects of identity come into conflict. Despite crises and challenges, most people develop a solid identity, and other people know them for their unique characteristics.

KEY TERMS

PART FIVE

The Social and Cultural Domain

© *Arthimedes/Shutterstock.com RF*

In the social and cultural domain, the emphasis is on personality as it is affected by and expressed through social institutions, social roles and expectations, and relationships with other people in our lives.

We saw in Chapter 3 that several taxonomies of traits emphasize interpersonal traits, such as dominance versus submissiveness, or love versus hate. Indeed, most of the important trait adjectives in language are important for describing how people behave with others. Interpersonal traits have long-term outcomes in our lives. For example, whether a person is controlling or easy-going affects such different aspects of life as conflicts with spouse and work partners and the

V

strategies used to achieve goals. Whether a person tends to be nervous or optimistic affects the likelihood of diverse social outcomes, such as divorce or success in a sales career. Many of the most important individual differences and personality traits are played out in our interpersonal relationships.

We describe three key processes whereby personality affects social interactions. The first process is through *selection,* in which people may choose specific social environments according to their personalities. A second process is evocation. We examine how people evoke distress, as well as positive feelings, in others. A final process whereby personality affects social interactions is through *manipulations* for influencing others. What are the strategies that people use to get what they want from others?

One important interpersonal context concerns relationships between men and women. An essential part of our social identity is our gender. Differences between men and women in terms of personality have long been of interest to personality psychology. Some researchers prefer to minimize the differences between men and women, emphasizing that sex differences are small and that the variability within a sex

exceeds the variability between the sexes. Other researchers focus on the differences between the sexes and emphasize that some are large and are found in different cultures. Men tend to score higher on aggressiveness, whereas women tend to score higher on measures of trust and nurturance. Where do sex differences come from?

Much of what we call gender may have its origins in culture, that is, in how society makes up different rules and expectations for men and women.

Other theories emphasize differences between men and women that may be due to hormones. Testosterone levels, for example, differ greatly between men and women, and testosterone has been reliably associated with the personality traits of dominance, aggression, and sexuality.

Another theory is evolutionary and suggests that men and women faced different challenges and have evolved solutions to these different challenges. Whatever their origins, gender differences have long been of interest to personality psychologists and are clearly part of the social and cultural domain because they refer to and are played out in interpersonal relations.

Another socially important difference among people derives from their culture, the system of social rules, expectations, and rituals in which a person is raised. For example, in one culture it might be expected that a crying baby is always picked up and comforted by its parents, whereas in another culture crying babies are left to cry. Could it be that being raised in these two different cultures results in differences in adult personality? Indeed, do people in different cultures have different personalities?

An important goal of personality psychology is to understand how cultures shape personality and how specific cultures are different from or similar to each other. Besides identifying ways in which people from different cultures differ, cultural personality psychologists have also looked for similarities among cultures. One example of a cultural universal appears to be the expression of specific emotions. Another aspect of personality that appears to show cultural universality is described by the five-factor model of traits.

In this part of the book, we focus on the broader social-interpersonal, gendered, and cultural aspects of personality.

© Arthimedes/Shutterstock.com RF

Personality and Social Interaction

15

Selection

Evocation

Manipulation: Social Influence Tactics

Panning Back: An Overview of Personality and Social Interaction

Summary and Evaluation
Key Terms

Sue and Joan sipped coffee while discussing their dates from the previous evening. "Michael seemed like a nice guy, at least at first," Sue noted. "He was polite, asked me what kind of food I liked, and seemed genuinely interested in knowing me as a person. But I was a little turned off by the rude way he talked to the waitress. He also insisted in choosing the food for me and selected a pork dish I didn't like. Then, over dinner, he talked about himself the whole time. At the end of the evening, he tried to invite himself back to my room, but I told him that I was tired and wanted to call it a night." "Did you kiss him?" asked Joan. "Well, yes, I started to give him a good-night kiss, but he began to get really aggressive with me, and I had to push him away. All the politeness disappeared, and he stormed off angry. I guess he wasn't such a nice guy after all. How did your date go?"

In the course of this conversation, Sue revealed a treasure trove of information about her date, Michael—information that figures prominently in the social decisions we make. Michael displayed aggressiveness, both toward the waitress and toward Sue during the good-night kiss. He displayed self-centeredness, focusing on himself during the course of the dinner. He showed a lack of empathy, as illustrated by his uncaring attitude toward the feelings of the waitress and his abrupt sexual aggressiveness. The thin veneer of politeness quickly gave way over the evening, revealing an abrasive interpersonal disposition that turned Sue off.

This episode illustrates several key ways in which personality influences social interaction. Personality interacts with situations in three ways: through selection, evocation, and manipulation of the situation. These three mechanisms can be applied to an understanding of how personality affects interpersonal situations. First, the personality characteristics of others influence whether we *select* them as our dates, friends, and even marriage partners. In this episode, Sue was turned off by Michael's aggressive and self-centered personality characteristics. People's personality characteristics also play a role in the kinds of interpersonal situations they select to enter and stay in. For example, someone with a personality different from Sue's might actually be attracted to a guy like Michael and could put up with his self-centeredness.

Second, the personality qualities of others *evoke* certain responses in us. Michael's aggressive displays upset Sue, evoking an emotional response that would not have been evoked if he had been kinder and more caring. Behaviors related to personality can evoke many responses in others, ranging from aggression to social support, and from marital satisfaction to marital infidelity.

Third, personality is linked to the ways in which we try to influence or *manipulate* others. Michael first tried the charm tactic. Then he pulled out the boasting tactic. Finally, he used coercion, trying to force himself on Sue. A man with a different personality would use different tactics such as reason or reward.

These three processes—selection, evocation, and manipulation—are key ways in which personality interacts with the social environment. Individuals in everyday life are not exposed to all possible social situations; individuals with certain personality dispositions seek out and avoid social situations selectively. Personality also influences how we evoke different reactions from other people and how others in turn evoke different responses from us, sometimes quite unintentionally. And personality affects how we purposefully influence, change, exploit, and manipulate the others with whom we have chosen to be associated.

Selection

In everyday life, people choose to enter some situations and avoid other situations. These forms of situation selection can hinge on personality dispositions and how we view ourselves. The following story illustrates the process of selection. In this example, a couple inadvertently entered a situation and then chose a rapid exit from it.

> Chip and Priscilla, a Yuppie couple from Chicago, have just moved to Dallas and are sampling some of the trendier nightspots on Lower Greenville Avenue. As they push through the swinging doors of what appears to be a quaint little Western saloon right out of the TV series Gunsmoke, they are confronted by six huge bikers from the motorcycle gang, who turn on their barstools to glare at them. The bikers have an average of more than two tattoos and three missing teeth. The fumes they emit smell flammable. Two of them stare with contempt at Chip, and one leers evilly at Priscilla. "This doesn't look like our kind of place," Chip says to Priscilla, as they prepare to beat a hasty retreat. (Ickes, Snyder, & Garcia, 1997, p. 165)

Social selections permeate daily life. These choices range in importance from the seemingly trivial ("Should I attend this party tonight?") to the profound ("Should I select this person as my marriage partner?"). Social selections are decision points that direct us to choose one path and avoid another. These decisions, which determine the nature of our social environments and social worlds, are often based on the personality characteristics of the selector. Extraverts choose to spend more time in social situations, whereas highly conscientious people select more work-related activities—choices that continue from adolescence through young adulthood (Wrzus, 2016). Agreeable people choose to spend more time looking at photos and media depicting positive images; disagreeable people expose themselves to more negative photos and media images (Bresin & Robinson, 2014).

Mate selection provides an especially dramatic example of the mechanism of selection. When you select a long-term mate, you place yourself into close and prolonged contact with one particular other. This alters the social environment to which you are exposed and in which you will reside. By selecting a mate, you are selecting the social acts you will experience and a network of friends and family.

In terms of personality characteristics, who do people seek as potential mates? Are there common personality characteristics that are highly desired by everyone? Do we look for potential mates who have personalities similar to our own or different from our own? And how is the choice of a mate linked to the likelihood that a couple will stay together over time?

Personality Characteristics Desired in a Marriage Partner

What do people want in a long-term partner? This was the focus of an international investigation of 10,047 individuals located on six continents and five islands from around the world (Buss et al., 1990). A total of 37 samples were chosen from 33 countries, representing every major racial group, religious group, and political system. Samples ranged from the coastal-dwelling Australians to the South African Zulu people. The economic status of the samples varied from middle- and upper-middle-class college students to lower socioeconomic groups, such as the Gujarati Indians and Estonians. Fifty researchers collected data. Standard questionnaires were translated into the language of each culture and then administered to the samples by native residents of each culture. This study, the largest conducted on what people want in a long-term mate, revealed that personality characteristics play a central role in mate selection. In the Exercise that follows, you can complete this questionnaire yourself and see how your selection preferences compare with those of the worldwide sample.

As you can see in Table 15.1, mutual attraction or love was the most favored characteristic, viewed as indispensable by almost everyone in the world. After mutual attraction or love, personality characteristics loom large in people's mate selection preferences—dependable character, emotional stability, and pleasing disposition. You may recall that these are quite close to the labels given to three of the factors in the five-factor model of personality (see Chapter 3). Dependability is close to Conscientiousness.

Exercise

INSTRUCTIONS: Evaluate the following factors in choosing a mate or marriage partner. If you consider the factor to be

indispensable, give it	3 points
important, but not indispensable, give it	2 points
desirable, but not very important, give it	1 point
irrelevant or unimportant, give it	0 points

Exercise (*Continued*)

___ 1. Good cook and housekeeper	___ 10. Desire for home and children
___ 2. Pleasing disposition	___ 11. Favorable social status
___ 3. Sociability	___ 12. Good looks
___ 4. Similar educational background	___ 13. Similar religious background
___ 5. Refinement, neatness	___ 14. Ambition and industriousness
___ 6. Good financial prospect	___ 15. Similar political background
___ 7. Chastity (no prior intercourse)	___ 16. Mutual attraction or love
___ 8. Dependable character	___ 17. Good health
___ 9. Emotional stability	___ 18. Education and intelligence

Now compare your ratings with the ratings given by the international sample of 10,047 men and women, shown in Table 15.1.

Table 15.1 Summary of Ratings by Sex Using Entire International Sample

	RATINGS BY MALES			RATINGS BY FEMALES		
Ranked Value	Variable Name	Mean	Std. Dev.	Variable Name	Mean	Std. Dev.
1.	Mutual attraction or love	2.81	0.16	Mutual attraction or love	2.87	0.12
2.	Dependable character	2.50	0.46	Dependable character	2.69	0.31
3.	Emotional stability and maturity	2.47	0.20	Emotional stability and maturity	2.68	0.20
4.	Pleasing disposition	2.44	0.29	Pleasing disposition	2.52	0.30
5.	Good health	2.31	0.33	Education and intelligence	2.45	0.25
6.	Education and intelligence	2.27	0.19	Sociability	2.30	0.28
7.	Sociability	2.15	0.28	Good health	2.28	0.30
8.	Desire for home and children	2.09	0.50	Desire for home and children	2.21	0.44
9.	Refinement, neatness	2.03	0.48	Ambition and industriousness	2.15	0.35
10.	Good looks	1.91	0.26	Refinement, neatness	1.98	0.49
11.	Ambition and industriousness	1.85	0.35	Similar education	1.84	0.47
12.	Good cook and housekeeper	1.80	0.48	Good financial prospect	1.76	0.38
13.	Good financial prospect	1.51	0.42	Good looks	1.46	0.28
14.	Similar education	1.50	0.37	Favorable social status or rating	1.46	0.39
15.	Favorable social status or rating	1.16	0.28	Good cook and housekeeper	1.28	0.27
16.	Chastity (no previous experience in sexual intercourse)	1.06	0.69	Similar religious background	1.21	0.56
17.	Similar religious background	0.98	0.48	Similar political background	1.03	0.35
18.	Similar political background	0.92	0.36	Chastity (no previous experience in sexual intercourse)	0.75	0.66

Source: Adapted from Buss et al. (1990), p. 19, Table 4.

Emotional stability is identical to the fourth factor on the five-factor model. And pleasing disposition is quite close to Agreeableness. Other personality factors rated highly include sociability, refinement and neatness, and ambition and industriousness.

Note that the respondents' top choices, except for love, were personality characteristics. Thus, personality factors play a central role in what people worldwide are looking for in a long-term mate—findings that have now been documented over many decades of research (e.g., Fletcher et al., 2004; Kamble et al., 2014; Lei et al., 2011; Souza et al., 2016). Moreover, the priority placed on personality traits such as Agreeableness, Conscientiousness, and Emotional Stability occur regardless of sexual orientation; they are as strong among non-heterosexual men and women as they are among heterosexual men and women (Valentova et al., 2016). Low scores on these personality traits tend to be relationship "dealbreakers" (Jonason et al., 2015).

Assortative Mating for Personality: The Search for the Similar

Over the past century, two fundamentally competing scientific theories have been advanced for who is attracted to whom. **Complementary needs theory** postulates that people are attracted to those who have different personality dispositions than they have (Murstein, 1976; Winch, 1954). People who are dominant, for example, might have a need for someone whom they can control and dominate. People who are submissive, according to complementary needs theory, choose a mate who can dominate and control them. One easy way to think about complementary needs theory is with the phrase "opposites attract."

In contrast, **attraction similarity theory** postulates that people are attracted to those who have similar personality characteristics. People who are dominant might be attracted to those who are also dominant because they like someone who "pushes back." People who are extraverted might like partners who are also extraverted so that they can party together. One easy way to remember this theory is with the phrase "birds of a feather flock together." Although there have been many proponents of both theories over the past century, the results are now in. They provide overwhelming support for the attraction similarity theory and no support for the complementary needs theory (Buss, 2016). Indeed, the only characteristic on which "opposites attract" that has been reliably documented is biological sex: Men tend to be attracted to women and women tend to be attracted to men. Although, of course, there will always be individual differences, the research shows that people are generally drawn to those who share their personalities.

People often are attracted to others who are similar to themselves. This refers to the concept of assortative mating.

© Andrew Rich/Vetta/Getty Images RF

One of the most common findings in the mate selection literature—that people are married to people who are similar to themselves—is a phenomenon known as **assortative mating**. For nearly every variable that has been examined—from single actions to ethnic status—people seem to select mates who are similar to themselves. Even for physical characteristics such as height, weight, and, astonishingly, nose breadth and earlobe length, couples show positive correlations. Even the perceived personality of individuals based on faces—personality trait assessment based solely on judgments of photographs—shows assortative mating (Little, Burt, & Perrett, 2006). Couples who have been together the longest appeared most similar in personality, a finding that results from the initial selection process and from dissimilar couples breaking up more often (e.g., Humbad et al., 2010).

But are these positive correlations caused by the active selection of mates who are similar? Or are these positive correlations merely byproducts of other causal processes? Sheer proximity, for example, could, in principle, account for some of the positive correlations. It is known that people tend to marry those who are close by. Notions of romantic love aside, the "one and only" often lives within driving distance, although internet dating sites have reduced this effect somewhat. And because people in close proximity may have certain common characteristics, the positive correlations found between married couples may be merely a side effect of mating with those who are close by rather than the active selection of partners who are similar. Cultural institutions, such as colleges and universities, may promote assortative mating by preferentially admitting those who are similar with respect to certain variables, such as intelligence, motivation, and social skills.

To test these competing predictions, Botwin and colleagues studied two samples of subjects: dating couples and newlywed couples (Botwin et al., 1997). The participants expressed their preferences for the personality characteristics in a potential mate on 40 rating scales, which were scored on five dimensions of personality: Extraversion, Agreeableness, Conscientiousness, Emotional Stability, and Intellect–Openness. The next step was to assess personality dispositions on these dimensions, using the same 40 rating scales. Three data sources were used for this second stage: self-reports; reports by their partners; and independent reports by interviewers. Correlations with mate preferences were computed between two sets of personality ratings: the ones made by the subject (self) and the average of the peer and interviewer ratings of the subject (aggregate).

As shown in Table 15.2, these correlations were consistently positive. Those who scored high on Extraversion wanted to select an extraverted person as a mate. Those who scored high on Conscientiousness desired a conscientious mate. The conclusions from this study, of course, must be qualified by one important consideration—perhaps the preferences people express for the personalities of their ideal mates might be influenced by the mates they already have. If an emotionally stable person is already mated to an emotionally stable person, perhaps the choice is justified by claiming that he or she is truly attracted to the person chosen. This could result in positive correlations between

Table 15.2 Personality Correlated with Mate Preferences

Trait	DATING COUPLES MEN Self	Aggregate	WOMEN Self	Aggregate	MARRIED COUPLES MEN Self	Aggregate	WOMEN Self	Aggregate
Extraversion	.33*	.42**	.59***	.35**	.20*	.15	.30**	.25**
Agreeableness	.37*	.17	.44***	.46***	.30**	.12	.44***	.31**
Conscientiousness	.34**	.45***	.59***	.53***	.53***	.49***	.61***	.53***
Emotional Stability	.29*	.36**	.52***	.30*	.27**	.21*	.32***	.27**
Intellect–Openness	.56***	.54***	.63***	.50***	.24*	.31**	.48***	.52****

$*p < .05$

$**p < .01$

$***p < .001$

Note: Each correlation in the table refers to the relationship between the personality trait of the individual and the corresponding personality trait desired in a mate. Thus, under Men, Self-Report column, the .33* indicates that men who are highly extraverted tend to prefer mates who are also extraverted. The fact that all the correlations in the table are positive, many significantly so, indicates that people generally want mates who are similar to themselves in personality.

Source: Botwin, Buss, & Shackelford (1997).

one's own personality and the personality people express for a desired mate. Nonetheless, studies of individuals who are not mated already find the same pattern of results—people prefer those who are similar to themselves (e.g., Buss, 2012), supporting the attraction similarity theory.

These data provide evidence that positive correlations on personality variables between husbands and wives are due, at least in part, to direct social preferences based on the personality characteristics of those doing the selecting. Subsequent studies have confirmed that people actively prefer romantic partners who are similar to themselves on Extraversion, Agreeableness, Conscientiousness, Emotional Stability, and Intellect–Openness. However, most people consider the "ideal" romantic partner personality to be someone who is higher on Extraversion, Conscientiousness, Agreeableness, and Emotional Stability than they are (Figueredo, Sefcek, & Jones, 2006). In sum, personality characteristics appear to play a pivotal role in the social mechanism of selection.

Do People Get the Mates They Want? And Are They Happy?

A fact of human life is that we do not always get what we want, and this is true of mate selection. You may want a mate who is kind, understanding, dependable, emotionally stable, and intelligent, but such desirable mates are always in short supply compared with the numbers of people who seek them. Therefore, many people end up mated with individuals who fall short of their ideals. It is reasonable to predict, therefore, that individuals whose mates deviate from their ideals will be less satisfied than those whose mates embody their desires.

Table 15.3 shows the correlations between the preferences that individuals express for the ideal personality characteristics of their mates and the actual personality characteristics of their obtained mates (Botwin et al., 1997, p. 127). Across three of the four subsamples—women who are dating, women who are married, and men who are married—there are modest but consistently positive correlations between the personality desired in a partner and the actual personality characteristics displayed by the partner. The correspondence between what one wants and what one gets is especially strong for Extraversion and Intellect–Openness. In short, as a general rule, people seem to get the mates they want in terms of personality.

Table 15.3 Personality Mate Preferences and Personality of Partner Obtained

| | DATING COUPLES | | | | MARRIED COUPLES | | | |
| | WOMEN'S PREFERENCES | | MEN'S PREFERENCES | | MEN'S PREFERENCES | | WOMEN'S PREFERENCES | |
Partner's Personality	Self	Aggregate	Self	Aggregate	Self	Aggregate	Self	Aggregate
Extraversion	.25	.39**	.28*	.24	.39***	.49***	.31***	.32**
Agreeableness	.28*	.32	.24	.02	.20*	.40***	.03	.25
Conscientiousness	.28*	.29*	.24	.26	.36***	.46***	.13	.24
Emotional Stability	.36**	.12	.40**	.10	.27**	.37**	.07	.12
Intellect–Openness	.33**	.41**	.40**	.11	.24**	.39***	.14	.39****

*p < .05
**p < .01
***p < .001
Source: Botwin, Buss, & Shackelford (1997).

Are people who get what they want happier with their marriages than people who do not? To examine this issue, Botwin and colleagues (1997) created difference scores between the preferences each individual expressed for the ideal personality of a mate and assessments of the spouse's actual personality. These difference scores were then used to predict satisfaction with the marriage, after first controlling for the main effects of the spouse's personality. The results were consistent—one's partner's personality had a substantial effect on marital satisfaction. Specifically, people were especially happy with their relationships if they were married to partners who were high on the personality characteristics of Agreeableness, Emotional Stability, and Intellect–Openness. But the difference scores between the partner's personality and one's ideal for that personality did *not* predict marital satisfaction. In other words, the key to marital happiness is having a partner who is agreeable, emotionally stable, and open, regardless of whether the partner departs in specific ways from what one wants (Luo et al., 2008).

The correlations between the participants' marital satisfaction scores and the partners' personality scores, obtained through the partners' self-reports, are shown in Table 15.4. Having a partner who is *agreeable* is an especially strong predictor of being happy with one's marriage for both men and women. People married to agreeable partners are more satisfied with their sex lives and view their spouses as more loving and affectionate, a source of shared laughter, and a source of stimulating conversation. People married to disagreeable partners are the most unhappy with the marriage and perhaps are most at risk of getting divorced.

The other personality factors that are consistently linked with marital satisfaction are Conscientiousness, Emotional Stability, and Intellect–Openness. Men whose wives score high on Conscientiousness are significantly more sexually satisfied with the marriage than are other husbands. Women whose husbands score high on Conscientiousness are generally more satisfied as well as happier with their spouses as sources of stimulating conversation—a finding replicated in a study of 125 long-wed couples (Claxton et al., 2011). Both men and women whose spouses score high on Emotional Stability are generally more satisfied, view their spouses as sources of encouragement and support, and enjoy spending time with their spouses. Low emotional stability scores are linked with relationship dissatisfaction among dating college students and among older adults in committed relationships (Slatcher & Vazire, 2009). Indeed, a meta-analysis of 19 samples found that emotional stability and agreeableness were the strongest predictors of satisfaction in intimate romantic relationships (Malouff et al., 2010). High neuroticism in one or both members of the couple leads to relationship dissatisfaction (Schaffjuser et al., 2014). On a positive note for those married to individuals low on emotional stability, one study found that having frequent sexual intercourse seems to protect couples from the negative marital consequences of neuroticism (Russell & McNulty, 2011).

Another link between personality and marital satisfaction emerges over the years following the newlywed year of marriage. As a general rule, in the newlywed year, people rate their spouses high on Agreeableness, Conscientiousness, Extraversion, and Intellect–Openness (Watson & Humrichouse, 2006). Over the ensuing two years, however, ratings of spouse's personalities become increasingly negative on these dimensions, illustrating a "honeymoon effect." And those who show the most marked negative ratings of their spouse's personality over time show the largest decreases in marital happiness. One speculation is that spouses in progressively unhappy marriages actually display progressively more unpleasant personalities, such as lower levels of Agreeableness, but only *within* the marital context itself. Those who maintain positive illusions about their partner's personality, in contrast, maintain high levels of satisfaction (Barelds & Dijkstra, 2011). Another key predictor of marital satisfaction is mate value—whether

Table 15.4 Facet of Marital Satisfaction and Spouse's Self-Reported Trait Ratings

Marital Satisfaction	SPOUSE'S SELF–REPORTED TRAIT RATINGS				
	E	A	C	ES	I–O
Husband's marital satisfaction					
General	.12	.32***	.06	.27**	.29**
Spouse as someone to confide in	−.05	.27**	.07	.11	.05
Sexual	−.08	.31**	.32***	.25**	.04
Spouse as source of encouragement and support	.03	.29**	.11	.26**	.18
Love and affection expressed	.07	.31**	.14	.21*	.26**
Enjoyment of time spent with spouse	.11	.30**	.13	.28**	.08
Frequency of laughing with spouse	.19*	.23*	.19	.11	.24**
Spouse as source of stimulating conversation	.06	.12	−.04	.21*	.17
Wife's marital satisfaction					
General	.07	.37***	.20*	.23*	.31***
Spouse as someone to confide in	.06	.25**	.15	.24**	.27**
Sexual	.08	.19*	.14	.09	.13
Spouse as source of encouragement and support	.04	.47***	.06	.20*	.31***
Love and affection expressed	−.04	.29**	.14	.28**	.33***
Enjoyment of time spent with spouse	.06	.27**	.06	.33***	.18
Frequency of laughing with spouse	−.02	.27**	−.02	.10	.08
Spouse as source of stimulating conversation	.23*	.24**	.25**	.18	.45***

Note: E = Extraversion; A = Agreeableness; C = Conscientiousness; ES = Emotional Stability; I–O = Intellect–Openness.
*p < .05
**p < .01
***p < .001
Source: Botwin, Buss, & Shackelford (1997).

one succeeds in selecting a mate whose personality embodies qualities most people want. Those mated with high mate-value individuals tend to be happier in their relationship than those mated with lower mate value individuals (Conroy-Beam et al., 2016).

In summary, the personality of one's spouse plays an important role in marital satisfaction. Those who select mates high on Agreeableness, Conscientiousness, Emotional Stability, and Intellect–Openness show the greatest happiness with their marriages. These are qualities linked with high mate value, since most people desire them. Those who select mates low on these personality factors are the most unhappy with their marriages. Differences from each person's individual ideal, however, do not appear to contribute to marital satisfaction.

Personality and the Selective Breakup of Couples

We have examined two ways in which personality plays a role in the mate selection process. First, there appear to be universal selection preferences—personality characteristics that everyone desires in a potential mate, such as dependability and emotional stability. Second, beyond the desires shared by everyone, people prefer partners who are similar to themselves in personality—dominant people prefer other dominant people, conscientious people prefer other conscientious people, and so on. But there is a third role that personality plays in the process of selection—its role in the selective breakup of marriages.

According to one theory of conflict between the sexes, breakups should occur more when one's desires are violated than when they are fulfilled (Buss, 2016). Following the **violation of desire** theory, we would predict that people married to others who lack desired characteristics, such as dependability and emotional stability, will more frequently dissolve the marriage. We would also predict, based on people's preferences for those who share their personality attributes, that the couples who are dissimilar on personality will break up more often than those who fulfill desires for similarity. Are these predictions borne out in the research findings?

Across a wide variety of studies, *emotional instability* has been the most consistent personality predictor of marital instability and divorce, emerging as a significant predictor in nearly every study that has included a measure of it (Kelly & Conley, 1987; Solomon & Jackson, 2014). One reason is that emotionally unstable individuals display high levels of jealousy—they worry more about a partner's infidelity, try to prevent social contact between their partner and others, and react more explosively when their partner does in fact engage in sex with others (Dijkstra & Barelds, 2008). Those high on Neuroticism also create more conflict and disagreement and their emotional upset after a fight tends to last longer (Solomon & Jackson, 2014). Low impulse control, or low conscientiousness (i.e., being impulsive and unreliable), particularly as exhibited by husbands, also emerges as a good predictor of marital dissolution (Bentler & Newcomb, 1978; Kelly & Conley, 1987). Low agreeableness predicts marital dissatisfaction and divorce, although this result is less consistent and less powerful than that found for emotional instability and low conscientiousness (Burgess & Wallin, 1953; Kelly & Conley, 1987). One reason for these breakups may be found in another link between personality and social behavior. A study of 52 nations found that the personality traits of low agreeableness and low conscientiousness (high impulsivity) were linked with higher rates of sexual infidelity in romantic relationships (Schmitt, 2004). Interestingly, extraversion and dominance are linked with higher levels of sexual promiscuity (Markey & Markey, 2007; Schmitt, 2004), although these personality traits are *not* related to marital satisfaction or breakups. A recent study of 8,206 individuals found that high Openness also predicted relationship breakups (Solomon & Jackson, 2014). The authors suggest that high Openness may lead to "a wandering eye," more sexual openness to others, and perhaps greater boredom with the relationship.

Being married to someone who lacks the personality characteristics that most people desire—dependability, emotional stability, and pleasing disposition—puts one most at risk for breakup. People actively seek mates who are dependable and emotionally stable, and those who fail to choose such mates are more at risk for divorce.

Another study examined the fate of 203 dating couples over the course of two years (Hill, Rubin, & Peplau, 1976). Over that time, roughly half of the couples broke up and half stayed together. Similarity in personality and values predicted staying together. Those who were most *dissimilar* were more likely to break up.

In summary, personality plays two key roles in mate selection. First, as part of the initial selection process, it determines the mates to whom we are attracted and the mates whom we desire. Second, personality affects satisfaction with one's mate and therefore determines the selective breakup of couples. Those who fail to select partners who are similar, agreeable, conscientious, and emotionally stable tend to break up more often than those who succeed in selecting such mates.

Shyness and the Selection of Risky Situations

Several other domains of selection have also been explored by personality researchers. One pertains to the effects of the personality disposition of shyness. **Shyness** is defined as a tendency to feel tense, worried, or anxious during social interactions or even when anticipating a social interaction (Addison & Schmidt, 1999). Shyness is a common phenomenon, and more than 90 percent of the population experience shyness at some point during their lives (Zimbardo, 1977). Some people, however, seem to be dispositionally shy—they tend to feel awkward in many social situations and so tend to avoid situations in which they will be forced to interact with people.

The effects of shyness on the selection of situations have been well documented. During high school and early adulthood, shy individuals tend to avoid social situations, resulting in a form of isolation (Schmidt & Fox, 1995). Shy women are also more likely to avoid going to the doctor for gynecological exams, and hence they put themselves at greater health risk (Kowalski & Brown, 1994). They are less likely to bring up the awkward issue of contraception with their partners before sexual intercourse, and so put themselves in potentially dangerous sexual situations (Bruch & Hynes, 1987).

Shyness also affects whether a person is willing to select risky situations in the form of gambles (Addison & Schmidt, 1999). In one experiment, shy people were identified through the Cheek (1983) shyness scale, which contains items such as "I find it hard to talk to strangers" and "I feel inhibited in social situations." On entry into the laboratory, each participant received the following instructions: "During this part of the experiment, you have a chance to win some money by picking a poker chip out of this

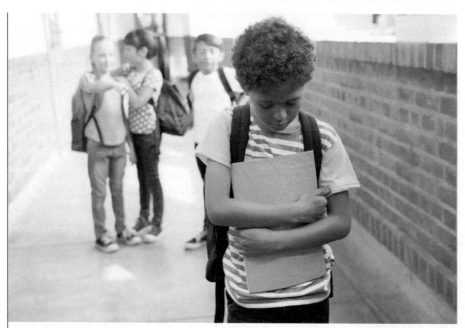

Shy individuals often feel tense or anxious in social situations and avoid entering situations in which they would be forced to interact with others.

© Wavebreakmedia/Getty Images RF

container. There are 100 poker chips in this box that are numbered from 1 to 100. . . ." The participants were given a choice to pick a gamble that they would most likely win (95 percent odds of winning) but from which they would receive only a small amount of money (e.g., 25¢), or to pick a riskier gamble, perhaps with only a 5 percent chance of winning but from which, if they won, they would receive $4.75. The experimenters also recorded the heart rate of the participants during their choice of gambles.

Shy women differed substantially from their nonshy counterparts in choosing the smaller bets that were linked with a higher likelihood of winning. The nonshy women, in contrast, chose the riskier bets with a lower likelihood of winning but with a larger payoff if they did win. During the task, the shy participants showed a larger increase in heart rate, suggesting that fearfulness might have led them to avoid the risky gambles.

These studies illustrate the importance of the personality disposition of shyness in the selection of, or avoidance of, certain situations. Shy women tend to avoid others, creating social isolation, and to avoid choosing risky gambles. Perhaps paradoxically, they also avoid going to the doctor for gynecological exams and avoid obtaining condoms, thus putting them at greater health risk than less shy women. Shyness, in short, appears to have a substantial impact on the selective entry into, or avoidance of, situations.

Other Personality Traits and the Selection of Situations

Other personality traits have been shown to affect selective entry into, or avoidance of, certain situations (Ickes et al., 1997). Those who are more empathic, for example, are more likely to enter situations such as volunteering for community activities (Davis et al., 1999). Those high on psychoticism seem to choose volatile and spontaneous situations more than formal or stable ones (Furnham, 1982). Those high on **Machiavellianism** prefer face-to-face situations, perhaps because these offer a better chance to ply their social manipulative skills to exploit others (Geis & Moon, 1981). People high on Extraversion tend to select more friends; however, people high on Agreeableness tend to be selected more often by others as friends (Selfhout et al., 2010).

High sensation seekers are more likely to volunteer for unusual experiments, such as studies involving drugs or sex (Zuckerman, 1978). High sensation seekers have been found to more frequently choose to enter risky situations (Donohew et al., 2000). High school students high in sensation seeking, more than their low sensation-seeking peers, more frequently attend parties where alcohol or marijuana is available to be consumed. They also more often have unwanted sex when drunk. Those who are high in sensation seeking also tend to select social situations characterized by high-risk sexual behavior (McCoul & Haslam, 2001). In a study of 112 heterosexual men, those who scored high on sensation seeking were more likely than their low-scoring peers to have unprotected sex more frequently. Even more striking, high sensation seekers had sexual intercourse with many more different partners than low sensation seekers ($r = .45$, $p < .001$). Those high on sensation seeking gravitate toward risky gambling bets and risky sexual situations (Webster & Crysel, 2012). Personality, in sum, affects the situations to which people are exposed through their selective entry into, or avoidance of, certain kinds of activities.

Evocation

Once we select others to occupy our social environment, a second class of processes is set into motion—the evocation of reactions from others. **Evocation** may be defined as the ways in which features of personality elicit reactions from others. Recall from

Chapter 3 the study of highly active children. Compared with their less active peers, highly active children tend to elicit hostility and competitiveness from others. Both parents and teachers tend to get into power struggles with these active children. The social interactions of less active children are more peaceful and harmonious. This is a perfect example of the process of evocation at work—a personality characteristic (in this case, activity level) evokes a predictable set of social responses from others (hostility and power struggles). Another example comes from the evocation of trust and cooperativeness by those high on Honesty-Humility (Thielmann & Hilbig, 2014). Perhaps because high scorers tend to trust others, they evoke trustworthy expectations in others.

Aggression and the Evocation of Hostility

It is well known that aggressive people evoke hostility from others (Dodge & Coie, 1987). People who are aggressive expect that others will be hostile toward them. One study has shown that aggressive people chronically interpret ambiguous behavior from others, such as being bumped into, as intentionally hostile (Dill et al., 1999). This is called a **hostile attributional bias**, the tendency to infer hostile intent on the part of others in the face of ambiguous behavior from them.

Because they expect others to be hostile, aggressive people tend to treat others in an aggressive manner. People who are treated in an aggressive manner often aggress back. In this case, the aggressive reactions of others confirm what the aggressive person suspected all along—that others have hostility toward him or her. But what the aggressive person fails to realize is that the hostility from others is a product of their making—the aggressor evokes it from others by treating them aggressively.

Evocation of Anger and Upset in Partners

There are at least two ways in which personality can play a role in evoking conflict in close relationships. First, a person can perform actions that cause an emotional response in a partner. A dominant person, for example, might act in a condescending manner, habitually evoking upset in the partner. Or a husband low in conscientiousness might neglect personal grooming and throw clothes on the floor, which might upset his wife. In short, personality characteristics can *evoke emotions* in others through the actions performed.

A second form of evocation occurs when a person elicits actions from another that in turn upset the original elicitor. An aggressive man, for example, might elicit the silent treatment from his mate, which in turn upsets him because she won't speak to him. A condescending wife might undermine the self-esteem of her husband and then become angry because he lacks self-confidence. In sum, people's personality characteristics can upset others either directly by influencing how they act toward others or indirectly by eliciting actions from others that are upsetting.

Research on these forms of evocation require studies that assesses the personality characteristics of both persons involved. In one study, the personality characteristics of both husbands and wives were assessed through three data sources: self-report, spouse-report, and independent reports by two interviewers (Buss, 1991a). An instrument assessed multiple sources of anger and upset in close relationships (Buss, 1989). A short version of this instrument is shown in the Exercise on page 474.

Statistical analyses determined which personality traits predicted that the spouse would become upset. The results were similar for men and women, so we will use men's personality traits that upset women to highlight the results.

Exercise

INSTRUCTIONS: We all do things that upset or anger other people from time to time. Think of a close romantic partner or close friend with whom you have been involved. Following is a list of things this person might have done that evoked anger or upset in you. Read the list, and place a check by the things your partner or close friend has done in the past year that have irritated, angered, annoyed, or upset you.

____   1. He/she treated me as if I were stupid or inferior.
____   2. He/she demanded too much of my time.
____   3. He/she ignored my feelings.
____   4. He/she slapped me.
____   5. He/she saw someone else intimately.
____   6. He/she did not help clean up.
____   7. He/she fussed too much with his/her appearance.
____   8. He/she acted too moody.
____   9. He/she refused to have sex with me.
____ 10. He/she talked about members of the opposite sex as if they were sex objects.
____ 11. He/she got drunk.
____ 12. He/she did not dress well or appropriately for a social gathering.
____ 13. He/she told me that I was ugly.
____ 14. He/she tried to use me for sexual purposes.
____ 15. He/she acted selfishly.

These acts represent items from the larger instrument of 147 acts that one can do to upset or anger a member of the opposite sex. The acts correspond to the following factors: (1) condescending, (2) possessive/jealous, (3) neglecting/rejecting, (4) abusive, (5) unfaithful, (6) inconsiderate, (7) physically self-absorbed, (8) moody, (9) sexually withholding, (10) sexualizing of others, (11) abusive of alcohol, (12) disheveled, (13) insulting of partner's appearance, (14) sexually aggressive, and (15) self-centered. It turns out that the personality of the person we are close to is a reasonably good predictor of whether that person will perform these upsetting acts.

Source: Buss (1991a).

The husbands high on dominance tended to upset their partners by being condescending—treating their wives' opinions as stupid or inferior and placing more value on their own opinions. The husbands who scored low on conscientiousness, in contrast, tended to upset their wives by having extramarital affairs—seeing someone else intimately or having sex with another woman. The husbands low on openness tended to evoke upset in their wives by acting rejecting (ignoring the wife's feelings), abusive (slapping or hitting the wife), physically self-absorbed (focusing too much on his face and hair), sexually withholding (refusing the wife's sexual advances), and abusive of alcohol (getting drunk).

By far the strongest predictors of evoked anger and upset, however, were the personality characteristics of disagreeableness and emotional instability. Disagreeable husbands evoked anger and upset in their wives in the following ways: being condescending,

The strongest predictors of a wife's anger and dissatisfaction with marriage are the personality traits of disagreeableness and emotional instability on the part of the husband.
© Stuart Jenner/Getty Images RF

such as treating them as if they were inferior; neglecting and rejecting them, such as failing to spend enough time with them and ignoring their feelings; abusing them, such as slapping, hitting, or spitting; committing infidelity; abusing alcohol; insulting her appearance, such as calling her ugly; and exhibiting self-centeredness. Indeed, low agreeableness of the husband was a better predictor of evoking upset in the wife than any other personality variable in the study. Another study found that low agreeable individuals, because of their anger, jealousy, and antisocial behavior, tend to evoke high levels of relationship conflict (Lemay & Dobush, 2014).

The emotionally unstable husbands also evoked anger and upset in their wives. In addition to being condescending, abusive, unfaithful, inconsiderate, and abusive of alcohol, these husbands also upset their wives by being moody (acting irritable) as well as jealous and possessive. For example, the emotionally unstable men tended to upset their wives by demanding too much attention, monopolizing the wife's time, being too dependent, and flying into jealous rages.

Several other studies have confirmed the important role of agreeableness and emotional stability in evoking or diminishing conflict in interpersonal relationships. In one study that used both hypothetical and daily diary assessments of conflict, those high in agreeableness tended to evoke less interpersonal conflict (Jensen-Campbell & Graziano, 2001). One reason might be that highly agreeable individuals tend to use "compromise" in dealing with conflict when it arises, whereas those low in agreeableness are less willing to compromise and are more likely to use verbal insults and physical force to deal with conflict. Married couples with highly agreeable wives tend to have more frequent sex, perhaps because they are receptive to, evoke more, sexual overtures (Meltzer & McNulty, 2016). The importance of low agreeableness in evoking conflict extends to a wide variety of interpersonal relationships, including those in the workplace (Bono et al., 2002).

These links between personality and conflict show up at least as early as early adolescence—young teenagers low in agreeableness not only evoke more conflict, but also are more likely to become victimized by their peers in high school (Jensen-Campbell et al., 2002). Agreeable individuals also tend to use effective conflict resolution tactics, a path leading to harmonious social interactions (Jensen-Campbell et al., 2003). Agreeable people tend to evoke trust and cooperation in laboratory-based economic games (Zhao & Smillie, 2015). Those high in negative emotionality (high neuroticism) were also likely to experience greater conflict in all their relationships, whereas those high in positive emotionality (a close cousin of agreeableness) experienced less conflict in all of their relationships (Robins, Caspi, & Moffitt, 2002). Indeed, studies from the United States, Australia, the Netherlands, and Germany reveal that *agreeableness* and *emotional stability* are the traits most consistently conducive to evoking satisfaction in relationships (Barelds, 2005; Donnellan, Larsen-Rife, & Conger, 2005; Heaven et al., 2003; Neyer & Voigt, 2004; White, Hendrick, & Hendrick, 2004).

In summary, personality plays a key role in the process of evocation—in this case, the evocation of anger and upset. By far, the strongest predictors of this upset are low agreeableness and emotional instability. It would be premature to conclude that this provides a recipe for choosing whom not to marry or whom not to choose as a close friend (in other words, avoid emotionally unstable and disagreeable people). But it does suggest that if you marry or befriend someone with these personality attributes, they will be likely to behave in anger-evoking ways.

Application

Psychologist John Gottman has been conducting research on married people for three decades. His main question has been "What distinguishes the happily married couple from the dissatisfied, unhappy couple?" After studying thousands of marital pairs, some of whom have been happily married for years and others of whom were applying for divorce, he has found many ways that the happy and unhappy couples differ. He distilled his research findings in an applied book on how to make marriage work (Gottman & Silver, 1999). His seven principles of positive relationships are summarized below. Several of these principles concern behaviors related to evoking responses in the partner.

1. Develop an empathic understanding of your partner (see Chapter 11 for a discussion of empathy). Get to know their "world," their preferences, and the important events in their life. As an example, once a day try to find out one important or significant event for your partner: what they are looking forward to or what important event happened to them. Trivial as it sounds, try asking, "How was your day?" each day.

2. Remain fond of each other and try to nurture your affection for your partner. Remember why you like this person, and tell her about it. As an example, keep a photo album together and go over it once in a while, reminding yourself of the fun times you had together and how much you enjoy being with this special person.

3. In times of stress, turn toward, rather than away, from each other. Also during the good times, do things together. In other words, don't take your partner for granted, and never ignore him, even in day-to-day life. Pay attention, stay connected, touch each other, and talk frequently.

4. Share power, even if you think you are the expert. Let your partner influence you. Ask her for help once in a while. Ask for her opinion. Let her know that her views matter to you.

5. You will undoubtedly have arguments. However, try to argue only about the solvable problems. When arguing:
   • Start gently
   • Proceed with respect
   • If feelings get hurt, stop and try to repair those hurt feelings
   • Be willing to compromise

6. Realize that some problems may never be solved. For example, perhaps one of you is religious and the other is not, and both intend to stay this way. Avoid gridlock on such unsolvable problems and don't let them become permanent topics of argument. Agree to disagree on certain issues.

7. Become a "we" instead of "I" and "I." Make the relationship important and consider it as well as your own wants and desires. Think about what is best for "us" rather than only what is best for "me."

Source: Adapted from Gottman & Silver, 1999.

Evocation of Likability, Pleasure, and Pain

One of the most important effects a person can have on the social world is the evocation of likability. Being liked by others is linked with higher levels of adjustment, mental health, and even academic performance (Wortman & Wood, 2011). Some personality traits consistently evoke likability in others—those linked with agreeableness, the sociable component of extraversion, and the honesty–humility factor (Wortman & Wood, 2011). People with these qualities evoke pleasure in others, leading to their liking (Saucier, 2010). Being extraverted increases likability even on online social networks (Stopfer et al., 2013). In contrast, people low on agreeableness and honesty–humility evoke pain in others. They cause others to be offended, annoyed, irritated, and even frightened and intimidated. Personality, in short, creates a footprint on one's social world by evoking liking, pleasure, or pain in other people.

Evocation Through Expectancy Confirmation

Expectancy confirmation is a phenomenon whereby people's beliefs about the personality characteristics of others cause them to evoke in others actions that are consistent with the initial beliefs. The phenomenon of expectancy confirmation has also been called self-fulfilling prophecy. Can mere beliefs have such a powerful role in evoking behavior from others?

In a study of expectancy confirmation, Snyder and Swann (1978) led individuals to believe that they would be dealing with a hostile and aggressive individual and then introduced the two individuals. They found that people's beliefs led them to act in an aggressive manner toward the unsuspecting target. Then the behavior of the unsuspecting target was examined. The intriguing finding was that the unsuspecting target actually acted in a more hostile manner, behavior that was evoked by the person who was led to expect hostility. In this example, beliefs about the personality of the other actually created the behavior that confirmed those initial beliefs (Snyder & Cantor, 1998).

Expectancies about personality may have widespread evocation effects in everyday life. After all, we often hear information about a person's reputation prior to, or following, actual encounters with the person. We hear that a person is smart, socially skilled, egocentric, a player, or manipulative. These beliefs about the personality characteristics of others may have far-reaching effects on evoking behavior that confirm our initial beliefs. It is sometimes said that, in order to change your personality, you must move to a place where people don't already know you. Through the process of expectancy confirmation, people who already know you may unwittingly evoke in you behavior that confirms their beliefs, thereby constraining your ability to change.

Manipulation: Social Influence Tactics

Manipulation, or social influence, includes all the ways in which people intentionally try to change the behavior of others. No malicious intent need be implied by the term *manipulation,* although such intent is not excluded either. A parent might influence a child not to cross between parked cars, but we would not call this behavior malicious. Indeed, part of social living is that we influence others all the time. Thus, the term *manipulation* is used here descriptively, with no negative connotation.

From an evolutionary perspective (see Chapter 8), natural selection favors people who successfully manipulate objects in their environment. Some manipulable objects are inanimate, such as the raw materials used to build shelters, tools, clothing, and weapons. Other manipulable objects are alive, including predators and prey of different species and mates, parents, children, rivals, and allies of the same species. The manipulation of other people can be summarized as the various means by which we influence the psychology and behavior of other people.

The process of manipulation can be examined from two perspectives within personality psychology. First, we can ask, "Are some individuals consistently more manipulative than others?" Second, we can ask, "Given that all people attempt to influence others, do stable personality characteristics predict the sorts of tactics that are used?" Do extraverted people, for example, more often use the charm tactic, whereas introverts use the silent treatment tactic?

A Taxonomy of Eleven Tactics of Manipulation

A **taxonomy** is simply a classification scheme—the identification and naming of groups within a particular subject field. Taxonomies of plants and animals, for example, have been developed to identify and name all the major plant and animal groups. The periodic table is a taxonomy of elements in the known universe. The Big Five personality traits that we examined in Chapter 3 is a taxonomy of major dimensions of personality. In this section, we look at the development of a taxonomy of tactics of manipulation—an attempt to identify and name the major ways in which people try to influence others in their social world.

A taxonomy of tactics of manipulation was developed through a two-step procedure: (1) nominations of acts of influence and (2) factor analysis of self-reports and observer-reports of the previously nominated acts (Buss, 1992; Buss et al., 1987). The act nomination procedure (see Chapter 2) was as follows: "We are interested in the things that people do to influence others in order to get what they want. Please think of your [romantic partner, close friend, mother, father, etc.]. How do you get this person to do something? What do you do? Please write down specific behaviors or acts that you perform in order to get this person to do things. List as many different sorts of acts as you can."

After this list was generated, the researchers converted it into a questionnaire that could be administered via self-report or observer report. You can see for yourself how this was done by taking the test in the Exercise below to find out what tactics of social influence you use.

Exercise

INSTRUCTIONS: When you want your partner to do something for you, what are you likely to do? Look at each of the following items and *rate how likely you are to do each when you are trying to get your partner to do something.* None of them will apply to all situations in which you want your partner to do something, so rate how likely you are, in general, to do what is described. If you are extremely likely to do it, write a "7" in the blank next to the item. If you are not at all likely to do it, write a "1" in the blank next to the item. If you are somewhat likely to do it, write a "4" in the blank. Give intermediate ratings for intermediate likelihood of performing the behaviors.

____ 1. I compliment her/him so that she/he will do it.
____ 2. I act charming so she/he will do it.
____ 3. I try to be loving and romantic when I ask her/him.
____ 4. I give her/him a small gift or card before I ask.
____ 5. I don't respond to her/him until she/he does it.
____ 6. I ignore her/him until she/he does it.
____ 7. I am silent until she/he does it.
____ 8. I refuse to do something she/he likes until she/he does it.
____ 9. I demand that she/he do it.
____ 10. I yell at her/him until she/he does it.
____ 11. I criticize her/him for not doing it.
____ 12. I threaten her/him with something if she/he does not do it.
____ 13. I give her/him reasons she/he should do it.
____ 14. I point out all the good things that will come from doing it.
____ 15. I explain why I want her/him to do it.
____ 16. I show her/him that I would be willing to do it for her/him.
____ 17. I pout until she/he does it.
____ 18. I sulk until she/he does it.
____ 19. I whine until she/he does it.
____ 20. I cry until she/he does it.
____ 21. I allow myself to be debased so that she/he will do it.
____ 22. I lower myself so that she/he will do it.
____ 23. I act humble so that she/he will do it.
____ 24. I act submissive so that she/he will do it.

You can find out your scores by simply adding up your scores in clusters of four: items 1–4 5 charm tactic; items 5–8 5 silent treatment tactic; items 9–12 5 coercion tactic; items 13–16 5 reason tactic; items 17–20 5 regression tactic; items 21–24 5 self-abasement tactic. The tactics you tend to use the most are those with the highest sums. The tactics you use the least are those with the lowest sums. This is an abbreviated version of the instrument used in the studies by Buss (1992).

A large number of participants completed versions of an expanded instrument, consisting of 83 acts of influence or tactics. Factor analysis was then used to identify clusters of acts of influence, or tactics. In all, 11 tactics were discovered through this procedure, as shown in Table 15.5. Although this taxonomy identifies manipulation tactics used across many contexts, it is important to remember that some tactics will depend on the goal of the tactician. For example, parents sometimes try to manipulate the mate choices of their sons and daughters, and use tactics specific to that context such as "chaperoning," for example, sticking around when the offspring is with a potential mate (Apostalou, 2014).

Sex Differences in Tactics of Manipulation

Do men and women differ in their usage of tactics of manipulations? Buss (1992) found that, by and large, the answer is no. Women and men equally performed almost all of the tactics of social influence. There was only one small exception: the regression tactic. In samples of dating couples and married couples, the women more than the men reported more frequent use of the regression tactic, including crying, whining, pouting, and sulking to get their way. The difference, however, was quite small, supporting the overall conclusion that men and women, in general, are similar in their performance of tactics of manipulation. Parents also use somewhat different tactics of manipulation with regard to the mate choices of their sons and daughters. They are more likely to monitor their daughters, control the clothing choices of their daughters, and outright prevent their daughters from seeing a potential mate the parents do not like (Apostalou & Papageorgi, 2014; Perilloux et al., 2008).

Personality Predictors of Tactics of Manipulation

The next interesting question is whether people with certain personality traits are more likely to use certain tactics of manipulation. A sample of more than 200 participants (Buss, 1992) rated each act of influence on the degree to which they used it in each of four

Table 15.5 Taxonomy of Eleven Tactics of Manipulation

Tactic	Sample Act
Charm	I try to be loving when I ask her to do it.
Coercion	I yell at him until he does it.
Silent treatment	I don't respond to her until she does it.
Reason	I explain why I want him to do it.
Regression	I whine until she does it.
Self-abasement	I act submissive so that he will do it.
Responsibility invocation	I get her to make a commitment to doing it.
Hardball	I hit him so that he will do it.
Pleasure induction	I show her how much fun it will be to do it.
Social comparison	I tell him that everyone else is doing it.
Monetary reward	I offer her money so that she will do it.

Note: These tactics then formed the basis for subsequent analyses, such as whether there are sex differences in the tactics of manipulation and whether personality traits are associated with the tactics of manipulation that people use.

A Closer Look

The Machiavellian Personality

The term *Machiavellian* originates from an Italian diplomat, Niccolo Machiavelli, who wrote a classic treatise, *The Prince,* in 1513 (Machiavelli, 1513/1966). Machiavelli observed, in his diplomatic role, that leaders come and go, rising and falling as they gain and lose power. *The Prince* is a book of advice on acquiring and maintaining power, which Machiavelli wrote to ingratiate himself with a new ruler after the one that he had served had been overthrown. The advice is based on tactics for manipulating others and is entirely lacking in traditional values, such as trust, honor, and decency. One passage in the book, for example, notes that "men are so simple and so much inclined to obey immediate needs that a deceiver will never lack for victims for his deceptions" (p. 63). Machiavellianism eventually came to be associated with a manipulative strategy of social interaction and with a personality

Niccolo Machiavelli, after whom the trait of Machiavellianism was named, wrote a book on strategies for manipulating others.
© *BeBa/Iberfoto/The Image Works*

style that uses other people as tools for personal gain.

Two psychologists—Richard Christie and Florence Geis—developed a self-report scale to measure individual differences in Machiavellianism (Christie & Geis, 1970). The following are some sample items from the test, with the Machiavellian direction noted in parentheses:

- *The best way to handle people is to tell them what they want to hear* (true).
- *Anyone who completely trusts anyone else is asking for trouble* (true).
- *Honesty is the best policy in all cases* (false).
- *Never tell anyone the real reason you did something unless it is useful to do so* (true).
- *Most people who get ahead in the world lead clean, moral lives* (false).
- *The biggest difference between most criminals and other people is that criminals are stupid enough to get caught* (true).
- *It is wise to flatter important people* (true).

As you can see from these items, the high scorer on the Machiavellianism scale (called a "high Mach") is manipulative, has a cynical worldview, treats other people as tools to be used for personal ends, does not trust other people, and lacks empathy. The low scorer on the Machiavellianism scale (called a "low Mach") is trusting, empathic, believes that things are clearly either right or wrong, and views human nature as basically good.

High and low scorers represent two alternative strategies of social conduct (Wilson, Near, & Miller, 1996). The high Mach represents an exploitative social strategy—one that betrays friendship and uses other people opportunistically. Theoretically, this strategy works best in social situations when there is room for innovation, rather than those that are highly constrained

by rules. Political consulting or the world of an independent entrepreneur might be relatively unconstrained, allowing much latitude for the high Mach to operate. The more structured world of universities, on the other hand, might allow fewer opportunities for the high Machs to ply their skills.

The low Mach, in contrast, represents a strategy of cooperation, sometimes called tit-for-tat. This strategy is based on reciprocity—you help me, and I'll help you in return, and we will both be better off as a result. This is a long-term social strategy, in contrast to the short-term strategy of the high Mach.

The success of the high Mach should depend greatly on the context. One study examined this prediction in a real-world setting by studying the sales performance of stockbrokers from two different organizational contexts (Shultz, 1993). One organizational context, the NYNEX, is a highly structured stock brokerage and rule bound, with little room for the salespeople to innovate or improvise. Employees are required to follow a two-volume manual of rules. The second organizational context, represented by stock brokerages such as Merrill Lynch, is more loosely structured and allows more opportunities for wheeling and dealing.

The sales success of stockbrokers was evaluated by the size of the commissions earned by the individuals in the two organizational contexts. In the loosely structured organizations, such as Merrill Lynch, the high Machs had more clients and earned fully twice as many commissions as the low Machs. On the basis of this impressive finding, one might be tempted to conclude that Machiavellianism is a successful strategy of social influence in general. However, in the more tightly structured organizations, the low Machs earned twice as much money on commissions as the high Machs. This study illustrates a key point

(Continued)

A Closer Look (*Continued*)

about the Machiavellian social strategy of influence—its success is highly context-dependent. Thus, Machiavellianism is not a social strategy that works all the time. Social situations with lots of rules do not allow high Machs to con others, tell lies, and betray those who trust them with impunity. In these situations, the high Machs get caught, sustain damage to their reputations, and often are fired. In more fluid occupational contexts, high Machs succeed because they can wheel and deal, move quickly from one situation to another, and exploit the opportunities available in these less rule-bound settings.

Machiavellianism is a social strategy in which practitioners are quick to betray others (Wilson et al., 1996). In one laboratory study, participants were given an opportunity to steal money in a worker-supervisor situation (Harrell & Hartnagel, 1976). The participants played the role of workers. They were supervised by a person who acted trustingly and who stated that he or she did not need to monitor the workers closely. A full 81 percent of the high Machs stole money, as contrasted with only 24 percent of the low Machs. Furthermore, the high Machs who did steal took a larger amount of money than those few low Machs who stole, they tended to conceal their theft, and they lied more often to the supervisor when questioned about the theft.

Not only do high Machs lie and betray others' trust more than low Machs, but there is also evidence that they make more believable liars (Exline et al., 1970; Geis & Moon, 1981). In one study, high and low Machs were instructed to cheat on a task and then to lie to the experimenter about having cheated (Exline et al., 1970). The experimenter then became increasingly suspicious and questioned the participants about whether they had cheated. The high Machs were able to maintain greater eye contact than the low Machs. Fewer of the high Machs than the low Machs confessed. Finally, the high Machs were judged to be better liars than the low Machs.

The manipulative tactics used by the high Machs extend to the romantic and sexual domains. High Machs, compared to their low Mach peers, are more likely to feign love in order to get sex (e.g., "I sometimes say 'I love you' when I don't really mean it to get someone to have sex with me"), get a partner drunk in order to induce the partner to have sex, and express a willingness to use force to achieve sex with an unwilling partner (McHoskey, 2001). They are more prone to committing sexual harassment (Zeigler-Hill et al., 2016). And they tend to maliciously gossip about their mating rivals (Gconcalves & Campbell, 2014; Lyons & Hughs, 2015). High Machs are more likely to cheat on their romantic

partner and to be sexually unfaithful with other people (Jones & Weiser, 2014). Interestingly, these links between Machiavellianism and specific tactics of manipulation are stronger for the male than for the female sample.

The Machiavellian strategy has many advantages, but it also has costs. By betraying, cheating, and lying, the high Mach runs the risk of retaliation and revenge by those who were exploited. Furthermore, the high Mach is more likely than the low Mach to incur damage to his or her reputation. Once people acquire reputations as exploitative, other people are more likely to avoid them and refuse to interact with them.

This discussion of the Machiavellian strategy also illustrates the three key processes by which personality affects social interaction, bringing us back full circle to the three central processes of personality and social interaction. First, the high Mach tends to *select* situations that are loosely structured, untethered by rules that would restrict the deployment of an exploitative strategy. Second, the high Mach tends to *evoke* specific reactions from others, such as anger and retaliation for having been exploited. Third, the high Mach tends to *manipulate* other people in predictable ways, using tactics that are exploitative, self-serving, and deceptive.

relationships: spouse, friend, mother, and father. Then, correlations were computed between the personality traits of the participants and their use of each tactic of manipulation.

Those scoring relatively high in dominance (extraversion) tended to use coercion, such as demanding, threatening, cursing, and criticizing, in order to get their way. Highly dominant people also tended to use responsibility invocation, getting others to commit to a course of action and saying that it was their duty to do it.

Those scoring low in dominance (relatively submissive individuals) used the self-abasement tactic as a means of influencing others. They lowered themselves, for example, or tried to look sickly to get others to do what they wanted. Interestingly, these submissive individuals also tended to use the hardball tactic—deception, lying, degradation, and even violence—more often than their dominant counterparts.

The two primary tactics of influence used by highly agreeable people are pleasure induction and reason. Agreeable individuals tell and show others how enjoyable the activity will be, explain the rationale for wanting others to engage in particular behaviors, and point out all the good things that will come from doing them. A study of how children manipulate their parents regarding their choice of a mate revealed that highly agreeable children used the reason tactic, and also convinced their parents to trust them (Apostolou et al., 2015).

Those who are disagreeable, in contrast, frequently use coercion and the silent treatment—results also found in a Croatian study (Butkovic & Bratko, 2007). Not only do they threaten, criticize, yell, and scream in order to get their way, they also give the stony silent look and refuse to speak to the other until he or she complies. Low-agreeable individuals are also likely to seek revenge on people who they perceive have wronged them; they use cost-inflicting rather than benefit-bestowing tactics of manipulation (McCullough et al., 2001). Low-agreeable individuals tend to be more selfish in their use of collective resources, whereas high-agreeable individuals exercise more self-restraint when the group's resources are scarce or threatened (Koole et al., 2001).

The personality disposition of conscientiousness is associated with only one tactic of social influence: reason. Conscientious individuals explain why they want the other person to do something, provide logical explanations for wanting it done, and explain the underlying rationale for doing it. One study found that low-conscientious individuals are more likely to use criminal strategies in gaining resources, as indicated by arrest records and recidivism (being rearrested after being let out of prison) (Clower & Bothwell, 2001).

The "silent treatment" is a manipulation strategy often employed by persons high on the trait of disagreeableness.

© Image Source/Getty Images RF

Emotionally unstable individuals use a wide variety of tactics to manipulate others—hardball and coercion, but also reason and monetary reward. The tactic most commonly used by emotionally unstable people, however, is regression. These people pout, sulk, whine, and cry to get their way (see Butkovic & Bratko, 2007). In a sense, this kind of behavior comes close to the core definition of emotional instability—the display of volatile emotions, some positive and some negative. But the fascinating part of these findings is that the emotional volatility is strategically motivated—it is used with the purpose of influencing others to get what they want.

What tactics do people high on Intellect–Openness use? Not surprisingly, these smart and perceptive people tend to use reason above all other tactics. They also use pleasure induction and responsibility invocation, however—findings that are not as intuitively obvious. Can you guess which tactic those *low* on Intellect–Openness use? They tend to use social comparison—saying that everyone else is doing it, comparing the partner with someone else who would do it, and telling others that they will look stupid if they do not do it.

A recent study examined the links between the "dark triad" personality traits (narcissism, psychopathy, and Machiavellianism) and tactics of social influence (Jonason & Webster, 2012). Those scoring high on these dark traits tended to manipulate others through a wide variety of tactics—coercion, hardball, reciprocity, social comparison, monetary reward, and even charm. High dark triad scorers were especially prone to using the hardball tactic, as illustrated by their tendency to bully other people with whom they are involved socially (Baughman et al., 2012).

In summary, these results provide strong evidence that personality dispositions are not static entities residing passively in the heads of people. They have profound implications for social interaction—in this case, for the tactics people use to manipulate others in their social environment.

Panning Back: An Overview of Personality and Social Interaction

The most important message from this chapter is that personality does not reside passively within individuals, but rather profoundly affects each person's social environment. The three processes by which personality can influence an individual's social environment—selection, evocation, and manipulation—are highlighted in Table 15.6.

These fundamental mechanisms operate in the physical as well as the social environment. Let's consider selection first. In the physical domain, an introvert is more likely to choose to live in a rural habitat, whereas an extravert is more likely to choose city living with all the opportunities for social interaction city life provides. In the social domain, an extravert is more likely to select a mate who is also extraverted, whereas an introvert is more likely to choose an introverted mate so that they can read books quietly side by side.

For the process of evocation, a loud, heavy person who treads heavily is more likely to evoke an avalanche while climbing a snowy mountain. In the social domain, narcissistic people evoke admiration from their followers and contempt from those who dislike their unbridled self-centeredness. For the process of manipulation, personality affects how people mold and modify the rooms in which they live (Gosling et al., 2002). Conscientious individuals, for example, keep their rooms tidy, neat, and free of clutter. Those low on Conscientiousness have more dirt, clutter, and mess in their rooms. Those high in Intellect–Openness decorate their rooms with stylish and unconventional objects and have many books and CDs that are highly varied in genre. Those low on Intellect–Openness have fewer and more conventional decorations, a narrower range of books, and a more delimited collection of CDs. In the social domain, disagreeable individuals are more likely than stable individuals to use "the silent treatment" as a tactic of manipulation. Those high in Intellect–Openness tend to use reason and rationality to get their way. And narcissists try to transfer blame for their failures onto others.

Personality, in short, affects the mates and friends a person chooses as well as the environments a person decides to enter or avoid (selection); the reactions elicited from

	Table 15.6 Causal Mechanisms That Create Links Between Personality and Environment: Examples from the Physical and Social Domains	
Mechanism	**Physical Environment**	**Social Environment**
Selection	Introvert selects rural habitat	Extravert chooses extraverted mate
	Avoidance of cold climates	Emotionally stable person chooses stable roommate
Evocation	Person who treads heavily elicits an avalanche	Disagreeable people evoke relationship conflict
	Clumsy person creates, elicits more noise and clatter	Narcissistic people evoke admiration from followers
Manipulation	Conscientious person creates clean, neat, uncluttered room	Disagreeable person uses "the silent treatment"
	Person high on openness creates stylish, colorful room with varied collection of books and CDs	Narcissists transfer blame to others

A Closer Look

Narcissism and Social Interaction

Narcissism is a personality dimension that involves, at the upper end, high levels of self-absorption and conceitedness, placing one's own wants and needs above those of others, displaying unusual grandiosity, showing a profound sense of entitlement, and lacking empathy for other people's feelings, needs, and desires (see Chapters 10 and 14; Raskin & Terry, 1988). Those high on narcissism tend to be *exhibitionistic* (e.g., flaunting money to impress others), *grandiose* (e.g., talking about how great they are), *self-centered* (e.g., taking the best piece of food for themselves), and *interpersonally exploitative* (e.g., using others for selfish ends) (Buss & Chiodo, 1991). Interestingly, female celebrities such as women on reality TV shows tend to be more narcissistic than average (Young & Pinsky, 2006). Nonetheless, it is also true that narcissistic individuals think they are hot (good looking), but empirical evidence suggests that they are only slightly more attractive than average (Bleske-Rechek, Remicker, & Baker, 2008; Holtzman & Strube, 2010). Personality psychologists have documented the impact of narcissism on social interaction, providing a fascinating illustration of the influence of personality on social selection, evocation, and manipulation.

In terms of *selection,* narcissists tend to choose people who admire them, who will reflect the extraordinarily positive view they hold about themselves. They don't want people around who will view them as anything other than as extraordinary, beautiful, or brilliant (Buss & Chiodo, 1991). In fact, because narcissists view themselves as "exceptional performers," they tend to select social situations in which they perceive that their "opportunity for glory" will be enhanced, and avoid situations in which their self-perceived magnificence will not be noticed by others (Wallace & Baumeister, 2002). Although they tend to appoint themselves to positions of power (Buss & Chiodo, 1991), they strenuously avoid social

situations that don't afford the chance to show off their brilliance (Wallace & Baumeister, 2002). Life, however, sometimes has a way of crashing in, and narcissists are sometimes rejected. When they are rejected, narcissists tend to lash out with great anger at those they perceive to have wronged them (Carpenter, 2012; Horton & Sedikides, 2009; Jones & Paulhus, 2010), perhaps because their self-esteem is a bit fragile in response to failure (Zeigler-Hill et al., 2010). Interestingly, narcissists are highly selective in their social perceptions—they view themselves as victims of interpersonal transgressions far more frequently than those low on narcissism (McCullough et al., 2003).

In the mating domain, the romantic partner selections of narcissists may be more precarious than those of others because they score low on commitment to their partner, perhaps because they view themselves as "better" or more desirable than their partner (Campbell & Foster, 2002; Campbell, Rudich, & Sedikedes, 2002). Narcissists do not doubt the commitment of their romantic partners (Foster & Campbell, 2005). When asked in an experiment to list possible reasons why their current romantic partner might be less committed than they are to the relationship, narcissists had great difficulty even completing the task! After the task, narcissists (compared with those low on narcissism) indicated substantially lower levels of their own commitment to their romantic partner and a greater willingness to accept a dating invitation from someone else. Narcissistic entitlement has also been linked to *an inability to forgive others,* a quality that could also impair the functioning of romantic relationships (Exline et al., 2004).

Narcissists also *evoke* predictable responses from others in their social environment. Because they are exhibitionistic and thrust themselves into the center of attention, narcissists sometimes split people in their evocations—some view them as brilliant, entertaining, and "not boring," whereas others view them as selfish and boorish (Campbell

et al., 2002). They sometimes evoke anger in others because of their self-aggrandizing actions, such as pulling rank on others to make a point. Narcissists evoke reactions from others through their behavior and dress. They tend to create Facebook pages that are more self-promoting (Buffardi & Campbell, 2008; Ong et al., 2011), including posting sexy images of themselves (DeWall et al., 2011). Narcissists post more "selfies," update their online profile photos more often, and spend more time on Instagram (Marshall et al., 2015; Moon et al., 2016; Sorokowski et al., 2015; Weiser, 2015). They are more likely to wear expensive and flashy clothes; and if they are female, they wear more makeup and show more cleavage—actions that may evoke sexual overtures in others (Vazire et al., 2008).

Narcissists also use a predictable set of tactics of *manipulation.* They are highly exploitative of others and would be described as "users." They use friends for their wealth or connections. When in positions of power, they use their positions to exploit subordinates and show no hesitation in pulling rank to humiliate someone else in front of others. They react to failure by derogating other people, possibly in an attempt to transfer the blame for their failure onto others (Park & Colvin, 2014; South, Oltmanns, & Turkheimer, 2003). In the mating domain, they engage in manipulative game-playing and are more likely to use sexually coercive and aggressive tactics (Blinkhorn et al., 2015; Haslam & Montrose, 2015). They also lash out in anger and aggression against others when confronted with their own failure. The entitlement and exploitativeness components of narcissism are especially good predictors of aggression (Reidy et al., 2008). In sum, the personality dimension of narcissism shows many links to the social selections they make, the reactions they evoke from others, and the tactics of manipulation they use to enhance their self-centered goals.

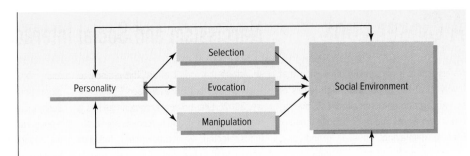

Figure 15.1

Personality and social interaction.

others and from the physical environment (evocation); and the ways in which one's physical and social environments are altered once inhabited (manipulation). These three processes are shown in Figure 15.1.

Further research is needed to determine whether the causal arrows in the figure run in both directions. Does the choice of a mate who is similar in personality, for example, create a social environment that reinforces that personality and makes it more stable over time (Neyer & Lehnart, 2007)? Does the conflict evoked by disagreeable people create a social environment in which they receive a lot of negative feedback, hence maintaining their disagreeable personality? Does the wide variety of manipulative tactics used by emotionally unstable individuals—from hardball to threats to sulking, whining, and pouting—create a social environment that is indeed rocked with greater turmoil, thus maintaining the personality disposition of neuroticism? Research within the next decade will undoubtedly answer these questions.

SUMMARY AND EVALUATION

The personality characteristics we carry with us affect the ways in which we interact with other people occupying our social world. The reciprocal influences of personality and social interactions have brought the fields of personality psychology and social psychology closer together (Swann & Selye, 2005).

This chapter described three key processes by which personality affects social interaction. First, we *select* people and environments, choosing the social situations to which we expose ourselves. In selecting a mate, for example, people worldwide look for mates who are dependable, are emotionally stable, and have a pleasing disposition. Furthermore, we tend to select mates who are similar in personality to ourselves, a process known as assortative mating. Complementary needs theory—the idea that opposites attract when it comes to human mating—has received no empirical support. Those who fail to get what they want—for example, ending up with mates who are emotionally unstable or disagreeable—tend to be unhappy with their marriages and tend to divorce more often than those who succeed in choosing what they want.

The process of selection extends beyond the choice of romantic partners. The personality trait of shyness, for example, is linked with avoiding gynecological exams, entering risky sexual situations by failing to bring up the topic of contraception, and avoiding risky situations that involve gambling money. Similarly, high sensation-seeking heterosexual males tend to choose risky sexual situations, such as having unprotected sex and sex with a larger number of partners.

Second, we *evoke* emotions and actions in others. These evocations are based, in part, on our personality characteristics. In a study of the ways in which men and women anger and upset their romantic partners, the strongest predictors of anger and upset are low Agreeableness and low Emotional Stability. Those low on Agreeableness, for example, tend to create a lot of conflict in their social situations, including with friends and romantic partners, and they tend to be socially victimized during their high school years. Furthermore, in a phenomenon known as expectancy confirmation, our beliefs about the personality characteristics of others sometimes evoke in others precisely the behaviors we expect. A belief that someone is hostile, for example, tends to elicit hostile behavior from that person.

Manipulation is the third process and is defined as the ways in which people intentionally influence and exploit others. Humans use many tactics for influencing others, including charm, silent treatment, coercion, reason, regression, and self-abasement. Men and women use these tactics approximately equally, with the exception of regression, which is used slightly more often by women. Personality characteristics play a key role in which tactics we use to influence others. Emotionally unstable people, for example, tend to use regression and the silent treatment. They also tend to use reason and monetary reward, though, suggesting some nonintuitive links between personality and tactics of manipulation. People high on Intellect–Openness tend to use reason; those low on this dimension tend to use the social comparison tactic.

One personality trait linked with manipulation tactics is called Machiavellianism. The high Mach tends to tell people what they want to hear, to use flattery to get what he or she wants, and to rely heavily on lying and deception. In the mating domain, for example, high Machs are more likely to feign love in order to get sex, use drugs and alcohol to render a potential sex partner more vulnerable, and even express a willingness to use force to get sex. High Machs also betray the trust of others, sometimes feigning cooperation before defecting. They are also more likely than low Machs to steal and then to lie about stealing when they are caught. The success of the high Mach seems to depend heavily on context. In loosely structured social situations and work organizations, high Machs can wheel and deal, using their manipulative, conning strategies to great effect. In more tightly structured, rule-bound situations, however, low Machs outperform high Machs.

All three processes have been documented with the personality disposition of narcissism. Narcissists tend to select others who admire them and avoid those who are skeptical of their claims of greatness. They selectively enter social situations in which there are opportunities for glory and avoid situations in which their brilliance will not be seen by others. Narcissists evoke admiration and respect from those who fawn over them, while evoking anger and disgust from those who are victims of their scorn and conceit. In terms of manipulation, narcissists are highly interpersonally exploitative, using friends for wealth or connections and transferring blame to others when things go wrong. Examining all these processes with respect to narcissists creates a fascinating portrait of the ways in which personality is strongly connected with the social interactions we create and the social environments we inhabit.

In summary, personality is predictably and systematically linked with social interaction through the ways in which we select our partners and social worlds, the ways in which we evoke responses from people we have initially chosen, and the ways in which we influence those people to attain our desired ends.

KEY TERMS

16

Sex, Gender, and Personality

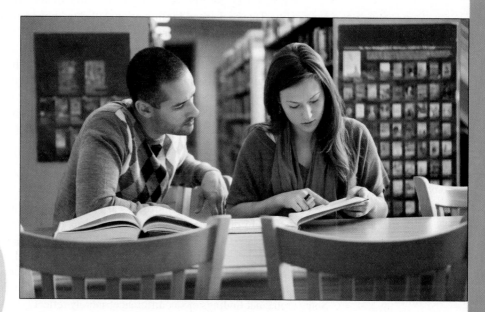

Some differences in personality between adult men and women are hypothesized to result from environmental events that occur during adolescence.
© Monashee Frantz/age fotostock RF

"Despite the advances of feminism, escalating levels of sexism and violence—from undervalued intelligence to sexual harassment in elementary school—cause girls to stifle their creative spirit and natural impulses, which ultimately destroys their self-esteem" (Pipher, 1994, bookjacket). This is a quotation from the book *Reviving Ophelia,* which remained on the best-seller list for an astonishing 135 weeks (Kling et al., 1999). The sentiment expresses widespread belief that women suffer lower self-esteem than men do and that this difference in adult personality is caused by destructive events during development.

Although we cannot know with certainty why *Reviving Ophelia* remained popular for so long, several possibilities warrant consideration. First, people are intrinsically fascinated with psychological **sex differences:** average differences between women and men in personality or behavior. Second, many people are concerned with the political implications of findings of sex differences. Will such findings be used to foster gender stereotypes? Will findings be used to oppress women? Third, people are concerned with the practical implications of sex differences for their everyday lives. Will knowledge of sex differences help people to understand and communicate better and reduce conflict between genders?

This chapter focuses centrally on the scientific issues, but it also discusses the broader debate about the scientific findings. Are women and men basically different or basically the same when it comes to personality? Have the differences been exaggerated because of stereotypes people have about what women and men are like? Which theories provide compelling explanations for sex-linked features of personality? As used in this book, the phrase *sex differences* simply refers to an average difference between women and men on certain characteristics, such as height, body fat distribution, or personality characteristics, with no prejudgment about the cause of the difference.

We begin by briefly sketching the history of the study of sex differences in personality. This background information will show how complex this topic is: we will see that the definition of **gender,** or social interpretations of what it means to be a man or a woman, can change over time. Next, we look at some of the techniques psychologists use to identify sex differences from research data. We examine sex differences in traits such as assertiveness, criminality, and sexuality, and use these differences to explore the fascinating topic of **gender stereotypes:** beliefs about how men and women differ or are supposed to differ, in contrast to what the actual differences are. Finally, we explore theories that attempt to explain the origins of these sex differences.

The Science and Politics of Studying Sex and Gender

Few topics generate as much controversy as the study of sex differences; "public debates about the nature of women and men are frequently in the spotlight, whether in media reports on the latest sex difference findings or in highly publicized legal cases involving single-sex educational institutions or sexual harassment" (Deaux & LaFrance, 1998, p. 788). Some worry, for example, that findings of sex differences might be used to support certain political agendas, such as excluding women from leadership or work roles. Some argue that findings of sex differences merely reflect gender stereotypes rather than real differences. Some psychologists argue that any discovery of sex differences merely reflects the biases of the scientists and are not objective descriptions of reality. Indeed, some psychologists, such as Roy Baumeister, have advocated stopping research on sex differences because findings of sex differences might conflict with ideals of egalitarianism (Baumeister, 1988), although he has since reversed his views on this (personal communication, May 17, 2006) and has published articles on sex differences.

Others argue, however, that both scientific psychology and social change will be impossible without coming to terms with the real sex differences that exist. Feminist psychologist Alice Eagly (1995), for example, argues that sex differences exist, they are consistent across studies, and they should not be ignored merely because they are perceived to conflict with certain political agendas. Indeed, Eagly argues that feminists who try to minimize these differences or pretend that they do not exist hamper the feminist agenda by presenting a dogma that is out of touch with reality. Still others, such as Janet Hyde, argue that sex differences have been exaggerated and that there is so much overlap between the sexes on most personality traits that the differences are minimal (Hyde, 2005; Hyde & Plant, 1995). We will examine these contrasting positions in more detail.

History of the Study of Sex Differences

Before 1973, relatively little attention was paid to sex differences. Indeed, in psychology research, it was common practice to use participants of only one sex, most often males. And even when both men and women were studied, few articles actually analyzed or reported whether the effects differed for men and women.

All of this changed in the early 1970s (Eagly, 1995; Hoyenga & Hoyenga, 1993). In 1974, Eleanor Maccoby and Carol Jacklyn published a classic book, *The Psychology of Sex Differences,* in which they reviewed hundreds of studies and drew several key conclusions about how men and women differed. They concluded that women were slightly better than men at verbal ability. Men were slightly better than women in mathematical ability (e.g., geometry, algebra) and spatial ability (e.g., ability to visualize what a three-dimensional object would look like if it were rotated in space by

90 degrees). In terms of *personality* characteristics, they concluded that only one sex difference existed: men were more aggressive than women. With other aspects of personality and social behavior, they concluded that there was not enough evidence to determine whether men and women differed. Overall, they concluded that sex differences were few in number and trivial in importance.

The *Psychology of Sex Differences* set off an avalanche of research on the topic. The book itself was criticized on various grounds. Some argued that many more sex differences existed than were portrayed by Maccoby and Jacklyn (Block, 1983). Others challenged the conclusion that men were more aggressive than women (Frodi, Macauley, & Thome, 1977). Furthermore, the methods by which the authors drew their conclusions, although standard practice at that time, were crude by today's standards.

Following the publication of *The Psychology of Sex Differences,* psychology journals changed their reporting practices. They started to require authors to calculate and report sex differences. Furthermore, protests that many of the findings in psychology were based primarily on studies of men led to calls for the greater inclusion of women as participants. There followed an explosion of research on sex differences. Literally thousands of studies were conducted on the ways in which men and women differed. Indeed, by 1992, the federal government had required members of both sexes to be represented in all federally funded research (unless, of course, there was a legitimate reason to limit the research to one sex, such as studies of ovarian or prostate cancer).

Since Maccoby and Jacklyn's early work, researchers have developed a more precise quantitative procedure for examining conclusions across studies and thus for determining sex differences, called meta-analysis. Recall that meta-analysis is a statistical method for summarizing the findings of large numbers of individual studies. Meta-analysis did not gain popularity until the mid-1980s. Meta-analysis allows researchers to calculate with greater objectivity and precision whether a particular difference—such as a sex difference—is consistent across studies. Furthermore, it allows researchers to estimate how large the difference actually is—called the **effect size**.

Calculation of Effect Size: How Large Are the Sex Differences?

The most commonly used statistic in meta-analysis is the effect size, or *d* statistic. The *d* statistic is used to express a difference in standard deviation units (see Chapter 2). A *d* of 0.50 means that the average difference between two groups is half a standard deviation. A *d* of 1.00 means that the difference between the groups is one full standard deviation. A *d* of 0.25 means that the difference between the groups is one-quarter of a standard deviation. An effect size can be calculated for each study of sex differences and then averaged across studies to give a more precise and objective assessment of whether the sexes differ and, if so, by how much.

Most meta-analyses have adopted a convention for interpreting effect sizes (Cohen, 1977):

d Score	Meaning
0.20 or −0.20	Small difference
0.50 or −0.50	Medium difference
0.80 or −0.80	Large difference

When comparing men to women, assume that positive *d* scores, such as 0.20 or 0.50, indicate that men score higher than women. Negative *d* scores, such as −0.20 or −0.50, indicate that women score higher than men. For example, a *d* score of −0.85 means that women score much higher on a particular trait.

When it comes to who can throw a ball farther, the effect size for the difference between men and women is 2.00, in favor of the men. Although this is a large difference in average ability, there will nevertheless be some women who can throw farther than most men because the distributions still overlap.

© *Design Pics/SuperStock RF*

To get a feel for various effect sizes, let's examine a few findings outside the realm of personality. Which sex can throw a ball farther, men or women? Although there are great individual differences within each sex, it is clear that men can, on average, throw farther than women. The *d* is approximately 2.00 (Ashmore, 1990). This means that the sexes differ, on average, by two full standard deviations, which is considered quite large. Which sex has a higher grade point average in college? The *d* for grade point average is −0.04, which is very close to zero. This means that men and women are essentially the same in their grade point average.

Which sex scores higher in verbal ability? It turns out that women are slightly better than men, but the *d* is only −0.11. Are men better at math? The *d* here also turns out to be quite small, only 0.15. These findings are in line with a vast literature that now documents that men and women are essentially the same (or do not differ by much) on most measures of cognitive ability (Hyde, 2005, 2014). About the only well-documented exception to this conclusion pertains to spatial rotation ability, such as the spatial ability involved in throwing a spear (or football) so that it correctly anticipates the trajectory of a moving object, such as an animal or a receiver. The *d* for this sort of spatial ability is 0.73, which comes close to the standard for "large" (Ashmore, 1990).

It is important to keep in mind that even large effect sizes for average sex differences do not necessarily have implications for any particular individual. Even with a *d* of 2.00 for throwing distance, some women can throw much farther than the average man, and some men cannot throw as far as the average woman. This overlap in the distributions of the sexes must be kept in mind when evaluating effect sizes (see Figure 16.1).

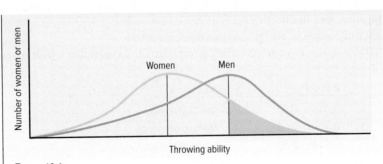

Figure 16.1

Overlap between the sexes in context of a mean difference. Even when one sex greatly exceeds the other in a particular ability, there is a large area of overlap. Women whose throwing ability falls in the shaded area exceed the throwing ability of the average man.

Minimalists and Maximalists

A central focus of the debate on sex differences follows from a consideration of effect sizes—on whether sex differences are small and relatively inconsequential or substantial and important. Those who describe sex differences as small and inconsequential take the **minimalist** position and offer two arguments. The first is that, empirically, most findings of sex differences show small magnitudes of effect (Deaux, 1984; Hyde, 2005, 2014; Hyde & Plant, 1995). Minimalists tend to emphasize that the distributions of men and women on any given personality variable show tremendous overlap, which reflect their small magnitude of effect (see Figure 16.1 for an example of distribution overlap). A second argument advanced by minimalists is that whatever differences exist do not have much practical importance for behavior in everyday life. If the sex differences are small and don't have consequences for people's lives, then perhaps we should concentrate on other psychological issues that are more important.

In contrast, those who take the **maximalist** position tend to argue that the magnitude of sex differences is comparable to the magnitude of many other effects in psychology and should not be trivialized (Eagly, 1995). Some sex differences tend to be small in magnitude, others are large in magnitude, and many are in the moderate range, according to this view. Furthermore, Eagly notes that even small sex differences can have large practical importance. A small sex difference in helping behavior, for example, could result in a large sex difference in the number of lives women and men aid over the long run. As you read through this chapter, you should keep in mind the range of positions psychologists have taken on sex differences, from the minimalist stance to the maximalist stance.

Sex Differences in Personality

We begin by examining sex differences in temperament in children. The five-factor model of personality provides a convenient framework for organizing a number of findings about sex differences in personality (see Table 16.1). Then we discuss sex differences in other domains of personality, such as sexuality, criminality and physical aggression, depression and psychopathy, and the interaction patterns of men and women in groups.

Temperament in Children

The importance of sex differences in temperament is aptly summarized by the authors of a meta-analysis: "The question of gender differences in temperament is arguably one of the most fundamental questions in gender differences research in the areas of personality and social behavior. Temperament reflects biologically based emotional and behavioral consistencies that appear early in life and predict—often in conjunction with other factors—patterns and outcomes in numerous other domains such as psychopathology and personality" (Else-Quest et al., 2006, p. 33). These authors conducted the most massive meta-analysis ever undertaken of sex differences in temperament in children ranging in age from 3 to 13.

The sex differences they discovered ranged from substantial to negligible. **Inhibitory control** showed the largest sex difference, with a $d = -0.41$, which is considered in the moderate range. Inhibitory control refers to the ability to control inappropriate responses or behaviors. A more recent study found very large gender differences on the trait of impulsivity, with boys being less able to control their impulses ($d = -0.72$) (Olino et al., 2013). As the authors summarize, "these findings may represent an overall better ability of girls to regulate or allocate their attention" and suppress socially undesirable behavior (Else-Quest et al., 2006, p. 61). **Perceptual sensitivity**—the ability to detect subtle stimuli from the environment—also showed a sex difference favoring girls ($d = -0.38$). Girls, on average, appear to be more sensitive than boys to subtle and low-intensity signals from their external world. Inhibitory control is related to the later development of the personality trait of Conscientiousness. Interestingly, the sex difference appears to fade, because adult men and women do not differ much in conscientiousness.

Surgency, a cluster including approach behavior, high activity, and impulsivity, showed a sex difference ($d = 0.38$), with boys scoring higher than girls. Perhaps the combination of high surgency and low inhibitory control accounts for the fact that boys tend to get into more disciplinary difficulties in school in the early years of their lives. Some subcomponents of surgency showed slightly smaller sex differences, such as activity level ($d = 0.33$) and high-intensity pleasure ($d = 0.30$), which is consistent with the finding that boys are more likely than girls to engage in rough-and-tumble play.

The combination of low inhibitory control and high surgency may account for another reliable gender difference—a difference in the domain of *physical aggressiveness*. Using an act frequency measure based on codings of actual behavior, Zakriski, Wright, and Underwood (2005) found a $d = 0.60$, indicating that boys were more physically aggressive than girls (approximate age 13).

In contrast to inhibitory control and surgency, girls and boys showed virtually no difference in a summary variable called **negative affectivity**, which includes components such as anger, difficulty, amount of distress, and sadness. A more fine-grained analysis of negative emotions, however, reveals that girls are higher on fearfulness ($d = -0.34$), whereas boys are higher on anger expression ($d = -0.34$) (Olino et al., 2013).

In summary, meta-analysis of temperament in children between the ages of 3 and 13 suggests a few gender differences of moderate magnitude. Girls show more inhibitory control and higher fearfulness. Boys show higher levels of surgency, higher levels of activity, more impulsivity, and more anger in the domain of emotional expression. These are average sex differences, however, which means that the distributions overlap considerably.

Five-Factor Model

The five-factor model provides a broad set of personality traits within which we can examine whether women and men differ.

Extraversion

Three facets of extraversion have been examined for sex differences: gregariousness, assertiveness, and activity. Women score slightly higher on gregariousness than men, but the difference is quite small. Similarly, men score slightly higher on activity level. A study of personality in 50 different cultures revealed a relatively small gender difference ($d = 0.15$) on extraversion (McCrae et al., 2005b). A facet analysis of gender differences in extraversion reveals a more interesting picture (De Bolle et al., 2015). Women score higher on the facets of Warmth ($d = -0.29$) and Gregariousness ($d = -0.26$), whereas men score higher on Assertiveness ($d = 0.24$) and Excitement Seeking ($d = 0.25$). A related finding, emerging from a study of 127 samples in 70 countries

($N = 77,528$), is that men place a greater importance on the *value of power* than do women (Schwartz & Rubel, 2005). That is, men tend to value social status and dominance over other people more than women.

The medium-size sex difference in assertiveness may show up in social behavior in group contexts. A number of studies suggest that men interrupt others in conversation more than women do in mixed-sex groups (Hoyenga & Hoyenga, 1993). An important source of conflict between the sexes—unwanted interruptions of dialogue—may stem from this moderate sex difference in assertiveness.

Studies show that women naturally smile more than men. Researchers disagree, however, on what this sex difference means; some suggest smiling is a sign of agreeableness, whereas others hold that smiling is a form of submissiveness or a way to ease tension in social situations.

© *Realistic Reflections RF*

Agreeableness

A study of 50 cultures revealed a small to medium gender difference ($d = -0.32$) on Agreeableness, indicating that women score higher than men (McCrae et al., 2005b; Schmitt et al., 2008). Older adults ranging in age from 65 to 98 also show a mean gender difference in Agreeableness ($d = -0.35$), with women scoring higher than men (Chapman et al., 2007; Wood, Nye, & Saucier, 2010). Two facets of agreeableness have been examined: trust and tender-mindedness. **Trust** is the proclivity to cooperate with others, giving others the benefit of the doubt, and viewing one's fellow human beings as basically good at heart. **Tender-mindedness** is a nurturant proclivity—having empathy for others and being sympathetic with those who are downtrodden. As you can see in Table 16.1, women score as more trusting than men. Women are also substantially more tender-minded than men (e.g., caring, giving), with a large effect size of -0.97, which is clearly well in the range considered to be large. Another facet of Agreeableness is Modesty; women are more modest than men in general ($d = -0.26$) (De Bolle et al., 2015). Recent research has focused on the context-specificity of these sex differences. Women seem to be more cooperative than men in mixed-sex social interactions (Balliet et al., 2011). In contrast, men are slightly more cooperative than women in same-sex social interactions (Balliet et al., 2011).

Another finding related to Agreeableness pertains to *smiling*. Meta-analyses show that women smile more often than men, with an effect size of -0.60 (Hall, 1984). If smiling reflects an agreeable personality disposition, we can conclude that women are more agreeable than men. However, some researchers view smiling as a sign of submissiveness rather than agreeableness (Eagly, 1995). Furthermore, some argue that it is low-status people who do a lot of smiling. It's possible that smiling reflects agreeableness in some contexts and submissiveness in other contexts.

Aggressiveness   Aggressiveness falls at the opposite end of agreeableness. It will not surprise you that men are more physically aggressive than women. This shows up in personality tests, in aggressive fantasies, and in actual measures of behavior (Hyde, 1986). In general, the effect sizes for aggression are largest for projective tests, such as the TAT ($d = 0.86$), the next largest for peer report measures of aggression ($d = 0.63$), and the smallest for self-report measures of aggression ($d = 0.40$). Fantasy measures of aggression, which assess how often people imagine aggressing against others, show large sex differences, with an effect size of 0.84.

These sex differences can have profound consequences for everyday life. The effect size for violent crimes is especially striking. Worldwide, men commit roughly

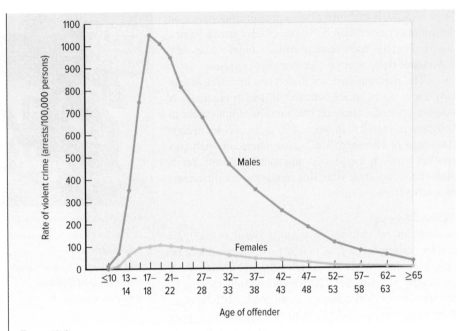

Figure 16.2

Arrest rates for violent crime in the United States as a function of age and gender.

90 percent of all homicides, and most of the victims of these homicides are other men (Buss, 2005b; Daly & Wilson, 1988). Furthermore, men commit more violent crimes of all sorts, ranging from assaults to gang wars. Figure 16.2 shows the arrest rate for violent crimes within the United States as a function of age and gender. As you can see, men commit these crimes far more than women. The largest sex differences in violent crimes show up just after puberty, peaking in adolescence and the early twenties. After age 50, violent crimes start to decline, and men and women become much more similar to each other in criminal aggressiveness.

These findings are not limited to the United States. In all cultures for which there are data, the vast majority of killings and other violent crimes are committed by young men (Daly & Wilson, 1988; Pinker, 2011). Psychologically, a key reason for the gender difference is that women are much more sensitive than men to punishment ($d = -.33$), whereas men seem more inclined to take risks, oblivious to the punishments they may receive (Cross, Copping, & Campbell, 2011). These culturally universal findings lend credence to theories that offer evolutionary explanations for some of the sex differences (see Chapter 8). It is important to keep in mind that these forms of aggression refer to physical violence. Other forms of aggression, specifically "relational aggression" such as verbal insults and gossip about others, show either no gender differences or a slight tendency for women to score higher (e.g., Hess et al., 2010; Ostrov & Godleski, 2010).

Conscientiousness

The 50-culture study revealed a negligible sex difference ($d = -0.14$) on overall levels of Conscientiousness (McCrae et al., 2005b). Only one facet of Conscientiousness has been scrutinized for sex differences—order. Women score slightly higher than men on order, with an effect size of only −0.13, although a larger cross-cultural study revealed a slightly larger gender difference in order ($d = -0.24$) (De Bolle et al., 2015). This is small enough to conclude that men and women are essentially the same on this dimension.

Nonetheless, even very small effects can sometimes have large cumulative effects over time. For example, a small difference in order between marriage partners may result in a large number of arguments about housecleaning over the course of a year.

Emotional Stability

Emotional Stability may be the most value-laden dimension of the five-factor model. As you will recall from Chapter 3, at one end of the dimension are those who are steady, calm, and stable. One can label this end "emotionally stable." The opposite end is characterized by volatility and changeability of mood. Although many have labeled this end of the dimension "emotionally unstable" or "neurotic," one could just as easily label it as "emotionally expressive." The important point to keep in mind is the psychological meaning of the dimension—the actual traits it includes—rather than the label given to either extreme.

The 50-culture study revealed that Emotional Stability shows the largest sex difference ($d = -0.49$) in the five-factor model, indicating that women are moderately lower than men on this dimension (McCrae et al., 2005b; see also Schmitt et al., 2008). A study of 10 Arab countries—Kuwait, Saudi Arabia, Emirates, Oman, Egypt, Syria, Lebanon, Palestine (Nablus and Gaza), Jordan, and Iraq—found similar sex differences using a measure of anxiety (Abdel-Khalek & Alansari, 2004). Older adults ranging in age from 65 to 98 also show a mean sex difference in Emotional Stability ($d = -0.52$), with women scoring lower than men (Chapman et al., 2007). The Anxiety facet of this factor shows the largest gender difference across cultures, with women scoring more in the anxious direction ($d = -0.54$) (De Bolle et al., 2015). And more detailed measures show that women are especially high on fearfulness ($d = -1.04$) (Campbell et al., 2016).

Intellect–Openness to Experience

The 50-culture study revealed essentially no sex differences ($d = -0.07$) in Intellect–Openness to experience (McCrae et al., 2005b), similar to a 55-culture study that found a $d = -0.05$ (Schmitt et al., 2008). Botwin and colleagues (1997) examined sex differences in Intellect–Openness to experience using three data sources: self-report, spouse-report, and independent interviewer reports (one male and one female interviewer). Separate analyses of these three data sources yielded no sex differences in Openness–Intellect. And a massive cross-cultural study of adolescents, college students, and adults reveals essentially no gender differences in Openness to Experience at the global trait level. Nonetheless, a facet analysis reveals that women score higher on two facets of Openness—Fantasy and especially Ideas (De Bolle et al., 2015). Table 16.1 summarizes the key findings of gender differences in the key facets of the five factor model of personality.

Basic Emotions: Frequency and Intensity

Emotions are central to personality, so much so that we devoted an entire chapter to them (Chapter 13). Research conducted on a cross-cultural scale has revealed precisely where the sexes differ in their experiences of emotions and where the sexes are essentially the same. The most extensive study examined 2,199 Australians and an international sample of 6,868 participants drawn from 41 different countries (Brebner, 2003). Eight fundamental emotions were examined, four "positive" emotions (Affection, Joy, Contentment, Pride) and four "negative" emotions (Fear, Anger, Sadness, Guilt). Participants used rating scales to indicate (1) how frequently they experienced each emotion and (2) the intensity with which they experienced each emotion. The basic findings are summarized in Table 16.2.

Table 16.1 Effect Sizes for Gender Differences in Facets of Personality within the Five Factor Model

Dimension	Effect Size
Extraversion	
Gregariousness	−0.26
Warmth	−0.29
Assertiveness	0.24
Activity	0.09
Excitement Seeking	0.25
Agreeableness	
Trust	−0.25
Tender-mindedness	−0.97
Modesty	−0.26
Aggressive Ideation	0.84
Conscientiousness	
Order	−0.24
Emotional Stability	
Anxiety	−0.54
Fearfulness	−1.04
Intellect-Openness	
Ideas	0.03
Fantasy	−0.31
Feelings	−0.42

Note: Positive numbers indicate that men score higher than women; negative numbers indicate that women score higher than men.

Table 16.2 Sex Differences in Experience of Emotions

Emotion	Frequency	Intensity
Positive Emotions	0.20	0.23
Affection	0.30	0.25
Joy	0.16	0.26
Contentment	0.13	0.18
Pride	ns	ns
Negative Emotions	0.14	0.25
Fear	0.17	0.26
Anger	0.05	0.14
Sadness	0.16	0.28
Guilt	ns	0.07

Note: Entries in the table are effect sizes (*d*). The designation "ns" indicates that the sex difference was not significant. Positive values indicate that women report experiencing the emotion more frequently or intensely than do men.

Source: Brebner (2003).

There are small, but statistically significant differences in the experience of emotions in this international sample. All point to women experiencing both positive emotions *and* negative emotions more frequently and intensely than do men. In the positive domain, affection and joy show the largest sex differences. Pride, in contrast, shows no sex difference in either frequency or intensity. In the negative domain, women experience fear and sadness more than men, especially in the reported intensity of the experience. Guilt, in contrast, shows a minimal gender difference in intensity and no difference in frequency—perhaps contradicting the stereotype that women are more guilt prone than men. These results must be qualified in two ways. First, the effect sizes are generally small. Second, other research has documented that more specialized explorations of emotions reveal some reversals of these sex differences, such as women experiencing more intense jealousy in response to the emotional infidelity of a partner (see Chapter 8).

One of the most common complaints that women express about men is that they don't express their emotions enough (Buss, 2016). Men, in contrast, often complain that women are too emotional. The results point to one possible reason for these complaints— perhaps men don't *express* their emotions because they literally don't *experience* emotions as frequently or as intensely as do women.

Other Dimensions of Personality

Several dimensions of personality are related to, but not directly subsumed by, the five-factor model of personality. We will examine three: self-esteem, sexuality and mating, and the people–things dimension.

Self-Esteem

A topic of major interest to women and men is self-esteem, or how good we feel about ourselves. This is reflected in the many popular books on the topic, such as *10 Simple Solutions for Building Self-Esteem* (Schiraldi, 2007). Although researchers have explored many facets of self-esteem, such as esteem of one's athletic abilities and esteem of one's social skills, by far the most frequently measured component is **global self-esteem**, defined as "the level of global regard that one has for the self as a person" (Harter, 1993, p. 88). Global self-esteem can range from highly positive to highly negative and reflects an overall evaluation of the self (Kling et al., 1999).

Global self-esteem is linked with many aspects of functioning and is central to mental health. Those with high self-esteem appear to cope better with the stresses and strains of daily life. In laboratory studies, when faced with negative feedback about one's performance, those with high self-esteem perform better on cognitive tasks. Those with high self-esteem tend to take credit for their successes but deny responsibility for their failures (Kling et al., 1999).

Meta-analyses have yielded an interesting pattern of sex differences (Feingold, 1994; Kling et al., 1999). The overall effect size is relatively small ($d = 0.21$), with males scoring slightly higher than females in self-esteem (Kling et al., 1999). The fascinating finding, however, emerged when the researchers analyzed sex differences in self-esteem according to the age of the participants. Young children (ages 7–10) showed only a slight sex difference in self-esteem ($d = 0.16$). As the children approached adolescence, however, the gap between the sexes widened. At ages 11–14, d was 0.23. And the sex difference peaked during the ages of 15–18 ($d = 0.33$). Females seem to suffer from lower self-esteem than males as they hit their mid- to late teens. The good news is that in adulthood the self-esteem gap starts to close. During the ages of 19–22, the effect size shrinks to 0.18. During the ages of 23–59, the sexes come even closer, with a d of 0.10.

And during older age, from 60 on up, the *d* is only −0.03, which means that the males and females are virtually identical in self-esteem.

The magnitudes of all these effects are relatively small, even during adolescence, when the gap between the sexes is the widest. The widespread fear that women's self-esteem is permanently damaged seems somewhat exaggerated in light of this empirical evidence. Nonetheless, even small differences in self-esteem can be extremely important to day-to-day well-being, so this sex difference should not be dismissed. It will be interesting for researchers to explore why females appear to lose self-esteem in adolescence relative to males and whether programs that attempt to raise self-esteem are successful.

When it comes to attitudes about casual sex, men tend to be more interested in women than women are in men, on average.

© *Jon Feingersh/Blend Images LLC RF*

Sexuality, Emotional Investment, and Mating

As we saw in Chapter 3, individual differences in sexuality show some overlap with the five-factor model of personality, but not perfect overlap (Schmitt & Buss, 2000). Two reviews concluded that there exist large sex differences in the desire for sexual variety (Schmitt et al., 2012; Petersen & Hyde, 2010). Men are more likely to have more permissive attitudes toward casual sex (*d* = .45) and view pornography more often (*d* = .63). Men more than women also desire a larger number of sex partners, have more frequent sexual fantasies, and are more willing to accept offers of sex from a stranger (Hald & Hogh-Olesen, 2010).

Can men and women be "just friends"? It turns out that men have more difficulty than do women in being friends with the opposite sex. Men are more likely than women to initiate friendship with someone of the opposite sex because they are sexually attracted to them; more likely to actually become sexually attracted to their opposite-sex friends; and more likely to dissolve such friendships if they do not result in sex (Bleske-Rechek & Buss, 2001).

Men are more likely than women to be sexually aggressive in the sense of trying to force women to have sex when women express an unwillingness to have sex (Buss, 2016). Nonetheless, not all men are sexually aggressive. Some studies have shown that men who indicate "hostile masculinity" (domineering and degrading attitudes toward women) and men who lack the personality disposition of empathy are most likely to report using sexual aggression (Wheeler, George, & Dahl, 2002). Furthermore, men who are narcissistic are especially likely to express rape-supportive beliefs and to lack empathy for rape victims (Bushman et al., 2003). So, although the sexes can be said to differ overall in sexual aggression, it really appears to be limited to a subset of men—those who are narcissistic, lack empathy, and display hostile masculinity.

If men score higher in desire for sexual variety, women typically score higher in "emotional investment," a cluster of items including *loving, lovable, romantic, affectionate, cuddlesome, compassionate,* and *passionate* (Schmitt & Buss, 2000). A study of 48 nations found an average effect size of −.39 (Schmitt et al., 2009). The authors interpret this sex difference as stemming from the evolution of sex differences in attachment, with women showing higher levels of emotional attachment both to children and to romantic partners (Schmitt et al., 2009). Women between the ages of 18 and 39 also report greater life longings for family and romantic partners (Kotter-Gruhn et al., 2009).

People–Things Dimension

Another dimension of personality has been labeled the **people–things dimension** (Lippa, 1998; Little, 1972a, 1972b). This refers to the nature of vocational interests. People who score toward the "things" end of the dimension prefer vocations that deal with impersonal objects—machines, tools, or materials. Examples include carpenters, auto mechanics, building contractors, tool makers, and farmers. Those scoring toward the "people" end of the dimension prefer social occupations, which involve thinking about others, caring for others, or directing others. Examples include high school teachers, social workers, nurses, and religious counselors.

As you might imagine, there are strong sex differences in these occupational preferences. The correlation between sex and the people–things dimension is .56, or a *d* of roughly 1.35, which means that men are more likely to score at the things end of the dimension, and women are more likely to score at the people end (Lippa, 1998). A study of more than half a million people found a *d* of 0.93, which is considered quite large (Su, Rounds, & Armstrong, 2009). When girls are asked to describe themselves spontaneously, they are more likely than boys to make references to their close relationships. They are more likely to value personal qualities linked to group harmony, such as sensitivity to others. And they are more likely to identify their personal relationships as central to their identity as a person (Gabriel & Gardner, 1999). The people–thing distinction is similar to the empathizing–systemizing distinction. **Empathizing** refers to tuning in to other people's thoughts and feelings. **Systemizing** is the drive to comprehend how things work, how systems are built, and how inputs into systems produce outputs (Baron-Cohen, 2003). Women score higher on empathizing, men higher on systemizing, which may partially explain gender differences in occupational preferences—women more than men prefer teaching and helping professions; men more than women gravitate toward construction and engineering (Wright et al., 2015).

Although these results are certainly not surprising in that they fit with our stereotypes of women and men, it is interesting that they were correctly identified more than a century ago: "[Researchers] found as the greatest difference between men and women that in the relative strength of the interest in things and their mechanisms [stronger in men] and the interest in persons and their feelings [stronger in women]" (Thorndike, 1911, p. 31).

These preferences are likely to have important consequences for the occupations women and men select and the pleasurable activities they pursue. Men, being more thing-oriented, are more likely to be found tinkering with engines or building wooden structures in their spare time. Women, being more people-oriented, are more likely to prefer planning weekend activities around other people.

Masculinity, Femininity, Androgyny, and Sex Roles

Women and men differ in a few dimensions: assertiveness, tender-mindedness, and anxiety, as well as in aggression, sexuality, and depression. But do these differences mean that there is such a thing as a masculine or feminine personality? This section explores conceptions of masculinity and femininity and how the treatment of these topics has changed over time.

In the 1930s, personality researchers began to notice that men and women differed in their responses to a number of personality items on large inventories. For example, when asked whether they preferred to take baths or showers, women indicated that they preferred baths, whereas men indicated that they preferred showers. Based on

A Closer Look   Sex Differences in Depression

Depression is marked by characteristics such as low self-esteem, pessimism (expecting the worst to happen), and the perception that one has little control over one's life. It's one of the most common psychological maladies of modern humans, and there is evidence that the rate of depression is increasing. Five studies comprised of 39,000 individuals living in five areas of the world revealed that young people are more likely than older people to have experienced at least one major episode of depression (Nesse & Williams, 1994). Moreover, the incidence of depression appears to be higher in more economically developed cultures (Nesse & Williams, 1994).

Adult men and women differ in the incidence of depression and in the nature of their depressive symptoms, but the sexes don't start out different. In childhood, there are no sex differences in depression. After puberty, however, women show a depression rate roughly twice that of men (Hoyenga & Hoyenga, 1993). Roughly 25 percent of all women have at least one depressive episode in their lifetimes. In contrast, only 10 percent of all men will have a depressive episode. The largest sex differences in depression show up between the ages of 18 and 44. After that, the sexes start to converge.

The following list contains some of the critical aspects of sex differences in depressive symptoms (Hoyenga & Hoyenga, 1993):

1. Depressed women more often than depressed men report excessive eating and weight gain as one of the symptoms (although loss of appetite is the most common symptom of depression in both sexes).
2. Women are more likely to cry when depressed and to confront their feelings directly; men are more likely to become aggressive when depressed.
3. Depressed women are more likely than men to seek treatment; depressed men are more likely simply to miss work.
4. Nervous activity (e.g., fidgeting) is more common in depressed women than in depressed men; inactivity is more common in depressed men than in depressed women.
5. Among depressed college students, men are more socially withdrawn, more likely to use drugs, and more likely to experience aches and pains; women are more likely to experience hurt feelings and a decline in self-esteem.
6. Men are more likely to commit suicide "successfully," perhaps because men are more likely to use guns as the method; women are more likely to make nonfatal suicide attempts, perhaps because they use less lethal methods, such as overdosing on pills.

One clue to the sex difference in the nature and rate of depression comes from a large-scale study of 1,100 community-based adults (Nolen-Hoeksema, Larson, & Grayson, 1999). The researchers speculated that women's greater vulnerability to depressive symptoms may stem from factors such as their lower power in the workplace, their relative lack of control over important areas of their lives, work overload, and lower status in heterosexual relationships. Because they are searching for ways to control their lives, women may start to *ruminate*. **Rumination** involves repeatedly focusing on one's symptoms or distress (e.g., "Why do I continue to feel so bad about myself?" or "Why doesn't my boss like me?"). Because their ruminations fail to lead to effective solutions, according to this theory, women continue to ruminate, and rumination is a key contributor to women's greater experience of depressive symptoms. Women ruminate more than men, and rumination in turn contributes to the perseverance of the depressive symptoms. Nonetheless, the gender difference in rumination is small ($d = -0.24$), and so unlikely to reveal the whole explanation (Johnson & Whisman, 2013).

Another theory is that the greater incidence of depression in women is caused by humans in the modern world living in isolated nuclear families, stripped of the extended kin and other social supports that characterize more traditional societies (Buss, 2000b).

Yet another theory is that women's greater depression is linked with entering mate competition and is caused by dissatisfaction with their physical appearance (Hankin & Abramson, 2001). Indeed, the onset of women's depression and the emergence of the sex difference appears around the age of 13, when heterosexual interactions start to increase. And it is well documented that men place a greater value on physical appearance in their mate selections worldwide, suggesting that women are under increased pressure to compete in the realm of attractiveness (Buss, 2016). Furthermore, body dissatisfaction increases in women around puberty, as does the onset of eating disorders such as binging and purging and dissatisfaction with current weight (Hankin & Abramson, 2001). The final link is that a woman's dissatisfaction with her body and physical appearance is linked with increases in depression. If a woman's self-worth is in part tied up in her physical appearance because of its importance in what men want in a mate, then women's pubertal onset of depression could stem in part from the intensity of mate competition after women hit puberty.

Whatever the origins, sex differences in depression represent one of the largest and most consequential differences in personality.

these sex differences, researchers assumed that the differences could be described by a single personality dimension, with *masculinity* at one end and *femininity* at the other end. A person who scored high on masculinity was assumed to score low on femininity, and vice versa. Researchers assumed that all people could be located on this single masculinity–femininity dimension. Items that showed large sex differences, such as "I enjoy reading *Popular Mechanics*" (men scored higher), and "I would enjoy the work of a librarian" (women scored higher), were used to construct a single scale of masculinity–femininity. But does a single scale with masculinity at one end and femininity at the other end really capture the important individual differences? Can't someone be both masculine *and* feminine? This question led to a new conception of sex-linked personality differences—androgyny.

The Search for Androgyny

In the early 1970s, with the rise of the feminist movement, researchers began to challenge the assumption of a single masculinity–femininity dimension. These new researchers instead started with the premise that masculinity and femininity are independent dimensions. Thus, one can be high on both masculinity and femininity, or low on both dimensions. Or one can be stereotypically masculine: high on masculinity, low on femininity; or one can be stereotypically feminine: high on femininity, low on masculinity. This shift represented a fundamental change in thinking about masculinity, femininity, and sex roles.

Two major personality instruments were published in 1974 to assess people using this new conception of sex roles (Bem, 1974; Spence, Helmreich, & Stapp, 1974). The **masculinity** dimension contained items reflecting assertiveness, boldness, dominance, self-sufficiency, and instrumentality. Those who agreed with personality trait terms connoting these qualities scored high on masculinity. The **femininity** dimension contained items that reflected nurturance, expression of emotions, and empathy. Those who agreed with personality trait terms connoting these qualities scored high on femininity. Those who scored high on both dimensions were labeled **androgynous**, to reflect the notion that a single person could possess both masculine and feminine characteristics. Table 16.3 shows the four possible scores these instruments can yield.

The researchers who developed these questionnaires viewed the androgynous person as the most highly developed. Androgynous persons were presumed to embody the most valuable elements of both sexes, such as the assertiveness to take positive steps in one's job and interpersonal sensitivity to the feelings of others. Furthermore, androgynous persons were presumed to be liberated from the shackles of traditional notions of sex roles. Before proceeding with our analysis, however, pause for a few minutes to determine where you are located on these measures. To find out, fill out the Exercise on pages 504–505.

The popularity of this new conception of sex roles is a testament to the influence of feminism in America. With the rise of the women's movement, traditional ideas about the roles of men and women were cast aside. Women started entering the

Table 16.3 Conception of Sex Roles Developed in the 1970s

	Low Masculinity	High Masculinity
Low Femininity	Undifferentiated	Masculine
High Femininity	Feminine	Androgynous

workforce in record numbers. Some men opted for more nurturant roles. John Lennon, of former Beatles fame, decided to stay at home and raise his son, Sean, while his wife, Yoko Ono, went to work, overseeing a massive financial empire (Coleman, 1992). Many people applauded Lennon for taking on this new liberated role. This political movement reinforced the idea that men were supposed to become more nurturant, caring, and empathic. At the same time, women were supposed to become more assertive as they entered many professions traditionally reserved for men. The psychological trend toward changing the conceptualization and measurement of sex roles reflected this larger political movement.

The new androgynous conception of sex roles, however, was not without its critics. One criticism pertained to the items on the inventories and their correlations with each other. Researchers seemed to assume that masculinity and femininity were single dimensions. Other researchers argued, however, that both constructs were actually multidimensional, containing many facets.

Another criticism goes to the heart of the androgyny concept. It turns out that several studies have found that masculinity and femininity indeed consist of a single, bipolar trait. Those who score high on masculinity, for example, tend to score low on femininity. Those who score high on femininity tend to score low on masculinity (e.g., Deaux & Lewis, 1984).

Exercise?

INSTRUCTIONS: Forty items follow. Each one contains a pair of statements describing contradictory characteristics; that is, you cannot be both at the same time, such as very artistic and not at all artistic. The letters form a scale between the two extremes. Select the letter that describes where you fall on the scale. For example, if you think that you are not at all aggressive, you would choose A. If you think you are very aggressive, you would choose E. If you are in between, you would choose C, or possibly B or D. Be sure to make a choice for every item. Mark your choice by drawing an X through the letter that you select.

1.	Not at all aggressive	A.....B.....C.....D.....E	Very aggressive
2.	Very whiny	A.....B.....C.....D.....E	Not at all whiny
3.	Not at all independent	A.....B.....C.....D.....E	Very independent
4.	Not at all arrogant	A.....B.....C.....D.....E	Very arrogant
5.	Not at all emotional	A.....B.....C.....D.....E	Very emotional
6.	Very submissive	A.....B.....C.....D.....E	Very dominant
7.	Very boastful	A.....B.....C.....D.....E	Not at all boastful
8.	Not at all excitable in a *major* crisis	A.....B.....C.....D.....E	Very excitable in a *major* crisis
9.	Very passive	A.....B.....C.....D.....E	Very active
10.	Not at all egotistical	A.....B.....C.....D.....E	Very egotistical
11.	Not at all able to devote self completely to others	A.....B.....C.....D.....E	Able to devote self completely to others
12.	Not at all spineless	A.....B.....C.....D.....E	Very spineless

Exercise (*Continued*)

13.	Very rough	A.....B.....C.....D.....E	Very gentle
14.	Not at all complaining	A.....B.....C.....D.....E	Very complaining
15.	Not at all helpful to others	A.....B.....C.....D.....E	Very helpful to others
16.	Not at all competitive	A.....B.....C.....D.....E	Very competitive
17.	Subordinates oneself to others	A.....B.....C.....D.....E	Never subordinates oneself to others
18.	Very home-oriented	A.....B.....C.....D.....E	Very worldly
19.	Very greedy	A.....B.....C.....D.....E	Not at all greedy
20.	Not at all kind	A.....B.....C.....D.....E	Very kind
21.	Indifferent to others' approval	A.....B.....C.....D.....E	Highly needful of others' approval
22.	Very dictatorial	A.....B.....C.....D.....E	Not at all dictatorial
23.	Feelings not easily hurt	A.....B.....C.....D.....E	Feelings easily hurt
24.	Doesn't nag	A.....B.....C.....D.....E	Nags a lot
25.	Not at all aware of feelings of others	A.....B.....C.....D.....E	Very aware of feelings of others
26.	Can make decisions easily	A.....B.....C.....D.....E	Has difficulty making decisions
27.	Very fussy	A.....B.....C.....D.....E	Not at all fussy
28.	Gives up very easily	A.....B.....C.....D.....E	Never gives up easily
29.	Very cynical	A.....B.....C.....D.....E	Not at all cynical
30.	Never cries	A.....B.....C.....D.....E	Cries very easily
31.	Not at all self-confident	A.....B.....C.....D.....E	Very self-confident
32.	Does not look out only for self, principled	A.....B.....C.....D.....E	Looks out only for self, unprincipled
33.	Feels very inferior	A.....B.....C.....D.....E	Feels very superior
34.	Not at all hostile	A.....B.....C.....D.....E	Very hostile
35.	Not at all understanding of others	A.....B.....C.....D.....E	Very understanding of others
36.	Very cold in relations with others	A.....B.....C.....D.....E	Very warm in relations with others
37.	Very servile	A.....B.....C.....D.....E	Not at all servile
38.	Very little need for security	A.....B.....C.....D.....E	Very strong need for security
39.	Not at all gullible	A.....B.....C.....D.....E	Very gullible
40.	Goes to pieces under pressure	A.....B.....C.....D.....E	Stands up well under pressure

Source: Spence et al. (1974).

In part as a response to these criticisms, the originators of the new conceptions of sex roles have changed their views. Janet Spence, author of one measure, no longer believes that her questionnaire assesses sex roles (Swann, Langlois, & Gilbert,

1999). Instead, she suggested that her scales really measure the personality characteristics of instrumentality and expressiveness. **Instrumentality** consists of personality traits that involve working with objects, getting tasks completed in a direct fashion, showing independence from others, and displaying self-sufficiency. **Expressiveness**, in contrast, is the ease with which one can express emotions, such as crying, showing empathy for the troubles of others, and showing nurturance to those in need.

Sandra Bem has also changed her views on sex roles. She considers her measure (the Bem Sex Role Inventory; Bem, 1974) to assess **gender schemata**, or cognitive orientations that lead individuals to process social information on the basis of sex-linked associations (Hoyenga & Hoyenga, 1993). According to this conception, the ideal is not to be androgynous but, rather, to be *gender-aschematic*. That is, the ideal is not to use gender at all in one's processing of social information.

Although most researchers assume that masculinity, femininity, and "gender schema" are personality attributes absorbed from socialization, parents, the media, or the culture, studies have challenged this view. Cleveland and his colleagues (2001) found that sex-typed behaviors and attitudes themselves tend to show moderate heritability within sex. Among women, for example, 38 percent of the variance in proclivity to engage in sex-typical behaviors such as crying, expressing emotions, sensitivity to the feelings of others, taking risks, and even fighting was explained by genetic differences. Another study found moderate (roughly 50 percent) heritabilities for measures of "gender atypicality" in boys and girls—that is, masculinity in girls and femininity in boys (Knafo, Iervolino, & Plomin, 2005). These findings still leave large room for environmental influences to affect sex roles, but they suggest that genes also play a causal role, even within each gender, in the degree to which the sex roles are adopted.

In summary, the movement that led to these new conceptions of sex roles proved to be problematic. The external validity of the measures is questionable. And the assumption that masculinity and femininity are unidimensional traits, and that masculinity and femininity are independent of each other, no longer seems tenable.

Research on masculinity and femininity is moving beyond these issues and beginning to explore the real-life consequences of masculinity and femininity. One study, for example, found that these dimensions affect sexual behavior and relationships (Udry & Chantala, 2004). Adolescent couples containing a highly masculine male and a highly feminine female tend to have sex sooner than other pairings. Couples in which both members are average for their sex tend to break up compared with other pairings. Future research can be expected to yield more interesting real-life consequences of masculinity and femininity.

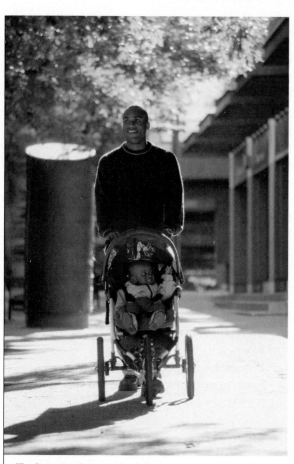

The distinctions between what behavior is appropriate for a woman and what behavior is appropriate for a man in our culture—social roles—have changed dramatically in the past few decades.

© Darren Greenwood/Design Pics RF

Gender Stereotypes

Much of this chapter so far has been concerned with the ways in which men and women differ. An important related topic pertains to the *beliefs* about how the sexes differ, regardless of whether these beliefs are accurate reflections of the sex differences that empirically exist. The beliefs that we hold about men and women are sometimes called gender stereotypes.

Gender stereotypes have three components (Hoyenga & Hoyenga, 1993). The first is *cognitive* and deals with the ways in which we form **social categories**. For example, we may categorize all men into "cads" or "dads," those who play around and are reluctant to commit versus those who are faithful and invest heavily in their children. The second component of gender stereotypes is *affective*. You may feel hostile or warm toward someone simply because you place that person in a particular social category. The third component of gender stereotypes is *behavioral*. For example, you may discriminate against someone simply because he belongs in a social category—in this case, "man." We discuss all three components of gender stereotypes—cognitive, affective, and behavioral—in the following sections, to illuminate how social categorizing shows up in everyday life.

Content of Gender Stereotypes

Although there are some variations from culture to culture, it is remarkable that the content of gender stereotypes—the attributes that we believe men and women possess—is highly similar across cultures. In the most comprehensive set of studies yet conducted, Williams and Best (1982, 1990) studied gender stereotypes in 30 countries around the world. In all these studies, men, compared with women, were commonly viewed as more aggressive, autonomous, achievement oriented, dominant, exhibitionist, and persevering. Women, compared with men, were commonly seen as more affiliative, deferent, heterosexual, nurturant, and self-abasing. These general gender stereotypes have a common theme. Women in all 30 countries tend to be perceived as more *communal*—oriented toward the group. Men, in contrast, are perceived to be more *instrumental*—asserting their independence from the group. These stereotypes correspond in many ways to the actual sex differences that have been discovered. Nonetheless, there is some evidence that people overestimate the magnitude of sex differences in personality, showing exaggerated beliefs about the size of sex differences that actually exist (Krueger, Hasman, et al., 2003; Wood & Eagly, 2010).

Stereotypic Subtypes of Men and Women

In addition to general gender stereotypes, studies show that most people have more finely differentiated stereotypic views of each sex. Six and Eckes (1991) examined the structure of their participants' cognitive categories of men and women and came up with several subtypes, as shown in Figure 16.3. Men were viewed as falling into five subtypes. The playboy subtype, for example, includes males who are cool, casual, "players," lady killers, and macho. The career man subtype includes men who are social climbers and managers. Stereotypes of women fell into a smaller number of subtypes. One might be called the "classically feminine" subtype, which includes housewives, secretaries, and maternal women. In the modern world, these women might be "soccer moms," highly devoted to their husbands and children. A second subtype is defined by short-term or overt sexuality. This subtype includes sex bombs, tarts, and vamps. These

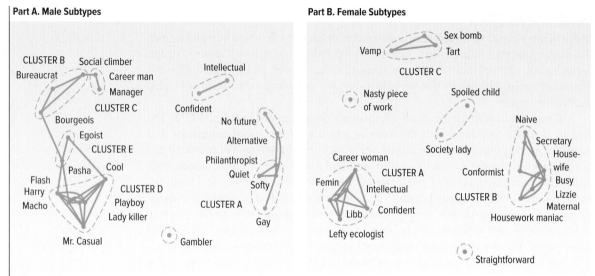

Part A. Male Subtypes

CLUSTER B   Social climber
Bureaucrat   Career man
                       Manager
           CLUSTER C
   Bourgeois
      Egoist
       CLUSTER E
   Pasha   Cool
Flash   CLUSTER D
Harry   Playboy
Macho   Lady killer
   Mr. Casual   Gambler

           Intellectual

Confident
           No future
           Alternative
   Philanthropist
   Quiet
           Softy
   CLUSTER A
           Gay

Part B. Female Subtypes

Vamp   Sex bomb
                   Tart
   CLUSTER C
   Nasty piece   Spoiled child
   of work
                         Naive
                         Secretary
           Society lady   House-
Career woman   Conformist   wife
   CLUSTER A   Busy
Femin   Intellectual   CLUSTER B   Lizzie
                              Maternal
   Libb   Confident   Housework maniac
Lefty ecologist

           Straightforward

Figure 16.3

The structure of cognitive sexual categories. The structure of cognitive categories of various male and female subtypes, where distance between subtypes on the graphs is assumed to correspond to cognitive "distances" in people's stereotypic concepts. Some subtypes are closely related to each other, as indicated by the dashed lines that surround them to form the various clusters.

Source: Six & Eckes, 1991.

two female subtypes correspond roughly to the "Madonna–whore" dichotomy, which is commonly made in everyday life (Buss, 2016). That is, these two stereotypes of women correspond to women who would make good mothers and women who give off the appearance of pursuing casual sex.

A third stereotype of women, however, involves a subtype that may have emerged relatively recently, perhaps over the past 20 or 30 years—the confident, intellectual, liberated career woman. Hillary Rodham Clinton would be a perfect illustration of this category—she scored at the top of her class in law school and developed an impressive influential career in politics. Also included in this cluster are feminist and lefty ecologist, perhaps suggesting that these political orientations tended to go along with independent, confident career women.

The key point is that, cognitively, most people do not hold only a single gender stereotype. Rather, cognitive categories are differentiated into subtypes of women and subtypes of men. It remains to be seen whether these stereotypical subtypes have any empirical basis. That is, are "playboy" men actually cooler, more casual, and more macho than other men? Are homemakers more naive, busy, and conformist than other women? Answers to these questions must await future research.

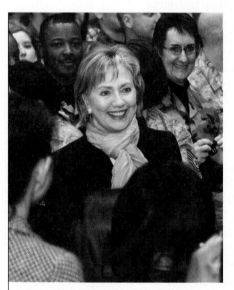

Hillary Rodham Clinton illustrates a relatively new gender stereotype—women who are intellectual, assertive, liberated, and career-minded.

Source: Airman Devin Doskey/USAF

Prejudice and Gender Stereotypes

Categories of gender, and the stereotypes associated with them, are not merely cognitive constructions that rattle around inside people's heads. They have real-world consequences. Prejudiced behavior is one damaging consequence of gender stereotypes. These damaging effects can be found in many important activities: in legal decisions, medical treatment, car purchases, check cashing, and job hunting (Wood & Eagly, 2010).

In wrongful death lawsuits, for example, the families of the victim receive more money if a man was killed than if a woman was killed (Goodman et al., 1991). In medicine, men are more likely to be recommended for coronary bypass surgery than women, even when they show the same amount of heart damage (Khan et al., 1990). A study in which men and women called car dealerships to request prices for particular cars found that the women were quoted higher prices than were the men for exactly the same car (Larrance et al., 1979). Women more than men are subjected to sexual harassment in the workplace, another form of gender discrimination (Buss, 2016).

Not all sex discrimination, however, favors men. In a study of book reviews published in the journal *Contemporary Psychology,* male authors were at the receiving end of more negative reviews (Moore, 1978). Interestingly, the male authors received more negative reviews than the women authors, whether the reviewer was a man or a woman. In another study of reviews by men and women of manuscripts submitted to refereed journals for publication, women gave more positive reviews to women authors than to men authors (Lloyd, 1990). Men reviewers did not show this bias.

In summary, gender stereotypes can have important consequences for men and women. These consequences can damage people where it counts most—in their health, their jobs, their chances for advancement, and their social reputations.

Theories of Sex Differences

So far in this chapter, we have seen that there are some differences in personality between the sexes but also many similarities. We have also seen that people hold stereotypes of sex differences that may go beyond the actual differences—stereotypes that can have lasting consequences for people's day-to-day lives. This section examines the major theories that have been proposed for explaining how sex differences arise. These include traditional theories of socialization and more complex theories of social roles and other notions of "gendered environments," hormonal theories, and theories anchored in evolutionary psychology.

Socialization and Social Roles

Socialization theory, the notion that boys and girls become different because boys are reinforced by parents, teachers, and the media for being "masculine," and girls for being "feminine," is probably the most widely held theory of sex differences in personality. The theory can be summarized as follows: Boys are given baseball bats and trucks. Girls are given dolls. Boys are praised for engaging in rough-and-tumble play. Girls are praised for being cute and obedient. Boys are punished for crying. Girls are comforted when they cry. Over time, according to socialization theory, children learn behaviors deemed appropriate for their sex.

Both socialization and social learning theories hold that gender roles have their roots in early sex-differentiated learning experiences—in short, boys are encouraged in one direction, and girls are encouraged in another direction.
© Michael Bridwell/PhotoEdit

In Bandura's (1977) **social learning theory**, a variant of socialization theory, boys and girls also learn by observing the behaviors of others, called *models,* of their own sex. Boys watch their fathers, male teachers, and male peers. Girls watch their mothers, female teachers, and female peer models. Boys see their fathers work. Girls see their mothers cook. Over time, even in the absence of direct reinforcement, these models provide a guide to behaviors that are masculine or feminine.

Some empirical evidence exists to support socialization and social learning theories of sex differences. Studies of socialization practices have found that both mothers and fathers encourage dependency more in girls than in boys (Block, 1983). Parents encourage girls to stay close to home, whereas boys are permitted or even encouraged to roam. Fathers engage in more physical play with their sons than with their daughters (Fagot & Leinbach, 1987). Finally, parents provide "gendered toys" to their children. Boys generally receive a greater variety of toys, more cars and trucks, more sports equipment, and more tools than girls do (Rheingold & Cook, 1975). Girls receive more dolls, pink clothing and furnishings, strollers, swings, and household appliances. This empirical evidence is consistent with socialization and social learning theories.

Cross-cultural evidence for different treatment of boys and girls exists as well. In many cultures, fathers do not interact with their daughters as much as with their sons (Whiting & Edwards, 1988). Girls in most cultures tend to be assigned more domestic chores than boys. Boys are permitted in most cultures to stray farther from home than are girls (Hoyenga & Hoyenga, 1993). Finally, boys in most cultures are socialized to be more competitive than are girls (Low, 1989). In a large study of socialization practices across cultures, Low (1989) found that in 82 percent of the cultures, the girls were trained to be more nurturant than the boys. In the majority of the cultures, the girls were socialized to be more sexually restrained than the boys—the parents tried to teach their daughters to delay having sexual intercourse (Perilloux et al., 2011), whereas the boys were encouraged to have sexual intercourse (Low, 1989). These patterns are also found among modern college populations (Perilloux et al., 2008), explained by what has been called the "daughter-guarding hypothesis."

One potential difficulty, however, pertains to the direction of effects—whether parents are socializing children in sex-linked ways or whether children are eliciting their parents' behavior to correspond to their existing sex-linked preferences (e.g., Scarr & McCartney, 1983). Perhaps the interests of the children drive the parents' behavior rather than the other way around. Parents may start out by giving a variety of toys to their children; however, if boys show no interest in dolls and girls show no interest in trucks, then over time parents may stop purchasing masculine toys for their daughters and feminine toys for their sons. The theory that the causal arrow runs one way—from parents to children—is open to question.

Another problem for traditional theories of socialization is that they provide no account of the *origins* of differential parental socialization practices. Why do parents want their boys and girls to grow up differently? Ideally, a comprehensive theory of the origins of sex differences should be able to account for the origins of sex-linked socialization practices. In sum, parents undoubtedly treat boys and girls differently, supporting the theory of sex-linked socialization of personality, but the origins of these practices currently remain a mystery.

A theory closely related to traditional socialization theories is **social role theory** (Eagly, 1987; Eagly & Wood, 1999; Wood & Eagly, 2010). According to social role theory, sex differences originate because men and women are distributed differently into different occupational and family roles. Men, for example, are expected to assume the breadwinning role. Women are expected to assume the homemaker role. Over time, children presumably learn the behaviors that are linked to these roles. Girls learn to be nurturing and emotionally supportive because these qualities are linked with the maternal role. Boys learn to be tough and aggressive, qualities expected of the breadwinner.

There is some evidence supporting social role theory (Eagly, 1987, 1995). Men and women in the United States have assumed different occupation and family roles, with women found more often in domestic and child care roles, and men more often in occupational roles. An event-sampling procedure explored how men's and women's behavior varied as a function of the social role to which they were assigned—a supervisor role, a coworker role, or the role of someone being supervised by someone else. Social role assignment had a large impact on the dominant behaviors that were expressed. The men and women assigned to the supervisor role displayed significantly more dominance, whereas those assigned the supervisee role displayed significantly more submissiveness (Moskowitz, Suh, & Desaulniers, 1994). When the roles were reversed, the people who formerly displayed dominance displayed submissiveness when they were put in a supervisee role, whereas the people who formerly were submissive became more dominant when they were assigned to the supervisor role.

Like socialization theory, however, social role theory fails to provide an account of the origins of sex-linked roles (Gangestad et al., 2006). Who assigns the different roles? Why should men and women passively accept the roles they are assigned? Why don't children follow the role of sitting quietly on airplanes or eating their spinach? Why do women assume domestic roles more than men? Are these roles found in all cultures?

Social role theory, however, is becoming increasingly testable as family and occupational roles change. Women are assuming breadwinning roles more often than in the past, and men are assuming greater responsibility for domestic duties. With these changes, if social role theory is correct, sex differences should diminish as well. Interestingly, the largest test of this prediction, a study of 17,637 individuals in 55 different cultures, has found precisely the opposite pattern (Schmitt et al., 2008). The most sexually egalitarian countries—those with the most equal access to education and knowledge and the greatest levels of economic wealth—show the largest, not the smallest, sex differences in personality. This surprising result appears to contradict the social role theory of sex differences in personality.

Hormonal Theories

Hormonal theories of sex differences argue that men and women differ not because of the external social environment, but rather because men and women have different underlying hormones. Physiological differences, not differential social treatment, causes boys and girls to diverge over development. Thus, some studies have sought to identify links between hormones such as testosterone (present in greater amounts in men) and sex-linked behavior.

There is some evidence that hormonal influences on sex differences begin in utero. The hormonal bath that the developing fetus is exposed to, for example, might affect both the organization of the brain and consequently the gendered interests and activities of the individual. Some of the best evidence for this comes from a condition called congenital adrenal hyperplasia (CAH), in which the female fetus has an overactive adrenal gland. This results in the female being hormonally masculinized. Young girls with CAH show a marked preference for "male" toys, such as Lincoln logs and trucks (Berenbaum & Beltz, 2011; Berenbaum & Snyder, 1995; Cohen-Bendahan

Testosterone is associated with dominance and aggressiveness, as well as with the massive buildup of muscular tissue. Here, U.S. olympic weightlifter Tim McRae rejoices after setting a new U.S. record in the snatch of 145 kg, a feat no woman in his weight class is likely to ever match. Olympic athletes are tested to make sure their testosterone levels are within normal ranges for their sex.
© *Kathy Willens/AP Images*

et al., 2005). As adults, CAH females show superiority in traditionally masculine cognitive skills, such as spatial rotation ability and throwing accuracy, as well as preferring traditionally masculine occupations (Kimura, 2002). These findings suggest that fetal exposure to hormones can have lasting effects on gender-linked interests and abilities.

Men and women do differ in their levels of circulating hormones. Women's level of circulating testosterone typically falls between 200 and 400 picograms per milliliter of blood at the lowest part of the menstrual cycle and between 285 and 440 at the highest part of the menstrual cycle (just prior to ovulation) (Hoyenga & Hoyenga, 1993). Men, in contrast, have circulating testosterone levels ranging from 5,140 to 6,460 picograms per milliliter of blood. Following puberty, there is no overlap between the sexes in their levels of circulating testosterone. Men typically show more than 10 times the level of women.

These sex differences in circulating testosterone are linked with some of the traditional sex differences found in behavior, such as aggression, dominance, and career choice. In women, high levels of testosterone are linked with pursuing a more masculine career and having greater success within the chosen career. Among lesbian women, testosterone has been associated with erotic role identification; more "masculine" lesbian partners having higher levels of testosterone than more "feminine" partners (Singh et al., 1999). Higher testosterone levels are associated with greater dominance and aggressiveness in both sexes. Female prison inmates who had more frequent disciplinary infractions also had higher testosterone (Dabbs & Hargrove, 1997). And Dabbs and colleagues (Dabbs, Hargrove, & Heusel, 1996) found that members of college fraternities who were more rambunctious had higher average levels of testosterone than those in fraternities who were better behaved.

Sexual desire is linked to levels of circulating testosterone, but only in women (van Anders, 2012). Women's testosterone levels peak just prior to ovulation, and women report a peak in their sexual desire at precisely the same time. At this peak, women report more female-initiated sexual intercourse and more desire for sexual intercourse (Sherwin, 1988). One study found that just thinking about sex increases testosterone in women, but not in men (Goldey & van Anders, 2012). So the links between hormones and sexuality are more complicated that scientists initially believed (van Anders, 2012).

These findings do not prove that the differences between men and women in sexuality, dominance, aggression, and career choices result from differences in testosterone levels. Correlation does not mean causation. Indeed, there is some evidence in nonhuman primates that rises in testosterone levels *follow* rises in status and dominance within the group rather than lead to them (Sapolsky, 1987). Furthermore, sexual arousal itself can result in an increase in testosterone level (Hoyenga & Hoyenga, 1993). A study on sports fans found that those whose team had just won an event had higher levels of testosterone than those fans whose team had just lost (Bernhardt et al., 1998). These results suggest that the link between hormones and behavior is bidirectional (Edwards, Wetzel, & Wyner, 2006). Higher testosterone may result from, as well as cause, behavior changes.

An additional limitation of hormonal theories of sex differences in personality is one shared with socialization theories—namely, neither of these theories identifies the *origins* of the differences. Precisely why do men and women differ so dramatically in their levels of circulating testosterone? Is this merely an incidental effect of being male versus being female? Or, is there a systematic process that causes men and women to differ in testosterone precisely because testosterone differences lead to behavioral differences in dominance and sexuality? One theoretical perspective that argues for this possibility is evolutionary psychology.

Evolutionary Psychology Theory

According to the evolutionary psychology perspective (see Chapter 8), men and women differ only in some domains of personality and show large similarities in most domains. The sexes are predicted to be similar in all the domains in which they have faced similar *adaptive problems* over human evolutionary history. The sexes are predicted to differ only in the domains in which men and women have confronted different adaptive challenges over human evolutionary history (Buss & Schmitt, 2011).

Adaptive problems are problems that need to be solved in order for an individual to survive and reproduce, or whose solution increases overall reproductive success. For example, both sexes have similar taste preferences for sugar, salt, fat, and protein. That's why fast-food restaurants are so popular—they package food with fat and sugar that both men and women desire. Food preferences reflect a solution to an important adaptive problem—getting calories and nutrients to survive.

In the domains of mating and sexuality, according to evolutionary psychologists, men and women have confronted somewhat different adaptive problems (Buss, 1995b). In order to reproduce, women must carry and gestate a fetus for nine months. Men, in contrast, can reproduce through a single act of sex. As a consequence, women historically faced the adaptive problem of securing resources to carry them through harsh winters or droughts, when resources might be scarce and a woman's mobility might be restricted by the burden of pregnancy. The costs of making a poor choice of a mate, according to this logic, would have been more damaging to women than to men. Because of the heavy investment women require for reproduction, they are theorized to have evolved exacting mate preferences for men who showed signals of the ability and willingness to invest in them and their children.

This line of reasoning predicts that men will be more sexually indiscriminate and more aggressive with other men about pursuing opportunities for sexual access to women. Because of women's heavy investment, they become the extraordinarily valuable reproductive resource over which men compete. Women, on the other hand, are predicted to be more selective about sex partners—being more discerning about who they are willing to have sex with. A woman who had made a hasty or poor mate choice in the past would have been faced with the difficulties of bearing and raising a child without the help of an investing man. A motivation for casual sex, in short, was more reproductively beneficial to ancestral men than to ancestral women.

Some of the empirical evidence for sex differences indeed corresponds to these predictions. Men clearly have a greater desire for sexual variety than women do (Buss & Schmitt, 1993, 2011; Symons, 1979). Men desire a larger number of sex partners, seek sex after a shorter time period has elapsed in knowing a potential partner, and have more fantasies about casual sex than do women (Schmitt et al., 2012). Furthermore, men tend to take more risks to secure the resources and status that women find desirable in marriage partners (e.g., Byrnes, Miller, & Schafer, 1999; Wilson & Daly, 2004). Thus, the findings that men are more aggressive, more willing to take physical risks, and more interested in casual sex are precisely the findings predicted by evolutionary psychology (Archer, 2009).

Despite this support, evolutionary psychology theory, like the other theoretical perspectives, leaves unanswered questions: What accounts for individual differences within each sex? Why are some women keenly interested in casual sex? Why are some men meek, dependent, and nurturing, whereas others are callous and aggressive? Some of these questions are beginning to be answered. It turns out, for example, that some women benefit greatly from pursuing a short-term sexual strategy, which can result in obtaining more and better resources, switching to a mate who is better than her regular mate, and possibly securing better genes for her offspring (Buss, 2016; Gangestad & Cousins, 2002; Gangestad & Thornhill, 2008). Ultimately, a comprehensive theory of sex differences must account for these differences within each sex, as well as the average differences between the sexes.

An Integrated Theoretical Perspective

The theoretical accounts we have examined seem very different, but they are not necessarily incompatible. Indeed, to some extent, they operate at different levels of analysis. Evolutionary psychology suggests *why* the sexes differ, but it does not specify *how* they became different. Hormonal and socialization theories specify *how* the sexes became different but do not specify *why* the sexes are different.

An integrated theory of sex differences would take all of these levels of analysis into account because they are clearly compatible with each other. Parents, for example, clearly have an interest in socializing boys and girls differently, and these socialization differences are, to some degree, universal (Low, 1989; Periloux et al., 2008). Furthermore, there is evidence that both men and women change their behavior as a function of the roles they adopt. Both sexes become more dominant when in supervisory roles; both become more submissive when being supervised. Socialization, in short, must play a role in any integrated theory of sex differences although some evidence contradicts social role theory.

Men and women clearly differ in circulating testosterone levels, and these differences are linked with differences in sexuality, aggression, dominance, and career interests (Edwards et al., 2006; Hoyenga & Hoyenga, 1993). Nonetheless, we cannot ignore the causal possibility, for which there is some evidence, that being in a dominant position actually causes testosterone to rise. Thus, social roles and hormones may be closely linked, and these links may be necessary for an integrated theory of sex differences.

These proximate paths—socialization and hormones—might provide the answers for *how* the sexes differ, whereas evolutionary psychology provides the answers for *why* the sexes differ. Are there evolutionary reasons that parents encourage greater aggressiveness and dominance in boys but more nurturance in girls? Are there evolutionary reasons for surges in testosterone when a person ascends a dominance hierarchy? At this point in the history of the science of sex differences, there are no answers to these questions. Nonetheless, it's a good bet that all three levels of analysis—social factors, hormonal and other physiological influences, and evolutionary processes—are needed for a complete understanding of gender and personality.

SUMMARY AND EVALUATION

The study of sex, gender, and personality has provoked heated debate over the past several decades. Perhaps in no other area of personality psychology do politics and values get so intermingled with science. Some researchers, called minimalists, emphasize the great similarities between the sexes, pointing out that the effect size differences are small and the distributions overlapping. Other researchers, called maximalists, emphasize that sex differences are real and replicable and stress the effect size differences rather than the overlap of the distributions.

When we take a step back, it is possible to gain a more accurate understanding of sex, gender, and personality. The past few decades have witnessed an explosion of research on sex differences, along with the development of meta-analytic statistical procedures, which allow for firm conclusions grounded in empirical data.

Some sex differences are real and not artifacts of particular investigators or methods. Some sex differences have remained relatively constant over generations and across cultures. Nonetheless, the magnitudes of sex differences vary tremendously. When questions about sex differences are posed, therefore, we must always ask the question "In what domains?"

The domains that show large and small sex differences are now fairly clear. Men score consistently higher on the personality attributes of assertiveness, aggressiveness (especially physical aggressiveness), and casual sexuality. Women consistently score higher on measures of anxiety, trust, and tender-mindedness (nurturance). Women are more likely than men to experience both positive emotions (e.g., affection, joy) and negative emotions (e.g., fear, sadness), although the magnitude of these differences is not large. Men are more likely to be sexually aggressive, trying to force women to have sex, although these findings appear to be limited to a subset of men—those who are narcissistic, lack empathy, and show hostile masculinity. Women tend to score higher on emotional investment—a cultural universal likely linked to attachment and bonding in romantic and other social relationships. Although no sex differences are reported in depression rates prior to puberty, at around age 13 women tend to show higher rates of depression than do men. This sex difference has been tied to theories suggesting that women ruminate more than men and theories linked to the importance of physical appearance in the domain of mate competition. Men tend to score toward the things end of the people–things dimension, whereas women tend to score more toward the people end. Within each of these domains, however, there is overlap. Some women are more assertive, aggressive, and things oriented than the majority of men. Some men are more anxious, tender minded, and people oriented than the majority of women.

In the 1970s, much attention was focused on the concept of androgyny. However, it became clear as more empirical evidence was gathered that masculinity and femininity were not independent, as the androgyny researchers had asserted. Those who score high on masculinity, or instrumentality, tend to score low on femininity, or expressiveness, and vice versa. Furthermore, many of the original androgyny researchers came to believe that these dimensions capture the essence of sex differences. Men tend to be more instrumental. Women tend to be more expressive. Nonetheless, there is much overlap, and many women are highly instrumental and many men are expressive.

Another important topic centers on gender stereotypes, or beliefs that people hold about each sex, regardless of their accuracy. Cross-cultural research has revealed some universality of gender stereotypes. In all cultures, men are believed to be more aggressive, autonomous, dominant, achievement oriented, and exhibitionistic, and women are believed to be more affiliative, deferent, nurturing, and self-abasing. These stereotypes about the sexes correspond in many ways to the actual sex differences that have been discovered. People also hold stereotypes about the subtypes within each sex. Men are viewed as playboys, career men, or losers. Women are viewed as feminists, housewives, or sex bombs.

Traditional theories of sex differences have emphasized social factors—socialization by parents, observational learning from social models, and social roles. There is some support for the importance of the social environment. Cross-cultural studies have revealed that boys are universally socialized more than girls to be achievement strivers, and girls are universally socialized to be more restrained than boys, especially in the sexual domain.

Studies of hormones suggest that social factors do not tell the whole story. Testosterone, for example, has been implicated in the personality factors of dominance, aggression, and sexuality. Because men and women differ substantially in their levels of circulating testosterone, it is possible that some of the personality differences are caused by hormonal differences.

According to evolutionary psychologists, men and women differ in domains in which the sexes have faced different adaptive problems over human evolutionary history. In other domains, the sexes are the same or highly similar. Aggression and orientation toward casual sex are two domains in which the sexes should differ, according to this theory, and these predictions are empirically supported. What is needed is an integrative theory of sex, gender, and personality that takes into account all of these factors: social factors, physiological factors, and evolutionary factors.

KEY TERMS

sex differences 489
gender 490
gender stereotypes 490
effect size 491
minimalist 493
maximalist 493
inhibitory control 493
perceptual sensitivity 494
surgency 494
negative affectivity 494

trust 495
tender-mindedness 495
global self-esteem 499
people–things dimension 501
empathizing 501
systemizing 501
rumination 502
masculinity 503
femininity 503
androgynous 503

instrumentality 506
expressiveness 506
gender schemata 506
social categories 507
socialization theory 509
social learning theory 510
social role theory 510
hormonal theories 511

© Arthimedes/Shutterstock.
com RF

Culture and Personality

17

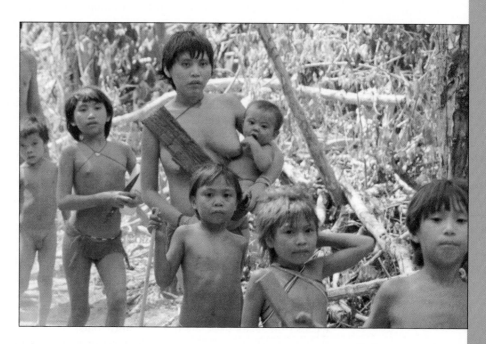

The Yanomamö Indian tribes are among the last truly traditional societies on earth, living a huntergatherer existence in the isolated jungles of Venezuela.
© John Maier/The Image Works

The Yanomamö Indians of Venezuela set up temporary shelters, from which they forage for food and hunt for game. When these shelters become depleted of food, they push on and settle elsewhere. On one particular day, the men gather at early dawn, preparing to raid a neighboring village. The group is tense. The men in the raiding party risk injury, and a fearful man might turn back, excusing himself from the raid by telling the others that he has a thorn in his foot. Men who do this too often risk damaging their reputation (Chagnon, 1983).

Not all Yanomamö men are the same. There are at least two discernible groups that differ profoundly in personality. The lowland Yanomamö men are highly aggressive. They do not hesitate to hit their wives with sticks for "infractions" as minor as serving tea too slowly. They often challenge other men to club fights or ax fights. And they sometimes declare war on neighboring groups, attempting to kill the enemy men and capture their wives. Yanomamö men shave the tops of their heads to reveal the scars from club fights, sometimes painting the scars red to display them as symbols of courage. Indeed, one is not regarded as a true man until one has killed another man—acquiring the honor of being called an *unokai*. The men who are unokai have the most wives (Chagnon, 1988).

In the highlands reside a different group of Yanomamö. These people are more peaceful and dislike fighting. The high levels of agreeableness can be seen on their faces. These Yanomamö do not raid neighboring villages, do not engage in ax fights, and rarely engage in club fights. They stress the virtues of cooperation. Unfortunately, though, food resources are more plentiful in the lowlands, where the aggressive Yanomamö dominate.

How can we understand cultural differences in personality between the highland and lowland Yanomamö? Did those who were temperamentally more disposed to aggression drive those who were more agreeable up to the highlands and away from the food resources? Or did the two groups start out the same, and only subsequently did cultural values take hold in one group different from those that took hold in the other? These questions form the subject matter of this chapter. What is the effect of culture on personality? What is the effect of personality on culture? And how can we understand patterns of cultural variation amid patterns of human universals?

Personality psychologists explore personality across cultures for several important reasons (Allik & Realo, 2009; Church, 2000; Paunonen & Ashton, 1998). One is to discover whether concepts of personality in one culture, such as American culture, are also applicable in other cultures. A second is to find out whether cultures differ, on average, in the levels of particular personality traits. Are Japanese, for example, really more agreeable than Americans, or is this merely a stereotype? A third reason is to discover whether the factor structure of personality traits varies across cultures or is universal. Will the five-factor model of personality discovered in American samples, for example, be replicated in Holland, Germany, and the Philippines? A fourth reason is to discover whether certain features of personality are universal, corresponding to the human nature level of personality analysis (see Chapter 1).

In this chapter, we explore which features of personality are common to everyone but differentially elicited only in some cultures; which features of personality are transmitted so that they become characteristic of some local groups, but not others; and which features of personality are common to everyone in all cultures. We start by examining just how different cultures can be.

Cultural Violations: An Illustration

Consider the following events:

1. One of your family members eats beef regularly. (your beef-eating family member)
2. A young married woman goes alone to see a movie without informing her husband. When she returns home, her husband says, "If you do it again, I will beat you black and blue." She does it again; he beats her black and blue. (the wife-beating husband)
3. A poor man goes to the hospital after being seriously hurt in an accident. The hospital refuses to treat him because he cannot afford to pay. (the refusing hospital)

Now examine each event and decide whether you think the behavior on the part of the person or institution in parentheses is morally wrong. If so, is it a serious violation, a minor offense, or not a violation at all?

If you are a Brahman Hindu, you are likely to believe that the first event—eating beef—is a serious violation but that the second event—the husband beating the wife for disobeying him—is not (Shweder, Mahapatra, & Miller, 1990). If you are an American, however, the odds are that your views are the reverse: unless you are a vegetarian, you see nothing wrong with eating beef, but you view it as very wrong for the husband to beat his wife. Both Brahman Hindus and Americans, however, agree that the hospital that denies treatment to the badly injured man is committing a serious violation.

This example highlights a fascinating question for personality psychologists. Some aspects of personality (including attitudes, values, and self-concepts) are highly variable across cultures. But other aspects of personality are universal—features that are shared by people everywhere. The central questions addressed by this chapter are "How do people from different cultures differ in personality, and how are people from all cultures the same?"

What Is Cultural Personality Psychology?

Before proceeding further, it is useful to briefly define culture. Let's start with an observation: "Humans everywhere show striking patterns of local within-group similarity in their behavior and thought, accompanied by profound intergroup differences" (Tooby & Cosmides, 1992, p. 6). Within-group similarities and between-group differences can be of any sort—physical, psychological, behavioral, or attitudinal. These phenomena are called **cultural variations**.

Consider the example of eating beef. Beef eating is common among Americans but is rare and viewed with abhorrence among Hindus. Among Hindus in India, the values and behaviors are shared for the most part. But they differ from the widely shared American attitudes toward beef eating. This difference—a local within-group similarity and between-group difference—is an example of a cultural variation.

Attaching the label of "culture" or "cultural variation" to phenomena such as these is best treated as a description, not an explanation. Labeling attitudes toward beef eating as "cultural" certainly describes the phenomenon. It tells us that we are dealing with a within-group similarity and a between-group difference. But it doesn't explain what has *caused* the cultural difference or *why* the groups differ. **Cultural personality psychology** generally has three key goals: (1) to discover the principles underlying the cultural diversity; (2) to discover how human psychology shapes culture; and (3) to discover how cultural understandings in turn shape our psychology (Fiske et al., 1997).

Three Major Approaches to Culture

Certain traits are common to all people, but others display remarkable variation. Cultural variants are the personality attributes that vary from group to group. Psychologists have developed three major approaches to explaining and exploring personality across cultures: evoked culture, transmitted culture, and cultural universals.

Evoked Culture

Evoked culture is defined as cultural differences created by differing environmental conditions activating a predictable set of responses. Consider the physical examples of skin calluses and sweat. There are undoubtedly cultural differences in the thickness and distribution of calluses and in the amount people sweat. The traditional !Kung Bushmen of

Botswana, for example, tend to have thicker calluses on their feet than most Americans because they walk around without shoes. These differences are aspects of evoked culture—different environments have different effects on people's callus-producing mechanisms. People who live near the equator, for example, are exposed to more intense heat than those who live in more northern climates, such as Canada. The observation that residents of Zaire sweat more than residents of Canada is properly explained as an environmentally evoked difference that operates on sweat glands, which all humans possess.

Note that two ingredients are necessary to explain cultural variations: (1) a universal underlying mechanism (in this case, sweat glands possessed by all people), and (2) environmental differences in the degree to which the underlying mechanism is activated (in this case, by differences in ambient temperature). Neither element alone is adequate for a complete explanation.

The same explanatory logic applies to other environmentally triggered phenomena shared by members of one group, but not by other groups. Drought, plentiful game, and poisonous snakes are all environmental events that affect some groups more than others. These events activate mechanisms in some groups that lie dormant in others. In the next section, we discuss several psychological examples of evoked culture and show how they may result in differences in personality traits among groups.

Evoked Cooperation

Whether someone is cooperative or selfish is a central part of personality, but these proclivities may differ from culture to culture. A concrete example of evoked culture is the patterns of cooperative food sharing found among different bands of hunter-gatherer tribes (Cosmides & Tooby, 1992). Different classes of food have different variances in their distribution. High-variance foods differ greatly in their availability from day to day. For example, among the Ache tribe of Paraguay, meat from hunting is a high-variance resource. On any given day, the probability that a hunter will come back with meat is only 60 percent. On any particular day, therefore, one hunter will be successful, whereas another hunter will come back empty-handed. Gathered food, on the other hand, is a lower-variance food resource. The yield from gathering depends more on the skill and effort a person expends than on luck. Under **high-variance conditions**, there are tremendous benefits to sharing. You share your meat today with an unlucky hunter, and next week he or she will share meat with you. The benefits of engaging in cooperative food sharing increase under conditions of high variance. In this example, the benefits of sharing are also increased by the fact that a large game animal contains more meat than one person, or even one family, can consume. Thus, some of the meat would spoil if it were not shared with others.

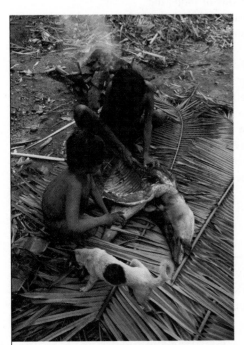

Yanomamö Indians butchering a giant anteater. In their culture, the successful hunter shares his catch with the whole group. The benefits of such cooperative food sharing are high in their environment (Chagnon, 1983).

© Claudia Andujar/Science Source

Kaplan and Hill (1985) found that, indeed, within the Ache tribe, meat is communally shared. Hunters deposit their kill with a "distributor," a person who allocates portions to various families, based on family size. In the same group, however, gathered food is not shared outside the family. In short, cooperative sharing seems to be evoked by the environmental condition of high food variance.

Halfway around the world, in the Kalahari Desert, Cashden (1980) found that some San groups are more egalitarian than others. The degree of **egalitarianism** is closely correlated with the variance in food supply. The !Kung San's food supply is highly variable, and they share food and express egalitarian beliefs. To be called a "stinge" (stingy) is one of the worst insults, and the group imposes strong social sanctions for stinginess and gives social approval for food sharing. Among the Gana San, in contrast, food variance is low, and they show great economic inequality. The Gana San tend to hoard their food and rarely share it outside their extended families.

Environmental conditions can activate some behaviors, such as cooperation and sharing. Everyone has the capacity to share and cooperate, but cultural differences in the degree to which groups do share and cooperate depend, to some extent, on the external environmental conditions, such as variance in the food supply.

Early Experience and Evoked Mating Strategies

Another example of evoked culture comes from the work of Jay Belsky and his colleagues (Belsky, 2000; Belsky et al., 2012). They argue that harsh, rejecting, and inconsistent child-rearing practices, erratically provided resources, and marital discord foster a personality of impulsivity and a mating strategy marked by early reproduction. In contrast, sensitive, supportive, and responsive child rearing, combined with reliable resources and spousal harmony, foster a personality of conscientiousness and a mating strategy of commitment, delayed reproduction, and stable marriage. Children in uncertain and unpredictable environments, in short, seem to learn that they cannot rely on a single mate and, so, opt for a sexual life that starts early and inclines them to seek multiple mates. In contrast, children growing up in stable homes with parents who predictably invest in their welfare opt for a strategy of long-term mating because they expect to attract a stable, high-investing mate. The evidence from children of divorced homes supports this theory. Such children tend to be more impulsive, tend to reach puberty earlier, engage in sexual intercourse earlier, and have more sex partners than do their peers from intact homes.

The sensitivity of personality and mating strategies to early experiences may help explain the differences in the value placed on chastity across cultures. In China, for example, marriages are lasting, divorce is rare, and parents invest heavily in their children over extended periods (Lei et al., 2011). In Sweden, many children are born out of wedlock, divorce is common, and fewer fathers invest consistently over time. These cultural experiences may evoke in the two groups different mating strategies, with the Swedes more than the Chinese tending toward short-term mating and more frequent partner switching (Buss, 2016).

Although more evidence is needed to confirm this theory, this example illustrates how a consistent pattern of individual differences can be evoked in different cultures, producing a local pattern of within-group similarities and between-group differences. All humans presumably have within their mating menu a strategy of short-term mating, marked by frequent partner switching, and a strategy of long-term mating, marked by enduring commitment and love (Buss, 2016). These mating strategies may be differentially evoked in different cultures, resulting in enduring cultural differences in mating strategies.

Honors, Insults, and Evoked Aggression

Why are people in some cultures prone to aggression at the slightest provocation, whereas people in other cultures resort to aggression only reluctantly as a last resort? Why do people in some cultures kill one another at relatively high rates, whereas people in other cultures kill one another at relatively low rates? Nisbett (1993) has proposed a theory to account for these cultural differences—a theory based on the notion of evoked culture.

Nisbett has proposed that the economic means of subsistence of a culture affects the degree to which the group develops a **culture of honor**. In cultures of honor, insults are viewed as highly offensive public challenges, which must be met with direct confrontation and physical aggression. The theory is that differences in the degree to which honor becomes a central part of the culture rests ultimately with economics—specifically, the manner in which food is obtained. In herding economies, one's entire stock could be lost suddenly to thieves. Cultivating a reputation as willing to respond with violent force—for example, by displaying physical aggression when publicly insulted— presumably deters thieves and others who might steal one's property. In more settled agricultural communities, the cultivation of an aggressive reputation is less important because one's means of subsistence cannot be rapidly undermined.

Nisbett tested his theory by using homicide statistics from different regions within the United States and experiments in which subjects from the northern and southern United States were insulted. Interestingly, the southerners (historically using animal herding for subsistence) did not endorse more positive attitudes toward the use of violence in general, compared with the northerners (historically using farming or agriculture for subsistence). The southerners, however, were indeed more likely to endorse violence for the purposes of *protection* and in response to *insults*. Furthermore, the homicide rates in the South were far higher than those in the North, particularly for murders triggered by efforts to defend one's reputation.

Nisbett found a similar pattern in the laboratory, where the northern and southern participants were insulted by an experimenter. In this study, the experimenter intentionally bumped into the participants and then said "asshole." Subsequently, the participants were asked to complete a series of incomplete word stems, such as "h _____." The southerners who had been insulted wrote down more aggressive words, such as *hate,* than did the northerners who had been insulted, suggesting that the insults had evoked in the southerners a higher level of aggression. When southerners and northerners were threatened in a laboratory setting, southerners had higher elevations of testosterone and responded with greater aggression (Nisbett & Cohen, 1996).

Presumably, all humans have the capacity to develop a high sensitivity to public insults and a capacity to respond with violence. These capacities are evoked in certain cultures, however, and presumably lie dormant in others.

Cultural Differences in Conformity

Pressures to conform with social norms are widespread. Individuals sometimes pay a steep social price for deviating from the group. Children are expected to obey parents and are sometimes punished if they rebel. On the other hand, uniqueness and novelty are sometimes celebrated, and those who resist the tyrannical dictates of a culture are sometimes seen as heroes. Could cultural differences in conformity be an example of evoked culture?

One hypothesis stems from evolutionary psychology, and suggests that the prevalence of disease-causing pathogens cause cultural pressure to conform (Murray et al., 2011). The logic is that infectious diseases historically posed a great threat to human survival. Consequently, humans have evolved defenses to defend against disease-causing pathogens. These include physiological defenses such as the immune system. They also include a "behavioral immune system" that functions to prevent contact with disease-causing agents. These may include avoiding people who with open sores, people who cough, or those who otherwise show signs of disease. When the threat of pathogen infection becomes especially salient, people become more introverted, avoiding contact with other people (Murray et al., 2011).

Similarly, conformity to group norms may also help to avoid diseases. Deviating from cultural norms of food preparation, for example, may increase one's risk of a food-born disease. In an innovative set of four studies, Murray and colleagues (2011) found that people in cultures with a high prevalence of pathogens tended to be substantially more conformist than those with a lower pathogen prevalence. And in cultures with low pathogen prevalence, there was substantially greater tolerance for nonconformity. If further tests confirm these results, they suggest that group differences in conformity may be a prime example of evoked culture—one that rests on a universal evolved psychology that is differentially activated by environmental differences in pathogen prevalence.

The concept of evoked culture provides one model for understanding and explaining cultural variations in personality traits, such as conformity, cooperativeness, or aggression. It rests on the assumption that all humans have the same potentials or capabilities. The aspects of these potentials that get evoked depend on features of the social or physical environment.

Transmitted Culture

Transmitted culture consists of ideas, values, attitudes, and beliefs that exist originally in at least one person's mind that are transmitted to other people's minds through their interaction with the original person (Tooby & Cosmides, 1992). The view that it is wrong to eat beef, for example, is an example of transmitted culture. This value presumably originated in the mind of one person, who then transmitted it to others. Over time, the view that eating beef is a serious violation came to characterize Hindus. Although we do not know much about how culture is transmitted or why certain ideas spread but others do not, the discovery of large cultural differences in seemingly arbitrary values provides circumstantial evidence for the existence of transmitted culture. Whereas people in some cultures view the eating of beef as wrong, people in other cultures view the eating of pork as wrong. Others see nothing wrong with eating beef or pork, others eat no meat at all, and others avoid all meat and all dairy products.

Cultural Differences in Moral Values

Cultures differ in their beliefs about what is morally right and wrong. As an example, consider whether you agree or disagree with the following statement: "It is immoral for adults to disobey their parents" (Rozin, 2003, p. 275). If you are a Hindu Indian, the odds are great that you will agree with this statement (80 percent of the Hindu women and 72 percent of the Hindu men). If you are an American, however, the odds are strong that

Exercise

Read each of the following items and decide whether the behavior described is wrong. Use the following four-point scale to indicate how serious the violation is (in parentheses is the person who committed the potential violation).

   a: Not a violation
   b: A minor offense
   c: A somewhat serious offense
   d: A very serious offense

Exercise (*Continued*)

___   **1.** The day after his father's death, the eldest son had a haircut and ate chicken.

___   **2.** One of your family members eats beef regularly.

___   **3.** One of your family members eats dog meat regularly.

___   **4.** A widow in your community eats fish two or three times a week.

___   **5.** Six months after the death of her husband, a widow is wearing jewelry and brightly colored clothes.

___   **6.** A woman cooks rice for her husband and his elder brother. Then she eats with them. (the woman)

___   **7.** A woman cooks food for her family members and sleeps in the same bed with her husband during her menstrual period. (the woman)

___   **8.** A man had a wife who was sterile. He wanted to have two wives. He asked his first wife and she said she did not mind, so he married a second woman, and the three of them lived happily in the same house. (the man)

___   **9.** A brother and sister decide to get married and have children.

___   **10.** The day after the birth of his first child, a man entered his temple (church) and prayed to God.

___   **11.** A woman is playing cards at home with her friends. Her husband is cooking rice for them. (the husband)

___   **12.** At night a wife asked her husband to massage her legs. (the wife)

Researchers interviewed Brahman Indian and American respondents about their reactions to the previous items (Shweder et al., 1990). To illustrate the cultural differences, consider the following responses from a Brahman to questions about the widow who eats fish two or three times a week (adapted from Shweder et al., 1990, p. 168):

Interviewer: Is the widow's behavior wrong?
Brahman: Yes. Widows should not eat fish, meat, onions or garlic, or any "hot" foods. They must restrict their diet to "cool" foods: rice, dal, ghee, vegetables.
Interviewer: How serious is the violation?
Brahman: A very serious violation. She will suffer greatly if she eats fish.
Interviewer: Is it a sin?
Brahman: Yes. It is a great sin.
Interviewer: What if no one knew this had been done?
Brahman: It is [still] wrong. A widow should spend her time seeking salvation—seeking to be reunited with the soul of her husband. Hot foods will distract her. They will stimulate her sexual appetite. She will lose her sanctity. She will want sex and behave like a whore. . . . She will offend his spirit if she eats fish.

Now consider the responses from an American interviewee (Shweder et al., 1990, p. 168):

Interviewer: Is the widow's behavior wrong?
American: No. She can eat fish if she wants to.
Interviewer: How serious is the violation?
American: It's not a violation.
Interviewer: Is it a sin?
American: No.
Interviewer: What if no one knew this had been done?
American: It is not wrong, in private or public.

Americans and Brahman Indians disagree with one another not just about eating fish, but about a host of other activities. The following are a few activities that Brahmans believe are wrong but that Americans believe are not wrong: a wife's eating with the husband's elder brother; eating beef; a wife's requesting a foot massage; addressing one's father by his first name; cutting one's hair and eating chicken after one's father's death; a widow wearing bright clothes; and a widow remarrying. In contrast, the following are activities that Americans believe to be wrong but that Brahmans believe are not wrong: having unequal inheritance, with more going to males than females; beating a disobedient wife for going to the movies; and caning (beating with a stick) an errant child.

Source: Shweder et al., 1990. Appeared originally in Shweder, R. A., Mahapatra, M., and Miller, J. G. (1987). Culture and moral development. In *The emergence of morality in young children,* Jerome Kagan and Sharon Lamb (Eds.), pp. 40–41, 43, 44. © 1987 by The University of Chicago. Reprinted by permission of University of Chicago Press.

you will disagree (only 13 percent of American women and 19 percent of American men agree). To get a concrete feel for these differences, complete the following exercise.

Culturally variable views of morality are apparently transmitted to children early in life. American 5-year-old children, for example, make almost identical judgments about right and wrong, showing a correlation between the two groups of 0.89 (Shweder et al., 1990). As adults, the groups differ tremendously.

Views of moral behavior—what is right and what is wrong—are important psychological principles that guide behavior, and they are central to personality. Cultures clearly differ in their views of what is right and wrong, sometimes in seemingly arbitrary ways. Among the Semang of Malaysia, for example, it is considered sinful to comb one's hair during a thunderstorm, to watch dogs mate, to tease a helpless animal, to kill a sacred wasp, to have sexual intercourse during the daytime, to draw water from a fire-blackened vessel, or to act casually or informally with one's mother-in-law (Murdock, 1980).

There may also be universals in what is considered right and wrong. Both Brahman Indians and Americans, for example, agree about the following wrongs: ignoring an accident victim, breaking a promise, kicking a harmless animal, committing brother-sister incest, and stealing flowers (Shweder et al., 1990). Most cultures consider it wrong to kill without cause. Most cultures consider it wrong to commit incest (Lieberman & Lobel, 2012). But even these seeming universals are violated in some cultures. Among certain subcultures, for example, killing is viewed as justified if one has been publicly insulted (Nisbett, 1993). In certain royal dynasties, to take another example, incest between brother and sister was actively encouraged as a way to preserve the family's wealth and power. Statements about universality are relative in the sense that there are always some cultural or subcultural exceptions.

The key point is that many moral values are specific to particular cultures and are likely to be examples of transmitted culture. They appear to be passed from one generation to the next, not through genes but through the teachings of parents and teachers or through observations of the behavior of others within the culture. Now we turn to another possible example of transmitted culture—the self-concept.

Cultural Differences in Self-Concept

The ways in which we define ourselves—our self-concepts—are the core components of human personality. Self-concepts influence behavior. A woman who defines herself as conscientious, for example, may take pains to show up for classes on time, return all

A Closer Look

Reaching Across the Great Divide: The Psychology of Cross-Cultural Marriages

What happens when people from different cultures meet and fall in love? We might expect that the more differences between the cultures, the greater the potential difficulties in the marriage. Large cultural differences—those in language, religion, race, politics, and class—may create major divides that may separate a cross-cultural couple.

Sociologists Rosemary Breger and Rosanna Hill (1998) present a detailed look at cross-cultural marriages. Throughout the book, the emphasis is on how cultural differences create challenges in marriages. For example, many cultural rituals surround food and eating. In some cultures, men are served first and begin eating before women. A man from a different culture might politely wait and not touch his food until his wife begins to eat. If the wife comes from a culture in which men eat first, she might suspect that her husband is dissatisfied with the meal because he is not eating before her. A polite social behavior in one culture can thus be seen as a signal of dissatisfaction in another.

In some cultures, the extended family becomes a large part of the couple's life, sometimes to the point of expecting to share sleeping space in their bedroom. In some cultures, you don't just marry the person; you marry his or her extended family as well.

According to Larsen and Prizmic-Larsen (1999), one of the largest challenges in cross-cultural marriages results from differences in native languages. They report a case where the wife, who was from Eastern Europe, said to the husband, "You are boring," when her real intent was to ask, "Are you bored?" Good communication is essential to any marriage. However, when one person has to conduct his or her marriage in a foreign language, there exists a minefield of potential misunderstandings between the spouses. Moreover, the presence of a heavy accent can lead to verbal misunderstandings, even when the content of a communication is accurate. Communicating in a foreign language also takes mental effort and, when tired or angry, one may not be able to communicate very well in a second language.

There are at least two lines of inquiry that interest personality psychologists about cross-cultural marriages. One question concerns who is the most likely to marry outside of his or her own culture. Are some personality variables involved in being attracted to others who are very different from oneself? A second line of inquiry concerns process. What happens in cross-cultural marriages that might make them different from monocultural marriages? How do two people who have cultural differences come to accommodate and adapt to each other? Are there ways that people can free themselves of cultural bonds and more easily function in a cross-cultural relationship? How do people maintain their identities and sense of self,

© Ingram Publishing RF

© Darren Greenwood/Design Pics RF

Relationships that bridge two cultures bring unique challenges, as well as unique opportunities, to the couple.
© Don Hammond/Design Pics RF

even when living in a foreign country and conducting their marriage in a foreign language?

Cross-cultural marriages have existed throughout history. However, the problems facing cross-cultural couples are changing. In the past, the difficulties were most likely connected with social class differences (e.g., Romeo and Juliet), nonacceptance by one's extended family, religion, or race. Throughout much of the twentieth century, interracial marriage was illegal in many U.S. jurisdictions, but today it is widely regarded as a matter of personal choice and widely accepted.

In many ways, boundaries between cultures are becoming more permeable, especially in the European community. On the other hand, there are many wars and ethnic conflicts based on animosities associated with cultural differences. Those animosities may deter opportunities or even the acceptability of certain cultural combinations in marriage. A good example can be found in the countries of former Yugoslavia, where cross-cultural marriages between, say, Muslims and Serbs or between Serbs and Croats were once common and acceptable. However, the conflicts set in motion in 1991 with the breakup of former Yugoslavia, and continuing in Kosovo, Bosnia, and Montenegro, have resulted in a reversal of social diversity in this area of the world. A new term has even entered the English language: **Balkanization,** meaning social re-segregation following a time of peaceful integration and social diversity. Balkanization in various countries around the world may make life difficult for cross-cultural marriages.

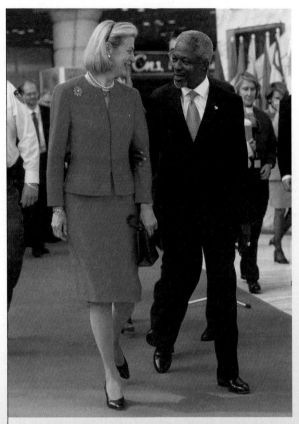

Former United Nations Secretary General Kofi Annan, born in Ghana, met Swedish attorney Nane Lagergren when they both worked for the U.N. High Commissioner for Refugees. They have been married since 1984.
© Javi Rodriguez/The Image Works

phone calls from friends, and remember to spell-check her term paper. A man who defines himself as agreeable may ensure that the wishes of others are taken into account when deciding where to eat, may give much to charity, and may wait until all others have feasted at the buffet table before helping himself. Our self-concepts, in short, affect how we present ourselves to others and how we behave in everyday life. Research shows that self-concepts differ substantially from culture to culture.

Markus and Kitayama (1991, 1994, 1998) propose that each person has two fundamental "cultural tasks," which have to be confronted. The first is communion, collectivism, or **interdependence**. This cultural task involves how you are affiliated with, attached to, or engaged in the larger group of which you are a member. Interdependence includes your relationships with other members of the group and your embeddedness within the group. The second task—agency, individualism, or **independence**—involves how you differentiate yourself from the group. Independence includes your unique abilities, your personal internal motives and personality dispositions, and the ways you separate yourself from the group.

People from different cultures differ profoundly in how they balance these two tasks. Western cultures, according to this theory, are characterized by independence. Conversations emphasize individual choices (e.g., "Where do you want to eat tonight?"). The system of salaries puts a premium on individual merit—your salary is specifically pegged to *your* performance.

In contrast, many non-Western cultures, such as Japan and China, are characterized by interdependence. These cultures emphasize the fundamental interconnectedness among those within the group. The self is meaningful, according to this view, only with reference to the larger group of which the person is a part. The major cultural tasks in these cultures are to fit in and to promote harmony and group unity. Personal desires are to be constrained rather than expressed in a selfish manner (e.g., "Where do *we* want to eat tonight?"). Conversational scripts emphasize sympathy, deference, and kindness. Pay is often determined by seniority rather than by individual performance.

To illustrate the contrasting orientations of independence and interdependence, consider the following descriptions, the first from an American student and the second from a Japanese student, in response to the instruction "describe yourself briefly":

> *I like to live life with a lot of positive energy. I feel like there is so much to do and see and experience. However, I also know the value of relaxation. I love the obscure. I play ultimate Frisbee, juggle, unicycle, and dabble on the recorder and concertina. I have a taste for the unique. I am very friendly and in most situations very self-confident. (Markus & Kitayama, 1998, p. 63)*

> *I cannot decide quickly what I should do, and am often swayed by other people's opinions, and I cannot oppose the opinions of people who are supposed to be respected because of age or status. Even if I have displeasure, I compromise myself to the people around me without getting rid of the displeasure. Also, I am concerned about how other people think about me. (p. 64)*

Notice the different themes that run through the self-descriptions of these two individuals. The American student tends to use global and largely context-free trait descriptions, such as *friendly, self-confident,* and *happy.* The Japanese student tends to use self-descriptions that are embedded in a social context, such as responding to elders or those who are higher in status and even using the social group as a method of calming down. These illustrate the themes of independence and interdependence. The independence theme is characterized by a self-view as autonomous, stable, coherent, and free from the influences of others. The interdependence theme is characterized by a self-view as connected, interpersonally flexible, and committed to being bound to others (Markus & Kitayama, 1998).

Is there empirical evidence that the way in which we define ourselves—something so fundamental to personality—depends on the culture in which we reside? Using the Twenty Statements Test, researchers have discovered that North American participants tend to describe themselves using abstract internal characteristics, such as *smart, stable, dependable,* and *open-minded* (Rhee et al., 1995). Chinese participants, in contrast, more often describe themselves using social roles, such as "I am a daughter" or "I am Jane's friend" (Ip & Bond, 1995).

Another study administered the Twenty Statements Test to samples of Asians in Seoul, Korea; to Asian Americans in New York City; and to European Americans in New York City (Rhee et al., 1995). The study was designed to examine cultural differences in self-concept, but with an interesting twist: Do Asians living in New York who

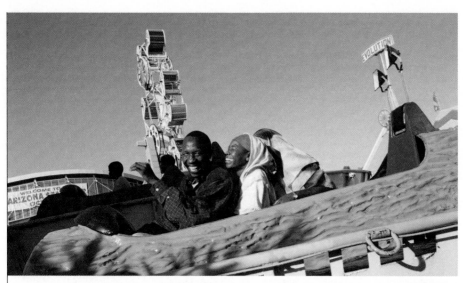

A refugee family from Somalia experiences the Arizona State Fair. After entering a new culture, acculturation is the process of adopting the ways of life and beliefs common in that culture.

© Christophe Calais/Corbis via Getty Images

self-identify as Asian differ in self-concept from Asians living in the same place who do not self-identify as Asian? In other words, do some people shift their self-concepts and adopt self-concepts similar to those of the adopted culture? The process of adapting to the ways of life in one's new culture is called **acculturation**.

The results were conclusive. The Asian Americans living in New York who did *not* self-identify as Asian described themselves using highly abstract and autonomous self-statements, similar to the responses of European Americans residing in New York. These Asian Americans used even more trait terms in their self-descriptions (45 percent) than did the European Americans (35 percent).

In contrast, in the study the New York–dwelling Asians who identified themselves as Asian used more socially embedded self-descriptions, much as the Chinese respondents did. They often referred to themselves by describing their role status (e.g., student) and their family status (e.g., son). Moreover, they were more likely to qualify their self-concepts with contextual information. Rather than describing themselves as *reliable,* they described themselves as "reliable when I'm at home."

Another study asked Japanese and American college students to complete the Twenty Statements Test in four social contexts: alone, with a friend, in a classroom with other students, and in a professor's office (Cross et al., 1995). The Japanese college students tended to describe themselves in all four conditions using preferences (e.g., "I like frozen yogurt") and context-dependent activities (e.g., "I like to listen to rock music on the weekends"). The American students, as in previous studies, more often used abstract, context-independent trait terms, such as *friendly* and *assertive.* Furthermore, the Japanese students, but not the American students, tended to characterize themselves differently in different contexts. In the professor's office, for example, Japanese students described themselves as "good students," but they did not mention this role in the other three contexts. The American students' responses tended to be more constant across different contexts.

Another study examined how frequently Japanese and European American students endorsed a variety of attributes as descriptive of themselves (Markus &

Table 17.1 Most Frequently Endorsed Attributes "I am"

EUROPEAN AMERICANS		JAPANESE	
Attribute	Percentage of Responses	Attribute	Percentage of Responses
Responsible	100%	Happy	94%
Persistent	100	Fun-loving	94
Cooperative	98	Relaxed	92
Special	96	Direct	92
Happy	95	Assertive	90
Unique	95	Laid-back	86
Fun-loving	93	Calm	86
Sympathetic	93	Free-spirited	86
Hardworking	93	Undisciplined	84
Ambitious	93	Ordinary	84
Reliable	93		
Independent	93		

Source: Adapted from Markus & Kitayama (1998), p. 79, Table 1.

Kitayama, 1998). A full 84 percent of the Japanese students described themselves as *ordinary*, whereas only 18 percent of the American students used this self-description. Conversely, 96 percent of the Americans described themselves as *special*, whereas only 55 percent of the Japanese described themselves with this term (see Table 17.1).

This theme of standing out and being unique versus fitting in and going along with the group is seen in the folk sayings of American and Japanese cultures. In American culture, people sometimes say, "The squeaky wheel gets the grease," signifying that standing out and asserting oneself as an individual is the way to pursue one's interests. In Japan, it is sometimes said that "the nail that stands out gets pounded down," which suggests that the American social strategy would fail in Japan. These themes even show up in language usage. Those with an interdependent/collectivist orientation tend to use "we," whereas those with an independent/individualistic orientation tend to use "I" (Na & Choi, 2009).

These cultural differences may be linked to the ways in which people process information. Japanese, compared with Americans, tend to explain events **holistically**—with attention to relationships, context, and the links between the focal object and the field as a whole (Nisbett et al., 2001). Americans, in contrast, tend to explain events **analytically**—with the object detached from its context, attributes of objects or people assigned to categories, and a reliance on rules about the categories to explain behavior. When watching animated scenes of fish swimming around, for example, the Japanese made more statements than did Americans about contextual information, linking the fish's behavior to their surroundings (Masuda & Nisbett, 2001). Thus, the cultural differences in the personality attributes of independence–interdependence may be linked to underlying cognitive proclivities in the ways in which individuals *attend to,* and *explain,* events in their world.

In sum, there is empirical support for the claim that people in different cultures have different self-concepts. Presumably, these different self-concepts are transmitted through parents and teachers to children.

Criticisms of the Interdependence–Independence and Collectivist–Individualist Concepts

Several authors have criticized the Markus-Kitayama theory that Western views of self are independent, whereas Asian views of self are interdependent, both on theoretical and evidentiary grounds. Matsumoto (1999) and Church (2009) contend that the evidence for the theory comes almost exclusively from North America and East Asia (notably, Japan) and may not generalize to other cultures. Furthermore, there is far more overlap in the self-concepts of people from different cultures than Markus and Kitayama imply. Many individuals in collectivist cultures, for example, do use global traits (e.g., *agreeable, fun-loving*) when describing themselves. Many in individualist cultures use relational concepts (e.g., "I am the daughter of . . .") when describing themselves. The cultural differences are more a matter of degree.

On theoretical grounds, Church (2000) notes that "attempts to characterize cultures of individuals in terms of such broad cultural dichotomies may be overly simplistic" (p. 688). Views of the self in all cultures appear to incorporate both independent and interdependent self-construals, and self-concepts in all cultures vary somewhat across social contexts.

A meta-analysis of dozens of studies suggests even more caution in generalizing about cultural differences in individualism and collectivism (Oyserman, Coon, & Kemmelmeier, 2002a). It found that although European Americans tended to be somewhat more individualistic (valuing independence) and less collectivistic (valuing interdependence) than those from *some* other cultures, the effect sizes proved to be small and qualified by important exceptions. European Americans were *not* more individualistic than either African Americans or Latinos, for example. Nor were European Americans less collectivistic than Japanese or Koreans—two cultures presumed to anchor one end of the interdependence continuum. Indeed, the Chinese, rather than the Japanese or Koreans, stood out as being unusually collectivistic and nonindividualistic in self-concept. Still other studies have found little support for the influence of transmitted culture on self-concept. One study of two presumably individualistic (United States, Australia) and two presumably collectivistic (Mexico, Philippines) cultures found that (1) people in all four cultures described themselves in trait terms with a high level of frequency; and (2) people in all four cultures mentioned *personal* rather than *social* or *collective* identity to be more important to their sense of self (del Prado et al., 2007).

Characterizations such as independent–interdependent also have been criticized on the grounds that they are too general (Chen & West, 2008), combining different kinds of social relationships and ignoring the context-specificity in which they are expressed (Fiske, 2002). Americans, for example, may be individualistic and independent while playing computer games, but interdependent while with their families or in church.

Despite these criticisms, there are real differences across cultures, and these must be explained. Most researchers have assumed that cultural differences in dimensions such as independence–interdependence are instances of transmitted culture—ideas, attitudes, and self-concepts that are passed from one mind to another within a culture, down through the generations. Others have proposed a different explanation involving evolutionary psychology and evoked culture (Oyserman, Coon, & Kemmelmeier, 2002b). They hypothesize that humans have evolved psychological mechanisms for *both* types of self-concepts and can switch from one mode to another, depending on fitness advantages. Specifically, when one's group is low in mobility, is limited in resources, and has many relatives in close proximity, it has paid survival dividends to be highly collectivistic and interdependent. One's genetic relatives, often the recipients of these collectivist proclivities, tend to benefit. On the other hand, when mobility is high and people move frequently from place to place, when resources are relatively abundant, and when few genetic relatives live close by, it has paid survival dividends to adopt a more individualistic and independent proclivity. This hypothesis is best summed up by its authors: "Thus, an evolutionary perspective suggests both the 'basicness' of independent and interdependent processing as well as the likelihood that all social systems are inhabited by individuals who can do both and draw on one or the other depending on their immediate contexts" (Oyserman et al., 2002b, p. 116). Research is increasingly exploring this fascinating fusion of evolutionary psychology and cultural psychology (e.g., Henrich, 2015).

Toshiyuki Tanaka, an umpire in the Japanese baseball league, during an interview. In his culture, harmony is valued over conflict. To keep the peace during a heated game, Tanaka often plays the role of diplomat. He rarely penalizes a team or ejects a player or coach from the game, events that are fairly common in American baseball. Moreover, Tanaka sometimes admits it when he makes a mistake, which is practically unheard of among American umpires.
© *Itsuo Inouye/AP Images*

Cultural Differences in Self-Enhancement

Self-enhancement is the tendency to describe and present oneself using positive or socially valued attributes, such as *kind, understanding, intelligent,* and *industrious.* Tendencies toward self-enhancement tend to be stable over time (Baumeister, 1997). Many studies have documented that North Americans tend to maintain a generally positive evaluation of themselves (Fiske et al., 1997). One study showed that the self-concepts of American adults contain more than four times as many positive attributes as negative ones (Herzog et al., 1995). The Japanese tend to make far fewer spontaneous positive statements about themselves. The Japanese score lower than Americans on translations of self-esteem scales (Fiske et al., 1997). Japanese respondents tend to give more negative descriptions of themselves, such as "I think too much" and "I'm a somewhat selfish person" (Yeh, 1995). Even the positive self-descriptions of the Japanese respondents tend to be in the form of negations, such as "I'm not lazy." American respondents would express a similar sentiment with the phrase "I'm a hard worker."

Similar cultural differences have been discovered between Korean and American respondents (Ryff, Lee, & Na, 1995). Korean respondents are more likely to endorse negative statements about themselves, whereas American respondents are more likely to endorse positive statements. Differences in self-enhancement also show up in parents' self-descriptions of the quality of their parenting practices (Schmutte, Lee, & Ryff, 1995). American parents describe their parenting practices in generally glowing terms; Korean parents give mostly negative self-evaluations. Another study found that Chinese individuals showed less of a tendency to self-enhance than USA Americans, but only one some traits and not others (Church et al., 2014).

Cultural differences in self-enhancement extend to evaluations of one's group compared with evaluations of other groups. Heine and Lehman (1995) asked Japanese and Canadian students to compare their own university with a rival university within their own culture. Among the Canadian respondents, there was a strong tendency toward in-group enhancement, with the rival university evaluated negatively by comparison. Among the Japanese respondents, there was no favoritism in the evaluation of one's own university in comparison with the rival university. Japanese and Asian-Canadians also tend to be more self-critical than Euro-Canadians (Falk et al., 2009), again suggesting cultural differences in self-enhancement.

Psychologists have advanced two explanations for cultural differences in self-enhancement. One is that the Asians are engaging in impression management (see Chapter 4)—deep in their hearts, perhaps, they truly evaluate themselves positively, but to express these views publicly would damage their reputation. A second explanation is that these cultural differences accurately reflect people's deep experiences. Asians, according to this view, due to profound cultural differences in values, truly evaluate themselves more negatively than do North Americans. There has been only one empirical test of these competing explanations (Fiske et al., 1997). When self-evaluations are made in conditions of total anonymity, where no one would be able to identify the respondent, researchers still found that the self-enhancement commonly seen among Americans does not occur among Asian respondents. This supports the theory that cultural differences reflect the actual subjective experiences and are not merely surface differences due to impression management by Asians.

Cultural differences are matters of degree; people in all cultures appear to display a self-enhancement bias to some extent (Kurman, 2001). In a study of three cultures—Singaporeans, Druze Israelis, and Jewish Israelis—Kurman (2001) asked participants whether they considered themselves to be below average or above average for the sex and age group on six traits: intelligence, health, and sociability (agentic traits) and cooperation, honesty, and generosity (communal traits). Although the Singaporeans showed slightly more self-enhancement than the other two cultures, it applied only to the agentic traits, and people in *all* cultures showed a self-enhancement bias. On the communal traits, 85 percent of the participants in all three cultures viewed themselves as "above average" for their age and sex group. On the agentic traits, although the Druze and Jewish Israeli samples showed a self-enhancement level of 90 percent and 87 percent, respectively, the Singaporeans showed a self-enhancement level of nearly 80 percent. Thus, people across cultures show a self-enhancement bias, so the cultural differences must be interpreted within the context of this overall similarity.

Do Cultures Have Distinctive Personality Profiles?

People have long been fascinated with the question of whether cultures have distinctive personality profiles. Are people from the Mediterranean region of Europe really more emotionally expressive, or is this merely an incorrect stereotype? Are people from Scandinavia really more calm and stoic, or is this merely an incorrect stereotype? Most studies reveal that stereotypes about national personality rarely correspond to average levels of actual assessed personality (Allik, 2012).

Robert McCrae and 79 colleagues from around the world studied the personality profiles of 51 different cultures, using 12,156 participants (McCrae et al., 2005a). They translated the Revised NEO Personality Inventory into the appropriate language for each culture and then examined the aggregate Big Five personality scores for each culture. The largest difference they found across cultures centered on Extraversion. Americans and Europeans scored higher than Asians and Africans. A few examples will illustrate these differences. With the cross-cultural average set to 50, the average Extraversion score was 52.3 for Americans, 53.8 for Australians, 53.7 for the English, and 52.2 for Belgians. In contrast, the average Extraversion scores were 46.5 for Ugandans, 47.0 for Ethiopians, and 46.6 for People's Republic Chinese. Some have questioned the validity of these findings because they rely exclusively on self-report (Ashton, 2007; Perugini & Richetin, 2007).

Recent studies confirm personality stereotypes in some domains but not in other domains. For example, stereotypes about gender differences across culture appear to be fairly accurate (Lockenhoff et al., 2014). Women are stereotyped as a bit more agreeable, conscientious, and anxious in a study of 26 cultures, and findings from both self-report and observer-report studies bear this out. On the other hand, many national character stereotypes appear to be inaccurate (McCrae et al., 2013). Some Chinese people stereotype Malays as "friendly, but lazy," but the empirical findings do not support this. A study of 26 countries found little support for national character stereotypes (McCrae et al., 2013). It is important to bear in mind that even when cultural differences in personality are found, they are relatively small. Most of the differences in personality occur *within* cultures, not among cultures. Indeed, the most striking finding from this study is how similar the 51 cultures actually are in their overall scores on the five-factor model.

Personality Variations Within Culture
Another dimension of transmitted culture pertains to **within-culture variations**, although these have not received the same degree of attention as cross-cultural variations. Within-culture variations can arise from several sources, including differences in growing up in various socioeconomic classes, differences in historical era, and differences in local evoked or transmitted culture.

There is some evidence, for example, that **social class** within a culture can have an effect on personality (Kohn et al., 1990). Lower-class parents tend to emphasize the importance of obedience to authority, whereas higher-status parents tend to emphasize self-direction and nonconformity to the dictates of others. According to Kohn, these socialization practices stem from the sorts of occupations that parents expect their children to enter. Higher-status jobs (e.g., manager, start-up company founder, doctor, lawyer) often require greater self-direction, whereas lower-status jobs (e.g., factory worker, gas station employee) more often require the need to follow rules and permit less latitude for innovation. In studies of American, Japanese, and Polish men, men from higher social classes in all cultures tended to be more self-directed, showed lower levels of conformity, and had greater intellectual flexibility than men from lower social classes. Interestingly, those from lower classes tend to be more generous and charitable than those in the upper classes, giving more even though they have less (Piff et al., 2010).

These findings are correlational, so, of course, direction of effects cannot be assumed. Perhaps people with personalities marked by self-direction and intellectual flexibility gravitate toward the higher social classes. Or perhaps the socialization practices of higher-social-class parents produce children with personalities that are different from the personalities of lower-social-class children. In either case, this example highlights the importance of within-culture differences. Figure 17.1 shows the distribution of individualism–collectivism in two

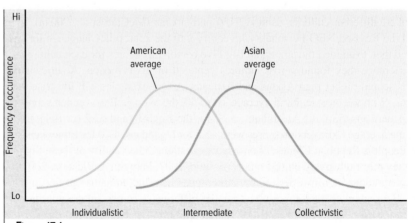

Figure 17.1

Individualism versus collectivism in American and Asian cultures. The distribution of two groups may be significantly different from each other in terms of the group mean yet have a high proportion of overlap. This means that many individuals from one group are higher (or lower) than many members of the other group, in a pattern opposite that of the mean difference. Asians score higher on collectivism than Americans do, yet there will always be some Americans who score higher than some Asians (those in the shaded area) on this measure.

cultures. The shaded part shows the overlap among cultures. Consequently, even though cultures can differ in their average level on a particular trait, many individuals within the one culture can be higher (or lower) than many individuals in the other culture.

Another type of within-culture variation pertains to the effects of **historical era** on personality. People who grew up during the Great Depression of the 1930s, for example, might be more anxious about job security, adopting a more conservative spending style. Those who came of age during the sexual revolution of the 1960s and 1970s might show a greater openness to experimentation. Those growing up in the age of the Internet spend more time interacting with others in distant places, expanding social horizons in ways that might influence personality. Many people in modern times find mates through internet dating sites, a phenomenon virtually absent a generation ago (Buss, 2016). Disentangling the effects of historical era on personality is an extremely difficult task because most currently used personality measures were not in use in earlier eras. One recent exception examined changes in average personality scores over a period of 25 years in the Netherlands (Smits et al., 2011). Researchers found small but consistent increases in Extraversion, Agreeableness, and Conscientiousness, and small decreases in Neuroticism.

Cultural Universals

A third approach to culture and personality is to attempt to identify features of personality that appear to be universal, or present in most or all human cultures. As described in Chapter 1, these universals constitute the human nature level of analyzing personality.

In the history of the study of personality and culture, the study of **cultural universals** has long been in disfavor. For most of the twentieth century, the focus was almost exclusively on cultural differences. This emphasis was fueled by anthropologists who reported on seemingly exotic cultures. Margaret Mead, for example, purported to discover cultures entirely lacking in sexual jealousy, cultures in which sex roles were reversed and adolescence was not marked with stress and turmoil (Mead, 1928, 1935). On sex roles, for example, Mead presumed to discover "a genuine reversal of the sex-attitudes of our culture, with the woman the dominant, impersonal, managing partner, the man the less responsible and the emotionally dependent person" (Mead, 1935, p. 279). Human nature was assumed to be infinitely variable, infinitely flexible, and not constrained by a universal human nature: "We are forced to conclude that human nature is almost unbelievably malleable, responding accurately and contrastingly to contrasting cultural conditions" (p. 280).

Over the past few decades, the pendulum has swung toward a more moderate view. Anthropologists who visited the islands Mead had visited failed to confirm Mead's findings (e.g., Freeman, 1983). In cultures in which sexual jealousy was presumed to be entirely absent, it turned out that sexual jealousy was the leading cause of spousal battering and spousal homicide. In cultures such as the Chambri, where the sex roles were presumed to be reversed, anthropologists instead found that men were considered to be in charge (Brown, 1991; Gewertz, 1981). Furthermore, the Chambri considered men to be more aggressive than women and women to be more submissive than men. Behavioral observations of social interactions among the Chambri confirmed these conceptions (Gewertz, 1981). All available evidence back to 1850, including some of Mead's recorded observations (as opposed to the inferences she made), suggest that the Chambri's sex roles are, in fact, strikingly similar to those of Western cultures. Brown (1991) and Pinker (1997) have a list of practices and attitudes that are good candidates for cultural universals—see Table 17.2.

Table 17.2   Culturally Universal Practices and Attitudes

Incest avoidance

Facial expressions of basic emotions

Favoritism toward in-group members

Favoritism toward kin over non-kin

Collective identities

Division of labor by sex

Revenge and retaliation

Self distinguished from others

Sanctions for crimes against the collectivity

Reciprocity in relationships

Envy, sexual jealousy, and love

Source: Brown, 1991; Pinker, 1997.

In this section, we consider three examples of cultural universals: beliefs about the personality characteristics of men and women, the expression of emotion, and the possible universality of the five-factor model of personality traits.

Beliefs About the Personality Characteristics of Men and Women

In the most massive study undertaken to examine beliefs about the personality characteristics of men and women, Williams and Best (1990) examined 30 countries over a period of 15 years. These included western European countries such as Germany, the Netherlands, and Italy; Asian countries such as Japan and India; South American countries such as Venezuela; and African countries such as Nigeria. In each country, university students examined 300 trait adjectives (e.g., *aggressive, emotional, dominant*) and indicated whether each trait is more often linked with men, women, or both sexes. The responses of the subjects within each culture were then summed. When the results came in, the big shock was this: many of the trait adjectives were highly associated with one or the other sex, and there proved to be tremendous consensus across cultures. Table 17.3 shows sample trait adjectives most associated with men and with women across cultures.

How can we summarize and interpret these differences in beliefs about men and women? Williams and Best (1994) scored each of these adjectives on the following dimensions: *favorability* (How desirable is the trait?), *strength* (How much does the trait indicate power?), and *activity* (How much does the trait signify energy?). These dimensions originate from older classical work in the field that discovered three universal semantic dimensions of *evaluation* (good–bad), *potency* (strong–weak), and *activity* (active–passive) (Osgood, Suci, & Tannenbaum, 1957). Overall, the traits ascribed to men and women are equally favorable. Some "masculine" traits, such as *serious* and *inventive*, were viewed as favorable, whereas others, such as *arrogant* and *bossy*, were viewed as unfavorable. Some "feminine" traits, such as *charming* and *appreciative*, were viewed as favorable, whereas others, such as *fearful* and *affected*, were viewed as unfavorable.

How can we interpret these cultural universals in beliefs about the personality characteristics of men and women? One way is that these beliefs represent stereotypes based on the roles men and women assume universally. Williams and Best (1994) argue

Table 17.3 Pancultural Traits Linked with Men or Women

Traits Associated with Men		Traits Associated with Women	
Active	Loud	Affected	Modest
Adventurous	Obnoxious	Affectionate	Nervous
Aggressive	Opinionated	Appreciative	Patient
Arrogant	Opportunistic	Cautious	Pleasant
Autocratic	Pleasure-seeking	Changeable	Prudish
Bossy	Precise	Charming	Sensitive
Coarse	Quick	Dependent	Sentimental
Conceited	Reckless	Emotional	Softhearted
Enterprising	Show-off	Fearful	Timid
Hardheaded	Tough	Forgiving	Warm

Source: Adapted from Williams & Best, 1994. Cross-cultural views of women and men. In Walter J. Lonner and Roy S. Malpass (Eds.), *Psychology and culture,* 1st edition, p. 193, © 1994. Reprinted by permission of Pearson Education, Inc., Upper Saddle River, New Jersey.

that society assumes that men are stronger than women and therefore assigns men to roles and occupations such as soldier and construction worker.

A second possibility is that the traits ascribed to men and women in all 30 cultures reflect actual observations of real sex differences in personality. Studies of the five-factor model, for example, do find that women score lower on Emotional Stability, suggesting that they are more fearful and emotional. And does anyone really doubt that men are, on average, more physically aggressive or violent than women (see Chapter 16)? In short, the universal beliefs about the differences between men and women in personality may reflect actual differences in personality.

Expression of Emotion

It is commonly believed that people in different cultures experience different emotions. As a consequence, personality psychologists have argued that different cultures have different words to describe emotional experience. The Tahitians, some have argued, do not experience the emotions of grief, longing, or loneliness, so they have no words in their language to express these emotions. For example, when a Tahitian boy dies in combat, according to legends reported by anthropologists, the parents smile and experience no grief, unlike the profound sadness felt by people in the modern Western world who experience similar events. Cultural variability in the presence or absence of emotional words has been interpreted by some personality psychologists to mean that cultures differ in the presence or absence of actual experiences of these emotions.

However, are emotions really this culturally variable? Or are there cultural universals in the experience of emotions? Psychologist Steven Pinker summarizes the evidence in this way: "Cultures surely differ in how often their members express, talk about, and act on various emotions. But that says nothing about what their people feel. The evidence suggests that the emotions of all normal members of our species are played on the same keyboard" (Pinker, 1997, p. 365).

The earliest evidence of cultural universals in emotions came from Charles Darwin. In gathering evidence for his book on emotions, *The Expression of Emotions in Man and Animals,* Darwin (1872/1965) asked anthropologists and travelers who interacted with peoples on five continents to give detailed information about how the natives expressed various emotions, such as grief, contempt, disgust, fear, and jealousy. He summarized the answers he received: "The same state of mind is expressed throughout the world with remarkable uniformity; and this fact is in itself interesting as evidence of the close similarity in bodily structure and mental disposition of all the races of mankind" (Darwin, 1872/1965, pp. 15, 17).

Darwin's methods, of course, were crude by today's scientific standards, but subsequent research has confirmed his basic conclusions. Psychologist Paul Ekman created a set of photographs of people expressing six basic emotions and then showed them to people in various cultures (Ekman, 1973). Some cultures in his study, such as the Fore foragers of New Guinea, had had almost no contact with Westerners. The Fore spoke no English, had seen no TV or movies, and had never lived with Caucasians. He also administered the tests to people in Japan, Brazil, Chile, Argentina, and the United States. Ekman asked each subject to label the emotion expressed in each photograph and to make up a story about what the person in the photograph had experienced. The six emotions—happiness, sadness, anger, fear, disgust, and surprise—were universally recognized by people in the various cultures. These findings have been subsequently replicated in other countries, such as Italy, Scotland, Estonia, Greece, Germany, Hong Kong, Sumatra, and Turkey (Ekman et al., 1987). Further research by Ekman and his colleagues has expanded the list of universal emotions to include contempt, embarrassment, and shame (Ekman, 1999).

In addition to finding that people of different cultures effortlessly recognized the emotions expressed on the faces in the photographs, Ekman reversed the procedure. He asked the Fore participants to act out scenarios, such as "Your child has died" and "You are angry and about to fight," and then photographed them. The emotions expressed in these photographs were easily recognized by facial expressions and were strikingly similar to the expressions of the same emotions seen in the photographs of the Caucasian participants. Further evidence for the universality, and possible evolutionary origins, of these basic emotions comes from the finding that children who are blind from birth display the same facial expressions of emotions that those with full sight display (Lazarus, 1991).

Pinker notes that whether a language has a word for a particular emotion or not matters little if the question is whether people *experience* the emotion in the same way: Tahitians are said not to have a word for grief; however, "when a Tahitian woman says 'My husband died and I feel sick,' her emotional state is hardly mysterious; she is probably not complaining about acid indigestion" (Pinker, 1997, p. 367).

Another example is the German word *Schadenfreude:* "When English-speakers hear the word *Schadenfreude* for the first time, their reaction is not, 'Let me see . . . pleasure in another's misfortunes . . . what could that possibly be? I cannot grasp the concept; my language and culture have not provided me with such a category.' Their reaction is, 'You mean there's a word for it? Cool!'" (Pinker, 1997, p. 367). People universally may experience the emotion of pleasure in an enemy's misfortunes in the same way, even if all cultures do not have a single word in their language to capture it.

The view that language is not necessary for people to experience emotions may be contrasted with what has been called the **Whorfian hypothesis of linguistic relativity**, which contends that language *creates* thought and experience. In the extreme view, the Whorfian hypothesis argues that the ideas that people can think and the emotions they feel are constrained by the words that happen to exist in their language and culture (Whorf, 1956).

Disgust appears to be an emotion universally experienced by humans.
© Tetra Images/Shutterstock.com RF

The difference between *experiencing* an emotion and *expressing* that emotion in public may be critical to resolving this debate. Ekman (1973) performed an ingenious experiment to explore the difference between the experience of emotion and its expression in public. He secretly videotaped the facial expressions of Japanese and American students while they watched a graphic film of a primitive puberty rite involving genital mutilation. In one condition, an experimenter wearing a white lab coat was present in the room. In the other condition, the participants were alone. When the experimenter was present (a public context), the Japanese students smiled politely during the film, but the American students expressed horror and disgust. If this were the only condition run, we might conclude that Japanese and American students experience the emotion of disgust differently. However, when the students were filmed when they were alone in the room watching the film, both the Japanese and American faces showed equal horror. This result suggests that Japanese and American students *experience* this emotion in the same way, even if they differ in their expression of it in a more public setting. More recent cross-cultural work has confirmed the universality of some basic forms of emotional expression. One study compared non-verbal emotional vocalizations (e.g., "yuck," "huh") of the "basic emotions" of anger, disgust, fear, joy, sadness, surprise) among Namibian and Western participants (Sauter et al., 2010). These vocal expressions were bi-directionally recognized—Namibiams correctly identified the emotion that corresponded with the non-verbal vocalizations uttered by Westerners and vice-versa. These findings lend further support to the notion that some emotions are universal across cultures.

Five-Factor Model of Personality

A fascinating question is whether there is a universal structure of personality, such as the five-factor model, or whether different factorial models exist in different cultures. To examine this issue, it is helpful to outline the conceptual positions that have been advanced.

According to some psychologists, even the concept of personality lacks universality. Hsu, for example, argues that "the concept of personality is an expression of the Western ideal of individualism" (Hsu, 1985, p. 24). Shweder, a well-known cultural psychologist, argues that "the data gathered from . . . personality inventories lends illusory support to the mistaken belief that individual differences can be described in language consisting of context-free global traits, factors, or dimensions" (Shweder, 1991, pp. 275–276).

These views have been elaborated on: "Universal [personality] structure does not by itself imply that 'personality' as understood within a European-American framework is a universal aspect of human behavior . . . nor does it imply that the variability that appears as an obvious feature of human life is a function of an internal package of attributes called 'personality'" (Markus & Kitayama, 1998, p. 67). Finally, cultural anthropologist Lawrence Hirschfeld argues that "in many, perhaps most, cultures there is a marked absence of discourse that explains human behavior in terms of transsituationally stable motivational (or intentional) properties captured by explanations of trait and disposition" (Hirschfeld, 1995, p. 315).

What is reflected in these quotations is a fundamental challenge to personality psychology—whether the core concept of traits is universal or, instead, is a local concept applicable only in Western cultures. The most extreme of these perspectives suggests that the very notion of personality, as an internal set of psychological characteristics, is an arbitrary construction of Western culture (Church, 2000). If this extreme position were really true, then any attempt to identify and measure personality traits in non-Western cultures would be doomed to failure (Church, 2000). At the other extreme is the position that personality traits are universal in their applicability and that precisely the same personality structure will emerge across cultures. As two personality research- ers noted, "The most important dimensions . . . [of] personality judgment are the most invariant and universal dimensions" (Saucier & Goldberg, 2001, p. 851).

The first source of evidence bearing on this debate pertains to the existence of trait terms in other cultures. Many non-Western psychologists have, in fact, described traitlike concepts that are indigenous to non-Western cultures and that appear strikingly like those that appear in Western cultures. Following are some examples: the Filipino concepts of *pakikiramdam* (sensitivity, empathy) and *pakikisama* (getting along with others); the Korean concept of *chong* (human affection); the Japanese concept of *amae* (indulgent dependence); the Chinese concept of *ren qin* (being relationship oriented); and the Mexican concept of *simpatico* (being harmonious and avoiding conflict) (Church, 2000). Many non-Western cultures, in short, appear to have traitlike concepts embedded in their lan- guages in much the same way that the American culture and English language do.

A second source of evidence bearing on the debate concerns whether the same factor structure of personality traits is found across cultures. That is, do different cul- tures have roughly the same broad categories of traits? The trait perspective on person- ality, of course, does not require the existence of precisely the same traits in all cultures. Indeed, the trait perspective might be extremely useful even if cultures were to differ radically in terms of which trait dimensions they used. Nonetheless, the most powerful support for the trait perspective across cultures would occur if the structure of personal- ity traits were found to be the same across cultures (Church, 2000).

Two approaches have been taken to exploring this issue. In the first approach, which can be labeled the "transport and test" strategy, psychologists have translated existing questionnaires into other languages and then have administered them to native residents in other cultures. This strategy has generated some findings supporting the five-factor model. The five-factor model (Extraversion, Agreeableness, Conscientiousness, Emotional Sta- bility, and Intellect–Openness) has now been replicated in France, Holland, and the Philippines and in languages from entirely different language families, such as Sino-Tibetan, Hamito-Semitic, Uralic, and Malayo-Polynesian (McCrae et al., 1998). The five-factor model also has been replicated in Spain (Salgado, Moscoso, & Lado, 2003) and in Croatia (Mlacic & Ostendorf, 2005). A study of 13 different countries—from Japan to Slovakia—also found support for the five-factor model (Hendriks et al., 2003).

Perhaps the most impressive was a massive study of 50 different cultures (McCrae et al., 2005b). This study, involving 11,985 participants, had college-age individuals rate someone they knew well using the Revised NEO Personality Inventory. Factor analyses of observer-based ratings yielded the five-factor model, with only minor variations in factor structure across cultures. This study suggests that cross-cultural evidence for the five-factor model is not limited to self-report data, but extends to observer-based data as well. Using the transport and test strategy, the five-factor structure of personality appears to be general across cultures. Table 17.4, for example, shows the factor structure from a Filipino sample.

A more powerful test of generality, however, would come from studies that start out using indigenous personality dimensions first, then testing whether the five-factor structure still emerges. This approach has been tried in Dutch, German, Hungarian, Italian, Czech, and Polish (De Raad et al., 1998). In each case, the trait terms in the language were identified. Although the absolute numbers of personality trait terms varied from language to language—Dutch has 8,690 trait terms, whereas Italian has only 1,337 trait terms—the percentage of words in each language that constituted trait terms was remarkably consistent, averaging 4.4 percent of all dictionary entries. You may recall the lexical hypothesis from Chapter 3, which states that the most important individual differences have been encoded within the natural language.

Table 17.4 Factor Analysis of the Filipino NEO-PI-R

NEO-PI-R Facet Scale	N	E	O	A	C
N1: Anxiety	**76**	−08	00	00	06
N2: Angry hostility	**67**	−19	01	−44	−10
N3: Depression	**73**	−23	03	−02	−25
N4: Self-consciousness	**68**	−14	−15	22	−04
N5: Impulsiveness	**40**	20	04	−37	−47
N6: Vulnerability	**70**	−22	−23	04	−30
E1: Warmth	−21	**69**	17	28	08
E2: Gregariousness	−29	**65**	−02	07	04
E3: Assertiveness	−28	**42**	23	−29	35
E4: Activity	−15	**51**	10	−24	25
E5: Excitement seeking	−08	**51**	26	−29	−12
E6: Positive emotions	−16	**66**	14	15	01
O1: Fantasy	16	27	**47**	−06	−27
O2: Aesthetics	14	20	**65**	14	22
O3: Feelings	30	32	**53**	03	12
O4: Actions	−39	−03	**46**	01	04
O5: Ideas	−04	−01	**69**	01	30
O6: Values	−13	−06	**62**	−05	−16
A1: Trust	−20	41	09	**52**	−10
A2: Straightforwardness	−03	−22	−02	**57**	10
A3: Altruism	−12	27	13	**65**	31
A4: Compliance	−20	−10	−09	**75**	12
A5: Modesty	18	−27	−03	**55**	−13
A6: Tender-mindedness	22	27	09	**49**	20
C1: Competence	−38	22	16	−10	**69**
C2: Order	−04	−15	−08	10	**73**
C3: Dutifulness	−08	12	07	21	**69**
C4: Achievement striving	−12	06	01	11	**83**
C5: Self-discipline	−24	02	00	07	**81**
C6: Deliberation	−27	−20	03	24	**65**

Note: $N = 696$. Decimal points are omitted; loadings greater than 40 in absolute magnitude are given in boldface;
N = Neuroticism, E = Extraversion, O = Openness, A = Agreeableness, C = Conscientiousness.
Source: McCrae, Costa, del Pilar, et al., 1998.

The next step in the De Raad and colleagues study was to reduce this list to a manageable number of several hundred trait terms, identified as indigenous to each culture, which could then be tested in each culture. Factor analyses of each sample within each culture showed that there was tremendous replicability of four of the five factors of the five-factor model: Extraversion (*talkative, sociable versus shy, intro-verted*), Agreeableness (*sympathetic, warm versus unsympathetic, cold*), Conscientiousness (*organized, responsible versus disorganized, careless*), and Emotional Stability (*relaxed, imperturbable versus moody, emotional*).

Despite cross-cultural agreement on these four factors, this study found some differences in what constituted the fifth factor, as noted in Chapter 3. In some cultures, such as Polish and German, the fifth factor resembled the American fifth factor (Intellect–Openness), with *intelligent* and *imaginative* anchoring one end and *dull* and *unimaginative* anchoring the other end. One study conducted in the Philippines also found a replicated five-factor model, including the fifth factor resembling Intellect–Openness, although there are a few indigenous constructs that are less successfully subsumed by the Big Five, such as social curiosity, obedience, and capacity for understanding (Katigbak et al., 2002). Other languages, however, revealed different fifth factors. In Dutch, for example, the fifth factor seemed more like a dimension of political orientation, ranging from *conservative* at one end to *progressive* at the other. In Hungarian, the fifth factor seemed to be one of truthfulness, with *just, truthful,* and *humane* anchoring at one end and *greedy, hypocritical,* and *pretending* at the other (De Raad et al., 1998). The fifth factor, in summary, appeared to be somewhat variable across cultures.

Cross-cultural research using the lexical approach, as you may recall from Chapter 3, has found compelling evidence for *six* factors, rather than five (Ashton et al., 2004; Saucier et al., 2005). The new sixth factor—honesty–humility—represents a major discovery across cultures (Ashton & Lee, 2010). By starting with the natural language within each culture, these researchers were able to capture an important dimension of personality that may have been bypassed using the "transport and test" research strategy.

Clearly, further indigenous tests are needed to determine whether the five-factor trait model of personality structure is universal. Based on the existing data, however, we can conclude that the truth is somewhere between the extreme positions outlined at the beginning of this section but closer to those that argue for universality. Trait terms appear to be present in all languages. Factor structures based on instruments developed in the United States, and then translated and transported to other cultures, show great similarity across cultures. Using the more rigorous standard of instruments developed indigenously, four of the five factors emerge consistently across cultures. The fifth factor is somewhat variable across cultures and therefore may reflect an important lack of universality of personality trait structure. And a sixth factor, honesty-humility, has been revealed by at least some studies using the indigenous strategy.

SUMMARY AND EVALUATION

People living in different cultures differ in key personality traits, such as self-concept, the prevailing levels of aggressiveness, and the moral values they hold. The differences are called cultural variations—patterns of local within-group similarity and between-group difference.

There are two major approaches to examining cultural variations. The first, evoked culture, involves the capabilities present in all people that are elicited only in some cultural contexts. Evoked cooperation provides one example—people tend to share food when there is high variability in success at obtaining it. Presumably, all people have the capacity to cooperate and share, but these dispositions are evoked only in certain cultural circumstances. Evoked aggression provides a second example of evoked culture. All people have the capacity to be aggressive at times; however, if one grows up in a culture of honor, then aggression is more likely to be evoked in response to public insults.

The second major way of conceptualizing cultural variants is called transmitted culture—representations originally in the mind of one or more people that are transmitted to the minds of other people. Three examples of cultural variants that appear to be forms of transmitted culture are differences in moral values, self-concept, and levels of self-enhancement. Patterns of morality, such as whether it is considered appropriate to disobey one's parents or to eat beef, or wrong for a wife to go to the movies without her husband, are specific to certain cultures. These moral values appear to be transmitted from person to person within the culture. Cultural differences in self-concept are another example of transmitted culture. Many Asian cultures, for example, appear to foster self-concepts that are highly interdependent and contextual, emphasizing the embeddedness of the self within the group. European American culture, in contrast, appears to promote a self-concept that is more independent, stressing the separateness of the person from the group.

The cross-cultural work on interdependence–independence has been criticized on several grounds. First, the magnitudes of effect are sometimes quite small. Second, the dichotomies may be overly simplistic because they ignore the context specificity of the tendencies (e.g., Americans might be independent at work and interdependent at home with their families) as well as individual differences within culture (e.g., some Koreans are more individualistic, others more collectivistic). Nonetheless, some cultural differences are real and must be explained. Most researchers have assumed that these differences are instances of transmitted culture. An alternative explanation proposes that all humans have evolved psychological mechanisms capable of acting both individualistically and collectively, as well as a mechanism that allows them to switch from one mode to the other, depending on the fitness advantages. This fascinating fusion of evolutionary psychology and cultural psychology holds much promise.

The culture in which we reside appears to influence our self-concepts. Using a procedure known as the Twenty Statements Test, researchers have found that North Americans tend to describe themselves using abstract internal characteristics, such as "I am smart," "I am dependable," and "I am friendly." Asians, in contrast, tend to define themselves more often using social roles, such as "I am the son of . . ." or "I am Liu's friend." These differences in self-concept appear to be examples of transmitted culture, passed down from person to person through the generations. It's important to keep in mind that these cultural differences are a matter of degree. People in collectivist cultures use some global traits to describe themselves, and people in individualist cultures use some relational terms to describe themselves.

Another reliable cultural difference pertains to self-enhancement, or the tendency to view oneself using positive or socially valued attributes. Korean and Japanese respondents are more likely than American respondents to endorse negative statements about themselves, such as "I am lazy" or "I am a somewhat selfish person." Americans, in contrast, tend to endorse more positive statements about themselves, such as "I'm a hard worker" or "I'm quite creative." Another study found that Chinese individuals tend to be somewhat less self-enhancing than Americans. These differences in self-enhancement also appear to be examples of transmitted culture.

In addition to cultural variations, some elements of personality appear to be culturally universal. One example of a cultural universal is people's beliefs about the personality traits that characterize men and women. Worldwide, people tend to regard men as having personalities that are more active, loud, adventurous, obnoxious, aggressive, opinionated, arrogant, coarse, and conceited. Women, in contrast, are regarded as having personalities that are more affectionate, modest, nervous, appreciative, patient, changeable, charming, fearful, and forgiving. There is some evidence that these cross-cultural gender stereotypes are accurate.

Another cultural universal appears to be the experience and recognition of specific emotional states, such as fear, anger, happiness, sadness, disgust, and surprise. People from Italy to Sumatra can recognize and describe these emotions when presented with photographs of others expressing them, even if the photographs are of people from other cultures. There is also evidence for the cross-cultural recognition of nonverbal vocal expressions of emotions such as anger, disgust, and joy.

Finally, there is some evidence that the structure of personality traits, as represented by the five-factor model of personality, may be universal, at least for four of the five traits—Extraversion, Agreeableness, Conscientiousness, and Emotional Stability. There is also evidence for the five-factor model using the "transport and test" strategy model of personality, using observer-based data from 50 cultures. Nonetheless, studies that begin with the natural language within each culture, using the lexical strategy to identify important trait terms, have discovered a six-factor structure. In addition to the five major factors, the new *honesty–humility* factor is in contention for being a fundamentally important personality factor. This discovery attests to the importance of cross-cultural research, particularly research that uses a strategy that begins *within* each culture.

KEY TERMS

cultural variations 521
cultural personality psychology 521
evoked culture 521
high-variance conditions 522
egalitarianism 522
culture of honor 524
transmitted culture 525

Balkanization 529
interdependence 529
independence 529
acculturation 531
holistic 532
analytic 532
self-enhancement 534

within-culture variations 536
social class 536
historical era 537
cultural universals 537
whorfian hypothesis of linguistic
    relativity 540

PART SIX

The Adjustment Domain

© Colin Anderson/Blend Images LLC RF

This domain is different from the others discussed in the book so far. The first five domains each referred to a collection of specific explanations of personality. That is, each gave a perspective on, and a collection of knowledge about, the causes of personality and individual differences. In this last domain—the Adjustment Domain—we examine some of the consequences of personality. We focus on adjustment because, in many ways, personality functions to help us adjust to the challenges and demands of life, albeit in a unique way for each of us. We focus on two important outcomes in this domain: physical health and mental health.

Day by day, all of us are adjusting to the demands of life and reacting to life events. Some of us might even think there is too much stress in our lives. However, stress is not "out there" in our lives; rather, stress mostly refers to how we respond to life events. How we interpret some event determines whether we feel it as stressful. The tendency to interpret events in a way that evokes a stress response is influenced by our personalities. Personality plays a key role in how we appraise and interpret events and cope, adapt, and adjust to the ebb and flow in our day-to-day lives. Moreover, some people display patterns of behavior, emotion, and interpersonal relations that create problems for them and for those around them. These problematic personality profiles form the collection of personality disorders. These two areas—coping with stress and disorders of personality—define the adjustment domain because they refer to how effectively people interact with and cope with challenges from the environment.

Considerable evidence has been accumulating that personality is linked with important health outcomes, such as heart disease. Psychologists have developed several theories for how and why these relationships exist, as well as have offered ways to change health-harming behavior patterns. Personality is also linked with a variety of health-related behaviors such as smoking, drinking, and risk taking. Some research has even demonstrated that personality is correlated with how long we live (Peterson, 1995, 2000).

We also introduce two important new concepts in the material on health: moderation and mediation. These concepts describe two specific ways that variables work together to produce some effect. Moderation is where two variables are related (for example, stress and illness) yet the degree of relationship is influenced by a third variable, for example, personality (say the link between stress and illness is stronger for some people than others). Mediation is where the influence of one variable on another (say personality and longivity) works by going through a third variable (say health behaviors, such that personality predicts longevity because personality is associated with behaviors that lead to a longer life, such as exercise and proper diet). While we discuss mediation and moderation within the context of personality and health, these are general ideas that can be found in other areas of personality psychology as well.

In addition to maintaining health and coping with stress, many of the important problems in living can be traced to personality. In this domain of knowledge there is the concept of disorder, the idea that certain personality profiles can be so abnormal or problematic that they create clear difficulties in the person's life, particularly in terms of work and social relationships. Certain personality features related to poor adjustment and poor outcomes in life are described as personality disorders. We devote an entire chapter to the personality disorders, such as the antisocial personality and the narcissistic personality. We believe that an understanding of "normal" personality functioning can be enhanced by examining what can go wrong with personality. This is similar to the field of medicine, in which an understanding of normal physiological functioning is often illuminated by the study of disorders and disease. We begin our coverage of the adjustment domain with the topics of stress, coping, adjustment, and health.

18

Stress, Coping, Adjustment, and Health

An AIDS patient in an advanced stage of the disease. Although AIDS is caused by a virus, its transmission from person to person occurs through specific behaviors.
© Sergei Supinsky/AFP/ Getty Images

For much of history, humans have been battling microbes in an effort to overcome disease and illness. The list of germ-borne illnesses is long, and there have been many epidemics. For example, in 1520, the Spanish conquistadors landed in Mexico with several slaves brought from Spanish Cuba. One of the slaves had smallpox. The illness spread to the native Aztec tribes, who had no immunity to smallpox. It quickly killed half of the Aztec people, including their emperor, Cuitlahuac. Aided by the microbe that causes smallpox, the Spanish had no trouble conquering all of Mexico. Imagine how helpless the Aztecs must have felt as the mysterious disease killed *only* them, sparing the Spaniards, who had developed immunity. The Aztecs must have thought the Spaniards were invincible. The native population of Mexico, estimated at 20 million when the Spaniards arrived, fell to 1.6 million in less than 100 years (Diamond, 1999).

The world recently experienced another epidemic of an infectious disease: the HIV virus, which causes AIDS. The microbe that causes AIDS resides in bodily fluids and passes from person to person whenever bodily fluids containing the microbe are exchanged. A cure for AIDS has not yet been discovered, though medicine has been able to extend the lives of people living with this disease by treating secondary symptoms. When it first began in the 1980s the explosive spread of this infectious disease had surprised even medical researchers.

The epidemic of AIDS illustrates a very important distinction; although its cause is a virus, its transmission is through specific behaviors. For example, unsafe sex practices (e.g., not using condoms) greatly increase the likelihood of transmitting AIDS. Another high-risk behavior is that of drug addicts sharing intravenous needles. While medical researchers search for a vaccination and cure, psychologists are searching for the best ways to change people's high-risk behavior.

This is only one example of the importance of behavior in understanding illness. In earlier centuries, most of the serious illnesses that afflicted humans were caused by microbe infection, including such diseases as tuberculosis, influenza, leprosy, polio, bubonic plague, cholera, smallpox, malaria, measles, rabies, and diphtheria. As modern medicine developed effective vaccines, these microbial diseases pretty much disappeared as major causes of death (at least in the United States). Today, many of the leading causes of death and disease are related not to microbes as much as to lifestyle factors, such as smoking, poor diet, inadequate exercise, and stress. In other words, now that we are curing microbial infections, behavioral factors have emerged as important contributors to the development of illness.

The realization that psychological and behavioral factors can have important health consequences has given rise to the field of **health psychology**. Researchers in this area of psychology study the relationship between the mind and the body, as well as the ways in which these two components respond to challenges from the environment (e.g., stressful events, germs) to produce either illness or health. Many of the psychological variables of interest have to do with stable patterns of behavior—for example, whether a person copes well with stress, exercises some or not at all, sleeps seven to eight hours each night, drinks alcohol only in moderation, routinely wears a seat belt, keeps his or her weight at a desirable level, avoids drugs, practices safe sex, and avoids unnecessary risks. Researchers find that such behaviors, called health behaviors, are correlated with life expectancy. In fact, in the United States, researchers suggest that health behavior deficits contribute to more than half of all premature deaths—that is, death before age 65 (Taylor, 1991).

Personality can have an impact on health in many ways, and personality psychologists are developing new methodological approaches to the study of this link. Current research is based on detailed models of the mechanisms underlying the links between personality and health (Smith & Spiro, 2002; Smith, Williams, & Segerstrom, 2015). Life-span studies show that personality can have lifelong effects on health, though the effects differ depending on the traits being considered (Aldwin et al., 2001) or the specific health outcomes under investigation, such as the cancer-prone personality characterized by being unassertive and emotionally inhibited, or the coronary-prone personality characterized by being hostile and aggressive (Eysenck, 2000).

In this chapter, we focus on the portion of the field of health psychology that concerns personality and individual differences. Some main research questions in this area are the following: "Are some people more likely than others to become ill?" "Do some people recover faster?" "Are some people more able than others to tolerate stress?" Understanding the nature and consequences of such differences among people is the focus of this chapter. We begin by discussing various ways of thinking about how personality influences health.

Models of the Personality–Illness Connection

Researchers have proposed several ways of thinking about how personality can relate to health. These models can take the form of diagrams of key variables, with the causal relations among those variables depicted by arrows. Models are useful to researchers in guiding their thinking about specific variables and especially in thinking about how those variables influence one another (Smith, 2006; Wiebe & Smith, 1997). In most of the models we will discuss, one variable—stress—will be important. **Stress** is the subjective feeling produced by events that are uncontrollable or threatening. It is important to realize that stress is a *response* to the perceived demands in some situation. Stress is not in the situation; stress refers to how people respond to a particular situation.

An early model of the personality health relationship, called the **interactional model**, is depicted in Figure 18.1(a). This model suggests that objective events happen to people, but personality factors determine the impact of those events by influencing people's ability to cope. In this model, personality has its effects on coping responses—that is, on how people respond to the event. It is called the interactional model because personality is assumed to moderate (influence) the relationship between stress and illness. Events such as exposure to microbes or chronic stress cause illness, but personality factors make a person more or less vulnerable to those events. For example, if a person were infected with a cold virus but had a hard-driving, competitive personality, such that the person would not rest, would not take time off from work, and would not do other behaviors necessary to quickly recover from a cold, this person could become very ill, perhaps with the cold turning into pneumonia, because the person's personality influenced how well he or she coped with the viral infection.

The interactional model has been very useful for conceptualizing how personality can influence risk for specific illnesses. One of its limitations, however, is that it does not specifically explain the mechanisms underlying the interactions (Lazarus, 1991). As such, researchers developed a second model—the **transactional model**, depicted in Figure 18.1(b). In this model, personality has three potential effects: (1) It can influence coping, as in the interactional model; (2) it can influence how the person appraises or interprets the events; and (3) it can influence the events themselves. These last two processes deserve special attention.

In the above paragraph we stated; "personality is assumed to moderate (influence) the relationship between stress and illness." Because moderation is an important concept, we want to take some time to explain what this term means. A variable is called a **moderator** when it influences the direction or degree of relationship between two other variables. So, for example, if stress is correlated with illness, yet this correlations is stronger for some people compared to others (say those high in neuroticism), then we would say that the personality trait of neuroticism is a moderator of the relationship between stress and illness. The interactional model of personality and health essentially holds that personality is a moderator. Examples of moderator effects are common in personality and health. For example, a strong predictor of whether a person will use illegal drugs is if they have friends who use illegal drugs (self use and peer use is correlated). However, for people low on the personality trait of sensation seeking, this correlation is not found, and so the trait of sensation seeking is said to moderate the relationship between own use and peer use of illegal drugs (Marschall-Levesque, Castellanos-Ryan, Vitaro, & Seguin, 2014). A moderator is sometimes thought of as a risk multiplier; in this case, the trait of high sensation seeking multiplies the risk of having peers who use drugs on the probability that the person will themselves use drugs. While we introduce the concept of personality as a moderator in the context of health psychology, the concept of moderation is general and can be found in other areas of personality psychology. For example, Senf and Liau (2013) developed a program to increase peoples gratitude, hypothesizing that being more thankful would make people happier. The gratitude training program worked and people were happier on average after the training, but it worked especially so for extraverts. In this case, the personality trait of extraversion moderated

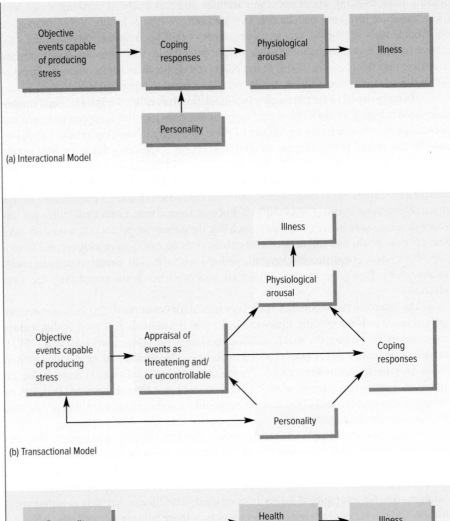

(a) Interactional Model

(b) Transactional Model

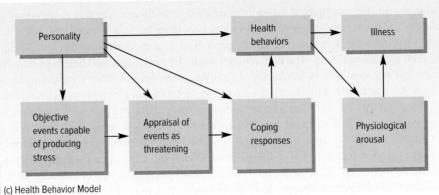

(c) Health Behavior Model

Figure 18.1

Three models specifying the role of personality in moderating the effects of stress on illness: (a) the interactional model, which specifies that personality influences how people cope; (b) the transactional model, which specifies that personality influences how people cope, as well as how they appraise and influence situations; and (c) the health behavior model, which specifies that personality influences how people cope, appraise, and influence situations, as well as the likely health behaviors that people practice.

the relation between gratitude training and happiness, with extraverts being more happy following the gratitude training than introverts.

In the transactional model, it is not the event itself that causes stress but how the event is appraised, or interpreted, by the person. You will recall from Chapter 12 that interpretation is important in determining behavior. An event, such as getting stuck in traffic on the way to a job interview, can happen to two people, yet the two people can interpret the event differently and thus experience it differently. One person might interpret getting stuck as a major frustration and hence might respond with a great deal of worry, stress, and anxiety. The other might interpret getting stuck in traffic as an opportunity to relax, enjoy some music on the radio, and use their cell phone to reschedule the job interview. This person does not experience the same level of stress.

The third point on the transactional model at which personality can have an impact consists of the events themselves. That is, people don't just respond to situations; they also create situations through their choices and actions, as we discussed in Chapter 4. People choose to be in certain kinds of situations; they evoke certain responses from those situations, especially from the persons in the situations; and they manipulate the people in those situations, all in ways that may reflect their personalities. For example, a high-neuroticism person, someone who complains all the time, may create situations in which others frequently avoid him or her. Or a disagreeable person may create interpersonal situations in which he or she gets into a lot of arguments.

These two parts of the transactional model—appraisal and the person's influence on events—are why the model is called transactional. These two elements of the model imply that stressful events don't just influence persons; persons also influence events. And this influence comes about through the appraisal of events, as well as the selection and modification of events. This reciprocal influence of persons and events makes this a more complicated, though perhaps more realistic, model of how the process actually works.

A third model, the **health behavior model**, adds another factor to the transactional model. It is important to realize that so far the two models are simply extensions of the theme that personality influences the stress–illness link. In the third model, which is depicted in Figure 18.1(c), personality does not directly influence the relationship between stress and illness. Instead, in this model, personality affects health indirectly through health-promoting or health-degrading behaviors. Everyone knows that poor health behaviors, such as eating too much fat, smoking, and practicing unsafe sex, increase the risk of developing certain illnesses. This model suggests that personality influences the degree to which a person engages in various health-promoting or health-degrading behaviors. For example, individuals who are low in the trait of conscientiousness engage in a variety of health-damaging behaviors, including smoking, unhealthy eating habits, dangerous driving, and lack of exercise (Bogg & Roberts, 2004).

This brings us to the concept of mediation. **Mediation** is similar to moderation, in that both describe specific ways that three variables are related to one another. Mediation is different, however, in that it specifies that the effect of one variable on another "goes through" a third variable. So, for example, the effect of conscientiousness on longevity goes through, or is due to, specific health behaviors. Mediation is a way of understanding the observed relationship (i.e., that conscientiousness is correlated with longevity) by specifying the underlying mechanism or process captured by the mediator variable (i.e., health behavior). This is not just a made up example. Turiano and colleagues (2015) used a national sample of over 6,000 people over a 14-year period, and found that Conscientiousness predicted a 13% reduction in mortality in the time period. Moreover, when health behaviors were examined as mediators, they found that heavy drinking, smoking, and greater waist circumferences (all negatively related to conscientiousness) significantly mediated the conscientiousness-mortality association. Findings such as these show how mediation can be a powerful way to explain how personality effects might work. Like moderation, mediation is often used in personality and health research, but its application as a way of thinking about how personality might have its effects extends to many other areas of personality psychology. As an example, among grade school children, the more extraverted ones tend to be more popular; extraversion and popularity are correlated. However, the effects of extraversion on popularity are mediated by oral fluency (Ilmarinen, Vainikainen, Verkasalo, & Lonnqvist, 2015). Consequently, it is not extraversion that directly affects popularity, but rather the effects of extraversion are indirect, going though verbal skills; extraverts are better verbalizers, at least at this age, and therefore become more popular with their peers.

To return to personality and health, conscientiousness is a personality trait that is reliably related to good health (e.g., Hill & Roberts, 2011). As a personality trait, conscientiousness is manifest in such behaviors as making lists before grocery shopping, keeping a calendar to plan activities, keeping one's work area neat and tidy, using a to-do list, and dressing up for special occasions. A list of several hundred behavioral indicators of conscientiousness can be found in Jackson and colleagues (2010). Why is it that conscientiousness predicts health and living longer? Researchers conclude that conscientious persons are also conscientious about their health behaviors. They tend to floss and brush regularly, take regular exercise, watch their diets, and adhere to other behaviors that are linked to better health. Conscientiousness thus appears to affect health primarily through a mediation mechanism described by the health behavior model.

A fourth model of the link between personality and health, the **predisposition model,** is shown in Figure 18.2(a). The previous three models were all variations on the same theme that personality influences the relationship between stress and illness either directly (interactional and transactional models) or indirectly (health behavior model). The fourth model is completely different and holds that personality and illness are both expressions of an underlying predisposition. This model is a very simple conception, suggesting that associations exist between personality and illness because of a third variable, which is causing them both. For example, enhanced sympathetic nervous system reactivity may be the cause of subsequent illnesses, *as well as* cause the behaviors and emotions that lead a person to be called neurotic. The predisposition model has not been the topic of much systematic study, though it seems likely that this model will guide investigators interested in the genetic basis of illnesses. It may well turn out that some genetic predispositions are expressed both in terms of a stable individual difference and in terms of susceptibility to specific illnesses (Bouchard et al., 1990). For example, some researchers speculate that there is a genetic cause of novelty seeking (a trait like sensation seeking) and that this genetic sequence also causes, or makes a person more likely to develop, an addiction to drugs (Cloninger, 1999). Consequently, the correlation between the novelty-seeking personality trait and addiction to drugs such as cocaine, meth, or heroin may be due to the fact that these two variables are both independently caused by a third variable—genes. This simple model may be useful as the human genome project (see Chapter 6) progresses from mapping the genome to understanding what specific genes control.

Conscientiousness has its effects on health through its association with health behaviors, such as brushing and flossing regularly.
© moodboard-Mike Watson Images/Brand X/Getty Images RF

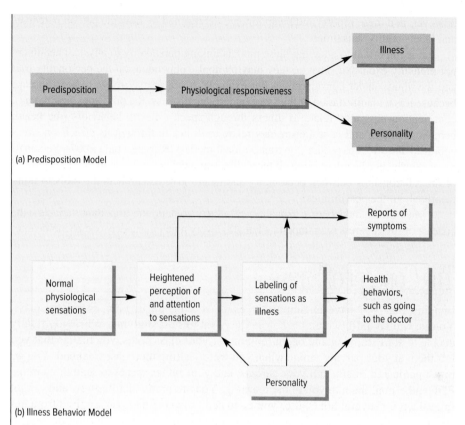

(a) Predisposition Model

(b) Illness Behavior Model

Figure 18.2

Additional models of the relationship between personality and health: (a) the predisposition model, which holds that personality and health are related due to a common predisposition; and (b) the illness behavior model, which specifies how personality might influence whether a person would seek medical attention or report illness symptoms.

The final model for our consideration—called the **illness behavior model**—is not a model of illness per se, but rather a model of illness behavior. Illness itself is defined as the presence of an objectively measurable abnormal physiological process, such as fever, high blood pressure, or a tumor. Illness behavior, on the other hand, is the action that people take when they think they have an illness, such as complaining to others about their symptoms, going to a doctor, taking the day off from school or work, or taking medication. Illness behaviors are related to actual illnesses, but not perfectly. Some individuals may tough out an illness, stoically refusing to engage in illness behaviors (e.g., refusing to take the day off from work when ill). Other people engage in all sorts of illness behaviors even in the absence of actual illness.

Figure 18.2(b) portrays the illness behavior model. It suggests that personality influences the degree to which a person perceives and pays attention to bodily sensations and the degree to which the person interprets and labels those sensations as an illness. The way in which a person perceives and labels those sensations, then, influences the person's illness behaviors, such as reporting the symptoms and going to a doctor. As discussed in Chapter 13, the personality trait of neuroticism is associated with a tendency to complain about physical symptoms. Self-reports of physical symptoms and illness behaviors may be influenced by factors other than actual illness, however, and these reports and behaviors are determined by how the person perceives and labels bodily sensations.

It is important to note that these models linking personality to physical health are not mutually exclusive. That is, they may all apply, depending on the personality trait and the illness under consideration. For example, hostility may relate to heart disease because it is a manifestation of the same underlying process (the predisposition model), conscientiousness may relate to illness through specific health behaviors (the health behavior model), and neuroticism may relate to ill health through its effects on stress appraisal and stress exposure (the transactional model) (Roberts et al., 2007). Personality may influence health through all these different mechanisms, and the various models of the relationships between personality and health give researchers the tools to think clearly about the possibilities.

Most of the models of personality and illness contain one important variable—the concept of stress. Stress is an important but also a very much misunderstood phenomenon.

The Concept of Stress

Imagine that you have an important exam coming up in your chemistry class. You've waited until two nights before the exam to start studying. When you finally decide to start studying and begin looking for your class notes, you realize that you left them at your parents' home when you were visiting there last weekend. You go into a panic and finally call your parents, and your father agrees to scan them into a PDF and e-mail them to you in the morning. You are pretty anxious now and cannot fall asleep for several hours after you go to bed. The next day you are tired from not sleeping well. The class notes arrive, but you have other classes during the day, so you will have to study that night at your apartment. That night, as you are getting ready to study, your roommate reminds you of the party he had planned for this evening, which you have forgotten about. Now you have to go somewhere else to study, an unfamiliar environment, such as the library. You rush to the library and settle into a secluded area to study. Although it is quiet in the library, you are so tired and anxious that you cannot seem to concentrate on the material. At midnight, the library closes, and you rush back to your apartment. The party is still going, and it continues until 2:00 a.m. Meanwhile, you are impatiently trying to study in your room but are distracted by the people and the music. Finally, you feel so overloaded, you just give up and go to bed after the people leave. But even now you cannot sleep. You are anxious and frustrated and feeling totally unprepared for the important exam you have in the morning. In fact, you see that the exam will be held in just a few hours. Things are out of your control. You notice that you have a painful headache, and even though you are lying in your bed, your heart is pounding and the palms of your hands are sweaty. You are not sure what to do. You want to study, but you also know it would be good to sleep a few hours. And you cannot seem to do either.

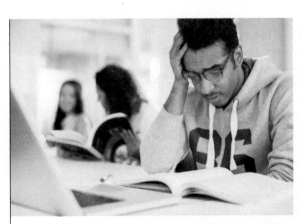

Studying for an exam can be stressful or not, depending on whether the situation controls you or you control the situation. Stress occurs when events seem uncontrollable and threatening. Taking control by keeping up with homework, planning each day, and preparing in a timely fashion can make studying less stressful.

© Caia Image/Glow Images RF

This is stress. It is a feeling of being overwhelmed by events that you cannot seem to control. Events that cause stress are called **stressors**, and they appear to have several common attributes:

1. Stressors are extreme, in the sense that they produce a state of feeling overwhelmed or overloaded, that one just cannot take it much longer.
2. Stressors often produce opposing tendencies, such as wanting and not wanting an activity or object—as in wanting to study but also wanting to put it off as long as possible.
3. Stressors are uncontrollable, outside our power to influence, such as an exam we cannot avoid.

Stress Response

When a stressor appears, people typically experience a pattern of emotional and physiological reactions. For example, if someone were to startle you by honking an automobile horn as you walked in front of the car, you would experience some startle; your heart would beat faster and your blood pressure would go up; and your palms and the soles of your feet would begin to sweat. This pattern of reaction has commonly been called the fight-or-flight response. This physiological response is controlled by an increase of sympathetic nervous system activity (see Chapter 7 for more details on nervous system responses). The increase in heart rate and blood pressure prepares you for action, such as fighting or running away. The sweaty palms and feet are perhaps a preparation for fighting or running away. This physiological response is usually very brief, and if the stressor is as minor as someone honking a car horn to see you jump, then perhaps you return to your normal state in a minute or less.

If, however, a person is exposed to a particular stressor day in and day out, then this physiological fight-or-flight response is just the first step in a chain of events termed the **general adaptation syndrome (GAS)** by Hans Selye (1976), a pioneer in stress research. Selye proposed that the GAS followed a stage model, as depicted in Figure 18.3. The first stage, called the **alarm stage**, consists of the fight-or-flight response of the sympathetic nervous system and the associated peripheral nervous system reactions. These include the release of hormones that prepare the body for challenge. If the stressor continues, then the next stage begins, the **resistance stage**. The body is using its resources at an above average rate, even though the immediate fight-or-flight response has subsided. At this point, stress is being resisted, but it is taking a lot of effort and energy. If the stressor remains constant, the person eventually enters the third stage, the **exhaustion stage**. Selye felt that this was the stage in which a person is most susceptible to illness and disease, as his or her physiological resources are depleted.

Figure 18.3

The three stages of the general adaptation syndrome proposed by Selye.

Major Life Events

What are some common stressors, events that are likely to evoke stress in most persons? Holmes and Rahe (1967) studied various **major life events**, those events that require people to make major adjustments in their lives. In their research, Holmes and Rahe wanted to estimate the potential stress value of a wide variety of life events. They started with a long list of events such as the death of a family member, loss of a job, or being put in jail. They then had a large number of subjects rate each of the events for how much stress each was likely to provoke. Each event was then associated with so many stress "points," and by counting up the events a person had experienced and adding up the stress points for all of those events, a good estimate of the amount of stress experienced by that person could be obtained.

In Table 18.1, we present a student version of the stressful event schedule based on the original Holmes and Rahe research. It has been modified for teaching purposes to apply to college-age adults and should be considered a rough indication of stress levels. In this scale, the number following the event refers to the stress "points" associated with that event. You can see that death of a close family member, death of a friend, and divorce of parents are the events likely to evoke the most stress. Interestingly, getting married is also likely to be stressful, as are other "positive" events, such as starting college or making some major achievement. This highlights the fact that stress is the subjective response to an event and that even though an event is positive, it may have the three characteristics associated with stressors: intensity, conflict, and uncontrollability.

If you take the Student Stress Test in Table 18.1 and turn out to have high levels of stress, there are several things you can do. First, monitor for early signs of stress, such as recurring stomachaches or headaches. Avoid negative thinking, pessimism, or catastrophizing. Arm your body against stress by eating nutritiously and getting enough sleep and exercise. Practice a relaxation technique regularly. Turn to friends and relatives for support when you need it.

In their initial research, Holmes and Rahe tallied up the stress points that each of the research participants had accumulated in the prior year. They found that the persons with the most stress points were also the most likely to have a serious illness during that year. This research was among the first systematic demonstrations that elevated stress—a psychological phenomenon—was associated with elevated risk for a number of illnesses. These findings persuaded medical researchers to take seriously the notion that factors other than microbes and organ malfunctions contribute to illness. Researchers following Holmes and Rahe have consistently found linkages between major life events and illness (reviewed in Schwarzer & Luszczynska, 2013).

Other researchers have taken a more experimental approach to see if stress is related to susceptibility to disease. For example, Cohen, Tyrrell, and Smith (1997) obtained reports of stressful life events for a group of volunteers and were able to score each participant along the lines of Holmes and Rahe's criteria for stressful points for various events. With the permission of the participants,

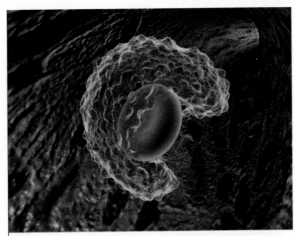

Illustration detail of a macrophage cell engulfing a particle, probably a leukemia-related pathogen.

© Purestock/SuperStock RF

Table 18.1 The Student Stress Test

DIRECTIONS: On the list below, check off each event that has happened to you in the past year. To determine your stress score, add up the number of points corresponding to the events you have experienced in the past year. If your score is 300 or higher, you are at risk for developing a health problem from stress. If your score is between 150 and 300, you have a 50-50 chance of experiencing a health problem in the next few years if the stress persists. If your score is below 150, you have a relatively low risk of a serious health change due to stress (DeMeuse, 1985; Insel & Roth, 1985).

STUDENT STRESS SCALE

	Event		Points
1.	Death of a close family member	_____	100
2.	Death of a close friend	_____	73
3.	Divorce between parents	_____	65
4.	Jail term	_____	63
5.	Major personal injury or illness	_____	63
6.	Marriage	_____	58
7.	Fired from job	_____	50
8.	Failed important course	_____	47
9.	Change in health of a family member	_____	45
10.	Pregnancy	_____	45
11.	Sex problems	_____	44
12.	Serious argument with a close friend	_____	40
13.	Change in financial status	_____	39
14.	Change of major at college	_____	39
15.	Trouble with parents	_____	39
16.	New girl- or boyfriend	_____	38
17.	Increased workload	_____	37
18.	Outstanding personal achievement	_____	36
19.	First quarter/semester in college	_____	35
20.	Change in living conditions	_____	31
21.	Serious argument with instructor	_____	30
22.	Lower grades than expected	_____	29
23.	Change in sleeping habits	_____	29
24.	Change in social activities	_____	29
25.	Change in eating habits	_____	28
26.	Chronic car trouble	_____	26
27.	Change in number of family get-togethers	_____	26
28.	Too many missed classes	_____	25
29.	Change of college	_____	24
30.	Dropped more than one class	_____	23
31.	Minor traffic violations	_____	20
		TOTAL _____	

Source: Based on "The Social Adjustment Rating Scale," by T. H. Holmes and R. H. Rahe, 1967, *Journal of Psychosomatic Research,* vol. 11, pp. 213–217.

these researchers then tried to infect half the participants with a cold by giving them nose drops containing the cold virus. The other half of the research participants were given plain nose drops; they served as the control group in this experiment. What happened? The participants with more negative life events in the previous year, who indicated they were experiencing a lot of life stress, were more likely to develop a cold after being given the cold virus than were the participants with fewer stressors in their lives, who were more resistant to the cold virus. The researchers interpreted this finding as consistent with the general adaptation syndrome: persons under chronic stress eventually deplete bodily resources and become vulnerable to microbial infections.

The relationship between increased stress and lowered resistance to viral and bacterial infection has been demonstrated repeatedly (e.g., Cohen et al., 1995). Currently, most researchers interpret such findings as illustrating the effects of stress on the immune system. That is, stress is thought to lower the functional ability of the immune system to mount an effective response to the presence of microbes, thereby leading to lowered immunity to infection and resulting illness (Marsland et al., 2001; Miller & Cohen, 2001).

Daily Hassles

Although the results of research on major life events are fascinating, many researchers on stress have gone on to new questions. One new line of research starts with the observation that major life events are, thankfully, fairly infrequent in our lives. It seems that the major sources of stress in most people's lives are what are termed **daily hassles** (Delongis, Folkman, & Lazarus, 1988; Lazarus, 1991). Although only minor, daily hassles can be chronic and repetitive. Examples of daily hassles are having too much to do all the time, having to fight the crowds while shopping, getting stuck regularly in heavy traffic, having to wait in lines all the time, having an unpleasant boss at work, having a long commute, and having to worry over money. Such daily hassles can be chronically irritating, though they do not initiate the same general adaptation syndrome evoked by some major life events. The results of research on daily hassles have shown that, similar to major life events, persons with a lot of minor stress in their lives suffer more than expected from psychological and physical symptoms. The top 10 most common daily hassles are listed in Table 18.2.

Table 18.2 The 10 Most Commonly Experienced Daily Hassles

Hassles	Percentage*
Concerns about weight	52%
Health of a family member	48
Rising prices of common goods	43
Home maintenance	43
Too many things to do	39
Misplacing or losing things	38
Yard work or outside home maintenance	38
Property, investment, or taxes	37
Crime	37
Physical appearance	36

*Over a nine-month period, these percentages represent the average percentages of people indicating that the hassle was a significant source of stress.

Source: Adapted from Kanner et al., 1991.

Varieties of Stress

Stress is a physical and psychological response to perceived demands and pressures. In the stress response, people mobilize physical and emotional resources to cope with the demands and pressures. Psychologists distinguish four varieties of stress:

- **Acute stress** is what most people associate with the term *stress*. Acute stress results from the sudden onset of demands and is experienced as tension headaches, emotional upsets, gastrointestinal disturbances, feelings of agitation, and pressure. September 11, 2001, was a day of acute stress for many people. Even for persons not directly involved in the terrible events of that day, many experienced the stress that comes from feeling that events are not under control (Peterson & Seligman, 2003).

- **Episodic acute stress** is more serious, in the sense that it refers to repeated episodes of acute stress, such as a weekend job that is stressful or having to meet a deadline each month. Episodic acute stress can lead to migraines, hypertension, stroke, anxiety, depression, or serious gastrointestinal distress.

- **Traumatic stress** refers to a massive instance of acute stress, the effects of which can reverberate for years or even a lifetime (e.g., Bunce, Larsen, & Peterson, 1995). Traumatic stress differs from acute stress mainly in terms of the symptoms associated with the stress response. This collection of symptoms, called **posttraumatic stress disorder (PTSD)**, is a syndrome that occurs in some persons after experiencing or witnessing life-threatening events, such as military combat, natural disasters, terrorist incidents, serious accidents, or violent personal assaults such as rape. Many persons in the United States experienced symptoms of PTSD after the September 11 terrorist tragedy. A study of refugees fleeing the war in Kosovo found that over 60 percent of them showed symptoms of PTSD (Ai, Peterson, & Ubelhor, 2002). People who suffer from PTSD often relive the experience through nightmares or intense flashbacks, have difficulty sleeping, have physical complaints, have flattened emotions, and feel detached or estranged from others. These symptoms can be severe enough and last long enough to significantly impair the person's daily life, such as having trouble with personal relationships or difficulty holding down a job.

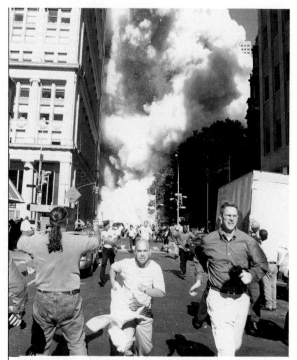

On September 11, 2001, many people in and around the World Trade Center in New York experienced traumatic stress. Many of them went on to develop posttraumatic stress disorder.
© Doug Kanter/AFP/Getty Images

- **Chronic stress** is another serious form of stress. It refers to stress that does not end. Day in and day out, chronic stress grinds us down until our resistance is gone. Serious systemic illnesses, such as those associated with decreased immune system functioning, or cardiovascular disease, can result from chronic stress.

Health psychologists believe that stress has **additive effects**; that is, the effects of stress add up and accumulate in a person over time. Stress affects each person differently. We each perceive demands and pressures differently and have different resources or coping skills. Such individual differences in the stress process form a core issue for psychologists who study personality and health.

Primary and Secondary Appraisal

Not all people respond to stressors in the same way. Two people can experience the same event, yet one is devastated and completely overwhelmed, whereas the other accepts the event as a challenge and is mobilized into positive action. Differences among people in how they respond to the same event are possible because stress is not "out there" in the environment. Rather, stress is in the *subjective reaction* of the person to potential stressors (Lazarus & Folkman, 1984). This is worth emphasizing, because many people refer to an event as stressful, as if stress were a characteristic of the event. Instead, stress is actually the response to that event. For example, two people are taking the same organic chemistry course; they take the same exam, and they both fail. One person may be very stressed by this event, whereas the other may take it in stride and not feel at all stressed by the failure. How can the same event happen to two people, yet one responds with stress and the other does not?

According to psychologist Richard Lazarus (1991), in order for stress to be evoked for a person, two cognitive events must occur. The first cognitive event, which Lazarus called **primary appraisal**, is for the person to perceive that the event is a threat to his or her personal goals. The second necessary cognitive event, **secondary appraisal**, is when the person concludes that he or she does not have the resources to cope with the demands of the threatening event. If either of these appraisals is absent—if the person does not perceive the event as threatening, or if the person feels he or she has plenty of resources for coping with the threat—then stress is not evoked. For example, if an event, such as an upcoming exam, is perceived as threatening to someone's goals, yet the person feels he or she has the resources demanded by that event (i.e., person has been studying and otherwise preparing for the exam), then the person might experience the event more as a challenge than as stress. Alternatively, the person might feel he or she does not have the resources demanded by the event (secondary appraisal) but might not think that the event is important to his or her long-term goals (primary appraisal) and so might not respond with stress.

What might lead some individuals to consistently avoid the stress response? What are some of the strategies that people use to overcome stress and the accompanying anxiety and feelings of being overwhelmed? Next we consider several personality dimensions that have been associated with resistance to stress.

Coping Strategies and Styles

Everyone has unpleasant events happen in their lives. We all have temporary setbacks, losses, and frustrations in our day-to-day lives. However, some people seem better able to cope, to get over stressful events, or to somehow see such events as challenges rather than as sources of stress. One personality dimension that has been studied in relation to stress is attributional style.

Attributional Style

Attributional style is a dispositional way of explaining the causes of bad events. One way to think about attributional style is in terms of the following question: "Where does the person typically place the blame when things go wrong?" As introduced in Chapter 12, the three important dimensions of attribution are external versus internal, unstable versus stable, and specific versus global. Various measures have been developed for assessing people's typical attributional style. One such measure is the Attributional Style Questionnaire (ASQ), developed by psychologist Chris Peterson[1] and his colleagues (1982). However, another very useful technique for scoring attributional style is by analyzing the content of people's written or spoken explanations. People often spontaneously provide explanations for events in their everyday conversations or writings, for example, Facebook posts, blogs, etc. It is possible to find these explanations in verbatim material and to rate them along the attributional dimensions of internality, stability, and globality. This technique for measuring attributional style was also developed by Peterson and his colleagues (1992), who called it the Content Analysis of Verbatim Explanations (CAVE).

Exercise?

Find an on-line article or blog post in which a person is explaining an event—perhaps a story about an accident, a natural disaster, or some sporting event. Analyze the story, paying particular attention to quotes from various people, to find examples of each of the three dimensions of explanatory style:

- Internal versus external
- Stable versus unstable
- Global versus specific

Come up with a characterization of the views on this event in terms of how people attribute responsibility.

The CAVE technique has the advantage of allowing the researcher to study participants who are either not available or not willing to participate in typical research, provided that such participants have made public some material containing causal explanations (Peterson, Seligman, & Vaillant, 1988). For example, presidential speeches, particularly State of the Union addresses, often contain explanations for a great many events. As another example, movie stars often do interviews that contain explanations for events in their lives. Psychotherapy tapes can be analyzed with CAVE, as they often contain persons' attributions for why things happened to them. Similarly, song lyrics, children's stories, descriptions of sports events, and myths and religious texts all contain explanations for events that can be rated for how internal, stable, and global they are.

Peterson, who has done a great deal of research on attributional style, prefers the term *optimism* to refer to this individual difference construct (Peterson, 2000). Persons who make stable, global, and internal explanations for bad events are seen as pessimists, whereas persons who make unstable, specific, and external explanations for bad events are seen as optimists. Optimism/pessimism is viewed as a traitlike dimension along which people differ. Optimists believe that life events are unstable and specific and that

---

[1]While completing the 5th edition of this textbook, Chris Peterson passed away suddenly in Ann Arbor, Michigan. Chris was a friend to both of us, and we will miss him. More importantly, the field of personality psychology has lost a creative and consistent contributor, one who was fascinated with the distinctly human part of human nature.

Following the events of September 11, 2001, the then mayor of New York City—Rudolph Giuliani—
exhibited a public coping style that included making attributions for the events that were external, temporary,
and specific.

© Henny Ray Abrams/AFP/Getty Images

what they do actually influences outcomes in life. Pessimists, on the other hand, believe that they are pretty helpless when it comes to bad events, that bad events have long-lasting causes that adversely affect many aspects of their lives (i.e., they blow things out of proportion). Consequently, pessimists believe that their behavior is not related to the outcomes in life.

Optimism has several different definitions, and distinctions can be made among the different underlying constructs (Peterson & Chang, 2003). For example, the optimism construct employed by Peterson and colleagues (e.g., Peterson & Steen, 2002) refers to the explanatory style for bad events being to blame them on temporary, specific, and external causes. However, a slightly different definition of optimism is offered by Scheier and Carver (1985; Carver & Scheier, 2000). These researchers emphasize **dispositional optimism** as the expectation that good events will be plentiful in the future, and that bad events will be rare in the future. For example, optimists are likely to believe that they will achieve success in most areas of their lives. This definition emphasizes not explanatory style but expectations for the future.

Another concept related to optimism, called self-efficacy, was developed by Bandura (1986). As discussed in Chapter 12, self-efficacy is the belief that one can do the behaviors necessary to achieve a desired outcome. Self-efficacy also is the confidence one has in one's ability to perform the actions needed to achieve a specific outcome. For example, someone's belief and confidence that he or she can climb Mt. Everest—this subjective feeling, the positive expectation about performing the behaviors necessary to climb the mountain—is self-efficacy.

Finally, a fourth concept related to optimism concerns perceptions of risk. Imagine being asked to estimate the probability of various events happening to you, using a scale from 0 to 100; 0 means "it will never happen to me" and 100 means "it is certain

A Closer Look

The Role of Positive Emotions in Coping with Stress

The vast majority of the research on personality and health focuses on negative emotions and how they contribute to stress and illness. However, in recent years, some researchers have taken an interest in the positive emotions, and positive appraisals, as well as how these can have a protective function (for a review, see Tedeschi, Park, & Calhoun, 1998). The general hypothesis is that positive emotions and positive appraisals may lead to a lowered impact of stress on health (Lyubomirsky, 2001).

Several decades ago, Lazarus, Kanner, and Folkman (1980) speculated that positive emotions played three important roles in the stress process: (1) they may sustain coping efforts; (2) they may provide a break from stress; and (3) they may give people time and opportunity to restore depleted resources, including the restoration of social relationships. However, no one in the health psychology research area gave serious attention to these ideas for almost two decades.

Psychologist Barbara Fredrickson has led the way in the search for the effects of positive emotions on stress and illness. She has proposed a "broaden and build model" of positive emotions, suggesting that positive emotions broaden the scope of attention, cognition, and action. This helps the person see more options in stressful situations, think about alternatives, and try different ways of coping with the stress. The "build" part of her model suggests that positive emotions help a person build up reserves of energy, as well as build up social resources, especially in terms of how positive emotions help a person build a social support network. She proposes that positive emotions are important in facilitating adaptive coping and adjustment to stress (Fredrickson, 1998,

2000). In experimental research, Fredrickson and Levenson (1998) found that the experience of positive emotions, following a period of acute stress, facilitated recovery from that stress. Specifically, these researchers examined cardiovascular reactivity to anxiety and threat manipulations, and they found that the participants who underwent a positive emotion following this stress showed faster heart rate and blood pressure recovery than did the participants who did not get the positive mood induction.

Psychologists Susan Folkman and Judith Moskowitz (2000) have built on Fredrickson's ideas and have suggested several important mechanisms in determining whether people will experience positive emotions during periods of severe stress. They give examples of these positive coping mechanisms from their study of gay men who were caregivers of partners dying from AIDS. Caring for someone with a chronic debilitating disease, such as AIDS or Alzheimer's disease, can be extremely stressful and often leads the caregiver to suffer physical costs from the stress and strain. From their study of such caregivers, Folkman and Moskowitz have identified three coping mechanisms that are capable of generating positive emotion during stress, as opposed to coping strategies that mainly provide relief from negative emotions.

The first positive emotion coping strategy is called **positive reappraisal**, a cognitive process whereby a person focuses on the good in what is happening or has happened. Forms of this positive coping strategy include seeing opportunities for personal growth and seeing how one's own efforts can benefit other people. By changing how they interpret what is

happening to them, people actually change the meaning of situations such that the adversity, in fact, gives them strength. In their study of AIDS caregivers, Folkman and Moskowitz found that the caregivers who were able to positively reappraise the situation (e.g., "I will emerge from this challenge a stronger and better person") showed better adjustment both during caregiving and even after the death of their partners (Moskowitz et al., 1996).

The second positive coping strategy identified by Folkman and colleagues (1997) is **problem-focused coping**, using thoughts and behaviors to manage or solve the underlying cause of the stress. It has typically been assumed that this strategy is useful in situations in which a person has some control over the outcomes. However, Folkman and Moskowitz note how this strategy can be useful in situations that, on the surface, appear uncontrollable. In the AIDS caregiver study, many of the caregivers were caring for partners who were dying, a situation that could not be stopped, reversed, or even slowed. However, even in these seemingly uncontrollable conditions, some caregivers were able to focus on the things they could control. For example, many created "to-do" lists of little things, such as getting prescriptions filled, administering medications, and changing their partners' bed linens. Keeping such lists, and ticking off the completed items, gave the caregivers opportunities to feel effective and in control in an otherwise overwhelming situation. In short, focusing on solving problems, even little ones, can give a person a positive sense of control even in the most stressful and uncontrollable circumstances.

A Closer Look (*Continued*)

The third positive coping mechanism is called **creating positive events** and is defined as creating a positive time-out from the stress. This can be done in a number of ways. Often, all it takes is to pause and reflect on something positive, such as a compliment received, a pleasing or humorous memory, or a sunset. These sorts of time-outs can give a person a momentary respite from the chronic stress. Many of the AIDS caregivers took time to remember positive events or to plan positive events, such as taking their partners for scenic drives. Some of the caregivers reported using humor to find some positive relief. It has long been thought that humor can be a tension reducer and that it may contribute to mental and physical health (Menninger, 1963).

This focus on positive emotions and their role in health and illness is new, and the research is in very early stages. Many of the early findings are intriguing but also raise new questions for research. For example, do different kinds of positive emotions—such as excitement, happiness, or contentment—play different roles in the stress process? Are the positive emotions most helpful in coping with particular kinds of stress? And, finally, of particular interest to personality psychologists are questions about differences among people in the ability to generate positive emotions while coping with stress (Affleck & Tennen, 1996). Who are the people who can generate humor, for example, during periods of coping? Are specific personality traits, such as extraversion or optimism, uniquely related to positive emotion coping styles? Can psychologists develop brief and targeted interventions to increase positive affect for persons experiencing serious life stress? Preliminary studies suggest that positive affect interventions are feasible and may be effective at helping people cope with stress (Moskowitz, 2011). These important questions point the way for the personality researchers of the future, who will undertake the necessary studies to understand why it is that some people manage to survive disaster, hardship, and misfortune with some degree of positivity.

to happen to me." The events you are asked to estimate are such things as dying in a plane crash, being diagnosed with cancer, having a heart attack, being killed in a terrorist attack, and being hit by lightning. Optimists perceive that they are at lower risk for such negative events than the average person is. What is interesting, however, is that most people generally underestimate their risks, with the average person rating his or her risk as below what is the true probability. This has been referred to as the **optimistic bias**, and it may actually lead people in general to ignore or minimize the risks inherent in life or to take more risks than they should. Nevertheless, people differ dramatically from each other in their perceptions of the risks associated with everyday life, with pessimistic persons overestimating the risks, relative to optimistic persons.

Optimism and Physical Well-Being

Many theorists using the various optimism constructs have examined the correlation between this individual difference and physical health and well-being. Research on optimism and health has been reviewed in detail by Peterson and colleagues (Peterson & Bossio, 1991; Peterson & Seligman, 1987). As a summary, optimism in general has been shown to predict good health as measured by self-report, ratings of general health made by the participants' physicians, the number of visits to the doctor, survival time after heart attacks, immune system functioning, faster rehabilitation after breast cancer surgery, and longer life (Carver et al., 1993; Scheier & Carver, 1992; Scheier et al., 1999). Moreover, optimism is found to correlate with a number of positive health behaviors, such as exercising regularly, avoiding fatty foods, drinking only in moderation or not at all, and responding to a cold with appropriate action (e.g., resting and taking fluids).

As with much personality research, the typical correlations between optimism and health or health behaviors tend to run between .20 and .30. Moreover, because this research is correlational, we cannot really know the causal mechanisms involved in the health–optimism link. For example, optimism may relate to a lower likelihood of becoming ill, to developing an illness of a lesser severity, to a faster recovery, or to a decreased likelihood of relapse.

As an in-depth example of research on optimism and health, let's look at a study by Peterson, Seligman, and colleagues (1998). This study examined more than 1,000 individuals over almost a 50-year period. The researchers found that the participants who scored in the more pessimistic direction were more likely to die at an earlier age than the optimistic participants were. Because Peterson and colleagues had such a large sample, the researchers were able to look at various causes of death to see where optimists and pessimists most differed. The researchers thought that the biggest differences might be in deaths due to cancer and heart disease, and they predicted that pessimists would have more of these lethal medical problems. This was not the case, however. The researchers found that the real difference between the optimists and pessimists, in terms of the causes of death, was in the frequency of accidents and violent deaths, with pessimists having more accidental deaths and deaths due to violent causes, resulting in a generally shorter life span, on average, than that of the optimists. This effect was especially strong for the men in this sample.

It seems that pessimists, especially male pessimists, have a habit of being in the wrong place at the wrong time. This research does not actually tell us specifically what the participants were doing when they accidentally or violently died. However, it seems likely that they were in the wrong situation, and moreover it is likely that pessimists, especially males, frequently choose to be in the wrong situation. An anecdote told by Peterson and Bossio (2001) is about a person who says, "I broke my nose in two places," and someone responds, "Well, I'd stay out of those two places if I were you." Pessimists, it appears, are frequently in those wrong places.

This result has been replicated, with pessimistic explanatory style correlating with the frequency of occurrence of accidents (Peterson & Bossio, 2001). The link between pessimism and a greater likelihood of mishaps appeared to be due to a preference for potentially hazardous situations and activities on the part of pessimists. Perhaps pessimists are motivated to escape their gloomy moods by choosing exciting but risky situations and activities.

Because of optimism's obvious health benefits, psychologist Marty Seligman and his colleagues are attempting to develop therapeutic ways to increase people's level of optimism (2002; Seligman & Peterson, 2003). In particular, Seligman has introduced a "pessimism prevention" program for use in grade schools, the details of which can be found in Weissberg, Kumpfer, and Seligman (2003) as well as at Dr. Seligman's Authentic Happiness Web site, hosted by the University of Pennsylvania, http://www.authentichappiness.sas.upenn.edu. The program teaches cognitive and social problem-solving skills that are based on optimistic principles. The program has been found to be effective at preventing symptoms of depression in low-income minority middle-school students (Cardemil, Reivich, & Seligman, 2002) and mainland Chinese adults (Yu & Seligman, 2002).

Management of Emotions

Sometimes we have emotions, and sometimes emotions have us. Emotions, especially negative ones, can be particularly difficult to control. Nevertheless, we can try to inhibit the expression of negative emotions, especially under certain circumstances. Imagine that your school team just lost an important championship, and you are really unhappy, distressed, and in an irritable mood, angry at the referees and disappointed by your team. However, you have an important exam tomorrow, so you must inhibit your distracting unpleasant emotions and concentrate on studying. You can think of similar examples of **emotional inhibition**, such as controlling your anxiety or hiding the fact that you are disappointed. For example, have you ever received a gift you really didn't like? Perhaps you suppressed your disappointment and replaced it with some positive false emotions, smiled, and said, "Thanks a lot; I really wanted one of those."

We all have to cover up such disappointments once in a while. But what about people who routinely suppress their emotions, who keep everything inside? What are the consequences of chronically inhibiting one's emotions? Some theorists suggest that emotional inhibition leads to undesirable consequences. For example, Sigmund Freud (see Chapter 9) believed that most psychological problems were the result of inhibited negative emotions and motivations. That is, repression and the other defense mechanisms are ways of preventing an unacceptable emotion from surfacing and being directly experienced and expressed. The early psychoanalysts saw this suppression of emotion, the pushing of unacceptable desires or urges into the unconscious, as the root of all psychological problems. Psychoanalytic therapy, or the talking cure, was designed to bring unconscious emotion into conscious awareness, so that it could be experienced and expressed in a mature manner. Moreover, the therapeutic relationship was seen as a place to experience and express emotions that had long been inhibited. There are other therapies that might be called "expressive therapies" because their goal is to get the person to release inhibited emotions.

Other theorists see emotional inhibition more positively. From a developmental perspective, the ability to inhibit emotions is acquired at an early age, at around 3 years, and is seen as a major developmental achievement. This is when children, though sad, are able to stop themselves from crying or, when angry, can inhibit themselves from striking back (Kopp, 1989; Thompson, 1991). The ability to inhibit negative emotion is seen as a very useful skill to learn in childhood. Children need to learn to control temper outbursts, such as the urge to hit someone who takes a toy from them. We have all seen adults who don't do a very good job of controlling disappointment or frustration, and their behavior (e.g., an adult temper tantrum) is often seen as childish. Some people are, however, very good at inhibiting negative emotions, even strong emotions.

What does the research reveal about the effects of chronically inhibited emotion? Surprisingly, there have been only a few well-done studies that directly address this question. For example, psychologists James Gross and Robert Levenson (1993, 1997; Gross, 2002) designed studies in which some of the participants were asked to suppress the expression of any emotions they were feeling while they watched a video designed to evoke the emotions of happiness (a comedy routine), then sadness (scenes from the funeral of a child, showing a distraught and highly emotional mother). Half of the participants were randomly assigned to the suppression condition, in which they were told, "If you have any feelings as you watch the [video] please try your best not to let those feelings show. In other words, try to behave in a way that a person watching you would not know you were feeling anything at all." The other half of the participants were assigned to the no-suppression condition, in which they were simply told to watch the video and were given no instructions to inhibit their emotions.

While the participants watched the video, the researchers videotaped them to determine how much they expressed their emotions while watching it. The researchers also collected

Which woman is genuinely happy? The woman on the left, Kelli Bradshaw from North Carolina, reacts to hearing her name called as the first runner-up (second place) in the Miss America Pageant in 1998. By implication, the woman on the right, Nicole Johnson from Virginia, simultaneously realizes that she is the next Miss America.
© Charles Rex Arbogast/AP Images

several physiological measures, such as those we discussed in Chapter 7. They also asked the participants to report on their feelings after each segment of the video.

Results showed that the participants who were instructed to suppress their emotions showed increased levels of physiological arousal, even before the video began, compared with the no-suppression participants. This widespread physiological arousal was interpreted as indicating that the participants were preparing for the effort necessary to suppress their emotions. The suppression participants also showed heightened physiological activity during the video, indicating increased sympathetic nervous system arousal, compared with the no-suppression participants. The researchers suggested that suppression of emotion takes effort and exerts physiological costs above and beyond the emotional arousal. The participants in the suppression condition showed less *outward* expression of emotion than did the control participants, as you would imagine. For example, the facial expressions of the suppression participants displayed little emotion, suggesting that they were, in fact, inhibiting the outward expression of their emotions, as instructed. As for the self-report, the suppression participants reported slightly less amusement in the amusement condition, but not less sadness in the sadness condition, compared with the no-suppression participants.

In an interesting line of research on emotion, Gross and colleagues (Ochsner et al., 2002) attempted to locate the emotional control center in the brain. They used fMRI to scan participants' brains while the participants tried to reinterpret a highly negative scene in unemotional terms. They found that several brain areas were associated with the successful regulation of negative emotions. These areas were mainly in the prefrontal cortex of the brain. This frontal part of the brain, which is also involved in planning and executive control, appears to be active when people are controlling their emotions. Interestingly, this is the area that was destroyed in the case of Phineas Gage, discussed in Chapter 7. Recall that Mr. Gage, after his accident, had difficulty controlling his negative emotions, took up cursing in public, was quick to anger, and frequently insulted people.

Sometimes it is necessary to inhibit feelings. Perhaps you do not want to hurt someone's feelings; perhaps you do not want to antagonize someone in a position of power; or perhaps you do not want to anger someone who is already acting aggressively (Larsen & Prizmic, 2004). For example, your boss may be upset with you for the wrong reason, and you may feel angry toward her. However, you cannot act out that anger because she is your boss and has a lot of power over you in terms of raises, workload, and working conditions. Quite simply, there are some situations in life in which it is wise to choose to hide feelings.

However, problems can arise when emotional inhibition becomes chronic, when a person routinely hides emotions. Someone who characteristically inhibits the free expression of emotion may suffer the effects of chronic sympathetic nervous system arousal. For example, Levy and colleagues (1985) have shown that people who keep their negative emotions to themselves are more likely than expressive persons to have a higher mortality rate, a greater likelihood of recurrence of cancer after treatment, and a suppressed immune system. Cancer patients who express their negative emotions, and who emotionally fight their disease, sometimes live longer than patients who accept their situation, inhibit their emotions, and quietly accept their treatment (Levy, 1990; Levy & Heiden, 1990).

The importance of emotional expression was illustrated in a study done by Noller (1984) on emotional expressiveness in romantic relationships. Noller found that the more people expressed their feelings to their partners, the fewer problems they reported in their relationships. Knowing how another feels allows you to adjust your behavior accordingly. If your partner never expresses how he or she feels, then it is difficult to know what makes him or her happy or sad or angry.

Example of an fMRI brain scan. Brighter colors, such as red, indicate areas with increased metabolic activity. This scan shows increased activity in the frontal area, an area of the brain important for the regulation of emotions.

© James Cavallini/Science Source

Other studies suggest that emotional expressiveness is good for our psychological health and general adjustment. King and Emmons (1990) had participants keep daily records of how they were feeling each day for three consecutive weeks. The participants completed a questionnaire measure of emotional expressiveness. The researchers found that emotional expressiveness correlated with higher levels of happiness over the three weeks, as well as with lower levels of anxiety and guilt. A similar study by Katz and Campbell (1994) found that emotional expressiveness was correlated with higher self-esteem.

Disclosure

Related to emotional expressiveness is the topic of **disclosure**, or telling someone about a private aspect of oneself. Many theorists have suggested that keeping things to ourselves, not opening up to other people, may be a source of stress and ultimately may lead to psychological distress and physical disease. These theorists have further argued that being open to others with our feelings may be curative, that talk therapy may work in part because through it we uncover secrets and reveal what we have been keeping to ourselves.

Psychologist James Pennebaker has been a pioneer in researching the effects of disclosure. In a typical study, he asks participants to think of an upsetting or traumatic event that has happened to them, something they have not discussed with anyone. He asks them to write down these secrets. People write about many different unpleasant events, such as various embarrassing moments, sexual indiscretions, illegal or immoral behaviors, humiliations, and so on. It is interesting that *all* participants quickly come up with a secret that they have been keeping. This suggests that probably all of us have some secrets.

Pennebaker argues that *not* discussing traumatic, negative, or upsetting events can lead to problems. It takes physical energy, he says, to inhibit the thoughts and feelings associated with such events. In other words, it is not easy to keep a secret to ourselves, and keeping something in, especially if it is a major trauma, is upsetting and takes a lot of energy. Over time, this stress builds and, like all stress, can increase the likelihood of stress-related problems, such as trouble sleeping, irritability, physical symptoms (e.g., stomachaches and headaches), and even illness resulting from lowered immune system functioning. Telling the secret, according to Pennebaker, relieves this stress. Confronting the traumatic memory by telling someone or even writing about it releases the person from the work of keeping the secret.

Pennebaker and his colleagues have conducted many studies on the topic of disclosure. In one study (Pennebaker & O'Heeron, 1984), they contacted participants who had lost a spouse through accident or suicide. Clearly, such a sudden and complete loss of a loved one through an unexpected and traumatic death must have a huge impact on the surviving spouse (recall that death of a spouse was the most stressful life event on the Holmes and Rahe list). The survivors were asked how much they discussed the tragedy with friends, family, or other helping professionals, such as a priest, rabbi, minister, or therapist. The researchers also did a thorough assessment of the participants' health since the death of the spouse. They discovered that the more the participants had talked about the tragedy with others, the better their subsequent health. In other words, those who kept the trauma to themselves tended to suffer more health problems than those who disclosed their feelings to others. Of course, this is correlational research, so we cannot know for certain if talking about one's problems causes better health. To pin this down, researchers need to do experiments where disclosure is randomly assigned. We now review some of these experiments.

Research started by psychologist Jammie Pennebaker has repeatedly shown that sharing ones difficulties and traumas with others is better than keeping your problems to yourself.
© Roanld Wixman RF

In an experimental study on this topic (Pennebaker, 1990), the participants were college students randomly assigned to one of two groups. One group was asked to recall and write about an experience that they found distressing. The other group was asked to write about a trivial topic, such as what they normally ate for breakfast. The students wrote about their assigned topic for 15 minutes each night for four consecutive nights. The participants writing about the traumatic event reported feeling more distress and discomfort while writing, and measures of blood pressure taken while writing suggested they were feeling more stress than was the trivial topic group. Six months later, the participants were contacted again and a health history was obtained. Students who had written about a trauma for those four days had had fewer illnesses in the subsequent six months, compared with the students who had written about trivial topics. Moreover, student records from the health services showed that the participants who had written about trauma had indeed gone to the campus health center less often than the participants who had written about trivial topics. Interestingly, just the act of writing about an upsetting event, even if no one ever reads the writing, may have a beneficial effect on health.

In another study by Pennebaker, Colder, and Sharp (1990), the participants were just starting college. For three nights in a row, they were asked to write about their difficulties and their feelings about the challenges of leaving family and friends at home and starting an independent life at college. Other participants (the control group) wrote about trivial topics. Health measures were then obtained after the students had been in college for at least a semester: the students who had written about their feelings and problems had gone to the student health center fewer times during the subsequent semester than had those who had written about trivial topics.

Other studies show that people who keep unpleasant information about themselves a secret are more likely to develop anxiety or depression than are those who tell someone (Larson & Chastain, 1990). Often, psychotherapists will ask their clients, especially those who have experienced a trauma or another extreme event, to talk or write about that trauma. Some psychologists even recommend keeping a diary of the events in one's life and how one is reacting to those events. Such a daily self-disclosure helps put one's feelings into perspective and make some sense out of the events in one's life. The process provides insight into oneself and the events in one's life.

Exercise

Try conducting a small experimental test of Pennebaker's hypothesis that disclosing secrets, even in writing, is associated with better health. Keep a record of your health every day for two weeks. Record each day whether you have a stomachache, a headache, muscle aches, a sore throat, or a runny nose. After this baseline period of recording your health, try keeping a diary each day for two weeks, writing down and describing all the stresses you experience each day and reflecting on how these make you feel. Pay attention to any difficulties, stress, or even embarrassing or trying moments. When the two weeks are over, stop keeping the diary and begin recording your daily health again. Although this is not a true experiment (you are both the subject and the experimenter, which is not done in true experiments), you can nevertheless get a feel for how research on this topic is done, and you might see a change in your health for the better as a function of keeping a diary.

How does disclosure work to promote healthy adjustment? Pennebaker's first theory of the mechanism concerned the relief that results from telling a secret. In other words, keeping the information inside takes effort and is stressful, and disclosing that information removes the effort and relieves the stress (Niederhoffer & Pennebaker, 2002). This explanation basically says that disclosure reduces the cost of having to inhibit this information. More recently, Pennebaker (2003a) has put forward a second explanation for how disclosure promotes adjustment. This explanation concerns how writing about an event allows a person to reinterpret and reframe the meaning of that event. In other words, a person writing or talking about a past traumatic event can try to better understand that event, search for some positive meaning in the event (the positive re-appraisal process discussed in the A Closer Look on pages 567–568), and integrate that event into her or his current situation. Both processes—relief from inhibition and reinterpretation of the event—may be occurring, and so both explanations may be correct. Indeed, Pennebaker (2003b) has speculated that this combination may be the basic ingredient that underlies most forms of successful talking therapy.

In summary, research on disclosure suggests that keeping traumatic events and the feelings about those events to ourselves can be stressful. Expressing our emotions in words can, in fact, produce some stress-reducing effects. Moreover, it appears that it does not matter how we put our feelings into words—whether we talk to a trusted friend or relative, go to a caring psychotherapist, go to confession at our church or have a talk with our minister or rabbi, have a discussion with our husband or wife, or write it in a diary. One study, designed to test how little disclosure is necessary to still achieve health benefits, found that two minutes of writing on two consecutive days produced measurable health benefits assessed four to six weeks later (Burton & King, 2008). Whatever form it takes, the disclosure of traumatic events, and our reactions to them, is much better for our health than keeping it all to ourselves.

Type A Personality and Cardiovascular Disease

Cardiovascular disease is one of the most frequent causes of death and disability in the United States. Health professionals have been searching for the factors that put people at risk for this disease. Known risk factors for developing cardiovascular disease include high blood pressure, obesity, smoking, family history of heart disease, inactive lifestyle, and high cholesterol. In the 1970s, physicians began to consider a new risk factor, a specific personality trait. As mentioned in Chapter 13, this grew out of the observation by some physicians that the patients who had had heart attacks often behaved differently, and they seemed to have different personalities compared with other patients. The heart attack patients were often more competitive and aggressive, more active and energetic in their actions and speaking, and more ambitious and driven (Friedman & Rosenman, 1974). They called this collection of behaviors the Type A personality.

Before examining some of the research findings on Type A, let us look at a few misconceptions. Although researchers often refer to Type A and Type B persons, it is not true that people come in these two distinct categories. As noted in Chapter 4, few personality variables are truly categorical, whereby people fall into distinct categories. Biological sex is an example of a categorical variable; blood type is another. However, very few personality traits are categorical. Instead, most are dimensional, ranging from one extreme to the other, with most people falling somewhere around the middle. The Type A/Type B distinction is like this, with Type As defining one end and Type Bs the other, and a large number of people in the middle, who are neither clearly A or B. Thus, the Type A personality variable is a trait, or disposition, as discussed in Chapter 3. It is distributed normally, as in Figure 18.4(a), not as a category variable. Psychologists describe normally distributed traits by reference to one end (e.g., Type A). However, by describing the characteristics of people at one end, it is implied that people at the other end (so-called Type B) have the opposite characteristics.

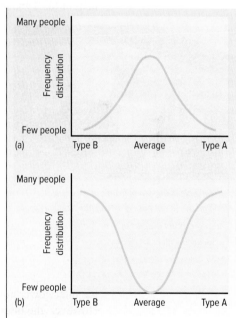

Figure 18.4

Type A and Type B are not really types at all and do not refer to categories of people. Rather, *Type A* refers to a normal distribution of people, anchored at one end by persons showing a lot of Type A behavior and at the other end by persons showing very little (a). Most people, however, are in the middle, or average, range. This is the case with almost all personality traits. A true type, or categorical variable, would be distributed as in (b), with most people at one end or the other and very few people in the middle. This is not the case with the Type A personality.

Another misconception is that Type A is a single trait; in actuality, Type A is a syndrome of several traits. More specifically, it is a collection of three subtraits, which together make up the Type A personality. One of these three subtraits is **competitive achievement motivation**. Type A persons like to work hard and achieve goals. They like recognition, power, and the defeat of obstacles. And they feel that they are at their best when competing with others. For example, a person who shows up at a charity bike-a-thon ready for the Tour de France bicycle race is exhibiting competitive achievement motivation. **Time urgency** is the second subtrait of the Type A behavior pattern. Type A persons hate wasting time. They are always in a hurry and feel under pressure to get the most done in the least amount of time. Often, they do two things at once, such as eat while reading a book. Red lights are their enemies, and they hate to wait in line for anything. The third subtrait of Type A is **hostility**. When blocked from attaining their goals, which is the definition of **frustration**, Type A persons can be hostile and aggressive. They get frustrated easily, and this frustration can make them act in an unfriendly or even malicious manner. The guy you see yelling at and pounding on a vending machine is perhaps displaying the hostile component of his Type A personality style.

Frequently doing two activities at once is a component of the Type A personality. Time urgency, however, is not the part of Type A that is most associated with heart disease.
© *Martinan/Getty Images RF*

Early studies of the Type A personality found that it was an independent risk factor for developing cardiovascular disease. An independent risk factor operates independently from other known risk factors, such as being overweight or smoking. Thus, for example, it is not true that Type A persons necessarily smoke more and that their smoking causes the heart disease. Instead, the Type A personality is independent of smoking, and someone who is Type A and smokes is at more of a risk for heart disease than someone who just smokes or who is just Type A. In fact, one study found that the Type A personality was a better predictor of heart disease than the person's history of smoking or the person's cholesterol level (Jenkins, Zyzanski, & Rosenman, 1976), although high cholesterol and smoking also contribute independently to heart disease.

Physicians conducted most of the early studies of Type A personality, and to measure this personality variable they developed a structured interview. Standard questions were asked, and the interviewer noted the participants' answers and how they reacted to the questions. However, the interviewer was also very interested in the behavior of the participants. For example, what was the tempo of their speech? Did they frequently interrupt the interviewer or put words in the interviewer's mouth? Did they fidget during the interview? Did they make frequent and vigorous gestures with their hands and heads? In one part of the interview, the interviewer tries to aggravate the participants by...talking....very......slowly. Type A people are especially aggravated when other people talk slowly, and they interrupt, talk out of turn, or finish sentences for people in order to speed them up.

As research on Type A personality gained momentum in the 1980s, researchers tried to devise a more efficient measure. Interviews are slow; they can measure only one person at a time, and it takes one interviewer to measure each participant. In short, interviewing is a relatively expensive and time-consuming way to measure any personality variable. Questionnaires are much cheaper because they are generally faster, they can be given to whole groups of participants, and can be administered on-line and scored automatically. Thus, researchers in this area put some effort into developing a questionnaire measure for Type A personality. Subsequently, one of the most widely used question-naire measures of Type A personality is the Jenkins Activity Survey. It contains ques-tions that tap into each of the three components of the Type A syndrome—for example, "My work improves as the deadline approaches," "I have been told that I eat too fast," and "I enjoy a good competition."

Early researchers using the structured interview often found a relationship between Type A personality and risk for heart attack and cardiovascular disease. Later research, mostly using the Jenkins questionnaire, often failed to replicate this finding. This puzzled researchers for several years. Some wondered if Type A personality was a risk factor for heart attacks at one time, but then things changed so that it no longer was a risk factor. Other psychologists began to take a close look at the studies, search-ing for a reason that some found a relationship but others didn't. Quickly the pattern emerged that the studies using the questionnaire measure were less likely to find a relationship between Type A and heart disease than the studies using the structured interview (Suls & Wan, 1989; Suls, Wan, & Costa, 1996). Researchers have con-cluded that the questionnaire measure taps into different aspects of Type A behavior than does the structured interview measures. Apparently, the structured interview gets more at the lethal component of Type A. But what part of the Type A behavior pattern is the most lethal, the part that is most related to heart disease?

Hostility: The Lethal Component of the Type A Behavior Pattern

When the interview measures of Type A were developed by physicians, they tended to emphasize the assessment of hostility and aggression. For example, it assessed whether the participants got frustrated when the physicians talked slowly, whether they swore during the interview, or whether they actively gestured or pounded the table. Later, when questionnaire measures were developed, more of an emphasis was placed on the time urgency and achievement components. For example, did the participants say they were always in a hurry, that they worked better as deadlines got closer, or that they achieved more than their peers?

As researchers began to use the questionnaires more and more (because they were faster, easier, and cheaper to administer than the interviews), evidence began to accu-mulate, showing that general Type A personality did not predict heart disease. Research-ers then compared the interviews with the questionnaires and learned that the interview method tapped more of the hostility component than the questionnaire method. As such, researchers began testing the hypothesis that it was really the more specific trait of hos-tility, rather than the general syndrome of Type A personality, that was the better predic-tor of heart disease.

What do researchers mean by the trait of hostility? People high in hostility are not necessarily violent or outwardly aggressive. They are not necessarily even assertive or demanding of others. Instead, such people are likely to react disagreeably to disappoint-ments, frustrations, and inconveniences. Frustration can be understood as the subjective feeling that comes when you are blocked from an important goal. For example, you want a cold drink from the vending machine and it takes your money but does not give you the drink you request. This is frustrating. A hostile person reacts to such frustrations with disagreeable behavior, attacking the machine or swearing and kicking the garbage can as he or she sulks away. Hostile people are easily irritated, even by small frustra-tions, such as when they misplace their car keys or have to wait in line at the grocery store. In such situations, hostile people can become visibly upset, sometimes even becoming rude and uncooperative or even antagonistic.

Several studies have now established that hostility is a strong predictor of cardiovascular disease (see meta-analysis by Chida & Steptoe, 2009). In fact, psychologists Dembrowski and Costa (1987) have demonstrated that even a questionnaire measure of the specific trait of hostility is a better predictor of artery disease than are questionnaire measures of Type A. Recent studies have also shown that hostility is associated with systemic inflammation, as indicated by elevated blood **leukocyte** counts, also known as white blood cell counts (Surtees et al., 2003). Physicians have long known that chronic inflammation is related to risk for coronary disease, and so have recommended that persons at risk take an aspirin a day, because aspirin reduces inflammation. Chronic inflammation may be one pathway whereby hostility is linked to the health endpoint of cardiovascular disease.

The good news about this research is that not everything about being Type A is bad for the heart and arteries. Given that hostility is apparently the lethal component, can we envision a "healthy" version of the Type A personality? It seems okay to strive for success and achievement, but don't be hostile and aggressive along the way. It's okay to strive to attain goals and even to be a workaholic, but don't get frustrated by the inevitable setbacks that come with everyday life. It's okay to be in a hurry and strive to get as much done as possible, but don't get frustrated and angry when you can't accomplish everything. And it's okay to enjoy a competition as long as it's friendly, not hostile. And sometimes it may be good therapy to get into the longest and slowest line at the store and just try to relax, take it easy, and not feel hostile or angry in such situations (Wright, 1988). Davidson and colleagues (2007) estimate that brief hostility-management therapy can result in cost savings for hospitals by reducing hospitalization expenses associated with coronary care.

A Closer Look   Type D Personality and Heart Disease

The Type A trait, and especially the hostility component, shows a modest correlation with the risk of developing coronary artery disease. Researchers have nevertheless been examining other personality factors that might relate to heart disease, especially in terms of how quickly the disease progresses once it starts or the survival rate after suffering a heart attack. Many people have early-stage indicators of heart problems, such as high blood pressure, minor artery blockage, or even progressive heart failure. Some of these people, but not all, will go on to full-blown heart attacks or death from their heart disease. Researchers are asking whether specific personality factors, other than Type A, predict the progression of heart disease once it has started.

A trait receiving a good deal of attention currently is called **Type D personality,** or "distressed" personality (e.g., Denollet, 2000). Just like Type A, the Type D trait is not truly a type; instead, it refers to a dimension along which individuals differ. In the case of Type D, it refers to two underlying traits. One of the traits is *negative affectivity,* defined as the tendency to frequently experience negative emotions across time and situations, including such unpleasant emotions as tension, worry, irritability, and anxiety. It is very similar to the trait of neuroticism and includes, in addition to a high frequency of negative emotions, a negative view of oneself, a tendency to complain, and finding oneself reacting more than usual to stressful situations. The second trait underlying the Type D construct is *social inhibition,* or the tendency to inhibit the expression of emotions, thoughts, and behaviors in social interactions. People high on social inhibition feel insecure or apprehensive in the company of others and worry about social evaluation and being the target of disapproval from others. Consequently, they inhibit themselves when around others and keep people at a distance. They are less likely to seek social support when they have problems.

Denollet (2005) has published a brief 14-item self-report personality questionnaire to measure the Type D construct. Items that assess the negative affectivity part of this construct include "I often make a fuss about unimportant things," "I am often in a bad mood," and "I often find myself worrying about something." Items that assess the social inhibition component of Type D include "I find it hard to start a conversation," "I often feel inhibited in social interactions," and "When socializing, I don't find the right things to talk about." Because this scale is short and convenient to use, its publication has stimulated research on the Type D personality dimension.

Research on Type D suggests that these two traits—negative affectivity and social inhibition—act synergistically to put cardiac patients at risk for further adverse cardiac events (Denollet et al., 2006). This means that high levels of *both* traits have to be found in the same person to put that individual at risk for further cardiac problems. For example, Denollet and colleagues (2003) studied 400 cardiac outpatients (aged 31–79 years) who had some degree of coronary artery blockage. These patients were followed up 6 to 10 years later to determine survival status. During this time, 38 patients had died, mostly of cardiac

disease. Patients who were high on the Type D trait were about four times more likely to die during this follow-up time period compared to the cardiac patients low on the Type D trait.

Kupper and Denollet (2007) review several studies conducted by Denollet and colleagues showing that among persons with coronary artery disease, the Type D personality dimension is associated with poorer outcomes, such as increased mortality and faster progression of the disease. A meta-analysis of 15 studies concluded that Type D personality has a small though reliable association with major adverse cardiac events (O'Dell et al., 2011). Other researchers have found similar results. For example, Pelle and colleagues (2008) examined 368 patients with coronary artery disease who were undergoing a program in cardiac rehabilitation (e.g., prescribed exercises, stress management techniques, improving diet, weight loss, and smoking cessation). Most patients showed some improvement in health after completing the cardiac rehabilitation program. However, patients high on the Type D dimension had poorer health status after the rehabilitation program than did patients low on Type D.

Given that cardiac patients high on the Type D personality dimension show greater risk for poor outcomes than patients who are low on this dimension, an important question concerns the mechanism underlying this effect: How is it that the personality trait increases the risk for

negative outcomes? Ongoing research is attempting to answer this question, and two mechanisms appear to be likely candidates. One mechanism involves disturbances in the brain's stress response, with high Type D persons showing an exaggerated stress response evidenced by higher levels of cortisol in their blood. Cortisol is a hormone released during the stress response and if high levels occur over time, it can increase inflammation in the arteries, leading to the buildup of blockages in the arteries (Whitehead et al., 2007). The association between Type D and physical health is mediated by measures of inflammatory burden (Mommersteeg et al., 2012). A second mechanism whereby the Type D personality dimension may result in poorer outcomes for cardiac patients is through lifestyle factors, including health-related behaviors and social support. For example, Williams and colleagues (2008) found that Type D subjects were less likely to eat sensibly, spent less time outdoors, were more bothered by events in their daily lives, and were less likely to get medical checkups than persons low on the Type D scale. Just as important, people with the Type D personality dimension reported lower levels of perceived social support compared to non-Type D persons. Other findings suggest that the Type D trait may affect health through poorer health behaviors and lower social support (Gilmour & Williams, 2012). Understanding if and how personality affects cardiac health is an active and exciting area of research.

How the Arteries Are Damaged by Hostile Type A Behavior

How does Type A behavior, particularly the hostility component, produce its toxic effects on the heart and arteries? Strong feelings of hostility and aggression produce the fight-or-flight response. Part of this response is an increase in blood pressure, accompanied by a constriction of the arteries, plus an increase in heart rate and in the amount of blood pumped out with each heartbeat. In short, the person's body suddenly pumps more blood through smaller arteries. These changes can produce

A cross-section of a human coronary artery, the artery that feeds the heart muscle itself, showing extreme arteriosclerosis. Here the artery diameter has narrowed dramatically by the buildup of plaque on the inside artery wall.
© Marc Phares/Science Source

wear and tear on the inside lining of the arteries, causing microscopic tears and abrasions. These abrasions then become sites at which cholesterol and fat can become attached. In addition to this mechanical wear and tear on the artery walls, stress hormones released into the blood during the fight-or-flight response may lead to artery damage and subsequent buildup of fatty deposits on the artery walls. As these fat molecules build up on the inside of the arteries, the arteries become progressively narrower. This is called **arteriosclerosis,** or hardening or blocking of the arteries. When the arteries that feed the heart muscle itself become blocked, the subsequent shortage of blood to the heart is called a heart attack.

In summary, research on the Type A personality has taken some interesting twists and turns. It all began with a couple of cardiologists noticing certain personality differences between heart attack patients and other medical patients. This led them to define the Type A personality as consisting of three characteristics: competitive achievement motivation, time urgency, and hostility. After several decades of research, psychologists have found that trait hostility is the most toxic component of the Type A personality, and most research on cardiovascular disease and personality today is focusing on this specific trait. Understanding how hostility develops and is maintained, how exactly it damages the arteries, how it is evoked by specific situations, and how it can be overcome or managed are all important questions for future personality researchers.

SUMMARY AND EVALUATION

This chapter focused on the part of personality psychology related to physical adjustment and health. We began with several models of the personality and illness link. We also introduced the important concepts of moderation and mediation, which describe specific ways that personality can produce its effects on health and other variables. We then examined the concept of stress as the subjective reaction to extreme events, which often involve conflicting feelings, and over which one has little or no control. The stress response comes in four distinct varieties: acute, episodic acute, chronic, and traumatic. Traumatic stress can evolve into a disorder, called posttraumatic stress disorder, in which the person experiences nightmares or flashbacks, difficulties sleeping and other somatic problems, and feelings of being detached from reality or estranged from other people. It is important to realize that stress is not in the event but in how one appraises the event. Primary appraisal concerns an evaluation of how threatening the event is with respect to a person's goals and desires. Secondary appraisal concerns an evaluation of the person's own resources for meeting the challenge of the threatening event. Both of these appraisals are important for understanding how events come to elicit the stress response. Research is exploring the role of positive emotions in coping with chronic stress.

Much of the work on personality and stress began with a focus on major life events, such as losing a loved one or getting fired from one's job. Although serious, such events are relatively rare. More insidious are daily hassles, the relatively minor but frequent frustrations and disappointments of daily life. Stress researchers have begun to focus on these daily stressors in terms of their impact on health.

Personality psychologists have been concerned with understanding why some people appear more resistant to stress than others. That is, some people appear to take frustration and disappointment more in stride and do not suffer the deleterious health consequences often associated with chronic stress. One personality dimension in this regard is optimism, which has a wealth of findings associating it with stress resistance, good health, competent immune functioning, and longer life expectancy. Psychologists are developing grade school programs to train people to be more optimistic. Some related personality characteristics associated with generally better health prognosis are emotional expressivity and personal disclosure.

This chapter also focused on a specific disease, cardiovascular disease, one of the most common serious diseases in the United States. We covered the history of the search for a personality dimension that might be a risk factor for developing heart disease. Type A personality provides an interesting example of progressive research, in which findings are gradually refined until the field becomes more and more certain about an effect. In the case of Type A personality, most researchers now agree that the hostility component is most associated with the tendency to develop heart disease. Fortunately, people can be competitive workaholics and strive to do more and more in less and less time, just as long as they do not have the hostile part of the Type A syndrome.

KEY TERMS

health psychology 552
stress 553
interactional model 553
moderator 553
transactional model 553
health behavior model 555
mediation 555
predisposition model 556
illness behavior model 557
stressors 559
general adaptation syndrome (GAS) 559
alarm stage 559
resistance stage 559

exhaustion stage 559
major life events 560
daily hassles 562
acute stress 563
episodic acute stress 563
traumatic stress 563
posttraumatic stress disorder (PTSD) 563
chronic stress 563
additive effects 563
primary appraisal 564
secondary appraisal 564
dispositional optimism 566
positive reappraisal 567

problem-focused coping 567
creating positive events 568
optimistic bias 568
emotional inhibition 569
disclosure 572
competitive achievement
    motivation 576
time urgency 576
hostility 576
frustration 576
leukocyte 578
Type D personality 578
arteriosclerosis 580

© Colin Anderson/Blend Images
LLC RF

Disorders of Personality

19

Kody Scott grew up in South Central Los Angeles. When he was 12 years old, he was initiated into the Eight-Tray Gangster CRIPS street gang. He shot his first victim the night he was initiated. He went on to earn the nickname "Monster" for particularly violent beatings he inflicted on people. For example, as a young teenager, Kody severely beat a victim who resisted when Kody attempted to mug him. Kody beat him far beyond what was necessary to make the victim submit. In fact, Kody seemed to enjoy hurting other people.

Kody's biological father was a professional football player with whom his mother had had a brief affair. His mother had an unstable and violent marriage with Kody's stepfather, who left the home for good when Kody was six. Kody's mother raised her six children in a two-bedroom house in a gang-infested ghetto neighborhood.

Kody was an intelligent and muscular boy who enjoyed thrills and excitement. He might have gone on to become a professional athlete, or he could have succeeded in a career involving adventure and plenty of action, such as a policeman, a soldier, or maybe even an astronaut. Instead, Kody grew up to become Monster, a violent individual who feared nothing, had no feelings of guilt or remorse, and craved excitement.

Kody Scott was one of the most notorious gangbangers in South Central L.A. For the early part of his life, he aspired to be the most feared member of the CRIPS. He was sent to prison in 1993 to serve a seven-year sentence for shooting a drug dealer in the kneecaps. In prison, he was classed as a maximum threat to security and was housed away from other inmates. He wrote his autobiography, *Monster: The Autobiography of an L.A. Gang Member,* while in solitary confinement in San Quentin prison, under the name Sanyika Shakur (1994), which is also the name of his Facebook page. Even after attaining celebrity status for his book, which sold over 100,000 copies, Kody Scott could not escape the gang culture or his own violent personality. In 2007, already wanted by the L.A. police for parole violations, Scott was arrested again, this time for beating an acquaintance, taking the keys to his Jaguar, and leaving the scene in the victim's vehicle. In May of 2008, Kody Scott, age 44, was convicted of carjacking and robbery and sentenced to another six years in Pelican Bay State Prison. He was released two years early, in 2012, and it 2013 published a book of essays.

We open this chapter with the case of Kody Scott (aka Sanyika Shakur) because he illustrates one of the personality disorders: the antisocial personality disorder. In fact, his book "Monster" is an articulate look into the mind and inner workings of a sociopath.

The Building Blocks of Personality Disorders

Many of the topics we have covered in previous chapters come together in helping to describe and understand the various personality disorders. The symptoms of personality disorders can be seen as maladaptive variations within several of the domains we have covered. These include traits, emotions, cognitions, motives, interpersonal behavior, and self-concepts. The 10 personality disorders we present in this chapter are built on the foundation of these broader concepts, and so we briefly discuss the relevance of each to this chapter.

Traits of personality describe consistencies in behavior, thought, or action and represent meaningful differences among persons, as we described in Chapter 4. Personality disorders can be thought of as maladaptive variations or combinations of normal personality traits. Widiger and colleagues describe how extremes on either end of specific trait dimensions can be associated with personality disorders (Widiger, Costa, & McCrae, 2002a; Widiger et al., 2002b). For example, a person with extremely low levels of trust and extremely high levels of hostility might be disposed to paranoid personality disorder. A person very low on sociability but very high on anxiety might be prone to avoidant personality disorder. A person with the opposite combination—extremely high on sociability and low on anxiety—might be prone to histrionic personality disorder. Thus, the concept of traits, such as the five-factor model of traits, can be especially useful for describing personality disorders (Trull & McCrae, 2002).

Motivation is another basic building block of personality that is important to understanding personality disorders. Motives describe what people want and why they behave in particular ways. In the intrapsychic domain, Chapters 9 to 11, we discussed several different kinds of motives, ranging from the sexual and aggressive basis of Freud's theory to modern research on the need for intimacy, achievement, and power. A common theme in several personality disorders concerns maladaptive variations on these common motives, especially need for power and intimacy. One important variation concerns an extreme lack of motivation for intimacy, which is seen in certain personality disorders. Another theme is an exaggerated need for power over others, which, at an extremely high level, can result in a maladaptive personality disorder. Other motives can be involved in personality disorders, such as the extreme need to be superior and receive the praise of others that is found in narcissistic personality disorder. The person with obsessive-compulsive personality disorder might be seen as having an extremely high motivation for order and devotion to detail.

Cognition also provides a building block for understanding personality disorders. As covered in Chapter 12, cognition consists of mental activity involved in perceiving, interpreting, and planning. These processes can become distorted in personality disorders. Some disorders involve routine and consistent misinterpretations of the intentions of others. Personality disorders typically involve an impairment of social judgment, such as when the paranoid thinks others are out to get her, or when the histrionic person thinks others actually like being with him. The person with a borderline personality disorder may misinterpret innocent comments as signs of abandonment or criticism or rejection. In various ways, each of the personality disorders involves some distortion in the perception of other persons and altered social cognition.

Emotion is another area that is important to understanding personality disorders. We discussed normal range individual differences in emotion in Chapter 13. With several personality disorders there is extreme variation in experienced emotions. Some disorders involve extreme volatility in emotions (e.g., borderline), whereas other disorders involve extremes of specific emotions, such as anxiety (avoidant personality disorder), fear (paranoid personality disorder), or rage (narcissistic personality disorder). Most personality disorders have an emotional core that is an important component to understanding that disorder.

The self-concept is another building block in personality disorders. As described in Chapter 14, the self-concept is the person's own collection of self-knowledge— one's understanding of oneself. With most personality disorders, there is some distortion in the self-concept. Most of us are able to build and maintain a stable and realistic image of ourselves; we know our own opinions, we know what we value, and we know what we want out of life. With many of the disorders, there is a lack of stability in the self-concept, such that the person may feel she or he has no "core" or has trouble making decisions or needs constant reassurance from others. Self-esteem is also an important part of the self, and some disorders are associated with extremely high (e.g., narcissism) or extremely low (e.g., dependent personality disorder) levels of self-esteem. The self provides an important perspective on understanding personality disorders.

Social relationships are frequently disturbed or maladaptive in personality disorders. Thus, the material we covered in the social and cultural domain, Chapters 15 through 17, is important for understanding and describing personality disorders. For example, a successful sexually intimate relationship with another person involves knowing when sexual behavior is appropriate and expected and when it is inappropriate and unwanted. Problems with intimacy, either staying too distant from others or becoming too intimate too quickly, are frequent features of several personality disorders. An important element of interpersonal skill involves empathy, knowing how the other person is feeling. Most personality disorders involve a deficit in empathy, such that the disordered person either misinterprets others or does not care about the feelings of others. Many disorders involve what might be called poor social skills, such as the schizoid person who stares at people without starting a conversation, or the histrionic person who behaves in an inappropriately flirtatious manner.

Biology can also form the building blocks of several of the personality disorders. The material covered in the biological domain, Chapters 6 through 8, is thus relevant.

Some of the personality disorders have been found to have a genetic component. Others have been studied via physiological components, such as examining the brain functioning of antisocial persons. There has even been an evolutionary theory proposed to explain the existence of personality disorders (Millon, 2000a).

Most personality textbooks do not cover personality disorders. We feel, however, that knowing about how something can become broken can tell us about how it works normally. Plus, we believe that the concept of personality disorders really ties together all the different components and domains of personality. As such, it is a fitting topic with which to end this book because it applies much of what has come before to an understanding of how the human personality can become disordered.

The Concept of Disorder

Today, a psychological **disorder** is a pattern of behavior or experience that is distressing and painful to the person, that leads to disability or impairment in important life domains (e.g., problems with work, marriage or relationship difficulties), and that is associated with increased risk for further suffering, loss of function, death, or confinement (American Psychiatric Association, 1994). The idea that something can go wrong with a person's personality has a long history. Some of the earliest writings in medical psychiatry included classifications and descriptions of personality and mental disorders (e.g., Kraeplin, 1913; Kretschmer, 1925). A very early concept derived by French psychiatrist Philippe Pinel was *manie sans delire,* or madness without loss of reason. This was applied to individuals who demonstrated disordered behavior and emotions but who did not lose contact with reality (Morey, 1997). A related concept, popular in the early 1900s, was called "moral insanity," to emphasize that the person did not suffer any impairment of intellect, but rather was impaired in terms of feelings, temperament, or habits. An influential psychiatrist named Kurt Schneider (1958) proposed the term *psychopathic personality* to refer to behavior patterns that caused the person and the community to suffer. Schneider also emphasized statistical rarity, along with behaviors that have an adverse impact on the person and the community in which that person lives. This definition highlights the notion that all forms of personality disorder involve impaired social relationships; other people suffer as much as or more than the person with the disorder.

A disorder is a conceptual entity that, although abstract, is nevertheless useful. It helps guide thinking about the distinction between what is normal and what is abnormal, or pathological. The field of **abnormal psychology** is the study of the various mental disorders, including thought disorders, emotional disorders, and personality disorders. In this chapter, we focus on disorders of personality and the ways in which they affect functioning.

What Is Abnormal?

There are many ways to define **abnormal**. One simple definition is that whatever is different from normal is abnormal. This is a statistical definition in the sense that researchers can statistically determine how often something occurs and, if it is rare, call it abnormal. In this sense, color blindness or polydactyly (having more than 10 fingers) is considered abnormal. Another definition of abnormal is a social definition based on what society tolerates (Shoben, 1957). If we define the term in this sense, behaviors that society deems unacceptable are labeled as abnormal. In this sense, incest and child abuse are both considered abnormal. Both the statistical and the social definitions of abnormality suffer from changing times and changing social or cultural norms (Millon, 2000a, 2000b). Behaviors deemed offensive or socially inappropriate 20 years ago might be acceptable today. For example, 20 or 30 years ago, homosexuality was considered to be both rare and socially unacceptable, a form of abnormal behavior or even a mental illness. Today, homosexuality is not considered abnormal in itself (American Psychiatric Association, 1994) and is protected under civil rights laws in the United States. Thus, the statistical and social definitions of abnormality are always somewhat tentative because society changes.

Psychologists have consequently looked to other ways of identifying what is abnormal in behavior and experience. They have looked within persons, inquiring about subjective feelings, such as anxiety, depression, dissatisfaction, and feelings of loneliness. They have looked at how people think and experience themselves and their worlds. Psychologists have found that some people have disorganized thoughts, disruptive perceptions, or unusual beliefs and attitudes that do not match their circumstances. They have identified ways in which people fail to get along with one another and ways people have trouble living in the community. They have analyzed patterns of behavior that represent ineffective efforts at coping or that put people at higher risk for other problems, behaviors that harm more than help. From a psychological perspective, any of these may be considered abnormal.

Combining all these approaches to abnormality (statistical, social, and psychological), psychologists and psychiatrists have developed the field of **psychopathology**, or the study of mental disorders. The diagnosis of mental disorders is both a scientific discipline and an important part of the clinical work of many psychiatrists and psychologists. Knowing how to define and how to identify a disorder is the first step in devising treatment or in designing research on that disorder.

The *Diagnostic and Statistical Manual of Mental Disorders*

The most widely used system for diagnosing mental disorders, including personality disorders, is the *Diagnostic and Statistical Manual of Mental Disorders*, published by the American Psychiatric Association (APA) and currently in its fifth edition (called the *DSM-5*). The *DSM-5* sets the standard for diagnoses, and its system is the one taught by almost all psychiatry and psychology doctoral training programs, the one that appears in hospital records systems, and the one most insurance companies demand for reimbursement purposes.

Because society standards change over time and because new research accumulates, the *DSM* undergoes revision from time to time. The current version—the *DSM-5*—was published in 2013. The APA began working on this revision a decade earlier and appointed various working groups of experts to assist in each broad area of mental disorders. The personality disorders working group consisted of active personality psychologists and psychiatrists. During the decade they worked on the revision for *DSM-5*, the personality disorders working group considered several broad changes to personality disorders that might be incorporated into *DSM-5*.

One change the personality disorders working group considered was to make diagnosis less categorical and more dimensional. The previous edition—*DSM-IV*—was based on a **categorical view** of personality disorders; one either had the disorder or did not have the disorder. The categorical view held that there is a qualitative break between people who are, for example, antisocial and people who are not. And this concept was applied to all the personality disorders, viewing disorders as distinct and qualitatively different from normal extremes on each personality trait.

In contrast to this categorical view is the **dimensional view** of personality disorders. In the dimensional view, each disorder is seen as a continuum, ranging from normality at one end to severe disability or disturbance at the other. According to this view, people with and without the disorder differ in degree only. For example, part of being antisocial is disregarding the rights of others. But there are degrees to which this disregard can manifest in behavior. For example, some people might simply be aloof and unconcerned about the feelings of others. Farther out on this dimension, a person might lack a desire to help others, being both aloof and uncaring. Even farther out on this dimension is the person who actively hurts or takes advantage of others. And finally, at the greatest extreme of disregard for others is someone like "Monster," the person introduced at the beginning of this chapter, who takes pleasure in harming or terrorizing others.

The dimensional view implies that certain patterns of behavior, in various amounts, comprise each of the personality disorders. It is only at the extreme ends of the dimensions that the person becomes a problem to themselves and to others. Moreover, extremes of different personality traits can combine in ways that create unique forms of disorder. For example, someone who has an obsessive compulsive personality would score extremely high on the Five Factor traits of conscientiousness and neuroticism. Modern personality theorists (e.g., Costa & Widiger, 1994; Widiger, 2000) argued that the dimensional view provides a more reliable and meaningful way to describe the personality disorders.

In 2012, a year before the DSM-5 was to be published, the well-regarded Journal of Personality released a special issue dedicated to the latest research on whether a dimensional view of personality disorders was scientifically valid and clinically useful. Every paper in this special issue provided strong support for the dimensional view. For example, Mullins-Sweatt (2012) discussed the clinical utility of a Five Factor Model view on disorders, and concluded that such an approach was more efficient to use, easier to communicate, and provided more specific guidance as to treatment. Similarly, Miller (2012) pointed out the many advantages of using the Five Factor Model to characterize degrees of personality disorders, as opposed to simply concluding that a person does or does not have a disorder. In various ways, and using a variety of data and theorizing, every other article published in this 2012 special issue pointed to the advantages of applying a dimensional view to personality disorders (see especially Trull, 2012; Widiger & Costa, 2012).

As the *DSM-5* revision work progressed, the personality disorders working group considered this, and several other, changes to the way personality disorders are defined and diagnosed. The top personality psychologists and psychiatrists were involved, many meetings were held, data were collected, public input was solicited and obtained, and many proposals were written and considered. However, to make a long story very short, the final outcome of the revision effort was the decision, on the part of the APA Board of Trustees, to make no changes to the way personality disorders are defined. The *DSM-5* therefore maintains the categorical model of personality disorders and retains the criteria for 10 specific personality disorders that were described in the previous edition. The *DSM-5* does contain a section—Section III—that describes which issues need further research. It is in this section—essentially an appendix to the *DSM-5*—were the dimensional model of personality disorders is detailed and a call for further research on the utility of viewing personality disorders as dimensions rather than distinct categories is issued. Later in this chapter, we work through the 10 personality disorders that are included in the *DSM-5*, but first we consider the general notion of "disorder."

What Is a Personality Disorder?

A **personality disorder** is an enduring pattern of experience and behavior that differs greatly from the expectations of the individual's culture (*DSM-5*). As discussed in Chapter 3, traits are patterns of experiencing, thinking about, and interacting with oneself and the world. Traits are observed in a wide range of social and personal situations. For example, a person who is high on Conscientiousness is hardworking and persevering. If a trait becomes maladaptive and inflexible and causes significant impairment or distress, then it is considered to be a personality disorder. For example, if someone were so conscientious that he or she checked the locks on the door 10 times each night and checked every appliance in the house 5 times before leaving in the morning, then we might consider the possibility of a disorder.

The essential features of a personality disorder, according to the *DSM-5*, are presented in Table 19.1. A personality disorder is usually manifest in more than one of the following areas: in how people think, in how they feel, in how they get along with others, or in their ability to control their own behavior. The pattern is rigid and is displayed across a variety of situations, leading to distress or problems in important areas in life, such as at work or in relationships. For example, an overly conscientious man might drive his wife crazy with his constant checking of his household appliances. The pattern of behavior that defines the personality disorder typically has a long history in the person's life and can often be traced back to manifestations in adolescence or even childhood. To be classed as a personality disorder, the pattern must not result from drug abuse, medication, or a medical condition, such as head trauma.

Culture, Age, and Gender: The Effect of Context

A person's social, cultural, and ethnic background must be taken into account whenever there is a question about personality disorders. Immigrants, for example, often have problems fitting into a new culture. Persons who originate in a different culture often have customs, habits, expressions, and values that are at odds with, or that create social problems within, a new culture. For example, the U.S. culture is very individualistic, and it values and rewards individuals for standing out from the

Table 19.1 General Criteria for Personality Disorders

1. A personality order shows an enduring pattern of inner experience and behavior that deviates markedly from the expectations of the individual's culture. This pattern is manifest in two or more of the following areas:
   - Cognition (i.e., ways of perceiving and interpreting the self, others, and events)
   - Affectivity (i.e., the range, intensity, ability, and appropriateness of emotional responses)
   - Interpersonal functioning
   - Impulse control
2. The enduring pattern is inflexible and pervasive across a broad range of personal and social situations.
3. The enduring pattern leads to clinically significant distress or impairment in social, occupational, or other important areas of functioning.
4. The pattern is stable and of long duration, and its onset can be traced back to adolescence or early adulthood.
5. The enduring pattern is not better accounted for as a manifestation or consequence of another mental disorder.
6. The enduring pattern is not due to the direct physiological effects of a substance (e.g., a drug of abuse, a medication) or a general medical condition, such as head trauma.

Source: American Psychiatric Association, 2013.

crowd. To societies that are more collectivistic and value fitting in with the group, efforts to stand out from the crowd might be interpreted as self-centered and individualistic in an unwanted sense. Indeed, the U.S. culture has been called a narcissistic culture; therefore, efforts to draw attention to the self are not socially abnormal in this society.

Before judging that a behavior is a symptom of a personality disorder, we must first become familiar with a person's cultural background, especially if it is different from the majority culture. A study of Third World immigrants to Norway (Sam, 1994) found that many exhibited adjustment problems that might have appeared to be personality disorders. Many young male immigrants, for example, exhibited antisocial behaviors. These behaviors tended to diminish as the immigrants acculturated to their new social environment.

Age also is relevant to judgments about personality disorder. Adolescents, for example, often go through periods of instability that may include identity crises (see Chapter 14), a symptom that is often associated with certain personality disorders. Most adolescents experiment with various identities yet do not have a personality disorder. For this reason, the American Psychiatric Association (1994) cautions against diagnosing personality disorders in persons under age 18. Also, adults who undergo severe loss, such as the death of a spouse or the loss of a job, sometimes undergo periods of instability or impulsive behavior that may look like a personality disorder. For example, a person who has experienced such a traumatic event may become violent or may impulsively enter into sexual relationships. A person's age and life circumstances must therefore be considered to be sure that the person is not simply going through a developmental stage or reacting to a traumatic life event.

Finally, gender is another context in which to frame our understanding of personality disorders. Certain disorders, such as the antisocial personality disorder, are diagnosed much more frequently in men than women. Other personality disorders are diagnosed more frequently in women than men. These gender differences may reflect underlying gender differences in how people cope. For example, in a study of more than 2,000 individuals, Huselid and Cooper (1994) found that males exhibit externalizing problems, such as fighting and vandalism, whereas females tend to exhibit relatively more internalizing problems, such as depression and self-harm. Similar findings were obtained by Kavanagh and Hops (1994). These differences in how men and women cope with problems most likely contribute to gender differences in the behaviors associated with the personality disorders. Psychologists need to be careful not to look for evidence of certain kinds of disorders just because of a person's gender.

Exercise ?

In this chapter, you will read about specific personality disorders. For each, try to think of examples of how culture, gender, or age might influence whether a person's behavior is seen as evidence of a disorder. For example, are persons from low socioeconomic groups likely to be seen by others as having particular disorders? How does this correspond to the topic of stereotypes and prejudice? How does this fit with the use of "profiles" by police and other law enforcement agencies?

Specific Personality Disorders

The following sections describe specific personality disorders, including the criteria for diagnosing someone as possessing each disorder. We focus this material on describing the characteristics of each personality disorder and by giving examples.

The Erratic Cluster: Ways of Being Unpredictable, Violent, or Emotional

Persons who are diagnosed with disorders belonging to the erratic group tend to have trouble with emotional control and to have specific difficulties getting along with others. People with one of these disorders often appear dramatic and emotional and are unpredictable. This group consists of four disorders: *antisocial, borderline, histrionic,* and *narcissistic* personality disorders.

Antisocial Personality Disorder

The antisocial person shows a general disregard for others and cares very little about the rights, feelings, or happiness of other people. The antisocial person has also been referred to as a sociopath or a psychopath (Zuckerman, 1991a). Adults with this disorder typically had a childhood that was fraught with behavioral problems. Such early childhood behavioral problems generally take the form of violating the rights of others (such as minor thefts) and breaking age-related social norms (such as smoking at an early age or fighting with other children). Other common childhood behavioral problems include behaving aggressively or cruelly toward animals, threatening and intimidating younger children, destroying property, lying, and breaking rules. Behavioral problems in childhood are often first noticed in school, but such children also come to the attention of the police and truant officers. Sometimes even very young children, during an argument with another child, use a weapon that can cause serious physical harm, such as a baseball bat or a knife.

Once childhood behavioral problems become an established pattern, the possibility of an **antisocial personality disorder** becomes more likely (American Psychiatric Association, 1994). As a child with behavioral problems grows up, the problems tend to worsen as the child develops physical strength, cognitive power, and sexual maturity. Minor problems, such as lying, fighting, and shoplifting, evolve into more serious ones, such as breaking and entering and vandalism. Severe aggression, such as rape or cruelty to a theft victim, might also follow. Some children with these behavioral problems rapidly develop to a level of dangerous and even sadistic behavior. For example, we sometimes hear in the news about preteen children (usually male) who murder other children in cold blood and without remorse. In one study, children who grew into severe delinquency as teenagers were already identifiable by kindergarten teachers' ratings of impulsiveness and antisocial behavior at age five (Tremblay et al., 1994). Studies of children ages 6–13 also find that some children exhibit a syndrome of antisocial behaviors, including impulsivity, behavioral problems, callous social attitudes, and lack of feelings for others (Frick et al., 1994).

If a child exhibits no signs of conduct problems by age 16, it is unlikely that he or she will develop an antisocial personality as an adult. Moreover, even among children *with* conduct problems, the majority simply grow out of them by early adulthood (American Psychiatric Association, 1994). However, some children with conduct problems go on to develop full-blown antisocial personality disorder in adulthood. Children with earlier-onset conduct problems (e.g., by age six or seven) are much more likely to grow into an antisocial personality disorder as an adult than are children who displayed a few conduct problems in high school (Laub & Lauritsen, 1994).

The antisocial adult continues with the same sorts of conduct problems started in childhood, but on a much grander scale. The term *antisocial* implies that the person has a *lack of concern for social norms.* Antisocial persons have very little respect for laws and may repeatedly engage in acts that are grounds for arrest, such as harassing others, fighting, destroying property, and stealing. "Cold-hearted" is a good description of their interactions with others. Antisocial persons may manipulate and deceive others to gain rewards or pleasure (e.g., money, power, social advantage, or sex).

Repeated lying is another feature of the antisocial personality. The pattern of lying starts early in life with minor deceptions and grows into a pattern of deceitfulness. Lying becomes a common part of social interaction for the antisocial personality. Some make a living conning others out of money. "Getting over" on people, especially authorities, through deception may even be pleasurable to the antisocial person.

Another common characteristic of the antisocial personality is *impulsivity,* which is often manifested as a failure to plan ahead. The antisocial person might start a chain of behavior without a clear plan or sequence in mind: For example, the person might enter a gas station and decide on the spot to rob the attendant, even though he or she has not planned a getaway. Prisoners with antisocial personalities often complain that their lack of planning led to their arrest, and they are often more remorseful about getting caught than about committing the crime.

A more common form of impulsivity is to simply make everyday decisions without much forethought or without considering consequences. For example, an antisocial man might leave his wife and baby for several days without calling to say where he is. This often results in trouble in relationships and trouble in employment settings. Generally, antisocial persons change jobs often, change relationships often, and move often.

Antisocial persons also tend to be *easily irritated* and to respond to even minor frustrations with aggression. Losing some coins in a vending machine might be all it takes for such a person to fly into a rage. Antisocial persons tend to be *assaultive,* particularly to those around them, such as spouses or children. Fights and physical attacks are common. *Recklessness* is another characteristic, with antisocial persons showing little regard for their own safety and that of others. Driving while intoxicated or speeding is indicative of recklessness, as is having unprotected sex with multiple partners.

Irresponsibility is another key feature of the antisocial personality. Antisocial persons get bored easily and find monotony or routine to be stressful. An antisocial person may, for example, decide on the spur of the moment to abandon his or her job, with no plan for getting another right away. Repeated unexplained absences from work are a common sign of the antisocial character. Irresponsibility in financial matters is

Application

Kenneth Lay was the founder and former CEO of Enron, a large energy company that went bankrupt in 2001, creating $60 billion in investment losses and wiping out $2.1 billion in the pension plans of thousands of workers. Lay was charged with 11 counts of conspiracy, insider trading, securities fraud, and lying to auditors. Prosecutors charged that he knew his company was in deep trouble and was aware of fraudulent accounting practices, and that he hid losses from investors until the company collapsed. During this time, Lay began dumping his own stock before Enron collapsed, even while encouraging others, including company workers, to buy more. During his trial, Lay claimed he never knew of the accounting fraud. He portrayed himself as a trusting man who was let down by corrupt staff, especially former finance chief Andrew Fastow, who served over five years in prison for his role in the Enron collapse. At times during his trial, Lay became combative and hostile, insisting that others were responsible. At other times he claimed that the collapse of Enron was the most painful experience of his life, even going so far as to say the experience was equivalent to the death of a loved one. In 2006, he was convicted and might have served up to 45 years in jail if he had not died suddenly of a heart attack before sentencing took place.

Kenneth Lay exhibited several characteristics consistent with the antisocial personality and psychopathy. He was a charming person who could convince others to buy his company's stock, even though he knew his company was in deep trouble and was secretly selling his own shares. Self-assured and confident, he used his personal charisma to dupe others out of billions of dollars. He repeatedly tried to shift the blame for his company's collapse onto others. When faced with evidence of his responsibility, he became combative and hostile and was easily irritated on the witness stand. He expressed no remorse for destroying the life savings of thousands of Enron workers. And finally, he tried to play the "poor me" card to garner sympathy from the jury by pointing out all the pain and suffering he had endured.

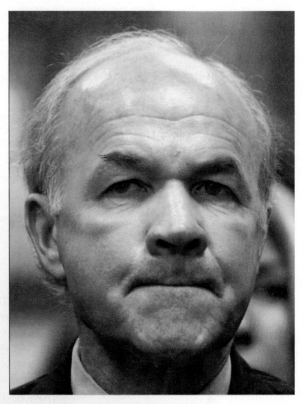

© Ron Edmonds/AP Images

also common, with the antisocial person often running up unpayable debts, or borrowing money from one person to pay a debt owed to another, staying one step ahead of the bill collector. Such a person may squander the money needed to feed his or her children or gamble away the money needed to buy necessities.

Lack of remorse and guilt feelings and indifference to the suffering of others are the hallmarks of the antisocial mind. The antisocial person can be ruthless, without the normal levels of human compassion, charity, or social concern. See A Closer Look on pages 596–597 for current theories and research on how people become antisocial and the psychological forces that keep them that way. Table 19.2 summarizes the key characteristics of the antisocial personality disorder. Also included are typical beliefs or thoughts that someone with this disorder might have.

A concept related to antisocial personality disorder is *psychopathy,* which was a term coined toward the middle of the twentieth century (Cleckley, 1941) to describe people who are superficially charming and intelligent, but are also deceitful, unable to feel remorse or care for others, impulsive, and lacking in shame, guilt, and fear. Psychopathy and antisocial personality are similar notions, but there are important distinctions so they should not be used interchangeably. The antisocial personality designation places emphasis on observable behaviors, such as chronic lying, repeated criminal behavior, and conflicts with authority. The psychopathy designation places emphasis on more subjective characteristics, such as the incapacity to feel guilt, a high degree of superficial charm, or having callous social attitudes. The distinction can get blurred because the *DSM*-5 also includes a subjective criterion, "lack of remorse," in its definition of antisocial personality

Table 19.2 Characteristics of Persons with Antisocial Personality Disorder

Fails to conform to social norms, e.g., breaks the law
Repeated lying or conning others for pleasure or profit
Impulsivity
Irritable and aggressive, e.g., frequent fights
Reckless disregard for safety of others and self
Irresponsible, e.g., truant from school, cannot hold a job
Lack of remorse, e.g., indifferent to pain of others, rationalizes having hurt or mistreated others

Typical Thoughts Associated with the Antisocial Personality
"Laws don't apply to me."
"I'll say whatever it takes to get what I want."
"I think I'll skip work today and go to the racetrack."
"That guy I beat up deserved every bit of it."
"She had it coming, she asked for it . . ."
"I'm the one you should feel sorry for here . . ."

disorder. However, the concept of psychopathy is mainly a research construct, pioneered by the scientific work of psychologist Robert Hare. He developed a measure of the construct called the Psychopathy Checklist, which contains two major clusters of symptoms. One cluster refers to emotional and interpersonal traits, such as incapacity for fear, superficial charm, lack of empathy and care for others, being egocentric, and having callous social attitudes and shallow emotions. The second cluster assesses the social deviance associated with an antisocial lifestyle, such as being impulsive, displaying poor self-control, possessing a high need for excitement, and having early and chronic behavioral problems. The major distinction between psychopathy and antisocial personality disorder mainly lies in the first cluster of emotional and interpersonal traits that define psychopathy. Consequently, most extreme psychopaths would meet criteria for a diagnosis of antisocial personality disorder, but not all people with antisocial personality disorder are psychopaths (if they don't have the subjective characteristics of superficial charm, egocentricity, lack of empathy, and shallow emotions).

One interesting concept is the notion of the "successful" psychopath (Smith, Watts, & Lillenfeld, 2014). Certainly there are some features of psychopathy that may be adaptive in some circumstances, such as interpersonal charm and charisma, fearlessness, and a willingness to take calculated risks. Some psychologists have speculated that these features of psychopathy may facilitate success in certain professions, such as financial consulting, politics, and contact sports. A recent review of research on the "successful" psychopath (Lillenfeld, Watts, & Smith, 2015) concludes that it is a controversial and elusive concept, fought with alternative interpretations, and requires

Exercise?

For the next week, read through at least one online newsmagazine each day. Look for stories on persons who might be good examples of the antisocial personality disorder, such as murderers, white-collar criminals, and con artists. Clip the stories and bring them in for discussion. Look for evidence from the person's life and actual behaviors that match the characteristics of the antisocial personality listed in Table 19.2.

additional research to determine if a positive manifestation of psychopathy can exist without the truly maladaptive and negative elements.

When evaluating the antisocial personality profile, it is good to keep in mind the social and environmental contexts in which some people live. Psychologists have expressed concern that the *antisocial* label is sometimes applied to people who live in settings where socially undesirable behaviors (such as fighting) are viewed as protective. For example, in a high-crime area, some of the antisocial attitudes may safeguard people against being victimized. Thus, the term *antisocial* should be used only when the behavior pattern is indicative of dysfunction and is not simply a response to the immediate social context. For example, youths who emigrate from war-ravaged countries, where aggressive behaviors are necessary to survive each day, should not be considered antisocial. The economic and social contexts must be taken into account when deciding whether undesirable behaviors are signs of dysfunction.

Borderline Personality Disorder

The lives of persons with **borderline personality disorder** are marked by *instability*. Their relationships are unstable, their behavior is unstable, their emotions are unstable, and even their images of themselves are unstable. Let's consider each of these, starting with relationships.

The relationships of borderline individuals tend to be intense, emotional, and potentially violent. They suffer from strong fears of abandonment. If such persons sense separation or rejection in an important relationship, profound changes in their self-image and in how they behave may result, such as becoming very angry at other people. Borderline individuals show marked difficulties in their relationships. When others leave them, they feel strong abandonment fears and sometimes become angry or *aggressive*. Sometimes, in their efforts to manipulate people back into their relationships, they engage in *self-mutilating behavior* (burning or cutting themselves) or suicide attempts. A study of 84 hospital patients with a diagnosis of borderline personality disorder found that 72 percent had a history of attempting suicide (Soloff, Lis, Kelly, & Cornelius, 1994). In fact, among this sample, the average borderline patient had attempted suicide on at least three occasions. The relationships of borderline individuals are unpredictable and intense. They may go from idealizing the other to ridiculing the other. They are prone to sudden shifts in their views of relationships, behaving at one time in a caring manner and at another time in a punishing and cruel manner. They may go from being submissive to being an avenger for past wrongs. The movie *Fatal Attraction* contains a character with several features of the borderline personality disorder. See A Closer Look on page 599 for a discussion of how this personality disorder was portrayed in that Oscar-nominated movie from 1987.

Borderline persons also have *shifting views of themselves*. Their values and goals are shallow and change easily. Their opinions may change suddenly. They may experiment with different kinds of friends or with different sexual orientations. Usually, they view themselves as, at heart, evil or bad. Self-harming acts are common and increase when others threaten to leave or demand that the borderline person assume some new responsibilities.

Strong emotions are common in the borderline personality, including panic, anger, and despair. Mostly, these emotions are caused by interpersonal events, especially abandonment or neglect. When stressed by others, the borderline person may lash out, becoming bitter, sarcastic, or aggressive. Periods of anger are often followed by shame,

A Closer Look

Theories of the Psychopathic Mind

Here we compare two theories about the origins of psychopathy: a biological explanation and a social learning explanation. Many psychologists have argued that psychopathy is caused by a biological deficit or abnormality (e.g., Cleckley, 1988; Fowles, 1980; Gray, 1987a, 1987b). Research along these lines has focused on the idea that psychopaths are deficient in their ability to experience fear (Lykken, 1982). Being deficient in fear would help explain why psychopaths do not learn as well from punishment as from reward (Newman, 1987). Psychopaths may pursue a career in crime and lawlessness because, in part, they are simply not afraid of the punishment because they are insensitive to fear.

The theory of Jeffrey Gray (1990) has been influential on a number of researchers looking for a biological explanation of psychopathy. Recall from Chapter 7 that Gray proposed a system in the brain that is responsible for inhibiting behavior. The behavioral inhibition system (BIS) acts as a psychological brake, responsible for interrupting ongoing behavior when cues of punishment are present. According to Gray, the BIS is the part of the brain that is especially sensitive to signals of punishment coming from the environment. People who sense that a punishment is likely to occur typically stop what they are doing and look for ways to avoid the punishment.

Researchers are beginning to examine the emotional lives of psychopaths, especially with respect to their experience of anxiety and other negative emotions. Psychologist Chris Patrick and his colleagues are following an interesting line of research. One study examined a group of prisoners, all of whom were convicted of sexual offenses (Patrick, Bradley, & Lang, 1993). Even in this group of severe offenders, some individuals were more psychopathic than others, as measured by Hare's Psychopathy Checklist (Hare, Hart, & Harpur, 1991). Patrick and his colleagues had the prisoners look at unpleasant pictures (e.g., injured people, threatening animals) to try to bring about feelings of anxiety. While they were looking at the pictures, the prisoners were startled by random bursts of a loud noise. People typically blink their eyes when they are startled by a loud noise. Moreover, a person who is in an anxious or fearful state when startled will blink faster and harder than a person in a normal emotional state. This means that eye-blink speed when startled may be an objective physiological measure of how anxious or fearful a person is feeling. That is, the **eye-blink startle method** may allow researchers to measure how anxious persons are without actually having to ask them.

The results from this study of prisoners showed that the more psychopathic offenders displayed *less* of the eye-blink effect when startled, indicating that they were experiencing relatively *less* anxiety to the same unpleasant pictures. However, when *asked* about how distressing the pictures were, both the psychopaths and the nonpsychopaths reported that the pictures were distressing. Overall, these results suggest that psychopaths will say that they are feeling anxious or distressed, yet direct nervous system measures suggest that they are actually *experiencing* less anxiety than nonpsychopaths in the same situation.

In another study, Patrick, Cuthbert, and Lang (1994) again used a group of prisoners who differed from each other in terms of antisocial behaviors. This time, the prisoners were asked to imagine fearful scenes such as having to undergo an operation. The low- and high-antisocial prisoners did not differ in terms of their self-reports of fear and anxiety—all reported more of these emotions in response to the fear images than in response to neutral images such as walking across the yard. Large differences, however, were found in their *physiological* responses to the fear images. The less antisocial prisoners were more aroused by the fear imagery than were the antisocial subjects. In other words, the antisocial prisoners displayed a deficit in fear responding when their fear responses were assessed with physiological measures, which are less susceptible to being faked than the self-report measures. These results are consistent with the idea that the

This is the kind of image used in the study by psychologist Chris Patrick, who found that psychopaths did not exhibit the normal fear response to such threatening stimuli.
© PM Images/Getty Images RF

psychopath is deficient in the ability to experience fear and anxiety. In a review of the literature, Patrick (1994) argued that the core problem with psychopaths is a deficit in the fear response. As a consequence, the psychopath is not motivated to interrupt his or her ongoing behavior to avoid punishment or other unpleasant consequences.

Other researchers have de-emphasized biological explanations for psychopathy and argue instead that the emotional unresponsiveness of the psychopath is learned (Levenson, Kiehl, & Fitzpatrick, 1995). The observed fearlessness of the psychopath may be the result of a desensitization process. If a person is repeatedly exposed to violence or other antisocial behavior (such as childhood abuse or gang activities), he or she may become desensitized to such behaviors. That is, the callous disregard for others—the hallmark of psychopathy—may result from desensitization, a well-known form of learning. A prospective study of more than 400 victims of childhood abuse found that, compared with a control group, the abused children had significantly higher rates of psychopathy 20 years later (Luntz & Widom, 1994). By being victims of abuse, the argument goes, people learn that abusing others is a means of achieving power and control and obtaining what they want. Many psychopaths are motivated by interpersonal dominance and appear to enjoy having power over others. This can sometimes be seen in board meetings of corporations, in police stations, in politics, and wherever else one person has an opportunity to bully others. The point of this research, however, is that people who grow up to be bullies were themselves frequently bullied and abused as children.

Levenson (1992) has used results such as these to argue for a social learning model of psychopathy. He holds that at some point people decide to engage in antisocial behavior because they have learned from observing others that this is one way to get what they want.

Psychologists are currently debating the relative merits of viewing psychopathy as biological or as learned. Whatever the cause of psychopathy, the frequency and severity of antisocial behaviors almost always decrease as a person ages. It has been said that the best therapy for the psychopath is to grow older while in prison. The incidence of antisocial behaviors dramatically decreases in persons age 40 and older (*DSM-5*). It has been widely known that, among criminals, those who make it to their fourth decade are much less likely to be rearrested for antisocial acts than are those in their twenties or thirties. For example, a study of 809 male prison inmates aged 16–69 found that deviant social behaviors, impulsivity, and antisocial acts were much less prevalent in the older prisoners (Harpur & Hare, 1994). There was less of an age decline in antisocial beliefs and callous social attitudes. Thus, although older psychopaths still don't care much about other people or their feelings, they nevertheless are less likely to impulsively act out these beliefs or to engage in actual antisocial behaviors.

guilt, and feelings of being evil or bad. Borderline persons often complain of feeling empty. They also have a way of undermining their own best efforts, such as dropping out of a training program just before finishing or destroying a caring relationship just when it starts going smoothly.

The borderline person is characterized by huge vacillations in both mood and feelings about the self and others. People with borderline personality disorder can shift quickly from loving another to hating that same person. They are very demanding on their friends, relatives, lovers, and therapists. They are also manipulative toward others. For example, they may threaten or even try suicide when they don't get their way.

Table 19.3 lists the major features of the borderline personality disorder, along with examples of beliefs and thoughts that persons with this disorder might commonly have. Persons with borderline personality disorder, compared with those without, have a higher incidence rate of childhood physical or sexual abuse, neglect, or early parental loss. Many researchers believe that borderline disorder is caused by an early loss of love from parents, as may happen in parental death, abuse, severe neglect, or parental drug or alcohol abuse (Millon et al., 2000). Early loss may affect a child's capacity to form relationships. Children in such circumstances may come to believe that others are not to be trusted. Although borderline persons have difficulty with relationships, they may form stable relationships if given enough structure and support. If they find someone who is accepting and stable, who is very

Table 19.3 Characteristics of Borderline Personality Disorder

Instability of relationships, emotions, and self-image
Fears of abandonment
Aggressiveness
Proneness to self-harm
Strong emotions

Typical Thoughts or Beliefs Associated with the Borderline Personality
"I'm nothing without you."
"I'll just die if you leave me."
"If you go, I'll kill myself."
"I hate you, I hate you, I HATE YOU."
"I love you so much that I'll do anything or be anything for you."
"I feel empty inside, as if I don't know who I am."

patient, who meets their expectations for commitment, and who is caring and can diffuse trouble as it occurs, then the borderline personality may experience a satisfying relationship.

Histrionic Personality Disorder

The hallmarks of **histrionic personality disorder** are *excessive attention seeking* and *emotionality.* Often such persons are overly dramatic, preferring to be the center of attention. They may appear charming or even flirtatious. Many are inappropriately seductive or provocative. And this *sexually provocative* behavior is often undirected and occurs in inappropriate settings, such as in professional settings. Physical appearance is often very important to histrionic persons, and they work to impress others and obtain compliments. Often, however, they overdo it and appear gaudy or flamboyant.

Histrionic individuals express their opinions frequently and dramatically. However, their *opinions are shallow* and easily changed. Such a person may say, for example, that some political official is a great and wonderful leader yet be unable to give any supporting details or actual examples of leadership. Such persons prefer impressions to facts and often act on intuition (Millon et al., 2000). They may *display strong emotions in public,* sometimes to the embarrassment of friends and family. They may throw temper tantrums over minor frustrations or cry uncontrollably over a sentimental little event. To others, their emotions appear insincere and exaggerated, to the point of being theatrical. Histrionic individuals are also highly *suggestible.* Because their opinions are not based on facts, they can be easily swayed.

Socially, histrionic individuals are difficult to get along with, due to their *excessive need for attention.* They may become upset and act impulsively when not given the attention they think they deserve. Such persons may use suicidal gestures and threats to get attention from others and to manipulate others into caring for them. Their seductiveness may put them at risk for sexual victimization. Other social difficulties arise out of their shallow emotional style. That is, they crave excitement and novelty, and although they may start relationships or projects with great enthusiasm, their interest does not last long. They may forgo long-term gains to make way for short-term excitement. Histrionic traits are maladaptive because

A Closer Look   Fatal Attraction

The thriller *Fatal Attraction* stars Michael Douglas and Glenn Close. Douglas plays Dan, a rich and powerful lawyer who is happily married to a beautiful woman. The couple have a wonderful daughter whom they both love. At a business dinner, Dan meets Glenn Close's character, Alex, who is an attractive, intriguing, single woman who catches Dan's eye. Dan is with his wife, however, and nothing happens with Alex at the dinner. A few weeks later, Dan is on a business trip without his wife one weekend and he sees Alex again. They flirt for some time, and there is definitely some attraction between them. Dan does not know at this point, but it is a fatal attraction. During the weekend, Dan and Alex have sex several times, and they appear to enjoy each other very much. In one scene, Dan and Alex are together in bed after sex, and the camera turns to a pot of coffee that is boiling on the stove. This is a subtle visual hint of the dangerous consequences being set into motion with their adulterous affair are about to boil over.

After this weekend infidelity, Dan returns to his wife. Alex is upset that Dan just seems to want to forget about her. She feels she loves him, yet she hates him at the same time for leaving her. Over the next several weeks, she calls Dan at his home and even stalks him on several occasions. Finally, she confronts Dan and tells him she is pregnant

with his baby and feels he should leave his wife for her. Dan, however, tells Alex to get an abortion and to forget about his ever leaving his wife. He makes it clear that he does not want to be a part of her life. She then alternates between extreme love and extreme hate for him. She wants Dan for herself and decides that the best way to get him is to destroy what is standing between her and Dan, which is his wife and child. The movie becomes a thriller when Alex begins terrorizing Dan and his family.

When this movie first came out, many reviewers referred to the Alex character incorrectly as a "psycho lover" or as "a nutcase." In fact, Alex exhibits several of the symptoms of borderline personality disorder. She exhibits the incredible relationship difficulties that are the hallmark of the borderline style. She vacillates between wanting to have and then wanting to destroy those she loves. She poses on the edge between destroying herself and harming those who are causing her emotional troubles. She becomes progressively angrier during the movie, and we don't know if she will direct this anger toward harming herself or harming others. All of this is triggered by feelings of abandonment, another hallmark of the borderline character. Being left out, left behind, or abandoned is a critical issue for persons with this disorder.

Because they often define themselves in terms of their relationships ("I'm nothing without you"), they fear losing those relationships. However, because of their strong and unpredictable emotions, their relationships tend to be unstable and unsatisfying and end prematurely. They bring about that which they fear.

In the movie Fatal Attraction, *Glenn Close plays the character Alex, who has many of the characteristics of borderline personality disorder.*
© *AF archive/Alamy Stock Photo*

they can interfere with relationships and cause difficulties with the individual being a productive member of society.

Table 19.4 lists the main characteristics of histrionic personality disorder, along with typical beliefs and thoughts persons with this disorder, might have. As with all personality disorder criteria, the standards for appropriate behavior differ greatly among cultures, generations, and genders. Therefore, we must ask whether specific behaviors cause social impairment or distress before concluding that those behaviors are signs or symptoms of histrionic personality disorder. For example, behavior that is considered seductive in one culture may be viewed as acceptable

Table 19.4 Characteristics of Histrionic Personality Disorder

Excessive attention seeking
Excessive and strong emotions
Sexual provocativeness
Shallow opinions
Suggestibility
Strong need for attention

Typical Thoughts or Beliefs Associated with the Histrionic Personality
"Hey, look at me!"
"I am happiest when I am the center of attention."
"Boredom is the pits."
"I usually go with my intuition; I don't have to think things through."
"I can amuse, impress, or entertain anyone, mainly because I am so interesting and exciting."
"If I feel like doing something, I go ahead and do it."

behavior in another. A woman from the southern coast of Italy may appear flirtatious in the United States, when, in fact, in her culture people are much more friendly and at ease with each other, and teasing flirtation is a common form of interaction. Consider also the culture of gender. The expression of histrionic personality disorder may depend on gender stereotypes. A male with this personality may behave in a "hyper-macho" fashion and attempt to be the center of attention by boasting of his skills in seduction or how much influence and power he has in his workplace. A woman with the histrionic style may express it with hyperfemininity,

Application

A case of histrionic personality disorder. Roxann was a student who also worked in the evenings as a dancer at an adult club. She would tell people that this was temporary and that she was different from the other women who worked there. She readily admitted, however, that the job met her two most important needs: money and attention, "two things I cannot live without." Roxann decided to take some psychology courses for self-improvement. She typically showed up to classes dressed to kill and seemed out of place even among students her own age. Once she went to her professor's office yet did not seem to have any direct questions to discuss. Instead, she seemed just to want to talk about herself and her extracurricular job. After this meeting, she was overheard telling other students that she was on a first-name basis with her professor and that he was actually her good friend. In class, she frequently behaved in ways that drew attention to herself, such as sighing loudly when the professor made a point, or blurting out answers to rhetorical questions. Toward the end of the course, Roxann quit going to class and missed the final exam. She e-mailed the professor, saying that she had been experiencing a debilitating condition and frequently had to lie down to avoid fainting. She said she had been to several doctors, but none were able to find any medical basis for her condition. The professor never heard from her again.

seeking to be the center of attention by adorning herself with bright, sexy clothes and wearing lots of gaudy accessories and makeup.

Narcissistic Personality Disorder

The calling cards of **narcissistic personality disorder** are a strong *need to be admired,* a strong sense of *self-importance,* and a *lack of insight into other people's feelings.* Narcissists see themselves in a very favorable light, inflating their accomplishments and undervaluing the work of others. Narcissists daydream about prosperity, victory, influence, adoration from others, and power. They routinely expect adulation from others, believing that homage is generally long overdue. They exhibit feelings of *entitlement,* believing that they should receive special privileges and respect, even though they have done nothing in particular to earn that special treatment.

A sense of *superiority* also pervades the narcissistic personality. They feel that they are special and should associate only with others who are similarly unique or gifted. Because they associate with special people, their own views of themselves are further enhanced. Such a person may insist on having the best lawyer or attending the best university, viewing him- or herself as unique, different from, and better than everyone else.

People with this personality expect a lot from those around them. They must receive regular praise from others and devoted admiration from those close to them. Many narcissistic persons prefer as friends those who are socially weak or unpopular so that they will not compete with the narcissists for attention. The narcissistic paradox is that although narcissists have high self-esteem, their *grandiose self-esteem is actually quite fragile.* That is, even though they appear self-confident and strong, they need to prop themselves up with admiration and attention from others. You might think that someone with truly high self-esteem would not have such an unreasonable need for praise and admiration from others. When narcissists show up at a party, they expect to be welcomed with great fanfare. When they go to a restaurant or store, they assume that waiters or clerks will rush to their attention. Narcissists thus depend on others to validate their self-importance.

To say that narcissists' self-esteem is vulnerable does not mean that they are covering up low self-esteem, but rather that they are exquisitely sensitive to criticism, that they can fly into a rage when they don't get what they think they deserve. Their self-esteem is full-blown and real; narcissists fully expect others to recognize how special, unique, and superior they are, even in the absence of any objective supportive evidence. Their vulnerability is exhibited as a thin-skinned, bristling kind of sensitivity, similar to childish temper tantrums and pouting.

Further making the narcissist socially difficult is an *inability to recognize the needs or desires of others.* In conversation, they tend to talk mostly about themselves— "I" this and "my" that. Narcissists use first-person pronouns (*I, me, mine*) more frequently in everyday conversation than does the average person (Raskin & Shaw, 1987). Psychologists Richard Robins and Oliver John (1997) have found that persons scoring high on a narcissism questionnaire evaluate their performances much more positively than those performances are evaluated by others, demonstrating the self-enhancement component of narcissism. People who are in a relationship with a narcissist often complain that narcissists are self-centered and unwilling to reciprocate in the normal give-and-take of a relationship.

A final social difficulty that creates problems for narcissists is the ease with which they become *envious of others.* When hearing of the success or accomplishment of

Table 19.5 Characteristics of Narcissistic Personality Disorder

Need to be admired
Strong sense of self-importance
Lack of insight into other people's feelings and needs
Sense of entitlement
Sense of superiority
Self-esteem that is strong but paradoxically fragile
Envy of others

Typical Thoughts or Beliefs Associated with the Narcissistic Personality
"I'm special and deserve special treatment."
"The typical rules don't apply to me."
"If others don't give me the praise and recognition I deserve, they should be punished."
"Other people should do my bidding."
"Who are *you* to criticize *me*?"
"I have every reason to expect that I will get the best that life has to offer."

acquaintances, narcissists may disparage that achievement. They may feel that they deserve the success more than the persons who worked to attain it. Narcissists may disdain others' accomplishments, particularly in public. A veneer of snobbery may hide strong feelings of envy and rage over the successes of others.

Table 19.5 lists the main characteristics of the narcissistic personality disorder, along with examples of some typical beliefs and thoughts persons with this disorder might have. Narcissists sometimes reach positions of high achievement, due primarily to their self-confidence and ambition. Nevertheless, their interpersonal lives are usually fraught with the problems that come with feelings of entitlement, an excessive need for praise and recognition, and an impaired recognition of others' needs. They have difficulty maintaining intimate relationships.

Exercise

Everyone knows someone who is a narcissist. Think of the most narcissistic person you know. List five of his or her characteristics or behaviors that make you think that this person is a narcissist. How do the acts and characteristics you have listed fit with the symptoms of the narcissistic personality disorder?

The Eccentric Cluster: Ways of Being Different

A second cluster of personality disorders contains traits that combine to make people ill at ease socially and just plain odd. Most of the oddness in these disorders has to do with how the person interacts with others. Some people have no interest in others; some are extremely uncomfortable with others; and some are suspicious of others. When carried to extremes, these interpersonal styles form the three personality disorders known as the schizoid, schizotypal, and paranoid personalities.

Schizoid and **schizotypal personality disorders** both take their root from schizophrenia and are closely tied to the history of this diagnostic category. *Schizophrenia* literally means cutting the mind off from itself and from reality. It is a serious mental illness that involves hallucinations, delusions, and perceptual aberrations. The personality disorders of schizoid and schizotypal exhibit some low-grade nonpsychotic symptoms of schizophrenia. For example, the schizotype is eccentric and is interested in odd and unusual beliefs, whereas the schizoid displays social apathy. Schizophrenics display both of these characteristics *plus* delusions or hallucinations. Thus these personality disorders have much in common with this more severe mental illness. In the case of schizotypal disorders, persons are likely to possess the genotype that makes them vulnerable to schizophrenia. A large proportion of the family members of persons with schizophrenia exhibit odd and unusual behaviors that would contribute to a diagnosis of schizotypal personality disorder.

Schizoid Personality Disorder

The schizoid personality is split off (schism), or *detached, from normal social relations.* The schizoid person simply appears to have no need or desire for intimate relationships or even friendships. Family life usually does not mean much to such people, and they do not obtain satisfaction from being part of a group. They have few or no close friends, and they would rather spend time by themselves than with others. They typically choose hobbies that can be done and appreciated alone, such as stamp collecting. They also typically choose solitary jobs, often with mechanical or abstract tasks, such as machinists or computer programmers. Usually, the schizoid personality experiences *little pleasure* from bodily or sensory experiences, such as eating or having sex. The person's emotional life is typically constricted.

At best, the schizoid person appears indifferent to others, neither bothered by criticism nor buoyed by compliments. "Bland" would be one description of such a person's emotional life. Often, the schizoid person does not respond to social cues and so appears *inept* or *socially clumsy*. For example, such a person may walk into a room where there is another person and simply stare at that person, apparently not motivated

Application

The case of Roger, a schizoid research assistant. Roger was an undergraduate who had volunteered to help out in the laboratory of one of his psychology professors. He was responsible, showing up on time and doing the work he was given. However, he seemed detached from the work, never getting too excited or appearing to be even interested, though he volunteered to work for several semesters. Roger often worked in the lab at night. On several occasions, some of the graduate students complained to the professor that Roger was "staring" at them. When pressed for details, these students said that, when they left their office doors open, they would sometimes turn around and find Roger standing in the doorway, looking at them. Several female graduate students complained that he was "spooky" and kept their office doors locked.

Roger lived with his younger brother, who also went to the same university. The brother apparently handled all the daily chores, such as dealing with the landlord, buying

Application (*Continued*)

groceries, and arranging for utilities. Roger thus had a protected life and spent most of his time studying, reading, or exploring the Internet. In class, he never talked or participated in discussion. Outside of class, he appeared to have no friends, nor did he participate in any extracurricular activities. The professor he worked for thought he might be on medication but, after inquiring, learned that Roger took no medication. After graduating with a degree in psychology, Roger returned to live with his parents. He remodeled the space above his parents' garage and has been living there, rent-free, for the past 15 years. Every few years, he e-mails his professor with an update on his rather stable life, although the professor's return e-mails bounce back with the message that "no such e-mail address exists." Apparently, Roger has found a way to keep his e-mail address secret.

to start a conversation. Sometimes the schizoid person is *passive* in the face of unpleasant happenings and does not respond effectively to important events. Such a person may appear directionless.

People from some cultures react to stress in a way that looks like schizoid personality disorder. That is, without actually having the disorder, some people under stress may appear socially numb and passive. For example, people who move out of extremely rural environments into large cities may react in a schizoid fashion for several weeks or

The famous surrealist painter Salvador Dali displayed many of the characteristics associated with the schizotypal personality disorder.
© *Ingram Publishing RF*

months. Such a person, overwhelmed by noise, lights, and overcrowding, may prefer to be alone, have constricted emotions, and manifest other deficits in social skills. Also, people who emigrate from other countries are sometimes seen as cold, reserved, or aloof. For example, people who emigrated from Southeastern Asia during the 1970s and 1980s were sometimes seen as being hostile or cold by people in mainstream urban American culture. These are cultural differences and should not be interpreted as personality disorders.

Schizotypal Personality Disorder

Whereas the schizoid person is indifferent to social interaction, the schizotypal person is acutely uncomfortable in social relationships. Schizotypes are *anxious in social situations,* especially if those situations involve strangers. Schizotypal persons also feel that they are different from others or that they do not fit in with the group. Interestingly, when such persons have to interact with a group, they do not necessarily become less anxious as they become more familiar with the group. For example, while attending a group function, the schizotype will not become less anxious as time wears on, but instead will become more and more tense. This is because schizotypes tend to be *suspicious of others* and are not prone to trust others or to relax in their presence.

Another characteristic of people with schizotypal personalities is that they are *odd* and *eccentric*. It is not unusual for them to harbor many superstitions such as believing in ESP and many other psychic or paranormal phenomena that are outside of the norms for their culture. They may believe in magic or that they possess some magical or extraordinary power, such as the ability to control other people or animals with their thoughts. They may have *unusual perceptions* that border on hallucinations, such as feeling that other people are looking at them or hearing murmurs that sound like their names.

Because of their suspiciousness of others, social discomfort, and general oddness, schizotypal persons have difficulty with social relationships. They often violate common social conventions in such ways as not making eye contact, dressing in unkempt clothing, and wearing clothing that does not go together. In many ways, the schizotype simply does not fit into the social group.

Because of their similarity in terms of avoiding social relations, the characteristics of schizoid and schizotypal personality disorders are presented together in Table 19.6. Some beliefs and thoughts, mostly concerned with other people, which characterize persons with these disorders, are also listed.

Mason, Claridge, and Jackson (1995) published a questionnaire for assessing schizotypal traits and validated it in several British samples. One of the scales contains items that get at the presence of *unusual experiences:* "Are your thoughts sometimes so strong you can almost hear them? Have you sometimes had the feeling of gaining or losing energy when certain people look at you or touch you? Are you so good at controlling others that it sometimes scares you?" Another scale contains items that assess *cognitive disorganization:* "Do you ever feel that your speech is difficult to understand because the words are all mixed up and don't make any sense? Do you frequently have difficulty starting to do things?" Another set of items measures the *tendency to avoid people:* "Are you much too independent to really get involved with people? Can you usually let yourself go and enjoy yourself

Table 19.6 Characteristics of Schizoid and Schizotypal Personality Disorders

Schizoid
Detached from normal social relationships
Pleasureless life
Inept or socially clumsy
Passive in the face of unpleasant events

Schizotypal
Anxious in social relations and avoids people
"Different" and nonconforming
Suspicious of others
Eccentricity of beliefs, such as in ESP or magic
Unusualness of perceptions and experiences
Disorganized thoughts and speech

Typical Thoughts or Beliefs Associated with the Schizoid and Schizotypal Personalities
"I hate being tied to other people."
"My privacy is more important to me than being close to others."
"It's best not to confide too much in others."
"Relationships are always messy."
"I manage best on my own and set my own standards."
"Intimate relations are unimportant to me."

A Closer Look

The Unabomber: Comorbidity of Personality Disorders

In 1996, Theodore Kaczynski was arrested for murder in a long line of bombings. He had been mailing bombs to unsuspecting university professors and scientists (hence his FBI code name—Unabomber) for 17 years. Many of his targets were computer scientists, but he did injure one psychology professor with a mail bomb (Professor James McConnell at the University of Michigan). Police knew the bombs were all from the same person, but they had no idea of his motives or why he was targeting university professors. After a 17-year period of anonymous killing and maiming from a distance, he decided to make the nature of his grievances clear. He sent several taunting letters to the FBI, and a long rambling manifesto to the *Washington Post* and *The New York Times,* which published his diatribe against technology and modern society. This was his undoing. Kaczynski's brother recognized the nature of the complaints in the manifesto and notified the police, who arrested Kaczynski at his isolated 10-by-12-foot shack in Montana.

A reporter—Maggie Scarf—writing in the *New Republic* magazine (June 10, 1996, p. 20), presented her view that Ted Kaczynski most likely had a narcissistic personality disorder. Scarf used the *DSM-IV* description of narcissistic disorder to explain Kaczynski's behavior. For example, as an undergraduate at Harvard, Kaczynski isolated himself so severely that none of his classmates can remember anything about him. He saw himself as a misunderstood genius whom the world would one day recognize. As a mathematics graduate student at the University of Michigan, he isolated himself even more. In his isolation he probably nurtured fantasies of prestige and power and revenge on those who refused to praise him. As a promising young professor of mathematics at U.C.–Berkeley, he suddenly bolted from his faculty position in 1969. No one, apparently, was recognizing his superiority. People did not realize, as he did, that he possessed a phenomenal intellect and superior vision of how everything worked. His colleagues were fools, he must have concluded, because they could not see his obvious superiority. His students, however, complained loudly about his teaching style. In their course evaluations, they indicated that his lectures were boring and useless and that he ignored questions from the students. They too must be fools, Kaczynski probably concluded.

In her article Scarf argued that when Kaczynski struck out at society, he was really saying, "I'm special and I deserve your respect." When he began taunting the police to try to capture him, he was really saying, "I am so extraordinary that I operate with impunity; you haven't been able to catch me for 17 years and you never will." Finally, when he gave his manifesto to the world, he was really saying, "You had better realize you are dealing with someone unprecedented in the history of the human race. I am so clever and powerful and smart that I will tell you all the problems with the world and how to fix them, and if you ignore my commands you do so at your own risk." His entire ranting manifesto is easily located on the World Wide Web by entering "Unabomber" in a search engine.

Scarf is a journalist, not a psychologist, so her diagnosis is based on her speculation. Kaczynski certainly does

Former University of California at Berkeley math professor Theodore Kaczynski was convicted in several of the "Unabomber" attacks, which occurred over a 17-year period. Kaczynski displays characteristics associated with a number of personality disorders.
© *Ralf-Finn Hestoft/CORBIS/Corbis via Getty Images*

have some features of the narcissistic personality disorder, but most narcissists are not serial murderers. What other possible clues might we have to his abnormal behavior? It turns out that the entire text of the court-appointed psychiatrist's report on Ted Kaczynski is available on the Web at http://www.paulcooijmans.com/psychology/unabombreport.html (as of February 2013). This report, prepared by government-appointed psychiatrist Sally Johnson, provides another perspective on Kaczynski. While at Harvard, Kaczynski was involved in a study by Henry Murray, whom we discussed in Chapter 11. Personality test results from his undergraduate days at Harvard indicate that he was extremely introverted and somewhat depressive, even at that early age. During his psychological evaluation 30 years later, the main finding was that he suffered from schizophrenia, paranoid type, which is a severe mental illness. However, he also had an IQ of 136, which puts him in the top 1 percent of the population. As for personality disorders, the psychiatrist concluded that Kaczynski had paranoid personality disorder along with many features of the avoidant and antisocial personality disorders as well. The following is a quote from her official report:

Mr. Kaczynski is also diagnosed as suffering from a Paranoid Personality Disorder with Avoidant and Antisocial Features. Review of his developmental history, adolescence and early adult life draws a picture consistent with the symptomatology associated with this type of personality disorder. Consistent with this type of *personality disordered function, Mr. Kaczynski historically has shown pervasive distrust of others such that their motives are interpreted as malevolent. Symptoms consistent with Paranoid Personality Disorders that are evident in Mr. Kaczynski's presentation include that he suspects, without sufficient basis, that others are exploiting, harming, or deceiving him; that he reads demeaning or threatening meanings into benign remarks or events; that he persistently bears grudges and is unforgiving of insults, injuries or slights; and that he perceives attacks on his character or reputation that are not apparent to others, and is quick to react angrily or to counterattack.*

In addition to meeting the criteria for Paranoid Personality Disorder, Mr. Kaczynski also has features of two other personality disorder types. Support for Avoidant Personality Disorder Traits includes that he has demonstrated a pervasive pattern of social inhibition, feelings of inadequacy and hypersensitivity to negative evaluations, beginning in his early life. Consistent with this, he has shown restraint within intimate relationships because of his fear of being shamed or ridiculed; he has been preoccupied with being criticized or rejected in social situations; and is inhibited in new interpersonal situations because of feelings of inadequacy. Consistent with Antisocial Personality Disorder Traits is his pervasive pattern of disregard for and violation of the rights of others. This includes his failure to conform to social norms with *respect to lawful behaviors, as indicated by repeatedly performing acts that are grounds for arrest. This description is based on his own account of his behavior in his writings and interviews. Also consistent with his Antisocial Personality Traits is the characteristic of deceitfulness, as indicated by his persistent and elaborate efforts to conceal his behaviors. He has demonstrated a reckless regard for the safety of others. He demonstrates a lack of remorse as indicated in his writings by being indifferent to having hurt, mistreated, or stolen from others. Mr. Kaczynski falls short of carrying a diagnosis of Antisocial Personality Disorder in that he does not have evidence of a conduct disorder before the age of 15. (Excerpted from the report of Sally C. Johnson, M.D., Chief Psychiatrist, Associate Warden of Health Services, Federal Correctional Institution, Butner, North Carolina, January, 1996.)*

Kaczynski shows features of at least four different personality disorders, with the prominent personality disorder being paranoid personality disorder. This disorder occurred along with paranoid schizophrenia, which involves delusions and elaborate belief systems. The presence of two or more disorders in one person is called comorbidity. Comorbidity can occur when two or more personality disorders exist, or when two or more disorders of any type coexist in the same person. Comorbidity is fairly common, and it makes for difficulty in diagnosing disorders (Krueger & Markon, 2006).

at a party?" And, finally, there is a scale for assessing the *nonconformity* aspect of schizotypy: "Do you often feel like doing the opposite of what people suggest, even though you know they are right? Would you take drugs that might have strange or dangerous effects?"

Exercise

Many famous persons have been odd or eccentric. Artists (e.g., Salvador Dali), writers (e.g., Tennessee Williams), musicians, film stars, and even politicians have exhibited some fairly eccentric behaviors. Can you think of examples of public figures who have displayed odd beliefs or actions recently? Would they fit the rest of the characteristics of the schizotypal personality?

Paranoid Personality Disorder

Whereas the schizotype is uncomfortable with others, the paranoid person is extremely *distrustful of others* and sees others as a constant threat. Such persons assume that others are out to exploit and deceive them, even though there is no good evidence to support this assumption. Paranoid persons feel that they have been injured by others and are preoccupied with doubts about the motivations of others.

People with this personality typically do not reveal personal information to others, fearing that the information will be used against them. Their reaction to others is "Mind your own business." The paranoid person often *misinterprets social events.* For example, someone makes an off-hand comment and the paranoid interprets it as a demeaning or threatening remark (e.g., wondering, "What did he mean by *that*?"). Paranoids are constantly on the lookout for hidden meanings and disguised motivations in the comments and behaviors of others.

The person with a **paranoid personality disorder** often holds *resentments toward others* for slights or perceived insults. Such a person is reluctant to forgive and forget even minor altercations. Paranoid persons often become involved in legal disputes, suing others for the slightest reasons. Sometimes paranoid persons plead with those in power to intervene on their behalf, such as writing to congresspersons or calling the local police chief day after day.

Pathological jealousy is a common manifestation of paranoid personality disorder. For example, a pathologically jealous woman suspects that her husband or partner is unfaithful, even though there is no objective evidence of infidelity. She may go to great lengths to find support for her jealous beliefs. She may restrict the activities of her partner or constantly question him as to his whereabouts. She may not believe her partner's accounts of how he spent his time or believe his claims of faithfulness.

People with paranoid personality disorder are at risk of harming those who threaten their belief systems. Their *argumentative and hostile nature* may provoke others to a combative response. This hostile response from others, in turn, validates the paranoids' original suspicion that others are out to get them. Their extreme suspiciousness and the unreasonableness of their beliefs make people with this disorder particularly difficult in social relations. Table 19.7 presents the main characteristics of the paranoid personality disorder, along with some examples of beliefs and thoughts commonly found among persons with this disorder.

The Anxious Cluster: Ways of Being Nervous, Fearful, or Distressed

The final cluster of personality traits consists of patterns of behavior that are geared toward avoiding anxiety. The disorders in this cluster, like all the other disorders, illustrate the **neurotic paradox:** Although a behavior pattern successfully solves one problem for the person, it may create or maintain another equally or more severe problem.

Table 19.7 Characteristics of Paranoid Personality Disorder

Is distrustful of others
Misinterprets social events as threatening
Harbors resentments toward others
Is prone to pathological jealousy
Is argumentative and hostile

Typical Thoughts or Beliefs Associated with the Paranoid Personality
"Get them before they get you."
"Other people always have ulterior motives."
"People will say one thing but do another."
"Don't let them get away with anything."
"I have to be on guard all the time."
"When people act friendly toward you, it is probably because they want something. Watch out!"

Avoidant Personality Disorder

The major feature of the **avoidant personality disorder** is a pervasive *feeling of inadequacy* and *sensitivity to criticism* from others. Clearly, no one likes to be criticized. However, avoidant persons will go to great lengths to avoid situations in which others may have opportunities to criticize their performance or character, such as in school, at work, or in other group settings. The main reason for this anxiety about performance is an extreme fear of criticism or rejection from others. Such persons may avoid making new friends or going to new places, through fear of criticism or disapproval. Friends may have to plead and promise lots of support and encouragement in order to get them involved in new activities.

Application

The case of Ellen, avoidant university student. Ellen is a 21-year-old university student who has gone to the university's psychological clinic with the general complaint that she is uncomfortable in social settings. Because she is so shy and nervous, she keeps her contact with others to a minimum. She is worried about starting new classes next semester and having to be in rooms with total strangers. She is especially worried about her psychology courses, where "they might find out I am a nutcase." She adds, "They are going to think I am a dysfunctional idiot because I am so shy and I go into a panic at the thought of speaking up in a group of strangers." She adds that she is thinking of switching her major from psychology to computer science. Although she is curious about people, and therefore likes psychology, she nevertheless feels awkward around them. Computers, she thinks, are much easier to get along with.

Ellen reports that, as a child, she was teased mercilessly by the other children in her school. She remembers withdrawing from others at about this time in her life. She says that in grade school she would try to make herself small and inconspicuous, so others would not notice her. As a teenager, she took some jobs babysitting, but she has never held a real job. At the university, she apparently has no friends, or at least cannot name any. She says she is afraid others will not like her "when they find out what I am really like," so she avoids social contact. In fact, she never once makes eye contact with the interviewer at the clinic.

Application (*Continued*)

At the university, Ellen follows a pattern of letting work pile up, then works hard to get it all done. She tries to do a few errands each day, keeps her apartment neat, and goes to the grocery store twice a month. She describes her life as "not very happy, but at least predictable." She likes exploring the Internet on her home computer. She says she enjoys going to chat rooms on the Internet, but when pressed on this, she confesses that she just watches and has never actually interacted with anyone over the Internet. She likes staying in the background, watching others interact: "when they don't even know I'm there, then I can be pretty sure they are not laughing at me."

Because avoidant persons fear criticism, they may *restrict their activities* to avoid potential embarrassments. For example, an avoidant man may cancel a blind date at the last minute because he can't find just the right clothes to wear. Avoidant individuals cope with anxiety by avoiding the risks of everyday social life. However, by avoiding the anxiety, they create other problems, often in the form of missed opportunities. In addition, avoidant individuals are typically seen by others as meek, quiet, shy, lonely, and solitary.

Avoidant persons are sensitive to what others think of them. Their feelings are easily hurt, and they appear vulnerable and inhibited in social interactions, withholding their own views, opinions, or feelings out of fear of being ridiculed. They typically have very *low self-esteem* and feel inadequate to many of life's day-to-day challenges. Because of their social isolation, they typically do not have many sources of social support. Even though they typically desire to be involved with others, and may even fantasize about relationships, they tend to avoid intimate contact out of their fear of rejection and criticism. The paradox is that, in avoidantly coping with their social anxiety, they shun the supportive relationships with caring others that could actually help boost their self-esteem. Table 19.8 presents the main features of the avoidant personality disorder, along with several examples of thoughts and beliefs that might occur in someone with this disorder.

Dependent Personality Disorder

Whereas the avoidant person avoids others to an extreme, the dependent person seeks out others to an extreme. The hallmark of the **dependent personality disorder**

Table 19.8 Characteristics of Avoidant Personality Disorder

Feelings of inadequacy
Sensitive to criticism
Activities are restricted to avoid embarrassment
Low self-esteem

Typical Thoughts or Beliefs Associated with the Avoidant Personality
"I am socially inept and undesirable."
"I wish you would like me, but I think you really hate me."
"I can't stand being criticized; it makes me feel so unpleasant."
"I must avoid unpleasant situations at all costs."
"I don't want to attract attention to myself."
"If I ignore a problem, it will go away."

is an *excessive need to be taken care of,* to be nurtured, coddled, and told what to do. Dependent persons act in *submissive* ways so as to encourage others to take care of them or take charge of the situation. Such individuals need lots of encouragement and advice from others and would much rather turn over responsibility for their decisions to someone else. Where should they live, what schools should they attend, what courses should they take, with whom should they make friends? The dependent personality has great difficulty making such decisions, and *seeks out reassurance from others.* However, such a person tends to seek advice about even minor decisions, such as whether to carry an umbrella today, what color clothes to wear, and what entree to order at a restaurant. The dependent person *rarely takes the initiative.*

Because of their fear of losing the help and advice of others, dependent persons *avoid disagreements* with those on whom they are dependent. Because of their extreme need for support, dependent personalities might even agree with decisions or opinions that they feel are wrong to avoid angering the persons on whom they depend.

Because of their low self-confidence and need for constant reassurance, dependent persons may *not work well independently.* They may wait for others to start projects or may need direction often during a task. They may demonstrate how inept they are, so as to trick others into assisting them. They may avoid becoming proficient at a task, so as to keep others from seeing that they are competent to work by themselves. It is too bad that a person who relies on others to solve problems may never learn the skills of living or working independently.

Persons with dependent personalities *may tolerate extreme circumstances to obtain reassurance and support from others.* Such people may submit to unreasonable demands, may tolerate abuse, or may stay in a distorted relationship. People who believe that they are unable to take care of themselves may tolerate a lot of abuse in order to maintain bonds with people who will take care of them. The unfortunate aspect of the dependent personality is that by giving over responsibility and depending on other people, dependent persons may never discover that they can take care of themselves. Table 19.9 presents the main characteristics of the dependent personality disorder along with associated beliefs and thoughts that persons with this disorder might have.

Table 19.9 Characteristics of Dependent Personality Disorder

Has an excessive need to be taken care of
Is submissive
Seeks reassurance from others
Rarely takes initiative and rarely disagrees with others
Does not work well independently
May tolerate abuse from others to obtain support

Typical Thoughts or Beliefs Associated with the Dependent Personality
"I am weak and need support."
"The worst possible thing would be to be abandoned and left alone."
"I must not offend those on whom I depend."
"I must be submissive to obtain their help."
"I need help making decisions."
"I hope someone will tell me what to do."

Application

The case of Edward, a dependent personality. Edward was a University Professor who had achieved some success in his field. One day, a psychologist friend stopped by his office to invite Edward and his wife to dinner. Edward said he had to call his wife to see if they could go, and his wife agreed and told Edward to invite the friend to stop by their house for a drink before going to dinner. That night, the friend arrived at the house before Edward was ready, and he noticed Edward asked his wife for advice on what to wear. It was raining that night, and Edward asked his wife if he should wear a jacket or a raincoat. At dinner, the friend noticed that Edward asked his wife what he should drink and, as he looked over the menu, Edward asked his wife what he should order for dinner. Edward even asked his wife; "What kind of food do I like?" At this point, the psychologist friend began to think Edward was displaying signs of a dependent personality disorder.

Obsessive-Compulsive Personality Disorder

The obsessive-compulsive person is *preoccupied with order* and *strives to be perfect.* The high need for order can manifest itself in the person's attention to details, however trivial, and fondness for rules, rituals, schedules, and procedures. Such persons may, for example, plan out which clothes they will wear every day of the week or clean their apartments every Saturday and Wednesday from 5 until 7 p.m. People with **obsessive-compulsive personality disorder** *hold very high standards for themselves.* However, they may work so hard at being perfect that they are never satisfied with their work. For example, a student might never turn in a research paper because it is never quite perfect enough. The desire for perfection can actually stifle a person's productivity.

Another characteristic is a *devotion to work at the expense of leisure and friendships.* Obsessive-compulsive persons tend to work harder than they need to. They may work at night and on weekends and rarely take time off. In his book on adult personality development, George Vaillant (1977) saw it as a sign of positive mental adjustment when his adult subjects reported taking at least a one-week vacation each year. Obsessive-compulsives tend not to meet this criterion for adjustment. When they do take time off for recreation, they prefer serious tasks such as stamp collecting or chess. For hobbies, they pick very demanding tasks or activities that require great attention to detail, such as cross-stitch sewing or computer programming. Even their play looks a lot like work.

The obsessive-compulsive person may also appear *inflexible* with regard to ethics and morals. Such persons set high principles for themselves and tend to follow the letter of the law. They are highly conscientious and expect others to be that way as well. There is usually only one right way to do something—their way. They often have trouble working with others because they are reluctant to delegate tasks; "If you want something done right, you have to do it yourself" is a common complaint from obsessive-compulsive persons. They become irritated when others don't take their work as seriously as they do.

A few other odd characteristics are often present in the obsessive-compulsive person. One is the preference to hang on to worn-out or useless things; many obsessive-compulsive people have trouble throwing things away. Many are *miserly*

Table 19.10   Characteristics of Obsessive-Compulsive Personality Disorder

Preoccupied with order
Perfectionistic
Devoted to work, seeking little leisure time or friendship
Frequently miserly or stingy
Rigid and stubborn

Typical Thoughts or Beliefs Associated with the Obsessive-Compulsive Personality
"I believe in order, rules, and high standards."
"Others are irresponsible, casual, and self-indulgent."
"Details are important; flaws and mistakes are intolerable."
"My way is the only right way to do things."
"If you can't do it perfectly, don't do it at all."
"I have only myself to depend on."

or stingy, hoarding their money and resources. And finally, along with being inflexible, obsessive-compulsives can be frustratingly *stubborn.* They may stubbornly insist, for example, that they cannot complete their work because of the imperfections of others. As you might imagine, they often cause difficulties for others at the workplace. Table 19.10 presents the essential features of obsessive-compulsive personality disorder, along with some typical beliefs and thoughts that characterize persons with this disorder.

There is another disorder—obsessive-compulsive disorder (OCD)—that is often confused with obsessive-compulsive personality disorder (OCPD). OCD is an anxiety disorder that is, in several ways, more serious and debilitating than OCPD. In OCD a pattern of unwanted and intrusive thoughts is recurrent and troubling to the person, such as the persistent thought that he or she may harm someone. In addition, OCD is characterized by the presence of ritualistic behaviors, such as frequent hand washing or the tendency to repeat actions a set number of times (e.g., having to touch an object three times before leaving a room, or repeating words to oneself three times). Obsessive-compulsive personality disorder, on the other hand, really involves a collection of traits, such as excessive need for order or extremely high conscientiousness. Nevertheless, people with OCPD are at risk for developing OCD as well as other kinds of anxiety disorders (Oltmanns & Emery, 2004).

Many of the characteristics of obsessive-compulsive personality can be adaptive in some respects. For example, wanting to perform a task as perfectly as possible is, up to a point, desirable and rewarded. Holding one's opinions firm is, up to a point, desirable and indicates character. Keeping everything neat and orderly is, up to a point, useful. How can one tell, however, when some of these characteristics and behaviors indicate an obsessive-compulsive personality? How can we tell the difference between a high level of conscientiousness and the disorder of obsessive-compulsiveness? The clearest way to know when obsessiveness is becoming a disorder is when this pattern of behavior starts to interfere with a person's ability to be productive or to maintain satisfying relationships. In the case study of Rita presented below, you'll see that her obsessive and compulsive personality led her to behave in ways that seriously interfered with both of these aspects of her life.

Application

The case of Rita, an obsessive-compulsive personality. Rita was a 39-year-old computer programmer who had been married for 18 years. She was always orderly and kept a very neat house. It was so neat, in fact, that she noticed when the books were in the wrong order on the bookshelves or if a knick-knack had been moved on a table or shelf. She vacuumed the house every day, whether it needed it or not. This resulted in the need for a new vacuum cleaner almost every year. Her husband thought this odd but concluded that she simply had a low threshold for what counted as dirty. She was constantly nagging him or angry at him because he did not seem to care as much as her that things be so neat, clean, and orderly. They did not have children because, according to Rita, children would be too much additional work for her, and she certainly could not count on her husband to do anything right in terms of taking care of children or the house. Besides, children would disrupt the order and neatness of her life.

Over the years, Rita added to her list of things she needed to do each day but never took anything off the list. In addition to vacuuming, she added dusting each day. Then she added cleaning the sinks with strong cleaners each day. She had to get up earlier in the mornings to get all of this cleaning done before work.

Her boss often complained that she was slow. The boss did not appreciate the fact that Rita checked her work over and over again before turning it in. Rita also had difficulties working as part of a team because none of the other workers met her standards. They did not check their work often enough, she thought, and were sloppy and imprecise. Her boss eventually had to isolate her and give her independent work because she could not get along with her coworkers.

Before leaving the house each morning, Rita checked the windows and doors, the gas, the water faucets, and all the light fixtures. After a few months of this, one check was not sufficient, and she began to check everything twice. Her husband complained about this, so she started making him wait in the car while she checked each sink, light, door, window, and so on. Her husband dutifully waited each day, but as the months went on, the wait grew longer and longer. He was now sitting in the car for an hour each morning, waiting for Rita to finish checking everything in the house. One morning, after checking the house thoroughly, she went outside to find that her husband had left without her. That afternoon she received an e-mail from him saying that he could not take it any longer and had decided to divorce her.

Prevalence of Personality Disorders

Figure 19.1 indicates the prevalence rates of the 10 personality disorders. **Prevalence** is a term that refers to the total number of cases that are present within a given population during a particular period of time. The data in Figure 19.1 are based on summaries of several community samples (Mattia & Zimmerman, 2001) and refer to prevalence rates at the time of sampling (e.g., at any given time, how many people are diagnosable with paranoid personality disorder?). These results show that obsessive-compulsive personality disorder is the most common, at just over 4 percent prevalence rate. Next most common are the schizotypal, histrionic, and dependent personality disorders, approximately 2 percent prevalence each. The least common is narcissistic personality disorder, affecting only 0.2 percent of the population. However, these diagnoses were all based on interviews, and it may be that narcissists are least likely to admit to the more disordered features of their condition. In fact, Oltmanns and colleagues have shown that

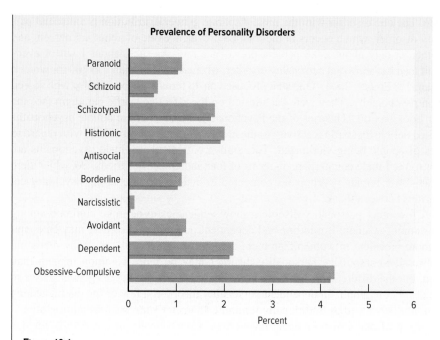

Figure 19.1

Estimates of the prevalence of personality disorders.

Source: Adapted from Epidemiology, by J. I. Mattia and M. Zimmerman, 2001, in *Handbook of Personality Disorders: Theory, Research, and Treatment,* edited by W. J. Livesley, New York: Guilford.

self-reports of narcissism correlate weakly with peer reports of narcissism, even though with most other personality traits there are modest to substantial correlations between self-report and peer report (Clifton, Turkheimer, & Oltmanns, 2004; Klonsky, Oltmanns, & Turkheimer, 2002; Oltmanns et al., 2004). These findings suggest that, because the data in Figure 19.1 are based on self-report through structured interviews, they may actually underestimate the prevalence of some of the disorders, especially narcissism.

The total prevalence rate for having at least one personality disorder is about 13 percent. That is, at any given time, approximately 13 percent of the population is diagnosable with a personality disorder of one or more types. This brings up the issue of comorbidity, which we also mentioned in our A Closer Look on the Unabomber. A substantial proportion, between 25 and 50 percent, of the people who meet the criteria for a diagnosis on one personality disorder will also meet the criteria for diagnosis on another personality disorder (Oltmanns & Emery, 2004). Many of the personality disorders contain common features. For example, several disorders involve social isolation, including schizotypal, schizoid, avoidant, and, in many cases, obsessive-compulsive disorder. Uninhibited and irresponsible behavior is one of the criteria for a diagnosis of borderline, histrionic, and antisocial personality disorders. As such, differential diagnoses are often challenging in personality disorders. A **differential diagnosis** is one in which, out of two or more possible diagnoses, the clinician searches for evidence in support of one diagnostic category over all the others.

Gender Differences in Personality Disorders

The overall prevalence rate for personality disorders is fairly equal in men and women. A few specific disorders, however, show a tendency to be more prevalent in men or in women. The one disorder with the most disparate gender distribution is antisocial personality disorder, which occurs in men with a prevalence rate of about 4.5 percent and in women at only about a 0.8 percent prevalence rate. As such, about 1 out of every 20 adult men has antisocial personality disorder, whereas it is less than 1 in 100 for women (Oltmanns & Emery, 2004). One study focused on 48 female prison inmates who scored high on psychopathy. They were each tested on the affective startle paradigm (see the Closer Look box on "Theories of the Psychopathic Mind"). These female psychopaths exhibited deficits in startle reactivity to the unpleasant images, especially with regard to images of people being victimized. This study confirms that female psychopaths are similar to their male counterparts in terms of fear and empathy deficits. So, while there are a lot fewer female psychopaths compared to males, they are strong psychological similarities between them.

A few other personality disorders show tendencies to be more common among men or among women. Borderline and dependent personality disorders may be somewhat more prevalent in women than men, though the evidence is not strong. Paranoid and obsessive-compulsive personality disorder may be more common in men than women, but the difference is not large. One important issue concerns gender biases in diagnoses. For example, in dependent personality disorder, a few of the distinguishing traits might be viewed as traditionally feminine characteristics, such as putting others' needs ahead of one's own or being unassertive. Consequently, if the criteria for this disorder are based on feminine stereotypes, then it might be relatively easier for women than men to meet the criteria for this diagnosis, even if a particular woman is not suffering significant impairment from those particular traits. Clinicians need to be aware of how stereotypes affect the ways they diagnose their clients.

A related issue is gender differences in the manifestation of the different disorders. For example, in histrionic personality disorder a main issue concerns excessive attention seeking. A woman might pursue this through hyperfemininity, perhaps even being sexually seductive. A male might pursue this through hypermasculinity, perhaps through shows of strength and bragging about accomplishments. Each is engaging in excessive attention seeking but doing it in ways that are gender stereotyped.

Dimensional Model of Personality Disorders

As discussed at the beginning of this chapter, modern theorists are arguing for a dimensional, as opposed to a categorical, view of personality disorders. In the dimensional model of personality, the only distinctions made between normal personality traits and disorders are in terms of extremity, rigidity, and maladaptiveness. For example, Widiger (1997) argues that disorders simply are maladaptive variants and combinations of normal-range personality traits. The personality traits most studied as sources of disorders are the five traits of the five-factor model, which we reviewed in Chapter 3. Costa and Widiger (1994) edited an influential book supporting the idea that the Big Five traits provide a useful framework for understanding disorders. Widiger (1997) presents data arguing that, for example, borderline personality disorder is extreme narcissism, and schizoid disorder is extreme introversion accompanied by low neuroticism (Emotional Stability). Extreme introversion accompanied by extremely high neuroticism, on the other hand, results in avoidant personality disorder. Histrionic disorder is characterized as extreme extraversion. Obsessive-compulsive disorder is a maladaptive form of extreme conscientiousness. Schizotypal personality disorder is a complex combination of introversion, high neuroticism, low agreeableness, and extreme openness.

The dimensional view is somewhat like chemistry: Add a little of this trait and some of that trait, amplify to extremely high (or low) levels, and the result is a specific disorder. Dimensional models may have certain advantages, such as accounting for why people in the same diagnostic category can be so different from each other in how they express the disorder. In addition, the dimensional model allows for a person to have multiple disorders of personality. The dimensional model also explicitly acknowledges that the distinction between what is normal and what is abnormal is more a matter of degree than a clear and qualitative break. One line of research that is currently underway is developing measures of the Five Factor Model that have higher precision at the tails of the distributions; that is, at the extremely high and extremely low ends (Miller & Lynam, 2015; Samuels & Gore, 2012). The original measures of the Five Factor Model were developed with the most precision in the middle of the distribution, which is where most people are (picture a normal curve, with its bell-shaped distribution). However, if one is interested in the extreme on these personality traits, then new measures will need to be developed that have adequate discrimination and accuracy way out on the tails of the distribution, at the extremes. This is currently an active area of research.

As mentioned above, the American Psychiatric Association has decided to continue its application of a categorical view in the definition and diagnosis of personality disorders. The decade of work that went into revising the *DSM-IV* into the *DSM-5* has amounted to essentially "no change" to the way we understand personality disorders. The report of the personality disorders working group does, however, appear in Section III the *DSM-5*. Moreover, the APA changed the numbering system for the *DSM* to numerical rather than roman numbers so that they can introduce more frequent though smaller updates with decimals, similar to software updates, for example, *DSM-5.1, DSM-5.2,* and so on. Perhaps one of the minor updates in the future will concern how personality disorders are conceptualized as dimensional rather than categorical.

Causes of Personality Disorders

The material covered in this chapter so far has been mainly descriptive, drawing from and expanding on the diagnostic criteria in the *DSM-5*. Abnormal psychology is a strongly descriptive science, and efforts are mainly to develop classification systems and taxonomies of disorders. This does not mean, however, that there are no attempts to understand how personality disorders develop or what causes one person to have a particular disorder. Researchers generally examine both biological and environmental factors that contribute to the development of personality disorders (Nigg & Goldsmith, 1994). For example, it is clear that persons who suffer with borderline personality disorder experienced poor attachment relationships in childhood (Kernberg, 1975, 1984; Nigg & Goldsmith, 1994), and that many borderline persons were the target of sexual abuse in childhood (Westen, 1990). There is abundant evidence that most people with borderline personality disorder grew up in chaotic homes, with a lot of exposure to the impulsive behavior of adults (Millon, 2000b).

It appears that genetic factors play little role in borderline personality disorder. Instead, most of the evidence implicates loss of, or neglect by, the parents in early childhood (Guzder et al., 1996).

When it comes to schizotypal personality disorder, the evidence is more in line with genetic causes. A variety of family, twin, and adoption studies suggest that schizotypal disorder is genetically similar to schizophrenia (Nigg & Goldsmith, 1994). Moreover, the first-degree relatives of persons with schizophrenia are much more likely to exhibit features of schizotypal personality disorder than persons in the general

Table 19.11 The Personality Disorders Described According to Unique Characteristics Associated with Self-Concept, Emotional Life, Behavior, and Social Relations

Specific Disorders	Self-Concept	Emotion
Antisocial Personality	Self as unfettered by rules	Lack of remorse, quick-tempered, easily irritated, aggressive
Borderline Personality	Self as vague, diffuse, changing, unstable, with no strong feeling of identity	Unstable, intense, with anger, shame, and guilt
Histrionic Personality	Self as desirable and charming	Flamboyant in public displays
Narcissistic Personality	Self as unique, admirable, special	Feelings of entitlement, vengeful when not recognized
Schizoid Personality	Self as loner, without ambition	Bland, taking little pleasure in life
Schizotypal Personality	Self as different from others, special	Uncomfortable, suspicious
Paranoid Personality	Self as victim	Feels threatened, argumentative, jealous
Avoidant Personality	Self as inadequate	Frequently embarrassed, fearing criticism and rejection
Dependent Personality	Self as needy, lacking self-direction	Meek, indecisive
Obsessive-Compulsive Personality	Self as rigid, with high standards and expectations	Easily irritated, stubborn, without much pleasure

population. However, prevalence rates for paranoid and avoidant personality disorders were also elevated among the relatives of the schizophrenia patients, suggesting that these disorders may be genetically related to schizophrenia (Kendler et al., 1993).

Antisocial personality disorder also has several explanatory theories. For example, many antisocial persons were themselves abused and victimized as children (Pollock et al., 1990), leading to social learning and psychoanalytic theories of the cause of this disorder. A high proportion of antisocial persons also abuse multiple illegal drugs or alcohol, leading some researchers to propose that biological changes associated with drug abuse are responsible for antisocial behavior. There are also clear familial trends suggesting that antisocial personality disorder is due, in part, to genetic causes (Lykken, 1995). Others have proposed learning theories of antisocial personality disorder, due mainly to research showing that such persons are deficient in learning through punishment (e.g., Newman, 1987).

The neurological underpinnings of antisocial and psychopathic traits are also being investigated. A useful model here is the triarchic model, which characterizes psychopaths in terms of three distinguishable components: boldness, meanness, and lack of inhibition (Patrick, Drislane, & Strickland, 2012). A new measure of this triarchic model provides better coverage of these three components than previous inventories (Drislane, Patrick, & Arsal, 2014). Moreover, this new measure correlates with neuroscience findings in quite sensible ways. For example, "boldness" is related to an

Behavior	Social Relations
Reckless, impulsive, irresponsible	Callous and indifferent to rights of others
Unpredictable, perhaps harmful to self or others	Intense, volatile, unstable, fearing abandonment
Attention seeking, extravagant	Attention seeking
Self-displaying, admiration seeking	Envious, lacking in empathy
Passive	Detached, socially inept, having no or few friends
Odd, eccentric with unusual beliefs	Socially anxious, avoiding others
Distrustful, self-protective, resentful	Sensitive, prone to misinterpretations, with many enemies
Quiet, shy, solitary	Withdrawing, sensitive to criticism
Reassurance seeking, rarely taking initiative	Submissive, needs nurturance, avoids conflict
Workaholic, likes repetition, details	No time for friends, others don't meet standards

underreactivity in the brain's defensive motivational system. The "lack of inhibition" component is related to deficits in the frontal cortical regions involved in self-regulation, cognitive control, and moral reasoning. Both of these components—boldness and lack of inhibition—are also associated with brain circuits that process rewards (Seara-Cardoso & Viding, 2015). The third component—"meanness"—is thought to be related to dysfunction in brain systems important to empathy, perspective taking, and perhaps even to lower levels of oxytocin, and neurochemical related to social bonding.

Explanations of the other personality disorders also follow this pattern. There are biological explanations, learning explanations, psychodynamic explanations, and cultural explanations. There may be some truth to each of these views, that personality disorders, like normal-range personality variables, have multiple causes. Moreover, it is very difficult to separate biology from learning, to separate nature from nurture. For example, an individual's early experiences—such as with an abusive parent—may lead to neurological changes in certain brain centers, such as the abnormalities in the hypothalamus and pituitary functioning (e.g., Mason et al., 1994). Consequently, it does not make sense to speak of early childhood abuse as a strictly experiential or learning factor when biological changes can follow from such abusive experiences.

Most of the research on personality disorders is descriptive or correlational. True experiments, where people would be randomly assigned to either have or not have a disorder, are impossible. Because the research is mostly correlational, it cannot pin down the causal direction of relationships that are identified. For example, suppose people with a specific disorder are found to have a high level of a particular neurotransmitter in their system. From these results we know something descriptive, but we don't know whether having a high level of that neurotransmitter causes the disorder, or whether having the disorder causes high levels of the neurotransmitter (or whether a third unknown variable causes both the neurotransmitter changes and the disorder). Consequently, when you read the literature on the "causes" of personality disorders, much of the evidence has to be interpreted with caution because correlational data can rarely prove causality (as we discussed in Chapter 2).

Clearly, biology and experience are tightly intermingled, making it difficult to attribute a disorder to only one kind of cause. Efforts to reduce the cause of personality disorders to one factor—say, genetics—are likely to be an oversimplification. Thus, we have to be comfortable with the notion that something as complicated as the human personality—and its disorders—has multiple causes. Table 19.11 presents all of the personality disorders along with descriptions of the self-concept, emotional life, behavior, and social relations of persons who have the disorder.

SUMMARY AND EVALUATION

We began this chapter with a discussion of how disorders of personality draw on almost all the other topics studied so far. The concept of disorder relies on making a distinction between what is normal and what is abnormal. There are several definitions of abnormality. One is statistical and relies on how frequently a condition appears among a population of people. Another definition is sociological and has to do with how much a society tolerates particular forms of behavior. A psychological definition emphasizes to what extent a behavior pattern causes distress for the person or for others. For example, is the behavior associated with disorganization in the person's own thoughts, emotions, or social relations? The hallmark of the psychological definition of abnormal is anything that prevents a person from having satisfying relationships or from carrying on productive work. Most of the personality disorders result in problems with relationships because they impair the person's ability to get along with others. Many of the disorders also impair the person's ability to engage in productive work. We saw that all of the personality disorders refer to symptoms that cause problems with relationships or with work, or both.

The study of abnormal psychology, also called psychopathology, has evolved into a distinct discipline within psychology and psychiatry. A major goal of this discipline is to develop reliable taxonomies for mental disorders. The most widely used system for classifying abnormal psychological conditions, at least in the United States, is the *Diagnostic and Statistical Manual of Mental Disorders,* fourth edition (*DSM-IV*). This sourcebook is undergoing revision, and the *DSM-5* will be released in early 2013. No major changes will be made, however, in how personality disorders are defined or diagnosed.

Personality disorders are enduring patterns of experience and behavior that differ greatly from the norm and the expectations of the individual's social group. Disorders typically show up in abnormalities in how people think, in how they feel, in how they get along with others, or in their ability to control their own actions. The patterns are typically displayed across a variety of situations, leading to distress, for either themselves or others, in important areas in life, such as at work or in relations with others.

Personality disorders typically have a long history in a person's life and can often be traced back to adolescence or childhood.

In this chapter, we covered the 10 personality disorders contained in the *DSM-IV* (and likely to be retained in the *DSM-5*). We organized these 10 disorders into three clusters: the erratic cluster (disorders pertaining to ways of being unpredictable or violent), the eccentric cluster (disorders pertaining to ways of being odd), and the anxious cluster (disorders pertaining to ways of being nervous or distressed). Each disorder consists of a unique combination of ways of thinking, experiencing, and acting. Future research is likely to emphasize the dimensional view of personality disorders, which sees disorders as simply extreme levels of normal personality traits, or combinations of extreme levels of various traits.

KEY TERMS

disorder 586
abnormal psychology 586
abnormal 586
psychopathology 587
categorical view 587
dimensional view 588
personality disorder 589
antisocial personality disorder 591

borderline personality disorder 595
eye-blink startle method 596
histrionic personality disorder 598
narcissistic personality disorder 601
schizoid personality disorder 603
schizotypal personality disorder 603
paranoid personality disorder 608
neurotic paradox 608

avoidant personality disorder 609
dependent personality disorder 610
obsessive-compulsive personality
   disorder 612
prevalence 614
differential diagnosis 615

Summary and Future Directions

20

CONCLUSION

Understanding the whole behind all the parts is the ultimate goal of personality psychology.
© *Peter Horree/Alamy Stock Photo*

After having read the first 19 chapters of this book, you should be able to provide answers the next time someone asks, "Why does that person behave that way?" Why do the things people do sometimes seem like a mystery? Personality psychology seeks to open this mystery to scientific investigation. If you are fascinated by the variety of human behavior, by the clever or silly things that people do, by the ways people solve or create problems for themselves, or by the variety of potential explanations for people's behavior, then you have something in common with personality psychologists—a deep curiosity about human nature.

Understanding the whole of human nature may seem like an impossible mission, but this is the ultimate goal of personality psychology. However, understanding the whole is quite a challenge. Psychologist Charles Carver (1996) said that "personality is a topic that's just too large to hold in the mind at once" (p. 330). When confronted with a large and difficult task, it is sometimes useful to partition the task into smaller, more manageable domains. This is the approach taken by modern medical science. Medical researchers specialize—there are dermatologists who focus on the skin, heart specialists, lung specialists, and so on. This is the approach we have taken in this book, based on the assumption that progress can be made in understanding human personality by focusing on each of the major domains of functioning. Clearly, these domains of functioning are linked with one another, just as there are important connections between the heart and the skin (e.g., the heart pumps blood that nourishes skin cells). A full understanding of human personality will eventually require not merely understanding each domain of functioning, but also understanding the ways in which the domains are connected and integrated with each other to form the whole functioning person. We have highlighted these links where such knowledge exists, such as the fascinating links between culture and evolutionary biology (Chapter 17).

Current Status of the Field

This is an exciting time for the field of personality psychology. Advances have led to some consensus regarding the nature, structure, and development of personality, resulting in several decades of sustained growth. The field is thriving. One hallmark that a field is hitting its stride is the existence of a handbook. Personality psychology has several handbooks (e.g., Buss & Hawley, 2011; Cooper & Larsen, 2014), as well as handbooks in personality disorders. Another indicator that a field is thriving is the existence of professional societies dedicated to its improvement. In personality psychology there are several societies, including the Society for Personality and Social Psychology, the European Society of Personality Psychology, and the Association for Research in Personality. This latter society, founded in 2001, is devoted especially to the interdisciplinary study of personality. It promotes scientific research on personality through an annual conference and through the official scientific journal of the association, the *Journal of Research in Personality.*

Personality psychologists doing research today typically focus on specific components of personality, such as self-esteem; specific traits, such as Extraversion or Agreeableness; or specific processes, such as the unconscious processing of information. This is the direction toward which the field of personality psychology has shifted over the past 100 years. The early personality theorists, such as Sigmund Freud, constructed theories about the whole person. These grand theories focused on universal properties of human nature, such as Freud's theory that all behavior is motivated by sexual or aggressive impulses.

Starting about 50 years ago, personality psychologists began turning away from grand theories of personality. In their place, personality psychologists began constructing mini-theories of specific parts of personality. They began to focus on distinct components of the whole person. This allowed psychologists to focus their research on very specific questions. For example, how do people develop and maintain self-esteem? In what ways do high- and low-self-esteem persons differ from each other? Why do females drop in self-esteem shortly after puberty? How might a person with low self-esteem increase self-esteem? Certainly, self-esteem is only part of personality. Nevertheless, understanding self-esteem contributes to knowledge about the whole person.

The whole of personality is the sum of its parts and the connections among those parts. Understanding the parts is required for an understanding of the whole. Most of the research in personality today is on specific parts of the proverbial elephant. When these parts are put together—from the dispositional to the biological, to the intrapsychic, to the cognitive/experiential, to the social and cultural, to the adjustment domains—then we have the foundation for understanding the whole personality.

To the extent that understanding the whole elephant requires understanding all of its parts, then the blind men, working together, could begin to assemble a reasonable understanding of the whole elephant. They could communicate to each other and work together to build a reasonable understanding of what a whole elephant is like. They could be systematic in their approach to the elephant, using diverse methods and approaches and communicating clearly with each other about how they see the elephant. Personality psychologists are like these blind men in that they typically focus only on one domain of personality at a time. However, personality psychologists do an excellent job of working together. Many psychologists working in one domain are aware of what is going on in other domains. We can get an idea of the whole by knowing the diverse domains of knowledge about human nature.

All of the contemporary research and theorizing appears to fit into the six major domains of knowledge. Because they formed the basic structure of this book, let's briefly review each domain that you have read about.

Domains of Knowledge: Where We've Been, Where We're Going

Each of the six domains of knowledge represents a specialty within the field of personality psychology. When any field of knowledge grows large and complex, workers in that field are forced to specialize. For example, there once was a time when the field of medicine was more simple and limited than it is now, and all doctors were general practitioners. The knowledge base of medicine was small enough so that each practitioner could generally master all of it. Today the field of medicine is so large and complicated that no one person can know it all, so most doctors today are specialists. Personality psychology is much the same—a field in which people tend to specialize in one of the six domains of knowledge outlined in this book. In the remainder of this chapter, we review the main features of each of these domains of knowledge, ending with some predictions about likely developments in each domain.

Dispositional Domain

The dispositional domain concerns the aspects of personality that are stable and that make people different from each other. For example, some people are outgoing and talkative; others are introverted and shy. Some are emotionally reactive and moody; others are calm and cool. Some people are conscientious and reliable; others are undependable. There are many ways in which people differ from one another, and many of these differences can be described as personality traits.

Major questions for psychologists working in this domain include these: How many personality traits exist? How can we discover and measure them? How do personality traits develop? and How do traits interact with situations to produce behaviors?

Trait psychologists will continue to focus on the interaction of persons and situations. Psychologists have realized that behaviors always occur within a context. A formulation offered by psychologists Shoda and Mischel (1996) is the idea of "if . . . then . . ." relations. Shoda and Mischel argue that personality is a specific pattern of "if . . . then . . ." relationships. For example, if an adolescent is aggressive, it means that certain behaviors (e.g., verbal insults) are likely to occur if certain situations are created (e.g., teased by a peer). Individual persons may be characterized by distinct

Personality psychologists will likely refine their understanding of the conditions or situations under which certain behaviors, such as arguing, will be evoked in people with certain traits, such as hostility.

© Latin Stock Collection/Corbis RF

profiles of "if . . . then . . ." relationships. What are the conditions under which a particular person will become depressed, angry, or frustrated? Each person has a distinct psychological signature in terms of specific "if . . . then . . . " relationships: The person will do behavior *A* when situation *Z* occurs, but behavior *B* when situation *Z* does not occur. Two people may be equally high on aggressiveness, but the situations that trigger their aggression may be different. This is one formulation of person-by-situation interaction.

A major emphasis of the dispositional domain concerns the accurate measurement of traits and abilities. The dispositional domain emphasizes quantitative techniques for measuring personality. This trend will probably continue, with trait psychologists developing new methods for measuring personality characteristics, as well as new statistics for evaluating personality research. Future developments in measurement theory are likely to have an impact on how measures of personality traits are developed and evaluated. For example, efforts are under way that will allow test makers to assess the accuracy and validity of individual items on a personality test. Other statistical developments are enabling personality researchers to examine causal connections between variables, even in the absence of experimental procedures. Continued progress in statistics, measurement, and testing will be a part of the dispositional domain of the future.

Different trait theories are associated with different procedures for identifying the most important individual differences. Some use the lexical strategy—starting with the thousands of trait terms embedded within language. Others use statistical techniques to identify important individual differences. The future will see cooperation among these researchers to test whether specific trait structures are found using different procedures. Indeed, the search will continue for other traits not yet identified by these strategies. For example, in the lexical approach, early researchers deleted adjectives related to sex or that were sex-linked (applied to one sex more than to the other). As a consequence of deleting these adjectives, researchers may have missed one or more traits related to sexuality or sex differences. The recent discovery of a sixth factor, *Honesty–Humility,* obtained from extensive cross-cultural research, represents an exciting new discovery in the dispositional domain.

Biological Domain

The core assumption of biological approaches to personality is that humans are biological systems. This domain concerns the factors within the body that influence or are related to personality as well as the evolutionary causal processes responsible for creating those bodily mechanisms. This domain is not any more fundamental than the other domains, nor is knowledge about this domain any closer to the truth about personality than is the knowledge in other domains. The biological domain simply contains the physical elements and biological systems that influence or are influenced by behaviors, thoughts, feelings, and desires. Biological processes may give rise to observable individual differences, or they may simply correlate with observable individual differences. In addition, biological differences among people cause personality differences (as in the biological theory of extraversion) or may be the result of personality differences (as in heart disease being the long-term consequence of the hostile Type A personality style).

One area of research that is likely to be active in the future concerns the psychology of approach and avoidance. Many current researchers on biological bases of behavior recognize two tendencies that underlie human behavior and emotion: (1) the tendency to feel positive emotions and to approach, and (2) the tendency to feel negative emotions and to avoid or withdraw. Much of the research reviewed in Chapter 7 concerns examples of this theme. Some examples include the work on separate brain areas associated with positive and negative emotions, Gray's theory about behavioral approach and behavioral inhibition, and the work on sensitivity to reward and punishment. These areas of research will most likely further converge, and the motives to approach and to avoid will become prominent themes in personality psychology.

Another major physical element within the body that influences personality is genes. Our genetic makeup contributes to whether we are tall or short, have blue eyes or brown eyes, or tend toward being skinny or overweight. It also appears that our genetic makeup influences behavior patterns associated with personality, such as how active we are, whether we are aggressive, and whether we like to be with others or prefer to spend time by ourselves. Understanding how genetics contributes to personality falls squarely within the biological domain.

Behavioral genetics research has come a long way from the simple nature versus nurture question. Most of the major personality traits are now known to show some moderate amount of heritability (in the range of .30 to .50). With 30 to 50 percent of the variance in these traits due to genetic differences, that leaves 50 to 70 percent due to either measurement error or the environment. The environment can be broken down into shared and nonshared components. The shared environment is what siblings have in common, such as the same parents, the (presumably) same parental rearing style, the same schools and religious institutions, and so on. The nonshared environment consists of such factors as different friends or peers outside the family, different teachers, different parental treatment, and random factors, such as accidents and illnesses. Researchers are pinpointing shared and nonshared environmental factors that appear important to personality. Thus, we will see the counterintuitive scenario in which genetics researchers will focus on identifying environmental influences.

Other researchers will concentrate on genetics at the molecular level. The Human Genome Project, which began in the 1990s, is one of the largest and most expensive scientific projects ever undertaken in the course of human history. The goal of this project is to map the entire human genome, to use molecular techniques to learn what every strand of DNA is responsible for. Twin and adoption studies, the primary methods of behavioral genetics, use indirect methods that only estimate the genetic component of traits by assessing the resemblance of relatives. Molecular genetic studies, on the other hand, are able to directly identify the DNA markers of genetic differences among individuals. Already, researchers have begun to focus these molecular techniques on the search for genes related to alcoholism, certain cognitive abilities, criminality, and impulse control. It is likely that researchers will find that genes are responsible for synthesizing specific neurotransmitters, and those neurotransmitters are in turn related to specific traits. Personality psychologists team with molecular geneticists to locate specific genes, and especially interactions among genes and interactions between

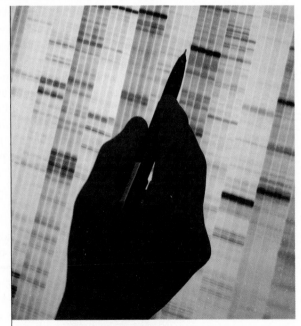

A technician works with DNA sequence information.
© Don Farrall/Getty Images RF

genes and environments, that will relate to personality dimensions (Plomin & Davis, 2009). Nonetheless, the genetics of personality is turning out to be much more complicated than initially envisioned. Hundreds of genes contribute small amounts to explaining each personality dimension, defying simple single-gene explanations. Perhaps we should not be surprised that human nature is so fascinatingly complex.

The biological domain also includes evolutionary perspectives on personality. From the perspective of evolutionary psychology, personality can be analyzed at three levels: human nature, sex differences, and individual differences. At each of these levels, an evolutionary perspective poses two related questions: What adaptive problems have humans confronted over the long expanse of human evolutionary history? What psychological solutions have evolved in response to these adaptive problems?

Because adaptive problems tend to be specific—for example, the problem of food selection differs from the problem of mate selection—the psychological solutions also tend to be specific. Thus, an evolutionary perspective leads us to expect that personality will be quite complex, consisting of a large collection of evolved psychological mechanisms, each corresponding to a specific adaptive problem. Specific mate preferences, jealousy, fears and phobias, altruistic feelings toward kin, and dozens more all may be parts of evolved psychological mechanisms, according to the evolutionary perspective.

This perspective, however, does not claim that humans are optimally adapted, or even well adapted, to the conditions of modern living. Given the slow pace of evolution, we possess Stone Age brains inhabiting a New Age world of the Internet, global travel, and modern medical miracles. Thus, problems can arise when large discrepancies exist between the ancient world in which our adaptations evolved, and the modern world that we have created.

The evolutionary perspective will continue to gain in importance, although it will not supplant other perspectives (Buss & Hawley, 2011). Instead, evolutionary psychology will add a new layer of questions and hence a necessary set of insights when these questions are answered empirically. Perhaps most critically, an evolutionary perspective asks, "What is the adaptive function of each psychological mechanism?" Posing questions about adaptive function will result in the discovery that human personality is even more complex and contains even more psychological mechanisms about which we are currently unaware. Rather than being motivated merely by sex and aggression, as Freud envisioned, humans will be found to be motivated by a dozen or more drives. But it should not surprise us that human personality will turn out to be so complex. After all, if personality were really simple, consisting of a small number of easily understood psychological mechanisms, then this book would be a lot shorter than it is.

Intrapsychic Domain

The intrapsychic domain concerns the factors within the mind that influence behavior, thoughts, and emotions. The pioneer of this domain was Sigmund Freud, though new perspectives have advanced beyond his original ideas. This domain deals with the basic psychological mechanisms of personality, many of which operate outside the realm of conscious awareness. Theories within this domain often start with fundamental assumptions about the motivational system—for example, the sexual and aggressive forces that Freud presumed energized much of human activity. Research has shown that motives, even those outside of awareness, can be powerful and that their manifestations in actual behavior can be studied empirically. The intrapsychic domain also includes defense mechanisms, such as repression, denial, and projection, some of which have been examined in laboratory studies.

In this book, the ideas and contributions of psychoanalysis were divided into two areas: classical psychoanalytic theory, as put forward by Freud and his disciples; and contemporary psychoanalytic theory, consisting of extensions of and changes to these basic ideas. For example, newer views emphasize social crises rather than sexual conflict as the tasks of personality development. Modern views in psychoanalysis also emphasize the importance of internalized representations of important relationships. These views retain the notion that childhood is crucial to understanding the adult personality, but the emphasis is now on relationships, such as the attachment between an infant and the primary caregiver.

A fundamental assumption of psychologists working in the intrapsychic domain is that there are areas of the mind that are outside of awareness. Within each person, there is a part of the mind that even the individual does not know about, called the unconscious. In classical psychoanalysis, the unconscious mind is thought to have a life of its own. It has its own motivation, its own will, and its own energy. It can interfere with the functions of the rest of the mind. In fact, it is thought to be the source of all psychological problems. Modern research on motives (e.g., the power motive, achievement motive, and intimacy motive) also draws on the notion that motive forces can operate outside of conscious awareness.

Psychologists will continue to be interested in unconscious psychological processes. Many psychologists view the unconscious as an automatic information-processing mechanism, which can influence conscious awareness. And they have developed impressive methods for studying the unconscious, such as priming and subliminal exposure. We are on the verge of learning a great deal about just how much cognitive activity occurs outside of awareness and the extent to which these unconscious thoughts influence behavior.

Cognitive/Experiential Domain

The cognitive/experiential domain centers on subjective experience and other mental processes, such as thoughts, feelings, beliefs, and desires about oneself and others. One of the central concepts in this domain is the self. Some aspects of the self describe how we view ourselves: our knowledge of ourselves, our images of past selves, and our images of possible future selves. Do we see ourselves as good or as evil? Are our past successes or past failures prominent in our self-views? Do we envision ourselves in a positive future? Psychologists will continue to focus their attention on self-concept and identity. Moreover, psychologists will incorporate the idea that identity is like a story, and a narrative or case history approach to understanding will continue to be a part of personality psychology.

A modern metaphor informing personality psychology is the information-processing, or computer, metaphor. Humans take in sensory information; process it through an elaborate cognitive system, which selects and modifies from the vast array of information available; then store it in memories, which do not bear a one-to-one

American actor Richard Gere, who often plays violent characters on film, leads a very different private life. As a practicing Buddhist, Gere believes in the principle of nonviolence. He is shown here speaking at an event for the National Day of Action for Tibet, 1998, in Washington, D.C. The development of the self and social identity, especially in complex and contradictory lives, will continue to fascinate personality psychologists.
© Mark Reinstein/The Image Works

relationship with the original events. At every step along the way—from attention and perception to memory and recall—there are opportunities for personality to influence the process. Psychologists will continue to take seriously the notion that people construct their experiences. Understanding how this works, and what it says about personality, will be one objective in this domain.

A somewhat different aspect of the cognitive/experiential domain pertains to the goals people strive for. This tradition approaches personality through the personal projects that individuals are trying to accomplish. Goal concepts will continue to be important within personality psychology. Goals have cognitive, emotional, and behavioral components. Goals are often individual expressions of social or institutional norms or standards, so the goal concept may be one route whereby psychologists can study relationships between individuals and broader social systems.

Yet another aspect of subjective experience entails emotions. Is a person habitually happy or sad? What makes a person angry or fearful? The joy, the sadness, feelings of triumph, and feelings of despair are essential elements in our subjective experience subsumed by the cognitive-experiential domain. If you want to learn what is important to a person, really important, ask about his or her emotions. When was the last time he or she was angry? What makes him or her sad? What does he or she fear? Emotions are likely to continue to be important concepts in personality.

Social and Cultural Domain

One of the novel features of this book is an emphasis on the social and cultural aspects of personality. Personality is not something that merely resides within the heads, nervous systems, and genes of individuals. Rather, personality affects, and is affected by, the significant others in our lives.

Humans are not passive recipients of their environments, and personality plays a key role in social interaction. We selectively enter some interpersonal environments and selectively avoid others. We actively choose our mates and friends. We evoke reactions from others, sometimes quite unintentionally. And we actively influence or manipulate those occupying our social worlds. Personality influences these processes of selection, evocation, and manipulation. Emotionally unstable individuals, for example, tend to choose similarly unstable persons as romantic partners; they evoke predictable forms of anger in those partners through their moodiness; and they more often use the "silent treatment" as a tactic for influencing their partners. Personality, in short, expresses itself through our social selections, evocations, and manipulations.

One important social sphere concerns relations between men and women. Personality may operate differently for men than for women in some domains. An essential part of our identity is gender. Much of what we call gender may have its origins in culture, in how society makes up different rules, roles, and expectations for men and women. Other aspects of gender may lie in evolved behavior patterns that represent adaptations to different pressures that faced men and women in the past. Gender differences will continue to be a compelling interest of personality psychologists. In an effort to understand gender differences, it is likely that personality psychologists will enlist the help of specialists from other disciplines, such as anthropologists, animal behaviorists, sociologists, and biopsychologists.

At the cultural level, it is clear that groups differ from one another. Some cultures are individualistic: people prefer to make their own decisions and to be responsible primarily for themselves. Other cultures are more collectivistic or more

Interacting with people from different cultures is a fact of daily life in many parts of the world. Understanding how people from different cultures are different from, or similar to, each other will continue to be an important part of personality psychology.

© *Rawpixel.com/Shutterstock.com RF*

interdependent: people prefer to see themselves as part of a social group and do not think of their individual needs as more important than their group's needs. Personality differences among these groups may be instances of transmitted culture or evoked culture. Some psychologists assume that they are caused by transmitted culture—ideas, values, and representations passed on from parents and others to children within their culture, down the generations. Other psychologists, however, propose that these are instances of evoked culture. According to this view, everyone may have the evolved capacity to be individualistic and preoccupied with the self. And everyone may also have the evolved capacity to be communal and concerned with the greater good of the group. Which of these capacities any one individual displays may depend on whether one lives in a culture that is highly mobile, with few genetic kin in close proximity (evoking an individualistic proclivity), or highly stable, with many genetic kin in close proximity (evoking a collectivistic proclivity). Even environmental variables such as pathogen prevalence may influence our evoked culture of conformity. This fascinating new direction represents a theoretical fusion of cultural psychology and evolutionary psychology.

The study of culture and cross-cultural differences and similarities will continue to grow in personality psychology. Our world is increasingly becoming a global community. Diversity is a fact of daily life in many areas. Many of us encounter persons from different cultures on a regular basis at our schools, jobs, and communities. There is a growing interdependence among people from different backgrounds. An important goal of personality psychology will be to understand how cultures shape personality and how specific cultures are different from, or similar to, each other.

Adjustment Domain

Personality plays a key role in how we cope, adapt, and adjust to the ebb and flow of events in our lives. Personality is linked with important health outcomes, such as heart disease. Personality is linked to a variety of health-related behaviors, such as smoking, drinking, and risk taking. Personality is even linked to how long we live. The role of personality in relation to health and well-being will occupy personality psychologists of the future. There has been a shift toward looking at the role of positive emotions, and this emphasis on the positive in psychology is likely to be a part of personality psychology. In addition, several longitudinal studies were started decades ago in various communities around the United States. Participants in this research are now adults, and researchers are beginning to learn about the long-term effects of lifestyles and personality on longevity and health.

Some important problems in coping and adjustment can be traced to personality disorders. An understanding of "normal" personality functioning can be deepened by examining disorders of personality, and vice versa. Psychologists have applied the trait approach to understanding personality disorders. This is likely to continue to sharpen our understanding of the nature of personality disorders.

Integration: Personality in the Twenty-First Century

The domains of knowledge should be viewed as complementary, not as conflicting. People have many facets, and these facets can be observed and studied from many different perspectives. To say that people have evolved psychological mechanisms to solve social problems does not imply that the principles of psychoanalysis are wrong. Similarly, to say that a portion of the variance in personality traits is due to genetics does not in any way imply that people do not develop or change their personalities in adulthood.

Exciting personality research will occur at the boundaries of domains. Examples include collaborations among brain researchers using functional magnetic resonance imaging (fMRI) technology to conduct brain scans and psychologists studying interpersonal dispositions; collaborations between cultural and evolutionary psychologists to study the causal origins and nature of cultural differences; and collaborations between dispositional researchers and cognitive psychologists to study the information-processing mechanisms underlying stable individual differences. The most interesting work will happen as researchers expand the theories surrounding each domain and try to make connections among domains or between personality psychology and other scientific fields.

Progress in this millennium will depend on researchers' willingness and ability to reach across domains. The most exciting progress will occur when researchers, perhaps working on multidisciplinary teams, combine different levels of analysis and different methods in approaching central questions of importance to the field. Building bridges that link domains of knowledge together in new and interesting ways will have the most impact on how human nature is understood.

If we look around the field of personality psychology today, we can find examples of bridges that are already being built among domains. For example, with regard to the topic of approach and avoidance motivation, psychologists are studying this phenomenon through brain activity, exploring the developmental course of these motives, examining cultural differences evoked by predictable environmental factors, and delving into how these traits contribute to disorders. It is likely that centers of research will be a model for progress, with groups of diverse scientists—such as trait psychologists, biological psychologists, cultural psychologists, and health psychologists—all working together on questions important to the field of personality psychology. It is not hard to imagine interesting possibilities. For example, it probably won't be long before psychologists interested in repressed memories approach the topic with fMRI brain scans or before psychologists interested in self-esteem begin looking both at neuro-chemistry and at cultural and evolutionary influences. As we move forward in the twenty-first century, the possibilities for increasing our knowledge of human nature are truly exciting.

Glossary

a

abnormal Broadly defined, the term *abnormal* is based on current levels of societal tolerance. In this sense, behaviors that society deems unacceptable would be labeled as abnormal (e.g., incest and child abuse). Because tolerance levels (e.g., toward homosexuality) can change over time, psychologists have started directing their attention toward people's subjective views and experiences. Anxiety, depression, and feelings of loneliness may be linked to disorganized thought patterns, disruptive perceptions, or unusual beliefs. These may inhibit a person's ability to work or socialize, and may all be considered abnormal. 586

abnormal psychology The study of the various mental disorders, including thought disorders (such as schizophrenia), emotional disorders (such as depression), and personality disorders (such as the antisocial personality). 586

acculturation The process of, after arriving in a new culture, adapting to the ways of life and beliefs common in that new culture. 531

achievement view of intelligence The achievement view of intelligence is associated with educational attainment—how much knowledge a person has acquired relative to others in his or her age cohort. 388

acquiescence (also known as yea saying) A response set that refers to the tendency to agree with questionnaire items regardless of the content of those items. 39

action tendencies Increases in the probabilities of certain behaviors that accompany emotions. The activity, or action tendency, associated with fear, for example, is to flee or to fight. 396

active genotype–environment correlation Occurs when a person with a particular genotype creates or seeks out a particular environment. 177

actometer A mechanical motion-recording device, often in the form of a watch attached to the wrist. It has been used, for example, in research on the activity level of children during several play periods. Motoric movement activates the recording device. 130

acute stress Results from the sudden onset of demands or events that seem to be beyond the control of the individual. This type of stress is often experienced as tension headaches, emotional upsets, gastrointestinal disturbances, and feelings of agitation and pressure. 563

adaptations Inherited solutions to the survival and reproductive problems posed by the hostile forces of nature. Adaptations are the primary product of the selective process. An adaptation is a "reliably developing structure in the organism, which, because it meshes with the recurrent structure of the world, causes the solution to an adaptive problem" (Tooby & Cosmides, 1992, p. 104). 9

adaptive problem Anything that impedes survival or reproduction. All adaptations must contribute to fitness during the period of time in which they evolve by helping an organism survive, reproduce, or facilitate the reproductive success of genetic relatives. Adaptations emerge from and interact with recurrent structures of the world in a manner that solves adaptive problems and hence aids in reproductive success. 227

additive effects The effects of different kinds of stress that add up and accumulate in a person over time. 563

adjacency In Wiggins circumplex model, adjacency indicates how close the traits are to each other on the circumference of the circumplex. Those variables that are adjacent or next to each other within the model are positively correlated. 73

adjustment domain Personality plays a key role in how we cope, adapt, and adjust to the ebb and flow of events in our day-to-day lives. In addition to health consequences of adjusting to stress, certain personality features are related to poor social or emotional adjustment and have been designated as personality disorders. 17

adoption studies Studies that examine the correlations between adopted children and their adoptive parents, with whom they share no genes. These correlations are then compared to the correlations between the adopted children and their genetic parents, who had no influence on the environments of the children. Differences in these correlations can indicate the relative magnitude of genetic and environment contributions to personality traits. 165

affect intensity Larsen and Diener (1987) describe high affect intensity individuals as people who typically experience their emotions strongly and are emotionally reactive and variable. Low affect intensity individuals typically experience their emotions only mildly and with only gradual fluctuations and minor reactions. 423

aggregation Adding up or averaging several single observations, resulting in a better (i.e., more reliable) measure of a personality trait than a single observation of behavior. This approach implies that personality traits refer to average tendencies in behavior, how people behave on average. 92

Agreeableness Agreeableness is the second of the personality traits in the five-factor model, a model which has proven to be replicable in studies using English-language trait words as items. Some of the key adjective markers for Agreeableness are "good natured," "cooperative," "mild/gentle," "not jealous." 78

alarm stage The first stage in Selye's general adaptation syndrome (GAS). The alarm stage consists of the flight-or-fight response of the sympathetic nervous system and the associated peripheral nervous system reactions. These include the release of hormones, which prepare our bodies for challenge. 559

alpha and beta press Murray introduced the notion that there is a real environment (what he called alpha press or objective reality) and a perceived environment (called beta press or reality as it is perceived). In any situation, what one person "sees" may be different from what another "sees." If two people walk down a street and a third person smiles at each of them, one person might "see" the smile as a sign of friendliness while the other person might "see" the smile as a smirk. Objectively (alpha press), it is the same smile; subjectively (beta press), it may be a different event for the two people.   332

alpha wave   A particular type of brain wave that oscillates 8 to 12 times a second. The amount of alpha wave present in a given time period is an inverse indicator of brain activity during that time period. The alpha wave is given off when the person is calm and relaxed. In a given time period of brain wave recording, the more alpha wave activity present the more we can assume that part of the brain was less active.   216

ambivalently attached   Ambivalently attached infants, as determined by Ainsworth's strange situation paradigm, are very anxious about the mother leaving. They often start crying and protesting vigorously before the mother even gets out of the room. While the mother is gone, these infants are difficult to calm. Upon her return, however, these infants behave ambivalently. Their behavior shows both anger and the desire to be close to the mother; they approach her but then resist by squirming and fighting against being held.   319

ambivalent relationship style   In Hazan and Shaver's ambivalent relationship style, adults are vulnerable and uncertain about relationships. Ambivalent adults become overly dependant and demanding on their partners and friends. They display high levels of neediness in their relationships. They are high maintenance partners in the sense that they need constant reassurance and attention.   320

Americans with Disability Act (ADA)   The ADA states that an employer cannot conduct a medical examination, or even make inquiries as to whether an applicant has a disability, during the selection process. Moreover, even if a disability is obvious, the employer cannot ask about the nature or severity of that disability.   111

amygdala   A section of the limbic or emotional system of the brain that is responsible for fear.   438

anal stage   The second stage in Freud's psychosexual stages of development. The anal stage typically occurs between the ages of 18 months and three years. At this stage, the anal sphincter is the source of sexual pleasure, and the child obtains pleasure from first expelling feces and then, during toilet training, from retaining feces. Adults who are compulsive, overly neat, rigid, and never messy are, according to psychoanalytic theory, likely to be fixated at the anal stage.   283

analytic   To describe something analytically is to explain the event with the object detached from its context, attributes of objects or people assigned to categories, and a reliance on rules about the categories to explain behavior.   532

androgynous   In certain personality instruments, the masculinity dimension contains items reflecting assertiveness, boldness, dominance, self-sufficiency, and instrumentality. The femininity dimension contains items that reflect nurturance, expression of emotions, and empathy. Those persons who scored high on both dimensions are labeled androgynous, to reflect the notion that a single person can possess both masculine and feminine characteristics.   503

anterior cingulate   Located deep toward the center of the brain, the anterior cingulate cortex most likely evolved early in the evolution of the nervous system. In experiments utilizing fMRI to trace increased activation of parts of the brain, the anterior cingulate cortex seems to be an area of the brain associated with affect, including social rejection.   415

antisocial personality disorder   A person suffering from antisocial personality disorder has a general disregard for others and cares very little about the rights, feelings, or happiness of other people. Also referred to as a sociopath or psychopath, a person suffering from antisocial personality disorder is easily irritated, assaultive, reckless, irresponsible, glib or superficially charming, impulsive, callous, and indifferent to the suffering of others.   591

anxiety   An unpleasant, high-arousal emotional state associated with perceived threat. In the psychoanalytic tradition, anxiety is seen as a signal that the control of the ego is being threatened by reality, impulses from the id, or harsh controls exerted by the superego. Freud identified three different types of anxiety: neurotic anxiety, moral anxiety, and objective anxiety. According to Rogers, the unpleasant emotional state of anxiety is the result of having an experience that does not fit with one's self-conception.   202, 354

apperception   The notion that a person's needs influence how he or she perceives the environment, especially when the environment is ambiguous. The act of interpreting the environment and perceiving the meaning of what is going on in a situation.   332

aptitude view of intelligence   The aptitude view of intelligence sees intelligence less as the product of education and more as an ability to become educated, as the ability or aptitude to learn.   388

arousal level and arousability   In Eysenck's original theory of extraversion, he held that extraverts had lower levels of cortical or brain arousal than introverts. More recent research suggests that the difference between introverts and extraverts lies more in the arousability of their nervous systems, with extraverts showing less arousability or reactivity than introverts to the same levels of sensory stimulation.   198, 200

arteriosclerosis   Hardening or blocking of the arteries. When the arteries that feed the heart muscle itself become blocked, the subsequent shortage of blood to the heart is called a heart attack.   580

ascending reticular activating system (ARAS)   A structure in the brain stem thought to control overall cortical arousal; the structure Eysenck originally thought was responsible for differences between introverts and extraverts.   198

assortative mating   The phenomenon whereby people marry people similar to themselves. In addition to personality, people also show assortative mating on a number of physical characteristics, such as height and weight.   465

attachment   Begins in the human infant when he or she develops a preference for people over objects.

Then the preference begins to narrow to familiar persons so that the child prefers to see people he or she has seen before, compared to strangers. Finally the preference narrows even further so that the child prefers the mother or primary caretaker over anyone else.   318

attraction similarity theory   States that individuals are attracted to those whose personalities are similar to their own. In other words, "birds of a feather flock together" or "like attracts like." As of 2003, attraction similarity has been proven to be the dominant attraction theory except in biological sex choices (i.e., women tend to be attracted to men and vice versa).   465

autonomic nervous system (ANS) That part of the peripheral nervous system that connects to vital bodily structures associated with maintaining life and responding to emergencies (e.g., storing and releasing energy), such as the beating of the heart, respiration, and controlling blood pressure. There are two divisions of the ANS: the sympathetic and parasympathetic branches.   191

average tendencies   Tendency to display a certain psychological trait with regularity. For example, on average, a high-talkative person will start more conversations than a low-talkative person. This idea explains why the principle of aggregation works when measuring personality.   5

avoidantly attached   Avoidantly attached infants in Ainsworth's strange situation avoided the mother when she returned. Infants in this group typically seemed unfazed when the mother left and did not give her much attention when she returned. Avoidant children seem to be aloof from their mothers. Approximately 20 percent of infants fall into this category.   319

avoidant personality disorder   The major feature is a pervasive feeling of inadequacy and sensitivity to criticism from others. The avoidant personality will go to great lengths to avoid situations in which others may have opportunities to criticize his or her performance or character, such as school or work or other group settings. Such a person may avoid making new friends or going to new

places because of fear of criticism or disapproval.   609

avoidant relationship style   In Hazan and Shaver's avoidant relationship style, the adult has difficulty learning to trust others. Avoidant adults remain suspicious of the motives of others, and they are afraid of making commitments. They are afraid of depending on others because they anticipate being disappointed, let down, abandoned, or separated.   320

b

Balancing selection   When genetic variation is maintained by selection because different levels of a personality trait are adaptive in different environments.   254

Balkanization   Social resegregation following a time of peaceful integration and social diversity. The term is derived from the breakup of Yugoslavia on the Balkan peninsula during the 1990s, in which national groups split apart and resegregated the formerly integrated countries in the Balkans.   529

Barnum statements   Generalities or statements that could apply to anyone. A good example is the astrology column published in daily newspapers.   103

behavioral activation system (BAS) In Gray's reinforcement sensitivity theory, the system that is responsive to incentives, such as cues for reward, and regulates approach behavior. When some stimulus is recognized as potentially rewarding, the BAS triggers approach behavior. This system is highly correlated with the trait of extraversion.   201

behavioral inhibition system (BIS)   In Gray's reinforcement sensitivity theory, the system responsive to cues for punishment, frustration, and uncertainty. The effect of BIS activation is to cease or inhibit behavior or to bring about avoidance behavior. This system is highly correlated with the trait of neuroticism.   201

Beliefs   See Theories and Beliefs.   19

belongingness needs   The third level of Maslow's motivation hierarchy. Humans are a very social species, and most people possess a strong need to belong to groups. Being accepted by others and welcomed into a group

represents a somewhat more psychological need than the physiological needs or the need for safety.   348

beta press   See *alpha and beta press*.   332

biological domain   The core assumption of biological approaches to personality is that humans are, first and foremost, collections of biological systems, and these systems provide the building blocks (e.g., brain, nervous system) for behavior, thought, and emotion. Biological approaches typically refers to three areas of research within this general domain: the genetics of personality, the psychophysiology of personality, and the evolution of personality.   15

bipolarity   In Wiggins circumplex model, traits located at opposite sides of the circle and negatively correlated with each other. Specifying this bipolarity is useful because nearly every interpersonal trait within the personality sphere has another trait that is its opposite.   73

blindsight   Following an injury or stroke that damages the primary vision center in the brain, a person may lose some or all of his or her ability to see. In this blindness the eyes still bring information into the brain, but the brain center responsible for object recognition fails. People who suffer this "cortical" blindness often display an interesting capacity to make judgments about objects that they truly cannot see.   268

borderline personality disorder The life of the borderline personality is marked by instability. Their relationships are unstable, their emotions are unstable, their behavior is unstable, and even their image of themselves is unstable. Persons with borderline personality disorder, compared to those without, have a higher incidence rate of childhood physical or sexual abuse, neglect, or early parental loss.   595

byproducts of adaptations Evolutionary mechanisms that are not adaptations, but rather are byproducts of other adaptations. Our nose, for example, is clearly an adaptation designed for smelling. But the fact that we use our nose to hold up our eyeglasses is an incidental byproduct.   228

C

cardiac reactivity   The increase in blood pressure and heart rate during times of stress. Evidence suggests that chronic cardiac reactivity contributes to coronary artery disease.   193

case study method   Examining the life of one person in particular depth, which can give researchers insights into personality that can then be used to formulate a more general theory that is tested in a larger population. They can also provide in-depth knowledge of a particularly outstanding individual. Case studies are useful when studying rare phenomena, such as a person with a photographic memory or a person with multiple personalities—cases for which large samples would be difficult or impossible to obtain.   49

castration anxiety   Freud argued that little boys come to believe that their fathers might make a preemptive Oedipal strike and take away what is at the root of the Oedipal conflict: the boy's penis. This fear of losing his penis is called castration anxiety; it drives the little boy into giving up his sexual desire for his mother.   284

categorical approach   Researchers who suggest emotions are best thought of as a small number of primary and distinct emotions (anger, joy, anxiety, sadness) are said to take the categorical approach. Emotion researchers who take the categorical approach have tried to reduce the complexity of emotions by searching for the primary emotions that underlie the great variety of emotion terms. An example of a categorical approach to emotion is that of Paul Ekman, who applies criteria of distinct and universal facial expressions, and whose list of primary emotions contains disgust, sadness, joy, surprise, anger, and fear.   397

categorical view   In psychiatry and clinical psychology today, the dominant approach to viewing personality disorders in distinct categories. There is a qualitative distinction made in which people who have a disorder are in one category, whereas people who do not have the disorder are in another category.   587

causal attribution   A person's explanation of the cause of some event.   382

chronic stress   Stress that does not end, like an abusive relationship that grinds the individual down until his or her resistance is eroded. Chronic stress can result in serious systemic diseases such as diabetes, decreased immune system functioning, or cardiovascular disease.   563

circadian rhythm   Many biological processes fluctuate around an approximate 24- to 25-hour cycle. These are called circadian rhythms (circa = around; dia = day). Circadian rhythms in temporal isolation studies have been found to be as short as 16 hours in one person, and as long as 50 hours in another person (Wehr & Goodwin, 1981).   212

client-centered therapy   In Rogers's client-centered therapy, clients are never given interpretations of their problem. Nor are clients given any direction about what course of action to take to solve their problem. The therapist makes no attempts to change the client directly. Instead, the therapist tries to create an atmosphere in which the client may change him- or herself.   357

cognition   A general term referring to awareness and thinking as well as to specific mental acts such as perceiving, interpreting, remembering, believing, and anticipating.   367

cognitive approaches   Differences in how people think form the focus of cognitive approaches to personality. Psychologists working in this approach focus on the components of cognition, such as how people perceive, interpret, remember, and plan, in their efforts to understand how and why people are different from each other.   366

cognitive-experiential domain   This domain focuses on cognition and subjective experience, such as conscious thoughts, feelings, beliefs, and desires about oneself and others. This domain includes our feelings of self, identity, self-esteem, our goals and plans, and our emotions.   16

cognitive schema   A schema is a way of processing incoming information and of organizing and interpreting the facts of daily life. The cognitive schema involved in depression, according to Beck, distorts the incoming information in a negative way that makes the person depressed.   418

cognitive social learning approach   A number of modern personality theories have expanded on the notion that personality is expressed in goals and in how people think about themselves relative to their goals. Collectively these theories form an approach that emphasizes the cognitive and social processes whereby people learn to value and strive for certain goals over others.   384

cognitive triad   According to Beck, there are three important areas of life that are most influenced by the depressive cognitive schema. This cognitive triad refers to information about the self, about the world, and about the future.   419

cognitive unconscious   In the cognitive view of the unconscious, the content of the unconscious mind is assumed to operate just like thoughts in consciousness. Thoughts are unconscious because they are not in conscious awareness, not because they have been repressed or because they represent unacceptable urges or wishes.   306

cohort effects   Personality change over time as a reflection of the social times in which an individual or group of individuals live. For example, American women's trait scores on assertiveness have risen and fallen depending on the social and historical cohort in which they have lived. Jean Twenge has posited that individuals internalize social change and absorb the cultural messages they receive from their culture, all of which, in turn, can affect their personalities.   143

combinations of Big Five variables   "Traits" are often examined in combinations. For example, two people high in extraversion would be very different if one was an extraverted neurotic and the other was extraverted but emotionally stable.   81

comorbidity   The presence of two or more disorders of any type in one person.   207

compatibility and integration across domains and levels   A theory that takes into account the principles and laws of other scientific domains that may affect the study's main subject. For example, a theory of biology that violated known principles of chemistry would be judged fatally flawed.   20

competitive achievement motivation
Also referred to as the need for achievement, it is a subtrait in the Type A behavior pattern. Type A people like to work hard and achieve goals. They like recognition and overcoming obstacles and feel they are at their best when competing with others. 576

complementary needs theory
Theory of attraction that postulates that people are attracted to people whose personality dispositions differ from theirs. In other words, "opposites attract." This is especially true in biological sex choices (i.e., women tend to be attracted to men and vice versa). Other than biological sex choices, the complementary needs theory of attraction has not received any empirical support. 465

comprehensiveness One of the five scientific standards used in evaluating personality theories. Theories that explain more empirical data within a domain are generally superior to those that explain fewer findings. 19

conditional positive regard
According to Rogers, people behave in specific ways to earn the love and respect and positive regard of parents and other significant people in their lives. Positive regard, when it must be earned by meeting certain conditions, is called conditional positive regard. 353

conditions of worth According to Rogers, the requirements set forth by parents or significant others for earning their positive regard are called conditions of worth. Children may become preoccupied with living up to these conditions of worth rather than discovering what makes them happy. 353

confirmatory bias The tendency to look only for evidence that confirms a previous hunch, and not to look for evidence that might disconfirm a belief. 301

Conscientiousness The third of the personality traits in the five-factor model, which has proven to be replicable in studies using English-language trait words as items. Some of the key adjective markers for Conscientiousness are "responsible," "scrupulous," "persevering," "fussy/tidy." 79

conscious That part of the mind that contains all the thoughts, feelings, and images that a person is presently aware

of. Whatever a person is currently thinking about is in his or her conscious mind. 265

conscious goals A person's awareness of what he or she desires and believes is valuable and worth pursuing. 368

consistency Trait theories assume there is some degree of consistency in personality over time. If someone is highly extraverted during one period of observation, trait psychologists tend to assume that she will be extraverted tomorrow, next week, a year from now, or even decades from now. 91

construct A concept or provable hypothesis that summarizes a set of observations and conveys the meaning of those observations (e.g., gravity). 376

construct validity A test that measures what it claims to measure, correlates with what it is supposed to correlate with, and does not correlate with what it is not supposed to correlate with. 42

constructive memory It is accepted as fact that humans have a constructive memory; that is, memory contributes to or influences in various ways (adds to, subtracts from, etc.) what is recalled. Recalled memories are rarely distortion-free, mirror images of the facts. 302

content The content of emotional life refers to the characteristic or typical emotions a person is likely to experience over time. Someone whose emotional life contains a lot of pleasant emotions is someone who might be characterized as happy, cheerful, and enthusiastic. Thus the notion of content leads us to consider the *kinds* of emotions that people are likely to experience over time and across situations in their lives. 400

continuity Identity has an element of continuity because many of its aspects, such as gender, ethnicity, socioeconomic status, educational level, and occupation, are constant. Having an identity means that others can count on you to be reliable in who you are and how you act. 450

contrast Identity contrast means that a person's social identity differentiates that person from other people. An identity is the combination of characteristics that makes a person unique in the eyes of others. 450

convergent validity Whether a test correlates with other measures that it should correlate with. 42

core conditions According to Carl Rogers, in client-centered therapy three core conditions must be present in order for progress to occur: (1) an atmosphere of genuine acceptance on the part of the therapist; (2) the therapist must express unconditional positive regard for the client; and (3) the client must feel that the therapist understands him or her (empathic understanding). 357

correlation coefficient (its direction and magnitude) Researchers are interested in the direction (positive or negative) and the magnitude (size) of the correlation coefficient. Correlations around .10 are considered small; those around .30 are considered medium; and those around .50 or greater are considered large (Cohen & Cohen, 1975). 46

correlational method A statistical procedure for determining whether there is a relationship between two variables. In correlational research designs, the researcher is attempting to directly identify the relationships between two or more variables, without imposing the sorts of manipulations seen in experimental designs. 46

cortisol A stress hormone that prepares the body to flee or fight. Increases in cortisol in the blood indicate that the animal has recently experienced stress. 217

counterbalancing In some experiments, manipulation is within a single group. For example, participants might get a drug and have their memory tested, then later take a sugar pill and have their memory tested again. In this kind of experiment, equivalence is obtained by counterbalancing the order of the conditions, with half the participants getting the drug first and sugar pill second, and the other half getting the sugar pill first and the drug second. 44

creating positive events Creating a positive time-out from stress. Folkman and Moskowitz note that humor can have the added benefit of generating positive emotional moments even during the darkest periods of stress. 568

criterion validity Whether a test predicts criteria external to the test. 42

cross-cultural universality In the lexical approach, cross-cultural universality states that if a trait is sufficiently important in all cultures so that its members have codified terms within their own languages to describe the trait, then the trait must be universally important in human affairs. In contrast, if a trait term exists in only one or a few languages but is entirely missing from most, then it may be of only local relevance. 63

cultural context of intelligence Looks at how the definition of intelligent behavior varies across different cultures. Because of these considerations, intelligence can be viewed as referring to those skills valued in a particular culture. 390

cultural personality psychology Cultural personality psychology generally has three key goals: (1) to discover the principles underlying the cultural diversity; (2) to discover how human psychology shapes culture; and (3) to discover how cultural understandings in turn shape our psychology (Fiske et al., 1997). 521

cultural universals Features of personality that are common to everyone in all cultures. These universals constitute the human nature level of analyzing personality and define the elements of personality we share with all or most other people. 537

cultural variations Within-group similarities and between-group differences can be of any sort—physical, psychological, behavioral, or attitudinal. These phenomena are often referred to as cultural variations. Two ingredients are necessary to explain cultural variations: (1) a universal underlying mechanism and (2) environmental differences in the degree to which the underlying mechanism is activated. 521

culture A set of shared standards for many behaviors. It might contain different standards for males and females, such that girls should be ashamed if they engage in promiscuous sex, whereas boys might be proud of such behavior, with it being culturally acceptable for them to even brag about such behavior. 314

culture of honor Nisbett proposed that the economic means of subsistence of a culture affects the degree to which the group develops what he calls "a culture of honor." In cultures of honor,

insults are viewed as highly offensive public challenges that must be met with direct confrontation and physical aggression. The theory is that differences in the degree to which honor becomes a central part of the culture rests ultimately with economics, and specifically with the manner in which food is obtained. 524

d

daily hassles The major sources of stress in most people's lives. Although minor, daily hassles can be chronic and repetitive, such as having too much to do all the time, having to fight the crowds while shopping, or having to worry over money. Such daily hassles can be chronically irritating though they do not initiate the same general adaptation syndrome evoked by some major life events. 562

deductive reasoning approach The top-down, theory-driven method of empirical research. 231

defense mechanisms Strategies for coping with anxiety and threats to self-esteem. 274

defensive pessimism Individuals who use a defensive pessimism strategy have usually done well on important tasks but lack self-confidence in their ability to handle new challenges. A defensive pessimist controls anxiety by preparing for failure ahead of time; they set low expectations for their performance and often focus on worse-case outcomes. This strategy overcomes anticipatory anxiety and transforms it into motivation. 448

deliberation-without-awareness The notion that, when confronted with a decision, if a person can put it out of their conscious mind for a period of time, then the "unconscious mind" will continue to deliberate on it, helping the person to arrive at a "sudden" and often correct decision some time later. 268

denial When the reality of a particular situation is extremely anxiety provoking, a person may resort to the defense mechanism of denial. A person in denial insists that things are not the way they seem. Denial can also be less extreme, as when someone reappraises an anxiety-provoking situation so that it seems less

daunting. Denial often shows up in people's daydreams and fantasies. 276

density distribution of states Refers to the idea that traits are distributions of states in a person's life over time, and the mean of that distribution is the person's level of the trait. 100

dependent personality disorder The dependent personality seeks out others to an extreme. The hallmark of the dependent personality is an excessive need to be taken care of, to be nurtured, coddled, and told what to do. Dependent persons act in submissive ways so as to encourage others to take care of them or take charge of the situation. Such individuals need lots of encouragement and advice from others and would much rather turn over responsibility for their decisions to someone else. 610

depression A psychological disorder whose symptoms include a depressed mood most of the day; diminished interest in activities; change in weight, sleep patterns, and movement; fatigue or loss of energy; feelings of worthlessness; inability to concentrate; and recurrent thoughts of death and suicide. It is estimated that 20 percent of Americans are afflicted with depression at some time in their lives (American Psychiatric Association, 1994). 418

developmental crisis Erikson believed that each stage in personality development represented a conflict, or a developmental crisis, that needed to be resolved before the person advanced to the next stage of development. 309

diathesis-stress model of depression Suggests that a preexisting vulnerability, or diathesis, is present among people who become depressed. In addition to this vulnerability, a stressful life event must occur in order to trigger the depression, such as the loss of a loved one or some other major negative life event. The events must occur together—something bad or stressful has to happen to a person who has a particular vulnerability to depression—in order for depression to occur. 418

differences among groups See *group differences.* 11

differential diagnosis A differential diagnosis is arrived at when, out of two or more possible diagnoses, the clinician searches for evidence in support of one diagnostic category over all the others. 615

differential gene reproduction
Reproductive success relative to others. The genes of organisms who reproduce more than others get passed down to future generations at a relatively greater frequency than the genes of those who reproduce less. Because survival is usually critical for reproductive success, characteristics that lead to greater survival get passed along. Because success in mate competition is also critical for reproductive success, qualities that lead to success in same-sex competition or to success at being chosen as a mate get passed along. Successful survival and successful mate competition, therefore, are both part of differential gene reproduction.   226

differential psychology   Due to its emphasis on the study of differences between people, trait psychology has sometimes been called differential psychology in the interest of distinguishing this subfield from other branches of personality psychology (Anastasi, 1976). Differential psychology includes the study of other forms of individual differences in addition to personality traits, such as abilities, aptitudes, and intelligence.   89

dimensional approach   Researchers gather data by having subjects rate themselves on a wide variety of emotions, then apply statistical techniques (mostly factor analysis) to identify the basic dimensions underlying the ratings. Almost all the studies suggest that subjects categorize emotions using just two primary dimensions: how pleasant or unpleasant the emotion is, and how high or low on arousal the emotion is.   398

dimensional view   The dimensional view approaches a personality disorder as a continuum that ranges from normality at one end to severe disability and disturbance at the other end. According to this view, people with and without the disorder differ in degree only.   588

directionality problem   One reason correlations can never prove causality. If A and B are correlated, we do not know if A is the cause of B, or if B is the cause of A, or if some third, unknown variable is causing both B and A.   49

disclosure   Telling someone about some private aspect of ourselves. Many theorists have suggested that keeping

things to ourselves may be a source of stress and ultimately may lead to psychological distress and physical disease.   572

discriminant validity,   What a measure should not correlate with.   42

disorder   A pattern of behavior or experience that is distressing and painful to the person, leads to some disability or impairment in important life domains (e.g., work, marriage, or relationship difficulties), and is associated with increased risk for further suffering, loss of function, death, or confinement.   586

disparate impact   Any employment practice that disadvantages people from a protected group. The Supreme Court has not defined the size of the disparity necessary to prove disparate impact. Most courts define disparity as a difference that is sufficiently large that it is unlikely to have occurred by chance. Some courts, however, prefer the 80 percent rule contained in the Uniform Guidelines on Employee Selection Procedures. Under this rule, adverse impact is established if the selection rate for any race, sex, or ethnic group is less than four-fifths (or 80 percent) of the rate for the group with the highest selection rate.   110

displacement   An unconscious defense mechanism that involves avoiding the recognition that one has certain inappropriate urges or unacceptable feelings (e.g., anger, sexual attraction) toward a specific other. Those feelings then get displaced onto another person or object that is more appropriate or acceptable.   277

dispositional domain   Deals centrally with the ways in which individuals differ from one another. As such, the dispositional domain connects with all the other domains. In the dispositional domain, psychologists are primarily interested in the number and nature of fundamental dispositions, taxonomies of traits, measurement issues, and questions of stability over time and consistency over situations.   15

dispositional optimism   The expectation that in the future good events will be plentiful and bad events will be rare.   566

distortion   A defense mechanism in Roger's theory of personality; distortion refers to modifying the

meaning of experiences to make them less threatening to the self-image.   354

dizygotic twins   (also called fraternal twins) Twins who are not genetically identical. They come from two eggs that were separately fertilized ("di" means two; so dizygotic means "coming from two fertilized eggs"). Such twins share only 50 percent of their genes with their co-twin, the same amount as ordinary brothers and sisters. Fraternal twins can be of the same sex or of the opposite sex.   164

domain of knowledge   A specialty area of science and scholarship, where psychologists have focused on learning about some specific and limited aspect of human nature, often with preferred tools of investigation.   14

domain specific   Adaptations are presumed to be domain specific in the sense that they are "designed" by the evolutionary process to solve a specialized adaptive problem. Domain specificity implies that selection tends to fashion specific mechanisms for each specific adaptive problem.   229

dopamine   A neurotransmitter that appears to be associated with pleasure. Dopamine appears to function something like the "reward system" and has even been called the "feeling good" chemical (Hamer, 1997).   210

DRD4 gene   A gene located on the short arm of chromosome 11 that codes for a protein called a dopamine receptor. The function of this dopamine receptor is to respond to the presence of dopamine, which is a neurotransmitter. When the dopamine receptor encounters dopamine from other neurons in the brain, it discharges an electrical signal, activating other neurons.   178

dream analysis   A technique Freud taught for uncovering the unconscious material in a dream by interpreting the content of a dream. Freud called dreams "the royal road to the unconscious."   287

dynamic   The interaction of forces within a person.   330

e

effect size   How large a particular difference is, or how strong a particular correlation is, as averaged over several experiments or studies.   491

effective polygyny   Because female mammals bear the physical burden of gestation and lactation, there is a considerable sex difference in minimum obligatory parental investment. This difference leads to differences in the variances in reproduction between the sexes: most females will have some offspring, whereas a few males will sire many offspring, and some will have none at all. This is known as effective polygyny.   239

egalitarianism   How much a particular group displays equal treatment of all individuals within that group.   522

ego   The part of the mind that constrains the id to reality. According to Freud, it develops within the first two or three years of life. The ego operates according to the reality principle. The ego understands that the urges of the id are often in conflict with social and physical reality, and that direct expression of id impulses must therefore be redirected or postponed.   270

ego depletion   When exertion of self-control results in a decrease of psychic energy.   272

ego psychology   Post-Freudian psychoanalysts felt that the ego deserved more attention and that it performed many constructive functions. Erikson emphasized the ego as a powerful and independent part of personality, involved in mastering the environment, achieving one's goals, and hence in establishing one's identity. The approach to psychoanalysis started by Erikson was called ego psychology.   307

Electra complex   Within the psychoanalytic theory of personality development, the female counterpart to the Oedipal complex; both refer to the phallic stage of development.   284

electrode   A sensor usually placed on the surface of the skin and linked to a physiological recording machine (often called a polygraph) to measure physiological variables.   191

electrodermal activity   (also known as galvanic skin response or skin conductance) Electricity will flow across the skin with less resistance if that skin is made damp with sweat. Sweating on the palms of the hands is activated by the sympathetic nervous system, and so electrodermal activity is a way to directly measure changes

in the sympathetic nervous system.   191

electroencephalograph (EEG)   The brain spontaneously produces small amounts of electricity, which can be measured by electrodes placed on the scalp. EEGs can provide useful information about patterns of activation in different regions of the brain that may be associated with different types of information processing tasks.   216

emotions   Emotions can be defined by their three components: (1) emotions have distinct subjective feelings or affects associated with them; (2) emotions are accompanied by bodily changes, mostly in the nervous system, and these produce associated changes in breathing, heart rate, muscle tension, blood chemistry, and facial and bodily expressions; (3) emotions are accompanied by distinct action tendencies or increases in the probabilities of certain behaviors.   396

emotional inhibition   Suppression of emotional expressions; often thought of as a trait (e.g., some people chronically suppress their emotions).   569

emotional intelligence   An adaptive form of intelligence consisting of the ability to (1) know one's own emotions; (2) regulate those emotions; (3) motivate oneself; (4) know how others are feeling; and (5) influence how others are feeling. Goleman posited that emotional intelligence is more strongly predictive of professional status, marital quality, and salary than traditional measures of intelligence and aptitude.   355

emotional stability   The fourth of the personality traits in the five-factor model, which has proven to be replicable in studies using English-language trait words as items. Some of the key adjective markers for Emotional Stability are "calm," "composed," "not hypochondriacal," "poised."   79

emotional states   Transitory states that depend more on the situation or circumstances a person is in than on the specific person. Emotions as states have a specific cause, and that cause is typically outside of the person (something happens in the environment).   397

emotional traits   Stable personality traits that are primarily characterized by specific emotions. For example, the

trait of neuroticism is primarily characterized by the emotions of anxiety and worry.   397

empathizing   Tuning in to other people's thoughts and feelings.   501

empathy   In Rogers's client-centered therapy, empathy is understanding the person from his or her point of view. Instead of interpreting the meaning behind what the client says (e.g., "You have a harsh superego that is punishing you for the actions of your id."), the client-centered therapist simply listens to what the client says and reflects it back.   357

enduring   When psychological traits are stable over time.   7

environment   Environments can be physical, social, and intrapsychic (within the mind). Which aspect of the environment is important at any moment in time is frequently determined by the personality of the person in that environment.   9

environmentalist view   Environmentalists believe that personality is determined by socialization practices, such as parenting style and other agents of society.   180

environmentality   The percentage of observed variance in a *group* of individuals that can be attributed to environmental (nongenetic) differences. Generally speaking, the larger the heritability, the smaller the environmentality. And vice versa, the smaller the heritability, the larger the environmentality.   160

episodic acute stress   Repeated episodes of acute stress, such as having to work at more than one job every day, having to spend time with a difficult in-law, or needing to meet a recurring monthly deadline.   563

equal environments assumption   The assumption that the environments experienced by identical twins are no more similar to each other than are the environments experienced by fraternal twins. If they are more similar, then the greater similarity of the identical twins could plausibly be due to the fact that they experience more similar environments rather than the fact that they have more genes in common.   165

Erikson's eight stages of development   According to Erikson, there are eight stages of development: trust versus mistrust, autonomy versus shame and doubt, initiative versus guilt, industry versus inferiority, identity versus role confusion, intimacy versus isolation, generativity versus stagnation, and integrity versus despair.   308

esteem needs   The fourth level of Maslow's motivation hierarchy. There are two types of esteem: esteem from others and self-esteem, the latter often depending on the former. People want to be seen by others as competent, as strong, and as able to achieve. They want to be respected by others for their achievements or abilities. People also want to feel good about themselves. Much of the activity of adult daily life is geared toward achieving recognition and esteem from others and bolstering one's own self-confidence.   348

eugenics   The notion that the future of the human race can be influenced by fostering the reproduction of persons with certain traits, and discouraging reproduction among persons without those traits or who have undesirable traits.   157

evocation   A form of person–situation interaction discussed by Buss. It is based on the idea that certain personality traits may evoke consistent responses from the environment, particularly the social environment.   97, 472

evoked culture   A way of considering culture that concentrates on phenomena that are triggered in different ways by different environmental conditions.   521

evolutionary byproduct   Incidental effects evolved changes that are not properly considered adaptations. For example, our noses hold up glasses, but that is not what the nose evolved for.   228

evolutionary noise   Random variations that are neutral with respect to selection.   228

evolutionary-predicted sex differences   Evolutionary psychology predicts that males and females will be the same or similar in all those domains where the sexes have faced the same or similar adaptive problems (e.g., both sexes have sweat glands because both sexes have faced the adaptive problem of thermal regulation) and different when men and women have faced substantially different adaptive problems (e.g., in the physical realm, women have faced the problem of childbirth and have therefore evolved adaptations that are lacking in men, such as mechanisms for producing

labor contractions through the release of oxytocin into the bloodstream).   238

exhaustion stage   The third stage in Selye's general adaptation syndrome (GAS). Selye felt that this was the stage where we are most susceptible to illness and disease, as our physiological resources are depleted.   559

expectancy confirmation   A phenomenon whereby people's beliefs about the personality characteristics of others cause them to evoke in others actions that are consistent with the initial beliefs. The phenomenon of expectancy confirmation has also been called self-fulfilling prophecy and behavioral confirmation.   477

experience sampling   People answer some questions, for example, about their mood or physical symptoms, every day for several weeks or longer. People are usually contacted electronically ("beeped") one or more times a day at random intervals to complete the measures. Although experience sampling uses self-report as the data source, it differs from more traditional self-report methods in being able to detect patterns of behavior over time.   27

experimental methods   Typically used to determine causality—to find out whether one variable influences another variable. Experiments involve the manipulation of one variable (the independent variable) and random assignment of subjects to conditions defined by the independent variable.   44

explanatory style   Whenever someone offers a cause for some event, that cause can be analyzed in terms of the three categories of attributions: internal–external, stable–unstable, and global–specific. The tendency a person has to employ certain combinations of attributions in explaining events (e.g., internal, stable, and global causes) is called their explanatory style.   382

expressiveness   The ease with which one can express emotions, such as crying, showing empathy for the troubles of others, and showing nurturance to those in need.   506

external locus of control   Generalized expectancies that events are outside of one's control.   379

extraversion   The first fundamental personality trait in the five-factor model, a taxonomy which has proven to be replicable in studies using

English-language trait words as items. Some of the key adjective markers for Extraversion are "talkative," "extraverted" or "extraverted," "gregarious," "assertive," "adventurous," "open," "sociable," "forward," and "outspoken."   78

extreme responding   A response set that refers to the tendency to give endpoint responses, such as "strongly agree" or "strongly disagree" and avoid the middle part of response scales, such as "slightly agree," "slightly disagree," or "am indifferent."   39

eye-blink startle method   People typically blink their eyes when they are startled by a loud noise. Moreover, a person who is in an anxious or fearful state will blink faster and harder when startled than a person in a normal emotional state. This means that eye-blink speed when startled may be an objective physiological measure of how anxious or fearful a person is feeling. The eye-blink startle method may allow researchers to measure how anxious persons are without actually having to ask them.   596

f

face validity   Whether the test, on the surface, measures what it appears to measure.   42

factor analysis   A commonly used statistical procedure for identifying underlying structure in personality ratings or items. Factor analysis essentially identifies groups of items that covary (i.e., go together or correlate) with each other, but tend not to covary with other groups of items. This provides a means for determining which personality variables share some common underlying property or belong together within the same group.   64

factor loadings   Indexes of how much of the variation in an item is "explained" by the factor. Factor loadings indicate the degree to which the item correlates with or "loads on" the underlying factor.   65

faking   The motivated distortion of answers on a questionnaire. Some people may be motivated to "fake good" in order to appear to be better off or better adjusted than they really are. Others may be motivated to "fake bad" in order to appear to be worse off or more maladjusted than they really are.   102

false consensus effect   The tendency many people have to assume that others are similar to them (i.e., extraverts think that many other people are as extraverted as they are). Thinking that many other people share your own traits, preferences, or motivations.   281

false memories   Memories that have been "implanted" by well-meaning therapists or others interrogating a subject about some event.   300

false negative and false positive   There are two ways for psychologists to make a mistake when making decisions about persons based on personality tests (e.g., when deciding whether or not to hire a person, to parole a person, or that the person was lying). When trying to decide whether a person's answers are genuine or faked, the psychologist might decide that a person who was faking was actually telling the truth (called a false positive). Or they might conclude that a truthful person was faking. This is called a false negative.   103

family studies   Family studies correlate the degree of genetic overlap among family members with the degree of personality similarity. They capitalize on the fact that there are known degrees of genetic overlap between different members of a family in terms of degree of relationship.   163

fear of success   Horney coined this phrase to highlight a gender difference in response to competition and achievement situations. Many women, she argued, feel that if they succeed, they will lose their friends. Consequently, many women, she thought, harbor an unconscious fear of success. She held that men, on the other hand, feel that they will actually gain friends by being successful and hence are not at all afraid to strive and pursue achievement.   314

female underprediction effect   On average, college entrance exam scores underpredict grade point average for women relative to men. Women tend to do better in college than one would predict from their entrance exam scores.   108

feminine   Traits or roles typically associated with being female in a particular culture.   314

femininity   A psychological dimension containing traits such as nurturance, empathy, and expression of emotions (e.g., crying when sad). Femininity traits refer to gender roles, as distinct from biological sex.   503

field dependent and field independent   In Witkin's rod and frame test, if a participant adjusts the rod so that it is leaning in the direction of the tilted frame, that person is said to be dependent of the visual field, or field dependent. If a participant disregards the external cues and instead uses information from his body in adjusting the rod to upright, he is said to be independent of the field, or field independent; appearing to rely on his own sensations, not the perception of the field, to make the judgment. This individual difference may have implications in situations where people must extract information from complex sensory fields, such as in multimedia education.   369

five-factor model   A trait taxonomy that has its roots in the lexical hypothesis. The first psychologist to use the terms "five-factor model" and "Big Five" was Warren Norman, based on his replications of the factor structure suggesting the following five traits: Surgency (or extraversion), Neuroticism (or emotional instability), Agreeableness, Conscientiousness, and Intellect-Openness to Experience (or intellect). The model has been criticized by some for not being comprehensive and for failing to provide a theoretical understanding of the underlying psychological processes that generate the five traits. Nonetheless, it remains heavily endorsed by many personality psychologists and continues to be used in a variety of research studies and applied settings.   74

fixation   According to Erikson, if a developmental crisis is not successfully and adaptively resolved, personality development could become arrested and the person would continue to have a fixation on that crisis in development. According to Freud, if a child fails to fully resolve a conflict at a particular stage of development, he or she may get stuck in that stage. If a child is fixated at a particular stage, he or she exhibits a less mature approach to obtaining sexual gratification.   282

flow   A subjective state that people report when they are completely involved in an activity to the point of forgetting time, fatigue, and everything else but the activity itself. While flow experiences are somewhat rare, they occur under specific conditions; there is a balance between the person's skills and the challenges of the situation, there is a clear goal, and there is immediate feedback on how one is doing.   351

forced-choice questionnaire   Test takers are confronted with pairs of statements and are asked to indicate which statement in the pair is more true of them. Each statement in the pair is selected to be similar to the other in social desirability, forcing participants to choose between statements that are equivalently socially desirable (or undesirable), and differ in content.   40

free association   Patients relax, let their minds wander, and say whatever comes into their minds. Patients often say things that surprise or embarrass them. By relaxing the censor that screens everyday thoughts, free association allows potentially important material into conscious awareness.   286

free running   A condition in studies of circadian rhythms in which participants are deprived from knowing what time it is (e.g., meals are served when the participant asks for them, not at prescheduled times). When a person is free running in time, there are no time cues to influence behavior or biology.   213

frequency–dependent selection   In some contexts, two or more heritable variants can evolve within a population. The most obvious example is biological sex itself. Within sexually reproducing species, the two sexes exist in roughly equal numbers because of frequency–dependent selection. If one sex becomes rare relative to the other, evolution will produce an increase in the numbers of the rarer sex. Frequency–dependent selection, in this example, causes the frequency of men and women to remain roughly equal. Different personality extremes (e.g., introversion and extraversion) may be the result of frequency dependent selection.   251

frontal brain asymmetry   Asymmetry in the amount of activity in the left and right part of the frontal hemispheres of the brain. Studies using EEG measures have linked more relative left brain activity with pleasant emotions and more relative right brain activity with negative emotions.   217

frustration   The high-arousal unpleasant subjective feeling that comes when a person is blocked from attaining an important goal. For example, a thirsty person who just lost his last bit of money in a malfunctioning soda machine would most likely feel frustration.   576

fully functioning person   According to Rogers, a fully functioning person is on his or her way toward self-actualization. Fully functioning persons may not actually *be* self-actualized yet, but they are not blocked or sidetracked in moving toward this goal. Such persons are open to new experiences and are not afraid of new ideas. They embrace life to its fullest. Fully functioning individuals are also centered in the present. They do not dwell on the past or their regrets. Fully functioning individuals also trust themselves, their feelings, and their own judgments.   353

functional analysis   In *The Expression of the Emotions in Man and Animals,* Charles Darwin proposed a functional analysis of emotions and emotional expressions focusing on the "why" of emotions and expressions. Darwin concluded that emotional expressions communicate information from one animal to another about what is likely to happen. For instance, a dog baring its teeth, growling, and bristling the fur on its back is communicating to others that he is likely to attack. If others recognize the dog's communication, they may choose to back away to safety.   396

functional magnetic resonance imaging (fMRI)   A noninvasive imaging technique used to identify specific areas of brain activity. As parts of the brain are stimulated, oxygenated blood rushes to the activated area, resulting in increased iron concentrations in the blood. The fMRI detects these elevated concentrations of iron and prints out colorful images indicating which part of the brain is used to perform certain tasks.   33

functionality   The notion that our psychological mechanisms are designed to accomplish particular adaptive goals.   229

fundamental attribution error   When bad events happen to others, people have a tendency to attribute blame to some characteristic of the person, whereas when bad events happen to oneself, people have the tendency to blame the situation.   277

g

gender   Social interpretations of what it means to be a man or a woman.   490

gender differences   The distinction between gender and sex can be traced back to Horney. Horney stressed the point that, while biology determines sex, cultural norms determine what is acceptable for typical males and females in that culture. Today we use the terms *masculine* and *feminine* to refer to traits or roles typically associated with being male or female in a particular culture, and we refer to differences in such culturally ascribed roles and traits as gender differences. Differences that are ascribed to being a man or a woman per se are, however, called sex differences.   314

gender schemata   Cognitive orientations that lead individuals to process social information on the basis of sex-linked associations (Hoyenga & Hoyenga, 1993).   506

gender stereotypes   Beliefs that we hold about how men and women differ or are supposed to differ, which are not necessarily based on reality. Gender stereotypes can have important real-life consequences for men and women. These consequences can damage people where it most counts—in their health, their jobs, their odds of advancement, and their social reputations.   490

general adaptation syndrome (GAS)   GAS has three stages: When a stressor first appears, people experience the alarm stage. If the stressor continues, the stage of resistance begins. If the stressor remains constant, the person eventually enters the third stage, the stage of exhaustion.   559

general intelligence   Early on in the study of intelligence, many psychologists thought of intelligence in traitlike terms, as a property of the individual. Individuals were thought to differ from each other in how much intelligence they possessed. Moreover, intelligence was thought of as a single broad factor, often called "g" for general intelligence. This stands in contrast to those views of intelligence as consisting of many discrete factors, such as social intelligence, emotional intelligence, and academic intelligence.   388

generalizability   The degree to which a measure retains its validity across different contexts.   43

generalized expectancies   A person's expectations for reinforcement that hold across a variety of situations (Rotter, 1971, 1990). When people encounter a new situation, they base their expectancies about what will happen on their generalized expectancies about whether they have the abilities to influence events.   378

genes   Packets of DNA that are inherited by children from their parents in distinct chunks. They are the smallest discrete unit that is inherited by offspring intact, without being broken up.   226

genetic junk   The 98 percent of the DNA in human chromosomes that are not protein-coding genes; scientists believed that these parts were functionless residue. Recent studies have shown that these portions of DNA may affect everything from a person's physical size to personality, thus adding to the complexity of the human genome.   156

genital stage   The final stage in Freud's psychosexual stage theory of development. This stage begins around age 12 and lasts through one's adult life. Here the libido is focused on the genitals, but not in the manner of self-manipulation associated with the phallic stage. People reach the genital stage with full psychic energy if they have resolved the conflicts at the prior stages.   285

genome   The complete set of genes an organism possesses. The human genome contains somewhere between 20,000 and 30,000 genes.   156

genotype–environment correlation   The differential exposure of individuals with different genotypes to different environments.   176

genotype–environment interaction   The differential response of individuals with different genotypes to the same environments.   175

genotypic variance   Genetic variance that is responsible for individual differences in the phenotypic expression of specific traits.   159

global self-esteem   By far the most frequently measured component of self-esteem; defined as "the level of global regard that one has for the self as a person" (Harter, 1993, p. 88). Global self-esteem can range from highly positive to highly negative, and reflects an overall evaluation of the self at the broadest level (Kling et al., 1999). Global self-esteem is linked with many aspects of functioning and is commonly thought to be central to mental health.   499

good theory   A theory that serves as a useful guide for researchers, organizes known facts, and makes predictions about future observations.   18

Griggs v. Duke Power   Prior to 1964, Duke Power Company had used discriminatory practices in hiring and work assignment, including barring blacks from certain jobs. After passage of the Civil Rights Act of 1964, Duke Power instituted various requirements for such jobs, including passing certain aptitude tests. The effect was to perpetuate discrimination. In 1971 the Supreme Court ruled that the seemingly neutral testing practices used by Duke Power were unacceptable because they operated to maintain discrimination. This was the first legal case where the Supreme Court ruled that any selection procedure could not produce disparate impact for a group protected by the Act (e.g., racial groups, women).   108

h

happiness   Researchers conceive of happiness in two complementary ways: in terms of a judgment that life is satisfying, as well as in terms of the predominance of positive compared to negative, emotions in one's life (Diener, 2000). It turns out, however, that people's emotional lives and their judgments of how satisfied they are with their lives are highly correlated. People who have a lot of pleasant emotions relative to unpleasant emotions in their lives tend also to judge their lives as satisfying, and vice versa.   401

harm avoidance   In Cloninger's tridimensional personality model, the personality trait of harm avoidance is associated with low levels of serotonin. People low in serotonin are sensitive to unpleasant stimuli or to stimuli or events that have been associated with punishment or pain. Consequently, people low in serotonin seem to expect that harmful and unpleasant events will happen to them, and they are constantly vigilant for signs of such threatening events.   211

health behavior model   Personality does not directly influence the relation between stress and illness. Instead, personality affects health indirectly, through health-promoting or health-degrading behaviors. This model suggests that personality influences the degree to which a person engages in various health-promoting or health-demoting behaviors.   555

health psychology   Researchers in the area of health psychology study relations between the mind and the body, and how these two components respond to challenges from the environment (e.g., stressful events, germs) to produce illness or health.   552

heritability   A statistic that refers to the proportion of observed variance in a group of individuals that can be explained or "accounted for" by genetic variance (Plomin, DeFries, & McClearn, 1990). It describes the degree to which genetic differences between individuals cause differences in some observed property, such as height, extraversion, or sensation seeking. The formal definition of heritability is the proportion of phenotypic variance that is attributable to genotypic variance.   159

heuristic value   An evaluative scientific standard for assessing personality theories. Theories that steer scientists to important new discoveries about personality are superior to those that fail to provide this guidance.   19

hierarchy of needs   Murray believed that each person has a unique combination of needs. An individual's various needs can be thought of as existing at a different level of strength. A person might have a high need for dominance, an average need for intimacy, and a low need for achievement. High levels of some needs interact with the amounts of

various other needs within each person.   330

high-variance conditions   One key variable triggering communal food sharing is the degree of variability in food resources. Specifically, under high-variance conditions, there are substantial benefits to sharing.   522

historical era   One type of intracultural variation pertains to the effects of historical era on personality. (People who grew up during the great economic depression of the 1930s, for example, might be more anxious about job security or adopt a more conservative spending style.) Disentangling the effects of historical era on personality is an extremely difficult endeavor because most current personality measures were not in use in earlier eras.   537

histrionic personality disorder   The hallmark of the histrionic personality is excessive attention seeking and emotionality. Often such persons are overly dramatic and draw attention to themselves, preferring to be the center of attention or the life of the party. They may appear charming or even flirtatious. Often they can be inappropriately seductive or provocative.   598

Hogan Personality Inventory (HPI) A questionnaire measure of personality based on the Big Five model but modified to emphasize the assessment of traits important in the business world, including the motive to get along with others and the motive to get ahead of others.   118

holistic   A way of processing information that involves attention to relationships, contexts, and links between the focal objects and the field as a whole.   532

hormonal theories   Hormonal theories of sex differences argue that men and women differ not because of the external social environment but because the sexes have different amounts of specific hormones. It is these physiological differences, not differential social treatment, that causes boys and girls to diverge over development.   511

hostile attributional bias   The tendency to infer hostile intent on the part of others in the face of uncertain or unclear behavior from others. Essentially, people who are aggressive expect that others will be hostile toward them.   473

hostile forces of nature Hostile forces of nature are what Darwin called any event that impedes survival. Hostile forces of nature include food shortages, diseases, parasites, predators, and extremes of weather. 224

hostility A tendency to respond to everyday frustrations with anger and aggression, to become irritable easily, to feel frequent resentment, and to act in a rude, critical, antagonistic, and uncooperative manner in everyday interactions (Dembrowski & Costa, 1987). Hostility is a subtrait in the Type A behavior pattern. 421, 576

human nature The traits and mechanisms of personality that are typical of our species and are possessed by everyone or nearly everyone. 10

humanistic tradition Humanistic psychologists emphasize the role of choice in human life, and the influence of responsibility on creating a meaningful and satisfying life. The meaning of any person's life, according to the humanistic approach, is found in the choices that people make and the responsibility they take for those choices. The humanistic tradition also emphasizes the human need for growth and realizing one's full potential. In the humanistic tradition it is assumed that, if left to their own devices, humans will grow and develop in positive and satisfying directions. 345

i

id The most primitive part of the human mind. Freud saw the id as something we are born with and as the source of all drives and urges. The id is like a spoiled child: selfish, impulsive, and pleasure loving. According to Freud, the id operates strictly according to the pleasure principle, which is the desire for immediate gratification. 270

id psychology Freud's version of psychoanalysis focused on the id, especially the twin instincts of sex and aggression, and how the ego and superego respond to the demands of the id. Freudian psychoanalysis can thus be called id psychology, to distinguish it from later developments that focused on the functions of the ego. 307

ideal self The self that a person wants to be. 441

identification A developmental process in children. It consists of

wanting to become like the same-sex parent. In classic psychoanalysis, it marks the beginning of the resolution of the Oedipal or Electra conflicts and the successful resolution of the phallic stage of psychosexual development. Freud believed that the resolution of the phallic stage was both the beginning of the superego and morality and the start of the adult gender role. 284

identity conflict According to Baumeister, an identity conflict involves an incompatibility between two or more aspects of identity. This kind of crisis often occurs when a person is forced to make an important and difficult life decision. Identity conflicts are "approach–approach" conflicts, in that the person wants to reach two mutually contradictory goals. Although these conflicts involve wanting two desirable identities, identity conflicts usually involve intense feelings of guilt or remorse over perceived unfaithfulness to an important aspect of the person's identity. 453

identity confusion A period when a person does not have a strong sense of who she or he really is in terms of values, careers, relationships, and ideologies. 311

identity crisis Erikson's term refers to the desperation, anxiety, and confusion a person feels when he or she has not developed a strong sense of identity. A period of identity crisis is a common experience during adolescence, but for some people it occurs later in life, or lasts for a longer period. Baumeister suggests that there are two distinct types of identity crises, which he terms identity deficit and identity conflict. 307

identity deficit According to Baumeister, an identity deficit arises when a person has not formed an adequate identity and thus has trouble making major decisions. When people who have an identity deficit look toward their social identity for guidance in making decisions (e.g., "What would a person like me do in this situation?"), they find little in the way of a foundation upon which to base such life choices. Identity deficits often occur when a person discards old values or goals. 452

identity foreclosure A person does not emerge from a crisis with a firm

sense of commitment to values, relationships, or career but forms an identity without exploring alternatives. An example would be young people who accept the values of their parents or their cultural or religious group without question. 311

idiographic The study of single individuals, with an effort to observe general principles as they are manifest in a single life over time. 12

"if . . . then . . ." propositions A component of Walter Mischel's theory referring to the notion that, if situation A, the person does X, but if situation B, then the person does Y. Personality leaves its signature, Mischel argues, in terms of the specific situational ingredients that prompt behavior from the person. 387

illness behavior model Personality influences the degree to which a person perceives and pays attention to bodily sensations, and the degree to which a person will interpret and label those sensations as an illness. 557

imagination inflation effect A memory is elaborated upon in the imagination, leading the person to confuse the imagined event with events that actually happened. 301

implicit motivation Motives as they are measured in fantasy-based (i.e., TAT) techniques, as opposed to direct self-report measures. The implied motives of persons scored, for example, from TAT stories, is thought to reveal their unconscious desires and aspirations, their unspoken needs and wants. McClelland has argued that implicit motives predict long-term behavioral trends over time, such as implicit need for achievement predicting long-term business success. 334

impulsivity A personality trait that refers to lowered self-control, especially in the presence of potentially rewarding activities, the tendency to act before one thinks, and a lowered ability to anticipate the consequences of one's behavior. 202

inclusive fitness theory Modern evolutionary theory based on differential gene reproduction (Hamilton, 1964). The "inclusive" part refers to the fact that the characteristics that affect reproduction need not affect the personal production of offspring; they can affect the survival and reproduction of genetic relatives as well.   226

independence   Markus and Kitayama propose that each person has two fundamental "cultural tasks" that have to be confronted. One such task, agency or independence, involves how you differentiate yourself from the larger group. Independence includes your unique abilities, your personal internal motives and personality dispositions, and the ways in which you separate yourself from the larger group.   529

independence training   McClelland believes that certain parental behaviors can promote high achievement motivation, autonomy, and independence in their children. One of these parenting practices is placing an emphasis on independence training. Training a child to be independent in different tasks promotes a sense of mastery and confidence in the child.   339

individual differences   Every individual has personal and unique qualities that make him or her different from others. The study of all the ways in which individuals can differ from others, the number, origin, and meaning of such differences, is the study of individual differences.   11

inductive reasoning approach   The bottom-up, data-driven method of empirical research.   231

influential forces   Personality traits and mechanisms are influential forces in people's lives in that they influence our actions, how we view ourselves, how we think about the world, how we interact with others, how we feel, our selection of environments (particularly our social environment), what goals and desires we pursue in life, and how we react to our circumstances. Other influential forces include sociological and economic influences, as well as physical and biological forces.   8

information processing   The transformation of sensory input into mental representations and the manipulation of such representations.   367

infrequency scale   A common method for detecting measurement technique problems within a set of questionnaire items. The infrequency scale contains items that most or all people would answer in a particular

way. If a participant answered more than one or two of these unlike the rest of the majority of the participants, a researcher could begin to suspect that the participant's answers do not represent valid information. Such a participant may be answering randomly, may have difficulty reading, or may be marking his or her answer sheet incorrectly.   102

inhibitory control   The ability to control inappropriate responses or behaviors.   493

insight   In psychoanalysis, through many interpretations, a patient is gradually led to an understanding of the unconscious source of his or her problems. This understanding is called insight.   289

inspection time   A variable in intelligence research; the time it takes a person to make a simple discrimination between two displayed objects or two auditory intervals that differ by only a few milliseconds. This variable suggests that brain mechanisms specifically involved in discriminations of extremely brief time intervals represent a sensitive indicator of general intelligence.   391

instincts   Freud believed that strong innate forces provided *all* the energy in the psychic system. He called these forces instincts. In Freud's initial formulation there were two fundamental categories of instincts: self-preservation instincts and sexual instincts. In his later formulations, Freud collapsed the self-preservation and sexual instincts into one, which he called the life instinct.   265

instrumentality   Personality traits that involve working with objects, getting tasks completed in a direct fashion, showing independence from others, and displaying self-sufficiency.   506

integrity tests   Because the private sector cannot legally use polygraphs to screen employees, some companies have developed and promoted questionnaire measures to use in place of the polygraph. These questionnaires, called integrity tests, are designed to assess whether a person is generally honest or dishonest.   105

Intellect–Openness   The fifth personality trait in the five-factor model, which has proven to be replicable in studies using

English-language trait words as items. Some of the key adjective markers for Openness are "creative," "imaginative," "intellectual." Those who rate high on Openness tend to remember their dreams more and have vivid, prophetic, or problem-solving dreams.   81

interactional model   Objective events happen to a person, but personality factors determine the impact of those events by influencing the person's ability to cope. This is called the interactional model because personality is assumed to moderate (that is, influence) the relation between stress and illness.   553

interdependence   Markus and Kitayama propose that each person has two fundamental "cultural tasks" that have to be confronted. The first is communion or interdependence. This cultural task involves how you are affiliated with, attached to, or engaged in the larger group of which you are a member. Interdependence includes your relationships with other members of the group and your embeddedness within the group.   529

internal locus of control   The generalized expectancy that reinforcing events are under one's control, and that one is responsible for the major outcomes in life.   379

internalized   In object relations theory, a child will create an unconscious mental representation of his or her mother. This allows the child to have a relationship with this internalized "object" even in the absence of the "real" mother. The relationship object internalized by the child is based on his or her developing relationship with the mother. This image then forms the fundamentals for how children come to view others with whom they develop subsequent relationships.   317

interpersonal traits   What people do to and with each other. They include *temperament* traits, such as nervous, gloomy, sluggish, and excitable; *character* traits, such as moral, principled, and dishonest; *material* traits, such as miserly or stingy; *attitude* traits, such as pious or spiritual; *mental* traits, such as clever, logical, and perceptive; and *physical* traits, such as healthy and tough.   72

interpretation   One of the three levels of cognition that are of interest to personality psychologists. Interpretation is the making sense of, or explaining, various events in the world. Psychoanalysts offer patients interpretations of the psychodynamic causes of their problems. Through many interpretations, patients are gradually led to an understanding of the unconscious source of their problems.   289, 368

inter-rater reliability   Multiple observers gather information about a person's personality, then investigators evaluate the degree of consensus among the observers. When different observers agree with one another, the degree of inter-rater reliability increases. When different raters fail to agree, the measure is said to have low inter-rater reliability.   28

intersexual selection   In Darwin's intersexual selection, members of one sex choose a mate based on their preferences for particular qualities in that mate. These characteristics evolve because animals that possess them are chosen more often as mates, and their genes thrive. Animals that lack the desired characteristics are excluded from mating, and their genes perish.   225

intrapsychic domain   This domain deals with mental mechanisms of personality, many of which operate outside the realm of conscious awareness. The predominant theory in this domain is Freud's theory of psychoanalysis. This theory begins with fundamental assumptions about the instinctual system—the sexual and aggressive forces that are presumed to drive and energize much of human activity. The intrapsychic domain also includes defense mechanisms such as repression, denial, and projection.   16

intrasexual competition   In Darwin's intrasexual competition, members of the same sex compete with each other, and the outcome of their contest gives the winner greater sexual access to members of the opposite sex. Two stags locking horns in combat is the prototypical image of this. The characteristics that lead to success in contests of this kind, such as greater strength, intelligence, or attractiveness to allies, evolve because the victors are able to mate more often and hence pass on more genes.   225

j

job analysis   When assisting a business in hiring for a particular job, a psychologist typically starts by analyzing the requirements of the job. The psychologist might interview employees who work in the job or supervisors who are involved in managing the particular job. The psychologist might observe workers in the job, noting any particular oral, written, performance, or social skills needed. He or she may also take into account both the physical and social aspects of the work environment in an effort to identify any special pressures or responsibilities associated with the job. Based on this job analysis, the psychologist develops some hypotheses about the kinds of abilities and personality traits that might best equip a person to perform well in that job.   112

l

latency stage   The fourth stage in Freud's psychosexual stages of development. This stage occurs from around the age of six until puberty. Freud believed few specific sexual conflicts existed during this time, and was thus a period of psychological rest or latency. Subsequent psychoanalysts have argued that much development occurs during this time, such as learning to make decisions for oneself, interacting and making friends with others, developing an identity, and learning the meaning of work. The latency period ends with the sexual awakening brought about by puberty.   284

latent content   The latent content of a dream is, according to Freud, what the elements of the dream actually represent.   287

learned helplessness   Animals (including humans), when subjected to unpleasant and inescapable circumstances, often become passive and accepting of their situation, in effect learning to be helpless. Researchers surmised that if people were in an unpleasant or painful situation, they would attempt to change the situation. However, if repeated attempts to change the situation failed, they would resign themselves to being

helpless. Then, even if the situation did improve so that they could escape the discomfort, they would continue to act helpless.   380

leukocyte   A white blood cell. When there is an infection or injury to the body, or a systematic inflammation of the body occurs, there is an elevation in white blood cell counts. Surtees et al., in a 2003 study, established a direct link between hostility and elevated white blood cell counts.   578

lexical approach   The approach to determining the fundamental personality traits by analyzing language. For example, a trait adjective that has many synonyms probably represents a more fundamental trait than a trait adjective with few synonyms.   63

lexical hypothesis   The lexical hypothesis—on which the lexical approach is based—states that important individual differences have become encoded within the natural language. Over ancestral time, the differences between people that were important were noticed and words were invented to communicate about those differences.   63

libido   Freud postulated that humans have a fundamental instinct toward destruction and that this instinct is often manifest in aggression toward others. The two instincts were usually referred to as libido, for the life instinct, and thanatos, for the death instinct. While the libido was generally considered sexual in nature, Freud also used this term to refer to any need-satisfying, life-sustaining, or pleasure-oriented urge.   265

life-outcome data (L-data) Information that can be gleaned from the events, activities, and outcomes in a person's life that are available to public scrutiny. For example, marriages and divorces are a matter of public record. Personality psychologists can sometimes secure information about the clubs, if any, a person joins; how many speeding tickets a person has received in the last few years; whether the person owns a handgun. These can all serve as sources of information about personality.   35

Likert rating scale   A common rating scale that provides numbers that are attached to descriptive phrases, such as 0 = disagree strongly, 1 = disagree slightly, 2 = neither agree nor disagree, 3 = agree slightly, 4 = strongly agree.   25

limbic system The part of the brain responsible for emotion and the "flight-fight" reaction. If individuals have a limbic system that is easily activated, we might expect them to have frequent episodes of emotion, particularly those emotions associated with flight (such as anxiety, fear, worry) and those associated with fight (such as anger, irritation, annoyance). Eysenck postulated that the limbic system was the source of the trait of neuroticism. 414

locus of control A person's perception of responsibility for the events in his or her life. It refers to whether people tend to locate that responsibility internally, within themselves, or externally, in fate, luck, or chance. Locus of control research started in the mid-1950s when Rotter was developing his social learning theory. 377

longitudinal study Examines individuals over time. Longitudinal studies have been conducted that have spanned as many as four and five decades of life and have examined many different age brackets. These studies are costly and difficult to conduct, but the information gained about personality development is valuable. 130

m

Machiavellianism A manipulative strategy of social interaction referring to the tendency to use other people as tools for personal gain. "High Mach" persons tend to tell people what they want to hear, use flattery to get what they want, and rely heavily on lying and deception to achieve their own ends. 481

major life events According to Holmes and Rahe, major life events require that people make major adjustments in their lives. Death or loss of a spouse through divorce or separation are the most stressful events, followed closely by being jailed, losing a close family member in death, or being severely injured. 560

manifest content The manifest content of a dream is, according to Freud, what the dream actually contains. 287

Manipulation in Person-Situation Interaction A form of person-situation interaction in which the person intentionally behaves in ways to influence those around them. Common tactics of manipulation include coercion, the silent treatment, and charm or flattery. 92

manipulation Researchers conducting experiments use manipulation in order to evaluate the influence of one variable (the manipulated or independent variable) on another (the dependent variable). 44, 98

masculine Traits or roles typically associated with being male in a particular culture. 314

masculinity Traits that define the cultural roles associated with being male. Two major personality instruments were published in 1974 to assess people using this new conception of gender roles (Bem, 1974; Spence, Helmreich, & Stapp, 1974). The masculinity scales contain items reflecting assertiveness, boldness, dominance, self-sufficiency, and instrumentality. Masculinity traits refer to gender roles, as distinct from biological sex. 503

maximalist Those who describe sex differences as comparable in magnitude to effect sizes in other areas of psychology, important to consider, and recommend that they should not be trivialized. 493

mean level change Within a single group that has been tested on two separate occasions, any difference in group averages across the two occasions is considered a mean level change. 125

mean level stability A population that maintains a consistent average level of a trait or characteristic over time. If the average level of liberalism or conservatism in a population remains the same with increasing age, we say that the population exhibits high mean level stability on that characteristic. If the average degree of political orientation changes, then we say that the population is displaying mean level change. 125

mediation Describes a situation whereby the effects of one variable on another "go through" a third variable (the mediator). For example, we know that conscientiousness in correlated with longevity. However, it is not conscientiousness in itself that causes a longer life. Instead, researchers have determined that, in this relation to longevity, the effects of conscientiousness go through (are mediated by) various health behaviors such as exercising regularly and eating a sensible diet. 555

minimalist Those who describe sex differences as small and inconsequential. 493

modeling By seeing another person engage in a particular behavior with positive results, the observer is more likely to imitate that behavior. It is a form of learning whereby the consequences for a particular behavior are observed, and thus the new behavior is learned. 385

moderation Describes a situation whereby one variable (the moderator) influences the degree or correlation between two other variables. For example, if people high in neuroticism showed a strong correlation between stress and illness, and people low in neuroticism showed a weak or no correlation between stress and illness, then we would say that neuroticism is a moderator of the stress-illness relationship. 553

molecular genetics Techniques designed to identify the specific genes associated with specific traits, such as personality traits. The most common method, called the association method, identifies whether individuals with a particular gene (or allele) have higher or lower scores on a particular trait measure. 178

monoamine oxidase (MAO) An enzyme found in the blood that is known to regulate neurotransmitters, those chemicals that carry messages between nerve cells. MAO may be a causal factor in the personality trait of sensation seeking. 209

monozygotic twins Identical twins that come from a single fertilized egg (or zygote, hence monozygotic) that divides into two at some point during gestation. Identical twins are always the same sex because they are genetically identical. 164

mood induction In experimental studies of mood, mood inductions are employed as manipulations in order to determine whether the mood differences (e.g., pleasant versus unpleasant) effect some dependent variable. In studies of personality, mood effects might interact with personality variables. For example, positive mood effects might be stronger for persons high on extraversion, and negative mood effects might be stronger for persons high on neuroticism. 410

mood variability Frequent fluctuations in a person's emotional life over time. 427

moral anxiety Caused by a conflict between the id or the ego and the superego. For example, a person who suffers from chronic shame or feelings of guilt over not living up to "proper" standards, even though such standards might not be attainable, is experiencing moral anxiety. 275

moratorium The time taken to explore options before making a commitment to an identity. College can be considered a "time out" from life, in which students may explore a variety of roles, relationships, and responsibilities before having to commit to any single life path. 311

morningness–eveningness The stable differences between persons in preferences for being active at different times of the day. The term was coined to refer to this dimension (Horne & Osterberg, 1976). Differences between morning- and evening-types of persons appear to be due to differences in the length of their underlying circadian biological rhythms. 212

motivated unconscious The psychoanalytic idea that information that is unconscious (e.g., a repressed wish) can actually motivate or influence subsequent behavior. This notion was promoted by Freud and formed the basis for his ideas about the unconscious sources of mental disorders and other problems with living. Many psychologists agree with the idea of the unconscious, but there is less agreement today about whether information that is unconscious can have much of an influence on actual behavior. 267, 306

motives Internal states that arouse and direct behavior toward specific objects or goals. A motive is often caused by a deficit, by the lack of something. Motives differ from each other in type, amount, and intensity, depending on the person and his or her circumstances. Motives are based on needs and propel people to perceive, think, and act in specific ways that serve to satisfy those needs. 328

multi-motive grid Designed to assess motives, it uses 14 pictures representing achievement, power, or intimacy and a series of questions about important motivational states to elicit answers from test subjects. In theory, the motives

elicited from the photographs would influence how the subject answers the test questions. 333

multiple intelligences Howard Gardner's theory of multiple intelligences includes several forms: interpersonal intelligence (social skills, ability to communicate and get along with others), intrapersonal intelligence (insight into oneself, one's emotions and motives), kinesthetic intelligence (the abilities of athletes, dancers, and acrobats), and musical intelligence. There are several other theories proposing multiple forms of intelligence. This position is in contrast to the theory of "g," or general intelligence, which holds that there is only one form of intelligence. 388

multiple social personalities Each of us displays different sides of ourselves to different people—we may be kind to our friends, ruthless to our enemies, loving toward a spouse, and conflicted toward our parents. Our social personalities vary from one setting to another, depending on the nature of relationships we have with other individuals. 28

Myers-Briggs Type Indicator (MBTI) One of the most widely used personality tests in the business world. It was developed by a mother-daughter team, Katherine Briggs and Isabel Myers, based on Jungian concepts. The test provides information about personality types by testing for eight fundamental preferences using questions in a "forced-choice" or either/or format. Individuals must respond in one way or another, even if their preferences might be somewhere in the middle. Although the test is not without criticism, it has great intuitive appeal. 113

n

narcissism A style of inflated self-admiration and the constant attempt to draw attention to the self and to keep others focused on oneself. Although narcissism can be carried to extremes, narcissistic tendencies can be found in normal range levels. 315

narcissistic paradox The fact that, although narcissistic people appear to have high self-esteem, they actually have doubts about their self-worth. While they appear to have a grandiose sense of self-importance, narcissists are

nevertheless very fragile and vulnerable to blows to their self-esteem and cannot handle criticism well. They need constant praise, reassurance, and attention from others, whereas a person with truly high self-esteem would not need such constant praise and attention from others. 315

narcissistic personality disorder The calling card of the narcissistic personality is a strong need to be admired, a strong sense of self-importance, and a lack of insight into other people's feelings. Narcissists see themselves in a very favorable light, inflating their accomplishments and undervaluing the work of others. Narcissists daydream about prosperity, victory, influence, adoration from others, and power. They routinely expect adulation from others, believing that homage is generally long overdue. They exhibit feelings of entitlement, even though they have done nothing in particular to earn that special treatment. 601

natural selection Darwin reasoned that variants that better enabled an organism to survive and reproduce would lead to more descendants. The descendants, therefore, would inherit the variants that led to their ancestors' survival and reproduction. Through this process, the successful variants were selected, and unsuccessful variants weeded out. Natural selection, therefore, results in gradual changes in a species over time, as successful variants increase in frequency and eventually spread throughout the gene pool, replacing the less successful variants. 224

naturalistic observation Observers witness and record events that occur in the normal course of the lives of their participants. For example, a child might be followed throughout an entire day, or an observer may record behavior in the home of the participant. Naturalistic observation offers researchers the advantage of being able to secure information in the realistic context of a person's everyday life, but at the cost of not being able to control the events and behavioral samples witnessed. 29

nature-nurture debate The ongoing debate as to whether genes or environment are more important determinants of personality. 161

need for achievement According to McClelland, the desire to do better, to be successful, and to feel competent. People with a high need for achievement obtains satisfaction from accomplishing a task or from the anticipation of accomplishing a task. They cherish the process of being engaged in a challenging task. 336

need for intimacy McAdams defines the need for intimacy as the "recurrent preference or readiness for warm, close, and communicative interaction with others" (1990, p. 198). People with a high need for intimacy want more intimacy and meaningful human contact in their day-to-day lives than do those with a low need for intimacy. 343

need for power A preference for having an impact on other people. Individuals with a high need for power are interested in controlling situations and other people. 340

needs States of tension within a person; as a need is satisfied, the state of tension is reduced. Usually the state of tension is caused by the lack of something (e.g., a lack of food causes a need to eat). 328

negative affectivity Includes components such as anger, sadness, difficulty, and amount of distress. 494

negative identity Identities founded on undesirable social roles, such as "gangstas," girlfriends of street toughs, or members of street gangs. 311

negligent hiring A charge sometimes brought against an employer for hiring someone who is unstable or prone to violence. Employers are defending themselves against such suits, which often seek compensation for crimes committed by their employees. Such cases hinge on whether the employer should have discovered dangerous traits ahead of time, before hiring such a person into a position where he or she posed a threat to others. Personality testing may provide evidence that the employer did in fact try to reasonably investigate an applicant's fitness for the workplace. 107

neurotic anxiety Occurs when there is a direct conflict between the id and the ego. The danger is that the ego may lose control over some unacceptable desire of the id. For example, a man who worries excessively that he might blurt out some unacceptable thought or desire in public is beset by neurotic anxiety. 275

neurotic paradox The fact that people with disorders or other problems with living often exhibit behaviors that exacerbate, rather than lessen, their problems. For example, borderline personality disordered persons, who are generally concerned with being abandoned by friends and intimate others, may throw temper tantrums or otherwise express anger and rage in a manner that drives people away. The paradox refers to doing behaviors that make their situation worse. 608

neuroticism A dimension of personality present, in some form, in every major trait theory of personality. Different researchers have used different terms for neuroticism, such as emotional instability, anxiety-proneness, and negative affectivity. Adjectives useful for describing persons high on the trait of neuroticism include moody, touchy, irritable, anxious, unstable, pessimistic, and complaining. 413

neurotransmitters Chemicals in the nerve cells that are responsible for the transmission of a nerve impulse from one cell to another. Some theories of personality are based directly on different amounts of neurotransmitters found in the nervous system. 208

neurotransmitter theory of depression According to this theory, an imbalance of the neurotransmitters at the synapses of the nervous system causes depression. Some medications used to treat depression target these specific neurotransmitters. Not all people with depression are treated successfully with drugs. That suggests that there may be varieties of depression; some are biologically based, while others are more reactive to stress, physical exercise, or cognitive therapy. 420

nomothetic The study of general characters of people as they are distributed in the population, typically involving statistical comparisons between individuals or groups. 12

noncontent responding (also referred to as the concept of response sets) The tendency of some people to respond to the questions on some basis that is unrelated to the question content. One example is the response set of acquiescence or yea saying. This is the tendency to simply agree with the questionnaire items, regardless of the content of those items. 39

nonshared environmental influences Features of the environment that siblings do not share. Some children might get special or different treatment from their parents, they might have different groups of friends, they might be sent to different schools, or one might go to summer camp while the other stays home each summer. These features are called "nonshared" because they are experienced differently by different siblings. 173

norepinephrine A neurotransmitter involved in activating the sympathetic nervous system for flight or fight. 211

novelty seeking In Cloninger's tridimensional personality model, the personality trait of novelty seeking is based on low levels of dopamine. Low levels of dopamine create a drive state to obtain substances or experiences that increase dopamine. Novelty and thrills and excitement can make up for low levels of dopamine, and so novelty-seeking behavior is thought to result from low levels of this neurotransmitter. 211

O

objectifying cognition Processing information by relating it to objective facts. This style of thinking stands in contrast to personalizing cognitions. 367

objective anxiety Fear occurs in response to some real, external threat to the person. For example, being confronted by a large, aggressive-looking man with a knife while taking a shortcut through an alley would elicit objective anxiety (fear) in most people. 275

objective self-awareness Seeing oneself as an object of others' attention. Often, objective self-awareness is experienced as shyness, and for some people this is a chronic problem. Although objective self-awareness can lead to periods of social sensitivity, this ability to consider oneself from an outside perspective is the beginning of a social identity. 436

object relations theory Places an emphasis on early childhood relationships. While this theory has several versions that differ from each other in emphasis, all the versions have at their core a set of basic assumptions: that the internal wishes, desires, and urges of the child are not as important as his or her developing relationships with significant external others, particularly parents, and that the others, particularly the mother, become internalized by the child in the form of mental objects.   317

observer-report data (O-data)   The impressions and evaluations others make of a person whom they come into contact with. For every individual, there are dozens of observers who form such impressions. Observer-report methods capitalize on these sources and provide tools for gathering information about a person's personality. Observers may have access to information not attainable through other sources, and multiple observers can be used to assess each individual. Typically, a more valid and reliable assessment of personality can be achieved when multiple observers are used.   27

obsessive-compulsive personality disorder   The obsessive-compulsive personality is preoccupied with order and strives to be perfect. The high need for order can manifest itself in the person's attention to details, however trivial, and fondness for rules, rituals, schedules, and procedures. Another characteristic is a devotion to work at the expense of leisure and friendships. Obsessive-compulsive persons tend to work harder than they need to.   612

oedipal conflict   For boys, the main conflict in Freud's phallic stage. It is a boy's unconscious wish to have his mother all to himself by eliminating the father. (Oedipus is a character in a Greek myth who unknowingly kills his father and marries his mother.)   284

optimal level of arousal   Hebb believed that people are motivated to reach an optimal level of arousal. If they are underaroused relative to this level, an increase in arousal is rewarding; conversely, if they are overaroused, a decrease in arousal is rewarding. By optimal level of arousal, Hebb meant a level that is "just right" for any given task.   205

optimistic bias   Most people generally underestimate their risks, with the average person rating his or her risk as below what is the true average. This has been referred to as

the optimistic bias, and it may actually lead people in general to ignore or minimize the risks inherent in life or to take more risks than they should.   568

optimistic explanatory style   A style that emphasizes external, temporary, and specific causes of events.   382

oral stage   The first stage in Freud's psychosexual stages of development. This stage occurs during the initial 18 months after birth. During this time, the main sources of pleasure and tension reduction are the mouth, lips, and tongue. Adults who still obtain pleasure from "taking in," especially through the mouth (e.g., people who overeat or smoke or talk too much) might be fixated at this stage.   283

organized and enduring   "Organized" means that the psychological traits and mechanisms for a given person are not simply a random collection of elements. Rather, personality is coherent because the mechanisms and traits are linked to one another in an organized fashion. "Enduring" means that the psychological traits are generally consistent over time, particularly in adulthood, and over situations.   7

orthogonality   Discussed in terms of circumplex models, orthogonality specifies that traits that are perpendicular to each other on the model (at 90 degrees of separation, or at right angles to each other) are unrelated to each other. In general, the term "orthogonal" is used to describe a zero correlation between traits.   73

ought self   A person's understanding of what others want them to be.   441

overt and covert integrity measures   Both are self-report measures of integrity used in business and industry. Overt measures include questions directly related to past violations of workplace integrity, such as excessive absenteeism or theft. Covert measures include questions that are indirectly related to integrity, such as questions about personality traits that are correlated with workplace integrity, such as conscientiousness.   107

P

pain tolerance   The degree to which people can tolerate pain, which shows wide differences between persons. Petrie believed that individual

differences in pain tolerance originated in the nervous system. She developed a theory that people with low pain tolerance had a nervous system that amplified or augmented the subjective impact of sensory input. In contrast, people who could tolerate pain well were thought to have a nervous system that dampened or reduced the effects of sensory stimulation.   373

paranoid personality disorder   The paranoid personality is extremely distrustful of others and sees others as a constant threat. Such a person assumes that others are out to exploit and deceive them, even though there is no good evidence to support this assumption. Paranoid personalities feel that they have been injured by other persons and are preoccupied with doubts about the motivations of others. The paranoid personality often misinterprets social events and holds resentments toward others for slights or perceived insults.   608

parsimony   The fewer premises and assumptions a theory contains, the greater its parsimony. This does not mean that simple theories are always better than complex ones. Due to the complexity of the human personality, a complex theory—that is, one containing many premises—may ultimately be necessary for adequate personality theories.   20

passive genotype–environment correlation   Occurs when parents provide both genes and environment to children, yet the children do nothing to obtain that environment.   176

penis envy   The female counterpart of castration anxiety, which occurs during the phallic stage of psychosexual development for girls around 3 to 5 years of age.   284

people–things dimension   Brian Little's people–things dimension of personality refers to the nature of vocational interests. Those at the "things" end of the dimension like vocations that deal with impersonal tasks—machines, tools, or materials. Examples include carpenter, auto mechanic, building contractor, tool maker, or farmer. Those scoring toward the "people" end of the dimension prefer social occupations that involve thinking about others, caring for others, or directing others. Examples include high school teacher, social worker, or religious counselor.   501

percentage of variance   Individuals vary or are different from each other, and this variability can be partitioned into percentages that are related to separate causes or separate variables. An example is the percentages of variance in some trait that are related to genetics, the shared environment, and the unshared environment. Another example would be the percentage of variance in happiness scores that are related to various demographic variables, such as income, gender, and age.   159

perception   One of the three levels of cognition that are of interest to personality psychologists. Perception is the process of imposing order on the information our sense organs take in. Even at the level of perception, what we "see" in the world can be quite different from person to person.   367

perceptual sensitivity   The ability to detect subtle stimuli from the environment.   494

person–environment interaction   A person's interactions with situations include perceptions, selections, evocations, and manipulations. *Perceptions* refer to how we "see" or interpret an environment. *Selection* describes the manner in which we choose situations—such as our friends, our hobbies, our college classes, and our careers. *Evocations* refer to the reactions we produce in others, often quite unintentionally. *Manipulations* refer to the ways in which we attempt to influence others.   8

person–situation interaction   The person–situation interaction trait theory states that one has to take into account both particular situations (e.g., frustration) and personality traits (e.g., hot temper) when understanding a behavior.   92

personal construct   A belief or concept that summarizes a set of observations or version of reality, unique to an individual, which that person routinely uses to interpret and predict events.   376

personal project   A set of relevant actions intended to achieve a goal that a person has selected. Psychologist Brian Little believes that personal projects make natural units for understanding the working of personality, because they reflect how people face up to the

serious business of navigating through daily life.   383

personality   The set of psychological traits and mechanisms within the individual that are organized and relatively enduring and that influence his or her interactions with, and adaptations to, the environment (including the intrapsychic, physical, and social environment).   4

personality coherence   Changes in the manifestations of personality variables over time, even as the underlying characteristics remain stable. The notion of personality coherence includes both elements of continuity and elements of change: continuity in the underlying trait but change in the outward manifestation of that trait. For example, an emotionally unstable child might frequently cry and throw temper tantrums, whereas as an adult such a person might frequently worry and complain. The manifestation might change, even though the trait stays stable.   125

personality-descriptive nouns   As described by Saucier, personality-descriptive nouns differ in their content emphases from personality taxonomies based on adjectives and may be more precise. In Saucier's 2003 work on personality nouns, he discovered eight factors, including "Dumbbell," "Babe/Cutie," "Philosopher," "Lawbreaker," "Joker," and "Jock."   83

personality development   The continuities, consistencies, and stabilities in people over time, and the ways in which people change over time.   124

personality disorder   An enduring pattern of experience and behavior that differs greatly from the expectations of the individual's culture. The disorder is usually manifest in more than one of the following areas: the way a person thinks, feels, gets along with others, or controls personal behavior. To be classed as a personality disorder, the pattern must *not* result from drug abuse, medication, or a medical condition such as head trauma.   589

personalizing cognition   Processing information by relating it to a similar event in your own life. This style of processing information occurs when people interpret a new event in a personally relevant manner. For example, they might see a car accident

and start thinking about the time they were in a car accident.   367

personnel selection   Employers sometimes use personality tests to select people especially suitable for a specific job. Alternatively, the employer may want to use personality assessments to deselect, or screen out, people with specific traits. In both cases an employer is concerned with selecting the right person for a specific position from among a pool of applicants.   106

perspective taking   A final unfolding of the self-concept during the teen years; the ability to take the perspectives of others, or to see oneself as others do, to step outside of one's self and imagine how one appears to other people. This is why many teenagers go through a period of extreme self-consciousness during this time, focusing much of their energy on how they appear to others.   436

pessimistic explanatory style   Puts a person at risk for feelings of helplessness and poor adjustment, and emphasizes internal, stable, and global causes for bad events. It is the opposite of optimistic explanatory style.   382

phallic stage   The third stage in Freud's psychosexual stages of development. It occurs between three and five years of age, during which time the child discovers that he has (or she discovers that she does not have) a penis. This stage also includes the awakening of sexual desire directed, according to Freud, toward the parent of the opposite sex.   284

phenotypic variance   Observed individual differences, such as in height, weight, or personality.   159

physiological needs   The base of Maslow's need hierarchy. These include those needs that are of prime importance to the immediate survival of the individual (the need for food, water, air, sleep) as well as to the long-term survival of the species (the need for sex).   347

physiological systems   Organ systems within the body; for example, the nervous system (including the brain and nerves), the cardiac system (including the heart, arteries, and veins), and the musculoskeletal system (including the muscles and bones which make all movements and behaviors possible).   186

pleasure principle   The desire for immediate gratification. The id operates according to the pleasure principle; therefore, it does not listen to reason, does not follow logic, has no values or morals (other than immediate gratification), and has very little patience.   270

positive illusions   Some researchers believe that part of being happy is to have positive illusions about the self—an inflated view of one's own characteristics as a good, able, and desirable person—as this characteristic appears to be part of emotional well-being (Taylor, 1989; Taylor et al., 2000).   402

positive reappraisal   A cognitive process whereby a person focuses on the good in what is happening or has happened to them. Folkman and Moskowitz note that forms of this positive coping strategy include seeing opportunities for personal growth or seeing how one's own efforts can benefit other people.   567

positive regard   According to Rogers, all children are born wanting to be loved and accepted by their parents and others. He called this inborn need the desire for positive regard.   353

positive self-regard   According to Rogers, people who have received positive regard from others develop a sense of positive self-regard; they accept themselves, even their own weaknesses and shortcomings. People with high positive self-regard trust themselves, follow their own interests, and rely on their feelings to guide them to do the right thing.   354

possible selves   The notion of possible selves can be viewed in a number of ways, but two are especially important. The first pertains to the desired self—the person we wish to become. The second pertains to our feared self—the sort of person we do not wish to become.   440

postmodernism   In personality psychology, the notion that reality is a construct, that every person and culture has its own unique version of reality, and that no single version of reality is more valid or more privileged than another.   376

posttraumatic stress disorder (PTSD)   A syndrome that occurs in some individuals after experiencing or witnessing life-threatening events, such as military combat, natural disasters, terrorist attacks, serious accidents, or violent personal assaults (e.g., rape). Those who suffer from PTSD often relive the trigger experience for years through nightmares or intense flashbacks; have difficulty sleeping; report physical complaints; have flattened emotions; and feel detached or estranged from others. These symptoms can be severe and last long enough to significantly impair the individual's daily life, health, relationships, and career.   563

power stress   According to David McClelland, when people do not get their way, or when their power is challenged or blocked, they are likely to show strong stress responses. This stress has been linked to diminished immune function and increased illness in longitudinal studies.   342

preconscious   Any information that a person is not presently aware of, but that could easily be retrieved and made conscious, is found in the preconscious mind.   266

predictive validity   Whether a test predicts criteria external to the test (also referred to as criterion validity)   42

predisposition model   In health psychology, the predisposition model suggests that associations may exist between personality and illness because a third variable is causing them both.   556

prefrontal cortex   Area of the brain found to be highly active in the control of emotions. Many people who have committed violent acts exhibit a neurological deficit in the frontal areas, portions of the brain assumed to be responsible for regulating negative emotions.   415

press   Need-relevant aspects of the environment. A person's need for intimacy, for example, won't affect that person's behavior without an appropriate environmental press (such as the presence of friendly people).   331

prevalence   The total number of cases that are present within a given population during a particular period of time.   614

prevention focus   One focus of self-regulation where the person is concerned with protection, safety, and the prevention of negative outcomes and failures. Behaviors with a prevention focus are characterized by vigilance, caution, and attempts to prevent negative outcomes.   386

Price Waterhouse v. Hopkins   A Supreme Court case in which Ann Hopkins sued her employer, Price Waterhouse, claiming that they had discriminated against her on the basis of sex in violation of Title VII of the Civil Rights Act, on the theory that her promotion denial had been based on sexual stereotyping. The Supreme Court accepted the argument that gender stereotyping does exist and that it can create a bias against women in the workplace that is not permissible under Title VII of the Civil Rights Act. By court order Ann Hopkins was made a full partner in her accounting firm.   109

primary appraisal   According to Lazarus, in order for stress to be evoked for a person, two cognitive events must occur. The first cognitive event, called the primary appraisal, is for the person to perceive that the event is a threat to his or her personal goals. See also *secondary appraisal*.   564

primary process thinking   Thinking without the logical rules of conscious thought or an anchor in reality. Dreams and fantasies are examples of primary process thinking. Although primary process thought does not follow the normal rules of reality (e.g., in dreams people might fly or walk through walls), Freud believed there were principles at work in primary process thought and that these principles could be discovered.   270

priming   Technique to make associated material more accessible to conscious awareness than material that is not primed. Research using subliminal primes demonstrates that information can get into the mind, and have some influence on it, without going through conscious experience.   306

private self-concept   The development of an inner, private self-concept is a major but often difficult development in the growth of the self-concept. It may start out with children developing an imaginary friend, someone only they can see or hear. This imaginary friend may actually be children's first attempt to communicate to their parents that they know there is a secret part, an inner part, to their understanding of their self. Later, children develop the full realization that only they have access to their own thoughts, feelings, and desires, and that no one else can know this part of them unless they choose to tell them.   435

problem-focused coping   Thoughts and behaviors that manage or solve the underlying cause of stress. Folkman and Moskowitz note that focusing on solving problems, even little ones, can give a person a positive sense of control even in the most stressful and uncontrollable circumstances.   567

projection   A defense mechanism based on the notion that sometimes we see in others those traits and desires that we find most upsetting in ourselves. We literally "project" (i.e., attribute) our own unacceptable qualities onto others.   280

projective hypothesis   The idea that what a person "sees" in an ambiguous figure, such as an inkblot, reflects his or her personality. People are thought to project their own personalities into what they report seeing in such an ambiguous stimulus.   288

projective techniques   A person is presented with an ambiguous stimulus and is then asked to impose some order on the stimulus, such as asking what the person sees in an inkblot. What the person sees is interpreted to reveal something about his or her personality. The person presumably "projects" his or her concerns, conflicts, traits, and ways of seeing or dealing with the world onto the ambiguous stimulus. The most famous projective technique for assessing personality is the Rorschach inkblot test.   34

promotion focus   One focus of self-regulation whereby the person is concerned with advancement, growth, and accomplishments. Behaviors with a promotion focus are characterized by eagerness, approach, and "going for the gold."   386

psychic energy   According to Sigmund Freud, a source of energy within each person that motivates him or her to do one thing and not another. In Freud's view, it is this energy that motivates all human activity.   264

psychoanalysis   A theory of personality and a method of psychotherapy (a technique for helping individuals who are experiencing some mental disorder or even relatively minor problems with living). Psychoanalysis

can be thought of as a theory about the major components and mechanisms of personality, as well as a method for deliberately restructuring personality.   285

psychological mechanisms   Similar to traits, except that mechanisms refer more to the *processes* of personality. For example, most personality mechanisms involve some information-processing activity. A psychological mechanism may make people more sensitive to certain kinds of information from the environment (input), may make them more likely to think about specific options (decision rules), or may guide their behavior toward certain categories of action (outputs).   6

psychological traits   Characteristics that describe ways in which people are unique or different from or similar to each other. Psychological traits include all sorts of aspects of persons that are psychologically meaningful and are stable and consistent aspects of personality.   5

psychological types   A term growing out of Carl Jung's theory implying that people come in types or distinct categories of personality, such as "extraverted types." This view is not widely endorsed by academic or research-oriented psychologists because most personality traits are normally distributed in the population and are best conceived as dimensions of difference, not categories.   114

psychopathology   The study of mental disorders that combines statistical, social, and psychological approaches to diagnosing individual abnormality.   587

psychopathy   A term often used synonymously with the antisocial personality disorder. It is used to refer to individual differences in antisocial characteristics.   252

psychosexual stage theory   According to Freud, all persons pass through a set series of stages in personality development. At each of the first three stages, young children must face and resolve specific conflicts, which revolve around ways of obtaining a type of sexual gratification. Children seek sexual gratification at each stage by investing libidinal energy in a specific body part. Each stage in the developmental process is named

after the body part in which sexual energy is invested.   282

psychosocial conflicts   As posited by Erik Erikson, psychosocial conflicts occur throughout a person's lifetime and contribute to the ongoing development of personality. He defined psychosocial conflicts as the crises of learning to trust our parents, learning to be autonomous from them, and learning from them how to act as an adult.   309

r

race or gender norming   The Civil Rights Act of 1991 forbids employers from using different norms or cutoff scores for different groups of people. For example, it would be illegal for a company to set a higher threshold for women than men on their selection test.   111

random assignment   Assignment in an experiment that is conducted randomly. If an experiment has manipulation between groups, random assignment of participants to experimental groups helps ensure that each group is equivalent.   44

rank order stability   Maintaining one's relative position within a group over time. Between ages 14 and 20, for example, most people become taller. But the rank order of heights tends to remain fairly stable because this form of development affects all people pretty much the same. The tall people at 14 fall generally toward the tall end of the distribution at age 20. The same can apply to personality traits. If people tend to maintain their position on dominance or extraversion relative to the other members of the group over time, then we say that there is high rank order stability to the personality characteristic. Conversely, if people fail to maintain their rank order, we say that the group has displayed rank order instability or rank order change.   124

rank order stability   The maintenance of individual position within the group.   91

rationalization   A defense mechanism that involves generating acceptable reasons for outcomes that might otherwise be unacceptable. The goal is to reduce anxiety by coming up with an explanation for some event that is easier to accept than the "real" reason.   280

reaction formation   A defense mechanism that refers to an attempt to stifle the expression of an unacceptable urge; a person may continually display a flurry of behavior that indicates the opposite impulse. Reaction formation makes it possible for psychoanalysts to predict that sometimes people will do exactly the opposite of what you might otherwise think they would do. It also alerts us to be sensitive to instances when a person is doing something in excess. One of the hallmarks of reaction formation is excessive behavior.   280

reactive genotype–environment correlation   Occurs when parents (or others) respond to children differently depending on their genotype.   176

reactively heritable   Traits that are secondary consequences of heritable traits.   250

reality principle   In psychoanalysis, it is the counterpart of the pleasure principle. It refers to guiding behavior according to the demands of reality and relies on the strengths of the ego to provide such guidance.   271

reciprocal causality   The notion that causality can move in two directions; for example, helping others can lead to happiness, and happiness can lead one to be more helpful to others.   404

reducer/augmenter theory   Petrie's reducer/augmenter theory refers to the dimension along which people differ in their reaction to sensory stimulation; some appear to reduce sensory stimulation, some appear to augment stimulation.   373

reinforcement sensitivity theory   Gray's biological theory of personality. Based on recent brain function research with animals, Gray constructed a model of human personality based on two hypothesized biological systems in the brain: the behavioral activation system (which is responsive to incentives, such as cues for reward, and regulates approach behavior) and the behavioral inhibition system (which is responsive to cues for punishment, frustration, and uncertainty).   201

reliability   The degree to which an obtained measure represents the "true" level of the trait being measured. For example, if a person has a "true" IQ of 115, then a perfectly reliable measure of IQ will yield a score of 115 for that person. Moreover, a truly reliable

measure of IQ would yield the same score of 115 each time it was administered to the person. Personality psychologists prefer reliable measures so that the scores accurately reflect each person's true level of the personality characteristic being measured.   38

repeated measurement   A way to estimate the reliability of a measure. There are different forms of repeated measurement, and hence different versions of reliability. A common procedure is to repeat the same measurement over time, say at an interval of a month apart, for the same sample of persons. If the two tests are highly correlated between the first and second testing, yielding similar scores for most people, then the resulting measure is said to have high test-retest reliability.   38

Repetition Compulsion   The idea that people recreate or repeat their interpersonal problems over and over with different people in their lives. This notion underlies the psychoanalytic transference, wherein the patient recreates the interpersonal difficulties they have in their everyday life with the analyst during the course of their treatment.   290

repression   One of the first defense mechanisms discussed by Freud; refers to the process of preventing unacceptable thoughts, feelings, or urges from reaching conscious awareness.   276

resistance   When a patient's defenses are threatened by a probing psychoanalyst, the patient may unconsciously set up obstacles to progress. This stage of psychoanalysis is called resistance. Resistance signifies that important unconscious material is coming to the fore. The resistance itself becomes an integral part of the interpretations the analyst offers to the patient.   289

resistance stage   The second stage in Selye's general adaptation syndrome (GAS). Here the body is using its resources at an above-average rate, even though the immediate fight-or-flight response has subsided. Stress is being resisted, but the effort is making demands on the person's resources and energy.   559

response sets   The tendency of some people to respond to the questions on

some basis that is unrelated to the question content. Sometimes this is referred to as noncontent responding. One example is the response set of acquiescence or yea saying. This is the tendency to simply agree with the questionnaire items, regardless of the content of those items.   39

responsibility training   Life experiences that provide opportunities to learn to behave responsibly, such as having younger siblings to take care of while growing up. Moderates the gender difference in impulsive behaviors associated with need for power.   341

restricted sexual strategy   According to Gangestad and Simpson (1990), a woman seeking a high-investing mate would adopt a restricted sexual strategy marked by delayed intercourse and prolonged courtship. This would enable her to assess the man's level of commitment, detect the existence of prior commitments to other women and/or children, and simultaneously signal to the man the woman's sexual fidelity and, hence, assure him of his paternity of future offspring.   251

reward dependence   In Cloninger's tridimensional personality model, the personality trait of reward dependence is associated with low levels of norepinephrine. People high on this trait are persistent; they continue to act in ways that produced reward. They work long hours, put a lot of effort into their work, and will often continue striving after others have given up.   211

right to privacy   Perhaps the largest issue of legal concern for employers using personality testing is privacy. The right to privacy in employment settings grows out of the broader concept of the right to privacy. Cases that charge an invasion-of-privacy claim against an employer can be based on the federal constitution, state constitutions and statutes, and common law.   111

rite of passage   Some cultures and religions institute a rite of passage ritual, usually around adolescence, which typically is a ceremony that initiates a child into adulthood. After such ceremonies, the adolescent is sometimes given a new name, bestowing a new adult identity.   311

Rod and Frame Test (RFT)   An apparatus to research the cues that people use in judging orientation in space. The participant sits in a darkened room and is instructed to watch a glowing rod surrounded by a glowing square frame. The experimenter can adjust the tilt of the rod, the frame, and the participant's chair. The participant's task is to adjust the rod by turning a dial so that the rod is perfectly upright. To do this accurately, the participant has to ignore cues in the visual field in which the rod appears. This test measures the personality dimension of field dependence–independence.   369

rumination   Repeatedly focusing on one's symptoms or distress (e.g., "Why do I continue to feel so bad about myself?" or "Why doesn't my boss like me?"). Rumination is a key contributor to women's greater experience of depressive symptoms.   502

S

safety needs   The second to lowest level of Maslow's need hierarchy. These needs have to do with shelter and security, such as having a place to live and being free from the threat of danger. Maslow believed that building a life that was orderly, structured, and predictable also fell under safety needs.   347

schizoid personality disorder   The schizoid personality is split off (schism) or detached from normal social relations. The schizoid person simply appears to have no need or desire for intimate relationships or even friendships. Family life usually does not mean much to such people, and they do not obtain satisfaction from being part of a group. They have few or no close friends, and they would rather spend time by themselves than with others.   603

schizotypal personality disorder
Whereas the schizoid person is indifferent to social interaction, the schizotypal personality is acutely uncomfortable in social relationships. Schizotypes are anxious in social situations, especially if those situations involve strangers. Schizotypal persons also feel that they are different from others, or that they do not fit in with the group. They tend to be suspicious of others and are seen as odd and eccentric.   603

scientific standards for evaluating personality theories   The five key standards are comprehensiveness, heuristic value, testability, parsimony,

and compatibility and integration across domains and levels.   19

secondary appraisal   According to Lazarus, in order for stress to be evoked for a person, two cognitive events must occur. The second necessary cognitive event, called the secondary appraisal, is when the person concludes that he or she does not have the resources to cope with the demands of the threatening event. See *primary appraisal*.   564

secondary process thinking   The ego engages in secondary process thinking, which refers to the development and devising of strategies for problem solving and obtaining satisfaction. Often this process involves taking into account the constraints of physical reality, about when and how to express some desire or urge. See *primary process thinking*.   271

secure relationship style   In Hazan and Shaver's secure relationship style, the adult has few problems developing satisfying friendships and relationships. Secure people trust others and develop bonds with others.   320

securely attached   Securely attached infants in Ainsworth's strange situation stoically endured the separation and went about exploring the room, waiting patiently, or even approaching the stranger and sometimes wanting to be held by the stranger. When the mother returned, these infants were glad to see her, typically interacted with her for a while, then went back to exploring the new environment. They seemed confident the mother would return. Approximately 66 percent of infants fall into this category.   319

selective breeding   One method of doing behavior genetic research. Researchers might identify a trait and then see if they can selectively breed animals to possess that trait. This can occur only if the trait has a genetic basis. For example, dogs that possess certain desired characteristics, such as a sociable disposition, might be selectively bred to see if this disposition can be increased in frequency among offspring. Traits that are based on learning cannot be selectively bred for.   162

selective placement   If adopted children are placed with adoptive parents who are similar to their birth parents, this may inflate the

correlations between the adopted children and their adoptive parents. In this case, the resulting inflated correlations would artificially inflate estimates of environmental influence because the correlation would appear to be due to the environment provided by the adoptive parent. There does not seem to be selective placement, and so this potential problem is not a problem in actual studies (Plomin et al., 1990).   166

self-actualization need   Maslow defines self-actualization as becoming "more and more what one idiosyncratically is, to become everything that one is capable of becoming" (1970, p. 46). The pinnacle of Maslow's need hierarchy is the need for self-actualization. Maslow was concerned with describing self-actualization; the work of Carl Rogers was focused on how people achieve self-actualization.   348

self-attributed motivation
McClelland argued that self-attributed motivation is primarily a person's self-awareness of his or her own conscious motives. These self-attributed motives reflect a person's conscious awareness about what is important to him or her. As such, they represent part of the individual's conscious self-understanding. McClelland has argued that self-attributed motives predict responses to immediate and specific situations and to choice behaviors and attitudes. See *implicit motivation*.   334

self-complexity   The view that each of us has many roles and many aspects to our self-concepts. However, for some of us, our self-concepts are rather simple, being made up of just a few large categories. Other people may have a more complex or differentiated self-concept. For people with high self-complexity, a failure in any one aspect of the self (such as a relationship that breaks apart) is buffered because there are many other aspects of the self that are unaffected by that event. However, for persons low in self-complexity, the same event might be seen as devastating because they define themselves mainly in terms of this one aspect.   445

self-concept   The way a person sees, understands, and defines himself or herself.   431

self-efficacy   A concept related to optimism and developed by Bandura. The belief that one can behave in ways necessary to achieve some desired outcome. Self-efficacy also refers to the confidence one has in one's ability to perform the actions needed to achieve some specific outcome.   385

self-enhancement   The tendency to describe and present oneself using positive or socially valued attributes, such as kind, understanding, intelligent, and industrious. Tendencies toward self-enhancement tend to be stable over time, and hence are enduring features of personality (Baumeister, 1997).   534

self-esteem   "The extent to which one perceives oneself as relatively close to being the person one wants to be and/ or as relatively distant from being the kind of person one does not want to be, with respect to person-qualities one positively and negatively values" (Block & Robbins, 1993, p. 911).   139

self-esteem variability   An individual difference characteristic referring to how much a person's self-esteem fluctuates or changes over time. It is uncorrelated with mean level of self-esteem.   449

self-fulfilling prophecy   The tendency for a belief to become reality. For example, a person who thinks he or she is a "total failure" will often act like a total failure and may even give up trying to do better, thus creating a self-fulfilling prophecy.   420

self-guides   The ideal self and the ought self act as self-guides, providing the standards that one uses to organize self-relevant information and motivate appropriate behaviors to bring the self in line with these self-guides.   441

self-handicapping   Situations in which people deliberately do things that increase the probability that they will fail.   448

self-report data (S-data) Information a person verbally reveals about themselves, often based on questionnaire or interview. Self-report data can be obtained through a variety of means, including interviews that pose questions to a person, periodic reports by a person to record the events as they happen, and questionnaires of various sorts.   24

self-schema   (schemata is plural, schema is singular) The specific knowledge structure, or cognitive

representation, of the self-concept. Self-schemas are the network of associated building blocks of the self-concept.   440

self-serving bias   The common tendency for people to take credit for success yet to deny responsibility for failure.   315

sensation seeking   A dimension of personality postulated to have a physiological basis. It refers to the tendency to seek out thrilling and exciting activities, to take risks, and to avoid boredom.   205

sensory deprivation   Often done in a sound-proof chamber containing water in which a person floats, in total darkness, such that sensory input is reduced to a minimum. Researchers use sensory deprivation chambers to see what happens when a person is deprived of sensory input.   205

separation anxiety   Children experiencing separation anxiety react negatively to separation from their mother (or primary caretaker), becoming agitated and distressed when their mothers leave. Most primates exhibit separation anxiety.   318

serotonin   A neurotransmitter that plays a role in depression and other mood disorders. Drugs such as Prozac, Zoloft, and Paxil block the reuptake of serotonin, leaving it in the synapse longer, leading depressed persons to feel less depressed.   210

sex differences   An average difference between women and men on certain characteristics such as height, body fat distribution, or personality characteristics, with no prejudgment about the cause of the difference.   489

sexual selection   The evolution of characteristics because of their mating benefits rather than because of their survival benefits. According to Darwin, sexual selection takes two forms: intrasexual competition and intersexual selection.   225

sexually dimorphic   Species that show high variance in reproduction within one sex tend to be highly sexually dimorphic, or highly different in size and structure. The more intense the effective polygyny, the more dimorphic the sexes are in size and form (Trivers, 1985).   239

shared environmental influences Features of the environment that siblings share; for example, the number

of books in the home, the presence or absence of a TV and VCR, quality and quantity of the food in the home, the values and attitudes of the parent, and the schools, church, synagogue, or temple the parents send the children to.   173

shyness   A tendency to feel tense, worried, or anxious during social interactions, or even when anticipating a social interaction (Addison & Schmidt, 1999). Shyness is a common phenomenon, and more than 90 percent of the population reports experiencing shyness at some point during their lives (Zimbardo, 1977). Some people, however, seem to be dispositionally shy—they tend to feel awkward in most social situations and so tend to avoid situations in which they will be forced to interact with people.   471

situational selection   A form of interactionism that refers to the tendency to choose or select the situations in which one finds oneself. In other words, people typically do not find themselves in random situations in their natural lives. Instead, they select or choose the situations in which they will spend their time.   96

situational specificity   The view that behavior is determined by aspects of the situation, such as reward contingencies.   94

situationism   A theoretical position in personality psychology that states that situational differences, rather than underlying personality traits, determine behavior. For example, how friendly a person will behave or how much need for achievement a person displays will depend on the situation, not the traits a person possesses.   92

skin conductance   The degree to which the skin carries (or conducts) electricity, which locate depends on the amount of water present in the skin.   191

social and cultural domain Personality affects, and is affected by, the social and cultural context in which it is found. Different cultures may bring out different facets of our personalities in manifest behavior. The capacities we display may depend to a large extent on what is acceptable in and encouraged by our culture. At the level of individual differences within cultures, personality plays itself out in the social sphere. One important social sphere concerns relations between men and women.   17

social anxiety   Discomfort related to social interactions, or even to the anticipation of social interactions. Socially anxious persons appear to be overly concerned about what others will think. Baumeister and Tice propose that social anxiety is a species-typical adaptation that functions to prevent social exclusion.   232

social attention   The goal and payback for surgent or extraverted behavior. By being the center of attention, the extravert seeks to gain the approval of others and, in many cases, through tacit approval controls or directs others.   78

social categories   The cognitive component that describes the ways individuals classify other people into groups, such as "cads" and "dads." This cognitive component is one aspect of stereotyping.   507

social class   Variability between people based primarily on economic, educational, and employment variables. In terms of within-culture variation, social class can have an effect on personality (Kohn et al., 1990). For example, lower-class parents tend to emphasize the importance of obedience to authority, whereas higher-status parents tend to emphasize the importance of self-direction and not conforming to the dictates of others.   536

social comparison   When people compare their skills and abilities with others   434

social desirability   Socially desirable responding refers to the tendency to answer items in such a way as to come across as socially attractive or likable. People responding in this manner want to make a good impression, to appear to be well adjusted, to be a "good citizen."   39

social identity   Identity refers to the social aspects of the self, that part of ourselves we use to create an impression, to let other people know who we are and what can be expected from us. Identity is different from the self-concept because identity refers mainly to aspects of the self that are socially observable or publicly available outward, such as ethnicity or gender or age. Nevertheless, the social aspects of identity can become important aspects of the self-concept.   431

social learning theory   A general theoretical view emphasizing the ways in which the presence of others influence people's behavior, thoughts, or feelings. Often combined with learning principles, the emphasis is on how people acquire beliefs, values, skills, attitudes, and patterns of behavior through social experiences.   510

social power   Horney, in reinterpreting Freud's concept of penis envy, taught that the penis was a symbol of social power rather than some organ that women actually desired. Horney wrote that girls realize, at an early age, that they are being denied social power because of their gender. She argued that girls did not really have a secret desire to become boys. Rather, she taught, girls desire the social power and preferences given to boys in the culture at that time.   314

social role theory   According to social role theory, sex differences originate because men and women are distributed differentially into occupational and family roles. Men, for example, are expected to assume the breadwinning role. Women are expected to assume the housewife role. Over time, children presumably learn the behaviors that are linked to these roles.   510

socialization theory   The notion that boys and girls become different because boys are reinforced by parents, teachers, and the media for being "masculine," and girls for being "feminine." This is probably the most widely held theory of sex differences in personality.   509

sociosexual orientation   According to Gangestad and Simpson's theory of sociosexual orientation, men and women will pursue one of two alternative sexual relationship strategies. The first mating strategy entails seeking a single committed relationship characterized by monogamy and tremendous investment in children. The second sexual strategy is characterized by a greater degree of promiscuity, more partner switching, and less investment in children.   66

spreading activation   Roediger and McDermott applied the spreading activation model of memory to account for false memories. This model holds that mental elements (like words or images) are stored in memory along with associations to other elements in memory. For example, *doctor* is associated with *nurse* in most people's memories because of the close connection or similarity between these concepts. Consequently, a person recalling some medical event might falsely recall a nurse rather than a doctor doing something.   302

stability coefficients   The correlations between the same measures obtained at two different points in time. Stability coefficients are also called test-retest reliability coefficients.   131

stage model of development Implies that people go through stages in a certain order, and that a specific issue characterizes each stage.   309

state levels   A concept that can be applied to motives and emotions, state levels refer to a person's momentary amount of a specific need or emotion, which can fluctuate with specific circumstances.   333

statistical approach   Having a large number of people rate themselves on certain items, and then employing a statistical procedure to identify groups or clusters of items that go together. The goal of the statistical approach is to identify the major dimensions or "coordinates" of the personality map.   63

statistically significant   Refers to the probability of finding the results of a research study by chance alone. The generally accepted level of statistical significance is 5 percent, meaning that, if a study were repeated 100 times, the particular result reported would be found by chance only 5 times.   45

strange situation procedure Developed by Ainsworth and her colleagues for studying separation anxiety and for identifying differences between children in how they react to separation from their mothers. In this procedure, a mother and her baby come into a laboratory room. The mother sits down and the child is free to explore the room. After a few minutes an unfamiliar though friendly adult enters the room. The mother gets up and leaves the baby alone with this adult. After a few minutes, the mother comes back into the room and the stranger leaves. The mother is alone with the baby for several more minutes. All the while, the infant is being videotaped so that his or her reactions can later be analyzed.   318

stress   The subjective feeling that is produced by uncontrollable and threatening events. Events that cause stress are called stressors.   553

stressors   Events that cause stress. They appear to have several common attributes: (1) stressors are extreme in some manner, in the sense that they produce a state of feeling overwhelmed or overloaded, that one just cannot take it much longer; (2) stressors often produce opposing tendencies in us, such as wanting and not wanting some activity or object, as in wanting to study but also wanting to put it off as long as possible; and (3) stressors are uncontrollable, outside of our power to influence, such as the exam that we cannot avoid.   559

strong situation   Certain situations that prompt similar behavior from everyone.   95

structured and unstructured   Self-report can take a variety of forms, ranging from open-ended questions to forced-choice true or false questions. Sometimes these are referred to as *unstructured* (open-ended, such as "Tell me about the parties you like the most") and *structured* ("I like loud and crowded parties"; answer true or false) personality tests.   24

style of emotional life   How emotions are experienced. For example, saying that someone is high on mood variability is to say something about the style of his or her emotional life, that his or her emotions change frequently. Compare to the content of emotional life.   400, 423

sublimation   A defense mechanism that refers to the channeling of unacceptable sexual or aggressive instincts into socially desired activities. For Freud, sublimation is the most adaptive defense mechanism. A common example is going out to chop wood when you are angry rather than acting on that anger or even engaging

in other less adaptive defense mechanisms such as displacement.   281

subliminal perception   Perception that bypasses conscious awareness, usually achieved through very brief exposure times, typically less than 30 milliseconds.   306

superego   That part of personality that internalizes the values, morals, and ideals of society. The superego makes us feel guilty, ashamed, or embarrassed when we do something wrong, and makes us feel pride when we do something right. The superego sets moral goals and ideals of perfection and is the source of our judgments that something is good or bad. It is what some people refer to as conscience. The main tool of the superego in enforcing right and wrong is the emotion of guilt.   271

surgency   A cluster of behaviors including approach behavior, high activity, and impulsivity.   494

symbols   Psychoanalysts interpret dreams by deciphering how unacceptable impulses and urges are transformed by the unconscious into symbols in the dream. (For example, parents may be represented as a king and queen; children may be represented as small animals.)   287

Sympathetic Nervous System   That branch of the autonomic nervous system that supports the fight-or-flight response. The sympathetic nervous system is activated when a person feels threatened or experiences strong emotions such as anxiety, guilt, or anger.   191

synonym frequency   In the lexical approach, synonym frequency means that if an attribute has not merely one or two trait adjectives to describe it, but rather six, eight, or ten words, then it is a more important dimension of individual difference.   63

Systemizing   The drive to comprehend how things work, how systems are built, and how inputs into systems produce outputs.   501

t

taxonomy   A technical name given to a classification scheme—the identification and naming of groups within a particular subject field.   478

telemetry   The process by which electrical signals are sent from

electrodes to a polygraph using radio waves instead of wires.   191

temperament   Individual differences that emerge very early in life, are likely to have a heritable basis, and are often involved in behaviors linked with emotionality or arousability.   129

tender-mindedness   A nurturant proclivity, having empathy for others, and being sympathetic with those who are downtrodden.   495

test data (T-data)   A common source of personality-relevant information comes from standardized tests (T-data). In these measures, participants are placed in a standardized testing situation to see if different people react or behave differently to an identical situation. Taking an exam, like the Scholastic Aptitude Test, would be one example of T-data as a measure used to predict success in school.   29

testability   The capacity to render precise predictions that scientists can test empirically. Generally, the testability of a theory is dependent upon the precision of its predictions. If it is impossible to test a theory empirically, the theory is generally discarded.   19

thanatos   Freud postulated that humans have a fundamental instinct toward destruction and that this instinct is often manifest in aggression toward others. The two instincts were usually referred to as libido, for the life instinct, and thanatos, for the death instinct. While thanatos was considered to be the death instinct, Freud also used this term to refer to any urge to destroy, harm, or aggress against others or oneself.   265

thematic apperception test   Developed by Murray and Morgan, this is a projective assessment technique that consists of a set of black and white ambiguous pictures. The person is shown each picture and is told to write a short story interpreting what is happening in each picture. The psychologist then codes the stories for the presence of imagery associated with particular motives. The TAT remains a popular personality assessment technique today.   332

theoretical approach   The theoretical approach to identifying important dimensions of individual differences starts with a theory, which then determines which variables are important. The theoretical strategy dictates in a specific manner which variables are important to measure.   63

theoretical bridge   The connection between two different variables (for instance, dimensions of personality and physiological variables).   191

theoretical constructs   Hypothetical internal entities useful in describing and explaining differences between people   42

theories and beliefs   Beliefs are often personally useful and crucially important to some people, but they are based on leaps of faith, not on reliable facts and systematic observations. Theories, on the other hand, are based on systematic observations that can be repeated by others and that yield similar conclusions.   19

third variable problem   One reason correlations can never prove casuality. It could be that two variables are correlated because some third, unknown variable is causing both.   49

time urgency   A subtrait in the Type A personality. Type A persons hate wasting time. They are always in a hurry and feel under pressure to get the most done in the least amount of time. Often they do two things at once, such as eat while reading a book. Waiting is stressful for them.   576

Title VII of the Civil Rights Act of 1964   A specific section of the Civil Rights Act of 1964 that requires employers to provide equal employment opportunities to all persons, regardless of sex, race, color, religion, or national origin.   107

trait-descriptive adjectives   Words that describe traits, attributes of a person that are reasonably characteristic of the individual and perhaps even enduring over time.   4

trait levels   A concept that can be applied to motives and emotions, trait levels refer to a person's average tendency, or his or her set point, on the specific motive or emotion. The idea is that people differ from each other in their typical or average amount of specific motives or emotions.   333

transactional model   In the transactional model of personality and health, personality has three potential effects: (1) it can influence coping, as in the interactional model; (2) it can influence how the person appraises or interprets the events; and (3) it can

influence exposure to the events themselves.   553

transference   A term from psychoanalytic therapy. It refers to the patient reacting to the analyst as if he or she were an important figure from the patient's own life. The patient displaces past or present (negative and positive) feelings toward someone from his or her own life onto the analyst. The idea behind transference is that the interpersonal problems between a patient and the important people in his or her life will be reenacted in the therapy session with the analyst. This is a specific form of the mechanism of evocation, as described in the material on person-situation interaction.   290

transmitted culture   Representations originally in the mind of one or more persons that are transmitted to the minds of other people. Three examples of cultural variants that appear to be forms of transmitted culture are differences in moral values, self-concept, and levels of self-enhancement. Specific patterns of morality, such as whether it is considered appropriate to eat beef or wrong for a wife to go to the movies without her husband, are specific to certain cultures. These moral values appear to be transmitted from person to person within the culture.   525

traumatic stress   A massive instance of acute stress, the effects of which can reverberate within an individual for years or even a lifetime. It differs from acute stress mainly in terms of its potential to lead to posttraumatic stress disorder.   563

tridimensional personality model   Cloninger's tridimensional personality model ties three specific personality traits to levels of the three neurotransmitters. The first trait is called novelty seeking and is based on low levels of dopamine. The second personality trait is harm avoidance, which he associates with low levels of serotonin. The third trait is reward dependence, which Cloninger sees as related to low levels of norepinephrine.   211

trust   The proclivity to cooperate with others, giving others the benefit of the doubt, and viewing one's fellow human beings as basically good at heart.   495

twin studies   Twin studies estimate heritability by gauging whether identical twins, who share 100 percent of their genes, are more similar to each other than fraternal twins, who share only 50 percent of their genes. Twin studies, and especially studies of twins reared apart, have received tremendous media attention.   163

type A personality   In the 1960s, cardiologists Friedman and Rosenman began to notice that many of their coronary heart disease patients had similar personality traits—they were competitive, aggressive workaholics, were ambitious overachievers, were often hostile, were almost always in a hurry, and rarely relaxed or took it easy. Friedman and Rosenman referred to this as the Type A personality, formally defined as "an action-emotion complex that can be observed in any person who is aggressively involved in a chronic, incessant struggle to achieve more and more in less and less time, and if required to do so, against the opposing efforts of other things or other persons" (1974, p. 37). As assessed by personality psychologists, Type A refers to a syndrome of several traits: (1) achievement motivation and competitiveness; (2) time urgency; and (3) hostility and aggressiveness.   193

Type D personality   A dimension along which individuals differ on two underlying traits: (1) negative affectivity, or the tendency to frequently experience negative emotions across time and situations (e.g., tension, worry, irritability, and anxiety); and (2) social inhibition, or the tendency to inhibit the expression of emotions, thoughts, and behaviors in social interactions. People high on both of these traits are said to have the Type D personality, which places them at risk for poor outcomes once they develop cardiac disease.   578

U

unconditional positive regard   The receipt of affection, love, or respect without having done anything to earn it. For example, a parent's love for a child should be unconditional.   354

unconscious   The unconscious mind is that part of the mind about which the conscious mind has no awareness.   266

Uniform Guidelines on Employee Selection Procedures   The purpose of the guidelines is to provide a set of principles for employee selection that meet the requirements of all federal laws, especially those that prohibit discrimination on the basis of race, color, religion, sex, or national origin. They provide details on the proper use of personality tests and other selection procedures in employment settings.   108

unrestricted mating strategy   According to Gangestad and Simpson (1990), a woman seeking a man for the quality of his genes is not interested in his level of commitment to her. If the man is pursuing a short-term sexual strategy, any delay on the woman's part may deter him from seeking sexual intercourse with her, thus defeating the main adaptive reason for her mating strategy.   251

V

validity   The extent to which a test measures what it claims to measure.   42

validity coefficients   The correlations between a trait measure and measures of different criteria that should relate to the trait. An example might be the correlation between a self-report measure of agreeableness, and the person's roommate reports of how agreeable they are.   131

violation of desire   According to the violation of desire theory of conflict between the sexes, breakups should occur more frequently when one's desires are violated than when they are fulfilled (Buss, 2003). Following this theory, we would predict that people married to others who lack desired characteristics, such as dependability and emotional stability, will more frequently dissolve the marriage.   470

W

Ward's Cove Packing Co. v. Atonio   Ward's Cove Packing Co. was a salmon cannery operating in Alaska. In 1974 the non-White cannery workers started legal action against the company, alleging that a variety of the company's hiring and promotion practices were responsible for racial stratification in the workplace. The claim was advanced under the disparate impact portion of Title VII of the Civil Rights Act. In 1989 the Supreme Court decided on the case in favor of Ward's Cove. The court decided that, even if employees can prove discrimination, the hiring practices may still be considered legal if they serve "legitimate employment goals of the employer." This decision allowed disparate impact if it was in the service of the company. This case prompted Congress to pass the Civil Rights Act of 1991, which contained several important modifications to Title VII of the original act. Most important, however, the new act shifted the burden of proof onto the employer by requiring that it must prove a close connection between disparate impact and the ability to actually perform the job in question.   109

Whorfian hypothesis of linguistic relativity   In 1956, Whorf proposed the theory that language creates thought and experience. According to this hypothesis, the ideas that people can think and the emotions they feel are constrained by the need locate words that happen to exist in their language and culture and with which they use to express them.   540

wish fulfillment   If an urge from the id requires some external object or person, and that object or person is not available, the id may create a mental image or fantasy of that object or person to satisfy its needs. Mental energy is invested in that fantasy and the urge is temporarily satisfied. This process is called wish fulfillment, whereby something unavailable is conjured up and the image of it is temporarily satisfying.   270

within-culture variation   Variations within a particular culture that can arise from several sources, including differences in growing up in various socioeconomic classes, differences in historical era, or differences in the racial context in which one grows up.   536

within the individual   The important sources of personality reside within the individual—that is, people carry the sources of their personality inside themselves—and hence are stable over time and consistent over situations.   7

working models   Early experiences and reactions of the infant to the parents, particularly the mother, become what Bowlby called "working models" for later adult relationships. These working models are internalized in the form of unconscious expectations about relationships.   319

X

xenophobia   The fear of strangers. Characteristics that were probably adaptive in ancestral environments, such as xenophobia, are not necessarily adaptive in modern environments. Some of the personality traits that make up human nature may be vestigial adaptations to an ancestral environment that no longer exists.   228

References

Abdel-Khalek, A. M., and Alansari, B. M. (2004). Gender differences in anxiety among undergraduates from ten Arab countries. *Social Behavior and Personality, 32,* 649–656.

Abe, J.A.A. (2005). The predictive validity of the five-factor model of personality with preschool age children: A nine year follow-up study. *Journal of Research in Personality, 39,* 423–442.

Abelson, R. P. (1985). A variance explanation paradox: When a little is a lot. *Psychological Bulletin, 97,* 129–133.

Abrahamson, A. C., Baker, L. A., and Caspi, A. (2002). Rebellious teens? Genetic and environmental influences on the social attitudes of adolescents. *Journal of Personality and Social Psychology, 83, 6,* 1392–1408.

Ackerman, J. M., and Bargh, J. A. (2010). The purpose-driven life: Commentary on Kenrick et al. (2010). *Perspectives on Psychological Science, 5,* 323–326.

Aczel, B., Lukacs, B., Komlos, J., and Aitken, M.R.F. (2011). Unconscious intuition or conscious analysis? Critical questions for the deliberation-without-attention paradigm. *Judgment and Decision Making, 6,* 351–358.

Adan, A. (1991). Influence of morningness-eveningness preference in the relationship between body temperature and performance: A diurnal study. *Personality and Individual Differences, 12,* 1159–1169.

Adan, A. (1992). The influence of age, work schedule and personality on morningness dimension. *International Journal of Psychophysiology, 12,* 95–99.

Addison, T. L., and Schmidt, L. A. (1999). Are women who are shy reluctant to take risks? Behavioral and psychophysiological correlates. *Journal of Research in Personality, 33,* 352–357.

Affleck, G., and Tennen, H. (1996). Construing benefits from adversity: Adaptational significance and dispositional underpinnings. *Journal of Personality, 64,* 899–922.

Aharon, I., Etcoff, N., Ariely, D., Chabris, C. F., O'Connor, E., and Breiter, H. C. (2001). Beautiful faces have variable reward value: fMRI and behavioral evidence. *Neuron, 32,* 537–551.

Ai, A. L., Peterson, C., and Ubelhor, D. (2002). War-related trauma and symptoms of posttraumatic stress disorder among adult Kosovar refugees. *Journal of Traumatic Stress, 15,* 157–160.

Aigner, M., Eher, R., Fruenhwald, S., Frottier, P., Gutierrez-Lobos, K., and Dwyer, S. M. (2000). Brain abnormalities and violent behavior. *Journal of Psychology and Human Sexuality, 11,* 57–64.

Ainsworth, M. D. (1979). Infant-mother attachment. *American Psychologist, 34,* 932–937.

Ainsworth, M. D., Bell, S. M., and Stayton, D. J. (1972). Individual differences in the development of some attachment behaviors. *Merrill-Palmer Quarterly, 18,* 123–143.

Ainsworth, M. D., and Bowlby, J. (1991). An ethological approach to personality development. *American Psychologist, 46,* 333–341.

Aknin, L. B., Barrington-Leigh, C. P., Dunn, E. W., Helliwell, J. F., Burns, J., Biswas-Diener, R., and . . . Norton, M. I. (2013). Prosocial spending and well-being: Cross-cultural evidence for a psychological universal. *Journal of Personality and Social Psychology, 104*(4), 635–652.

Aldwin, C. M., Spiro, A., III, Levenson, M. R., and Cupertino, A. P. (2001). Longitudinal findings from the normative aging study: III. Personality, individual health trajectories, and mortality. *Psychology and Aging, 16,* 450–465.

Alessandri, G., Caprara, G. V., and De Pascalis, V. (2015). Relations among EEG-alpha asymmetry and positivity personality trait. *Brain and Cognition, 97,* 10–21.

Alexander, R. D., Hoodland, J. L., Howard, R. D., Noonan, K. M., and Sherman, P. W. (1979). Sexual dimorphisms and breeding systems in pinnipeds, ungulates, primates, and humans. In N. A. Chagnon and W. Irons (Eds.), *Evolutionary biology and human social behavior.* North Scituate, MA: Duxbury Press.

Algom, D., Chajut, E., and Lev, S. (2004). A rational look at the emotional Stroop phenomenon: A generic slowdown, not a Stroop effect. *Journal of Experimental Psychology: General, 133,* 323–338.

Alleman, M., Zimprich, D., and Hertzon, C. (2007). Cross-sectional age differences and longitudinal age changes in middle adulthood and old age. *Journal of Personality, 75,* 323–358.

Allemand, M., Gomez, V., and Jackson, J. J. (2010). Personality trait development in midlife: Exploring the impact of psychological turning points. *European Journal of Aging, 7,* 147–155.

Allik, J. (2012). National differences in personality. *Personality and Individual Differences, 53,* 114–117.

Allik, J., and Realo, A. (2009). Editorial: Personality and Culture. *European Journal of Personality, 23,* 149–152.

Allport, G. W. (1937). *Personality: A psychological interpretation.* New York: Holt, Rinehart and Winston.

Allport, G. W. (1961). *Pattern and growth in personality.* New York: Holt, Rinehart and Winston.

Allport, G. W., and Odbert, H. S. (1936). Trait-names: A psycho-lexical study. *Psychological Monographs, 47* (1, Whole No. 211).

Almagor, M., Tellegen, A., and Waller, N. G. (1995). The big seven model: A cross-cultural replication and further exploration of the basic dimensions of natural language trait descriptors. *Journal of Personality and Social Psychology, 69,* 300–307.

Alston, W. P. (1975). Traits, consistency and conceptual alternatives for personality theory. *Journal for the Theory of Social Behavior, 5,* 17–48.

Amelang, M., Herboth, G., and Oefner, I. (1991). A prototype strategy for the construction of a creativity scale. *European Journal of Personality, 5,* 261–285.

American Psychiatric Association. (2013). *Diagnostic and statistical manual of mental disorders* (5th ed.). Washington, DC: Author.

Anastasi, A. (1976). *Psychological testing.* New York: Macmillan.

Anderson, C., and Kilduff, G. J. (2009). Why do dominant personalities attain influence in face-to-face groups? The competence-signaling effects of trait dominance. *Journal of Personality and Social Psychology, 96,* 491–503.

Ando, J., Ono, Y., Yoshimura, K., Onoda, N., Shinohara, M., Kanba, S., and Asai, M. (2002). The genetic structure of Cloninger's seven-factor model of temperament and character in a Japanese sample. *Journal of Personality, 70, 5,* 583–610.

Andrews, J. D. W. (1967). The achievement motive in two types of organizations. *Journal of Personality and Social Psychology, 6,* 163–168.

Angier, N. (1999). *Woman: An intimate geography.* Boston: Houghton Mifflin.

Angleitner, A., and Demtroder, A. I. (1988). Acts and dispositions: A reconsideration of the act frequency approach. *European Journal of Psychology, 2,* 121–141.

Angleitner, A., Buss, D., & Demtröder, A. I. (1990). A cross-cultural comparison using the act frequency approach (AFA) in West Germany and the United States. *European Journal of Personality, 4,* 187–207.

Anusic, I., Lucas, R. E., and Donnellan, M. B. (2012). Cross-sectional age differences in personality: Evidence from nationally representative samples from Switzerland and the United States.

Journal of Research in Personality, 46, 116–120.

Apostolou, M., and Papageorgi, I. (2014). Parental mate choice manipulation tactics: exploring prevalence, sex and personality effects. *Evolutionary Psychology, 12,* 588–620.

Apostolou, M., Zacharia, M., and Frantzides, N. (2015). Children's tactics of mate choice manipulation: Exploring sex differences and personality effects. *Personality and Individual Differences, 80,* 6–11.

Archer, J. (2009). Does sexual selection explain human sex differences in aggression? *Behavioral and Brain Sciences, 32,* 249–311.

Archer, J., and Thanzami, V. (2009). The relation between mate value, entitlement, physical aggression, size and strength among a sample of young Indian men. *Evolution and Human Behavior, 30,* 315–321.

Archontaki, D., Lewis, G. J., and Bates, T. C. (2013). Genetic influences on psychological well-being: A nationally representative twin study. *Journal of Personality, 81*(2), 221–230.

Aron, A., Aron, E. N., Tudor, M., and Nelson, G. (2004). Close relationships as including other in the self. In H. T. Reis and C. E. Rustbult (Eds.), *Close relationships: Key readings* (pp. 365–379). Philadelphia: Taylor and Francis.

Aschoff, J. (1965). Circadian rhythms in man. *Science, 143,* 1427–1432.

Asendorpf, J. B., and Scherer, K. R. (1983). The discrepant repressor: Differentiation between low anxiety, high anxiety, and repression of anxiety by autonomic-facial-verbal patterns of behavior. *Journal of Personality and Social Psychology, 45,* 1334–1346.

Asendorpf, J. B., and Van Aken, M.A.G. (2003). Validity of five personality judgments in childhood: A 9-year longitudinal study. *European Journal of Personality, 32,* 649–656.

Ashmore, R. D. (1990). Sex, gender, and the individual. In L. A. Pervin (Ed.), *Handbook of personality: Theory and research* (pp. 486–526). New York: Guilford Press.

Ashton, M. C. (2007). Self-reports and stereotypes: A comment on McCrae et al. *European Journal of Personality, 21,* 983–986.

Ashton, M. C., and Lee, K. (2005). A defense of the lexical approach to the study of personality. *European Journal of Personality, 19,* 5–24.

Ashton, M. C., Lee, K., and de Vries, R. E. (2014). The HEXACO honesty-humility, agreeableness, and emotionality factors a review of research and theory. *Personality and Social Psychology Review, 18*(2), 139–152.

Ashton, M. C., Lee, K., and Paunonen, S. V. (2002). What is the central feature of extraversion? Social attention versus reward sensitivity. *Journal of Personality and Social Psychology, 83, 1,* 245–252.

Assor, A. (1989). The power motive as an influence on the evaluation of high and low status persons. *Journal of Research in Personality, 23,* 55–69.

Augustine, A. A., Larsen, R. J., Walker, M. S., and Fisher, E. B. (2008). Personality predictors of the time course for lung cancer onset. *Journal of Research in Personality, 42,* 1448–1455.

Averill, J. R. (1975). A semantic atlas of emotional concepts. *Catalog of Selected Documents in Psychology, 5,* 30.

Avinun, R., and Knafo, A. (2013). Parenting as a reaction evoked by children's genotype a meta-analysis of children-as-twins studies. *Personality and Social Psychology Review, 18,* 87–102.

Back, M. D., Schmukle, S. C., and Egloff, B. (2008). How extraverted is honey.bunny77@hotmail.de? Inferring personality from email addresses. *Journal of Research in Personality, 42,* 1116–1122.

Bagby, R. M., Vachon, D. D., Bulmash, E. L., Toneatto, T., Quilty, L. C., and Costa, P. T. (2007). Pathological gambling and the five-factor model of personality. *Personality and Individual Differences, 43,* 873–880.

Bailey, J. M., Dunne, M. P., and Martin, N. G. (2000). Genetic and environmental influences on sexual orientation and its correlates in an Australian twin sample. *Journal of Personality and Social Psychology, 78,* 524–536.

Bailey, S. L., and Heitkemper, M. M. (1991). Morningness–eveningness and early-morning salivary cortisol levels. *Biological Psychology, 32,* 181–192.

Bailey, J. M., Kirk, K. M., Zhu, G., Dunne, M. P., and Martin, N. G. (2000). Do individual differences in sociosexuality represent genetic or environmentally contingent strategies? Evidence from the Australian Twin Registry. *Journal of Personality and Social Psychology, 78,* 537–545.

Bailey, J. M., Pillard, R. C., Neale, M. C., and Agyei, Y. (1993). Heritable factors influence sexual orientation in women. *Archives of General Psychiatry, 50,* 217–223.

Baker, R. A. (1992). *Hidden memories.* Buffalo, NY: Prometheus Books.

Balliet, D., Li, N. P., Macfarlan, S. J., and Van Vugt, M. (2011). Sex differences in cooperation: A meta-analytic review of social dilemmas. *Psychological Bulletin, 137,* 881–909.

Bandura, A. (1977). *Social learning theory.* Englewood Cliffs, NJ: Prentice Hall.

Bandura, A. (1986). The explanatory and predictive scope of self-efficacy theory. *Journal of Social and Clinical Psychology, Special Issue: Self-efficacy theory in contemporary psychology, 4,* 359–373.

Bandura, A. (1989). Human agency in social cognitive theory. *American Psychologist, 44,* 1175–1184.

Bandura, A. (1997). *Self-efficacy: The exercise of control.* New York: Freeman.

Barelds, D.P.H. (2005). Self and partner personality in intimate relationships. *European Journal of Personality, 19,* 501–518.

Barelds, D.P.H., and Dijkstra, P. (2011). Positive illusions about a partner's personality and relationship quality. *Journal of Research in Personality, 45,* 37–43.

Barenbaum, N. B., and Winter, D. G. (2003). Personality. In D. K. Freedheim (Ed.), *Handbook of psychology: History of psychology* (pp. 177–203). New York: Wiley.

Bargh, J. A. (2005). Bypassing the will: Toward demystifying the nonconscious control of social behavior. In R. R. Hassin, J. S. Uleman, and J. A. Bargh (Eds.), *The new unconscious* (pp. 37–60). New York: Oxford University Press.

Bargh, J. A. (2006). *The new unconscious.* New York: Oxford University Press.

Bargh, J. A. (2008). Free will is un-natural. In J. Baer, J. C. Kaufman, & R. F. Baumeister (Eds.), Are we free? Psychology and free will (pp. 128–154). New York: Oxford University Press.

Bargh, J. A., and Morsella, E. (2008). The unconscious mind. *Perspectives on Psychological Science, 3,* 73–79.

Bargh, J. A., and Morsella, E. (2010). Unconscious behavioral guidance systems. In C. R. Agnew, D. E. Carlston, W. G. Graziano, and J. R. Kelly (Eds.), *Then a miracle occurs: Focusing on behavior in social psychological theory and research* (pp. 89–118). New York, NY: Oxford University Press.

Baron, M. (1993). Genetics and human sexual orientation. *Biological Psychology, 33,* 759–761.

Bar-On, R. (2001). Emotional intelligence and self-actualization. In J. Ciarrochi and J. P. Forgas (Eds.), *Emotional intelligence in everyday life: A scientific inquiry* (pp. 82–97). Philadelphia, PA: Psychology Press.

Baron, R. A. (1977). *Human aggression.* New York: Plenum Press.

Barrantes-Vidal, N., and Kwapil, T. R. (2014). The application of experience sampling methodology for the study of individual differences in real life. *Personality and Individual Differences, 60,* S6.

Barrett, H. C., Frederick, D., Haselton, M., and Kurzban, R. (2006). Can manipulations of cognitive load be used to test evolutionary hypotheses? *Journal of Personality and Social Psychology, 91,* 513–518.

Barrick, M. R., and Mount, M. K. (1991). The Big Five personality dimensions and job performance: A meta-analysis. *Personnel Psychology, 44,* 1–25.

Barron, J. W., Eagle, M. N., and Wolitzky, D. L. (1992). *Interface of psychoanalysis and psychology.* Washington, DC: American Psychological Association.

Bartels, M. (2015). Genetics of wellbeing and its components satisfaction with life, happiness, and quality of life: A review and meta-analysis of heritability studies. *Behavior Genetics, 45*(2), 137–156.

Bass, E., and Davis, L. (1988). *The courage to heal: A guide for women survivors of child sexual abuse.* New York: Perennial Library/Harper and Row.

Bastone, L. M., and Wood, H. A. (1997). Individual differences in the ability to decode emotional facial expressions. *Psychology: A Journal of Human Behavior, 34,* 32–36.

Bauer, J. J., Schwab, J. R., and McAdams, D. P. (2011). Self-actualizing: Where ego development finally feels good? *The Humanistic Psychologist, 39,* 121–136.

Baughman, H. M., Dearing, S., Giammarco, E., and Vernon, P. A. (2012). Relationship between bullying behaviours and the Dark Triad: A study with adults. *Personality and Individual Differences, 52,* 571–575.

Baumeister, R. F. (1986). *Identity: Cultural change and the struggle for self.* New York: Oxford University Press.

Baumeister, R. F. (1988). Should we stop studying sex differences altogether? *American Psychologist, 43,* 1092–1095.

Baumeister, R. F. (1991). The self against itself: Escape or defeat? In R. C. Curtis (Ed.), *The relational self: Theoretical convergences in psychoanalysis and social psychology* (pp. 238–256). New York: Guilford Press.

Baumeister, R. F. (1997). Identity, self-concept, and self-esteem: The self lost and found. In R. Hogan, J. Johnson, and S. Briggs (Eds.), *Handbook of personality psychology* (pp. 681–711). New York: Academic Press.

Baumeister, R. F. (2014). Self-regulation, ego depletion, and inhibition. *Neuropsychologia, 65,* 313–319.

Baumeister, R. F., Bratslavsky, E., Muraven, M., and Tice, D. M. (1998). Ego depletion: Is the active self a limited resource? *Journal of Personality and Social Psychology, 74,* 1252–1265.

Baumeister, R. F., Bushman, B. J., and Campbell, W. K. (2000). Self-esteem, narcissism, and aggression: Does violence result from low self-esteem or from threatened egotism? *Current Directions in Psychological Science, 9,* 26–29.

Baumeister, R. F., Campbell, J. D., Krueger, J. I., and Vohs, K. D. (2003). Does high self-esteem cause better performance, interpersonal success, happiness, or healthier lifestyles? *Psychological Science in the Public Interest, 4,* 1–44.

Baumeister, R. F., Dale, K., and Sommer, K. L. (1998). Freudian defense mechanisms and empirical findings in modern social psychology: Reaction formation, projection, displacement, undoing, isolation, sublimation, and denial. *Journal of Personality, 66,* 1061–1081.

Baumeister, R. F., and Leary, M. R. (1995). The need to belong: Desire for interpersonal attachments as a fundamental human motivation. *Psychological Bulletin, 117,* 497–529.

Baumeister, R. F., and Muraven, M. (1996). Identity as adaptation to social, cultural and historical context. *Journal of Adolescence, 19,* 405–416.

Baumeister, R. F., and Tice, D. M. (1990). Anxiety and social exclusion. *Journal of Social and Clinical Psychology, 9,* 165–195.

Baumeister, R. F., Tice, D. M., and Hutton, D. G. (1989). Self-presentational motivations and personality differences in self-esteem. *Journal of Personality, 57,* 547–579.

Baumeister, R. F., and Vohs, K. (2004). *Handbook of self-regulation.* New York: Guilford Press.

Baumeister, R. F., Vohs, K. D., & Tice, D. M. (2007). The strength model of self-control. *Current Directions in Psychological Science, 16,* 396–403.

Beaty, R. E., Kaufman, S. B., Benedek, M., Jung, R. E., Kenett, Y. N., Jauk, E., and . . . Silvia, P. J. (2016). Personality and complex brain networks: The role of openness to experience in default network efficiency. *Human Brain Mapping, 37*(2), 773–779.

Beauducel, A., Debener, S., Brocke, B., & Kayser, J. (2000). On the reliability of augmenting/reducing: Peak amplitudes and principal component analysis of auditory evoked potentials. *Journal of Psychophysiology, 14,* 226–240.

Beauregard, M., Levesque, J., and Bourgouin, P. (2001). Neural correlates of conscious self-regulation of emotion. *Journal of Neuroscience, 21,* RC165 (1–6).

Bechara, A., Dolan, S., Denbrug, N., Hindes, A., Anderson, S. W., and Nathan, P. E. (2001). Decision-making deficits, linked to a dysfunctional ventromedial prefrontal cortex, revealed in alcohol and stimulant abusers. *Neuropsychologica, 39,* 376–389.

Bechara, A., Tranel, D., and Damasio, H. (2005). Characterization of the decision-making deficit of patients with ventromedial prefrontal cortex lesions. *Brain, 123,* 2189–2202.

Beck, A. T. (1976). *Cognitive therapy and the emotional disorders.* New York: International Universities Press.

Beer, J. S., and Lombardo, M. V. (2007). Patient and neuroimaging methods. In R. W. Robins, R. C. Fraley, and R. F. Krueger (Eds.), *Handbook of research methods in personality psychology* (pp. 360–369). New York: Guilford Press.

Bègue, L., Beauvois, J. L., Courbet, D., Oberlé, D., Lepage, J., and Duke, A. A. (2015). Personality predicts obedience in a Milgram paradigm. *Journal of Personality, 83*(3), 299–306.

Belle, D., Doucet, J., Harris, J., Miller, J., and Tan, E. (2000). Who is rich? Who is happy? *American Psychologist, 55,* 116–117.

Belsky, J. (2000). Conditional and alternative reproductive strategies: Individual differences in susceptibility to rearing experience. In. J. Rodgers, D. Rowe, and W. Miller (Eds.), *Genetic influences on human fertility and sexuality: Theoretical and empirical contributions from the biological and behavioral sciences* (pp. 127–146). Boston: Kluwer.

Belsky, J., Steinberg, L., and Draper, P. (1991). Childhood experience, interpersonal development, and reproductive strategy: An evolutionary theory of socialization. *Child Development, 62,* 647–670.

Bem, D. J. (1996). Exotic becomes erotic: A developmental theory of sexual orientation. *Psychological Review, 103,* 320–333.

Bem, S. L. (1974). The measurement of psychological androgyny. *Journal of Consulting and Clinical Psychology, 42,* 153–162.

Bendixen, M., Kennair, L. E. O., and Buss, D. M. (2015). Jealousy: Evidence of strong sex differences using both forced choice and continuous measure paradigms. *Personality and Individual Differences, 86,* 212–216.

Benet-Martinez, V., Donnellan, M. B., Fleeson, W., Fraley, R. C., Gosling, S. D., King, L. A., Robins, R. W., and Funder, D. C. (2015). Six visions for the future of personality psychology. In L. Cooper and R. J. Larsen (Eds.), *Handbook of personality and social psychology: Personality processes and individual differences* (pp. 665–690). Washington, DC: American Psychological Association.

Benjamin, J., Li, L., Patterson, C., Greenberg, B. D., Murphy, D. L., and Hamer, D. H. (1996). Population and familial association between the D4 dopamine receptor gene and measures of novelty seeking. *Nature Genetics, 12,* 81–84.

Bentler, P. M., and Newcomb, M. D. (1978). Longitudinal study of marital success and failure. *Journal of Consulting and Clinical Psychology, 46,* 1053–1070.

Berant, E. (2009). Attachment styles, the Rorschach, and the Thematic Appercaption Test: Using traditional projective measures to assess aspects of attachment. In J. J. Obegi and E. Berant (Eds.), *Attachment theory and research in clinical work with adults* (pp. 181–206). New York, NY: Guilford Press.

Berenbaum, S. A., and Beltz, A. M. (2011). Sexual differentiation of human behavior: effects of prenatal and pubertal organizational hormones. *Frontiers in neuroendocrinology, 32*(2), 183–200.

Berenbaum, S. A., and Snyder, E. (1995). Early hormonal influences on childhood sex-typed activity and playmate preferences: Implications for the development of sexual orientation. *Developmental Psychology, 31,* 31–42.

Berman, S., Ozkaragoz, T., Yound, R. M., and Noble, E. P. (2002). D2 dopamine receptor gene polymorphism discriminates two kinds of novelty seeking. *Personality and Individual Differences, 33,* 867–882.

Bernhardt, P. C., Dabbs, J. M., Jr., Fielden, J., and Lutter, C. (1998). Testosterone changes during vicarious experiences of winning and losing among fans at sporting events. *Physiology and Behavior, 65,* 59–62.

Bernstein, D. M., and Loftus, E. F. (2009). How to tell if a particular memory is true or false. *Perspectives on Psychological Science, 4,* 370–374.

Berry, D. S., and Miller, K. M. (2001). When boy meets girl: Attractiveness and the five-factor model in opposite-sex interactions. *Journal of Research in Personality, 35,* 62–77.

Berry, C. M., Sackett, P. R., & Wiemann, S. (2007). A review of recent developments in integrity test research. *Personnel Psychology, 60,* 271–301.

Bian, M., and Leung, L. (2015). Linking loneliness, shyness, smartphone addiction symptoms, and patterns of smartphone use to social capital. *Social Science Computer Review, 33*(1), 61–79.

Birley, A. J., Gillespie, N. A., Heath, A. C., Sullivan, P. F., Boomsma, D. I., and Martin, N. G. (2006). Heritability and nineteen-year stability of long and short EPQ-R Neuroticism scales. *Personality and Individual Differences, 40,* 737–747.

Bjork, R. A., and Druckman, D. (1991). *In the mind's eye: Enhancing human performance.* Washington, DC: National Academy Press.

Blachnio, A., Przepiorka, A., and Díaz-Morales, J. F. (2015). Facebook use and chronotype: Results of a cross-sectional study. *Chronobiology International, 32*(9), 1315–1319.

Black, J. (2000). Personality testing and police selection: Utility of the Big Five. *New Zealand Journal of Psychology, 29,* 2–9.

Bleidorn, W. (2012). Hitting the road to adulthood short-term personality development during a major life transition. *Personality and social psychology bulletin, 38*(12), 1594–1608.

Bleske-Rechek, A. L., and Buss, D. M. (2001). Opposite-sex friendship: Sex differences and similarities in initiation, selection, and dissolution. *Personality and Social Psychology Bulletin, 27, 10,* 1310–1323.

Bleske-Rechek, A., Remiker, M. W., and Baker, J. P. (2008). Narcissistic men and women think they are so hot—but they are not. *Personality and Individual Differences, 45,* 420–424.

Blinkhorn, V., Lyons, M., and Almond, L. (2015). The ultimate femme fatale? Narcissism predicts serious and aggressive sexually coercive behaviour in females. *Personality and Individual Differences, 87,* 219–223.

Block, J. (1971). *Lives through time.* Berkeley, CA: Bancroft Books.

Block, J. (1977). Advancing the psychology of personality: Paradigmatic shift or improving the quality of research. In D. Magnusson and N. S. Endler (Eds.), *Personality at the crossroads* (pp. 37–63). Hillsdale, NJ: Erlbaum.

Block, J. H., and Block, J. (1980). *The California Child Q-Set.* Palo Alto, CA: Consulting Psychologists Press.

Block, J. (2010). The five-factor framing of personality and beyond: Some ruminations. *Psychological Inquiry, 21,* 2–25.

Block, J., and Robbins, R. W. (1993). A longitudinal study of consistency and change in self-esteem from early adolescence to early adulthood. *Child Development, 64,* 909–923.

Block, J. H. (1983). Differential premises arising from differential socialization of the sexes: Some conjectures. *Child Development, 54,* 1335–1354.

Blonigen, D. M., Carlson, M. D., Hicks, B. M., Kreuger, R. F., and Iacono, W. G. (2008). Stability and change in personality traits from late adolescence to early adulthood: A longitudinal twin study. *Journal of Personality, 76,* 229–266.

Blonigen, D. M., Carlson, S. R., Krueger, R. F., and Patrick, C. J. (2003). A twin study of self-reported psychopathic personality traits. *Personality and Individual Differences, 35,* 179–197.

Blonigen, D. M., Hicks, B. M., Krueger, R. F., Patrick, C. J., & Iacono, W. G. (2006). Continuity and change in psychopathic traits as measured via normal-range personality: A longitudinal–biometric study. *Journal of Abnormal Psychology, 115, 1,* 85.

Bochner, S. (1994). Cross-cultural differences in the self-concept: A test of Hofstede's individualism/collectivism distinction. *Journal of Cross-Cultural Psychology, 25,* 273–283.

Bogg, T. (2008). Conscientiousness, the transtheoretical model of change, and exercise: A neo-socioanalytic integration of trait and social-cognitive frameworks in the predictions of behavior. *Journal of Personality, 76,* 775–802.

Bogg, T., and Roberts, B. W. (2004). Conscientiousness and health behaviors: A meta-analysis of the leading behavioral contributors to mortality. *Psychological Bulletin, 130,* 887–919.

Bohart, A. C. (2013). The actualizing person. In M. Cooper, M. O'Hara, P. F. Schmid, A. C. Bohart, M. Cooper, M. O'Hara, . . . A. C. Bohart (Eds.), *The handbook of person-centred psychotherapy and counselling* (2nd ed.) (pp. 84–101). New York, NY: Palgrave Macmillan.

Bolkan, C., Hooker, K., and Coehlo, D. (2015). Possible selves and depressive symptoms in later life. *Research On Aging, 37*(1), 41–62.

Bollich, K. L., Doris, J. M., Vazire, S., Raison, C. L., Jackson, J. J., and Mehl, M. R. (2016). Eavesdropping on character: Assessing everyday moral behaviors. *Journal of Research in Personality, 61,* 15–21.

Bolt, T. S., Hampton, R. S., Furr, R. M., Fleeson, W., Laurienti, P. J., and Dagenbach, D. (2016). Integrating personality/character neuroscience with network analysis. In J. R. Absher, J. Cloutier, J. R. Absher, J. Cloutier (Eds.), *Neuroimaging personality, social cognition, and character* (pp. 51–69). San Diego, CA, US: Elsevier Academic Press.

Bonanno, G. A. (1990). Repression, accessibility, and the translation of private experience. *Psychoanalytic Psychology, 7,* 453–473.

Bonanno, G. A., Wortman, C. B., Lehman, D. R., Tweed, R. G., Haring, M., Sonnega, J., Carr, D., and Nesse, R. M. (2002). Resilience to loss and chronic grief: A prospective study from preloss to 18-months postloss. *Journal of Personality and Social Psychology, 83, 5,* 1150–1164.

Bono, J. E., Boles, T. L., Judge, T. A., and Lauver, K. J. (2002). The role of personality in task and relationship conflict. *Journal of Personality, 70,* 311–344.

Boomsma, D. I., Koopmans, J. R., Van Doorren, L.J.P., and Orlebeke, J. M. (1994). Genetic and social influences on starting to smoke: A study of Dutch adolescent twins and their parents. *Addiction, 89,* 219–226.

Borkenau, P., Riemann, R., Angleitner, A., and Spinath, F. M. (2001). Genetic and environmental influences on observed personality: Evidence from the German observational study of adult twins. *Journal of Personality and Social Psychology, 80, 4,* 655–668.

Bornstein, R. F. (1999). Source amnesia, misattribution, and the power of unconscious perceptions and memories. *Psychoanalytic Psychology, 16,* 155–178.

Bornstein, R. F. (2005). The dependent patient: Diagnosis, assessment, and treatment. *Professional Psychology: Research and Practice, 36,* 82–89.

Botwin, M. D., and Buss, D. M. (1989). Structure of act-report data: Is the five-factor model of personality recaptured? *Journal of Personality and Social Psychology, 56,* 988–1001.

Botwin, M., Buss, D. M., and Shackelford, T. (1997). Personality and mate preferences: Five factors in mate selection and marital satisfaction. *Journal of Personality, 65,* 107–136.

Bouchard, T. J., and Loehlin, J. C. (2001). Genes, evolution, and personality. *Behavior Genetics, 31,* 243–273.

Bouchard, T. J., Lykken, D. T., McGue, M., and Segal, N. L. (1990). Sources of human psychological differences: The Minnesota study of twins reared apart. *Science, 250,* 223–228.

Bouchard, T. J., and McGue, M. (1990). Genetic and rearing environmental influences on adult personality: An analysis of adopted twins reared apart. *Journal of Personality, 58,* 263–292.

Bowlby, J. (1969a). *Attachment and loss: Vol. 1: Attachment.* New York: Basic Books.

Bowlby, J. (1969b). *Attachment and loss: Vol. 2: Separation, anger, and anxiety.* New York: Basic Books.

Bowlby, J. (1980). *Attachment and loss: Vol. 3: Loss, sadness, and depression.* New York: Basic Books.

Bowlby, J. (1988). *A secure base: Parent-child attachment and healthy human development.* New York: Basic Books.

Boyce, C. J., Wood, A. M., and Brown, G.D.A. (2010). The dark side of conscientiousness: Conscientious people experience greater drops in life satisfaction following unemployment. *Journal of Personality, 44,* 535–539.

Boyle, G. J. (1995). Myers-Briggs Type Indicator (NBTI): Some psychometric limitations. *Australian Psychologist, 30,* 71–74.

Bradberry, T. (2007). *The personality code.* New York: Putnam.

Brand, C. R., and Egan, V. (1989). The "Big Five" dimensions of personality? Evidence from ipsative, adjectival self-attributions. *Personality and Individual Differences, 10,* 1165–1171.

Branje, S.J.T., van Lieshout, C.F.M., and Geris, J.R.M. (2006). Big Five personality development in adolescence and adulthood. *European Journal of Personality, 21,* 45–62.

Brase, G. L., Caprar, D. V., and Voracek, M. (2004). Sex differences in responses to relationship threats in England and Romania. *Journal of Social and Personal Relationships, 21,* 763–778.

Braun, K. A., Ellis, R., and Loftus, E. F. (2002). Make my memory: How advertising can change our memories of the past. *Psychology and Marketing, 19,* 1–23.

Brebner, J. (2003). Gender and emotions. *Personality and Individual Differences, 34,* 387–394.

Brebner, J., and Cooper, C. (1978). Stimulus- or response-induced excitation: A comparison of the behavior of introverts and extraverts. *Journal of Research in Personality, 12,* 306–311.

Bredemann, T. M. (2012). Estrogen increases stress resilience and hippocampal synaptic physiology in the learned helplessness model of depression in female rats. *Dissertation Abstracts International: Section B: The Sciences and Engineering, 72*(12-B), 7734.

Breger, R., and Hill, R. (Eds.). (1998). *Cross-cultural marriage: Identity and choice.* New York: Berg.

Brendl, C. M., Markman, A. B., and Messner, C. (2001). How do indirect measures of evaluation work? Evaluating the inference of prejudice in the Implicit Association Test. *Journal of Personality and Social Psychology, 81,* 760–773.

Brennan, K. A., and Shaver, P. R. (1993). Attachment styles and parental divorce. *Journal of Divorce and Remarriage, 21,* 161–175.

Brennan, P. A., and Raine, A. (1997). Biosocial bases of antisocial behavior: Psychophysiological, neurological, and cognitive factors. *Clinical Psychology Review Special Issue: Biopsychosocial Conceptualizations of Human Aggression, 17,* 589–604.

Bresin, K., and Robinson, M. D. (2015). You are what you see and choose: Agreeableness and situation selection. *Journal of personality, 83*(4), 452–463.

Bretherton, I., and Main, M. (2000). Obituary: Mary Dinsmore Salter Ainsworth (1913–1999). *American Psychologist, 55,* 1148–1149.

Brickman, P., Coates, D., and Janoff-Bulman, R. J. (1978). Lottery winners and accident victims: Is happiness relative? *Journal of Personality and Social Psychology, 36,* 917–927.

Briley, D. A., and Tucker-Drob, E. M. (2014). Genetic and environmental continuity in personality development: A meta-analysis. *Psychological Bulletin, 140*(5), 1303–1331.

Brooks, S. J., and Stein, D. J. (2014). Unconscious influences on decision making: Neuroimaging and neuroevolutionary perspectives. *Behavioral and Brain Sciences, 37*(1), 23–24.

Brody, J. E. (1996, March 27). Personal health. *The New York Times,* Section B.

Brose, L. A., Rye, M. S., Lutz-Zois, C., and Ross, S. R. (2005). Forgiveness and personality traits. *Personality and Individual Differences, 39,* 35–46.

Brown, D. E. (1991). *Human universals.* New York: McGraw-Hill.

Brown, J. D., and Dutton, K. A. (1995). The thrill of victory, the complexity of defeat: Self-esteem and people's emotional reactions to success and failure. *Journal of Personality and Social Psychology, 68,* 712–722.

Brown, J. D., and Smart, S. A. (1991). The self and social conduct: Linking self-representations to prosocial behavior. *Journal of Personality and Social Psychology, 60,* 368–375.

Brown, R. P., and Zeigler-Hill, V. (2004). Narcissism and the non-equivalence of self-esteem measures: A matter of dominance. *Journal of Research in Personality, 38,* 585–592.

Bruce, J., Davis, E. P., Gunnar, M. R. (2002). Individual differences in children's cortisol response to the beginning of a new school year. *Psychoneuroendocrinology, 27,* 635–650.

Bruch, M. A., and Hynes, M. J. (1987). Heterosexual anxiety and contraceptive behavior. *Journal of Research in Personality, 21,* 343–360.

Bruggemann, J. M., and Barry, R. J. (2002). Eysenck's P as a modulator of affective and electrodermal responses to violent and comic film. *Personality and Individual Differences, 32,* 1029–1048.

Brummett, B. H., Babyak, M. A., Williams, R. B., Barefoot, J. C., Costa, P. T., and Siegler, I. C. (2006). NEO personality domains and gender predict levels and trends in body mass index over 14 years during midlife. *Journal of Research in Personality, 40,* 222–236.

Buday, S. K., Stake, J. E., and Peterson, Z. D. (2012). Gender and the choice of a science career: The impact of social support and possible selves. *Sex Roles, 66,* 197–209.

Buerkle, J. V. (1960). Self attitudes and marital adjustment. *Merrill-Palmer Quarterly, 6,* 114–124.

Buffardi, L. E., and Campbell, W. K. (2008). Narcissism and social networking web sites. *Personality and Social Psychology Bulletin, 34,* 1303–1314.

Bullock, W. A., and Gilliland, K. (1993). Eysenck's arousal theory of introversion-extraversion: A converging measures investigation. *Journal of Personality and Social Psychology, 64,* 113–123.

Bunce, S. C., Larsen, R. J., and Peterson, C. (1995). Life after trauma: Personality and daily life experiences of traumatized persons. *Journal of Personality, 63,* 165–188.

Burgess, E. W., and Wallin, P. (1953). *Engagement and marriage.* New York: Lippincott.

Burke, R. J., Mattheiesen, S. B., and Pallesen, S. (2006). Personality correlates of workaholism. *Personality and Individual Differences, 40,* 1223–1233.

Burns, M. O., and Seligman, M. E. (1989). Explanatory style across the life span: Evidence for stability over 52 years. *Journal of Personality and Social Psychology, 56,* 471–477.

Burnstein, E., Crandall, C., and Kitayama, S. (1994). Some neo-Darwinian decision rules for altruism: Weighing cures for inclusive fitness as a function of the biological importance of the decision. *Journal of Personality and Social Psychology, 67,* 773–789.

Burt, S. A. (2009). A mechanistic explanation of popularity: Genes, rule breaking, and evocative gene-environment correlations. *Journal of Personality and Social Psychology, 96,* 783–794.

Burt, S. A., McGue, M., Iacono, W., Comings, D., and MacMurray, J. (2002). An examination of the association between DRD4 and DRD2 polymorphisms and personality traits. *Personality and Individual Differences, 33,* 849–859.

Burton, C. M., and King, L. A.(2008). Effects of (very) brief writing on health: The two-minute miracle. *British Journal of Health Psychology, 13,* 9–14.

Bush, G., Luu, P., and Posner, M. I. (2000). Cognitive and emotional influences in anterior cingulated cortex. *Trends in Cognitive Sciences, 4,* 215–222.

Bushman, B., and Baumeister, R. (1998). Threatened egotism, narcissism, self-esteem, and direct and displaced aggression: Does self-love or self-hate lead to violence? *Journal of Personality and Social Psychology, 75,* 219–229.

Bushman, B. J., and Baumeister, R. F. (2002). Does self-love or self-hate lead to violence? *Journal of Research in Personality, 36,* 543–545.

Bushman, B. J., Bonacci, A. M., van Dijk, M., and Baumeister, R. F. (2003). Narcissism, sexual refusal and aggression: Testing a narcissistic reactance model of sexual coercion. *Journal of Personality and Social Psychology, 84, 5,* 1027–1040.

Buss, A. H. (1989). Personality as traits. *American Psychologist, 44,* 1378–1388.

Buss, D. M. (1981). Predicting parent-child interactions from children's activity level. *Developmental Psychology, 17,* 59–65.

Buss, D. M. (1984). Toward a psychology of person-environment (PE) correlation: The role of spouse selection. *Journal of Personality and Social Psychology, 47,* 361–377.

Buss, D. M. (1987). Selection, evocation, and manipulation. *Journal of Personality and Social Psychology, 53,* 1214–1221.

Buss, D. M. (1989). Sex differences in human mate preferences: Evolutionary hypotheses tested in 37 cultures. *Behavioral and Brain Sciences, 12,* 1–49.

Buss, D. M. (1990). The evolution of anxiety and social exclusion. *Journal of Social and Clinical Psychology, 9,* 196–201.

Buss, D. M. (1991a). Conflict in married couples: Personality predictors of anger and upset. *Journal of Personality, 59,* 663–688.

Buss, D. M. (1991b). Evolutionary personality psychology. *Annual Review of Psychology.* Palo Alto, CA: Annual Reviews, Inc.

Buss, D. M. (1992). Manipulation in close relationships: Five personality factors in interactional context. *Journal of Personality, 60,* 477–499.

Buss, D. M. (1993). Strategic individual differences: The role of personality in creating and solving adaptive problems. In J. Hettema and I. Deary (Eds.), *Social and biological approaches to personality* (pp. 175–189) New York: Wiley.

Buss, D. M. (1995a). Evolutionary psychology: A new paradigm for psychological science. *Psychological Inquiry, 6,* 1–49.

Buss, D. M. (1995b). Psychological sex differences: Origins through sexual selection. *American Psychologist, 50,* 164–168.

Buss, D. M. (1996). Social adaptation and five major factors of personality. In J. S. Wiggins (Ed.), *The five-factor model of personality: Theoretical perspectives* (pp. 180–207). New York: Guilford Press.

Buss, D. M. (2000a). *The dangerous passion: Why jealousy is as necessary as love and sex.* New York: Free Press.

Buss, D. M. (2000b). The evolution of happiness. *American Psychologist, 55,* 15–23.

Buss, D. M. (2005a). *The handbook of evolutionary psychology.* New York: Wiley.

Buss, D. M. (2005b). *The murderer next door: Why the mind is designed to kill.* New York: Penguin.

Buss, D. M. (2009a). The great struggles of life: Darwin and the emergence of evolutionary psychology. *American Psychologist, 64,* 140–148.

Buss, D. M. (2009b). How can evolutionary psychology successfully explain personality and individual differences? *Perspectives in Psychological Science, 5.*

Buss, D. M. (2011). Personality and the adaptive landscape: The role of individual differences in creating and solving social adaptive problems. In D.M. Buss & P. Hawley (Eds.)(2011). *The evolution of personality and individual differences* (pp. 29–60). New York: Oxford University Press.

Buss, D. M. (2012). *Evolutionary psychology: The new science of the mind* (4th ed.). Boston: Allyn & Bacon.

Buss, D. M. (2016). *The evolution of desire: Strategies of human mating* (Revised and updated ed.). New York: Basic Books.

Buss, D. M., Abbott, M., Angleitner, A., Asherian, A., Biaggio, A., et al. (1990). International preferences in selecting mates: A study of 37 cultures. *Journal of Cross-Cultural Psychology, 21,* 5–47.

Buss, D. M., and Barnes, M. L. (1986). Preferences in human mate selection. *Journal of Personality and Social Psychology, 50,* 559–570.

Buss, D. M., Block, J. H., and Block, J. (1980). Preschool activity level: Personality correlates and developmental implications. *Child Development, 51,* 401–408.

Buss, D. M., and Chiodo, L. M. (1991). Narcissistic acts in everyday life. *Journal of Personality, 59, 2,* 179–215.

Buss, D. M., and Craik, K. H. (1983). The act frequency approach to personality. *Psychological Review, 90,* 105–126.

Buss, D. M., and Duntley, J. D. (2006). The evolution of aggression. In M. Schaller, D. T. Kenrick, and J. A. Simpson (Eds.), *Evolution and social psychology* (pp. 263–286). New York: Psychology Press.

Buss, D. M., Gomes, M., Higgins, D. S., and Lauterbach, K. (1987). Tactics of manipulation. *Journal of Personality and Social Psychology, 52,* 1219–1229.

Buss, D. M., and Greiling, H. (1999). Adaptive individual differences. *Journal of Personality, 67,* 209–243.

Buss, D. M., and Haselton, M. G. (2005). The evolution of jealousy. *Trends in Cognitive Science, 9,* 506–507.

Buss, D. M., and Hawley, P. (2011). *The evolution of personality and individual differences.* New York: Oxford University Press.

Buss, D. M., and Hawley, P. (Eds.) (2011). *The evolution of personality and individual differences.* New York: Oxford University Press.

Buss, D. M., Larsen, R. J., Semmelroth, J., and Westen, D. (1992). Sex differences in jealousy: Evolution, physiology, and psychology. *Psychological Science, 3,* 251–255.

Buss, D. M., and Schmitt, D. P. (1993). Sexual strategies theory: An evolutionary perspective on human mating. *Psychological Review, 100,* 204–232.

Buss, D. M., Shackelford, T. K., Kirkpatrick, L. A., Choe, J., Hasegawa, M., Hasegawa, T., and Bennett, K. (1999). Jealousy and the nature of beliefs about infidelity: Tests of competing hypotheses about sex differences in the United States, Korea, and Japan. *Personal Relationships, 6,* 125–150.

Buss, D. M., & Schmitt, D. P. (1993). Sexual strategies theory: An evolutionary perspective on human mating. *Psychological Review, 100,* 204–232.

Buss, D. M., and Schmitt, D. P. (2011). Evolutionary psychology and feminism. *Sex Roles, 64,* 768–787.

Buss, K. A., Schumacher, J.R.M., Dolski, I., Kalin, N. H., Goldsmith, H. H., and Davidson, R. J. (2003). Right frontal brain activity, cortisol, and withdrawal behavior in 6-month-old infants. *Behavioral Neuroscience, 117,* 11–20.

Butkovic, A., and Bratko, D. (2007). Family study of manipulation tactics. *Personality and Individual Differences, 43,* 791–801.

Butler, A. C., Hokanson, J. E., and Flynn, H. A. (1994). A comparison of self-esteem lability and low trait self-esteem as vulnerability factors for depression. *Journal of Personality and Social Psychology, 66,* 166–177.

Button, T.M.M., Stallings, M. C., Rhee, S. H., Corley, R. P., and Hewitt, J. K. (2011). The etiology of stability and change in religious values and religious attendance. *Behavior Genetics, 41,* 201–210.

Buunk, B., Angleitner, A., Oubaid, V., and Buss, D. M. (1996). Sexual and cultural differences in jealousy: Tests from the Netherlands, Germany, and the United States. *Psychological Science, 7,* 359–363.

Byrne, K. A., Silasi-Mansat, C. D., and Worthy, D. A. (2015). Who chokes under pressure? The Big Five personality traits and decision-making under pressure. *Personality and Individual Differences, 74,* 22–28.

Byrnes, J. P., Miller, D. C., and Schafer, W. D. (1999). Gender differences in risk taking: A meta-analysis. *Psychological Bulletin, 125,* 367–383.

Cafferty, T. P., Davis, K. E., Medway, F. J., O'Hearn, R. E., and Chappell, K. D. (1994). Reunion dynamics among couples separated during Operation Desert Storm: An attachment theory analysis. In K. Bartholomew and D. Perlman (Eds.), *Attachment processes in adulthood* (pp. 309–330). Philadelphia, PA: Jessica Kingsley.

Campbell, A., Coombes, C., David, R., Opre, A., Grayson, L., and Muncer, S. (2016). Sex differences are not attenuated by a sex-invariant measure of fear: The situated fear questionnaire. *Personality and Individual Differences, 97,* 210–219.

Campbell, J. B., and Hawley, C. W. (1982). Study habits and Eysenck's theory of extraversion-introversion. *Journal of Research in Personality, 16,* 139–146.

Campbell, W. K., and Foster, C. A. (2002). Narcissism and commitment in romantic relationships: An investment model analysis. *Personality and Social Psychology Bulletin, 28, 4,* 484–495.

Campbell, W. K., Rudich, E. A., and Sedikides, C. (2002). Narcissism, self-esteem, and the positivity of self-views: Two portraits of self-love. *Personality*

and Social Psychology Bulletin, 28, 3, 358–368.

Canache, D., Hayes, M., Mondak, J. J., and Wals, S. C. (2013). Openness, extraversion and the intention to emigrate. *Journal of Research in Personality, 47*(4), 351–355.

Canli, T. (2008). Toward a neurogenetic theory of neuroticism. In D. W. Pfaff and B. L. Kieffer (Eds.), *Molecular and biophysical mechanisms of arousal, alertness, and attention* (pp. 153–174). Malden: Blackwell.

Canli, T., and Amin, Z. (2002). Neuroimaging of emotion and personality: Scientific evidence and ethical considerations. *Brain and Cognition, 50,* 414–431.

Cann, A., Mangum, J. L., and Wells, M. (2001). Distress in response to relationship infidelity: The roles of gender and attitudes about relationships. *Journal of Sex Research, 38,* 185–190.

Cantor, N. (1990). From thought to behavior: "Having" and "doing" in the study of personality and cognition. *American Psychologist, 45,* 735–750.

Caplan, S. E. (2002). Problematic Internet use and psychosocial well-being: Development of a theory-based, cognitive-behavioral measurement instrument. *Computers in Human Behavior, 18,* 553–575.

Caprara, G. V., Alessandri, G., De Giunta, L., Panerai, L., and Eisenberg, N. (2010). The contribution of agreeableness and self-efficacy beliefs to prosociality. *European Journal of Personality, 24,* 36–55.

Caprara, G. V., Barbaranelli, C., Consiglio, C., Picconi, L., and Zimbardo, P. G. (2003). Personalities of politicians and voters: Unique and synergistic relationships. *Journal of Personality and Social Psychology, 84, 4,* 849–856.

Caprara, G. V., and Perugini, M. (1994). Personality described by adjectives: Generalizability of the Big Five to the Italian lexical context. *European Journal of Psychology, 8,* 357–369.

Caputi, P. (2012). An introduction to grid-based methods. In P. Caputi, L. L. Viney, B. M. Walker, and N. Crittenden (Eds.), *Personal construct methodology* (pp. 149–158). Hoboken, NJ: John Wiley & Sons.

Cardemil, E. V., Reivich, K. J., and Seligman, M. E. P. (2002). The prevention of depressive symptoms in low-income minority middle school students. *Prevention and Treatment, 5,* np.

Carli, V., and Durkee, T. (2016). Pathological use of the Internet. In D. Mucic, D. M. Hilty, D. Mucic, D. M. Hilty (Eds.), *e-Mental health* (pp. 269–288). Cham, Switzerland: Springer International Publishing.

Carlo, G., Okun, M. A., Knight, G. P., and de Guzman, M.R.T. (2005). The

interplay of traits and motives on volunteering: Agreeableness, extraversion and prosocial value motivation. *Personality and Individual Differences, 38,* 1293–1305.

Carpenter, C. J. (2012). Narcissism on Facebook: Self-promotional and anti-social behavior. *Personality and Individual Differences, 52,* 482–486.

Carrasco, M., Barker, E. D., Trembley, R. E., and Vitaro, J. (2006). Eysenck's personality dimensions as predictors of male adolescent trajectories of physical aggression, theft, and vandalism. *Personality and Individual Differences, 41,* 1309–1320.

Carron, A. V., Shapcott, K. M., and Martin, L. J. (2014). The relationship between team explanatory style and team success. *International Journal of Sport And Exercise Psychology, 12*(1), 1–9.

Carter, R. (1999). *Mapping the mind.* Berkeley: University of California Press.

Carver, C. S. (1996). Emergent integration in contemporary personality psychology. *Journal of Research in Personality, 30,* 319–334.

Carver, C. S., Pozo, C., Harris, S. D., Noriega, V., Scheier, M. F., Robinson, D. S., Ketcham, A. S., Moffat, F. L., and Clark, K. C. (1993). How coping mediates the effect of optimism on distress: A study of women with early stage breast cancer. *Journal of Personality and Social Psychology, 65,* 375–390.

Carver, C. S., and Scheier, M. F. (2000). Autonomy and self regulation. *Psychological Inquiry, 11,* 284–291.

Carver, C. S., Sutton, S. K., and Scheier, M. F. (1999). Action, emotion, and personality: Emerging conceptual integration. *Personality and Social Psychology Bulletin, 26,* 741–751.

Carver, C. S., and White, T. L. (1994). Behavioral inhibition, behavioral activation, and affective responses to impeding reward and punishments: The BIS/BAS scales. *Journal of Personality and Social Psychology, 67,* 319–333.

Cashden, E. (1980). Egalitarianism among hunters and gatherers. *American Anthropologist, 82,* 116–120.

Caspi, A., Elder, G. H., Jr., and Bem, D. J. (1987). Moving against the world: Life-course patterns of explosive children. *Developmental Psychology, 23,* 308–313.

Caspi, A., Harrington, H., Milne, B., Amell, J. W., Theodore, R. F., and Moffitt, T. E. (2003). Children's behavioral styles at age 3 are linked to their adult personality traits at age 26. *Journal of Personality, 71,* 495–513.

Caspi, A., and Herbener, E. S. (1990). Continuity and change: Assortative mating and the consistency of personality in adulthood. *Journal of Personality and Social Psychology, 58,* 250–258.

Caspi, A., Roberts, B. W., and Shiner, R. L. (2005). Personality development: Stability and change. *Annual Review of Psychology, 56,* 453–458.

Caspi, A., Sugden, K., Moffitt, T., Taylor, A., Craig, I. W., Harringon, H., et al. (2003). Influence of life stress on depression: Moderation by a polymorphism in the 5-HTT gene. *Science, 301,* 386–389.

Cassidy, J., and Shaver, P. (1999). *Handbook of attachment: Theory, research, and clinical applications.* New York: Guilford Press.

Cattell, R. B. (1943). The description of personality: Basic traits resolved into clusters. *Journal of Abnormal and Social Psychology, 38,* 476–507.

Cattell, R. B. (1973). *Personality and mood by questionnaire.* San Francisco: Jossey-Bass.

Cattell, R. B., Eber, H. W., and Tatsouoka, M. M. (1970). *Handbook for the 16 PF.* Champaign, IL: Institute for Personality and Ability Testing.

Chagnon, N. (1983). *Yanomamö: The fierce people* (3rd ed.). New York: Holt, Rinehart and Winston.

Chagnon, N. (1988). Life histories, blood revenge, and warfare in a tribal population. *Science, 239,* 985–992.

Chamorro-Premuzic, T., and Furnham, A. (2003a). Personality predicts academic performance: Evidence from two longitudinal university samples. *Journal of Research in Personality, 37,* 319–338.

Chamorro-Premuzic, T., and Furnham, A. (2003b). Personality traits and academic examination performance. *European Journal of Personality, 17,* 237–250.

Chan, W., McCrae, R. R., De Fruyt, F., Jussim, L., Löckenhoff, C. E., De Bolle, M., . . . and Nakazato, K. (2012). Stereotypes of age differences in personality traits: Universal and accurate? *Journal of Personality and Social Psychology, 103,* 1050–1066.

Chapman, B. P., Dubestein, P. R., Sorensen, S., and Lyness, J. M. (2007). Gender differences in five factor model of personality traits in an elderly cohort. *Personality and Individual Differences, 43,* 1594–1603.

Chapman, B. P., and Goldberg, L. R. (2011). Replicability and 40-year predictive power of childhood ARC types. *Journal of Personality and Social Psychology, 101,* 593–606.

Charles, S. T., Reynolds, C. A. and Gatz, M. (2001). Age-related differences and change in positive and negative affect over 23 years. *Journal of Personality and Social Psychology, 80, 1,* 136–151.

Chavira, D. A., Stein, M. B., and Malcarne, V. L. (2002). Scrutinizing the relationship between shyness and social phobia. *Journal of Anxiety Disorders, 16,* 585–598.

Cheek, J. M. (1983). *The revised Cheek and Buss Shyness Scale.* Unpublished manuscript, Department of Psychology, Wellesley College, Wellesley, MA.

Cheek, J. M. (1989). *Conquering shyness.* New York: Dell.

Cheek, J. M., and Buss, A. H. (1981). Shyness and sociability. *Journal of Personality and Social Psychology, 41,* 330–339.

Cheek, J. M., and Krasnoperova, E. N. (1999). Varieties of shyness in adolescence and adulthood. In L. A. Schmidt and J. Schulkin (Eds.), *Extreme fear, shyness, and social phobia: Origins, biological mechanisms, and clinical outcomes* (pp. 224–250). London: Oxford University Press.

Cheek, J. M., and Melchior, L. A. (1990). Shyness, self-esteem, and self-consciousness. In H. Leitenberg (Ed.), *Handbook of social and evaluation anxiety* (pp. 47–82) New York: Plenum Press.

Cheit, R. E., Shavit, Y., and Reisse-Davis, Z. (2010). Magazine coverage of child sexual abuse, 1992–2004. *Journal of Child Sexual Abuse: Research, Treatment, & Program Innovations for Victims, Survivors, and Offenders, 19,* 99–117.

Chen, C., Burton, M., Greenberger, E., and Dmitrieva, J. (1999). Population migration and the variation of dopamine D4 receptor (DRD4) allele frequencies around the globe. *Evolution and Human Behavior, 20,* 309–324.

Chen, F. F., and West, S. G. (2008). Measuring individualism and collectivism: The importance of considering differential components, reference groups, and measurement invariance. *Journal of Research in Personality, 42,* 259–294.

Chen, F. S., and Johnson, S. C. (2012). An oxytocin receptor gene variant predicts attachment anxiety in females and autism-spectrum traits in males. *Social Psychological and Personality Science, 3,* 93–99.

Cheng, H., and Furnham, A. (2003). Personality, self-esteem, and demographic predictions of happiness and depression. *Personality and Individual Differences, 34,* 921–942.

Chen, S., Su, X., and Wu, S. (2012). Need for achievement, education, and entrepreneurial risk-taking behavior. *Social Behavior and Personality, 40,* 1311–1318.

Chida, Y., and Steptoe, A. (2009). The association of anger and hostility with future coronary heart disease: A meta-analytic review of prospective evidence. *Journal of the American College of Cardiology, 53,* 774–778.

Chioqueta, A. P., and Stiles, T. C. (2005). Personality traits and the development of depression, hopelessness, and suicidal ideation. *Personality and Individual Differences, 38,* 1283–1291.

Chodorow, N. J. (1989). *Feminism and psychoanalytic theory.* New Haven, CT: Yale University Press.

Choi, J. K., and Ji, Y. G. (2015). Investigating the importance of trust on adopting an autonomous vehicle. *International Journal of Human-Computer Interaction, 31*(10), 692–702.

Chow, J. T., and Lau, S. (2015). Nature gives us strength: Exposure to nature counteracts ego-depletion. *The Journal of Social Psychology, 155*(1), 70–85.

Christ, S. E., White, D., Brunstrom, J. E., and Abrams, R. A. (2003). Inhibitory control following perinatal brain injury. *Neuropsychology, 17,* 171–178.

Christie, R., and Geis, F. L. (1970). *Studies in Machiavellianism* (pp. 53–76). New York: Academic Press.

Chu, J. A. (1998). *Rebuilding shattered lives: The responsible treatment of complex post-traumatic and dissociative disorders.* New York: Wiley.

Church, A. T. (2000). Culture and personality: Toward an integrated cultural trait psychology. *Journal of Personality, 68,* 651–703.

Church, A. T. (2009). Prospects for an integrated trait and cultural psychology. *European Journal of Personality, 23,* 153–182.

Church, A. T., Katigbak, M. S., Mazuera Arias, R., Rincon, B. C., Vargas-Flores, J. D. J., Ibáñez-Reyes, J., . . . and Ortiz, F. A. (2014). A four-culture study of self-enhancement and adjustment using the social relations model: Do alternative conceptualizations and indices make a difference? *Journal of Personality and Social psychology, 106,* 997–1014.

Church, A. T., Katigbak, M. S., Miramontes, L. G., del Prado, A. M., and Cabrera, H. F. (2007). Culture and the behavioural manifestations of traits: An application of the act frequency approach. *European Journal of Personality, 21,* 389–417.

Clapper, R. L. (1990). Adult and adolescent arousal preferences: The revised reducer augmenter scale. *Personality and Individual Differences, 11,* 1115–1122.

Clapper, R. L. (1992). The reducer-augmenter scale, the revised reducer augmenter scale, and predicting late adolescent substance use. *Personality and Individual Differences, 13,* 813–820.

Claridge, G. S., Donald, J., and Birchall, P. M. (1981). Drug tolerance and personality: Some implications for Eysenck's theory. *Personality and Individual Differences, 2,* 153–166.

Clark, R. D. (1990). The impact of AIDS on gender differences in willingness to engage in casual sex. *Journal of Applied Social Psychology, 20,* 771–782.

Clark, R. D., and Hatfield, E. (1989). Gender differences in receptivity to sexual offers. *Journal of Psychology and Human Sexuality, 2,* 39–55.

Claxton, A., O'Rourke, N., Smith, J. Z., and DeLongis, A. (2011). Personality traits and marital satisfaction within enduring relationships: An intra-couple discrepancy approach. *Journal of Social and Personal Relationships, 29,* 375–396.

Cleckley, H. (1941). *The mask of sanity: An attempt to reinterpret the so-called psychopathic personality.* Oxford, England: Mosby.

Cleckley, H. (1988). *The mask of sanity.* Augusta, GA: Emily S. Cleckley.

Cleveland, H. H., Udry, J. R., and Chantala, K. (2001). Environmental and genetic influences on sex-types behaviors and attitudes of male and female adolescents. *Personality and Social Psychology Bulletin, 27, 12,* 1587–1598.

Clewley, N., Chen, S. Y., and Liu, X. (2011). Mining learning preferences in Web-based instruction: Holists vs. serialists. *Journal of Educational Technology and Society, 14,* 266–277.

Clifton, A., Turkheimer, E., and Oltmanns, T. F. (2004). Contrasting perspectives on personality problems: Descriptions from the self and others. *Personality and Individual Differences, 36,* 1499–1514.

Cloninger, C. R. (1986). A unified biosocial theory of personality and its role in the development of anxiety states. *Psychiatric Developments, 3,* 167–226.

Cloninger, C. R. (1987). A systematic method for clinical description and classification of personality variants: A proposal. *Archives of General Psychiatry, 44,* 573–588.

Cloninger, C. R. (1999). *Personality and psychopathology.* Washington, DC: American Psychiatric Press.

Cloninger, C. R., Svrakic, D. M., and Przybeck, T. R. (1993). A psychobiological model of temperament and character. *Archives of General Psychiatry, 50,* 975–990.

Clower, C. E., and Bothwell, R. K. (2001). An exploratory study of the relationship between the Big Five and inmate recidivism. *Journal of Research in Personality, 35,* 231–237.

Coan, J. A., and Allen, J. B. (2004). Frontal EEG asymmetry as a moderator and mediator of emotion. *Biological Psychology, 67*(1-2), 7–49.

Coan, J. A., and Gottman, J. M. (2007). Sampling, experimental control, and generalizability in the study of marital process models, *Journal of Marriage and Family, 69,* 73–80.

Cohen, J. (1977). *Statistical power analysis for the behavioral sciences.* San Diego, CA: Academic Press.

Cohen, J., and Cohen, P. (1975). *Applied multiple regression/correlation analysis for the behavioral sciences.* Hillsdale, NJ: Erlbaum.

Cohen, S., Doyle, W. J., Skoner, D. P., Fireman, P., Gwaltney, J. M., Jr., and Newsom, J. T. (1995). State and trait negative affect as predictors of objective and subjective symptoms of respiratory viral infections. *Journal of Personality and Social Psychology, 68,* 159–169.

Cohen, S., Tyrrell, D. A. J., and Smith, A. P. (1997). Psychological stress in humans and susceptibility to the common cold. In T. W. Moller (Ed.), *Clinical disorders and stressful life events* (pp. 217–235). Madison, CT: International Universities Press.

Cohen-Bendahan, C. C., van de Beek, C., and Berenbaum, S. A. (2005). Prenatal sex hormone effects on child and adult sex-typed behavior: methods and findings. *Neuroscience & Biobehavioral Reviews, 29*(2), 353–384.

Coleman, R. (1992). *Lennon: The definitive biography.* New York: Perennial.

College Board Online. (2009). *SAT validity studies.* Retrieved from http://professionals.collegeboard.com/data-reports-research/sat/validity-studies.

Collins, J. N. (1994). Some fundamental questions about scientific thinking. *Research in Science and Technological Education, 12,* 161–173.

Confer, J. C., Easton, J. E., Fleischman, D. S., Goetz, C., Lewis, D. M., Perilloux, C., and Buss, D. M. (2010). Evolutionary psychology: Controversies, questions, prospects, and limitations. *American Psychologist, 65,* 110–126.

Conley, J. J. (1984a). The hierarchy of consistency: A review and model of longitudinal findings on adult individual differences in intelligence, personality, and self-opinion. *Personality and Individual Differences, 5,* 11–25.

Conley, J. J. (1984b). Longitudinal consistency of adult personality: Self-reported psychological characteristics across 45 years. *Journal of Personality and Social Psychology, 47,* 1325–1333.

Conley, J. J. (1985). Longitudinal stability of personality traits: A multitrait-multimethod-multioccasion analysis. *Journal of Personality and Social Psychology, 49,* 1266–1282.

Conley, J. J., and Angelides, M. (1984). *Personality antecedents of emotional disorders and alcohol abuse in men: Results of a forty-five-year prospective study.* Unpublished manuscript: Wesleyan University, Middletown, CT.

Connelly, B. S., and Ones, D. S. (2010). Another perspective on personality: Meta-analytic integration of observers' accuracy and predicative validity. *Psychological Bulletin, 136,* 1092–1122.

Connolly, I., and O'Moore, M. (2003). Personality and family relations of children who bully. *Personality and Individual Differences, 35,* 559–567.

Conrad, M. A. (2006). Aptitude is not enough: How personality and behavior predict academic performances. *Journal of Research in Personality, 40,* 339–346.

Conroy-Beam, D., Buss, D. M., Pham, M. N., and Shackelford, T. K. (2015). How sexually dimorphic are human mate preferences? *Personality and Social Psychology Bulletin, 41,* 1082–1093.

Conroy-Beam, D., Goetz, C. D., & Buss, D. M. (2016). What predicts romantic relationship satisfaction and mate retention intensity: mate preference fulfillment or mate value discrepancies? *Evolution and Human Behavior.*

Cooper, M. L., Wood, P. K., Orcutt, H. K., and Albino, A. (2003). Personality and the predisposition to engage in risky or problem behaviors during adolescence. *Journal of Personality and Social Psychology, 84, 2,* 390–410.

Cooper, S. H. (1998). Changing notions of defense within psychoanalytic theory. *Journal of Personality, 66,* 947–965.

Corcoran, D. W. J. (1964). The relation between introversion and salivation. *American Journal of Psychology, 77,* 298–300.

Cosmides, L., and Tooby, J. (1992). Cognitive adaptations for social exchange. In J. Barkow, L. Cosmides, and J. Tooby (Eds.), *The adapted mind* (pp. 163–228). New York: Academic Press.

Costa, P. T., and McCrae, R. R. (1980). Influence of extraversion and neuroticism on subjective well-being: Happy and unhappy people. *Journal of Personality and Social Psychology, 38,* 668–678.

Costa, P. T., and McCrae, R. R. (1985). Hypochondriasis, neuroticism, and aging: When are somatic complaints unfounded? *American Psychologist, 40,* 19–28.

Costa, P. T., Jr., and McCrae, R. R. (1988). Personality in adulthood: A six-year longitudinal study of self-reports and spouse ratings on the NEO Personality Inventory. *Journal of Personality and Social Psychology, 54,* 853–863.

Costa, P. T., Jr., and McCrae, R. R. (1989). *The NEO-PI/NEO-FFI manual supplement.* Odessa, FL: Psychological Assessment Resources.

Costa, P. T., Jr., and McCrae, R. R. (1992). Trait psychology comes of age. In T. B. Sonderegger (Ed.), *Nebraska symposium on motivation: Psychology and aging* (pp. 169–204). Lincoln: University of Nebraska Press.

Costa, P. T., Jr., and McCrae, R. R. (1994). Set like plaster? Evidence for the stability of adult personality. In T. F. Heatherton and J. L. Weinberger (Eds.), *Can personality change?* Washington, DC: American Psychological Association.

Costa, P. T., Jr., and McCrae, R. R. (1995). Solid ground in the wetlands of personality: A reply to Block. *Psychological Bulletin, 117,* 216–220.

Costa, P. T., Jr., and McCrae, R. R. (2005). The NEO-PI-3: A more readable revised NEO personality inventory. *Journal of Personality, 84,* 261–270.

Costa, P. T., McCrae, R. R., and Zonderman, A. B. (1987). Environmental and dispositional influences on well-being: Longitudinal follow-up of an American national sample. *British Journal of Psychology, 78,* 299–306.

Costa, P. T., and Widiger, T. A. (Eds.). (1994). *Personality disorders and the five-factor model of personality.* Washington, DC: American Psychological Association.

Costa, P. T., and Widiger, T. A. (Eds.). (2002). *Personality disorders and the five-factor model of personality.* (2nd ed.). Washington, DC: American Psychological Association.

Coutts, L. M. (1990). Police hiring and promotion: Methods and outcomes. *Canadian Police College Journal, 14,* 98–122.

Cox, K., and McAdams, D. P. (2012). The transforming self: Service narratives and identity change in emerging adulthood. *Journal of Adolescent Research, 27,* 18–43.

Craik, K. H. (1986). Personality research methods: An historical perspective. *Journal of Personality, 54,* 18–51.

Craik, K. H. (2008). *Reputation: A network analysis.* New York: Oxford University Press.

Cramer, P. (1991). *The development of defense mechanisms: Theory, research, and assessment.* New York: Springer-Verlag.

Cramer, P. (2000). Defense mechanisms in psychology today: Further processes for adaptation. *American Psychologist, 55,* 637–646.

Cramer, P. (2002). Defense mechanisms, behavior, and affect in young adulthood. *Journal of Personality, 70,* 103–126.

Cramer, P. (2012). Psychological maturity and change in adult defense mechanisms. *Journal of Research in Personality, 46,* 306–316.

Cramer, P., and Davidson, K. (1998). Defense mechanisms in contemporary personality research. *Special Issue of the Journal of Personality, 66.*

Crandall, V., Dewey, R., Katkovsky, W., and Preston, A. (1964). Parents' attitudes and behaviors and grade-school children's academic achievements. *Journal of Genetic Psychology, 104,* 53–66.

Crede, M., Tynan, M.C., and Harms, P.D. (in press). Much ado about Grit: A meta-analytic synthesis of the Grit literature. *Journal of Personality and Social Psychology.*

Creswell, J. D., Bursley, J. K., and Satpute, A. B. (2013). Neural reactivation links unconscious thought to decision-making performance. *Social Cognitive and Affective Neuroscience, 8*(8), 863–869.

Crocker, J., and Major, B. (1989). Social stigma and self-esteem: The self-protective properties of stigma. *Psychological Review, 96,* 608–630.

Cronbach, L. J., and Gleser, G. C. (1965). *Psychological tests and personnel decisions.* Urbana: University of Illinois Press.

Cronbach, L. J., and Meehl, P. E. (1955). Construct validity in psychological tests. *Psychological Bulletin, 52,* 281–302.

Crone, E. A., Vendel, I., and van der Molen, M. W. (2003). Decision-making in disinhibited adolescents and adults: Insensitivity to future consequences or driven by immediate reward? *Personality and Individual Differences, 35,* 1625–1641.

Cross, C. P., Copping, L. T., and Campbell, A. (2011). Sex differences in impulsivity: A meta-analysis. *Psychological Bulletin, 137,* 97–130.

Cross, S. E., Kanagawa, C., Markus, H. R., and Kitayama, S. (1995). *Cultural variation in self-concept.* Unpublished manuscript, Iowa State University, Ames.

Crowne, D. P., and Marlowe, D. (1964). *The approval motive: Studies in evaluation dependence.* New York: Wiley.

Cruce, S. E., Pashak, T. J., Handal, P. J., Munz, D. C., and Gfeller, J. D. (2012). Conscientious perfectionism, self-evaluative perfectionism, and the five-factor model of personality traits. *Personality and Individual Differences, 53,* 268–273.

Cruz, M., and Larsen, R. J. (1995). Personality correlates of individual differences in electrodermal lability. *Journal of Social Behavior and Personality, 23,* 93–104.

Csikszentmihalyi, M. (1999). If we are so rich, why aren't we happy? *American Psychologist, 54,* 821–827.

Csikszentmihalyi, M. (2000). *Beyond boredom and anxiety* (25th anniversary ed.). San Francisco: Jossey-Bass. (Original work published 1975)

Csikszentmihalyi, M., Abuhamdeh, S., and Nakamura, J. (2005). Flow. In A. J. Elliot and C. S. Dweck (Eds.), *Handbook of competence and motivation* (pp. 598–608). New York: Guilford Press.

Curtis, V., Aunger, R., and Rabie, T. (2004). Evidence that disgust evolved to protect from risk of disease. *Proceedings of the Royal Society of London B: Biological Sciences, 271*(Suppl 4), S131–S133.

Curtis, V., and Biran, A. (2001). Dirt, disgust, and disease: Is hygiene in our genes? *Perspectives in Biology and Medicine, 44*(1), 17–31.

Cutler, S. S., Larsen, R. J., and Bunce, S. C. (1996). Repressive coping style and the experience and recall of emotion: A naturalistic study of daily affect. *Journal of Personality, 65,* 379–405.

Dabbs, J. M., Jr., and Dabbs, M. G. (2000). *Heroes, rogues and lovers: Testosterone and behavior.* New York: McGraw-Hill.

Dabbs, J. M., Jr., and Hargrove, M. F. (1997). Age, testosterone, and behavior among female prison inmates. *Psychosomatic Medicine, 59,* 477–480.

Dabbs, J. M., Jr., Hargrove, M. F., and Heusel, C. (1996). Testosterone differences among college fraternities: Well-behaved vs. rambunctious. *Personality and Individual Differences, 20,* 157–161.

Dalgleish, T. (1995). Performance on the emotional Stroop task in groups of anxious, expert, and control subjects: A comparison of computer and card presentation formats. *Cognition and Emotion, 9,* 341–362.

Daly, M., and Wilson, M. (1988). *Homicide.* New York: Aldine de Gruyter.

Damasio, A. R. (1994). *Descartes' error: Emotion, reason, and the human brain.* New York: Putnam.

Danner, D. D., Snowdon, D. A., and Friesen, W. V. (2001). Positive emotions in early life and longevity: Findings from the nun study. *Journal of Personality and Social Psychology, 80,* 804–813.

Darwin, C. (1859) *The origin of species.* London: Murray.

Darwin, C. (1872/1965). *The expression of the emotions in man and animals.* Chicago: University of Chicago Press.

Davidson, K. W., Gidron, Y., Mostofsky, E., and Trudeau, K. J. (2007). Hospitalization cost offset of a hostility intervention for coronary heart disease patients. *Journal of Consulting and Clinical Psychology, 75,* 657–662.

Davidson, R. J. (1991). Cerebral asymmetry and affective disorders: A developmental approach. In D. Cicchetti and S. L. Toth (Eds.), *Internalizing and Externalizing Expressions of Dysfunction: Rochester Symposium and Developmental Psychopathology* (Vol. 2, pp. 123–154). Hillsdale, NJ: Erlbaum.

Davidson, R. J. (1993). The neuropsychology of emotion and affective style. In M. Lewis and J. M. Haviland (Eds.), *Handbook of emotions* (pp. 143–154). New York: Guilford Press.

Davidson, R. J. (2000). Affective style, psychopathology, and resilience: Brain mechanisms and plasticity. *American Psychologist, 55,* 1196–1214.

Davidson, R. J., Ekman, P., Saron, C. D., Senulis, J. A., and Friesen, W. V. (1990). Approach/withdrawal and cerebral asymmetry: Emotional expression and brain physiology. I. *Journal of Personality and Social Psychology, 58,* 330–341.

Davidson, R. J., Kabat-Zinn, J., Schumacher, J., Rosenkranz, M., Muller, D., Santorelli, S. F., Urbanowski, F., Harrington, A., Bonus, K., and Sheridan, J. F. (2003). Alterations in brain and immune function produced by mindfulness meditation. *Psychosomatic Medicine, 65,* 564–570.

Davidson, R. J., Scherer, K. R., and Goldsmith, H. H. (2003). *Handbook of affective sciences.* New York: Oxford University Press.

Davis, M. H., Luce, C., and Kraus, S. J. (1994). The heritability of characteristics associated with dispositional empathy. *Journal of Personality, 62,* 369–391.

Davis, M. H., Mitchell, K. V., Hall, J. A., Lothert, J., Snapp, T., and Meyer, M. (1999). Empathy, expectations, and situational preferences: Personality influences on the decision to participate in volunteer helping behaviors. *Journal of Personality, 67,* 469–503.

Davis, P. J. (1987). Repression and the inaccessibility of affective memories. *Journal of Personality and Social Psychology, 53,* 585–593.

Davis, P. J., and Schwartz, G. E. (1987). Repression and the inaccessibility of affective memories. *Journal of Personality and Social Psychology, 52,* 155–162.

De Raad, B. (1998). Five big, big five issues: Rationale, content, structure, status, and crosscultural assessment. *European Psychologist, 3,* 113–124.

De Raad, B., and Barelds, D.P.H. (2008). A new taxonomy of Dutch personality traits based on a comprehensive and unrestricted list of descriptors. *Journal of Personality and Social Psychology, 94,* 347–364.

De Raad, B., Barelds, D. P. H., Levert, E., Ostendof, F., Mlacic, B., De Blas, L., Hrebickova, M., et al. (2010). Only three factors of personality description are fully replicable across languages: A comparison of 14 trait taxonomies. *Journal of Personality and Social Psychology, 98,* 1060–1173.

De Raad, B., Perugini, M., Hrebickova, M., and Szarota, P. (1998). Lingua Franca of personality: Taxonomies and structures based on the psycholexical approach. *Journal of Cross-Cultural Psychology, 29,* 212–232.

De Vries, J., and Van Heck, G. L. (2002). Fatigue: Relationships with basic personality and temperament dimensions. *Personality and Individual Differences, 33,* 1311–1324.

Del Giudice, M., and Belsky, J. (in press). The development of life history strategies: Toward a multi-stage theory. In D. M. Buss and P. Hawley (Eds.), *The evolution of personality and individual differences.* New York: Oxford University Press.

del Prado, A. M., Church, A. T., Katigbak, M. S., Miramontes, L. G., Whitty, M. T., Curtis, G. J., et al. (2007). Culture, method, and the content of self-concepts: Testing trait, individual-self primacy, and cultural psychology perspectives. *Journal of Research in Personality, 41,* 1119–1160.

DeAngelis, T. (1991). Honesty tests weigh in with improved ratings. *APA Monitor, 22,* 6.

De Bolle, M., De Fruyt, F., McCrae, R. R., Löckenhoff, C. E., Costa Jr, P. T., Aguilar-Vafaie, M. E., . . . and Avdeyeva, T. V. (2015). The emergence of sex differences in personality traits in early adolescence: A cross-sectional, cross-cultural study. *Journal of Personality and Social Psychology, 108,* 171–185.

Deaner, R. O., Goetz, S. M. M., Shattuck, K., and Schnotala, T. (2012). Body weight, not facial width-to-height ratio, predicts aggression in pro hockey players. *Journal of Research in Personality, 46,* 235–238.

Deaux, K. (1984). From individual differences to social categories: Analysis of a decade's research on gender. *American Psychologist, 39,* 105–116.

Deaux, K., and LaFrance, M. (1998). Gender. In D. T. Gilbert, S. T. Fiske, and G. Lindzey (Eds.), *The handbook of social psychology* (vol. 1, 4th ed., pp. 788–827). Boston: McGraw-Hill.

Deaux, K., and Lewis, L. L. (1984). Structure of gender stereotypes: Interrelationships among components and gender label. *Journal of Personality and Social Psychology, 46,* 991–1004.

Decuyper, M., De Bolle, M., & De Fruyt, F. (2012). Personality similarity, perceptual accuracy, and relationship satisfaction in dating and married couples. *Personal Relationships, 19,* 128–145.

Deiner, C. I., and Dweck, C. S. (1978). An analysis of learned helplessness: Continuous changes in performance, strategy, and achievement cognitions following failure. *Journal of Personality and Social Psychology, 36,* 451–462.

Deiner, C. I., and Dweck, C. S. (1980). An analysis of learned helplessness (II): The processing of success. *Journal of Personality and Social Psychology, 39,* 940–952.

Del Giudice, M., and Belsky, J. (2011). The development of life history strategies: Toward a multi-stage theory. In D.M. Buss and P. Hawley (Eds.), *The evolution of personality and individual differences.* New York: Oxford University Press.

Delongis, A., Folkman, S., and Lazarus, R. S. (1988). The impact of daily stress on health and mood: Psychological and social resources as mediators. *Journal of Personality and Social Psychology, 54,* 986–995.

Dembrowski, T. M., and Costa, P. T. (1987). Coronary-prone behavior: Components of the Type A pattern and hostility. *Journal of Personality, 55,* 211–235.

Demerath, P. (2001). The social cost of acting "extra": Students' moral judgments of self, social relations, and academic success in Papua New Guinea. *American Journal of Education, 108,* 3.

DeMeuse, K. (1985). The relationship between life events and indices of classroom performance. *Teaching of Psychology, 12,* 146–149.

Denissen, J. J. (2014). A roadmap for further progress in research on personality development. *European Journal of Personality, 28,* 213–215.

Denissen, J. J. A., and Penke, L. (2008a). Motivational individual reaction norms underlying the five-factor model of personality: First steps toward a theory-based conceptual framework. *Journal of Research in Personality, 42,* 1285–1302.

Denissen, J. J. A., and Penke, L. (2008b). Neuroticism predicts reactions to cues of social exclusion. *European Journal of Personality, 22,* 497–517.

Denissen, J., Penke, L., Schmitt, D. P., and van Aken, M. (2008). Self-esteem reactions to social interactions: Evidence for sociometer mechanisms across days, people, and nations. *Journal of Personality and Social Psychology, 95,* 181–196.

Denollet, J. (2000). Type D personality: A potential risk factor refined. *Journal of Psychosomatic Research, 49,* 255–266.

Denollet, J. (2005). DS14: Standard assessment of negative affectivity, social inhibition, and Type D personality. *Psychosomatic Medicine, 67,* 89–97.

Denollet, J., Conraads, V. M., Brutsart, D. L., De Clerck, L. S., Stevens, W. J., and Brints, C. J. (2003). Cytokines and immune activation in systolic heart failure: The role of Type D personality. *Brain, Behavior, and Immunity, 17,* 304–309.

Denollet, J., Pedersen, S. S., Ong, A. T., Erdman, R. A., Serruys, P. W., and van Domburg, R. T. (2006). Social inhibition modulates the effects of negative emotions on cardiac prognosis following percutaneous coronary intervention in the drug-eluting stent era. *European Heart Journal, 27,* 171–177.

DePaulo, B. (2006). *Singled out: How singles are stereotyped, stigmatized, and ignored, and still live happily ever after.* New York: St. Martin's Press.

DePaulo, B. M., Dull, W. R., Greenberg, J. M., and Swaim, G. (1989). Are shy people reluctant to ask for help? *Journal of Personality and Social Psychology, 56,* 834–844.

DePaulo, B. M., Kenny, D. A., Hoover, C. W., Webb, W., and Oliver, P. V. (1987). Accuracy of person perception: Do people know what kinds of impressions they convey? *Journal of Personality and Social Psychology, 52,* 303–315.

DePrince, A. P., Brown, L. S., Cheit, R. E., Freyd, J. J., Gold, S. N., Pezdek, K., and Quina, K. (2012). Motivated forgetting and misremember: Perspectives from betrayal trauma theory. In R. F. Belli (Ed.), *True and false recovered memories: Toward a reconciliation of the debate* (pp. 193–242). New York: Springer.

Depue, R. A. (1996). A neurobiological framework for the structure of personality and emotion: Implications for personality disorders. In J. Clarkin and M. Lenzenweger (Eds.), *Major theories of personality disorders* (pp. 347–390). New York: Guilford Press.

Depue, R. A. (2006). Interpersonal behavior and the structure of personality: Neurobehavioral foundations of agentic extraversion and affiliation. In T. Canli (Ed.), *Biology of personality and individual differences* (pp. 60–92). New York: Guilford Press.

Depue, R. A., and Collins, P. F. (1999). Neurobiology of the structure of personality: Dopamine, facilitation of incentive motivation, and extraversion. *Behavioral and Brain Sciences, 22,* 491–517.

DeSteno, D. A., Bartlett, M. Y., Salovey, P., and Braverman, J. (2002). Sex differences in jealousy: Evolutionary mechanisms of experimental artifact? *Journal of Personality and Social Psychology, 83,* 1103–1116.

Depue, R. A., and Fu, Y. (2013). On the nature of extraversion: Variation in conditioned contextual activation of dopamine-facilitated affective, cognitive, and motor processes. *Frontiers in Human Neuroscience, 7.*

Derakshan, N., Eysenck, M. W., and Myers, L. B. (2007). Emotional information processing in repressors: The vigilance-avoidance theory. *Cognition and Emotion, 21*(8), 1585–1614.

DeSteno, D. A., and Salovey, P. (1996). Evolutionary origins of sex differences in jealousy: Questioning the "fitness" of the model. *Psychological Science, 7,* 367–372.

DeWall, C. N., Baumeister, R. F., Stillman, T. F., and Gailliot, M. T. (2007). Violence restrained: Effects of self-regulatory capacity and its depletion on aggressive behavior. *Journal of Experimental Social Psychology, 33,* 1547–1558.

DeWall, C. N., Buffardi, L. E., Bosner, I., and Campbell, W. K. (2011). Narcissism and implicit attention seeking: Evidence from linguistic analyses of social networking and online presentation. *Personality and Individual Differences, 51,* 57–62.

DeYoung, C. G. (2010). Personality neuroscience and the biology of traits. *Social and Personality Psychology Compass, 4,* 1165–1180.

DeYoung, C. G. (2015). Openness/Intellect: A dimension of personality reflecting cognitive exploration. In L. Cooper and R. J. Larsen (Eds.), *Handbook of personality and social psychology: Personality*

processes and individual differences (369–400). Washington, DC: American Psychological Association.

DeYoung, C. G., Grazioplene, R. G., and Peterson, J. B. (2012). From madness to genius: The openness/intellect trait domain as a paradoxical simplex. *Journal of Research in Personality, 46,* 63–78.

DeYoung, C. G., Hirsh, J. B., Shane, M.S., Rajeevan, N., and Gray, J. R. (2010). Testing predictions from personality neuroscience: Brain structure and the big five. *Psychological Science, 21,* 820–828.

DeYoung, C. G., Shamosh, N. A., Green, A. E., Braver, T. S., and Gray, J. R. (2009). Intellect as distinct from openness: Differences revealed by fMRI of working memory. *Journal of Personality and Social Psychology, 97,* 883–892.

Di Blas, L. (2005). Personality-relevant attribute-nouns: A taxonomic study in the Italian language. *European Journal of Personality, 19,* 537–557.

Di Blas, L. (2007). A circumplex model of interpersonal attributes in middle childhood. *Journal of Personality, 75,* 863–897.

Diamond, J. (1999). *Guns, germs, and steel.* New York: Norton.

Diener, E. (2000). Subjective well-being: The science of happiness and a proposal for a national index. *American Psychologist, 55,* 34–43.

Diener, E., and Biswas-Diener, R. (2002). Will money increase subjective well-being? A literature review and guide to needed research. *Social Indicators Research, 57,* 119–169.

Diener, E., and Biswas-Diener, R. (2008). *Happiness: Unlocking the mysteries of psychological wealth.* Malden, MA: Blackwell.

Diener, E., and Diener, M. (1995). Cross-cultural correlates of life satisfaction and self-esteem. *Journal of Personality and Social Psychology, 68,* 653–663.

Diener, E., Diener, M., and Diener, C. (1995). Factors predicting the subjective well-being of nations. *Journal of Personality and Social Psychology, 69,* 851–864.

Diener, E., Emmons, R. A., Larsen, R. J., and Griffin, S. (1985). The Satisfaction With Life Scale. *Journal of Personality Assessment, 49,* 71–75.

Diener, E., Ng, W., Harter, J., and Arora, R. (2010). Wealth and happiness across the world: Material prosperity predicts life evaluation, whereas psychosocial prosperity predicts positive feeling. *Journal of Personality and Social Psychology, 99,* 52–61.

Diener, E., Horowitz, J., and Emmons, R. A. (1985). Happiness of the very wealthy. *Social Indicators Research, 16,* 263–274.

Diener, E., and Larsen, R. J. (1984). Temporal stability and cross-situational consistency of affective, behavioral, and cognitive responses. *Journal of Personality and Social Psychology, 47,* 871–883.

Diener, E., Larsen, R. J., and Emmons, R. A. (1984). Person X situation interactions: Choice of situations and congruence response models. *Journal of Personality and Social Psychology, 47,* 580–592.

Diener, E., Larsen, R. J., Levine, S., and Emmons, R. A. (1985). Intensity and frequency: Dimensions underlying positive and negative affect. *Journal of Personality and Social Psychology, 48,* 1253–1265.

Diener, E., Lucas, R. E., and Larsen, R. J. (2003). Measuring positive emotions. In C. R. Snyder, and S. J. Lopez (Eds.), *The handbook of positive psychological assessment* (pp. 201–218). Washington, DC: American Psychological Association.

Diener, E., Oishi, S., and Lucas, R. E. (2003). Personality, culture, and subjective well-being: Emotional and cognitive evaluations of life. *Annual Review of Psychology, 54,* 403–425.

Diener, E., Sandvik, E., Seidlitz, L., and Diener, M. (1993). The relationship between income and subjective well-being: Relative or absolute? *Social Indicators Research, 28,* 195–223.

Diener, E., and Scollon, C. N. (2002). Our desired future for personality psychology. *Journal of Research in Personality, 36,* 629–637.

Diener, E., and Seligman, M. E. P. (2002). Very happy people. *Psychological Science, 13,* 80–83.

Diener, E., Suh, E. M., Lucas, R. E., and Smith, H. L. (1999). Subjective well-being: Three decades of progress. *Psychological Bulletin, 125,* 276–302.

Digman, J. M., and Inouye, J. (1986). Further specification of the five robust factors of personality. *Journal of Personality and Social Psychology, 50,* 116–123.

Dijksterhhuis, A., Bos, M. W., Nordgren, L. F., and van Baaren, R. B. (2006). On making the right choice: The deliberation-without-attention effect. *Science, 311,* 1005–1007.

Dijkstra, P., and Barelds, D.P.H. (2008). Self and partner personality and responses to relationship threat. *Journal of Research in Personality, 42,* 1500–1511.

Dijkstra, P., and Buunk, B. P. (2001). Sex differences in the jealousy-evoking nature of a rival's body build. *Evolution and Human Behavior, 22,* 335–341.

Dill, K. E., Anderson, C. A., Anderson, K. B., and Deuser, W. E. (1999). Effects of aggressive personality on social expectations and social perceptions. *Journal of Research in Personality, 31,* 272–292.

Dixon, W. A., Mauzey, E. D., and Hall, C. R. (2003). Physical activity and exercise: Implications for counselors. *Journal of Counseling and Development, 81,* 502–505.

Dodge, K. A., and Coie, J. D. (1987). Social-information-processing factors in reactive and proactive aggression in children's peer groups. *Journal of Personality and Social Psychology, 53,* 1146–1158.

Donhauser, P. W., Rösch, A. G., and Schultheiss, O. C. (2015). The implicit need for power predicts recognition speed for dynamic changes in facial expressions of emotion. *Motivation and Emotion, 39*(5), 714–721.

Donnellan, M. B., Kenny, D. A., Trzesniewski, K. H., Lucas, R. E., and Conger, R. D. (2012). Using trait-state models to evaluate the longitudinal consistency of global self-esteem from adolescence to adulthood. *Journal of Research in Personality, 46,* 634–645.

Donnellan, M. B., Larsen-Rife, D., and Conger, R. D. (2005). Personality, family history, and competence in early adult romantic relationships. *Journal of Personality and Social Psychology, 88,* 562–576.

Donnellan, M. B., Trzesniewski, K. H., and Robins, R. W. (2009). An emerging epidemic of narcissism or much ado about nothing? *Journal of Research in Personality, 43,* 498–501.

Donohew, L., Zimmerman, R., Cupp, P. S., Novak, S., Colon, S., and Abell, R. (2000). Sensation seeking, impulsive decision-making, and risky sex: Implications for risk-taking and design interventions. *Personality and Individual Differences, 28,* 1079–1091.

Dreber, A., Apilcella, C. L., Eisenberg, D. T. A., Garcia, J. R., Zamore, R. S., Lum, J. K., and Campbell, B. (2009). The 7R polymorphism in the dopamine receptor D4 gene (DRD4) is associated with financial risk taking in men. *Evolution and Human Behavior, 30,* 85–92.

Drislane, L. E., Patrick, C. J., and Arsal, G. (2014). Clarifying the content coverage of differing psychopathy inventories through reference to the Triarchic Psychopathy Measure. *Psychological Assessment, 26*(2), 350–362.

Dubbert, Patricia M. (2002). Physical activity and exercise: Recent advances and current challenges. *Journal of Consulting and Clinical Psychology Special Issue: Behavioral medicine and clinical health psychology, 70,* 526–536.

Duckworth, A. L., Peterson, C., Matthews, M. D., and Kelly, D. R. (2007). Grit: Perseverance and passion for long-term goals. *Journal of Personality and Individual Differences, 92,* 1087–1101.

Dudley, N. M., Orvis, K. A., Lebiecki, J. E., and Cortina, J. M. (2006). A meta-analytic investigation of conscientiousness in the prediction of job performance: Examining the intercorrelations and the incremental validity of narrow traits. *Journal of Applied Psychology, 91,* 40–57.

Dunbar, R. I. M. (1993). Coevolution of neocortical size, group size, and language in humans. *Behavioral and Brain Sciences, 16,* 681–735.

Dunlop, P. D., Lee, K., Ashton, M. C., Butcher, S. B., and Dykstra, A. (2015). Please accept my sincere and humble apologies: The HEXACO model of personality and the proclivity to apologize. *Personality and Individual Differences, 79,* 140–145.

Dunn, E. W., Aknin, L. B., and Norton, M. I. (2008). Spending money on others promotes happiness. *Science, 319,* 1687–1688.

Dweck, C. S. (1999a). Caution—praise can be dangerous. *American Educator, 23,* 4–9.

Dweck, C. S. (1999b). *Self-theories: Their role in motivation, personality, and development.* Philadelphia: The Psychology Press.

Dweck, C. S. (2002). Beliefs that make smart people dumb. In R. J. Sternberg (Ed.), *Why smart people can be so stupid* (pp. 24–41). New Haven, CT: Yale University Press.

Dweck, C. S. (2006). *Mindset.* New York: Random House.

Dweck, C. S., Chiu, C., and Hong, Y. (1995). Implicit theories and their role in judgments and reactions: A world from two perspectives. *Psychological Inquiry, 6,* 267–285.

Dweck, C. S., and Master, A. (2009). Self-theories and motivation: Students' beliefs about intelligence. In K. R. Wenzel, A. Wigfield, K. R. Wenzel, A. Wigfield (Eds.), *Handbook of motivation at school* (pp. 123–140). New York, NY, US: Routledge/Taylor & Francis Group.

Eagly, A. H. (1987). *Sex differences in social behavior: A social-role interpretation.* Hillsdale, NJ: Erlbaum.

Eagly, A. H. (1995). The science and politics of comparing women and men. *American Psychologist, 50,* 145–158.

Eagly, A., and Wood, W. (1999). A social role interpretation of sex differences in human mate preferences. *American Psychologist, 54,* 408–423.

Easterlin, R. A. (1974). Does economic growth improve the human lot: Some empirical evidence. In P. A. David and W. R. Levin (Eds.), *Nations and households in economic growth* (pp. 98–125). Palo Alto, CA: Stanford University Press.

Easterlin, R. A. (1995). Will raising the incomes of all increase the happiness of all? *Journal of Economic Behavior and Organization, 27,* 35–47.

Ebstein, R., Novick, O., Umansky, R., Priel, B., Osher, Y., Blaine, D., Bennett, E. R., Nemanov, L., Katz, M., and Belmaker, R. H. (1996). Dopamine D4 receptor (D4DR) exon III polymorphism associated with the human personality trait of novelty seeking. *Nature Genetics, 12,* 78–80.

Edmundson, M., Berry, D. R., High, W. M., Shandera-Ochsner, A. L., Harp, J. P., and Koehl, L. M. (2015). A meta-analytic review of Minnesota Multiphasic Personality inventory—2nd edition (mmpi-2) profile elevations following traumatic brain injury. *Psychological Injury And Law.*

Edwards, D. A., Wetzel, K., and Wyner, D. R. (2006). Intercollegiate soccer: Saliva cortisol and testosterone are elevated during competition, and testosterone is related to status and social connectedness with teammates. *Physiology and Behavior, 30,* 135–143.

Egan, S., and Stelmack, R. M. (2003). A personality profile of Mount Everest climbers. *Personality and Individual Differences, 34,* 1491–1494.

Eid, M., and Larsen, R. J. (2008). *The science of subjective well-being.* New York: Guilford Press.

Eisenberg, D.T.A., Campbell, B., Gray, P. B., and Soronson, M. D. (2008). Dopamine receptor genetic polymorphisms and body composition in undernourished pastoralists: An exploration of nutrition indices among nomadic and recently settled Ariaal men of northern Kenya. *BMC Evolutionary Biology, 8,* 173.

Eisenberg, N., Guthrie, I. K., Cumberland, A., Murphy, B. C., Shepard, S. A., Zhou, Q., and Carlo, G. (2002). Prosocial development in early adulthood: A longitudinal study. *Journal of Personality and Social Psychology, 82, 6,* 993–1006.

Ekman, P. (1973). Cross-cultural studies of facial expression. In P. Ekman (Ed.), *Darwin and facial expression: A century of research in review* (pp. 169–222). New York: Academic Press.

Ekman, P. (1992a). An argument for basic emotions. *Cognition and Emotion, 6,* 169–200.

Ekman, P. (1992b). Facial expressions of emotion: New findings, new questions. *Psychological Science, 3,* 34–38.

Ekman, P., (1999). In T. Dalgleish and M. Power (Eds.), *Handbook of Cognition and emotion.* Sussex, U.K: John Wiley & Sons.

Ekman, P., Friesen, W. V., and Ellsworth, P. (1972). *Emotion in the human face: Guidelines for research and an integration of findings.* New York: Pergamon Press.

Ekman, P., Friesen, W. V., O'Sullivan, M., Chan, A., Diacoyanni-Tarlatzis, I., Heider, K., Krause, R., et al. (1987). Universals and cultural differences in the judgments of facial expressions of emotions. *Journal of Personality and Social Psychology, 53,* 712–717.

Elder, G. H., and Clipp, E. C. (1988). Wartime losses and social bonding: Influence across 40 years in men's lives. *Psychiatry, 51,* 117–198.

Elfenbein, H. H., Curhan, J. R., Eisenkraft, N., Shirako, A., and Baccaro, L. (2008). Are some negotiators better than others? Individual differences in bargaining outcomes. *Journal of Research in Personality, 42,* 1463–1475.

Elkins, I. J., King, S. M., McGue, M., and Iacono, W. G. (2006). Personality traits and the development of nicotine, alcohol, and illicit drug disorders: Prospective links from adolescence to young adulthood. *Journal of Abnormal Psychology, 115,* 26–39.

Elliot, A. J., and Dweck, C. S. (2005). *Handbook of competence and motivation.* New York: Guilford Press.

Ellis, B. J., Simpson, J. A., and Campbell, L. (2002). Trait-specific dependence in romantic relationships. *Journal of Personality, 70,* 611–660.

Ellis, L., and Bonin, S. L. (2003). Genetics and occupation-related preferences. Evidence from adoptive and nonadoptive families. *Personality and Individual Differences, 35,* 929–937.

Else-Quest, N. M., Hyde, J. S., Goldsmith, H. H., and Van Hulle, C. A. (2006). Gender differences in temperament: A meta-analysis. *Psychological Bulletin, 132,* 33–72.

Emmons, R. A. (1987). Narcissism: Theory and measurement. *Journal of Personality and Social Psychology, 52,* 11–17.

Emmons, R. A. (1989). The personal striving approach to personality. In L. Pervin et al. (Eds.), *Goal concepts in personality and social psychology* (pp. 87–126). Hillsdale, NJ: Erlbaum.

Endler, N. S., and Magnusson, D. (1976). Toward an interactional psychology of personality. *Psychological Bulletin, 83,* 956–974.

Engelhard, I. M., van den Hout, M. A., and Kindt, M. (2003). The relationship between neuroticism, pre-traumatic stress, and post-traumatic stress: A prospective study. *Personality and Individual Differences, 35,* 381–388.

Englert, C., and Bertrams, A. (2014). The effect of ego depletion on sprint start reaction time. *Journal of Sport & Exercise Psychology, 36*(5), 506–515.

Entwisle, D. R. (1972). To dispel fantasies about fantasy-based measures of achievement motivation. *Psychological Bulletin, 77,* 377–391.

Epstein, S. (1979). The stability of behavior: I. On predicting most of the people much of the time. *Journal of Personality and Psychology, 37,* 1097–1126.

Epstein, S. (1980). The stability of behavior: II. Implications for psychological research. *American Psychologist, 35,* 790–806.

Epstein, S. (1983). Aggregation and beyond: Some basic issues on the prediction of behavior. *Journal of Personality, 51,* 360–392.

Erdelyi, M. H., and Goldberg, B. (1979). Let's not sweep repression under the rug: Toward a cognitive psychology of repression. In J. G. Kihlstrom and F. J. Evans (Eds.), *Functional disorders of memory* (pp. 355–402). Hillsdale, NJ: Erlbaum.

Erdheim, J., Wang, M., and Zickar, M. J. (2006). Linking the Big Five personality constructs to organizational commitment. *Personality and Individual Differences, 41,* 959–970.

Erikson, E. H. (1963). *Childhood and society* (2nd ed.). New York: Norton. (Original work published 1950)

Erikson, E. H. (1968). *Identity: Youth and crisis.* New York: Norton.

Erikson, E. H. (1975). *Life history and the historical moment.* New York: Norton.

Evans, C. A., Nelson, L. J., and Porter, C. L. (2009). Making sense of their world: Sensory reactivity and novelty awareness as aspects of temperament and correlates of social behaviours in early childhood. *Dissertation Abstracts International: Section B: The Sciences and Engineering, 69*(10-B), 6450.

Evans, C., Richardson, J. E., and Waring, M. (2013). Field independence: Reviewing the evidence. *British Journal Of Educational Psychology, 83*(2), 210–224.

Exline, J. J., Baumeister, R. F., Bushman, B. J., Campbell, W. K., and Finkel, E. J. (2004). Too proud to let go: Narcissistic entitlement as a barrier to forgiveness. *Journal of Personality and Social Psychology, 87,* 894–912.

Exline, R. V., Thiabaut, J., Hickey, C. B., and Gumpart, P. (1970). Visual interaction in relation to expectations, and situational preferences: Personality influences on the decision to participate in volunteer helping behaviors. *Journal of Personality, 67,* 470–503.

Eysenck, H. J. (1967). *The biological basis of personality.* Springfield, IL: Charles C Thomas.

Eysenck, H. J. (Ed.). (1981). *A model for personality.* Berlin: Springer-Verlag.

Eysenck, H. J. (1985). *The decline and fall of the Freudian empire.* London: Viking Press.

Eysenck, H. J. (1990). Biological dimensions of personality. In L. Pervin (Ed.), *Handbook of personality theory and research* (pp. 244–276). New York: Guilford Press.

Eysenck, H. J. (1991). Biological dimensions of personality. In L. A. Pervin (Ed.), *Handbook of personality* (pp. 244–276). New York: Guilford Press.

Eysenck, H. J. (2000). Personality as a risk factor in cancer and coronary heart disease. In D. T. Kenny and J. G. Carlson (Eds.), *Stress and health: Research and clinical applications* (pp. 291–318). Amsterdam, Netherlands: Harwood Academic.

Eysenck, H. J., and Eysenck, M. W. (1985). *Personality and individual differences: A natural science approach.* New York: Plenum Press.

Eysenck, H. J., and Eysenck, S. B. (1967). On the unitary nature of extraversion. *Acta Psychologica, 26,* 383–390.

Eysenck, H. J., and Eysenck, S. B. G. (1972). *Manual of the Eysenck Personality Questionnaire.* San Diego: Educational and Industrial Testing Service.

Eysenck, H. J., and Eysenck, S. B. G. (1975). *Eysenck personality questionnaire manual.* San Diego: Educational and Industrial Testing Service.

Eysenck, S. B. G., Eysenck, H. J., and Barrett, P. (1985) A revised version of the Psychoticism scale. *Personality and Individual Differences, 6,* 21–29.

Fagot, B. I., and Leinbach, M. D. (1987). Socialization of sex roles within the family. In D. B. Carter (Ed.), *Current conceptions of sex roles and sex typing.* New York: Praeger.

Falk, C. F., Heine, S. J., Yuki, M., and Takemura, K. (2009). Why do Westerners self-enhance more than East Asians? *European Journal of Personality, 23,* 183–203.

Feingold, A. (1994). Gender differences in personality: A meta-analysis. *Psychological Bulletin, 116,* 429–456.

Fenichel, O. (1945). *The psychoanalytic theory of neurosis.* New York: Norton.

Fenigstein, A., and Peltz, R. (2002). Distress over the infidelity of a child's spouse: A crucial test of evolutionary and socialization hypotheses. *Personal Relationships, 9,* 301–312.

Fetchenhauer, D., Groothuis, T., and Pradel, J. (2010). Not only states but traits—Humans can identify permanent altruistic dispositions in 20 s. *Evolution and Human Behavior, 31,* 80–86.

Fiddick, L., Brase, G. L., Ho, A. T., Hiraishi, K., Honma, A., and Smith, A. (2016). Major personality traits and regulations of social behavior: Cheaters are not the same as the reckless, and you need to know who you're dealing with. *Journal of Research in Personality, 62,* 6–18.

Figueredo, A. J., de Baca, T. C., and Woodley, M. A. (2012). The measurement of Human Life History strategy. *Personality and Individual Differences, 55,* 251–255.

Figueredo, A. J., Sefcek, J. A., and Jones, D. N. (2006). The ideal romantic personality. *Personality and Individual Differences, 41,* 431–441.

Figueredo, A. J., Sefcek, J. S., Vasquez, G., Brumbach, B. H., King, J. E., and Jacobs, W. J. (2005a). Evolutionary personality psychology. In D. M. Buss (Ed.), *The handbook of evolutionary psychology* (pp. 851–877). New York: Wiley.

Figueredo, A. J., Vasquez, G., Brumbach, B. H., Sefcek, J. A., Kirsner, B. R., and Jacobs, W. J. (2005b). The K-factor: Individual differences in life history strategy. *Personality and Individual Differences, 39,* 1349–1360.

Fine, S. (2010). Cross-cultural integrity testing as a marker of regional corruption rates. *International Journal of Selection and Assessment, 18,* 251–259.

Fineman, S. (1977). The achievement motive and its measurement: Where are we now? *British Journal of Psychology, 68,* 1–22.

Finger, F. W. (1982). Circadian rhythms: Implications for psychology. *New Zealand Psychologist, 11,* 1–12.

Fink, B., Weege, B., Pham, M. N., and Shackelford, T. K. (2016). Handgrip strength and the Big Five personality factors in men and women. *Personality and Individual Differences, 88,* 175–177.

Fischer, C. S. (2008). What wealth-happiness paradox? A short note on the American case. *Journal of Happiness Studies, 9*(2), 219–226.

Fiske, A. P. (2002). Using individualism and collectivism to compare cultures: A critique of the validity and measurement of the constructs. *Psychological Bulletin, 128,* 78–88.

Fiske, A. P., Kitayama, S., Markus, H., and Nisbett, R. E. (1997). The cultural matrix of social psychology. In D. Gilbert, S. Fiske, and G. Lindzey (Eds.), *Handbook of social psychology* (3rd ed.). New York: McGraw-Hill.

Fiske, D. W. (1949). Consistency of the factorial structures of personality ratings from different sources. *Journal of Abnormal and Social Psychology, 44,* 329–344.

Fitzgerald, C. J., and Colarelli, S. M. (2009). Altruism and reproductive limitations. *Evolutionary Psychology, 7*(2), 234–252.

Fleeson, W. (2001). Toward a structure- and process-integrated view of personality: Traits as density distributions of states. *Journal of Personality and Social Psychology, 80,* 1011–1027.

Fleeson, W. (2004). Moving personality beyond the person-situation debate: The challenge and the opportunity of within-person variability. *Current Directions, 13,* 83–87.

Fleeson, W., and Gallagher, P. (2009). The implications of Big Five standing for the distribution of trait manifestation in behavior: Fifteen experience-sampling studies and a meta-analysis. *Journal of Personality and Social Psychology, 97,* 1097–1114.

Fleeson, W., and Law, M. K. (2015). Trait enactments as density distributions: The role of actors, situations, and observers in explaining stability and variability. *Journal of Personality and Social Psychology, 109,* 1090–1104.

Fleeson, W., Malanos, A. B., and Achille, N. M. (2002). An intraindividual process approach to the relationship between extraversion and positive affect: Is acting extraverted as "Good" as being extraverted? *Journal of Personality and Social Psychology, 83, 6,* 1409–1422.

Fleeson, W., and Noftle, E. E. (2009). The end of the person-situation debate: An emerging synthesis in the answer to the consistency question. *Social and Personality Compass, 2,* 1667–1684.

Fletcher, G.J.O., Tither, J. M., O'Loughlin, C., Friesen, M., and Overall, N. (2004). Warm and homely or cold and beautiful? Sex differences in trading off traits in mate selection. *Personality and Social Psychology Bulletin, 30,* 659–672.

Flett, G. L., Blankstein, K. R., and Hewitt, P. L. (1991). Factor structure of the Short Index of Self-Actualization. *Journal of Social Behavior and Personality Special Issue: Handbook of self-actualization, 6,* 321–329.

Floderus-Myrhed, B., Pedersen, N., and Rasmuson, I. (1980). Assessment of heritability for personality based on a short form of the Eysenck Personality Inventory: A study of 12,898 twin pairs. *Behavior Genetics, 10,* 153–162.

Flynn, F. J. (2005). Having an open mind: The impact of openness to experience on interracial attitudes and impression formation. *Journal of Personality and Social Psychology, 88,* 816–826.

Flynn, J. R. (1984). The mean IQ of Americans: Massive gains 1932 to 1978. *Psychological Bulletin, 95,* 29–51.

Flynn, J. R. (2007). *What is intelligence? Beyond the Flynn effect.* New York: Cambridge University Press.

Flynn, J. R. (2012). *Are we getting smarter? Rising IQ in the twenty-first century.* New York, NY: Cambridge University Press.

Foa, U. G., and Foa, E. B. (1974). *Societal structures of the mind.* Springfield, IL: Charles C Thomas.

Fodor, E. M. (1985). The power motive, group conflict, and physiological arousal. *Journal of Personality and Social Psychology, 49,* 1408–1415.

Fodor, E. M. (2009). Power motivation. In M. R. Leary, R. H. Hoyle, M. R. Leary, R. H. Hoyle (Eds.), *Handbook of individual differences in social behavior* (pp. 426–440). New York, NY, US: Guilford Press.

Folkman, S., and Moskowitz, J. T. (2000). Stress, positive emotion, and coping. *Current Directions in Psychological Science, 9,* 115–118.

Folkman, S., Moskowitz, J. T., Ozer, E. M., and Park, C. L. (1997). Positive meaningful events and coping in the context of HIV/AIDS. In B. H. Gottlieb (Ed.), *Coping with chronic stress* (pp. 293–314). New York: Plenum Press.

Fordyce, M. W. (1978). *Prospectus: The self-descriptive inventory.* Unpublished manuscript, Edison Community College, Fort Myers, FL.

Fordyce, M. W. (1988). A review of results on the happiness measures: A 60-second index of happiness and mental health. *Social Indicators Research, 20,* 355–381.

Foster, J. D., and Campbell, W. K. (2005). Narcissism and resistance to doubts about romantic partners. *Journal of Research in Personality, 39,* 550–557.

Fowles, D. C. (1980). The three arousal model: Implications of Gray's two-factor learning theory for heart rate, electrodermal activity, and psychopathy. *Psychophysiology, 17,* 87–104.

Fox, N. A., Bell, M. A., and Jones, N. A. (1992). Individual differences in response to stress and cerebral asymmetry. *Developmental Neuropsychology, 8,* 165–184.

Fox, N. A., and Calkins, S. D. (1993). Multiple-measure approaches to the study of infant emotion. In M. Lewis and J. M. Haviland (Eds.), *Handbook of emotions* (pp. 167–185). New York: Guilford Press.

Fox, N. A., and Davidson, R. J. (1986). Taste-elicited changes in facial signs of emotion and the asymmetry of brain electrical activity in human newborns. *Neuropsychologia, 24,* 417–422.

Fox, N. A., and Davidson, R. J. (1987). Electroencephalogram asymmetry in response to the approach of a stranger and maternal separation. *Developmental Psychology, 23,* 233–240.

Fox, N. A., and Polak, C. P. (2004). The role of sensory reactivity in understanding infant temperament. In R. DelCarmen-Wiggins and A. Carter (Eds.), *Handbook of infant, toddler, and preschool mental health assessment* (pp. 105–119). New York, NY: Oxford University Press.

Fraley, R. C. (2002a). Attachment stability from infancy to adulthood: Meta-analysis and dynamic modeling of developmental mechanisms. *Personality and Social Psychology Review, 6,* 123–151.

Fraley, R. C. (2002b). Introduction to the special issue: The psychodynamics of adult attachments—Bridging the gap between disparate research traditions. *Attachment and Human Development Special Issue: The psychodynamics of adult attachments—Bridging the gap between disparate research traditions, 4,* 131–132.

Fraley, R. C. (2007). A connectionist approach to the organization and continuity of working models of attachment. *Journal of Personality, 75,* 1157–1180.

Fraley, R. C., Hudson, N. W., Heffernan, M. E., & Segal, N. (2015). Are adult attachment styles categorical or dimensional? A taxometric analysis of general and relationship-specific attachment orientations. *Journal of Personality and Social Psychology, 109*(2), 354–368.

Fraley, R. C., and Roisman, G. I. (2015). Early attachment experiences and romantic functioning: Developmental pathways, emerging issues, and future directions. In J. A. Simpson, W. S. Rholes, J. A. Simpson, W. S. Rholes (Eds.), *Attachment theory and research: New directions and emerging themes* (pp. 9–38). New York, NY, US: Guilford Press.

Fraley, R. C., Roisman, G. I., and Haltigan, J. D. (2013). The legacy of early experiences in development: Formalizing alternative models of how early experiences are carried forward over time. *Developmental Psychology, 49,* 109–126.

Fraley, R. C., and Tancredy, C. M. (2012). Twin and sibling attachment in a nationally representative sample. *Personality and Social Psychology Bulletin, 38,* 308–316.

Fraley, R. C., Vicary, A. M., Brumbaugh, C. C., and Roisman, G. I. (2011). Patterns of stability in adult attachment: An empirical test of two models of continuity and change. *Journal of Personality and Social Psychology, 101,* 974–992.

Fransella, F. (2003). *International handbook of personal construct psychology.* New York: Wiley.

Fransella, F., and Neimeyer, R. A. (2003). George Alexander Kelly: The man and his theory. In F. Fransella (Ed.), *International handbook of personal construct psychology* (pp. 21–31). New York: Wiley.

Fraser, S. (1995). *The bell curve wars: Race, intelligence, and the future of America.* New York: Basic Books.

Fredrickson, B. L. (1998). What good are positive emotions? *Review of General Psychology, 2,* 300–319.

Fredrickson, B. L. (2000). Cultivating positive emotions to optimize health and well-being. *Prevention and Treatment* (online), 2. Retrieved from http://journals.apa.org/prevention.

Fredrickson, B. L., and Levenson, R. W. (1998). Positive emotions speed recovery from the cardiovascular sequelae of negative emotions. *Cognition and Emotion, 12,* 191–220.

Freeman, D. (1983). *Margaret Mead and Samoa: The making and unmaking of an anthropological myth.* Cambridge, MA: Harvard University Press.

Freshwater, S. M., and Golden, C. J. (2002). Personality changes associated with localized brain injury in elderly populations. *Journal of Clinical Geropsychology, 8,* 251–277.

Freud, A. (1936/1992). The ego and mechanisms of defense. In Vol. 2 of *The writings of Anna Freud.* New York: International Universities Press.

Freud, S. (1900/1913). *The interpretation of dreams.* New York: Macmillan.

Freud, S. (1915/1957). The unconscious. In J. Strachey (Ed. and Trans.), *The standard edition of the complete psychological works of Sigmund Freud* (vol. 14, pp. 166–204). London: Hogarth Press.

Freud, S. (1916/1947). *Leonardo da Vinci, a study in psychosexuality.* New York: Random House.

Frick, P. J., O'Brien, B. S., Wootton, J. M., and McBurnett, K. (1994). Psychopathy and conduct problems in children. *Journal of Abnormal Psychology, 103,* 700–707.

Friedman, H. S., Tucker, J. S., Schwartz, J. E., Tomlinson-Keasey, C., and Martin, L. R., et al. (1995). Psychosocial and behavioral predictors of longevity. *American Psychologist, 50,* 69–78.

Friedman, M., and Rosenman, R. H. (1974). *Type A behavior and your heart.* New York: Knopf.

Frijda, N. H. (1986). *The emotions.* New York: Cambridge University Press.

Frisell, T., Pawitan, Y., Langstrom, N., and Lichtenstein, P. (2012). Heritability, assortative mating and gender differences in violent crime: Results from a total population sample using twin, adoption, and sibling models. *Behavior Genetics, 42,* 3–18.

Frodi, A., Macauley, J., and Thome, P. R. (1977). Are women always less aggressive than men? A review of the experimental literature. *Psychological Bulletin, 84,* 634–660.

Funder, D. C. (2002). Personality psychology: Current status and some issues for the future. *Journal of Research in Personality, 36,* 638–639.

Funder, D. C. (2006). Towards a resolution of the personality triad: Persons, situations, and behaviors. *Journal of Research in Personality, 40,* 21–34.

Furnham, A., Richards, S. C., and Paulhus, D. L. (2013). The Dark Triad of personality: A 10 year review. *Social and Personality Psychology Compass, 7*(3), 199–216.

Furmark, T. (2002). Social phobia: Overview of community surveys. *Acta Psychiatrica Scandinavica, 105,* 84–93.

Furnham, A. (1982). Psychotocism, social desirability, and situation selection. *Personality and Individual Differences, 3,* 43–51.

Furr, R. M. (2009). Personality psychology as a truly behavioural science. *European Journal of Personality, 23,* 369–401.

Gable, S. L., and Nezlak, J. B. (1998). Level and instability of day-to-day psychological well-being and risk for depression. *Journal of Personality and Social Psychology, 74,* 129–138.

Gabriel, S., and Gardner, W. L. (1999). Are there "his" and "hers" types of interdependence? The implications of gender differences in collective versus relational interdependence for affect, behavior, and cognition. *Journal of Personality and Social Psychology, 77,* 642–655.

Gailliot, M. T., and Baumeister, R. F. (2007). Self-regulation and sexual restraint: Dispositionally and temporarily poor self-regulatory abilities contribute to failures at restraining sexual behavior. *Personality and Social Psychology Bulletin, 33,* 173–186.

Gale, A. (1983). Electroencephalographic studies of extraversion-introversion: A case study in the psychophysiology of individual differences. *Personality and Individual Differences, 4,* 371–380.

Gale, A. (1986). Extraversion-introversion and spontaneous rhythms of the brain: Retrospect and prospect. In J. Strelau, F. Farley, and A. Gale (Eds.), *The biological basis of personality and behavior* (vol. 2). Washington, DC: Hemisphere.

Gale, A. (1987). The psychophysiological context. In A. Gale and B. Christie (Eds.), *Psychophysiology and the electronic workplace* (pp. 17–32). Chichester, England, UK: Wiley.

Gale, C. R., Batty, G. D., and Deary, I. J., (2008). Locus of control at age 10 years and health outcomes and behaviors at age 30 years: The 1970 British cohort study. *Psychosomatic Medicine, 70,* 397–403.

Galic, Z., Jerneic, Z., and Kovacic, M. P. (2012). Do applicants fake their personality questionnaire responses and how successful are their attempts? A case of military pilot cadet selection. *International Journal of Selection and Assessment, 20,* 229–241.

Gallup, A. C., O'Brien, D. T., White, D. D., and Wilson, D. S. (2009). Peer victimization in adolescence has different effects on the sexual behavior of male and female college students. *Personality and Individual Differences, 46,* 611–615.

Gallup, G. G. (1977a). Self-recognition in primates: A comparative approach to the bidirectional properties of consciousness. *American Psychologist, 32,* 329–338.

Gallup, G. G. (1977b). Absences of self-recognition in a monkey (*Macaca fascicularis*) following prolonged exposure to a mirror. *Developmental Psychobiology, 10,* 281–284.

Gangestad, S. W., and Cousins, A. J. (2002). Adaptive design, female mate preferences, and shifts across the menstrual cycle. *Annual Review of Sex Research.*

Gangestad, S. W., Haselton, M. G., and Buss, D. M. (2006). Evolutionary foundations of cultural variation: Evoked culture and mate preferences. *Psychological Inquiry, 17,* 75–95.

Gangestad, S. W., and Simpson, J. A. (1990). Toward an evolutionary history of female sociosexual variation. *Journal of Personality, 58,* 69–96.

Gangestad, S. W., and Thornhill, R. (2008). Human oestrus. *Proceedings of the Royal Society of London, B, 275,* 991–1000.

Garbarino, E., Slonim, R., and Snydor, J. (2011). Digit ratios (2D:4D) as predictors of risky decision making for both sexes. *Journal of Risk and Uncertainty, 42,* 1–26.

Garber, J., and Seligman, M. E. P. (1980). *Human helplessness: Theory and applications.* New York: Academic Press.

Gardner, H. (1983). *Frames of mind: The theory of multiple intelligences.* New York: Basic Books.

Gardner, H. (1999). *Intelligence reframed: Multiple intelligences for the 21st century.* New York: Basic Books.

Gardner, W. I., and Martinko, M. J. (1996). Using the Myers-Briggs Type Indicator to study managers: A literature review and research agenda. *Journal of Management, 22,* 45–83.

Gauguin, P. (1985). *Noa Noa: The Tahitian Journal.* Mineola, NY: Dover.

Geary, D. C., DeSoto, M. C., Hoard, M. K., Skaggs, S., and Cooper, M. L. (2001). Estrogens and relationship jealousy. *Human Nature, 12,* 299–320.

Geen, R. (1984). Preferred stimulation levels in introverts and extraverts: Effects on arousal and performance. *Journal of Personality and Social Psychology, 46,* 1303–1312.

Geer, J. H., and Head, S. (1990). The sexual response system. In J. T. Cacioppo and L. G. Tassinary (Eds.), *Principles of psychophysiology* (pp. 599–630). Cambridge, England: Cambridge University Press.

Geis, F. L., and Moon, T. H. (1981). Machiavellianism and deception. *Journal of Personality and Social Psychology, 41,* 766–775.

Gelade, G. A. (2008). IQ, cultural values, and the technological achievement of nations. *Intelligence, 36,* 711–718.

George, C., and Solomon, J. (1996). Representational models of relationships: Links between caregiving and attachment. *Infant Mental Health Journal, 17,* 198–216.

Gergen, K. J. (1992). Toward a postmodern psychology. In S. Kvale (Ed.), *Psychology and postmodernism* (pp. 17–30). London: Sage.

Gerring, J. P., and Vasa, R. A. (2016). Head injury and externalizing behavior. In T. P. Beauchaine, S. P. Hinshaw, T. P. Beauchaine, S. P. Hinshaw (Eds.), *The Oxford handbook of externalizing spectrum disorders* (pp. 403–415). New York, NY, US: Oxford University Press.

Gerson, M. W., and Fernandez, N. (2013). PATH: A program to build resilience and thriving in undergraduates. *Journal of Applied Social Psychology, 43*(11), 2169–2184.

Gewertz, D. (1981). A historical reconsideration of female dominance among the Chambri of Papua New Guinea. *American Ethnologist, 8,* 94–106.

Gibbs, W. (2003). The unseen genome: Gems among the junk. *Scientific American, 289,* 49.

Gigy, L. L. (1980). Self-concept in single women. *Psychology of Women Quarterly, 5,* 321–340.

Gilmour, J., and Williams, L. (2012). Type D personality is associated with maladaptive health-related behaviours. *Journal of Health Psychology, 17,* 471–478.

Giluk, T. L., and Postlethwaite, B. E. (2015). Big Five personality and academic dishonesty: A meta-analytic review. *Personality and Individual Differences, 72,* 59–67.

Gladden, P. R., Figueredo, A. J., and Jacobs, W. J. (2009). Life history strategy, psychopathic attitudes, personality, and general intelligences. *Personality and Individual Differences, 46,* 270–275.

Gladwell, M. (2008). *Outliers: The story of success.* New York: Little, Brown.

Glenn, A. L., and Raine, A. (2014). Neurocriminology: Implications for the punishment, prediction and prevention of criminal behavior. *Nature Reviews Neuroscience, 15*(1), 54–63.

Glicksohn, J., and Bozna, M. (2000). Developing a personality profile of the bomb-disposal expert: The role of sensation seeking and field dependence–independence. *Personality and Individual Differences, 28*(1), 85–92.

Gnambs, T. (2015). What makes a computer wiz? Linking personality traits and programming aptitude. *Journal of Research in Personality, 58,* 31–34.

Goldberg, L. R. (1981). Language and individual differences: The search for universals in personality lexicons. In L. Wheeler (Ed.), *Review of personality and social psychology* (vol. 2, pp. 141–165). Beverly Hills, CA: Sage.

Goldberg, L. R. (1990). An alternative "description of personality": The Big-Five factor structure. *Journal of Personality and Social Psychology, 59,* 1216–1229.

Goldey, K. L., & van Anders, S. M. (2012). Sexual arousal and desire: Interrelations and responses to three modalities of sexual stimuli. *Journal of Sexual Medicine, 9,* 2315–2329.

Golding, S. L. (1978). Toward a more adequate theory of personality: Psychological organizing principles. In H. London (Ed.), *Personality: A new look at metatheories* (pp. 69–96). New York: Wiley.

Goldsmith, H. H., Aksan, N., and Essex, M. (2001). Temperament and socioemotional adjustment to kindergarten: A multi-informant perspective. In T. Wachs and G. A. Kohnstamm (Eds.), *Temperament in context* (pp. 103–138). Mahwah, NJ: Erlbaum.

Goldsmith, H. H., and Rothbart, M. K. (1991). Contemporary instruments for assessing early temperament by questionnaire and in the laboratory. In J. Strelau and A. Angleitner (Eds.), *Explorations in temperament.* New York: Plenum Press.

Goleman, D. (1995). *Emotional intelligence: Why it can matter more than IQ.* New York: Bantam.

Goncalves, M. K., and Campbell, L. (2014). The Dark Triad and the derogation of mating competitors. *Personality and Individual Differences, 67,* 42–46.

Goodman, G., and Kaufman, J. C. (2014). Gremlins in my head: Predicting stage fright in elite actors. *Empirical Studies of the Arts, 32*(2), 133–148.

Goodman, J., Lofts, E. F., Miller, M., and Greene, E. (1991). Money, sex, and death: Gender bias in wrongful death damage awards. *Law and Society Review, 25,* 263–285.

Gorbaniuk, O., Budzińska, A., Owczarek, M., Bożek, E., and Juros, K. (2013). The factor structure of Polish personality-descriptive adjectives: An alternative psycho-lexical study. *European Journal of Personality, 27*(3), 304–318.

Gordon, R. A. (1997). Everyday life as an intelligence test: Effects of intelligence and intelligence context. *Intelligence, 24,* 203–320.

Gosling, S. D. (2001). From mice to men: What can we learn about personality from animal research? *Psychological Bulletin, 127,* 45–86.

Gosling, S. D., John, O. P., Craik, K. H., and Robins, R. W. (1998). Do people know how they behave? Self-reported act frequencies compared with on-line codings by observers. *Journal of Personality and Social Psychology, 74,* 1337–1349.

Gosling, S. D., Ko, S. J., Mannarelli, T., and Morris, M. E. (2002). A room with a cue: Personality judgments based on offices and bedrooms. *Journal of Personality and Social Psychology, 82,* 379–398.

Gosling, S. D., Kwan, V.S.Y., and John, O. P. (2003). A dog's got personality: A cross-species comparative approach to evaluating personality judgments. *Journal of Personality and Social Psychology, 85,* 1161–1169.

Gosling, S. D., and Mason, W. (2015). Internet research in psychology. *Annual Review of Psychology, 66,* 877–902.

Gottman, J. (1994). *Why marriages succeed or fail.* New York: Simon and Schuster.

Gottman, J., Levenson, R., and Woodin, E. (2001). Facial expressions during marital conflict. *Journal of Family Communication, 1,* 37–57.

Gottman, J. M., and Silver, N. (1999). *The seven principles for making marriage work.* New York: Three Rivers Press.

Gough, H. G. (1957/1987). *California Psychological Inventory: Administrator's guide.* Palo Alto, CA: Consulting Psychologists Press.

Gough, H. G. (1980). *The Adjective Check List manual.* Palo Alto, CA: Consulting Psychologists Press.

Gough, H. G. (1996). *California psychological inventory manual* (3rd ed.). Palo Alto, CA: Consulting Psychologists Press.

Grano, N., Virtanen, M., Vahtera, J., Elovainio, M., and Kivimaki, M. (2004). Impulsivity as a predictor of smoking and alcohol consumption. *Personality and Individual Differences, 37,* 1693–1700.

Granqvist, P., Mikulincer, M., Gewirtz, V., and Shaver, P. R. (2012). Experimental findings on God as an attachment figure: Normative processes and moderating effects of internal working models. *Journal of Personality and Social Psychology, 103,* 804–818.

Grant, H., and Higgins, E. T. (2003). Optimism, promotion pride, and prevention pride as predictors of quality of life. *Personality and Social Psychology Bulletin, 29,* 1521–1532.

Grant, J. D., and Grant, J. (1996). Officer selection and the prevention of abuse of force. In W. Geller and H. Toch (Eds.), *Police violence: Understanding and controlling police abuse of force* (pp. 150–164). New Haven, CT: Yale University Press.

Gray, J. (1990). Brain systems that mediate both emotion and cognition. *Motivation and Emotion, 4,* 269–288.

Gray, J. A. (1972). *The psychology of fear and stress.* New York: McGraw-Hill.

Gray, J. A. (1975). *Elements of a two-process theory of learning.* Oxford, England: Academic Press.

Gray, J. A. (1982). *The neuropsychology of anxiety.* Oxford, England: Oxford University Press.

Gray, J. A. (1987a). *The psychology of fear and stress.* Cambridge, England: Cambridge University Press.

Gray, J. A. (1987b). Perspectives on anxiety and impulsivity: A commentary. *Journal of Research in Personality, 21,* 493–509.

Gray, J. A. (1991). The neuropsychology of temperament. In J. Strelau and A. Angleitner (Eds.), *Explorations in temperament: International perspectives on theory and measurement* (pp. 105–128). New York: Plenum Press.

Grayson, D. K. (1993). Differential mortality and the Donner Party disaster. *Evolutionary Anthropology, 2,* 151–159.

Graziano, W. G., (2003). Personality development: An introduction toward process approaches to long-term stability and change in persons. *Journal of Personality, 71,* 893–903.

Graziano, W. G., and Tobin, R. M. (2002). Agreeableness: Dimension of personality or social desirability artifact? *Journal of Personality, 70,* 695–727.

Greenberg, D. M., Müllensiefen, D., Lamb, M. E., and Rentfrow, P. J. (2015). Personality predicts musical sophistication. *Journal of Research in Personality, 58,* 154–158.

Greenberg, J. R., and Mitchell, S. (1983). *Object relations in psychoanalytic theory.* Cambridge, MA: Harvard University Press.

Greenwald, A. G., and Farnham, S .D. (2000). Using the Implicit Association Test to measure self-esteem and self-concept. *Journal of Personality and Social Psychology, 79,* 1022–1038.

Gregg, A. P., and Sedikides, C. (2010). Narcissistic fragility: Rethinking its links to explicit and implicit self-esteem. *Self and Identity, 9,* 142–161.

Gregory, T., Nettelbeck, T., Howard, S., & Wilson, C. (2008). Inspection time: A biomarker for cognitive decline. *Intelligence, 36,* 664–671.

Gregory, T., Nettelbeck, T., and Wilson, C. (2009). Inspection time and everyday functioning: A longitudinal study. *Personality and Individual Differences, 47,* 999–1002.

Greiling, H., and Buss, D. M. (2000). Women's sexual strategies: The hidden dimension of extra-pair mating. *Personality and Individual Differences, 28,* 929–963.

Grigorenko, E. L. (2002). In search of the genetic engram of personality. In D. Cervone and W. Michele (Eds.), *Advances in personality science* (pp. 29–82). New York: Guilford Press.

Griskevicius, V., Tybur, J. M., Gangestad, S. W., Perea, E. F., Shapiro, J. R., and Kenrick, D. T. (2009). Aggress to impress: Hostility as an evolved context-dependent strategy. *Journal of Personality and Social Psychology, 96,* 980–994.

Gross, J. J. (2002). Emotion regulation: Affective, cognitive, and social consequences. *Psychophysiology, 39,* 281–291.

Gross, J. J., and Levenson, R. W. (1993). Emotional suppression: Physiology, self-report, and expressive behavior. *Journal of Personality and Social Psychology, 64,* 970–986.

Gross, J. J., and Levenson, R. W. (1997). Hiding feelings: The acute effects of inhibiting positive and negative emotions. *Journal of Abnormal Psychology, 106,* 95–103.

Gross, J. J., Sutton, S. K., & Ketelaar, R. (1998). Relations between affect and personality: Support for the affect-level and affective reactivity views. *Personality and Social Psychology Bulletin, 24,* 279–288.

Grosskurth, P. (1991). *The secret ring: Freud's inner circle and the politics of psychoanalysis.* Reading, MA: Addison-Wesley.

Guéguen, N. (2011). Effects of solicitor sex and attractiveness on receptivity to sexual offers: A field study. *Archives of Sexual Behavior, 40*(5), 915–919.

Gunderson, E. A., Gripshover, S. J., Romero, C., Dweck, C. S., Goldin-Meadow, S., and Levine, S. C. (2013). Parent praise to 1- to 3-year-olds predicts children's motivational frameworks 5 years later. *Child Development, 84*(5), 1526–1541.

Guzder, J., Paris, J., Zelkowitz, P., and Marchessault, K. (1996). Risk factors for borderline personality in children. *Journal of the American Academy of Child and Adolescent Psychiatry, 35,* 26–33.

Hacher, S. L., Nadeau, M. S., Walsh, L. K., and Reynolds, M. (1994). The teaching of empathy for high school and college students: Testing Rogerian methods with the Interpersonal Reactivity Index. *Adolescence, 29,* 961–974.

Hagerty, M. R. (1999). Testing Maslow's hierarchy of needs: National quality-of-life across time. *Social Indicators Research, 46,* 249–271.

Hahn, E., Johnson, W., and Spinath, F. M. (2013). Beyond the heritability of life satisfaction–The roles of personality and twin-specific influences. *Journal of Research in Personality, 47*(6), 757–767.

Hair, E. C., and Graziano, W. G. (2003). Self-esteem, personality, and achievement in high school: A prospective longitudinal study in Texas. *Journal of Personality, 71,* 971–994.

Hald, G. M., and Hogh-Olesen, H. (2010). Receptivity to sexual invitations from strangers of the opposite gender. *Evolution and Human Behavior, 31,* 453–458.

Hall, C., Smith, K., and Chia, R. (2008). Cognitive and personality factors in relation to timely completion of a college degree. *College Student Journal, 42,* 1087–1098.

Hall, J. A. (1984). *Nonverbal sex differences.* Baltimore: Johns Hopkins University Press.

Hamer, D. (1997). The search for personality genes: Adventures of a molecular biologist. *Current Directions in Psychological Science, 6,* 111–114.

Hamer, D., and Copeland, P. (1994). *The science of desire: The search for the gay gene and the biology of behavior.* New York: Simon and Schuster.

Hamilton, L. D., Rellini, A. H., and Meston, C. M. (2008). Cortisol, sexual arousal, and affect in response to sexual stimuli. *Journal of Sexual Medicine, 5,* 2111–2118.

Hamilton, W. D. (1964). The evolution of social behavior. *Journal of Theoretical Biology, 7,* 1–52.

Hamm, A. O., Weike, A. I., Schupp, H. T., Treig, T., Dressel, A., and Kessler, C. (2003). Affective blindsight: Intact fear conditioning to a visual cue in a cortically blind patient. *Brain, 126, 2,* 267–275.

Hammack, S. E., Cooper, M. A., and Lezak, K. R. (2012). Overlapping neurobiology of learned helplessness and conditioned defeat: Implications for PTSD and mood disorders. *Neuropharmacology, 62,* 565–575.

Hampshire, S. (1953). Dispositions. *Analysis, 14,* 5–11.

Hampson, S. E., Andrews, J. A., Barckley, M., and Peterson, M. (2007). Trait stability and continuity in childhood: Relating sociability and hostility to the five-factor model of personality. *Journal of Research in Personality, 41,* 507–523.

Hampson, S. E., Goldberg, L. R., Vogt, T. M., and Dubanoski, J. P. (2006). Forty years on: Teachers' assessments of children's personality traits predict self-reported health behaviors and outcomes at midlife. *Health Psychology, 25,* 57–64.

Hampson, S. E., Severson, H. H., Burns, W. J., Slovic, P., and Fisher, K. J. (2001). Risk perception, personality factors and alcohol use among adolescents. *Personality and Individual Differences, 30,* 167–181.

Hankin, B. L., and Abramson, L. Y. (2001). Development of gender differences in depression: An elaborated cognitive vulnerability transactional stress theory. *Psychological Bulletin, 127, 6,* 773–796.

Hansen, C. H., Hansen, R. D., and Schantz, D. W. (1992). Repression at encoding: Discrete appraisals of emotional stimuli. *Journal of Personality and Social Psychology, 63,* 1026–1035.

Hansen, R. D., and Hansen, C. H. (1988). Repression of emotionally tagged memories: The architecture of less complex emotions. *Journal of Personality and Social Psychology, 55,* 811–818.

Hare, R. D., Hart, S. D., and Harpur, T. J. (1991). Psychopathy and the DSM-IV criteria for antisocial personality disorder. *Journal of Abnormal Psychology Special Issue: Diagnosis, dimensions, and DSM-IV; The science of classification, 100,* 391–398.

Hardison, H. G., and Neimeyer, R. A. (2012). Assessment of personal constructs: Features and functions of constructivist techniques. In P. Caputi, L. L. Viney, B. M. Walker, and N. Crittenden (Eds.), *Personal construct methodology* (pp. 3–51). Hoboken, NJ: John Wiley & Sons.

Harenski, C. L., Kim, S. H., and Hamann, S. (2009). Neuroticism and psychopathy predict brain activation during moral and nonmoral emotion regulation. *Cognitive, Affective and Behavioral Neuroscience, 9,* 1–15.

Hargrave, G. E., and Hiatt, D. (1989). Use of the California Psychological Inventory in law enforcement officer selection. *Journal of Personality Assessment, 53,* 267–277.

Haring, M. J., Stock, W. A., and Okun, M. A. (1984). A research synthesis of gender and social class as correlates of subjective well-being. *Human Relations, 37,* 645–657.

Harlow, H. F. (1958). The nature of love. *American Psychologist, 13,* 673–685.

Harlow, H. F., and Suomi, S. J. (1971). Production of depressive behaviors in young monkeys. *Journal of Autism and Childhood Schizophrenia, 1,* 246–255.

Harlow, H. F., and Zimmermann, R. R. (1959). Affectionate responses in the infant monkey. *Science, 130,* 421–432.

Harpending, H., and Cochran, G. (2002). In our genes. *Proceedings of the National Academy of Sciences of the United States of America, 99,* 10–12.

Harpur, T. J., and Hare, R. D. (1994). Assessment of psychopathy as a function of age. *Journal of Abnormal Psychology, 103,* 604–609.

Harrell, W. A., and Hartnagel, T. (1976). The impact of Machiavellianism and the trustfulness of the victim on laboratory theft. *Sociometry, 39,* 157–165.

Harris, C. R. (2000). Psychophysiological responses to imagined infidelity: The specific innate modular view of jealousy reconsidered. *Journal of Personality and Social Psychology, 78,* 1082–1091.

Harris, J. R. (2007). *No two alike: Human nature and human individuality.* New York: Norton.

Harter, S. (1993). Causes and consequences of low self-esteem in children and adolescents. In R. Baumeister (Ed.), *Self-esteem: The puzzle of low self-regard* (pp. 87–111). New York: Plenum Press.

Haslam, C., and Montrose, V. T. (2015). Should have known better: The impact of mating experience and the desire for marriage upon attraction to the narcissistic personality. *Personality and Individual Differences, 82,* 188–192.

Hartshorne, H., and May, M. A. (1928). *Studies in the nature of character: Vol. 1. Studies in deceit.* New York: Macmillan.

Hatemi, P. K., Medland, S. E., Klemmensen, R., Oskarsson, S., Littvay, L., Dawes, C. T., . . . & Christensen, K. (2014). Genetic influences on political ideologies: Twin analyses of 19 measures of political ideologies from five democracies and genome-wide findings from three populations. *Behavior genetics, 44*(3), 282–294.

Hawes, S. W., Perlman, S. B., Byrd, A. L., Raine, A., Loeber, R., and Pardini, D. A. (2016). Chronic anger as a precursor to adult antisocial personality features: The moderating influence of cognitive control. *Journal of Abnormal Psychology, 125*(1), 64–74.

Hazan, C., and Shaver, P. R. (1987). Romantic love conceptualized as an attachment process. *Journal of Personality and Social Psychology, 52,* 511–524.

Hazan, C., and Shaver, P. R. (1994). Attachment as an organizational framework for research on close relationships. *Psychological Inquiry, 5,* 1–22.

Heath, A. C., Bucholz, K. K., Dinwiddie, S. H., Madden, P.A.F., and Slutske, W. W. (1994). *Pathways from the genotype to alcoholism risk in women.* Paper presented at the annual meeting of the Behavioral Genetics Association, Barcelona, Spain.

Heatherton, T. E., and Polivy, J. (1991). Development and validation of a scale for measuring state self-esteem. *Journal of Personality and Social Psychology, 60,* 895–910.

Heaven, P. C. L., Crocker, D., Edwards, B., Preston, N., Ward, R., and Woodbridge, N. (2003). Personality and sex. *Personality and Individual Differences, 35,* 411–419.

Hebb, D. O. (1955). Drives and the CNS (conceptual nervous system). *Psychological Review, 62,* 243–259.

Heckhausen, H. (1982). The development of achievement motivation. In W. W. Hartup (Ed.), *Review of child development research* (vol. 6, pp. 600–668). Chicago: University of Chicago Press.

Heidemeier, H., and Göritz, A. S. (2013). Perceived control in low-control circumstances: Control beliefs predict a greater decrease in life satisfaction following job loss. *Journal of Research in Personality, 47,* 52–56.

Heine, S. J., and Lehman, D. R. (1995). Cultural variation in unrealistic optimism: Does the West feel more invulnerable than the East? *Journal of Personality and Social Psychology, 68,* 595–607.

Helson, R., and Picano, J. (1990). Is the traditional role bad for women? *Journal of Personality and Social Psychology, 59,* 311–320.

Helson, R., and Stewart, A. (1994). Personality change in adulthood. In T. F. Heatherton and J. L. Weinberger (Eds.), *Can personality change?* Washington, DC: American Psychological Association.

Helson, R., and Wink, P. (1992). Personality change in women from the early 40s to the early 50s. *Psychology and Aging, 7,* 46–55.

Henderson, L., and Zimbardo, P. (2001a). Shyness as a clinical condition: The Stanford model. In W. R. Crozier and L. E. Alden (Eds.), *International handbook of social anxiety: Concepts, research and interventions relating to the self and shyness* (pp. 431–447). New York: Wiley.

Henderson, L., and Zimbardo, P. (2001b). Shyness, social anxiety, and social phobia. In S. G. Hofmann and P. M. DiBartolo (Eds.), *From social anxiety to social phobia: Multiple perspectives* (pp. 46–85). Needham Heights, MA: Allyn and Bacon.

Henderson, N. D. (1982). Human behavioral genetics. *Annual Review of Psychology, 33,* 403–440.

Hendriks, A. A. J., Perugini, M., Angleitner, A., Ostendorf, F., Johnson, J. A., De Fruyt, F., Hrebickova, M., et al. (2003). The five-factor personality inventory: Cross-cultural generalizability across 13 countries. *European Journal of Personality, 17,* 347–373.

Hennig, K. H., and Walker, L. J. (2008). The darker side of accommodating others: Examining the interpersonal structure of maladaptive constructs. *Journal of Research in Personality, 42,* 2–21.

Henrich, J. (2015). *The secret of our success: how culture is driving human evolution, domesticating our species, and making us smarter.* Princeton, NJ: Princeton University Press.

Herbert, T. B., and Cohen, S. (1993). Depression and immunity: A meta-analytic review. *Psychological Bulletin, 113,* 472–486.

Herrington, J. D., Koven, N. S., Miller, G. A., and Heller, W. (2006). Mapping the neural correlates of dimensions of personality, emotion, and motivation. In T. Canli (Ed.), *Biology of personality and individual differences* (pp. 133–156). New York: Guilford Press.

Herrnstein, R., and Murray, C. (1994). *The bell curve: Intelligence and class structure in American life.* New York: Free Press.

Herzog, A. R., Franks, X., Markus, H. R., and Holmberg, X. (1995). *The American self in its sociocultural variations.* Unpublished manuscript.

Hess, N., Helfrecht, C., Hagen, E., Sell, A., and Hewlett, B. (2010). Interpersonal aggression among Aka hunter-gatherers of the Central African Republic: Assessing the effects of sex, strength, and anger. *Human Nature, 21,* 330–354.

Hibbard, S., Porcerelli, J., Kamoo, R., Schwartz, M., Abell, S. (2010). Defense and object relational maturity on Thematic Apperception Test Scales indicate levels of personality organization. *Journal of Personality Assessment, 92,* 241–253.

Higgins, E. T. (1987). Self-discrepancy: A theory relating self to affect. *Psychological Review, 94,* 319–340.

Higgins, E. T. (1996). The "self digest": Self-knowledge serving self-regulatory functions. *Journal of Personality and Social Psychology, 71,* 1062–1083.

Higgins, E. T. (1997). Beyond pleasure and pain. *American Psychologist, 52,* 1280–1300.

Higgins, E. T. (1999). Persons and situations: Unique explanatory principles or variability in general principles? In D. Cervone and Y. Shoda (Eds.), *The coherence of personality* (pp. 61–93). New York: Guilford Press.

Higgins, E. T. (2012). Regulatory focus theory. In P. A. M. Van Lange, A. W. Kruglanski, and T. E. Higgins (Eds.), *Handbook of theories of social psychology* (pp. 483–504). Thousand Oaks, CA: Sage.

Hilbig, B. E., Heydasch, T., and Zettler, I. (2014). To boast or not to boast: Testing the humility aspect of the Honesty–Humility factor. *Personality and Individual Differences, 69,* 12–16.

Hill, C. T., Rubin, Z., and Peplau, L. A. (1976). Breakups before marriage: The end of 103 affairs. *Journal of Social Issues, 32,* 147–168.

Hill, P. L., and Roberts, B. W. (2011). The role of adherence in the relationship between conscientiousness and perceived health. *Health Psychology, 30,* 797–804.

Hill, P. L., Turiano, N., Hurd, M. D., Mroczek, D. K., and Roberts, B. W. (2011). Conscientiousness and longevity: An examination of possible mediators. *Health Psychology, 30,* 536–541.

Hiroto, D. S., and Seligman, M. E. P. (1975). Generality of learned helplessness in man. *Journal of Personality and Social Psychology, 102,* 311–327.

Hirschfeld, L. A. (1995). Anthropology, psychology, and the meaning of social causality. In D. Sperber, D. Premack, and A. J. Premack (Eds.), *Causal cognition: A multidisciplinary debate* (pp. 313–344). Oxford, England: Clarendon Press.

Hirsh, J. B. (2015). Extraverted populations have lower savings rates. *Personality and Individual Differences, 81,* 162–168.

Hirsh, J. B., and Peterson, J. B. (2009). Extraversion, neuroticism, and the prisoner's dilemma. *Personality and Individual Differences, 46,* 254–256.

Hirsh, S. K., and Kummerow, J. M. (1990). *Introduction to type in organizations* (2nd ed.). Palo Alto, CA: Consulting Psychologists Press.

Hirsh, J. B., & Peterson, J. B. (2009). Extraversion, neuroticism, and the prisoner's dilemma. *Personality and Individual Differences, 46, 2,* 254–256.

Hofer, J., Bond, M. H., and Li, M. (2010). The implicit power motive and sociosexuality in men and women: Pancultural effects of responsibility. *Journal of Personality and Social Psychology, 99,* 380–394.

Hoffman, W., Baumeister, R. F., Forster, G., and Vohs, K. E. (2012). Everyday temptations: An experience sampling study of desire, conflict, and self-control. *Journal of Personality and Social Psychology, 102,* 1318–1335.

Hoffmann, W., Vohs, K. D., and Baumeister, R. F. (2012). What people desire, feel conflicted about, and try to resist in everyday life. *Psychological Science, 23,* 582–588.

Hogan, J., and Holland, B. (2003). Using theory to evaluate personality and job performance relations. *Journal of Applied Psychology, 88,* 100–112.

Hogan, R. (1983). A socioanalytic theory of personality. In M. Page and R. Dienstbier (Eds.), *Nebraska Symposium on motivation, 1982* (pp. 55–89). Lincoln: University of Nebraska Press.

Hogan, R. (2005). In defense of personality measurement: New wine for old whiners. *Human Performance, 18,* 331–341.

Hogan, R., & Hogan, J. (2002). The Hogan personality inventory. In B. de Raad and M. Perugini (Eds.), *Big Five assessment* (pp. 329–346). Ashland, OH: Hogrefe & Huber Publishers.

Hogan, R. & Chamorro-Premuzic, T. (2015). Personality and career success. In L. Cooper and R. Larsen (Eds.), *Handbook of personality and social psychology: Personality processes and individual differences* (pp. 619–638). Washington, DC, American Psychological Association.

Hokanson, J. E., Burgess, M., and Cohen, M. F. (1963). Effect of displaced aggression on systolic blood pressure. *Journal of Abnormal and Social Psychology, 67,* 214–218.

Holland, A. S., Fraley, R. C., and Roisman, G. I. (2012). Attachment styles in dating couples: Predicting relationship functioning over time. *Personal Relationships, 19,* 234–246.

Hollmann, E. (2001). *Paul Gaugin: Images from the South Seas.* New York: Prestel USA.

Holmes, D. (1990). The evidence for repression: An examination of sixty years of research. In J. Singer (Ed.), *Repression and dissociation: Implications for personality, theory, psychopathology, and health* (pp. 85–102). Chicago: University of Chicago Press.

Holmes, T. H., and Rahe, R. H. (1967). The Social Readjustment Rating scale. *Journal of Psychosomatic Research, 11,* 213–218.

Holroyd, K. A., and Coyne, J. (1987). Personality and health in the 1980s: Psychosomatic medicine revisited? *Journal of Personality, 55,* 359–375.

Holtzman, N. S., and Strube, M. J. (2010). Narcissism and attractiveness. *Journal of Research in Personality, 44,* 133–136.

Honekopp, J. (2011). Relationships between digit ratio 2D:4D and self-reported aggression and risk taking in an online study. *Personality and Individual Differences, 51,* 77–80.

Hong, R. Y., and Paunonen, S. V. (2009). Personality traits and health-risk behaviours in University students. *European Journal of Personality, 23,* 675–696.

Honomichl, R. D., and Donnellan, M. B. (2012). Dimensions of temperament in preschoolers predict risk taking and externalizing behaviors in adolescents. *Social Psychological and Personality Science, 3,* 14–22.

Hooper, J. L., White, V. M., Macaskill, G. T., Hill, D. J., and Clifford, C. A. (1992). Alcohol use, smoking habits and the Junior Eysenck Personality Questionnaire in adolescent Australian twins. *Acta Genetica Med. Gemellol. 41,* 311–324.

Hoover, E. (2013). Colleges seek "noncognitive" gauges of applicants. *The Chronicle of Higher Education, 56,* 1.

Hopkins, A. B. (1996). *So ordered: Making partner the hard way.* Amherst: University of Massachusetts Press.

Hopwood, C. J., Ansell, E .B., Pincus, A. L., Wright, A. G. C., Lukowitsky, M. R., and Roche, M. J. (2011). The circumplex model of interpersonal sensitivities. *Journal of Personality, 79,* 707–739.

Hormuth, S. E. (1986). The sampling of experiences in situ. *Journal of Personality, 54,* 262–293.

Horne, J. A., and Ostberg, O. (1976). A self-assessment questionnaire to determine morningness–eveningness in human circadian rhythms. *International Journal of Chronobiology, 4,* 97–110.

Horne, J. A., and Ostberg, O. (1977). Individual differences in human circadian rhythms. *Biological Psychology, 5,* 179–190.

Horney, K. (1937). *The neurotic personality of our time.* New York: Norton.

Horney, K. (1939). *New ways in psychoanalysis.* New York: Norton.

Horney, K. (1945). *Our inner conflicts: A constructive theory of neurosis.* New York: Norton.

Horney, K. (1950). *Neurosis and human growth: The struggle toward self-realization.* New York: Norton.

Horton, R. S., and Sedikedes, C. (2009). Narcissistic responding to ego threat: When the status of the evaluator matters. *Journal of Personality, 77,* 1493–1526.

Hotard, S. R., McFatter, R. M., McWhirter, R. M., and Stegall, M. E. (1989). Interactive effects of extraversion, neuroticism, and social relationships on subjective well-being. *Journal of Personality and Social Psychology, 57,* 321–331.

Howard, A., and Bray, D. (1988). *Managerial lives in transition: Advancing age and changing times.* New York: Guilford Press.

Hoyenga, K. B., and Hoyenga, K. T. (1993). *Gender-related differences: Origins and outcomes.* Boston: Allyn and Bacon.

Hsu, F. K. K. (1985). The self in cross-cultural perspective. In J. J. Marsella, G. De Vos, and F. L. K. Hsu (Eds.), *Culture and self* (pp. 24–55). London: Tavistock.

Hua, H., and Epley, C. H. (2012). Putting the "personal" into personal construct theory. *Journal of Constructivist Psychology, 25,* 269–273.

Hudson, N. W., & Fraley, R. C. (2015). Volitional personality trait change: Can people choose to change their personality traits? *Journal of personality and social psychology, 109*(3), 490–507.

Hudson, N. W., and Roberts, B. W. (2016). Social investment in work reliably predicts change in conscientiousness and agreeableness: A direct replication and extension of Hudson, Roberts, and Lodi-Smith (2012). *Journal of Research in Personality, 60,* 12–23.

Huan, V. S., Ang, R. P., Chong, W. H., and Chye, S. (2014). The impact of shyness on problematic Internet use: The role of loneliness. The Journal of Psychology: *Interdisciplinary and Applied, 148*(6), 699–715.

Hudziak, J. J., van Beijsterveldt, C. E. M., Bartels, M., Rietveld, J. J. J., Rettew, D. C., Derks, E. M., and Boomsma, D. I. (2003). Individual differences in aggression: Genetic analyses by age, gender, and informant in 3-, 7-, and 10-year-old Dutch twins. *Behavior Genetics, 33,* 575–589.

Humbad, M. N., Donnellan, M. B., Iacono, W. G., McGue, M., and Burt, S. A. (2010). Is spousal similarity for personality a matter of convergence or selection? *Personality and Individual Differences, 49,* 827–830.

Hunsley, J., Lee, C. M., and Wood, J. M. (2003). Controversial and questionable assessment techniques. In S. O. Lilienfeld, S. J. Lynn, and J. M. Lohr (Eds.), *Science and pseudoscience in clinical psychology* (pp. 39–76). New York: Guilford Press.

Hunt, E., and Wittmann, W. (2008). National intelligence and national prosperity. *Intelligence, 36,* 1–9.

Huprich, S. K. (2008). TAT oral dependency scale. In S. R. Jenkins (Ed.), *A handbook of clinical scoring systems for thematic apperceptive techniques* (pp. 385–398). Mahwah, NJ: Erlbaum.

Huselid, R. F., and Cooper, M. L. (1994). Gender roles as mediators of sex differences in expressions of pathology. *Journal of Abnormal Psychology, 103,* 595–603.

Hyde, J. S. (1986). Gender differences in aggression. In J. S. Hyde and M. C. Linn (Eds.), *The psychology of gender: Advances through meta-analysis.* Baltimore: Johns Hopkins University Press.

Hyde, J. S. (2005). The gender similarities hypothesis. *American Psychologist, 60,* 581–592.

Hyde, J. S. (2014). Gender similarities and differences. *Annual Review of Psychology, 65,* 373–398.

Hyde, J. S., and Kling, K. C. (2001). Women, motivation, and achievement. *Psychology of Women Quarterly, 25,* 364–378.

Hyde, J. S., and Plant, E. A. (1995). Magnitude of psychological gender differences: Another side to the story. *American Psychologist, 50,* 159–161.

Hyman, I. E., and Loftus, E. F. (2002). False childhood memories and eyewitness memory errors. In M. L. Eisen (Ed.), *Memory and suggestibility in the forensic interview* (pp. 63–84). Mahwah, NJ: Erlbaum.

Ickes, W., Snyder, M., and Garcia, S. (1997). Personality influences on the choice of situations. In R. Hogan, J. A. Johnson, and S. Briggs (Eds.), *Handbook of personality psychology* (pp. 165–195). San Diego: Academic Press.

Ilmarinen, V., Vainikainen, M., Verkasalo, M., and Lönnqvist, J. (2015). Why are extraverts more popular? Oral fluency mediates the effect of extraversion on popularity in middle childhood. *European Journal of Personality, 29*(2), 138–151.

Immelman, A. (2002). The political personality of U.S. president George W. Bush. In L. O. Valenty and O. Feldman (Eds.), *Political leadership for the new century: Personality and behavior among American leaders* (pp. 81–103). Westport, CT: Praeger.

In Den Bosch-Meevissen, Y. C., Peters, M. L., and Alberts, H. M. (2014). Dispositional optimism, optimism priming, and prevention of ego depletion. *European Journal of Social Psychology, 44*(6), 515–520.

Inglehart, R. (1990). *Culture shift in advanced industrial society.* Princeton, NJ: Princeton University Press.

Insel, P., and Roth, W. (1985). *Core concepts in health* (4th ed.). Palo Alto, CA: Mayfield.

Ip, G. W. M., and Bond, M. H. (1995). Culture, values, and the spontaneous self-concept. *Asian Journal of Psychology, 1,* 30–36.

Irwin, M. (2002). Psychoneuroimmunology of depression: Clinical implications. *Brain, Behavior, and Immunity, 16,* 1–16.

Ishihara, K., Miyake, S., Miyasita, A., and Miyata, Y. (1992). Morningness-eveningness preference and sleep habits in Japanese office workers of different ages. *Chronobiologia, 19,* 9–16.

Ishihara, K., Saitoh, T., and Miyata, Y. (1983). Short-term adjustment of oral temperature of 8-hour advanced-shift. *Japanese Psychological Research, 25,* 228–232.

Ishikawa, S. S., Raine, A., Lencz, T., Bihrle, S., and LaCasse, L. (2001). Increased height and bulk in antisocial personality disorder and its subtypes. *Psychiatry Research, 105,* 211–219.

Ivcevic, Z. (2007). Artistic and everyday creativity: An act-frequency approach. *The Journal of Creative Behavior, 41,* 271–290.

Izard, C. E. (1977). *Human emotions.* New York: Plenum Press.

Izard, C. E., Libero, D. Z., Putnam, P., and Haynes, O. M. (1993). Stability of emotion experiences and their relations to traits of personality. *Journal of Personality and Social Psychology, 64,* 847–860.

Jackson, D. N. (1967). *Personality research form manual.* Goshen, NY: Research Psychologists Press.

Jackson, D. N., and Messick, S. (1967). *Problems in human assessment.* New York, McGraw-Hill.

Jackson, J. J., Bogg, T., Walton, K. E., Wood, D., Harms, P. D., Lodi-Smith, J., Edmonds, G. W., and Roberts, B. W. (2009). Not all conscientiousness scales change alike: A multimethod, multisample study of age differences in the facets of conscientiousness. *Journal of Personality and Social Psychology, 96,* 446–459.

Jackson, J. J., Wood, D., Bogg, T., Walton, K. E., Harms, P. D., and Roberts, B. W. (2010). What do conscientious people do? Development and validation of the Behavioral Indicators of Conscientiousness (BIC). *Journal of Research in Personality, 44,* 501–511.

Jacoby, R., and Glauberman, N. (1995). *The bell curve debate: History, documents, opinions.* New York: Random House.

James, W. (1884). What is an emotion? *Mind, 9,* 188–205.

Jang, K. L., Dick, D. M., Wolf, H., Livesley, W. J., and Paris, J. (2005). Psychosocial adversity and emotional instability: An application of gene-environment interaction models. *European Journal of Personality, 19,* 359–372.

Jang, K. L., Livesley, W. J., Angleitner, A., Riemann, R., and Vernon, P. A. (2002). Genetic and environmental influences on the covariance of facets defining the domains of the five-factor model of personality. *Personality and Individual Differences, 33,* 83–101.

Jenkins, S. R. (1994). Need for power and women's careers over 14 years: Structural power, job satisfaction, and motive change. *Journal of Personality and Social Psychology, 66,* 155–165.

Jenkins, C. D., Zyzanski, S. J., and Rosenman, R. H. (1976). Risk of new myocardial infarction in middle age men with manifest coronary heart disease. *Circulation, 53,* 342–347.

Jensen, A. R. (2011). The theory of intelligence and its measurement. *Intelligence, 39,* 171–177.

Jensen-Campbell, L. A., Adams, R., Perry, D. G., Workman, K. A., Furdella, J. Q., and Egan, S. K. (2002). Agreeableness, extraversion, and peer relations in early adolescence: Winning friends and deflecting aggression. *Journal of Research in Personality, 36,* 224–251.

Jensen-Campbell, L. A., Gleason, K. A., Adams, R., and Malcolm, K. T. (2003). Interpersonal conflict, agreeableness, and personality development. *Journal of Personality, 71,* 1059–1085.

Jensen-Campbell, L. A., and Graziano, W. G. (2001). Agreeableness as a moderator of interpersonal conflict. *Journal of Personality, 69,* 323–362.

Jeronimus, B. F., Riese, H., Sanderman, R., and Ormel, J. (2014). Mutual reinforcement between neuroticism and life experiences: A five-wave, 16-year study to test reciprocal causation. *Journal of Personality and Social Psychology, 107,* 751–764.

Jerskey, B. A., Panizzon, M. S., Jacobson, K. C., Neale, M. C., Grant, M. D., Schultz, M., Eisen, S., et al. (2010). Marriage and divorce: A genetic perspective. *Personality and Individual Differences, 49,* 473–478.

John, O. P. (1990). The "Big Five" factor taxonomy: Dimensions of personality in the natural language and questionnaires. In L. A. Pervin (Ed.), *Handbook of personality* (pp. 66–100). New York: Guilford Press.

John, O. P., Naumann, L. P., and Soto, C. J. (2010). Paradigm shift to the integrative Big Five trait taxonomy: History, measurement, and conceptual issues. In O. P. John, R. W. Robins, and L. A. Pervin (Eds.), *Handbook of personality* (pp. 114–158). New York: Guilford Press.

John, O. P., Robins, R. W., and Pervin, L. A. (2010). *Handbook of personality: Theory and research* (3rd ed.). New York: Guilford Press.

Johnson, D. P., and Whisman, M. A. (2013). Gender differences in rumination: A meta-analysis. *Personality and Individual Differences, 55*(4), 367–374.

Johnson, M. K., Rowatt, W. C., and Petrini, L. (2011). A new trait on the market: Honesty-humility as a unique predictor of job performance. *Personality and Individual Differences, 50,* 857–862.

Johnson, R. E. (1970). Some correlates of extramarital coitus. *Journal of Marriage and the Family, 32,* 449–456.

Johnson, W. (2007). Genetic and environmental influences on behavior: Capturing all the interplay. *Psychological Review, 114,* 423–440.

Johnson, W., and Deary, I. J. (2011). Placing inspection time, reaction time, and perceptual speed in the broader context of cognitive ability: The VPR model in the Lothian Birth Cohort 1936, *Intelligence, 39,* 405–417.

Johnson, W., Hicks, B. M., McGue, M., and Iacono, W. G. (2007). Most of the girls are alright, but some aren't: Personality trajectory groups from ages 14–24 and some associations with outcomes. *Journal of Personality and Social Psychology, 93,* 266–284.

Johnson, W., McGue, M., and Krueger, R. F. (2005). Personality stability in late adulthood: A behavior genetic analysis. *Journal of Personality, 73,* 523–551.

Johnson, W., McGue, M., Krueger, R. F., and Bouchard, T. J., Jr. (2004). Marriage and personality: A genetic analysis. *Journal of Personality and Social Psychology, 86,* 285–294.

Johnson, W., Penke, L., and Spinath, F. M. (2011). Heritability in the era of molecular genetics: Some thoughts for understanding genetic influences on behavioural traits: Understanding heritability. *European Journal of Personality, 25,* 254–266.

Johnston, M. (1999). *Spectral evidence: The Ramona case: Incest, memory, and truth on trial in Napa Valley.* Boulder, CO: Westview Press.

Jokela, M. (2009). Personality predicts migration within and between U.S. states. *Journal of Research in Personality, 43,* 79–83.

Jokela, M., Kivimaki, M., Elovainio, M., and Keltikangas-Jarvinen, L. (2009). Personality and having children: A two-way relationship. *Journal of Personality and Social Psychology, 96,* 218–230.

Jonason, P. K., Garcia, J. R., Webster, G. D., Li, N. P., and Fisher, H. E. (2015). Relationship deal breakers traits people avoid in potential mates. *Personality and Social Psychology Bulletin, 41*(12), 1697–1711.

Jonason, P. K., and Webster, G. D. (2012). A protean approach to social influence: Dark Triad personalities and social influence tactics. *Personality and Individual Differences, 52,* 521–526.

Jones, A., and Crandall, R. (1986). Validation of a short index of self-actualization. *Personality and Social Psychology Bulletin, 12,* 63–73.

Jones, D. N., and Paulhus, D. L. (2010). Different provocations trigger aggression in narcissists and psychopaths. *Social Psychological and Personality Science, 1,* 12–18.

Jones, D. N., and Weiser, D. A. (2014). Differential infidelity patterns among the Dark Triad. *Personality and Individual Differences, 57,* 20–24.

Jordan, C. H., Spencer, S. J., Zanna, M. P., Hoshino-Browne, E., and Correll, J. (2003). Secure and defensive high self-esteem. *Journal of Personality and Social Psychology, 85,* 969–978.

Judge, D. S., and Hrdy, S. B. (1992). Allocation of accumulated resources among close kin: inheritance in Sacramento, California, 1890–1984. *Ethology and Sociobiology, 13*(5), 495–522.

Judge, T., and Larsen, R. J. (2001). Dispositional sources of job satisfaction: A review and theoretical extension. *Organizational Behavior and Human Decision Processes, 86,* 67–98.

Jung, I., Lee, H., and Cho, B. (2004). Persistent psychotic disorder in an adolescent with a past history of butane gas dependence. *European Psychiatry, 19,* 519–520.

Kagan, J. (1981). *The second year: The emergence of self-awareness.* Cambridge, MA: Harvard University Press.

Kagan, J. (1994). *Galen's prophecy: Temperament in human nature.* New York: Basic Books.

Kagan, J. (1999). Born to be shy? In R. Conlan (Ed.), *States of mind* (pp. 29–51). New York: Wiley.

Kagan, J., and Moss, H. (1962). *Birth to maturity: A study in psychological development.* New York: Wiley.

Kagan, J., and Snidman, N. (1991). Infant predictors of inhibited and uninhibited profiles. *Psychological Science, 2,* 40–44.

Kamakura, T., Ando, J., and Ono, Y. (2007). Genetic and environmental effects on the stability and change in self-esteem during adolescence. *Personality and Individual Differences, 42,* 181–190.

Kamble, S., Shackelford, T. K., Pham, M., and Buss, D. M. (2014). Indian mate preferences: Continuity, sex differences, and cultural change across a quarter of a century. *Personality and Individual Differences, 70,* 150–155.

Kammrath, L. K., and Scholer, A. A. (2011). The Pollyanna myth: How highly agreeable people judge positive and negative relational acts. *Personality and Social Psychology Bulletin, 37,* 1172–1184.

Kandler, C., Bleidorn, W., Spinath, F. M., and Riemann, R. (2010). Sources of cumulative continuity in personality: A longitudinal multiple-rater twin study. *Journal of Personality and Social Psychology, 98,* 995–1008.

Kanner, Allen D., Feldman, S., and Weinberger, D. A. (1991). Uplifts, hassles, and adaptational outcomes in early adolescents. In A. Monat and R. S. Lazarus (Eds.), *Stress and coping: An anthology* (3rd ed.) (pp. 158–181). New York: Columbia University Press.

Kaplan, H., and Hill, K. (1985). Food-sharing among Ache foragers: Tests of evolutionary hypotheses. *Current Anthropology, 26,* 223–246.

Kapogiannis, D., Sutin, A., Davatzikos, C., Costa, P. J., and Resnick, S. (2013). The five factors of personality and regional cortical variability in the Baltimore longitudinal study of aging. *Human Brain Mapping, 34*(11), 2829–2840.

Karantzas, G. C., and Simpson, J. A. (2015). Attachment and aged care. In J. A. Simpson and W. S. Rholes (Eds.), *Attachment theory and research: New directions and emerging themes* (pp. 319–345). New York, NY, US: Guilford Press.

Katigbak, M. S., Church, A. T., Guanzon-Lapena, M. A., Carlota, A. J., and del Pilar, G. H. (2002). Are indigenous personality dimensions culture-specific? Philippine inventories and the five-factor model. *Journal of Personality and Social Psychology, 82,* 1, 89–101.

Katz, I. M., and Campbell, J. D. (1994). Ambivalence over emotional expression and well-being: Nomothetic and idiographic tests of the stress-buffering hypothesis. *Journal of Personality and Social Psychology, 67,* 513–524.

Kaufman, S. B., Quilty, L. C., Grazioplene, R. G., Hirsh, J. B., Gray, J. R., Peterson, J. B., and DeYoung, C. G. (2015). Openness to experience and intellect differentially predict creative achievement in the arts and sciences. *Journal of Personality, 82,* 248–258.

Kavanagh, K., and Hops, H. (1994). Good girls? Bad boys? Gender and development as contexts for diagnosis and treatment. *Advances in Clinical Child Psychology, 16,* 45–79.

Kawamoto, T. (2016). Cross-sectional age differences in the HEXACO personality: Results from a Japanese sample. *Journal of Research in Personality, 62,* 1–5.

Kelley, H. H. (1992). Common-sense psychology and scientific psychology. In M. R. Rosensweig and L. W. Porter (Eds.), *Annual review of psychology* (vol. 43, pp. 1–23). Palo Alto, CA: Annual Reviews.

Kelly, E. L., and Conley, J. J. (1987). Personality and compatibility: A prospective analysis of marital stability and marital satisfaction. *Journal of Personality and Social Psychology, 52,* 27–40.

Kelly, G. A. (1955). *The psychology of personal constructs* (vols. 1 and 2). London: Routledge.

Keltikangas-Järvinen, L., Elovainio, M., Kivimäki, M., Lichtermann, D., Ekelund, J., and Leena Peltonen, L. (2003). Association between the Type 4 dopamine receptor gene polymorphism and novelty seeking. *Psychosomatic Medicine, 65,* 471–476.

Kendler, K. S., McGuire, M., Gruenberg, A. M., O'Hare, A., Spellman, M., and Walsh, D. (1993). The Roscommon Family Study III: Schizophrenia-related personality disorders in relatives. *Archives of General Psychiatry, 50,* 781–788.

Kendler, R. S., Heath, A. C., Neale, M. C., Kessler, R. C., and Eaves, L. J. (1992). A population-based twin study of alcoholism in women. *Journal of the American Medical Association, 268,* 1877–1882.

Kenrick, D. T., Griskevicius, V., Neuberg, S. L., and Schaller, M. (2010). Renovating the pyramid of needs: Contemporary extensions built upon ancient foundations. *Perspectives on Psychological Science, 5,* 292–314.

Kenrick, D. T., and Luce, C. L. (2004). *The functional mind: Readings in evolutionary psychology.* Boston: Allyn and Bacon.

Kerkhof, G. A. (1985). Inter-individual differences in the human circadian system: A review. *Biological Psychology, 20,* 83–112.

Kernberg, O. (1975). *Borderline conditions and pathological narcissism.* New York: Jason Aronson.

Kernberg, O. F. (1984). *Severe personality disorders.* New Haven, CT: Yale University Press.

Kernis, M. H., Grannemann, B. D., and Barclay, L. C. (1992). Stability of self-esteem: Assessment, correlates, and excuse making. *Journal of Personality, 60,* 621–643.

Kernis, M. H., Grannemann, B. D., and Mathis, L. C. (1991). Stability of self-esteem as a moderator of the relation between level of self-esteem and depression. *Journal of Personality and Social Psychology, 61,* 80–84.

Kesebir, S., Graham, J., Oishi, S. (2010). A theory of human needs should be human-centered, not animal-centered: Commentary on Kenrick et al. (2010). *Perspectives on Psychological Science, 5,* 315–319.

Ketelaar, T. (1995). *Emotion as mental representations of fitness affordances: I. Evidence supporting the claim that the negative and positive emotions map onto fitness costs and benefits.* Paper presented at the annual meeting of the Human Behavior and Evolution Society, Santa Barbara.

Khan, S. S., Nessim, S., Gray, R., Czer, L. S., Chaux, A., and Matloff, J. (1990). Increased mortality of women in coronary artery bypass surgery: Evidence for referral bias. *Annals of Internal Medicine, 112,* 561–567.

Kihlstrom, J. F. (1999). The psychological unconscious. In L. A. Pervin and O. P. John (Eds.), *Handbook of personality: Theory and research* (pp. 424–442). New York: Guilford Press.

Kihlstrom, J. F. (2003a). Freud is dead weight on psychology. In E. E. Smith, S. Nolen-Hoeksema, B. L. Fredrickson, G. R. Loftus, D. J. Bem, and S. Maren, *Introduction to psychology* (p. 487). Belmont, CA: Wadsworth/Thomson Learning.

Kihlstrom, J. F. (2003b). Hypnosis and memory. In J. F. Byrne (Ed.), *Learning and memory* (2nd ed., pp. 240–242). Farmington Hills, MI: Macmillan.

Kihlstrom, J. F. (2013). The person-situation interaction. In D. E. Carlston (Ed.), *The Oxford handbook of social cognition* (pp. 786–805). New York: Oxford University Press.

Kihlstrom, J. F., Barnhardt, T. M., and Tataryn, D. J. (1992). The psychological unconscious: Found, lost, and regained. *American Psychologist, 47,* 788–791.

Kim, E. (2002). Agitation, aggression, and disinhibition syndromes after traumatic brain injury. *NeuroRehabilitation, 17,* 297–310.

Kim, K., Smith, P. K., and Palermiti, A. (1997). Conflict in childhood and reproductive development. *Evolution and Human Behavior, 18,* 109–142.

Kim-Cohen, J., Caspi, A., Taylor, A., Williams, B., Newcombe, R., Craig, I. W., et al. (2006). MAOA, maltreatment, and gene-environment interaction predicting children's mental health: New evidence and a meta-analysis. *Molecular Psychiatry, 11,* 903–913.

Kimura, D. (2002). Sex hormones influence human cognitive pattern. *Neuroendocrinology Letters, 23* (Suppl. 4): 67–77.

Kjærgaard, A., Leon, G. R., and Venables, N. C. (2015). The 'right stuff' for a solo sailboat circumnavigation of the globe. *Environment And Behavior, 47*(10), 1147–1171.

King, L. A. (1995). Wishes, motives, goals, and personal memories: Relations and correlates of measures of human motivation. *Journal of Personality, 63,* 985–1007.

King, L. A., and Emmons, R. A. (1990). Conflict over emotional expression: Psychological and physical correlates. *Journal of Personality and Social Psychology, 58,* 864–877.

King, L. A., and Hicks, J. A. (2012). Positive affect and meaning in life: The intersection of hedonism and eudaimonia.

In P. T. P Wong (Ed.), The human quest for meaning: Theories, research and applications (2nd ed., pp. 125–141). New York, NY: Routledge/Taylor & Francis Group.

Kintz, B. L., Delprato, D. J., Mettee, D. R., Parsons, D. E., and Schappe, R. H. (1965). The experimenter effect. *Psychological Bulletin, 63,* 223–232.

Kipnis, D. (1971). *Character structure and impulsiveness.* New York: Academic Press.

Kling, K. C., Hyde, J. S., Showers, C. J., and Buswell, B. N. (1999). Gender differences in self-esteem: A meta-analysis. *Psychological Bulletin, 125,* 470–500.

Klinger, E. (1977a). The nature of fantasy and its clinical uses. *Psychotherapy: Theory, Research, and Practice, 14,* 223–231.

Klinger, E. (1977b). *Meaning and void: Inner experience and the incentives in people's lives.* Minneapolis: University of Minnesota Press.

Klonsky, E. D., Oltmanns, T. F., and Turkheimer, E. (2002). Informant reports of personality disorder: Relation to self-reports and future research directions. *Clinical Psychology: Science and Practice, 9,* 300–311.

Klucken, T., Kruse, O., Schweckendiek, J., and Stark, R. (2015). Increased skin conductance responses and neural activity during fear conditioning are associated with a repressive coping style. *Frontiers in Behavioral Neuroscience, 9.*

Kluckhohn, C., and Murray, H. A. (1948). *Personality in nature, society, and culture.* New York: Knopf.

Knafo, A., Iervolino, A. C., and Plomin, R. (2005). Masculine girls and feminine boys: Genetic and environmental contributions to atypical gender development in early childhood. *Journal of Personality and Social Psychology, 88,* 400–412.

Knutson, B., and Bhanji, J. (2006). Neural substrates for emotional traits? In T. Canli (Ed.), *Biology of personality and individual differences* (pp. 116–132). New York: Guilford Press.

Knutson, B., Wolkowitz, O. M., Cole, S. W., Chan, T., Moore, E. A., Johnson, R. C., Terpestra, J., et al. (1998). Selective alteration of personality and social behavior by serotonergic intervention. *American Journal of Psychiatry, 155,* 373–378.

Koenig, L. B., McGue, M., Krueger, R. F., and Bouchard, T. J., Jr. (2005). Genetic and environmental influences on religiousness ratings. *Journal of Personality, 73,* 471–488.

Koestner, R., and McClelland, D. C. (1990). Perspectives on competence motivation. In L. A. Pervin (Ed.), *Handbook of personality: Theory and research* (pp. 527–548). New York: Guilford Press.

Kofman, S. (1985). *The enigma of woman: Woman in Freud's writings.* Ithaca, NY: Cornell University Press.

Kohn, M. L., Naoi, A., Schoenbach, C., Schooler, C., and Slomczynski, K. M. (1990). Position in the class structure and psychological functioning in the United States, Japan, and Poland. *American Journal of Sociology, 95,* 964–1008.

Kohut, H. (1977). *The restoration of the self.* Madison, CT: International Universities Press.

Koole, S. L., Jager, W., van den Berg, A. E., Vlek, C.A.J., and Hofstee, W.K.B. (2001). On the social nature of personality: Effects of extraversion, agreeableness, and feedback about collective resource use on cooperation in a resource dilemma. *Personality and Social Psychology Bulletin, 27, 3,* 289–301.

Koopmans, J. R., and Boomsma, D. I. (1993). Bivariate genetic analysis of the relation between alcohol and tobacco use in adolescent twins. *Psychiatric Genetics, 3,* 172.

Kopp, C. B. (1989). Regulation of distress and negative emotions: A developmental view. *Developmental Psychology, 25,* 343–354.

Kosslyn, S. M., Cacioppo, J. T., Davidson, R. J., Hugdahl, K., Lovallo, W. R., Spiegel, D., and Rose, R. (2002). Bridging psychology and biology: The analysis of individuals in groups. *American Psychologist, 57,* 341–351.

Kosslyn, S. M., and Rosenberg, R. S. (2004). *Psychology: The brain, the person, the world.* Boston: Allyn and Bacon.

Kotov, R., Gamez, W., Schmidt, F., and Watson, D. (2010). Linking "big" personality traits to anxiety, depressive, and substance use disorders: A meta-analysis. *Psychological Bulletin, 136,* 768–821.

Kotter-Gruhn, D., Wiest, M., Zurek, P. P., and Scheibe, S. (2009). What is it we are longing for? Psychological and demographic factors influencing the contents of Sehnsucht (life longings). *Journal of Research in Personality, 43,* 428–437.

Kowalski, R. M., and Brown, K. J. (1994). Psychosocial barriers to cervical cancer screening: Concerns with self-presentation and social evaluation. *Journal of Applied Social Psychology, 24,* 941–958.

Kraeplin, E. (1913). *Psychiatrie: Ein Lehrbuch* (8th ed.). Leipzig: Barth.

Krasno, J. (2015). William Jefferson Clinton: Promise, persistence, and the will to be adored. In J. Krasno, S. LaPides, J. Krasno, S. LaPides (Eds.), *Personality, political leadership, and decision making: A global perspective* (pp. 295–318). Santa Barbara, CA, US: Praeger/ABC-CLIO.

Kretschmer, E. (1925). *Physique and char- acter.* London: Kegan Paul.

Krueger, J. I., Hasman, J. F., Acevedo, M., and Villano, P. (2003). Perceptions of trait typicality in gender stereotypes: Examining the role of attribution and categorization processes. *Personality and Social Psychology Bulletin, 29, 1,* 108–116.

Krueger, R. F., and Markon, K. E. (2006). Reinterpreting comorbidity: A model- based approach to understanding and classifying psychopathology. *Annual Review of Clinical Psychology, 2,* 111–133.

Krueger, R. F., Markon, K. E., and Bouchard, T. J., Jr. (2003). The extended genotype: The heritability of personality accounts for the heritability of recalled family environments in twins reared apart. *Journal of Personality, 71, 5,* 809–834.

Krueger, R. F., South, S., Johnson, W., and Iacono, W. (2008). The heritability of personality is not always 50%: Gene- environment interactions and correla- tions between personality and parenting. *Journal of Personality, 76,* 1485–1522.

Kuhl, J., and Kazén, M. (2008). Motivation, affect, and hemispheric asymmetry: Power versus affiliation. *Journal of Per- sonality and Social Psychology, 95,* 456–469.

Kuhle, B. X. (2011). Did you have sex with him? Do you love her? An in vivo test of sex differences in jealous interrogations. *Personality and Individual Differences, 51,* 1044–1047.

Kuhle, B. X., Smedley, K. D., and Schmitt, D. P. (2009). Sex differences in the motivation and mitigation of jealousy- induced interrogations. *Personality and Individual Differences, 46,* 499–502.

Kuhn, M., and McPartland, T. S. (1954). An empirical investigation of self-attitudes. *American Sociological Review, 19,* 68–76.

Kupper, N., & Denollet, J. (2007). Type D personality as a prognostic factor in heart disease: Assessment and mediating mechanisms. *Journal of Personality Assessment, 89,* 265–276.

Kurman, J. (2001). Self-enhancement: Is it restricted to individualistic cultures? *Personality and Social Psychology Bulletin, 27, 12,* 1705–1716.

Krasno, J. (2015). William Jefferson Clin- ton: Promise, persistence, and the will to be adored. In J. Krasno, S. LaPides, J. Krasno, S. LaPides (Eds.), *Personality, political leadership, and decision mak- ing: A global perspective* (pp. 295–318). Santa Barbara, CA, US: Praeger/ ABC-CLIO.

Kwapil, T. R., Wrobel, M. J., and Pope, C. A. (2002). The five-factor personality structure of dissociative experiences.

Personality and Individual Differences, 32, 431–443.

Kwon, P., Campbell, D. G., and Williams, M. G. (2001). Sociotropy and autonomy: Preliminary evidence for construct valid- ity using TAT narratives. *Journal of Personality Assessment Special Issue: More data on the current Rorschach controversy, 77,* 128–138.

Kyl-Heku, L., and Buss, D. M. (1996). Tac- tics as units of analysis in and personal- ity psychology: An illustration using tactics of hierarchy negotiation. *Person- ality and Individual Differences, 21,* 497–517.

Laham, S. M., Gonsalkorale, K., and von Hippel, W. (2005). Darwinian grandpar- enting: Preferential investment in more certain kin. *Personality and Social Psy- chology Bulletin, 31,* 63–72.

Lajunen, T. (2001). Personality and acci- dent liability: Are extraversion, neuroti- cism and psychoticism related to traffic and occupational fatalities? *Personality and Individual Differences, 31,* 1365–1373.

Lalumiere, M. L., Chalmers, L. J., Quinsey, V. L., and Seto, M. C. (1996). A test of the mate deprivation hypothesis of sex- ual coercion. *Ethology and Sociobiology, 17,* 299–318.

Lalumiere, M. L., Harris, G. T., and Rice, M. E. (2001). Psychopathy and develop- mental instability. *Evolution and Human Behavior, 22,* 75–92.

Langens, T. A. (2001). Predicting behavior change in Indian businessmen from a combination of need for achievement and self-discrepancy. *Journal of Research in Personality, 35,* 339–352.

Langens, T. A., and Schmalt, H. D. (2008). Motivational traits: New directions and measuring motives with the multi- motive grid (MMG). In G. J. Boyle, G. Matthews, and D. H. Saklofske (Eds.), *The SAGE handbook of personality the- ory and assessment, vol. 1: Personality theories and Models* (pp. 523–544). Thousand Oaks, CA: Sage.

Langevin, R., Bain, J., Wortzman, G., and Hucker, S. (1988). Sexual sadism: Brain, blood, and behavior. *Annals of the New York Academy of Science, 528,* 163–171.

Langford, P. H. (2003). A one-minute mea- sure of the Big Five? Evaluating and abridging Shafer's (1999) Big Five markers. *Personality and Individual Dif- ferences, 35,* 1127–1140.

Langner, C. A., and Winter, D. G. (2001). The motivational basis of concessions and compromise: Archival and labora- tory studies. *Journal of Personality and Social Psychology, 81,* 711–727.

Lanning, K. (1994). Dimensionality of observer ratings on the California Adult Q-set. *Journal of personality and social psychology, 67, 1,* 151.

Larrance, D., Pavelich, S., Storer, P., Polizzi, M., Baron, B., Sloan, S., Jordan, R., and Reis, H. T. (1979). Com- petence and incompetence: Asymmetric responses to women and men on a sex- linked task. *Personality and Social Psy- chology Bulletin, 5,* 363–366.

Larsen, R. J. (1984). Theory and measurement of affect intensity as an individual differ- ence characteristic. *Dissertation Abstracts International, 45, 7-B.* (UMI No. 2297).

Larsen, R. J. (1985). Individual differences in circadian activity rhythm and person- ality. *Personality and Individual Differ- ences, 6,* 305–311.

Larsen, R. J. (1987). The stability of mood variability: A spectral analytic approach to daily mood assessments. *Journal of Personality and Social Psychology, 52,* 1195–1204.

Larsen, R. J. (1989). A process approach to personality: Utilizing time as a facet of data. In D. Buss and N. Cantor (Eds.), *Personality psychology: Recent trends and emerging directions* (pp. 177–193). New York: Springer-Verlag.

Larsen, R. J. (1991). Personality and emo- tion. In V. Derlega, B. Winstead, and W. Jones (Eds.), *Contemporary research in personality* (pp. 407–432). Chicago: Nelson-Hall.

Larsen, R. J. (1992). Neuroticism and selec- tive encoding and recall of symptoms: Evidence from a combined concurrent- retrospective study. *Journal of Personal- ity and Social Psychology, 62,* 480–488.

Larsen, R. J. (2000a). Toward a science of mood regulation. *Psychological Inquiry, 11,* 129–141.

Larsen, R. J. (2000b). Maintaining hedonic balance. *Psychological Inquiry, 11,* 218–225.

Larsen, R. J. (2009). Affect intensity. In M. R. Leary and R. H. Hoyle (Eds.), *Hand- book of individual differences in social behaviors* (pp. 241–254). New York: Guilford Press.

Larsen, R. J., Billings, D., and Cutler, S. (1996). Affect intensity and individual differences in cognitive style. *Journal of Personality, 64,* 185–208.

Larsen, R. J., Chen, B., and Zelenski, J. (2003). *Responses to punishment and reward in the emotion Stroop paradigm: Relations to BIS and BAS.* Unpublished manuscript.

Larsen, R. J., and Cowan, G. S. (1988). Internal focus of attention and depres- sion: A study of daily experience. *Moti- vation and Emotion, 12,* 237–249.

Larsen, R. J., and Diener, E. (1985). A multitrait-multimethod examination of affect structure: Hedonic level and emo- tional intensity. *Personality and Individual Differences, 6,* 631–636.

Larsen, R. J., and Diener, E. (1987). Affect intensity as an individual difference characteristic: A review. *Journal of Research in Personality, 21,* 1–39.

Larsen, R. J., and Diener, E. (1992). Problems and promises with the circumplex model of emotion. *Review of Personality and Social Psychology, 13,* 25–59.

Larsen, R. J., Diener, E., and Cropanzano, R. S. (1987). Cognitive operations associated with individual differences in affect intensity. *Journal of Personality and Social Psychology, 53,* 767–774.

Larsen, R. J., Diener, E., and Emmons, R. A. (1986). Affect intensity and reactions to daily life events. *Journal of Personality and Social Psychology, 51,* 803–814.

Larsen, R. J., Diener, E., and Lucas, R. (2002). Emotion: Models, measures, and individual differences. In R. Lord, R. Klimoski, and R. Kanfer (Eds.), *Emotions at work* (pp. 64–106). San Francisco: Jossey-Bass.

Larsen, R. J., and Fredrickson, B. L. (1999). Measurement issues in emotion research. In D. Kahneman, E. Diener, and N. Schwarz (Eds.), *Understanding quality of life: Scientific perspectives on enjoyment and suffering* (pp. 40–60). New York: Sage.

Larsen, R. J., and Kasimatis, M. (1990). Individual differences in entrainment of mood to the weekly calendar. *Journal of Personality and Social Psychology, 58,* 164–171.

Larsen, R. J., and Ketelaar, T. (1989). Extraversion, neuroticism, and susceptibility to positive and negative mood induction procedures. *Personality and Individual Differences, 10,* 1221–1228.

Larsen, R. J., and Ketelaar, T. (1991). Personality and susceptibility to positive and negative emotional states. *Journal of Personality and Social Psychology, 61,* 132–140.

Larsen, R. J., Mercer, K. A., and Balota, D. A. (2006). Lexical characteristics of words used in emotion Stroop tasks. *Emotion, 6,* 62–72.

Larsen, R. J., and Prizmic, Z. (2004). Affect regulation. In R. Baumeister and K. Vohs (Eds.), *Handbook of self-regulation research* (pp. 40–60). New York: Guilford Press.

Larsen, R. J., & Prizmic, Z. (2006). Multimethod measurement of emotion. In M. Eid and E. Diener (Eds.), *Handbook of measurement: A multimethod perspective* (pp. 337–352). Washington, DC: American Psychological Association.

Larsen, R. J., and Prizmic-Larsen, Z. (1999). Marrying a culture when you marry a person. *Contemporary Psychology, 44,* 538–540.

Larsen, R. J., and Zarate, M. A. (1991). Extending reducer/augmenter theory into the emotion domain: The role of affect in regulating stimulation level. *Personality and Individual Differences, 12,* 713–723.

Larson, D. G., and Chastain, R. L. (1990). Self-concealment: Conceptualization, measurement, and health implications. *Journal of Social and Clinical Psychology, 9,* 439–455.

Lassek, W. D., and Gaulin, S. J. C. (2009). Costs and benefits of fat-free muscle mass in men: Relationship to mating success, dietary requirements, and native immunity. *Evolution and Human Behavior, 30,* 322–328.

Lassiter, G. D., Lindberg, M. J., Gonzalez-Vallejo, C., Bellezza, F. S., & Phillips, N. D. (2009). The deliberation-without-attention effect: Evidence for an artifactual interpretation. Psychological Science, 20, 671–675.

Laub, J. H., and Lauritsen, J. L. (1994). The precursors of criminal offending across the life course. *Federal Probation, 58,* 51–57.

Lawton, M. P., Moss, M. S., Winter, L., and Hoffman, C. (2002). Motivation in later life: Personal projects and well-being. *Psychology and Aging, 17,* 539–547.

Lazarus, R. S. (1991). *Emotion and adaptation.* Oxford, England: Oxford University Press.

Lazarus, R. S., and Folkman, S. (1984). *Stress, appraisal and coping.* New York: Springer.

Lazarus, R. S., Kanner, A. D., and Folkman, S. (1980). Emotions: A cognitive-phenomenological analysis. In R. Plutchik and H. Kellerman (Eds.), *Theories of emotion* (pp. 189–217). New York: Academic Press.

Leary, M. R., and Kowalski, R. M. (1995). Social anxiety. New York: Guilford Press.

Le Boeuf, B. J., and Reiter, J. (1988). Lifetime reproductive success in northern elephant seals. In T. H. Clutton-Brock (Ed.), *Reproductive success* (pp. 344–362). Chicago: University of Chicago Press.

Lee, C., Corte, C., Stein, K. F., Finnegan, L., McCreary, L. L., and Park, C. G. (2015). Expected problem drinker possible self: Predictor of alcohol problems and tobacco use in adolescents. *Substance Abuse, 36*(4), 434–439.

Lee, B. W., and Leeson, P. C. (2015). Online gaming in the context of social anxiety. *Psychology of Addictive Behaviors, 29*(2), 473–482.

Lee, D., Kelley, K. R., and Edwards, J. K. (2006). A closer look at relationships among trait procrastination, neuroticism, and conscientiousness. *Personality and Individual Differences, 40,* 27–37.

Lee, K., and Ashton, M. C. (2008). The HEXACO personality factors in the indigenous personality lexicons of English and 11 other languages. *Journal of Personality, 76,* 1011–1054.

Lee, K., Ogunfowora, B., and Ashton, M. C. (2005). Personality traits beyond the Big Five: Are they within the HEXACO space? *Journal of Personality, 73,* 1437–1463.

Lee-Ross, D. (2015). Personality characteristics of the self-employed: A comparison using the world values survey data set. *Journal of Management Development, 34*(9), 1094–1112.

Leeuwis, F. H., Koot, H. M., Creemers, D. M., & van Lier, P. C. (2015). Implicit and explicit self-esteem discrepancies, victimization and the development of late childhood internalizing problems. *Journal of Abnormal Child Psychology, 43*(5), 909–919.

Lee-Won, R. J., Herzog, L., and Park, S. G. (2015). Hooked on Facebook: The role of social anxiety and need for social assurance in problematic use of Facebook. *Cyberpsychology, Behavior, and Social Networking, 18*(10), 567–574.

Lehmann, R., Denissen, J. J., Allemand, M., and Penke, L. (2013). Age and gender differences in motivational manifestations of the Big Five from age 16 to 60. *Developmental Psychology, 49,* 365–383.

Lei, C., Wang, Y., Shackelford, T. K., and Buss, D. M. (2011). Chinese mate preferences: Cultural evolution and continuity across a quarter century. *Personality and Individual Differences, 50,* 678–683.

Leikas, S., Lonnqvist, J., and Verkasalo, M. (2012). Persons, situations, and behaviors: Consistency and variability of different behaviors in four interpersonal situations. *Journal of Personality and Social Psychology, 103,* 1007–1022.

Leitner, J. B., Hehman, E., Deegan, M. P., and Jones, J. M. (2014). Adaptive disengagement buffers self-esteem from negative social feedback. *Personality and Social Psychology Bulletin, 40*(11), 1435–1450.

Lemay, E. P., and Dobush, S. (2015). When do personality and emotion predict destructive behavior during relationship conflict? The role of perceived commitment asymmetry. *Journal of Personality, 83*(5), 523–534.

Leopold, D. A. (2012). Primary visual cortex: Awareness and blindsight. *Annual Review of Neuroscience, 35,* 91–109.

LeVay, S. (1991). A difference in hypothalamic structure between heterosexual and homosexual men. *Science,* pp. 1034–1037.

LeVay, S. (1993). *The sexual brain.* Cambridge, MA: MIT Press.

LeVay, S. (1996). *Queer science: The use and abuse of research into homosexuality.* Cambridge, MA: MIT Press.

Levy, B. R., Slade, M. D., and Ranasinghe, P. (2009). Causal thinking after a tsunami wave: Karma beliefs, pessimistic explanatory style and health among Sri Lankan survivors. *Journal of Religion and Health, 48*(1), 38–45.

Levenson, M. R., Kiehl, K. A., and Fitzpatrick, C. M. (1995). Assessing psychopathic attributes in a noninstitutionalized population. *Journal of Personality and Social Psychology, 68,* 151–158.

Levenson, R. W. (1983). Personality research and psychophysiology: General considerations. *Journal of Research in Personality, 17,* 1–21.

Levenson, R. W. (2003). Autonomic specificity and emotion. In R. J. Davidson, K. R. Scherer, and H. H. Goldsmith (Eds.), *Handbook of affective science* (pp. 212–224). New York: Oxford University Press.

Levesque, J., Fanny, E., and Joanette, Y. (2003). Neural circuitry underlying voluntary suppression of sadness. *Biological Psychiatry 53,* 502–510.

Levy, S. M. (1990). Psychosocial risk factors and cancer progression: Mediating pathways linking behavior and disease. In K. D. Craig and S. M. Weiss (Eds.), and *Health enhancement, disease prevention, and early intervention: Biobehavioral perspectives* (pp. 348–369). New York: Springer.

Levy, S. M., and Heiden. L. A. (1990). Personality and social factors in cancer outcome. In H. S. Friedman (Ed.), *Personality and disease* (pp. 254–279). New York: Wiley.

Levy, S. M., Herberman, R., Maluish, A., Achlien, B., and Lippman, M. (1985). Prognostic risk assessment in primary breast cancer by behavioral and immunological parameters. *Health Psychology, 4,* 99–113.

Li, N. P., Valentine, K. A., & Patel, L. (2011). Mate preferences in the U.S. and Singapore: A cross-cultural test of the mate preference priority model. *Personality and Individual Differences, 50,* 291–294.

Lewis, M., and Ramsay, D. (2004). Development of self-recognition, personal pronoun use, and pretend play during the second year. *Child Development, 75,* 1821–1831.

Li, H., Zhang, Y., Wu, C., and Mei, D. (2016). Effects of field dependence-independence and frame of reference on navigation performance using multi-dimensional electronic maps. *Personality and Individual Differences, 97,* 289–299.

Lieberman, D., and Lobel, T. (2012). Kinship on the Kibbutz: Coresidence duration predicts altruism, personal sexual aversions and moral attitudes among communally reared peers. *Evolution and Human Behavior, 33*(1), 26–34.

Lilienfeld, S. O. (2002). When worlds collide: Social science, politics and the Rind et al. (1998) Child abuse meta-analysis. *American Psychologist, 57,* 177–187.

Lilienfeld, S. O., Watts, A. L., and Smith, S. F. (2015). Successful psychopathy:

A scientific status report. *Current Directions in Psychological Science, 24*(4), 298–303.

Lin, S., Ma, J., and Johnson, R. E. (2016). When ethical leader behavior breaks bad: How ethical leader behavior can turn abusive via ego depletion and moral licensing. *Journal of Applied Psychology, 101*(6), 815–830.

Linville, P. W. (1987). Self-complexity as a cognitive buffer against stress-related illness and depression. *Journal of Personality and Social Psychology, 52,* 663–676.

Lippa, R. (1998). Gender-related individual differences and the structure of vocational interests: The importance of the people-things dimension. *Journal of Personality and Social Psychology, 74,* 996–1009.

Lishman, W. A. (1972). Selective factors in memory. Part 1: Age, sex, and personality attributes. *Psychological Medicine, 2,* 121–138.

Little, A. C., Burt, D. M., and Perrett, D. I. (2006). Assortative mating for perceived facial personality traits. *Personality and Individual Differences, l 40,* 973–984.

Little, B. R. (2011). Personal projects and motivational counseling: The quality of lives reconsidered. In W. M. Cox and E. Klinger (Eds.), *Handbook of motivational counseling: Goal-based approaches to assessment and intervention with addiction and other problems* (2nd ed., pp. 73–87). Hoboken, NJ: Wiley-Blackwell.

Little, B. R. (1972a). *Person-thing orientation: A provisional manual for the T-P scale.* Oxford, England: Oxford University, Department of Experimental Psychology.

Little, B. R. (1972b). Psychological man as scientist, humanist, and specialist. *Journal of Experimental Research in Personality, 6,* 95–118.

Little, B. R. (1999). Personality and motivation: Personal action and the cognitive revolution. In L. A. Pervin and O. P. John (Eds.), *Handbook of personality: Theory and research* (pp. 501–524). New York: Guilford Press.

Little, B. R. (2007). Prompt and circumstance: The generative contexts of personal projects analysis. In B. Little, K. Salmela-Aro, and S. D. Phillips (Eds.), *Personal project pursuit: Goals, action, and human flourishing* (pp. 3–49). Mahwah, NJ: Erlbaum.

Little, B. R. (2011). Personal projects and motivational counseling: The quality of lives reconsidered. in W. M. Cox and E. Klinger (Eds.), Handbook of motivational counseling: Goal-based approaches to assessment and intervention with addiction and other problems (2nd ed.). New York: Wiley-Blackwell.

Little, B. R., and Gee, T. L. (2007). The methodology of personal projects analysis: Four modules and a funnel. In B. Little, K. Salmela-Aro, and S. D. Phillips (Eds.), *Personal project pursuit: Goals, action, and human flourishing* (pp. 51–94). Mahwah, NJ: Erlbaum.

Little, B. R., Lecci, L., and Watkinson, B. (1992). Personality and personal projects: Linking Big Five and PAC units of analysis. *Journal of Personality, 60,* 501–525.

Little, B. R., Salmela-Aro, K., and Phillips, S. D. (2007). *Personal project pursuit: Goals, action, and human flourishing.* Mahwah, NJ: Erlbaum.

Lloyd, M. E. (1990). Gender factors in reviewer recommendations for manuscript publication. *Journal of Applied Behavior Analysis, 23,* 539–543.

Löckenhoff, C. E., Chan, W., McCrae, R. R., De Fruyt, F., Jussim, L., De Bolle, M., ... and Nakazato, K. (2014). Gender stereotypes of personality: universal and accurate? *Journal of Cross-Cultural Psychology,* 0022022113520075.

Loehlin, J. C. (2010). Is there an active gene-environment correlation in adolescent drinking behavior? *Behavior Genetics, 40,* 447–451.

Loehlin, J. C. (2012). The differential heritability of personality item clusters. *Behavior Genetics, 42,* 500–507.

Loehlin, J. C., Neiderhiser, J. M., and Reiss, D. (2003). The behavior genetics of personality and the NEAD Study. *Journal of Research in Personality, 37,* 373–387.

Loehlin, J. C., and Nichols, R. C. (1976). *Heredity, environment and personality.* Austin: University of Texas Press.

Loftus, E. F. (1992). When a lie becomes memory's truth: Memory distortion after exposure to misinformation. *Current Directions in Psychological Science, 1,* 121–123.

Loftus, E. F. (1993). The reality of repressed memories. *American Psychologist, 48,* 518–537.

Loftus, E. F. (2000). Remembering what never happened. In E. Tulving (Ed.), *Memory, consciousness, and the brain: The Tallinn Conference* (pp. 106–118). Philadelphia, PA: Psychology Press.

Loftus, E. F. (2003). Memory in Canadian Courts of Law. *Canadian Psychology, 44,* 207–212.

Loftus, E. (2011). Intelligence gathering after post-9/11. American Psychologist, 66, 532–541.

Loftus, E. F. (2011). Intelligence gathering post-9/11. American Psychologist, 66, 532–541.

London, H., and Exner, J. E., Jr. (Eds.). (1978). *Dimensions of personality.* New York: Wiley.

Lönnqvist, J. E., and Itkonen, J. V. (2016). Homogeneity of personal values and personality traits in Facebook social networks. *Journal of Research in Personality, 60,* 24–35.

Lönnqvist, J. E., Itkonen, J. V., Verkasalo, M., and Poutvaara, P. (2014). The five-factor model of personality and degree and transitivity of Facebook social networks. *Journal of Research in Personality, 50,* 98–101.

Lounsbury, J. W., Sundstrom, E., Loveland, James M., and Gibson, L. W. (2003). Intelligence, "Big Five" personality traits, and work drive as predictors of course grade. *Personality and Individual Differences, 35,* 1231–1239.

Low, B. (1989). Cross-cultural patterns in the training of children: An evolutionary perspective. *Journal of Comparative Psychology, 103,* 311–319.

Lowenstein, L. F. (2002). Ability and personality changes after brain injuries. *Criminal Lawyer, 120,* 5–8.

Lowry, P. E. (1997). The assessment center process; New directions. *Journal of Social Behavior and Personality, 12,* 53–62.

Lucas, R. E. (2007). Personality and the pursuit of happiness. *Social and Personality Psychology Compass, 1,* 168–182.

Lucas, R. E. and Baird, B. M. (2004). Extraversion and emotional reactivity. *Journal of Personality and Social Psychology, 86,* 473–485.

Lucas, R. E., Le, K., and Dyrenforth, P. S. (2008). Explaining the extraversion/positive affect relation: Sociability cannot account for extraverts' greater happiness. *Journal of Personality, 76,* 385–414.

Lucas, R. E., and Schimmack, U. (2009). Income and well-being: How big is the gap between the rich and the poor? *Journal of Research in Personality, 43,* 75–78.

Ludeke, S. G., and Carey, B. (2015). Two mechanisms of biased responding account for the association between religiousness and misrepresentation in Big Five self-reports. *Journal of Research in Personality, 57,* 43–47.

Ludtke, O., Trautwein, U., and Husemann, N. (2009). Goal and personality trait development in a transitional period: Assessing change and stability in personality development. *Personality and Social Psychology Bulletin, 35,* 428–441.

Lukaszewski, A. W. (2013). Testing an adaptationist theory of trait covariation: Relative bargaining power as a common calibrator of an interpersonal syndrome. *European Journal of Personality, 27*(4), 328–345.

Lukaszewski, A. W., Larson, C. M., Gildersleeve, K. A., Roney, J. R., and Haselton, M. G. (2014). Condition-dependent calibration of men's uncommitted mating orientation: Evidence from multiple samples. *Evolution and Human Behavior, 35*(4), 319–326.

Lukaszewski, A. W., and Roney, J. (2010). Kind toward whom? Mate preferences for personality traits are target-specific. *Evolution and Human Behavior, 31,* 28–38.

Lukaszewski, A. W., and Roney, J. (2011). The origins of extraversion: Joint effects of facultative calibration and genetic polymorphism. *Personality and Social Psychology Bulletin, 37,* 409–421.

Lund, O. C. H., Tamnes, C. K., Moestue, C., Buss, D. M., and Vollrath, M. (2006). Tactics of hierarchy negotiation. *Journal of Research in Personality, 41,* 25–44.

Luntz, B. K., and Widom, C. S. (1994). Antisocial personality disorder in abused and neglected children grown up. *American Journal of Psychiatry, 151,* 670–674.

Luo, S., Chen, H., Yue, G., Zhang, G., Zhaoyang, R., and Xu, D. (2008). Predicting marital satisfaction from self, partner, and couple characteristics: Is it me, you, or us? *Journal of Personality, 76,* 1231–1266.

Lykken, D. T. (1982, September). Fearlessness. *Psychology Today,* pp. 6–10.

Lykken, D. T. (1995). *The antisocial personalities.* Hillsdale, NJ: Erlbaum.

Lynn, R. (2008). *The global bell curve: Race, IQ and inequality worldwide.* Augusta, GA: Washington Summit.

Lynn, R., & Harvey, J. (2008) The decline of the world's IQ. *Intelligence, 36,* 112–120.

Lynn, S. J., Lock, T., Loftus, E. F., Krackow, E., and Lilienfeld, S. O. (2003). The remembrance of things past: Problematic memory recovery techniques in psychotherapy. In S. O. Lilienfeld and S. J. Lynn (Eds.), *Science and pseudoscience in clinical psychology* (pp. 205–239). New York: Guilford Press.

Lyons, M. T., and Hughes, S. (2015). Malicious mouths? The Dark Triad and motivations for gossip. *Personality and Individual Differences, 78,* 1–4.

Lytton, H., Martin, N. G., and Eaves, L. (1977). Environmental and genetical causes of variation in ethological aspects of behavior in two-year-old boys. *Social Biology, 24,* 200–211.

Lyubomirsky, S. (2001). Why are some people happier than others? The role of cognitive and motivational processes in well-being. *American Psychologist, 56,* 239–249.

Lyubomirsky, S. (2007). *The how of happiness: A scientific approach to getting the life you want.* New York, NY, US: Penguin Press.

Lyubomirsky, S., King, L., and Diener, E. (2005). The benefits of frequent positive affect: Does happiness lead to success? *Psychological Bulletin, 131,* 803–855.

Ma, V., and Schoeneman, T. J. (1997). Individualism versus collectivism: A comparison of Kenyan and American self-concepts. *Basic and Applied Social Psychology, 19,* 261–273.

MacAndrew, C., and Steele, T. (1991). Gray's behavioral inhibition system: A psychometric examination. *Personality and Individual Differences, 12,* 157–171.

Maccoby, E. E., and Jacklin, C. N. (1974). *The psychology of sex differences.* Stanford, CA: Stanford University Press.

MacDonald, G., and Leary, M. R. (2005). Why does social exclusion hurt? The relationship between social and physical pain. *Psychological Bulletin, 131,* 202–223.

Machiavelli, N. (1966). *The prince.* New York: Bantam. (Original work published 1513)

MacLaren, V. V., Best, L. A., Dixon, M. J., and Harrigan, K. A. (2011). Problem gambling and the five factor model in university students. *Personality and Individual Differences, 50,* 335–338.

Macmillan, M. B. (2000). Restoring Phineas Gage: A 150th retrospective. *Journal of the History of the Neurosciences, 9,* 42–62.

Madsen, E. A., Tunney, R. J., Fieldman, G., Plotkin, H. C., Dunbar, R. I., Richardson, J. M., and McFarland, D. (2007). Kinship and altruism: A cross-cultural experimental study. *British Journal of Psychology, 98*(2), 339–359.

Magnavita, J. J. (2003). *Handbook of personality disorders: Theory and practice.* New York: Wiley.

Malcolm, J. (1981). *Psychoanalysis: The impossible profession.* New York: Knopf.

Maleva, V., Westcott, K., McKellop, M., McLaughlin, R., Widman, D., and College, J. (2014). Optimism and college grades: Predicting GPA from explanatory style. *Psi Chi Journal of Psychological Research, 19*(3), 129–135.

Malone, J. C., Weston, D., and Levendosky, A. (2011). Personalities of adults with traumatic childhood separations. *Journal of Clinical Psychology, 67,* 1259–1282.

Malouff, J. M., Thorsteinsson, E. B., Schutte, N. S., Bhullar, N., and Rooke, S. E. (2010). The five-factor model of personality and relationship satisfaction of intimate partners: A meta-analysis. *Journal of Research in Personality, 44,* 124–127.

Maltby, J., Wood, A. M., Day, L., Kon, T. W. H., Colley, A., and Linley, P. A., (2008). Personality predictors of levels of forgiveness two and a half years after the transgression. *Journal of Research in Personality, 42,* 1088–1094.

Maner, J. K., and Shackelford, T. K. (2008). The basic cognition of jealousy: An evolutionary perspective. *European Journal of Personality, 22,* 31–36.

Marangoni, C., Garcia, S., Ickes, W., and Teng, G. (1995). Empathic accuracy in a clinically relevant setting. *Journal of Personality and Social Psychology, 68,* 854–869.

Marcia, J. E. (1966). Development and validation of ego-identity status. *Journal of Personality and Social Psychology, 3,* 551–558.

Marcia, J. E. (2002). Identity and psychosocial development in adulthood. *Identity, 2,* 7–28.

Markey, C. N., Markey, P. M., and Tinsley, B. J. (2003). Personality, puberty, and preadolescent girls' risky behaviors: Examining the predictive value of the five-factor model of personality. *Journal of Research in Personality, 37,* 405–419.

Markey, P. M., and Markey, C. N. (2007). The interpersonal meaning of sexual promiscuity. *Journal of Research in Personality, 41,* 1199–1212.

Markus, H. (1983). Self-knowledge: An expanded view. *Journal of Personality, 51,* 543–565.

Markus, H., and Nurius, P. (1986). Possible selves. *American Psychologist, 41,* 954–969.

Markus, H., and Nurius, P. (1987). Possible selves: The interface between motivation and the self concept. In K. Yardley and T. Honness (Eds.), *Self and identity: Psychosocial perspectives* (pp. 157–172). Chichester, England: Wiley.

Markus, H. R., and Kitayama, S. (1991). Culture and the self: Implications for cognition, emotion, and motivation. *Psychological Review, 98,* 224–253.

Markus, H. R., and Kitayama, S. (1994). A collective fear of the collective: Implications for selves and theories of selves. *Personality and Social Psychology Bulletin, 20,* 568–579.

Markus, H. R., and Kitayama, S. (1998). The cultural psychology of personality. *Journal of Cross-Cultural Psychology, 29,* 63–87.

Marsh, Herbert W. (1996). Positive and negative global self-esteem: A substantively meaningful distinction or artifactors? *Journal of Personality and Social Psychology, 70,* 810–819.

Marschall-Lévesque, S., Castellanos-Ryan, N., Vitaro, F., and Séguin, J. R. (2014). Moderators of the association between peer and target adolescent substance use. *Addictive Behaviors, 39*(1), 48–70.

Marshall, T. C., Lefringhausen, K., and Ferenczi, N. (2015). The Big Five, self-esteem, and narcissism as predictors of the topics people write about in Facebook status updates. *Personality and Individual Differences, 85,* 35–40.

Marsland, A. L., Cohen, S., Rabin, B. S., and Manuck, S. B. (2001). Associations between stress, trait negative affect, acute immune reactivity, and antibody response in hepatitis B injection in healthy young adults. *Health Psychology, 20,* 4–11.

Martin, M., Ward, J. C., and Clark, D. M. (1983). Neuroticism and the recall of positive and negative personality information. *Behavior Research and Therapy, 21,* 495–503.

Martins, A., and Calheiros, M. M. (2012). Construction of a self-complexity scale for adolescents. *Psychological Assessment, 24,* 973–982.

Maslow, A. H. (1968). *Toward a psychology of being* (2nd ed.). New York: Harper and Row. (Original work published 1954)

Maslow, A. H. (1970). *Motivation and personality.* New York: Harper and Row. (Original work published 1954)

Maslow, A. H. (1987). *Motivation and personality.* New York: Harper and Row. (Original work published 1954)

Maslow, A. H., and Hoffman, E. (1996). *Future visions: The unpublished papers of Abraham Maslow.* Thousand Oaks, CA: Sage.

Mason, A., and Blankenship, V. (1987). Power and affiliation motivation, stress, and abuse in intimate relationships. *Journal of Personality and Social Psychology, 52,* 203–210.

Mason, J., Southwick, S., Yehuda, R., Wang, S., Riney, S., Bremner, D., Johnson, D., Lubin, H., Blake, D., and Zhou, G. (1994). Elevation of serum free triiodothyronine, total triiodothyronine, thyroxine-binding globulin, and total thyroxine levels in combat-related posttraumatic stress disorder. *Archives of General Psychiatry, 51,* 629–641.

Mason, O., Claridge, G., and Jackson, M. (1995). New scales for the assessment of schizotypy. *Personality and Individual Differences, 18,* 7–13.

Masson, J. M. (1984). *The assault on truth: Freud's suppression of the seduction theory.* New York: Farrar, Straus and Giroux.

Masuda, T., and Nisbett, R. E. (2001). Attending holistically versus analytically: Comparing the context sensitivity of Japanese and Americans. *Journal of Personality and Social Psychology, 81,* 5, 922–934.

Matsumoto, D. (1999). Culture and self: An empirical assessment of Markus and Kitayama's theory of independent and interdependent self-construals. *Asian Journal of Social Psychology, 2,* 289–310.

Matthes, J., Wirth, W., Schemer, C., and Kissling, A. K. (2011). I see what you don't see: The role of individual differences in field dependence-independence as a predictor of product placement recall and brand liking. *Journal of Advertising, 40,* 85–89.

Matthews, G. (2000). Attention, automaticity, and affective disorder. *Behavior Modification, 24,* 69–93.

Matthews, G., Derryberry, D., and Siegle, G. J. (2000). Personality and emotion: Cognitive science perspectives. In S. E. Hampson (Ed.), *Advances in personality psychology* (vol. 1, pp. 199–237). Philadelphia: Taylor and Francis.

Matthews, G., and Gilliland, K. (1999). The personality theories of H. J. Eysenck and J. A. Gray: A comparative review. *Personality and Individual Differences, 26,* 583–626.

Matthews, G., and Oddy, K. (1993). Recovery of major personality dimensions from trait adjective data. *Personality and Individual Differences, 15,* 419–431.

Mattia, J. I., and Zimmerman, M. (2001). Epidemiology. In W. J. Livesley (Ed.), *Handbook of personality disorders: Theory, research and treatment.* New York: Guilford Press.

Maynard Smith, J. (1982). *Evolution and the theory of games.* Cambridge, England: Cambridge University Press.

McAdams, D. P. (1990). Motives. In V. Derlega, B. Winstead, and W. Jones (Eds.), *Contemporary research in personality* (pp. 175–204). Chicago: Nelson-Hall.

McAdams, D. P. (1999). Personal narratives and the life story. In L. A. Pervin and O. P. John (Eds.), *Handbook of personality: Theory and research* (2nd ed., pp. 478–500). New York: Guilford Press.

McAdams, D. P. (2008). Personal narratives and the life story. In O. John, R. Robins, and L. A. Pervin, *Handbook of personality: Theory and research* (pp. 241–261). New York: Guilford Press.

McAdams, D. P. (2011). Narrative identity. In S. J. Schwartz, K. Luyckx, and V. L. Vignoles (Eds.), *Handbook of identity theory and research* (vols. 1 & 2, pp. 99–115). New York, NY: Springer Science + Business Media.

McAdams, D. P. (2016). Life authorship in emerging adulthood. In J. J. Arnett, J. J. Arnett (Eds.), *The Oxford handbook of emerging adulthood* (pp. 438–446). New York, NY, US: Oxford University Press.

McAdams, D. P., and Bryant, F. B. (1987). Intimacy motivation and subjective mental health in a nationwide sample. *Journal of Personality, 55,* 395–413.

McAdams, D. P., Hoffman, B. J., Mansfield, E. D., and Day, R. (1996). Themes of agency and communion in significant autobiographical scenes. *Journal of Personality, 64*(2), 339–377.

McAdams, D. P., and Vaillant, G. E. (1982). Intimacy motivation and psychosocial adjustment: A longitudinal study. *Journal of Personality Assessment, 46,* 586–593.

McCarley, N. G., and Clarskadon, T. G. (1983). Test-retest reliabilities of the scales and subscales of the Myers-Briggs

Type Indicator and of criteria for clinical interpretive hypotheses involving them. *Research in Psychological Type, 6,* 24–36.

McClelland, D. C. (1958). Risk-taking in children with high and low need for achievement. In J. W. Atkinson (Ed.), *Motives in fantasy, action, and society* (pp. 306–327). Princeton, NJ: Van Nostrand.

McClelland, D. C. (1965). N achievement and entrepreneurship: A longitudinal study. *Journal of Personality and Social Psychology, 1,* 389–392.

McClelland, D. C. (1979). Inhibited power motivation and high blood pressure in men. *Journal of Abnormal Psychology, 88,* 182–190.

McClelland D. C. (1982). The need for power, sympathetic activation, and illness. *Motivation and Emotion, 6,* 31–41.

McClelland, D. C. (1985). How motives, skills, and values determine what people do. *American Psychologist, 40,* 812–825.

McClelland, D. C., Alexander, C., and Marks, E. (1982). The need for power, stress, immune function, and illness among male prisoners. *Journal of Abnormal Psychology, 91,* 61–70.

McClelland, D. C., and Jemmott, J. B. (1980). Power motivation, stress, and physical illness. *Journal of Human Stress, 6,* 6–15.

McClelland, D. C., Koestner, R., and Weinberger, J. (1989). How do self-attributed and implicit motives differ? *Psychological Review, 96,* 690–702.

McClelland, D. C., and Pilon, D. A. (1983). Sources of adult motives in patterns of parent behavior in early childhood. *Journal of Personality and Social Psychology, 44,* 564–574.

McConnell, A. R., Strain, L. M., Brown, C. M., and Rydell, R. J. (2009). The simple life: On the benefits of low self-complexity. *Personality and Social Psychology Bulletin, 35,* 823–835.

McCoul, M. D., and Haslam, N. (2001). Predicting high risk sexual behaviour in heterosexual and homosexual men: The roles of impulsivity and sensation seeking. *Personality and Individual Differences, 31,* 1303–1310.

McCrae, R. R., Chan, W., Jussim, L., De Fruyt, F., Löckenhoff, C. E., De Bolle, M., . . . and Allik, J. (2013). The inaccuracy of national character stereotypes. *Journal of Research in Personality, 47*(6), 831–842.

McCrae, R. R., and Costa, P. T., Jr. (1985). Updating Norman's "adequate taxonomy": Intelligence and personality dimensions in natural language and questionnaires. *Journal of Personality and Social Psychology, 49,* 710–721.

McCrae, R. R., and Costa, P. T. (1991). Adding liebe und arbeit: The full five-factor model and well-being. *Personality and Social Psychology Bulletin, 17,* 227–232.

McCrae, R. R., and Costa, P. T., Jr. (1997). Personality trait structure as a human universal. *American Psychologist, 52,* 509–516.

McCrae, R. R., and Costa, P. T., Jr. (1999). A five-factor theory of personality. In L. A. Pervin and O. John (Eds.), *Handbook of personality: Theory and research* (2nd ed.). New York: Guilford Press.

McCrae, R. R., and Costa, P. T., Jr. (2008). The five factor theory of personality. In O. P. John, R. W. Robins, and L. A. Pervin (Eds.), *Handbook of personality* (pp. 159–181). New York: Guilford Press.

McCrae, R. R., Costa, P. T., Jr., del Pilar, G. H., Rolland, J., and Parker, W. D. (1998). Cross-cultural assessment of the five-factor model: The Revised NEO Personality Inventory. *Journal of Cross-Cultural Psychology, 29,* 171–188.

McCrae, R. R., Costa, Jr, P. T., and Martin, T. A. (2005). The NEO–PI–3: A more readable revised NEO personality inventory. *Journal of Personality Assessment, 84*(3), 261–270.

McCrae, R. R., Costa, P. T., Jr., Terracciano, A., Parker, W. D., Mills, C. J., De Fruyt, F., and Mervielde, I. (2002). Personality trait development from age 12 to age 18: Longitudinal, cross-sectional, and cross-cultural analyses. *Journal of Personality and Social Psychology, 83,* 1456–1468.

McCrae, R. R., and John, O. P. (1992). An introduction to the five-factor model and its applications. *Journal of Personality, 60,* 175–215.

McCrae, R. R., Terracciano, A., and 78 Members of the Personality Profiles of Cultures Project. (2005a). Personality profiles of cultures: Aggregate personality traits. *Journal of Personality and Social Psychology, 89,* 407–425.

McCrae, R. R., Terracciano, A., and 78 Members of the Personality Profiles of Cultures Project. (2005b). Universal features of personality traits from the observer's perspective: Data from 50 cultures. *Journal of Personality and Social Psychology, 88,* 547–561.

McCullough, M. E., Bellah, C. G., Kilpatrick, S. D., and Johnson, J. L. (2001). Vengefulness: Relationships with forgiveness, rumination, well-being, and the Big Five. *Personality and Social Psychology Bulletin, 27, 5,* 601–610.

McCullough, M. E., Emmons, R. A., Kilpatrick, S. D., and Mooney, C. N. (2003). Narcissists as "victims": The role of narcissism in the perception of transgressions. *Personality and Social Psychology Bulletin, 29, 7,* 885–893.

McDaniel, M. J., Beier, M. E., Perkins, A. W., Goggin, S., and Frankel, B. (2009). An assessment of fakeability of self-report and implicit personality measures. *Journal of Research in Personality, 43,* 682–685.

McDaniel, S. R., and Zuckerman, M. (2003). The relationship of impulsive sensation seeking and gender to interest and participation in gambling activities. *Personality and Individual Differences, 35,* 1385–1400.

McGrath, R. E., and Carroll, E. J. (2012). The current status of "projective" "tests." In H. Cooper, P. M. Camic, D. L. Long, A. T. Panter, D. Rindskopf, and K. J. Sher (Eds.), *APA handbook of research methods in psychology, vol. 1: Foundations, planning, measures, and psychometrics* (pp. 329–348). Washington, DC: American Psychological Association.

McHoskey, J. W. (2001). Machiavellianism and sexuality: On the moderating role of biological sex. *Personality and Individual Differences, 31,* 779–789.

McLoyd, V. S. (1998). Socioeconomic disadvantage and child development. *American Psychologist, 53,* 188–204.

Mead, M. (1928). *Coming of age in Samoa.* New York: Morrow.

Mead, M. (1935). *Sex and temperament in three primitive societies.* New York: Morrow.

Mealey, L. (1995). The sociobiology of sociopathy: An integrated evolutionary model. *Behavioral and Brain Sciences, 18,* 523–599.

Mecacci, L., Scaglione, M. R., and Vitrano, I. (1991). Diurnal and monthly variations of temperature and self-reported activation in relation to sex and circadian typology. *Personality and Individual Differences, 12,* 819–824.

Megargee, E. I. (1969). Influence of sex roles on the manifestation of leadership. *Journal of Applied Psychology, 53,* 377–382.

Mehl, M. R., and Pennebaker, J. W. (2003). The social dynamics of a cultural upheaval: Social interactions surrounding September 11, 2001. *Psychological Science, 14,* 579–585.

Meltzer, A. L., and McNulty, J. K. (2016). Who is having more and better sex? The Big Five as predictors of sex in marriage. *Journal of Research in Personality, 63,* 62–66.

Mendle, J., Moore, S. R., Briley, D. A., and Harden, K. P. (2016). Puberty, socioeconomic status, and depression in girls evidence for gene× environment interactions. *Clinical Psychological Science, 4*(1), 3–16.

Menninger, K. (1963). *The vital balance: The life process in mental health and illness.* New York: Viking Press.

Messick, S. (1994). The matter of style: Manifestations of personality in cognition, learning, and teaching. *Educational Psychologist, 29,* 121–136.

Michalos, A. C. (1991). *Global report on student well-being. Vol. 1: Life satisfaction and happiness.* New York: Springer-Verlag.

Mike, A., Jackson, J. J., & Oltmanns, T. F. (2014). The conscientious retiree: The relationship between conscientiousness, retirement, and volunteering. *Journal of research in personality, 52,* 68–77.

Mikulincer, M., and Florian, V. (1995). Appraisal and coping with a real-life stressful situation: The contribution of attachment styles. *Personality and Social Psychology Bulletin, 69,* 1203–1215.

Mikulincer, M., Florian, V., and Weller, A. (1993). Attachment styles, coping strategies, and posttraumatic psychological distress: The impact of the Gulf War in Israel. *Journal of Personality and Social Psychology, 64,* 817–826.

Miller, A. L. (2007). Creativity and cognitive style: The relationship between field-dependence-independence, expected evaluation, and creative performance. *Psychology of Aesthetics, Creativity, and the Arts, 1,* 243–246.

Miller, G. E., and Cohen, S. (2001). Psychological interventions and the immune system: A meta-analytic review and critique. *Health Psychology, 20,* 47–63.

Miller, J. D. (2012). Five-Factor Model personality disorder prototypes: A review of their development, validity, and comparison to alternative approaches. *Journal of Personality, 80*(6), 1565–1591.

Miller, J. D., and Lynam, D. R. (2015). Understanding psychopathy using the basic elements of personality. *Social and Personality Psychology Compass, 9*(5), 223–237.

Miller, J. D., Lynam, D., Zimmerman, R. S., Logan, T. K., Leukefeld, C., and Clayton, R. (2004). The utility of the five factor model in understanding risky sexual behavior. *Personality and Individual Differences, 36,* 1611–1626.

Miller, S. L., and Maner, J. K. (2009). Sex differences in response to sexual versus emotional infidelity: The moderating role of individual differences. *Personality and Individual Differences, 46,* 287–291.

Miller, T.W.K., Smith, T. W., Turner, C. W., Guajardo, M. L., and Hallet, A. J. (1996). A meta-analytic review of research on hostility and physical health. *Psychological Bulletin, 119,* 322–348.

Millon, T. (1990). *Toward a new personology: An evolutionary model.* New York: Wiley-Interscience.

Millon, T. (1999). Reflections on psychosynergy: A model for integrating science, theory, classification, assessment, and therapy. *Journal of Personality Assessment, 72,* 437–456.

Millon, T. (2000a). Reflections of the future of DSM Axis II. *Journal of Personality Disorders, 14,* 30–41.

Millon, T. (2000b). Sociocultural conceptions of the borderline personality. *Psychiatric Clinics of North America Special Issue: Borderline Personality Disorder, 23,* 123–136.

Millon, T., Davis, R., Millon, C., Escovar, L., and Meagher, S. (2000). *Personality disorders: Current concepts and classical foundations.* New York: Wiley.

Mischel, W. (1968). *Personality and assessment.* New York: Wiley.

Mischel, W. (1984). Convergences and challenges in the search for consistency. *American Psychologist, 39,* 351–364.

Mischel, W. (1990). Personality dispositions revisited and revised: A view after three decades. In L. Pervin (Ed.), *Handbook of personality: Theory and research* (pp. 111–134). New York, Guilford Press.

Mischel, W. (2000). A cognitive-affective system theory of personality: Reconceptualizing situations, dispositions, dynamics, and invariance in personality structure. In E. T. Higgins and A. W. Kruglanski (Eds.), *Motivational science: Social and personality perspectives* (pp. 150–176). New York: Psychology Press.

Mischel, W. (2004). Toward an integrative science of the person. *Annual Review of Psychology, 55,* 1–22.

Mischel, W. (2010). The situated person. In B. Mesquita, L. F. Barrett, and E. R. Smith (Eds.), The mind in context (pp. 149–173). New York: Guilford Press.

Mischel, W., and Peake, P. K. (1982). Beyond déjà vu in the search for cross-situational consistency. *Psychological Review, 89,* 730–755.

Mischel, W., and Shoda, Y. (2010). The situated person. In B. Mesquita, L. F. Barrett, and E. R. Smith (Eds.), *The mind in context* (pp. 149–173). New York, NY: Guilford.

Mischel, W., Shoda, Y., and Mendoza-Denton, R. (2002). Situation-behavior profiles as a locus of consistency in personality. *Current Directions in Psychological Science, 11,* 50–54.

Mittler, P. (1971). *The study of twins.* Harmondsworth, England: Penguin Books.

Mlacic, B., and Ostendorf, F. (2005). Taxonomy and structure of Croatian personality-descriptive adjectives. *European Journal of Personality, 19,* 117–152.

Moffitt, T. E. (2005). The new look of behavioral genetics in developmental psychopathology: Gene-environment interplay in antisocial behaviors. *Psychological Bulletin, 131,* 533–554.

Mommersteeg, P. M. C., Pelle, A. J., Ramakers, C., Szabó, B. M., Denollet, J., and Kupper, N. (2012). Type D personality and course of health status over 18 months in outpatients with heart failure: Multiple mediating inflammatory biomarkers. *Brain, Behavior, and Immunity, 26,* 301–310.

Monk, T. H., Leng, V. C., Folkard, S., and Weitzman, E. D. (1983). Circadian rhythms in subjective alertness and core body temperature. *Chronobiologia, 10,* 49–55.

Montemayor, R., and Eisen, M. (1977). The development of self-conceptions from childhood to adolescence. *Developmental Psychology, 13,* 314–319.

Moon, J. H., Lee, E., Lee, J. A., Choi, T. R., and Sung, Y. (2016). The role of narcissism in self-promotion on Instagram. *Personality and Individual Differences, 101,* 22–25.

Moore, M. (1978). Discrimination or favoritism? Sex bias in book reviews. *American Psychologist, 33,* 936–938.

Moore, M., Schermer, J. A., Paunonen, S.V., and Vernon, P. A. (2010). Genetic and environmental influences on verbal and nonverbal measures of the Big Five. *Personality and Individual Differences, 48,* 884–888.

Moretti, R. J., and Rossini, E. D. (2004). The Thematic Apperception Test (TAT). In M. J. Hilsenroth and E. L. Segal (Eds.), *Comprehensive handbook of psychological assessment, Vol. 2: Personality assessment* (pp. 356–371). Hoboken, NJ: Wiley.

Morey, L. C. (1997). Personality diagnosis and personality disorders. In R. Hogan, J. A. Johnson, and S. R. Briggs (Eds.), *Handbook of personality psychology* (pp. 919–946). San Diego: Academic Press.

Morgan, C. D., and Murray, H. A. (1935). A method of investigating fantasies. *Archives of Neurological Psychiatry, 34,* 289–306.

Morgan, C. A., Southwick, S., Steffian, G., Hazlett, G. A., and Loftus, E. F. (2012). Misinformation can influence memory for recently experienced, highly stressful events. *International Journal of Law and Psychiatry, 36,* 11–17.

Moskowitz, D. S. (1993). Dominance and friendliness: On the interaction of gender and situation. *Journal of Personality, 61,* 387–409.

Moskowitz, J. T. (2011). Coping interventions and the regulation of positive affect. In S. Folkman (Ed.), *The Oxford handbook of stress, health, and coping* (pp. 407–427). New York, NY: Oxford University Press.

Moskowtiz, D. S., and Fournier, M. A. (2015). The interplay of persons and situations: Retrospect and prospect. In L. Cooper and R. J. Larsen (Eds.),

Handbook of personality and social psychology: Personality processes and individual differences. Washington, DC: American Psychological Association.

Moskowitz, D. S., Suh, E. J., and Desaulniers, J. (1994). Situational influences on gender differences in agency and communion. *Journal of Personality and Social Psychology, 66,* 753–761.

Moskowitz, J. T., Folkman, S., Collette, L., and Vittinghoff, E. (1996). Coping and mood during AIDS-related caregiving and bereavement. *Annals of Behavioral Medicine, 18,* 49–57.

Mower, O. H. (1960). *Learning theory and behavior.* New York: Wiley.

Mroczek, D. K., and Spiro, A., III. (2003). Modeling intraindividual change in personality traits: Findings from the Normative Aging Study. *Journals of Gerontology Series B-Psychological Sciences & Social Sciences, 58B,* P153–P165.

Mroczek, D. K., Spiro, A., III., and Turiano, N. A. (2009). Do health behaviors explain the effect of neuroticism on mortality? Longitudinal findings from the VA Normative Aging Study. *Journal of Research in Personality, 43,* 653–659.

Mufson, D. W., and Mufson, M. A. (1998). Predicting police officer performance using the Inwald Personality Inventory: An illustration from Appalachia. *Professional Psychology: Research and Practice, 29,* 59–62.

Mullins-Sweatt, S. N., and Lengel, G. J. (2012). Clinical utility of the Five-Factor Model of personality disorder. *Journal of Personality, 80*(6), 1615–1639.

Multon, K. D., Brown, S. D., and Lent, R. W. (1991). Relation of the self-efficacy beliefs to academic outcomes: A meta-analytic investigation. *Journal of Counseling Psychology, 38,* 30–38.

Munafo, M. R., Yalcin, B., Willis-Owen, S. A., and Flint, J. (2008). Association of the dopamine D4 receptor (DRD4) gene and approach-related personality traits: Meta-analysis and new data. *Biological Psychiatry, 63,* 197–206.

Murdock, G. P. (1980). *Theories of illness: A world survey.* Pittsburgh: University of Pittsburgh Press.

Murphy, K. R. (1995). Integrity testing. In N. Brewer and C. Wilson (Eds.), *Psychology and policing* (pp. 205–229). Hillsdale, NJ: Erlbaum.

Murphy, S. M., Vallacher, R. R., Shackelford, T. K., Bjorklund, D. F., and Yunger, J. L. (2006). Relationship experience as a predictor of romantic jealousy. *Personality and Individual Differences, 40,* 761–769.

Murray, D. R., Trudeau, R., and Schaller, M. (2011). On the origins of cultural differences in conformity: Four tests of the pathogen prevalence hypothesis.

Personality and Social Psychology Bulletin, 37, 318–329.

Murray, G., Allen, N.B., and Trinder, J. (2002). Longitudinal investigation of mood variability and neuroticism predicts variability in extended states of positive and negative affect. *Personality and Individual Differences, 33,* 1217–1228.

Murray, H. (1948). *Assessment of men: Selection of personnel for the Office of Strategic Services.* New York: Rinehart.

Murray, H. A. (1933). The effect of fear upon estimates of the maliciousness of other personalities. *Journal of Social Psychology, 4,* 310–329.

Murray, H. A. (1938). *Explorations in personality.* New York: Oxford University Press.

Murray, H. A. (1967). Autobiography (the case of Murr). In E. G. Boring and G. Lindzey (Eds.), *History of psychology in autobiography* (vol. 5, pp. 285–310). New York: Appleton-Century-Crofts.

Murstein, B. I. (1976). *Who will marry whom? Theories and research in marital choice.* New York: Springer.

Myers, D. G. (1993). *The pursuit of happiness.* New York: Avon Books.

Myers, D. G. (2000). The funds, friends, and faith of happy people. *American Psychologist, 55,* 56–67.

Myers, D. G., and Diener, E. (1995). Who is happy? *Psychological Science, 6,* 10–19.

Myers, I. B., McCaulley, M. H., Quenk, N. L., and Hammer, A. L. (1998). *Manual: A guide to the development and use of the Myers-Briggs Type Indicator.* Palo Alto: Consulting Psychologists Press.

Myers, L. B. (2010). The importance of the repressive coping style: Findings from 30 years of research. *Anxiety, Stress & Coping: An International Journal, 23*(1), 3–17.

Myers, L. B., and Derakshan, N. (2015). The relationship between two types of impaired emotion processing: Repressive coping and alexithymia. *Frontiers in Psychology, 6.*

Myrseth, H., Pallesen, S., Molde, H., Johnsen, B. H., and Lorvik, I. M. (2009). Personality factors as predictors of pathological gambling. *Personality and Individual Differences, 47,* 933–937.

Na, J., and Choi, I. (2009). Culture and first-person pronouns. *Personality and Social Psychology Bulletin, 35,* 1492–1499.

Nasby, W., and Read, N. W. (1997). The life voyage of a solo circumnavigator: Integrating theoretical and methodological perspectives. *Journal of Personality, 65,* 785–1068.

Nash, M. R. (1987). What, if anything, is regressed about hypnotic age regression: A review of the empirical literature. *Psychological Bulletin, 102,* 42–52.

Nash, M. R. (1988). Hypnosis as a window on regression. *Bulletin of the Menninger Clinic, 52,* 383–403.

Nash, M. R. (1999). The psychological unconscious. In V. J. Derlega, B. A. Winstead, and W. H. Jones (Eds.), *Personality: Contemporary theory and research* (pp. 197–228). Chicago: Nelson-Hall.

Nash, M. R. (2001). The truth and the hype of hypnosis. *Scientific American* (July), 47–55.

Nathanson, C., Paulhus, D. L., and Williams, K. M. (2006). Personality and misconduct correlates of body modification and other cultural deviance markers. *Journal of Research in Personality, 40,* 779–802.

Neisser, U. (1998). *The rising curve: Long-term gains in IQ and related measures.* Washington, DC: American Psychological Association.

Nelson, E., Hoffman, C. L., Gerald, M. S., and Schultz, S. (2010). Digit ratio (2D:4D) and dominance rank in female rhesus macaques (*Macaca mulatta*). *Behavioral ecology and sociobiology, 64,* 1001–1009.

Nesse, R., and Williams, G. C. (1994). *Why we get sick.* New York: New York Times Books.

Nettle, D. (2006). The evolution of personality variation in humans and other animals. *American Psychologist, 61,* 622–631.

Nettle, D., and Liddle, B. (2008). Agreeableness is related to socio-cognitive, but not socio-perceptual, theory of mind. *European Journal of Personality, 22,* 323–335.

Newell, B. R., and Shanks, D. R. (2014). Unconscious influences on decision making: A critical review. *Behavioral and Brain Sciences, 37*(1), 1–18.

Newman, J. P. (1987). Reaction to punishment in extraverts and psychopaths: Implications for the impulsive behavior of disinhibited individuals. *Journal of Research in Personality, 21,* 464–480.

Newman, J. P., Widom, C. S., and Nathan, S. (1985). Passive avoidance and syndromes of disinhibition: Psychopathy and extraversion. *Journal of Personality and Social Psychology, 48,* 1316–1327.

Newman, P. R., and Newman, B. M. (1988). Differences between childhood and adulthood: The identity watershed. *Adolescence, 23,* 551–557.

Newton, N. J., and Stewart, A. J. (2013). The road not taken: Women's life paths and gender-linked personality traits. *Journal of Research in Personality, 47,* 306–316.

Neyer, F. J. (2006). Editorial: EJP special edition on personality change. *European Journal of Personality, 20,* 419–420.

Neyer, F. J., and Lehnart, J. (2007). Relationships matter in personality development: Evidence from an 8-year longitudinal study across young adulthood. *Journal of Personality, 75,* 535–568.

Neyer, F. J., and Voigt, D. (2004). Personality and social network effects on romantic relationships: A dyadic approach. *European Journal of Personality, 18,* 279–299.

Nicolaou, A., and Xistouri, X. (2011). Field dependence/independence cognitive style and problem posing: An investigation with sixth grade students. *Educational Psychology, 31,* 611–627.

Niederhoffer, K. G., and Pennebaker, J. W. (2002). Sharing one's story: On the benefits of writing or talking about emotional experience. In C. R. Snyder and S. J. Lopez (Eds.), *Handbook of positive psychology* (pp. 573–583). London: Oxford University Press.

Niederle, M., and Vesterlund, L. (2005). *Do women shy away from competition? Do men compete too much?* Working paper # 11474, National Bureau of Economic Research, Cambridge, MA.

Nietzsche, F. (1891/1969). *Thus spoke Zarathustra: A book for everyone and no one.* Translated with an introduction by R. J. Hollingdale. New York: Penguin Books.

Nigg, J. T., and Goldsmith, H. H. (1994). Genetics of personality disorders: Perspectives from personality and psychopathology research. *Pathological Bulletin, 115,* 346–380.

Nisbett, R., and Cohen, D. (1996). *Culture of honor.* Boulder, CO: Westview Press.

Nisbett, R. E. (1993). Violence and U.S. regional culture. *American Psychologist, 48,* 441–449.

Nisbett, R. E., Peng, K., Choi, I., and Norenzayan, A. (2001). Culture and systems of thought: Holistic vs. analytic cognition. *Psychological Review, 108,* 291–310.

Niv, S., Tuvbld, C., Raine, A., Want, P., and Baker, L. A. (2012). Heritability and longitudinal stability of impulsivity in adolescence. *Behavior Genetics, 42,* 378–392.

Noftle, E. E., and Robins, R. W. (2007). Personality predictors of academic outcomes: Big Five correlates of GPA and SAT scores. *Journal of Personality and Social Psychology, 93,* 116–130.

Nolen-Hoeksema, S., Larson, J., and Grayson, C. (1999). Explaining gender differences in depressive symptoms. *Journal of Personality and Social Psychology, 77,* 1061–1072.

Noller, P. (1984). *Nonverbal communication and marital interaction.* Oxford, England: Pergamon Press.

Norem, J. K. (1995). The power of negative thinking: Interview with psychology professor Julie Norem. *Men's Health, 10,* June, p. 46.

Norem, J. K. (1998). Why should we lower our defenses about defense mechanisms? *Journal of Personality Special Issue: Defense mechanisms in contemporary personality research, 66,* 895–917.

Norem, J. K. (2001). Defensive pessimism, optimism, and pessimism. In E. Change (Ed.), *Optimism and pessimism: Implications for theory, research, and practice* (pp. 77–100). Washington, DC: American Psychological Association.

Norman, W. T. (1963). Toward an adequate taxonomy of personality attributes: Replicated factor structure in peer nomination personality ratings. *Journal of Abnormal Psychology, 66,* 574–583.

Norman, W. T. (1967). *2800 personality trait descriptors: Normative operating characteristics in a university population.* Ann Arbor: Department of Psychology, University of Michigan.

Nudelman, A. E. (1973). Bias in the Twenty-Statements Test: Administration time, incomplete protocols, and intelligence. *Psychological Reports, 33,* 524–526.

Nusbaum, E. C., and Silva, P. J. (2011). Are openness and intellect distinct aspects of Openness to Experience? A test of the O/I model. *Personality and Individual Differences, 51,* 571–574.

Oaten, M., Stevenson, R. J., and Case, T. I. (2009). Disgust as a disease-avoidance mechanism. *Psychological Bulletin, 135*(2), 303–321.

Oatley, K., and Johnson-Laird, P. N. (1987). Towards a cognitive theory of emotions. *Cognition and Emotion, 1,* 29–50.

Ochsner, K. N., Bunge, S. A., Gross, J. J., and Gabrieli, J. D. E. (2002). Rethinking feelings: An fMRI study of the cognitive regulation of emotion. *Journal of Cognitive Neuroscience, 14,* 1215–1229.

O'Connell, D., and Marcus, D. K. (2016). Psychopathic personality traits predict positive attitudes toward sexually predatory behaviors in college men and women. *Personality and Individual Differences, 94,* 372–376.

O'Donnell, J. R., and Rutherford, J. (2016). *Trumped!: The Inside Story of the Real Donald Trump—His Cunning Rise and Spectacular Fall.* Crossroad Press.

O'Connell, M., and Sheikh, H. (2011). "Big Five" personality dimensions and social attainment: Evidence from beyond the campus. *Personality and Individual Differences, 50,* 828–833.

Ode, S., Robinson, M. D., and Wilkowski, B. M. (2008). Can one's temper be cooled? A role for agreeableness in moderating neuroticism's influence on anger and aggression. *Journal of Research in Personality, 42,* 295–311.

O'Dell, K. R., Masters, K. S., Spielmans, G. I., and Maisto, S. A. (2011). Does type-D personality predict outcomes among patients with cardiovascular disease? A meta-analytic review. *Journal of Psychosomatic Research, 71,* 199–206.

Oerlemans, W. G., and Bakker, A. B. (2014). Why extraverts are happier: A day reconstruction study. *Journal of Research in Personality, 50,* 11–22.

Ofshe, R. J. (1992). Inadvertent hypnosis during interrogation: False confession due to dissociative states: Misidentified multiple personality and the satanic cult hypothesis. *International Journal of Clinical and Experimental Hypnosis, 40,* 125–156.

Oishi, S., and Kesebir, S. (2015). Income inequality explains why economic growth does not always translate to an increase in happiness. *Psychological Science, 26*(10), 1630–1638.

Oishi, S., Talhelm, T., and Lee, M. (2015). Personality and geography: Introverts prefer mountains. *Journal of Research in Personality, 58,* 55–68.

Olino, T. M., Durbin, C. E., Klein, D. N., Hayden, E. P., and Dyson, M. W. (2013). Gender differences in young children's temperament traits: Comparisons across observational and parent-report methods. *Journal of Personality, 81*(2), 119–129.

Oliver, M. B., and Hyde, J. S. (1993). Gender differences in sexuality: A meta-analysis. *Psychological Bulletin, 114,* 29–51.

Olson, J. (2002). *"I": The creation of a serial killer.* New York: St. Martin's Paperbacks.

Oltmanns, T. F., and Emery, R. E. (2004). *Abnormal psychology* (4th ed.). Upper Saddle River, NJ: Prentice Hall.

Oltmanns, T. F., Friedman, J. N., Fiedler, E. R., and Turkheimer, E. (2004). Perceptions of people with personality disorders based on thin slices of behavior. *Journal of Research in Personality, 38,* 216–229.

Olweus, D. (1978). *Bullies and whipping boys.* Washington, DC: Hemisphere.

Olweus, D. (1979). Stability of aggressive reaction patterns in males: A review. *Psychological Bulletin, 86,* 852–875.

Olweus, D. (2001). *Olweus' core program against bullying and antisocial behavior: A teacher handbook.* Research Center for Health promotion (Hemil Center). Bergen, Norway.

Ones, D. S., and Viswesvaran, C. (1998). Integrity testing in organizations. *Monographs in Organizational Behavior and Industrial Relations, 23,* 243–276.

Ong, E.Y.L., Ang, R. P., Ho, J.C.M., Lim, J. C. Y., Goh, D. H., Lee, C. S., and Chua, A.Y.K. (2011). Narcissism, extraversion and adolescents' self-presentation on Facebook. *Personality and Individual Differences, 50,* 180–185.

Oniszczenko, W., Zawadzki, B., Strelau, J., Reimann, R., Angleitner, A., and Spinath, F. M. (2003). Genetic and environmental determinants of temperament: A comprehensive study based on Polish and German samples. *European Journal of Personality, 17,* 207–220.

Ortony, A., and Turner, T. J., (1990). What's basic about basic emotions. *Psychological Review, 97,* 315–331.

Osgood, C. E., Suci, G. J., and Tannenbaum, P. H. (1957). *The measurement of meaning.* Urbana: University of Illinois Press.

Osmon, D. C., and Jackson, R. (2002). Inspection time and IQ: Fluid or perceptual aspects of intelligence? *Intelligence, 30,* 119–128.

Ostendorf, F. (1990). *Language and personality structure: Towards the validity of the five-factor model of personality.* Regensburg, Germany: Roderer-Verlag.

Ostrov, J. M., and Godleski, S. A. (2010). Toward an integrated gender-linked model of aggression subtypes in early and middle childhood. *Psychological Review, 117,* 233–242.

Oughton, J. M., and Reed, W. M. (1999). The influence of learner differences on the construction of hypermedia concepts: A case study. *Computers in Human Behavior, 15,* 11–50.

Oyserman, D., Coon, H. M., and Kemmelmeier, M. (2002a). Rethinking individualism and collectivism: Evaluation of theoretical assumptions and meta-analyses. *Psychological Bulletin, 128,* 1, 3–72.

Oyserman, D., Coon, H. M., and Kemmelmeier, M. (2002b). Cultural psychology, a new look: Reply to Bond (2002), Fiske (2002), Kitayama (2002), and Miller (2002). *Psychological Bulletin, 128,* 1, 110–117.

Oyserman, D., Destin, M., and Novin, S. (2016). The context-sensitive future self: Possible selves motivate in context, not otherwise. In C. Tsekeris, C. Tsekeris (Eds.), *Revisiting the self: Social science perspectives* (pp. 99–114). New York, NY, US: Routledge/Taylor & Francis Group.

Oyserman, D., and Markus, H. (1990). Possible selves in balance: Implications for delinquency. *Journal of Social Issues, 46,* 141–157.

Oyserman, D., and Saltz, E. (1993). Competence, delinquency, and attempts to attain possible selves. *Journal of Personality and Social Psychology, 65,* 360–374.

Ozer, D. J., and Benet-Martinez, V. (2006). *Annual Review of Psychology, 57,* 401–421.

Ozer, D. J., and Buss, D. M. (1991). Two views of behavior: Agreement and disagreement in married couples. In A. Stewart, J. Healy, and D. Ozer (Eds.), *Perspectives in personality psychology* (pp. 93–108). London: Jessica Kingsley.

Palys, T. S., and Little, B. R. (1983). Perceived life satisfaction and the organization of personal project systems. *Journal of Personality and Social Psychology, 44,* 1221–1230.

Panksepp, J. (2005). Why does separation distress hurt? Comment on MacDonald and Leary (2005). *Psychological Bulletin, 131,* 224–230.

Paradis, C. M., Horn, L., Lazar, R. M., and Schwartz, D. W. (1994). Brain dysfunction and violent behavior in a man with a congenital subarachnoid cyst. *Hospital and Community Psychiatry, 45,* 714–716.

Park, J. H., van Leeuwen, F., and Stephen, I. D. (2012). Homeliness is in the disgust sensitivity of the beholder: relatively unattractive faces appear especially unattractive to individuals higher in pathogen disgust. *Evolution and Human Behavior, 33*(5), 569–577.

Park, S. W., and Colvin, C. R. (2015). Narcissism and other-derogation in the absence of ego threat. *Journal of Personality, 83*(3), 334–345.

Parkes, K. R., and Razavi, T. D. B. (2004). Personality and attitudinal variables as predictors of voluntary union membership. *Personality and Individual Differences, 37,* 333–347.

Patrick, C. J. (1994). Emotion and psychopathy: Startling new insights. *Psychophysiology, 31,* 319–330.

Patrick, C. J. (Ed.). (2005). *The handbook of psychopathy.* New York: Guilford Press.

Patrick, C. J., Bradley, M. M., and Lang, P. J. (1993). Emotion in the criminal psychopath: Startle reflex modulation. *Journal of Abnormal Psychology, 102,* 82–92.

Patrick, C. J., Cuthbert, B. N., and Lang, P. J. (1994). Emotion in the criminal psychopath: Fear image processing. *Journal of Abnormal Psychology, 103,* 523–534.

Patterson, C. H. (2000). *Understanding psychotherapy: Fifty years of client-centred theory and practice.* Ross-on-Wye, England: PCCS Books Ltd.

Paulhus, D. L. (1984). Two component models of socially desirable responding. *Journal of Personality and Social Psychology, 46,* 598–609.

Paulhus, D. L. (1990). Measurement and control of response bias. In J. P. Robinson, P. R. Shaver, and L. Wrightsman (Eds.), *Measures of personality and social-psychological attitudes* (pp. 17–59). San Diego, CA: Academic Press.

Paulhus, D. L., and Vazire, S. (2007). The self-report method. In R. W. Robins, R. C. Fraley, and R. F. Krueger (Eds.), *Handbook of Research Methods in Personality Psychology* (pp. 224–239). New York: Guilford.

Paulhus, D. L., and Williams, K. M. (2002). The Dark Triad of personality: Narcissism, Machiavellianism, and psychopathy. *Journal of Research in Personality, 36,* 556–563.

Paunesku, D., Walton, G. M., Romero, C., Smith, E. N., Yeager, D. S., and Dweck, C. S. (2015). Mind-set interventions are a scalable treatment for academic underachievement. *Psychological Science, 26*(6), 784–793.

Paunonen, S. V. (2002). *Design and construction of the Supernumerary Personality Inventory* (Research Bulletin 763). London, Ontario: University of Western Ontario.

Paunonen, S. V. (2003). Big Five factors of personality and replicated predictions of behavior. *Journal of Personality and Social Psychology, 84,* 2, 411–424.

Paunonen, S. V., and Ashton, M. C. (1998). The structured assessment of personality across cultures. *Journal of Cross-Cultural Psychology, 29,* 150–170.

Paunonen, S. V., Haddock, G., Forsterling, F., and Keinonen, M. (2003). Broad versus narrow personality measures and the prediction of behaviour across cultures. *European Journal of Personality, 17,* 413–433.

Paunonen, S. V., and Hong, R. Y. (2015). In defense of personality traits. In L. Cooper and R. J. Larsen (Eds.), *Handbook of personality and social psychology: Personality processes and individual differences* (pp. 233–260). Washington, DC: American Psychological Association.

Paunonen, S. V., and O'Neil, T. A. (2010). Self-reports, peer ratings, and construct validity. *European Journal of Personality, 24,* 189–206.

Pedersen, N. L. (1993). Genetic and environmental change in personality. In T. J. Bouchard and P. Proping (Eds.), *Twins as a tool of behavioral genetics* (pp. 147–162). West Sussex, England: Wiley.

Pelle, A. J., Erdman, R.A.M., van Domburg, R. T., Spiering, M., Kazemier, M., and Pedersen, S. S. (2008). Type D patients report poorer health status prior to and after cardiac rehabilitation compared to non-Type D patients. *Annals of Behavioral Medicine, 36,* 167–175.

Penke, L., and Asendorpf, J. B. (2008a). Beyond global sociosexual orientations: A more differentiated look at sociosexuality and its effects on courtship and romantic relationships. *Journal of Personality and Social Psychology, 95,* 1113–1135.

Penke, L., and Asendorpf, J. B. (2008b). Evidence for conditional sex differences in emotional but not in sexual jealousy at the automatic level of cognitive processing. *European Journal of Personality, 22,* 3–30.

Penke, L., Denissen, J.J.A., and Miller, G. F. (2007). The evolutionary genetics of personality. *European Journal of Personality, 21,* 549–587.

Pennebaker, J. W. (1990). *Opening up: The healing powers of confiding in others.* New York: Morrow.

Pennebaker, J. W. (2003a). The social, linguistic and health consequences of emotional disclosure. In J. Suls and K. A. Wallston (Eds.), *Social psychological foundations of health and illness* (pp. 288–313). Malden, MA: Blackwell.

Pennebaker, J. W. (2003b). Writing about emotional experiences as a therapeutic process. In P. Salovey and A. J. Rothman (Eds.), *Social psychology of health* (pp. 362–368). New York: Psychology Press.

Pennebaker, J. W., and Chung, C. K. (2011). Expressive writing: Connections to physical and mental health. *Oxford handbook of health psychology* (417–437). New York: Oxford University Press.

Pennebaker, J. W., Colder, M., and Sharp, L. K. (1990). Accelerating the coping process. *Journal of Personality and Social Psychology, 58,* 528–537.

Pennebaker, J. W., and O'Heeron, R. C. (1984). Confiding in others and illness rates among spouses of suicide and accidental-death victims. *Journal of Abnormal Psychology, 93,* 473–476.

Perilloux, C., Fleischman, D. S., and Buss, D. M. (2008). The daughter-guarding hypothesis: Parental influence on children's mating behavior. *Evolutionary Psychology, 6,* 217–233.

Perilloux, C., Fleischman, D. S., and Buss, D. M. (2011). Meet the parents: Parent-offspring convergence and divergence in mate preferences. *Personality and Individual Differences, 50,* 253–258.

Perry, V. G. (2008). Giving credit where credit is due: The psychology of credit ratings. *Journal of Behavioral Finance, 9,* 15–21.

Perugini, M., and Richetin, J. (2007). In the land of the blind, the one-eyed man is king. *European Journal of Personality, 21,* 977–981.

Petersen, J. L., and Hyde, J. S. (2010). A meta-analytic review of research on gender differences in sexuality, 1993–2007. *Psychological Bulletin, 136,* 21–38.

Peterson, B. E., Winter, D. G., and Doty, R. M. (1994). Laboratory tests of a motivational-perceptual model of conflict escalation. *Journal of Conflict Resolution, 38,* 719–748.

Peterson, C. (1991). The meaning and measurement of explanatory style. *Psychological Inquiry, 2,* 1–10.

Peterson, C. (1995). Explanatory style and health. In G. M. Buchanan and M.E.P. Seligman (Eds.), *Explanatory style* (pp. 233–246). Hillsdale, NJ: Erlbaum.

Peterson, C. (2000). The future of optimism. *American Psychologist, 55,* 44–55.

Peterson, C., and Bossio, L. M. (1991). *Health and optimism.* New York: Free Press.

Peterson, C., and Bossio, L. M. (2001). Optimism and physical well-being. In E. C. Chang (Ed.), *Optimism and pessimism: Implications for theory, research, and practice* (pp. 127–145). Washington, DC: American Psychological Association.

Peterson, C., and Chang, E. C. (2003). Optimism and flourishing. In C. L. Keyes and J. Haidt (Eds.), *Flourishing: Positive psychology and the life well-lived* (pp. 55–79). Washington, DC: American Psychological Association.

Peterson, C., Maier, S. F., and Seligman, M.E.P. (1993). *Learned helplessness: A theory for the age of personal control.* New York: Oxford University Press.

Peterson, C., and Park, N. (2010). What happened to self-actualization? Commentary on Kenrick et al. (2010). *Perspectives on Psychological Science, 5,* 320–322.

Peterson, C., Schulman, P., Castellon, C., and Seligman, M.E.P. (1992). CAVE: Content analysis of verbatim explanations. In C. P. Smith (Ed.), *Motivation and personality: Handbook of thematic content analysis* (pp. 383–392). New York: Cambridge University Press.

Peterson, C., and Seligman, M.E.P. (1987). Explanatory style and illness. Special issue: Personality and physical health. *Journal of Personality, 55,* 237–265.

Peterson, C., and Seligman, M. E. P. (2003). Character strengths before and after September 11. *Psychological Science, 14,* 381–384.

Peterson, C., Seligman, M.E.P., and Vaillant, G. E. (1988). Pessimistic explanatory style is a risk factor for physical illness: A thirty-five-year longitudinal study. *Journal of Personality and Social Psychology, 55,* 23–27.

Peterson, C., Seligman, M.E.P., Yurko, K. H., Martin, L. R., and Friedman, H. S. (1998). Catastrophizing and untimely death. *Psychological Science, 9,* 49–52.

Peterson, C., Semmel, A., von Baeyer, C., Abramson, L. Y., Metalsky, G. I., and Seligman, M.E.P. (1982). The Attributional Style Questionnaire. *Cognitive Therapy and Research, 6,* 287–299.

Peterson, J. B., Smith, K. W., and Carson, S. (2002). Openness and extraversion are associated with reduced latent inhibition: Replication and commentary. *Personality and Individual Differences, 33,* 1137–1147.

Peterson, C., and Steen, T. A. (2002). Optimistic explanatory style. In C. R. Snyder and S. J. Lopez (Eds.), *Handbook of positive psychology* (pp. 244–256). London: Oxford University Press.

Petrie, A. (1967). *Individuality in pain and suffering.* Chicago: University of Chicago Press.

Petrill, S. A. (2002). The case for general intelligence: A behavioral genetic perspective. In R. J. Sternberg and E. L. Grigorenko (Eds.), *The general factor of intelligence: How general is it?* (pp. 281–298). Mahwah, NJ: Erlbaum.

Pickering, A. D., Corr, P. J., and Gray, J. A. (1999). Interactions and reinforcement sensitivity theory: A theoretical analysis of Rusting and Larsen (1997). *Personality and Individual Differences, 26,* 357–365.

Pickering, A., Farmer, A., Harris, T., Redman, K., Mahmood, A., Sadler, S., and McGuffin, P. (2003). A sib-pair study of psychoticism, life events and depression. *Personality and Individual Differences, 34,* 613–623.

Piedmont, R. L. (2001). Cracking the plaster cast: Big Five personality change during intensive outpatient counseling. *Journal of Research in Personality, 35,* 500–520.

Piff, P. K., Kraus, M. W., Côté, S., Cheng, B. H., and Keltner, D. (2010). Having less, giving more: the influence of social class on prosocial behavior. *Journal of Personality and Social Psychology, 99*(5), 771–784.

Pietrzak, R., Laird, J. D., Stevens, D. A., and Thompson, N. S. (2002). Sex differences in human jealousy: A coordinated study of forced-choice, continuous rating-scale, and physiological responses on the same subjects. *Evolution and Human Behavior, 23,* 83–94.

Pincus, J. H. (2001). *Base instincts: What makes killers kill?* New York: Norton.

Pinker, S. (1997). *How the mind works.* New York: Norton.

Pinker, S. (2012). *The better angels of our nature.* New York: Viking.

Pipher, M. (1994). *Reviving Ophelia: Saving the selves of adolescent girls.* New York: Ballantine Books.

Piquero, A. R., Carriaga, M. L., Diamond, B., Kazemian, L., and Farrington, D. P. (2012). Stability in aggression revisited. *Aggression and Violent Behavior, 17*(4), 365–372.

Pittenger, D. J. (2005). Cautionary comments regarding the Myers-Briggs Type Indicator. *Consulting Psychology Journal: Practice and Research, 57,* 210–221.

Plavcan, J. M. (2012). Sexual size dimorphism, canine dimorphism, and male-male competition in primates. *Human Nature, 23,* 45–67.

Plomin, R. (2002). Individual differences research in a postgenomic era. *Personality and Individual Differences, 33,* 909–920.

Plomin, R., and Crabbe, J. (2000). DNA. *Psychological Bulletin Special Issue: Psychology in the 21st Century, 126,* 806–828.

Plomin, R., and Davis, O.S.P. (2009). The future of genetics in psychology and psychiatry: Microarrays, genome-wide association, and non-coding RNA. *Journal of Child Psychology and Psychiatry, 50,* 63–71.

Plomin, R., and DeFries, G. E. (1985). *Origins of individual differences in infancy: The Colorado Adoption Project.* New York: Academic Press.

Plomin, R., DeFries, J. C., and Fulker, D. W. (1988). *Nature and nurture during infancy and early childhood.* New York: Cambridge University Press.

Plomin, R., DeFries, J. C., and Loehlin, J. C. (1977). Genotype-environment interaction and correlation in the analysis of human behavior. *Psychological Bulletin, 84,* 309–322.

Plomin, R., DeFries, J. C., and McClearn, G. E. (1990). *Behavioral genetics: A primer* (2nd ed.). New York: W. H. Freeman.

Plomin, R., DeFries, J. C., McClern, G. E., and McGuffin, P. (2001). *Behavioral genetics* (4th ed.). New York: Worth.

Plomin, R., DeFries, J. C., Knopik, V. S., & Neiderheiser, J. (2013). *Behavioral genetics.* Basingstoke, UK: Palgrave Macmillan.

Plutchik, R. (1980). A general psychoevolutionary theory of emotion. In R. Plutchik and H. Kellerman (Eds.), *Emotion: Theory, research, and experience: Vol. 1: Theories of emotion* (pp. 3–31). New York: Academic Press.

Pollock, V. E., Briere, J., Schneider, L., Knop, J., Mednick, S., and Goodwin, D. W. (1990). Childhood antecedents of antisocial behavior: Parental alcoholism and physical abusiveness. *American Journal of Psychiatry, 147,* 1290–1293.

Poropat, A. E. (2009). A meta-analysis of the five-factor model of personality and academic performance. *Psychological Bulletin, 135,* 322–338.

Post, J. M. (Ed.). (2003). *The psychological assessment of political leaders.* Ann Arbor: University of Michigan Press.

Preckel, F., Lipnevich, A. A., Schneider, S., and Roberts, R. D. (2011). Chronotype, cognitive abilities, and academic achievement: A meta-analytic investigation. *Learning And Individual Differences, 21*(5), 483–492.

Price, M. E., Cosmides, L., and Tooby, J. (2002). Punitive sentiment as an anti–free rider psychological device. *Evolution and Human Behavior, 23,* 203–231.

Prior, H., Schwarz, A., and Güntürkün, O. (2008). Mirror-induced behavior in the magpie (*Pica pica*): Evidence of self-recognition. *Public Library of Science: Biology, 6*(8), 202 (doi:10.1371/ journal.pbio.0060202).

Promislow, D. (2003). Mate choice, sexual conflict, and evolution of senescence. *Behavior Genetics, 33,* 191–201.

Pullmann, H., Raudsepp, L., and Allik, J. (2006). Stability and change in adolescents' personality: A longitudinal study. *European Journal of Personality, 20,* 447–459.

Rabbie, J. M., and Horwitz, M. (1969). Arousal of ingroup-outgroup bias by a chance win or loss. *Journal of Personality and Social Psychology, 13,* 269–277.

Rafaeli-Mor, E., and Steinberg, J. (2002). Self-complexity and well-being: A review and research synthesis. *Personality and Social Psychology Review, 6,* 31–58.

Raine, A. (2002). Biosocial studies of antisocial and violent behavior in children and adults: A review. *Journal of Abnormal Child Psychology, 30,* 311–326.

Raine, A., Meloy, J. R., and Bihrle, S. (1998). Reduced prefrontal and increased subcortical brain functioning assessed using positron emission tomography in predatory and affective murderers. *Behavioral Sciences and the Law Special Issue: Impulsive aggression, 16,* 319–332.

Rammsayer, T. H., and Brandler, S. (2002). On the relationship between general fluid intelligence and psychophysical indicators of temporal resolution in the brain. *Journal of Research in Personality, 36,* 507–530.

Rammstedt, B., Goldberg, L. R., and Borg, I. (2010). The measurement equivalence of Big-Five factor markers for persons with different levels of education. *Journal of Research in Personality, 44,* 53–61.

Ramona v. Isabella, California Superior Court, Napa, C61898, 1994.

Randler, C., and Jankowski, K. S. (2014). Evidence for the validity of the Composite Scale of Morningness based on students from Germany and Poland— Relationship with sleep–wake and social schedules. *Biological Rhythm Research, 45*(4), 653–659.

Randler, C., and Kretz, S. (2011). Assortative mating in morningness-eveningness. *International Journal of Psychology, 46*(2), 91–96.

Randler, C., Baumann, V. P., and Horzum, M. B. (2014). Morningness–eveningness, Big Five and the BIS/BAS inventory. *Personality And Individual Differences, 66,* 64–67.

Rantanen, J., Metsäpelto, R. L., Feldt, T., Pulkkinen, L. E. A., and Kokko, K. (2007). Long-term stability in the Big Five personality traits in adulthood. *Scandinavian Journal of Psychology, 48*(6), 511–518.

Raskin, J. D. (2001). The modern, the postmodern, and George Kelly's personal construct psychology. *American Psychologist, 56,* 368–369.

Raskin, R., and Hall, C. S. (1979). A narcissistic personality inventory. *Psychological Reports, 45,* 590.

Raskin, R., and Shaw, R. (1987). *Narcissism and the use of personal pronouns.* Unpublished manuscript.

Raskin, R., and Terry, H. (1988). A principle-components analysis of the narcissistic personality inventory and further evidence of its construct validity. *Journal of Personality and Social Psychology, 54,* 890–902.

Rattan, A., Good, C., and Dweck, C. S. (2012). "It's OK—Not everyone can be good at math": Instructors with an entity theory comfort (and demotivate) students. *Journal of Experimental Social Psychology, 48,* 731–737.

Rattan, A., Savani, K., Chugh, D., and Dweck, C. S. (2015). Leveraging mindsets to promote academic achievement: Policy recommendations. *Perspectives on Psychological Science, 10*(6), 721–726.

Rauthmann, J., and Denissen, J. J. A. (2011). I often do it vs. I like doing it: Comparing a frequency- and valency-approach to extraversion. *Personality and Individual Differences, 50,* 1283–1288.

Rawlings, D. (2003). Personality correlates of liking for "unpleasant" paintings and photographs. *Personality and Individual Differences, 34,* 395–410.

Regan, P. C., and Atkins, L. (2006). Sex differences and similarities in frequency and intensity of sexual desire. *Social Behavior and Personality, 34,* 95–102.

Reidy, D. E., Zeichner, A., Foster, J. D., and Martinez, M. A. (2008). Effects of narcissistic entitlement and exploitativeness on human physical aggression. *Personality and Individual Differences, 44,* 685–875.

Renner, W., Kandler, C., Bleidorn, W., Riemann, R., Angleitner, A., Spinath, F. M., and Menschik-Bendele, J. (2012). Human values: Genetic and environmental effects on five lexically derived domains and their facets. *Personality and Individual Differences, 52,* 89–93.

Renshon, S. A. (1998). Analyzing the psychology and performances of presidential candidates at a distance: Bob Dole and the 1996 presidential campaign. *Leadership Quarterly, 9,* 377–395.

Renshon, S. A. (2005). George W. Bush's cowboy politics: An inquiry. *Political Psychology, 26,* 585–614.

Revelle, W., Humphreys, M. S., Simon, L., and Gilliland, K. (1980). The interactive effect of personality, time of day, and caffeine: A test of the arousal model. *Journal of Experimental Psychology: General, 109,* 1–31.

Rhee, E., Uleman, J., Lee, H., and Roman, R. (1995). Spontaneous self-descriptions and ethnic identities in individualistic and collectivist cultures. *Journal of Personality and Social Psychology, 69,* 142–152.

Rheingold, H. L., and Cook, K. V. (1975). The contents of boys' and girls' rooms as an index of parents' behavior. *Child Development, 46,* 459–463.

Rhodenwalt, F., and Morf, C. (1998). On self-aggrandizement and anger: A temporal analysis of narcissism and affective reactions to success and failure. *Journal of Personality and Social Psychology, 74,* 672–685.

Richardson, J. A., and Turner, T. E. (2000). Field dependence revisited I: Intelligence. *Educational Psychology, 20,* 255–270.

Richardson, M., and Abraham, C. (2009). Conscientiousness and achievement motivation predict performance. *European Journal of Personality, 23,* 589–605.

Ridley, M. (1999). *Genome: The autobiography of a species in 23 chapters.* New York: HarperCollins.

Rind, B., Tromovitch, P., and Bauserman, R. (1998). A meta-analytic examination of assumed properties of child sexual abuse using college samples. *Psychological Bulletin, 124,* 22–53.

Rindermann, H. (2008). Relevance of education and intelligence at the national level for the economic welfare of people. *Intelligence, 36,* 127–142.

Ritter, V., Leichsenring, F., Strauss, B. M., and Stangier, U. (2013). Changes in implicit and explicit self-esteem following cognitive and psychodynamic therapy in social anxiety disorder. *Psychotherapy Research, 23*(5), 547–558.

Ritts, V., and Patterson, M. L. (1996). Effects of social anxiety and action identification on impressions and thoughts in interaction. *Journal of Social and Clinical Psychology, 15,* 191–205.

Ritvo, L. B. (1990). *Darwin's influence on Freud: A tale of two sciences.* New Haven, CT: Yale University Press.

Roberts, B. W., Caspi, A., and Moffitt, T. E. (2001). The kids are alright: Growth and stability in personality development from adolescence to adulthood. *Journal of Personality and Social Psychology, 81, 4,* 670–683.

Roberts, B. W., Caspi, A., and Moffitt, T. E. (2003). Work experiences and personality development in young adulthood. *Journal of Personality and Social Psychology, 84, 5,* 582–593.

Roberts, B. W., and DelVecchio, W. F. (2000). The rank-order consistency of personality traits from childhood to old age: A quantitative review of the longitudinal studies. *Psychological Bulletin, 126,* 3–25.

Roberts, B. W., Kuncel, N. R., Shiner, R., Caspi, A., and Goldberg, L. R. (2007). The power of personality: The comparative validity of personality traits, socioeconomic status, and cognitive ability for predicting important life outcomes. *Perspectives on Psychological Science, 2,* 313–345.

Roberts, B. W., Walton, K. R., and Viechtbauer, W. (2006). Patterns of mean-level change in personality traits across the life course: A meta-analysis of longitudinal studies. *Psychological Bulletin, 132,* 1–25.

Roberts, J. E., and Monroe, S. M. (1992). Vulnerable self-esteem and depressive symptoms: Prospective findings comparing three alternative conceptualizations. *Journal of Personality and Social Psychology, 62,* 804–812.

Roberts, W. B., and Robins, R. W. (2004). Person-environment fit and its implications for personality development: A longitudinal study. *Journal of Personality, 72,* 89–110.

Robins, R. W., Caspi, A., and Moffitt, T. E. (2002). It's not just who you're with, it's who you are: Personality and relationship experiences across multiple relationships. *Journal of Personality, 70,* 925–964.

Robins, R. W., Fraley, R. C., Roberts, B. W., and Trzesniewski, K. H. (2001). A longitudinal study of personality change in young adulthood. *Journal of Personality, 69, 4,* 617–640.

Robins, R. W., and John, O. P. (1997). Self-perception, visual perspective, and narcissism: Is seeing believing? *Psychological Science, 8,* 37–42.

Robins, R. W., Noftle, E. E., Trzesniewski, K. H., and Roberts, B. W. (2005). Do people know how their personality has changed? Correlates of perceived and actual personality change in young adulthood. *Journal of Personality, 73,* 489–521.

Roediger, H. L., Balota, D. A., and Watson, J. M. (2001). Spreading activation and arousal of false memories. In Henry L. Roediger, III, and James S. Nairne (Eds.), *The nature of remembering: Essays in honor of Robert G. Crowder* (pp. 95–115). Washington, DC: American Psychological Association.

Roediger, H. L., and McDermott K. B. (1995). Creating false memories: Remembering words not presented in lists. *Journal of Experimental Psychology: Learning, Memory, and Cognition, 21,* 803–814.

Roediger, H. L., McDermott, K. B., and Robinson, K. J. (1998). The role of associative processes in creating false memories. In M. A. Conway, S. E. Gathercole, and C. Cornoldi (Eds.), *Theories of memory II* (pp. 187–246). Hove, Sussex, England: Psychological Press.

Rogers, C. R. (1957). The necessary and sufficient conditions of therapeutic personality change. *Journal of Consulting Psychology, 21,* 95–103.

Rogers, C. R. (1975). Empathic: An unappreciated way of being. *The Counseling Psychologist, 5,* 2–10.

Rogers, C. R. (2002). *Carl Rogers: The quiet revolutionary, an oral history.* Roseville, CA Penmarin Books.

Rogness, G. A., and McClure, E. B. (1996). Development and neurotransmitter-environment interactions. *Development and Psychopathology, 8,* 183–199.

Romero, C., Master, A., Paunesku, D., Dweck, C. S., and Gross, J. J. (2014). Academic and emotional functioning in middle school: The role of implicit theories. *Emotion, 14*(2), 227–234.

Romero, E., Luengo, M. T., Carrillo-de-la-Pena, T., and Otero-Lopez, J. M. (1994). The act frequency approach to the study of impulsivity. *European Journal of Personality, 8,* 119–134.

Rosch, E. (1975). Cognitive reference points. *Cognitive Psychology, 7,* 532–547.

Rose, R. J. (1995). Genes and behavior. *Annual Review of Psychology, 46,* 625–654.

Rosenzweig, S. (1986). Idiodynamics vis-à-vis psychology. *American Psychologist, 41,* 241–245.

Rosenzweig, S. (1994). *The historic expedition to America (1909): Freud, Jung, and Hall the king-maker.* St. Louis, MO: Rana House.

Rosenzweig, S. (1997). "Idiographic" vis-à-vis "idiodynamic" in the historical perspective of personality theory: Remembering Gordon Allport, 1897–1997. *Journal of the History of the Behavioral Sciences, 33,* 405–419.

Ross, K. M., Liu, S., Tomfohr, L. M., and Miller, G. E. (2013). Self-esteem variability predicts arterial stiffness trajectories in healthy adolescent females. *Health Psychology, 32*(8), 869–876.

Ross, L., Greene, D., and House, P. (1977). The false consensus effect: An egocentric bias in social perception and attribution processes. *Journal of Experimental Social Psychology, 13,* 279–301.

Ross, S. R., Canada, K. E., and Rausch, M. K. (2002). Self-handicapping and the five factor model of personality: Mediation between neuroticism and conscientiousness. *Personality and Individual Differences, 32,* 1173–1184.

Rothbart, M. K. (1981). Measurement of temperament in infancy. *Child Development, 52,* 569–578.

Rothbart, M. K. (1986). Longitudinal observation of infant temperament. *Developmental Psychology, 22,* 356–365.

Rothbart, M. K., and Hwang, J. (2005). Temperament. In A. J. Elliot and C. S. Dweck (Eds.), *Handbook of competence & motivation* (pp. 167–184). New York: Guilford.

Rotter, J. B. (1971). Generalized expectancies for interpersonal trust. *American Psychologist, 26,* 443–452.

Rotter, J. B. (1982). *The development and application of social learning theory.* New York: Praeger.

Rotter, J. B. (1990). Internal versus external control of reinforcement: A case history of a variable. *American Psychologist, 45,* 489–493.

Rowe, D. C. (2001). *Biology and crime.* New York: Roxbury.

Rozin, P. (1996). Towards a psychology of food and eating: From motivation to module to model to marker, morality, meaning, and metaphor. *Current Directions in Psychological Science, 5*(1), 18–24.

Rozin, P. (2003). Five potential principles for understanding cultural differences in relation to individual differences. *Journal of Research in Personality, 37,* 273–283.

Ruchkin, V. V., Koposov, R. A., Eisemann, M., and Hagglof, B. (2002). Alcohol use in delinquent adolescents from Northern Russia: The role of personality, parental rearing and family history of alcohol abuse. *Personality and Individual Differences, 32,* 1139–1148.

Rule, A. (2000). *The stranger beside me.* New York: Norton.

Runyon, W. M. (1983). Idiographic goals and methods in the study of lives. *Journal of Personality, 51,* 413–437.

Rushton, J. P. (1985). Differential K theory: The sociobiology of individual and group differences. *Personality and Individual Differences, 6,* 441–452.

Rushton, J. P., Cons, T. A., and Hur, Y-M. (2008). The genetics and evolution of the general factor of personality. *Journal of Research in Personality, 42,* 1173–1185.

Russell, V. M., and McNulty, J. K. (2011). Frequent sex protects intimates from the negative implications of their neuroticism. *Social Psychological and Personality Science, 2,* 220–227.

Rusting, C. L., and Larsen, R. J. (1997). Extraversion, neuroticism, and susceptibility to positive and negative affect: A test of two theoretical models. *Personality and Individual Differences, 22,* 607–612.

Rusting, C. L., and Larsen, R. J. (1998a). Diurnal patterns of unpleasant mood: Associations with neuroticism, depression, and anxiety. *Journal of Personality, 66,* 85–103.

Rusting, C. L., and Larsen, R. J. (1998b). Personality and cognitive processing of affective information. *Personality and Social Psychology Bulletin, 24,* 200–213.

Rusting, C. L., and Larsen, R. J. (1999). Clarifying Gray's theory of personality: A response to Pickering, Corr, and Gray. *Personality and Individual Differences, 26,* 367–372.

Ryan, R. M., and Deci, E. L. (2000). Self-determination theory and the facilitation of intrinsic motivation, social development, and well-being. *American Psychologist, 55,* 68–78.

Ryff, C., Lee, Y., and Na, K. (1995). *Through the lens of culture: Psychological well-being at mid-life.* Unpublished manuscript, University of Michigan, Ann Arbor.

Sagarin, B. J. (2005). Reconsidering evolved sex differences in jealousy: Comment on Harris (2003). *Personality and Social Psychology Review, 9,* 62–75.

Sagarin, B. J., Becker, D. V., Guadagno, R. E., Nicastle, L. D., and Millevoi, A. (2003). Sex differences (and similarities) in jealousy: The moderating influence of infidelity experience and sexual orientation. *Evolution and Human Behavior, 24,* 17–23.

Sagarin, B. J., Martin, A. L., Clutinho, S. A., and Edlund, J. E. (2009). *A meta-analysis of studies examining sex differences in jealousy using continuous measures.* Paper presented to the Evolutionary Psychology Preconference, Annual Meeting of the Society of Personality and Social Psychology, Tampa, Florida.

Sagarin, B. J., Martin, A. L., Coutinho, S. A., Edlund, J. E., Patel, L., Skowronski, J. J., and Zengel, B. (2012). Sex differences in jealousy: A meta-analytic examination. *Evolution and Human Behavior, 33,* 595–613.

Sagie, A., and Elizur, D. (1999). Achievement motive and entrepreneurial orientation: A structural analysis. *Journal of Organizational Behavior, 20,* 375–387.

Sakuta, A., and Fukushima, A. (1998). A study on abnormal findings pertaining to the brain in criminals. *International Medical Journal, 5,* 283–292.

Salgado, J. F., Moscoso, S., and Lado, M. (2003). Evidence of cross-cultural invariant of the Big Five personality dimensions in work settings. *European Journal of Personality, 17,* S67–S76.

Salovey, P., and Mayer, J. D. (1990). Emotional intelligence. *Imagination, Cognition, and Personality, 9,* 185–211.

Sam, D. L. (1994). The psychological adjustment of young immigrants in Norway. *Scandinavian Journal of Psychology, 35,* 240–253.

Samuel, D. B., and Gore, W. L. (2012). Maladaptive variants of conscientiousness and agreeableness. *Journal of Personality, 80*(6), 1669–1696.

Sandvik, E., Diener, E., and Seidlitz, L. (1993). Subjective well-being: The convergence and stability of self-report and non-self-report measures. *Journal of Personality, 61,* 317–342.

Santayana, G. (1905/1980). *Reason in common sense: The life of reason, vol. 1.* New York, NY: Dover.

Sapienza, P., Zingales, L., and Maestripieri, D. (2009). Gender differences in financial risk aversion and career choices are affected by testosterone. *Proceedings of the National Academy of Science, USA, 106,* 15268–15273.

Sapolsky, R. M. (1987). Stress, social status, and reproductive physiology in free-living baboons. In D. Crews (Ed.), *Psychobiology of reproductive behavior: An evolutionary perspective.* Englewood Cliffs, NJ: Prentice Hall.

Saroglou, V. (2002). Religion and the five factors of personality: A meta-analytic review. *Personality and Individual Differences, 32,* 15–25.

Satterfield, J. H., and Schelle, A. M. (1984). Childhood brain function differences in delinquent and non-delinquent hyperactive boys. *Electroencephalography and Clinical Neurophysiology, 57,* 199–207.

Saucier, G. (2003). Factor structure of English-Language personality Type-nouns. *Journal of Personality and Social Psychology, 85, 4,* 695–708.

Saucier, G. (2009). Recurrent personality dimensions in inclusive lexical studies: Indications for a Big Six structure. *Journal of Personality, 77,* 1577–1614.

Saucier, G. (2010). The structure of social effects: Personality as impact on others. *European Journal of Personality, 24,* 222–240.

Saucier, G., Georgiades, S., Tsaousis, I., and Goldberg, L. R. (2005). The factor structure of Greek personality adjectives. *Journal of Personality and Social Psychology, 5,* 856–875.

Saucier, G., and Goldberg, L. R. (1996). The language of personality: Lexical perspectives on the five-factor model. In J. S. Wiggins (Ed.), *The five-factor model of personality: Theoretical perspectives* (pp. 21–50). New York: Guilford Press.

Saucier, G., and Goldberg, L. R. (1998). What is beyond the Big Five? *Journal of Personality, 66,* 495–524.

Saucier, G., and Goldberg, L. R. (2001). Lexical studies of indigenous personality factors: Premises, products, and prospects. *Journal of Personality, 69, 6,* 847–879.

Saudino, K. J., and Plomin, R. (1996). Personality and behavioral genetics: Where have we been and where are we going? *Journal of Research in Personality, 30,* 335–347.

Sauter, D. A., Eisner, F., Ekman, P., and Scott, S. K. (2010). Cross-cultural recognition of basic emotions through nonverbal emotional vocalizations. *Proceedings of the National Academy of Sciences, 107*(6), 2408–2412.

Scarf, M. (1996). The mind of the unabomber. The New Republic, June 10, 1996, p. 20.

Scarr, S. (1968). Environmental bias in twin studies. *Eugenics Quarterly, 15,* 34–40.

Scarr, S., and Carter-Saltzman, L. (1979). Twin method: Defense of a critical assumption. *Behavior Genetics, 9,* 527–542.

Scarr, S., and McCartney, K. (1983). How children make their own environments: A theory of genotype environment effects. *Child Development, 54,* 424–435.

Scealy, M., Phillips, J. G., and Stevenson, R. (2002). Shyness and anxiety as predictors of patterns of Internet usage. *CyberPsychology and Behavior, 5,* 507–515.

Scelza, B. A. (2014). Jealousy in a small-scale, natural fertility population: the roles of paternity, investment and love in jealous response. *Evolution and Human Behavior, 35*(2), 103–108.

Schacter, D. L. (1997). *Searching for memory: The brain, the mind, and the past.* New York: Basic Books.

Schaffhuser, K., Allemand, M., and Martin, M. (2014). Personality traits and relationship satisfaction in intimate couples: Three perspectives on personality. *European Journal of Personality, 28*(2), 120–133.

Schaller, M. (2016). The behavioral immune system. In D.M. Buss (Ed.), *The handbook of evolutionary psychology.* Hoboken, NJ: Wiley.

Schaller, M., Neuberg, S. L., Griskevicius, V., and Kenrick, D. T. (2010). Pyramid power: A reply to commentaries. *Perspectives on Psychological Sciences, 5,* 335–337.

Scheier, M. F., and Carver, C. S. (1992). Effects of optimism on psychological and physical well-being: Theoretical overview and empirical update. *Cognitive Therapy and Research, 16,* 201–228.

Scheier, M. F., Matthews, K. A., Owens, J. F., Schulz, R., Bridges, M. W., Magovern, G. J., and Carver, C. S. (1999). Optimism and rehospitalization following coronary artery bypass graft surgery. *Archives of Internal Medicine, 159,* 829–835.

Schinka J. A., Letsch, E. A., and Crawford, F. C. (2002). DRD4 and novelty seeking: Results of meta-analyses. *American Journal of Medical Genetics, 114,* 643–648.

Schiraldi, G. (2007). *10 simple solutions for building self-esteem.* Oakland, CA: New Harbinger.

Schmalt, H. (1999). Assessing the achievement motive using the grid technique. *Journal of Research in Personality, 33,* 109–130.

Schmidt, L. A., and Fox, N. A. (1995). Individual differences in young adults' shyness and sociability: Personality and health correlates. *Personality and Individual Differences, 19,* 455–462.

Schmidt, L. A., and Fox, N. A. (2002). Individual differences in childhood shyness: Origins, malleability and developmental course. In D. Cervone and W. Mischel (Eds.), *Advances in personality science* (pp. 83–105). New York: Guilford Press.

Schmidt, L. A., Fox, N. A., Rubin, K. H., Hu, S., and Hamer, D. H. (2002). Molecular genetics of shyness and aggression in preschoolers. *Personality and Individual Differences, 33,* 227–238.

Schmitt, D. P. (2004). The Big Five related to risky sexual behavior across 10 world regions: Differential personality associations of sexual promiscuity and relationship infidelity. *European Journal of Personality, 18,* 301–319.

Schmitt, D. P., and Buss, D. M. (2000). Sexual dimensions of person description: Beyond or subsumed by the Big Five? *Journal of Research in Personality, 34,* 141–177.

Schmitt, D. P., and Buss, D. M. (2001). Human mate poaching: Tactics and temptations for infiltrating existing relationships. *Journal of Personality and Social Psychology, 80,* 894–917.

Schmitt, D. P., Jonason, P. K., Byerley, G. J., Flores, S. D., Illbeck, B. E., O'Leary, K. N., and Qudrat, A. (2012). A reexamination of sex differences in sexuality: New studies reveal old truths. *Current Directions in Psychological Science, 21,* 135–139.

Schmitt, D. P., and 118 Members of the International Sexuality Description Project. (2003). Universal sex differences in the desire for sexual variety: Tests from 52 nations, 6 continents, and 13 islands. *Personality and Social Psychology, 85,* 85–104.

Schmitt, D. P., Realo, A., Voracek, M., and Allik, J. (2008). Why can't a man be more like a woman? Sex differences in Big Five personality traits across 55 cultures. *Journal of Personality and Social Psychology, 94,* 168–182.

Schmitt, D. P., Youn, G., Bond, B., Brooks, S., Frye, H., Johnson, S., Klesman, J., et al. (2009). When will I feel love? The effects of culture, personality, and gender on the psychological tendency to love. *Journal of Research in Personality, 43,* 830–846.

Schmutte, P. S., Lee, Y. H., and Ryff, C. D. (1995). *Reflections on parenthood: A cultural perspective.* Unpublished manuscript, Madison: University of Wisconsin.

Schneider, K. (1958). *Psychopathic personalities.* London: Cassell.

Schüler, J. , Sheldon, K. M., and Fröhlich, S.M. (2010). Implicit need for achievement moderates the relationship between competence need satisfaction and subsequent motivation. *Journal of Research in Personality, 44,* 1–12.

Schultheiss, O. C. (2013). The hormonal correlates of implicit motives. *Social & Personality Psychology Compass, 7*(1), 52–65.

Schultheiss, O. C., and Brunstein, J. C. (2001). Assessment of implicit motives with a research version of the TAT: Picture profiles, gender differences, and relations to other personality measures. *Journal of Personality Assessment Special Issue: More data on the current Rorschach controversy, 77,* 71–86.

Schultheiss, O. C., Liening, S., and Schad, D. (2008). The reliability of a Picture Story Exercise measure of implicit motives: Estimates of internal consistency, retest reliability, and ipsative stability. *Journal of Research in Personality, 42,* 1560–1571.

Schultheiss, O. C., and Pang, J. S. (2007). Measuring implicit motives. In R. W. Robins, R. C. Fraley, & R. Krueger (Eds.), *Handbook of research methods in personality psychology* (pp. 322–344). New York: Guilford Press.

Schultheiss, O. C., and Schultheiss, M. (2014). Implicit motive profile analysis: An if-then contingency approach to the picture-story exercise. *Social & Personality Psychology Compass, 8*(1), 1–16.

Schultheiss, O. C., Wiemers, U. S., and Wolf, O. T. (2014). Implicit need for achievement predicts attenuated cortisol responses to difficult tasks. *Journal of Research in Personality, 48,* 84–92.

Schumann, K., Zaki, J., and Dweck, C. S. (2014). Addressing the empathy deficit: Beliefs about the malleability of empathy predict effortful responses when empathy is challenging. *Journal of Personality and Social Psychology, 107*(3), 475–493.

Schutzwohl, A. (2008). Relief over the disconfirmation of the prospect of sexual and emotional infidelity. *Personality and Individual Differences, 44,* 668–678.

Schutzwohl, A., Fuchs, A., McKibbin, W. F., and Shackelford, T. K. (2009). How willing are you to accept sexual requests from slightly unattractive to exceptionally attractive imagined requestors? *Human Nature, 20,* 282–293.

Schutzwohl, A., and Koch, S. (2004). Sex differences in jealousy: The recall of cues to sexual and emotional infidelity in adaptively relevant and irrelevant context conditions. *Evolution and Human Behavior, 25,* 249–257.

Schuyler, B. S., Kral, T. A., Jacquart, J., Burghy, C. A., Weng, H. Y., Perlman, D. M., and ... Davidson, R. J. (2014). Temporal dynamics of emotional responding: Amygdala recovery predicts emotional traits. *Social Cognitive and Affective Neuroscience, 9*(2), 176–181.

Schwartz, C. E., Wright, C. I., Shin, L. M., Kagan, J., and Rauch, S. L. (2003). Inhibited and uninhibited infants "grown up": Adult amygdalar response to novelty. *Science, 300,* 1952–1953.

Schwartz, S. H., and Rubel, T. (2005). Sex differences in value priorities: Cross-cultural and multimethod studies. *Journal of Personality and Social Psychology, 89,* 1010–1028.

Schwarzer, R., and Luszczynska, A. (2013). Stressful life events. In A. M. Nezu, C. M. Nezu, P. A. Geller, and I. B. Weiner (Eds.), *Handbook of psychology, vol. 9: Health psychology* (2nd ed., pp. 29–56). Hoboken, NJ: John Wiley & Sons.

Schwerdtfeger, A. (2007). Individual differences in auditory, pain, and motor stimulation: The case of augmenting/reducing. *Journal of Individual Differences, 28,* 165–177.

Schwerdtfeger, A., and Baltissen, R. (1999). Augmenters vs. reducers: Cortical and autonomic reactivity in response to increasing stimulus intensity. *Zeitschrift fuer Differentielle und Diagnostische Psychologie, 20,* 247–262.

Schwerdtfeger, A., and Baltissen, R. (2002). Augmenting-reducing paradox lost? A test of Davis et al.'s (1983) hypothesis. *Personality and Individual Differences, 32,* 257–271.

Schwerdtfeger, A., Heims, R., and Heer, J. (2010). Digit ratio (2D:4D) is associated with traffic violations for male frequent car drivers. *Accident Analysis and Prevention, 42,* 269–274.

Scott, W. A., and Johnson, R. C. (1972). Comparative validities of direct and indirect personality tests. *Journal of Consulting and Clinical Psychology, 38,* 301–318.

Sear, R., and Mace, R. (2008). Who keeps children alive? A review of the effects of kin on child survival. *Evolution and Human Behavior, 29,* 1–18.

Seara-Cardoso, A., and Viding, E. (2015). Functional neuroscience of psychopathic personality in adults. *Journal of Personality, 83*(6), 723–737.

Segal, N. L. (1999). *Entwined lives: Twins and what they tell us about human behavior.* New York: Plume.

Seidlitz, L., and Diener, E. (1993). Review of the Satisfaction with Life Scale. *Psychological Assessment, 5,* 164–172.

Selfhout, M., Burk, W., Branje, S., Denissen, J., van Aken, M., and Meeus, W. (2010). Emerging late adolescent friendship networks and Big Five personality traits:

A social network approach. *Journal of Personality, 78,* 509–538.

Seligman, M., and Hager, J. (1972). *Biological boundaries of learning.* New York: Appleton-Century-Crofts.

Seligman, M. E. P. (1992). *Helplessness: On depression, development, and death.* New York: Freeman.

Seligman, M. E. P. (1994). *What you can change and what you can't.* New York: Knopf.

Seligman, M.E.P. (2002). Positive psychology, positive prevention, and positive therapy. In C. R. Snyder and S. J. Lopez (Eds.), *Handbook of positive psychology* (pp. 3–9) London: Oxford University Press.

Seligman, M.E.P., and Csikszentmihalyi, M. (2000). Positive psychology: An introduction. *American Psychologist, 55,* 5–14.

Seligman, M.E.P., and Peterson, C. (2003). Positive clinical psychology. In L. G. Aspinwall and U. M. Staudinger (Eds.), *A psychology of human strengths: Fundamental questions and future directions for a positive psychology* (pp. 305–317). Washington, DC: American Psychological Association.

Sell, A., Hone, L. S. E., and Pound, N. (2012). The importance of physical strength to human males. *Human Nature, 23,* 30–44.

Sell, A., Tooby, J., and Cosmides, L. (2009). Formidability and the logic of human anger. *Proceedings of the National Academy of Science, 106,* 15073–15078.

Selye, H. (1976). *The stress of life.* New York: McGraw-Hill.

Senf, K., and Liau, A. K. (2013). The effects of positive interventions on happiness and depressive symptoms, with an examination of personality as a moderator. *Journal of Happiness Studies, 14*(2), 591–612.

Servaas, M. N., van der Velde, J., Costafreda, S. G., Horton, P., Ormel, J., Riese, H., and Aleman, A. (2013). Neuroticism and the brain: A quantitative meta-analysis of neuroimaging studies investigating emotion processing. *Neuroscience and Biobehavioral Reviews, 37*(8), 1518–1529.

Shackelford, T. K., Buss, D. M., and Bennett, K. (2002). Forgiveness or breakup: Sex differences in responses to a partner's infidelity. *Cognition and Emotion, 16,* 299–307.

Shackelford, T. K., Goetz, A., Buss, D. M., Euler, H. A., and Hoier, S. (2005). When we hurt the ones we love: Predicting violence against women from men's mate retention. *Personal Relationships, 12,* 447–463.

Shackelford, T. K., Voracek, M., Schmitt, D. P., Buss, D. M., Weekes-Shackelford, V. A., and Michalski, R. L. (2004).

Romantic jealousy in early adulthood and in later life. *Human Nature, 15,* 59–76.

Shafer, A. B. (2001). The Big Five and sexuality trait terms as predictors of relationships and sex. *Journal of Research in Personality, 35,* 313–338.

Shakur, S. (1994). *Monster: The autobiography of an L.A. gang member.* New York: Penguin.

Shatz, S. M. (2008). IQ and fertility: A cross-national study. *Intelligence, 36,* 109–111.

Sheldon, K. M., and Kasser, T. (2001). Getting older, getting better? Personal strivings and psychological maturity across the life span. *Developmental Psychology, 37,* 491–501.

Sheppard, K. E., and Boon, S. D. (2012). Predicting appraisals of romantic revenge: The roles of honest-humility, agreeableness, and vengefulness. *Personality and Individual Differences, 52,* 128–132.

Sheppard, L. D., and Vernon, P. A. (2008). Intelligence and speed of information-processing. *Personality and Individual Differences, 44,* 535–551.

Shiner, R. L., Masten, A. S., and Roberts, J. M. (2003). Childhood personality foreshadows adult personality and life outcomes two decades later. *Journal of Personality, 71,* 1145–1170.

Shiner, R. L., Masten, A. S., and Tellegen, A. (2002). A developmental perspective on personality in emerging adulthood: Childhood antecedents and concurrent adaptation. *Journal of Personality and Social Psychology, 83,* 5, 1165–1177.

Shneidman, E. S. (1981). *Endeavors in psychology: Selections from the personology of Henry A. Murray.* New York: Harper and Row.

Shoben, E. J. (1957). Toward a concept of the normal personality. *American Psychologist, 12,* 183–189.

Shoda, Y., and Mischel, W. (1996). Toward a unified, intra-individual dynamic conception of personality. *Journal of Research in Personality, 30,* 414–428.

Shoda, Y., Mischel, W., and Wright, J. C. (1994). Intra-individual stability in the organization and patterning of behavior: Incorporating psychological situations into the idiographic analysis of personality. *Journal of Personality and Social Psychology, 67,* 674–687.

Shoda, Y., Wilson, N. L., Chen, J., Gilmore, A. K., and Smith, R. E. (2013). Cognitive-affective processing system analysis of intra-individual dynamics in collaborative therapeutic assessment: Translating basic theory and research into clinical applications. *Journal of Personality, 81*(6), 554–568.

Shoda, Y., Wilson, N. L., Whitsett, D. D., Lee-Dussud, J., and Zayas, V. (2015). The person as a cognitive-affective processing system: Quantitative ideography as an integral component of cumulative science. In M. Mikulincer, P. R. Shaver, M. L. Cooper, R. J. Larsen, M. Mikulincer, P. R. Shaver, ... and R. J. Larsen (Eds.), *APA handbook of personality and social psychology, Volume 4: Personality processes and individual differences* (pp. 491–513). Washington, DC, US: American Psychological Association.

Shultz, J. S. (1993). Situational and dispositional predictions of performance: A test of the hypothesized Machiavellianism X structure interaction among salespersons. *Journal of Applied Social Psychology, 23,* 478–498.

Shweder, R. A. (1991). *Thinking through cultures: Expeditions in cultural psychology.* Cambridge, MA: Harvard University Press.

Shweder, R. A., Mahapatra, M., and Miller, J. G. (1990). Culture and moral development. In J. W. Stigler, R. A. Shweder, and G. Herdt (Eds.), *Cultural psychology: Essays on comparative human development* (pp. 130–204). Cambridge, MA: Cambridge University Press.

Sibley, C. G., Osborne, D., and Duckitt, J. (2012). Personality and political orientation: Meta-analysis and test of a Threat-Constraint Model. *Journal of Research in Personality, 46*(6), 664–677.

Siegel, J. (1997). Augmenting and reducing of visual evoked potentials in high- and low-sensation seeking humans, cats, and rats. *Behavior Genetics, 27,* 557–563.

Siegel, J., and Driscoll, P. (1996). Recent developments in an animal model of visual evoked potential augmenting/reducing and sensation seeking behavior. *Neuropsychobiology, 34,* 130–135.

Siegel, J. M. (1986). The Multidimensional Anger Inventory. *Journal of Personality and Social Psychology, 51,* 191–200.

Sigusch, V., and Schmidt, G. (1971). Lower-class sexuality: Some emotional and social aspects in West German males and females. *Archives of Sexual Behavior, 1,* 29–44.

Sih, A., Mathot, K. J., Moirón, M., Montiglio, P. O., Wolf, M., and Dingemanse, N. J. (2015). Animal personality and state–behaviour feedbacks: A review and guide for empiricists. *Trends in Ecology & Evolution, 30*(1), 50–60.

Silas, F. A. (1984). Fit for the job? Testing grows—gripes too. *American Bar Association Journal,* July, p. 34.

Silverthorne, C. (2001). Leadership effectiveness and personality: A cross-cultural evaluation. *Personality and Individual Differences, 30,* 303–309.

Silvia, P. J., Nusbaum, E. C., and Beaty, R. E. (2014). Blessed are the meek? Honesty–Humility, Agreeableness, and the HEXACO structure of religious beliefs, motives, and values. *Personality and Individual Differences, 66,* 19–23.

Simonton, D. K. (1991). Emergence and realization of genius: The lives and works of 120 classical composers. *Journal of Personality and Social Psychology, 61,* 829–840.

Simpson, J. A., and Gangestad, S. W. (1991). Individual differences in sociosexuality: Evidence for convergent and discriminant validity. *Journal of Personality and Social Psychology, 60,* 870–883.

Simpson, J. A., and Rholes, W. S. (1998). *Attachment theory and close relationships.* New York: Guilford Press.

Simpson, J. A., Rholes, W. S., Orinea, M. M., and Grich, J. (2002). Working models of attachment, support giving, and support seeking in a stressful situation. *Personality and Social Psychology Bulletin, 28,* 598–608.

Singh, D., Vidaurri, M., Zambarano, R. J., and Dabbs, J. M., Jr. (1999). Behavioral, morphological, and hormonal correlates to erotic role identification among lesbian women. *Journal of Personality and Social Psychology, 76,* 1035–1049.

Singh, S. (1978). Achievement motivation and entrepreneurial success: A follow-up study. *Journal of Research in Personality, 12,* 500–503.

Six, B., and Eckes, T. (1991). A closer look at the complex structure of gender stereotypes. *Sex Roles, 24,* 64.

Slatcher, R. B., and Vazire, S. (2009). Effects of global and contextualized personality on relationship satisfaction. *Journal of Research in Personality, 43,* 624–633.

Slutske, W. S., Caspi, A., Moffitt, T. E., and Poulton, R. (2005). Personality and problem gambling. *Archives of General Psychiatry, 62,* 769–775.

Slutske, W. S., Eisen, S. A., True, W. R., Lyons, M. J., Goldberg, J., and Tsuang, M. T. (2005). Common genetic vulnerability for pathological gambling and alcohol dependence in men. *Archives of General Psychiatry, 57,* 666–673.

Smillie, L. D., Cooper, A. J., Wilt, J., and Revelle, W. (2012). Do extraverts get more bang for the buck? Refining the affective-reactivity hypothesis of extraversion. *Journal of Personality and Social Psychology, 103,* 306–326.

Smillie, L. D., and Wacker, J. (2014). Dopaminergic foundations of personality and individual differences. *Frontiers In Human Neuroscience, 8.*

Smillie, L. D., Yeo, G. B., Furnham, A. F., and Jackson, C. J. (2006). Benefits of all work and no play: The relationship

between neuroticism and performance as a function of resource allocation. *Journal of Applied Psychology, 91,* 139–155.

Smith, C. P., and Atkinson, J. W. (1992). *Motivation and personality: Handbook of thematic content analysis.* New York: Cambridge University Press.

Smith, G. M. (1967). Usefulness of peer ratings of personality in educational research. *Educational and Psychological Measurement, 27,* 967–984.

Smith, P., Caputi, P., and Crittenden, N. (2013). Measuring optimism in organizations: Development of a workplace explanatory style questionnaire. *Journal of Happiness Studies, 14*(2), 415–432.

Smith, R. E., and Shoda, Y. (2009). Personality as a cognitive-affective processing system. In P. J. Corr and G. Matthews (Eds.), *The Cambridge handbook of personality psychology* (pp. 473–487). New York, NY: Cambridge University Press.

Smith, R. E., Shoda, Y., Cumming, S .P., and Smoll, F. L. (2009). Behavioral signatures at the ballpark: Intraindividual consistency of adults' situation-behavior patterns and their interpersonal consequences. *Journal of Research in Personality, 43,* 187–195.

Smith, S. M., Nichols, T. E., Vidaurre, D., Winkler, A. M., Behrens, T. J., Glasser, M. F., and ... Miller, K. L. (2015). A positive-negative mode of population covariation links brain connectivity, demographics and behavior. *Nature Neuroscience, 18*(11), 1565–1567.

Smith, T. W., Williams, P. G., and Segerstrom, S. C. (2015). Personality and physical health. In L. Cooper and R. J. Larsen (Eds.), *Handbook of personality and social psychology: Personality processes and individual differences.* Washington, DC: American Psychological Association.

Smith, T. W. (1979). Happiness: Time trends, seasonal variations, intersurvey differences, and other mysteries. *Social Psychology Quarterly, 42,* 18–30.

Smith, T. W. (2006). Personality as risk and resilience in physical health. *Current Directions in Psychological Science, 15,* 227–231.

Smith, T. W., Pope, M. K., Rhodewalt, F., and Poulton, J. L. (1989). Optimism, neuroticism, coping, and symptom reports: An alternative interpretation of the Life Orientation Test. *Journal of Personality and Social Psychology, 56,* 640–648.

Smith, T. W., and Spiro, A. III. (2002). Personality, health, and aging: Prolegomenon for the next generation. *Journal of Research in Personality, 36,* 363–394.

Smith, T. W., Williams, P. G., and Segerstrom, S. C. (2015). Personality and physical health. In M. Mikulincer,

P. R. Shaver, M. L. Cooper, R. J. Larsen, M. Mikulincer, P. R. Shaver, . . . R. J. Larsen (Eds.), *APA handbook of personality and social psychology, Volume 4: Personality processes and individual differences* (pp. 639–661). Washington, DC, US: American Psychological Association.

Smits, I.A.M., Dolan, C. V., Vorst, H.C.M., Wicherts, J. M., and Timmerman, M. E. (2011). Cohort differences in Big Five personality factors over a period of 25 years. *Journal of Personality and Social Psychology, 100,* 1124–1138.

Snitz, B. E., Weissfeld, L. A., Cohen, A. D., Lopez, O. L., Nebes, R. D., Aizenstein, H. J., and . . . Klunk, W. E. (2015). Subjective cognitive complaints, personality and brain amyloid-beta in cognitively normal older adults. *The American Journal of Geriatric Psychiatry, 23*(9), 985–993.

Snyder, J. K., Fessler, D.M.T., Tiokhin, L., Frederick, D. A., Lee, S. W., and Navarrete, C. D. (2011). Trade-offs in a dangerous world: Women's fear of crime predicts preferences for aggressive and formidable mates. *Evolution and Human Behavior, 32,* 127–137.

Snyder, M. (1983). The influence of individuals on situations: Implications for understanding the links between personality and social behavior. *Journal of Personality, 51,* 497–516.

Snyder, M., and Cantor, N. (1998). Understanding personality and social behavior: A functionalist strategy. In D. T. Gilbert, S. T. Fiske, and G. Lindzey (Eds.), *The handbook of social psychology* (vol. 1, 4th ed., pp. 635–679). Boston: McGraw-Hill.

Snyder, M., and Gangestad, S. (1982). Choosing social situations: Two investigations of self-monitoring processes. *Journal of Personality and Social Psychology, 43,* 123–135.

Sokolowski, K., Schmalt, H., Langens, T. A., and Puca, R. M. (2000). Assessing achievement, affiliation, and power motives all at once: The Multi-Motive Grid (MMG). *Journal of Personality Assessment, 74,* 126–145.

Soloff, P. H., Lis, J. A., Kelly, T., and Cornelius, J. (1994). Risk factors for suicidal behavior in borderline personality disorder. *American Journal of Psychiatry, 151,* 1316–1323.

Solomon, B. C., and Jackson, J. J. (2014). Why do personality traits predict divorce? Multiple pathways through satisfaction. *Journal of Personality and Social Psychology, 106*(6), 978–996.

Solomon, Z., Berger, R., and Ginzburg, K. (2007). Resilience of Israeli body handlers: Implications of repressive coping style. *Traumatology, 13*(4), 64–74.

Somer, O., and Goldberg, L. R. (1999). The structure of Turkish trait-descriptive adjectives. *Journal of Personality and Social Psychology, 76,* 431–450.

Sorokowski, P., Sorokowska, A., Oleszkiewicz, A., Frackowiak, T., Huk, A., and Pisanski, K. (2015). Selfie posting behaviors are associated with narcissism among men. *Personality and Individual Differences, 85,* 123–127.

South, S. C., and Krueger, R. F. (2008). An interactionist perspective on genetic and environmental contributions to personality. *Social and Personality Psychology Compass, 2,* 929–948.

South, S. C., Krueger, R. F., Elkins, I. J., Iacono, W. G., and McGue, M. (2016). Romantic relationship satisfaction moderates the etiology of adult personality. *Behavior Genetics, 46*(1), 124–142.

South, S. C., Krueger, R. F., Johnson, W., and Iacono, W. G. (2008). Adolescent personality moderates genetic and environmental influences on relationships with parents. *Journal of Personality and Social Psychology, 94,* 899–912.

South, S. C., Oltmanns, T. F., and Turkheimer, E. (2003). Personality and the derogation of others: Descriptions based on self- and peer report. *Journal of Research in Personality, 37,* 16–33.

Sowislo, J. F., and Orth, U. (2013). Does low self-esteem predict depression and anxiety? A meta-analysis of longitudinal studies. *Psychological Bulletin, 139,* 213–240.

Souza, A. L., Conroy-Beam, D., and Buss, D. M. (2016). Mate preferences in Brazil: Evolved desires and cultural evolution over three decades. *Personality and Individual Differences, 95,* 45–49.

Spangler, W. D. (1992). Validity of questionnaire and TAT measures of need for achievement: Two meta-analyses. *Psychological Bulletin, 112,* 140–154.

Spanos, N. P., and McLean, J. (1986). Hypnotically created false reports do not demonstrate pseudomemories. *British Journal of Experimental and Clinical Hypnosis, 3,* 167–171.

Spearman, C. (1910). Correlation calculated from faulty data. *British Journal of Psychology, 3,* 271–295.

Specht, J., Bleidorn, W., Denissen, J. J., Hennecke, M., Hutteman, R., Kandler, C., . . . and Zimmermann, J. (2014). What drives adult personality development? A comparison of theoretical perspectives and empirical evidence. *European Journal of Personality, 28,* 216–230.

Specht, J., Egloff, B., and Schmukle, S. C. (2011). Stability and change of personality across the life course: The impact of age and major life events on mean-level and rank-order stability of the Big Five. *Journal of Personality and Social Psychology, 101,* 862–882.

Spence, J. T., Helmreich, R., and Stapp, J. (1974). The Personal Attributes Questionnaire: A measure of sex-role stereotypes and masculinity and femininity. *Journal Supplement Abstract Service Catalog of Selected Documents in Psychology, 4,* 42 (No. 617).

Spengler, M., Lüdtke, O., Martin, R., and Brunner, M. (2013). Personality is related to educational outcomes in late adolescence: Evidence from two large-scale achievement studies. *Journal of Research in Personality, 47*(5), 613–625.

Spies, R. A., and Plake, B. S. (2005). *The Sixteenth Mental Measurements Yearbook.* Lincoln, NE: Buros Institute of Mental Measurements.

Spilker, B., and Callaway, E. (1969). Augmenting and reducing in averaged visual evoked responses to sine wave light. *Psychophysiology, 6,* 49–57.

Spinath, F. M., and O'Connor, T. G. (2003). A behavioral genetic study of the overlap between personality and parenting. *Journal of Personality, 71, 5,* 785–808.

Spinath, F. M., Wolf, H., Angleitner, A., Borkenau, P., and Riemann, R. (2002). Genetic and environmental influences on objectively assessed activity in adults. *Personality and Individual Differences, 33,* 633–645.

Spotts, E. L., Lichtenstein, P., Pedersen, N., Neiderhiser, J. M., Hansson, K., Cederblad, M., and Reiss, D. (2005). Personality and Marital Satisfaction: A Behavioural Genetic Analysis. *European Journal of Personality, 19,* 205–227.

Spotts, E. L., Neiderhiser, J. M., Towers, H., Hansson, K., Lichtenstein, P., Cederblad, M., and Pedersen, N. L. (2004). Genetic and environmental influences on marital relationships. *Journal of Family Psychology, 18,* 107–119.

Srivastava, S., John, O. P., Gosling, S. D., and Potter, J. (2003). Development of personality in early and middle adulthood: Set like plaster or persistent change? *Journal of Personality and Social Psychology, 84, 5,* 1041–1053.

Stake, J. E., Huff, L., and Zand, D. (1995). Trait self-esteem, positive and negative events, and event specific shifts in self-evaluation and affect. *Journal of Research in Personality, 29,* 223–241.

Steel, P., and Ones, D. S. (2002). Personality and happiness: A national-level analysis. *Journal of Personality and Social Psychology, 83, 3,* 767–781.

Steger, M. F., Hicks, B. M., Kashdan, T. B., Krueger, R. F., and Bouchard, T. J., Jr. (2007). Genetic and environmental influences on the positive traits of the values in action classification, and biometric covariance with normal personality. *Journal of Research in Personality, 41,* 524–539.

Stein, A. A. (1976). Conflict and cohesion: A review of the literature. *Journal of Conflict Resolution, 20,* 143–172.

Steinberg, L., Albert, D., Cauffman, E., Banich, M., Graham, S., and Woolard, J. (2008). Age differences in sensation seeking and impulsivity as indexed by behavior and self-report: evidence for a dual systems model. *Developmental Psychology, 44*(6), 1764–1778.

Steiner, A. W., and Coan, J. A. (2011). Prefrontal asymmetry predicts affect, but not beliefs about affect. *Biological Psychology, 88*(1), 65–71.

Steiner, M., Allemand, M., and McCullough, M. E. (2012). Do agreeableness and neuroticism explain age differences in the tendency to forgive others? *Personality and Social Psychology Bulletin, 38,* 441–453.

Stelmack, R. M. (1990). Biological basis of extraversion: Psychophysiological evidence. *Journal of Personality, 58,* 293–311.

Stelmack, R. M., and Stalkas, A. (1991). Galen and the humour theory of temperament. *Personality and Individual Differences, 12,* 255–263.

Sternberg, R. J. (1985). *Beyond IQ: A triarchic theory of human intelligence.* New York: Cambridge University Press.

Stevenson, R. J., Hodgson, D., Oaten, M. J., Moussavi, M., Langberg, R., Case, T. I., and Barouei, J. (2012). Disgust elevates core body temperature and up-regulates certain oral immune markers. *Brain, Behavior, and Immunity, 26*(7), 1160–1168.

Stewart, M. E., Donaghey, C., Deary, I. J., and Ebmeier, K. P. (2008). Suicidal thoughts in young people: Their frequency and relationships with personality factors. *Personality and Individual Differences, 44,* 809–820.

Stewart, M. E., Ebmeier, K. P., and Deary, I. J. (2005). Personality correlates of happiness and sadness: EPQ-R and TPQ compared. *Personality and Individual Differences, 38,* 1085–1096.

Stocker, S. (1997). Don't be shy: Advice for becoming more outgoing. *Prevention,* p. 96.

Stoeber, J., Otto, K., and Dalbert, C. (2009). Perfectionism and the Big Five: Conscientiousness predicts longitudinal increases in self-oriented perfectionism. *Personality and Individual Differences, 47,* 363–368.

Stopfer, J. M., Egloff, B., Nestler, S., and Back, M. D. (2013). Being popular in online social networks: How agentic, communal, and creativity traits relate to judgments of status and liking. *Journal of Research in Personality, 47*(5), 592–598.

Strauss, K., Griffin, M. A., and Parker, S. K. (2012). Future work selves: How salient hoped-for identities motivate proactive career behaviors. *Journal of Applied Psychology, 97,* 580–598.

Strelan, P. (2007). Who forgives others, themselves, and situations? The roles of narcissism, guilt, self-esteem, and agreeableness. *Personality and Individual Differences, 42,* 259–269.

Stroop, J. R. (1935). Studies of interference in serial verbal reactions. *Journal of Experimental Psychology, 18,* 643–661.

Strout, S. L., Laird, J. D., Shafer, A., and Thompson, N. S. (2005). The effect of vividness of experience on sex differences in jealousy. *Evolutionary Psychology, 3,* 263–274.

Stucke, T. S., and Baumeister, R. F. (2006). Ego depletion and aggressive behavior: Is the inhibition of aggression a limited resource? *European Journal of Social Psychology, 36,* 1–13.

Su, R., Rounds, J., and Armstrong, P. I. (2009). Men and things, women and people: A meta-analysis of sex differences in interests. *Psychological Bulletin, 135,* 859–884.

Suls, J., and Wan, C. K. (1989). The relation between Type A behavior and chronic emotional distress: A meta-analysis. *Journal of Personality and Social Psychology, 57,* 503–512.

Suls, J., Wan, C. K., and Costa, P. T., Jr. (1996). Relationship of trait anger to resting blood pressure: A meta-analysis. *Health Psychology, 14,* 444–456.

Surtees, P., Wainwright, N., Khaw, K. T., Luben, R., Brayne, C., and Day, N. (2003). Inflammatory dispositions: A population-based study of the association between hostility and peripheral leukocyte counts. *Personality and Individual Differences, 35,* 1271–1284.

Sutin, A. R., Ferrucci, L., Zonderman, A. B., and Terracciano, A. (2011). Personality and obesity across the adult life span. *Journal of Personality and Social Psychology, 101,* 579–592.

Sutton, S. K. (2002). Incentive and threat reactivity: Relations with anterior cortical activity. In D. Cervone and W. Mischel (Eds.), *Advances in personality science* (pp. 127–150). New York: Guilford Press.

Sverko, B., and Fabulic, L. (1985). Stability of morningness-eveningness: Retest changes after seven years. *Revija za Psihologiju, 15,* 71–78.

Swanbrow, D. (1989, August). The paradox of happiness. *Psychology Today,* pp. 37–39.

Swann, W. B., Langlois, J. H., and Gilbert, L. A. (Eds.). (1999). *Sexism and stereotypes in modern society: The gender science of Janet Taylor Spence.* Washington, DC: American Psychological Association.

Swann, W. R., Jr., and Selye, C. (2005). Personality psychology's comeback and its emerging symbiosis with social psychology. *Personality and Social Psychology Bulletin, 31,* 155–165.

Symons, D. (1979). *The evolution of human sexuality.* New York: Oxford.

Symons, D. (1992). On the use and misuse of Darwinism in the study of human behavior. In J. Barkow, L. Cosmides, and J. Tooby (Eds.), *The adapted mind* (pp. 137–159). New York: Oxford University Press.

Szepsenwol, O., Simpson, J. A., Griskevicius, V., and Raby, K. L. (2015). The effect of unpredictable early childhood environments on parenting in adulthood. *Journal of Personality and Social Psychology, 109*(6), 1045–1067.

Tackett, J. L., Krueger, R. F., Iacono, W. G., and McGue, M. (2008). Personality in middle childhood: A hierarchical structure and longitudinal connections with personality in late adolescence. *Journal of Research in Personality, 42,* 1456–1462.

Tamir, M., Robinson, M. D., and Solberg, E. C. (2006). You may worry, but can you recognize threats when you see them? Neuroticism, threat identification, and negative affect. *Journal of Personality, 74,* 1481–1506.

Tamir, Y., and Nadler, A. (2007). The role of personality in social identity: Effects of field-dependence and context on reactions to threat to group distinctiveness. *Journal of Personality, 75,* 927–954.

Tarantolo, D., Lamptev, P. R., and Moodie, R. (1999). The global HIV/AIDS pandemic: Trends and patterns. In L. Gibney and R. J. DiClemente (Eds.), *Preventing HIV in developing countries: Biomedical and behavioral approaches* (pp. 9–41). New York: Kluwer Academic/Plenum Publishers.

Tate, J. C., and Shelton, B. L. (2008). Personality correlates of tattooing and body piercing in a college sample: The kids are alright. *Personality and Individual Differences, 45,* 281–285.

Taylor, S. (1991). *Health psychology* (2nd ed.). New York: McGraw-Hill.

Taylor, S. E. (1989). *Positive illusions: Self-deception and the healthy mind.* New York: Basic Books.

Taylor, S. E., Kemeny, M. E., Reed, G. M., Bower, J. E., and Gruenewald, T. L. (2000). Psychological resources, positive illusions, and health. *American Psychologist, 55,* 99–109.

Teasdale, T. W., and Owen, D. R. (2008). Secular declines in cognitive test scores: A reversal of the Flynn effect. *Intelligence, 36,* 121–126.

Tedeschi, R. G., Park, C. L., and Calhoun, L. (1998). Posttraumatic growth: Conceptual issues. In R. G. Tedeschi and P. L. Crystal (Eds.), *Posttraumatic growth:*

Positive changes in the aftermath of crisis (pp. 1–22). Mahwah, NJ: Erlbaum.

Telama, R., Yang, X., Viikari, J., Välimäki, I., Wanne, O., and Raitakari, O. (2005). Physical activity from childhood to adulthood: A 21-year tracking study. *American Journal of Preventive Medicine, 28*(3), 267–273.

Tellegen, A., Lykken, D. T., Bouchard, T. J., Wilcox, K., Segal, N., and Rich, S. (1988). Personality similarity in twins reared apart and together. *Journal of Personality and Social Psychology, 54,* 1031–1039.

Templer, D. I. (2008). Correlational and factor analytic support for Rushton's differential K life history theory. *Personality and Individual Differences, 45,* 440–444.

Terman, L. M. (1938). *Psychological factors in marital happiness.* New York: McGraw-Hill.

Theakston, J. A., Stewart, S. H., Dawson, M. Y., Knowlden-Loewen, S. A. B., and Lehman, D. R. (2004). Big Five personality domains predict drinking motives. *Personality and Individual Differences, 37,* 971–984.

Thielmann, I., and Hilbig, B. E. (2014). Trust in me, trust in you: A social projection account of the link between personality, cooperativeness, and trustworthiness expectations. *Journal of Research in Personality, 50,* 61–65.

Thomas, A. K., Bulevich, J. B., and Loftus, E. F. (2003). Exploring the role of repetition and sensory elaboration in the imagination inflation effect. *Memory and Cognition, 31,* 630–640.

Thompson, R. A. (1991). Emotional regulation and emotional development. *Educational Psychology Review, 3,* 269–307.

Thorndike, E. L. (1911). *Individuality.* Boston: Houghton Mifflin.

Thornhill, R., and Gangestad, S. W. (2008). *The evolutionary biology of human female sexuality.* New York: Oxford University Press.

Thrash, T. M., and Elliot, A. J. (2002). Implicit and self-attributed achievement motives: Concordance and predictive validity. *Journal of Personality, 70,* 729–755.

Thrash, T. M., Elliot, A. J., and Schultheiss, O. C. (2007). Methodological and dispositional predictors of congruence between implicit and explicit need for achievement. *Personality and Social Psychology Bulletin, 33,* 961–974.

Tice, D. M. (1991). Esteem protection or enhancement? Self-handicapping motives and attributions differ by trait self-esteem. *Journal of Personality and Social Psychology, 60,* 711–725.

Tice, D. M. (1993). The social motivations of people with low self-esteem. In R. F.

Baumeister (Ed.), *Self-esteem: The puzzle of low self-regard* (pp. 37–53). New York: Plenum Press.

Tice, D. M., and Baumeister, R. F. (1990). Self-esteem, self-handicapping, and self-presentation: The strategy of inadequate practice. *Journal of Personality, 58,* 443–464.

Tice, D. M., and Bratslavsky, E. (2000). Giving in to feel good: The place of emotion regulation in the context of general self-control. *Psychological Inquiry, 11,* 149–159.

Tolea, M. I., Terracciano, A., Simonsick, E. M., Metter, E. J., Costa, P. T., Jr., and Ferrucci, L. (2012). Associations between personality traits, physical activity level, and muscle strength. *Journal of Research in Personality, 46,* 264–270.

Tomarken, A. J., Davidson, R. J., and Henriques, J. B. (1990). Resting frontal brain asymmetry predicts affective responses to films. *Journal of Personality and Social Psychology, 59,* 791–801.

Tomkins, S. S. (2008). *Affect, imagery, consciousness: The complete edition* (vols. 1–4). New York: Springer.

Tooby, J., and Cosmides, L. (1990). On the universality of human nature and the uniqueness of the individual: The role of genetics and adaptation. *Journal of Personality, 58,* 17–68.

Tooby, J., and Cosmides, L. (1992). Psychological foundations of culture. In J. Barkow, L. Cosmides, and J. Tooby (Eds.), *The adapted mind* (pp. 19–136). New York: Oxford University Press.

Tooke, J., and Camie, L. (1991). Patterns of deception in intersexual and intrasexual mating strategies. *Ethology and Sociobiology, 12,* 345–364.

Tremblay, R. E., Pihl, R. O., Vitaro, F., and Dobkin, P. L. (1994). Predicting early onset of male antisocial behavior from preschool behavior. *Archives of General Psychiatry, 51,* 732–739.

Trinkaus, E., and Zimmerman, M. R. (1982). Trauma among the Shanidar Neanderthals. *American Journal of Physical Anthropology, 57,* 61–76.

Trivers, R. (1985). *Social evolution.* Menlo Park, CA: Benjamin/Cummings.

Trivers, R. L. (1972). Parental investment and sexual selection. In B. Campbell (Ed.), *Sexual selection and the descent of man: 1871–1971* (pp. 136–179). Chicago: Aldine.

Trobst, K. K., Herbst, J. H., Masters, H. L., and Costa, P. T. (2002). Personality pathways to unsafe sex: Personality, condom use, and HIV risk behaviors. *Journal of Research in Personality, 36,* 117–133.

Trull, T. J. (2012). The Five-Factor Model of personality disorder and DSM-5. *Journal of Personality, 80*(6), 1697–1720.

Trull, J. J., and McCrae, R. M. (2002). A five-factor perspective on personality disorder research. In P. T. Costa, Jr., and T. A. Widiger (Eds.), *Personality disorders and the five factor model of personality* (2nd ed., pp. 45–58). Washington, DC: American Psychological Association.

Trzesniewski, K. H., Donnellan, M. B., and Robins, R. W. (2003). Stability of self-esteem across the life span. *Journal of Personality and Social Psychology, 84, 1,* 205–220.

Tsai, A., Loftus, E., and Polage, D. (2000). Current directions in false-memory research. In D. F. Bjorklund (Ed.), *False-memory creation in children and adults: Theory, research, and implications* (pp. 31–44). Mahwah, NJ: Erlbaum.

Tuerlinckz, F., De Boeck, P., and Lens, W. (2002). Measuring needs with the Thematic Apperception Test: A psychometric study. *Journal of Personality and Social Psychology, 82,* 448–461.

Tupes, E. C., and Christal, R. C. (1961). *Recurrent personality factors based on trait ratings.* USAF ASD Technical Report, No. 61–97, U.S. Air Force, Lackland Air Force Base, TX.

Turiano, N. A., Chapman, B. P., Gruenewald, T. L., and Mroczek, D. K. (2015). Personality and the leading behavioral contributors of mortality. *Health Psychology, 34*(1), 51–60.

Turiano, N. A., Whiteman, S. D., Hampson, S. E., Roberts, B. W., and Mroczek, D. K. (2012). Personality and substance use in midlife: Conscientiousness as a moderator and the effects of trait change. *Journal of Research in Personality, 46,* 295–305.

Turkheimer, E., Pettersson, E., and Horn, E. E. (2014). A phenotypic null hypothesis for the genetics of personality. *Annual Review of Psychology, 65,* 515–540.

Twenge, J. M. (2000). The age of anxiety? Birth cohort change in anxiety and neuroticism, 1952–1993. *Journal of Personality and Social Psychology, 79,* 1007–1021.

Twenge, J. M. (2001a). Changes in women's assertiveness in response to status and roles: A cross-temporal meta-analysis, 1931–1993. *Journal of Personality and Social Psychology, 81,* 133–145.

Twenge, J. M. (2001b). Birth cohort changes in extraversion: A cross-temporal meta-analysis, 1966–1993. *Personality and Individual Differences, 30,* 735–748.

Twenge, J. M., Konrath, S., Foster, J. D., Campbell, W. K., and Bushman, B. J. (2008). Egos inflating over time: A cross-temporal meta-analysis of the Narcissistic Personality Inventory. *Journal of Personality, 76,* 875–902.

Tybur, J. M., & de Vries, R. E. (2013). Disgust sensitivity and the HEXACO model of personality. *Personality and Individual Differences, 55*(6), 660–665.

Tybur, J. M., Lieberman, D., and Griskevicius, V. (2009). Microbes, mating, and morality: Individual differences in three functional domains of disgust. *Journal of Personality and Social Psychology, 97*(1), 103–122.

Udry, J. R., and Chantala, K. (2004). Masculinity-femininity guides sexual union formation in adolescence. *Personality and Social Psychology Bulletin, 30,* 44–55.

Uher, R., Caspi, A., Houts, R., Sugden, K., Williams, B., Poulton, R., and Moffitt, T. E. (2011). Serotonin transporter gene moderates childhood maltreatment's effects on persistent but not single-episode depression: Replications and implications for resolving inconsistent results. *Journal of Affective Disorders, 135,* 55–65.

U.S. Department of Health and Human Services, Administration on Children, Youth and Families. (2008). *Child Maltreatment 2006.* Washington, DC: U.S. Government Printing Office.

U.S. News & World Report, September 29, 2003.

Vaidya, J. G., Gray, E. K., Gaig, J. R., Mroczek, D. K., and Watson, D. (2008). Differential stability and individual growth trajectories of Big Five and affective traits during young adulthood. *Journal of Personality, 76,* 267–304.

Vaidya, J. G., Gray, E. K., Haig, J., and Watson, D. (2002). On the temporal stability of personality: Evidence for differential stability and the role of life experiences. *Journal of Personality and Social Psychology, 83, 6,* 1469–1484.

Vaillant, G. E. (1977). *Adaptation to life.* Boston: Little Brown.

Vaillant, G. E. (1994). Ego mechanisms of defense and personality psychopathology. *Journal of Abnormal Psychology, 103,* 44–50.

Valentova, J. V., Štěrbová, Z., Bártová, K., and Varella, M. A. C. (2016). Personality of ideal and actual romantic partners among heterosexual and non-heterosexual men and women: A cross-cultural study. *Personality and Individual Differences, 101,* 160–166.

van Anders, S. M. (2012). Testosterone and sexual desire in healthy women and men. *Archives of Sexual Behavior, 41,* 1471–1484.

Van Beijsterveldt, C.E.M., Bartels, M., Hudziak, J. J., and Boomsma, D. I. (2003). Causes of stability of aggression from early childhood to adolescence: A longitudinal genetic analysis of Dutch twins. *Behavior Genetics, 33,* 591–605.

Van Den Berg, S. M., de Moor, M. H., McGue, M., Pettersson, E., Terracciano, A., Verweij, K. J., ... & Hansell, N. K. (2014). Harmonization of Neuroticism and Extraversion phenotypes across inventories and cohorts in the Genetics of Personality Consortium: an application of Item Response Theory. *Behavior genetics, 44*(4), 295–313.

van Den Berg, S. M., de Moor, M. H., Verweij, K. J., Krueger, R. F., Luciano, M., Vasquez, A. A., ... & Gordon, S. D. (2016). Meta-analysis of Genome-Wide Association Studies for Extraversion: Findings from the Genetics of Personality Consortium. *Behavior genetics, 46*(2), 170–182.

Van Eck, R. N., Fu, H., and Drechsel, P. J. (2015). Can simulator immersion change cognitive style? Results from a cross-sectional study of field-dependence–independence in air traffic control students. *Journal of Computing in Higher Education, 27*(3), 196–214.

Van der Linden, D., Figueredo, A. J., de Leeuw, R. N. H., Scholte, R. J. J., and Engels, R. C. M. E. (2012). The general factor of personality (GFP) and parental support: Testing a prediction from Life History Theory. *Evolution and Human Behavior, 33,* 537–546.

van Scheppingen, M. A., Jackson, J. J., Specht, J., Hutteman, R., Denissen, J. J., and Bleidorn, W. (2016). Personality trait development during the transition to parenthood a test of social investment theory. *Social Psychological and Personality Science, 7*(5), 452–462.

Vando, A. (1974). The development of the R-A scale: A paper-and-pencil measure of pain tolerance. *Personality and Social Psychology Bulletin, 1,* 28–29.

Vazire, S. (2010). Who knows what about a person? The self-other knowledge asymmetry (SOKA) model. *Journal of Personality and social Psychology, 98,* 281–300.

Vazire, S., and Gosling, S. D. (2003). The role of animal research in bridging psychology and biology. *American Psychologist, 58,* 407–408.

Vazire, S., and Mehl, M. R. (2008). Knowing me, knowing you: The accuracy and unique predictive validity of self and other ratings of daily behavior. *Journal of Personality and Social Psychology, 95,* 1207–1216.

Vazire, S., Naumann, L. P., Rentfrow, P. J., and Gosling, S. D. (2008). Portrait of a narcissist: Manifestations of narcissism in physical appearance. *Journal of Research in Personality, 42,* 1439–1447.

Veenhoven, R. (1988). The utility of happiness. *Social Indicators Research, 20,* 333–354.

Veenhoven, R. (1991a). Questions on happiness: Classical topics, modern answers, blind spots. In F. Strack and M. Argyle (Eds.), *Subjective well-being: An interdisciplinary perspective* (pp. 7–26). Oxford, England: Pergamon Press.

Veenhoven, R. (1991b). Is happiness relative? *Social Indicators Research, 24,* 1–34.

Vernon, P., Villani, V. C., Vickers, L. C., and Harris, J. A. (2008). A behavioral genetic investigation of the Dark Triad and the Big 5. *Personality and Individual Differences, 44,* 445–452.

Veroff, J., Atkinson, J. W., Feld, S. C., and Gurin, G. (1960). The use of thematic apperception to assess motivation in a nationwide interview study. *Psychological Monography, 74,* 32.

Verona, E., Bresin, K., and Patrick, C. J. (2013). Revisiting psychopathy in women: Cleckley/Hare conceptions and affective response. *Journal of Abnormal Psychology, 122*(4), 1088–1093.

Veselka, L., Schermer, J. A., and Vernon, P. A. (2012). The Dark Triad and an expanded framework of personality. *Personality and Individual Differences, 53,* 417–425.

Vidacek, S., Kaliterna, L., Radosevic-Vidacek, B., and Folkard, S. (1988). Personality differences in the phase of circadian rhythms: A comparison of morningness and extraversion. *Ergonomics, 31,* 873–888.

Vignoles, V. L., Regalia, C., Manzi, C., Golledtge, J., and Scabini, E. (2006). Beyond self-esteem: Influence of multiple motives on identity construction. *Journal of Personality and Social Psychology, 90,* 308–333.

Vining, D. (1982). On the possibility of the reemergence of a dysgenic trend with respect to intelligence in American fertility differentials. *Intelligence, 6,* 241–264.

Vitaro, F., Arsenault, L., and Tremblay, R. E. (1997). Dispositional predictors of problem gambling in male adolescents. *American Journal of Psychiatry, 154,* 1769–1770.

von Rueden, C. R., Lukaszewski, A. W., and Gurven, M. (2015). Adaptive personality calibration in a human society: effects of embodied capital on prosocial traits. *Behavioral Ecology, 26*(4), 1071–1082.

Vrij, A., van der Steen, J., and Koppelaar, L. (1995). The effects of street noise and field independence on police officers' shooting behavior. *Journal of Applied Social Psychology, 25,* 1714–1725.

Vukasović, T., and Bratko, D. (2015). Heritability of personality: A meta-analysis of behavior genetic studies. *Psychological Bulletin, 141*(4), 769–785.

Wachtel, P. L. (1973). Psychodynamics, behavior therapy, and the implacable experimenter: An inquiry into the consistency of personality. *Journal of Abnormal Psychology, 82,* 324–334.

Wacker, J., Mueller, E. M., and Stemmler, G. (2012). Prenatal testosterone and personality: Increasing the specificity of trait assessment to detect consistent associations with digit ratio (2D:4D). *Journal of Research in Personality,* online first posting, digital online identifier: 10.1016/j.jrp.2012.10.007.

Wacker, J., and Smillie, L. D. (2015). Trait extraversion and dopamine function. *Social and Personality Psychology Compass, 9*(6), 225–238.

Wagner, J., Becker, M., Lüdtke, O., and Trautwein, U. (2015). The first partnership experience and personality development: A propensity score matching study in young adulthood. *Social Psychological and Personality Science, 6,* 455–463.

Wagner, J., Lüdtke, O., Jonkmann, K., and Trautwein, U. (2013). Cherish yourself: Longitudinal patterns and conditions of self-esteem change in the transition to young adulthood. *Journal of Personality and Social Psychology, 104,* 148–163.

Wagstaff, G. F., Vella, M., and Perfect, T. (1992). The effect of hypnotically elicited testimony on jurors' judgments of guilt and innocence. *Journal of Social Psychology, 132,* 591–595.

Wahba, M. A., and Bridwell, L. (1973). Maslow's need hierarchy theory: A review of research. *Proceedings of the Annual Convention of the American Psychological Association (1973).* 571–572.

Wagner, J., Lüdtke, O., and Trautwein, U. (2015). Self-esteem is mostly stable across young adulthood: Evidence from latent starts models. *Journal of Personality (serial online).*

Wagner, J., Lüdtke, O., Jonkmann, K., and Trautwein, U. (2013). Cherish yourself: Longitudinal patterns and conditions of self-esteem change in the transition to young adulthood. *Journal of Personality and Social Psychology, 104*(1), 148–163.

Wallace, H. M., and Baumeister, R. F. (2002). The performance of narcissists rises and falls with perceived opportunity for glory. *Journal of Personality and Social Psychology, 82, 5,* 819–834.

Waller, N. (1994). The importance of nongenetic influences on romantic love styles. *Psychological Science, 9,* 268–274.

Walton, G. M., Paunesku, D., and Dweck, C. S. (2012). Expandable selves. In M. R. Leary and J. P. Tangney (Eds.), *Handbook of self and identity* (2nd ed., pp. 141–154). New York, NY: Guilford Press.

Watson, D. (2000). *Mood and temperament.* New York: Guilford Press.

Watson, D. (2003). To dream, perchance to remember: Individual differences in dream recall. *Personality and Individual Differences, 34,* 1271–1286.

Watson, D., and Clark, L. A. (1984). Negative affectivity: The disposition to experience aversive emotional states. *Psychological Bulletin, 96,* 465–490.

Watson, D., and Humrichouse, J. (2006). Personality development in emerging adulthood: Integrating evidence from self-ratings and spouse ratings. *Journal of Personality and Social Psychology, 91,* 959–974.

Watson, D., and Pennebaker, J. W. (1989). Health complaints, stress, and distress: Exploring the central role of negative affectivity. *Psychological Review, 96,* 234–254.

Watson, D. C. (2001). Procrastination and the five-factor model: A facet level analysis. *Personality and Individual Differences, 30,* 149–158.

Watson-Jones, R. E., Whitehouse, H., and Legare, C. H. (2015). In-group ostracism increases high-fidelity imitation in early childhood. *Psychological Science, 27,* 34–42.

Watts, B. L. (1982). Individual differences in circadian activity rhythms and their effects on roommate relationships. *Journal of Personality, 50,* 374–384.

Webster, G. D., and Crysel, L. C. (2012). "Hit Me, Maybe, One More Time": Brief measures of impulsivity and sensation seeking and their prediction of blackjack bets and sexual promiscuity. *Journal of Research in Personality, 46*(5), 591–598.

Wechsler, D. (1949). *The Wechsler Intelligence Scale for Children.* New York: Psychological Corporation.

Wegmann, E., Stodt, B., and Brand, M. (2015). Addictive use of social networking sites can be explained by the interaction of Internet use expectancies, Internet literacy, and psychopathological symptoms. *Journal of Behavioral Addictions, 4*(3), 155–162.

Wehr, T. A., and Goodwin, F. K. (1981). Biological rhythms and psychiatry. In S. Arieti and H. K. Brodie (Eds.), *American handbook of psychiatry: Advances and new directions* (vol. 7). New York: Basic Books.

Weinberger, D. S., Schwartz, G. E., and Davidson, R. J. (1979). Low-anxious, high-anxious, and repressive coping styles: Psychometric patterns and behavioral and physiological responses to stress. *Journal of Abnormal Psychology, 88,* 369–380.

Weinberger, J. (2003). Freud's influence on psychology is alive and vibrant. In E. E. Smith, S. Nolen-Hoeksema, B. L. Fredrickson, G. R. Loftus, D. J. Bem, and S. Maren, *Introduction to psychology* (p. 486). Belmont, CA: Wadsworth/Thomson Learning.

Weinberger, J., and McClelland, D. C. (1990). Cognitive versus traditional motivational models: Irreconcilable or complementary? In E. T. Higgins and R. M. Sorrentino (Eds.), *Handbook of motivation and cognition* (vol. 2, pp. 562–597). New York: Guilford Press.

Weinberger, J., and Westen, D. (2007). *RATS, we should have used Clinton: Subliminal priming in political campaigns.* Paper presented at the annual meeting of the International Society of Political Psychology, Portland, Oregon. *USA Online.* Retrieved February 3, 2009, from www.allacademic.com/meta/p204661_index.html

Weinstein, A., Dorani, D., Elhadif, R., Bukovza, Y., Yarmulnik, A., and Dannon, P. (2015). Internet addiction is associated with social anxiety in young adults. *Annals of Clinical Psychiatry, 27*(1), 4–9.

Weinstock, L. M., and Whisman, M. A. (2006). Neuroticism as a common feature of the depressive and anxiety disorders: A test of the revised integrative hierarchical model in a national sample. *Journal of Abnormal Psychology, 115,* 68–74.

Weiser, E. B. (2015). # Me: Narcissism and its facets as predictors of selfie-posting frequency. *Personality and Individual Differences, 86,* 477–481.

Weiss, A., King, J. E., and Enns, R. M. (2002). Subjective well-being is heritable and genetically correlated with dominance in chimpanzees *(Pan troglodytes). Journal of Personality and Social Psychology, 83, 5,* 1141–1149.

Weissberg, R. P., Kumpfer, K. L., and Seligman, M. E. P. (2003). Prevention that works for children and youth: An introduction. *American Psychologist Special Issue: Prevention that works for children and youth, 58,* 425–432.

Weller, H. G., Repman, J., Lan, W., and Rooze, G. (1995). Improving the effectiveness of learning through hypermedia-based instruction: The importance of learner characteristics. Special Issue: Hypermedia: Theory, research, and application. *Computers in Human Behavior, 11,* 451–465.

Wertsch, J., and Kanner, B. (1992). A sociocultural approach to intellectual development. In R. Sternberg and C. A. Berg (Eds.), *Intellectual development* (pp. 328–349). New York: Cambridge University Press.

Wessman, A. E., and Ricks, D. F. (1966). *Mood and personality.* New York: Holt, Rinehart, and Winston.

West, S. G. (2002). Some methodological and training/funding perspectives on the future of personality research. *Journal of Research in Personality, 36,* 640–648.

Westen, D. (1990). Psychoanalytic approaches to personality. In L. A.

Pervin (Ed.), *Handbook of personality: Theory and research* (pp. 21–65). New York: Guilford Press.

Westen, D. (1992). The cognitive self and the psychoanalytic self: Can we put our selves together? *Psychological Inquiry, 3*, 1–13.

Westen, D. (1998). The scientific legacy of Sigmund Freud: Toward a psychodynamically informed psychological science. *Psychological Bulletin, 124*, 333–371.

Westen, D., and Gabbard, G. O. (2002a). Developments in cognitive neuroscience: I. Conflict, compromise, and connectionism. *Journal of the American Psychoanalytic Association, 50*, 53–98.

Westen, D., and Gabbard, G. O. (2002b). Developments in cognitive neuroscience: II. Implications for theories of transference. *Journal of the American Psychoanalytic Association 50*, 99–134.

Westen, D., Ludolph, P., Misle, B., and Ruffins, S. (1990). Physical and sexual abuse in adolescent girls with borderline personality disorder. *American Journal of Orthopsychiatry, 60*, 55–66.

Wever, R. A. (1979). *The circadian system of man: Results of experiments under temporal isolation.* New York: Springer.

Whalen, P. J., Bush, G., and McNally, R. J. (1998). The emotional counting Stroop paradigm: A functional magnetic resonance imaging probe of the anterior cingulate affective division. *Biological Psychiatry, 44*, 1219–1228.

Wheeler, J. G., George, W. H., and Dahl, B. J. (2002). Sexually aggressive college males: Empathy as a moderator in the "Confluence Model" of sexual aggression. *Personality and Individual Differences, 33*, 759–775.

Wheeler, R. W., Davidson, R. J., and Tomarken, A. J. (1993). Frontal brain asymmetry and emotional reactivity: A biological substrate of affective style. *Psychophysiology, 30*, 82–89.

White, J. K., Hendrick, S. S., and Hendrick, C. (2004). Big Five personality variables and relationship constructs. *Personality and Individual Differences, 37*, 1519–1530.

Whitehead, D. L., Perkins-Porras, L., Strike, P. D., Magid, K., and Steptoe, A. (2007). Cortisol awakening response is elevated in acute coronary syndrome patients with Type D personality. *Journal of Psychosomatic Research, 62*, 419–425.

Whiting, B., and Edwards, C. P. (1988). *Children of different worlds.* Cambridge, MA: Harvard University Press.

Whorf, B. L. (1956). *Language, thought, and reality.* Cambridge, MA: MIT Press.

Wicker, F. W., Brown, G., Weihe, J. A., Hagen, A. S., and Reed, J. L. (1993). On reconsidering Maslow: An examination of the deprivation/domination proposition. *Journal of Research in Personality, 27*, 118–133.

Wickman, S. A., and Campbell, C. (2003). An analysis of how Carl Rogers enacted client-centered conversation with Gloria. *Journal of Counseling and Development, 81*, 178–184.

Widiger, T. A. (1997). Personality disorders as maladaptive variants of common personality traits: Implications for treatment. *Journal of Contemporary Psychotherapy Special Issue: Personality disorders, 27*, 265–282.

Widiger, T. A. (2000). Personality disorders in the 21st century. *Journal of Personality Disorders, 14*, 3–16.

Widiger, T. A., and Costa, P. T. (2012). Integrating normal and abnormal personality structure: The Five-Factor Model. *Journal of Personality, 80*(6), 1471–1506.

Widiger, T. A., Costa, P. T., Jr., and McCrae, R. M. (2002a). A proposal for Axis II: Diagnosing personality disorders using the five-factor model. In P. T. Costa Jr. and T. A. Widiger (Eds.), *Personality disorders and the five-factor model of personality* (2nd ed., 431–456). Washington, DC: American Psychological Association.

Widiger, T. A., Trull, T. J., Clarkin, J. F., Sanderson, C., and Costa, P. T., Jr. (2002b). A description of the *DSM-IV* personality disorders with the five-factor model of personality. In P. T. Costa Jr. and T. A. Widiger (Eds.), *Personality disorders and the five-factor model of personality* (2nd ed., 89–102). Washington, DC: American Psychological Association.

Wiebe, D. J., and Smith, T. (1997). Personality and health: Progress and problems in psychosomatics. In R. Hogan, J. Johnson, and S. Briggs (Eds.), *Handbook of personality psychology* (pp. 892–918). San Diego, CA: Academic Press.

Wiederman, M. W., and Kendall, E. (1999). Evolution, gender, and sexual jealousy: Investigation with a sample from Sweden. *Evolution and Human Behavior, 20*, 121–128.

Wiggins, J. S. (1973). *Personality and prediction: Principles of personality assessment.* Menlo Park, CA: Addison-Wesley.

Wiggins, J. S. (1979). A psychological taxonomy of trait-descriptive terms: I. The interpersonal domain. *Journal of Personality and Social Psychology, 37*, 395–412.

Wiggins, J. S. (1996). *The five-factor model of personality: Theoretical perspectives.* New York: Guilford Press.

Wiggins, J. S. (2003). *Paradigms of personality assessment.* New York: Guilford Press.

Wiggins, J. S., Phillips, N., and Trapnell, P. (1989). Circular reasoning about interpersonal behaviour: Evidence concerning some untested assumptions underlying diagnostic classification. *Journal of Personality and Social Psychology, 56, 2,* 296–305.

Willerman, L. (1979). Effects of families on intellectual development. *American Psychologist, 34*, 923–929.

Willerman, L., Loehlin, J. C., and Horn, J. M. (1992). An adoption and a cross-fostering study of the Minnesota Multiphasic Personality Inventory (MMPI) Psychopathic Deviate scale. *Behavior Genetics, 22*, 515–529.

Williams, D. E., and Page, M. M. (1989). A multi-dimensional measure of Maslow's hierarchy of needs. *Journal of Research in Personality, 23*, 192–213.

Williams, J. E., and Best, D. L. (1982). *Measuring sex stereotypes: A thirty-nation study.* Beverly Hills: Sage.

Williams, J. E., and Best, D. L. (1990). *Measuring sex stereotypes: A multi-nation study.* Newbury Park, CA: Sage.

Williams, J. E., and Best, D. L. (1994). Cross-cultural views of women and men. In W. J. Lonner and R. Malpass (Eds.), *Psychology and culture* (pp. 191–196). Boston: Allyn and Bacon.

Williams, J.M.G., Mathews, A., and MacLeod, C. (1996). The emotional Stroop task and psychopathology. *Psychological Bulletin, 120*, 3–24.

Williams, L., O'Connor, R. C., Howard, S., Hughes, B. M., Johnston, D. W., Hay, J. L., O'Connor, et al. (2008). Type D personality mechanisms of effect: The role of health-related behavior and social support. *Journal of Psychosomatic Research, 64*, 63–69.

Williams, P. G., O'Brien, C. D., and Colder, C. R. (2004). The effects of neuroticism and extraversion on self-assessed health and health-relevant cognition. *Personality and Individual Differences, 37*, 83–94.

Wilson, D. S., Near, D., and Miller, R. R. (1996). Machiavellianism: A synthesis of the evolutionary and psychological literatures. *Psychological Bulletin, 119*, 285–299.

Wilson, M., and Daly, M. (1985). Competitiveness, risk-taking, and violence: The young male syndrome. *Ethology and Sociobiology, 6*, 59–73.

Wilson, M., and Daly, M. (2004). Do pretty women inspire men to discount the future? *Proceedings of the Royal Society of London, B (Suppl.), 271*, S177–S179.

Winch, R. F. (1954). The theory of complementary needs in mate selection: An analytic and descriptive study. *American Sociological Review, 19*, 241–249.

Winjgaards-de Meij, L., Stroebe, M., Schut, H., Stroebe, W., van den Bout, J., van der Heijden, P., and Dijkstra, I. (2007). Neuroticism and attachment insecurity as predictors of bereavement outcome. *Journal of Research in Personality, 41,* 498–505.

Wink, P., Ciciolla, L., Dillon, M., and Tracy, A. (2007). Religiousness, spiritual seeking, and personality: Findings from a longitudinal study. *Journal of Personality, 75,* 1051–1070.

Winter, D. G. (1973). *The power motive.* New York: Free Press.

Winter, D. G. (1988). The power motive in women—and men. *Journal of Personality and Social Psychology, 54,* 510–519.

Winter, D. G. (1993). Power, affiliation, and war: Three tests of a motivational model. *Journal of Personality and Social Psychology, 65,* 532–545.

Winter, D. G. (1998). A motivational analysis of the Clinton first term and the 1996 presidential campaign. *Leadership Quarterly, 9,* 367–376.

Winter, D. G. (1999). Linking personality and "scientific" psychology: The development of empirically derived Thematic Apperception Test measures. In Gieser and M. I. Stein (Eds.), *Evocative images: The Thematic Apperception Test and the art of projection* (pp. 107–124). Washington, DC: American Psychological Association.

Winter, D. G. (2002). The motivational dimensions of leadership: Power, achievement, and affiliation. In R. E. Riggio and S. E. Murphy (Eds.), *Multiple intelligences and leadership* (pp. 119–138). Mahwah, NJ: Erlbaum.

Winter, D. G., and Barenbaum, N. B. (1985). Responsibility and the power motive in women and men. *Journal of Personality, 53,* 335–355.

Winter, D. G., John, O. P., Stewart, A. J., Klohnen, E. C., and Duncan, L. E. (1998). Traits and motives: Toward an integration of two traditions in personality research. *Psychological Review, 105,* 230–250.

Witkin, H. A. (1973). A cognitive-style perspective on evaluation and guidance. *Proceedings of the Invitational Conference on Testing Problems,* 21–27.

Witkin, H. A. (1977). Role of the field-dependent and field-independent cognitive styles in academic evolution: A longitudinal study. *Journal of Educational Psychology, 69,* 197–211.

Witkin, H. A., Dyk, R. B., Fattuson, H. F., Goodenough, D. R., and Karp, S. A. (1962). *Psychological differentiation: Studies of development.* New York: Wiley.

Witkin, H. A., and Goodenough, D. R. (1977). Field dependence and interpersonal behavior. *Psychological Bulletin, 84,* 661–689.

Witkin, H. A., Lewis, H. B., Hertzman, M., Machover, K., Meissner, P. B., and Wapner, S. (1954). *Personality through perception: An experimental and clinical study.* New York: Harper.

Witkin, H. A., Moore, C. A., Goodenough, D. R., and Cox, P. W. (1977). Field-dependent and field-independent cognitive styles and their educational implications. *Review of Educational Research, 47,* 1–64.

Woike, B. A. (1995). Most memorable experiences: Evidence for a link between implicit and explicit motives and social cognitive processes in everyday life. *Journal of Personality and Social Psychology, 68,* 1081–1091.

Wood, A. C., Saudino, K. J., Rogers, H., Asherson, P., and Kuntsi, J. (2007). Genetic influences on mechanically-assessed activity level in children. *Journal of Child Psychology and Psychiatry, 48,* 695–702.

Wood, A. H., and Eagly, A. H. (2010). Gender. In S. Fiske, D. Gilbert, & G. Lindzey (Eds.), *Handbook of Social Psychology* (5th ed., vol. 1, pp. 629–667). New York: Wiley.

Wood, D. (2015). Testing the lexical hypothesis: Are socially important traits more densely reflected in the English lexicon? *Journal of personality and social psychology, 108*(2), 317–335.

Wood, D., Nye, C. D., and Saucier, G. (2010). Identification and measurement of a more comprehensive set of person-descriptive trait markers from the English lexicon. *Journal of Research in Personality, 44,* 258–272.

Wood, J. J., McLeod, B. D., Sigman, M., Hwang, W. C., and Chu, B. C. (2003). Parenting and childhood anxiety: Theory, empirical findings, and future directions. *Journal of Child Psychology and Psychiatry and Allied Disciplines, 44,* 134–151.

Wood, J. M., Nezworski, M. T., Lilienfeld, S. O., and Garb, H. N. (2003). *What's wrong with the Rorschach? Science confronts the controversial inkblot test.* San Francisco: Jossey-Bass.

Wood, J. M., Nezworski, M. T., and Stejskal, J. W. (1996). The comprehensive system for the Rorschach: A critical examination. *Psychological Science, 7,* 3–10.

Wortman, J., and Wood, D. (2011). The personality traits of liked people. *Journal of Research in Personality, 45,* 519–528.

Wright, C. I., Williams, D., Feczko, E., Barrett, L. F., Dickerson, B. C., Schwartz, C. E., and Wedig, M. M. (2006). Neuroanatomical correlates of extraversion and neuroticism. *Cerebral Cortex, 16*(12), 1809–1819.

Wright, D. B., Eaton, A. A., and Skagerberg, E. (2015). Occupational

segregation and psychological gender differences: How empathizing and systemizing help explain the distribution of men and women into (some) occupations. *Journal of Research in Personality, 54,* 30–39.

Wright, L. (1988). The Type A behavior pattern and coronary artery disease. *American Psychologist, 43,* 2–14.

Wrulich, M., Stadler, G., Brunner, M., Keller, U., and Martin, R. (2015). Childhood intelligence predicts premature mortality: Results from a 40-year population-based longitudinal study. *Journal of Research in Personality, 58,* 6–10.

Wrzus, C., Wagner, G. G., and Riediger, M. (2016). Personality-situation transactions from adolescence to old age. *Journal of Personality and Social Psychology, 110*(5), 782.

Wu, K. D., and Clark, L. A. (2003). Relations between personality traits and self-reports of daily behavior. *Journal of Research in Personality, 37,* 231–256.

Yarkoni, T. (2015). Neurobiological substrates of personality: A critical overview. In L. Cooper and R. J. Larsen (Eds.), *Handbook of Personality and Social Psychology: Personality Processes and Individual Differences* (pp. 61–84). Washington, DC: American Psychological Association.

Yeh, C. (1995). *A cultural perspective on interdependence in self and morality: A Japan-U.S. comparison.* Unpublished manuscript, Department of Psychology, Stanford University, Stanford, CA.

Yik, M. S. M., and Russell, J. A. (2001). Predicting the big two of affect from the Big Five of personality. *Journal of Research in Personality, 35,* 247–277.

Yildirim, I., and Zengel, R. (2014). The impact of cognitive styles on design students' spatial knowledge from virtual environments. *TOJET: The Turkish Online Journal of Educational Technology, 13*(3), 210–215.

Young, S. M., and Pinksky, D. (2006). Narcissism and celebrity. *Journal of Research in Personality, 40,* 463–471.

Yu, D. L., and Seligman, M. E. P. (2002). Preventing depressive symptoms in Chinese children. *Prevention and Treatment, 5,* np.

Zagorsky, J. L. (2007). Do you have to be smart to be rich? The impact of IQ on wealth, income, and financial distress. *Intelligence, 35,* 489–501.

Zaki, J. (2011) What, me care? Young are less empathetic. *Scientific American Mind, 21,* 14–15.

Zakriski, A. L., Wright, J. C., and Underwood, M. K. (2005). Gender similarities and differences in children's social behavior: Finding personality in contextualized patterns of adaptation. *Journal*

of Personality and Social Psychology,
88, 844–855.

Zarevski, P., Bratko, D., Butkovic, A., and Lazic, A. (2002). Self-reports and peer-ratings of shyness and assertiveness. *Review of Psychology, 9,* 13–16.

Zeidner, M., Matthews, G., Roberts, R. D., and MacCann, C. (2003). Development of emotional intelligence: Towards a multi-level investment model. *Human Development, 46,* 69–96.

Zeigler-Hill, V., Besser, A., Morag, J., & Campbell, W. K. (2016). The Dark Triad and sexual harassment proclivity. *Personality and Individual Differences, 89,* 47–54.

Zeigler-Hill, V., Myers, E. M., and Clark, C. B. (2010). Narcissism and self-esteem reactivity: The role of negative achievement events. *Journal of Research in Personality, 44,* 285–292.

Zelenski, J. M., and Larsen, R. J. (1999). Susceptibility to affect: A comparison of three personality taxonomies. *Journal of Personality, 67,* 761–791.

Zelenski, J. M., and Larsen, R. J. (2000). The distribution of emotions in everyday life: A state and trait perspective from experience sampling data. *Journal of Research in Personality, 34,* 178–197.

Zengel, B. Edlund, J. E., and Sagarin, B. J., (2013). Sex differences in jealousy in response to infidelity: Evaluation of demographic moderators in a national random sample. *Personality and Individual Differences, 54,* 47–51.

Zettler, I., and Hilbig, B. E. (2010). Honesty-humility and person-situation interaction at work. *European Journal of Personality, 24,* 569–582.

Zhao, K., & Smillie, L. D. (2014). The role of interpersonal traits in social decision making exploring sources of behavioral heterogeneity in economic games. *Personality and Social Psychology Review,* 1088868314553709.

Zhu, B., Chen, C., Loftus, E .F., He, Q., Chen, C., Lei, X., Lin, C., and Dong, Q. (2012). Brief exposure to misinformation can lead to long-term false memories. Applied Cognitive Psychology, *26,* 301–307.

Zilcha-Mano, S., Mikulincer, M., and Shaver, P. R. (2012). Pets as safe havens and secure bases: The moderating role of pet attachment orientations. *Journal of Research in Personality, 46,* 571–580.

Zimbardo, P. G. (1977). *Shyness: What it is and what to do about it.* New York: Symphony.

Zinovieva, I. L. (2001). Why do people work if they are not paid? An example from Eastern Europe. In D. R. Denison (Ed.), *Managing organizational change in transition economies* (pp. 325–341). Mahwah, NJ: Erlbaum.

Zuckerman, M. (1974). The sensation seeking motive. In B. Maher (Ed.), *Progress in experimental personality research* (vol. 7, pp. 79–148). New York: Academic Press.

Zuckerman, M. (1978). Sensation seeking. In H. London and J. E. Exner (Eds.), *Dimensions of personality* (pp. 487–559). New York: Wiley Interscience.

Zuckerman, M. (1984). Sensation seeking: A comparative approach to a human trait. *Behavioral and Brain Sciences, 7,* 413–471.

Zuckerman, M. (1991a). *Psychobiology of personality.* New York: Cambridge University Press.

Zuckerman, M. (1991b). Sensation-seeking trait. *Encyclopedia of Human Biology, 6,* 809–817.

Zuckerman, M. (2005). The neurobiology of impulsive sensation seeking: Genetics, brain physiology, biochemistry, and neurology. In C. Stough and C. Stough (Eds.), *Neurobiology of exceptionality* (pp. 31–52). New York, NY, US: Kluwer Academic/Plenum Publishers.

Zuckerman, M. (2006). Biosocial bases of sensation seeking. In T. Canli (Ed.), *Biology of personality and individual differences* (pp. 37–59). New York: Guilford Press.

Zuckerman, M. (2012). Psychological factors and addiction: Personality. In H. J. Shaffer, D. A. LaPlante, S. E. Nelson, H. J. Shaffer, D. A. LaPlante, and S. E. Nelson (Eds.), *APA addiction syndrome handbook, Vol. 1: Foundations, influences, and expressions of addiction* (pp. 175–194). Washington, DC, US: American Psychological Association.

Zuckerman, M., and Aluja, A. (2015). Measures of sensation seeking. In G. J. Boyle, D. H. Saklofske, G. Matthews, G. J. Boyle, D. H. Saklofske, and G. Matthews (Eds.), *Measures of personality and social psychological constructs* (pp. 352–380). San Diego, CA, US: Elsevier Academic Press.

Zuckerman, M., and Haber, M. M. (1965). Need for stimulation as a source of stress response to perceptual isolation. *Journal of Abnormal Psychology, 70,* 371–377.

Zuckerman, M., and Kuhlman, D. M. (2000). Personality and risk-taking: Common biosocial factors. *Journal of Personality, 68,* 999–1029.

Name Index

Marsland, A. L., 416, 562
Martin, A. L., 244
Martin, L. J., 383
Martin, L. R., 147, 569
Martin, M., 415
Martin, N. G., 165, 167, 171, 172, 249
Martin, R., 147, 148
Martinez, M. A., 485
Martinko, M. J., 114, 116
Martins, A., 445
Maslow, A. H., 66, 346, 347
Mason, A., 341
Mason, J., 619
Mason, O., 605
Masson, J. M., 268
Masten, A. S., 145, 147
Master, A., 385
Masters, H. L., 79, 82
Masters, K. S., 579
Masuda, T., 532
Mathews, A., 417
Mathis, L. C., 141, 142, 449
Mathot, K. J., 16
Matloff, J., 509
Matsumoto, D., 533
Mattheiesen, S. B., 78
Matthews, G., 65, 200, 389, 417
Matthews, K. A., 568
Matthews, M. D., 79, 147
Mattia, J. I., 614, 615
Mauzey, E. D., 421
May, M. A., 99
Mayer, J. D., 389
Maynard Smith, J., 251
Mazuera Arias, R., 534
McAdams, D. P., 308, 333, 335, 343,
    344, 348
McBurnett, K., 591
McCarley, N. G., 116
McCartney, K., 177, 510
McCaulley, M. H., 113
McClelland, D. C., 334, 335, 336, 337, 338,
    339, 342
McClelland, D. C., 342
McClern, G. E., 159, 160
McClure, E. B., 210
McConnell, A. R., 445
McCoul, M. D., 472
McCrae, R. M., 583, 584
McCrae, R. R., 26, 63, 74, 75, 76, 77, 83,
    132, 134, 135, 136, 140, 406, 407,
    410, 416, 494–497, 495, 496, 497,
    535, 542
McCreary, L. L., 441
McCullough, M. E., 82, 483, 485
McDaniel, M. J., 41
McDaniel, S. R., 42, 207
McDermott, K. B., 302
McDermott, K. B., 302
McFarland, D., 235
McFatter, R. M., 407
McGrath, R. E., 333
McGue, M., 132, 137, 147, 168, 169, 170,
    172, 176, 179, 465, 556
McGuffin, P., 71, 159, 160
McGuire, M., 618
McHoskey, J. W., 71, 482

McKellop, M., 383
McKibbin, W. F., 247
McLaughlin, R., 383
McLean, J., 301
McLeod, B. D., 288, 437
McLoyd, V. S., 408
McNally, R. J., 414
McNulty, J. K., 468, 475
McPartland, T. S., 25
McWhirter, R. M., 407
Mead, M., 537
Meagher, S., 597, 598
Mealey, L., 252
Mecacci, L., 214
Medland, S. E., 170
Mednick, S., 618
Medway, F. J., 320
Meehl, P. E., 42
Meeus, W., 472
Megargee, E. I., 30
Mehl, M. R., 27, 28, 32
Meissner, P. B., 368
Melchior, L. A., 438
Meloy, J. R., 422
Meltzer, A. L., 475
Mendoza-Denton, R., 387
Menninger, K., 568
Menschik-Bendele, J., 170
Mercer, K. A., 417
Mervielde, I., 136
Messick, S., 102, 371
Meston, C. M., 33
MetsΣpelto, R. L., 134
Mettee, D. R., 31
Metter, E. J., 78
Meyer, M., 472
Michalos, A. C., 404
Michalski, R. L., 244
Mike, A., 79
Mikulincer, M., 323, 324
Miller, A. L., 372
Miller, D. C., 514
Miller, G. A., 194
Miller, G. E., 197, 449, 562
Miller, G. F., 179, 248, 253, 254
Miller, J., 408
Miller, J. D., 82, 588, 617
Miller, J. G., 521, 526, 527
Miller, K. L., 196
Miller, K. M., 78
Miller, M., 509
Miller, R. R., 481, 482
Miller, S. L., 240
Miller, T. W. K., 147
Millevoi, A., 244
Millon, C., 597, 598
Millon, T., 252, 586, 587, 597, 598, 617
Mills, C. J., 136
Milne, B., 132
Miramontes, L. G., 60, 62, 533
Mischel, W., 7, 92, 94, 381, 387, 625
Mitchell, K. V., 472
Mitchell, S., 299
Mittler, P., 164
Miyake, S., 216
Miyasita, A., 216
Miyata, Y., 214, 216

Mlacic, B., 78, 542
Moestue, C., 62, 79
Moffat, F. L., 568
Moffitt, T., 176, 180
Moffitt, T. E., 132, 137, 146, 147, 176, 180,
    207, 476
Moirón, M., 16
Molde, H., 82
Mommersteeg, P. M. C., 579
Mondak, J. J., 82
Monk, T. H., 214
Monroe, S. M., 142, 449
Montemayor, R., 435
Montiglio, P. O., 16
Montrose, V. T., 485
Moon, J. H., 27, 32, 485
Moon, T. H., 472, 482
Mooney, C. N., 485
Moore, C. A., 369, 371
Moore, E. A., 210
Moore, M., 167, 168, 509
Morag, J., 482
Moretti, R. J., 333
Morey, L. C., 586
Morf, C., 316
Morgan, C. A., 301
Morgan, C. D., 332
Morris, M. E., 484
Morsella, E., 307
Moscoso, S., 542
Moskowitz, D. S., 95, 511
Moskowitz, J. T., 567, 568
Moskowtiz, D. S., 95
Moss, H., 338
Moss, M. S., 384
Mostofsky, E., 578
Mount, M. K., 112
Moussavi, M., 237
Mower, O. H., 399
Mroczek, D. K., 135, 137, 146, 147, 148, 555
Mueller, E. M., 188
Mufson, D. W., 113
Mufson, M. A., 113
Müllensiefen, D., 81
Muller, D., 202, 217
Mullins-Sweatt, S. N., 588
Multon, K. D., 385
Munafo, M. R., 179
Muncer, S., 497
Munz, D. C., 79
Muraven, M., 272, 450
Murdock, G. P., 527
Murphy, B. C., 135
Murphy, D. L., 178–179
Murphy, K. R., 104
Murphy, S. M., 244
Murray, C., 180, 390
Murray, D. R., 524, 525
Murray, G., 80
Murray, H., 10
Murray, H. A., 4, 10, 330, 332
Murstein, B. I., 465
Myers, D. G., 402, 404, 405, 406, 408
Myers, E. M., 485
Myers, I. B., 113
Myers, L. B., 279
Myrseth, H., 82

Subject Index

Note: **Boldface** page numbers indicate key terms.
Italic page numbers indicate figures or tables.